Middle East Countries BASIC DATA

COUNTRY Capital	Area in 1000 Sq. Km.	Popula- tion in millions (1995)	Avg. Annual Growth % pop. (1990-94)	GDP in $US billions (1994)	GDP per capita in $US (1994)	GNP per capita: real growth rate (%) (1985-94)	External debt in $US billions (1995)	Lit- eracy % of pop.	Density per Sq. Km	Avg. Life Expect- ancy
Morocco Rabat	446.5	29.1	2.1	31.5	1,182	1.1	20.5	50	36.7	68.9
Oman Musqat	212.4	2.1	4.2	10.8	5,152	0.6	3	35	6.8	70.2
Qatar Doha	11	0.533	2.74	7.9	16,455	-0.8	1.5	76	51.9	70
Saudi Arabia Riyadh	1960.5	18.7	2.2	123.7	6,819	-1.2	18.9	62	7.6	68.5
Somalia Mogadishu	637.6	7.3	15.58	1.4	164	-1.2	1.9	24	11.4	55.74
Sudan Khartoum	2505.8	30.1	2.35	6.6	242	-0.2	17	32	12	54.7
Syria Damascus	185.1	15.4	3.4	42.0	3,016	-2.4	19.4	64	74.6	66.81
Tunisia Tunis	163.6	8.8	2.2	15.9	1,844	1.8	7.7	57	57.9	73.2
Turkey Ankara	780.5	63.4	1.97	149[3]	2,450[4]	1.5	66.6	79	79.1	71.4
UAE Abu Dhabi	75.5	1..95	2.6	37.0	16,923	0.2	11.6	71	30.6	72.5
Yemen San`a	527.9	14.2	5.1	18.7	1,272		7	38	27.2	62.5
West Bank & Gaza Strip	6.220	2.4	4..5	2.6	1,416				1246	71.2

POLITICAL
ENCYCLOPEDIA
OF THE
MIDDLE EAST

POLITICAL ENCYCLOPEDIA

OF THE

MIDDLE EAST

Avraham Sela, Editor

CONTINUUM • NEW YORK

1999

The Continuum Publishing Company
370 Lexington Avenue
New York, NY 10017

Copyright © 1999 by G.G. The Jerusalem Publishing House Ltd.,
39 Tchernichovski Street,
Jerusalem

Printed in China

Library of Congress Cataloging-in-Publication Data

Political encyclopedia of the Middle East / edited by Avraham Sela.
    p.   cm.
  ISBN 0-8264-1053-7
  1. Middle East–Politics and government–Encyclopedias.   2. Middle
East–History–20th century–Encyclopedias.   1. Sela, Avraham.
DS62 . 8 . P64 1988
956 . 04′ 03–dc21   97-51280
                                                                   CIP

FOREWORD

This new political encyclopedia of the Middle East is an updated and useful source of knowledge on one of the most crucial regions of world affairs in our time. It brings to the reader a wealth of information and scholarly insight on this region, in a historical perspective, with emphasis on the two recent decades, which were marked by cataclysmic events both in and out of the region. Among the more conspicuous events during these two decades were: the Israel-Egypt peace treaty (1979); the Islamic revolution in Iran (1979); the eight-year-long Iran-Iraq war (1980-88); the Iraqi invasion of Kuwait and the Gulf war (1990-91); the collapse of the Soviet Union and the end of the Cold War (1991); and the breakthrough in Arab-Israel peacemaking (1993-94). Related to these events were the volatile price of oil, the major natural resource in the Middle East; the intensified demographic and economic predicaments of many states in the region; the gap between the quest for political participation and liberalization, and the political reality of authoritarian, security-obsessed, and politically restrictive regimes; and the rising tide of Islamic radicalism, which has become the primary social and political force in the region.

This encyclopedia takes a special interest in the post-Gulf War and post-Cold War resumption of the Arab-Israeli peacemaking process and its dramatic breakthrough, represented by the Israel-PLO Declaration of Principles of September 1993 on the establishment of the Palestinian Authority in the Gaza Strip and the West Bank, followed by the Israel-Jordan peace treaty of October 1994. This breakthrough was above all a reflection of the changing political structures, of both a domestic and inter-state politics, of the Middle East, i.e., the erosion of regional ethno-religious identities rooted in supra-national pan-Arabism and Islam, to increasingly state-based identities and hence, to more pragmatic politics. These changes also brought modest reconsideration of the wrapped up in term "Middle East" regarding its geographical boundaries and cultural essence.

Indeed, despite the prevalent use of the term "Middle East" (Near East in Europe), for decades students and institutions of the international academic community have been divided over the very validity of the term and even more so over its geographical boundaries. Area specialists tended to point to the historical, linguistic and religious commonality of the Middle East peoples, defining the region as one marked by dominant Arab-Islamic identity, which excluded Israel as an alien and non-regional actor. They rejected the term "Middle East" as a reflection of imperialists viewpoint and interests. Some Arab scholars have defined the region as an all-Arab national system of states, arguing that the term "Middle East" was deliberately introduced by Western imperialists to legitimize the existence of Israel in the heart of the Arab homeland. Indeed, the Arab world, "from the [Atlantic] Ocean to the [Persian] Gulf," constitutes the major part of the Middle East land and population. Israel is indeed an alien entity in this region in terms of its cultural, religious, social and economic characteristics, even though about half of its Jewish population is Middle Eastern by origin. However, from the end of World War I, the nascent political Jewish community in Palestine, and later the state of Israel, has played an indispensable role in shaping the map of the contemporary Middle East. Furthermore, the Arab Israel conflict has left its imprint on the region's political thought and practice, reflecting mainly the Arab-Muslim response to the religious, cultural, territorial and political challenge that the Jewish state constituted to its neighbors. Obviously, Israel played a key role in the region's strategic and international affairs, even though for most of its fifty years of existence Israel's relations with most of the Middle East states were marked by ideological hostility and a practical state of war.

The 1990s also witnessed the growing incorporation of Turkey in the Middle East setting, underlined by intensified ethnic (primarily concerning the Kurds) and water conflicts with its Arab south and south-eastern neighbors, shared economic interests with Iraq and Iran, and a newly established strategic alliance with Israel. At the same time, Iran has maintained its interest and penetration in the Arab-Muslim Middle East, boosted by its Islamic revolution in 1979.

This volume thus defines the Middle East as a region encompassing the whole Arab world, from the Maghreb in North Africa to the Persian Gulf (including nominally Arab states, hence briefly reviewed—Mauritania, Somalia, Eritrea and Djibouti) as well as non-Arab states: Israel, Turkey and Iran. While this definition derives mainly from a common Muslim identity of the vast majority of the peoples in the region, and their sense of shared regional identity, for the purposes of this encyclopedia it is also necessary to conceive the region in the context of long-term structural interactions among states, as well as the existence of cross-national institutions, trends, and shared economic, security, and political links. Thus, in addition to entries on each state in the region (reviewing land, people, culture, and political history, both domestic and international), major elements of regional significance are amply discussed in this encyclopedia through substantive entries that constitute short essays on issues, such as: Arab Nationalism; Arab-Israel Conflict; Arab-Israel Peacemaking; Islamic Radicalism and Movements; Water Politics; Military Forces; Oil; Non-Conventional Weapons; Refugees and Migrants; Terrorism; and Women. Other entries of regional importance relate to ethnic and religious groups, such as Arabs, Kurds, Druze, Jews, Alawis, Copts, Circassians, Maronites, as well as Muslims (Sunnis, Shi`is, Isma`ilis, etc.), Christians (Greek Orthodox, Greek Catholic, Latin, etc.). In addition, the encyclopedia also includes short entries on leading political figures, parties and movements.

The encyclopedia is arranged in an alphabetical order, with cross-references designed to help the reader find entries close or related to the issue searched. To ease the search, cross-references appear in small caps, non-English words and terms, as well as original names of movements, parties, and ideas, appear in italics. An annexed table provides basic updated data on the Middle East states, such as area, economic growth and main resources, population and population growth, gross domestic product and per capita income, and more.

A short note on transliteration: the approach adopted in this volume is "user friendly," that is, regarding Arabic names, we used the customary way of spelling names and places in the English-speaking world, with a tendency toward a phonetic rather than precise transliteration from Arabic. Al (with capital A) is rarely used as part of a dynasty's name, denoting "The house (family) of...", as opposed to the usual al-, denoting the definite article. In the case of Turkish and Iranian names, we took the closest spelling to the phonetic pronunciation.

I would like to thank all the contributors to this volume: Menashe Amir, Oren Barak, Alexander Bligh, Ela Greenberg, Shiela Hattis, Nurit Kliot, David Kushnir, Meir Litvak, Bruce Maddy-Weizman, Arie Oded, Galit Peleg, Paul Rivlin, Yudith Ronen, Malka Rosin, Barry Rubin, David Sagiv, Yiftah Shafir, Amir Weisbrod, and Danny Zissenwine. I also wish to thank Shoshana Lewis for her dedication and care in handling the technical aspects that such a project entails. I am especially indebted to Rachel Gilon, who masterfully conducted the production of this volume, coordinated, inspired, and encouraged the contributors, copy editors, and typesetters, and made sure that this volume saw the light of day.

Jerusalem   A.S.

CONTRIBUTORS

Iran	Menashe Amir, B.A. Head of the Persian Department, Israeli Broadcasting Authority, Jerusalem
Arabs in Israel	Haidar Aziz, Ph.D. Professor of Sociology, Alquds University, Jerusalem Chairman of the Arab Association of Sociology Fellow Researcher at The Harry Truman Institute, The Hebrew University of Jerusalem
Lebanon Syria	Oren Barak, Ph.D. candidate Fellow Researcher at The Harry Truman Institute for the Development of Peace, and Instructor, Department of Middle Eastern Studies, The Hebrew University of Jerusalem
Jordan Yemen United Arab Republic	Alex Bligh, Ph.D. Senior Lecturer at the Jezreel College, Israel
Women in the Middle East	Ela Greenberg, Ph.D. candidate Middle Eastern Studies, The Hebrew University of Jerusalem Graduate of the Department of Middle Eastern Studies, Chicago University
Water Politics	Nurit Kliot, Ph.D. Professor at the Department of Geography, Haifa University
Turkey	David Kushner, Ph.D. Professor at the Department of Middle Eastern Studies, Haifa University
Israel	Sheila Hattis, Ph.D. Researcher in the Knesset and Middle East Market Research Institute, Tel Aviv, Weekly column in the Jerusalem Post, Political commentator on foreign radio and television network
Algeria	Meir Litvak, Ph.D. Fellow Researcher, The Moshe Dayan Center for Middle Eastern and African Studies, Tel Aviv University Senior Lecturer, Middle Eastern and African Studies, Tel Aviv University
Morocco	Bruce Maddy-Weitzman, Ph.D. Fellow Researcher, The Moshe Dayan Center for Middle Eastern and African Studies, Tel Aviv University Senior Lecturer, Middle Eastern and African Studies, Tel Aviv University

Relations between African and Arab countries	Arye Oded, Ph.D. Former Israeli Ambassador in several African states Senior Lecturer on African Studies, The Hebrew University of Jerusalem
Oil and OPEC	Paul Rivlin, Ph.D. Fellow Researcher, The Moshe Dayan Center for Middle Eastern and African Studies, Tel Aviv University
Water Politics	Yehudit Ronen, Ph.D. Senior Associate Researcher at The Moshe Dayan Center, Tel Aviv University Lecturer of Middle Eastern and African History, Tel Aviv University
European Commonwealth	Malka Rosin, Ph.D. candidate Department of International Relations, The Hebrew University of Jerusalem
Terrorism	Barry Rubin, Ph.D. Senior Resident Scholor, BESA Center for Strategic Studies, Bar Ilan University, Ramat Gan and Editor of the Middle East Review of International Affairs
Egypt	David Sagiv, Ph.D. Fellow Researcher at The Harry Truman Institute, The Hebrew University of Jerusalem Lecturer at Bar Ilan University, Ramat Gan
Palestinians	Avraham Sela, Ph.D. Senior Fellow Researcher at The Harry Truman Institute, The Hebrew University of Jerusalem Senior Lecturer, Department of International Relations, The Hebrew University of Jerusalem
Nuclear Weapons	Yiftah Shapir Fellow Researcher at the Jaffee Center for Strategic Studies, Tel Aviv University
Iraq	Amir Weissbroad Graduate of the Department of Middle Eastern Studies at The Hebrew University of Jerusalem, and Political Analyst at the Research Branch of the Israel Foreign Ministry
Tunisia	Danny Zisenwine, M.A. Graduate of Middle Eastern Studies and General History The Hebrew University of Jerusalem

A

ABBAS, MAHMUD (nickname: *Abu Mazen*) (b. 1933)   Prominent Palestinian leader in the PALESTINE LIBERATION ORGANIZATION (PLO) and, since 1994, in the PALESTINIAN AUTHORITY. Born in Safed, following the exodus from Mandatory Palestine, and educated in JORDAN, he worked in QATAR. From there he joined the founders of *Fatah* in KUWAIT. Following the take-over of the PLO by *Fatah* in the late 1960s, Abbas held various political, financial and diplomatic positions. From the mid-1970s he became increasingly involved in Israeli affairs and contacts between PLO figures and leftist Israelis. In 1983, after Issam Sirtawi was assassinated, Abbas was appointed direct supervisor of *Fatah's* relations with the Israeli left. This led him to numerous meetings with Israeli leftist figures, primarily in Bucharest and Budapest. Such exposure to domestic Israeli affairs (especially to Ashkenazi-Sephardic cultural divergences), along with a sense of deprivation among Sephardic JEWS in ISRAEL, resulted in the development of his thesis—the potential alignment of Middle East Jews and Palestinians. In his capacity as head of the Department of the Occupied Land, he was sent in 1990 to Moscow for talks with its leaders. This was motivated by an attempt to prevent the wave of Soviet Jewish immigration to Israel. After the killing of Khalil al-Wazir (*Abu Jihad*) in 1988, he was appointed head of the PLO delegation to the negotiations with Jordan on the WEST BANK and Gaza. Furthermore, he led the PLO talks with the Jordanian regime following King HUSSEIN's proclamation of disengagement from the West Bank on 31 July 1988.

During the 1980s, Abbas became one of the prominent pragmatists in the PLO. He supported a two-state solution, but continued to write and speak in terms of the "bankruptcy of ZIONISM" and near "collapse of Israel." In 1993, Abbas coordinated the secret talks with Israel in Oslo, which culminated in the signing of the Oslo Agreement. His role was acknowledged in his participation in the ceremony of the signing of the agreement on the White House lawn on 13 September 1993, together with Yasser ARAFAT. With the establishment of the Palestinian Authority in Gaza, disagreement erupted between him and Arafat, apparently over his position in the new system of government. However, in 1995 he resumed his position as Chief Coordinator of the negotiations with Israel during the first phases of the Oslo Agreement. Through this position he became Arafat's "number two" in the Palestinian Authority's negotiations with Israel. At the same time, he maintained his position as Secretary of the Executive Committee of the PLO.

Abbas maintains close relations with EGYPT and the Gulf states, traveling there occasionally to enlist material and political support. Abbas belongs to the group of Palestinian pragmatist technocrats who lack the mythical image and manneristic behavior of Arafat and leading combatants of the Palestinian national movement.

ABDALLAH IBN ABDEL AZIZ (b. 1923)   Saudi prince, one of the sons of IBN SA'UD (his mother came from the RASHID clan of the Shammar tribes—whose state the Saudis overpowered in 1921); Crown-Prince and First Deputy Prime Minister of SAUDI ARABIA since 1982. Abdallah is considered to head a conservative faction (as opposed to those identified with strong American orientation). He served for some time as Governor of Mecca and, in 1962–1963, as Deputy Minister of Defense. Since 1963 he has been the Commander of the National Guard. When Prince Khaled became King and Prime Minister in 1975, Abdallah was appointed Second Deputy Prime Minister. With Khaled's death and the accession of King FAHD in June 1982, he became Crown Prince and First Deputy Prime Minister. He is therefore supposed to accede to the throne when Fahd dies—but some foresee a potential struggle with Prince Sultan Ibn Abdel Aziz. Abdallah is married to a Syrian woman (said to belong to the ALAWI sect and a relative of President ASAD). In recent years he has advocated closer Saudi cooperation with the Arab states, including the radical ones (e.g., SYRIA). He has also become more active in Arab politics and tried, without much success, to mediate in the Lebanese crisis, the Syrian-Iraqi dispute, and between Syria and the United States.

ABDALLAH IBN HUSSEIN (1882–1951) Emir (governor) of Transjordan (1921–1946), King and founder of the HASHEMITE Kingdom of JORDAN (1946–1951). Born in Mecca, second son of Sharif Hussein Ibn Ali, scion of the Prophet Muhammad's Hashemite clan of the *Quraishi* tribe. Educated in Istanbul, where he lived from 1891 to 1908 with his father under Ottoman surveillance. Abdallah was active in Arab cultural circles and in contact with semi-clandestine Arab nationalist groups in Istanbul. When his father was allowed to return to Mecca as Emir, after the Revolution of the YOUNG TURKS, Abdallah went with him. He remained in Istanbul again, as Deputy for Mecca in the Ottoman Parliament (1912–1914). When his father launched the ARAB REVOLT in June 1916, Abdallah took a leading part in it. From 1917 he also served his father, who had assumed the title of King of HIJAZ, as political advisor and Foreign Minister. (Nonetheless, it was his younger brother FEISAL who was fostered by the British agents in the Middle East as the leading figure in the Hashemite family and who represented Hussein in the peace negotiations.)

In March 1920, at an Arab nationalist congress in Damascus that proclaimed Feisal King of SYRIA, a group of Iraqi nationalists offered Abdallah the crown of IRAQ. This corresponded to vague Hashemite ideals of three Arab Kingdoms—GREATER SYRIA; Iraq; and Hijaz, ruled by Hussein's sons and federated under King Hussein. In July 1920 the French forces entered Damascus and compelled Feisal to flee from Syria. The British, whose zone of power was to include Iraq, preferred Feisal over Abdallah as ruler of Iraq. In March 1921 Abdallah arrived in Amman from Hijaz with troops, declaring his intention to restore Arab-Hashemite rule to Syria. As the British wished to avoid an armed clash between their Hashemite client and the French, and perceiving Abdallah to be a useful agent of BRITAIN's interests in Transjordan, the then Colonial Secretary Winston Churchill offered Abdallah the title of Emir over the territory of Transjordan. This was in re-

turn for renouncing his plans regarding Syria as well as his claims to the Iraqi crown which Abdallah accepted. In April 1920 the League of Nations endorsed that settlement, within the Palestine MANDATE given to Britain—with a clause, suggested by Britain, making the "Jewish National Home" inapplicable to Transjordan. Britain recognized Transjordan in May 1923 as an autonomous Emirate. Under British supervision, Abdallah gradually established an administration, aligning with BEDUIN tribal chiefs and fostering their allegiance to his status as a patriarch figure. This comprised a government, an army (the Arab Legion, British-run), a constitution (1928), and representative institutions (later developing into a bicameral Parliament). He remained closely linked to the British, dependent on their financial aid, and proved his loyalty during World War II, when he sent Arab Legion forces to assist in the suppression of Rashid Ali's rebellion in Iraq (1941).

From the outset, Abdallah fostered aspirations for the throne of Greater Syria, i.e., a union of Syria, LEBANON, Palestine and Transjordan—under his crown—and a Fertile Crescent Federation of Greater Syria with Iraq. He also sought to cultivate Syrian and Palestinian-Arab politicians who might support his scheme. Abdallah publicized these plans mainly after World War II. Some elements in Syria, Iraq and Palestine supported them but Arab political elites in these countries were mostly hostile. EGYPT, Syria and SAUDI ARABIA strongly opposed any "revisionist" plans to change the inter-Arab status quo, while Abdallah's Hashemite cousins in Iraq competed him for the same union, but under their leadership. The French rejected the Greater Syria scheme as a British plot. While some British service branches seem to have supported Abdallah's aspirations to some extent, official British policy never fully backed them.

Abdallah maintained good relations with the leaders of the Zionist Movement and the Jewish *Yishuv*. In the early 1930s he invited Jewish settlement in Transjordan—but Arab nationalist outcries and the British Palestine administration foiled these plans. It is against this backdrop that Arab nationalists regarded Abdallah as a British puppet, and most Arab regimes doubted his independence even after it was formally granted by Britain in May 1946, when Abdallah assumed the title of King and changed Transjordan's name to The Hashemite Kingdom of Jordan.

From 1946 towards the final Palestine crisis, Abdallah's contacts with the Zionist leaders intensified and finally led to a secret unwritten and vague understanding. Abdallah, though preferring an autonomous Jewish entity within a Palestinian-Jordanian Kingdom under his crown, would not resist or impede the partition of Palestine and the creation of a Jewish state (in accordance with a UN decision then expected), while the JEWS and nascent ISRAEL would not hinder Abdallah from taking over the Arab part of Palestine. In fact, while they would not actually assist him, they encouraged such a take-over, and cooperation would be maintained. Reports of that agreement inevitably reached Abdallah's Arab adversaries. They wanted to foil it and prevent him from taking over part of Palestine with or without the Jews. This played an important role in the collective Arab decision-making regarding their involvement in the 1948 Palestine war (see ARAB-ISRAEL CONFLICT).

With the intensifying Arab-Jewish hostilities in Palestine in early 1948, Abdallah proved unable to fully keep his pledge. He told his Zionist contacts (Golda MEIR) who met him on 11 May 1948, that he could not resist the pressure to join the all-Arab military action regarding Palestine. The British government secretly backed his efforts to take over the Arab part of Palestine designated to a separate Palestinian state by the United Nations partition resolution, ostensibly in concert with all-Arab moves. He sent his army into Palestine along with the other Arab forces after being appointed titular Commander-in-Chief of all the invading forces. Abdallah's Arab Legion took over the Arab-inhabited central mountainous area later to be known as the WEST BANK, meeting virtually no resistance. In line with the British warnings, but also due to his military limitations, Abdallah avoided attacking Israel in the areas allotted to it by the UN partition plan. Fighting did take place in JERUSALEM, its vicinity and on the road leading to it, areas not allotted to Israel by the UN plan (and not covered by Abdallah's tacit understanding with the Zionist leaders). When hostilities ceased, Abdallah resumed contacts with Israel. In late March-early April 1949, while official armistice talks were being held in Rhodes between Israeli and Jordanian military delegations, the most difficult points were settled in secret negotiations directly with the King. Following the signing of the armistice agreement between the two countries, relations continued to be close and, in November 1949, the two governments began talks with the purpose of reaching a peace treaty. Due to domestic and regional Arab constraints, however, these talks led only to a draft of a non-aggression pact, which was initialled by the two sides in February 1950, but was never ratified. Abdallah could not persuade even his closest aides to ratify the agreement, and three prime ministers resigned consecutively to avoid implementation of the King's will. Finally, mounting pressure by the Arab states, which culminated in a threat to expel Jordan from the ARAB LEAGUE if it would sign a separate accord with Israel, forced the King to drop the idea. In return for Abdallah's renunciation of the pact with Israel, the Arab states acquiesced (but never formally recognized) in the annexation of Arab Palestine by Jordan which they had violently opposed.

Already before the end of the war, Abdallah began implementing a series of administrative measures designated to establish his authority in the occupied area and tighten his control of the population. Late in 1948 Abdallah had begun to turn the military take-over of the Arab part of Palestine into full annexation. He was invited to do so by congresses of Palestinian-Arab notables, orchestrated by his longstanding supporters from among the Nashashibi—led opposition, and unopposed by an extremist leadership totally discredited by the defeat of 1948. The formal act of annexation was proclaimed in April 1950 under the slogan of "Unity of the Two Banks" (of the River Jordan). Although the Arab Legion effectively salvaged part of Arab Palestine from falling into the hands of the Jews, Abdallah became the scapegoat of the Arab collective failure in the war and responsibility to the "loss of Palestine."

Abdallah's post-1948 years in power were marked by political turmoil and increasing domestic difficulties. The incorporation of the PALESTINIAN ARABS introduced modern nationalist politics and a highly active, fermenting, traumatized population which seriously restricted the King's powers and ability to adopt domestic and foreign policies without consideration of public opinion. In addition, many regarded Abdallah as a collaborator with the British and the Jews, and as a traitor. Abdallah was assassinated in July 1951 by a Palestinian from the HUSSEINI clan while entering al-Aqsa Mosque in Jerusalem for prayer.

ABDEL HAMID II (1842–1918)   The twenty-fourth sultan of the OTTOMAN EMPIRE. Abdel Hamid was the son of Sultan Abdel Meçid, and began his reign in 1876, after his brother Murad V was deposed because of mental illness. The Ottoman Empire was then going through a most difficult period. In 1875–1876, having suppressed insurrections in Bosnia, Herzegovina and Bulgaria, it entered into war with Serbia and Montenegro and encountered strong European pressure for reforms. It also collapsed financially and was unable to pay its growing debts. Abdel Hamid took the throne with the support of the reformist circles in the Empire and, in December 1876, promulgated the first Ottoman constitution, introducing a Parliamentary system to the state. But this did not prevent a declaration of war by RUSSIA in April 1877, and by early the following year Russian troops had advanced to the proximity of Istanbul, forcing the Ottomans to call for an armistice. The Treaty of Berlin, signed in July 1878, imposed on the Ottoman Empire heavy territorial concessions, depriving it of many of its possessions in the Balkans and Eastern Anatolia. Cyprus was handed over to BRITAIN in a separate agreement.

During the rest of Abdel Hamid's reign, peace was disrupted only by a short war with Greece over an insurrection in Crete in 1897. Nevertheless, the Ottoman Empire continued to lose territories (Tunis and Thessaly, 1881 and EGYPT, 1882), and had to contend with rebellion and restlessness in many of its provinces. Abdel Hamid was particularly harsh in putting down disorders caused by ARMENIAN nationalists in the 1890s, and had to deal with the growing insurgency in Macedonia. In order to curb the spread of nationalist ideas among ARABS and other Muslim subjects, Abdel Hamid followed a clear PAN-ISLAMIC policy, enhancing his religiously sanctioned position as CALIPH of all Muslims and supporting Islamic institutions. His most celebrated project was the completion of the Hijaz Railway to Medina in 1908.

Abdel Hamid furthered the modernization of the Ottoman Empire in his development of the judicial system, industry, communications, public services and education. With the help of the Public Debt Administration, which he created in 1881, he also significantly improved the state finances. But he went back on his early support for a liberal order and, using the war with Russia as a pretext, suspended the constitution in 1878, and henceforth ruled the Empire as an autocrat. His regime, increasingly arbitrary and ruthless, led directly to the establishment of the movement of the YOUNG TURKS and to the revolution they carried out in July 1908. Abdel Hamid restored the constitutional order and was allowed to remain enthroned but was deposed in April 1909 and sent into house arrest after being implicated in an attempted coup.

ABDEL ILAH IBN ALI (1912–1958)   Regent (1939–1953) and Crown Prince (1953–1958) of IRAQ. Born in HIJAZ to Sharif Ali, the eldest son of Sharif Hussein, later King of Hijaz. Abdel Ilah moved to Baghdad in 1925, when Hijaz was conquered by IBN SA'UD. When King Ghazi of Iraq, his cousin and brother-in-law, died in 1939, he became Regent of Iraq on behalf of the infant Prince FEISAL. When Feisal attained his maturity in 1953, Abdel Ilah assumed the title of Crown Prince, retaining considerable influence. In 1941, he was forced to flee from Iraq by the nationalist anti-British revolt led by Rashid Ali al-Keilani. He was able to restore his reign after the British forces had occupied Iraq and repressed the revolt. He was strongly pro-British, considered by anti-British opinion on the right and left as a symbol of subservience to imperialist domination. Abdel Ilah fostered abortive plans for a Fertile Crescent Federation and was believed, in the 1950s, to aspire to the throne of SYRIA. Abdel Ilah was murdered during the military coup of July 1958.

ABDEL MAJID, AHMAD ISMAT (b. 1923) Egyptian diplomat, Secretary General of the ARAB LEAGUE since May 1991. Born in Alexandria, he graduated the Faculty of Law, University of Alexandria (1944) and specialized in International Law, in which he received his Ph.D. from the University of Paris (1951). Abdel Majid held various Egyptian diplomatic and political positions: *inter alia*, Ambassador to Paris (1970); Minister of State for Cabinet Affairs (1970–1972); Ambassador at the UN (1972–1983); Minister of Foreign Affairs (1983); Deputy Prime Minister and Foreign Minister (until May 1991). He represented EGYPT in numerous conferences and meetings, participating in the Egyptian delegation to the negotiations concerning the withdrawal of British forces from the SUEZ CANAL (1954–1956). He headed the Egyptian delegation to the preliminary talks for a peace conference, held in ISMA'ILIYYA (1977), shortly after Anwar al-SADAT's visit to JERUSALEM. In addition he led the Egyptian delegation to the twentieth session of the heads of states and prime ministers of the Organization of African Unity (1984). He is the author of several books on Arab politics and international law.

ABDEL NASSER, GAMAL (1918–1970) Egyptian officer and statesman, President of EGYPT (1956–1970). He graduated from the military academy in 1938 and served in SUDAN, and from 1941 as instructor at the academy. He took part in Egypt's expeditionary forces in the 1948 Palestine war.

Nasser was founder and leader of the "Free Officers," a clandestine group conspiring to depose Egypt's royal regime whom they held responsible for the humiliating defeat of 1948, and other Egyptian ills. On 22 July 1952, they mounted a successful coup and took power, forming a Revolutionary Council with General Muhammad Nagib as its official head. A power struggle soon erupted between Nagib and Nasser. Nasser won and this resulted in the establishment of an army-led populist one-party regime. In January 1953, all political parties were banned and a single organization established, with Nasser as its Secretary-General. In May 1953, Nasser also became Deputy Secretary-General of the Revolutionary Council, and in June—Deputy Premier and Minister of the Interior (with Nagib as President and Premier).

In February 1954 the struggle between Nasser and Nagib came to a head, with demonstrations and counter-demonstrations and rival army units moving into combat positions. In April the struggle was resolved: Nasser became Prime Minister, while Nagib remained President but was stripped of any real power. In November 1954 he was dismissed and put under house arrest. Nasser took action against the remnants of the old political parties by conducting purges and trials. An attempt on Nasser's life in October 1954 was ascribed to the MUSLIM BROTHERHOOD who were severely suppressed; their leaders were put on public trials and some of them executed.

For Nasser's reforms from 1952, and his measures of nationalization, (see EGYPT). Under a new January 1956 constitution, Nasser was elected, in a June referendum President for a six-year term. With the merger of Egypt and SYRIA in February 1958, he

was elected President of the UNITED ARAB REPUBLIC (UAR). After its dissolution in September 1961 he retained for Egypt its official name and remained President of the UAR until his death. The UAR's breakup led Nasser to initiate radical measures of nationalization, declaring war against the bourgeoisie. In 1962 Nasser founded a new ruling party—the ARAB SOCIALIST UNION—and formulated a National Charter as the basic doctrine of the party and the nation.

In his first years of power, Nasser had appeared moderate and pragmatic in his foreign and inter-Arab policies. In 1954 he reached an agreement with BRITAIN that had eluded all previous governments. He obtained the abolition of the Treaty of 1936, evacuation of British forces and the termination of all special privileges for Britain. Nasser also conceded, in 1952–1953, to the Sudan the right of self-determination which all former rulers had denied. Even in ISRAEL he was at first seen as a moderate with whom a *modus vivendi* appeared possible.

In the mid-1950s, Nasser began adopting increasingly militant, populist, revolutionary, and anti-Western policies. This soon made him an Arab national hero, especially in the Fertile Crescent countries. His growing identification with the "Third World" neutralism led him to oppose plans for a Middle East defense alliance linked to the West, the Baghdad Pact. The ensuing confrontation with the West coincided with Nasser's first appearance as a leading actor on the international scene. This was at the BANDUNG CONFERENCE of Asian leaders, (1955), in which he emerged with Tito and Nehru as one of the architects of a neutralist bloc. It also led him to conclude an arms deal with Czechoslovakia (1955)—marking a budding alliance with the Soviet Bloc.

In 1956 the US retaliated by denying Egypt aid to the ASWAN DAM, Nasser's ambitious project (and inducing the World Bank to do likewise). This step led Nasser to obtain the aid denied by the West from the USSR, and to nationalize the SUEZ CANAL. The confrontation with the West culminated in the Anglo-French invasion of the Suez Canal zone in October 1956. Israel's participation in that invasion convinced Nasser that no peace with Israel was possible. From that crisis of 1956 Nasser emerged triumphant, as the leader of a small newly-independent nation that had successfully withstood imperialist aggression, and his Arab and international standing sky-rocketed.

In December 1957, a first (non-governmental) Afro-Asian solidarity conference was held in Cairo. In 1961, Nasser took part in the founding conference of the Casablanca Bloc, and in a neutralist summit meeting in Belgrade. In 1963, he participated in a summit conference founding the Organization for African Unity—which held its second congress in 1964 in Cairo. Later in 1964, Nasser hosted leaders of non-aligned states in Cairo for their second conference. In 1958, Nasser paid his first visit to the Soviet Union.

From the mid-1950s, Nasser took an increasingly activist line in inter-Arab affairs with the unhidden intention of establishing Egypt's status as a hegemonic regional power. In his booklet *The Philosophy of the Revolution* (1954) Nasser described Egypt's position at the center of three circles: Arab, Islamic and African. Gradually, Nasser's inter-Arab policies assumed a compulsory nature, tending to impose Egyptian leadership and nationalist values on other Arab states by fostering Nasserist pressure groups in the Arab countries. This was to be done by subversion and, if needed, by violence. Following the collapse of the UAR, Nasser declared war against both his conservative and revolutionary Arab adversaries in the name of his version of socialist revolution. This policy, which culminated in Egypt's military intervention in YEMEN in 1962, aggravated inter-Arab disputes and led to the deterioration of Egypt's and Nasser's posture in the Arab world.

In late 1963, while his army had been involved in a costly and hopeless war in Yemen, Nasser was confronted with Syrian threats to entangle Egypt in an untimely war with Israel. Consequently, Nasser was forced to shift priorities and adopt a truce in his relations with the conservative Arab regimes that would preserve his Arab leadership and prevent war with Israel. Nasser shifted temporarily the center of gravity of his regional policy from Arab-centered Pan-Arab national revolution to collective Arab endeavor in the struggle against Israel. Nasser thus sponsored a series of ARAB SUMMIT CONFERENCES (1964–1965) which resulted in the foundation of the PALESTINE LIBERATION ORGANIZATION (PLO), a Joint Arab Command, and a plan for the diversion of the Jordan river's tributaries to prevent Israel from using them in its national water carrier. The new regional Arab

role adopted by Nasser called for restricting his interventionist activities in the Arab states. However, this policy proved fragile and temporary. It brought no relief to Nasser's predicaments in the Yemen war or in preventing uncontrolled escalation with Israel. His cooperation with the conservative regimes brought him under attack from both conservative and revolutionary regimes, which stood at the backdrop of his reversion from the cooperative inter-Arab strategy back to aggressive, revolutionary policy.

It was against this backdrop that in 1966–1967 Nasser revived and reinforced his alliance with Syria's neo-BA'TH regime. With this he hoped to enhance Syria's sense of security and prevent untimely war with Israel. However, in May 1967, Nasser was dragged into a crisis with Israel which made war inevitable, following acts of introducing massive forces into SINAI, ordering the withdrawal of the UN Emergency Force from Sinai, proclaiming a blockade of the Straits of TIRAN, and signing a military alliance with JORDAN. The May 1967 crisis initiated by Nasser's escalating steps toward Israel aroused tremendous mass enthusiasm which brought Nasser to the pinnacle of his all-Arab leadership. All the Arab countries fervently backed him, many sending troops or equipment to aid Egypt. When the war turned into defeat, Nasser claimed personal responsibility and resigned, but stormy mass demonstrations—carefully staged—"forced" him to retract the resignation.

In the three years after 1967, Nasser's policies were less flamboyant and more collaborative in terms of his inter-Arab policy. His weakened leadership, along with the urgent need for financial support from the oil-rich conservative states to recover Sinai from Israeli occupation, compelled him to depart from his interventionist Arab policies and redefine national priorities. Still, he would not accept a peace settlement or negotiations with Israel. Nonetheless he consented to the UN Security Council 242 Resolution, which included an implicit, de-facto recognition of the State of Israel. Given his wounded prestige and loss of national territory, Nasser conducted a strategy of limited war against Israel (1969–1970) in order to restore his army's morale and speed up the international peace efforts in the Middle East conflict, even at the cost of inviting Soviet air and air-defense units to deploy on Egyptian soil. Egypt's growing dependence on the Soviet Union, with thousands of technicians and advisors, represented a departure from Nasser's hitherto sacrosanct principle of absolute sovereignty.

Having been the sponsor of the PLO in 1964, following the 1967 debacle, Nasser gave his full support to the PLO's new leadership of *Fatah* and helped the build-up of its political and military posture in the Arab world. He exerted his influence on Jordan and LEBANON, allowing the Palestinian guerrilla forces to entrench and effectively create a state within a state, and refrain from taking effective measures against them. Nasser mediated the "Cairo Agreement" between the Lebanese government and the PLO (November 1969) which established the PLO's rights in maintaining military activity on Lebanese soil. When the coexistence broke down in Jordan and King HUSSEIN confronted the PLO by armed force in September 1970, Nasser convened an Arab summit conference and called the fighting parties to cease fire and join his efforts of mediation.

Nasser died on 20 September 1970, the day the summit was concluded, and after bringing Jordan and the PLO to agree on working principles for the continued presence of the Palestinian guerrillas on Jordanian soil. His image had dimmed somewhat since his death, because of among other reasons, the departure of his successors—Anwar al-SADAT and MUBARAK—from his social and nationalist ideologies. Since the mid-1990s, Nasser's legacy has seen a revival, in response to the ARAB-ISRAEL PEACEMAKING and decline of Pan-Arabism (see also NASSERISM).

Nasser was endowed with unusual charisma and wielded an immense, though controversial, influence throughout the Arab world. He was a towering figure among the leaders of modern Egypt and the Arab world and has left a distinctive mark on the history of his country and on the Middle East as a whole.

ABDEL RAHMAN OMAR (b. 1938) Egyptian Islamic scholar (Sheikh), born in al-Manzala, Dakahliyya District. He studied in the Islamic University of AL-AZHAR in Cairo, where he received his Ph.D. degree in Theology, and later taught there.

Abdel Rahman is the leader of one of the most fanatic Egyptian Islamic groups called *al-Jama'a al-Islamiyya*. He is considered a leading spiritual figure by the JIHAD Organization in Upper EGYPT. In the late 1970s he issued a FATWA, which was interpreted as giving licence to assassinate Anwar SADAT, stating that he was "not a ruler by what was commanded by Allah."

After Sadat's assassination in 1981, Abdel Rahman was appointed Emir (leader) of the Jihad Organization. The military court, which tried him and other members of the Jihad, released him due to insufficient evidence.

Immediately after his release he published his book "*Kalimat Haqq*" (Word of Truth), including his speech in self-defense before the military court, in which he strongly attacked MUBARAK's regime. In the mid-1980s he was hunted by the Egyptian authorities for his involvement in terrorist attacks against COPTS and security forces, but he fled to SUDAN. From there he managed to obtain a visa to the US. Before his arrival to the US he visited IRAN, where he preached for his extremist opinions. In 1990, he settled in Jersey City, where he founded a religious center. After the explosion at the World Trade Center in New York in 1992, some members of his congregation were subsequently tried and sentenced to long-term imprisonment. Later on, Abdel Rahman himself was tried and similarly sentenced.

ABDEL SHAFI, HAIDAR (b. 1918) Palestinian politician, son of a notable family in Gaza. Educated in the Arab College in JERUSALEM and graduated in 1943 from the American University of Beirut in Medicine. After 1948, he practiced public health under the Egyptian military government. By 1955 he had become Head of Public Health Administration in the GAZA STRIP. He refused to collaborate with the Israeli military government during the short occupation of the Gaza Strip in 1956–1957 and, together with others, founded the national military organization (The National Front Against Imperialism and ZIONISM).

Abdel Shafi's activity against the Israeli occupation helped his promotion under the Egyptian government when it resumed power. In 1958 he was elected member in the newly established Constitutional Council, meant to serve as a nucleus of Palestinian self-rule, and one of its fifteen-member executive committee. In 1960, he was elected to the executive committee of the Palestinian National Union—a new political organization established by ABDEL NASSER. This was meant to constitute the basis for the Palestinian entity. In 1962, Abdel Shafi was re-elected to the Constitutional Council. A year later he became its President. With the establishment of the PALESTINE LIBERATION ORGANIZATION (PLO) in 1964, he supported Ahmad al-SHUQEIRI; participated in the founding assembly of the organization in Jerusalem, and became amember of its executive committee (1964–1968). Abdel Shafi was active in promoting the law which established the Palestinian Liberation Army in 1965, while continuing his practice as a physician. With the establishment of the Palestinian RED CRESCENT Society in 1969 by the PLO, he became Director of its branch in the Gaza Strip, a position he has continued to assume. Between the Madrid Peace Conference (October 1991) and the Israel-PLO Oslo Agreement (September 1993) Abdel Shafi led the Palestinian delegation to the talks with ISRAEL. He became critical of the PALESTINIAN AUTHORITY (PA) for its peacemaking policy and conduct on human rights. In January 1996 he was elected as an independent member of the Palestinian Authority's Council, but resigned his position in late summer 1997 in protest to the stalemated peacemaking process and the marginalization of the Council by the PA.

ABU- - - (Arabic: Father of - - -) Calling a man Father of his first-born son as an honorific added to his name, is a widespread custom in Arab society. In most cases, the honorific is known only to close acquaintances. In some, it becomes public knowledge—particularly in underground organizations, where the honorific name serves as a *nom de guerre* or ia even used as the actual name (Abu Ammar—Yasser ARAFAT, ABU NIDAL—Sabri al-Banna; and many other PALESTINE LIBERATION ORGANIZATION (PLO) activists). There were also many family names with "Abu - - -"—such as Abu-(a)l-Huda, Abu-(a)l-Fath, or in North African form (usually with the French transcription) BOURGUIBA, Bouteflika, Boucetta. These stay in the family, in contrast to the honorifics and *noms de guerre* which are tied to the person bearing them.

ABU DHABI The largest and most populous of the seven sheikhdoms of the TRUCIAL COAST (Trucial Oman) federated since 1971 as the UNITED ARAB EMIRATES (UAE). Abu Dhabi's territory—some 29,000 sq. miles (75,000 sq. km.)—is mostly unsettled desert saline or covered by sand. Its borders are in several areas disputed by its neighbors. In one such

dispute, with SAUDI ARABIA, Abu Dhabi in 1955 occupied al-BURAIMI oasis by British-led military action (together with OMAN, which acquiesced half of the oasis); Saudi Arabia reluctantly relinquished its claim in 1974. Other disputes, with QATAR and DUBAI, were settled amicably in the 1960s. In the 1974 agreement, Abu Dhabi ceded to Saudi Arabia, in return for Buraimi, a 30 mile (50 km.)-long strip in its extreme west. This gave Saudi access to the PERSIAN GULF between Abu Dhabi and Qatar.

Abu Dhabi's population was given a variety of estimates, until the 1960s, at 20,000–40,000; a census of 1968 put it at 46,600. By the late 1980s it had grown, in the wake of the rapid development of its oil economy, to an estimated 450,000. Most of this, according to some estimates, comprised up to eighty percent foreign workers and migrants (Arab, and mainly Pakistani). Of the less than 1 million residents of Abu Dhabi in the late 1990s, a majority live in the capital, Abu Dhabi. The modernization processes since the 1970s and the large proportion of foreign workers have created serious social problems.

The Sheikh of Abu Dhabi, of the Al-NUHAYAN family, was under British protection from the nineteenth century, with a British political officer stationed in Abu Dhabi. The present ruler, Sheikh Zayed Ibn Sultan, assumed power in 1966 with British help toppling his brother Sheikh Shakbut who had, in 1928, overthrown his uncle.

Since 1966, Abu Dhabi has maintained a small military force. In 1971, BRITAIN withdrew and Abu Dhabi formed, with the other six sheikhdoms, an independent federation; the United Arab Emirates (UAE). It became—in constant rivalry with Dubai—the dominant power within the federation. Abu Dhabi city is the temporary capital of the UAE (a new federal capital is to be built on the Abu Dhabi-Dubai border). Sheikh Zayed was elected by the Council of Rulers as President of the UAE, and re-elected every five years. His son, the Crown Prince, became Deputy Premier and, from 1977, Deputy Commander-in-Chief, another member of the family taking over his cabinet post. Generally Abu Dhabi's leaders want the federation to tighten and strengthen *vis-a-vis* its component parts (while Dubai prefers it to remain loose). Apart from the Sheikh's traditional informal consultations, Abu Dhabi has not developed representative institutions of its own. (An appointed Consultative Council represents the UAE as a whole.) Strict Islamic law is in force.

OIL concessions were granted in 1939 and 1953, and oil was struck in and first exported in 1962. In spite of low oil prices in the 1980s and 1990s, Abu Dhabi citizens enjoy one of the highest Gross Domestic Product (GDP) per capita in the world.

Economic development remained mainly linked to the oil and petrochemical sector—though various other schemes were being planned. A network of modern roads was built, as was a port, which was opened in 1972 and became one of the leading ports in the Gulf area. Social services and institutions—schools, hospitals, etc.—were also energetically developed. In 1971 an "Arab Development Fund" was established. Abu Dhabi dispenses aid and credits through this—mainly to Arab, but also to some Asian and African countries. In 1996, a free zone was inaugurated on one of the islands not far from Abu Dhabi. The investment of 3 billion dollars is supposed to be covered by the income from this new enterprise.

ABU MAZEN   see ABBAS MAHMUD.

ABU MUSSA A small island in the PERSIAN GULF located in the Straits of HORMUZ and rich in OIL; disputed between IRAN and SHARJA, one of UNITED ARAB EMIRATES (UAE)'s sheikhdoms. In 1906 BRITAIN compelled the Sheikh of Sharja, one of the TRUCIAL COAST sheikhdoms, to cancel an iron-oxide mining concession in Abu Mussa granted to a German company. During the twentieth century, Sharja's ownership of Abu Mussa has been disputed by both the Trucial Ccast sheikhdom of UMM AL-QAIWAN and Iran. Umm al-Qaiwan mainly claimed offshore oil rights, but also granted a concession to an American company, which contradicted a concession given by Sharja to a competing American company. Iran claimed territorial possession of the island. When Britain's protectorate over the Trucial Coast came to its end in 1971, Iran and Sharja reached an agreement allowing Iranian deployment on the island while recognizing Sharja's sovereignty and sharing oil revenues. Iran did station military units on the island, but concurrently occupied the near by Tunb island belonging to RAS AL-KHAIMA (one of the UAE's emirates). Iran continued to endorse, however, the offshore oil concession previously granted by Sharja.

Offshore production began in 1974 and has since been the only source of oil for Sharja. In the wake of the IRAN-IRAQ WAR, the KUWAIT crisis and the war launched by the international coalition against IRAQ in 1990–1991, Iran decided to build the island as a strategic stronghold from which the closure of the Hormuz straits would be launched if necessary. In 1992, Iran took a series of moves to re-assert her presence on the island: in March, she expelled the foreigners from the island and in September declared full sovereignty over the three islands. In 1995, Iran increased its troops to 4,000 and deployed surface-to-air missiles, artillery, and anti-ship missiles. Iran opened an airport on the island in March 1996. For all practical purposes, the island has become Iranian territory.

ABU NIDAL (al-Banna Sabri Khalil) (b. 1939) Palestinian leader of a terrorist group. From 1974, General Secretary of *Fatah* Revolutionary Council (FRC); a dubious group which had never been part of the PALESTINE LIBERATION ORGANIZATION (PLO). Born in Jaffa, 1939, Abu Nidal moved to SAUDI ARABIA after the 1967 War to work there as a teacher. He joined the *Fatah* in the mid 1960s and in 1969 was in charge of the Khartoum branch. Later he headed the Baghdad PLO office. Following the October 1973 War and consequent willingness of the PLO to accept the diplomatic option in the conflict with ISRAEL, Abu Nidal rebeled against *Fatah's* new attitude and, backed by Iraqi intelligence, he conspired to assassinate *Fatah* leader Yasser ARAFAT for his new political attitude. Abu Nidal was sentenced to death by the military court of *Fatah* for that conspiracy, but managed to escape to IRAQ. In early 1974 he announced from Baghdad the establishment of an alternative organization under the title "*Fatah*-Revolutionary Council" (*majlis fateh al-thawry*), claiming to be the authentic representative of the organization's principles, namely, the armed struggle against Israel, following their betrayal by Arafat. Abu Nidal's group was fully supported by the Iraqi regime and, in return, became the executive instrument of Iraqi subversive policy during the 1970s, mainly toward SYRIA and the PLO. During those years the Abu Nidal group committed several terrorist acts against Syrian targets within Syria and abroad. From 1978 it began to attack the growing trend of pragmatism within *Fatah's* ranks, expressed by the willingness to accept a Palestinian state in the WEST BANK and GAZA STRIP, alongside Israel. The group adopted a policy of assassination of Palestinian figures who led the PLO's diplomatic offensive in Europe in this direction and had met with leading Israeli leftists, with Arafat's tacit backing.

In 1979, Abu Nidal left Baghdad against the backdrop of *rapprochement* between the Iraqi regime and the PLO, and moved to Damascus where he began serving his new hosts in their subversive activity against Iraq, the PLO and JORDAN. One of the victims of this offensive was Isam Sirtawi, head of the PLO office in Brussels, who was murdered in 1983, in the midst of the Syria-PLO dispute and the Syrian-inspired split within *Fatah*. Other Palestinian and Jordanian diplomats were among the victims of the terrorist activity of the group.

In early June 1982 the Abu Nidal group made an attempt on the life of Israel's ambassador in London. This gave the Israeli government the pretext it had been looking for to justify a major military operation in LEBANON against the Palestinians. Given the Israeli proclaimed threats to take such action if any JEW anywhere would be hurt by Palestinians, the attempt might have been deliberately directed to trigger such conflagration. In 1985 Abu Nidal moved to South Lebanon, near his military training camp and began his contacts with LIBYA. In 1989 some senior members of his organization left the group, accusing Abu Nidal personally of the killing of 150 members of the FRC, among them fifteen senior members who had been suspected by him of plotting against his leadership. The Abu Nidal group was held responsible for assassinating *Fatah's* second in command, Abu Iyad (Salah Khalaf), and security chief Abu al-Hawl in Tunis (1991).

The FRC is currently headquartered in Libya with branches in the Biqa' of Lebanon and a few Palestinian refugee camps in Lebanon, and also has presence in SUDAN. Its operations have taken place so far in the Middle East, Asia and Europe. The main financial sources of the organization come from patron states, graft and blackmail, and also its own network of business companies and front organizations. For political reasons, the FRC has no formal or permanent patron state, except for Libya where, according to rumors from ALGERIA, Abu Nidal's present location and home base are situated.

Although the group was successively supported by Iraq, Syria and Libya, it apparently maintained a level of financial and operational freedom. While many of its operations may have coincided with the interests of the hosting states, the group also conducted independent operations. Since the mid-1970s the Abu Nidal group has committed dozens of major attrocities, which have claimed the lives of many officials and innocent people in the Middle East, Western Europe, Romania, TURKEY, Austria, and India. Among the group's salient attacks were: machine-gunning a Vienna synagogue, killing 2 and wounding 17 (1981); bombing the office of British Airways and Alia Airlines in Madrid, killing a woman and wounding 29 (1985); hijacking an Egyptian airliner to Malta, where 60 people were killed in the rescue operation conducted by an Egyptian commando unit (1985); hijacking a Pan Am airliner in Karachi, Pakistan, killing 17 and injuring over 150 (1986); attacking synagogue worshipers in Istanbul, killing 22 (1987); detonating a car bomb in Nicosia, Cyprus, near the Israeli Embassy, killing 3 and injuring 17 (1988); killing 8—mostly British citizens—and wounding 21, in an attack on the Acropol Hotel and the Sudan Club in Khartoum (1988). See also TERRORISM.

ADEN Town and harbor at the western end of the south coast of the Arabian peninsula. Acquired by BRITAIN in 1839 and developed as a coaling and supply station for ships, Aden was administered by the government of Bombay province until 1932, the government of India 1923–1937, and as a separate Crown Colony from 1937. In 1963 Aden joined the short-lived Federation of South Arabia as one of its member-states and its Governor's title was changed to High Commissioner. In 1967, when the Federation was transformed into the independent People's Republic of SOUTH YEMEN, Aden became part of the new state and served as its capital until 1990. With the unification of South Yemen and YEMEN, Aden kept her central place in Yemen's economy due to its refinery, port facilities, and continuous contact with international trade. (With the transfer of all government functions to San'a in Yemen in the united country). In 1994 Aden was the center of South Yemeni fighting in an attempt to re-establish independence. The Northern army bombed Aden during the fighting causing many casualties. In spite of the North's victory, Aden has continued to occupy its traditional position in Yemeni economy.

Aden colony had an area of 75 sq. miles (194 sq. km.) and occupied two peninsulas around a natural bay—Aden on the eastern side, "Little Aden" on the western side, and Sheikh Uthman at the head of the bay; there, and farther inland on territory of the sheikhdom of Aqrabi, a new town—*al-Ittihad* (Union), renamed Madinat al-Sha'b (People's Town) in 1967—was built as the capital of the South Arabian Federation and later of South Yemen. Aden harbor—a free port since 1850—became, after the opening of the SUEZ CANAL, one of the busiest ports of the world (with over 6,200 ships per annum docking in the mid-1960s), until its decline in the late 1960s. An OIL refinery was built in 1952–1954 by the Anglo-Iranian Oil Company and later expanded; by the late 1970s its capacity reached 8 million tons per annum. Aden also served as a principal British air and naval base until 1967.

Aden was a small fishing village in 1839. The bunkering station and British base, and later the oil refinery and the growing trading center, caused an increasing influx from the tribal hinterland, Yemen and other countries. Aden's population grew to 47,000 in the 1940s, over 200,000 in the 1950s, roughly 340,000 in the mid 1980s, and 562,000 in 1995. Aden hosted a small Jewish community of approximately 1,000—mainly of Yemenite JEWS, most of whom had left by 1967, after anti-Jewish disturbances and the British evacuation. The urban population of Aden town provided the main growing ground for the national feeling and political movements of the late 1950s and the 1960s that led to the creation of independent South Yemen.

In the hinterland of Aden, petty sultans, sheikhs and emirs were gradually brought under British protection during the nineteenth and twentieth centuries, and became known as the "Western" and "Eastern" Aden Protectorates—most of which joined the Federation of South Arabia. All of them were absorbed in 1967 in the People's Republic of South Yemen.

Aden colony and Protectorate also included the Red Sea islands of QAMARAN and Perim, as well as Socotra and the Kuria Muria islands in the Arabian sea. Qamaran went to Yemen; Perim and Socotra—to South Yemen; Kuria Muria—to OMAN (see also SOUTH YEMEN).

AFLAQ, MICHEL (1910–1989) Syrian thinker and politician, co-founder (with Salah al-Din al-

Bitar) and chief ideologist of the BA'TH Party. Born in Damascus, a GREEK ORTHODOX Christian, Aflaq studied in Paris and was close to the COMMUNIST PARTY. In the late 1930s he consolidated his own brand of revolutionary Arab nationalism, stressing the aim of immediate all-Arab unity. In the 1940s he organized, together with Salah al-Din al-Bitar (1912–1980), who was a SUNNI-Muslim, a group of like-minded students and young intellectuals as the Arab Renaissance Party (*hizb al-ba'th al-'arabi*). The party first appeared on the political scene in the Syrian elections of 1947: Aflaq stood as a candidate, but failed. In 1949 he served briefly as Minister of Education (in Hashem al-ATASSI's government, following the Sami Hinawi coup), but was again defeated when he stood for Parliament. He remained Secretary-General of the *Ba'th* Party when it merged, in 1953, with Akram Hourani's Arab Socialist Party, to create the Arab Renaissance Socialist Party (*hizb al-ba'th al-'arabi al-ishtiraki*) which became a major actor in SYRIA's domestic politics. In 1959 Aflaq formulated the party's doctrine in his book entitled "For the Cause of the Ba'th" (*fi sabil al-ba'th*) which, like most of the *Ba'th* political thought, was markedly utopian and lacked a clear political program. Aflaq played a key role in pushing Syria to a unity of merger with EGYPT in February 1958 under the UNITED ARAB REPUBLIC, assuming that this unity would enhance his party's stance in Syria. When his hopes had been frustrated, however, he led the party, as of mid-1959, to oppose ABDEL NASSER's centralized domination of Syria, which came to an end following the latter's coup and cessation in September 1961. In the factional struggles that split the party after it came to power through the coup of March 1963, Aflaq sided (together with Bitar) with the "civilian wing," considered more moderate, serving occasionally in the government and retaining his moral stature as the founding father of the regime's declared ideology, though the real power had been increasingly shifting in favor of the military. In February 1966, a new military coup brought to power a new brand of militant Ba'thism, bringing to an end the era of Aflaq and Bitar who found refuge in IRAQ. Aflaq continued to lead the "National" (i.e. all-Arab) Leadership of the *Ba'th* seated in Beirut and Baghdad, which the new Syrian *Ba'th* denied, establishing its own National Leadership. In 1967, Aflaq emigrated to Brazil; but late in 1968 he went to Baghdad to resume his position of leadership. In 1970 he left Baghdad in protest against Iraq's failure to send troops against JORDAN in support of the Palestinian guerrillas; in 1974 a reconciliation was effected and he returned to Iraq. But while highly respected as an ideologist and party intellectual, Aflaq no longer retained much influence on party and state policies (determined by a junta of officer-politicians rather than by doctrine or party institutions). Aflaq died in 1989 and was buried in Iraq. Following his death, the *Ba'th* Party in Iraq announced he had secretly converted to ISLAM, an act that, if true, seems quite inconsistent with the secular nature of the *Ba'th* Party and its ideology.

AFRO-ARAB RELATIONS Relations between the Arabs and Black Africa date back to ancient history. Already in the second century C.E., long before the appearance of ISLAM, Arab traders used to sail from the Arabian peninsula to the eastern coast of Africa. Some of them settled there and mixed with the indigenous Bantu population, contributing to the creation of the Swahili community and culture along the coasts of SOMALIA, Kenya and Tanzania. Arab traders reached the Sahil (coast) region in Western Africa in the ninth century, and under their influence the spread of Islam began. Arabs were also amongst the most prominent participants in the African slave trade, and as early as the seventh century, slaves from Ethiopia could be purchased in Mecca. This trade formally continued well into the nineteenth century, and there were some vestiges of it in the twentieth century.

In modern times Egyptian President Gamal ABDEL NASSER acted to strengthen the status of EGYPT and of the Arab world in Africa, taking advantage of the fact that about one-third of the inhabitants of the African continent are Muslims. In his struggle against the West and ISRAEL, Nasser politicized Islam by establishing institutions and apparatuses for political action amongst the Muslims of Africa. In cooperation with the well-established al-AZHAR University, hundreds of teachers, preachers and IMAMS were sent to the African states in order to disseminate his political positions.

In his book *The Philosophy of Revolution*, Nasser expressed his belief that Egypt and the Arab world should take advantage of Islam for political purposes, emphasizing the need to operate in the African circle, side by side with the Islamic circle and the Arab circle.

In the 1950s and 1960s Egypt turned into the center for African underground leaders from various countries fighting against the colonial regimes, and radio messages were broadcasted from Cairo in various African languages.

Following Abdel Nasser's footsteps, Libyan President Mu'ammar al-QADHAFI has been acting since the1970s to strengthen Islam in Africa and the world, and to spread his political views against the West and Israel. *Inter alia* Qadhafi set up the "Jihad Fund," for financing the dispatch of preachers and propagandists, and the "Islamic Legion," made up of soldiers mobilized in Africa, to take part in his wars, using them primarily in his wars against Chad.

As a result of the struggle by the Arab states against Israel, and in reaction to Israel's diplomatic breakthrough into Africa as of the late 1950s, additional Arab states entered the circle of political activity in Africa. These included the Arab oil-producing states SAUDI ARABIA, KUWAIT, UNITED ARAB EMIRATES (UAE) and ALGERIA, as well as the ARAB LEAGUE and the PALESTINE LIBERATION ORGANIZATION (PLO). This enhanced activity manifested itself in the establishment of an extensive network of Arab embassies, which were engaged in political and propaganda activities, as well as the establishment of Islamic centers and the granting of financial loans and grants.

However, the main Arab political influence in Africa was exerted through the Organization of African Unity (OAU), established in 1963, nine members of which—Egypt, SUDAN, LIBYA, Algeria, TUNISIA, MOROCCO, DJIBOUTI, Somalia and MAURITANIA—are also members of the Arab League. The Arab states gradually managed to get the meetings of this organization to pass increasingly frequent and strong anti-Israeli resolutions within the Middle East context. Already before 1973 a number of black African states severed their diplomatic relations with Israel. The rest of the African states followed this line in the course of the October 1973 war (see ARAB-ISRAEL CONFLICT) in response to the OAU's resolution—adopted at Egypt's request—that called on the African states to break their diplomatic relations with Israel. Only Malawi, Swaziland and Lesotho did not act accordingly.

After the 1973 War the financial assistance promised by the Arab states to Africa became a major factor in strengthening the Arab posture in the continent. The Arab states set up multilateral and bilateral financial institutions to assist Africa, the most active of which is the Arab Bank for Economic Development in Africa. The multilateral and bilateral Arab aid to Africa reached its peak at the end of the 1970s, when the Arab pledges to the states of Black Africa reached a billion dollars per annum. About a third of these pledges were actually paid up, and in the case of several poor African states this aid was of the greatest importance. However, since the early 1980s the Arab aid has progressively decreased, both because of the plunge of oil prices and revenues of the oil-producing states, and as a result of the IRAN-IRAQ WAR; and its relative importance, compared to that provided the European states, the US and Japan, has progressively fallen.

Within the Arab political-Islamic activities, the IS-LAMIC CONFERENCE ORGANIZATION (ICO) was set up in 1969. It is an inter-governmental organization centered in Jedda in Saudi Arabia. Over the years eighteen African states have joined this organization—including states which do not have a Muslim majority such as Uganda, Cameroon and Gabon. The latter were interested in becoming members of the organization because the Islamic Development Bank (IDB), established in 1974, with its center in Jedda, provides loans and grants only to members of the ICO. The decisions in the annual meetings of this organization have consistently supported the Arab states on all issues concerning the Middle East, while publishing strongly worded condemnations of Israel. In 1981 the ICO set up an Islamic Office for the Boycott of Israel, to supplement the activities of the Central Boycott Office in Damascus (see ARAB BOYCOTT).

In order to introduce into the circle of activity in Africa additional Arab states, especially those that produce OIL but are not located on the African continent, a summit conference, meeting in Cairo in March 1977, established the Afro-Arab Organization, in which all the Arab and Black African states are members. In the course of the summit conference, the African states conditioned their agreement to set up the organization on the Arab states increasing their financial support, and Arab oil producers agreed, under pressure, to do so. Given the rise of oil prices, they undertook to grant the African states about one and a half billion dollars.

The summit conference in Cairo also agreed to set up Afro-Arab institutions in the economic, political, cultural and information spheres, and to convene a summit conference every three years. The resolutions adopted by the summit made it clear that the two sides, the Arabs and the Africans, undertook to mutually support each other. Apart from financial aid, the Arabs would support the African struggle for the independence of Zimbabwe and Namibia, and strove towards putting an end to the apartheid regime in South Africa, in return for African support for the Arab struggle, and especially the Palestinian struggle against Israel.

It should be noted that, to the present day, no other Afro-Arab summit conference has convened, especially because of differences of opinion between the Africans and Arabs, as will be described below. Nevertheless, from time to time Afro-Arab sub-committees representing attorneys, students, women, writers, etc. have met. The effect of these meetings has been primarily on the political or information levels.

In the mid-1970s the aggravating economic crisis in many Black African states due to the rising oil prices led to intensified criticism by the African states of the Arab oil-producing states for not helping their African "brethren" in their distress. The fact that the Arab states did not realize all their financial promises to Africa led to overt disappointment of many African leaders at the volume of the aid and embittered Afro-Arab relations. Indeed, the fact that investments by Arab states in Africa have been extremely limited compared to their investments in financial institutions, industry and real estate in North America and Western Europe, and the visible political strings attached to whatever aid was provided, was also a cause for growing dissatisfaction. In the course of the 1980s, Black African leaders repeatedly sounded their disappointment at the level of Afro-Arab cooperation, which did not translate into investments in agricultural and industrial projects. Another complaint was that in those Muslim states in Africa that did receive financial aid, this was invariably earmarked for the preservation of the ARABIC language and the strengthening of Islam through the construction of mosques and Islamic universities, as in the cases of Niger and Uganda. The Africans pointed out that only one percent of Arab foreign aid went to Africa.

Even after the Arab states had undertaken to increase the aid at the Afro-Arab summit conference in Cairo in 1977, the bitter criticism continued and the Arabs were chastized for failing to distinguish in their policies between "brothers and imperialists," or to give the Africans any concessions. Indeed, to many African states the use of oil as a political weapon dealt a more terrible blow than to the Western capitalists, because of the latter's economic resilience.

Repeated threats by the Arab League in the course of the 1980s, to the effect that any state that would renew its diplomatic relations with Israel would no longer receive aid from the Arabs, angered many African leaders. Thus, when Zaire re-established diplomatic relations with Israel in 1982, the Arab states broke off their diplomatic relations with it and stopped all aid. In reaction, the President of Zaire said that the Arab states had not been liberated from the mentality of treating the Black Africans as slaves, required to abide by the commands of their masters.

The insufficient Arab aid was only one of the issues that soured Afro-Arab relations. Other issues were: the memory of the Arab role in the slave trade, which has been brought up from time to time by African leaders and intellectuals, especially in times of political or economic dispute; and the ethnic difference between the "white" North African states and Black Africa, south of the Sahara (several African states even proposed setting up a Black Africa League, as a separate entity from the OAU, in which only Black African states would participate). Domestic and inter-state disputes also added to the bitterness marking Afro-Arab relations: the continuing war in Southern Sudan, and its objection to the Islamization and Arabization policies conducted by the North; the objection of most of the African states to Morocco's control over the WESTERN SAHARA and its support of the POLISARIO, for which the membership of Morocco in the OAU was suspended; and the objection of many states in Africa to the militant Islamic and political activity of several Arab states, especially Libya. In the course of the 1970s and 1980s, about twenty African states broke off their diplomatic relations with Libya or expelled Libyan diplomats. These included Senegal, Mali, Ghana, Nigeria, Kenya and Uganda. In 1991 Zambia closed the embassies of Iraq and Iran in its capital, accusing them of sabotage and militant Islamic activities. In general, the African states have started looking

upon the Islamic activities of the Arab states amongst the Muslims in their countries with suspicion, and have tried to limit this activity for fear of an extreme Muslim awakening.

Nevertheless, it should be noted that the Afro-Arab differences of opinion remained for a long period "inside the Afro-Arab family". Thus, during this period they did not have any effect on the attitude of the African states towards Israel, and did not lead to the renewal of relations with it. A change started to manifest itself only in 1982, nine years after relations with Israel had been broken off, and this, to a large extent was a result of the signing of the Egyptian-Israeli peace treaty (see ARAB-ISRAEL PEACE-MAKING) and the completion of the Israeli withdrawal from the SINAI. Zaire was the first Black African state to renew its relations with Israel in that year against this background, and it was followed by additional African states, including Cameroon, Ethiopia, the Ivory Coast and Liberia.

Developments in the Middle East, especially the signing of the Declaration of Principles between Israel and the PLO in September 1993 and the Jordanian-Israeli peace treaty in October 1994 (see ARAB-ISRAEL PEACEMAKING), further affected the states of Black Africa, most of which—with the exception of Chad, Guinea and Mali—established relations with Israel, including states whose population is mostly Muslim, such as Senegal, Gambia and in November 1996, Niger. All this happened despite the obstinate objection of the Arab states which viewed it as a blow to Afro-Arab unity and the resolutions of the OAU, and argued that as long as the Palestinian problem has not been resolved and Israel has not withdrawn from all the occupied territories, relations should not be renewed.

Despite the renewal of relations between the Black African states and Israel, the influence of the Arabs in the OAU is still strong, and the resolutions of the organization continue to support the Arab line on all Middle East issues. Thus, the OAU conference, which convened in 1996 in Cameroon, emphasized the importance of "Afro-Arab solidarity". The main difference in recent years in the resolutions of the OAU has been that on the basis of the recommendation of some of the more moderate African states, such as Kenya, the Ivory Coast and Cameroon, some of the more extreme condemnations of Israel have been removed from these resolutions, and more moderate ones have replaced them. However, support for the Arab positions on such issues as the Middle East, JERUSALEM and the Palestinians, remains. The situation is similar in the UN where the African bloc continues to support the Arabs on most of the resolutions regarding the Middle East.

AHMADIYYA

AHMADIYYA   A religious community derived from ISLAM, founded by Mirza Ghulam Ahmad of Qadian, India (1835–1908), who claimed to be a manifestation of Krishna, Jesus (who, according to him, died in India), Muhammad and all the prophets, and the MAHDI of Islam. After the death of his successor (*khalifa*), Hakim Nur al-Din, in 1914, the Ahmadiyya split into two main groups. The main faction, also called Qadiani, has its center in Rabwah, Pakistan, and branches in many countries, especially in India, Pakistan and West Africa. It engages in vigorous missionary activity. This group considers Mirza Ghulam Ahmad as the "Seal of the Prophets", i.e. the last prophet—a title usually accorded to Muhammad. The smaller faction, the Lahoris, centered in Lahore, Pakistan, and also active in missionary work, is closer to orthodox Islam and regards the founder as an innovative Islamic thinker rather than a prophet.

The Ahmadiyya claim to be the true community of Islam. They believe in the Qur'an—translated to English by one of their leaders, Muhammad Ali (d. 1951)—and the basic tenets and commandments of Islam (interpreting *jihad*—as do some orthodox Muslims—as "effort" for the sake of Islam rather than as "holy war". Muslim leaders generally denounce the Ahmadiyya and regard them as infidels, outside Islam. There have been instances of persecution and pogroms—e.g. in Pakistan in 1953 and again in 1974. Their activities have been banned and their institutions closed in SYRIA (1958), Uganda (1975) and Pakistan (1974)—though their community continues to exist. Estimates of the number of Ahmadiyya vary between 1 million and 5 million; the Ahmadiyya themselves claim to number 10 or even 20 million (4–5 million in Pakistan alone).

AJMAN

AJMAN   The smallest of the seven sheikhdoms of the TRUCIAL COAST (Trucial Oman) forming, since 1971, the UNITED ARAB EMIRATES (UAE). Its area is 97 sq. miles (250 sq.km.). Ajman's populace is mostly nomadic. Some are engaged in fishing. There were less than 5,000 inhabitants until the 1960s. The estimate is now approximately 120,000. The ruler belongs to the al-Nu'aimi family.

Since the nineteenth century, Ajman was under British protection. An OIL exploration concession granted in 1962 to a small American company expired in 1967. In 1970 a new concession was granted to the American Occidental Company. So far no oil strikes have been reported. To compensate for the lack of oil revenues, Ajman has developed a port and free zone adjacent to it. Ajman has also launched an ambitious development plan that will render it, in the early twenty-first century, the largest cattle growing center in the Gulf as well as a center of new industrial plants.

ALAWIS, ALAWITES

ALAWIS, ALAWITES   (Arabic: followers of Ali, the fourth CALIPH). An Islamic sect located in the north-western mountains of SYRIA. An offshoot of the Twelver SHI'A, the Alawis adhere to the idea that Imam Ali, the Prophet's cousin and son-in-law, was the sole legitimate heir who was deprived of his divine right to inherit Muhammad. The term Alawis evolved during the French Mandate, replacing the earlier term Nusseiris. In their religious bases the Alawis follow the Shi'a. Some elements of the Alawi religious concept apparently derived from the ISMA'ILIYYA version of the Shi'a although their rituals include Christian and Zoroastrian festivities as well. Little is known of their origin. Some view the Alawis as descendants of an ancient Canaanite people who, surviving in the isolated mountains of Syria, were only marginally influenced by Christianity and ISLAM and retained many pagan Syrian customs. They adopted the ARABIC language and the Islamic faith, in its Isma'ili version, in the Middle Ages. They then became a separate sect. Parts of their tenets are secret, known only to the initiates. They reportedly believe in a holy trinity of Ali, the Prophet Muhammad and Salman al-Farisi i.e., the Persian—one of the Companions (SAHABA) of the Prophet. Some Muslims regard them as marginal to, on the fringes of or even outside of, Islam. In Syria, however, they are generally regarded, for purposes of personal status jurisdiction, as Shi'i Muslims; their recognition as Muslims is at least implied in the fact that the Head of State—who must, according to the Constitution be a Muslim—is since 1971 an Alawi, Hafez al-ASAD (some SUNNI Muslim protests were voiced against his election). An addition to this recognition of the Alawis as Shi'i Muslims came in 1973, when the Lebanese Shi'i leader Mussa al-SADR recognized the Alawis in LEBANON (and as a consequence, the Alawis in Syria) as Shi'is, but this still does not prevent some Sunni-Muslims from regarding the Alawis as heretics.

Most of the Alawis—approximately seventy-five percent—live in Syria, while the rest are mainly in the ALEXANDRETTA (Hatay) and Cilicia regions of southern TURKEY, and some in northern Lebanon. In Syria, the Alawis are the largest minority group, between ten and twelve percent of the total population, over 1.5 million. Most of them live in mountain villages in the Ladhiqiyya district, on the north-western coast, also known as the Alawis region or the Mountain of the Nusseiris. They comprise approximately two-thirds of the district's population, though they are a minority in its capital, Ladhiqiyya.

Under Ottoman rule the Alawis enjoyed a measure of local autonomy. However, in the mid-nineteenth century, the Ottoman government began tightening its control (e.g., Alawis were now tried in Muslim-Sunni courts). When FRANCE established its Mandate in Syria, in 1920–1922, the Alawis region was recognized as an autonomous territory under a French governor, and the French endeavored to advance the Alawis economically and culturally. In 1936, the Alawi state became part of Syria, with partial autonomy. This special autonomous status ended with the departure of the French, in 1944–1946, and fulfillment of Syrian independence, arousing an Alawi revolt which was harshly suppressed.

Since the early 1960s, the Alawis constituted a disproportionately large group, serving in the officers' corps and high command of the Syrian military forces. This was partly due to French efforts to enlist members of the minorities to the "Special Forces" (*Troupes Spéciales*) they established. Many Alawis saw a military career as a way to social and economic mobility. Since the 1950s many Alawi officers joined the BA'TH Party and its cells in the officers' corps, as they were attracted by the party's emphasis on supra-national-secular values. When the *Ba'th* officers seized power in 1963, more Alawis joined. Since the mid-1960s, Alawi officers were salient in Syria's political and military echelons e.g., Salah JADID, Asad (President since 1971), Ibrahim Makhus, Ali Douba, Ali Haidar, Adnan Makhluf and Muhammad al-Khuli—

to a degree that many speak of Syria's "Alawi regime" or "Alawi rulers". Yet, the Alawis remain, economically and culturally, Syria's most backward community.

In northern Lebanon, Alawis form the backbone of the faction supporting Syria to the hilt. During the Civil War (1975–1990) they frequently fought Muslim-Sunni fundamentalist groups in Tripoli. Since 1992 they have been in the Lebanese Parliament (two seats), perhaps as a consequence of Syria's dominant position in this country. In Turkey, on the other hand, Alawis do not display strong communal cohesion or aspirations (non-Alawi Shi'i-Muslims are generally called ALEVI).

ALEVI Turkish for followers of Ali, the cousin and son-in-law of the Prophet Muhammad, and the fourth Muslim CALIPH. Alevi is the name given to an important sect in TURKEY. Exact statistics are lacking and estimates range between seven and thirty percent of the largely SUNNI population of Turkey. Members of the Alevi sect (distinct from the largely Syrian ALAWIS, as well as from the mainstream SHI'A) were, in the past, concentrated especially in the central and eastern parts of Anatolia. Today, due to migration, they can be found in all parts of the country. They are predominantly ethnic Turks, though KURDS and Arabs are also found amongst them, and in socio-economic terms, they are often of the lower social strata. They originate from some of the early Turkish tribes who settled Anatolia in the late Middle Ages and were susceptible to strong Shi'a and Sufi (mystical) influences. Their beliefs are accordingly a mixture of both, with their own unique set of principles and rites, and they are widely regarded as lax in terms of strict religious observance. Denounced by the Sunni establishment and often persecuted by the Ottoman authorities, they were accustomed to keep their beliefs secret (*taqiyya*).

With the establishment of the Turkish Republic, the Shi'is largely became adherents of secularism and supporters of the progressive Kemalist ideology, and in more recent times supported the Turkish leftist parties. A leftist and largely Alevi party, called the Turkey Unity Party, led by Mustafa Timisi, was formed in 1973, but it did not succeed in growing into a strong mass party. With the growth of social tensions in the country and the impact of Islamic fundamentalism in recent years, relations between the

Alevis and conservative or ultra-nationalist Sunnis greatly deteriorated. Beginning in the late 1970s, several riots erupted between them in various cities, adding to the already serious breakdown in law and order in the country. The worst incident took place in Kahramanmaras in December 1978, resulting in the killing of over 100 people. There were also bloody riots in Çorum in June 1980, claiming 30 victims. The September 1980 military coup for the most part cracked down on anarchy, but incidents between Alevis and Sunnis continued to erupt from time to time, demonstrating the persistence of the deep-rooted tensions between the two communities.

ALEXANDRETTA Province (in Turkish: Hatay) and port (in Turkish: Iskenderun) in South Turkey, at the head of the eastern Mediterranean Bay of Alexandretta. The area was included, as a district with special status *sanjaq*), in French-mandated SYRIA, 1921, and handed to TURKEY in 1939, after a protracted crisis. The Alexandretta district, under Syria, had an area of 1,814 sq. miles (4,704 sq. km.) and a population (in the late 1930s) of approximately 220,000, with about 30,000 in Alexandretta town. Of this population, forty percent were Turks, according to French estimates, while Turkey claimed a Turkish majority.

In the Franklin-Bouillon Agreement of 1921 that fixed the Syrian Turkish border, Alexandretta was allotted to the "State of Aleppo" within French-mandated Syria, as a district with a special regime and whose official language was Turkish. When, in 1924, the "State of Aleppo" merged with the "State of Damascus" into Syria, that special regime was retained. In 1936, when a Franco-Syrian treaty was negotiated providing for Syrian independence, Turkey opposed the inclusion of Alexandretta in an independent Syria, claiming she had ceded it to the French Mandate only, and demanded separate statehood for it, while FRANCE and Syria insisted on its retention by Syria. The dispute was raised at the League of Nations which decided in 1937 on a compromise: Alexandretta would form a separate entity, independent in internal affairs and with its own constitution, linked to Syria concerning currency, customs and foreign affairs only; ARABIC and Turkish would both be official languages, and Turkey would enjoy special rights in Alexandretta port; and no military bases or fortifications were to be constructed.

Attempts to implement this formula led to unrest and violence between Turks and Arabs in the district. While France, preoccupied with the mounting European crisis and eager to retain Turkish friendship, was a weak defender of Syria's position, Turkey acted systematically and forcefully to gain control of Alexandretta. Turkish armed forces entered the district in 1938. Under Turkish pressure an electoral law was passed that gave the Turkish inhabitants a majority in the House of Representatives. Turks were elected President and Premier of an all-Turkish government. Turkey abrogated her acceptance of the League of Nations' supervision. The district was given an official Turkish name, Hatay, linked to the Turkish currency and postal services, and subjected to Turkish law. In June 1939 France ceded the district to Turkey.

Turkey's annexation of Alexandretta caused an outcry in Syria; demonstrations against Turkey and France demanded the return of the territory, but to no avail. Syria has never recognized Turkey's possession of the district—its maps include Alexandretta within Syrian territory—and from time to time it demands its return. Usually, however, the dispute is dormant; it has not prevented Syria from establishing and maintaining normal relations with Turkey (implying, at least, a de facto acceptance of Turkey's territory and borders). The other Arab states, too, while verbally and in principle supporting Syria's claim, are usually silent and keep the dispute dormant.

ALGERIA (Arabic: *al-jaza'ir*, the islands) A republic on the southern coast of the western Mediterranean, over four-fifths of it in the western Sahara Desert. Most of the population is SUNNI-Muslim of the Maliki school, and the majority speak ARABIC, which is the official language. The remainder, mainly in the Kabylia highlands, speak Berber. (Those with Berber as their mother-tongue are estimated at 4–6 million; the number of those still conscious of BERBER descent is difficult to evaluate: estimates run from twenty-five to fifty percent, i.e., 5-10 million). Its capital is Algiers with 1,483,000 residents (1987 estimate).

Pre-Independence History

Until its conquest in 1830 Algeria's coastal plain was nominally part of the OTTOMAN EMPIRE. Local rebellions against the French were widespread—the most important, led by the Berber chieftain Abdel Qader (1807–1883), was finally suppressed in 1847; Abdel Qader was exiled to Damascus. He is regarded as a national hero and the father of Algerian nationalism.

Outbreaks of militant opposition to the French continued throughout the nineteenth century and reduced the Muslim population—according to some estimates by some 3 million. French and European colonists settled on Algeria's fertile lands, which were often confiscated or bought for them, occupying 6 million acres between the two world wars, or twenty-five to thirty percent of all cultivated land, including most of the best lands. French settlers also became dominant in trade, finance and industry. On the eve of World War I, French and European inhabitants numbered about 800,000—against a local Muslim population of 4.5–5 million.

Algeria was administered as part of FRANCE, but French citizenship was not granted to the local population—non-French in language, culture and ethnicity. An exception was made for the Jewish community which received French citizenship in 1870 under a decree of Justice Minister Adolphe Crémieux. Algeria's Muslims could obtain French citizenship on certain conditions, including defined educational levels and the renunciation of their status under Muslim personal laws; very few made use of that right. Representative bodies established in Algeria were limited to French citizens, and their powers were advisory.

In the twentieth century, the gap between the French and the local population widened. A growing group of Muslims who studied abroad and came in contact with European politics and Arab nationalism, started to politicize their grievances. In 1924 Hajj Ahmad Messali (Messali Hajj) founded a nationalist society in Paris, the "North African Star," and a leftist newspaper. The society's links with the Communists were severed in 1927 and Messali developed traditional Muslim tendencies. The French banned the society in 1929 and Messali was imprisoned several times. In 1933 he co-sponsored a congress which called for the independence of Algeria; in 1937 he founded the "Parti Populaire Algerien (PPA). Islamic circles were also active in nationalist politics, and in 1931 they founded a Society of (Religious) Scholars (jam'iyyat al-'ulama') which combined Muslim revival with Arab-Algerian nationalism. These early nationalist attempts had only a limited influence on the Muslim population.

The victory of the Popular Front in France in 1936 brought some hope for an integration with France on a basis of equality. But the Blum-Violette Plan for full citizenship for a growing number of Algerians was dropped due to the opposition of the French right-wing and the French settlers in Algeria.

World War II put a temporary halt to nationalist activities. The Vichy regime was hostile to Algerian nationalist sentiments. Antisemitism, however, was common to both groups. Anti-Jewish legislation of the Vichy administration and the cancellation of the 1870 Crémieux Decree in October 1940 were supported by the Muslims. (The Crémieux Decree was re-enacted in October 1943 after the Allies' takeover.)

Following the Allied Forces' landing in Algeria in November 1942, nationalist activity resumed. In December 1942 a group headed by Ferhat Abbas called for the establishment of an Algerian constituent assembly elected by all the population, as well as full equality for the Muslims. In a "National Manifesto," published in May 1943, the group demanded the creation of an Algerian state.

The Free French administration in Algeria rejected all these demands but tried to calm Muslim discontent with reforms. A statute of March 1944 granted some 60,000 Muslims the right to acquire French citizenship and take part in French elections, but only 32,000 Muslims registered. The Muslim share of seats in the mixed regional and municipal councils was set at forty percent. Abbas now founded a party, *Amis du Manifeste de la Libération* (AML), calling for the foundation of an autonomous Algerian republic, federally linked to France. The AML, supported mainly by middle-class Muslims, was banned in mid-1945. Abbas was arrested following the brutal suppression of riots at Setif in May 1945, which claimed the lives of many Muslims (an estimated 1,000–15,000 or more). In March 1946 Abbas was released and he established the *Union Démocratique du Manifeste Algérien* (UDMA), calling for the establishment of an autonomous, secular Algerian state within the French Union. Messali, who had returned to politics in 1944, set up the *Mouvement pour le Triomphe des Libertés Démocratique* (MTLD), which called for the creation of a separate Algeria and the evacuation of French troops.

A new constitution in September 1947 provided French citizenship and the right to vote to all, and recognized Arabic as an official language. It set up an Algerian Assembly divided into two "colleges" of sixty members each, one representing 1.5 million French citizens (including 60,000–70,000 Muslims), the other representing the rest of the population (some 9 million Muslims). A Governing Council was also established, composed of representatives of both colleges and nominated members.

The new constitution did not satisfy the nationalists, who by now aspired to independence. They gained a majority in the second college in the October 1947 municipal elections, but failed in the April 1948 elections for the Algerian Assembly: the MTLD won nine seats, the UDMA eight. The nationalists claimed that the French administration had rigged the elections.

Many nationalists despaired of achieving their aims through political-constitutional means. In 1947 younger members of the MTLD formed an *Organisation Secrète* (OS), which built up a network of cells throughout Algeria in preparation for an armed insurrection, and in 1949 launched an attack on Oran. In 1950 most of the OS leaders were arrested. A nucleus, however, survived in the Kabyla region, renowned as a stronghold for dissident activities. Among its leaders were Ahmad BEN BELLA, Hussein Ait-Ahmad, Muhammad Khidr and Belkacem Krim.

The establishment of the OS marked the growing split between traditional leaders represented by Messali Hadj and more militant younger nationalists. In March 1953 nine former OS members established a *Conseil Révolutionnaire pour l'Unité et l'Action* (CRUA), which advocated armed revolt. EGYPT had a profound influence on the CRUA and Cairo became the center of Algerian underground activities.

The revolt was launched on 1 November 1954 by the FRONT DE LIBÉRATION NATIONALE (FLN) formed from the CRUA. The MTLD failed in its attempt to form a military organization of its own (*Mouvement National Algérien*,—MNA), and most of the nationalist groups merged with the FLN. The FLN was headed by a nine-man command (among them Ben Bella, Rabah Bitat, Khidr, Muhammad Boudiaf, Hocine (Hussein) Ait-Ahmad and Belkacem Krim), and revolutionary Algeria was divided into six regions (*wilaya*), each headed by a military commander. The revolt, which started in the Aurès region, en-

gulfed all the settled areas of Algeria by the end of 1956.

As the rebellion progressed, a rift developed between the FLN leaders in Cairo and the command in the field. In August 1956 the FLN held a congress in the Soummam Valley in Kabylia, which formed a coordinating committee, composed mainly of the commanders of the six military regions, and a *Conseil National de la Révolution Algérienne* (CNRA) as a representative body of all the nationalist groups. Two-thirds of the CNRA members were to be from inside Algeria. The congress also drew up a socialist program for the future of Algeria.

The French tried to quell the revolt by force and also pressured Egypt to stop supporting it. France also tried to step up the political integration of Algeria, coupled with socio-economic reforms. But the bloody revolt, fought mercilessly by both sides, continued. In October 1956 five FLN leaders on their way from MOROCCO to TUNISIA were kidnapped to Algeria by their French pilot and arrested; they included Ben Bella, Khidr, Ait-Ahmad and Boudiaf (Rabah Bitat had been caught earlier).

The growing radicalism of the FLN caused a backlash from the Army and the French settlers. In May 1958 Army officers and settlers rebelled, bringing about the collapse of the French Fourth Republic and the return to power of General de Gaulle in the hope that he would enforce the complete integration of Algeria into France. At first, de Gaulle stepped up military operations against the FLN. But, realizing the strength of Algerian nationalism, he began moving toward accepting Algerian independence.

The FLN, while stepping up its operations, in September 1958 set up a *Gouvernement Provisionnel de la République Algérienne* (GPRA) in Tunis, headed by Ferhat Abbas (replaced in August 1961 by Ben Youssef Ben Khedda).

Since 1955 the Algerian problem was debated each year in the UN. No solution acceptable to both sides was reached, but the continued debate put much pressure on France and encouraged the rebels. In late 1958 de Gaulle ordered the release of the interned FLN leaders into house arrest in France. A new election law granted the Algerian Muslims a decisive majority among the deputies to be elected to the French National Assembly (forty-eight, against twenty-one Europeans). French proposals for ceasefire negotiations were rejected by the FLN leaders, who insisted on full discussion of Algeria's self-determination.

During 1959 de Gaulle realized that the policy of integration was futile. In September 1959 he offered the Algerian people a cease-fire and self-determination in the form of a referendum to decide on one of three solutions: full integration with France, autonomy within the French community, or independence with no links to France. The FLN government accepted it in principle, while the French colonists and right-wing rejected this proposal. In January 1960 the colonists in Algeria rebelled, but were suppressed within nine days. In January 1961 a referendum was held on de Gaulle's policy in Algeria, but following an FLN call to boycott the referendum, only fifty-eight percent of the electorate in Algeria participated, sixty-nine percent of whom supported de Gaulle.

Secret talks on self-determination were renewed in February. At first the negotiations failed, as the FLN insisted it would discuss future relations with France only after the referendum, and stop fighting only after an agreement on FLN demands. Right-wing elements within the Army and the colonists in Algeria had, in early 1961, formed an *Organisation Armée Secrète* (OAS) to resist a negotiated settlement and the transfer of power to Algerians. On 24 April 1961 four generals—Challe, Zeller, Jouhaud and Salan—staged an army coup in Algiers, but failed as most officers remained loyal to de Gaulle. Following the abortive Evian talks, both the FLN and the Army stepped up their operations, to which were added OAS attacks against local Muslims.

Negotiations with the FLN were resumed in October 1961. They concluded in Evian on 18 March 1962 with a cease-fire agreement and a declaration of future policy providing for the establishment of an independent Algeria after a transitional period. Rights of French citizens were safeguarded. France was to retain a naval base in Mers el-Kebir for fifteen years and nuclear testing grounds in the Sahara for five years. The cease-fire came into force the same day, and Ben Bella and his colleagues were released. A provisional government was established, headed by Abdel Rahman Fares, who remained in Paris until July. The OAS made a last attempt to foil these developments by implementing a "scorched earth" policy. Its commander, General Salan, was captured on 20 April. Following renewed FLN violence and

reprisals, some 200,000 Europeans and most of the Jewish community left Algeria for France. After secret negotiations with the FLN, the OAS decided on 17 June to end its resistance. In the referendum, on 1 July 1962, 99.7% voted for independence, and de Gaulle proclaimed Algeria independent on 3 July. The new state was admitted to the ARAB LEAGUE in August, and to the UN in October.

Independent Algeria

Domestic Affairs: The long war of independence claimed the lives of 300,000–500,000 Algerian Muslims, many of them killed by the FLN itself in internal purges and in punitive and terrorist actions against citizens suspected of collaborating with the French authorities. In addition, of close to a quarter of a million of recognized Muslim French collaborators known as the *Arki*, only 15,000 managed to find refuge in France, where they have been condemned to live in poverty and humiliating seclusion. A large part of the remainder, some 30,000–150,000, were executed or slaughtered shortly after the agreement on independence was reached, and even before the French troops withdrew. The lengthy war and the staggering number of casualties it claimed from the Algerian people became a central ethos and a national unifying memory for independent Algeria. Despite the different versions about the real price of the war for the Algerians, the FLN government adopted the legendary number of one million losses as a nation building symbol.

With independence splits, within the nationalist leadership became more evident between the FLN's GPRA and the Fares government established under the Evian Agreement, between various factions and between the politicians and the military commanders. The latter, in turn, were split between those entering Algeria from Morocco and Tunisia, commanded by Houari BOUMÉDIENNE, and the guerrilla leaders inside Algeria. Ben Bella and Khidr advocated Nasserist, leftist, anti-Western policies, while Boudiaf, Ait-Ahmad and Belkacem Krim were more moderate. The guerrilla formations inside Algeria were virtually independent of each other and, therefore, politically weak. Ben Bella and his followers were identified with the Army outside Algeria, while Krim, Boudiaf and Ait-Ahmad with the guerrillas inside. In June 1962, shortly before the declaration of independence, the wider Revolutionary Council (CNRA), which was convened by Ben Bella in Tripoli, proclaimed the "Tripoli Programme," which adopted a socialist platform and a neutralist anti-colonialist foreign policy. The FLN Politbureau was to be superior to the government. Following the declaration of independence, authority was divided between three bodies: the official Provisional government, headed by Fares; that of the FLN, headed by Ben Khedda; and the Politbureau of Ben Bella. In August 1962 Ben Bella and the Politbureau took governmental powers, with Ben Khedda's acquiescence, while the Fares government was eclipsed. Boumédienne and the "outside" forces, with Ben Bella's support, won against the "inside" guerrillas by a compromise which in fact established Ben Bella's primacy.

Elections were held on 20 September 1962. The FLN, all loyal to Ben Bella, listed 180 candidates, and made sure no rival list would challenge it; some ninety-nine percent voted in favor of this list. On 25 September, the Assembly was opened, and Ferhat Abbas became its President; the GPRA ceased to exist and Ben Bella became Prime Minister, with Boumédienne as Minister of Defense. In November 1962 the government banned Messali Hajj's PPA, the COMMUNIST PARTY, and Boudiaf and Ait-Ahmad's "Socialist Party". Ben Bella further consolidated his rule in April 1963 by taking the position of FLN Secretary-General. In August 1963 the National Assembly adopted a Presidential constitution, with a single party (the FLN), which was endorsed in a referendum in September. That same month Ben Bella, as the only candidate, was elected President retaining the Premiership. His main opponents inside the FLN had by now resigned their seats and positions, amongst them Khidr, Ferhat Abbas and Rabah Bitat. Resistance in the Kabylia mountains turned, in mid-1964, into armed rebellion. However, Ben Bella succeeded in dividing his rivals, wooing some to his side and capturing others. Boudiaf, Khidr and Ait-Ahmad were formally expelled from the FLN, the two former joined Belkacem Krim in exile; Ait-Ahmad was captured but released in spring 1965.

On 19 June 1965 Ben Bella was deposed by Boumédienne in a bloodless coup. Supreme authority passed to a twenty-six-member Revolutionary Council headed by Boumédienne. A Government was formed on 20 July, with Boumédienne as Prime Minister and Minister of Defense, and de facto President. The Army, under his control, remained the dominant center of power. Several opposition organizations were set up in exile in Europe. Their influence on Algerian politics was negligible, but a number of their leaders were assassinated, most likely by the regime's agents, including Khidr (1967) and Krim (1970). Several coup attempts in 1967–1968 failed, as most officers remained loyal to Boumédienne.

Boumédienne's regime was based on a technocratic-military alliance pursuing a socialist policy. During the 1970s he launched an ambitious industrialization project under government control based on growing revenues from the petroleum and gas reserves. It was accompanied with the redistribution of private estates and the nationalization of food distribution, which met considerable resistance. Students were involved in these conflicts, which in 1975 erupted into violent clashes at the Algiers University (with the speed and depth of "Arabization" of studies as another issue of conflict). The nationalization of foreign enterprises that had begun under Ben Bella continued.

In June 1976 a new National Charter, drafted by the FLN leadership and by a National Conference, was approved in a referendum, and in November a new constitution was endorsed (with no basic change from the one of 1963). In December 1976 Boumédienne was re-elected President (as single candidate).

On 27 December 1978 Boumédienne died. Within the FLN leadership, two men were seen as the chief candidates for succession: Foreign Minister Abdel Aziz Bouteflika, regarded as a moderate, and Muhammad Salah Yahyawi, the administrative head of the FLN, a more radical socialist. Yet the one finally chosen as President in February 1979 was Colonel Chadli BEN JEDID, the commander of the Oran military district. Ben Jedid's administration was less centralized then Boumédienne's, and constitutional changes adopted by the National Assembly by mid-1979 made the appointment of a Prime Minister obligatory. The new regime was lenient on the opposition and many political prisoners were released, including Ben Bella, who went into exile in October 1980. In 1980 the President's control over the FLN was strengthened. The Politbureau was reduced from twenty-one to seven members, all selected by the President as FLN Secretary-General. Many former leaders were dropped from prominent positions in the FLN and replaced by the President's men.

In elections in March 1982 the single list was still FLN-vetted, but only fifty-five of the 281 assembly members were said to be FLN activists. President Ben Jedid was re-elected in January 1984. Among the issues in dispute in the early 1980s was the intensifying effort for "Arabization" in all spheres of public life. At the same time Berber demands, centered in the Kabylia region, to allow a cultivation of Berber language and culture also intensified.

Gross economic mismanagement, widespread corruption and declining oil prices since 1982 caused heavy losses to Algeria's industries by the mid-1980s, leaving the country with staggering national debt, frequent food shortages and rising agricultural prices. Rapid population growth and the economic stagnation led to growing unemployment (estimated at thirty percent among the youth). Ben Jedid opted for economic liberalization. A new National Charter, adopted by an FLN congress in December 1985 and endorsed by a referendum in January 1986, emphasized agriculture and small industry, and recommended the dismantling of state-run giant conglomerates. It also sought to link Algeria's socialism to ISLAM and turned away from Marxist doctrines.

The crisis and economic liberalization widened the social disparities between the privileged elites, who used the socialist system to their advantage, and the masses, eroding support for the regime and for the FLN whose "revolutionary past" no longer appealed to the impoverished youth.

This growing disillusionment was reflected in the revival of Islamic groupings outside the authorized state structure since the mid-1970s, which called for an Islamic state ruled by the SHARI'A. A radical trend, led by Mustafa Bouyali, an ex-FLN fighter, attempted an armed insurrection in the countryside during 1984–1987. The regime crushed the group and arrested hundreds of Islamic activists.

Austerity measures adopted by Ben Jedid in 1988 destroyed the unwritten social contract in Algeria, ensuring the people's political submissiveness in return for social welfare and economic security, and precipitated mass riots in October 1988. The military suppression of the riots (which caused approximately 500 deaths), prompted Ben Jedid to implement political reforms in order to restore the regime's legitimacy, and enhance his own authority by weakening the moribund and discredited FLN. In February 1989 a national referendum approved a new constitution breaking Algeria's socialist tradition, separating state and party and legalizing opposition parties.

The new constitution led to the proliferation of new opposition parties (sixty in 1992), the most important of which was the ISLAMIC SALVATION FRONT (*Front Islamic du Salut*— FIS), which was founded on 18 February 1989, uniting several smaller Islamic groups. It was led by Dr. Abbasi Madani (b. 1931), a graduate of the Sorbonne and a teacher at the University of Algiers. His more radical deputy, Ali Ben Haj (b. 1956), who represented the younger impoverished generation, lacked formal education but was known as a charismatic orator. Madani, supported by younger activists of the *jazra'a* (Algerianization) trend, sought to replace the regime even by confrontation, whereas the older leaders of the *salafi* trend (see ISLAM) adopted a reformist approach. Advocating the creation of an Islamic state, the FIS spread throughout Algeria, using its network of 8,000 mosques and social and welfare institutions.

The first test of Algeria's political opening materialized in the local and regional elections held in June 1990. The FIS took control of fifty-five percent of the local councils and two-thirds of the regional particularly in the more populated northern regions. The 1991 GULF WAR postponed the scheduled elections but radicalized the FIS, which supported IRAQ and presented itself as the true heir of the 1954 revolution and openly attacked the regime and the military.

In March 1991 the National Assembly passed a bill increasing the number of Parliamentary seats and changing their distribution to achieve rural overrepresentation, where the FLN was strong, at the expense of the cities in the north, where the FIS was more popular. All opposition parties rejected the new law, and the FIS declared a national strike. Mass riots broke out on 5 June 1991 when the election campaign started. Ben Jedid imposed a martial law, dismissed the government and postponed the elections. Using state-of-siege constitutional decrees, the Army arrested thousands of FIS supporters, including Madani and Ben Haj. It also forced the resignation of Moulud Hamrouch's government for being lenient toward the Islamists.

In the first round of the general elections held on 26 December 1991, the FIS won 188 out of 430 seats in the Parliament, even though it lost 1 million votes compared to the 1990 elections, apparently to the smaller *Hamas (harakat al-mujtama' al-islami)*, led by Mahfuz Nahnah, and *al-nahda*, led by Abdallah Jaballah. The largely Berber *Front des Forces Socialistes* (FFS), led by Ait-Ahmad, won 25 seats, while the FLN only 16 (but 1,612,000 votes); forty-one percent of the eligible voters abstained. In the other undecided regions the FIS won forty-five to fifty percent of the votes.

With the FIS poised for victory in the second round, the Army, which feared for its position as the major power broker, declared a state of emergency. It forced Ben Jedid to dissolve the National Assembly and to resign on 11 January 1992. The army set up a five-member ruling body—High Council of State,(*Haut Comité d'État*— HCE)—and recalled Muhammad Boudiaf from exile to serve as President. The new regime's strongman was Defense Minister Lieutenant General Khalid Nizar (who retired in 1993 due to ill heath). The FIS was banned in March 1992 and thousands of its supporters were imprisoned. The arrests paved the way for younger and more radical activists, who advocated armed struggle against the regime. Boudiaf strove to avert a slide to violence by promising radical changes of the old order and criticizing the corruption which characterized the Ben Jedid period, while admonishing the FIS for politicizing Islam. While he managed to develop a popular constituency, Boudiaf lacked actual authority over the military, which was wary of his anti-corruption campaign. He was assassinated in June 1992 by his bodyguard, allegedly by order of senior military officers. He was replaced by Ali al-Kafi. Boudiaf's murder hastened the political polarization and escalation toward violent insurrection. Veterans of the Bouyali movement, led by Abdel Qader Shabuti (killed in 1994), organized a guerrilla force called Armed Islamic Movement (*Mouvement Islamique Armée*—MIA). In July 1994 the MIA and several other smaller Islamic armed groups formed the *Armée Islamique du Salut* (AIS) as the FIS military arm. Madani Merzaq, a veteran of the Afghan War, was appointed National Commander in March 1995. Since 1993 the FIS adopted a dual position of pursuing armed struggle against the military regime, while calling for a dialogue with the military in order to

end the violence, and aimed to restore the legal political process as the means to establish an Islamic state.

More radical and violent was *al-jama'a al-islamiyya al-musallaha (Group Islamique Armée—GIA)*, which was founded by volunteers of the Afghan War, and operated as an amalgam of separate groups maintaining a loosely unified formation. Drawing inspiration from the teachings of Sayyid Qutb (see ISLAMIC RADICALISM), the GIA advocated holy war as a means to establish an Islamic state, and regarded the military regime, and all those who collaborated with it in whatever form, as apostates deserving death. In addition to targeting the army and economic institutions, the GIA launched a terror campaign against the Westernized elites, killing hundreds of intellectuals, government employees, women who refused to veil and foreigners. Fighters for both the GIA and AIS came from the impoverished urban youths. The regime, on its part, employed brutal anti-insurgency measures, including mass arrests and indiscriminate killings of suspects. It also formed civil militias to combat the Islamists.

The military was divided between two factions: the "conciliators", headed by Defense Minister Major General al-Amin Zerwal (Liamine ZEROUAL) who espoused the use of military means and dialogue with the opposition without relinquishing the army's dominant role in politics, and the "eradicators", headed by Chief of Staff Muhammad al-Amari (Lamari), who advocated a military solution while rejecting any concession to the Islamists.

On 31 January 1994 the mandate of the five-man HCE was to expire. Following the collapse of the National Dialogue Conference in January, convened to decide on the succession to the HCE, the ruling Higher Security Council (*Haut Conseil de Securite*), i.e., the military high command, decided to appoint Zeroual President for a three-year transitional period.

The deterioration of the economic and security situation forced the military to seek an indirect dialogue with the FIS. Concurrently, the FIS formed a loose coalition with seven other smaller opposition parties, representing altogether eighty percent of the voters in the 1991 elections. In January 1995 the coalition issued the National Pact of Rome, calling for the rescission of the state of emergency, restoration of the democratic process, legalization of the FIS and the rejection of violence as a means to attain or hold power.

While Zeroual rejected the National Pact, he renewed his dialogue with the imprisoned FIS leaders in March 1995. The negotiations failed in June, when the FIS rejected Zeroual's demand to renounce violence as precondition for the release of its leadership. Despairing of the dialogue, Zeroual launched a process designed to endow Algeria with the legitimate political institutions it had lacked since the 1992 coup, and to secure the military's dominant role in politics by preventing the Islamist opposition from attaining power through elections. First, he scheduled presidential elections for November 1995 in order to attain legitimacy for the regime. While the FIS and the National Pact parties boycotted the elections, three candidates—Mahfuz Nahnah of *Hamas*, Sa'id Sa'di of the mainly Berber Rally for Culture and Democracy (RCD), and Nur al-Din Boukrouh of the Algerian Renewal Party (PRA)—ran against Zeroual.

The elections were conducted in a fairly free manner, with a 75.7% (12,087,281 out of 15,969,904) voter turnout. Zeroual won 61.3% (7,088,616) of the votes while Nahnah obtained 25.4% (2,971,974). Although the opposition parties initially claimed that the elections were rigged, they acknowledged the failure of the boycott and recognized the elections' validity.

With his position enhanced, Zeroual promulgated constitutional amendments, which enhanced the Presidency and prohibited the use of Islam, Berber identity and Arabism, the three components of Algerian identity, in the names and ideology of political parties. The amendments were ratified in a national referendum held on 28 November 1996 by an eighty-five percent majority, amidst charges of manipulation against the regime. The political achievement did not end the violent struggle, which reportedly had taken the lives of some 50,000 people by the end of 1996 and a similar number in the year 1997.

Thanks to growing oil prices and increased gas exports, as well as rescheduling its massive foreign debt, Algeria managed to avert a financial collapse. Concurrently, the regime's efforts to liberalize the economy and privatize the inefficient state-owned industries, met only partial success due to the resistance of the bureaucracy and the impact of on-going

violence. Unemployment remained high (twenty-five percent).

Foreign Affairs: Boumédienne tried to cultivate relations with both France and the USSR. In 1966 agreements were signed with France providing technical and educational aid for twenty years. Large numbers of Algerians worked in France, and France continued to assist the Algerian Army, which was also aided by the USSR. Diplomatic relations with the US were severed in 1967 and resumed only in 1974. Nevertheless, trade, some US investments, and the service of US experts, mainly in the development of oil and gas resources, continued. Boumédienne's anti-colonial line was most evident in his African policy. Gradually he adopted harder policies toward France. French military and naval bases had to be handed over, despite the Evian Agreement, by 1967–1968. In February 1971 Algeria took over a fifty-one percent holding in the two French companies who together accounted for some two-thirds of its oil production. This controversy aroused much ill feeling against the 700,000 Algerians working in France at the time (see also OIL).

Algeria's relations with Morocco were troubled by a border dispute over the Colomb-Bechar and Tindouf areas, and general antagonism concerning inter-Arab and international policies. The border dispute led, in the early 1960s, to armed clashes and, in 1963, to a brief war. The crisis was defused by mediation of the Organization of African Unity, but not finally solved; the disputed areas remained under Algerian sovereignty. Algerian-Moroccan relations were aggravated by the conflict over Western (formerly Spanish) Sahara: Algeria supported the establishment of an independent state and actively aided the liberation movement there, the POLISARIO; in 1976 Algeria recognized the Saharan Arab Democratic Republic (SADR), then in bitter conflict with Morocco who annexed this territory in 1976 and 1979. The Algeria-Morocco dispute over Western Sahara became a pivotal issue in the MAGHREB system relations, and to a large extent shaped Algeria's policies in the regional Arab system at large (see also WESTERN SAHARA CONFLICT.

Concerning the Palestine question, Algeria's stand was hard-line and militant. At the first ARAB SUMMIT CONFERENCE in Cairo in January 1964, Ben Bella supported the foundation of a Palestinian liberation organization along the lines of the FLN. Under

Boumédienne, Algeria was among the first Arab states to offer, as early as 1965, official representation for *Fatah* in Algiers as well as military support. Algeria sent troops to fight ISRAEL on the Egyptian front in 1967 and in its aftermath joined SYRIA's efforts to dissuade ABDEL NASSER from seeking a diplomatic solution to the loss of Arab territories to Israel, granting Egypt 200 million dollars for arms procurement to its demised Army. In 1973 an Algerian armored brigade arrived on the Egyptian front shortly after a cease-fire had been reached. Prior to the October 1973 war (see ARAB-ISRAEL CONFLICT) Algeria's President played a central role in mobilizing the political support of the non-aligned states for the Arab cause, and in the aftermath of the war, Boumédienne was recognized as one of the four prominent Arab leaders, along with presidents al-SADAT and ASAD, and King FEISAL. Algeria hosted the Arab summit conference in November 1973, and was the venue of many other important meetings of Palestinian and Arab leaders. However, given Morocco's assertive policy on Western Sahara (as of 1975) it aimed at annexing this area to its sovereign land, with Egyptian and Saudi support), Algeria moved to an antagonistic position in the regional Arab system. Hence, Algeria rejected Egyptian President Anwar Sadat's peace initiative of 1977, joined in the "Front of Steadfastness and Confrontation" established at the Tripoli summit of the radical Arab regimes, and suspended its diplomatic relations with Egypt. Algeria adhered to its radical line in the Palestine conflict through the 1980s, although unlike other radical states such as LIBYA and Syria, it remained sympathetic toward the PLO and its political decisions.

Algeria's international and inter-Arab policies in the 1980s became more moderate. Although it was among the last of the Arab states to renew its relations with Egypt in 1988, it gradually took a more cooperative role in the regional Arab states system, moving away from its antagonistic role as a member of the Front of Steadfastness and Confrontation since 1977, toward the mainstream led by Egypt. Algeria also improved its relations with the US and the European Community due to its economic crisis and the need for Western support against the Islamist challenge, even supporting the Western effort against Iraq in 1991. Algeria supported the international peace conference convened in Madrid in late October 1991, as well as the Israeli-Palestinian

Oslo Agreement. Relations with Morocco, however, remained tense, undermining the ARAB MAGHREB UNION established in 1989 to improve the Maghreb countries' economic integrations.

With the intensifying massacres committed by the Islamist radical groups, Algeria's government has come under growing European pressure to allow access to observers in order to help put an end to the bloodshed.

ALI IBN HUSSEIN   see HASHEMITES.

ALIYAH, JEWISH IMMIGRATION   see ISRAEL.

ALLON PLAN   see ARAB-ISRAEL PEACEMAKING.

AMAL   (Arabic: Hope; acronym of *afwaj al-muqawama al-lubnaniyya*: the Lebanese Resistance Battalions) Political organization and militia of the Shi'i community in LEBANON, mainly in South Lebanon and Beirut. Traditionally, the Shi'i community was led and represented, in addition to its religious-spiritual leaders, by notables of rival clans, and had no party (or a militia) of its own. In the mid-1970s, however, the combination of several factors brought about change: the increasing role played by militias organized by other communities (particularly the Christian-Maronite PHALANGES) in the Civil War that erupted in 1975; the growing domination of South Lebanon by the PALESTINIAN GUERRILLA ORGANIZATIONS, and the massive Israeli retaliation against it (sometimes even full invasion, such as the Litani Operation in 1978); the Islamic revolution in IRAN in 1979; and the weakening of the leftist movements in Lebanon, which in the past were a lodestone to many Shi'is. As a result, young Shi'i leaders felt the need to set up their own organization. Chief among them was Mussa al-SADR, the charismatic religious-political authority (who disappeared, and was probably murdered, in LIBYA in 1978). The organization first appeared under different names (e.g., "The Disinherited" or "The Oppressed") and was mainly local, with little centralized leadership, but in the late 1970s Amal emerged as a primarily Shi'i organization, representing the community's specific interests. At that time it also became a militia first and foremost. Its first political leader after Sadr's disappearance was Hussein al-Husseini, 1978–1980, who was later nominated Speaker (President) of the Lebanese Parliament. A relatively unknown lawyer, Nabih BERRI, replaced him as leader in 1980 and has retained this position ever since. In 1992, Berri became Speaker of the Lebanese Parliament.

During the first phase of the civil war, 1975–1976, Amal was not identified with either of the rival camps and took little part in the fighting, restricting itself to defending Shi'i villages and quarters. Compared to other Lebanese militias, it was inferior both politically and militarily, lacking a territorial power base, as Shi'i-populated areas were under control of more powerful forces: the Palestinian organizations in the south, the Syrian Army in the Biqa' and the leftist-Palestinian camp in West Beirut. In 1982, on the eve of ISRAEL's invasion, it had become more powerful, almost equal in number of armed men to its rivals—the Palestinian organizations (though not as equally trained as the latter). Following their expulsion from Lebanon by Israel in summer 1982, Amal became the strongest militia in the Shi'i areas in Beirut and South Lebanon.

The Shi'is had first welcomed the Israeli invaders, after long years of suffering under Palestinian rule. However, this soon changed into resistance, as Israel signalled that it intended to remain in Lebanon for the time being and secure the dominance of Lebanon by its allies, the Maronite-Christian Phalanges. Gradually, Amal moved closer to the "Leftist" Syria-oriented camp, and from 1983–1984 Berri was in alliance with the camp's leader, Walid JUNBLAT, though the alliance was uneasy, unstable, and sometimes shaken by bloody clashes. When the "Leftist" coalition formed, in 1984, a "Government of National Unity," Berri joined it, pressing for and obtaining the establishment of a special Ministry for South Lebanon with himself at its head. But while being a cabinet minister, he actually remained in opposition, foiling the government's effort to impose control on the areas controlled by Amal. In February 1984, and again in April 1985, Amal wrested control of West Beirut from opposing factions (mainly SUNNI-Muslim) and government forces, and though it later accepted a degree of army control, it remained the dominating force there, supported by SYRIA. These actions were mainly a consequence of the short-sighted policy of President Amin JUMAYYIL, who tried to suppress the Shi'is in Beirut, thus provoking Amal to act. From 1985 Amal forcibly resisted the re-establishment of PLO control over the Pales-

tinian camps in South Lebanon and Beirut, and bloody battles broke out and lasted—despite several cease-fire attempts—until January 1988 ("The Battle of the Camps"). Syria, at that time trying to weaken Yasser ARAFAT and strengthen the anti-Arafat pro-Syrian Palestinian factions, tried to impose a settlement but in fact assisted Amal in the fight against the PLO.

Since 1979, and particularly since the 1982 war, the Shi'i community has come under the increasing influence of extremist trends inspired and sometimes guided by the Shi'i-revolutionary regime in Iran—a radicalization manifested in attacks against American and French targets in Lebanon and also, from 1983 to 1984, in growing Shi'i guerrilla attacks on Israeli forces occupying South Lebanon. The radicals established, with Syria's connivance, an independent base in the Syrian-occupied Biqa' region. They appeared as "Islamic Amal"; "Hizballah," and "Islamic Jihad," which later left Amal altogether and formed a loose alliance, HIZBALLAH. Some of the top religious Shi'i leaders, headed by Sheikh Muhammad HUSSEIN FADALLAH provided a religious legitimacy to Hizballah. Ever since, Amal and Hizballah have been engaged in a bitter competition over the support of the Shi'i community in Lebanon, differing in the means to reach the goal of equality, social justice and greater representation to the Shi'i community, considered the largest in Lebanon. The end of the 1980s witnessed violent clashes between the two Shi'i movements over control of the Shi'i dominated areas, and while Hizballah was aided by Iran, Amal sought the help of Syria. The alliance with Syria bore fruit in the battlefield, where the Syrians tried to weaken the more radical (and therefore dangerous) Hizballah and help Amal win, as well as in the political field, where Nabih Berri was one of the pillars of the new political order in Lebanon established under Syrian auspices.

In December 1985 Nabih Berri and Walid Junblat agreed with Elie Hubeika, then leader of the Christian-Maronite "Lebanese Forces," on the Damascus Agreement—a plan for a new political structure for Lebanon, in line with Syria's conceptions and demands; but the agreement was rejected by the Christian leadership and remained abortive (see LEBANON). In 1989 Amal accepted the Ta'if Agreement and took part in the political and military effort to end the Civil War in Lebanon, handing over most of its heavy weapons to the Lebanese government. Since 1992, Berri has become—together with Lebanon's ambitious Sunni-Muslim Prime Minister Rafiq HARIRI—one of Lebanon's most powerful politicians. Amal participated successfully in the Lebanese Parliamentary elections of 1992 (a "Liberation List" led by Berri in the South, including, among others, candidates from *Hizballah*, did very well in these elections) and 1996 (in a list formed together with *Hizballah*), and has sent several deputies to the Lebanese Parliament. Offering a more moderate political program than that of *Hizballah* and maintaining close relations with Syria, Amal—the dominant factor in Lebanon—remains popular in the Shi'i community, despite its emphasis on political means as opposed to the military effort exercised by *Hizballah*. However, it does not rule out some military activity, and remains active—though in a much lesser extent than its Shi'i competitor—in military operations against Israels' declared "Security Zone" in South Lebanon.

AMERICAN POLICIES, INTEREST   see UNITED STATES.

AMIN, HUSSEIN AHMAD (b. 1932 in Cairo) Egyptian scholar, diplomat and political thinker, son of the well-known author, historian and journalist, Hussein Amin. He studied Law in the University of Cairo (1953); and served as lawyer and radio broadcaster (1954). He studied for a Ph.D in English Literature in Britain. In 1957–1992, Amin served in different diplomatic positions in Canada, the USSR, Germany, Brazil and ALGERIA. Amin has become reputable mainly for his liberal thought expressed in books and articles that deal mainly with issues concerning society and ISLAM. In his numerous publications he called for the separation of religion from state and for the return to the enlightened Islam, condemning the violent methods used by the Islamic militant groups to impose their ideas on society. He has also been critical of the Egyptian authorities who fail to struggle against the real reasons leading to religious extremism, relying on administrative measures to combat the militant Islamic groups and organizations.

ANTISEMITISM   The ARAB-ISRAEL CONFLICT brought about various manifestations of antisemitism

in the Middle East Arab-Muslim political culture. Arab governments and spokesmen usually assert that there can be no antisemitism among the Arabs, as they are themselves "Semites". This assertion, however, disregards the real problem. ARABIC is, no doubt, a Semitic language; and the European inventors of the doctrine of races, claiming the existence of a Semitic "race", would have to include the Arabs in that imaginary "race". But antisemitism means, specifically, anti-*Jewish* instincts, feelings or doctrines. And, though in the Middle Ages the fate of the Jews in the Arab countries—as a "protected people" (*ahl al-dhimma*) without civil rights—was better than that of the Jews in the Christian world, such anti-Jewish feelings do exist in the Arab countries. They have been intensified by the dispute over Palestine between Arab nationalism and Jewish nationalism (ZIONISM) and, since 1948, the Arab-Israel Conflict. Recent Arab history contains instances of pogroms, anti-Jewish violence, persecution (see JEWS), some of which were triggered by the Arab-Israel dispute. The two stock-in-trade props of antisemitism appear in Arab antisemitism, too: the blood libel (i.e. the horror-tale that Jews use the blood of non-Jewish children for baking their Passover bread) was raised in several nineteenth-century pogroms; and the belief in a world-wide Jewish, or Zionist, conspiracy to dominate the world is widespread. German Nazi propaganda in the 1930s and 1940s helped spread these notions. Arab antisemitism is noticeable after the end of World War II, as well. Antisemitic Nazi literature continues to be printed and distributed (German Nazi experts for some time served as advisers to Egyptian and Syrian information departments). Nazi-style caricatures of "The Jews" continue to appear in the press of Arab countries, including EGYPT—even after its peace agreement with ISRAEL. Hitler's *Mein Kampf* in Arabic translations is being reprinted; so are the *Protocols of the Elders of Zion*—a notorious forgery "documenting" the Jewish plot to take over the world. An antisemitic bias can be discerned in school textbooks and in indoctrination material of the armed forces. Arab top leaders avoid showing such bias and in recent years stress that they are fighting ZIONISM and Israel only, and not the Jews, and even invite Jews who left the Arab countries to come back. However, anti-Jewish clichés keep reappearing in speeches by Arab political and religious leaders, and in the press.

ARAB, ARABISM The Arabic term *al-'arab* originally referred to the nomads of the Arabian desert. Traces of this original usage survive to this day: all BEDUIN tribes are called "Arab al-" (Arab al-Tarabin Arab al-Ta'amira meaning the Beduin tribe of Tarabin or Ta'amira. Tribes of pure Arab descent sometimes resent the fact that the tribes of mixed descent, e.g. with Negro or Turcoman blood, are also called "Arab al-"). However, with the Arab-Muslim conquests of the seventh and eighth centuries and the spreading and gradual domination of the ARABIC language throughout the area conquered, the term acquired a new meaning, generally accepted today: all members of the Arab nation. There is no official, commonly accepted definition of that Arab nation. As it has absorbed, over the centuries, most of the pre-Arab inhabitants of different ethnic-national character, it cannot be defined in terms of ethnic (let alone "racial") descent. The reasonable working rule is to define Arabs as all those who speak Arabic as their mother tongue, feel themselves (and are seen by others) to be Arabs, and are formed by the heritage of Arab history and civilization (and do not possess, though speaking Arabic, a different national identity—such as the JEWS).

Arabs in that definition form the majority in the Arabian peninsula and its northern rim, the "Fertile Crescent"—with the exception of ISRAEL and the Kurdish regions of Iraq (all these countries are called *al-mashriq*, "The East"), and in the countries of North Africa, north and east of the Sahara (the countries west of Libya, sometimes defined to include Libya, are called *al-maghrib*, "The West"). In the MAGHREB strong pre-Arab and non-Arab BERBER elements survive, partly retaining their non-Arabic languages. Estimates vary as to their share in the population, the actual use of their language and the degree of their separate national consciousness. In any case, the Arabic language and Arab consciousness dominate. To a much lesser extent residues of a pre-Arab national consciousness survive in EGYPT (see PHARAONISM), among certain groups and tribes in SUDAN (even outside the wholly non-Arab South), in LEBANON, and among some of the ancient oriental Christian communities in SYRIA and Iraq—some of which used, until recent times, Syriac-Aramaic not only in their liturgy but also as a spoken tongue. In Iraq, the names assumed by some of the ancient Christian communities evoke pre-Arab national memories (ASSYRIANS,

CHALDEANS)—but there seems to be no conscious cultivation of pre-Arab national sentiments. Anyway, except for the Berbers, such non-Arab national memories are marginal and no counterweight to the complete domination of the Arab nation in its realm. Wholly non-Arab populations included in Arab states are, mainly, the KURDS of Iraq and the African tribes of Southern Sudan.

Beyond that Arab realm, Arab populations exist in Israel, in the Turkish province of Hatay (ALEXANDRETTA) and other border regions in southern TURKEY, and in Khozistan, the south-western part of IRAN (sometimes also called Arabistan). Semi-Arab populations—sometimes with Arabic as second language or *lingua franca*, though not as a mother-tongue—are found in several African countries bordering on the Arab domain, such as Chad, Niger, MAURITANIA, DJIBOUTI, SOMALIA AND ERITREA.

All the Arab states have achieved full political independence, most of them after a protracted struggle with colonial or semi-colonial protecting powers. Arab nationalists claim some of the areas with partly Arab or semi-Arab populations beyond their borders—such as the whole of Palestine (i.e. the elimination of Israel); Turkish Hatay; Iranian Khozistan; and the northern part of Chad. Mauritania, Somalia, Djibouti and the Komoro Islands have joined the ARAB LEAGUE and wish, presumably, to be counted among the Arab countries.

The Arab nation does not form one united Arab state but is politically divided into twenty-one separate states with a combined population of about 240 million (1984 estimate—including some 10 million in the three non-Arab member-states of the Arab League). Several powerful factors—a common classical language, literature and civilization (including the heritage of Arab ISLAM, though this is, in terms of religious belief, not shared by the non-Muslim parts of the nation), and a common national consciousness and history—unite the population of these twenty-one states and make of them one nation. Other elements—different spoken dialects, separate statehood and interests, divergent histories—make for the growth of particular entities, and many turn the Arabs in their various countries into separate peoples with increasingly unique national attributes (Egyptian, Syrian, Iraqi, Moroccan, etc.) Opinions differ as to whether the unifying or the dividing factors are stronger and which trend will prevail. All Arab political leaders, and many literary and cultural leaders, stress the unity of the Arab nation, and great efforts have been made to enhance that unity, give it political expression and increase inter-Arab cooperation (see ARAB NATIONALISM, PAN-ARABISM).

ARAB BA'TH SOCIALIST PARTY   see BA'TH.

ARAB BOYCOTT (of Israel) A major manifestation of the Arab-Israel conflict, especially since 1946. In the late 1920s, Palestinian-Arab leaders initiated an economic boycott of the Jewish community in Palestine as one of their weapons in the intensifying Palestine dispute. They campaigned through the 1930s for a complete boycott of Palestinian-Jewish products and services, and at times tried to enforce that boycott by violence. However, these efforts assumed a temporary and partial nature and failed to stifle the economic development of the Jewish community. In some fields the Arab boycott even stimulated it. In fact, many Arabs, Palestinian and non-Palestinian alike, ignored the boycott and continued using Palestinian-Jewish products, with a particular emphasis on Jewish services, such as physicians, hospitals, and lawyers. In December 1945, however, the newly established ARAB LEAGUE decided to apply (as of 1 January 1946) a complete economic boycott of the Jews of Palestine. Arab states were to enforce that decision. From the end of 1945 onwards the boycott was embodied in the legislation of all Arab states. The collective Arab boycott was officially presented as a measure of support for the Arab-Palestinians in their struggle against the Zionist aspirations in Palestine. The boycott was primarily geared to protect the building of Arab national economies and prevent the influx of Jewish industrial products into the Arab countries, which had already been considerable. Moreover, the Arab governments ignored the frequent complaints of the Palestinian Arabs that the indiscriminate boycott of Palestinian economy had turned into a costly burden. In 1948, the boycott was automatically transferred from the Jews of Palestine to the State of ISRAEL, and since the early 1950s it has been supervised by a special boycott office of the Arab League located in Damascus. In the absence of an effecive Arab military or political plan in the conflict with Israel, the economic and political boycott became the main feature of Arab hostility toward Israel.

The direct primary boycott of Israeli goods and services was fully implemented. It prevented all communications and trade. However, some Israeli products reach Arab markets camouflaged under foreign labels or smuggled in with labels removed. This rupture of all ties between Israel and its Arab neighbors—its natural trading area, undoubtedly damaged Israel's economy to an extent that cannot be estimated in figures, since it cannot be determined how much trade there would have been without the boycott.

The main efforts of the Arab boycott office were geared to implementing a secondary boycott: to persuade private and public enterprises in non-Arab countries to refrain from doing business with Israel. The boycott offices tended to acquiecse ordinary trading with Israel, but they requested foreign companies to supply them with information about their transactions with Israel, and about Jews among their shareholders, directors and employees. In some cases they used pressure to prevent even ordinary trade where even major enterprises (apprehensive of damage to their interests in Arab countries), submit to that pressure and refrain from exporting to Israel. The main object was to prevent foreign enterprises from investing in Israel, building plants, granting franchises, or any cooperation beyond trade. Companies that violate the instructions of the boycott offices were blacklisted and themselves threatened with boycott.

Several Western governments took steps against boycott pressures, by banning certain boycott practices and obliging their enterprises to report any request by boycott offices for information (e.g., the Ribicoff Amendment of 1976 to the US Internal Revenue Act, and 1977 and 1979 amendments to the US Export Administration Act; more modest French legislation of 1977, implemented only since 1984; and similar decrees in the Netherlands). But none has completely outlawed the submission to boycott demands. Boycott pressures were applied in a haphazard and inconsistent way. Some companies that insisted on their rights and refused to submit were not hurt, especially if they were large and powerful and the Arab states needed their cooperation. Others quietly found ways to circumvent the boycott by forming subsidiaries for their operations in Israel, or camouflaging such operations. Yet, some enterprises, over the years, submitted to the Arab boycott, closing their plants or refraining from operating in Israel. There was no way of determining what part the fear of the Arab boycott played in a foreign company's decision not to operate in Israel. The actual damage that was done to Israel cannot be estimated.

The Arab boycott was also applied to international shipping and aviation. Ships and airplanes calling at Israeli ports were barred from Arab ports (exceptions being made for some tourist cruise ships), and planes en route to or from Israel were prohibited from flying over Arab territory. However, attempts to impose a complete boycott on shipping companies and airlines that also serve Israel were not pursued when met with firm resistance. Attempts were made to extend the boycott to international conventions, congresses and organizations, also in a rather haphazard way. The boycott offices have also tried to boycott foreign artists and bar their films, records etc., if they were deemed to have too close ties to Israel.

Since 1967, the boycott apparatus has not found effective solutions for the problem posed by the Israel-occupied areas. So far they have failed to prevent the infiltration of Israeli goods among the Palestinian products of the WEST BANK and GAZA STRIP (that should not be boycotted), and to ensure that the Arabs of the occupied territories are not hurt by the boycott of Israel. During the mid-1980s Arab boycott operations slackened, with some Gulf Arab monarchies lifting the secondary boycott. Israel's peace treaty with EGYPT (March 1979) included the latter's commitment to abolish all sorts of boycott against Israel. The same practice was excercised in the case of the Oslo Agreement signed between Israel and the PALESTINE LIBERATION ORGANIZATION (PLO) (September 1993), as well as in the Israel-Jordan peace treaty of October 1994. In September 1994, the six member-states of the GULF COOPERATION COUNCIL renounced the indirect boycott against Israel. The establishment of low-level diplomatic relations between Israel and MOROCCO, MAURITANIA, OMAN and QATAR further eroded the Arab boycott. However, even without official commitment to the Arab economic boycott against Israel, positive economic relations with Israel remained dependent on the political atmosphere in the region, and a vulnerable object at times of Israeli-Arab tension and discord. Fear of Israeli economic domination, and strong public re-

sentment toward apparent Israeli commercial and economic activity (even in those Arab countries maintaining peace relations with Israel), underline the low profile and limited scope of Arab willingness to develop normal economic relations with Israel.

ARAB COOPERATION COUNCIL (ACC) (Arabic: *majlis al-ta'awun al-'arabi*) Regional framework of inter-Arab cooperation established in February 1989 by EGYPT, IRAQ, JORDAN and YEMEN, ostensibly to promote economic integration among the signatories, primarily in the fields of movement and work of ACC nationals within each other's territory, and trade. However, the haste in which the ACC came into being and the significance of politics involved in its foundation, underpinned the doubtful nature of the declared aims of the new inter-Arab bloc, as well as of its validity. Not only was there no full territorial continuity among the member states, there was little basis of sound economic cooperation—their similar economic production and resources, such as labor forces and consumer industries were bound to enhance competition rather than complement it. Despite its declaration that it was open to other states, it was perceived by Iraq as an instrument to isolate SYRIA, then in conflict with Iraq and an IRAN ally, and create a potential threat toward SAUDI ARABIA and other Gulf emirates. For Egypt, the ACC served as the final springboard to return to the ARAB LEAGUE—which was approved in the ARAB SUMMIT CONFERENCE held in Casablanca in September of that year—after most Arab states had resumed diplomatic relations with it. The absence of common substantive interests among the ACC members brought it to its demise in the wake of the Iraqi invasion of KUWAIT in August 1990 due to Egypt's strong objection to the Iraqi venture and decision to join the international coalition against Iraq.

ARABIA The Arabian Peninsula, with an area of 1.1 million sq. miles (2.9 million sq. km.) and an estimated population of 27 million, is mostly desert, except for the south-west (YEMEN) and the southeast (OMAN). Seventy-five percent of Arabia constitutes the Kingdom of SAUDI ARABIA. Other political entities are located along the southern and eastern coast: Yemen, the UNITED ARAB EMIRATES (UAE). QATAR and KUWAIT (and the offshore islands of BAHRAIN, usually considered part of Arabia).

ARABIC The language of the ARABS, a Semitic tongue which originated in the Arabian Peninsula and spread through most of the Middle East and North Africa, mainly after the Arab-Muslim conquests, from the seventh century. Written, literary Arabic shaped by pre-Islamic poetry and principally by the Koran (*Qur'an*) and medieval Islamic literature, retains the main structure and vocabulary of classical Arabic. Yet it has adapted itself to modern use with astonishing flexibility and has created a rich vocabulary answering the needs of contemporary scientific and social-political terminology. There is a great difference between written, literary Arabic (*fusha*)—pure, or *nahawi*—grammatical, correct) and spoken Arabic, divided into many dialects—so different that their speakers can hardly communicate unless they use *nahawi*.

Written Arabic is used in literature, official documents, the press, broadcasts and films, as well as in contacts between educated Arabs from different countries, at conferences and in speeches. In everyday life, even educated Arabs use the spoken tongue in its local form. There are, however, ways of slightly mixing the two levels of the language. Newscasters often add certain spoken forms or idioms to their generally literary Arabic, as do many leaders, each creating his own style. Some writers advocate the use of the spoken tongue in fiction. Plays have been written in dialect, and novelists increasingly use dialogues in the local spoken Arabic in their novels that are otherwise written in classical Arabic. This tendency underlines the growing localized nature of contemporary Arabic literature. Still, most Arabs insist on the use of pure classical Arabic, as the only language of writing and communication. The fact that written Arabic is a powerful factor uniting the Arab nation, while the cultivation of spoken dialects might lead to separatism, is an important element in that majority position, along with its fundamental respect for the heritage of Arab civilization and its continuity. Academies of Arabic in Cairo, Damascus and Baghdad cultivate the language and its development; their suggestions for new terms, and sometimes changes and corrections, are not, however, always found acceptable by the public.

ARAB-ISRAEL CONFLICT In 1948 the Arab-Zionist communal dispute in Palestine, beginning in the late nineteenth century, became an international conflict between ISRAEL and the Arab states. This development culminated three decades of growing convergence of interests, though not necessarily of identical purposes, between the PALESTINE-ARAB leadership and the ruling elites of the neighboring Arab countries. While the former strove to enlist the ARAB-Muslim world for their national cause, the latter viewed the intensifying Arab-Zionist conflict in Palestine with growing interest as a source of political legitimacy in their efforts to establish authority on both domestic and regional levels. Throughout its century-long history, the conflict not only widened to include other parts of the Arab and Muslim world, but also deepened in terms of the growing personal and collective losses, and the increased psychological barriers on both sides of the conflict. Hence any history of this conflict is subjective and might not represent other versions accepted by the other side, or within one's own political community.

Political History

1. Pre-Mandatory History (1882–1917) When Zionist settlement began in the 1880s, good neighborly relations were maintained in most cases with adjacent Arab villages. Arabs from other parts of Palestine wanted to settle near the Jewish villages seeking employment and trade. At the same time, violent Arab resistance to the new Jewish settlements, mostly non-political, was manifested by peasants, tenants or BEDUIN shepherds who feared the settlements might affect their tenancy or grazing habits. Bands of marauders also attacked the settlers. They were considered weak until they posted armed guards nucleus of later organized self-defense (*ha-shomer*). Such clashes were sporadic and did not become organized violence or a national struggle until after World War I. However, even before the War, Arab resistance to the Zionist enterprise had assumed an increasingly political shape. This was portrayed by urban notables and the incipient Arabic press as an existential threat to the indigenous Arab-Muslim population. Visionary as it was, ZIONISM's goal of reviving the Jewish homeland (gaining a majority of the population and establishing Jewish sovereignty over Palestine) was a growing source of concern among Arabs. This was expressed in meetings, pamphlets, articles in the press, and in petitions to the Ottoman authorities, in an attempt to prevent Jewish immigration and settlement. Apart from the immediate existential threat of such goals to the indigenous Arab inhabitants of the country, these expressions of opposition were motivated by the awakening Arab nationalism or by Muslim-Ottoman considerations. Both of them led to the same anti-Zionist conclusions. When Arab national associations began forming, from approximately 1908 in the Arab parts of the OTTOMAN EMPIRE, some of them inscribed opposition to Zionist aspirations on their program. The Zionist leadership, became aware of the need to compensate Arab peasants who lost their tenancy rights on lands sold by their Arab landlords to the Zionist organization. Moreover, before and during World War I, the Zionist movement established contacts with Arab leaders, mainly from EGYPT, Beirut and Istanbul, who had advocated decentralization of the Ottoman Empire and sought support for their national aspirations in the Zionist movement. However, these Zionist-Arab efforts to reach understanding and cooperation turned out to be futile.

2. The Palestine Conflict During the British Mandate (1917–1948)

A. Consolidation of the Inter-Communal Conflict

Both Arab and Jewish national aspirations entered a new phase with the dismemberment of the Ottoman Empire at the end of World War I, and the BALFOUR DECLARATION of 2 November 1917, in which Great BRITAIN officially undertook to support the establishment of a "Jewish National Home" in Palestine. In 1920, Palestine was defined by the victorious powers as a MANDATE territory entrusted to Britain, officially linked with the provisions of the Balfour Declaration regarding the establishment of a "Jewish National Home" in Palestine. Particularly for the Palestinian-Arabs, the decisive majority of the population in what became Mandatory Palestine under British rule (550,000 Arabs, mostly Muslims, against 50,000 JEWS), the shift was doubly hurtful: they lost their privileged status as Muslims in a Muslim state, and were confronted by the Zionist enterprise which enjoyed the full backing of a world power, which also happened to have been entrusted with the Mandate over Palestine.

The HASHEMITE King HUSSEIN of HIJAZ and his sons—perceived by Britain as senior agents of its imperial interests in the Fertile Crescent and Hijaz, and fostered as leaders of the Arab national movement and its claim to independence—were willing to regard the Zionists as their potential allies, hoping to attain world Jewry's support for their own aspirations for an Arab regional union under their lead. They were willing to accept the establishment of a Jewish autonomy in Palestine, which could be included in an independent Arab federation. In January 1919, after a number of meetings in Palestine and the Paris Peace Conference, Prince Feisal and the President of the Zionist Movement, Haim WEIZMANN, concluded an agreement. The Feisal-Weizmann Agreement held that the Arab and Jewish national movements recognized each other, pledging mutual support and cooperation. On several points the agreement was vague and open to ambiguous interpretations, but its essence was clear: the future Arab state and a Jewish Palestine were to be two separate entities which would cooperate, and the Arab nationalist movement and Zionist enterprise were to support each other.

From the outset, the validity of the agreement was not concrete. Feisal had added to it, personally, in ARABIC, that it would be valid only if all Arab national demands were attained, which was soon to be frustrated by Anglo-French arrangements. Furthermore, Feisal's mandate to represent the Arab nationalists of the Fertile Crescent countries was dubious. Most Arab nationalist leaders rallying under his banner, especially those of Palestine, rejected the agreement and its validity, claiming, alternatively, that it was a Zionist forgery; that Feisal was deceived by the British advisors and did not understand what he was signing; and that he was not entitled to speak for the Arab nationalist movement. Above all, the agreement was a product of the special circumstances that prevailed immediately after the war, marked by British interest to demonstrate to its allies the Arab and Zionist accord as a ploy to win Palestine and serve its own plans in the Fertile Crescent.

The Feisal-Weizmann Agreement left no real mark on the ensuing Arab-Zionist conflict over Palestine. The Arab federation in whose name Feisal spoke was never established, and Palestinian-Arab nationalist leaders, as well as other Arab nationalists and governments turned against the Zionist enterprise. Feisal himself—from 1921 as King of IRAQ—and his successors continued to seek ways in which to accommodate a Jewish autonomous community in Palestine within a greater Arab federation led by Iraq under the title "The Fertile Crescent Unity." A similar idea of regional Arab unity (GREATER SYRIA) was fostered by Feisal's brother Emir ABDALLAH, who, in March 1921, was instated by Britain as a semi-autonomous prince of Transjordan under the Palestine Mandate. Abdallah also tried to obtain the assistance of the Zionist movement and world Jewry to actualize his aspirations. In return he was willing to accept an autonomous Jewish entity in Palestine under his crown and restricted Jewish immigration.

Zionist leaders made continuous efforts to explore the possibility of an Arab-Zionist agreement that would allow uninterrupted growth of the Zionist enterprise in Palestine in terms of both land acquisition and Jewish immigration. However, except for marginal groups, the Zionist leadership was unified in its refusal to condition the future of their enterprise on Arab will. They perceived Britain as the overall power in Palestine, realizing that they would not receive from the Arabs better conditions than those given by London. In the absence of prospects for agreement, Zionist diplomacy toward the Arabs sought to attain tactical goals: temporary mitigation of the inter-communal tension to gain valuable time for additional growth of the Zionist enterprise; exploring new opportunities for land; intelligence for security; and dividing the political Palestinian-Arab community. To achieve these goals, propaganda in the Arabic language, welfare services, financial aid, and personal bribery, all served as a means in this policy. The Zionist Executive made efforts to foster moderate Arab leaders, primarily from the rural population, and organizations inside Palestine, as a preemptive strategy: to erode the image of Palestinian-Arab national resistance to the Zionist enterprise and to prevent the negative implications of such resistance on Britain's policy toward the "Jewish National Home."

Given the intransigent position of the Palestinian-Arab leadership to any such accommodation, Zionist efforts were focused on the Arab elites in the neighboring countries. In 1931, against the backdrop of the 1929 Arab riots in Palestine (see below), and consequential British White Paper (1930), which effectively threatened to bring the Zionist enterprise in Palestine to a halt, a decision was made by the Zionist Congress to open diplomatic contacts with the Arabs to reach a peace agreement. Yet the talks held theretofore by the leaders of the Jewish Agency—dominated, from 1931, by the Labor Movement—ended with the same futility as the previous

contacts. Especially after being appointed as Head of the Zionist Executive in 1933, David BEN GURION, drawing on the Pan-Arab idea of regional unity, held between 1934–1936 a series of meetings with leading Pan-Arab protagonists of the neighboring countries known for their Pan-Arab nationalist attitudes mostly Syrians, such as Shakib ARSALAN, Ihsan al-Jabiri, Habib Lutfallah and Riyad al-Sulh. Others, from Palestine, included Mussa al-Alami, George Antonius and Awni Abdel Hadi. These contacts also revealed the unbridgeable gap between the two sides. Some of the Arab leaders were willing to accept the Zionist support to achieve their goal of a unified Arab state, but none would exchange it for Ben Gurion's claim for attaining a Jewish majority in Palestine, even with his commitment to share representation and power with the Palestinian-Arabs on a parity basis.

Another direction of contacts was with MARONITE leaders in LEBANON, such as Presidents Emile Edde and Alfred Naqqash, and Patriarch Arida, in an attempt to forge an alliance of non-Muslim minorities. However, it had a minimal effect on the relations between the Zionist movement and Lebanon. The two sides represented non-sovereign entities, devoid of authority and power, which were in the hands of the respective Mandatory powers. The Maronite leaders were not accepted even as representatives of the whole Maronite community. Moreover, with the growing tide of Arab nationalism among the urban middle-class, students and professionals, and parallel to the process of politicization of the masses, the Arab-Jewish conflict in Palestine became an increasingly public matter, adopted by the political elite for domestic as well as inter-Arab political reasons.

The Balfour Declaration triggered the consolidation of Palestinian-Arab national movements whose main ideological basis and motivating power was the resistance toward Zionism and its political purposes. The total rejection of the Zionist political and moral premises and goals, as well as of the British Mandate based on the Balfour Declaration and its obligation to assist in creating a "Jewish National Home," soon became the trademark of Arab political life in Palestine. The ensuing Palestinian-Arab national movement argued that the country belonged to the people living in it, of whom the majority was Arab-Muslim, and was entitled to fulfil its right for self-determination by establishing national representative institutions and a government to obtain independence in the future, like other Mandate territories. No Jewish immigration or settlement was to take place without the consent of the country's Arab owners. The British and the world powers had no right to promise a land that was not theirs, and their promise to the Jews was null and void. Zionist counter-arguments—that the Jewish people had a historical right to the land; that it could only establish its homeland in Palestine to alter an historical injustice of two thousand years and to prevent further persecution; that the rights of the Arab majority should be weighed not against those of the Jews already in the country, but against those of the entire Jewish nation; that the development of the country would benefit both peoples; that the "Jewish National Home" was being created mostly in uninhabited swamps and deserts; and that no Arab had been, or would be, expelled, and that Arab civil rights and freedoms would be honored—failed to assuage Arab opposition.

Palestinian-Arab leaders rejected and boycotted the Mandate's proposals to establish representative institutions, on the grounds that such participation would imply a recognition of the Balfour Declaration and the Zionist policy of the British Mandate. However, in the course of the 1920s, the Palestinian-Arab national movement showed weakness and an inability to forge a collective consensus over agreed upon national goals. Poor organization was primarily due to the traditional and primordial structure of the society, as well as the geographical and factional fragmentation of the notables and projection of their rivalries on the national level. The Palestinian-Arab national institutions of the Executive Committee, representing the political leadership and the National Congress, were inactive, ill-financed and lacking effective authority. The government-based Supreme Muslim Council became a focal center of power due to its funds and employment capacity. Yet it could not function as a national leadership, although its President, the MUFTI of JERUSALEM al-Hajj Amin al-HUSSEINI, turned his position into a springboard for national leadership. Above all, the Palestinian-Arab leadership was deeply divided along family and geographic allegiances, and urban-rural populations. (These represented modernity and economic dynamism *vis-a-vis* traditionalism and declin-

ing economy.) Simultaneously, the Jewish community in Palestine under the Mandate (the *Yishuv*) developed its own social and economic infrastructure (embodied mainly by the *Histadrut*), representative (*Knesset* Israel) and executive institutions of both the world Zionist movement (the Jewish Agency) and of the Jewish community (*ha-va'ad ha-le'umi*: the national committee), coordinating between the Zionist movement and the local *Yishuv*; and sought to expand collaboration with the government in every possible aspect. From 1931, the *Yishuv's* self-defense organization of the *Hagana* had been reorganized as a national branch subordinated to a joint control of the Jewish Agency and the *Yishuv's* institutions.

The Palestinian-Arab national movement thus failed to create the means to underpin its total rejection of the government's Zionist policy. While collaboration with the government in a collective form was rejected, on an individual level, Palestinian-Arab leaders served in the administration and state institutions without inhibitions. This weakened their bargaining position *vis-a-vis* the government. In the absence of powerful or political means, the only possible way of affecting the government's policy for the Palestinian-Arabs (other than protests, petitions, and strikes) came in the form of short and sporadic, mostly uncontrolled, eruptions of violence against the Jews, culminating in the 1936–1939 Arab revolt. Arab violence led to Britain's reconsideration of its contradictory policy in Palestine. This led to reduced opportunities for the Zionist enterprise. In April 1920, the annual popular celebrations of the pilgrimage to Nabi Mussa (on the Jerusalem-Jericho road) turned into a violent eruption against Jews in Jerusalem. On 1 May 1921, Jewish demonstration triggered Arab riots, mainly in Jaffa and several Jewish colonies on the coastal plain. In August 1929, countrywide riots erupted, culminating in a year-long tension between the two communities as a result of Jewish attempts to expand their prayer rights at the Western Wall, and Muslim religious fears and incitement, claiming that the Jews sought control of the "Noble Sanctuary" (*al-haram al-sharif*—the Temple Mount). This time, the riots included indiscriminate attacks on Jewish (Zioinist) settlements as well as massacres of established Jewish communities, such as in Hebron and Safed. The riots led to a protracted inquiry of their causes followed by investigation of land and agrarian problems and the questioning of further Jewish settlement. The inquiries resulted in the White Paper of 1930s redefinition of British policy in Palestine. This effectively retreated from the Balfour Declaration by restricting Jewish immigration and land sales. However, following Zionist pressure, the Paper was effectively abolished by the British Prime Minister's letter to Weizmann in February 1931, giving a pro-Zionist interpretation of the White Paper. The riots of 1929 were a watershed in the history of the conflict, deepening processes of separation of the two communities in the spheres of residence, business, and socializing. The frustration caused by the shift of British policy intensified inclinations toward political militancy and violence among the Palestinians, especially with the young, educated, politicized generation. The lesson from the Jewish side was the necessity of a stronger and better organized self-defense force, settlement in contiguous, defensible areas, and rapid immigration of world Jewish youth.

During the early 1930s, the inter-communal dispute underwent a process of radicalization due to growing Jewish immigration, especially from Germany following the ascendancy of the Nazis to power in 1933, and the rise of new militant groups among the Palestinian-Arabs who sought to abandon the policy of protests and turn to force, primarily against Britain. The harbinger of this tendency was Sheikh 'Izz al-Din al-Qassam, a Syrian by origin, and preacher in Haifa since the late 1920s, who forged a group of adherents and led them to armed struggle as the fulfillment of Holy War (JIHAD) against the Jews and Britain—the infidels and invaders of the land of ISLAM. His death in late 1935 in a clash with the British forces was one of the turning points in the emergence of a new Palestinian-Arab leadership, comprised of the heads of the six parties which had been established since 1932. In November 1935, this leadership repeated the traditional demands for an immediate take-over by the Arab majority, with the Jewish minority frozen in its status, with no more immigration or acquisition of lands. This formula did not correspond to the facts of power and realities. The Zionist leadership maintained contacts with Arab leaders, inside and outside Palestine, even during the rebellion; but there was no breakthrough. Unofficial Jewish personalities suggested, in various versions, far-reaching concession by the Jews. These amounted to a renunciation of plans of a Jewish majority and a Jewish state, e.g. a bi-national state based on perpetual parity in all future government institutions. This idea was not welcomed by the mainstream Zionists. Yet had there been an Arab leadership willing to accept it, many Jews might have supported it, provided that immigration and settlement could continue within its framework—as a basis for fruitful negotiations. Other proposals, going even further by suggesting a predetermined ceiling for the Jewish population in absolute numbers or a percentage, were unacceptable to Jewish public opinion—the more so as the Arab notables contacted regarded a Jewish population of thirty-five percent or, at the utmost, forty percent as the ceiling. Nonetheless, the Palestinian-Arab leadership showed no interest in a bi-national or parity based solution. The Zionist leaders thus continued to search for a formula based on the old Feisal-Weizmann conception: a Jewish Palestine within a Pan-Arab or Middle Eastern framework that would satisfy Arab national demands, create a sense of Arab strength and security, and be able to accommodate a Jewish commonwealth. But this concept, too, proved unacceptable to most Arab leaders.

B. The Arab Revolt (1936–1939): The Palestine Conflict as a Regional Arab Issue There was an unprecedented rapid increase in Jewish immigration after Hitler's rise to power in Germany in 1933. This brought the Jewish population in 1936 to over 400,000, which was a third of the total population in the country. This aggravated tensions and led to further militancy on the part of the Palestinian-Arabs, especially in view of the neighboring Arab states' progress toward independence, while Mandatory Palestine still had neither representative institutions nor a national government. At the same time, growing economic depression of rural Palestinian-Arabs, coupled with the rise of an urban, educated and nationalist new generation, intensified militancy and inclination to resort to violence against both the British Mandate and Jewish community. The political leadership of the Palestinian-Arabs had been undergoing a shifting of the guards, with the long-dormant Arab Executive, headed by the aging Musa Kazem al-Husseini, which actually disappeared with the latter's death in 1934, even though it had a short awakening reflected in organizing mass demonstrations against the government in Jerusalem and Jaffa in 1933. In April 1936, mutual Arab-Jewish violence, and an eruption of political protest led by young Arab militant leaders triggered the formation of the Higher Arab Committee (HAC), comprised of the heads of Arab parties (representing mostly strong local clans) and headed by the Mufti, al-Hajj Amin al-Husseini, who had emerged as the top leader of Palestinian-Arabs since the late 1920s. Amidst growing violence, the HAC proclaimed a general Arab strike and a total boycott of all Jewish goods and services, which turned into a general Arab rebellion. Guerrilla groups (*isabat*) proliferated, and attempts were made to impose a centralized military command (see PALESTINIAN-ARABS). These measures were to continue until the government fulfilled the following demands: an end to Jewish immigration and land sales, and the establishment of a national government based on the Arab majority.

In August 1936 an armed force of several hundred Arab volunteers, mainly from SYRIA and Iraq, and organized and financed by the Iraqi government, under Fawzi al-Qawuqji—Lebanese-born, with a record of a rebel against the French, and current officer in the Iraqi army—penetrated Palestine and deployed in the Nablus-Jenin-Tulkarm "Triangle". Furthermore it established itself as a supreme commander of both local and foreign rebels. During the six months of the strike, the rebels attacked Jewish settlements as well as quarters in mixed towns and particularly inter-urban communications. The government reinforced its police force (largely composed of Arabs, some of whom sympathized and collaborated with the rebels) with some British troops. Its reaction was restrained and rather feeble. In view of the Arab rebellion, the Jewish Agency and the *Yishuv* leadership adopted a policy of restraint (*havlaga*) and static defense in response to Arab attacks. They also refrained from offensive reprisal action against the centers of Arab guerrilla bands in the villages. The policy of restraint derived mainly from political considerations, namely, to maintain and promote cooperation with the government and reap gains in terms of widening the opportunities for legal armed activity, establishing settlements and economic development. The restraint policy was justified by moral and ethical reasons, as reprisals would hurt innocent villages, women and children. This issue engendered much controversy and led to a split in the *Hagana*, with the more extremist advocates of an activist strategy seceding and

forming the National Military Organization (*Irgun Tzeva'i Le'umi* (IZL). In addition, the Jewish leadership offered its support to the government's efforts to maintain law and order in the country. The tightening of the understanding allowed the Jews to increase their settlement and immigration efforts and, in the face of the ARAB BOYCOTT, expand their economy to sectors hitherto exclusively in Arab hands. The underground and illegal self-defense organization, the *Hagana*, gradually began operations as a fully-fledged, though poorly equipped, military organization with a central command. The policy of cooperation with the Mandate government provided for legal mobilization, training and employment of thousands of Jewish additional policemen under official British command. This contributed immensely to the *Hagana* in terms of acquiring experience, familiarity with advanced military doctrines and, above all, increasing the amount of men with military experience.

The rebellion of 1936 failed to achieve its objectives due to a lack of resources, an ineffective and divided leadership, and the British government's strict policy of repression. The ongoing strike, which endured for over six months, hurt the Arab community more than either the Jews or the government. In the absence of political achievements, the Palestinian-Arab leadership—divided, lacking control of the rebels, and pressured by owners of citrus orchards to put an end to the strike—proved unable to call off the strike. The lengthening of the strike and the inability of the local Arab leadership to sponsor its halt, brought leading Arab figureson to the scene, primarily from Hashemite Iraq and Transjordan, offering their offices as mediators between the government and the HAC. This early Arab official involvement in the Palestine conflict was encouraged by Britain, whose main interest was to end the Arab armed resistance and strike. The Arab efforts to resolve the crisis aroused old-rooted inter-Arab rivalries and competition. These led to a collective appeal by the Arab monarchs in October 1936, which called upon the Palestinian-Arabs to stop the strike, promising to continue their efforts to support their cause. The appeal, on behalf of the Kings of Iraq and SAUDI ARABIA, and the Emir of Transjordan, with the IMAM of YEMEN, associated but not fully participating. (Egypt took no part in that all-Arab action; Syria and Lebanon were under French

Mandate.) The appeal was heeded, and the rebellion halted (temporarily, as it soon re-emerged). Qawuqji's volunteer army withdrew.

In July 1937, a British Royal Commission under Lord Peel published its recommendations. As both the Arab and the Jewish nations were entitled to independence in Palestine, and as an agreement on joint independence in a single state was unattainable, the Commission proposed to partition the country into a Jewish state, an Arab state that would be united with Transjordan under Abdallah's crown, and an extensive zone (including Jerusalem) to remain under British administration. The Zionists, while rejecting the specific, detailed boundaries proposed for the Jewish state, were prepared (following a majority decision of the Zionist Congress, after a bitter debate) to discuss the Peel scheme as a basis, i.e., they accepted the principle of Partition. The Arabs, however, rejected it, including the Nashashibi-led opposition faction. Yet given its growing links with Emir Abdallah of Transjordan and the threats posed against it by the alliance of the *Mufti* al-Hajj Amin al-Husseini with the traditional-rural population triggered by the rebellion, it might have acquiesced in Partition had it been firmly imposed. In the inter-Arab arena, the Peel Report met strong opposition as well. This reflected the growing inclination of the ruling elite to adopt the Palestinian-Arab cause to establish their own domestic, as well as, regional legitimacy. Egypt, having attained independence the previous year, now became increasingly involved in the Palestine issue, with Saudi Arabia, strongly opposed to the proposal to give to Emir Abdallah part of Palestine west of the River Jordan, reviving its territorial claims on Aqaba and the Ma'an areas along the Transjordan-Saudi border.

The struggle against the Partition proposal—which was approved by the British Cabinet—witnessed a growing convergence of interests and cooperation between Arab nationalists from Palestine and the neighboring countries regarding the Palestine cause. In September 1937, a non-official all-Arab conference was held in the Syrian resort town of Bludan. The decisions concluded there rejected the British proposals of Partition, insisting on putting an end to Jewish immigration and land sales to Jews, calling for independence of Palestine as an independent Arab state, and undertaking to extend financial and military aid—to be supervised by a permanent committee in Damascus—for the Palestinian-Arabs' armed struggle to attain those goals. That same month the Arab rebellion resumed, beginning with the murder of the British acting governor of the Galilee. The Mandatory government responded by outlawing the HAC and arresting its members. (The *Mufti*, al-Husseini, managed to escape along with many Palestinian-Arab nationalist leaders.) The Supreme Muslim Council was dissolved, and a firm policy of military repression of the rebellion launched. This policy shattered the fledgling Palestinian-Arab national leadership, identified with the *Mufti*, al-Hajj Amin, who, together with a few hundred family members and aids, began to guide the rebellion from Syria.

The Palestinian-Arab rebellion in its second stage, 1937–1939, became increasingly ferocious. There was increased internal Arab terrorism against dissidents, and counter-terror by Peace Gangs (see PALESTINE-ARABS). However, despite its military success in controlling large areas of the Galilee and the Jenin-Hebron mountainous area, by mid-1939 it had been fully suppressed. The Arab opposition to the Peel recommendations, however, reaped a political victory in the form of Britain's withdrawal from those recommendations (1938), and the adoption of an appeasing policy toward the Arab countries. This was the result of the increasing conviction among British foreign policy makers since 1936 that the Palestine question had become a regional Arab issue, affecting Britain's stature and interests in the Arab world, and even among the Muslims of India. These considerations were reinforced in view of the British weakness *vis-a-vis* the Fascist-Nazi Axis and the mounting European crisis and its implications on the Middle East.(Italy's conquest of Ethiopia in 1935, and growing anti-British propaganda and subversion). Against this backdrop, in early 1939. Britain issued invitations to the Arab governments of Egypt, Saudi Arabia, Iraq, Yemen and Transjordan, as well as to the Palestinian-Arab and Zionist leaderships, to a "round table" conference on Palestine in London. As the Arab leaders refused to recognize or conduct official talks with the Zionist delegation, the conference assumed the form of separate sessions of British officials with the Arab and Zionist delegates, with the operative emphasis on the Anglo-Arab consultation.

The result was the British White Paper of May 1939 which was rejected by both the *Mufti*-domi-

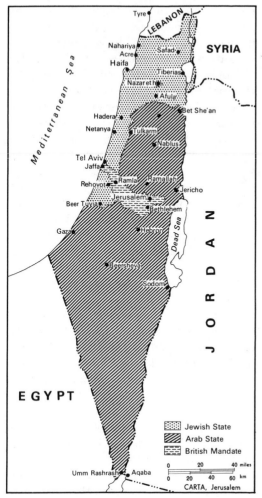

The Peel Commission partition plan, 1937.

tempted to convince the HAC to endorse it, to no avail.

The 1936–1939 Arab revolt in Palestine strongly motivated the Arab states to increase their active role in the Palestine conflict, assuming growing influence on this issue, especially in view of the political weakness demonstrated by the Palestinian-Arab leadership. Until the mid-1930s Arab interest in the Palestinian-Arab cause had assumed a public, non-official nature. This was expressed by moral, political and financial support from political movements. The most salient of these (since the early 1930s) was the MUSLIM BROTHERHOOD Society in Egypt which began to assume an increasingly official nature, directly involving the governments. As soon as the Palestine issue became high on the official agendas of Arab states, it became a matter of competition for regional leadership, nurtured particularly by the Hashemites in Iraq and Transjordan, and, as of the late 1930s, also by Egypt.

Thus, the dispatch of Qawuqji's volunteer force in 1936 was inspired and financed by the Iraqi government. The intervention of the Arab Kings in October 1936 (then without Egypt) was an important milestone. Inter-Arab congresses and popular committees in support of the Palestinian-Arabs proliferated and acquired a semi-official character, with increasing participation of Parliamentary and government representatives. Thus, in addition to the 1937 Bludan Conference, another all-Arab, semi-official conference was held in Cairo in October 1938 in support of the Palestinian-Arab cause, with the participation of the Prime Minister and blessing of King Farouq. The conference indicated Egypt's efforts to play a growing role in the Palestine conflict. Yet it was a way of promoting Egypt's regional Arab leadership, that had been fostered by the King and a growing group of Pan-Arab politicians. There was a gradual transfer of the decision-making from the Palestinian-Arab leadership to the Arab governments in those years. This was hardly resisted by the Palestinian-Arabs, exhausted by their struggle and internal terror and with their most prominent leaders in exile or detention. The London Conference of 1939, now including Egypt, led to British efforts to encourage, from 1936, this transfer of decision-making from the Palestinian-Arabs to the Arab states. The growing involvement of Arab states in the Palestine conflict, the inter-Arab competition, and re-

nated HAC (though not without disagreement), although it met the main Arab demands: Palestine was to become independent after ten years, and a national government based on its Arab majority was to be initiated following the end of violence and when peace was resumed; Jewish immigration was to be limited to 75,000 for the following five years, after which it would be stopped altogether; and land purchase was to be strictly limited, mainly to those areas already with a Jewish majority. The Zionist movement conceived the new White Paper as a total retreat from the Mandate ("The Paper of Treason") and as a death sentence to Zionist enterprise, proclaiming its indignation and practical revolt against the new British policy document. As for the Arab governments, although they never officially endorsed the White Paper, they virtually accepted it and at-

peated conferences and consultations regarding Palestine in which delegates from various Arab states participated, contributed significantly to the consolidation of collective Arab frameworks of action and coordination, as well as its essential role in formatting the Pan-Arab doctrine between the two World Wars.

C. Overtaking the Palestine Issue by the Arab States (1939–1947) During the war years, the Palestinian-Arab leadership continued to decline, losing control of its own political problem. The Palestinian-Arab political life had been dormant during this time, due to the post-rebellion exhaustion and British-enforced restrictions on political activity. Moreover, the hard core of the national leadership, headed by al-Hajj Amin al-Husseini, not only remained in exile, but rendered further disasters to the Palestinian-Arab cause. In April 1941, the *Mufti* was involved, alongside with the military junta dominating Iraq at the time, in the Iraqi nationalist, anti-British coup , which led to the temporary fleeing of the Royal Hashemite family and some of the leading pro-British politicians from the country, and was repressed by Britain within less than a month. The Hashemite regime was restored, while many of the *Mufti's* aids and companions were arrested or forced to go into exile. The *Mufti* himself managed to flee through IRAN and TURKEY and arrived in Rome. He was received by the Duce, and finally settled in Berlin. He became a close collaborator with Nazi Germany and its propaganda campaign against the allies. The *Mufti* encouraged the mobilization of Muslims (especially in Croatia and Bosnia-Herzogovina) to the Whermacht, and, as of late 1943, he became increasingly linked to the S.S. and attempts to prevent deals of exchanging Jews from the German-occupied central European countries for lorries and other material resources. The *Mufti's* records in Iraq and Nazi Germany became overwhelmingly restrictive when, following the end of the War in Europe, the *Mufti* returned to the Middle East and resumed leadership of the Palestinian-Arab community toward the ensuing war which was to decide the fate of Palestine. With Hashemite Iraq as one of the main Arab states involved in Palestine, and Britain's post-war weakness and urgent need for American financial support and strategic coordination, the *Mufti* was shunted aside, restricted and subverted against with far-reaching implications on the Palestine question in the 1948 War (see below).

In the absence of the Husseini leadership, their followers in Palestine rejected the establishment of an alternative Palestinian leadership (1943–1944). This rendered the political arena inactive and the parties practically non-existent. The Palestinian-Arabs were unable to participate in the inter-Arab consultations on Arab unity conducted in those years, despite repeated invitations issued to them. The obstacles were removed only temporarily in late 1944 when a compromise delegate, Mussa al-Alami was chosen to represent Palestine at the preparatory conference of Arab unity, held in Alexandria (see ARAB LEAGUE). However, political fragmentation and competition continued to prevent the establishment of a Palestinian-Arab official leadership until late 1945, when an Arab League commission arrived in the country and arbitrarily imposed a new form of HAC, with similar representation (of the 1930s' parties). The new HAC was to be headed by Jamal al-Husseini, who was later released from detainment in Rhodesia. Until then, the main Palestinian-Arab activity focused on preventing the sale of Arab-owned land to Jews. Two rival institutions were established for that purpose: a "National Fund" (*sunduq al-umma*), which offered to buy any land in danger of being sold to Jews; and Mussa Alami's "Constructive Project"(*al-mashru' al-insha'i*), financed by the Iraqi government which sought to foster him as its political agent and perhaps as an alternative to the *Mufti's* leadership. Neither of the two institutions achieved much success. The Arab League, which adopted the idea of financially supporting the Palestinian-Arabs in this venture, procrastinated its decision, and finally came up with a project of investment on a commercial basis which had no impact at all in Palestine.

With the establishment of the Arab League in March 1945, the Palestine conflict finally came to be patronized by this institution whose very *raison d'etre* as a watch-dog of the inter-Arab status quo necessitated collective control of this territorially and politically unresolved problem. Indeed, the cause of Palestine was the only case of a foreign-dominated Arab territory to be officially mentioned in a special annex of the Arab League's Charter, expressing recognition of and commitment to its independence as an Arab state. However, the Palestinian-Arabs were not given membership in the League's institution, only the right to participate in those sessions discussing the issue of Palestine. The establishment of the Arab League aggravated inter-Arab competition over Palestine. Frustrated by Egypt's victory in shaping and leading the Arab League and confronting growing nationalist and communist opposition, Hashemite Iraq turned the question of Palestine into a major foreign policy issue on the regional level. This was aimed at leading the collective Arab policy on Palestine by advocating extremist measures toward the UNITED STATES and Britain as the key powers in deciding the fate of Palestine.

Toward the end of World War II, the Arab governments raised the issue of Palestine with Britain and the US, in view of the growing Zionist propaganda and consequent public support for its demands. These had been formed since November 1942 as the "Biltmore Plan," aspiring to turn Palestine into a Jewish Commonwealth and opening the country to unrestricted Jewish immigration. The urgency and energy which characterized the Zionist effort in the US and Britain, and the general sympathy with its platform due to the Holocaust, became an ever-growing source of concern to the Arab ruling elite, mainly those confronted by strong militant opposition (Egypt, Syria, Lebanon, and Iraq) and identified with Britain (mostly Iraq). By late 1945, with the appointment of the Anglo-American Committee of Inquiry, the Palestinian issue became high on the international diplomatic agenda. In the following two years British diplomacy aimed to bring the Palestine conflict to a resolution, agreed by the rival parties, which would preserve Britain's strategic interests in the country, but to no avail, paving the road to the civil war that erupted in late 1947. The Committee's report in May 1946 recommended a future bi-national independence based on equal representation; an immediate immigration of 100,000 displaced Jewish persons in Europe; an abortive Anglo-American scheme (the "Morrison-Grady Plan," July 1946, recommending semi-autonomous Arab and Jewish cantons); another Anglo-Arab conference (boycotted by the Palestinian-Arab leaders in its first session, September 1946, but attended in its second session, January 1947); Britain's decision to hand over the Palestinian problem to the UN (February 1947); UN Special Committee on Palestine (UNSCOP, April–August 1947); and recommendations by a majority of its members of partition of Palestine and establishment of Arab and

Jewish states; the UN resolution of 29 November 1947 to partition Palestine and establish a Jewish state (on fifty-five percent of the Palestine territory) and an Arab state, to form an economic union, and an internationalized Jerusalem; and the Arab preparations for the final fight to prevent the implementation of that decision.

During World War II, the Jewish *Yishuv* grew stronger economically, militarily and demographically, despite the White Paper. The Jewish economy managed to benefit immensely from Britain's needs for food products, materials for fortifications, and infrastructure. Moreover, in 1941, the *Hagana's* mobilized striking force (*Palmah*) was established. This significantly contributed to the *Yishuv's* military capability. The Palestinian-Arabs, aware of the sharp growth of the Jewish economy—including the significant volume of its trade with the neighboring Arab countries—pressured since late 1944 to apply an economic boycott on Jewish products and services, as well as on raw material supplies, as a means to help the Palestinian-Arabs. However, shortly after the Arab governments applied, as of 1 January 1946, for the desired boycott, it hurt Jews and Arabs in Palestine without discrimination, and remained so, despite repeated Palestinian-Arab appeals and protests to the Arab League's office supervising the boycott. Indeed, the Arab governments were primarily motivated by the interest to build their national economies and to protect their products from Jewish competition. As it turned out, the Palestinian-Arabs largely ignored the boycott of the Jewish economy until the eruption of hostilities in late 1947.

In the summer of 1946, following the Morrison-Grady Plan, the Zionist movement's mainstream adopted the principle of Partition. They expressed their willingness to discuss the British government's "viable Jewish state" in Palestine. By then, no further contacts between Zionist and the mainstream Palestinian-Arab leadership were possible or desired. In the Arab camp, four conflicting attitudes were discernible in the years 1945–1948:

a) A few individual statesmen acquiesced in the establishment of a Jewish state or even supported the idea, such as former Prime Minister of Egypt Isma'il Sidqi; the Syrian ex-Premier Husni Barazi (who secretly recommended that solution to the Anglo-American Committee); some leaders of the Nashashibi-led Palestinian-Arab opposition (also in secret); and the leaders of the Catholic Maronite church in Lebanon (one of them, Archbishop Ignatius Mubarak, even in public in 1946). A secret written agreement was signed between the Zionist Executive's delegate and the Maronite Patriach Arida. This provided for cooperation between nascent Israel and the Lebanese Maronite community. But these dissenters had no influence on the course of events.

b) Some statesmen realized that the only realistic way to prevent total Jewish independence was to offer far-reaching autonomy, cantonal or confederal, within the framework of an Arab federation. The leading Iraqi politician Nuri al-SA'ID, who served numerous times as Prime Minister (including several months between 1946–1947), thought along these lines. His plan for a Fertile Crescent Federation, presented in a "Blue Book" in 1942, contained partial Jewish autonomy in Palestine. This idea, however, was rejected by both the Zionist leadership, which would not compromise the aspiration of establishing a Jewish independent state, and the Palestinian-Arab national movement, on the grounds of non-recognition of any political status of the Jewish community in Palestine. King Abdallah of JORDAN went much farther. Aspiring to lead a regional unity of "Greater Syria," with Palestine as a whole being part of it, he was realistically willing to settle for taking over the Arab part of partitioned Palestine if and when such partition was indeed effected. He was prepared to do that in cooperation with the Jews, and while he preferred Jewish autonomy or semi-independence under his crown, he accepted full Jewish independence in part of the country. In 1946–1947 he reached an informal and unwritten understanding along these principles with the Zionist leaders, with no detailed agreement on borders or the status of Jerusalem. He kept that accord secret, but it soon became widely rumored—the more so as Abdallah kept telling the Arab rulers that he reserved to himself "freedom of action" in Palestine when the Mandate ended. This was understood by everyone to mean the freedom to take over the Arab part of Palestine. Efforts to foil his plans played a significant role in Arab decision-making toward the 1948 War.

c) The mainstream, represented by the official Arab governments and the Arab League, in effect accepted the British White Paper of 1939, espe-

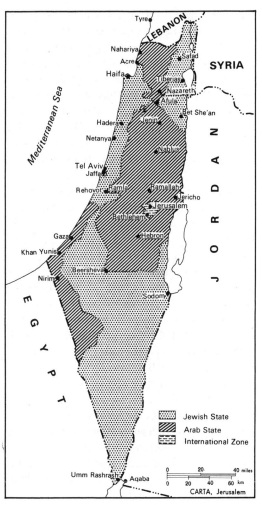

Palestine: the Jewish and Arab states according to the 1947 UN resolution.

cially in the aftermath of World War II. They maintained that Palestine should be an independent unitary state based on the Arab majority, with full civil rights for the Jews, but no autonomy, no further immigration and no land acquisition. (This policy met the expectations of the Arab constituencies but paid no heed to political realities.)

d) The Palestinian-Arab leadership insisted on immediate independence and was willing to assure only the civil rights of those Jews who had lived in Palestine before the Balfour Declaration (seven percent of the population). It also refused to assure the existing Jewish population civic and minority rights in the future Palestinian-Arab state.

In the course of 1946–1947 both Arab and Jewish leaders in Palestine became increasingly convinced that the final struggle would be decided by force of arms. The Jewish national militia, the *Hagana*, still underground and illegal, and reinforced by the regular *Palmah*, totalled by the end of 1947, 30,000–35,000 men, mostly trained but not fully armed. There were also the "dissidents," more extremist formations of the IZL and the LHI (*Lohamei Herut Israel*: Fighters for Freedom of Israel, entitled thus by the British "Stern Gang"), whose total number was some 4,000–6,000. The Arabs of Palestine formed major paramilitary youth organization in 1946: a real one *al-Najjada* closer to the opposition; and a virtual one the *Futuwwa*, identified with the Husseinis and aimed at swallowing al-Najjada. In late 1946, the Arab Higher Committee decided to merge the two, and in 1947 appointed an Egyptian officer as commander. However, the merger never got off the ground, causing the disintegration of the former organization, which had been the only hope for an effective Arab militia. Despite this gloomy reality on the Palestinian-Arab part, the *Mufti* adhered to the view that his people had been ready for war. He demanded that Britain end the Mandate and withdraw from Palestine so that the Palestinian-Arabs would settle the dispute with the Jews. From the Arab governments, the *Mufti* demanded only financial aid, arms and ammunition, not forces. In practical terms, the Palestinian Arabs were by no means ready to frustrate the Jewish hope for an independent state, hence help of the armed might of the Arab states turned out to be inevitable.

The Arab states had, indeed, declared, before and after the UN decision of November 1947, that they would resist and foil the partition of Palestine by all means, including military force. As UN members, however, they were reluctant to officially resist the organization's decision of partition. Moreover, they were unable to involve their regular military forces in Palestine as long as the British Mandate had not expired. Thus, with the beginning of Arab-Jewish hostilities in Palestine on the morrow of the UN partition resolution, the Arab governments adopted a policy of unofficial war, to be conducted by irregular, volunteer forces from Palestine and other Arab countries. The collective Arab policy on Palestine was shaped in emergency conferences held by the Arab League at Inshas in May 1946. (This was attended by the Arab heads of state.) There was a meeting of the Arab League's Political Committee at

Bludan (June 1946), Sofar (September 1947) and Aley (October 1947). In these meetings the Arab states made increasingly committed decisions in their support of the Palestinian-Arabs, providing them financial, logistic and arms aid, and volunteers. Yet they wanted to avoid the direct involvement of their regular armed forces. (The Bludan Conference added several secret decisions, threatening Britain and the US with economic and diplomatic sanctions if they supported a Zionist solution of the Palestine dispute.) In September 1947, a military committee was appointed by the Arab League's secretariat, headed by the Iraqi General Isma'il Safwat, with representatives from all Arab states and the Palestinian-Arabs. Although Safwat adhered to the view that only the Arab regular forces could defeat the Jewish community in Palestine, his recommendations remained unheeded and he became Commander-in-Chief of all volunteer forces with his headquarters in Damascus. The former Iraqi Premier and Defense Minister, General Taha al-Hashemi, served as Inspector-General of the volunteer forces effectively operating under Syrian President Quatli's guidance.

3. The 1948 War

Phase I: Prelude. The official Arab-Israeli War began a few hours after the proclamation of the State of Israel, on 15 May 1948. It was preceded, while Palestine was still under British administration, by bloody clashes between Arabs and Jews that gradually turned into a full civil war, which also involved volunteers from the Arab countries. Arab violence erupted on 30 November 1947, the day after the UN had adopted the partition resolution. Jewish buses were attacked. In Jerusalem a Jewish commercial quarter was burned and looted, and clashes soon spread. The pattern of violence was similar to the rebellion of 1936–1939. Local guerilla groups (*isabat*), frequently reinforced by men of neighboring villages or townquarters who were recruited *ad hoc* (*faz'a*), attacked Jewish traffic, isolated settlements and outlying quarters—usually by small-arms—sniping and bombs. While Jewish traffic was much affected, attempts to capture settlements failed. The *Hagana*, still underground, was at first mainly defensive, limiting retaliation to those directly involved in assaults, and only gradually moved to the offensive against centers of Arab military formations. The dissident *Irgun* tended to retaliate indiscriminately (e.g., by planting a bomb in an Arab market). British security forces only intervened sporadically, as Britain, on its way out, was unwilling to assume responsibility for enforcing partition or safeguarding security and order where it was not directly linked to the safety of its personnel and orderly withdrawal. Palestinian-Arabs serving in the British police and other military forces operating in Palestine perpetrated several terrorist attacks on Jewish targets, including the Jewish Agency buildings, the Palestine Post newspaper, and houses on a central Jerusalem street.

The eruption of violence in Palestine encouraged the Arab governments to organize military support for the Arabs of Palestine, under the supervision of an Arab League special military committee. The Arab states were to provide arms and volunteers in accordance with quotas allocated to each of them. The volunteers were to operate partly as a garrison in major mixed cities such as Jerusalem, Jaffa and Haifa, and partly as a mobile force (*Jaish al-Inqadh*—The Army of Deliverance) under the command of Fawzi al-Qawuqji. In January 1948 the first contingent of the Arab volunteer force entered Palestine and took over Arab areas in the north with further forces entering later, taking the area of Jenin-Ramallah in the mountainous center. Other volunteers, mainly Egyptian Muslim Brothers, began operating in the Negev from March 1948. The central coastal plain and Jerusalem was left for the local Palestinian-Arab armed forces loyal to the Mufti al-Hajj Amin al-Husseini, under the command of Hassan Salama in Jaffa-Ramle and Abd al-Qader al-Husseini in Jerusalem. Qawuqji's force increased to 5,000 by April. Yet this force failed in most of its operations to conquer a Jewish settlement (Tirat Tzvi, Mishmar Ha'emek, Ramat Yohanan), but scored some success in attacks on Jewish traffic along major routes, as had other guerrilla formations. From the outset, however, relations between the various Arab volunteer forces operating in Palestine were marked by rivalry and even hostility, with each trying to mobilize public and military support and expand its area of influence at the expense of the other, rendering military support and coordination largely impossible. With the diminishing British role of serving as a government in the areas predominantly inhabited by each of the rival communities in February–March 1948, armed clashes proliferated. By late March, Jewish Jerusalem was virtually cut off from the coastal

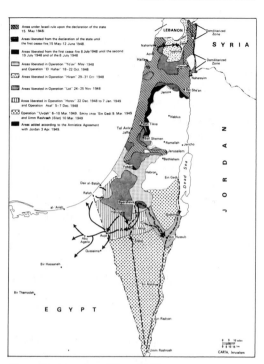

Map of Independence War, 1948.

plain (and from supplies and reinforcements), the Western Galilee was cut off from Haifa, and the Negev from Tel Aviv.

During the last week of March, the Jews sustained close to 100 losses in attacks on their supply convoys to Jerusalem and other isolated Jewish localities. This led to a decision of the Jewish High Command to seize the initiative to gain effective control of the territory allotted to the Jewish state by the UN partition plan and secure communications within and with Jewish settlements outside it, in accordance with "Plan D", which was shaped in March. The plan also included, for the first time, instructions regarding the expulsion of Palestinian-Arabs from their villages, securing control and security of the Jewish forces.

Early in April 1948 the *Hagana* Operation "Nahshon" reopened the road to besieged Jewish Jerusalem, taking over the hills and Arab villages overlooking the road to Jerusalem from Bab al-Wad eastward. The Jewish offensive caused the collapse of the Arab volunteers in the Jerusalem area and the fall of Abd al-Qader al-Husseini. Moreover, the offensive had a strong psychological effect on the Palestinian-Arab villagers whose tendency to leave under Jewish military pressure became a mass exodus.

As a result of the collapse of the Palestinian-Arab forces in Jerusalem and its approaches, the Arab League-based military committee assigned Qawuqji the command of the whole central area. They sent him two additional battalions of volunteers as a last available reinforcement. Due to limited capabilities, the *Hagana* could not capture and hold the road to Jerusalem all the way from the predominantly Jewish coastal plain to Jerusalem. This enabled Qawuqji in late April to close the road to Jerusalem in the Latrun-Bab al-Wad area. Once again this forced the *Hagana* unsuccessfuly to wage costly battles on the road. The *Hagana* offensive was far more successful in other sectors, capturing the mixed cities of Tiberias (18 April), Haifa (22 April), Safad (10 May), and Jaffa (13 May). In Jerusalem itself, the *Hagana* captured the Arab-inhabited neighborhoods of Qatamon and Sheikh Jarrah quarters in Jerusalem. (The last had to be re-evacuated following a British ultimatum.)

Before the end of the Mandate, the Western Galilee was taken over as was the Hula Valley. In April the exodus of Arabs from their towns and villages assumed mass dimensions. What had began in December 1947 as a limited departure of social elite families and foreign nationals (primarily labor migrants from the neighboring countries) grew steadily wider along with the intensified hostilities, the *Hagana* offensive and consequent collapse of the irregular Arab forces. The exodus was further accelerated and enlarged by reports of the massacre perpetrated by the IZL in the village of Deir Yassin near Jerusalem on 12 April. (The Arabs responded to this with a massacre of Jews on a convoy to the University Hospital on Mount Scopus two days later.) This was vehemently denounced by the *Hagana* and the Zionist leadership. Although there were many instances of forcible evacuation of Arabs, particularly in the villages involved in the hostilities and those which served as bases for Arab military operations, the exodus was fundamentaly a spontaneous movement, caused by an awareness of the Arab weakness and a fear of annihilation typical to civil wars. Moreover, an early visible departure of nearly all the leadership was clearly understood as a signal, if not as an outright instruction, despite efforts by the local Arab National Committees—representing the HAC—as well as by the Army of Deliverance, to instruct perseverance.

By mid-April 1948, it became clear that the all-Arab unofficial action fell far short of plans and was irresolute. Each state followed its own policies and tactics, and none fully trusted the others. Funds were allotted grudgingly; arms provided (mainly rifles) never matched the quantities requested and promised; the armed volunteers who did enter Palestine as of January 1948 lacked clear strategic instructions; and relations between Fawzi al-Qawuqji and the Palestinian-Arab irregulars under the *Mufti's* lieutenants were marked by competition and even hostility. The collapse of the Arab volunteer forces entailed a moral collapse and disintegration of the Palestinian-Arab community. By mid-May the number of Arab refugees reached 250–300 thousand, most of whom had remained in the Arab parts of Palestine, while a growing number of refugees arrived in the neighboring Arab countries. On the other hand, the Jewish military successes seemed to have practically created the basis for proclaiming the Jewish state. These developments resulted in growing domestic unrest and put pressure on the governments to take action to help the Palestinian-Arabs. Along with indications that King Abdallah of Jordan was planning to invade Palestine and take over its Arab part, possibly in agreement with the Jews the Arab states were encouraged to order their regular armies to intervene in Palestine immediately after the expiration of the British Mandate on 15 May. What boosted the option of collective Arab intervention was primarily the fall of Haifa (22–23 April). This was of utmost importance to Iraq as its main outlet to the sea, oil terminals and refineries.

Although inter-Arab political and military consultations began shortly afterwards, it was not clear, until a few days before 15 May, which of the Arab States would participate in the war and under what plan. It was especially unclear whether or not Egypt would take part in the war due to differences between Prime Minister Nuqrashi and King Farouq. The decision-making rested mainly with Egypt, Iraq and Syria, with the latter two pressing for action. Abdallah reserved his freedom of action. Lebanon had little military force and no interest in taking active part in the war, and Saudi Arabia and Yemen were on the sidelines.

The final decision on the invasion of Palestine, made on 13 May—a day after the Egyptian government had formally agreed to join the Arab coalition—was made against the advice of the Arab Chiefs of Staff who met for the first time on 30 April, in Amman. The latter maintained that the Arab regular armies were unable to sufficiently defeat the *Yishuv*. Arab leaders, especially the Secretary General of the Arab League, Abdel Rahman Azzam, were thus willing to consider options that would exempt them from the duty to intervene in a war for which they were unprepared, such as the prolongation of the Mandate, or truce and avoidance of the Zionist leadership to proclaim an independent Jewish state. However, as the Mandate approached its end, with the Jewish offensive gathering momentum, Arab domestic pressure of popular politicians grew stronger. This threatened the survival of the regimes in Iraq, Egypt, Syria, Jordan and Lebanon. The failure of the British and American efforts to mediate a truce in Palestine left the Arab leaders with no alternative but to take a collective decision to intervene militarily. In Egypt, it was King Farouq who, since mid-April, had strongly pressed for military intervention in Palestine, contrary to his government's reluctance, as a means to uphold his declining prestige, and pre-empt an independent action by King Abdallah. Urgent inter-Arab consultations were held on 13–14 May in Damascus to decide the joint military plan and allocate assignments to each Arab army. According to the initial plan, Egypt was to proceed northbound along the sea shore. The Jordanian and Iraqi forces were to cross the Jordan River at Gesher and Samakh, respectively. The Syrian force was to cross the northern border from Lebanon and connect with Safed. The Lebanese force was to proceed southbound along the shore. The plan, which was undoubtedly was intended to cut off the newly established Jewish state at the Jordan and Jezrel Valley and open the door to Haifa, was changed by King Abdallah, who insisted and received—obviously to keep him in the collective Arab line—the title of Supreme Commander of the Arab forces. Adballah dictated an amended plan more appropriately to fit his own plans to take over the Arab part of Palestine. Instead of entering Palestine at Gesher, the Jordanian force was assigned with crossing near Jericho, on the Alenby Bridge. Iraq was moved to the area of Gesher, and Syria to Samakh. Neither scheme set forward clear aims, a magnitude of force, or a schedule to implement the goals. The absence of a clear war aim accounted for the passive standing shown by most Arab forces during the months of the War. On 14 May, the People's Council and the People's Administration (established by the Zionist Executive on 18 April), proclaimed the foundation of the State of Israel under a Provisory government. Within a few hours, the new state was recognized de facto by the United States and the Soviet Union. Thus, when regular forces of Egypt, Iraq, Syria and Jordan crossed the borders of Mandatory Palestine at midnight of 14–15 May, they were invading an existing state, legitimized by the UN partition resolution, which was rapidly gaining international recognition.

Of all Arab states, Jordan was the only one with clear war aims: taking over the Arab part of Palestine and annexing it to the Kingdom. Abdallah had been fully—albeit secretly—supported by the British government in this respect, following official consultations which resulted in tight coordination since early February 1948. Accordingly, Abdallah was committed to restrict himself to the area allotted to a Palestinian state and refrain from violating the territory allocated to the Jewish state, so as not to embarrass his British patrons. Units of Jordan's Arab Legion, which had been employed by the British Mandate in security and guard missions in Palestine under the British military command, were to return to Jordan before 15 May and enter again as the Mandate ended. On their departure, however, some of these units attacked the Jewish block of settlements, Gush Etzion, south of Bethlehem, conquering it after two days of fighting (13–14 May), as well as two settlements north of Jerusalem. The Arab Legion also took over the power plant at the Jordan-Yarmuk confluence before 15 May; the evacuated Jewish settlement of Beit Ha'arava; and the Potash plant at the northern end of the Dead Sea. On 15 May, Tel Aviv was bombed by Egyptian planes, at a time when an Egyptian regular force began moving along the coastal plain, attacking Jewish settlements on its path and eventually capturing some (Yad Mordekhai, Nitzanim), while bypassing others, putting them under siege. The Egyptian advance was halted near Negba, 22 miles (35 km) from Tel Aviv (with the help of the first fighter planes which had arrived the same day from Czechoslovakia). The Egyptian expeditionary force included about a thousand volunteers of the Muslim Brotherhood, mostly from Egypt, but also from LIBYA, SUDAN and other Arab North African states, which moved along the Hebron-

Jerusalem road and engaged in heavy battles in Ramat Rachel, at the southern outskirts of Jerusalem. The Arab Legion, after occupying the Arab inhabited central Palestine without any fighting, entangled in heavy and costly battles in Jerusalem due to the Jewish successful offensive against the Arab irregular forces in the city, which had begun immediately after the British departure from the city on 14 May, threatening to conquer the Old City. The Arab Legion thus found itself obliged to deviate from its initial plan and respond to the Palestinians' urgent pleas to save Jerusalem and prevent it from falling into Israeli hands. In the absence of implementation of the UN decision that Jerusalem be a separate international area (*corpus separatum*), the Arab Legion did not cross the partition line or violate the British conditions. On 18 May a Jordanian force entered the Old City of Jerusalem, just when an Israeli force managed to break into the besieged Jewish Quarter and bring personnel and ammunition reinforcements. The Legion also occupied the Bab al-Wad-Latrun foothills which dominated the road from the coastal plain to Jerusalem. Henceforth, Jerusalem and its western approaches at Latrun became the main battlefield of the Arab Legion, which succeeded in repulsing repeated Israeli attempts to dislodge it from Latrun, but to no avail, leaving the road to besieged Jerusalem effectively blocked. (The IDF built an alternative road—nicknamed the "Burma Road"—through which Jerusalem was equipped with food, fuel, arms and ammunition.) On 28 May the Legion captured the besieged Jewish Quarter in the Old City after bitter fighting. It failed to capture Mount Scopus, and the Hebrew University and Hadassah Hospital remained in Israeli hands. The Arab Legion did not try to penetrate the new Jewish city, primarily because of its insufficient order of battle for such a mission, nor did it attempt to attack the area allotted by the UN to the Jewish state.

The Syrian army occupied some territory south of the Lake of Galilee, but was halted at the gates of Deganya and forced to retreat. Farther north, the Syrians succeeded in crossing the Jordan River south of the Huleh Lake, capturing Mishmar Hayarden and creating a bridgehead which sustained later Israeli attacks to dislodge it. The Lebanese army contented itself with a single company force attack on, and capture of Malikiyya (at the bend where the frontier turns sharply to the north), together with

the Army of Deliverance. The latter had withdrawn from the central sector immediately after the invasion of the regular forces and, after a short reorganization, was assigned with penetration into the Galilee to serve as the main Arab force in that area, under the direct supervision of the Syrian Army. Thereafter, the Lebanese army took a defensive position, undertaking to provide the Army of Deliverance with its logistic needs as well as serving as its rear headquarters. The Iraqi force, which failed in its attempts to cross the Jordan River at the Naharayim-Gesher sector, on 28 May entered and deployed in central Palestine at the Nablus-Tulkarm-Jenin "Triangle," replacing the Jordanian units which were necessary for defending the Legion's achievements in Jerusalem and its approaches. The Iraqi force took a passive position, refraining from attempts to advance into the coastal plain. On the other hand, a major Jewish attack on Jenin at the of June was repulsed despite its initial success.

The *Hagana,* now known as the Israel Defense Forces (IDF), exhausted by the fighting of the preceding months and as yet without an air force, artillery or armor, hastily mobilized its forces to contain the invasion. Although the Israeli High Command had based its plans on the assumption that it would confront regular Arab forces, and despite the initial success in halting the Syrian and Iraqi attacks, the military situation was critical during the first three weeks of the official war.

By early June the Arab offensive had lost momentum, with the Israeli forces taking the initiative and turning to the offensive in some sectors. Jewish forces had suffered heavy casualties but had not collapsed. They withheld most of the territory allotted to the Jewish state (except for the southern coastal areas taken by Egypt, and the Syrian bridgehead), and Jewish Jerusalem. At Britain's efforts, on 29 May, a Security Council resolution was passed. This imposed a total embargo on war material to the parties involved in the Palestine War, and ordered a truce of twenty-eight days, which went into effect on 10 June. The resolution also included the appointment of an international mediator (Count Folke Bernadotte), to supervise the truce and work out a peaceful settlement of the Palestine conflict. However, Bernadotte's efforts with the Arab and Israeli governments during the four-week truce, only served to underline the abyss between the Arabs and Israel regarding a peaceful solution. Israel refused to return to the UN partition borders or let the Palestinian-Arab refugees return to their homes, arguing that the issue must be resolved within the context of a permanent Arab-Israeli peace. In June, Israel's government decided to forbid the return of Palestinian-Arab refugees, perceiving it as part of the final settlement of the conflict with the Arab states. Israel also began to take action to effectively block the return of the refugees, by flattening abandoned villages and introducing Jewish immigrants into Arab homes in urban neighborhoods. At the same time, the Arab states refused to accept the mediator's proposal for recognizing a streamlined state of Israel (with the Western Galilee but without the Negev), with the Arab part of Palestine and Jerusalem at large to be annexed to Jordan. As the truce came to its end, only Jordan was in favor of its prolongation. Syria, Egypt and Iraq rejected it, indicating the resumption of hostilities. Once again, this decision reflected the fear of those governments, lest their acceptance of prolongation of the truce might arouse public sentiments against them, especially in view of their early promises to their peoples for a quick victory. No less important was the objection of those governments to the mediator's plan by which Abdallah was to be rewarded a significant territorial gain.

When fighting resumed on 8 July, the IDF which had consolidated and absorbed heavy equipment, took the initiative to expand the territory it controlled. In so doing, Israel finally abrogated its previous commitment to the UN blueprint-map which it considered obsolete, as it had been based on a peaceful implementation and an economic union and was indefensible in armed conflict. "Operation Dekel" led to the capture of the Lower Galilee, including Nazareth. "Operation Brosh" failed to eradicate the Syrian bridgehead at Mishmar Hayarden. An attempt to capture the Old City of Jerusalem also failed. However, Israel's strategic effort was directed at the central front. "Operation Dani" took Ramla and Lod (Lydda)—including the vital airfield—causing another wave of Arab refugees expelled from these two towns and the surrounding villages. Resumed efforts to take Latrun and the hills leading to Ramallah, and widen the corridor to Jerusalem, failed. In the south, the Egyptians again succeeded in closing the main road to the Negev. Israel devised a secret alternative route used at night, but failed to dislodge the Egyptians. Yet the initiative had passed to Israel. It was reported in response to an Arab request that the Security Council ordered a new truce, this time of unlimited duration. This came into effect on 18 July.

The truce was uneasy, and resumed efforts by the UN mediator to work out a political compromise plan remained unsuccessful. The truce witnessed increasing inter-Arab tension and division, primarily over Abdallah's measures of effective annexation in the areas occupied by the Arab Legion. In response, Egypt and Syria, with the active support of the Secretary General of the Arab League, Azzam, initiated the convening of a Palestinian Constituent Council and the establishment of the "All-Palestine Government" in Gaza City, in which the *Mufti* al-Hajj Amin al-Husseini, was elected President. The initiative was aimed at undermining Abdallah's efforts to annex parts of Palestine to his kingdom, rather than creating an effective Palestinian-Arab authority. However, for the Israeli decision-makers it was perceived detrimental to any future peaceful settlement of the conflict. Furthermore, Bernadotte's proposal to exclude the Negev from the Jewish state aggravated Israeli concern for it considered that area vital to its security and future development. In September, Bernadotte was assassinated in Jerusalem by a group of Lehi members, apparently in response to his earlier recommendations for territorial concessions to be made by Israel, though by then he had modified his plan, suggesting that Jerusalem be internationalized.

On 15 October, Israeli forces opened the largest military action ("Operation Yoav") since the beginning of the war. This was aimed at dislodging the Egyptian forces from the Negev. Israel succeeded in removing the siege on its settlements, capturing Be'er Sheva, and effectively ousted the Egyptian forces from the area allocated to the Jewish state, save a brigade-based enclave at Falujah (the "Falujah Pocket"). The Egyptian volunteer force in the Hebron mountains and south of Jerusalem were now isolated, with growing military presence of Jordanian forces who used the opportunity of the Israeli offensive to penetrate into the Bethlehem-Hebron area, establishing themselves as the responsible government in this area. Simultaneously, "Operation El Hahar" widened southward along the precarious narrow corridor to Jerusalem.

On 29–31 October, Israeli forces opened another offensive ("Operation Hiram"). This was aimed at expelling the irregular force of Qawuqj, who had never accepted the truce and continued harassing Jewish settlements in the Galilee. The IDF mounted a pincer attack, from Safed in the East and the coast in the West, and took western Upper Galilee, penetrating into Lebanon's area and capturing seventeen villages. In October–November, Israeli forces also reduced the area held by the Egyptians in the southern coastal plain. "Operation Horev" in December was designed to expel Egyptian forces from Palestine and force Egypt to enter negotiations with Israel on armistice, in accordance with the Security Council resolution of 16 November in this regard. The IDF flanked the Egyptians, advancing southwards through the desert, crossing into Sinai at Auja, capturing Abu Ageila and reaching the sea southwest of the GAZA STRIP. As Egyptian territory was now involved, Britain threatened to intervene against Israel, invoking the Anglo-Egyptian Treaty (which Egypt had not invoked). This led to the shooting down of five British aircrafts by Israeli pilots over Sinai. British-US pressure compelled Israel to withdraw from Sinai. Israel regrouped its troops east of the Gaza Strip, posing an obvious threat to the last main stronghold of Egyptian forces in Palestine. Despite repeated Israeli attacks, the Egyptian brigade at Falujah remained besieged (one of its staff officers was a young major named Gamal ABDEL NASSER).

On 5 January 1949, Egypt agreed to enter into indirect negotiations with Israel on armistice. As fighting on the other fronts had long ceased, the other Arab States followed suit. On 7 January a truce took effect, and on 13 January armistice negotiations began in Rhodes under the chairmanship of the acting UN mediator, Dr. Ralph Bunche.

A General Armistice Agreement with Egypt was signed on 24 February 1949. It served as a model for similar agreements signed with Lebanon (23 March, at the border point of Naqura), Jordan (3 April, in Rhodes) and Syria (20 July, at the border point of the Bridge of Jacob's Daughters).

The Armistice Agreements were based on the existing lines of the cease fire. They were defined as steps toward the restoration of peace, banned any "warlike or hostile act," affirmed "the right of each party to security and freedom from fear of attack," and laid down that "no aggressive action shall be undertaken, planned or threatened against the people or armed forces of the other side"; the Armistice line was not to be crossed. They would not, however, "prejudice the rights, claims and positions" of the parties as to the "ultimate peaceful settlement of the Palestine question" and the Armistice lines were "not to be construed in any sense as a political or territorial boundary." Mixed Armistice Commissions (MAC) were set up, chaired by UN-appointed officers and aided by UN observers.

The agreements also contained specific provisions that differed from case to case. With Egypt, the Armistice line was defined as identical with the southern international border of Palestine, apart from the Gaza Strip, which remained under Egyptian control. Al-Auja and its vicinity were demilitarized and designated as the seat of the Mixed Armistice Commission. The Egyptian brigade besieged at Faluja was evacuated. With Lebanon, too, the Armistice line was identical with the international border. Israel evacuated the area its forces had occupied during the fighting inside Lebanon.

Matters were more complicated with Jordan. Here, with no previous border, the whole length of the dividing line had to be negotiated. This issue was resolved behind the scene of the official Rhodes negotiations, in secret talks with King Abdallah. The King ceded, under Israeli military pressure, certain strips of territory in the coastal plain and the Wadi Ara hills that were not actually held by it. (They were held by Iraqi forces, but Iraq refused to negotiate an armistice and handed to Jordan the responsibility for the area occupied by it.) Jordan also gave up claims it had raised concerning the border in the southern Negev and accepted the line as requested by Israel, along the middle of the Arava valley. Several issues concerned Jerusalem, e.g. free movement on vital roads (the one from the coast to Jerusalem, via Latrun—for Israel; the East Jerusalem-Bethlehem road—for Jordan); free access for Israel to Jewish Holy Places in East Jerusalem (particularly the Western Wall), to the cemetery on the Mount of Olives, and to the University and Hospital on Mount Scopus (forming an enclave in Jordan-held territory); the operation of the Latrun pumping stations supplying water to Jerusalem, and of the railroad to Jerusalem; and the provision of electricity to the Old City of Jerusalem). On these problems agreement was reached in principle that a special committee would work out detailed arrangements. But this committee was never established and the matters listed were not resolved. The Hospital and University on Mount Scopus, could not operate, though they were maintained by Israeli caretaker crews supplied and rotated by UN-supervised convoys. Jews had no access to their Holy Places in Jerusalem.

Syria was the only Arab country to hold territory allotted to the Jewish State under the UN resolution, and it refused to hand it over. The deadlock was resolved by a deliberately vague formula establishing demilitarized zones in these areas, which were to be evacuated by Syrian forces. Elsewhere the Armistice line followed the international border. From 1949 to 1967, the Demilitarized Zones caused frequent clashes and a state of almost permanent crisis. Israel regarded them as part of its own sovereign territory, with limitations only on military forces and installations as specified, while Syria considered them as areas in which it had special rights and which did not belong to Israel. (It disputed, for instance, Israel's right to divert Jordanian waters in the Demilitarized Zone.) Syria also insisted that the Demilitarized Zones were under the jurisdiction of the Arab countries, which Israel denied (though conceding certain rights of supervision to its chairman but not to the commission itself, with its Syrian members). In the 1950s Israel stopped attending the commission.

4. Deepening of the Conflict (1949–1967)

A. Results of the 1948 War The results of the War were strictly reflected in the different meaning it was given by each of the parties involved. For Israel, it became the War of Independence, whilst the Arabs termed it the Palestine Catastrophe (*nakbat filastin*, or *al-nakba*). The war caused substantial Israeli casualties: over 6,000 dead (4,500 soldiers and over 1,500 civilians)—almost one percent of the population. Arab casualties have been estimated at about 2,000 for the invading regular armies and an unknown number of Palestinian civilians and irregular fighters. (The figure of 13,000 has been suggested but no reliable figures are available.)

The war resulted in three main phenomena which were to remain indivisible elements of the conflict:

a) In the course of operations, the Jewish forces exceeded the UN-proposed boundaries for the Jewish state, which were militarily indefensible (see map; the UN had, indeed, not considered defense needs, as-

Map of Armistice Lines, 1949.

suming that partition would be implemented in peace and mutual cooperation), expanding the territory allotted to the Jewish state by approximately 2,600 sq. miles (6,742 sq. km.) to the some 5,400 sq. miles (14,000 sq. km.) envisaged. Part of Palestine had now become Israel, while the area to be known as the WEST BANK—2,160 sq. miles (5,600 sq. km)—was annexed by Jordan (a fact since 1948–1949, formally proclaimed in April 1950), and what became the Gaza Strip—146 sq. miles (378 sq. km.)—remained militarily governed by Egypt.

b) The disastrous results of the war for the Palestinian-Arabs were strikingly reflected in the displacement and exodus of over half of them. 650,000–700,000 from the areas which became the state of Israel became refugees. Of the Arab population that had lived in this area before the war, only 160,000 remained and became citizens of the State of Israel, mainly in villages in the Galilee. The urban elite, including the upper-class, professionals and the intelligentsia, had left. About 750,000–800,000 Palestinian Arabs, half of whom were residents of the West Bank, became citizens of Jordan. (Over half of the refugees moved to reside in Jordan; approximately 200,000–250,000 were in the Gaza Strip (with no Egyptian citizenship), including 120,000–160,000 refugees from Israeli held areas; and 100,000–150,00 refugees were in Lebanon and Syria). The causes for the creation of the refugee problem became a pivotal dispute between Israel and its Arab neighbors. While the Arab version maintains that the refugees were forcibly expelled by the Jews in order to make room for the Jewish immigrants, Israel has always denied this, adhering to the argument that the Palestinian-Arabs had been called by the Arab states to leave in order to return when the situation normalizes.

c) The poor performance of the Arab regular forces in the war triggered intensified inter-Arab divisions and mistrust, boosting domestic upheavals and the rise of ultra-nationalist movements which called for radical socio-political changes in the Arab world toward the inevitable "second round" against Israel. In 1949, three military coups in Syria took place, as did the assassinations of Lebanon's and Egypt's Prime Ministers. In 1951 King Abdallah was assassinated and a year later a military coup took place in Egypt.

While these developments indicated the shifting attention of Arab politics inwardly, it disrupted the maintenance of the armistice agreements, preventing their promotion to peaceful coexistence. The domestic upheavals undergone by the Arab neighboring states led to intensified inter-Arab struggles for legitimacy and regional leadership which, regardless of the general rhetoric regarding the need for a "second round" of war against Israel in which the Arab states must be unified, deepened their divisions, weakening their ability to forge an agreed strategy of either war or peace concerning Israel. As a result, in the years 1949–1967 the conflict was marked by growing declarative hostility, which was not translated into practical operation. The Arab states adopted short-of-war measures such as tightening the economic and political boycott and im-

posing a strategic blockade on Israel, invariably encouraging guerrilla warfare across its borders.

The termination of the 1948 War, largely monitored and encouraged by the UN, led to a continuous international effort to bring the conflict to an agreed settlement between Israel and its Arab neighbors, but to no avail. The institutional and contextual bases for those efforts were shaped during the war, primarily by the late UN mediator Bernadotte (such as the establishment of a UN Truce Supervision and Observation Organization (UNTSO), culminating in the UN General Assembly Resolution 194 of December 1948). This resolution dealt with the Arab refugee problem, confirming the right of return of those refugees "wishing to live at peace with their neighbors"; internationalization of Jerusalem; and the establishment of a Palestine Conciliation Commission (PCC), composed of representatives of the United States, FRANCE and Turkey.

Following the realization of armistice agreements between Israel and its neighbors—save Syria—in April 1949, the PCC convened a conference in Lausanne but the Arab States refused to meet officially with Israel's delegates (unofficial meetings did occur). Although the parties signed (separately) a protocol providing for the UN blueprint map of 1947 to be regarded as a starting point for discussion, the Arabs interpreted that as an acceptance of the 1947 map, while considering it only as an opening for negotiations. Israel, on its part, ignored the protocol, adhering to its refusal to territorial concessions. Further efforts of the PCC were also unsuccessful, and while it was never officially disbanded, it gradually faded away (see ARAB-ISRAEL PEACEMAKING).

For the State of Israel, with its independence firmly established and recognized by most nations, the Arab-Jewish dispute over Palestine ended. The conflict became between Israel and the Arab states. However, Israel's hopes for a near peace settlement based on the territorial status quo were soon frustrated. While Israel was content with its territorial gains, with no claim but Arab recognition of its independence, the Arab states and the Palestinian-Arabs took a completely different position.

The Arab states insisted on two main demands: a) Israel should withdraw to the borders blueprinted by the UN plan of November 1947, and b) the refugees should be allowed to return. Israel rejected both demands, arguing that the new borders—

that could be changed, under the Armistice Agreements, by consent only—had been established as a result of war, and because the UN blueprint took no account of defense needs and was militarily untenable, there was no going back to that blueprint. As to the refugees, Israel was willing to allow an agreed number of them to return (the figure of 100,000 was proposed) and to pay compensation for land and housing left behind (tentative estimates of the value of that property were made by a UN commission, and Israel did not dispute its findings). A return of all the refuges, or a free choice for all those who wished to return, was, however, out of the question, not only because were they hostile to the Jewish state, they would also fundamentally alter the Jewish character of the state. Moreover, in view of the large-scale Jewish immigration from the Arab countries to Israel in the course of the 1950s and early 1960s, Israel argued that a population exchange had taken place. Throughout history, problems created by similar population movements had been solved not by repatriation and the re-creation of large hostile and disruptive national minorities, but by resettlement in the countries chosen by the refugees in the hour of decision. The bulk of the refugees should, in this case too, be resettled, with international help, in the Arab countries—the homeland of their own nation.

The Arab states rejected Israel's arguments and proposals on both moral and political grounds. Israel's emergence at the expense of the Palestinian-Arab society and its tragedy of expulsion and forcible exile was perceived as an unbearable manifestation of injustice. Growing domestic pressures on the ruling elites by militant nationalist, Islamic and socialist movements made the former all the more politically vulnerable. Hence they generally refused to meet with Israel in any direct negotiations, and were unable to provide domestic or regional acceptance of the demands from Israel.

The General Assembly and its committees, as well as UN special agencies, held incessant debates. The UN majority opinion was not favorable to Israel's policies. No clear stand was taken on the territorial question, but the UN tended to favor the refugee's right to choose between repatriation and compensation. In addition to General Assembly Resolution 194 of December 1948, confirming the right of return of those refugees—albeit conditionally—a resolution in 1950 recommended "the reintegration of the refugees into economic life of the Near East either by repatriation or resettlement." Similar resolutions were adopted year after year. While they were linked to a general desire to achieve peace in the Middle East, they did not stress or elaborate the basic issues of peace and coexistence or call for Arab-Israel negotiations. At any rate they had little effect.

In December 1949, the UN established the United Nations Work and Relief Agency (UNRWA) for the Palestinian REFUGEES. For nearly fifty years that agency has been providing housing (in camps), food rations, education and health services. Its efforts to advance to rehabilitation and resettlement yielded virtually no results, mainly because the Palestinians themselves resisted them. In 1949, when it was still believed that resettlement was politically feasible, in the framework of a major Middle Eastern development scheme, the PCC commissioned a group of experts to survey the economic prospects and work out such a general scheme. Its report—the "Clapp Report", represented in December 1949— envisaged the resettlement of the refugees linked with a regional development project, within one year. The Arab states, however, wanted no link between the refugee question and their economic development, and the Clapp Report was filed away.

While the official Arab policy toward Israel strictly shaped by collective decision-making was met with the uncompromising Israeli position on the territorial and refugee issues, secret bilateral contacts and negotiations toward separate agreements took place from the late summer of 1948, between Israel and Jordan and Egypt. Those with King Abdallah of Jordan were re-established while the war was still on. The Armistice with Jordan was in fact concluded in secret talks with the King himself behind the screen of the official negotiations in Rhodes. Continuing contacts yielded a secret draft non-aggression pact, initialled in February 1950 but not finally signed (see ARAB-ISRAEL PEACEMAKING, ABDALLAH.) Further contacts with Abdallah were cut short by his assassination in July 1951. In 1949, before Syria and Israel had reached an Armistice Agreement, Husni Za'im, Syria's new military leader, approached Israel indirectly, proposing to discuss a possible peace settlement in a meeting with Ben Gurion. However, while Ben Gurion refused to meet with Za'im, he approved contacts at the level of foreign ministers, which were never held because the Syrian Foreign Minister, Adel Arsalan, refused to meet with his Israeli counterpart, preferring to resign if forced to do that. The episode was cut short by Za'im's fall and execution. Secret intermittent contacts were also held with Egypt from September 1948, in which emissaries of King Farouq participated. However, these contacts led nowhere, mainly due to Egypt's claim on the Negev as a major condition for a settlement. These contacts continued after the July 1952 revolution with Nasser through various middlemen, but nothing came of them. One of the contributory reasons for that failure may have been an abortive attempt by Israel's secret service, in 1954, to foil a rapprochement between Egypt and the United States, and the evacuation of British troops, by covert sabotage acts against American institutions in Egypt. This caused a deep and protracted political crisis in Israel (see ISRAEL). Israel also maintained covert contacts with forces outside the Arab mainstream, such as the Christian Maronites in Lebanon and their paramilitary organization the PHALANGES, and exiled leaders of nationalist KURDS.

The hostility of the Arab states led them—beyond the political struggle and the propaganda linked with it—to take practical anti-Israel steps, such as a complete boycott (see ARAB BOYCOTT). Egypt also closed the SUEZ CANAL to Israeli shipping and to foreign ships *en route* to or from Israel. Against its obligation under the Convention of Constantinople of 1888, to keep the Canal open to ships of all nations, even in times of war, it cited article X of that Convention enabling it to take measures for its security. In September 1951, the UN Security Council condemned the closure of the Canal and called on Egypt to terminate it, but Egypt did not heed that (binding) decision. As of 1955, Egypt imposed a similar blockade on the Straits of TIRAN, the entrance to the Gulf of Aqaba. After acquiring the islands of Tiran and Sanafir from Saudi Arabia, in 1950 (promising, at the time, not to interfere with the freedom of navigation in the Gulf), it claimed the right to close the Gulf entrance as it was entirely within its territorial waters. Several attempts by ships of different flags to defy the blockade and reach Eilat, Israel's port at the head of the Gulf, failed and Eilat remained blockaded (until 1956).

The most significant security problems faced by Israel after 1948 were the frequent border clashes, that were caused by infiltration, terror and sabotage acts by individuals and small groups of Palestinian-Arabs. In the early 1950s, most of these infiltrations were haphazard, unorganized, and economically motivated, reflecting the existential hardships of the refugee population in the West Bank and Gaza Strip, for theft and grazing aims. Efforts made by the neighboring states to prevent those infiltrations were of limited success and even though only a small part of them involved violence, it triggered Israeli retaliatory policy against the country from which the infiltrators had come, gradually eroding the armistice order, further embittering the conflict. The first major reprisal publicly reported was in October 1953 against the border village of Qibya in the West Bank, in which many innocent citizens were killed, seriously staining Israel's moral standing. In 1954–1956, these acts grew increasingly organized by the Egyptian authorities from both the Gaza Strip and the West Bank, aimed at espionage, sabotage and terror, committed by self-sacrificers (*fida'iyyun*) guerrilla squads. Holding the neighboring Arab states responsible for these attacks, despite denials by the latter, Israel escalated its military retaliations against Egyptian and Jordanian targets in an attempt to force these governments to take effective preventive measures or suffer costly damage of their direct interests. A major retaliatory operation against Gaza in February 1955 apparently triggered Nasser's first arms deal with the Soviet Block in 1955, and was later cited by him as a turning point toward escalation in Egypt-Israel relations. Israel was repeatedly condemned, following Arab complaints about such reprisals to the Security Council, for breaching the armistice by its regular forces. As the sabotage intrusions that triggered those retaliations were on a much smaller scale and with no proof as to the Arab states' responsibility, Israel's claims could rarely be proved when aired at the Mixed Armistice Commissions. In any case, these commissions and UN observers could only record and censure breaches of the armistice, but had no power to prevent or counteract them. The commission's work was also frequently interrupted—thus Israel, from 1952 to 1957, participated only in emergency sessions of the Israel-Syrian commission, and from 1957 boycotted them completely. (Syria insisted that the commission also consider the Demilitarized Zones, which Israel held, to be outside its authority.) From 1956 to 1959 Israel boycotted the Israel-Jordan commission, and from 1956 perceived the Israel-Egypt commission to be abolished.

B. The Sinai Campaign (October 1956) In 1955–1956, Israel felt increasingly threatened by a siege engendered by increasing Palestinian guerrilla (*fida'iyyun*) attacks through the borders. The Egyptian blockade of Eilat, and the build-up of Egyptian forces, enhanced by the 1955 major arms deal with the Soviet Bloc, was accompanied by threatening Egyptian rhetoric, growing inter-Arab tension and struggle for power generated by the Baghdad Pact (signed by Turkey and Iraq in February 1955), and the crisis generated by Egypt's nationalization of the Suez Canal in June 1956. The prospects of renewed Western arms supplies to Iraq—and probably to other Arab states joining the pact—aggravated the fears of Israel due to the assumption that such an alliance might lead to American pressure on Israel to make concessions to the Arabs. Thus, Israel requested to join NATO. When this request was rejected, Israel made an official approach to the US government to reach a bilateral, mutual defense agreement. This was also rejected by Washington. When, in October 1956, Jordan joined a Syro-Egyptian military pact and a Joint Command was established, Israel felt that the siege was complete, posing an immediate mortal danger. Israel resorted to preemptive military action. This operation had been secretly coordinated with Britain and France, whose military plan was aimed at deposing Nasser on grounds of his conflict with Britain over the Suez Canal, and support for the Algerian armed struggle for national liberation against France.

On 29–30 October, Israeli parachutists seized the Mitla Pass. Subsequently, three columns set out across the Sinai desert, tactically supported by the air force. One, striking south from Eilat, took Sharm al-Sheikh, commanding the Straits of Tiran. Another advanced across central Sinai towards ISMA'IIYYA. The northern column outflanked the Gaza Strip, turned back to take it and mop up its Egyptian forces, and then turned southwest along the coastal road toward Qantara.

As the Egyptian air force was unable to intervene in full strength because of the simultaneous Anglo-French assault, Egypt's massive forces in Sinai were completely routed within 100 hours. An Egyptian destroyer was also captured off of Haifa. Other Arab

countries, defense pacts notwithstanding, did not participate in the War.

Heeding a pre-arranged Anglo-French ultimatum, Israel's forces halted 10 miles (16 km.) east of the Suez Canal. As the Security Council was paralyzed because of the veto power of the two permanent members themselves involved, the UN General Assembly, with the USA and the USSR in a rare show of unanimity, called on 2 November, and again on 7 November, for the immediate withdrawal of Israeli forces to the armistice lines, along with that of the Anglo-French forces which had in the meantime invaded the Canal Zone. The USSR threatened to use force if the resolution was not heeded. On 4 November the Assembly created a UN Emergency Force (UNEF) to replace the withdrawing troops. On 8 November Israel withdrew upon the conclusion of the arrangements with the UN concerning UNEF. By 22 January 1957, it had evacuated all the territory occupied except for the Gaza Strip (Egyptian-occupied since 1948, but not Egyptian territory) and the eastern coast of Sinai facing the Straits of Tiran. Concerning these areas, Israel insisted on safeguards for free navigation, and freedom from attacks and sabotage raids across the lines. In March 1957 the UNEF was deployed along the borders, including the Gaza Strip, and in Sharm al-Sheikh, to prove such safeguards, though its terms of reference in that respect were rather vague. Israel also obtained certain diplomatic assurances, but those given by the Secretary-General of the UN were vague and non-committal (a face-saving formula rather than a binding guarantee) and separate US assurances also fell short of full guarantees. When Israel completed its withdrawal in March 1957, the Gaza Strip was, contrary to Israel's expectations, immediately handed over to Egypt, and hostile incursions were soon resumed, though on a much lower scale than before the Sinai Campaign. Israel's casualties in the Sinai campaign were about 170. In retrospect, the operation provided Israel with a decade of relatively calm Egyptian border and the freedom of navigation through the Straits of Tiran (when its closure again by Egypt was among the main causes of the June 1967 War). Together with the prestige of a swift military success, these were Israel's only achievements in the Sinai Campaign. On the other hand, Israel's collaboration with Britain's and France's offensive against Egypt confirmed its image in Arab

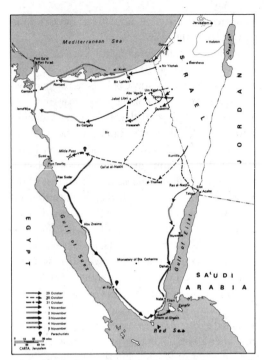

Map of Sinai Campaign, Sinai War, 1956

to-air HAWK missiles, indicating further arms deals, including offensive weapons. At the same time Israel continued to receive arms supplies from France. Following Israel's launching of an experimental missile to the atmosphere in the summer of 1961, Egypt initiated a costly project of developing ground-to-ground missiles with the help of German scientists. Although the missiles turned out to be militarily useless for lacking navigation systems, they became another source of concern to the Israeli decision makers who made major covert efforts to foil the Egyptian plan. Although the arms race was discernible regarding other Arab states involved in the conflict with Israel, it was the Israeli-Egyptian arms race that motivated other Arab countries to fulfill their own share in this race. In the case of the monarchic regimes this was due to a sense of threat from Egypt no less than from Israel.

By late 1963, two new elements appeared in the Arab-Israel conflict, which were to shift the focus of regional politics from the inter-Arab ideological enmities and violent struggles back to the Arab-Israel conflict.

First, the problem of sharing the waters of the Jordan River became an acute, critical issue. It had come close to an agreed solution in the mid-1950s when experts on both Israel and the Arab states agreed to the Johnston Plan. (It was named after Eric Johnston, the American Presidential envoy on this issue.) The agreement had then been rejected by the Arab leaders for political reasons. Israel decided to implement its part of the scheme—unilaterally, but conforming to the principles and water-quantities of the Johnston Plan—and in 1958 began implementing its plan to build a National Water Carrier from the Sea of Galilee to the Negev (see WATER POLITICS). In 1959, the issue became part of the Arab League agenda and a Technical Committee began examining ways to prevent the use of water by Israel, ending up with a plan to divert the Jordan River's tributaries—the Banyas in Syria and the Hasbani in Lebanon. However, the proposal remained unattended until late 1963 when Syria—immersed in bitter rivalry with Nasser—revived this issue, pointing to the imminent inauguration of the Israeli project (said to be completed in late 1964). Syria called to go to war against Israel to prevent the use of the water, challenging Nasser's leadership and commitment to the Palestine cause. That year the

eyes as an aggressive entity, spearhead of Western imperialism and sworn enemy of Arab national liberation. In terms of attitude and official policy, Arab-Israel relations after 1956–1957 remained much as they had been before—adamantly hostile. However, border clashes and intrusions and sabotage acts ceased, at least from Egyptian territory. At the same time, the build-up of forces by the Arab states continued, first and foremost by Egypt.

C. The Road to the June 1967 War Despite relative calmness on the Israeli-Egyptian border, Israel's sense of siege was aggravated by the February 1958 merger of Egypt and Syria into a UNITED ARAB REPUBLIC (UAR), triggering a wave of solidarity and Arab nationalism throughout the region. Furthermore, the intensified Cold War in the Middle East in the late 1950s and early 1960s, led a renewed arms race between the Superpowers to their allies in the Middle East. Even before its military intervention in Yemen, Egypt embarked on an ambitious five-year plan to double its military forces, for which new Soviet arms deals were to be signed. The Yemen War instigated these efforts, leding Israel to request military and diplomatic support from the US. The Kennedy Administration responded positively, and for the first time agreed to provide Israel with ground-

BA'TH Party, which had come to power in March 1963, proclaimed its adherence to the idea of "popular armed struggle" against Israel, challenging Nasser's procrastination of war against Israel until Arab unity had been reached and the regular armies were ready for a swift and decisive war.

Second, since 1959, the Palestinian issue had become increasingly discussed in the Arab political discourse, with growing manifestations of an emergence of Palestinian nationalism, accompanied by unrest among the Palestinian refugees in the Gaza Strip. Apparently, under the impact of the decolonization process in Asia and Africa, the idea of a Palestinian Entity (al-kiyan al-filastini) appeared. This expressed an aspiration of reviving the world cognition to the existence of a Palestinian-Arab people and its national cause. In mid-1959 Nasser adopted the idea, calling for the establishment of a Palestinian Entity, as a political expression of the Palestinian people, followed by his arch-Arab rival—QASSEM of Iraq—calling Nasser to turn the Egyptian-held Gaza Strip into a base of popular Palestinian war against Israel. That year, a secret group of young, educated Palestinian refugees established itself in KUWAIT under the name Fatah (meaning conquest in opposite reading). Fatah maintained that the Palestinians should play a vanguard role in a popular war for the liberation of Palestine, following which the Arab states would join under pressure of their masses. Fatah preached Palestinian self-reliance and changing the commonly accepted order in the Arab strategy toward Israel: popular war would lead to Arab unity. Ba'th Syria thus became Fatah's natural ally when the organization turned into armed action against Israel in early 1965, directing its first sabotage operation against the Israel National Water Carrier.

Nasser was bogged-down in the Yemen civil war, and his prestige in the inter-Arab arena was in decline since the break-up of the UAR. He faced growing economic difficulties, and was being pushed by his Syrian rivals to an undesirable war with Israel. He thus initiated a truce in his troubled relations with the Arab conservative regimes, and called for coordination of the Arab policy toward Israel as a way to resume all-Arab leadership, but mainly to prevent the danger of war with Israel. In January 1964, the heads of all Arab states convened in Cairo following Nasser's call for "unity of rank" over the issue of Palestine, leaving aside inter-Arab differences.

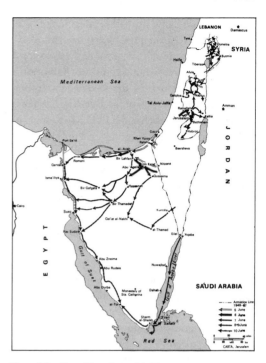

Map of Six-Day War, June 1967

Nasser's initiative meant to attain an all-Arab confirmation to his position that the time for war with Israel had not arrived and that in order to do that the Arabs would have to prepare themselves under a unified Arab command controlled by Egypt. The ARAB SUMMIT CONFERENCE approved the plan for the diversion of Jordan's tributaries and allocated the needed financial resources to implement it, and resolved to establish a Joint Arab Command (JAC) headed by an Egyptian general to supervise and coordinate Arab military preparations for future war with Israel, which could be a result of the Arab diversion plan. The summit also resolved to empower Ahmad al-SHUQEIRI, the representative of the Palestinian-Arabs in the Arab League, to examine the conditions and responses regarding the establishment of a political organization to represent the Palestinians and their cause. Although the summit had not empowered Shuqeiri to establish the organization, apparently with Nasser's backing and King Hussein's reluctant acquiescence, in May 1964, a constituent congress of Palestinians, mostly from Jordan, was held in Jerusalem, proclaiming the foundation of the PALESTINE LIBERATION ORGANIZATION (PLO).

The Cairo summit was a turning point in the history of the conflict. For the first time since 1948, the Arab states came up with a specific collective plan of action regarding the Palestinian issue.

The PLO was meant to be a political expression of the Palestinian entity, not a combat organization as claimed by Syria. In 1965 the second Arab summit approved the foundation of the Palestine Liberation Army (PLA). Nevertheless the PLO was to remain a faithful reflection of Nasser's regional policies, bereft of any military means. It was also confined to propagating the cause of Palestine as a problem of national liberation and to conduct their political mobilization in those Arab countries permitting the PLO to operate.

The new trend in regional Arab politics constituted a threat to Israel, which in June 1964 began operating its National Water Carrier uninterruptedly. However, the following year was marked by intensified Israeli-Syrian military clashes along their common border over the Jordanian waters. In March, Syria began implementing the diversion plan and the Demilitarized Zones, perceived by Israel as its sovereign territory. Israel made it clear that it would consider any diversion as an act of hostility, underscoring that warning by several deliberate strikes at the diversion points in Syria. When border incidents presented an opportunity, the Arab states backtracked. Syria, and particularly Lebanon, made the continuation of the diversion work conditional on full all-Arab military guarantees, which the Arab states were not prepared to give. Diversion works, while not officially canceled, therefore virtually ground to a halt. At the same time, Palestinian sabotage raids against Israeli border settlements and vital installations, mainly along the Lebanese and Jordanian border, became frequent. They were encouraged by Syria, who entangled Lebanon and Jordan in Israeli military retaliations.

The military escalation along the Israeli-Syrian borders had its roots in the internal struggle for power in Syria, and the latter's attempts to attain Egypt's support and recognition by imposing on Nasser its militant approach to the conflict with Israel. Nasser, however, repeatedly and publicly refused to be dragged into war with Israel. Egypt had not been prepared for this. Yet although 50,000–70,000 of his troops engaged in the Yemen civil war, Nasser could not ignore the repeated Syrian calls to remove the UNEF from Sinai and champion a joint Arab military response against Israel.

Nasser's attempt to gain time and postpone the undesirable war against Israel were only partly successful. He refused to send Syria any reinforcements and yet could not withstand the growing pressure on the part of his Arab adversaries to take the lead on the Palestine issue. Nasser's unresolved difficulties in the inter-Arab arena, primarily the Yemen war, and sense of siege by the Arab conservative regimes, in 1966 led to the collapse of the conciliatory atmosphere in inter-Arab relations, while the tension along Israel's northern borders had been constantly on the rise. In November 1966, Nasser signed a defense pact with Syria, resuming diplomatic relations for the first time since Syria's secession from the UAR in 1961. This was apparently due to Soviet efforts to this effect and as an attempt to calm the ultra-revolutionary Ba'th regime that had come to power in February of that year. However, the tension along Israel's northern borders continued to escalate. On 7 April, Israeli planes struck at Syrian artillery positions and shot down six Syrian MIGs. Syria complained bitterly to Egypt that it had not rushed to its aid, particularly in view of their newly signed defense pact. Nasser, however, adhered to his attitude that Egypt had not been ready for war and that he would not be entangled in a war as long as preparations for the decisive war remained incomplete. By mid-May 1967, statements by official Israeli spokesmen, especially the Chief of Staff, Yitzhak RABIN, were taken by both Arab and Russian circles as real threats against Syria. These resulted in Soviet intelligence reports suggesting that Israel had massed military forces along the Syrian border in preparation of an attack on Syria. These brought Nasser to announce that he would not tolerate any further Israeli action against Syria, and on 15 May began massing, rather demonstratively, most of the Egyptian order of battle into Sinai. Despite Israeli and UN observers' denial of the Soviet information, as well as a report verifying the Israeli position, written by the Egyptian Chief of Staff after visiting the Syrian front, the escalation on Egypt's part continued.

As Israel was taking precautionary measures by mobilizing part of its reserve forces and deploying them on the Egyptian front, on 16 May, Nasser requested the immediate withdrawal of the UN Emergency Force (UNEF) from the borders and the Straits of Tiran, and on 18 May, from the whole of Sinai. The UN Secretary-General complied with the request. On 21–22 May, Nasser reimposed a blockade on the Gulf of Aqaba, closing the Straits of Tiran to all shipping to and from Eilat—a step which Israel had repeatedly stated it would regard as *casus belli*. Accordingly, Israel fully mobilized its reserve forces, amid repeated announcements about the strictly defensive nature of these measures, and diplomatic appeals to the Powers to end the crisis. The Egyptian measures were accompanied by threatening, bellicose speeches, tauntingly challenging Israel to war and proclaiming that Egypt was now strong enough to win. Public opinion was deliberately inflamed and mass demonstrations excitedly called for war. Leaders of the other Arab states rallied around Egypt, making equally bellicose speeches. On 30 May, King HUSSEIN of Jordan, under intense domestic pressure, joined the Syro-Egyptian military pact and joint command. On 4 June, Iraq followed suit. The US and several other maritime nations proclaimed that they regarded the Straits of Tiran as an international waterway open to free passage of ships of all nations, and reserved their right to use it, but took no effective steps to make President Nasser change his decision, nor to break the blockade by force. Nasser, on his part, declared that any attempt to break the blockade would be considered an act of war. The blockade, itself an act of war, seemed to be a fact, and the encirclement appeared complete.

Nasser's intentions in initiating the crisis and bringing it to the brinks of war remained unclear. Anyway, it is doubtful that he had any clear military plan or specific war aims, and even when he himself estimated, following the closure of the Straits of Tiran, that war had become inevitable, he was probably expecting Israel to start war while Egypt would remain on the defensive. Whatever his intentions and aims had been, by putting Israel under an existential threat, with an unprecedented all-inclusive Arab war coalition, he effectively left no choice for Israel but to wage a preemptive war. On 5 June, with the international diplomatic efforts leading nowhere, Israeli airplanes mounted a rapid, massive attack against Egyptian air fields and air force concentrations, and Israeli armor moved into Sinai. Syrian airfields were attacked the same day, followed by similar action against the closest Iraqi airfield at H-3. A message was sent to King Hussein warning him to stay out of the war and pledging that Israel would initiate no action against Jordan. The warning went unheeded

and Jordan joined the war (moving, first, to occupy the UN Headquarters south of Jerusalem). During the first day, both the Egyptian, Syrian and Jordanian air forces were largely destroyed, losing over 400 planes (against 19 Israeli planes), and Israel won complete air superiority.

Simultaneously, Israeli forces attacked Gaza, where bitter fighting took place, and advanced into Sinai in three columns; towards al-Arish in the north; Abu Ageila and its elaborate fortifications in north-central Sinai (where a major battle was fought); and al-Qusseima in the center farther south. Sharm al-Sheikh was taken from the sea, and parachutists landed without opposition. At the end of 6 June, the Egyptian forces retreated in disarray, and when the third day of fighting ended, Israeli forces had taken all of Sinai, up to the Suez Canal, and the Gaza Strip.

Jordan's joining the war met swift Israeli counter-action. On 5 June, Israeli forces took the UN Headquarters and on the following day linked up with the isolated outpost on Mount Scopus. The next day they attacked Jordanian positions in East Jerusalem (restraining the inevitable artillery and armor operations out of respect for the Holy Places). On 7 June, East Jerusalem was taken in its entirety, including the Old City, as was most of the West Bank.

On 7 June, the Security Council, after much wrangling, called for a cease-fire. Israel accepted, as did Jordan; Egypt initially rejected it, but acceded on 8 June. Syria, however, which had intensively shelled border villages, refused to accept the cease-fire—relying on the tremendous tactical advantage of her heavily fortified positions on the crest and slopes of the Golan Heights which dominated all of eastern Upper Galilee. Israeli forces thereupon attacked Syrian positions, and after 20 hours of intensive uphill fighting, captured the Golan Heights up to and including Quneitra. Now Syria, too, accepted the cease-fire effective from 10 June.

In less than six days, Israel had routed the armies of three Arab states supported by several other Arab countries (with token contingents in same cases; Iraq sent four brigades, but played no major role). In addition to the 400-plus aircraft destroyed on the first day, more than 500 tanks were destroyed or captured; Arab military equipment lost included approximately seventy percent of the three armies' heavy armament. There were over 11,000 Egyptians killed, and 5,600 taken prisoner. King Hussein

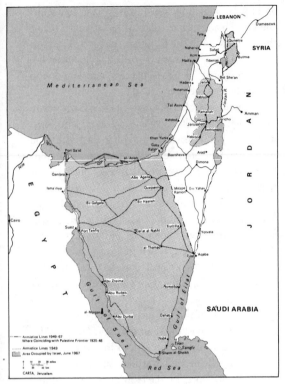

Cease-Fire lines, June 1967

claimed that Jordan had lost 6,000 men—though other estimates were considerably lower. Syria lost nearly 1,000 men. Israel lost over twenty airplanes and over sixty tanks, and its casualties were nearly 700 dead.

5. Between June 1967 and October 1973 Wars

A. Futile Diplomacy. The Six-Day War left Israel occupying an area over three times its pre-1967 size, with an Arab population of nearly one million (in addition to its own 400,000 Arab citizens). The occupied area included the whole of Sinai up to the Suez Canal (which was blocked by ships that had sunk, and kept closed by Egypt), the Syrian Golan Heights, and the Arab part of Palestine, i.e., Jordan's West Bank and Eastern Jerusalem, and the Egyptian-occupied Gaza Strip. The euphoria that prevailed in Israel and world Jewry following the swift victory was diametrically opposed to the sense of despair and disorientation in the Arab world. Israel made official proposals to the Arab states—submitted less than two weeks after the war through the US government—-for direct talks on permanent peace in return for its full withdrawal from the

occupied territories, save some modifications needed for security. Jerusalem, which had been annexed to the State of Israel a few days after the war and unified with Israel's West Jerusalem and the Gaza Strip was not included in the proposal. However, the suggested shift from endemic hostility to peaceful negotiations, especially following a humiliating Arab defeat, was adamantly refused by Egypt and Syria, which insisted on unconditional Israeli withdrawal to the pre-war lines. Especially for Nasser, such an option was impossible, given his wounded prestige, ruined armed forces, and unswerving commitment to Pan-Arab nationalism. Hence, the slogan he adopted following the war maintained that "what had been taken by force would be returned by force." While Nasser did not reject in principle a diplomatic settlement along the lines of the internationally sponsored arrangements which led to Israel's withdrawal from Sinai in 1957, he could not afford a shift toward direct negotiations with Israel, which under the current circumstances would be tantamount to capitulation. King Hussein of Jordan made—with Nasser's tacit backing—efforts to further explore the Israeli proposals through secret meetings with Israeli figures, which emphasized the unbridgeable gap between the two sides.

The Arab collective attitude regarding the results of the war was defined by the Khartoum summit conference held in late August-early September 1967. While proclaiming the adoption of political and diplomatic action in the international arena to "eliminate the traces of aggression," namely, the Israeli occupation of Arab lands, the summit restricted this strategy by three "nays:" no peace with Israel; no negotiations with Israel; and no recognition of Israel. The option chosen by the Arab states maintained a combination of international diplomatic efforts by the two Superpowers—later reinforced by Security Council Resolution 242, approved on 22 November 1967, which set the principles for a peaceful settlement of the Middle East conflict (see ARAB-ISRAEL PEACEMAKING)—-and an escalation of military pressure on Israel along its new borders, aimed at restoring their legitimacy and undermining the international efforts to force Israel to withdraw from the occupied territories.

However, the Arab front was now deeply divided over Resolution 242, which had been immediately accepted by Israel, Jordan and Egypt, but bluntly rejected by Syria. Thus, Nasser's efforts to bring his Arab partners to activate their own military fronts in a coordinated strategy of military pressure on Israel failed. Except for the Palestinian guerrilla operations, mostly across the Jordan River and the Lebanese border, the Jordanian and Syrian Armies remained relatively passive. Nonetheless, the Khartoum decisions and renewal of hostilities hardened Israel's position, underlining the significance of the newly occupied territories for Israel's security. Moreover, the return of Jews to the Old City of Jerusalem, the West Bank and Gaza Strip, and the Golan, aroused strong religious response. These were translated into political conclusions succinctly defined by the slogan "The Whole of the land of Israel" (*eretz Israel ha-shlema*), adopted by right-wing movements, security hard-liners within the Labor movement, and the religious-nationalist, messianic groups, perceiving the redemption of the Land of Israel as a step toward the redemption of the Jewish people and the advent of the Messiah. Yet despite calls on the part of the ideological right-wing to annex to the State of Israel all the occupied parts of Palestine as well as the Golan, the national coalition government refrained from officially changing the status of the occupied territories other than East Jerusalem.

The UN and the Great Powers renewed their efforts to find a formula for an Arab-Israel settlement soon after a cease-fire ordered by the Security Council had ended the War. These efforts were now even more difficult, as the Soviet Bloc, except for Romania, had severed relations with Israel. Six radical Arab states had broken relations with the US, whom they accused of collusion with Israel. Attempts by the Soviet Bloc and Third World countries to bring the UN to order an immediate Israeli withdrawal, with no settlement and no conditions, failed both in the Security Council and the General Assembly. However, the UN was nearly unanimous in condemning the annexation of East Jerusalem in Israel and demanding its annulment. On November 1967, the Security Council, after protracted wrangles, unanimously adopted Resolution 242. This became the principal document concerning the Arab-Israel conflict agreed to by the UN, the Great Powers and most of the states of the region. It stressed the need for "a just and lasting peace in which every state in the area can live in security," "the inadmissibility of the acquisition of territory by war," and the "right

of all states in the region to live in secure and recognized borders." The decision also called for the withdrawal of Israeli armed forces "from territories" ("the territories" according to the French version); the "termination of all claims or states of belligerency and respect for and acknowledgment of the sovereignty, territorial integrity and political independence of every state in the area"; guarantees for the freedom of navigation through international waterways; and a "just settlement of the refugee problem." Israel accepted Resolution 242, stressing that its English version called for withdrawal "from territories" and not from "*the*" or "*all*" territories occupied, and that the withdrawal was to be part of a negotiated peace settlement. Most Arab states accepted the Resolution, while Syria and other radical regimes, as well as the PLO rejected it (principally because it spoke of refugees only, without acknowledging Palestinian national rights to independence and statehood). But all Arab spokesmen interpreted it as ordering the withdrawal of Israel from *all the* territories occupied, and without the need for prior negotiations or peace agreements.

Resolution 242 also requested the UN Secretary-General to designate a "special representative" to promote agreement and assist peace efforts. He appointed the Swedish diplomat Gunnar Jarring. Such efforts were even more urgent as hostilities between Egypt and Israel were resumed soon after the war.

Israel adhered to its willingness for peace and, based on Resolution 242, insisted on direct Israeli-Arab negotiations to suggest its recognition by the Arab states, in return for most occupied territories. Israel maintained that the Armistice lines of 1949, explicitly defined as not final political borders, were not sacrosanct, and invalidated by the War of 1967, thus new agreed borders had to be negotiated. A general indication of what Israel might wish to retain (most of the Jordan Valley; the eastern slope of the Judean desert; the Etzion block of former settlements south of Jerusalem; Sharm al-Sheikh on the Straits of Tiran; and the East coast of Sinai connecting it to Eilat), was outlined in the "Allon Plan" which dominated the ruling Labor Party's thinking, though it was never formally adopted. Israel's territorial appetite and intentions, however, were explicitly expressed by its policy of establishing new settlements in the occupied areas. Initially these were semi-military, frontier settlements, along with the

Labor-Zionist ethos of the *Yishuv* and first decade of the state, and until 1977, mostly in those parts that Israel intended to retain under the Allon Plan. To "normalize" its rule over the West Bank, Israel also instituted a policy of "Open Bridges". This allowed economic links between the occupied West Bank and Jordan, imports and particularly exports, financial ties, and a constant, though controlled, movement of mutual visits. An influx of West Bank and Gaza Palestinian-Arabs into Israel became apparent for labor purposes, mostly in menial jobs in agriculture, construction and services. Within three years, those working in Israel were thirty-five to fifty percent of the West Bank and Gaza labor force, contributing twenty to twenty-five percent of the occupied areas' GNP. For the Arab states, on the other hand, Israel's withdrawal from all territories occupied in 1967 remained an essential pre-condition for any political settlement.

B. The Rise of the Palestinian Resistance

The aftermath of the 1967 War witnessed a surge of Palestinian nationalism and the strategy of popular armed struggle against Israel. Initially this was fully supported by the Arab regimes, adopting the Palestinian resistance to compensate for their inaction, and as a cure to their ruined prestige. As the West Bank and the Gaza Strip, the heartland of Arab Palestine, were now occupied by Israel, additional refugees, estimated at 250,000–350,000 (including more than 100,000 refugees from 1948) had left the area. Thus the potential for political mobilization to the newly mushrooming Palestinian guerrilla organizations was widely available, adopting *Fatah's* idea of Palestinian activism in the liberation War of the whole territory of Palestine. The PLO was taken over, in 1968–1969, by the various *fida'iyyun* guerilla groups, becoming an umbrella organization for them. With the removal of Shuqeiri and his colleagues from the PLO leadership, and the takeover by the guerrilla groups, the PLO Charter was amended, emphasizing its narrow Palestinian-nationalist nature (*watani*), unlike the previous Charter, which had carried a Pan-Arab (*qawmi*) inclination, defining the Palestinian goals with regards to territorial goals, the status of Jews in the future Palestinian state, and most important, the definition of the armed struggle as a strategy and not a tactic.

Indeed, the dominant phenomenon on Israel's borders with Lebanon, Syria and Jordan, in the wake of the 1967 War were frequent clashes, caused mostly by actions of the PALESTINIAN GUERRILLA ORGANIZATIONS and Israel's reprisals. Attempts to organize popular resistance within the occupied territories were curbed—in the West Bank by the end of 1967, and in Gaza by 1971–1972. While there were occasional incidents, the occupied areas were relatively quiet until the mid-1980s. Yet despite their proclaimed support for the PLO and the Palestinian guerrilla organizations, the Arab states could not ignore the impact of Palestinian military activity on their soil, triggering painful Israeli military retaliations against targets in their own sovereign territories. The Palestinian guerrilla organizations entrenched themselves in Jordan and Lebanon, particularly in the refugee camps, through 1967–1970, where they established their legitimate semi-autonomous status. A bitter violent conflict soon erupted between the state and the revolution in these countries. In November 1969, intensive armed clashes between Palestinian guerrillas and Lebanese military units (mostly Maronite Christians), combined with a long governmental crisis, led to Nasser's interference and mediation. This led to the Cairo Agreement which officially recognized their right for military presence on Lebanese territory, albeit with some geographic and operational limitations. Unlike their political victory in Lebanon, Jordan clashed with the Palestinian resistance organizations after preparations which included international coordination with the US and Israel. The Palestinian guerrilla groups sustained a total military defeat in two bloody confrontations ("Black September" 1970, and July 1971), following which they were expelled from the country, despite Arab outcries and attempts at diplomatic intervention. Syria kept the Palestinians on its soil under strict control, disallowing them any independent action. (see PLO, JORDAN, LEBANON, SYRIA). From that time on, Lebanon became the main and virtually only base for PLO operations.

As terrorist attacks increased in scope and intensity, so did Israel's counter-action—air raids, brief punitive incursions, commando operations—mainly in Jordan and Lebanon. In March 1968, a large scale Israeli raid against the Palestinian guerrilla bases at Karame turned into a confrontation with the Jordanian forces, causing significant losses to the Israeli force and enabling the PLO to present the battle as its own victory. Israel was frequently condemned for these incursions by the UN Security Council. In 1968 some Palestinian groups became involved in international TERRORISM, initially directed against Israeli targets—hijacking a civilian airliner in July—but increasingly against foreign ones, outside the Middle East, attacking planes and passengers in international airports. Operations of this kind culminated in the spectacular hijacking of several international airliners in September 1970 (timed to coincide with the decisive battle against Jordan) and a suicide attack (by Japanese terrorists allied with the PFLP) on passengers at Lod (Tel Aviv Airport) in May 1972. Following "Black September" *Fatah* also entered the arena of international terrorism, broadening the scope of this activity, aiming it also at Jordanian and Western targets. There were attacks on Israeli Embassies and official delegations; the assassination of Israeli athletes at the Munich Olympics, September 1972; and the seizure of the Saudi Embassy in Khartoum (with the murder of the American Ambassador and other foreign diplomats in March 1973). In 1974 the PLO's mainstream dissociated itself from international terrorism and air-hijacks and ordered them to stop. Nonetheless, extremist factions within *Fatah* and the PFLP continued these actions. Israel's secret servicesturned to methods of counter-terror, such as seeking out and killing terrorist leaders in covert operations or military raids on their headquarters in Lebanon (April 1973 in Beirut). (see also TERRORISM)

C. The War of Attrition (1969–1970) Border friction resumed soon after the cease-fire came into effect on 10 June 1967. It intensified, particularly along the Suez Canal where Egyptian artillery barrages responded in kind, and after the sinking of an Israeli destroyer by Egyptian missile boats, in October 1967, when Israel heavily shelled and destroyed the Suez oil refineries. While on the Lebanese, Syrian and Jordanian borders the main fighting against Israel was conducted by the Palestinian guerrillas, in 1968–1969 tension and military clashes intensified along the Egyptian front due to Egyptian artillery shelling and commando raids, to which Israel reacted by counter-shelling. This culminated, as of July 1969, in Israel increasing employment of its air force against Egyptian military targets. By early 1970 it engaged in in-depth attacks on strategic targets. In March 1969, Nasser declared a War of Attrition against Israel. This served as a prelude to the next

phase of an all-out war for the liberation of Sinai. Egypt, however, remained alone in the battlefield against Israel, with the other states invariably content with militant rhetoric, limited financial aid to Egypt, Jordan and the PLO, and reluctant support of the Palestinian resistance activity.

Even the fire set in August 1969 at the al-Aqsa Mosque by a Christian fanatic in Jerusalem failed to bridge the inter-Arab differences. Yet Arab and Islamic leaders refused to accept Israel's assurance that the arsonist was a demented foreign tourist. Rather they suspected it was an Israeli plot against *al-haram al-sharif* (the Temple Mount), the third most sacred shrine for Muslims all over the world. An Islamic summit conference was held in protest in Rabat, Morocco, and later became permanent under the name ISLAMIC CONFERENCE ORGANIZATION (ICO), whose main goals revolved around the defense of the Muslim holy shrines under Israeli occupation. Nonetheless, Nasser's efforts to use the event for rallying the Arab world around Egypt's lead and soliciting additional significant funds from the Arab oil-producers for the expansion of Egypt's military capabilities, remained unheeded, as he had insisted on maintaining both military and diplomatic options open.

In March 1969, Jarring suspended his efforts. Talks by the four Great Powers, and the two Super powers were also of no avail (particularly as the Soviet Union's proposals were entirely in line with the Arab position regarding the implementation of Resolution 242). In October 1969, the US Secretary of State, William Rogers, presented his proposals to the USSR and the Middle East disputing parties. These were published in December as the Rogers Plan. The plan was based on Israel's near-total withdrawal on the Egyptian and Jordanian fronts. (It did not deal with the Israeli-Syrian border, though its principles were similar on all fronts.) It comprised negotiations on certain details only, and on the choice of return for the refugees. The plan was bluntly rejected by Israel. It was also rejected by the Arab states and the USSR and was accused of being excessively pro-Israel.

The growing demoralization caused by the Israeli in-depth air raids forced Nasser to call, in April 1970, for urgent Soviet involvement in construction and operation of a comprehensive air defense system, comprising surface-to-air missiles, largely manned by

Soviet crews, which managed to down several of the raiding planes; and Soviet pilots reinforcing the Egyptian air force and participating in operative missions. The Soviet defense system proved to be effective, significantly raising the cost for Israeli air raids against Egypt. In addition, even though Israel had built a network of fortifications along the eastern bank of the Suez Canal, casualties were heavy.

In view of the danger of military escalation with Russian involvement, in June 1970 US Secretary of State William Rogers submitted to the parties his plan for a three-month cease-fire and military standstill on both sides (to be monitored by the Americans). During this the international mediator Gunnar Jarring would resume his peace-making mission based on Resolution 242. The plan, which had been discussed with the Soviets and had gained their approval, was accepted by Nasser on 22 July and became effective on 7 August shortly after the Israeli government gave its approval. This was not before far-reaching secret assurances had been given to it by President Nixon. However, it turned out that on the night the cease-fire came into force, the Egyptians moved forward surface-to-air missiles, near the Canal. This pre-planned action was intended to give the Egyptian air defense further depth and was part of the preparations for a future operation of major crossing of the Canal and creating a defensible bridgehead on the east bank. The revealed violation of the cease-fire led Israel to suspend the renewal of Jarring's mediatory talks until this violation was altered by the Egyptians. Egypt, however, refused to abide by the Israeli and American claims, stalemating the political situation. The end of the War of Attrition was of interest for both sides concerned due to the high price they were to pay for continuing this limited War. On Israel's side more than 1,000 were killed until the War ended in August 1970, while Egyptian casualties were estimated at over 10,000.

In September 1970 Nasser passed away and was replaced by Anwar al-SADAT who, on 4 February 1971 announced the prolongation of the cease-fire by another month. During this time Israeli forces would withdraw from the Suez Canal to the al-Arish-Ras Muhammad line, following which works to reopen the canal would begin. Sadat explained that this would be the first step in a comprehensive implementation of Resolution 242 according to an agreed timetable. A few days later, Israeli Prime Minister Golda MEIR publicly welcomed Sadat's initiative. However, Sadat's proposals remained an historical episode, perceived by many as a lost opportunity for peace that could have prevented the October 1973 War. Nevertheless, on 7 February, Jarring, launching his last mediation effort, submitted a plan to Egypt and Israel, initially requesting a clear Egyptian commitment to end all belligerency (including freedom of shipping through the Suez Canal and the Straits of Tiran) and an Israeli one to total withdrawal of the former Palestinian-Egyptian border. Egypt, now under President Sadat, replied favorably, though it hedged its commitment to the freedom of navigation by making it subject, for the Suez Canal, to the CONSTANTINOPLE CONVENTION OF 1888, and for the Straits of Tiran to "the principles of international law," both of which it had cited in the past to justify the denial of passage. Egypt also demanded a prior Israeli commitment to the repatriation of the refugees. Israel replied that it was committed to withdraw "to the secure, recognized and agreed boundaries to be established in the peace agreement," but would not withdraw to the pre-June 1967 lines. Concerning the refugees it was prepared to negotiate compensation and Israeli participation in the planning of their "rehabilitation in the region" (i.e., settlement in place, not repatriation). From 1971, Rogers attempted to mediate an interim agreement on the reopening of the Suez Canal based on a partial withdrawal and an agreed military de-escalation—a proposal which Sadat and Israel were prepared to discuss. Nothing came out of these efforts either.

Despite the failure of the international mediation, the post-1967 years witnessed the beginning of essential changes in the Arab position in the conflict with Israel:

a) Extremist slogans defining the Arab strategic goal in total terms, such as the elimination of the state of Israel, which had damaged the Arab case in world public opinion and deluded the public at home, were gradually discarded. The strategic goal was to be defined in terms of Israeli withdrawal from the occupied territories. Nonetheless, much ambiguity remained concerning the Arab claim for the restoration of Palestinian national rights. The acceptance of Resolution 242 by Egypt, Jordan and tacitly by other Arab states, indicated a de facto acceptance of Israel's existence, even though this was conditional on total Israeli withdrawal from the territories occupied in June 1967, which Israel adamantly rejected.

b) Israel's takeover of Arab national territories boosted inter-Arab diversity and care for one's own interest as opposed to the collective approach to Israel—content with essentially passive hostility and short-of-war measures—which had prevailed before 1967. Thus, although in terms of intensity the post-1967 years indicated a sharp rise of armed confrontation along the borders, the new situation created conditions for the beginning of a shift by those Arab states—namely, Egypt and Jordan—for whom the cost of the 1967 War triggered a self-searching regarding their position in the conflict with Israel, looking for ways to bring it to a reasonable end.

c) A claim for a mini-Palestinian state—in the West Bank and Gaza Strip—was increasingly supported by Palestinian elite figures in these territories, though until 1973, fiercely rejected by the PLO, employing terror and punishment against its advocates. Shortly after his ascendancy as President, Sadat began advocating this idea, trying to convince the PLO leaders to adopt a more realistic position on the future Palestinian state. Before 1967 the stress had been on the elimination of Israel, implying the establishment of an Arab-dominated Palestinian state on its ruins—but all references to the "West Bank" annexed by Jordan and forming half of the Kingdom, had been blurred so as not to antagonize Jordan, and no group or movement in the West Bank itself had explicitly advocated secession and the creation of a separate Palestinian independence. This restraint disappeared in the early 1970s, with most Arab states implicitly speaking of a Palestinian state in the West Bank and Gaza Strip, implying acquiescence in Israel's existence in its pre-1967 borders.

Jordan did not abandon its claim for the West Bank or for representing its Arab inhabitants, or Jordanian citizens. However, following the Jordanian-Palestinian confrontation of 1970–1971, and the consequent Hashemite loss of legitimacy in the Arab world, King Hussein had to accommodate Palestinian claims to self-determination, at least in part. In March 1972 he announced a federal structure for his kingdom, with the West Bank as a semi-independent constituency. This plan was strongly re-

jected by most Arab states, especially Egypt. Until the October 1973 War, the PLO had rejected the idea of a mini-Palestinian state alongside Israel, and insisted on its claim for the whole territory of historic Palestine. However, given the negative effect of the newly amended Palestinian National Charter (1968), which clearly spelled out but mainly implied in many of its articles, not only the illegitimacy of Israel, but also the decisive Jewish majority in Israel, stated that only those Jews who had lived in Palestine permanently before the beginning of the "Zionist invasion" (defined elsewhere as the year 1917), would be considered citizens of the Palestinian state. In 1969 the PLO officially adopted the idea of a democratic, non-sectarian Palestinian state in which Muslims, Christians and Jews would be living in peace and harmony. This was criticized by the radical ultra nationalist PFLP and other factions of its sort. Israel regarded the "secular and democratic" formula as a public relations ploy and did not take it seriously, but did, however, impress liberal and leftist circles in the West and the elites of the "Third World", many of whom supported the PLO in its quest for self-determination and independence for the Palestinians.

D. The October 1973 War (also called the "Yom Kippur War" in Israel and the West; the "October War," or the "Ramadan War" by the Arabs) The continued occupation of Sinai and the Golan Heights by Israel and the stalemated international mediation efforts since February 1971, laid the foundations for the military initiative taken by President Sadat, in coordination with Syria's new ruler Hafez al-ASAD, that led to the October War. Israel's leaders deluded themselves into thinking that the Bar-Lev line on the Suez Canal made an Arab military assault impossible, that Egypt and the Arab states would have to acquiesce in the occupation for a long time or accept its conditions for a settlement, and that Israel could sit it out. Sadat viewed the war as the last resort, adopting this option only when it had become clear that both Superpowers were comfortable with the "no war no peace" mode that had prevailed in the conflict with Israel, and that the only means to break the stalemate was a major military action. This estimate was clearly confirmed by secret talks held by President Sadat's and President Nixon's national security advisors prior to the War, as well as by the policy of reluctance and procrastination that

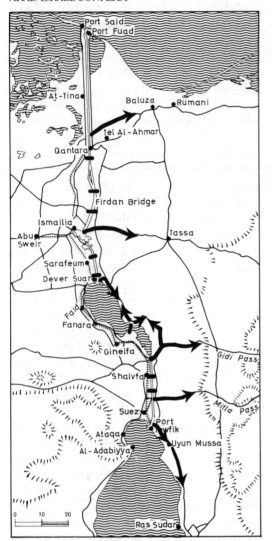

Yom Kippur War, 1973, Phase 1 — Egyptian attack

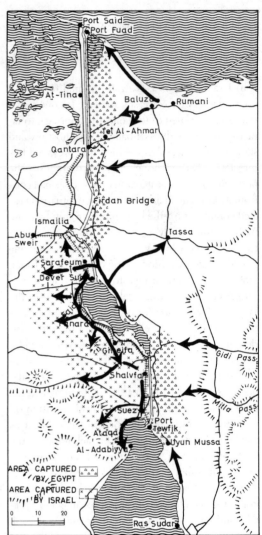

Phase 2 — Repulse of Egyptian army

marked the Soviet Union's response to Sadat's requests for the needed weapons and equipment that would enable Egypt to wage war against Israel. Preparations for a coordinated offensive on both Egyptian and Syrian fronts, and efforts to ensure military support from other Arab states in case of war, had been made since late 1972. To maximize their military prospects the Arab planners strove for strategic surprise, for which they worked out a deception plan that would confuse the Israeli intelligence and political decision makers. The military preparations were combined by political ones which were to ensure Third World support, as well as the use of the oil weapon by the Arab oil-rich countries. Indications in September 1973 of a major Arab build-up on both the

Egyptian and Syrian fronts were interpreted in Israel as part of military exercises (that were frequently staged, particularly on the Suez Canal front). This assessment supported Israeli intelligence estimates that the Arab armies were not ready for a major war, that their leadership was not capable of launching one, and that, anyway, an assault across the Suez Canal was not feasible. It also tallied with general conceptions of Israel's leaders who failed to conceive the urgent imperative for the Arab regimes to put an end to the occupation of their national territories. The military intelligence assessment was misled by deliberate successful Egyptian and Syrian deception plans.

At 14:00 on 6 October, Syria mounted air attacks and heavy artillery shelling, and moved three divi-

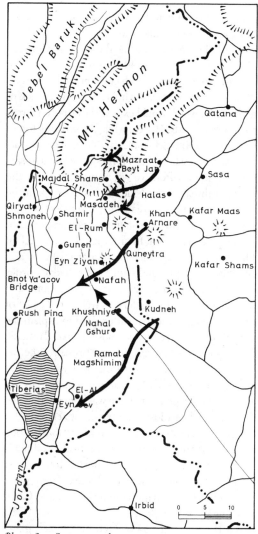

Phase 3 – Syrian attack

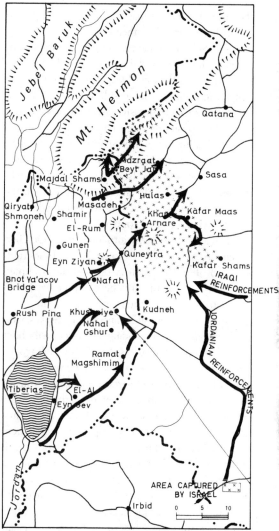

Phase 4 – Repulse of Syrian army

sions with some 1,400 tanks into the Golan, with two more divisions ready to follow. Facing them was an Israeli line of outposts, each with a small force of tanks—a total of, initially, two armor brigades. One of these posts on Mount Hermon was overrun by Syrian forces and surrendered. (This later caused a bitter controversy in Israel), and three were evacuated. Syrian forces advanced deep into the Golan, in two main thrusts. One advanced along the main northeast-to-southwest axis of the central Golan leading from Quneitra to the Bridge of Jacob's Daughters. This force reached the Nafah area, some 6 miles (10 km.) from the Bridge, with one of its companies reaching the Bridge itself but never crossing it. The other advanced along the parallel axis farther south—

the road leading from Rafid towards the Lake of Galilee. This force reached the area of El Al and also moved northwest, along the disused Tapline and the road parallel to it, to reinforce the first force in the Nafah area. However, Israeli counter attacks, from 8 October, leading to bitter fighting and heavy losses on both sides, succeeded in halting the Syrian advance on both axis and pushing the Syrians back. By 10 October Syrian forces had been pushed out of the Golan.

On 11 October Israeli forces continued their counter-attack into Syrian territory, in two thrusts: one in the north, crossing the lines in the area of Jubata, advanced up to Mazra'at Beit Jann; the other, farther south, in the central sector, advanced along the main Quneitra-Damascus road beyond Khan al-Arnabeh and turned southeast, reaching al-Kanaker and Kafr Shams. In that area they were attacked by two fresh Iraqi armored divisions which had just arrived in the battle area. Despite heavy fighting in which the Iraqis sustained substantial losses, they stopped the Israeli offensive. Israeli forces consolidated their positions when paratroopers captured the dominating hill of Tall Shams on 12 October. The lost position on Mount Hermon was recaptured on 21–22 October, and Israeli forces advanced, taking several Syrian outposts on the Mount. In the naval operations the Israelis destroyed much of the Syrian navy and gained control.

When a cease fire came into force on 22 October, Israeli forces had occupied some 231 sq. miles (600 sq. km.) of Syrian territory beyond the occupied Golan, with the entire area between the battlefield and Damascus within the range of their guns.

Egypt's attack were simultaneous with Syria's, with five Egyptian divisions crossing the Suez Canal, about 70,000 troops, against less than 500 Israeli troops holding the Bar-Lev Line in widely dispersed outposts. When Israeli armored forces, hastily mobilized, rushed to counter-attack, they found the Egyptians established on the eastern side of the Canal. They came under heavy attack, particularly by anti-tank missiles that caused heavy casualties. Egypt's dense anti-aircraft missile system frustrated operations by the Israeli air force, causing substantial casualties. Efforts to relieve small units besieged in isolated outposts of the Bar-Lev Line also led to severe casualties. By the third day, most of the Bar-Lev Line had been captured or abandoned. The most southerly one, at Port Tawfiq, held out for most of the week but surrendered after running out of ammunition and supplies. The first Israeli counter-attack, waged on 8 October, ended with heavy losses to the attacking force, with a battalion commander taken prisoner. The Egyptians set up three major bridgeheads across the Canal: one in the north, based in Qantara (the Second Army); one in the center, based in Isma'iliyya (Second Army), and one in the south, in the area of the Great Bitter Lake and opposite the town of Suez (Third Army). From the outset, the Egyptian military plan sought to attain a limited aim, namely, a viable bridgehead on the east bank of the Suez Canal, with 6–9 miles (10–15 km.) depth. The plan maintained (mainly in response to

Syria's demand) that this would constitute only the first phase. After awhile it would develop the offensive with the aim of capturing the strategic Mitla and Gidi Passes 25–28 miles (40-45 km.) from the Canal.

However, the Egyptian High Command was aware of its inability to wage such an offensive for lack of air defense, which would expose the armored forces to Israeli air raids. Hence, while the crossing forces continued to entrench in their positions and press farther east, and while Israeli forces were still in disarray, no major offensive was mounted. With the growing threat of the Israeli counter-attack in the north, Syrian appeals to Sadat to implement his commitment to develop the offensive eastward, brought the Egyptian President to order his General Staff on October 11 to wage such an offensive with the aim of taking the Mitla and Gidi Passes. Sadat's order aroused objection on the part of the Second and Third Armies' commanders, as well as the Chief of Staff, General Shazli, who attempted to explain the dangers of such an offensive, causing a two-day delay. However, under the President's pressure, the offensive did take place on 14 October with most of the armored order-of-battle participating in the thrust. The Egyptian offensive was contained by the Israelis with heavy losses among the attacking tanks. Egyptian attempts to advance southeastwards along the Gulf of Suez towards the Abu Rudeis oil fields were also foiled. Egypt was reported to have lost over 300 tanks in these two offensives, paving the way to the Israeli major counter-attack and Canal crossing westward.

On the night of 15–16 October, Israeli paratroopers crossed the Canal north of the Bitter Lake, establishing a bridgehead on its western side. The following day they were joined by elements of an armored brigade which began to widen the perimeter. Attempts to secure and widen a corridor on the eastern bank so that larger forces, including those moving down from the northern sector, could cross the Canal, met with surprisingly meager Egyptian resistance, clearly out of surprise and lack of sufficient armored forces in the border line between the two Egyptian Armies' sectors. The routes to the bridging area, and a corridor leading to them, were cleared by the northern division on 16–17 October. Bridges were built, and on 17–18 October the northern force crossed the Canal. On 19 October a division from the southern sector also crossed, bringing Israeli forces on the west bank to three divisions. The operations leading to the crossing, as well as the decision-making process, involved bitter controversy among the generals who commanded the crossing divisions, reaching the Israeli public. Egyptian counterattacks on the west bank, from Isma'iliyya southwards, on 17–18 October, failed. The growing presence of Israeli armored forces west of the Canal drove the Egyptian Chief of Staff to demand the withdrawal of Egyptian forces from the east bank to reinforce the defense of the area between the Canal and the Nile Valley. This demand was firmly rejected by President Sadat and led to the dismissal of Shazli from his post. During those days the Israeli air force also regained, in large-scale air battles, the upper hand.

Israeli forces on the east bank continued their efforts to clear widening areas of Egyptian troops and strongholds. There was partial success for this in the center and north; the Egyptian Third Army in the south, was surrounded and cut off. Nonetheless, those on the western bank advanced, amid heavy fighting. The southern forces reached, and cut, the Suez-Cairo road on 22 October, and the same day closed the ring by taking Adabiyya. They also entered Suez town, believing that firing had ceased there, but came up against Egyptian strong points and suffered heavy casualties. Except for Suez town, Israeli forces now held a continuous area of some 617 sq. miles (1,600 sq. km.) inside Egypt, from the outskirts of Isma'iliyya to Adabiyya on the Gulf of Suez. The Israeli navy also had, in several encounters, gained the upper hand and controlled both the coastal waters of the Mediterranean and the Gulf of Suez.

The War stretched for over two weeks, primarily due to the Superpowers' effort to air lift to their clients massive military supplies. The Russians, who had resumed large-scale military aid to Egypt after much controversy, implemented a huge arms deal signed in March 1973. They greatly increased their supplies in October by sea and in a massive airlift (reportedly 15,000 tons by air, in over 900 flights, and 63,000 tons by sea). The US began rushing supplies to Israel, after some controversy as to the timing and extent, in an airlift, from 14 October (reportedly 22,000 tons). Both Superpowers, and the other powers, were working in the UN Security Council for a cease-fire, with the USSR pressing for speedy decisions reportedly in response to a Syr-

ian request. There was confusion on that point, as Egypt objected to a cease-fire in the early stages of the War, when matters seemed to be going well, which Syria thereupon denied. After much wrangling, the Security Council decided on a cease-fire on 21 October. When the fighting did not stop, it reiterated its urgent call on 22 October, coupling it with another general-political resolution on peace in the Middle East—Resolution 338, reconfirming Resolution 242 of November 1967, adding a call for immediate negotiations between the parties concerned under appropriate auspices. Fighting still continued, with the Egyptian Third Army trying to break out of the Israeli ring and Israel consolidating its forces' positions around Suez-Adabiyya. On 24 October the Soviet Union, angry with the delay, reportedly threatened massive intervention. US forces were put on world-wide—including nuclear—alert against that threat. But on 24 October the fighting ceased. On 16 October, the Arab oil producers decided to sharply raise the oil prices, to impose an oil embargo on the US and Holland (for serving the airlift military support for Israel), and reduce oil production by five percent each month, until Israel had withdrawn from the territories it occupied in 1967. It was the first effective use of Arab oil as a political weapon in the Arab-Israeli conflict, with unprecedented psychological impact on Western public opinion and on the world as a whole. It was especially significant in view of the Arab limited military success, and the world energy crisis since the early 1970s.

The cease-fire left Egypt in possession of two major bridgeheads on the east bank of the Suez Canal, to a depth of some 6 miles (10 km.), an area of more than 386 sq. miles (1,000 sq. km.). However, its Third Army, in the southern sector (20,000 troops with some 300 tanks), was surrounded and cut off, but saved from total annihilation by the cease-fire. Israel was left in possession of the 995 mile (1,600 km.) area on the West Bank described above. The total losses of the two sides were relatively heavier than ever before. Syrian and Egyptian casualties were close to 15,000, and 8,000 troops were taken prisoner; Egypt and Syria lost 1800 tanks (forty percent of their tanks), 400 aircraft and 14 missile boats. Israeli losses on both fronts totalled 2,700 killed and 5,000 wounded. 305 Israeli soldiers were taken prisoner; 500 tanks were destroyed (another 500 were hit and repaired during the war); 120 aircraft, were downed and no missile boats were lost. On the Syrian front alone, Syria had over 3,000 fatalities (with some estimates much higher), losses of 600–800 tanks and 160 planes, and its elaborate ground-to-air missile system was largely destroyed. About 370 Syrian soldiers were taken prisoner. Israel had lost over 770 dead and some 250 tanks (of which some 150 could later be repaired); more than 2,400 soldiers were wounded, 65 were taken prisoner.

In purely military terms, the October War that began with heavy—even critical setbacks for Israel, culminated in a clear Israeli victory. Although Israel was denied its final fruits, namely, the elimination of the Egyptian Third Army, by the cease-fire imposed by the Superpowers and the Security Council, its military achievements played a significant role in convincing Sadat to enter a diplomatic process with Israel, beginning with the military talks at Kilometer 101 (from Cairo). This indicated a new phase in Israeli-Egyptian relations. In Israel, the circumstances under which the war broke out, the strategic surprise and the large scope of human losses, indeed no less, the psychological shock caused by the very Arab military initiative and performance, all resulted in soul-searching, official investigations, bitter controversy and a sense of a deep moral and political crisis. In contrast, the Arab world was in a state of euphoria, deriving from the wide participation of Arab states in the War by sending expeditionary forces, supplying weapons, or employing the oil weapon. Above all, the war resulted in a sense of victory at shattering the legend of Israel's military invincibility, and getting out of the dark tunnel through which the Arabs had been wandering since 1967. Egypt claimed credit for much of this success, first and foremost due to the crossing of the Suez Canal, which was seen as a brilliant feat of military valor. Egypt had proven the Arabs' ability to plan and execute a complex military operation, cleansed the Arabs' shield of honor of the stain of previous defeats, and restored a sense of Arab self-confidence. The War also broke the deadlock of Israel's immovable occupation of the territories captured in 1967 and established a significant Egyptian presence at least in part of these territories. It thus, politically and morally, broke through a psychological barrier and enabled Sadat to envisage steps toward a peaceful settlement (to begin with a settlement of

Egypt's own Sinai problem even before a comprehensive solution of Arab-Israeli issues was attained).

Although the war took the other Arab regimes by surprise, the initial success of Egyptian and Syrian forces and relative length of hostilities generated widespread manifestations of Arab solidarity, demonstrating the rallying power of war against Israel. Moreover, nine Arab states (Iraq, ALGERIA, Jordan, Libya, MOROCCO, TUNISIA, Kuwait, Sudan, and Saudi Arabia) dispatched forces and weaponry to the front, albeit token in some cases. Arab support by expeditionary forces had been discussed and concluded in principle prior to the war, but not all Arab states lived up to their commitments. Some did, and others even exceeded them. The total scope of the Arab expeditionary forces was significant: ten squadrons, one armored and one mechanized division (both Iraqi, sent to the Syrian front), five armored and two infantry brigades, and two infantry battalions. Jordan had been excused from direct, frontal participation in the war, but had sent an armored force to aid Syria, which sustained heavy losses. The Iraqi armored forces played a crucial role on the Syrian front, even though Iraq had not been asked to send forces, arriving in the front just in time to block the Israeli offensive from further advance toward Damascus.

6. The Peace Process (1973–1979)

A. Military Disengagement and Beyond (1973–1975)
The UN Security Council's Resolution 338 re-established UNEF which had existed in Sinai until 1967. The Council also reaffirmed Resolution 242 of 1967, adding a call for immediate Arab-Israel peace negotiations, under "appropriate auspices". The main diplomatic effort was exerted by US Secretary of State Henry Kissinger "shuttling" innumerable times as an untiring mediator between Cairo, Jerusalem and Damascus, and cajoling the disputing parties into partial settlements which evolved under his guidance. Egyptian and Israeli senior officers had been meeting under UN auspices since the end of October on the cease-fire line at Kilometer 101 on the Suez-Cairo road. In November a "Six Point Agreement" was reached, dealing with the reinforcement of the shaky cease-fire and with food and non-military supplies to the besieged Third Egyptian Army, east of the Suez Canal, and the town of Suez. Further talks ran into difficulties and were suspended. Late in December 1973,

a conference optimistically termed "Peace Conference" met in Geneva under the co-chairmanship of the Russian and American Foreign Ministers, and the UN Secretary-General. Egypt, Jordan and Israel attended (Syria refused to participate, and the PLO had not been invited). It achieved no progress. An Egyptian-Israeli Military Committee also met in Geneva to discuss an agreed disengagement of forces. Agreement on this, however, was reached not at Geneva, but under Kissinger's auspices, in January 1974, and implemented in February-March. Under its terms, Israel withdrew its forces from Egypt west of the Canal; accepted the presence of Egyptian forces in Sinai, east of the Canal, up to the line of the October cease-fire; and lifted the siege of the Egyptian Third Army. A 6 mile (10-km.) UNEF buffer-zone was established, to separate the two armies. In strips of east and west of that zone Egyptian and Is-raeli forces were "thinned out" and limitations were imposed on their equipment. In view of Sadat's sep-arate diplomacy, Syria renewed the fire along its front, as a means of pressure. The lifting of the Arab oil embargo—under strict American pressure—rendered Asad's position even more precarious re-garding similar military agreement with Israel. After tough negotiations mediated by Kissinger, a military disengagement agreement was eventually reached in late May 1974. Israel withdrew from Syrian terri-tory captured in October 1973, and from the empty town of Quneitra held since 1967. A buffer zone was manned by a UN Disengagement Observer Force (UNDOF), and limitations on the strength of forces and their equipment were accepted for a 6 mile (10-km.) strip and a further 16 miles (25-km.) zone on each side. Syria refused to pledge that it would pre-vent guerrilla infiltrations and attacks from its terri-tory, but was believed to have given an informal, verbal undertaking to Kissinger. (For the diplomat-ic process in the aftermath of the war, see ARAB-IS-RAEL PEACEMAKING.)

Efforts by Kissinger to proceed in the summer to a similar agreement on the Israel-Jordan front scored no success. Jordan's failure to enter the war on its own front, and the heavy regional Arab pressure in favor of the PLO, combined to weaken the legitimate basis of the Hashemite claim to represent the Palestinians in the West Bank. Israel, now under a new govern-ment headed by Yitzhak Rabin, was unwilling to dis-cuss territorial concessions in this area, mainly because it lacked sufficient support in the government to such an approach. Instead, Israel suggested "functional settlement," namely, the application of Jordanian authority over the Palestinian population, but with-out territorial sovereignty, in parts of the West Bank. The King's efforts at reaping a territorial achieve-ment in this territory aroused wide Arab resent-ment, particularly on the part of the PLO and Syria. This culminated in the resolution adopted by the Arab Summit Conference in Rabat (October 1974), recognizing the PLO as "the sole legitimate repre-sentative of the Palestinian people," and finally dis-qualifying Jordan to speak in the name of the West Bank.

From late 1974, Arab attempts to renew the peace process in a comprehensive framework, including the Palestinian issue to be represented by the PLO, proved to be impracticable in view of the Israeli and American strict rejection of the PLO. Israel pre-ferred to continue with the "step by step" peace process separately with Egypt, in order to drive a wedge between the largest and strongest Arab state and the rest of the Arab states. A new round of shut-tle diplomacy by Kissinger in February and March 1975 in an attempt to further Israeli-Egyptian agree-ment was frustrated, leading to a "reassessment" of the US policy toward Israel. On 5 June, the Suez Canal was reopened. This led to a renewal of nego-tiations under American auspices, and to the signing of an Israeli-Egyptian Interim Agreement in Sep-tember 1975. The agreement ("Sinai II") provided for a further withdrawal in Sinai and a new UN buffer zone. It moved further to the east with Egypt-ian forces moving east into what had previously been the buffer zone. Egypt and Israel each set up a sur-veillance and early-warning station in the new buffer zone, with a third such station manned by American civilian technicians. The oil fields and installations in the Abu Rudeis area on the Red Sea coast were re-stored to Egypt, demilitarized and with a civilian UNEF-supervised administration. The new agree-ment assumed new political elements tantamount to ending the state of war between the two coun-tries. The parties reaffirmed that they would not re-sort to the use or threat of force and that the conflict should be solved by peaceful means. The agreement was to remain valid until it was replaced by anoth-er; and a free passage through the Suez Canal of Is-rael-bound (non-military) cargoes on (non-Israeli ships) was now permitted. This Interim Agreement was made possible by new US secret assurances to Israel, set down in a formal "Memorandum of Understanding" (and balanced by parallel US assurances to Egypt). Aside from a commitment for further military and financial aid, the American administration undertook to refrain from holding any diplomatic contacts with the PLO as long as the organization had not renounced terrorism, accepted Resolution 242, and recognized the State of Israel.

There was no comparable progress in Israeli-Syrian relations. Secret and informal contacts with King Hussein of Jordan, based mainly along the general lines of the "Allon Plan", continued, but yielded no agreement. During those years, the political position and status of the PLO grew noticeably stronger, as outlined above. In June 1974, the PLO National Council's meeting decided to establish an "independent combatant national authority" on any liberated part of Palestine. This was interpreted by some as implying the PLO's readiness to be content with a Palestinian-Arab state in the West Bank and Gaza that would coexist with Israel—but such a readiness was not officially spelled out, nor did it lead to any change in the Palestinian National Charter. The post-1973 War witnessed Israel's increased isolation in the international arena, primarily as a reflection of the immense impact of Arab oil and wealth, particularly on Third World states and, to a lesser extent, also on Western Europe. This impact was manifested not only by the large number of African and Asian states that had severed their diplomatic relations with Israel shortly before and after the War, but also in the automatic decisive anti-Israeli majority in the United Nations and its organizations, which became instrumental in the Arab political warfare against Israel, spearheaded by the Palestinian issue. From 1969 on, it demanded the right of self-determination for the "Palestinians", i.e., the Palestinian-Arabs ("the inalienable rights of the Palestinian people"—December 1969). In November 1974, Yasser ARAFAT was invited to address the General Assembly. The PLO was accorded observer status and the right to participate in debates. The UN General Assembly and its special agencies, year after year condemned Israel's occupation of Arab territories; its practices as an occupying power; and its anti-terrorist reprisals and raids. The Assembly denounced Israeli settlements in the occupied areas

as illegal (July 1979, endorsed by the Security Council in March 1980, and since then reiterated). In November 1975 the Assembly even denounced ZIONISM, as a form of "racism".

Throughout these years, attacks by Lebanon-based Palestinian guerrilla groups against Israel continued, generally on civilian "targets" like schools, buses and apartment blocs, with occasional attacks abroad—e.g., at embassies or airports—and with the hijacking of airliners. These operations, many of which were aimed at emphasizing the Palestinian issue, especially in view of Israel's efforts to ignore and exclude the PLO from the peace process, triggered Israeli counter-operations, preventive, deterrent or punitive, particularly against targets on Lebanese territory. The Palestinian guerrilla warfare against Israel was hardly affected by the Lebanese civil war that had erupted in April 1975, and into which the mainstream *Fatah* organization joined by the end of the year. In July 1976, an Israeli commando operation at Entebbe, Uganda, rescued a hijacked French airliner with its captive, mostly Israeli, passengers. Raids on Palestinian guerrilla bases in south Lebanon culminated, in March 1978 (following *Fatah's* raid from the sea and killing of 32 Israeli citizens near Tel Aviv), in a three month occupation of a strip of Lebanese territory up to the Litani River. The UN Security Council Resolution 425 ordered Israel's withdrawal and created a UN force, UNIFIL, to supervise it and help prevent further hostilities. Israel ostensibly implemented the UN resolution, withdrawing to the international border, but in fact handing over control of the border strip to a Lebanese militia, mostly Christian, equipped and trained by Israel. Since 1976, Israel's northern border was kept nearly open—at "the Good Fence"—for the inhabitants of South Lebanon's border zone to sell their produce and seek supplies, medical help, and employment. Israel's secret ties with the Christian Phalanges also grew stronger and gradually came into the open.

B. The Israel-Egypt Peace Treaty (1977–1979) The Israel-Egypt Sinai II Agreement led to Egypt's isolation in the inter-Arab arena for over a year, especially deepening the cleavages with Syria and the PLO. The inter-Arab fences, mended by October 1976 on the occasion of the Syrian-Palestinian confrontation in Lebanon (see LEBANON), on grounds of another agreement to seek a comprehensive Israeli-Arab settlement, once again proved futile. In May 1977, an historic shift of power occurred in Israel with the right-wing Likud Party taking over for the first time in Israel's history. The new government adhered to continued Israeli possession of the West Bank and Gaza Strip, as part of the Jewish homeland—aspiring to incorporate them into Israel, with local autonomy to the Palestinian residents—and rejected withdrawal from most of the occupied territories. Attempts to reconvene the Geneva Peace Conference failed, primarily because Israel and the US refused to accord the PLO representation on an equal footing at the peace conference. The stalled peace process, previously led exclusively by the US Government, took a new direction when Soviet-American talks yielded a joint statement (1 October 1977) that was rejected by Israel, and apparently resented by President Sadat, who identified Soviet involvement in the peace process with rigid support of Syria and the PLO, anticipating a continued impasse.

The deadlock was dramatically broken by Egypt's President Anwar al-Sadat. In November 1977, after short secret preparations, he held an official visit to Jerusalem, shocking the whole world with his bold decision. The visit, that had been prepared in secret contacts (in which President Ceausescu of Rumania and King HASAN of Morocco allegedly had some part), turned into a dramatic and highly emotional state visit.

In addition to meeting Israel's leaders, government and opposition, Sadat addressed the Knesset, Israel's Parliament, offering peace (effectively, the end of the state of war) against Israel's withdrawal from all territories occupied in 1967 and—though he failed to mention the PLO—he insisted on a just solution to the Palestinian problem. In substance, Sadat's proposals were not very different from the position of the other moderate Arab states. His great achievement was, first, as he also himself put it, a psychological breakthrough, cutting off the vicious circle by directly meeting the Israeli "enemy" and talking to him face to face; and second, spelling out what other Arab leaders at best implied—a preparedness to accept Israel and coexist peacefully once Israel agreed to the far-reaching concessions he demanded. He made it clear, though, that he would not conclude a separate peace but would consider an eventual agreement as being within the context of, and a first

step toward, a comprehensive Israel-Arab settlement.

Sadat's historic visit ended with an agreement to negotiate a peace accord. In Egypt, Sadat's move and the agreements ensuing later were opposed by the Nasserist intelligentsia, the extreme Left and the Islamic fundamentalists. Yet public opinion in general seemed satisfied with the return of their whole national territory of Sinai. The radical Arab states, led by Syria and Libya, immediately began moves to ostracize and isolate Egypt. Most of the Arab states, however, with the Gulf oil monarchies, Jordan, Morocco, and Sudan, although critical of Sadat's separate moves, suggested a restrained "wait and see" policy in response.

Israeli-Egyptian negotiations proved difficult following the November 1977 euphoria. They were conducted with the mediation of the US administration and required a great deal of American persuasion and cajoling, with the personal involvement of President Carter. After several rounds of talks yielding no agreement, Sadat, Begin and Carter closeted themselves in September 1978 at the US President's residence "Camp David"—and there, after twelve days of hard negotiation, two Camp David Agreements were signed on 17 September. One was a "Framework for Peace in the Middle East," committing the parties to an active search for "a just, comprehensive and durable settlement of the Middle East conflict through the conclusion of peace treaties based on Security Council Resolutions 242 and 338" and respect for the "sovereignty, integrity and independence of every state in the area along with their right to live in peace within secure and recognized boundaries, free from threats or acts of force." To achieve this, and implement Resolution 242, negotiations were needed (as Israel had always insisted, and the Arabs had denied). Egypt and Israel agreed that for a transitional period of up to five years, an autonomous regime should be established in the West Bank and Gaza (for "the inhabitants," as Israel insisted, meaning: not for the territory). Jordan would be invited to join the negotiations on the details and the self-governing authority, and the Egyptian and Jordanian delegations might include Palestinians acceptable to all. The five-year transitional period would begin with the inauguration of the self-governing authority, whereupon Israeli armed forces would withdraw to "specified security locations." During that transitional period, Israel, Egypt, Jordan and the elected representatives of the inhabitants of the West Bank and Gaza would negotiate and agree on "the final status of the West Bank and Gaza and its relationship with its neighbors," while simultaneously, Israel and Jordan, "joined by the elected representatives of the West Bank and Gaza," would negotiate an Israeli-Jordanian peace treaty. The "solution" negotiated "must also recognize the legitimate rights of the Palestinian people and their just requirements".

A second agreement laid down a "framework for a peace treaty between Israel and Egypt." It provided for Egyptian sovereignty up to the international border between Egypt and Mandatory Palestine, along with the withdrawal of Israeli armed forces from Sinai. This followed the Israeli failure to obtain Sadat's assent to an Israeli presence at Sharm al-Sheikh and the east coast of Sinai—even in the form of a lease recognizing Egyptian sovereignty or as a joint Egyptian-Israeli presence—or to Israel's retention of an area of Israeli settlements in the northeastern corner of Sinai (with the new Israeli town of Yamit). Three major airfields built by Israel in Sinai were to be used by Egypt for civilian purposes only. The free passage of Israeli ships through the Suez Canal, the Gulf of Suez, the Straits of Tiran and the Gulf of Aqaba was assured. Certain limitations were imposed on the size and equipment of military forces in Sinai. UN forces were to be stationed in parts of Sinai (this was later changed to a "Multinational Force of Observers," US-directed and not under UN auspices). After the signature of the peace treaty, "complete, normal relations" would be established between Egypt and Israel, "including diplomatic, economic and cultural relations." Furthermore, "economic boycotts and barriers to the free movement of goods and people" would be terminated.

The Camp David Accords were accompanied by several letters exchanged by the Egyptian, Israeli and US heads of government. In one of them, Sadat insisted that "Arab Jerusalem is an integral part of the West Bank" and "should be under Arab sovereignty," and, while the city should be undivided and under a joint municipal council, "all the measures taken by Israel are null and void and should be rescinded." In December 1978 Sadat and Begin jointly received the Nobel Peace Prize.

Sadat's efforts to entice other Arab states into the Egyptian-Israeli framework of negotiations failed. Late in November 1978, an invitation issued by Sadat to Jordan, Syria and Lebanon, as well as the USSR, to join a Cairo Conference preliminary to the resumption of the dormant "Geneva Conference," was attended only by Egypt, Israel and the US, and still ended with a deadlock. All the Arab States and the Soviet Bloc rejected the Camp David Agreement. The radical regimes had taken steps to ostracize and boycott Egypt since December 1977. A new inter-Arab Syrian-Iraqi alignment now led the Arab world as a whole to adopt a series of sanctions against Egypt, should it insist on implementing them. An agreed draft of the Peace Treaty had been almost completed by November 1978. Certain differences remained unresolved until another personal intervention of President Carter, visiting Cairo and Jerusalem in March 1979 to mediate these issues and bring them to final conclusion, and the ceremonial signing in Washington of the Treaty of Alliance between the two states took place on 26 March 1979. It conformed to the framework of the Camp David Accords, and was accompanied by several annexes, agreed minutes and letters. After much wrangling, this stated that "in the event of a conflict between obligations under the present Treaty and other obligations, (the former) will be binding." A joint letter committed Sadat and Begin to start, a month after ratification, negotiations on the "modalities for establishing the elected self-governing authority (administrative council)" for the West Bank and Gaza—with Jordan, if it accepted the invitation to join—to be completed within one year. Most of the Arab states immediately responded with severing their relations with Egypt, and joining the collective sanctions resolved by the Baghdad summit conference of November 1978 and the following conference of Arab foreign and economic ministers in March 1979, expelling Egypt from the Arab League and other inter-Arab forums, ceasing all sorts of official financial aid, and applying an economic boycott against Egypt.

The Peace Treaty was ratified, and went into effect, on 25 April 1979. Israel's withdrawal from half of Sinai, set for December 1979, was duly implemented. The town of al-Arish was handed over in advance, in May. The total withdrawal was completed in April 1982. Yamit and the settlements were dismantled and bulldozed by Israel. Israeli flag ships began passing through the Suez Canal in April 1979. The normalization of relations went into effect in January 1980. Ambassadors were exchanged in February. The boycott laws were repealed by Egypt's National Assembly the same month, and some trade began to develop, albeit less than Israel had hoped for. In March 1980 regular airline flights were inaugurated. Egypt also began supplying Israel crude oil. A US-led Multinational Force of Observers (MFO), with early warning stations etc., replacing UNEF (which had ended operations in July 1979) was in place in March 1982, but no major incidents called for its intervention.

Thus there was peace between Egypt and Israel. Egypt, since October 1981 under President Husni MUBARAK, continued Sadat's policy despite Arab pressures and strong interest to rejoin the "Arab fold" and resume its leadership, and despite disappointing vicissitudes and crises in Egypt-Israel relations. The growth of normal, friendly relations—beyond an official state of peace—had hit obstacles which the two parties have thus far been unable to overcome. Talks on the autonomy regime for the West Bank and Gaza were stalled soon after they opened in 1979, both on the substance of the autonomy envisaged and on procedure (e.g., Israel's insistence that some sessions be held in Jerusalem, which Egypt refused), and were, despite several attempts to revive them, not resumed. A dispute on the small area of Taba, adjacent to Eilat was resolved only in 1986, in an arbitrary agreement. Egypt resented legislation finalizing the annexation of East Jerusalem (July 1980) and the extension of Israeli law to the Golan, i.e. its de facto annexation (December 1981), as well as the Israeli air raid on the Iraqi nuclear reactor in June 1981, and the invasion of Lebanon in June 1982. In September 1982, following the massacre of Palestinians by the Phalanges in the refugee camps of Sabra and Shatila in Beirut, at the tacit consent of the Israeli High Command, Egypt was forced to recall its ambassador, leaving the Embassy headed by a lower-level diplomat, and virtually freeze the process of normalization and the cultivation of trade, and cultural relations, etc. It also saw a violation of the spirit, if not the letter, of the peace agreement in the halting of the normalization process, and complained of that even before September 1982. Egypt had permitted its press and public organiza-

tions to conduct vicious anti-Israel propaganda, and had hampered efforts to cultivate trade and cultural relations. American efforts to mediate or informally assist in an improvement, an unfreezing of relations, were only partial successful. Only in September 1986, did Egypt's President and Israel's Premier meet—for the first time in five years—with the former agreeing to appoint a new Egyptian ambassador, after Israel, having withdrawn from Lebanon, agreed to submit the Taba dispute to arbitration. This, however, could not change the basic nature of relations between the two countries, best defined as "cold peace," with minimal elements of normalization except for the official diplomatic relations.

7. Israel's Lebanon War (1982–1985) The Egypt-Israel peace agreement remained isolated, with no progress on other Arab-Israel fronts. With Egypt expelled from the Arab League, politically and economically boycotted, the Arab world proved to be paralyzed, extremely fragmented, and absent of a leading power. The Shi'i revolution in Iran (February 1979), and consequent eruption, in September 1980, of the IRAN-IRAQ WAR, revived the Syrian-Iraqi hostility and aggravated the Gulf monarchies' sense of insecurity, leaving them with no real option of following Egypt or restoring their relations with it given the Syrian-Iranian alliance and desire to preserve their friendly relations with Syria as a shield toward revolutionary Iran. While the Israeli-Jordanian front was quiet and the "open-bridges" policy of close Jordan-West Bank relations was maintained, PLO military infrastructure in South Lebanon grew stronger, especially in view of the gathering forces of the Maronite-Christians in this country in a growing secret alliance with Israel. Israeli counter-operations, commando and air raids against the PLO establishment in Lebanon, which inevitably also hurt the Palestinian and Lebanese civilian populations, were intensified. They often led to clashes and air battles with Syrian forces stationed in the East Lebanon Biqa'. Thus Syrian planes were shot down in air battles in June 1979 and April 1981. In the latter clash, near Zahla, Israel let itself be drawn into the fray to protect and assist its Maronite-Christian Lebanese Forces (the name adopted by the unified Maronite militias under Bashir JUMAYYIL's lead). In July 1981, after two weeks of Israeli-provoked heavy artillery exchanges between Israel and the Palestinian forces in South Lebanon, an American-mediated cease-fire was informally concluded. This provided for a halt in attacks from Lebanon on Israel. However, the Israeli government—led by political and military hard-liners—resented this arrangement and looked for a pretext to eradicate the Palestinian military buildup in Lebanon as a whole, in conjunction with its Maronite allies in their country.

Although Israel's invasion of Lebanon was ostensibly launched in response to the attempt on the life of Israel's ambassador in London—perpetrated by the ABU-NIDAL terrorist faction—it had long been pre-planned for a long time at the highest level, and discussed in principle with the US government. The intended war set far-reaching political aims, namely, to eliminate the PLO politically and militarily; to support Israel's Maronite-Christian allies to establish themselves in power, and to expel the Syrians—over a division-size force—from this country. The war, was termed in Israel as "war by choice." This indicated the poor legitimacy it received in the divided Israeli public, and for the first time in Israel's history shattered the consensus over national security. On 6 June 1982, Israeli forces invaded South Lebanon in a large scale operation designed—so Israel announced—to liquidate the PLO's military-terrorist establishment entrenched there and to halt approximately 25 miles (40 km.) from the border. The local population, including its Shi'i-Muslim majority, largely welcomed the invading troops as liberators from the near-domination of South Lebanon by the PLO that had become oppressive. However, Israeli troops continued their advance, occupying most of the Shuf, the mountainous region southeast of Beirut with its mixed, DRUZE and Christian population, advancing in the Biqa', reaching the southern outskirts of Beirut, and cutting the Beirut-Damascus highway in several places. When a cease-fire took hold, on 24 June (a first cease-fire on 11-12 June had been inffective), Israeli troops joined Christian Phalange forces and reached the coast northeast of Beirut, encircling the capital. The Israeli forces advanced northward on three axes: one along the Mediterranean coast; one in the central mountain region; and one in the eastern sector, near the Lebanese-Syrian border. A fourth important axis would later develop in the Biqa' valley. The operational instructions to the forces were to avoid con-

frontation with Syrian forces in the Biqa'. As it turned out, this instruction had not been genuine, at least as far as Defense Minister SHARON and the IDF command were concerned.

On 9 June, the invasion of Lebanon became a full-scale confrontation with the Syrian force in the Biqa', particularly in the air and in raids against the air-defense system. In a pre-emptive strike, the Israeli Air Force destroyed 17 of the 19 SAM batteries which Syria had installed in the Biqa'. An unprecedented air battle also took place, with the participation of 150 fighter aircraft; 29 Syrian MIG-21s and MIG-23s were shot down. Armored warfare took place in the Qar'un Lake area, both south of Jezzin and in areas southeast of Qar'un, and heavy fighting took place in the vicinity of Ein Zhalta, with very slow Israeli progress. On the following day, a full scale confrontation with Syria developed on the ground as well. In the early morning, the largest tank battle of the war began north and northeast of Lake Qar'un, between an Israeli armored corps and a Syrian armored division. The IDF prevailed, its forces moving north towards Jubb Jenin. In another large-scale air battle, some twenty-five Syrian MIGs were shot down. The IDF continued its slow advance along the coastal axis, meeting Syrian and PLO resistance north of Khaldeh, 2 miles (3 km.) south of Beirut Airport. On the central front, Israel's tank forces were halted by heavy Syrian resistance in the mountain passes of the Ein Zehalta region.

Thus when a cease-fire came into effect at noon on 11 June, Israeli forces were positioned about 2 miles (3 km.) south of Beirut Airport on the coastal front; a few miles south of the Beirut-Damascus highway in the Ein Zehalta area; in the vicinity of Jubb Jenin—well below the highway—in the Biqa'; and in Kafr Quq on the eastern axis near the Lebanese-Syrian border.

The cease-fire declared by Israel and Syria on 11 June did not end Israel's operations against the Palestinian armed units. There was now a "crawling" stage, initially meaning Israeli movement to cut off the PLO in West Beirut from its Syrian suppliers. Initially this involved artillery exchanges between the IDF and the PLO forces south of Beirut. On 13 and 14 June, Israeli tank and paratroop units completed the encirclement of Beirut by linking up with the Lebanese forces led by Bashir Jumayyil in East Beirut. They also won control of Beirut's exit to the

Beirut-Damascus highway, reaching the proximity of the presidential palace at Ba'abdah and the outskirts of Beirut Airport. This was achieved through a tough battle, involving Syrian tank and anti-tank commando forces. However, already at this stage, the Lebanese Forces were reluctant at actively collaborating with Israel's forces, taking a passive position to refrain from demonstrating their close alliance with Israel. On 20 June, the PLO and Syria withdrew their forces from Beirut Airport, and Israeli forces gained control of the airport without a battle.

The second part of the "crawling" stage began on 21 June with a major battle initiated by the IDF against Syria's reinforced tank and commando units in an effort to gain control of the Beirut-Damascus highway in the Alley-Bhamdun area. Israel's advance was slowly gaining momentum. The battle raged for almost a week. When it ended, Israel had gained control of the highway to a point just east of Beirut, putting under siege its western part, aiming to force the PLO and the Syrian forces to evacuate the city.

The US had not opposed UN Security Council calls for a cease-fire and the withdrawal of Israeli troops. It did however, condone Israel's operation in its first limited version, being somewhat sympathic to its expanded, grand-design version. In June again sent a senior diplomat, Philip Habib, to mediate. In July it announced that Marines would be sent to supervise the evacuation of PLO forces. Efforts were increased, in concert with Saudi Arabia and Syria, to reach an agreement on that evacuation. Israel intensified its pressure, shelling and bombing West Beirut—thereby arousing much condemnation and strong US objections. The siege endured throughout July and most of August, employing artillery, naval and air bombardment of the PLO positions in Beirut, as well as incremental advances into the western parts of the city. On 11 and 12 August, the air force conducted a massive bombardment of Beirut. The following day, the PLO agreed (under pressure from the Lebanese and Arab governments) to withdraw under the protection of a multi-national force. The withdrawal of Palestinian and Syrian forces from Beirut commenced on 25 August; PLO chairman Yasser Arafat left Beirut on 30 August, as did the Syrian brigade positioned in the city. By 4 September, the evacuation of the PLO military personnel and Syrian forces was completed. 8,000 Palestinians left by sea, and 6,000 Syrian and

loyal Palestinian forces left the city by land to the Biqa' area, under the auspices of the multi-national force. In August, the Israeli grand design seemed to approach realization when—the term of Lebanon President SARKIS having expired—the militant young Phalange leader Bashir Jumayyil was elected President. However, on 14 September these hopes were shattered with the assassination of President-elect Jumayyil, apparently on Syria's instructions. Despite the Israeli government's decision not to enter West Beirut, on September 14–15, Israeli forces captured West Beirut. This was followed by a massacre conducted by Phalange forces at the Palestinian refugee camps of Sabra and Shatila, with the tacit consent of the Israeli military command. Following the worldwide outcry against the massacre, the "multi-national" forces that had withdrawn from Beirut in mid-September now returned. Israeli troops evacuated Beirut late in September, maintaining a liaison office in a suburb. On 21 September, Amin Jumayyil replaced his murdered brother Bashir as President.

The massacre stained Israel with moral responsibility due to its partnership with the Phalange, arousing an international world-wide protest, as well as in Israel, where the government was forced to establish a Committee of Enquiry to investigate the events. This led to the dismissal of Defense Minister Ariel Sharon, an end of the Chief of Staff's term, and the disqualification of the local commanding officer for further assignments of field command. For the next year, the IDF's main task was to hold on to its positions pending the outcome of the negotiations.

The new Lebanese President was less militant as a Phalangist fighter for Christian predominance. He wanted a compromise and national reconciliation, and an accommodation with Syria. He was also less identified with, and sympathetic to, Israel. When Israel-Lebanon talks on the withdrawal of Israeli forces began in December 1982, the new regime no longer shared the basic conception that Israel's withdrawal would be accompanied by—even conditional on—a formal agreement on border security and the prevention of terrorism from Lebanese soil, as well as a non-belligerent coexistence or a de facto peace with close liaison and possibly open borders and normalized relations. Negotiations were protracted and required much American mediation. The agreement, finally signed on 17 May 1983, fell short of Israel's expectations, but satisfied some of its minimum requirements. The state of war was terminated and mutual respect for the two countries' independence and territorial integrity proclaimed. The "existence or organization of irregular forces, armed bands, organizations, bases, offices or infrastructure" aiming at "incursions into or any act of terrorism in" the other party's territory were to be prevented, as were "entry into, deployment in, or passage through" the parties' territory, air space and territorial waters of "military forces or equipment hostile to the other party." Previous Lebanese agreements enabling such activities were declared null and void. Israeli forces were to withdraw from all Lebanese territory within three months after the ratification of the agreement, simultaneously with Syrian and PLO forces. (This last condition was not spelled out but informally understood, and confirmed in an Israeli-US exchange of letters.) Lebanon would establish a special security zone, whose southern part, a 9 mile (15-km.) wide strip from the Israeli border nearly to the Litani (and de facto a further area up to the Zahrani river), would be policed by an "Army Territorial Brigade" incorporating "existing local units" (i.e., Major Haddad's Southern-Lebanese forces, set up and maintained by Israel), while its northern part, a further 30 km wide, up to the Awali river, was to be policed by a regular army brigade. UNIFIL would be transferred to that northern area. A Joint Liaison Committee, with US participation, would supervise these measures, with joint supervisory patrols. Israel would maintain a Liaison Office in Lebanon, and Lebanon was granted the right to do likewise in Jerusalem. An agreement would be negotiated on the "movement of goods, products and persons" (i.e. de facto normalization). In the meantime existing patterns of such movements would continue.

The agreement of May 1983 was never ratified by Lebanon and thus did not go into effect. It was vehemently opposed by Syria and its allies within Lebanon, headed by the Druze and Shi'i leaders. As President Jumayyil aspired to a compromise with his adversaries and a government of national unity, the demand for its annulment was a main issue at the lengthy negotiations on intra-Lebanese reconciliation (Jumayyil had been unenthusiastic about it in the first place). Eventually, when a conciliation agreement under a government of national unity was established (February 1984, see LEBANON), the May 1983 Agreement was formally annulled by Lebanon

on 5 March 1984. The Israeli Liaison Office, transferred in 1983 to a northern suburb of Beirut in the Christian area controlled by the Phalanges, was ordered to close down in July. Israel's vision of coordination and friendly, near-normal relations with Lebanon had been shattered.

Militarily and politically, Israel's presence in Lebanon still had to cope with three types of threats. First, was Syria's entrenched military forces in Lebanon, which now included some three divisions (two armored, one mechanized) and a number of independent brigades and commando units, totalling the equivalent of over four divisions. Against some 350 tanks in Lebanon before the war, Syria now had some 1,200 tanks positioned in the Biqa', both north and south of the Beirut-Damascus highway. Although this force still lacked air and air-defense cover, its inferiority in these realms was alleviated to some degree by the introduction of Soviet SA-5 systems into Syria in late 1982. Overall, the Syrians enjoyed an impressive defensive capability against the IDF in Biqa'.

The second problem the IDF had to face was the intense conflict between the Christian-Maronites and the Leftist Druze, led by Walid JUNBLAT in the Shuf mountains. Since the area was under Israeli control from late June 1982 for over a year, the Lebanese forces, as Israel's allies, strove to take control of the Shuf—a traditional stronghold of the Druze. The IDF found itself in a cross-fire between the warring factions, without being able to settle their differences. Against this backdrop, from the summer of 1983, with the May 1983 Agreement inoperative and eventually abortive, Israel had to envisage a unilateral withdrawal of its troops—if possible, in coordination with the Lebanese government and army. Efforts to attain such coordination, however, failed. The Lebanese government, now under strong Syrian influence, was unwilling to agree with Israel, insisting on a total and unconditional withdrawal. It was also incapable of taking over and imposing its rule on the rival militias. Israel therefore, in September 1983, withdrew from the Shuf and the Kharrub district (southwest of it, including the coastal area) to a new line on the Awali River, north of Sidon (positions in the east, the Biqa', were maintained). That unilateral withdrawal was then blamed for the anarchy, the bloody fighting, and the mutual massacres between Christians and Druze that broke out in the Shuf and ended with the full take-over of the region by the Druze and the elimination of much of its Christian population.

Finally, the IDF had to cope with an escalation of armed resistance waged increasingly by the Shi'i militia AMAL, and its militant-fundamentalist off-shoot, HIZBALLAH. Some small armed Palestinian units still remained in the Israeli-held territories of Lebanon. Others infiltrated through the areas held by the Syrians, the Christians, and the multi-national force. Since June 1982, a growing Iranian influence within the Shi'is in the Biqa', due to the arrival of some 1500 Revolutionary Guards (PASDARAN), led to the consolidation of *Hizballah*, which was responsi-ble for a seires of suicide bombings during the last few months of 1983 against the American embassy in Beirut, the Multi-National Force Headquarters, and Israeli headquarters and bases. Over 400 men, mostly Americans were killed. The result was that while the War relieved the towns of northern Israel (at least temporarily) from the danger of Palestinian guerrilla attacks, the IDF came under attack by armed Shi'i resistance in Lebanon. One account noted 256 guerrilla attacks against the IDF in Lebanon between September 1982 and April 1983. Resistance con-tinued after Israel's unilateral withdrawal to the Awali river in September 1983. On 4 November, a sui-cide bombing conducted by Syrian-backed Shi'is destroyed the IDF's headquarters in Tyre, killing 36 Israelis.

In November 1984, military talks between Israel and Lebanon began in Naqura under the chair-manship of UNIFIL's Commander, and convoca-tion of the UN Secretary General. By mid-January, the talks proved to be futile as the parties had in-compatible conceptions. Israel insisted on security arrangements that would prevent the return of Lebanon into a military base for hostile guerrilla ac-tivity. Israel doubted whether the Lebanese army— barely in control of all Beirut since July 1984, and unable to move into the Shuf and the coastal plain south of Beirut—could ensure security and prevent hostilities. Israel thus proposed a southern zone in which the Israeli-backed SOUTH LEBANON ARMY (SLA) would be responsible for security in coordination with Israel, and a northern zone where the UN force would be stationed. While the Lebanese delegation accepted the Israeli demand to enforce security and prevent any hostile activity from its territory, it in-sisted that this was the exclusive duty of the Lebanese

army, rejecting any role for Israeli-based force and the transfer of UNIFIL from its designated area of deployment (according Resolution 425) along the border, further northward. The Lebanese delega-tion insisted on a total and unconditional withdrawal, with no coordinated security arrangements and no "gains derived from the invasion."

As pressure mounted on the Israeli home front to speed up the withdrawal and extricate the coun-try from an operation that had failed, and no agree-ment with the Lebanese government had been achieved, Israel announced in January 1985 its de-cision to withdraw unilaterally, in three phases, with arrangements to be imposed unilaterally. Withdrawal from the Sidon area was completed in mid-Febru-ary 1985; from the Tyre region, to the Litani, the central area of South Lebanon around Jezzin and Nabatiyya, and the southern Biqa'—in April 1985. The last stage, completed in June 1985, left Israel in control of a "Security Zone" 3–6 miles (5–10 km.) wide, with a population of about 150,000, mostly Shi'i, policed by the 2,000–2,500 strong SLA, with Israeli forces sending patrols but keeping no per-manent positions. (UNIFIL was stationed in parts of the same area.) Lebanon protested and demanded the complete evacuation of all Lebanese territory, and the UN repeatedly supported that demand. The SLA's main assignment was to prevent infiltrations of hos-tile elements into Israeli territory.

In January 1985, the official Israeli casualty toll in Lebanon since June 1982 reached 609. By late 1997, more than 200 additional soldiers were killed, as well as another hundred casualties caused by ac-cidents in, or on the way to the security zone. The annual cost of maintaining the Israeli occupation of Lebanese territory in the years 1983–1984 was 240 million dollars, and the total cost of the 1982 Lebanon War for Israel was estimated at 6–7 billion dollars. Since the actual withdrawal of the IDF from most of the occupied Lebanese territory (May 1985), Shi'i guerrilla operations against the SLA and the Israeli forces in the security zone, and occasional shellings of Israel's northern settlements and towns, contin-ued. As of the early 1990s, *Hizballah* took the lead in waging this guerrilla warfare against Israel's pres-ence in South Lebanon. Under these circumstances, and for sheer military reasons, Israel deepened the Security Zone and enlarged its force employed in this area to an average size of two battalions, to compensate for the SLA's inability to confront the Shi'i guerrilla attacks (see SOUTH LEBANON ARMY, LEBANON).

Hizballah guerrillas sometimes escalated their shelling by Katyusha rockets of towns and villages in northern Israel (from positions in or near villages in northern Lebanon, across the "Security Zone"). Israel reacted with major raids beyond the Security Zone, including the seizure of more Lebanon territory for some time—thus in the Biqa' in May 1988 and in "Operation Accounting" in South Lebanon in July 1993. The latter ended with a cease-fire secretly negotiated by US envoys and accompanied by a secret unwritten agreement. The *Hizballah* would not shell Israeli territory and would not mount attacks from Lebanese villages beyond the Security Zone, while Israel would not attack Lebanon territory beyond the Security Zone (this implied a legitimacy of *Hizballah* resistance, and Israeli counter-operations, inside the Israeli occupied zone). But this secret agreement was not fully kept. Clashes and breaches from both sides continued. These escalated in April 1996 with another major Israeli attack, and seizure of territory in South Lebanon ("Operation Grapes of Wrath"). This culminated in a new cease-fire, again arranged by US envoys, and renewed mutual commitments, de facto identical with those of 1993—but this time in writing. Syria was part of these commitments and indeed encouraged both the Lebanese government and *Hizballah* to accept them. Furthermore, Syria made it clear that any Israeli-Lebanese settlement such as an Israeli proposal to withdraw from all Lebanese territory against Lebanese guarantees of security and the disarming of *Hizballah* (rejected by Lebanon) was feasible only with Syria's approval—indeed a part of a Syrian–Israeli settlement.

8. Return to Peacemaking Efforts (1982–1987)

By the summer of 1981, the deadlock in the peacemaking efforts concerning the interim autonomy for the Palestinians in the West Bank and Gaza, agreed upon at Camp David, had become undeniable. At the same time, there were increased regional threats to the stability and national security of the Gulf oil states—growing Soviet presence and influence in Ethiopia and SOUTH YEMEN, and particularly the Shi'i revolution in Iran and the eruption of the Iraq-Iran war. The Arab states remained divided over the issue of peacemaking with Israel, with the radicals—Syria and Libya—rejecting any

compromise with Egypt. Egypt remained excommunicated and boycotted, though informally wielding great influence. The moderates—Jordan, Tunisia, Morocco, and the Gulf oil monarchies—although compromising the majority of Arab states, were too vulnerable to act along the Egyptian-Israeli line. It was against this backdrop that in August 1981, Crown Prince FAHD presented an eight-point peace plan most important of which were: total withdrawal from all the occupied territories, including East Jerusalem; all Israeli settlements in the occupied territories to be dismantled; Palestinian refugees to have the right to return or receive compensation; the UN to take over the West Bank and Gaza Strip for a transitory period of a few months; the establishment of an independent Palestinian state with East Jerusalem as its capital; the right of all states in the region to live in peace "would be recognized." The UN would ensure the implementation of these principles. The plan represented a shift in Saudi Arabia's regional policies. However, efforts to have the plan approved by the summit conference held at Fez in November of that year led to its suspension after a few hours, due to intransigent Syrian objection. The plan was discussed again at the Fez Arab summit in November 1982, shortly after the siege of Beirut had been lifted and the evacuation of the Palestinian and Syrian armed forces from Beirut had been completed.

Meanwhile, Israel's Lebanon War led to a new American initiative with the aim of renewing the peace talks over the West Bank and Gaza. Israel's aim at the destruction of the Palestinian military infrastructure in Lebanon and expulsion of the PLO and its military apparatuses from besieged Beirut were not incompatible with the interests of most Arab states, including Syria and Saudi Arabia—manifested in their active participation in the diplomatic contacts to facilitate the Palestinian exodus. However, no doubt remained as to their concerns about, and interest in, promoting a settlement of the Palestinian issue as a key regional matter.

On 1 September, President Reagan announced his plan. He proposed a five-year transitional regime of "full autonomy" for the West Bank and Gaza Strip, under an elected self-governing Palestinian authority. Israeli settlement in these areas was to be frozen. During the transitional period, final solutions were to be negotiated by the parties concerned.

The American plan opposed both annexation to Israel and the establishment of an independent Palestinian state, stating that "self-government ... in association with Jordan" offered "the best chances for a ... just and lasting peace." The conflict should be resolved, on the basis of Resolution 242, "through negotiations involving an exchange of land for peace"; the "extent to which Israel should be asked to give up territory (would) be heavily affected by the extent of true peace and normalization and the security arrangements offered in return." Jerusalem was to remain undivided, but its final status was to be decided through negotiations.

The Reagan Plan was rejected by most Arab states, the PLO and Israel. However, in view of the challenge posed by the Reagan Plan, the PLO's loss of its territorial basis in Lebanon, and the need to use the momentum created by the Lebanon War in favor of a renewed peacemaking effort, the Arab summit conference held at Fez in November 1982 renewed their discussion of the Fahd plan. An amended peace plan emerged, adopted by all Arab participants, stressing the status of the PLO as the sole legitimate representative of the Palestinian people, with one major amendment compared to the original formula, which dropped the point of recognition of the right of all states in the region to live in peace and, instead, stated that "the UN Security Council will give guarantees for peace, which will prevail among all states in the region, including the independent Palestinian state."

However, despite the preferred decisions, the PLO now sought to open a political dialogue with Jordan, in an attempt to improve its international and regional position which had been severely undermined by the Lebanon War, and the growing rift with Syria. On the other hand, King Hussein had vested interest to come to terms with the PLO as the only possible alternative to the current standstill, conceived by the Hashemite Kingdom as a danger to its very existence due to the intensified Israeli settlement policy in the West Bank and fear of a mass exodus of Palestinians from this territory to Jordan. The Jordan-PLO political dialogue was expedited by the advent of a Labor-led government in Israel, in August 1984, headed by Shimon PERES, a strong advocate of the "Jordanian Option." The expectations for enhanced American efforts to promote the peace process led Jordan to renew its diplomatic relations with Egypt in September, breaching the Arab summit resolutions of 1979. In February 1985, amid a terrorist Syrian-inspired campaign against the PLO mainstream and Jordanian targets world-wide—executed by Abu Nidal's terrorist group—King Hussein and Arafat signed the Amman Agreement. The agreement avoided the problem of the PLO's rejection of Resolution 242 by adopting the principle of "land for peace, as mentioned in the UN resolutions, including the Security Council resolutions." Rather it called for peace talks under the auspices of an international peace conference, sponsored by the Security Council's five permanent members, and invited all parties to the conflict, including the PLO, within a joint Jordanian-Palestinian delegation, to participate in it. The agreement, which constituted a departure from the Fez Plan, was rejected by the radical regimes, primarily Syria, but was also criticized by the PLO mainstream organization, *Fatah*, insisting on the equal status of the PLO in any peace conference, and on an independent Palestinian state before joining a Jordanian-Palestinian confederation.

The Amman Agreement, however, never took off the ground. Israel rejected the participation of PLO members in any peace conference as long as the PLO had not renounced terrorism and recognized Resolution 242. Arafat failed to fulfill this, and was unable to get the Amman Agreement endorsed by the PLO. In February 1986, King Hussein suspended the agreement, blaming the PLO for not standing by its commitments. In April 1987 the PLO abrogated the agreement, reiterating its rejection of Resolution 242 and its demand for an international Middle Eastern conference in which it would be independently represented. Efforts to bring about an international peace conference continued. The US had come round to support it, and the Labor Party section of Israel's coalition government acquiesced in an international conference as an umbrella, "accompanying" and endorsing direct negotiations, though the right-wing opposed it. As Prime Minister, Peres indeed made relentless efforts to break the stalemate in the peace process. Apart from bringing the issue of Taba to an agreed arbitration and improving relations with Egypt, in July 1986 Peres made a surprising visit to Morocco to meet King Hasan II, culminating a decade of secret contacts and mutual interests between the two states. The public visit was especially significant in view of King Hasan's position as President of the Islamic Conference Organization. The generally restrained Arab reaction to the visit (apart from Syria and Libya which broke their diplomatic relations with Morocco), indicated the deep transition of the Arab attitude toward Israel and the peace process. In April 1987 Israeli Foreign Minister Peres and King Hussein reached a secret agreement in London on attending such a conference. No approval or participation of the PLO in the conference was mentioned. Jordan did not demand Israel's full withdrawal from the occupied territories as a prerequisite. However, the agreement encountered strong opposition of Israel's Prime Minister SHAMIR, and remained another monument of the futile peace efforts.

9. The Palestinian Uprising (1987–1993) As the PLO had apparently lost both the military and the political option of action, in the mid-1980s the center of Palestinian national activity increasingly moved into the West Bank and Gaza Strip. As in the West Bank and Gaza, the occupation continued with no solution in sight. Settlements kept spreading and there was a growing sense of frustration and bitterness, along with increasing small-scale violence. In December 1987, a popular uprising began (INTIFADA). This soon captured international media attention and world public opinion, and led to renewed American effort to establish peace in the region. These efforts, however, based on a combination of elements from the Camp David Autonomy Plan and the Reagan Plan, proved to be obsolete and unrealistic. Even though the *Intifada* was initiated by the Palestinians of the occupied territories, it strongly emphasized the PLO's status as the only legitimate representative of the Palestinians. Moreover, within a few weeks, the PLO took over the *Intifada's* management and guidance, blocking any separate initiative of, or coordination with, the local leadership. The growing support of the PLO by the uprising Palestinians in the West Bank and Gaza Strip, as well as by the Arab world, along with fears of a spill-over of violence into Jordan, led to King Hussein's decision in late July 1988 to announce Jordan's disengagement from the West Bank. He officially abrogated the annexation of this area to Jordan, stating his recognition of the Palestinian people's right to fulfill its right to self-determination as an independent state of its own under the PLO's leadership. The

Jordanian decision paved the way to the declaration of the Independent Palestinian State at the Algiers session of the Palestinian National Council in November 1988, on the basis of the UN partition resolution of November 1947. The decision triggered a wave of euphoria among the Palestinians, and cemented the Hashemite regime's determination to reshape Jordan's identity as a separate state, though without abandoning its interest in the West Bank and Gaza Strip.

The achievements of the *Intifada* culminated in the American decision in December 1988—following Arafat's condemnation of terrorism and acceptance of Resolution 242—to begin a diplomatic dialogue with the PLO at the level of ambassadors. However, the dialogue was fruitless and soon came to a stalemate. In May 1990, a terrorist attack from the sea was perpetrated by the Palestine Liberation Front—one of the PLO's member factions—at Nitzanim. Arafat refused to deplore this, which led to the suspension of the dialogue with the US. In the course of 1989–1990, Arafat and King Hussein of Jordan closed ranks, indicating their mutual interests and need for each other's support. The two leaders shared a repeated complaint against the oil-rich Arab monarchies, which had decreased, or entirely ignored, their commitments for financial aid to the PLO (despite promises to support the *Intifada*) and Jordan (experiencing an economic crisis in the spring of 1989). One of these common concerns was the rapid rise of HAMAS (the Islamic Resistance Movement), established at the beginning of the *Intifda* in Gaza and which had spread into the West Bank, with a strong basis of support within the Islamic movement in Jordan. Especially for Arafat's PLO, the rise of an Islamic *Jihad* movement in the occupied territories and claim to constitute a moral and political alternative to the PLO, endangered the latter's exclusive status as the only legitimate symbol of the Palestinian state in the making. By 1990, competition between the two movements intensified, reaching in some cases violent clashes between their members. *Hamas*, however, refused to join the PLO on the latter's terms.

Meanwhile, the popular, all-inclusive, nature of the *Intifada* began gradually declining, reflecting primarily economic and psychological exhaustion of the Palestinian population, and the burden of Israeli repression, giving way to a sense of impasse. However, the *Intifada* still continued, culminating from time to time in major violent events, such as the killing of seventeen Palestinians on the Temple Mount in October 1990 by Israeli Border Guard police. The length and persistence of mass protest, violence, and willingness to suffer the losses they entailed, demonstrated by the Palestinians, could hardly be ignored by Israeli public opinion, which tended to become more polarized than ever before over the Palestinian issue and the occupied territories. In May 1989, the national coalition government—at its second term with Prime Minister Shamir at the helm—approved Defense Minister Rabin's plan which aimed at breaking the diplomatic stalemate on the Palestinian issue.

The government initiative suggested that violence cease, and that elections should be held in the West Bank and Gaza for a political delegation with whom Israel would come to terms regarding the implementation of Palestinian interim self-governing authority in these areas. The initiative, unprecedented in its definition of the Palestinians as the essential element in the negotiations over the West Bank and Gaza Strip, constituted a departure from the traditional tendency of Zionism and the State of Israel to circumvent the Palestinian national movement and prefer a dialogue with the neighboring Arab states. Israel's initiative was welcomed by the US and Egypt (which had resumed its Arab leadership since late 1987 when most Arab states resumed diplomatic relations with it) but not by the PLO, which insisted on acknowledging him as the only authority to represent the Palestinians. Efforts by the US and Egypt's President Mubarak to find a compromise formula failed. In March 1990, Shamir's Likud-Labor national coalition government collapsed and was dismissed in a no-confidence vote, but later reinstated itself on a narrow right-wing basis, without the Labor Party, which effectively buried the peace efforts. In contrast to the gloomy peacemaking prospects, as of late 1989 a rising tide of Jewish immigration from the Soviet Union began. This triggered new Arab fears of massive settlement of the newcomers in the West Bank and an emptying of its Palestinian inhabitants. In early 1990, the PLO and Jordan, most susceptible to be affected by this wave of immigration, called for a summit conference to be held to discuss the existential danger posed by the newcomers. Given Egypt's reluctance to handle the

issue, and Iraq's increasing militancy against Israel—in early April Saddam HUSSEIN revealed that Iraq possessed a binary chemical weapon, threatening to retaliate with it and "burn half of Israel" if it dared to attack Iraq—Saddam Hussein came to be regarded by many Palestinians as their hero and savior and the only Arab leader committed to their cause.

10. The Gulf War and Return to Peacemaking (1990–1991) In the course of 1990, regional and international attention increasingly focused on Iraq's intensive efforts to acquire advanced military-oriented technologies (allegedly, chemical and biological weapons, ground-to-ground missiles, a "super-canon," and nuclear capability). Iraq, which in 1988 ended its eight-year war with Iran—economically exhausted and with no tangible achievement—embarked on an aggressive policy against Syria (Iran's ally), by extending military support to General AWN, the Maronite-Christian leader who had declared war against the Syrian presence in Lebanon.

Moreover, the Iraqi regime demonstrated growing impatience with Kuwait, blaming it for stealing oil from Iraq, and causing the latter's economy heavy losses by exceeding the quota of oil production allotted to it. Although the crisis—culminating in the Iraqi invasion of Kuwait and its annexation to Iraq—derived purely from Iraqi and inter-Arab causes, Saddam Hussein soon involved Israel in his rhetoric and diplomacy, claiming equivalence between his occupation of Kuwait and Israel's occupation of the Palestinian territories. During the six months of the crisis, until the end of the GULF WAR (January-February 1991), Saddam Hussein did everything he could to involve Israel in it, initially by his flamboyant language, appealing to the Arab-Muslim world's sentiments to arouse it against those Arab regimes that had "conspired" against the Arab nation and Islam by joining the American-led international military coalition against Iraq. Indeed, the Iraqi invasion was by and large unacceptable to most Arab regimes, reflected by the decisions of the Cairo Arab Summit Conference held on 10 August, 1990. Nonetheless, Saddam Hussein's Islamic rhetoric, call for Holy War against the "new Crusade," and the linking of the Iraqi withdrawal from Kuwait to Israel's withdrawal from the occupied territories of 1967, all represented an attempt to incite Arab opposition movements (primarily Islamic ones) against their

Arab governments. Saddam's attempts to drag Israel into the fray as a ploy to foil Arab participation in the international coalition against him peaked during the "Desert Storm" (the code name of the international offensive against Iraq's occupation of Kuwait) when Iraq launched at Israel's cities 39 SCUD missiles with conventional warheads. These mainly caused only panic and material damage, and exposed Israel's vulnerability to this weapon. Israel, however, remained calm, primarily due to American pressures to this effect, though the military, backed by Defense Minister Moshe Arens, supported a military retaliation.

With the end of the Gulf War, the PLO's posture seemed lower than ever before due to the public solidarity its leaders manifested to Iraq. Yet, although the PLO was punished by the Gulf monarchies, ceasing financial aid to the organization and the occupied territories, already during the War but also after, they made a significant effort to secure a renewal of the peacemaking process when the War ended. Indeed, as the War came to an end—with the US now looming as the only world superpower following the break-up of the Soviet Union and end of the Cold War—American Secretary of State Baker embarked on an intensive effort to convince all the parties concerned to participate in an international peace conference. Jordan, economically overburdened by a wave of hundreds of thousands of Palestinian and Jordanian immigrants who had been returning from the Gulf countries following the Gulf War, was the first to accept the American proposals and agree to participate in the conference. Still, no less than eight months and seven shuttle trips to the Middle East capitals, and a US-Soviet Agreement, were needed to forge the Madrid framework based on Resolutions 242 and 338, and Israel's initiative of May 1989. The PLO, bankrupt due to the end of Arab financial aid, threatened by *Hamas's* growing popularity, and severely criticized by Palestinian figures for its political behavior during the Gulf crisis, had no choice but to accept Israel's harsh conditions regarding the Palestinian representation—no separate Palestinian delegation and no participation by the PLO, Jerusalemites or expelled figures. Furthermore, the talks were to revolve on Palestinian self-government only. The Arabs accepted the principle of direct and bilateral negotiations with Israel without foreign interference, and the goal of reaching a contractual

agreement of peace between Israel and each of the Arab parties concerned. This track was to be reinforced by a multilateral track of negotiations on key regional issues (such as refugees, regional development and environment, and arms control), serving as a confidence-building measure toward normalized relations among the Middle Eastern nations.

The Madrid Peace Conference began on 30 October 1991. It reflected a significant progress in the willingness of the Arabs to negotiate publicly with Israel, or openly support such negotiations by being present at the ceremonial opening. Indeed, most Arab states were represented in the conference, including Syria which since late 1989 had been moving toward the moderate Arab bloc headed by Egypt, primarily due to the weakening of its Soviet ally. Egypt—still the only Arab state with a peace agreement with Israel—and Saudi Arabia, were particularly active in encouraging Syria and the PLO to accept the American proposed formula and attend the conference. In spite of opposition to the Madrid Conference, primarily from Iran and Iraq, the event and consequent negotiations indicated the beginning of a new era in the Middle East, interpreted against the backdrop of the Gulf War, collapse of Pan-Arab nationalism as manifested in that war, and expectations for a "new world order" dominated by the United States and the Western democratic world. A new order in the Middle East came to be perceived by some Arab intellectuals. It was based on interests and mutual respect of sovereignty and independence, regardless of ethnicity or religion, which would include (in addition to the Arab states, Turkey and Iran) Israel as well.

The bilateral talks that followed between Israel and each of the Arab delegations (Jordanian-Palestinian, Syrian and Lebanese) in Washington soon after the ceremonial opening, demonstrated Syria's attempts to acquire control over the pace and essence of the negotiations, by holding frequent meetings in Damascus with all other delegations. Syria's complete domination of the Lebanese government effectively unified the Lebanese and Syrian fronts, preventing any possibility of a separate Israeli-Lebanese settlement, even though the two states had no territorial dispute, other than the one from the existence of the Security Zone. Coordination with Jordan and the PLO (the real authority guiding the Palestinian delegation of West Bankers and Gazans), turned out to be more precarious, revealing competition and mistrust, with each side watching the other lest they gain more or proceed faster on their bilateral track with Israel. Syria insisted on non-participation in the multilateral talks as long as Israel had not committed itself to full withdrawal from the occupied Golan Heights, imposing this position on Lebanon as well. Jordan and the Palestinians, however, overburdened by economic difficulties, did take part in the multilateral talks, along with Egypt, Morocco, Tunisia, and the Gulf oil monarchies. To ensure its leverage on the PLO, Syria continued to support those Palestinian factions, leftist as well as Islamist, rejecting the peace process and challenging Arafat's policy in this respect.

In the West Bank and Gaza Strip, the struggle between *Hamas* and the PLO intensified, with the Palestinian participation in the fruitless negotiations portrayed by *Hamas* and the leftist opposition as indications of the PLO's bankruptcy and irrelevance. *Hamas's* continued armed struggle in the name of the full liberation of Palestine certainly attracted more support for the Islamic movement in the Palestinian public. The Islamic acts of terror led Israel, in late 1992, to expel 425 Palestinians—all leading and activist figures of Hamas and the Islamic *jihad*— to Lebanon, following the kidnapping and murder of an Israeli soldier. The unprecedented mass expulsion, criticized throughout the world, paradoxically aggravated the PLO's predicament, forcing it to identify with *Hamas* and stop the negotiations with Israel until the expelled Islamists were allowed to return.

As long as the Shamir government had been in power, no progress was achieved in either of the tracks. However, in early 1992, Israel agreed to conduct separate talks with the Palestinian delegations, fully aware of its link and subordination to the PLO. Israel adopted a rigid opposition to discuss any substantive territorial withdrawal from occupied Golan, rendering any progress in this track practically impossible.

Syria's attempts to exercise its veto power over its weak Arab partners ended in a fiasco, once the latter had been facing a critical decision regarding a settlement. This came when, in the elections of June 1992, the Labor Party, led by Yitzhak Rabin, won. Rabin's commitment during the election campaign to reach agreement on interim autonomy with the Palestinians within six to nine months, and his willingness to apply the principle of "land for peace" on the Golan, and consider Israeli withdrawal "in the Golan," created a new basis for possible progress in the Washington talks. However, despite attempts to speed up the talks with Syria, the gap between the two sides remained unabridged regarding the depth of Israel's withdrawal and Syria's concept of peace. Faced with unexpected opposition at home to a major withdrawal in the Golan (including within the Labor Party) and unconvinced that Asad had become truly committed to peace as a strategic choice, Rabin focused on reaching an agreement on security measures first, before any discussion over the depth of withdrawal was to occur. Intensive mediation efforts by US President Clinton and Secretary of State Christopher, helped to advance negotiations to the level of direct meetings between Israel's and Syria's Ambassadors to Washington, and in the spring of 1995, even between their Chiefs of Staff, but with no tangible progress.

A breakthrough was made in the least expected track—with the Palestinians. By early 1993, a new channel of secret talks, first conducted by academics and then fully supported by the foreign ministry under Shimon Peres, became more productive, and finally broke the deadlock. On 13 September 1993, on the White House lawn, Israeli Prime Minister Rabin and PLO Chairman Arafat, in the presence of President Clinton and the Russian Foreign Minister, officially signed the Declaration of Principles (DOP), with mutual recognition at the core. The DOP shaped the principles for a prospective process of the establishment of a five-year interim self-governing authority, first in the Gaza Strip and the town of Jericho in the Jordan Valley. This was to be expanded later to other parts of the West Bank, and included the election of a Palestinian Council. The PLO undertook to abolish from the Palestinian National Charter all statements denying Israel's legitimacy or calling for war against it. The permanent status of the self-governed territory, borders, Israeli settlements, Jerusalem and the Palestinian refugees were left open without being prejudged by the interim arrangements.

The implementation of the first stage of the DOP in May 1994, and Arafat's arrival in the Gaza Strip in June of that year, set in motion a state formation process, with financial aid from Western donors and Japan.

The Israel-PLO Accord strongly critized Syria, as well as radical Palestinian groups, particularly *Hamas*. However, the agreement was internationally welcomed, leading to manifestations of acceptance of Israel by other Arab states, and boosting Israel's prestige in the region. Given the direct implications of the DOP on Jordan, King Hussein was now prompted to seek his own settlement with Israel. On 14 September, Israel and Jordan signed a framework for a peace accord but the King remained hesitant to go forward separately without Syrian consent, preferring to let Syria go first and pursue its settlement. However, after almost a year of continued Israeli-Syrian negotiations without agreement, and growing implications of the Israeli-Palestinian peace process, Jordan decided to follow the pattern of separate settlement.

On 26 October, Jordan signed a Treaty of Alliance with Israel, witnessed—as in the case of the Israel-PLO agreement—by US President Clinton.

Syria's criticism notwithstanding, the Oslo Agreement had far-reaching implications on Israel's position in the region, especially among the Gulf monarchies and the MAGHREB states. On 30 September the GULF COOPERATION COUNCIL member states decided to abolish the indirect boycott on Israel. This was followed by decisions of Morocco, Tunisia, MAURITANIA, OMAN, and later QATAR, to establish low level diplomatic relations with Israel, without heeding Syria's protests. In October 1994, the Middle East Economic Summit was convened in Casablanca under the auspices of the American and Russian Presidents, with participants from most Arab states and Israel, reflecting Peres's vision of a New Middle East, based on economic cooperation and development. Similar conferences were held in each year at the same month in Amman, 1995; Cairo, 1996; and Doha, 1997; though with deteriorating success rates due to the gradual stumbling on the Israeli-Palestinian Oslo process. However, the ongoing peacemaking process led to increased foreign investments in Israel and an economic boom, combined with the continuing absorption of the Russian immigration into the Israeli economy.

The impact of the Oslo Agreement on Israel's position in the region confirmed the significance of the Palestinian issue as the heart of the Arab-Israel conflict and key element in Middle Eastern politics. However, Israel's breakthrough into the Arab world became a source of concern to Arab opponents of the normalization with Israel, nationalists and Islamists alike. Israel's economic, technological, and military might loomed larger and more threatening than ever before. This was presented in the Arab public debate as a warning. It was argued that the peace process must be slowed down, to prevent a wholesale of Arab assets and values for the sake of peace, from which Israel would reap the main benefits and gain economic domination throughout the Middle East.

However, the new trend in Israeli-Palestinian relations also entailed a wave of violence by religious fanatics on both sides. In February 1994, an Israeli settler in Hebron massacred twenty-nine Muslim worshippers in the Cave of the Patriarchs during prayer (he was also killed). This was followed by a series of suicide bombings launched by *Hamas* and the Islamic *Jihad* against Israelis, mostly citizens. The wave of Islamic terror against Israeli citizens was a blow to the Labor-led government which had based its policy on the premise that the PALESTINIAN AUTHORITY (PA), committed to combating terror from the territory under its jurisdiction, would be able to fulfill this duty. Thus, apart from growing criticism of the Government by the right-wing parties and movements for the serious flows of the Oslo Agreement and its danger to Israel's national security, the occasional suicide bombings by the Islamic opposition helped the Israeli opposition undermine the shaky majority in the Israeli public that had initially supported the Oslo process, adopting an increasingly insightful and delegitimizing tone against the government, especially Prime Minister Rabin.

In September 1995, Israel and the PLO signed the Taba Agreement. According to this Israel was to withdraw from six major towns in the West Bank, as a first stage in its redeployment and transfer of authorities to the PA, but retain overall responsibility for domestic as well as external security. The West Bank was divided by the agreement into three zones: Zone A (three percent of the West Bank territory), in which the PA enjoys full self-governing power, including domestic security; Zone B (twenty-seven percent of the West Bank), in which Israeli and Palestinian forces shared responsibility for security; and Zone C (seventy percent of the territory), which Israel continued to govern directly. The agreement was fully implemented by the Israeli government under Rabin (and following his assassination on 4 November 1995, under Peres), except for the city of Hebron. Due to the complex problem of a large Jewish population there, this was postponed until after the general elections, which were to be held on 29 May 1996.

Meanwhile, the transfer of Palestinian cities to the PA boosted the protest and bitter opposition on the Israeli Right. This brought into the debate religious verdicts of nationalist Rabbis claiming that the transfer of parts of *Eretz Ysrael* to foreigners contradicted the *Halacha*, and some even suggested that those in charge of committing that crime were to be executed. The assassination of Rabin by an Israeli fanatic was a national shock for Israeli society, but not for long. A renewed cycle of Israeli-Syrian talks under US auspices had apparently brought the two parties closer than ever to an agreement (with Israeli consent, in principle, to withdraw from the whole of occupied Golan in return for full normalization of relations with Syria). However, the Syrian President still hesitated. In February–March 1996, a new series of suicide bombings led to renewed attacks on the government, now led by Peres. The US administration led an anti-terror international conference at Sharm al-Sheikh, with many heads of state taking part, but without President Asad. (Syria was still considered a state supervising terrorism.) This apparently put an end to the Israeli-Syrian current phase of negotiations.

The Peres government's troubles were doubled by *Hizballah's* intensified attacks on Israeli and SLA positions in the Security Zone, as well as massive shellings of northern Israel from the Lebanese territory. This dragged Israel to initiate a new version of Operation Accounting (named "Grapes of Wrath" Operation) of mass shelling against the *Hizballah* bases, including those in the villages of the south, to force the Lebanese and Syrian governments to put an end to *Hizballah* activity against Israel. In the course of the Operation, the IDF, apparently by mistake, hit a group of Lebanese civilians who found refuge in the vicinity of one of the UNIFIL bases at Kafr Kana, killing about a hundred and injuring many more. Thanks to US mediation, a new understanding was reached, undertaken this time by Syria as well, in which Israel and the IDF would refrain from shelling each other's civilians. This legitimized *Hizballah's* combat of Israel's military presence in the Security Zone. However, despite the foundation of a

follow-up committee, the activity of *Hizballah* continued, without an effective Israeli response. In the summer of 1997, a grass-roots movement (the Four Mothers) and other groups began stating a claim for unilateral withdrawal to the international border. The Netanyahu government, through Defense Minister Mordechai, proposed a separate settlement with Lebanon, based on full Israeli implementation of the 1978 Security Council Resolution 425. However, Syria rejected these proposals as an Israeli gimic aimed at dividing the Syrian-Lebanese front and avoiding withdrawal from the Golan.

The victory of Binyamin NETANYAHU in the general elections, in the first exercise of the new law of direct election of the Prime Minister, shifted at once Israel's peacemaking policy regarding both the PA and Syria. Although Netanyahu had promised that Israel would be faithful to its international commitments, including the Oslo Agreements, his ultra-right fragmented coalition government was reluctant. Some of its components were even unwilling to adhere to the commitments already given by Israel to the Palestinians. The significance of the transfer of power in Israel from the Labor to the Likud was well reflected in Egypt's initiative to hold—for the first time in six years—an Arab summit conference in Cairo, to discuss the changing government in Israel. Egypt was motivated by its permanent aim to play a leading role in the Arab arena, taking advantage of the concern expressed by Syria and other Arab states over the advent of Netanyahu and his government. The summit ended with a clear call to the Israeli government to adhere to the peace process.

While the summit clearly emphasized that the Arab world had chosen peace as a strategy, it also made it clear that in the case of a continued stalemate, the process of normalization between Israel and the Arab states would be frozen. Indeed, despite Netanyahu's visits in Cairo and Amman, meetings with Mubarak and King Hussein, respectively, and the Israeli Premier's success in creating a positive impression with his hosts, the following year and a half witnessed a growing abyss of mistrust and hostility between these Arab rulers and Netanyahu. Thus the Cairo summit's decision, linking the normalization to progress in the peacemaking, primarily on the Palestinian front, became a guiding line for Arab states, bringing to a halt the movement of Arab states toward Israel, especially in the Gulf, and a continued restriction of the already achieved normalization between Israel and the Arab states, especially Morocco, Qatar, and Oman. One of the commitments undertaken by Israel in the Oslo II Agreement, concerned the Israeli pledge to redeploy its forces in Hebron, which the PA now insisted on implementing. In September 1996, however, the government's decision to open the Hasmonean Tunnel near the Temple Mount caused violent clashes, resulting in over sixty Palestinian and fifteen Israeli casualties. The clashes brought for the first time to the Israeli cognition the new reality created by the Oslo Agreements namely the presence of an armed police force of approximately 30,000 Palestinians, whose behavior could easily shift from collegial to hostile. The serious clashes brought President Clinton to call Netanyahu, Arafat and King Hussein to a summit meeting at the White House. This ended with deep differences, but with Netanyahu's willingness to negotiate a new agreement on Hebron. This agreement was signed in January 1997, creating an extremely precarious situation, with a small Jewish community in the heart of this Palestinian-Muslim city.

The agreement also set the time table for three phases of Israeli redeployment in the West Bank in accordance with the Oslo Agreement. However, Netanyahu's government coalition comprised of hard-line parties opposed to any further withdrawal from the West Bank, threatened to foil the government if it had ceded any piece of land to the PA. Indeed, Israel's offer of the first redeployment was rejected by the PA as ridiculously insignificant, and the second, slated for November 1997, but procrastinated by the Israeli government, was reportedly far below the PA's expectations, and with no definite date of when it was to be implemented. This policymaking was accompanied by repeated arguments by the Israeli government regarding violations of the PA's commitment to Israel—primarily, insufficient combat of Palestinian terrorism; non-extradition of terrorists to Israel; failure to abolish the hostile articles in the Palestinian National Charter; and the conduct of illegal activity in Jerusalem— explaining that the redeployment was conditional on repairing those violations and fulfilling others in accordance with the signed agreements between the two parties. The PA, on its part, also complained that Israel was violating its commitments, primarily the on-going con-fiscation of land and creation of new facts prejudicing the final status negotiations; the delays in operating the airport and harbor in the Gaza Strip, as well as the safe passage between Gaza and the West Bank; ignoring the 1994 Paris Agreement on economic cooperation; and the on-going policy of closure.

Following the signing of the Oslo II Agreement, Israel's regional and international posture improved immensely. This brought Israel and Turkey to close ranks in the course of 1996–1997, building growing strategic cooperation, including mutual top level visits, a multi-million dollar deal of refining Turkish aircraft, exchanging air force deployment and training flights on each other's territory, and joint training. The tightening Israeli-Turkish alliance, perceived as a threat by Syria, Iraq and Egypt, became another stumbling block in Israel's relations with its Arab neighbors, joining other reasons of criticism of Israel's regional policy. During the year that followed the agreement on Hebron, relations between Israel and the PA kept deteriorating, in view of the seeming Israeli attempt to avoid another redeployment and ceding any further territory to the PA.

ARAB-ISRAEL PEACEMAKING Ever since the beginning of the ARAB-ISRAEL CONFLICT efforts have been made to mitigate, if not to settle this conflict. Historically, these efforts have been manifested through various goals and means:

• the advocacy of idealistic solutions to the Arab-Jewish conflict in Palestine before the foundation of the State of ISRAEL;

• futile Arab-Zionist and Arab Israeli diplomacy;

• diplomatic initiatives and mediation efforts by foreign powers and the United Nations;

• Israeli ideas concerning the future status of the territories occupied in the Six-Day War (see ARAB-ISRAEL CONFLICT) in the context of peacemaking with the Arabs;

• military agreements between Israel and its neighbors following hostilities and wars;

• peace plans and initiatives announced by Israel and the Arabs;

• non-final agreements of principles and formal peace treaties between Israel and its Arab neighbors.

From its outset the Arab-Zionist conflict over Palestine was marked by a symmetry of approaches from each side, each claiming its exclusive national right regarding Palestine/*Eretz Yisrael* and denying any such right to its adversary. This symmetry, justified and defined by religious and cultural tenets, underpinned the perception of this conflict as a zero-sum game and the exclusion of the possibility of peaceful coexistence between the disputed parties, which prevailed for most of the twentieth century. While the Arab political approach to peaceful coexistence with Israel remained by and large rigidly negative until 1967, on the Zionist/Israeli side an effort to mitigate the conflict if not to resolve it through dialogue with the Arabs was, from the outset, a matter of political debate and action. The effort reflecting existential anxiety and moral unease regarding the PALESTINE-ARAB hositility and its repercussions on British Mandatory policy. Zionist individuals and political movements made occasional efforts, especially following outbreaks of Arab violence, to reach agreements with influential Arab leaders, both in Palestine and neighboring countries, but without conceding their right to unimpeded Jewish immigration, land and settlement.

Partition: The first de facto partition of Mandatory Palestine occurred in 1922 when the area of Transjordan (see JORDAN, HASHEMITE KINGDOM OF), constituting seventy-four percent of the territory of the MANDATE, was separated administratively from the rest of Palestine, and the "Jewish National Home" provisions of the Mandate were no longer applied to it. The territory of Transjordan was designated to remain Arab under Emir ABDALLAH IBN HUSSEIN. Ideas and plans for partitioning Palestine remained linked with that part of historic Palestine which in 1946 became the independent Hashemite Kingdom of Jordan.

The first partition plan for western Palestine was proposed in 1932 by the Zionist representative in Geneva, Victor Jacobson, but was never seriously considered. Five years later, the Peel Commission, headed by Earl Peel, concluded in its July 1937 report that the mandate for Palestine was, in fact, unworkable, and proposed the partition of Palestine into a Jewish state, an Arab state and a British mandatory zone. The small Jewish state was to include the coastal plain from a point south of Jaffa northward, the northern valleys and Galilee. The British zone was to have included the holy cities of JERUSALEM and Bethlehem, an enclave connecting them to Jaffa and the port of Haifa, and the Arab towns of Lydda and

Ramleh. The rest of Palestine, together with Transjordan, was to constitute an Arab state. The proposal was rejected by the Arabs and accepted, as a basis for discussion, by the 1937 Zionist Congress. However, after the Woodhead Commission, sent to Palestine by the British government in 1938 to further investigate partition, the plan was shelved as impractical.

The principles of the Peel partition plan were in fact adopted by the British War Cabinet under Churchill's premiership in 1943–1944, but for political considerations it was to remain secret and its implementation to be postponed until the end of the war. After the war the plan was dropped due to fear of violent Arab reaction and damage to Britain's position in the Middle East, though it remained a theoretical option. Partition was again proposed by the UN Special Committee on Palestine (UNSCOP), sent out to investigate the problem of Palestine in April 1947. The committee submitted its conclusions to the General Assembly on 31 August 1947. The majority report proposed that Palestine be partitioned into a Jewish state and an Arab state, which should be linked in an economic union. The Jewish state was to include the coastal plane from near Ashkelon to Acre, the northern valleys, eastern Galilee and a certain area in southern Galilee, as well as much of the Negev. The Arab state was to include the rest of the country, except Jerusalem, which was to become a "corpus seperatum" under UN trusteeship. The majority report was adopted by the UN General Assembly in resolution 181 on 27 November 1947, by a vote of thirty-three in favor, thirteen against and ten abstentions.

The plan was essentially accepted by the mainstream Zionist movement and most of the *Yishuv* (the Jewish community in Palestine) but rejected by the Arabs, who decided to forestall its implementation by armed force. As a result of the 1948–1949 War (see ARAB-ISRAEL CONFLICT), Israel ended up with a territory significantly larger than that allotted to it in the plan—with the addition of the western Galilee, and almost the entire Negev. The vast majority of the Arab population in the areas that became part of the State of Israel were forced into exile. Of the areas to have constituted the Arab state, the GAZA STRIP was occupied by EGYPT and the WEST BANK was occupied by and later annexed to Jordan. Jerusalem was partitioned de facto between Israel and Jordan during the war. It was only in November 1988 that the Palestine National Council (PNC) (see PALESTINE LIBERATION ORGANIZATION (PLO), which proclaimed a Palestinian state, relayed its decision to UN resolution 181 as a source of international legitimacy.

Most of the peace plans proposed in the aftermath of the 1967 War, which spoke of Israeli withdrawal from all or part of the occupied West Bank and Gaza Strip, were in fact proposing the repartition of Palestine, though what exactly was to become of these areas after Israel's withdrawal and to whom they were to be handed were not always clarifed. Though the Israeli-Palestinian Declaration of Principles (DOP) did not deal with permanent settlement, the underlying assumption was that the process would lead to the repartition of the country, and that side by side with the State of Israel a "Palestinian entity" would emerge.

Bi-nationalism: While the concept of partition was based on the belief that separation between JEWS and Arabs was the only practical solution to the conflict, the bi-national idea sought to preserve the unity of the country.

The bi-national idea, most of whose proponents before 1948 were Jewish intellectuals who defined themselves as socialists or humanists, was based on the premise that both the Jews and the Arabs had a right to live in Palestine and that neither nation should dominate the other. Most of the plans for a bi-national state were based on the principle of parity in government, irrespective of the numerical strength of either side, and the right of each people to autonomy in its internal affairs. Amongst the specific propositions raised were federal and confederal plans and measures that sought to preserve Palestine as a unitary state in which bi-nationalism would be based on the concept of communal or personal autonomy.

Bi-nationalism was never officially adopted as a policy by neither the Arabs or the Zionists, though the idea was considered by the latter. For a short period (1946–1947) Britain's interest to preserve Palestine's unitary form, led its government to adopt de-facto bi-nationalism as a preferable solution to the problem. The Arabs were unwilling to consider it because they rejected the notion that the Jews had any political rights in Palestine, and were willing to offer the Jews only minority status in a Palestinian state at best. Though at various stages several prominent

Zionist leaders, including David BEN GURION in 1929, were willing to consider bi-nationalism as a last resort solution, the idea was unpopular because the Zionist goal was the establishment of a Jewish state in order to solve the Jewish problem. Thus a state in part of Palestine was considered preferable to a binational state in the whole of Palestine. After the War the latter became one of the main arguments of those advocating a territorial compromise, especially within the Israeli Labor Party. In 1969 the PLO adopted the idea that Palestine should become a secular democratic state in which Muslims, CHRISTIANS and Jews will live in equality and non-discrimination. This idea was, however, bereft of any expressed recognition of Jewish political rights in the envisioned democratic state and was utterly rejected by Israel as nothing more than propaganda.

Middle East federations: Jewish leaders such as David BEN GURION and Haim WEIZMANN considered the idea that Palestine would turn into a Jewish state or autonomy within the framework of a Middle East federation, in which the Arabs would constitute a vast majority. The idea drew on ambitions to lead a regional Arab unity fostered by the HASHEMITE rulers of Iraq and Transjordan since the 1920s, who attempted to attract Britain's support, *inter alia* as a panacea to the Arab-Zionist conflict in Palestine. The Hashemite willingness to accept Jewish autonomy in Palestine—and a limited measure of continued Jewish immigration into the country—as an integral part of the plan was utterly rejected by the Arab-Palestinian leadership that objected to victimizing its homeland for the goal of Pan-Arab unity. Indeed, Zionist proponents attempted to market the idea mainly among non-Palestinian Arab leaders, the most conspicuous attempt of which was Ben Gurion's series of talks with Arab leaders in the years 1934–1936 in which he proposed a quid pro quo deal: the Arabs would accept the establishment of a Jewish state in Palestine in return for Zionist support for the Arab aspiration to Pan-Arab unity with which the Jewish state would maintain federative relations. The Hashemites' plans and the idea of an Arab-Zionist federation never took off the ground though they had a discernible impact on British decision making circles during World War II in conjunction with envisioned post-war settlements in the Middle East and securing Britain's position in the region. (see also ARAB UNITY)

Territorial compromise: The most prevalent Israeli principle for peaceful settlement with the Arabs following the 1967 War was territorial compromise, drawing on the newly occupied Arab territories. The most famous plan was the Allon Plan, developed over several years following the Six-Day War by Yigal Allon (1918–1980), one of the leaders of the Israel Labor Party. The plan called for the return by Israel of the densely populated areas in the West Bank and Gaza Strip to a Jordanian-Palestinian state, the return of most of the Sinai to Egypt, and a limited area in the GOLAN HEIGHTS to SYRIA. According to this plan Israel was to remain in control of the Jordan Rift Valley and the first mountain ridge to its west, where it would maintain settlements and early warning defense systems. Jerusalem, the Gush Etzion area and Kiryat Arba outside Hebron were to come under Israeli sovereignty, and a few additional border changes were also to leave such areas as Latrun in Israeli hands. The area in the West Bank which would be returned to Arab sovereignty, was to have been connected to Jordan by means of a wide corridor around Jericho, and the Gaza Strip was to be connected to it by means of a highway. In Sinai, Israel was to have retained control over the Rafa Salient and its town of Yamit, the west bank of the bay of Aqaba, leading south from Eilat to Sharm al-Sheikh and two military airfields constructed close to the old international border. The rest of the Sinai Peninsula was to be returned to Egypt. Most of the Golan Heights was also to have remained in Israeli hands.

The plan was based on the premise that for Israel to remain both Jewish and democratic, it could not continue to rule over the 1.2 million Palestinians who lived in the territories occupied by Israel in 1967. On the other hand, Israel had genuine security concerns that had to be addressed, which called for the demilitarization of all Arab territories west of the Jordan River and Israel's maintaining a military and civilian presence on the Golan Heights, along the Jordan Valley and the Red Sea. The plan was entirely unrealistic as far as the Arabs were concerned and probably never meant to serve as a basis for Arab-Israeli settlement.

The Allon Plan as such was never adopted as the official policy of the government of Israel, but during the Labor-led governments until 1977, all the Jewish settlement activities in the West Bank, Gaza Strip, Golan Heights and Sinai were within the parameters of the plan. In 1973 the principles of the Allon Plan were included in the Labor Party platform, and some of them still constitute the basis for Labor Party thinking regarding the permanent settlement with the Palestinians today. The Allon Plan served as the main basis for the Labor Party's long-lived concept of peacemaking with Jordan, known as the "Jordanian Option". However, no Arab regime, including the Hashemite king of Jordan who conferred with Israel's leaders on numerous occasions after 1967, was willing to consider the Allon Plan as a basis for negotiations, and the Egyptian-Israel peace treaty was based on a total Israeli withdrawal from the SINAI PENINSULA. Syria, in its talks with Israel since the 1991 Madrid Conference also insisted on total Israeli withdrawal from the Golan Heights.

While the Palestinians, since the Madrid Conference, formally called for total Israeli withdrawal from the West Bank and Gaza Strip, the Beilin-Abu Mazen document of 1 November 1995, reportedly suggested that the Palestinians might be willing to accept a territorial compromise solution, if indeed the result would be the establishment of a Palestinian state in most of the West Bank and Gaza Strip territory. The document, formulated by Yossi BEILIN and ABBAS MAHMUD (nicknamed Abu Mazen) in the course of some twenty meetings which began in October 1993, dealt with possible parameters for a permanent settlement between Israel and the Palestinians. The document proposed that a demilitarized Palestinian state be established in the Gaza Strip and ninety percent of the territory of the West Bank, whose capital would be in the Arab neighborhood Abu-Dis, east of Jerusalem; that Jerusalem remain united, but the Palestinian flag fly over the Temple Mount; that Israel hand over to the Palestinians the Halutza sand dunes—an area in the northern Negev—in return for the annexation to Israel of about ten percent of the West Bank in which most of the Jewish settlements are concentrated and in which about seventy percent of the settlers live; and that the Jordan Valley and the northern part of the Dead Sea be handed over to the Palestinians in the year 2007. The document was never adopted by neither the Israeli nor Palestinian leaderships, but its principles are certain to surface when Israel and the Palestinians discuss the permanent settlement. Since 1967 the idea of territorial compromise in the West Bank and

Gaza Strip faced ever-growing objection of the supporters of GREATER ISRAEL, namely, the religious-nationalist stream, as well as staunch advocates of ultimate national security based on territorial depth. The main instrument—vastly used by Israeli right wing governments (1977–1984, 1990–1992)—to prevent such a solution was to establish massive Jewish settlement all over the West Bank and Gaza Strip in order to make such a solution impractical.

Functional compromise: Another Israeli idea, associated with Moshe DAYAN, proposed that the West Bank and Gaza Strip be administered in condominium by Israel and Jordan, where each of the two would have certain powers and responsibilities. This idea, like the Allon Plan, assumed that a "Jordanian option" for solving the Palestinian problem existed. To a certain extent one might argue that the various interim arrangements within the framework of the Oslo process imply a functional compromise between Israel and the PALESTINIAN AUTHORITY.

History of the peacemaking efforts since 1948

1948–1967: On 29 May 1948, two weeks after the proclamation of the State of Israel and invasion of Palestine by Arab armies, a UN Security Council resolution initiated by Britain imposed an embargo on arms deliveries to the Middle East, and called for a truce to end hostilities and enable international mediation to resolve the dispute. Count Folke Bernadotte (1895–1948), a Swedish nobleman and president of the Swedish Red Cross, was appointed UN Mediator for Palestine. In the course of the four months which he spent in Palestine, he supervised the implementation of the Arab-Israeli truces and cease-fires imposed by the UN Security Council in the course of the 1948–1949 war. To do so Bernadotte established a UN Truce Supervision Organization (ONTSO) comprised of military observers (mainly American, French, Belgian and Scandinavian officers), which remained a permanent phenomenon in the country ever since. Bernadotte's main mission was to work out a peaceful settlement between Israel and its Arab neighbors, an effort which had an influence on the warring parties' considerations and decisions. Bernadotte recommended the integration of the Arab part of Palestine with Jordan; the annexation of the Negev (which was allotted to the Jewish state) to Jordan in exchange for western Galilee (which had been allotted to the Arab

state, but was conquered by Israeli forces); and the repatriation of all the Arab REFUGEES who had fled or were expelled from the areas under Israeli control. The first version of Bernadotte's plan proposed that Jerusalem also be annexed to Jordan. The second version called for its internationalization. Bernadotte also recommended that the port of Haifa be turned into an international port and that the airport at Lydda (Lod, today Ben Gurion airport) be turned into an international airport.

The second version of the plan was submitted to the UN in September 1948, a short time before Bernadotte was assassinated on 17 September 1948, by Jewish members of the ultra-nationalist Lehi underground movement. The plan was, however, rejected by the Political Committee of the UN General Assembly early in December 1948, after it became clear that neither Israel nor the Arabs were willing to accept it. The British Foreign Office, which had shaped much of Bernadotte's suggestions, was also behind shaping the UN General Assembly Resolution 194 (11 December 1948), stipulating the internationalization of Jerusalem; recognizing the right of the Palestinian-Arab refugees "who would want to live in peace with their neighbors" to return to their homes; and establishing the Palestine Conciliation Commission (PCC) in order to help work out a peaceful settlement to the Arab-Israel Conflict.

The five permanent members of the UN Security Council chose the US, FRANCE and TURKEY to be members of the Commission. In April 1949 a conference was convened by the PCC in Lausanne (without SYRIA, but with the unofficial participation of Palestinian-Arab refugee representatives). As was the rule in Arab political practice since the late 1920s, their representatives refused to hold direct official talks with the Israelis (although some of them did maintain informal meetings with the Israeli delegates). Thus, the members of the Commission held separate meetings with the Israeli and Arab representatives. On 12 May 1949 a protocol was agreed upon by Israel, EGYPT, LEBANON and Jordan, which established the procedural basis and principles for the continuation of the talks. According to the protocol the Arab governments accepted the UN partition plan as a basis for any settlement of the conflict while Israel tacitly accepted the right of Palestinian refugees to repatriation. It soon became clear that the protocol was far from representing genuine intentions on either part. Within a few weeks, the talks in Lausanne were stalemated.

In the course of the 1950s the PCC continued its activity—with limited success—on several issues such as Jerusalem, Palestinian-Arab property and deposits frozen in Israeli banks, family reunification and other issues. In the late 1950s the PCC presented a plan to try to resolve the problem of the Palestinian refugees. It proposed a solution on three levels: that some of the refugees be repatriated to Israel, that others be settled in the Arab countries, and that the remainder be absorbed in other countries. In 1961 Dr. Joseph E. Johnson of the Carnegie Foundation was sent to the Middle East to investigate the issue. Johnson submitted his first report towards the end of 1961, and his final report in September 1962. The report was shelved by the PCC because neither side was willing to discuss it. Though the PCC was never officially dismantled, it ceased to function in 1962.

The 1948–1949 War ended formally with four separate Armistice Agreements signed by Israel and its four Arab neighbors—Lebanon, Syria, Jordan and Egypt. The agreements regulated the relations between them in the absence of peace, and defined the international boundaries between Israel and Lebanon and Egypt (except along the Gaza Strip); the "Green Line" between Israel and Syria, Jordan and the Gaza Strip; zones considered "no man's land"; and demilitarized or limited zones. Mixed armistice commissions, with UN chairmen, were set up to deal with problems arising from and related to the agreements.

The agreements were negotiated primarily in Rhodes, under the auspices of UN mediator Ralph Bunche. The agreement with Egypt was signed on 24 February 1949, with Lebanon on 23 March 1949, with Jordan on 3 April 1949 and with Syria on 20 July 1949. No agreement was signed with Iraq, even though Iraqi troops had participated in the war (but left shortly before the armistice with Jordan was signed). Only on the Lebanese front did the borders drawn in the Armistice Agreements survive the Six-Day War.

The Armistice Agreement between Jordan and Israel was the only one which was followed by an attempt by the two sides to move on to a more substantial agreement. On 5 May 1949 Israeli foreign minister Moshe Sharett visited Abdallah, to discuss the common rejection of the internationalization of Jerusalem and the issue of an outlet to the Mediterranean for Transjordan.

On 24 February 1950, a document laying down the principles of a five-year non-aggression agreement between Israel and Jordan was initiated. It dealt with the armistice lines, no-man's land, joint committees on economic and territorial issues, a free zone for Jordan in the port of Haifa, trade cooperation and financial compensation for persons who had lost their property in Jerusalem as a result of the partition of the city. However, although the Israeli government approved the agreement, it never ratified it.

The separate agreement with Israel was fiercely rejected by the other Arab neighboring states thus Jordan had no choice but to follow suit.. On 3 April 1950, the ARAB LEAGUE decided to expel any Arab state which reached a separate economic, political or military agreement with Israel. On 20 July 1951, King Abdallah was assassinated in Jerusalem, bringing an end to his life-long effort to effect a settlement with his Jewish neighbors to the west.

In 1953 US President Dwight Eisenhower requested that businessman Eric Johnston (1896–1963) draft an agreement for a unified or coordinated regional water development plan for the exploitation of the waters of the Jordan River to the benefit of the riparian countries (Lebanon, Syria, Jordan and Israel). The mission was another attempt since 1948 to resolve the Palestinian refugee problem by resettlement in the neighboring Arab countries. After protracted negotiations, Johnston presented a plan in 1955 for the distribution of the Jordan waters approved by the technical experts from the states concerned (and in Israel's case, by the political authorities as well). However, the Johnston Plan floundered when brought before the Arab League for collective approval, mainly because of Syria's refusal to recognize formally any scheme in which Israel was also a part. Israel and Jordan proceeded to implement unilateral water development projects, which took the Johnston Plan into consideration.

In the first four months of 1956 an American mediator, Robert Anderson, a personal friend of President Eisenhower, made four trips between Jerusalem and Cairo, in an attempt to bring about some agreement between Israel and Egypt. The mediatory efforts came to naught.

Israeli withdrawal from Sinai in the aftermath of the 1956 Sinai Campaign (see ARAB-ISRAEL CONFLICT) was not accompanied by any efforts to establish peace between Israel and Egypt, though a UN Emergency Force was stationed in the Gaza Strip, along the border in Sinai and in Sharm al-Sheikh (the southeastern tip of the peninsula) to secure free navigation through the straits of Aqaba. In fact, there was no significant peacemaking effort in the period from 1956 to 1967, even though there were diplomatic efforts which sought to avert the June 1967 War.

1967–1973: Most of the post-1967 peace plans and peacemaking efforts alluded to UN Security Council Resolution 242, passed on 22 November 1967. The resolution was based on a British-American initiative and included two basic principles for the establishment of a just and lasting peace in the Middle East. These were the call for the "withdrawal of Israeli armed forces from territories occupied" by Israel in the course of the 1967 War (some confusion was caused by the fact that the French version of the resolution spoke of "*les territoires*", whereas the English version only mentioned "territories"); and the "termination of all claims or states of belligerency and respect for the acknowledgment of the sovereignty, territorial integrity and political independence of every state in the area and their right to live in peace within secure and recognized boundaries, free from threats or acts of force." The resolution further affirmed the necessity "for guaranteeing freedom of navigation through international waterways in the area; for achieving a just settlement of the refugee problem (in later years the PLO strongly objected to having the Palestinian problem referred to in these terms); for guaranteeing the territorial inviolability and political independence of every state in the area, through measures including the establishment of demilitarized zones." Finally it requested "the Secretary General of the UN to designate a special representative to proceed to the Middle East to establish and maintain contacts with the states concerned in order to promote agreement and assist efforts to achieve a peaceful and accepted settlement in accordance with the provisions and principles" of the resolution.

It was on the basis of the last provision that the Swedish Ambassador Dr. Gunnar Jarring (b. 1907) was chosen as special envoy to the Middle East by the Secretary General of the UN. Because the Arab states refused to hold direct talks with Israel, Jarring was obliged to commute between Jerusalem and the Arab capitals. His talks were suspended in the spring of 1969 without results when the representatives of the four Great Powers began to discuss the Middle East issue—an effort which also came to naught.

International mediation efforts in this period revealed an unbridgeable gap between Israel and its Arab neighbors whose positions regarding a settlement with Israel varied significantly. Israel aspired for a contractual peace with its neighbors, insisting on direct negotiations with them as an essential step toward recognizing its legitimacy, and was unwilling to accept full withdrawal to the 5 June borders on grounds of security. Although Jordan and Egypt accepted the Resolution 242 (Syria accepted it only in 1972), they were struggling with domestic pressures and inter-Arab competition which narrowed their freedom to maneuver, especially regarding symbolic concessions to Israel. The three "nays" (to negotiations and peace with, or recognition of, Israel) adopted by the Arab summit of Khartoum in early September 1967, and the rise of Palestinian national claims stifled these regimes' capability to enter into any substantial diplomatic effort that would not secure an unconditional withdrawal of Israel from the occupied territories. On 9 December 1969, in the midst of the War of Attrition (see ARAB-ISRAEL CONFLICT), US Secretary of State William Rogers initiated a plan for breaking the deadlock of the Arab-Israeli conflict. The plan called for Israel to withdraw to the international boundary with Egypt. The status of the Gaza Strip and Sharm al-Sheikh would be negotiated, but they would not remain under Israeli control. Jerusalem would remain united but under the administration of the three religious communities, and freedom of navigation for Israeli shipping would be ensured in the SUEZ CANAL. This plan was rejected by Egypt as being excessively pro-Israel, and by Israel for not ensuring its security not calling for direct negotiations toward a formal peace treaty,; and not ensuring that Jerusalem remain under Israeli control. On 18 December a proposal by the permanent US representative to the UN, Charles W. Yost, expanded the Rogers Plan to the Jordanian front, proposing that Israel would withdraw to the 1949 Armistice Lines, with slight border revisions. The Arab refugees were to be accorded the choice of returning to Israel or accepting compensation.

Repeating the already rejected proposals on Jerusalem, the Yost Document called for Israel and Jordan to enjoy an equal status in Jerusalem in the religious, economic and civil spheres. Freedom of navigation in the Gulf of Aqaba would be ensured for Israeli shipping. This proposal was tacitly accepted by Jordan but rejected by Israel on 22 December 1969.

In June 1970 Rogers initiated a second plan, which proposed negotiations between Egypt and Israel under the auspices of Ambassador Gunnar Jarring. The new negotiations were aimed at reaching an agreement on a just and lasting peace, to be based on mutual recognition of each country's sovereignty, territorial integrity and political independence, and on an Israeli withdrawal from territories occupied in 1967 in accordance with Security Council Resolution 242. As a first step Rogers proposed that the cease-fire between Israel and Egypt be renewed. On 21 June the Israeli cabinet rejected the new plan. On 22 July Egypt, apparently concerned by the possibility of further escalation of the War of Attrition, accepted the proposals. US pressure then intensified on Israel. President Nixon sent clarifications to Prime Minister Golda MEIR confirming that Israel's withdrawal would be to secure agreed borders, not the pre-June 1967 borders; that no withdrawal would be demanded until a contractual and binding peace had been signed; that the Arab refugee problem would be solved such that it would not impair the Jewish character of the State of Israel; that the US would ensure the integrity, sovereignty and security of Israel; and that the balance of arms would be preserved. On 31 July 1970 Israel agreed to consider the plan. This agreement led to the Herut— Liberal block (*Gahal*) decision to leave the National Unity Government. The cease-fire between Egypt and Israel came into force on 7 August 1970.

The Jarring talks were resumed soon thereafter. However, Israel suspended the talks when it became apparent that Egypt had, with Soviet assistance, violated the cease-fire agreement by moving anti-aircraft missiles close to the Suez Canal. On 4 February Anwar al-SADAT announced the prolongation of the cease-fire by another month, suggesting an immediate Israeli withdrawal to the el-Arish-Ras Muhammad line, following which works to reopen the Suez Canal would start. Sadat explained that these steps were to be part of a comprehensive settlement in accordance with Resolution 242. Although Israeli Prime

Minister Meir responded publicly in favor of Sadat's proposal, it was another futile initiative. On 8 February Jarring submitted his own proposals for a peace arrangement which went far beyond Sadat's initiative. These proposals involved an Israeli commitment to withdraw its forces from occupied Arab territory "to the former international boundary between Egypt and the British mandate of Palestine," on the understanding that satisfactory arrangements were made for the establishment of demilitarized zones and freedom of navigation through the Suez Canal, and practical security arrangements in the Sharm al-Sheikh area to guarantee freedom of navigation through the Straits of Tiran. Egypt, according to the proposals, would commit itself to entering a peace agreement with Israel, in which it would undertake, on a mutual basis: to terminate the state of belligerency; to acknowledge and respect the other side's independence; to acknowledge and respect Israel's right to live in peace within secure and recognized boundaries; to do everything possible to prevent any act of belligerence or hostility from its territory against the population, citizens and property of the other party; to refrain from interfering in the affairs of the other side.

The proposal was accepted in principle by Egypt, but turned down by Israel, since the agreement called for its withdrawal to the 1967 borders. Israel wanted direct negotiations without preconditions. For all intents and purposes this brought the Jarring Mission to an end. A third Rogers Plan for an interim agreement along the Suez Canal was rejected by Israel on 4 October 1971, several hours after being delivered, since it did not ensure that such an agreement would be followed by peace moves.

1973–1991: Security Council Resolution 338, passed on 22 October 1973, two days before the formal end of the Yom Kippur War, called for a cease-fire, "the implementation of Security Council Resolution 242 in all its parts, and the beginning of negotiations" between the parties concerned under appropriate auspices, aimed at establishing a just and durable peace in the Middle East.

On 6 November 1973, under the influence of the oil crisis, the nine members of the European Community published the first of numerous Middle East statements. This statement listed four principles for resolving the Arab-Israel conflict. These were: inadmissibility of acquisition of territory by force; the need for Israel to end the territorial occupation which it had maintained since the war in 1967; respect for the sovereignty, territorial integrity and independence of every state in the region and its right to live in peace within secure and recognized boundaries; and recognition that in the establishment of a just and lasting peace, the legitimate rights of the Palestinians must be taken into account.

On the basis of Security Council Resolution 338, the US and the USSR convened a Middle East peace conference, which was to meet in Geneva under the auspices of the UN. Egypt and Jordan agreed to participate, on condition that additional states would be present and they would not be obliged to hold direct negotiations with Israel. Their official excuse for conferring with Israel under the same roof—the first such occasion in the history of the Arab-Israel conflict—was that this was a means of attaining an Israeli withdrawal from the territories it had occupied in 1967. While Israel declared that it would not meet with the Syrians until they published the list of Israeli prisoners of war captured in the course of the Yom Kippur War, Syria refused to participate without the PLO being represented—a demand utterly rejected by Israel and the US. Lebanon was not invited. Egypt and Jordan wanted France and Great Britain to participate in the talks, but Israel and the Superpowers objected.

The Geneva Conference opened on 21 December 1973 with the presence of UN Secretary General Kurt Waldheim, and the Foreign Ministers of the two Superpowers who acted as co-chairmen. Due to the Arab refusal to sit with Israel at a round table, the participating delegations sat at separate tables arranged as a hexagon, with one table left empty for the Syrian delegation. Under the full glare of televion cameras and the press, the six participants gave their opening speeches. Following this ceremony, the conference was adjourned until after the Israeli elections to the eighth Knesset, which were to take place on 31 December. The Geneva Conference was never reconvened, though Arab states, the USSR and various European states continued to argue that the Geneva Conference was the desirable framework for attaining a comprehensive settlement in the Middle East. Nonetheless, the Geneva Conference served as an official umbrella for the coming Israeli agreements on disengagement of forces with Egypt and Syria.

Following the opening session of the Geneva Conference, an Egyptian-Israeli military committee began meeting in Geneva on 26 December 1973, to discuss a disengagement agreement, but the negotiations were finally pursued through the mediation of US Secretary of State Henry Kissinger. What came to be known as "Kissinger's shuttle diplomacy", which involved the Secretary of State flying back and forth between Jerusalem and various Arab capitals, resulted in the signing of the Egyptian-Israeli Disengagement Agreement on 18 January 1974 and the Syrian-Israeli Disengagement Agreement on 31 May 1974. The two agreements dealt with the disposition and reduction of military forces on both sides of the cease-fire lines, and Israeli withdrawal from certain areas. The agreement between Israel and Egypt provided for the withdrawal of Israeli forces from Sinai, west of the Suez Canal; accepted the presence of Egyptian forces in the Sinai Peninsula up to the October cease-fire line; and lifted the Israeli siege of the Egyptian Third Army. It also established a 6 miles (10-km.), buffer zone under the UN Emergency Forces (UNEF), with the reduction of Israeli and Egyptian forces on either side of this line and the limitation of their military equipment. The agreement between Israel and Syria provided for Israeli withdrawal from some of the Syrian territories occupied in October 1973, from the town of Kuneitra and an adjacent area held since 1967, which was to be reinhabited by the Syrians. A buffer zone was set up, manned by the UN Disengagement Observer Force (UNDOF), while limitations were imposed on the strength and equipment of forces within 6 miles (10-km.), and a further 16 miles (25 km.) on either side of the cease-fire line.

Efforts to negotiate a disengagement agreement between Israel and Jordan (even though Jordan had not formally participated in the Yom Kippur War), failed. In the summer of 1974 the possibility of an Israeli-Jordanian agreement along the Jordan River was discussed, namely, the Jericho Plan, by which Israel would return Jericho and its environs to Jordan in return for an arrangement similar to the agreements with Egypt and Syria. The plan, which was promoted by Yigal Allon Israeli Minister for Foreign Affairs and discussed with Secretary of State Henry Kissinger, was rejected by King Hussein of Jordan. It is doubtful that the Rabin coalition government dependent on the Religious-Nationalist Party (*Maf-*

dal)—would have been able to deliver such a concession. In any event, the possibility of an Israeli-Jordanian Agreement was strictly blocked by the Rabat ARAB SUMMIT CONFERENCE of October 1974, which declared the PLO the sole representative of the Palestinian people and the only body entitled to negotiate on its behalf. In principle, the Rabat Conference cancelled Israeli Labor Party's so-called "Jordanian option", which sought to solve the Palestinian problem through negotiations with the Hashemite Kingdom of Jordan, though in practice, this option would survive until King Hussein's disengagement from the West Bank on 31 July 1988.

On 4 September 1975 Israel and Egypt signed the Sinai II Agreement in Geneva, known as the Interim Agreement, which like the previous agreement was based on "a little piece of territory for a little bit of peace." The agreement provided for Israeli withdrawal from the Suez front to the eastern ends of the strategic Mitla and Giddi Passes. Most of the vacated territory was to become a new UN buffer zone 12–26 miles wide, (19–42 km.) while the old buffer zone became part of the existing Egyptian limited-force zone. Israel was to evacuate the Abu Rudeis and Ras Sudar oil fields and a narrow strip along the Gulf of Suez connecting the oil fields to Egyptian-controlled territory south of Suez, with joint UN-Egyptian administration and no military forces stationed within the evacuated area. A joint effort was to be made to refrain from the use or threat of force or military blockade, to observe the cease-fire scrupulously and to renew the mandate of the UN Emergency Force (UNEF) annually. The passage of non-military Israeli cargoes through the Suez Canal (which was reopened to navigation on 5 June 1975) was to be provided for and American-manned electronic early-warning stations in the area of the Mitla and Giddi Passes were to be installed. A joint Israeli-Egyptian commission was to deal with problems as they arose and assist the UNEF;. Finally a military work group which would meet in Geneva to draw up a protocol establishing in detail the implementation stages of the agreement. The signatories also agreed that the accord would remain in force until it was replaced by another one. The Interim Agreement entailed an American memorandum of understanding with Israel, undertaking, to provide Israel with further financial support and arms supplies, and not to conduct any dialogue with the PLO

as long as it had not recognized Israel's existence and Resolution 242, and renounced TERRORISM.

The Sinai II Agreement triggered a crisis in Egypt's relations with Syria and the PLO. Not only was it a separate and partial agreement, but it assumed significant political elements, particularly the commitment to refrain from the use of force in future disputes. After the 1973 War, Sadat attempted to take advantage of the American mediation to recover as much as possible of occupied Sinai from Israel, regardless of the repercussions of such a strategy on other Arab interests in similar progress on their own fronts, namely Syria and the PLO. The latter's efforts to establish an all-Arab commitment to a joint diplomatic Arab action regarding the peacemaking process with Israel—which was approved by the Arab summit conference at Rabat (October 1974)—were repeatedly foiled by Sadat's autonomous diplomacy. In late 1976, Sadat managed to mend his fences with Syria and the PLO, with a view to working together toward a comprehensive settlement of the Arab-Israeli conflict with the newly elected US President Jimmy Carter. However, the attempts to re-convene the Geneva Conference stumbled, mainly due to the unresolved problem of Palestinian representation: Israel and the US utterly rejected PLO representation at the conference. In the summer of 1977, the peace process seemed to have been deadlocked. The unprecedented victory of the right-wing Likud Party in Israel, in the May 1977 general elections, seemed to have further narrowed the prospects for progress. It was this deadlock, coupled by Carter's attempt to bring the USSR back into the diplomatic stage, that drove Sadat to seek an outlet, resulting in a major breakthrough in the peace process. Through the good offices of various foreign leaders, including President Ceausescu of Romania, Israeli Foreign Minister Moshe Dayan met the Egyptian Vice President Dr. Hasan al-Tuhami in MOROCCO, soon after the new Israeli government, led by Menachem BEGIN was formed. Despite its significance, this meeting failed to create a common basis for further dialogue. It was the Joint American-Soviet Declaration of 1 October that led the Egyptian President Anwar al-Sadat to initiate his historical peacemaking visit to Jerusalem, during which he delivered a speech to the Knesset on 20 November. Sadat's visit to Jerusalem opened a series of Israeli-Egyptian negotiations which soon reached an impasse, calling on the US to return to its mediating role in the peace process. The Arab world was split by Sadat's initiative, revealing how far from conform the Arab attitude to Israel actually was. The standstill was caused by unbridgeable gaps mainly regarding Israel's required withdrawal to the lines of 5 June 1967, as well as by Sadat's insistence on a concept of comprehensive settlement, which would include the Palestinian front. Israel submitted a plan for interim autonomy for the Palestinians in the West Bank and Gaza Strip, yet by the summer of 1978, the peace process slowed dramaticly.

A turning point in the peacemaking process was the Camp David Accords, signed by Sadat and Begin as well as by US President Jimmy Carter, who played a major mediatory role. The two accords were signed on 17 September 1978, after a thirteen-day meeting at Camp David. The first formulated a framework for peace in the Middle East, which stated that Security Council Resolution 242 was to be the basis for such peace. It addressed the West Bank and Gaza Strip, calling for the implementation of an autonomy plan to be followed after five years by a permanent settlement, leaving open the question of sovereignty over these territories. It then delineated a process of normalization in the relations between Egypt and Israel, to be followed by similar agreements between Israel and its other neighbors. The second accord constitued a framework for the conclusion of a peace treaty between Egypt and Israel, based on a complete withdrawal of Israel from the Sinai Peninsula "up to the internationally recognized border between Egypt and mandatory Palestine," to be followed by the establishment of normal relations, which were to include mutual recognition, diplomatic, economic and cultural relations, "the termination of economic boycotts (see the ARAB BOYCOTT) and barriers to free movement of goods and people, and the mutual protection of citizens by the due process of law."

Egypt insisted that its peace process with Israel be linked to an agreement regarding the future of the West Bank and Gaza Strip, in order to avoid accusations by the Arab world of having concluded a separate peace with Israel and "selling out" the Palestinian cause. Israel's main concern was not to appear to be giving up its claim for control over the West Bank and Gaza Strip. But in fact, Egypt did conclude a separate peace with Israel, while Israel was obliged to concede that the negotiations regarding the permanent status of the West Bank and Gaza Strip "must also recognize the legitimate rights of the Palestinian people and their just requirements," and that Jordan would be actively involved in the area in which the autonomy was to be implemented during the interim period. The signed Accords were accompanied by an exchange of letters regarding Jerusalem, in which Begin declared Jerusalem to be indivisible and the capital of Israel, while Sadat declared Arab Jerusalem to be an indivisible part of the West Bank, which should be returned to Arab sovereignty. Carter also verified that Begin had informed him that Israel took the terms "Palestinians" and "Palestinian people" to mean "the Arabs of *Eretz Yisrael*."

The translation of the Camp David Accords to an Egyptian-Israeli peace treaty stretched over the next six months and stumbled over symbolic and secondary issues, creating again a threatening deadlock. A US presidential visit to Cairo and Jerusalem in March 1979 was necessary to rescue the peace process and conclude a final peace treaty, signed on 26 March 1979, on the White House lawn in Washington D.C. Once again, the three signatories were Carter, Sadat and Begin. The treaty brought about an immediate termination of the state of war between the parties, provided for a gradual withdrawal of Israeli forces from the remainder of the Sinai (the withdrawal ended in April 1982), and for the establishment of "normal and friendly relations" between the two states, including full recognition, diplomatic, economic and cultural relations, termination of boycotts and discriminatory barriers to the free movement of people and goods, and a guarantee of full mutual enjoyment of the due process of law by each other's citizens. Egypt and Israel undertook recognizing and respect of each other's right to live in peace within secure and recognized boundaries, to "refrain from the threat or use of force, directly or indirectly, against each other" and to "settle disputes between them by peaceful means." Disputes arising out of the treaty itself were to be settled by means of negotiations, conciliation or arbitration. The treaty also provided for limited free zones on both sides of the international boundary, the presence of UN forces and observers, and unimpeded passage of Israeli ships through the Suez Canal and the Straits of Tiran.

The process of normalization did not proceed as anticipated by the treaty, and though ambassadors were exchanged between the two countries, the Egyptian Ambassador was recalled as a result of the Lebanese War (see ARAB-ISRAEL CONFLICT) and returned only in September 1986, following the resolution of the Taba dispute. The dispute over Taba, a tiny piece of territory on the Red Sea south of Eilat, soured the relations between the two states until finally settled by means of arbitration on 29 September 1988, following which the disputed area was returned by Israel to Egypt. Even though the peace between the two countries remained a "cold peace," there was never any question of its abrogation from either side.

The relatively successful military results of the Yom Kippur War, at least from Egypt's viewpoint, and the effective use of the Arab oil weapon during that war (see OIL) had brought about a change in Egyptian thinking that made the 1974 and 1975 agreements possible. These, in turn, helped pave the way toward the more dramatic agreements of 1978 and 1979. However, it was primarily the continued economic and social crisis in Egypt that drove Sadat in the direction of peace.

The Egyptian-Israeli peace treaty did not lead to further progress in the Middle East peacemaking process. On the contrary, it led to Egypt's being expelled from the Arab League, economically punished and formally ostracized by most of the Arab states. On 6 October 1981 Sadat was assassinated by Muslim extremists in the context of their Holy War against the infidel ruler. His successor, Husni MUBARAK, sought to adhere to Sadat's peace policy toward Israel, and yet striving to restore Egypt's relations with the rest of the Arab states, as well as its leading regional position.

Though there was no progress in the peacemaking process, in the following years peacemaking efforts initiated by both Arab and foreign circles continued, focusing on the Palestinian issue. This trend resulted largely from the collapse of the Israel-Egyptian autonomy talks in the course of 1979–1980, the European Community's anxiety concerning their oil interests in the Arab world following the Shi'i revolution in IRAN, and the increasing military clashes between Israel and the Palestinian armed guerrillas in Lebanon, which culminated in Israel's invasion of that country and nine-week siege of Beirut. On 30 June 1980 the European Community published its Venice Declaration, which supported the Palestinian's right to self-determination and stated, inter alia, that the PLO must be incorporated in peace negotiations.

The growing international interest in the Palestinian issue was echoed in Israel as well. In the mid-1970s, talks began between a group of leftist Israeli public figures—though without political influence—and representatives of the PLO's mainstream Fatah organization. Prime Minister Yitzhak RABIN was informed of the content of these talks, but did not approve them. The Israeli-Palestinian contacts became possible in view of the PLO's June 1974 PNC decision which expressed willingness to accept less than the whole territory of Palestine, and interest in advancing its international legitimacy as an equal partner in the peac making process (see PALESTINE LIBERATION ORGANIZATION). Though the Israeli personalities involved had only very limited effect over Israeli public opinion at the time, they played an important role in the gradual change in the thinking of leading personalities within the PLO. However, it was to take close to two decades before the Israeli and Palestinian leaderships finally came to terms with each other. Although Yasser ARAFAT himself sanctioned tacitly contacts between top Fatah members and Israeli public figures, they were subjected to attempts on their lives and actual assassinations were implemented by radical factions, such as of ABU NIDAL, who was sponsored at the time by IRAQ.

Meanwhile, the anti-Egypt Arab front fell apart, manifesting its paralysis without Egypt's lead. The weakness and disarray in the Arab world were further aggravated by threats to the domestic and regional security of the Gulf oil monarchies posed by the Iranian Shi'i revolution, the Soviet invasion of Afghanistan (January 1980) and the offset of the IRAN-IRAQ WAR (September 1980). It was under these circumstances that Saudi Crown Prince (later King) FAHD IBN ABDEL AZIZ proposed a framework for peace in the Middle East, which was meant to win international approval and replace the Camp David Accords. The Saudi peace plan, the first of its kind, was published on 7 August 1981. It called for Israeli withdrawal from all Arab territories occupied in 1967, including East Jerusalem and the removal of Israeli settlements established on Arab lands since 1967. It guaranteed freedom of worship in the holy places for all religions and affirmed the right of the Palestinian people to return to their homes, and compensation to those who decide not to do so. It also called for UN control over the West Bank and Gaza Strip for a transitional period not exceeding a few months, the establishment of an independent Palestinian state with Jerusalem as its capital and the right of all states in the region to live in peace. Furthermore it proposed that the UN or some of its members guarantee and implement these principles.

Israel rejected the Saudi plan and also expressed doubts as to whether the Saudis were really willing to recognize Israel. The Arab states were divided over the plan. Those that accepted the Fahd Plan asserted that it implied recognition of the State of Israel under its affirmation of the right of all states in the region to live in peace. This was also precisely why Syria stood up against it and, leading a block of radical Arab states, exerted vehement pressures to co-opt Lebanon and the PLO into its own line. PLO Chairman Arafat at first tacitly agreed with the plan as a basis for negotiations. But in view of Syria's (and Iraq's) opposition at the Arab summit conference, convened in Fez (Morocco) on 25 November 1981, to discuss the plan, Arafat was obliged to renounce it. The summit adjourned without the heads of state having even discussed the plan.

The Fahd Plan was followed by an American plan—the Reagan Plan, which was published on 1 September 1982, two days after the evacuation of West Beirut by the PLO. Clearly, the American statement came in response to Israel's long siege of Beirut and Arab appeals to Washington during that siege to renew its mediating role in the conflict with Israel. The statement, issued by President Ronald Reagan, put the US clearly on record as favoring Israeli withdrawal from territories it had occupied in June 1967, and the association of an autonomous West Bank and Gaza Strip with Jordan. The President stated that "the United States will not support the establishment of an independent Palestinian state in the West Bank and Gaza, and we will not support annexation or permanent control by Israel."

The Reagan Plan repeated the American commitment to Israel not to recognize or negotiate with the PLO unless it accepted Security Council Resolutions 242 and 338. It called for a freeze of all Israeli settlement activities in the territories, the status

of existing Israeli settlement to be determined in the course of negotiations on the final status of the territories. The Palestinians, including those residing in East Jerusalem, would be allowed to play a leading role in determining their own future through the provisions of the Camp David Accords. During the transitional period a self-governing authority would be elected in the territories, to assume real powers over the population, the land and its resources. It would assume progressive responsibility over internal security subject to its performance and the degree of its control over the situation. The status of East Jerusalem would be determined through negotiations.

In Israel, the government rejected the initiative the day after it was made public. The Arabs responded more favorably but could not accept Jordan's leading role in a negotiated settlement with Israel, certainly not after their poor performance during the Lebanon War and tacit collaboration with the PLO's expulsion from Beirut. The Arab summit conference held at Fez on 8 September 1982 adopted a modified version of a peacemaking plan—the Fez Plan—based on the Fahd Plan. It differed from the latter in that Israeli withdrawal and the dismantling of settlement no longer referred to 1967, implying the possibility that these two sections may also refer to settlements within the Green Line. It spoke of the Palestinian right to self-determination and of the PLO as being the sole representative of the Palestinians, while the Fahd Plan spoke merely of the right of the Palestinians to return to their homes and did not mention the PLO. The most controversial article of the Fahd Plan namely an affirmation of the right of all states in the region to live in peace was also changed, speaking now of a UN Security Council guarantee for the peace and security of all states in the region. Finally, the Fez Plan called for a Security Council guarantee of the plan's implementation, whereas the Fahd plan left an option open for guarantees by some of the UN members, i.e., the Western powers only. Although Israel entirely rejected the Fez Plan it was the first time in the history of the Arab-Israel conflict that the Arab world came on its own initiative with a peacemaking plan.

Unlike previous wars, the Lebanon War did not help to advance the peacemaking process, at least not in the immediate aftermath of hostilities. This derived from the anarchic nature of the Lebanese state after seven years of civil war, collapse of the state's institutions and foreign interference in its domestic affairs. Israel clearly sought to reap the benefits from the expulsion of the PLO's armed personnel and Syrian units from Beirut to formalize its clandestine alliance with the Maronite militias through an official "peace treaty." Thus, even though Israel and Lebanon signed, with the help of American mediation, a peace agreement on 17 May 1983, it was worthles, and eventually backfired. Not only the Muslim factions, strongly supported by Syria, rejected the treaty with Israel. Even the new President, Amin JUMAYYIL, held reservations regarding the treaty, which was in fact forced on him by Israel. Above all, Lebanon had no capability of delivering the commitments it had undertaken by the treaty with Israel. The agreement spoke of complete Israeli withdrawal from Lebanon, in return for an implied Lebanese promise that it would take responsibily to prevent all acts of terror from its territory against Israel and a withdrawal of Syrian forces from Lebanon. It was also agreed that an international peace-keeping force would be posted in Lebanon; the South Lebanese Army would be integrated in the Lebanese Army; and that the relations between the two countries would be normalized. If anything, the Israel-Lebanon peace agreement convinced Syria to accelerate its indirect campaign against any Israeli influence in Lebanon by playing the divided Lebanese communities against the President, portraying him as a communal leader and the multi-national peace-keeping force. On 5 March 1984 Lebanese President Amin Jumayyil announced its abrogation.

The aftermath of the Lebanon War witnessed a joint Jordanian-Palestinian effort to bring a renewal of the peace process by working out an agreed formula for political action, taking into consideration the PLO's political weakness after its expulsion from Lebanon, and yet, its status as the sole representative of the Palestinian people, and the Reagan Plan which designated Jordan as Israel's partner for a settlement on the occupied West Bank and Gaza Strip. In February 1985 King Hussein and Arafat signed in Amman an accord which adopted a formula of "land for peace as mentioned in the UN resolutions, including the Security Council resolutions," circumventing the problem of PLO recognition of Resolution 242. The agreement spoke of a Jordanian-Palestinian confederation, rather than a separate Palestinian state, as the framework within which Palestinian independence would be materialized. Finally, it called for peace talks under the auspices of an international conference as an overall basis for a comprehensive peace in which the PLO's status as an equal participant would be recognized.

The Amman Accord, which came shortly after a national unity government was formed in Israel by Shimon PERES revived the idea of convening an international peace conference for the Middle East. The basic idea was that the conference would serve as an umbrella for direct talks between Jordan and Israel. In August 1985 the Arab summit conference in Casablanca expressed support for an international peace conference including the UN Security Council's permanent members. Prime Minister Peres also adopted the idea and in his speech at the UN in October 1985, expressed Israeli consent to Palestinians constituting part of a joint Jordanian-Palestinian delegation. However, in February 1986 the Amman Accord was suspended by Jordan's King Hussein due to the PLO's refusal to accept Resolution 242, indicating the collapse of the Amman Accord.

In April 1987 King Hussein and Peres (then Foreign Minister in a national unity government headed by Yitzhak SHAMIR) reached a secret agreement in London on the international conference. The London Agreement spoke of a UN-sponsored international conference, including the five permanent members of the Security Council and all parties involved in the Arab-Israel conflict, to negotiate a settlement based on Security Council Resolutions 242 and 338 with the goal of achieving a comprehensive settlement. The conference was to serve as an umbrella for direct and bilateral negotiations between the parties concerned, but would neither impose a settlement nor veto any agreement reached by the parties to the conflict. The agreement specified that the objective of the negotiations would be to solve all aspects of the Palestinian problem in all its aspects and that the Palestinians would be represented by a joint Jordanian-Palestinian delegation. In early May the London Agreement was voted against in the Likud-led Israeli government on grounds that the international conference would be a "trap" for Israel.

With the eruption of the Palestinian uprising (INTIFADA) in the West Bank and Gaza Strip in December 1987, the long diplomatic standstill came to an end, returning the Palestinian issue back to center stage. In February 1988, Secretary of State George Shultz presented his proposal which included elements from the Camp David Accord on Palestinian autonomy, the Amman and London agreements. The Shultz plan suggested, *inter alia*, an international convention in April 1988, with the participation of the parties to the conflict and the five permanent members of the UN Security Council, followed by direct negotiations between Israel, Jordan and the Palestinians on an interim autonomy agreement for the West Bank and Gaza Strip, to be implemented as of October for a three-year period. In December 1988 talks were to begin on the permanent solution, between Israel and a Jordanian-Palestinian delegation that would include the autonomy administration. The permanent solution would be based on the "land for peace" formula. Non-resident Palestinians would be allowed to participate on condition that they accepted Resolutions 242 and 338.

In Israel the plan was welcomed by Peres but turned down by Prime Minister Shamir, because it did not condition the negotiations on the INTIFADA ending first, and because it ignored the Camp David Accords. On the Palestinian front, where the intifada had revived the PLO's stature and set the goal of a Palestinian independent state in the West Bank and Gaza, eliminating any remnant of allegiance to Jordan, the plan was outdated the moment it became public. Even King Hussein had to express reservations on the American plan. It was now the PLO's turn to translate the intifada into a political breakthrough in its relations with the US. At the Arab summit conference in Algiers held in June 1988, a "personal" document, formulated by Arafat's advisor, Bassam Abu Sharif, was informally presented to the participants, indicating acceptance of Resolutions 242 and 338, as well as direct negotiations with Israel in an international conference. The document reflected the growing influence of the Palestinians in the occupied territories on PLO decision-making, and pressure to adopt the goal of an independent Palestinian state in the West Bank and Gaza Strip. This trend culminated in the declaration of the Independent State of Palestine at the nineteenth PNC session in Algiers (November 1988), based on the UN Partition Resolution of 29 November 1947. Yet the PLO's new political program

was still far from meeting the US conditions for opening a dialogue with the PLO, namely, unreserved acceptance of Resolutions 242 and 338 and renouncing terrorism. These conditions were finally met a month later in Arafat's statement in Geneva, resulting in Washington's announcement that diplomatic dialogue with the PLO would begin.

In May 1989 Israel's second national unity government adopted a new peacemaking initiative backed jointly by Defense Minister Rabin and Prime Minister Shamir. The core of the initiative called for holding elections in the West Bank and Gaza Strip in order to elect a representation with whom Israel would negotiate a transitional self-government and later, a permanent settlement. The initiative, which had won the new US administration's support, was a historical shift from the traditional Zionist and Israeli policy of overlooking the national Palestinian leadership in favor of neighboring Arab partners. Even though the Israeli initiative did not preclude an active role of neighboring Arab states, it was the first time that an Israeli government named the Palestinians as the main partner for direct negotiations over the future of the West Bank and Gaza Strip. The Israeli plan might have intended to drive a wedge between the "inside" Palestinian leadership and the "outside" PLO establishment in Tunis. Yet, despite its strict objection to negotiations with the PLO, establishment of a Palestinian state in and Israeli withdrawal from the West Bank and Gaza Strip, the plan clearly indicated a change of heart within the Labor Party—unmatched by the Likud—regarding the Palestinian issue, triggered by the prolonged intifada.

In response to this plan, Egyptian President Husni Mubarak proposed that Israeli and Palestinian delegations meet in Cairo to open talks on the elections, and published his own ten-point program for the implementation of the Israeli initiative. Although the Egyptian program refrained from mentioning the PLO or a Palestinian state, it stumbled over the issue of participation of Palestinian residents of East Jerusalem in the elections, and the principle of land for peace, both of which were rejected by most of the Israeli government members.

The debate over Mubarak's ten points, indicating a substantive gap between the Likud's and Labor's positions, led to further indulgence in ostensibly procedural issues, which in fact had been of essential significance. On 6 December a five-point document published by US Secretary of State James Baker, which dealt with the procedures of the Israeli-Palestinian dialogue to be held in Cairo. The Israeli government, however, insisted on prior approval of the list of Palestinian representatives. This brought the American effort to a dead end in March 1990, and precipitated the downfall of the national unity government by a vote of no confidence initiated by the Labor Party.

1991–present: Even though the GULF WAR of January–February 1991 revolved around Iraq's aggression against KUWAIT, the six-month crisis underlined the organic link between Middle East regional politics and the issue of Palestine, regardless of the PLO's actual political weight. In fact, already in an early phase of building up the international coalition against Iraq, leading Arab proponents, such as the oil monarchies and Egypt, sought to legitimize their participation in the coalition against Iraq by extracting a joint US-Soviet commitment to convene an international peace conference after the liberation of Kuwait. Certainly, the collapse of the Soviet Union in 1991 and the emergence of the US as the sole world power, on the one hand, and the re-alignment of the Middle East actors following the war on the other hand, facilitated the efforts to resume the peace process.

Nonetheless, seven months of intensive shuttle diplomacy and eight rounds of visits to the Middle East by Secretary of State Baker were needed to obtain the agreement of all the parties directly involved in the Arab-Israel conflict to participate in an international conference in Madrid, which at Israel's insistence was to serve only as a preamble to direct bilateral and multilateral talks between Israel and its neighbors. Also accepted were the Israeli demands that the PLO should not be party to the negotiations, that only Palestinians from the territories (and no East Jerusalem residents), approved by Israel, should form part of a joint Jordanian-Palestinian delegation and that there should be no pre-conditions to the talks. That the PLO had to accept those conditions was a clear reflection of its weakened position due to its support for Iraq and the rift this had caused in its relations with the Arab oil monarchs, who consequently halted financial aid to the organization and the Palestinians in the occupied territories.

The Madrid Conference was sponsored by both the US and Soviet Presidents who also served as as co-chairman of the meeting. The historical significance of the conference was in the fact that all the parties directly involved in the Arab-Israeli conflict participated and sat at the same table, while all the other Arab states (except Iraq) were represented by observers.

Immediately after the conference ended the first meetings between Israel's negotiating teams and three separate Syrian, Lebanese and Jordanian-Palestinian teams took place in Madrid. These were followed by bilateral talks, held without observers, in Washington, the first round of which was opened on 10 December 1991. Parallel to the bilateral talks, a track of multilateral talks was created to encourage progress with the participation of many of the Arab states (Syria and Lebanon refused to take part in these talks in the absence of an agreement with Israel), Israel and countries outside the region. Separate committees were set up to deal with water resources, the environment, arms control and regional security, refugees and regional economic development.

The first five rounds of bilateral talks were held while the Likud was in power in Israel, dealing primarily with procedural matters with little substance. After Rabin formed a Labor-led government in July 1992, the talks continued with a clear tendency on the Israeli part to deal with substantial matters in order to reach agreement on either the Palestinian or the Syrian fronts. Thus, for the first time, Israel was officially willing to discuss a withdrawal in, though not from, the Golan. Yet despite the inter-Arab competition over the pace and substance of the negotiations, little progress was realized. Israel's separate talks with the Palestinian delegation bore no fruits; meanwhile the intifada in the occupied territories continued. The Palestinian delegation was in fact under the PLO's control and guidance, which, it seemed to Israel's government was increasingly adamant to block any possible progress in the Palestinian-Israeli talks. These talks were finally sidetracked, by the Oslo channel between Israel and the PLO, which led to the signing of the Declaration of Principles (DOP) on 13 September 1993, and high level secret talks between Israel and Jordan, which was followed by the signing of the Israel Jordan Peace Treaty on 27 October 1994.

The talks between Israel and Syria continued in Washington until the beginning of 1996, but came to an abrupt end after Binyamin NETANYAHU was elected Prime Minister of Israel on 29 May 1996, since Netanyahu refused to continue the talks from where they had been left off by the previous government—namely, an implied Israeli willingness to consider withdrawal from the Golan Heights in return for full peace and normalized relations with Syria. The Syrians argued that the Madrid Conference had established the principle of "land for peace," and that Israel could not retract from it. Despite an unprecedented number of shuttle visits by US Secretary of State Warren Christopher and one visit by President Bill Clinton to Damascus, Syria remained vague about its willingness to meet Israeli demands for security and full normalization. The talks between Israel and Lebanon came to a standstill in the course of 1994, since progress was dependent on Syria's consent, and the Syrians conditioned the talks between Lebanon and Israel on its own progress with Israel.

Although from late 1992 Prime Minister Rabin clearly emphasized the priority he gave to reaching an agreement with Syria, he seized the secret avenue opened by Israeli academics and PLO representatives in Oslo since January 1993, to come to terms with the PLO. The secret contacts initiated by the Norwegians were not the only track along which Israelis and PLO-based Palestinians conducted talks alongside the official Washington talks, clearly indicating the PLO's willingness to reach out to Israeli decision-makers. The main figure behind the secret Oslo talks was Yossi Beilin who, after assuming his new post as Deputy Minister for Foreign Affairs, approved and supervised the contacts, at first on an unofficial level. In February, Peres disclosed the existence of the talks to Prime Minister Rabin. The issue being discussed concerned Israeli withdrawal from Gaza and the transfer of economic authority in the territories to the Palestinians.

In May Rabin and Peres agreed to rise to the official level of the talks, while keeping the talks in Washington going. By the end of July an agreement started to crystallize, though it was only in August that Rabin was finally convinced that the talks were likely to end in an agreement, after he was informed that the Palestinians were willing to reach an interim settlement which would avoid dismantling any

Jewish settlements; would leave Jerusalem under full Israeli control; would leave the responsibility for the security of the Israelis in the territories and for external security in Israeli hands; and would leave all the options for the negotiations regarding the permanent settlement open. The agreement, known as the Declaration of Principles (DOP) was initialed in the presence of Peres and Norwegian Foreign Minister Johan Jurgen Holst in Oslo on 20 August. The signing ceremony took place in Washington on 13 September 1993.

Undoubtedly, the agreement signed with the PLO in Oslo was the most significant development in the Arab-Israeli peacemaking process since Sadat's visit to Jerusalem in November 1977. Similarly, the Oslo Agreement was a separate step by the PLO, which took Jordan and Syria by surprise but demonstrated the PLO's determination to shape its political course independently, regardless of Arab criticism. What the DOP involved was mutual recognition between Israel and the PLO and the transfer of most of the Gaza Strip and Jericho to Palestinian hands, as a first step toward a permanent peace settlement between the two sides. The mutual recognition between Israel and the PLO was effected by means of an exchange of letters between Rabin and Arafat on 9 September. Israel recognized the PLO as the representative of the Palestinian people, and announced its decision to open negotiations with it within the framework of the Middle East peace process. Arafat, in turn, recognized, in the name of the PLO, Israel's right to exist in peace and security, and reiterated his commitment to the Middle East peace process and to resolving the conflict between the two sides by peaceful means. He undertook to prevent the use of terror and other violent means, repeated his recognition of Security Council Resolutions 242 and 338, and took upon himself to bring to the approval of the Palestinian National Council (PNC) the abolition of those articles in the Palestine National Covenant incompatible with the letters exchanged between Israel and the PLO on 1 and 9 September, namely those articles calling directly or indirectly for the destruction of the State of Israel, or denying its right to exist.

The DOP stated that the goal of the negotiations which would follow between the two parties would establish a PALESTINIAN AUTHORITY in the West Bank and Gaza Strip for an interim period of no more than five years, and that a permanent settlement would be negotiated on the basis of Security Council Resolutions 242 and 338. It took another eight months before the agreement began to be implemented, following the signing of the Cairo Agreement on 4 May, 1994. The agreement paved the road to Arafat's move from Tunisia to Gaza in July, to take charge of the Palestinian Authority. The active role played by Egyptian President Mubarak in finalizing the Oslo and Cairo Agreements bolstered their legitimacy in the Arab world.

The Cairo Agreement defined the West Bank and Gaza Strip as a single territorial unit, while delineating the areas in the Gaza Strip and Jericho that would be handed over by Israel to the Palestinians in the first stage. The main issues agreed upon were a timetable for the Israeli withdrawal; the legislative powers of the Palestinian authority; the establishment of a strong Palestinian police force to preserve public order and internal security in the Gaza Strip and the Jericho area; and the Israeli responsibility regarding security in face of external threats. Agreement was also reached on the status and rights of Israelis living in the Gaza Strip; joint Israeli-Palestinian patrols along the horizontal roads in the Gaza Strip; and the need to take all the necessary steps to prevent acts of terror, crime and hostility directed at the other side. In late April 1994 an accord was reached in Paris between Israeli and Palestinian delegates regarding future economic relations between Israel and the Palestinian Authority, including the monetary system, trade, customs and tariffs.

The Oslo Agreement was both an incentive and obligation for King Hussein to conclude his own long-awaited agreement with Israel. However, regional and domestic constraints obliged the king to give way to a possible Syrian-Israeli Agreement first; only after it proved futile, he moved forward alone. On 25 July 1994, nearly three months after the Cairo Agreement was signed, King Hussein and Yitzhak Rabin appeared together publicly for the first time, and signed the Washington Declaration, regarding their intention to conclude a peace treaty. In the course of the twenty-four years before this date numerous secret meetings had been held between Hussein and various Israeli Prime Ministers, while cooperation on such issues as security and water had also quietly taken place for awhile a few years. On 26 October 1994, the Peace Treaty was signed at a cer-

emony which took place on the border between the two countries, in the Arava, in the presence of US President Clinton.

The Treaty was meant to resolve all the disputed issues between the two parties and constitute an obligation to work together toward full normalization of their diplomatic, strategic and economic relations. It stated that the boundary between the two states would be the border delineated in mandatory times between western Palestine and Transjordan—the territory east of the Jordan River, which had been included in the Mandate for Palestine. Within this framework Israel returned to Jordan an area of over 116 sq. miles (300 sq. km.), which it had taken over in the years 1968–1972 by moving the border fences eastward during the battle against terrorist attacks and hostile infiltrations from Jordanian territory. Jordan agreed to hand over to Israeli sovereignty 30 square kilometers of this territory, which included fields that had been cultivated by Israeli farmers during the previous twenty years, and in return Israel gave Jordan areas of equal size to the west of the old Mandatory border. In an additional ten locations, minor mutual border changes were made. The Treaty also included an Israeli undertaking to supply Jordan with 50 million cubic meters of water from Lake Tiberias and Beisan Valley in the short run, as well as an agreement that the two states would cooperate to increase the availability of water for Jordan by desalination of water in the vicinity of Lake Tiberias and construction of storage facilities on the Yarmuk and Lower Jordan in the Beit-She'an (Beisan) area.

Israel and Jordan agreed that the problem of the 1948 Palestinian refugees would be resolved on a bilateral basis, and the fact that after the establishment of the State of Israel Jews in many of the Arab states were forced by circumstance to leave their homes, was also mentioned. Regarding the 1967 refugees (the Palestinians who had escaped from the West Bank to Jordan during the Six-Day War), it was agreed that the issue would be discussed within the framework of the talks of the permanent committee, including Israel, Jordan, Egypt and the Palestinians.

The Treaty stipulated the abolition of the Arab boycott of Jordan, and the development of trade and tourism relations. As for Jerusalem, Israel undertook to respect the special status of the government of Jordan in the places holy to Islam in the city, and to give Jordan high priority in the negotiations on the permanent status of holy places. It was concluded that within one month from the ratification of the Treaty, full diplomatic and consular relations would be established between the two countries.

The agreement between Jordan and Israel was followed by Israel's establishment of formal, low-level diplomatic ties with Morocco and Tunisia in North Africa, and QATAR and OMAN in the Gulf. However, the lingering progress in the Israeli-Syrian negotiations was a constant obstacle to establishing normalization with other Arab oil monarchies who, under tacit threat or interest to secure Syria's valuable friendship in view of the Iranian threats, preferred to postpone rapprochement with Israel until progress was achieved in those negotiations.

Soon after the Jordanian-Israeli peace treaty was signed the first Middle East and North African (MENA) economic conference, with the participation of Arab, Israeli and non-regional countries was held in Casablanca (Morocco) under the auspices of the US and Russia. The conference brought together officials and private business figures with the idea of enhancing economic development and cooperation in the region. The overwhelming presence of Israeli business figures in the conference and the foreign backing given to Israeli efforts to be incorporated in the "New Middle East", triggered a wave of resentment toward what seemed an Israeli attempt to assume economic hegemony in the Middle East. Although these fears were by no means new in the history of the conflict, in late 1994 the sudden change in the strategic setting of the Middle East following Israel's agreements with the PLO and Jordan seemed to have created an Israeli-dominated economic block (with Jordan and the Palestinian Authority) with bridges to the Arab world.

The following year the conference—dealing primarily with concrete projects and business ventures—was held in Amman (Jordan), and in November 1996 it was held in Cairo (Egypt). The later conferences were characterized by growing tensions between Israel and Egypt due to the latter's insistence on maintaining its regional leadership and determining the pace of the peace process, which seemed to have gone out of Cairo's control , especially in the case of Jordan's peace agreement with Israel, and the Gulf Emirates independent relations with Israel.

Meanwhile, despite continued terrorist bombings committed against Israeli citizens by the Palestinian Islamic movements of HAMAS and the Islamic Jihad, Israel and the Palestinian Authority continued to proceed with the DOP. On 8 September 1995 the Taba Agreement, better known as Oslo II, was signed between Israel and the Palestinian Authority, another interim agreement between the two sides, on the way toward a permanent settlement. The agreement, included six appendices which dealt with security arrangements, elections for the Palestinian Authority, and the transfer of authority, legal issues, economic relations and cooperation between the two sides in various spheres.

The main goal of the agreement was to broaden the spheres of Palestinian self-government in the West Bank, as laid down in the Cairo Agreement, by means of elections for an eighty-two member Palestinian Council. It dealt with the elections for a Council and laid down that Palestinians living in Jerusalem would also be able to participate in the elections. According to the agreement, Israel was to hand over to the Palestinian Authority, after its establishment, powers and areas of responsibility both in the civilian and security spheres in the West Bank and Gaza Strip. The Israeli Civil Administration was to withdraw from the areas handed over to the Palestinians. The withdrawal of the IDF was to begin before the elections.

The agreement laid down three categories of areas in the West Bank: Area A—which included all the cities, except Hebron, in which the Palestinian Authority would have full responsibility for internal security and public order, as well as for civilian life; Area B—which included the Palestinian villages and towns, in which the Council was to receive full authority to run the civilian life and maintain public order, while Israel would continue to be responsible for general security; Area C—which included concentrated Jewish settlements and security zones in which the Palestinian population was sparse, and in which the Palestinian Authority will only have power in the civilian sphere over the Palestinian inhabitants.

Special provisions were made for Hebron, due to the presence of Jewish settlers in the center of the city, and in which the redeployment of the Israel Defense Forces (IDF) was to have ended by 26 March 1996. It was agreed that after the redeployment a high ranking committee would be set up to follow the security situation in the city and examine the arrangements in it, and that there should be a temporary international presence in the city.

The agreement also dealt with the stages of the redeployment of the IDF in the territories, which was to have been completed at the beginning of 1996. The timetable was not kept however, as a result of Rabin's assassination on 4 November 1995; the wave of Islamist suicide terrorist acts against Israeli citizens in February and March 1996; and the change of government in Israel in June 1996 following elections.

According to the agreement a Palestinian police force made up of twelve thousand policemen was to be set up. In fact various paramilitary units, with a much larger number of men, were established by the Palestinians, reaching close to forty thousand. The agreement dealt with the movement of Israelis in all the areas, responsibility for the holy places, the arrangements for the handing over of powers to the Palestinian Authority, increase in the quantity of water allocated by Israel to the Palestinians and the continuation of the release of Palestinian prisoners held by Israel.

The Palestinian Authority reconfirmed its undertaking to change the problematic articles in the Palestine National Covenant within several months of the establishment of the Palestinian Authority. However, the decisions made at the the PNC session held in Gaza in mid-May 1996, although welcomed by Prime Minister Peres, remained debated as to what extent they genuinely intended to meet the Palestinian commitment.

Since the redeployment of the IDF in Hebron was not terminated as scheduled, the issue became the subject of yet another agreement—the Hebron Agreement, signed between the Israeli government under Binyamin Netanyahu and the Palestinian Authority on 15 January 1997. Under the new Agreement Hebron was divided into two zones: one in which the Palestinian police received powers similar to those it has in Area A, and a Jewish enclave in the old city, in which Israel would continue to maintain full authority and responsibility for internal security and public order. Apart from setting security rules and arrangements between the two zones, it was agreed to take measures to normalize the economic life of the city which had been dormant due

to strict security measures taken by Israel. Israel would continue to be responsible for the overall security of Israelis throughout Hebron, but without the right to "hot pursuit". The Cave of the Patriarchs remained under the sole responsibility of Israel, but several other holy sites were passed to the Palestinians.

Beyond the agreement on Hebron itself, Israel undertook to continue its withdrawal from territories in the West Bank in three stages (to end by the middle of 1998), to continue to release Palestinian prisoners and to open negotiations on the permanent settlement. The Palestinians undertook to complete the process of amending the Palestine National Covenant, to continue fighting terror and prevent violence, not to diverge from the number of policemen permitted under previous agreements, and to carry on governmental activities only in those areas agreed upon in the Taba Agreement—in other words, not in Jerusalem. The agreement was accompanied by letters from US Secretary of State Christopher to Netanyahu and Arafat.

The ascendancy of a right-wing government headed by Netanyahu caused a growing mistrust among Arab leaders toward the genuine goals of the new Israeli government. Relations with the Palestinian Authority and Egypt grew more bitter due to Israel's declared policy of widening the Jewish population in the West Bank, the opening of a tunnel in the Old City of Jerusalem in September 1996 (which led to armed clashes between Israeli soldiers and Palestinian policemen, claiming a total of over seventy-five casualties), a policy of denying the right of residency to Palstinians who moved their residence out of the municipal area of Jerusalem, decisions on new Jewish construction projects in East Jerusalem, such as Har Homa on the southern outskirt of the municipal area, and the tiny territory which Israel was willing to hand over to the Palestinians from Area C (only two percent) as an implement of the first redeployment according to the Hebron Agreement. Above all, the ongoing closure imposed by Israel on Palestinians in the West Bank and Gaza Strip struck these areas with desperate economic depression, further embittering the relations between Arafat and the Israeli government. On the Israeli side, the Palestinian Authority was repeatedly accused of not fulfilling its undertakings, particularly in fighting Palestinian terrorism.

On 31 March 1997, under Palestinian and Syrian pressure, the Arab foreign ministers, meeting in Cairo, decided to freeze all normalization steps in the relations with Israel. This included closing the Israeli offices and missions in various Arab states and those of Arab states in Israel until Israel agreed to abide by the principle of "land for peace", the suspension of Arab participation in the multilateral talks; and the preservation of the primary boycott against Israel, until a comprehensive and just peace is attained in the region.

ARAB-ISRAEL WARS   see ARAB-ISRAEL CONFLICT.

ARAB LEAGUE (*jami'at al-duwal al arabiyya*) The League of Arab states was founded, after the Preparatory Conference at Alexandria (October 1944), in March 1945, in Cairo, by the seven Arab states independent or nearly independent: EGYPT, IRAQ, SAUDI ARABIA, YEMEN, Transjordan (from 1946: JORDAN), SYRIA and LEBANON. The following countries joined subsequently: LIBYA (1953), SUDAN (1956), TUNISIA, MOROCCO (1958), KUWAIT (1961), ALGERIA (1962) SOUTH YEMEN (1967-1990) BAHRAIN, QATAR the UNITED ARAB EMIRATES, OMAN (1971), MAURITANIA (1973), Somalia (1974) and DJIBOUTI (1977). From the founding conferences, the PALESTINE ARABS were represented at the Arab League (1945–1948, by the Higher Arab Committee; 1948–1964, by the All-Palestine government; from 1964, by the PLO), enjoying aobserver status. This lasted until 1976 when Palestine was accorded recognition as a full member of the Arab League. Thus the Arab League incorporated, since 1977, twenty-two members, including the PLO. Since the merger of Yemen and the PDRY in 1989, Arab League members number twenty-one.

The foundation of the Arab League was triggered by Hashemite Iraq and Transjordan ruler aspirations and competition for regional unity under their thrones, which accelerated by World War II and the expectations for the post-war settlements in the region. The HASHEMITES' aspirations faced tacit opposition of the national elites in Syria and Lebanon who resented the idea of giving away their newly achieved independence, as well as of Egyptian and Saudi leaders objecting to a Hashemite hegemony in the Fertile Crescent. Furthermore, before agreeing to join the Arab League, Lebanon requested and obtained a specific recognition of its independence and territorial integrity—against potential Syrian plans (suspected, but not spelled out) to annex it or its Muslim-majority North, South and East. This recognition formed an annex to the Alexandria Protocol which prepared the Arab League Charter.

The Palestine question also played a major role in triggering the foundation of the Arab League. Having acquired a major role in domestic and regional Arab politics between the two world wars as a focal all-Arab issue, the question of Palestine, as an open territorial and political problem, threatened the regional Arab status quo. The Arab League Charter not only included a unique annex on Palestine but also proclaimed commitment to support the Palestinian Arabs in their struggle for independence. In the years 1945–1948, the Arab League in fact appropriated the question of Palestine from the Palestinian Arab leadership and turned into a supreme authority shaping the collective Arab policy on this issue. Indeed, from the outset, the question of Palestine was the main issue on the Arab League agenda. This remained unchanged since the advent of the State of Israel.

The foundation of the Arab League was ostensibly a realization of the ARAB UNITY vision (see PAN-ARABISM). However, the institutional result of the inter-Arab official deliberations in 1943–1945 represented a loose regional organization of independent and sovereign states whose commitment to cooperate was defined in rather modest terms. Indeed, not only was the Arab League far from the federal union envisioned by the Iraqis, it had no binding power over its member-states. In fact, the Arab League is first and foremost a status-quo organization whose main goal is to regulate inter-Arab state relations on a basis of equality, mutual acceptance of state independence and sovereignty. Indeed, the Arab League Charter failed to mention even once the word "unity." It emphasized primarily the member-states' commitment to respect other members' independence and sovereignty and refrain from interfering with each other's domestic affairs. According to its Charter, only decisions accepted by consensus of its Council members are binding.

During its first few years the Arab League enjoyed a dignified status and prestige. This was illustrated by the high-level of Arab representatives participating in its Councils' sessions (prime ministers or foreign ministers). However, the Arab defeat in the 1948 war and the "loss of Palestine," related to the League which had conducted and coordinated the Arab political and military action on Palestine. This inflicted an incurable blow to this body and its first Secretary-General Abdel Rahman Azzam.

Egypt has been (except for 1979–1989, when its membership was suspended because of its peace agreement with ISRAEL), the most influential dominant power in the Arab League. The Arab League headquarters were in Cairo except in 1979–1990 when they were transferred to Tunis. During the years when the Arab League Secretary-General was the Tunisian KLIBI, Chedli (al-Shadhily al-Qulaibi), all Secretary-Generals were Egyptians: Abdel Rahman Azzam (1945–1952), Abdel Khaleq Hassuna (1952–1972), Mahmud RIYAD (1972–1979). According to the Charter, the budget is raised by the member-states according to a percentage scale that is adjusted from time to time to match the members' economic capabilities.

The Arab League had initiated many projects for all-Arab cooperation in the economic, cultural, social, technical, military and political fields. Many of these schemes have not—or not fully—materialized, but a limited degree of coordination in various spheres has been achieved. A Development Bank (from 1959), a Development Fund (1972–1973) a mining company (1975), a Monetary Fund (1977), a joint shipping company and a maritime transport corporation (oil tankers, 1972–1973), communications' satellites; an Organization of Arab Petroleum-exporting Countries (OAPEC) (1967–1968). An Economic Union was planned from 1964, designed to develop within ten years into a Common Market.

In the early 1980s, another project of Arab economic integration and complementarity was planned. None of these projects have materialized. Most of these projects were not under the direct auspices of the Arab League but were arranged by some of its members in various combinations. The Arab League however, was a clearing ground for many of them. It served as an institutional framework for Arab Summit Conferences since 1964. It was in this capacity that the Arab League arranged for aid to be given by the rich Arab Countries (mainly Saudi Arabia, Kuwait, and other oil principalities of the PERSIAN GULF) to the confrontation states e.g., those bordering on Israel (Egypt, Jordan, Syria, Lebanon), and the PLO,

between 1967 and 1978, and again in 1978–1987 (this time excluding Egypt).

In military matters, mainly the armed struggle with Israel, the Arab countries involved mostly preferred to follow their own policies and conclude bilateral or multilateral pacts with other Arab countries rather than operate through the League apparatuses. A "Collective Security Pact" was signed in 1950—intended mainly to give more binding power to League decisions. However, this Pact played no significant role until 1964, when Egypt's ABDEL NASSER led the Arab states to shape a military and political response to Israel's challenges by initiating a plan for the diversion of the Jordan river's tributaries and establishing a joint Arab Command to prepare for the imminent war against Israel. However, even in this case, inter-Arab military cooperation remained haphazardous and inefficacious. The Arab League did play a role in 1972–1973 in arranging for Arab states' commitment to share the war effort with Egypt by expeditionary forces or by lending armaments. This activity was conducted by Secretary-General Mahmud RIYAD in tandem with Egypt's Chief of Staff, Shazli. Most of the commitments undertaken by Arab states were implemented during the 1973 war.

Despite its weaknesses and failures, the League remained a central agency shaping collective Arab policies of ideological significance, primarily the Arab-Israel conflict and inter-Arab relations. Hence, it assumed the role of coordinating and presenting a common political front in the international arena and conducting information and propaganda efforts. Since 1950, it has enjoyed observer status at the UN, maintaining information offices in several capitals. Its propaganda centered mainly on issues and areas where Arab demands for national liberation had not been fully satisfied—Syria and Lebanon in the 1940s; Morocco, Tunisia and Algeria in the 1950s; ADEN and the Persian Gulf in the 1960s; and the Palestine problem and the Arab-Israel dispute since the League's inception. The Arab League directs and supervises the economic boycott of Israel and those trading with it (see ARAB BOYCOTT). Following the establishment of the PLO in 1964, the Arab League, namely, Egypt, supervised and financed the organization, until 1968 when it acquired more independence.

Within the Arab League, divergent or conflicting trends have always formed rival blocs which impeded the Arab League's functioning as an all-Arab body. In the 1940s and 1950s, the Egyptian-Syrian-Saudi bloc was guarding the inter-Arab status quo against the Hashemite Iraqi-Jordanian bloc with federalist-revisionist plans. As Hashemite federal schemes became obsolete after 1958, a Saudi-Jordanian rapprochement emerged. A new, different confrontation shaped rivalries throughout the 1960s: an Egypt-led socialist and neutralist bloc (Egypt, Syria, Iraq, Algeria, South Yemen), which was itself torn apart by political animosities, versus a conservative group (Saudi Arabia, Jordan, Morocco). It was now Egypt and its allies that were revisionist, fostering unionist schemes and revolutionary changes in the countries of the rival bloc. It is against this backdrop that the late 1950s and early 1960s were years of crisis for the Arab League. Since most inter-Arab disputes were linked to Egypt (the leading power in the Arab League), the organization became identified with Nasser's Arab politics which assumed an antagonistic and challenging stance.

A degree of inter-Arab reconciliation was achieved in the mid-1960s (with newly instituted summit conferences as the supreme, though informal, inter-Arab forum, beginning with the First Summit, 1964). The failure of Egypt's operations in Yemen and of its subversive schemes elsewhere had sobered Nasser's interventionist zeal, while the mounting Arab-Israel crisis caused all Arab countries to rally around Egypt.

The pre-1967 Arab alignment, shaped by ideology and power struggle, has however, changed dramatically following the military debacle of 1967. Arab confrontation states had to look for the recovery of their territories occupied by Israel, for which they desperately needed financial support from the conservative oil states, promoting inclinations of pragmatism and inter-Arab coexistence. Egypt's gradual return to more conservative, mainline inter-Arab policies, begun in Nasser's last years. It was now Nasser himself who, in order to help Egypt's cause, revived the role of the Arab League as an instrument of Arab collective action. This fully unfolded, after Nasser's death (1970), under his successors. However, during the War of Attrition (1969–1970) along the SUEZ CANAL, Nasser's efforts to canvass Arab military and financial support through the summit conferences proved futile, mainly because of uncertainty about his goals and bitter residues due to past inter-Arab friction.

When Egypt signed a peace treaty with Israel (March 1979), its membership in the Arab League was suspended by a summit conference decision, which also resolved to transfer the League headquarters to Tunis, and called to sever all official diplomatic and economic relations with Egypt. The boycott was never fully implemented (see EGYPT), and even political relations were maintained, at least with some Arab countries, by semi-official representatives or interest sections in foreign embassies. Some Arab states never severed their relations with Egypt (Sudan, Somalia and Oman) and others gradually restored their official relations with Cairo (the PLO in 1983, Jordan in 1984, Djibouti in 1986). A collective Arab summit decision (November 1987), legitimizing the resumption of diplomatic relations with Egypt, was needed to enable most Arab states to do so. Even this, however, was not enough to allow Egypt back into the Arab League and it took another two years to overcome the resistance of Syria and Libya to the return of Egypt to the Arab fold, following which the Arab League Headquarters were moved back to Cairo.

Throughout the years, the Arab League had to accommodate differences and rivalries among its members. Acute disputes frequently impeded its coherence. Thus the League sessions themselves were boycotted by Tunisia 1958–1961, Iraq 1961–1963, Egypt 1962–1963 and Libya several times. Even summit conferences were frequently boycotted, mainly by radical states (Libya and Iraq in 1973–1974; Syria, Libya, Algeria and PDRY in the 1980, 1985). The fact that diplomatic relations were frequently severed between various Arab countries also impeded their cooperation in the framework of the Arab League. As to the various inter-Arab disputes themselves, the League was usually unable to prevent, arbitrate or even mitigate them, and its Charter's provisions for arbitration have hardly been used. Thus the League had little say in the Yemen war (1962–1967). It did not mediate when Algerian and Moroccan troops fought each other (1963) or in the dispute over Western Sahara. All-Arab attempts to settle the clashes between the Palestinian guerrillas and Jordan and Lebanon (1968–1971) were not conducted by the League or within its framework. Complaints by Arab states against Egyptian or UAR subversion or aggression (Sudan 1958; Tunisia 1958 and onwards; Lebanon 1958; Jordan 1958 and onwards; Iraq 1959; Syria 1962; Saudia 1963; Morocco 1963) were useless—and the complainants frequently chose to turn to other bodies, such as the UN Security Council. The only inter-Arab clash in which the League directly mediated or assisted the wronged party was the defense of Kuwait against Iraqi threats (1961).

Thus, the efficacy and success of the Arab League has been limited both in inter-Arab political and military coordination and in the sphere of cooperation projects. Various measures have been proposed to amend its Charter so as to make it more effective e.g., to substitute majority decisions for the rule of unanimity and to make its decisions more binding; and to create an Arab Court of Justice; but nothing has come of such proposals. Suggestions have been made, periodically, to supplement, or even to replace, the League of Arab states by a League of Arab peoples ; in the early 1960s Egypt began to institutionalize such a body but did not persist and allowed the new organization to fade away. After the suspension of Egypt's membership, Sadat also proclaimed, in 1980, the foundation of a League of "Arab and Islamic Peoples" but his successor dropped the plan and dissolved that body in 1983. Anyway, the Arab League has been a useful instrument of Arab policies, and even its detractors have not seriously proposed its abolition.

ARAB LEGION   see JORDAN.

ARAB MAGHREB UNION (Arabic: *ittihad al-maghreb al-arabi*) Organization of regional economic cooperation signed in 1989 by MOROCCO, TUNISIA, ALGERIA, LIBYA and MAURITANIA. The establishment of the AMU reflected a discernible improvement of intra-Maghreb relations, especially between Tunisia and Libya, who in May 1988, agreed to establish a social and economic union. This led to several joint Tunisian-Libyan projects, increased Libyan tourism to Tunisia, and widened employment of Tunisians in Libya. It was especially due to Tunisian President BEN ALI's initiative that further efforts were made to establish a strong regional economic organization, that would enhance the Maghreb states' bargaining position toward the ensued conclusion of the European Union. In June 1988, at the Arab summit conference in Algiers, the heads of the Maghreb states met to discuss the idea, which was finally re-

alized in February 1989. The new union was to reflect, in addition to its economic goals, a common regional identity.

In the January 1990 meeting of the AMU Foreign Ministers, the Tunisian delegate suggested a series of measures that would create a unified energy market for the Maghreb, allowing free trade in electricity, petroleum and natural gas. In March 1990, a regional television service for the entire Maghreb was founded in Tunis. In July of that year, at a summit conference of the members' heads of state, a custom union was propounded as an intermediate objective. However, the AMU failed to evolve into an active regional organization, due to political frictions and minimal common economic interest. The idea of attaining economic integration through intra-regional trade failed due to the significant disequilibrium in the productive structures between oil-exporters (Libya and Algeria) and non-oil exporters (Morocco, Tunisia and Mauritania), as well as in intra-regional and extra-regional trade. Most of the export of the Maghreb states goes to extra-regional customers, and the proportion is even higher in imports; most of which comes from the developed countries. In addition to these structural causes, the AMU also suffered from the unresolved political tensions among the member states, emanating from different ideologies (which came to the fore regarding the Iraqi invasion of KUWAIT, the GULF WAR, the Madrid Peace Conference) domestic troubles (such as the Algerian Civil War), and the WESTERN SAHARA CONFLICT (see MOROCCO).

ARAB NATIONALISM Feelings of Arab-Islamic identity together with pride of its heritage and traditions, and resistance to foreign domination have been prevalent among Arabs. Like other nations it has become the foundation of nationalism. An Arab national movement in the modern sense, however is a movement based on the conception that "nations", and the Arab "nation" among them, were entitled to independence. Furthermore, states should be formed on the basis of "nations" (and not, for instance, religion or dynastic allegiance), and organizations with the defined aim of attaining independence and establishing an Arab nation-state (or states). This emerged only at the beginning of the twentieth century. It had been preceded by Egyptian nationalism and by the stirring of an Algerian national movement against French rule. But these were principally Muslim, Egyptian and Algerian rather than Arab in their conception and aims.

The Arab national movement was rooted in, and preceded by, a movement of cultural and literary renaissance in the nineteenth century. This was centered mainly in the Levant (and to some degree in EGYPT), strongly influenced by the penetration of Western civilization and inspired by European romantic nationalism and national liberation movements. Among the leaders of that renaissance were Christian-Arab intellectuals, such as the Lebanese Boutros Bustani (1818–1883) and Nassif Yazeji (1800–1871). European and American Christian missionaries also significantly contributed to that renaissance, particularly by the development of educational institutions and technical instruments (printing presses, textbooks). The national renaissance was later strongly influenced by the modernist Islamic revival movement (Jamal al-Din al-Afghani, 1839–1897; Muhammad Abduh, Rashid Rida, Abdel Rahman al-Kawakibi, 1849–1903)—perhaps without fully realizing the inherent conflict between the supra-national PAN-ISLAM and extra-religious, Arab Nationalism, two ideologies that run parallel or overlap in some areas.

A politically motivated Arab national movement began organizing in the first decade of the twentieth century. This took place in the Arabic-speaking parts of the OTTOMAN EMPIRE, primarily in the "Fertile Crescent" (the Levant and IRAQ). Students, young officers and officials from those areas (HIJAZ, (Egypt, and Arabic-speaking North Africa were, at that time, outside the scope and target-area of incipient Arab nationalism). The organizers were influenced by the revolt of the YOUNG TURKS (1908), which at first seemed to pave the way for a liberalized, de-centralized regime in the Ottoman capital.

When the new rulers imposed a centralist and Turkish-nationalist regime, some of the new Arab societies grew increasingly antagonistic and began envisaging full Arab independence and the dissolution of the Ottoman Empire. Others strove for Arab autonomy within a decentralized empire. This difference coincided with the divergence described between Islamic influences and Arab nationalist motivations. Radical Arab nationalism necessarily demanded a struggle for full independence and the abolition of Turkish rule. Islamists however, were

bound to be loyal to the Muslim empire, to the Ottoman Sultan in his capacity as Khalifa (CALIPH), the head of the whole Islamic community. This ideological dichotomy was never fully resolved, though in fact the loyalists seemed to have the upper hand in the Arab parts of the empire. Nor did the Arab societies in these initial stages clearly define their aims. Did they aspire to one national state for all the Arab countries?; to several separate states?; to a federation of several Arab states? Futhermore what precisely was the area covered by their Arab nationalism, what was the extent of their future independent state or states?

The Arab National Movement at its initial stage consisted of various clubs or societies—such as the "*Ligue de la patrie arabe*" (Paris 1904), headed by Najib Azuri; the "Literary Club" (*al-muntada al-adabi*) (Istanbul 1909); the "Decentralization Party" (Cairo 1912); the "Reform Committee" (Beirut 1912); *al-Qahtaniyya* (1909, founded by Azia Ali al Masri); the "Arab Pact" (*al-Ahd*, founded 1914, by the same, with its members mainly young army officers); the "Young Arab Society" (al-*Fatah*, Paris 1911—among its founders the Syrian Jamil Mardam and the Palestinian Awni Abdel Hadi); the last three were clandestine. Al-*Fatah* which called for full Arab independence, was perhaps the most important among these groups. In 1913 it organized an Arab nationalist conference in Paris which was seen as an important landmark. Members of these organizations later became prominent in the leadership of the Arab states. At the time, they were a small group, with an active membership hardly exceeding a hundred, a few hundred supporters, and little influence. They did not arouse any popular movement for Arab independence, let alone an insurrection against the Ottoman rulers—even during World War I, when the international and military situation presented an opportunity. Arrests and trials of their members and other Arab notables conducted by the Turkish authorities in 1916–1917 which resulted in a number of death sentences and executions, were preventive rather than punitive.

An Arab insurrection arose during World War I from a different source. HUSSEIN IBN ALI, the Sharif of Mecca, of the Hashemi clan, rebelled in 1916, after preliminary contacts with the British and with their support (see ARAB REVOLT). The Sharif, and particularly his sons FEISAL and ABDALLAH, had had contacts with the Arab nationalist societies. In his exchange of letters with the British, he stipulated the establishment of an independent Arab state, or Arab states, in the Arabian peninsula and the Fertile Crescent, after the dissolution of the Ottoman Empire. He obtained British support, though that support remained rather vague he envisaged a measure of British (and French) tutelage for the future Arab state(s), and was not finalized in a clear and official agreement. The Arab nationalists in the Fertile Crescent probably sympathized with the Sharif's revolt, but did not support it by a simultaneous rebellion in their countries. Only a handful of Arab officers in the Ottoman army joined the revolt, deserting their Ottoman units. Among them were Aziz Ali al-Masri, who became the revolt's chief-of-staff for a short time, the Iraqis Nuri al- SA'ID who succeeded him, Ja'far al-Askari, Jamil al-Midfa'i, Ali Jawdat al-Ayyubi, and the Syrian Nassib al-Bakri. In 1918, Prince Feisal and his troops, advancing into Transjordan and Syria as the right wing of the British and allied forces under General Allenby, were allowed to enter Damascus and establish their headquarters and an Arab administration there.

The character of Arab nationalism in the post-World War I period was determined by the settlement imposed by the allied powers. The Hashemite princes' design for one Arab state, or a Unity of Arab states in ARABIA and the Fertile Crescent under their rule was not implemented. Separate semi-independent states under British and French tutelage were set up instead in Iraq, Syria, LEBANON, and Transjordan (with Palestine under a British Mandate, to become a Jewish National Home, and Hashemi rule in Arabia contested by the rising Saudi power). National movements arose in each of the states created in the formerly Ottoman area, each struggling for full independence from BRITAIN and FRANCE—sympathetic to, and supporting, each other, but separate. For the PALESTINE ARABS, there was the additional struggle against ZIONISM and the JEWS of Palestine. This struggle was also supported by the emerging Arab states and the national movements. National movements and the independence struggle in Egypt and North Africa also gradually became part of, and involved in, Arab nationalism. This country-by-country fight for full independence achieved its main goal (in most cases in stages), by the 1940s and 1950s, except for the case of Palestine. By that time all Arab countries were fully independent (in South Arabia and the PERSIAN GULF this took place in the 1960s and 1970s). The last vestiges of foreign, imperial privileges, military bases, unequal treaties were eliminated.

The inter-war years was the formative period of the Arab national doctrine, combining political and socio-economic developments, alongside the growing autonomy of the newly established Arab political entities. Growing education and urbanization accelerated the politicization of the masses, which turned nationalism into Islamism in its values and symbols. The emergence of new middle class deepened the social cleavages and intensified the tendency to use nationalist, that is, xenophobic rhetoric, as well as slogans of social justice directed against the traditional leadership of notables. These trends within Arab societies, combined with the growing struggle for national liberation from European domination and the intensifying Arab-Jewish dispute in Palestine to define Arab nationalism in militant and compulsive terms. The growing role of the Palestine conflict in Arab domestic and regional politics in the 1930s and 1940s, and the proven power of this issue as a mobilizing and rallying slogan—due to its religious significance: the threat to the Muslim shrines in JERUSALEM—not only accelerated the incorporation of Islamic values into Arab nationalism but also turned the Palestine question into a central element in this emerging ideology.

The original plans of the Arab national movement for a greater, united all-Arab entity (see ARAB UNITY, PAN-ARABISM) continued to be fostered by Arab political writers and thinkers—such as the Egyptian Abdel Rahman Azzam and the Syrians Sati al-Husri and Constantine (Qusti) Zureiq. In terms of practical politics, they survived mainly in schemes of the Hashemite rulers of Iraq and Jordan for a Fertile Crescent Federation or a GREATER SYRIA. In the 1920s, a "Syria-Palestine" representation in Europe also spoke for Pan-Arab nationalism, This was vaguely linked to these Hashemite plans but had little political effect and gradually faded out. These Hashemite schemes were revived in the 1940s, but they found little support in the "target" countries of Syria, Lebanon and the Palestinian Arabs. British backing, always suspected by the French and many Arabs, was at best partial and half-hearted, and the Hashemite plans never got off the ground. They were, anyway, adamantly opposed by most Arab states, and particularly by Egypt, Syria and Saudi Arabia. When in 1945, the ARAB LEAGUE was founded, it was based on close cooperation between independent Arab states and the rejection of all "revisionist", federal schemes. Pan-Arab nationalism in its Hashemite version lost its relevance with the assassination of Kings Abdallah (1951) and Feisal II (1958) and the elimination of Hashemite rule in Iraq (1958).

From the 1950s, Pan-Arab nationalism appeared in a new, invigorated, radical version—postulating an all-Arab nationalism (*qawmiyya*) that transcended the patriotism of specific Arab countries (*wataniyya*). This concept followed the German example of cultural nationalism, based on language and common history, as the primary definition of territorial and social identity. The shock of the Arab defeat in Palestine, 1948, was a main catalyst in that re-emergence of all-Arab nationalism. The new trends were Leftist, Socialist in inclination, and partly inspired by "New Left", Maoist-Castroist. One of them was the "Movement of Arab Nationalists" (*harakat al-qawmiyyin, al-arab*), clandestinely organized from about 1949–1950, at first mainly among students, e.g., at the American University of Beirut. Among its underground and never clearly identified leaders, was the Palestinian George HABASH. The *qawmiyya* gradually moved further left, aiming at the elimination of the conservative Arab regimes and the creation of revolutionary Arab unity. They advocated violence and terrorism against foreign interests, Israel, Arab conservatives and dissenters. They were closely linked to Palestinian-Arab guerrilla groups, with Habash's Democratic Front For The Liberation of Palestine (DFLP) as their sister-organization, having some influence on the radical nationalists of SOUTH YEMEN, the ruling National Liberation Front. Factional splits among the *qawmiyyin* were frequent, and while their underground cells may still be active, little has been heard of them since the 1970s.

Another trend of Pan-Arab Leftist-revolutionary nationalism with a rather more elaborate ideology published in detail was the "Arab Renaissance" (al- BA'TH group). This faction regarded the existing Arab states as temporary entities only, bound to be merged into a united all-Arab state—by revolutionary violence or subversion if necessary. The *Ba'th* group (at its inception mainly students and young intellectuals) cultivated ties to younger officers, particularly in the Syrian and Iraqi armies. It was these clandestine officers' cells that transformed the little club of intellectuals into a politically significant faction. This enabled it first to push Syria into union with Egypt (1958), then to assist in Syria's secession from the union (1961), and finally to seize power, through military coups, in Syria (1963) and Iraq (1963 and, after losing power later the same year, again in 1968), It maintains branches outside Syria and Iraq, too, but except for Lebanon, these are illegal underground cells. Since the 1960s, the *Ba'th*, enmeshed in the power politics of the two countries it rules, has contributed very little to the development of all-Arab nationalism. For further developments concerning the *Ba'th*, its rule and its splits—see BA'TH.

Pan-Arab revolutionary nationalism in the 1950s and 1960s found its strongest expression in Egyptian NASSERISM and in the teachings of Libya's QAD-HAFI. The Egyptian officers' regime, in power since the coup of 1952, was at first moderate and restrained in its foreign policies. In the 1950s, under the leadership of Gamal ABDEL NASSER, it turned increasingly activist in inter-Arab affairs, attempting to impose on the other Arab states a regime in its image—"Arab Socialism", populist-totalitarian single-party state socialism, leftist-neutralist in international affairs. The ideology of "Arab Socialism"—called "Nasserism" by others, not by its own leaders—developed pragmatically. It developed out of Egyptian political needs, and was never laid down as a formal, complete doctrine. Though Nasser and his aides encouraged "Nasserist" factions in other Arab countries, no all-Arab Nasserist Party was ever created, and rival Nasserist factions often fought each other. Even in Egypt the regime was based on the state bureaucracy rather than on the single party (which never got off the ground). Nasserism had some affinities with *Ba'thism*, and the Syrian Arab Socialists pressed for union with Egypt, achieved in 1958, in the hope that a joint doctrine could be worked out and that the pragmatic Nasserists would accept *Ba'thist* ideological guidance. After the union, the Egyptian's determination to impose their centralist single-party system and state bureaucracy on the united state soon caused a clash with the Syrian *Ba'thists* and led to Syria's secession in 1961.

In the 1950s and the early 1960s, Egyptian Nasserism operated chiefly through subversion, causing innumerable inter-Arab complaints and disputes. Nasser justified such methods by repeatedly proclaiming that true inter-Arab cooperation and unity could be achieved only by "progressive" Arab-Socialist regimes and that conservative, "reactionary" regimes would have to be swept away. At the same time he was pragmatic enough to enable the Arab League, and cooperation with the self-same "reactionary" regimes, to continue. After the dissolution of the Syro-Egyptian union; the failure of all Egyptian-Nasserist attempts to topple conservative regimes and impose all-Arab unity according to Nasserist prescriptions; the frustration of Egypt's military intervention in Yemen (1962–1967), and finally, the military defeat of 1967 war, Nasser's all-Arab unionist fervor cooled considerably, and Nasserism lost much of its momentum. After Nasser's death in 1970, Egypt's rulers abandoned revolutionary Arab-Socialist unionism. Although Nasserist trends still have some influence in Egypt, and rival Nasserist factions exist in Syria and Lebanon under various Arab-Socialist or Socialist-Unionist labels, Nasserism has faded away or at least lost its impact.

Libya's Mu'ammar Qadhafi, in power since his military coup of 1969, developed his own version of Arab Nationalism. It was a mass-oriented populist-totalitarian semi-Socialism. It was fervently nationalist with strong Islamic emphasis, pressing for immediate moves towards all-Arab unity (and based, though strictly anti-Communist, on a firm alliance with the Soviet Bloc). Qadhafi's doctrine and policies, laid down in a "Green Book" (1976 and 1978), led him into unrelenting efforts to unite Libya with various Arab countries. Coupled with subversive, even terrorist, activities, this brought him into constant conflict with the very countries that he wanted to merge with Libya—Egypt, Sudan, Tunisia, and Morocco (see LIBYA, QADHAFI).

Arab Nationalism, the assertion of Arab independence and power (since World War II with strong leanings to non-alignment) and the construction of modern, stable, economically and socially developed nation-states (in many cases with populist or socialist tendencies), has remained the dominant force in Arab thinking, sentiment and policy. Arab Nationalism like other independent movements, has its difficulties with the process of nation-building. These include: the problems of regime and administration; good government; and social development.

It has not completely overcome, for the sake of the nation's unity, divergent or particularist allegiances—regional, tribal, and mainly communal-religious. Minority communities tend to feel a dominant, first priority allegiance to their community, while many simple, uneducated Muslim Arabs hardly distinguish between "Muslim" and "Arab", instinctively regarding only a Muslim Arab as wholly Arab. In recent years the upsurge of strong, radical Islamic trends, has added to this problem. Wide strata of the Muslim-Arab population do not, perhaps, perceive the intrinsic dialectic tension, and even contradiction, between extra-religious Arab Nationalism and supranational Islamism. Leaders, policy makers and intellectuals make this distinction. They try to cope with the problem in various ways—e.g., by emphasizing the basic link between Islam and the Arab nation, the fact that Islam became a world religion through the medium of the Arabs genius and their language, and the Arabs achieved greatness through Islam. In terms of ideology and doctrine, Arab Nationalism had never clearly resolved this issue. However, these problems do not detract from the dominant position of Arab nationalism in Arab thinking and politics.

All-Arab nationalism, (qawmiyya), Arab unionism, remains an aspiration, a potent emotion, a dominant ideological trend. Actually and historically, wataniyya (the nationalism of the various of Arab states) determines policies. The two trends go side-by-side in dialectical interplay, contradicting each other whilst simultaneously influencing and complementing each other. Some elements unite all Arabs from Morocco to the Persian Gulf, forging them into one nation. Other elements make for increasing divergence and the emergence of separate Arab nations—Egyptian, Syrian, Iraqi, Algerian, Moroccan etc. The historically dominant trend seems to be toward growing inter-Arab cooperation on the basis of equality and mutual respect of each other's independence and sovereignty and not under compelling principles of Pan-Arab nationalism at any price. Ideologically and emotionally the stress among the masses may be on all-Arab Nationalism and many Arabs may balk at the assumption that the separate Arab states are borne by separate Arab nationalisms. However, at least among social and political elites, actual Arab unity and the nationalism inspiring it are based, as the Arab League is, on the acceptance of, and respect for, the sovereignty and integrity of separate individual Arab nation-states.

ARAB REVOLT (also "The Revolt in the Desert") The Arab uprising wasled by HUSSEIN IBN ALI the Sharif of Meccan, and his sons ALI, ABDALLAH and FEISAL, of the HASHEMITE clan, against the Turkish-OTTTOMAN EMPIRE during World War I. It began in June 1916. The Arab Revolt was preceded by an exchange of letters between Hussein and Sir Henry McMahon, the British High Commissioner in EGYPT. He promised British support for Arab Independence after the war (for details see MCMAHON-HUSSEIN CORRESPONDENCE). Britain financed the Arab Revolt with 200,000 dollars per month and supplied arms, provisions and direct artillery support; it also sent experts of guerrilla warfare, among them T. E. Lawrence. The size of the Arab Revolt force remained uncertain, with estimates raging between seven to ten thousand Hijazi Bedouin, reinforced by a much larger number of semi-attached and recruited occasionally. Several Arab (Syrian and Iraqi) officers of the Ottoman Army—deserters or prisoners—joined the Arab Revolt, but their number remained very small. For a short time, the Egyptian Aziz ali al-Masri served as Chief-of-Staff, and for some time—the Iraqi Nuri al-SA'ID. The Revolt's contribution to the Allied war effort remained debated, glorified by Arab nationalists while doubted by British sources of that time. The rebels took Mecca (with British artillery support and Aqaba (with British naval support); al-Madina remained in Turkish hands, but was cut off. The Arab Revolt's main operation was sabotaging the Hijaz railway. The principal Turkish supply route to Western ARABIA. When the British and allied forces, under General Allenby, advanced into Palestine and SYRIA, 1917–1918, the rebel army formed their right wing. It was allowed to enter Damascus first, raise the Arab flag and establish an Arab administration, semi-coordinated with the allied military administration of occupied territories. Though this Arab government was suppressed and evicted in 1919–1920 by the French, the princes heading the Arab Revolt became the principal and recognized spokesmen for the Arab national cause at the peace conference. Their connection to the Arab nationalists of the Fertile Crescent was tenuous, and their claims and demands were not fully realized (see ARAB NATIONALISM, Syria, Hussein Ibn Ali, Feisal, Abdallah); yet the Arab Revolt to this day is seen as the birth of Arab national independence. Several of the officers of the Arab Revolt became spokesmen and leaders of the Arab states in the 1920s and 1930s, and they continued glorifying the memory of the revolt (helped by the impressive, though not quite reliable, writing of Lawrence) .

ARAB SOCIALISM The term Socialism (*ishtirakiyya*) is widely used in Arab political writings and appears in the names of numerous political movements and parties throughout the Arab world. Generally, however, Arab politicians and writers are not referring to the western-type Socialism as developed in the twentieth century, in contradistinction to COMMUNISM, as organized in the Socialist International—i.e., a Socialism based on multi-party parliamentary democracy and a liberal conception of human rights, non-revolutionary, and self-defined Social Democracy. In the Arab world the term implies a state Socialism, which denotes social justice and equality, in contrast to the exploitation and abhorrent inequality that had marked the ancient regime. Arab Socialism is often combined with a populist-revolutionary approach, single-party and semi-totalitarian regimes led by former or current army officers.

Before World War I, a measure of Western-type Socialist thinking could have been found in the ideas and writings of several Egyptian and Lebanese writers and politicians, but no Social-Democratic party or organization was formed. Traces of Social-Democracy may perhaps be seen in the left-wing of the Egyptian WAFD Party, in the Iraqi Ahali group (Kamel Chadirji), or in the Tunisian Neo-Destour Party. After the war, the Moroccan left wing (Ben Barka, the UNFP and USFP), and for some time Kamal JUNBLAT's PSP in LEBANON, may be added. Yet even in these groups Western-type Social Democracy did not mature, gradually changing into other types of Socialism. Yet the Socialist International was anxious to discover like-minded groups in the Arab countries and cultivate relations with them. They were particularly attracted by the Moroccan Left and the Lebanese PSP. The latter was even invited to join, and though its full adhesion never materialized, it was given the status of an observer, as was the Egyptian ARAB SOCIALIST UNION. Relations did not become close, and the two Arab parties did not become Social-

Democratic groups. The Socialist parties of Asia, coalescing in an "Asian Socialist Conference" in January 1953 (with the Socialist parties of Burma, India, and ISRAEL as the chief initiators), were also keen to associate sister-parties from the Arab countries and invited several of them to their conference. Israel's prominent role in that Asian organization induced the Arab parties to decline the invitation to the 1953 Conference and additional ones held until 1972.

Since the 1950s, populist-revolutionary state Socialism has become the ruling creed in many of the left-leaning Arab states. The Egyptian officers' regime founded in 1952, adopted it as a slogan from the mid-1950s, and in 1962 changed the name of its single ruling party into the ARAB SOCIALIST UNION (ASU). Under al-SADAT's guidance, the ASU was artificially divided into three "stages". (These later became fully-fledged parties.) The emphasis on Socialism declined; the mainstream group, the "National Democratic Party", no longer has Socialism in its name; but two smaller opposition parties in Egypt remained committed to the idea, at least in name: the "Socialist Labor Party" and the"Socialist Liberal Party". The Arab BA'TH (Renaissance) Party, that had originated in SYRIA, added the word "Socialism" to its name since its merger with Akram Hourani's "Arab Socialist Party" in 1953. It has ruled Syria since 1963 and Iraq since 1968. The ruling party in SOUTH YEMEN, formerly the NATIONAL LIBERATION FRONT FOR OCCUPIED SOUTH YEMEN (NLF), was called from 1978 the "Yemen Socialist Party". SUDAN's NUMEIRI called the single party he set up in 1971 the "Sudan Socialist Union". ALGERIA's FRONT DE LIBÉRATION NATIONAL (FLN), the single and ruling party, does not carry the term Socialist in its name, but belongs to the same trend of populist-revolutionary Socialism in TUNISIA's "Socialist Destour Party" (formerly Neo-Destour). It has ruled the country since independence, professes a socialism containing elements of both the populist brand and Western Social Democracy, but its practice did not conform to the latter. A more liberal faction that split from it in the 1970s, led by Ahmad Mestiri, called itself the "Democratic Socialist Movement" and seemed to have professed a Western-type Social Democracy. Junblat's "Progressive Socialism Party" in Lebanon has never been the ruling party but enjoyed much influence until the early 1990s. It also belongs to the populist brand of Socialism, and has remained mainly a DRUZE

formation, with Socialist ideology as a secondary element. On the Moroccan Left, one of the main factions identifies itself as the "Socialist Union of Popular Forces", USFP); it seems to belong to the populist brand of Socialism.

In the late 1950s and the 1960s, ABDEL NASSER and his followers (such as the ARAB NATIONALIST MOVEMENT) used to emphasize the Arab national character of their Socialism, calling their movement "Arab Socialism" and claiming that it had created a special, distinctive brand of Socialism. From 1962, Nasser elevated his revolutionary Arab Socialism to a prerequisite for ARAB UNITY. He used this to legitimize his intransigent hostility toward the monarchic Arab regimes. "Arab Socialism" has contributed very little to international Socialist ideology or doctrine; Since it was closely linked to Pan-Arab plans for an all-Arab union, most of its factions called themselves "Socialist-Unionist". They all declined after Nasser's death and the decline of NASSERISM.

ARAB SOCIALIST UNION From 1962 to 1976–1977, the only legal political organization in EGYPT. It was preceded, as the single party intended to provide popular support for the post-1952 officers' regime, by the "National Liberation Organization", 1953–1958, and the "National Union", 1957–1962, which were considered to have failed in their task. The Arab Socialist Union was closely integrated in the new constitution pattern devised by ABDEL NASSER (see EGYPT) following the breakup of the UNITED ARAB REPUBLIC (UAR) in 1961. Its leadership was chosen indirectly: village and township committees sent representatives to regional committees whose delegates formed district committees which in turn elected the national leadership. The Arab Socialist Union leadership nominated the single-party candidates for election to the National Assembly, as well as a single candidate as President of Egypt.

Their Executive Committee was comprised of President Nasser, his Vice-Presidents and the other top leaders of government. Its Secretary-General (sometimes styled chairman) was for sometime Nasser himself, for most of the time Ali SABRI. After Nasser's death in 1970 several Secretaries followed each other in rapid changes. The Arab Socialist Union, like its predecessors, remained part of the official establishment rather than an independent popular organization. It had little influence of its own, but in the late 1960s, Ali Sabri gradually shaped it into a power instrument for himself and his leftist faction (and was dismissed in 1969).

In the hidden struggle for the succession, after Nasser's death, the Arab Socialist Union was considered the center of "Nasserist" opposition to President SADAT, and in 1971 its leadership was purged and new functionaries were appointed. In the course of Sadat's liberalization moves, various trends and factions that had developed within the Arab Socialist Union began asserting themselves. In 1975, and in 1976 three trends (or "platforms", *minbar*, pl. *manabir*) were permitted to constitute themselves formally within the Arab Socialist Union: a Right-wing Liberal faction, a Leftist one (headed by Khaled Muhyi al-Din), and a center or mainstream (considered to be the government faction and headed by the Prime Minister). In the elections for the National Assembly, October 1976, candidates were presented by these Arab Socialist Union "platforms": the center won an overwhelming majority, the Rightist-Liberals twelve (of whom several immediately joined the center), and the Left two. Late in 1976, fully fledged parties were permitted, and a party law of June 1977 regulated their formation. The Arab Socialist Union thus lost its monopoly; its Right wing became the "Social Liberal Party", its Left—the "Progressive-Unionist Rally". In 1978, President Sadat established his own "National Democratic Party"—and the mainstream faction of the Arab Socialist Union, which by now called itself "Egypt Party" (*Misr*, decided to merge into it). It was formally dissolved in May 1980.

ARAB SUMMIT CONFERENCES Since 1964, the Heads of the Arab states have been meeting, irregularly, at the top level. These meetings have been in addition to the regular bi-annual sessions of the ARAB LEAGUE Council, held at the level of Foreign Ministers or Permanent Representatives. The resort to this forum came after a period of declining prestige and inefficacy of the Arab League, due to deep inter-Arab divisions and even violent conflicts. In the mid-1960s these culminated in EGYPT's military involvement in the Yemen War, and President ABDEL NASSER's efforts to impose his hegemony on other Arab ruling elites in the name of his revolutionary Pan-Arab nationalism.

The first summit conference was convened in January 1964 in Cairo, in an effort to revitalize collective Arab action. The idea was to shift attention to the Palestine conflict under Nasser's leadership, and provide the latter with mechanisms of control to prevent untimely war that had been strongly advocated by SYRIA and militant Palestinians. The first summit set the procedures and form of future plenary meetings of Arab heads of states, ostensibly held within the framework of the Arab League and confined to its member states. Effectively it reflected the regional inter-Arab balance of power and interests of the leading Arab states. Indeed, from the outset, ARAB SUMMIT CONFERENCES focused—in line with the Arab League's *raison d' tre*—on the conflict with ISRAEL and the Palestinian cause. By so doing, the summits represented a steady tendency to regulate inter-Arab relations and ensure regional stability by means of controlling the dangers of military escalation with Israel, rather than organizing the Arab world for such confrontation. Such regularity, however, was largely dependent on the validity and decisive weight of an Arab core coalition, normally with Egypt as its keystone, with the participation of one or more, of IRAQ (1964–1965, 1989), SAUDI ARABIA (1973–1976, 1987–1996) and Syria (1973–1976, 1990–1996). Arab summit conferences served as a mechanism for the equitable distribution of the financial burden entailed by preparations, or actual war against Israel. Hence, following the Arab defeat in the 1967 War and the employment of the OIL weapon by the Arab oil-producing states, Arab summits were instrumental in mitigating tensions between the confrontations states and the oil-rich states by assigning the latter with giving the former financial aid. This divided equitably the economic burden which the war against Israel entailed.

While the success of Arab summit meetings in resolving inter-Arab disputes was only partial—more success was achieved in managing such conflicts—these conferences served as the standard-bearer and supreme political arbitrator on disputed Arab national matters. Hence, such conferences strove to reach consensus on decisions such as effectively postponing the war against Israel (1964–1965); legitimized the diplomatic, peace-making process, with Israel after the October 1973 War; decided on sanctions against Egypt for its separate peace conference with Israel (1978–1980); legitimized the resumption of diplomatic relations with Egypt (1987); or legitimized Arab support for and joining of the US-led international coalition against Iraq in the wake of its invasion of KUWAIT (1990). Arab summit meetings shaped the collective Arab policies on Arab core issues, most prominently the Palestine issue. As such, these summits in fact accounted for redefinition of Arab strategies and positions on the conflict with Israel, shifting from established intransigent hostility to negotiated settlement; from a dispute over legitimacy to a dispute over territory. Despite decisions to hold a summit conference every year, this was not implemented, except between1978–1982, mainly due to inter-Arab disagreement over a common agenda. In 1964–1997 only twenty one Arab summit conferences, including regular and emergency meetings, had been held, attended by most Arab states, albeit not necessarily by the head of state. Following is a list of the Arab summit conferences, venue, and main debated issues:

1. Cairo, January 1964: Diversion of the River Jordan's tributaries to prevent their use by Israel; the Joint Arab Command; and the Palestinian Entity.

2. Alexandria, September 1964: Implementation of the Jordan Diversion Plan and the Joint Arab Command, the PALESTINE LIBERATION ORGANIZATION (PLO).

3. Casablanca, September 1965: The Diversion Plan and its difficulties; the Joint Arab Command; Arab Solidarity Charter.

4. Khartoum, September 1967: Shaping the Arab principles for coping with the results of the 1967 war; resolving the Egypt-Saudi conflict over Yemen; allocating financial aid from the oil-rich states to the confrontation states.

5. Rabat, December 1969: Egypt's long-range military plan and requirements for financial aid; support for the Palestinian Resistance Movement under the PLO leadership.

6. Cairo, September 1970 (emergency meeting): The Jordanian-Palestinian armed confrontation.

7. Algiers, November 1973: Shaping the Arab strategy of phases in the conflict (legitimating employment of diplomatic means) for the recovery of the 1967 occupied lands; deciding the PLO-Jordan conflict over representation of the Palestinians.

8. Rabat, October 1974: Representation of the Palestinian people (the PLO was recognized as the sole legitimate representative); principles of collective Arab action in the diplomatic process with Israel; and providing financial aid from the oil-rich states to the confrontation states as well as to the Palestinians.

9. Cairo, October 1976: Approving Syria's military presence and hegemony in Lebanon; putting an end to the Lebanese civil war; settling the PLO-Syrian conflict in Lebanon.

10. Baghdad, November 1978: Shaping the Arab response to Egypt-Israel Camp David Accords; applying Arab sanctions on Egypt.

11. Tunis, November 1979: The Lebanon-PLO dispute over south Lebanon; Arab financial aid for Lebanon's rehabilitation.

12. Amman, November 1980: The IRAN-IRAQ WAR; plans for long-range inter-Arab financial aid and economic integration.

13. Fez, November 1981: The Saudi Peace Plan ("Fahd Plan," see the ARAB-ISRAEL PEACEMAKING).

14. Fez, November 1982: Formulation of an Arab peace plan, based on the Saudi peace plan; the Reagan Plan; (see ARAB-ISRAEL PEACEMAKING) the results of Israel's Lebanon war.

15. Casablanca, August 1985: The Jordan-PLO accord; security of the Palestinians in Lebanon; The problem of inter-Arab terrorism.

16. Amman, November 1987 (emergency meeting): The Iranian threat for the Gulf Arab states; resumption of diplomatic relations with Egypt; the crisis in Lebanon.

17. Algiers, June 1988: The Palestinian uprising (INTIFADA).

18. Casablanca, May 1989 (emergency meeting): The resumed war in Lebanon; Egypt's return to the Arab League; financial aid to the Intifada.

19. Baghdad, May 1990 (emergency meeting): Russian-Jewish immigration to Israel and its dangers; Iraqi concerns and financial needs; Joranian and PLO requests for financial aid.

20. Cairo, August 1990 (emergency meeting): The Iraqi invasion of Kuwait and measures to resolve the crisis.

21. Cairo, June 1996: The Arab-Israel peace process in view of the advent of a right-wing Israeli government (see ISRAEL).

ARAB UNITY (Arabic: *wahda arabiyya*) One of the main principles of Arab nationalism (*qawmiyya*), and its final goal, as opposed to the political division of the Arab nations into numerous states, usually blaming the foreign rule for this reality. Plans to unite all or several Arab countries, in varying degrees of union (merger, federation, loose cooperation), were an integral part of ARAB NATIONALISM from its inception, until World War II, when they usually referred only to the formerly Ottoman countries of the Fertile Crescent, and sometimes also to HIJAZ, in the Arabian Peninsula, but did not include either EGYPT and the Arab areas of North Africa.

The HASHEMITE clan headed by Sharif HUSSEIN of Mecca, led the ARAB REVOLT of World War I. He also represented Arab nationalist claims in the post-war peace talks. These were intended—though they were never formulated clear-cut, detailed plans—to establish a federative Kingdom consisting of Arabia (effectively, Hijaz), historic SYRIA (bilad al-sham, including the later established MANDATE areas of Syria LEBANON, Palestine and Transjordan), and IRAQ. Each of the three territories was to be ruled by one of the Hashemite princes: FEISAL and ABDALLAH, the sons of Sharif HUSSEIN, with their father as overall King [Caliph]). Despite these plans, the area was divided into separate Mandatory areas under British and French rule. Feisal and Abdallah, appointed by BRITAIN as semi-independent rulers of Iraq and Transjordan, respectively, continued nurturing—separately, and competitively—-the idea of a regional Arab federation under their leadership, with Syria as their real goal. Feisal and his followers fostered the idea of Fertile Crescent unity, and submitted an official proposal to this effect as early as 1929. Nonetheless, Abdallah nurtured the idea of GREATER SYRIA. With the shifting balance of the war in favor of the Allies in late 1942, both branches of the Hashemite dynasty reasserted their schemes. In January 1943, the Iraqi statesman Nuri al-SA'ID presented to BRITAIN his "Blue Paper" which included a unity plan to include Iraq, Syria, Lebanon, Palestine and Transjordan, with autonomy to the Jews in Palestine and the Christians in Lebanon. A similar initiative was adopted by Emir (later King) Abdallah of Jordan, concerning his Greater Syria scheme. Until the mid-1930s, the Hashemite plans for a regional Arab union reflected dynastic and personal aspirations commanding little, if any, popular root in the political reality of the countries aimed to be unified, with a few exceptions. Antoun SA'ADEH and his SYRIAN SOCIAL NATIONALIST PARTY's idea of a Greater Syria,

inspired by a specifically Syrian nationalism and aspiring to a unitary, not a federal, state of an authoritarian, fascist oriented pattern. The Istiqlal Party, identified with King Feisal, with branches in the Fertile Crescent countries, also advocated the idea. However, the non-Hashemite Arab states of SAUDI ARABIA, Egypt (after it became active in inter-Arab affairs in the late 1930s), Syria, Lebanon as well as both Arab and Jewish communities of Palestine—all opposed the formation of a Hashemite-led regional unity, rejecting any change in the inter-Arab territorial and political status quo. Their position determined the character of the ARAB LEAGUE, founded in 1945, as a close alliance of independent states, whose main aim was to protect the sovereignty and territorial integrity of its member states rather than an instrument for unity of merger or federation and the revisionist unionist Hashemites acquiesced.

By the mid-1950s, the cause of Arab unity—adopting the concept of unity of merger-became increasingly advocated by radical nationalist movements in Syria, primarily the BA'TH Party, and later adopted by ABDEL NASSER of Egypt. With the traumatic experience of the 1948 War of Palestine in mind, and the growing wave of NASSERISM against foreign domination and influence, popular pressure for no less than full unity was advocated by revolutionary movements in the Arab world. True to their Leftist-revolutionary doctrines, abhorring compromises such as federative unity or less than that as petit bourgeois, they aspired to full union on a unitary pattern. Although Nasser himself was initially reluctant about the Ba'th proposal for full union with Syria, he eventually accepted their concept but imposed his own centralist rules. This made the new venture seem more like a takeover than a step toward a mutually rewarding merger. The UNITED ARAB REPUBLIC (UAR) of February 1958 allowed Yemen to join the union in a Federation—the "Federation (or union) of Arab states" (Ittihad al-Duwal al-Arabiyya. The ARABIC language, otherwise so immensely rich, has no separate terms for "Union and "Federation" using Ittihad for both), to be open for other Arab countries to join. The Federation never got off the ground.

Hashemite Iraq continued to make efforts to advance its unity scheme with Syria until the mid-1950s, and was supported mainly by the People's Party in Syria. As to Jordan, with the assassination of King Abdallah in July 1951, the Greater Syria scheme was entirely dropped from the Jordanian agenda. With the establishment of the UAR, the two Hashemite rulers rushed to proclaim on 14 February, the foundation of "The Arab Union" (al-Ittihad al-Arabi of Iraq and Jordan. The new union was meant to be a barrier against domestic and regional pressures to join the UAR under Nasser's leadership, rather than a step toward practical unity. In any case, in contrast to the UAR, the Hashemite union was shaped in federal terms and institutions with each component state to retain its identity and sovereignty. A Constitution, published in mid-March, appointed King Feisal II Head of State of Iraq, with Jordan's King Hussein as his deputy. Each would remain King in his own country; the capital would rotate semi-annually between Baghdad and Amman. A federal Parliament would be appointed from among the members of the two Parliaments, twenty from each state. Foreign affairs, defense and diplomatic representation would be a joint, federal matter. Citizenship would remain separate. This Constitution was endorsed by both Parliaments in March 1958 and Jordanian and Iraqi Constitutions were accordingly amended. The Federal Parliament met in May (with a Jordanian President and an Iraqi Vice-President), and a Federal government took office that same month. The Iraqi Nuri al-Sa'id was Prime Minister and the Jordanian Ibrahim Hashem as Deputy-Premier. The Iraqi Tawfiq al-Suweidi was Foreign Minister (with a Jordanian Deputy) whilst the Jordanian-Palestinian Suleiman Tuqan held the post of Minister of Defense (with an Iraqi Deputy). However, before the new "Arab Union" could make its mark, it was swept away by the Iraqi revolution of July 1958. Fears that the new Iraqi regime would insist on an Iraqi-Jordan federation and try to extend its revolution to Jordan proved unfounded, and Iraq acquiesced in the dissolution of the union.

The break-up of the UAR in 1961, with Syria seceding, was a traumatic event that shocked the Arab world and left the relations between Egypt and Syria irreparable for another five years. However, despite Nasser's loath of the Syrian Ba'th and their continued mutual recrimination, he could not turn down the request of both Iraq and Syria which, in February and March 1963, respectively, had become dominated by their Ba'th Party branches, to enter a tripartite union, this time on a federal basis. The federal pattern ostensibly represented a compromise between the Ba'thists' disappointing experience of full merger with Egypt and their persistent desire for closer union. However, as it turned out later, the main goal of the new Iraqi and Syrian regimes was to establish their power through attaining legitimacy from Nasser during their initial period in power. In April 1963, Egypt, Syria and Iraq agreed to form a new "United Arab Republic"—which was to be entirely federal in structure, leaving each member state its identity and institutions. Yemen again adhered to the federation in June 1963. By that time however, a bitter dispute had broken out between Nasser and the Ba'thists in Syria, and in July the agreement was abrogated.

In the fall of 1963 Syria and Iraq agreed on plans for an economic union and a joint command, toward a further federation without Egypt. These plans, too, were canceled in April 1964 (Iraq had ceased in November 1963, to be Ba'th ruled). Now it was Egypt's turn to try federation with Iraq—without Syria. Iin May 1964, Nasser and President Aref of Iraq agreed to establish a joint Presidential Council, political command and fully coordinate their economic and military polities towards full (federal) union within two years. Yemen again joined, in a separate agreement with Egypt. The joint Council was formally established and Aref began to adapt Iraq's policies and institutions to Egypt's, but after Iraq had again become Ba'thist, it was abolished in July 1968.

Nonetheless, a new attempt at establishing Arab unity, with Egypt at its center, was made from 1969–1970—this time with LIBYA (revolutionary and unionist since Colonel QADHAFI's coup of 1969) as a main partner. In December 1969 the leaders of Egypt, Libya and SUDAN (also populist-revolutionary since NUMEIRI's coup of 1969) proclaimed the "Tripoli Charter" under which the three countries would closely coordinate their policies. In November 1970 they announced plans for a fully-fledged federation, which Syria decided to join. In April 1971 the "Federation of Arab Republics" (FAR) (Ittihad al-Jumhuriyyat al-Arabiyya) of Egypt, Libya and Syria—Sudan had opted out at the last moment—was proclaimed. It was endorsed by plebiscites in three countries and went into effect on 1 January 1972. The FAR had a full range of federal institutions: a Constitution; a Presidential Council (the three Heads of State); a Federal Assembly (its members delegated by the National Assemblies in Egypt and

Syria; as Libya had no such assembly, the Revolutionary Council selected its delegates) and a Federal Council of Ministers. It was to have one common flag; a national anthem and a capital, a joint Defense Council and common diplomatic representation abroad; diplomatic representatives among its members were replaced by "liaison officers".

Though duly installed and officially existing, the FAR never got off the ground. All the regimes involved in the new federation had been newly established and needed legitimacy, yet none of them were willing to cede any of their authority for the sake of sharing a collective one. Apart from the intrinsic difficulties between states so different and so unequal, it was mainly Libyan-Egyptian relations that caused its failure. Colonel Qadhafi was pressing for full Libyan-Egyptian union within the FAR, and in August 1972 he persuaded President al-SADAT (who had replaced Nasser in 1970, between the time of the conception of the FAR and its birth) to agree to the proclamation of such a union, to be implemented by September 1973. As Sadat wanted to go slow, and probably had second thoughts on the plan itself any way. Qadhafi went to Egypt in June-July 1973, appealing directly to the Egyptian public behind the back of its government. Later in July he organized a "spontaneous" march of Libyan masses into Egypt. His fiery speech had little success in Egypt, where the whole operation was bitterly resented. In August 1973, Sadat reaffirmed the merger agreement—but it was clear by this stage that he had no intention of going through with it, and indeed it was never implemented. Relations deteriorated. There were bitter recriminations and accusations of Libyan plots and subversion which led to the severance of relations, border military clashes, and, in 1977, actual confrontation. After Sadat's visit to ISRAEL in November 1977, Libya was in the forefront of those Arab states denouncing Sadat and clamoring for Egypt's expulsion (as was Syria). In December 1977 Syria and Libya expelled Egypt from the Federation of Arab Republics, dismissed Sadat as its President and transferred its headquarters from Cairo to Tripoli. As Qadhafi continued referring to the validity of the FAR, Egypt's National Assembly in December 1984 passed a Bill abolishing it.

Plans for a Syro-Iraqi Federation were revived late in 1978. It was at this time that the two *Ba'th* regimes—having experienced a decade of bitter hostility and ideological dispute—both opposed Sadat's peace initiative toward Israel. Unity was apparently seen as a means of conciliation and of forging a united front against Egypt, but each of the two regimes had different needs to be served by such unity. Aware of Syria's anxiety of its being deserted by Egypt in the confrontation with Israel, Iraq pressed for closer unity and penetration into Syrian political arena, while Syria needed a strategic backing, without much willingness to exchange it for its sovereignty. This attempt, too, failed and was soon called off, despite the work put into forging a constitutional framework of the envisioned union. Efforts to effect a reconciliation between Syria and Jordan, embroiled in bitter conflict, also led, in 1975, to proposals for a Syro-Jordanian unity, and, in December 1976, even to an agreement in principle; but nothing came of it.

The most active and persistent protagonist of Arab unity plans was Colonel Mu'ammar Qadhafi of Libya. Following Nasser's death, he began to portray himself as Nasser's heir in pursuing Arab unity. Qadhafi's motivation was apparently derived from considerations of domestic insecurity, isolated position in the Arab arena—excluded by the Maghrib sub-system and threatened by Egypt's immense power—and his self-conceived revolutionary image. He worked, from 1969–1970 to consolidate the FAR with Egypt and Syria; pressed for full union with Egypt, 1972–1973; offered unity to Malta (1971); persuaded—or pressured—TUNISIA's President Bourguiba in January 1974 to agree to a Libyan-Tunisian union (abolished shortly afterwards). He pressed for full union with Syria. In 1980 this assumed the form of a declarative union, announced by al-ASAD and Qadhafi, which remained a mere declaration. In 1981 Qadhafi imposed unity on Chad amid military intervention. He repeatedly put out feelers to ALGERIA regarding the prospects for a unity of merger and, in August 1984, he agreed with the King of Morocco—with whom he had been in bitter dispute—to establish a Libyan-Moroccan union. This union, which did not initially appear realistic, was abrogated by MOROCCO in August 1986. In short, nothing emerged from Qadhafi's fervent unionist scheming. If anything, his repeated futile attempts seemed anachronistic and triggered contempt among other Arab states.

In contrast to these highly publicized unity plans, Egypt and Sudan in the mid-1970s and early 1980s, quietly strengthened their relations to a degree that amounted to near-confederal arrangements. Since the early 1920s, Egypt had regarded the "Unity of the Nile Valley" as one of its main national aims, endeavoring, in a bitter struggle with BRITAIN, to extend the reign of the Egyptian crown to Sudan, without consulting the Sudanese or granting them the right of self-determination. In 1954–1955 the revolutionary officers' regime, in agreement with the Sudanese political parties, conceded self-determination. Sudan chose independence. It may be assumed that Nasser and his associates did not really renounce Egypt's aspirations to union with Sudan, but wisely decided that they would be better served by friendly cooperation with an independent Sudan.

For some years Sudanese resentment and suspicions of Egyptian big-brother attitudes and the cultivation of pro-Egyptian factions marred relations; but gradually the moderate policy of 1954–1955 paid off. Numeiri's revolutionary regime of 1969 concluded an agreement of coordination, with federal intent that was announced in late 1970. Sudan's need for Egyptian assistance, political and military, against suspected Libyan plots, enhanced the trend toward closer cooperation. Although Sudan withdrew from the plan for unity with Egypt, Libya and Sudan in 1971, bilateral cooperation with Egypt grew. In July 1976 a Defense Pact was concluded finalizing a process of coordination agreed upon in 1974. In 1979 Sudan refused to tow the all-Arab line and break relations with Egypt. In October 1982, a ten-year agreement for "Integration" was signed in which a joint "Nile Valley Parliament" was established, with sixty members of each of the two National Assemblies delegated to meet twice a year in joint session. Arrangements did not amount to a Federation. (Policy coordination was far from complete. Egypt had, for instance, serious misgivings concerning Numeiri's enforcement of Islamic Law, since 1983). The trend was toward confederation. However, the overthrow of Numeiri in April 1985 cooled relations between Sudan's new regime and Egypt.

Relations with Egypt further deterioated with the ascendancy of power of Omar Hasan al-BASHIR and the Islamic Front in 1989.

Another case of a planned inter-state merger was the long-standing scheme for a union between Yemen and SOUTH YEMEN. Both countries have always regarded themselves, in principle, as part of greater

Yemen. While the British ruled that what later became South Yemen (then—Aden and the Aden Protectorates), Yemen claimed those territories and the nationalists in Aden strove ultimately to join Yemen. But when South Yemen attained independence, in 1967, and union with Yemen became feasible, it was not implemented. The two countries were too different in character and regime, and Yemen—rather conservative even under its post-1962 republican government—suspected that a union might turn into a take over by the Leftist revolutionaries of South Yemen. The decision to merge the two countries was reaffirmed in principle in 1970, 1972 and 1979, though tension sometimes led to armed clashes and twice, in 1972 and 1979, to actual war. Usually, South Yemen was pressing for union, while Yemen dragged its feet. (Its reluctance was enhanced by Saudi Arabia, on whose support and aid Yemen depends). The merger plan remained, with the two states occasionally confirming its principle, and joint committees and presidential meetings preparing the ground. Yet there was no progression toward its implementation until 1989. The driving force toward practical merger was South Yemen's economic predicament (see SOUTH YEMEN).

In 1971 seven small sheikhdoms of the Gulf, hitherto the British-protected principalities of the TRUCIAL COAST (Trucial Oman), attained independence as the United Arab Emirates (UAE)—the only Arab state that retains a federal structure. The idea of establishing a federal relationship between separate entities was proposed by King Hussein of JORDAN to be applied with the Palestinians of the WEST BANK and possibly also with the GAZA STRIP. The idea, in its confederal form, was also raised and discussed in the framework of the Jordanian-Palestinian dialogue (1983–1986), during which PLO leader ARAFAT and King Hussein reached the Amman Agreement on joint political action, describing their common goal as a joint confederation. However, this became a bone of contention as the PLO's mainstream *Fatah* insisted that such unity should be realized only after an independent Palestinian state had been established, so that the union would be between equally sovereign partners.

Most of the unity plans described concerned actually two or several states, though some of them were proclaimed open for additional Arab states to join, and were thus far removed from the original idea of Pan-Arab unity. Attempts at establishing Arab unity between various Arab states have been made from time to time—sometimes as a means to improve one's national or regional security, or counterbalance an external threat, rather than to cement existing relations. A proclaimed unity between states was usually seen as a threat or a blow to other, neighboring states, increasing inter-Arab tension. The break-up of the UAR (1961); the intensifying inter-Arab disputes with Egypt as their main hinge, deriving from Nasser's quest for all-Arab hegemony, and finally the 1967 Arab defeat in the war with Israel; all eroded the moral and political force of the idea of Arab unity, Nasser having been its undisputed symbol. By the mid-1970s, the idea of Arab unity became less and less apparent in Arab politics, though it remained a wishful goal among the masses. With the entrenchment of the state as a strong political power, relatively stable and territorially integrated, and the ruling elites' obsession with sovereignty and domestic security—given the economic, political and social discrepancies among Arab states—the idea seems to have become a vision of a distant ideal future—or phantom—rather than an attainable political goal.

It was against this backdrop that in the 1980s, three attempts at creating sub-regional frameworks of cooperation were made. Only one was successful. In May 1981, the six Gulf oil monarchies (Saudi Arabia, KUWAIT, QATAR, BAHRAIN, the UAE, and OMAN) established the GULF COOPERATION COUNCIL (GCC). Its main aim was to promote regional and domestic security, in view of the Iranian revolutionary threats to their stability. Since then, the GCC has managed to function increasingly as a regional organization of states, with relative success in resolving disagreements (mainly border disputes); coordinating foreign policies on shared issues, and as a forum of decision making on oil production and pricing policies. Other, less successful attempts were the Arab Maghrib Union (al-ittihad al-maghribi al-arabi) (AMU-combining Libya, Morocco, Algeria, Tunisia, and MAURITANIA) and the ARAB COOPERATION COUNCIL (majlis al-ta'awun al-arabi) (ACC-combining Egypt, Iraq, Jordan and Yemen), both established in 1989, with the promotion of economic cooperation as their main declarative goal. However, these two attempts did not survive for long and their achievements were short-lived political coordination among the mem-

ber states in each of these organizations. There was no discernible improvement of inter-state economic cooperation, and even in the political sphere relations deteriorated shortly after.

Efforts to promote Arab unity also included the economic and military spheres, which were no more successful than the political one. Agreements and charters were signed but never implemented. Repeated resolutions and agreements by the Arab League member states to promote economic cooperation by establishing free trade zone, a common currency, and joint institutions of planning, were effectively futile, with no discernible gains made by the respective signatories. In 1957, the Arab League's members signed the Agreement of Economic Union, which was to become operational in 1964, but it was never implemented. In 1964, the League decided to establish the Common Arab Market. This was intended to remove all custom barriers among Arab states, but it met with the same fate as its predecessor. Another attempt was made in 1980, when the Arab League's Council approved a plan for economic complementarity among Arab states. This was only partial adopted by the Arab summit held that year in Amman, and even this part remained unattended. If any economic cooperation had been achieved, it happened on a bilateral and not a multilateral level.

In the military sphere, in 1950 the Arab League's Council approved the Pact of Joint Defense and Economic Cooperation, known as The Arab Collective Security Pact. Similar to the Arab League itself, the new Pact was born out of inter-Arab rivalries such as Egypt's attempt to prevent Iraqi-Syrian unity which was allegedly on the grounds of Syria's security needs in view of Israel's threats. The Pact was tantamount to a multilateral collective defense pact, in which all Arab states guaranteed the security of each one of them against an external threat. This determined the establishment of several institutions to determine the coordination and ongoing military preparations of the Arab member states: a Permanent Military Committee, in charge of shaping collective defense plans, subjected to a Joint Defense Council composed of foreign and defense ministers and chiefs-of-staff of all member states. The new Pact went beyond the Arab League Pact in terms of creating closer relations cooperation among the League's members: a) Decisions approved by two-thirds of the votes were to be committal; b) The signatories undertook not to sign any international agreement, or conduct foreign policy, that could collide with the provisions of this Pact. However, nothing had been done to implement the Pact (Iraq and Jordan procrastinated its ratification until 1951 and 1953, respectively), until the late 1950s when those institutions stipulated by the Pact were established. Still, the recommendations made by these forums had to be discussed by the first ARAB SUMMIT CONFERENCE held in 1964 in Cairo, which led to the foundation of a Joint Arab Command in response to Israel's National Water Carrier. The Arab Defense Council was convened a number of times in the course of the late 1960s and early 1970s, but its discussions and resolutions were usually unheeded. Toward the October 1973 war this forum was instrumental for the Egyptian preparations for war, allowing the Secretary General of the Arab League and the Egyptian Chief-of-Staff to coordinate with the Arab states possible support to Egypt in case of war with Israel.

ARABIAN-AMERICAN OIL COMPANY   see ARAMCO.

ARAFAT YASSER (b. 1929)   Chairman of the PALESTINE LIBERATION ORGANIZATION (PLO) (since 1969), a founding father of the *Fatah* organization (1959) and President of the PALESTINIAN AUTHORITY since June 1994. His biography is a reflection of the Palestinian national history since the 1948 war.

A distant relative of the prominent HUSSEINI family, Arafat was educated in EGYPT and graduated from Cairo University as an Engineer. In the 1950s he was Chairman of the Palestinian Students' Union centered in Gaza. He later became politically active in KUWAIT while working there as an engineer, 1957–1960 (reportedly after briefly serving in the Egyptian Army in 1957). In the late 1950s, Arafat was a cofounder of the al-*Fatah* guerrilla group, which soon had branches among Palestinians residing in Arab countries and among students in Europe. He emerged in the 1960s as its chief leader. When in mid-1968 the PLO turned into a roof-organization of various guerrilla groups, with *Fatah* gaining effective control of the organization, Arafat was elected spokesman of the PLO. In February 1969 he became chairman of its Executive Committee and the PLO's main leader and commander-in-chief. In this capacity he was recognized by the Arab states as the top leader of the Palestinian people, and became increasingly involved in inter-Arab politics as an essential element in its shaky balance. His regional and international status continued to emerge in the early 1970s as a leading figure in Middle East politics, culminating in the October 1974 ARAB SUMMIT CONFERENCE in Rabat. This recognized the PLO as the sole legitimate representative of the Palestinian people. With the acceptance of Palestine as a full member of the League of Arab states (1976), ARAFAT became officially treated as a head of state in the Arab world. He attended all-Arab Summit Conferences since 1969 (apart from the one held in Amman in 1980), maintained frequent contact with Arab heads-of-state and political leaders—who endeavored to enlist political legitimacy by identifying with the Palestinian guerrilla movement, especially in the latter's years of glory (1967–1970). He was treated as a head-of-state in various third world organizations, such as those of the Non-Aligned and Islamic states. Already by the late 1960s Arafat became the symbol-figure of the Palestinian people, its national cause, and claim for statehood. In October 1974, under the impact of Arab oil in the international arena in the wake of the October 1973 war, Arafat was officially invited to address the UN General Assembly, an invitation he materialized a month later, despite strong criticism within the PLO against it.

As head of al-*Fatah*, Arafat was responsible for the planning and execution of continuous sabotage and terror operations committed by this organization in Israel. According to *Fatah* chronology, this began in January 1965, primarily through the Jordanian and Lebanese borders. From 1971, *Fatah* expanded its guerrilla operations to the Arab and international arena under the covert name of "Black September" (attacks on Jordanian, Israeli and Western targets, including aviation). Shortly after the 1967 war, Arafat infiltrated into the WEST BANK and spent a few weeks there in an attempt to organize a network of *Fatah* cells that would implement classical guerrilla warfare against ISRAEL. However, Arafat was compelled to flee to East Jordan after learning that Israeli security agents were persuing him. Shortly afterwards, Arafat's effort totally collapsed when the newly established guerrilla infrastructure was exposed and eliminated by Israel. As a result, *Fatah* and other guerrilla organizations had to launch their attacks against Israel from Jordanian territory. This led eventually to the establishment of armed Palestinian presence in JORDAN—a "state within a state"—which soon began to threaten the Jordanian regime and authority, culminating in the Jordanian monarch's decision to eliminate the armed Palestinian presence on his land. In the course of events that led to the showdown in September 1970, Arafat revealed his political limitations as head of one-albeit the largest-guerrilla organization, even though he made an effort to prevent a confrontation with the Jordanian regime.

With the beginning of the peace process in the Middle East after the 1973 war, Arafat and his mainstream faction ceased to commit hijacking and international terrorist operations against foreign targets, believing that such operations could harm the PLO's international interests. As chairman of the PLO he was unable to prevent such operations being implemented by other Palestinian organizations that comprised the PLO. These divergences often limited his power as the leader of the PLO, entangling him in confrontations with the hosting countries of the guerrilla movement (see PALESTINE LIBERATION ORGANIZATION, JORDAN, LEBANON). With the funds put at his disposal by the Arab oil-rich states, Arafat managed to turn the PLO from a feeble association of small guerilla groups into a strong national institution; a nucleus of the Palestinian state in the making; a multi-branched establishment conducting military, economic-financial, social, medical and educational operations.

Israel's Lebanon war, starting June 1982 (which accounted for the destruction of the PLO military and territorial stronghold in Lebanon) culminated in the expulsion of the PLO armed personnel and headquarters from West Beirut after nine weeks of siege by Israel. This was accompanied by bombings and shellings (see PALESTINE LIBERATION ORGANIZATION, LEBANON and ARAB-ISRAEL CONFLICT). The evacuation of the PLO personnel and headquarters to Yemen, ALGERIA, and TUNISIA—and not to SYRIA, the longstanding ally of the Palestinian guerrilla movement-signalled the growing animosity between President ASAD and Arafat. This surfaced during the long siege of Beirut. In May 1983, the Syrians instigated an anti-Arafat Fatah faction located in Syrian-occupied East Lebanon (the Biqa') to rebel and expel Arafat's loyalists from the Biqa'. Ostensibly this was on the grounds of mismanagement of the war and for seeking a peace policy with Jordan and Israel. Arafat's attempt to mend his fences with Damascus by visiting Syria in June of that year ended with a humiliating expulsion. In November of that year, those Fatah rebels, reinforced by Syrian-based Palestine Liberation Army units and heavy Syrian Army support, continued their combat against Arafat, who had returned to Lebanon and rallied his forces in Tripoli and the Palestinian camps around it to reestablish the PLO's and his own political position. In December, following a few weeks of heavy fighting, Arafat and his fellow-loyalists were once again expelled from Lebanon, this time by a Palestinian-Syrian coalition.

Arafat was always considered in Arab and Palestinian circles as a mainstream politician, balancing the right and left wings within his own organization Fatah. Arafat's early leadership of Fatah was marked by an extremely militant and intransigent ideology and action toward Israel—as reflected in the Palestinian National Charter of 1968 (see PALESTINE LIBERATION ORGANIZATION). He refused to accept any kind of compromise or coexistence with a Jewish state in historic Palestine. However, from the outset, Arafat demonstrated a unique ability of adjustment and flexibility regarding the PLO Arab policies, especially when compared to rival PLO factions, particularly the leftist ones of HABASH and HAWATMA (Popular Front for the Liberation of Palestine and Democratic Front for the Liberatin of Palestine, respectively) with their Marxist-Maoist doctrines, and those linked to militant Arab states which rejected the peace process in the Middle East as a whole.

Arafat's policy regarding opposition organizations within the PLO was that the unity of the Palestinian national movement must be maintained, at any cost, save its independent decision making. Thus, he advocated the postponement of all internal social-ideological struggles concerning political orientations. This position was traditionally considered by leftists as right-wing. Indeed, Arafat's own inclination was patently conservative, with a measure of Islamist tendencies.

Since the mid-1970s, Arafat led the PLO to a gradual pragmatization in its policy on the conflict with Israel. This demonstrated his political realism and ability to adjust to the PLO's regional and international constraints. Given the beginning of a peace process after the 1973 war, Arafat led the shift toward the strategy of phases adopted by the Arab states in the all-Arab summit meeting in Algiers (November 1973) toward Israel. This was vital to attain legitimacy for political settlements with Israel. Arafat was the main force behind the PLO's historic decision at the twelfth session of the Palestinian National Council (June 1974) which decided, *inter alia*, that the PLO would establish a combatant national Palestinian authority over any part of Palestine to be liberated from Israel. This indicated the first shift from a vision of retrieving the whole territory of Palestine to a pragmatic policy, acquiescing in the establishment of a Palestinian state in the West Bank and GAZA STRIP.

Toward the late 1970s, Arafat sanctioned a growing dialogue between the PLO and "progressive" (namely, non-Zionist and later, leftist) Israelis. Such contacts were based explicitly, on the acceptance of the Jews of Israel as individuals rather than as a political community that deserved to be defined in national terms and, implicitly, on the assumption that some settlement between Israel and the PALESTINIAN ARABS was feasible. (Again this was contrary to the PLO Charter.) Simultaneously, Arafat conducted growing efforts to mobilize European, in addition to third world, support for the acknowledgment of the PLO as an equal partner in the Middle East peacemaking. With the Arab-Israeli peace efforts occuring, Arafat came to oppose international terrorism by his own faction *Fatah*. Yet *Fatah* continued to maintain close collaborative relations with foreign underground guerrilla groups, providing them with training and military support. Nonetheless, Arafat's way to pragmatism was often implicated by contradictory pronunciations and statements, allowing everyone to interpret them as desired. In the late 1970s, he repeatedly emphasized his willingness to accept a political solution, implying that he would prefer a diplomatic struggle to military-terrorist operations. He spoke of joining the American-led international efforts to negotiate a settlement. He hinted that even Security Council Resolution 242, considered by most countries as the key to any settlement, might be acceptable if it was amended to recognize the national rights and aspirations of the Palestine Arabs, i.e., an independent state. Arafat was initially positive toward the Fahd Plan (1981) but later backtracked under Syrian and inside militant pressures. He supported the Fez Summit Res-

olution of 1982, advocating a settlement based on the recognition of the Palestinians' right to independent statehood and acquiescence in the peaceful existence of all states in the region, including Israel. However, given the Israeli (and the US) objection to consider a dialogue with the PLO, Arafat remained either vague or fluctuating between moderation and militancy in order to survive politically, both within the Palestinian and Arab arenas. He refused to commit himself to the recognition of Israel; to renounce terror; or to accept Resolution 242, as long as he remained anathema to Israel and the United States. On the contrary, he had frequently invalidated or counter-balanced moderate statements by renewed expressions of extremism.

Arafat's relations with the Arab regimes witnessed ups and downs. However he remained basically aligned with Egypt. Yet between 1977–1983, he boycotted AL-SADAT because of his peace policy toward Israel. This alignment was repeatedly demonstrated despite recurrent tensions and crises between Arafat and the Egyptian leadership (1970; 1977–1983; 1990). Arafat boycotted Egypt in accordance with collective Arab decisions in response to AL-SADAT's visit to JERUSALEM. This followed the Camp David Accords and the Peace Treaty with Israel. He then resumed, since 1983, close relations with President MUBARAK's Egypt to a point that there was talk of a "moderate bloc" formed by Egypt, Jordan and Arafat's mainstream of the PLO.

Despite the bitter residues of the bloody confrontation with the Hashemite Jordanian regime in September 1970, and the Rabat Arab summit resolution that the PLO was the sole legitimate representative of the Palestinian people, Arafat was aware of the PLO limitations to provide needed services to the Palestinian inhabitants of the West Bank. Hence he was willing to acquiesce in Jordan's continued functioning as the authority in charge of that population throughout the 1970s and most of the 1980s. In late 1978, Arafat arrived in Jordan for talks with King Hussein. This resulted in the establishment of the Joint Palestinian-Jordanian Committee for the Occupied Land. This took charge of distributing the financial aid provided by the Baghdad Summit (November 1978) to the West Bank and GAZA STRIP Palestinian inhabitants and continued to function until 1987. Since late 1982, Arafat negotiated with King Hussein of Jordan a joint formula of Palestinian-Jordanian political action to-ward renewal of the peace process. They reached an agreement in February 1985. This was rejected by the PLO radical factions, and adopted with reservations by *Fatah*. Here, too, Arafat was unable to accept the US conditions for a dialogue, or to concede to King Hussein's proposals. The accord's failure to bring about American change in its attitude toward the PLO led to its suspension by King Hussein in February 1986. It was later abrogated by the PLO in April 1987 (see PALESTINE LIBERATION ORGANIZATION, JORDAN. In April 1987 he had to accept the radicals' demand to abrogate the agreement for the benefit of renewed Palestinian unity.

Arafat's growing quest for participation in the peacemaking process and its flirtations with King Hussein in the late 1970s and early 1980s, brought Arafat into increasing tension with Syria, especially following the signing of a peace treaty between Israel and Egypt. Reports repeatedly appeared to the effect that Syria was interested in replacing Arafat as the PLO leader, culminating in a full confrontation between them in the aftermath of Israel's siege of Beirut and beginning of the PLO-Jordan dialogue in late 1982.

Arafat's status and position were repeatedly questioned after 1982, mainly due to his confrontation with Syria and loss of the PLO's territorial base in Lebanon. In fact, the immediate post-1982 years witnessed a reduction of the PLO, except for some indecisive military operations, to a feeble traveling diplomacy. His policies of rapprochment with Jordan and Egypt, deepened the rift with Syria. This had originated from the following: Arafat's refusal to submit to Syrian guidance; Syria's refusal to accord the PLO full freedom of action; and the extremist, Syria-based factions of the PLO. The *Fatah* rebellion of 1983 deprived Arafat of his last power base in the Biqa and the Tripoli area, causing an irreversible split within the PLO. It was fully supported by some of the extremist factions while the two leftist ones of Habash and Hawatma half-sympathized with it and tried to mediate. The rebels and their supporters demanded Arafat's dismissal, boycotting all meetings and sessions of Arafat's loyalist PLO. In November 1984, Arafat succeeded in convening, in Amman, the Palestinian National Council that was attended only by his loyalists. It endorsed Arafat's policies and his leadership. By 1985–1986, he had reestablished his leadership, despite near-constant

clashes with the Shi'i AMAL *militia*—a strong presence of his PLO wing in the Palestinian refugee camps in South Lebanon and Beirut. In April 1987, Arafat reached a reconciliation with some of the radical factions within the PLO. To achieve this, he had to accept some of the policy changes they demanded (mainly concerning PLO relations with Jordan and Egypt). Syria and the factions it guided were not reconciled with Arafat.

Under the circumstances that resulted from the 1991 Gulf crisis—the cease of financial aid by the oil-rich Arab monarchies to the PLO and the Palestinians, and the speedy rise of HAMAS in the West Bank and Gaza Strip as a moral and political alternative to the PLO—Arafat was willing to accept Israel's conditions for Palestinian participation in the Madrid Peace Conference (1991) and later on, to sign the Oslo Document of Principles (DOP) with Israel which accounted for mutual recognition between the state of Israel and the PLO, and principles of a process-oriented settlement between the signatories. Arafat was the driving force behind the scenes for concluding the agreement and effectively the decisive authority on the Palestinian side, through his senior negotiator Mahmud ABBAS MAHMUD (Abu Mazen). The signing of the DOP by Arafat culminated two decades of political pragmatism of the Palestinian leader, which had been camouflaged and confused by endless contradictory statements and actions. In May 1994, Arafat signed with Prime Minister RABIN the Cairo Agreement, which elaborated the specific arrangements for the establishment of the Palestinian Authority in Gaza Strip and Jericho. Later that year Arafat was awarded the Noble peace prize which he shared with Rabin and Shimon PERES. In September 1995 Arafat signed the Taba Agreement, by which Israel was to withdraw from the main Palestinian cities in the West Bank. This agreement paved the way to the first general, and free elections among the Palestinians in the whole area of the West Bank, Gaza Strip and East Jerusalem, to both the Palestinian Council and President of the Palestinian Authority, held on 20 January 1996. Arafat was elected President with eighty-three percent of the votes.

Despite the establishment of the Palestinian Authority under Arafat's leadership and his election as the Palestine Authority's President in January 1996, he preserved his position as Chairman of the PLO. In this capacity, Arafat convened the Palestinian National Council (PNC) in Gaza city in May 1996, for the first time since the Oslo DOP had been signed. The PNC was convened to ratify the Palestine Authority's peace policy, and-by Arafat's commitment at signing the DOP—to abolish those articles in the Palestinian National Charter that called for the destruction of the State of Israel or contradicted the Rabin-Arafat's exchange of letters prior to the singing of the DOP. The results of the session were considered successful for Arafat, but in Israel the vague decision made by the PNC regarding the Charter remained much controversial.

Arafat's image as a master of political maneuvers and arch-survivalist since the foundation of the Palestine Authority underlined his indecisive and infirm style of state—and nation-building, especially when dealing with the political opposition (Hamas) and repressing violence against Israel in accordance with his commitments in the Oslo Accords. By and large, Arafat demonstrated clear preference of containment and co-optation rather than confrontation, inclusion rather than exclusion, though not at the expense of his own political hegemony. It was only under extreme circumstances of threat to his political authority that he was willing to exert to violent repression, as in the case of the bloody clash with the Islamists on 18 November 1994 in the Palestine Mosque of Gaza. His need of survival has occasionally been reflected in appeals to the Palestinian populace with emotional messages, upholding Islamic and Palestinian nationalist symbols, such as JIHAD (Holy War), and East Jerusalem as the Palestinian capital, which could be interpreted to be colliding with his commitments to Israel.

Until the late 1980s, the PLO's leadership had assumed a collective nature. This was embodied by *Fatah's* hard core of founders, especially Arafat, Salah Khalaf (Abu Iyad), and Khalil al-Wazir (Abu Jihad). With the murder of the latter, allegedly by Israeli commando, in 1988 and the assassination of Abu Iyad in 1991 by a Palestinian opponent, Arafat remained the sole Palestinian leader. Decision making turned increasingly personal, of Arafat alone. The solitude of Arafat's leadership surfaced as a problem when in 1991, his plane crashed and his survival was questioned. The solitary and centralized nature of Arafat's leadership became particularly evident with the establishment of the Palestinian Authority (PA) in June 1994 in Gaza, following the

signing of the Israel-PLO Cairo Agreement (May 1994). The high expectations fostered by Western governments and international agencies for stability and economic boom in the Palestinian territories following the establishment of the Palestinian Authority in 1994, slowly faded up when it was revealed that Arafat's style of government was marked by ultra-centralization. Shortly after the foundation of the Palestinian Authority, it was heavily critized by both Palestinian opponents and foreign observers underlined the inefficacy, corruption, violation of human rights, and extreme mistrust on the part of Arafat toward his own aides. This mistrust was reflected in the multiplicity of security and police organizations, all subordinated to Arafat, and in entrusting the same administrative assignment to a number of figures.

ARAMCO (Arabian-American Oil Company). A consortium of American oil companies—Standard Oil of California; Texas Oil; Standard Oil of New Jersey (later ESSO, EXXON); and Socony Vacuum, formed in the mid 1940s to produce oil in SAUDIA ARABIA. See OIL in the Arab countries.

ARMED FORCES   Most states throughout history regarded the possession and development of armed forces as a chief attribute of statehood, needed to counter threats, both domestic and external, and as the main instrument of enforcing authority over a given territory and population. The modern Middle Eastern states are no exception, especially in view of the long tradition of martial feats and warrior pride consolidated through centuries of wars in the name of ISLAM. However, from the outset, armed forces in the contemporary Middle East, have also been largely conceived as a forerunner and major instrument of modernization and state formation.

The most conspicuous reality regarding armed forces in the Middle East has been their constant growth in personnel, armament and expenditures, to a level incomparable to other Third World countries. This fact clearly illustrates their essential role in the growth of body and capability of the state in the region. This reflects itself in the central role of the military in politics and state bureaucracy (see below). Middle Eastern states possess some of the largest armed forces in relation to their population and some of the most expensive in relation to their

Armed Forces of Middle East States 1994-1995

COUNTRY	Personnel			Tanks	AFVs	Artille
	Regular x 1000	Reserves x 1000	Total x 1000			
Algeria	152	150	302	1100	1780	(
Baharin	7.4	-	7.4	81	192	
Egypt	431	694	1125	2900	5180	2
Iran	383	1000	1383	1500	1000	1 to
Iraq	400	?	400	2100	3300	1
Israel	177	427	604.5	3845	8000	1
Jordan	94	60	154	1067	1565	
Kuwait	32	-	32	700	50	
Lebanon	52	-	52	350	670	
Libya	76	-	76	2700	3000	2 to
Morocco	141	-	141	415	1500	
Oman	29.5	-	29.5	156	142	
Qatar	10.3	-	10.3	24	310	
Saudi Arabia	161	-	161	1015	4050	
Sudan	86.5	-	86.5	450	950	
Syria	390	142	532	4800	4980	
Tunisia	35.5	-	35.5	200	316	
Turkey	515	-	515	4280	4046	
UAE	46.5	-	46.5	216	1100	
Yemen	62	-	62	1150	1320	

[1] Including the Revolutionary Guards
[2] Including army aviation

SSM Launchers	Combat Aircraft	Transport Aircraft	Helicopters	SAM Batteries	Naval Combat Vessels	Submarines
) - 35	205	76	108	30	68	
-	24	3 - 4	23	-	30	
24	497	43	221	122	128	8
15	214	119	275	-	177	3
34	350		300	60	93	
	677	83	269	41	36	3
-	85	12	60	14	12	
-	83	4	18 - 21	6	35	
-	16	1	40	-	9	
10	483	106	210	20	53	
-	74	48	127	-	25	
-	37	44	37	-	28	
-	14	7	41		55	
-12	256	76	180	23	129	
-	45	25	53	5	10	
62	515	23	285	108	48	
-	13	11	35	-	36	
-	434	62	260^2	29	86	16
-	66	36	85	5 - 7	131	
22	166	26	67	25	25	3

GDP (IRAQ, SYRIA, ISRAEL, TURKEY, IRAN, EGYPT). For example, in 1982, Iraq's military expenditure was 29.7 percent of its GDP; Syria, 13.7 percent and JORDAN, 11.3 percent. That same year, the armed forces of these three states represented 2.4–2.9 percent of their populations (compared to an international average of 0.5 percent).

Middle Eastern countries receive over half of the arms' deliveries to the Third World and more than a quarter of all world international arms sales. The average military expenditure continuously escalates in the Middle Eastern countries growing tenfold in value from 4.7 billion dollars in 1962, to 46.7 billion dollars in 1980 (nearly three times the world average). Military personnel however, increased by sixty-four percent from 1972 to 1982, rising from 2.1 million to 3.5 million. Some states in the Middle East (especially Israel, Egypt, Syria, LIBYA and Turkey) possess huge numbers of tanks (2,700–4,800 each) and combat aircraft (480-675 each) which equals or surpasses most major European powers. (For a breakdown of Arab armed forces and their equipment see the table).

The rapid growth of military expenditure and personnel in Middle Eastern countries has been the result of four main causes:

A. The proliferation of inter-state conflicts, some of which assume a protracted regional form, and global significance, primarily the ARAB-ISRAEL CONFLICT and the PERSIAN GULF disputes. Cycles of wars between Israel and the surrounding Arab states led, especially since the early 1960s, to an increasing arms race, which all but intensified in the aftermath of the 1967 War due to the occupation of national Arab territories by Israel and intensified confrontation along the new fronts, culminating in the 1973 War; the emergence of the Palestinian resistance movement and entrenchment in Jordan and LEBANON. This led to semi-civil armed confrontations, and culminating in Israel's invasion of Lebanon in 1982 and confrontation with the Syrian forces in that country. The growth of military expenditure of Israel and Egypt, for example, remained relatively high even after they signed a peace treaty in 1979. In fact, they could increase their military expenditure—especially for purchasing sophisticated arms—due to American financial aid designated for that purpose. Thus, in 1986–1987, Israel's military expenditure was about fifteen percent of its GDP, while Egypt's was

just slightly below this proportion.. In the Gulf area, the oil monarchies continued their relatively high expenditure in the 1980s, regardless of the shrinking oil revenues from 1982, and especially from the mid-1980s, due to the imminent threats of the Islamic revolution, the IRAN-IRAQ WAR (1980–1988) and the Gulf crisis of 1990–1991 caused by the Iraqi invasion of KUWAIT.

B. The Superpowers' competition for the Middle East during the Cold War, was expressed primarily in their race of arms supplies to their respective clients. The collapse of the Soviet Union and end of the Cold War brought little change, due to the urgent need of the ex-Soviet states for foreign currency, the relative removal of agreed East-West constraints regarding arms supplies to certain areas, and willingness to sell their surplus arsenals at dumping prices. Apart from the Cold War, sheer economic considerations motivated competition among European states, primarily FRANCE, BRITAIN, and Italy, for the giant capacity and appetite of Middle Eastern states for advanced arms systems. Thus, France was the main arms supplier of Iraq during its war with Iran. Furthermore, in the course of the 1980s, China and North Korea also entered into this market, especially with medium-range missile technology.

C. The availability of vast state-owned oil revenues at the disposal of Arab and Iranian rulers. From 1967, Arab oil producing states routinely—though not constantly regarding the scope of aid-supported arms procurement by Arab "confrontation states" (Egypt, Jordan, and, from 1973, Syria as well) and the Palestinian Resistance Movement. This aid, collectively negotiated and agreed between recipients and donors, remained valid until 1987 (for Egypt, until 1978). The rise of the revolutionary Islamic regime in Iran, and the eruption of the Iran-Iraq War, boosted the military expenditure of the Gulf oil monarchies, mainly for sophisticated arms systems from the West, though without augmenting their sense of security due to their small populations, vast territory (as in the case of SAUDI ARABIA), large migrant workers' populations, and wealth. Thus, Saudi Arabia's average expenditure from the 1980s was slightly over twenty percent of its GDP (around 20 billion dollars annually).

D. The prevalence of intra-state security problems: communal uprisings; civil wars; coup attempts; and the political role of the military as a core instrument of stability and regime security. Intra-state rebellions, some of them protracted strifes, struck many of the Middle Eastern countries, forcing the government to employ its armed forces to quell the rebels—SUDAN's Civil War against the rebelling South; Iraq's repeated confrontations with Kurdish rebellions; Turkey's military campaigns against the PKK since the late 1980s, including military incursions into Iraq for that purpose; Syrian military operation against the Muslim Brotherhood uprising in Hamah in 1982; Yemen's Civil War of 1962–1967; and 1994. Other Middle East regimes have to cope with increasingly threatening armed Islamic opposition groups (Egypt, Algeria, from the late 1980s).

Historical Background: Under the Abbasid Empire, a tradition developed of forming armed forces of militarily trained slaves (*mamluk*; plural, *mamalik*) to be the core of its military body. (This emerged as a military society which took power and established dynasties and rulers over large areas of Egypt and the Fertile Crescent in the thirteenth and eighteenth centuries). The Ottomans adopted a similar institution (*devshirme*) of militarily trained slaves (*yeniceris*) who constituted the "regular" army and upheld the Empire's wars with external enemies. However, with the beginning era of modernization in the Middle East, the traditional armed institutions had already declined and lost their credibility, along with the decline of the regions' Islamic powers—the Ottoman and Persian empires and MOROCCO. The technological eminence of the European powers and continued retreat of the traditional Muslim states of the Middle East under the European military pressure in the late eighteenth and nineteenth centuries, forced them to adopt a strategy of modernization. This initially focused on the armed forces, as a means to secure their political survival. Most armed forces in the Middle East were systematically modernized from the nineteenth century, usually under European guidance and supply of military weapons, technologies, and doctrines. This modernization, however, could not be limited to the military establishment. Rather, it entailed a radical change in a wide spectrum of spheres, such as languages and education, taxation and economy, and the administrative and judicial systems. Modernization of the armed forces in those Muslim states, or in semi-autonomous provinces that possessed armed forces (Egypt, TUNISIA), began in the early nineteenth

century. They often met with resistance necessitating the elimination of the existing military establishment in order to enable the formation of a European-modeled army. The modernized Egyptian Army, founded by Muhammad Ali in 1816, serving him and his descendants in their efforts to build a modern Egypt (semi-independent under Ottoman suzerainty). It became the role model for the Ottoman Sultan ten years later, as well as for other Muslim states. However, the modernized armies of the Muslim states remained largely inferior to their European rivals and were usually and repeatedly defeated in the battlefield. When these Muslim areas came under European domination—Tunisia in 1881, Egypt in 1882, Morocco in 1912—their armed forces were reorganized under the tutelage and command of the French or British colonial power.

Apart from Turkey and Iran, and to a lesser extent Egypt and Morocco, the armed forces of the Middle Eastern states were the product of the foreign European rule, with a nucleus of ex-Ottoman officers in Iraq. Under British and French tutelage, armed forces were rapidly established, primarily for domestic security purposes, initially under government control. Their transfer to full national control formed part of the nationalist struggle for the attainment of full independence. The Egyptian armed forces were officially commanded until 1924 by the British Governor-General of SUDAN, concurrently bearing the title *Sirdar* of the Egyptian armed forces. From 1924–1925, their command was fully Egyptian, but the British continued to exercise de facto control, at least until the conclusion of the Anglo-Egyptian Treaty of 1936 and in some measure even after it.

An Iraqi Army was established in 1921, under Iraqi command; but here, too, the British wielded a large measure of control, at least until the Anglo-Iraqi Treaty of 1930 recognized Iraq's full independence. The British also raised, outside the framework of the Iraqi armed forces, special "levies" for internal security. The "Arab Legion" established in Transjordan in 1920 gradually became Jordan's national Army; but it was British-commanded and financed until 1956. The "Sudan Defense Force", established in 1925 by the British, was also British-commanded. So were, later, paramilitary guards or levies set up by the British in the areas they still controlled in a semi-colonial way (the Western Aden Protectorate, 1937; the "Hadrami Legion" in the

Eastern ADEN Protectorate, 1940; the "Trucial Scouts' in TRUCIAL OMAN, 1955). The armed forces of independent Muscat and OMAN were also comanded British officers.

In Palestine, under the British Mandate no armed forces were established beyond the police and a small Palestinian-Transjordanian Frontier Force, TJFF. (Palestinian volunteer units in World War II—mostly Jewish, from September 1944; the "Jewish Brigade", and some 9,000 Arabs—were part of the British Army). The French in SYRIA and LEBANON kept even tighter direct control of the *"Troupes Spéciales"* they established in 1926. This colonial force was based to a large extent on minority groups (ALAWIS, KURDS, and DRUZE) in accordance with the policy of keeping the nationalist political Sunni and Christian elite under control , while encouraging separatist-autonomous tendencies of the minority groups. Of the countries of the Arabian peninsula not under formal foreign tutelage, Yemen had a small, primitive army. King HUSSEIN's Hijaz armed forces seem to have reverted to mainly tribal levies—and were overrun in 1924–1925 by the WAHHABI-Saudi conquest of HIJAZ. The Saudi forces conquering most of Arabia were tribal fighters and the Wahhabi *Ikhwan* (Order of the Brethren). Saudi Arabia began establishing modern, organized armed forces only after World War II.

The Arab armed forces under imperial tutelage, in the 1920s ad 1930s, served mostly internal purposes—the suppression of tribal unrest (e.g. in Iraq) or rebellious minorities (e.g. the Kurds in Iraq) and the prevention of BEDUIN incursions from the desert into these newly established political entities, smugglings and enforcement of law and order. Their leading officers also began appearing as contenders for power and staging the first military coups in Iraq, 1936. Foreign operations, exclusively inter-Arab, were confined to the Arabian Peninsula (Wahhabi-Hijazi clashes, 1919–1920; Wahhabi raids on Iraqi, Transjordanian and Persian Gulf border areas; the Wahhabi-Saudi conquest of Hijaz, 1924–1925; Saudi's war against Yemen, 1934). These were traditional tribal warfare and raids rather than military operations of modern armed forces. The Iraqi armed forces seem to have had a hand in the organization of Qawuqji's volunteer force for the Palestinian-Arab rebellion of 1936. No Arab armed forces were involved in World War II—except for operations of the Iraqi armed forces against their British ally that were suppressed in May 1941 in a short War, and the dispatch of units of Jordan's Arab Legion to support the British forces in that war.

After World War II, as imperial tutelage was drawing to its end, the Arab armed forces became instruments of fully independent states. British guidance and interference virtually ceased with regard to Egypt's and Iraq's armed forces.Jordan, independent since 1946, asserted growing control of its "Arab Legion", though it remained British—administrated and British-financed until 1956–1957. After a bitter struggle, France in 1945–1946 handed to Syria and Lebanon the command of its *Troupes Spéciales*, which became the two countries' national armies. Similar development in the MAGHREB. "French" North Africa, came later, from 1956–1957. The main preoccupation of the Arab armed forces in the later 1940s was their growing involvement in the Palestine struggle—preparations and the provision of training, arms, volunteers, logistic support from 1946–1947, and finally fuly armed intervention in May 1948 (see ARAB-ISRAEL CONFLICT).

The principal Arab armies were at that time comparatively small forces—Egypt: 30,000–35,000 increasing by 1949–1950 to 60,000–80,000; Iraq: 25,000–30,000; Syria: 10,000–15,000; Jordan: 6,000–10,000. These forces possessed the usual arms and branches, though the air forces, armor and mechanized units were still in the initial stages of development. (Jordan established an air force only in the 1950s. The armed forces command, in its angry efforts to explain the Palestinian defeat of 1948, particularly in Egypt, claimed, and tried to prove in trials that ended in convictions, that the procurement and supply of equipment had been sabotaged by corruption.

A tremendous upsurge in the strength of the Arab armed forces, and particularly in the modernization of their equipment, especially concerning the air force, armor, and advanced air defense systems, began in the mid-1950s and the early 1960s. In 1950 the UNITED STATES OF AMERICA, Britain and France agreed to keep the inter-Arab and Arab-Israel military balance, and coordinated and limited their sales of weapons. However, these limitations were breached by incipient Arab arms purchases from the Soviet Bloc, from 1955. They were soon eroded in the West, too. The permanent cause and target of Arab efforts to improve their armed forces and their equipment, was the increasingly bitter confrontation with Israel. The assertion of stiffening neutralist or non-aligned polices by Egypt and Syria (and Iraq, since 1958), and apprehensions that the Western powers might try to foil these independent policies, even by military intervention—apprehensions aggravated by the Anglo-French Suez campaign of 1956 an by continuous efforts to impose on the Arab states Western-led anti-Soviet defense pacts (see CENTO)—reinforced the will to develop the strongest possible armed forces. The fact that the countries concerned were ruled by military juntas, may have further strengthened that resolve.

From 1955–1956, Egypt and Syria increasingly turned to the Soviet Union as a source of weapons, military equipment, training, expert advice, instructors and technicians. Iraq joined that new orientation after 1958—as did ALGERIA and SOUTH YEMEN, after attaining independence (1962 and 1967) and Libya, after the coup of 1969. During the 1960s and particularly after the Six-Day War of 1967 and again during and after the October war of 1973, unprecedented quantities of Soviet arms and equipment flowed to Egypt and Syria, as well as to Iraq, Libya and Algeria. In Egypt, and even more so in Syria, entire sectors of the military establishment—e.g. sophisticated air defense and missile systems—were organized and supervised, and partly manned, by Soviet personnel. The number of Soviet military technicians and experts in Egypt were estimated before 1969–1970 at approximately 5,000. During the "War of Attrition". 1969–1970, the USSR sent, in response to President ABDEL NASSER's appeal, an air defense division, comprising Soviet-manned surface-to-air missiles (SAM) and 150 fighter aircraft. In the early 1970s, the number of Soviet military experts was estimated at 15,000–20,000 in Egypt and 5,000–7,000 in Syria. The huge supplies of Soviet arms depended mostly on Soviet credits and created an ever-increasing debt to the USSR.

In Syria, the flow of Soviet arms—and the resulting dependence of Soviet replacements, parts instructors, credits—continued throughout the 1970s and 1980s. Egypt under alSADAT, on the other hand, changed course in the 1970s. Sadat, complaining bitterly about the inadequacy of Soviet aid and bout increasing Soviet interference, in July 1972 terminated the services of over 15,000 Soviet technicians, i.e. ex-pelled them. Yet he had to depend on Soviet aid again in 1973, before and during the October War, and received new massive supplies of Soviet arms, including fighter planes, advanced surface-to-air missiles and rockets, and modern tanks (as did Syria). But Sadat increasingly turned to the West (France from 1972, Britain, and in the later 1970s mainly the USA) and began re-equipping Egypt's armed forces with American weapons (with US grants and credits). Iraq's dependence on Soviet arms had also been modified when the USSR took a neutral position in the Iran-Iraq War, since 1980, and the supply of Soviet weapons, and particularly the highly sophisticated systems Iraq required, was greatly reduced. Iraq therefore increasingly turned to France, and gradually to other Western powers (motivated also by political reasons—see IRAQ).

The Arab countries not allied with the Soviet Bloc, like Jordan, Saudi Arabia and Morocco after it attained its independence in 1956, also greatly increased the strength and modern equipment of their armed forces, but they did this later than Egypt, Syria and Iraq, and to a much smaller extent. Tunisia, Lebanon, Sudan and Yemen did not make similar efforts to build very large armed forces and equip them with hyper-modern weaponry—though both Sudan and Yemen received Soviet arms (where the armed forces played a decisive role in internal political events). Jordan, after a brief nationalist lurch in 1956–1957, which included the dismissal of the British commander of its Army and the termination of its special links with Britain, remained allied with the West and depends mainly on American military equipment. The strength of its armed forces grew to about 90,000 regular troops (in addition of some 60,000 reservists). Saudi Arabia transformed its tribal levies into a modern army in the 1950s, with US aid in training and instruction. It did not need financial aid, like the other Arab countries, and even aided others. Its oil income rose, in the 1960s and 1970s, enabling it to make large military purchases, equipping its armed forces with the most advanced and sophisticated defense systems from Western sources, mostly US but also British, French, Italian and German. So did Kuwait, on a much smaller scale, after attaining independence in 1961. However, Kuwait took a neutralist stance, though most of its equipment was British, and some American and French, and in the 1980s purchased some Soviet arms, too. As the other Persian Gulf principalities—BAHRAIN, QATAR the UNITED ARAB EMIRATES—attained independence in 1971, they also began building small armed forces with British, American and French equipment. In the mid-1980s, efforts were made to establish joint defense units of the GULF COOPERATION COUNCIL consisting of the three last-named countries, Saudi Arabia, Kuwait and Oman. The Sultanate of Oman also had its own small armed forces, built with British aid and officered by Britons under contract. All these Gulf countries had ample means to finance advanced equipment for their armed forces from their oil revenues.

On the whole, the military forces in the Middle East underwent a process of professionalization, unlike the early years of independence when armed forces were significantly more identified with politics, accounting for coups and revolutions. This trend became increasingly salient from the 1970s. Thus, Egypt's military defeat in the June 1967 War and the coup attempt of Marshal Amer against ABDEL NASSER, led to a professional reorganization of the Egyptian army removing its officers from politics apart from a symbolic representation of the military in the government by the Defense Minister who was usually a general in uniform. At the same time, the military expertise were promoted in terms of training, advanced equipment, and growing selection of the enlisted soldiers and officers. Hence, in 1985, sixty-six percent of the mobilized soldiers were high school graduates, twenty percent vocational schools graduates; and fourteen percent university graduates. The armed forces of Syria, Algeria and Iraq—where military officers had been involved in politics until the late 1960s—encountered a similar process, especially at the junior and medium levels of the officers.

A special case is that of Lebanon's armed forces. It had never been particularly strong (until the 1970s, 15,000–17,000 men, in the early 1980s, increased to a nominal 20,000–23,000, and in the mid-1990s, reaching close to 50,000), the Lebanese Army, based largely on confessional-territorial brigades (MARONITE-Christian, Sunni and Shi'i Muslims, and Druze), and serving mostly as an instrument of internal security, was hardly able to initiate war against a foreign enemy, and turned to be impotent even in maintaining its domestic duties. The Army was in danger of collapsingt whenever it was used in an inter-communal conflict, due to the non-proportional distribution of the top command positions, held mainly by the Maronites, while most of the rank and file were Shi'is. Indeed, apart from symbolic participation in the ARAB-ISRAEL CONFLICT of 1948, the Lebanese armed forces played no part in other Arab confrontations with Israel, and offered hardly any resistance to the Israeli forces in their repeated incursions into Lebanon (including the invasions of 1978 and 1982). From the late 1960s the Lebanese units failed also in enforcing the state's rules over the PALESTINIAN GUERRILLA ORGANIZATIONS, and finally disintegrated in the early phases of the Lebanese Civil War (1975–1976). Attempts at rebuilding the Lebanese Army following Israel's invasion (1983–1984) were short-lived, resulting in total failure despite a nominal growth of its personnel, due to the continued factional disputes. In the early 1990s, following the national conciliation Agreement of Ta'if (1989), and under Syrian supervision, the Lebanese Army was reorganized on non-confessional and non-territorial units, and significantly enlarged, with Shi'is as the single main group. During the 1990s, the Lebanese Army demonstrated unprecedented capabilities and efficiency in imposing law and order in various districts and communal populations of Lebanon.

In recent decades, the armed forces of the Arab states have also been used in several inter-Arab disputes. Saudi troops clashed in 1955 with a British-led Omani force, over possession of the al-BURAIMI oasis. Omani troops fought South Yemenite units aiding rebels in Dhofar in the 1960s. South Yemen was involved several times in border fighting with Yemen, which escalated in 1972 and again in 1979 into short wars (ended by all-Arab mediation). An all-Arab force composed of Saudi, Egyptian (UAR), Sudanese, Jordanian and Tunisian troops was dispatched in 1961 to Kuwait, to defend it against Iraqi annexation threats. In 1962, Egypt sent an expeditionary force to Yemen, intervening in that country's civil war and supporting its revolutionary republican regime (leading also to clashes, and nearly to war, with Saudia). The force was finally withdrawn in 1967. Algerian and Moroccan troops clashed in a brief border war in 1963. Syrian force crossed into Jordan in 1970, to intervene on the PALESTINE LIBERATION ORGANIZATION's (PLO) side in the Jordan-PLO fighting. It was repelled by the Jordanian armed forces and by American and Israeli threats of intervention. Since 1975, Moroccan troops have been operating against "POLISARIO"; the guerrilla of the "Sahara Arab Republic"—formerly Spanish Sahara, which Morocco claims as its own—operations that also created Moroccan-Algerian tension and sometimes lead to clashes. Repeated clashes between Libya and Egypt briefly escalated into warlike activities in 1977.

Syrian troops openly and massively intervened in 1976 in Lebanon's civil war, after protracted semi-clandestine intervention without regular troops. This Syrian intervention force was transformed, the same year, into an "Arab Deterrent Force" with troops from several Arab countries (Saudia, Sudan, Libya, Yemen, South Yemen). Some of these Arab troops were soon withdrawn, and all of them were out by 1979; but even while the force—variously reported to number 24,000–40,000 men—was nominally all-Arab, its bulk was Syrian. From 1979, the force was virtually Syrian only, though the ARAB LEAGUE continued extending its term as an "all-Arab" force—extensions from which several Arab states dissociated themselves. The government of Lebanon several times requested Syria to withdraw its troops, but as there was no formal Arab League decision to disband the "all-Arab" force, Syria did not comply. In the June 1982 Israeli invasion of Lebanon, Syrian troops clashed with Israeli ones; those in Beirut, Southern and Western Lebanon, were evacuated in September 1982. However, Syria maintained its troops in Northern and Eastern Lebanon (the Tripoli-Akkar region and the Biqa') and in effect occupied these areas.

Libya conducted military operations in neighboring Chad since the mid 1970s. In 1973 it occupied, and later annexed, a strip of territory—the "Aouzou Strip"—which it claimed as part of Libya. In the late 1970s, its support of one of the warring factions in Chad led it into full military intervention. Its forces continue occupying large parts of northern Chad—despite several agreements to end that occupation. In 1987, the Libyan forces were defeated and finally expelled from Chad. (This apparently involving French troops.) Iraq was involved in the longest War with Iran (1980–1988), which began with an Iraqi invasion of southwestern Iran (the SHATT AL-ARAB and southern Khuzistan). By 1986 this had spread to the Persian Gulf as a whole, especially the oil installations, terminals and tankers, culminating in mutual use of missiles launched to-

ward in-depth cities at times of stalemate on the battle fronts. Iraq was apparently encouraged to attack Iran by the turmoil Iran had been undergoing after its Islamic revolution; the disarray within its armed forces because of the massive purges and disintegration of the commanding officers corps, and its disconnection from the American source of arms supplies. Iraq had a distinct advantage in modern war-equipment and the personnel to operate it. Iran had three-times more territory and population, in addition to the revolutionary zeal instilled by the Islamic regime. This enabled Iran, against all odds, to defy the Iraqi offensive and roll it back into Iraq's land, though without being able to attain any decisive goal. This long war and side-effects on the region's oil industry and export capabilities, intensified the militarization of the Gulf countries as a whole, manifested in the increased military expenditures not only of Iran and Iraq but also of the Arab oil monarchies.

Except for the Arab-Israel wars and the Iran-Iraq war, inter-state military clashes in the Middle East were relatively minor. However, states perceive their armed forces ready to meet domestic as well as external threats. Saudi Arabia and the Gulf, emirates, for instance, felt responsible for the security of the Gulf and apprehensive of potential Iranian machinations; Jordan feared possible Syrian moves against it; the WESTERN SAHARA crisis led to near-constant tension between Morocco and Algeria and Libya's neighbors had to be alert for new Libyan schemes. Yet, it was principally the Arab-Israeli conflict that explains the historic growth of armed forces in, and security expenditure of both Israel and its neighboring Arab states. This has been attested to by the magnitude of armored, artillery and airfighters—unprecedented since World War II—operated in the 1973 War between Israel and the Egyptian-Syrian war coalition.

From the early-1980s, a growing number of Middle Eastern states purchased (from the Soviet Union, China, and North Korea) or developed NON-CONVENTIONAL WEAPONS—mostly chemical—and missiles with varying ranges and accuracy, in addition to those countries that had already possessed them (Egypt, and allegedly Israel). Chemical weaponry was first reported to have been used by Egypt in the Yemen War (1962–1967), and later on was more intensively used by the Iraqis in their War with Iran

(1980–1988), which also witnessed a vast use of missiles with conventional warheads. Ballistic missiles were also used by Iraq against Israel during the GULF WAR (1991), following which Iraq's arsenal of biological and chemical weapons, in addition to efforts to develop nuclear capability, were revealed (see NON-CONVENTIONAL WEAPONS, IRAQ).

The Military in Politics: The process of forming modern armed forces in Middle Eastern countries, initially subordinated the reformed armed forces to the civilian authority, as in the case of the OTTOMAN EMPIRE from the late 1820s. However, the reformed armed forces became a vanguard group in the process of modernization in the Middle East Muslim states (the Ottoman Empire, Morocco and Iran) and semi-independent provinces (Egypt, Tunisia). Furthermore, the professional officers corps, trained and educated in military academies, became a power group imbued with reformism and nationalism, a sense of mission, and leadership ambitions. These characteristics tended to be translated into action under various circumstances which had resulted from weak ruling authority, deterioration of law and order due to demonstrations, strikes or riots—often after having been employed by the government in restoring domestic security and order—or after a humiliating experience of the armed forces themselves. Hence, the involvement of military officers in Ottoman politics and eventual takeover of state power by military coups (1908, 1913, and 1920); the takeover by Reza Khan in Persia (later Iran) in 1921; and the military coups in Syria and Egypt in the aftermath of the Arab-Israel War of 1948.

The involvement of military officers in politics in the Middle East countries has been part of a prevalent phenomenon in the developing countries, deriving from their social and political realities. In the absence of established social and political institutions capable of mass mobilization and legitimization of authority, the military is often the sole institution with the potential to operate social and political change. Moreover, officers represented the emerging urban, educated middle class, whose frustrated expectations and strive for more equitable sharing of political power and economic resources—especially in view of the rigidity of social and political mobility in the Middle East countries—turned the military career the shortest way of achieving so-

cial status and political influence. As such, army officers often strove to incorporate civilians in the government, or even instating them as figureheads for legitimacy purposes, but more often, allying themselves with certain social or ethnic group with the aim of widening their political power base. Seeking legitimacy, officers in power often adopted a strategy of creating a civilian image to their regime, by replacing the uniform with a suit or appearing in a traditional dress.

The Turkish Army, the most modernized in the Middle East—played a decisive role in the shaping of modern Turkey, almost in every sense. Under Kemal Pasha's lead, the Turkish nationalist forces defied the humiliating conditions of the SÈVRES, TREATY OF, according to which Anatolia was to be divided among the Allied powers. The nationalists established an alternative system of government and representing institutions in Ankara (to that of the Sultan's regime in Istanbul), signed treaties with neighboring USSR, France and Italy; defeated the Greeks, and established a republican, secular, national regime. Since the early 1920s, the military in Turkey played a unique role in politics, as a watch dog of the Kemalist legacy but also as a central element in the Turkish social and political elite. The military leadership endeavored to refrain from directly interfering in politics. It conducted two major coups (1960, 1980), which were followed by a short period of military government and submission of power to the civilians, not before some precautionary measures, constitutional and political. However, former military officers led Turkey until 1950, and remained most conspicuous in politics since they toppled the Democratic Party's government in 1960. In 1997, the military again manifested its decisive weight in pressuring the Islamic Welfare Party-led government out of power and finally outlawing it on grounds of violating the principle of secularism (see TURKEY).

In Iran, the military played a minimal independent role in politics after the coup led by Reza Khan in 1921, following which the military became not only the main guarantee of the new order dictated by Reza Shah, but also a decisive instrument in the process of state formation and modernization conducted by the regime, backing the implementation of social and economic reforms and enforcing the government's authority over the huge and underdeveloped Iranian national territory. In the first two decades of Muhammad Pahlavi's reign (1941–1979), the army had initially remained primarily designed to respond to domestic security problems and challenges by tribes and opposition groups. However, from the mid-1960s the Shah began to establish Iran as a primary military power in the Gulf area. This led to rapid process of armament, increasing the scope of military personnel. However, the military was kept out of politics, increasingly bereft of autonomous decision-making and totally subordinated to the Shah's personal authority as the supreme commander of the Iranian armed forces. Hence, when the Shah opted to leave Iran in early 1979 under the growing turmoil and Islamic revolutionary agitation, the armed forces played no role in curbing the revolution, and soon collapsed and disintegrated. Later purges conducted by the *Shi'i* revolutionary regime in the ranks of the military officers, left this body weak and in a state of disarray for a long time. Moreover, despite the eruption of War with Iraq in 1980, the regime preferred to develop the "Revolutionary Guards"—the regime's initial militia and guarantor of its domestic security—as a parallel military force to the army, with all the components of navy, airforce, armored, and infantry forces. The "Revolutionary Guards" maintained their independence despite the damaging division and competition that emerged between them and the regular army. Attempts were made by the Iranian government before the end of the War with Iraq to merge them into one force. This led only to the creation of a coordinating body. Thus, despite the role of armed forces in the eight-year long War, the Iranian official Army remained out of politics, and often a secondary element in military decision making compared to the rival "Revolutionary Guards."

As the Arab countries became independent, they tended to follow the pattern of officers' coup set in Turkey (1908, 1920) and Iran (1921). A predecessor coup was staged in Egypt in 1881–1882 by Colonel Ahmad Urabi, though it was an anti-British revolt and not one staged against an indigenous government. (The main coups are described in the entries on the various Arab countries). A brief list of the main coups would include: Iraq 1936 (Bakr Sidqi), 1937; 1958 (QASSEM), 1963, 1968 (BA'TH); Egypt, 1952 (Abdel Nasser); Syria 1949 (Za'im; Hinnawi; Shishakli), 1951 (Shishakli), 1954,1962, 1963, 1966, 1970 (*Ba'th*); Sudan 1958 (Abbud), 1969 (NUMEIRI),

1986, 1989; Yemen 1962 (Sallal); Libya 1969 (QADHAFI); Algeria 1965 (BOUMÉDIENNE). All these coups involved purges and the detention and/or exile of deposed rulers. Some of them were bloody (e.g. Iraqi 1958).

Changes in the regimes set up after these coups could no longer be effected by political constitutional means but were usually semi-coups—such as the accessions to power by Iraqi juntas of colonels in the later 1930s (the "Golden Square") and their installation of the Rashid Ali al-Kilani government, 1941, al-ASAD's takeover in Syria in 1970, or al-Abdin's takeover in Tunisia in 1987. Such semi-coups, which cannot be precisely defined, have been frequent. A list of failed coups, including in the surviving monarchies, such as Jordan and Morocco, would also be extensive.

Many of the officers' coups had reformist tendencies, promising clean-handed and efficient government, and implementing fundamental economic and social reforms, often in the direction of state socialism-centralized economy; nationalization of major trade; financial and manufacturing firms, creating a large public sector. As such, many of them opted to build strong state machinery with excessively coercive systems of government, while adopting an assertive nationalist-neutralist line in their foreign policies with close relations to the Soviet block. Most of the military coups led to authoritarian regimes, based on a single-party system and People's Assembly, endorsed by plebiscites and personality cult of the head of state. Indeed, since the early 1970s the phenomenon of military coups in the region declined, indicating the entrenchment of the military bureaucracies in power by assuming civilian appearance, allying themselves with other social and economic forces, widening their popular base, building centralized and controlled economies.

ARMENIANS A sizeable group of Armenians live in several Arab countries, particularly SYRIA and LEBANON, and some in JERUSALEM. Most of them migrated from the Turkish parts of Armenia after the large scale massacres of Armenians in 1894–1896 and 1915–1916, and after the Arab-inhabited parts of Eastern Turkey were re-occupied by post war, Kemalist Turkey in 1920. More Armenians came in 1939 from ALEXANDRETTA when it was annexed by TURKEY. Of the estimated total of about 7 million

Armenians over 5 million live in the Armenian Republic (former Soviet Armenia) and 2 million in diaspora, half of which are in the Middle East: 25,000–30,000 in Syria, 150,000–200,000 in Lebanon, 40,000–50,000 in EGYPT, 45,000–50,000 in Turkey mostly in Istanbul, and a few thousand in IRAQ and JORDAN. (Of the rest, some 200,000 reside in IRAN. No Armenians have remained in the originally Armenian inhabited eastern parts of Turkey. About 1.5 million Armenians reside in the USA,d Latin Americ, and Western Europe, mostly FRANCE; Jerusalem has some 2,000 Armenians). After World War II, the Soviet Government encouraged the Armenians of the diaspora to return to Soviet Armenia. Some 200,000 did so, among them (according to unverified and conflicting reports), more than 100,000 from Arab countries. The return movement ceased after a few years.

The Armenians in the Arab countries are well integrated in the economic life of the host countries. Many have become citizens and most of them speak ARABIC. They have not become part of the Arab nations, as they jealously preserve the coherence of closely knit Armenian communities. In Lebanon, the Armenians are recognized, within the community structure of the state, as a community entitled to representation. In sixty-six-member and seventy-seven-member Parliaments, there were three Armenian-Orthodox deputies and one Armenian-Catholic. In the ninety-nine-member chamber there were four Armenian Orthodox and one Armenian-Catholic. Some Lebanese Governments contained an Armenian Minister. However, the Armenians take little part in Lebanese political struggles, such as the civil war since 1975.

The Armenians are Christians. Most of them belong to the Armenian Orthodox Church, which is MONOPHYSITE. The head of the church bears the title Catholicos and resides in Tchmiadzin in Soviet Armenia. In the late eleventh century the Catholicos moves to Sis, in Cilicia. When his successor later retuned to Etchmiadzin, the seat of Sis was maintained—with a measure of rivalry between two Catholici in their two seats. In the 1920s, the seat of Sis was transferred to Antalias in Lebanon. The Armenian-Orthodox Church has a Patriarch in Constantinople and one in Jerusalem. A minority of Armenians joined the Catholic Church, as a semi-autonomous community, from the twelfth century.

This "UNIATE" was reformalized in 1740. The number of Armenian-Catholics is estimated at approximately five percent of all Armenians. Most of them live in the European and American diaspora, and approximately 50,000 in the Arab countries—the majority in Lebanon. Under Ottoman rule the Armenians were among the first four religious communities accorded the status of MILLET.

The Armenians, particularly those in the Arab countries, maintain communal organizations of their own, including political parties. There are two main Parties: *Hantchak*, and *Tashnak*—both with shifting ideologies and allegiances. In recent times, *Hantchak* has been considered Leftist, sometimes with Communist leanings, while *Tashnak* is considered Right-wing and pro-Western and describes itself as Social-Democratic. A third Party is *Ramkavar* (about whose political tendencies reports differ). An Armenian terrorist organization, the "Armenian Secret Army for the Liberation of Armenia (ASALA)", operates against Turkish institutions, diplomats, etc., in Europe and America. It is said to cooperate with the PALESTINE LIBERATION ORGANIZATION (PLO) and international terrorist organizations.

ARMISTICE AGREEMENTS   see ARAB-ISRAEL PEACEMAKING.

ARSALAN (often spelled **Arslan**);   also called Yazbaki. Clan of Lebanese DRUZE notables, whose chiefs bear the hereditary title of Emir; until the late nineteenth century—the semi-feudal lords of the south-western regions of Mount Lebanon, centered in the al-Gharb area east of Beirut. Since the seventeenth and eighteenth centuries, the Arsalan clan headed one of the rival factions competing for the overall leadership of Lebanon's Druze community—mainly against the JUNBLAT clan. The Arsalan-Junblat rivalry became pronounced in the late nineteenth century, after the elimination of the semi-Druze Shihab dynasty, with whom the Arsalans had been allied. During the French Mandate, the Arsalans were usually in opposition to the Mandatory regime; some of them took an active part in the Pan-Arab nationalist movement and opposed Lebanon's separate status. Thus, Adel Arsalan (1882–1954), a right-wing Syrian politician, served briefly as Deputy Premier and Foreign Minister in 1949. Since 1943, however, the Arsalans have supported the unwritten "National Pact" and the Maronite-dominated establishment based mainly on a Maronite-SUNNI coalition (see LEBANON). Their leader was Majid Arsalan (1904–1983) who, from 1937, filled ministerial posts many times, mostly as Defense Minister. As the Junblats increasingly became the chief spokesmen of Druze demands and opposition, the Arsalans' influence declined, particularly during the civil war (1975–1990), in which they tried not to become involved and, in contrast to the Junblats, maintained no real organized militia. Since the death of their chief, Majid Arsalan, in 1983 and the succession of his son Feisal Arsalan (b. 1941), this decline has been aggravated by the lack of strong leadership and an organized military force. Feisal Arsalan's alliance with the Maronite-Christian PHALANGES under Bashir Jumayyil in the late 1970s and early 1980, undermined his position, especially after the clashes between the Lebanese forces and the Druze fighters in the Shuf in 1983–1984. Feisal's half-brother, Talal Arsalan (b. 1963), became leader of the clan and served as Minister of Tourism (1990–1992) and a member of the Lebanese parliament since 1991.

al-ASAD, HAFEZ (b. 1930) Syrian officer and politician, President of SYRIA since 1971. Born in Qardaha near Ladhiqiya to an ALAWI family, Asad became a professional officer in the Syrian Air Force. In the 1950s he joined the clandestine officers' cells linked to the BA'TH Party. He took a leading part in the *coup* of March 1963 that brought the *Ba'th* officers to power, and became commander of the Air Force (promoted to the rank of *Fariq*, Lieutenant-General, in 1968). From 1965 Asad was a member of the *Ba'th* High Command—both the "national", i.e., all-Arab, and the "regional"-Syrian one. In the incessant factional struggles that rocked the Syrian *Ba'th* and caused frequent changes in party, army and government leadership, Asad sided with the "military" faction of the extreme doctrinaire "Left" which opposed the AFLAQ-Bitar-Hafez faction then in power. He was one of the leaders of the coup of February 1966 carried out by the military wing and became a leading figure in the newly established regime, serving as Acting Defense Minister and commander of the Air Force. However, Asad soon fell out with Salah JADID, another Alawi officer, and the leading figure in the new ruling junta which adopted extremely militant and antagonistic domestic and regional policies. Asad formed his own nationalist faction and opposed Jadid's rigid revolutionary leftism which remained unaltered despite the debacle of the 1967 war. Asad represented a pragmatic approach to political and economic issues. He opposed total identification with the Soviet Union, chafed at Syria's growing isolation within the Arab world and aimed a closer all-Arab cooperation and a stronger emphasis on the struggle against ISRAEL. In February 1969, in a bloodless semi-coup, Asad gained control of the government and party leadership but accepted, reportedly on Egyptian and Russian advice, a compromise providing for a coalition and leaving some of his adversaries in positions of power (e.g., Nur al-Din al-ATASSI as President and Prime Minister). The power struggle between the military and civil factions of the ruling *Ba'th* party soon resumed, culminating in Asad's seizure of full control in a semi-coup in November 1970. This time Asad predominated, purging and dismissing his opponents and detaining their leaders. He assumed the premiership, retained the Defense Ministry, and became Secretary-General of the *Ba'th*. In February 1971 he nominated a "People's Council", which appointed him President, after the *Ba'th* leadership had nominated him. In March 1971 a plebiscite endorsed that election, with Asad as the only candidate and 99.2 percent of the votes in his favor. He was re-elected President, for seven year terms, by plebiscites in February 1978, February 1985 and December 1991—nominated, as the only candidate, by the *Ba'th* and the People's Council (National Assembly).

Since 1971 Asad has given Syria a regime of unprecedented stability, with the reins firmly in his own hands. He continued an economic policy of nationalization, a pragmatic state socialism, and kept Syria's economy on an even keel (in the late 1980s and early 1990s some economic reforms had been introduced, see Syria). He established firm constitutional patterns: a constitution was adopted in 1973 and elections for a People's Council were held, from 1973, every four years—with a *Ba'th*-led "National Progressive Front "(including the Communist Party) as the sole permitted party, but with *Ba'th* - approved independent candidates admitted. In fact, the *Ba'th* apparatus was in firm control with Asad himself as its undisputed chief. Behind the facade of semi-democratic and populist institutions the

regime in fact remained harshly authoritarian, underpinned by a powerful all-pervasive secret police.
Opposition, apart from exiled politicians, came mainly from fundamentalist Sunni-Muslim groups, such
as the outlawed MUSLIM BROTHERS, and it was aggravated by the fact that Asad, the Head of State, and
many of his close associates belong to the heretic
Alawite sect. Asad ruthlessly suppressed the Muslim Brothers and broke their resistance by massive
military means (see SYRIA). Other political and factional
struggles were conducted semi-clandestinely within the ruling army and party junta. In November
1983 Asad sustained serious physical exhaustion, or
a heart condition, which put him temporarily out
of control. His sudden absence from the political
structure of power which was so dependent on him
triggered an open struggle for the succession in which
his younger half-brother Rif'at (b. 1937) was involved, with other claimants, bringing the ruling
junta to the verge of a civil war (see SYRIA).

Asad's regime In contrast to the erratic flam-
boyance of Libya's QADHAFI, Asad's close ally for many
years, and to the miscalculated adventurism of Iraq's
Saddam HUSSEIN, his bitter rival, Asad conducted
both his authoritarian rule of Syria and his hard-line
foreign policies with cool calculation and suave tactics, earning him a reputation of master-politician.
Asad's regime, however, remained markedly closed,
demonstrating little interest in cultural, social or
economic exchange with Western countries. Asad
himself rarely has visited Western countries and does
not speak English. The problem of Asad's succession and the struggle between rival army and civilian
factions seems to remain unresolved. In the early
1990s, Asad was reported to be training his son,
Basil (b. 1962), as his successor, giving him an increasing role in Syrian politics, including Syria's complicated relations with Lebanon. However, Basil died
in January 1994 in what was reported to be a car
accident. Asad's younger son, Bashar (b. 1965) was
called to take his place, but although considered to
be the prominent candidate to replace Asad, he lacks
sufficient military and political experience.

In his foreign and inter-Arab policies, Asad soon
effected a measure of *rapprochement* with the all-
Arab main line, taking Syria out of her isolation. He
reinforced relations with EGYPT, joining in 1971 a
"Federation of Arab Republics" with it and LIBYA,
and entering a close partnership with al-SADAT of

Egypt towards and during the October 1973 war
against Israel. This partnership, however, underwent
repeated crises due to Asad and Sadat's different
priorities and constraints regarding the peace process
that followed the war. Differences with Egypt had
emerged even during the October War (see ARAB-
ISRAEL CONFLICT), when the Egyptians accepted a
cease-fire without consulting Syria. Asad needed
Egypt as his major ally both for war and peaceful
settlement with Israel. Yet Sadat's independent peace
diplomacy under US mediation struck Asad with a
lesson that Syria must build its own regional, self-reliant stature so as to enhance its bargaining position
and military immunity toward both Egypt and Israel, respectively. In 1974–1976 Asad made efforts
to build a Syrian-led coalition with JORDAN, the PLO
and LEBANON, which achieved only temporary results. In 1976 Asad obtained all-Arab endorsement
(and Israeli consent) for his military intervention in
Lebanon in return for a rapprochement with Egypt
and resumption of the concerted Arab peace strategy, which had been stalemated since the second Israeli-Egyptian settlement in Sinai a year earlier. But
as Sadat made his historical visit to Jerusalem in November 1977 and gradually moved towards separate peace with Israel, Asad adopted increasingly
hard-line militant policies, leading Syria back into
militant isolation in front of Israel from which he
had initially sought to extricate her. The Egypt-Israel
peace process deepened the rupture between Damascus and Cairo. In December 1977 Syria, together with other radical Arab regimes and the PLO,
established the Steadfastness and Confrontation
Front and became its mainstay. This led Sadat to
cut off diplomatic relations with all the Front's members. The Camp David accords (see ARAB-ISRAEL PEACE-
MAKING) signed in September 1978 confronted Syria
with a new reality concerning the Israeli threat. With
Egypt's defection from the Arab war coalition Syria
had no real alternative to an alliance with IRAQ. Thus,
even before Egypt and Israel signed a peace treaty
in March 1979, a Baghdad-Damascus axis became
the new regional Arab core coalition whose *raison
d'etre* was to isolate Egypt and prevent other Arab
participants from following Sadat's line. Under Syrian and Iraqi pressure most Arab states applied diplomatic and economic boycotts of Egypt, including
expulsion from the ARAB LEAGUE. The Syria-Iraq *rapprochement* and efforts to effect unity between their

regimes was short-lived. Tension and mutual hostility between the two Ba'th regimes soon resumed, leaving Syria again without a regional ally. Asad's persistent quest for preserving his regime's stability and survivability led him, in April 1982, to sign a formal alliance with IRAN against Iraq in the IRAN-IRAQ WAR, 1980–1988, contrary to all the principles of Arab solidarity so deeply rooted in the regime's ideology. Asad's hostility toward Iraq was no obstacle for continued financial aid from SAUDI ARABIA and other Gulf oil monarchies, who had also extended financial support to Iraq. Yet despite Syria's antagonistic inter-Arab policy in most of the 1980s, Asad was pragmatic enough to slowly shift back to the center due to growing economic difficulties resulting from unprecedented efforts at enhancing Syria's military power. With Egypt's return to the Arab League in 1989, renewed Iraqi subversion through Asad's Lebanese opponents, and especially in view of the declining Soviet commitment to Syria's strategic needs, in early 1990 Asad was the last Arab ruler to resume diplomatic relations with Egypt. In 1990–1991 Syria joined the multinational anti-Iraqi coalition and symbolically participated in the GULF WAR, paving the way for Syria's inclusion in the pro-Western, pro-American camp and the Arab-Israel peace process: the Madrid conference in 1991 and the bilateral Syrian-Israeli talks that followed.

In his views towards neighboring Lebanon, Asad adopted a policy aiming at the preservation of Lebanon (with some adjustments in the Lebanese political system) as a weak state that would not be allowed to endanger Syria politically or militarily—as a place d'armes for other armies. Syria's intervention in Lebanon in 1976 turned into a permanent occupation of northern and eastern Lebanon by some 30,000 Syrian troops, and though Asad took care not to be dragged into the Lebanese quagmire he became the arbiter of Lebanese internal affairs, through client militias and political leaders. By 1990 Syria acquired total political and military domination of Lebanon (except for Israel's self-declared "Security Zone" in the south) and put an end to the lingering Civil War, 1975–1990. This came after years of failing to reach a compromise between the many warring factions, after confronting the Israeli invasion by herself in 1982, and after the abrogation of the 17 May 1983 agreement between her and Lebanon. In 1991 Lebanon and Syria signed

agreements requiring cooperation and coordination between the two states in all areas, a clear achievement for Asad's Syria (for details see LEBANON).

Towards Israel Asad took a hard line—though he strictly maintained the disengagement agreement in the Golan Heights signed in May 1974. He also prevented terrorist attacks from Syrian soil (while allowing, and at times encouraging, such raids from Lebanese or Jordanian territory). He strove to attain a "Strategic Balance" with Israel, opposed American peace plans until the early 1990s, and vehemently objected to the Jordanian King's repeated efforts to work out a formula for peace negotiations. His relations with Jordan, aggravated by those efforts and by King Hussein's alliance with the PLO under ARAFAT, were anyhow far from friendly though there were ups and downs, and periods of rapprochement in 1975–1976 and again from late 1985. Asad's bitter dispute with Arafat, originating in the latter's refusal to accept his guidance and subject the PLO to Syrian dictates, was exacerbated by Arafat's moderate line and accommodation with Jordan. Asad cultivated PLO factions subservient to Syria, instigated and supported an armed revolt within the PLO's main faction al-Fatah, in 1983, and waged a war against the PLO forces loyal to Arafat, expelling them from Syria and Syrian-occupied eastern and northern Lebanon. In 1993 he strongly opposed the Oslo Accords between the PLO and Israel, and endorsed the setting up of an opposition Front comprising ten Palestinian organizations, based in Damascus. In 1996 he refused to denounce terrorist bombings in Israel, leading to the interruption of peace talks with Israel.

Despite his opposition to his predecessors' close alliance with the USSR, Asad further cemented that alliance and made Syria even more dependent on the Soviet Union, especially after the 1982 war when the Syrian Army's order of battle was substantially enlarged and equipped with advanced Soviet weapons. However, Soviet aid had considerably decreased since 1987, when Gorbachev made it clear to Asad that the USSR would not continue to back Syria's plans for a "Strategic Balance" and advised him to seek a peaceful resolution with Israel.

The disintegration of the USSR left Syria with no superpower backing, forcing Asad to seek help elsewhere, from the US (and at times from Iran and North Korea).

In terms of achievements, however, with the exception of Lebanon, Syria under Asad is still quite far from attaining her political objectives or from becoming a regional power. It has not yet managed to reach an agreement that will secure the return of the occupied GOLAN to Syria; it is still listed as a country giving refuge to terrorists and is therefore deprived of US economic aid; it had to accept the separate Israeli-Egyptian peace as well as Egyptian involvement and mediation in the ARAB-ISRAEL PEACE-MAKING; contrary to Asad's wishes, the PLO and Jordan have slipped away from Syria's grasp and made separate peace with Israel; some Gulf and North African states have established economic ties with Israel despite the absence of a Syrian-Israeli accord, leading to Syria's relative isolation in the Arab World; the relations between Syria and its northern neighbor, TURKEY, are unstable: Turkey threatens Syria's water supplies, its military ties with Israel have been considerably expanded, and it is furious over Syria's support for the Kurdish PKK.

ASALA Initials for the Armenian Secret Army for the Liberation of Armenia, an Armenian underground organization which was active particularly in the 1970s and 1980s, hitting Turkish officials and installations abroad. Asala was established in Beirut in 1975 by a young Armenian activist, Bedros Ohanessian ("Hagop Hagopian") from Mosul. It had a radical leftist-nationalist platform, and was committed to the establishment of Armenian rule in the "lost" Armenian areas in Anatolia. Through the use of violence, it hoped to bring the Armenian cause to the world's attention and to apply enough pressure on Turkey so as to force it to admit its responsibility for the massacres committed during World War I and concede to Armenian demands which included material compensation to the victims and, in the long run, "return" of territory.

Asala emerged as the strongest amongst all the Armenian underground organizations. It drew its supporters from the Armenian youth in LEBANON and other centers of the Armenian diaspora around the world, and entered into close cooperation with Lebanese and Palestinian organizations. Asala was reportedly supported by SYRIA as another instrument of pressure on Turkey in their disputed relations (see SYRIA). Having no territorial basis in TURKEY itself, it was forced to operate mostly outside the country, concentrating its activities in assaults on Turkish diplomats and official institutions. For almost a decade it was responsible for killing over thirty Turkish diplomats, wounding many more, and carrying out several attacks on Turkish missions and offices. By the mid 1980s its activities dwindled, probably a result of having lost its base in Lebanon (after 1982), internal struggles, and objections to its tactics within the Armenian community itself.

ASHMAWI, MUHAMMAD SA'ID (b. 1932) Egyptian judge and liberal thinker. Born in al-Giza district near Cairo. He graduated from the Faculty of Law, Cairo University where he was appointed assistant of District Attorney in Alexandria (1954); District Attorney (1956); Judge (1961); Chief Prosecuter (1971); State Counsellor for Legislation (1974); and High Court Judge (1978, during which he also studied at Harvard Law School). From 1981, he was Chief Justice of the High Court; Chief Justice of the High Court of Assizes; Chief Justice of the High Court for the Security of the State. Ashmawi's vast knowledge of Islamic law enabled him to stand firmly against religious extremism and to repel the fundamentalists' demand to impose the SHARI'A rule in EGYPT, and his views on Islamic extremism and Islamic law have been taken attentively by the Egyptian regime. He is the author of numerous books on controversial issues of Islamic law, ISLAM society and state law. In 1996, Ashmawi wrote a series of articles in the weekly October Magazine about the "Arab-Israeli Cultural Struggle," in which he expressed support for peace with Israel, though not without misgivings regarding Israel's position toward the Palestinians. He writes extensively in the Egyptian Press, primarily on matters of ISLAM, in which he vigorously challenges extremism and political violence, and insists that religion should be separated from politics.

ASHRAWI, HANAN (b. 1946) A prominent Palestinian woman, Minister of Higher Education in the PALESTINIAN AUTHORITY from 1996 onward. After being a women's rights activist in the occupied territories, she attained worldwide recognition for her speeches. She was speaker of the WEST BANK and GAZA STRIP Palestinian delegation to the Madrid Conference (October 1991) and Washington peace talks, until the signing of the Israel-PLO Oslo Agreement (1993). Afterwards, she resigned her position in protest, criticizing the agreement as insufficient for the Palestinians. Despite her criticism of the Oslo accords, Ashrawi remained within PLO's mainstream.

Ashrawi's position as an "inside" leader emerged following the eruption of the Palestinian uprising (INTIFADA) in the occupied territories in December 1987. Born in Ramallah to a Christian Anglican family, Ashrawi graduated with a Master's degree in English Literature at the American University of Beirut. She also received her Doctorate in English Language and Literature at the University of Virginia, USA. Before she became involved in politics, Ashrawi lectured in English Language and Literature at the University of Bir Zeit, and Dean of the university between 1986–1990. Following her election to the Legislative Council on January 20, 1996 elections as an independent delegate, she was appointed by ARAFAT as Minister of Higher Education in the Palestinian National Authority. Ashrawi is often sent by Arafat to diplomatic missions in the US and Europe, and spreads the Palestinian Authority's message in world media.

ASSYRIANS Alternative name for the Nestorian Christians—surviving, in the nineteenth century, mainly in the Zagros mountains of Kurdistan in eastern Antolia, between Lake Van and Lake Urmia, and in northern Mesopotamia (an area divided after World War I among TURKEY, IRAN and IRAQ.

The Nestorian Church seceded from the main body of Christianity after the Council of Ephesus, 431, when Nestorios, the Patriarch of Constantinople, and his followers rejected the doctrine of the divine nature of Christ confirmed at that Council. The description of the Nestorians as Assyrians came into use much later. The implied link to the Assyrians of antiquity has no proven historical basis (except that *all* inhabitants of northern Iraq may trace their origins in part to the Assyrians and Babylonians of old). The Nestorians-Assyrians spoke an Eastern Syriac-Aramaic tongue, but today its use is largely confined to their liturgy. Throughout the centuries, the Assyrians were divided into several tribes, becoming a small minority struggling for survival in their remote mountain strongholds, against the dominant Muslim populations and other hostile communities. Their number—estimated at ap-

proximately 100,000 in the nineteenth century, mostly in today's Iraq. Since then, their numbers have dwindled because of persecutions and defections to other Christian creeds—mainly to the Catholic Church, UNIATE (the CHALDEANS), and to Protestant churches. Currently most of the Assyrians live overseas and small communities still exist in Syria and Lebanon.

During World War I, they were suspected of having connections with enemy countries—BRITAIN, and mainly RUSSIA—and were harassed and persecuted by the OTTOMAN EMPIRE. After repeated attacks by Turks and KURDS, some 50,000–70,000 Assyrians crossed into Iran, led by their Patriarch, the Catholicos, and joined the Russian forces occupying northern Iran. When the Russians occupied parts of eastern Anatolia, the Assyrians collaborated with them, and when the Russians withdrew, they were exposed to Turkish retaliation. At the end of the war, more Assyrians left for Russian-governed areas of the Caucasus. A main group of Assyrians marched to join the British forces in Iraq, followed by their families, and some 50,000 of them were placed by the British in refugee camps in Iraq, where many perished. Many of the men were employed by the British as guards, which were later organized into special levies.

Vague plans, between the end of World War I and the victorious emergence of Kemalist Turkey, to form an independent state for a Syriac-language nation—the Assyrians, the Chaldeans and the Syrian-Orthodox JACOBITES—did not materalize. Assyrians who tried to return to their ancestral homes were soon reexpelled by the Turks. They settled in a few areas in northern Iraq vacated by Turks and Kurds, but these were too small to maintain all the Assyrians. In 1932, when the British Mandate in Iraq ended, many of them were practically still refugees.

In independent Iraq, the Assyrians met with considerable Iraqi animosity, as they were clamoring for autonomy and were, moreover, identified with the intensely unpopular armed levies employed by the British. Their Kurdish neighbors were also hostile. Soon, bloody clashes erupted, and in August 1933 hundreds of Assyrians were killed in a massacre. An exodus of thousands followed; some 4,000 migrated to America, about 6,000 to Syria, and some to Lebanon. The French, with the support of the League of Nations, tried to settle some of the Assyrians in

Syria, but independent Syria discontinued that project. Other settlement schemes proposed in the League of Nations did not materialize. 30,000–35,000 Assyrians remained in Iraq. Since Kurdish rebellions were resumed in northern Iraq in the 1950s, many of them gradually moved to Baghdad. Of those that settled in north-western Iran, many moved to the cities, primarily to Teheran. The Assyrians were not active in the Iraqi (or Iranian) nationalist movement or other political organizations. Some of them joined communist groups. In recent decades, no further crises have hit the Assyrians in Iraq and they seem to have settled down. Moreover, in April 1972 the Iraqi BAʿTH régime, in the course of efforts to come to terms with Iraq's restless minorities (and to create the impression that the partial autonomy given to the Kurds was part of a larger scheme), granted the Syriac-speaking communities—i.e., the Assyrians and Chaldeans—a measure of cultural autonomy. Little has been heard of the actual implementation of that decree.

The number of Nestorian Assyrians is estimated at 50,000 or more in the Soviet Union (where they have no republic or autonomous area of their own); some 80,000 in the Middle East 50,000 in Iraq, 30,000 in Iran, and approximately 15,000 in Syria; the rest reside in states of Europe and America (about 10,000 in the USA).

The Nestorian ecclesiastical hierarchy is headed by the Catholicos, who always bears the title "Mar Shamʿoun" (as the successor of the Apostle Simon Petrus) and whose office passes from uncle to nephew. The Catholicos' seat, since the eightth century in Baghdad, was in recent centuries in Mosul. However, in 1933 Mar Shamʿoun XXI Eshai fled (or was exiled) to Cyprus, from where he later went to the USA, maintaining little contact with his flock in the Middle East. His permanent absence—and also the fact that he broke the rule of celibacy by marrying—caused a schism, and in 1968 part of the Assyrian clergy in Iraq elected the Metropolitan Bishop of Baghdad as (rival) Catholicos. Mar Shamʿoun Eshai was assassinated in California in 1975.

ASWAN DAM The first dam on the Nile river in Upper EGYPT constructed by British engineers in 1898–1902 near Aswan. It is partially controlled by the Nile floods and enabled the transfer of large tracts of land from basin-flooding to permanent irrigation. Its height was raised in 1907–1912 and again in 1933–1935. Its storage lake held approximately 5,500 cubic meters. Several more recent development schemes were based on the original Aswan Dam, such as an electric power station and a fertilizer plant, which were both opened in 1960.

Egypts's most important and most publicized development project since the mid-1950s was the construction of a new, much bigger Aswan Dam (the "High Dam"); 5 miles(8 km.) south of the original structure.

Work was begun in 1960 and completed in 1970, and the High Dam and its power plant were formally opened in January 1971. One of the world's largest man-made lakes—Lake Nasser— formed behind it, 360 miles long, (579 km.) covering approximately 2,000 sq. miles (5,186 sq. km.) and holding 140,000–160,000 cubic meters. The regulated release of its waters added 1.5–2 million acres to Egypt's irrigated area and transformed additional areas, estimated at 700,000 acres to nearly 1 million acres, from partially irrigated one-crop land into permanently irrigated land with several crops each year.

The High Aswan Dam's power plant had a generating capacity of more that 2 million kilowatt, producing up to 6,000 million kilowatt hours per annum. Initial estimates of 10,000 million kilowatt hours proved excessive.) That power contributed significantly to Egypt's industrialization, with several plants constructed near the Aswan Dam and enabled the linking of all Egypt's villages to the national power grid. The cost of the construction of the Aswan Dam was estimated at some 1,5000 million dollars.

Lake Nasser flooded agricultural land and villages with a population of more than 100,000, mostly Nubian, about half of them in SUDAN. Egypt compensated to Sudan, and both countries resettled the displaced villages elsewhere. A large part of them later drifted back and re-established villages on both shores of Lake Nasser. The lake also inundated several sites of ancient Egyptian monuments; the best-known among them, the temple of Abu Simbel, was elevated, at tremendous cost, by an international operation with contributions from many nations.

The regulation of the Nile's seasonal floods through the High Dam and its storage lake, and the resulting expansion of perennial irrigation, have also had negative side-effects. In the absence of the silt deposited by the Nile in its annual flood before the Aswan Dam was erected, stronger erosion along the river and an increase in soil salinity have set in. It is also feared that Egypt's coastline might recede and sea-water might seep in. The incidence of *Bilharzia* has also increased. Sardine fishing off the Egyptian coast was also affected somewhat, although it remains unclear precisely how much. The government of Egypt is endeavoring to counteract such negative effects.

The Aswan Dam project in its initial stages was the subject of an international crisis. Following Egypt's arms deal of 1955 with the Soviet Bloc, the US and the International Bank in 1956 canceled plans to aid the project financially. Egypt reacted by nationalizing the SUEZ CANAL, declaring that its revenues would be used to finance the construction of the Aswan Dam. This culminated in the Anglo-French Suez War of 1956. Egypt also requested aid from the USSR—and the USSR responded. Soviet credits—variously estimated at 220–1,300 million rubles, 300–500 million or more, about one quarter of the cost—were the project's main source of foreign finance. Soviet Engineers and Technicians took a leading part in its design and construction, using mainly Soviet equipment and supplying most of the machinery needed. USSR President Podgorny attended the festive opening of the Aswan Dam. In the later 1970s much of the machinery turned out to be deficient. Most of the power turbines were not operating properly and in constant need of repair. After the change that had occurred in Egypt's political orientation, American experts began executing the repairs needed and replacing parts of the machinery with American equipment.

Lake Nasser The Lake created by the "High Dam" South of Aswan in Egypt and Sudan since the early 1970s.

al-ATASSI Syrian land-owning clan of notables which provided many leaders of modern SYRIA. It was centered in Homs and wielded considerable influence in all of northern Syria. When Syria had a parliamentary regime and political parties were operating, leaders of the Atassi clan were often in opposition to the mainstream of the nationalist movement and the Damascus Government. In the 1940s they were among the founders and leaders of the "People's Party". The following were prominent members of the family:

Hashem al-Atassi (1874?–1960) Politician, three times President of Syria. Educated in Istanbul, Atassi served as district governor in the Ottoman administration. In 1920 he chaired the nationalist Syrian-Arab Congress and was for a short time Prime Minister of the government Amir FEISAL established in Damascus. Under the French Mandate he was one of the leaders of the "National Bloc" which fought for Syrian independence. He headed the delegation which signed the Franco-Syrian Treaty of 1936 providing for Syria's independence with certain privileges to FRANCE, a treaty that was not ratified by France and remained abortive. He was President of Syria, 1936–1939. In the 1940s Atassi drifted away from the mainstream Damascus faction of the National Bloc. He took no active part in the final struggle for complete independence, 1945–1946, and the Syrian governments that ensued. In 1949, after Hinawi's coup, he became Prime Minister, and in December 1949, following Shishakli's coup, President; but Shishakli was the real ruler, behind the scenes, and the President's powers were limited, almost nominal. When the politicians failed in their struggle with the dictator, Atassi resigned in 1951 and began working for the overthrow of Shishakli. Following Shishakli's fall, Atassi returned to the Presidency in 1954; but as real power was again in the hands of shifting officers' cliques, he was frustrated, resigned in September 1955, and retired from politics.

Nur al-Din al-Atassi (1929–1992) Syrian politician. President of Syria 1966–1970. A physician (Damascus University, 1955), Atassi was close to the BA'TH group. After the *Ba'th* officers' coup of 1963 he became

Minister of Interior, 1963–1964, Deputy Prime Minister, 1964–1965, and a member of the Revolutionary Council and the Presidential Council, 1964. In the struggle between rival *Ba'th* factions he was close to the extremist Leftist "military" group, and after that faction came to power in the coup of February 1966, he was made President and Secretary-General of both the "national" (i.e., all-Arab) and "regional" (Syrian) leaderships of the *Ba'th* Party. From 1968 to 1970 Atassi also served as Prime Minister. In the struggle between the factions of Hafez al-ASAD and Salah JADID, he sided with the latter, but tried to mediate. After Asad's semi-coup of 1969, Atassi retained his posts, as part of a compromise settlement; but when Asad took full control in November 1970, Atassi was dismissed from his three posts as President, Prime Minister and Secretary-General, and imprisoned. In August 1992 he was released from prison and in December died in a Paris hospital.

Adnan al-Atassi (b. 1905) The son of Hashem al-Atassi—in the 1950s among the leaders of the "People's Party" and Minister in several governments. Accused, in 1956–1957, of playing a leading role in an "Iraqi-British-American plot", tried and sentenced to death in February 1957 (commuted to prison for life), pardoned by ABDEL NASSER in September 1960 and released into forced

residence in Cairo, he did not return to play an active part in Syrian politics.

Faidi al-Atassi Also a leader of the "People's Party" in the 1950s and a Minister in several governments. He was accused in 1956–1957 of involvement in the Iraqi plot mentioned mentioned above tried (in absentia, as he had fled) and acquitted. He was not active further in Syrian politics.

Feisal al-Atassi One of the leaders of the military coup which overthrew Adib Shishakli in February 1954, but not among the leaders of the regime that followed.

Dr. Jamal al-Atassi (b. 1922) Active as a young psychiatrist and lecturer in the *Ba'th* group and for some time editor of its organ *al-jumhuriyya* (closed in 1959 under Nasser's orders). He later drifted away from the Ba'th and became a leader of the Nasserist "Arab Socialist Union"; in the numerous factional splits of that group he headed, in the 1960s and 1970s, a faction that refused to cooperate with the *Ba'th* and its government and was one of the founders of an anti-*Ba'th* "National Progressive Front" in exile.

Colonel Louay al-Atassi (b. 1926) Close to the *Ba'th* officers' group, he was, after the *Ba'th* coup of 1963, briefly Chief-of-Staff and President of the Revolutionary Council, but was removed in July 1963 in the course of *Ba'th*-Nasserist and intra-*Ba'th* factional struggles.

ATATÜRK, KEMAL MUSTAFA (1881–1938)
Founder and first President of the Turkish Republic. Atatürk was born in Salonica. After studying in the military secondary school in his hometown (and in the military high school in Manastir), he enrolled in the War College in Istanbul and then in the Staff Academy, where he graduated in 1905 as staff captain. He took an early interest in the movement of the YOUNG TURKS, opposing Sultan ABDEL HAMID II's tyranny. On assignment in Damascus he founded a secret society of his own. He was transferred to Salonica, and after the Young Turks revolution in 1909, actively participated in crushing a counter coup in Istanbul which aimed at restoring the old regime.

Gradually, Atatürk grew disenchanted with the ruling party of the Young Turks—the Committee for Union and Progress—comprised largely of officers continuously meddling in politics. He devoted himself to his military assignments which took him to Tripoli (Libya) and then to Sofia as a military attaché. Upon the entry of the OTTOMAN EMPIRE into the War (which he opposed), he was promoted to colonel and appointed commander of the Second Army Corps, responsible for the defense of the Galipoli peninsula against invasion. He was later transferred to the Caucasian and Palestinian fronts, and, following the armistice of Mudros in 1918, returned to Istanbul where he was appointed (after several months) commander of the Ninth Army in Erzurum.

Arriving in Samsun in May 1919 he set out at once to organize and lead the Turkish resistance movement (which was rising all over Anatolia) against the Allies' intentions to divide large parts of the country between them. Resigning his military post, he led the two nationalist congresses in Erzurum and Sivas, and in April 1920 convened the Grand National Assembly in Ankara, cutting his last links with the Sultan's Government in Istanbul.

Overseeing the armed struggle to free the Turkish provinces from foreign occupation, he became the commander in chief of the armed forces in August 1921 and played a major role in halting the Greek advance on the Sakarya River, for which he was granted the title of *Ghazi* (fighter of the faith). Upon the end of the successful war of independence, Atatürk initiated the abolition of the *Ottoman Sultanate* in November 1922. Following the signing of the Treaty of Lausanne, he went on in October 1923 to move the capital to Ankara and announce the Turkish Republic. He was elected its first President, a post to which he was re-elected three times until his death in November 1938. He was elected whilst leading his own Party, the Republican People's Party.

After securing independence, Atatürk embarked upon an ambitious program to enhance Turkey's status in the world, and transform it into a modern nation on the Western model. His biography and the history of Turkey were closely interwoven (see TURKEY. He was greatly successful in improving relations between Turkey and its neighbors as well as with the world powers, under the formula "Peace at Home, Peace in the World". Internally, he was the moving spirit behind the secularization of state and society, bringing about the abolition of the *caliphate* and the religious seminaries (*medreses*) (1924), the closing of all religious orders (*tarikats*) (1925) · and the adoption of new European modeled codes of law (1926). He also initiated the prohibition of the wearing of the *fez* and religious garb; the adoption of the Latin alphabet and the reform of the Turkish language (see TURKEY), and the requirement to choose European style family names in 1934 (he himself chose Atatürk, meaning Father-Turk). Apart from these and other reforms, Atatürk gave top priority to economic development, particularly to industrialization and to the promotion of literacy and education. Ruling in effect as dictator, and harsh towards rebels and opponents, he attempted to abide by legal and democratic rules, and his stated goal remained to "reach the level of contemporary civilization" and establish a Western style order.

In Turkey Atatürk is revered first and foremost as a great war hero and the liberator of the nation. But his ideas and principles, known as *kemalism*, have also exercised a profound influence upon Turkish society, particularly the core of the secular elite made up of professionals, intellectuals, civil servants and military officers. The major principles of *kemalism*, known as the six "arrows" of the Republican People's Party, were written into the constitution in 1937. They included Republicanism, Nationalism, Secularism, Populism, Etatism and Reformism. Although Turkey has over the years deviated in many ways from the strict observance of Kemalist principles, and subsequent constitutions dropped most of them ,they are still taken as the prime guideline for the conduct of state and society. Both Atatürk and his teachings are mentioned in the constitution as models to be followed.

al-ATRASH   see DRUZE.

ATTRITION WAR (1969–1970)   see ARAB-IS-RAEL CONFLICT.

AWN, MICHEL (b. 1935)   Lebanese Maronite-Christian officer and politician, Prime Minister of LEBANON, 1988–1990. After graduating as an artillery Second Lieutenant from the Military Academy in 1958, Awn was sent for complementary and staff training in FRANCE (1958–1959 and 1966) and the USA (1978–1980). He rose through the ranks and in 1976, as Lieutenant-Colonel, commanded the artillery corps. In 1982 he was the Army commander of the Beirut area, considered pro-PHALANGES, and in 1983 commanded the Eighth Brigade (a unit with a clear Christian-Maronite majority) ordered to prevent the DRUZE militia from advancing and taking the Presidential palace in Ba'abda. In 1984, under President Amin JUMAYYIL, he was promoted to the rank of Brigadier-General and appointed Commander of the Lebanese Army, which had disintegrated in 1976 and was trying to avoid further involvement in the Civil War that had erupted in 1975. Awn, coming from a lower-middle-class family (his father was a farmer), had little tolerance for the traditional political bosses (the Zu'ama') or for the militias which took control of state functions. Neither did he feel committed to the Maronite establishment. In the Army Command's view, all these were responsible for the defeat of the army in 1983–1984, and were to step aside and let the army officers try to put things straight. Thus, in summer-autumn 1988, when President Amin Jumayyil's term neared its end and the Lebanese parliament was unable to meet and elect a new president, Awn declared that the army will not remain a mere spectator if elections will not take place. Considering the Lebanese army's traditional abstention from intervening in politics, this was a clear sign of change.

In the last minutes of President Jumayyil's term, in the night between 22 and 23 September 1988, the outgoing president appointed Awn Prime Minister of a military interim government that was to rule until the election of a new president. Although it was the outgoing president's constitutional right to appoint a temporary successor in the absence of a new elected president, the "National Pact" of 1943 determined that the prime minister must be a SUNNI-Muslim (and not a Maronite). This breach of tradition, as well as Awn's anti-Syrian views, aroused strong protest from the Muslim camp: acting Prime Minister Salim al-Huss disputed Awn's appointment, claiming that he and his government were the only legal authority, and formally dismissed Awn from his army command. The Syrians also objected to his nomination, fearing Iraqi (and possibly Israeli) involvement on his behalf. Iraq indeed supplied Awn with weapons as part of its efforts to undermine Asad's domination of Lebanon. Although Awn's military government controlled only Christian East Beirut and parts of the region surrounding it, he held the bulk of the army's fighting force and weapons under his command. What he needed next was to consolidate his rule and gain international support. However, soon he clashed with the Christian-Maronite "Lebanese Forces" (his potential allies) and suppressed them in bloody fighting in February 1989 and again in January 1990. In addition to this, from March 1989 he was involved in fierce battles with Druze militias southeast of Beirut, backed by Syrian troops, which imposed a tight blockade on his area. This pushed him to declare an all-out "war of liberation" against SYRIA, to defend Lebanon's independence—but with little outside support he could do little more than maintain control of East Beirut. In October 1989 the Lebanese Parliament met in Ta'if, SAUDI ARABIA, agreed on the Ta'if "National reconciliation pact", and in November elected a new President, Rene Mu'awwad, and after his assassination, Elias HARAWI, both pro-Syrian candidates. Awn refused to accept that election, held in a Syrian-controlled area and under Syrian auspices, and maintained that his was the only legal government.

All efforts to reach a compromise failed, and on 13 October 1990 the Syrian Army and the various militias arrayed against Awn attacked East Beirut and quickly overcame Awn's troops. (The "Lebanese Forces", his would-be allies, did not come to his help but reportedly took advantage of the situation to settle old scores). The attack was supported by an American "green light" given to Syria in return for its participation in the anti-Iraqi coalition. Awn himself escaped and sought asylum in the French Embassy, ordering his troops to reintegrate into the Lebanese Army and submit to its discipline. He stayed in the embassy until August 1991, due to the Lebanese Government's refusal to let him leave until he had repaid large amounts of money which he had unlawfully appropriated—according to government allegations. Since then he has resided in France, and although is not allowed to take part in public polit-

ical activities and may never return to Lebanon, he is one of the leaders of the Lebanese opposition, condemning the Syrians for occupying Lebanon and calling for the withdrawal of all foreign forces from its soil and for the boycott of the Lebanese parliamentary elections (in 1992 and in 1996).

AZERBAIJAN see IRAN.

al-AZHAR Official mosque of Cairo and the most important institution for the teaching of Islam in Cairo, attracting scholars and students from all over the Islamic world for over a thousand of years. Established in 970 (359 H) by Jawhar the Sicilian by order of the *Fatimid Caliph al-Mu'izz li-Din Allah* to a center of the Shi'te-ISMA'ILIS preaching. Although no official document exists with an explanation of the name of the mosque, it was probably named after Fatima al-Zahra, Prophet Muhammad's daughter, wife of Ali Ibn Abi Talib, the fourth Caliph. The mosque lost its official status under the SUNNI *Ayyubids*, but regained its activity and status during the reign of the Mamluk Sultan Baybars the First (1260-1277). Since the sixteenth century it has been regarded as a principal institution of Islamic theological teaching.

From the nineteenth century onward several attempts were made to reform its medieval methods of teaching. In the late nineteenth century al-Azhar came under sharp criticism for being old-fashioned in its style and content of education not only from the secular elite but also from Muslim reformers such as Muhammad Abdu. Abdu had been the Mufti of EGYPT since 1895 until his death in 1905, during which time he persuaded the Khedive of Egypt to convene an administrative council for reorganizing al-Azhar. Abdu was a member of this council, and in 1895 he implemented modern reforms into this old institution. In 1961, al-Azhar was transformed, according to "Law No. 103" into one of Egypt's five state Universities. From that time on women were admitted to al-Azhar, and several faculties of secular studies were added. Its main function, however, has remained that of teaching Islamic theology. Al-Azhar trains Muslim students from all parts of the world as judges, preachers and Muftis (official expounder of Islamic law), sending teachers abroad. It issues legal-religious opinions and decisions (FATWA), in response to questions from all over the Islamic world. It arranges conferences and publishes Islamic writings and periodicals, the best-known of which is the monthly *Majallat al-Azhar*, and it encourages Islamic missionary work, especially in Africa and the Far East. The *Uluma* (Muslim scholars) of al-Azhar are also involved in politics, promoting the domination of Islamic teachings and the Islamic law (the SHARI'A) in Egyptian society and legislation. Al-Azhar' council of *Ulama* often exercises its religious authority to censor and ban writings of liberal writers and thinkers, claiming that they contradict Islamic principles. Some of these liberal writers and thinkers recently voiced their protests against these measures.

The *Ulama* usually cooperate with the government. In ABDEL NASSER's days, for instance, they propounded the doctrine of Islamic Socialism, while in recent years they have strongly supported the efforts of Presidents AL-SADAT and MUBARAK to strengthen the country's conservative Islamic foundation, while combatting radical Islamic groups (like the MUSLIM BROTHERHOOD and more extremist groups). Al-Azhar also issued *Fatwas* serving Egypt's foreign policies—e.g., a decree denouncing IRAQ's anti-Egyptian and pro-Communist leaders (1959), and several *Fatwas* against ISRAEL. Al-Azhar's publications also contain anti-Israeli and anti-Jewish material. In 1979, however, the Mufti of al-Azhar issued a *Fatwa* which justified and endorsed Sadat's peace treaty with Israel. On the other hand, some of al-Azhar's *sheikhs*, who are paid by the government, collaborate with the Islamic extremist groups, supporting them. In recent years the average number of university students at al-Azhar was over 20,000. In addition, al-Azhar maintains religious schools at different levels in most parts of Egypt.

AZIZ, TAREQ Iraqi politician, a Christian of the Nestorian-Assyrian community. Born in Bashiya, a small village near Mosul. Aziz received his Masters degree in English from the University of Baghdad. He began working as a journalist from 1958 at *al-jumhuriyya*. Being close to the al-*Ba'th* group, he edited the *al-jamahir* and *al-Ishtiraki* papers, considered the party's mouthpieces after the *Ba'th* coup of 1963. From 1969, he edited its main organ, *al-Thawra*. In the 1970s, reportedly from 1972, Aziz was co-opted to the Revolutionary Command Council ruling Iraq—apparently since he had not been a major political leader and in order to have a representative of the Christian communities on the Council—as well as to the *Ba'th* Party High Command. From 1974 to 1977 Aziz was Minister of Information.

In 1979, following the rise to power of Saddam HUSSEIN, Aziz entered the highest echelons of the Iraqi political elite. Aziz was not a decision-making political leader but loyally represented Hussein's foreign policies to the outer world. In 1979 he became Deputy Prime Minister. From January 1983 to March 1991 he was Foreign Minister, and since March 1991 he has been again Deputy Prime Minister. During the Gulf crisis and war of 1990–1991 he was much in the limelight as Iraq's chief negotiator. Aziz conducted Iraq's main discussions with UNSCOM (the United Nations Special Committee that was monitoring Iraq's mass destruction weapons industry).

B

BA'ATH see BA'TH.

BABISM see BAHA'IS.

BAGHDAD PACT see CENTO.

BAHA'IS Adherents of an eclectic religion founded in Persia in 1862–1863 by Mirza Hussein Ali, Baha'ullah (1817–1892). *Baha'ism* grew out of *Babism*, a sectarian deviation of Shi'i ISLAM that was proclaimed in 1843 by Ali Muhammad of Shiraz (1819–1950) *Bab al-Din*, ("The Gate of the Faith") or "The Bab," the forerunner of salvation and the end of days. The Bab was considered a heretic and was executed, and his followers were persecuted and deported. The Baha'is, whose creed stresses the unity of all religious, world peace and universal education, are also considered by many Muslims as heretic deviators from Islam. They were sometimes banned and persecuted in Persia and other Islamic countries. Baha'ullah himself was deported and taken by the Ottoman authorities to Acre, in Palestine (1868). Today *Baha'ism* is outlawed in MOROCCO, EGYPT and SYRIA (since 1960), and IRAQ (since 1970). In IRAN the *Baha'is* are considered to be non-believers and are harassed or persecuted by the Islamic regime.

The Baha'is spiritual leadership is the "Universal House of Justice", composed of nine "Hands". The main leader or Guardian, after Baha'ullah's death, was his son Abbas Effendi, Abdel Baha' (1844–1921), who was succeeded by his grandson Shogi Effendi (1896–1957). The latter was followed by his uncle Amin Effendi (1881–1974), whose leadership was disputed. The *Baha'is* revere the tomb of the Bab in Haifa, and that of Baha'ullah, in Acre, as holy places. The *Baha'is* developed vigorous missionary activities and attracted many followers in the West. Their number is variously estimated at 5 million or more (they claim over 10 million) of whom 50,000–100,000 live in Iran (they claim 700,000 to 1 million) and a few thousand in Arab countries.

BAHRAIN Sheikhdom on the eastern part of the PERSIAN GULF, between the QATAR peninsula and the Saudi Arabian coast is comprised of thirty-three islands, the largest of which is about 12 miles (19 km.) from the coast. Area: 250 sq. miles (648 sq. km.). The population is estimated at less than 600,000 and resides mainly on two islands, Bahrain and Muharraq, which are connected by a causeway. Around one-third of the population are foreigners, mainly Asians, Arabs from other countries, and Iranians. The indigenous inhabitants are mostly Arab, though a considerable part claim Persian origin and an estimated ten to twenty percent speak Persian as their mother tongue. About three-quarters of the population belong to the SHI'A sect of ISLAM. More than half of the population lives in the two main cities: Manama, the capital, and Muharraq.

Bahrain Island has been settled since ancient times because of its springs and oases. Before the Arabs named it al-Bahrain (The Two Seas), it was known as Dilmun. Since the Middle Ages it has been famous for its pearl fishing. After some decades of Portuguese rule in the sixteenth century, Bahrain was ruled intermittently by Persia (1602–1782). While Persia continued claiming sovereignty, the ruler since 1783 has been an Arab Sheikh from the house of AL-KHALIFA. The present Amir is Sheikh Issa ibn Salman Al-Khalifa (b. 1933; ruler since 1961). In the nineteenth century Great Britain became the dominating power in the Gulf. By several treaties and particularly one of 1880, it established a Protectorate over Bahrain too. It also installed a military base and a naval base expanded in 1966, towards the liquidation of the British base in ADEN.

When BRITAIN announced, in 1968, its decision to renounce its Protectorate and withdraw its forces from the Persian Gulf in 1971, IRAN revived its old claim to sovereignty over Bahrain. It agreed, however, to a public opinion poll to be supervised by the Secretary-General of the UN. This took place in April 1970, and a decisive majority favored independence. Iran acquiesced. But under the new, Islamic-revolutionary regime, since 1979, it resumed claims and subversive activities, this time in the name of Islamic fundamentalism. Bahrain intended to join a federation of Arab Gulf principalities (TRUCIAL OMAN, UNITED ARAB EMIRATES). It later retreated, preferring independence—which it proclaimed in August 1971. Since 1981 it has been a member of the GULF COOPERATION COUNCIL (GCC) established that year by Saudia and the five Gulf principalities. The British base was officially evacuated in 1971, but Bahrain kept its facilities at Britain's disposal, though in a more limited way. Moreover, in 1971 it granted similar facilities to the US, amounting virtually to a naval base. This agreement was terminated in 1973. In mid-1977 the US base was handed over. Certain minor facilities, however, remained at the disposal of the US. The military connection with the US was revived as a result of the Iraqi invasion of KUWAIT in 1990 and the war that followed. This new rapprochement led to the signing, in October 1991, of an agreement granting the US access to Bahraini facilities and allowing it to pre-position war material on Bahrainian soil. Since 1995 Bahrain has served as headquarters for the renewed US fifth fleet.

Demands for a measure of popular government and free political organization have been voiced in Bahrain since the 1930s. However, attempts to establish elected councils were not entirely successful. In the 1950s and 1960s, such demands were renewed, and the ruler set up partly elected advisory councils for health, education and other areas. In the late 1960s and early 1970s, political agitation revived—supported or triggered by foreign workers with Nasserist, BA'TH, PLO leanings and by underground groups considered "Leftist", mainly Shi'a. These were partly based abroad and supported by foreign interests (SOUTH YEMEN, IRAQ). This led to unrest and riots that were suppressed. However, a government was formally constituted in 1971, with the ruler's brother, Sheikh Khalifa ibn Salman, as Prime Minister and several other members of the ruling family among the Ministers. Late in 1972 the ruler granted a measure of self-government. A constituent assembly was elected with government ministers and appointees of the Emir joining the twenty-two elected members. In 1973 a constitution was fully proclaimed. Under that constitution, elections for a National Assembly were held in December 1973. In 1974–1975, however, agitation was resumed by The Popular Front which the regime considered subversive, leftist and linked with foreign revolutionary plots, but had supporters within the National Assembly. In 1975 the Assembly was dissolved and has not been reconstituted since. The ruler has quoted several reasons from the Islamic Revolution in Iran (1979), to the first Gulf War (1980–1988) and the invasion of Kuwait and the second GULF WAR (1991) . However, the actual reason was an attempt to avert an election showdown with the opposition. In order to quiet the opposition, the Emir announced the establishment of a consultative council in 1992, all of whose members were appointed by him.

The friction between the Shi'a majority and the Sunni-led Government has been a constant constraint in Bahraini politics. In December 1981 an attempt to topple the regime and establish an Islamic republic on the KHOMEINI pattern—reportedly instigated and organized by Iran—was foiled. Since then sporadic waves of violence, at times pretty intense, flared up. One of the worst waves began in late 1994 and continued until the end of 1996. Bahrainian opposition is active from within, mainly by Iranian support and through local cells of HIZBAL-LAH, and from outside in the western hemisphere. The discovery of a cell of the Iranian supported *Hiz-ballah* led in 1996 to the recalling of the Bahraini ambassador to Tehran and the curtailingt of relations between the two countries.

Bahrain's economy, (historically focusing on fisheries and pearl fishing), has moved closer to oil since the 1930s. However, due to the limited oil reserves, Bahrain has tried to diversify its sources of income.

An American company discovered oil in 1932 and started production in 1933. After nationalization in 1979, and as a result of the changes in the oil market, oil revenues have declined since the early 1980s. (For dates of production and revenues see OIL). Yet it has provided the bulk of Bahrain's national income and government revenue and enabled the gradual development of other branches of the economy. Since the mid-1970s Bahrain has become a major financial center, with some seventy international banks operating—many of them as offshore banks. This source of income also declined due to the crisis in the oil market. A refinery (capacity: 250,000 barrels per day) and an aluminum plant (capacity: 180,000 metric tons annually), opened in 1971, which have added their share to the Bahrain economy.

BAKER FIVE POINTS   see ARAB-ISRAEL PEACE-MAKING.

BAKHTIAR, SHAHPUR (1914–1991) Iranian politician, the last Prime Minister before the Islamic revolution took over power in Iran. Graduated in international law and political science from Paris University, and completed his Ph.D. In 1940, while in FRANCE, Bakhtiar was enlisted to the French army for eighteen months and his participation in the war against the Nazis had a profound influence on his personality.

Bakhtiar returned to IRAN in 1946. Until 1948 he worked for the Ministry of Labor. He was associated with the leftist Iran Party. In 1951–1952 he joined Dr. Mohammad MOSSADDEQ's National Front government as Deputy Minister of Labor. After Mossaddeq's fall in 1953 he was forced to retire from public service. He began practicing law and remained active in opposition groups. He constantly criticized the Shah, comparing his rule to the Nazi regime and his secret police (SAVAK) to the Gestapo. His subsequent arrests only increased his hostility toward the regime.

In January 1979 the Shah's power was threatened by the Islamic forces. US advisers advised him to appoint a government not identified with his autocratic and corrupt regime. He was seen as a pro-Western Social-Democrat, and was appointed Prime Minister. Though he had struggled against the Shah for years, Bakhtiar did not call for his deposition, but for a constitutional monarchy based on the British model.

As a modernist, secularist and liberal, Bakhtiar opposed the growing influence of the Islamic clergy, and declined an alliance between his NATIONAL FRONT and the Islamic opposition headed by KHOMEINI. Bakhtiar abolished the Savak and declared that Iran would no longer be the policeman of the PERSIAN GULF. Neither the Islamic fundamentalists nor the left accepted him, seeing him as a representative of the old regime. He was expelled from the National Front. When the Islamic revolution was won in February 1979 and Khomeini returned to Iran, he was dismissed after only thirty-eight days in power. After his resignation was announced, Bakhtiar went underground and after several days managed to leave Iran. In July 1979 he turned up in Paris and announced the establishment of the National Resistance Movement of Iran with the goal of deposing the Islamic regime in Iran. Though he advocated cooperation among all the various opposition groups, he refused in fact to cooperate with some of them. He attacked Abul-Hassan BANI-SADR, Rajavi of the *Mujahiedin Khalqh*, and the left. The only one he cooperated with was the Shah's son.

Bakhtiar's struggle against the Shah had made him popular. However, he was swept aside by the Islamic revolution. His reported meetings with Iraq's Saddam HUSSEIN were searching for his support for the Iranian opposition on the eve of the IRAN-IRAQ WAR. His eagerness to initiate a counter-revolution, turned public opinion against him. In his Paris exile, he had little influence. In July 1980 Bakhtiar escaped an assassination attempt but was finally murdered in Paris in August 1991.

BALFOUR DECLARATION A statement of British policy conveyed by Foreign Secretary Arthur J. Balfour on 2 November 1917 to Lord Rothschild. Largely the result of the efforts of Zionist leader Chaim WEIZMAN, it stated that "His Majesty's government view with favour the establishment in Palestine of a national home for the Jewish people, and will use their best endeavours to facilitate the achievement of this object, it being clearly understood that nothing shall be done which may prejudice the civil and religious rights of existing non-Jewish communities in Palestine, or the rights and political status enjoyed by Jews in any other country." The state-

ment deliberately spoke of a "national home" rather than a state, and contrary to the earlier drafts, mentioned the "existing non-Jewish communities in Palestine."

The British issued the declaration in the hope that it would win over American Jewish support for the entry of the US into World War I; convince Russian Jews to support Bolshevik Russia's continued participation in the War; forestall any German effort to gain Jewish support by issuing a similar delcaration (the Germans did, in fact, issue a lukewarm delcaration on 5 January 1918); and improve British chances of retaining Palestine as a strategic asset. The Arabs argued that the British declaration constituted a British promise to the Jews of a land which was not theirs to dispose of, and that it contradicted the MCMAHON-HUSSEIN CORRESPONDENCE of July 1915–March 1916.

BANDUNG CONFERENCE In April 1955 the first conference of the independent states of Asia and Africa convened in Bandung, Indonesia. Its leading initiators were the Prime Ministers of India (Jawaharlal Nehru), Pakistan, Indonesia, Burma and Ceylon. High-ranking delegations from twenty-nine countries attended—twenty-three from Asia and six from Africa; of these, nine were Arab states: six from Asia and three from Africa. Among them were the major leaders of Asia and Africa—Nehru, Chou En-Lai, Sukarno, U Nu, Nkrumah, Sihanouk, Pham Van Dong and ABDEL NASSER. The participants included all the then independent Asian and African nations—except ISRAEL and Korea, who were deliberately excluded; "Nationalist China" (Taiwan), which would not attend a congress recognizing the People's Republic of China as representing China; the Asian republics of the USSR; and Mongolia. Both South and North Vietnam attended. The sponsors of the Bandung Conference, led by Nehru and the U Nu of Burma, wished to invite Israel; but when the Arab states threatened to boycott it if it was invited, they gave in.

The Bandung Conference was meant to mark a new era, the appearance on the stage of history of hitherto oppressed nations, and the end of colonialism. It deliberately avoided any discussion of controversial political issues and stressed mainly the newly won independence of the nations of Asia and Africa, their cooperation and the struggle against colonialism where it still ruled. It solemnly endorsed the "Five Principles" (*Panch Sila*) formulated by Nehru (in his joint statement with Chou En-Lai of China, June 1954): mutual respect for the territorial integrity and sovereignty of all states; nonaggression; noninterference in the internal affairs of other states; "equality and mutual benefit"; and peaceful coexistence. It called for economic and cultural cooperation and proclaimed its support for the principles of human rights and self-determination, the abolition of colonialism, and world peace. Among specific "anticolonial" struggles mentioned and supported was Yemen's position on ADEN and "the southern parts of Yemen known as the Protectorate." The final declaration expressed support for "the rights of the Arab people of Palestine" and called for the implementation of the UN resolutions on Palestine and a peaceful settlement.

It also denounced the "persistent denial to the peoples of North Africa of their right to self-determination," supporting the right of ALGERIA, MOROCCO and TUNISIA to independence, and called for the admission to the UN of Asian and African states not yet admitted (including, in the Arab world, JORDAN and LIBYA).

The countries participating in the Bandung Conference had differing political and ideological orientations. The Conference did not discuss these issues let alone adopt decisions concerning them, but the general trend was unmistakably towards neutralist attitudes, nonalignment. In fact, the borderline between Asian-African, i.e. geographical and non-ideological criteria, and the emergence of the Bandung Conference as the nucleus of a neutralist movement, was blurred. This double function of the Bandung Conference became even more evident in the years that followed it. Attempts to organize the nations of Asia and Africa in a permanent body failed, as did efforts to convene another gathering of all Asian-African governments, in a "second Bandung Conference" (while nongovernmental Afro-Asian organizations were established). A group of non-aligned nations, on the other hand, held several conferences and established a near-permanent bloc—and regarded these activities in large measure as a continuation of the Bandung Conference.

The Bandung Conference was the stage for the first appearance of several leaders in the international arena. Thus the People's Republic of China appeared for the first time at a major international gathering, and her Prime Minister, Chou En-Lai, made important contacts and emerged as a major leader on the world scene. The same goes for several Arab countries; particularly for Egypt's Gamal Abdel Nasser. The Bandung marked his first appearance on the international scene, his emergence as a major leader and co-founder of the neutralist bloc and the beginning of a more activist Egyptian foreign policy.

BANI-SADR, ABUL-HASSAN (b. 1931) The first President of the Islamic Republic of IRAN. Born in the town of Hamedan to a religious family. He studied economics and sociology at The University of Tehran. In the early 1950s he was active in the NATIONAL FRONT OF IRAN led by Mohammad MOSSADDEQ and participated in student demonstrations against the Shah. In 1963 he visited ISRAEL with a group of Iranian students by invitation of the Israeli government. In 1964 Bani-Sadr was arrested by the SAVAK. After his release, he moved to Paris for doctoral studies at the Sorbonne, where he carried on extensive activities within the framework of the Confederation of Iranian Students. Due to his religious inclinations, he joined the Islamic Students Organization within the framework of the Confederation. In 1977 he traveled to Najaf in IRAQ where KHOMEINI was in exile. Khomeini took a liking to him, and when Iraq decided to expel Khomeini by request of the Shah, and KUWAIT refused to receive him, Bani-Sadr proposed that he move to Paris. Once Khomeini was in Paris, Bani-Sadr became his Liaison Officer with the Western press and one of his close assistants. In November 1979, nine months after the Islamic revolution in Iran, Bani-Sadr was appointed Foreign Minister and later Minister of Economics and Finance. In the elections of January 1980, he was elected President of Iran by seventy-five percent of the voters, with the unqualified support of Khomeini, who saw in him a link between the religious leaders on the one hand, and the secularists and intellectuals on the other.

In February 1980 he was appointed Chairman of the Islamic Revolutionary Council. He ran the state until the elections to the Majlis in the spring of that year. Upon the outbreak of the war with Iraq, Khomeini appointed him Acting Supreme Commander of the Armed Forces (which according to the Islamic constitution, is reserved for the leader himself). However, his popularity started to wane after the religious camp in the Majlis stopped supporting him. A member of the Majlis Khamenei was the following year elected President and later on, Spiritual Leader. He spoke out against Bani-Sadr and demanded his expulsion. Bani-Sadr also angered Khomeini when he accused the institutions of the revolution of trampling over human rights. In June 1981 he was impeached by order of Khomeini and forced to escape to Paris dressed as a woman in an air force plan together with Mas'ud Rajavi, leader of the guerrilla organization MOJAHEDIN-E KHALQ-E. He settled in Versaille, in a castle put at his disposal by the French Government. Together with Rajavi he established the National Council of Resistance of Iran. However, in 1984 their roads parted—both against an ideological background and because of the willingness of the Mojahedin to transfer the center of their activity to Iraq, which was in a state of war with Iran.

Bani-Sadr still considers himself "the elected President" of Iran and actively opposes the regime. He was a major witness in the trial before a court in Berlin, in the case of the murder of four opponents of the Iranian regime (including the leader of the Kurdish Democratic Party of Iran) on German soil. The court ruled in April 1997 that the murders had been committed on the order of the highest echelons of the Islamic regime in Iran.

al-BANNA, HASSAN   see MUSLIM BROTHERS, BROTHERHOOD.

al-BANNA SABRI KAHALIL   see ABU NIDAL

BARAK (BRUG), EHUD (b. 1942)   The most highly decorated Israeli officer, a former Chief of Staff and politician. Born in Mishmar Hasharon, ISRAEL, he was enlisted to the IDF in 1959. After being appointed Deputy Chief of Staff in 1987, he became Chief of Staff in 1991.

In 1968 Barak completed a first degree in physics and mathematics at The Hebrew University in JERUSALEM, and in 1987, a second degree in systems analysis at Stanford University in California. As Chief of Staff he met the Syrian Chief of Staff in Washington, within the framework of the bilateral talks between Israel and SYRIA. He left the IDF on 1 January 1995, and spent a short time in the US. In July 1995,

after a brief period in business, Barak joined the government of Yitzhak RABIN as Minister of the Interior. Following Rabin's assassination, he was appointed Minister for Foreign Affairs in the government of Shimon PERES. He came in second in the Labor Party primaries toward the elections for the fourteenth Knesset (1996) and in the primaries to the Labor Party leadership, held in June 1997, Barak was elected from among four candidates by a 50.33% majority. Barak, who is highly knowledgeable on a large variety of subjects, is generally regarded as heir to Rabin's political heritage.

BARZANI (or **BARAZANI**) (see also KURDS)   Kurdish tribe and clan in northern IRAQ, leaders of Kurdish rebellions. Originally a branch of the (Sunni) Sufi Naqshabandi order (see DERVISH ORDERS, the Barzani's assumed the characteristics of a tribe in the nineteenth century. Their center is the village of Barzan, some 50 miles north of Arbil. The Barzani sheikhs, always involved in feuds with rival Kurdish clans, and in constant competition for predominance among their tribes, were traditionally semi-feudal, tribal-type leaders of their community, maintaining a sort of de facto autonomy in their mountain valleys, closely linked to related tribes across the border in IRAN. Through interaction with Kurdish nationalist groups in the towns or in exile, the Barzani tribal sheikhs gradually became involved in a revolutionary nationalist upheaval—though never uncontested—leaders. From 1915 the head of the tribe was Sheikh Ahmad Barzani (d. 1969), a religious eccentric, often considered mentally disturbed. In the 1930s and early 1940s he was identified with the leaders of the Kurdish rebellions, but later faded out of the political and military struggle.

The leader of the Kurds in their national struggle from the late 1930s was Sheikh Ahmad's younger brother, Mulla Mustafa Barzani (1903–1979). He was arrested with his brother Sheikh Ahmad in the early 1930s and spent the following years in and out of prison, and in exile (mainly in Iran). He returned in 1943 and assumed the leadership of a new rebellion. In 1945–1946 he again crossed into Iran and in 1946 he commanded the army of the short-lived Kurdish Republic of MAHABAD. After its collapse, he escaped with a band of followers to the USSR, which supported the Mahabad Republic regardless of its non-Communist ideology. He stayed in Russia until he was allowed to return to Iraq after QASSEM's coup of 1958. He and his men supported Qassem against both Nasserist and Communist attempts to take over the country, but he himself was not allowed to leave Baghdad. In 1960, when Kurdish hopes for a political reward in the form of Kurdish autonomy were disappointed by the Qassem regime and a new rebellion began fermenting, Barzani escaped to the Kurdish mountains and assumed the leadership of the rebellion that re-erupted in 1961. Barzani had obtained significant aid from the Shah of Iran and was able to use Iranian territory as a supply base and staging area. He also reportedly obtained military aid, including arms supplies and training, from Israel.

While Barzani's leadership remained essentially traditional and tribal, he maintained a firm alliance with political nationalist groups and formally headed the modernist-socialist Kurdish Democratic Party (KDP) that led the national struggle from the 1950s. Yet his leadership was beset by both tribal and political-factional rivalries and defections, and his rivals (such as Jalal TALABANI who headed a faction considered Marxist) frequently collaborated with the Iraqi authorities. Throughout the rebellion Barzani conducted negotiations with the Iraqi government, offering to end the rebellion in return for far-reaching autonomy for the Kurds. An agreement conceding a large part of Barzani's demands was reached in June 1966; but as it was not implemented, the rebellion re-erupted in 1968. A new agreement, even more far-reaching, was signed with the BA'TH regime in March 1970. The Kurds held that the agreement was not honestly implemented, and in March 1974 Barzani's fighters, the *Pesh Merga*, resumed fighting. But in March 1975, an agreement between Iraq and Iran stipulated *inter alia*, that the Shah would stop his aid to the Kurdish rebels, leading to the collapse of the Kurdish rebellion. On 20 March 1975, Barzani announced its end in defeat and he himself was among more than 100,000 refugees who escaped to Iran. He found refuge in the US, where he died in 1979. One of Barzani's sons, Ubaidullah, was reported to be collaborating with the Baghdad Government. Two others, Idris and mainly Mas'ud, continued from the late 1970s to try to rebuild the KDP and resume armed resistance through collaboration with KHOMEINI's Iran. Idris died in January 1987 and Mas'ud Barzani assumed the KDP leadership (with his nephew, Nechirvan, as his deputy).

Mas'ud Barzani (b. 1947) was brought up in Moscow during his father's exile following the collapse of the Kurdish Republic of Mahabad. Although he collaborated with Iran's Islamic regime—which helped him set up autonomous zones along the Iranian border during its war with Iraq—his relations with Teheran never developed into an alliance due to the secular nature of the KDP.

As the KDP leader, Mas'ud Barzani led the rapprochement with the Patriotic Union of Kurdistan (PUK), which resulted in an understanding in July 1987 on the creation of the Iraqi-Kurdistan front. However, the two rival Kurdish factions failed to maintain cooperation, continuing their traditional tribal squabbles over territory, power and resources, occasionally betraying each other by collaborating with one or more of the governments concerned with the Kurdish problem. Thus, while Talabani was supported by Iran and SYRIA, Barzani maintained secret ties with the Iraqi regime, and more overt alliances with the Turkish Government.

With the defeat of Iraq in 1991 by the international coalition, Mas'ud led the rebellion against Baghdad, which was swiftly repressed, resulting in another wave of Kurdish exiles—this time into Turkey—and intervention by the international anti-Iraq coalition and creation of a protected Kurdish zone. Mas'ud Barzani took part in the subsequent talks with the Iraqi government, which ended in failure. He later cooperated with other Kurdish factions, mainly Talabani's PUK, in holding elections for a Kurdish assembly in May 1992, following which the two main factions shared power in the protected zone. However, within two years, this arrangement came to an end due to renewed competition for power. Repeated attempts by the Turkish and US governments to effect a cease-fire between the warring factions proved to be short-lived. In August 1996, fearing the PUK's strengthening power, thanks to massive Iranian military support, Mas'ud Barzani colluded with Saddam HUSSEIN in initiating an offensive against PUK forces during which the KDP captured its rival's central cities, including Arbil and Sleimaniya. The PUK succeeded in recovering most of its strongholds—except for Arbil—but the deep cleavages between these two factions remained unresolved.

BASES, FOREIGN (MILITARY/NAVAL/AIR)

The right to maintain military forces and permanent military bases in the countries of the Middle East, was, for many years, an important policy aim of the great powers. It was to be attained either forcibly, through colonial or semi-colonial occupation, as usual until World War I, or by agreement with the host country, as preferred since World War I.

In the pre-World War I period, Great Britain maintained forces and military bases in EGYPT (since 1882), in Aden and several islands nearby (since 1839), and in the PERSIAN GULF (since the 1820s), as well as in Cyprus (since 1878) and Somaliland (since 1881) and MOROCCO (1912—de facto since the beginning of the century); Italy—in LIBYA (1912), as well as in SOMALIA and on the Etritrean coast of the Red Sea (since 1880s). Spain had bases in Morocco—under a protectorate imposed in 1912—and in several towns on Morocco's Mediterranean coast that it considered to be Spanish territory. The main development of foreign military bases occurred between the two world wars. Italy maintained its military base in Libya and ERITREA (also conquering Ethiopia in 1935–1936). BRITAIN kept and expanded its military base in Egypt (mainly in Alexandria port and the SUEZ CANAL Zone), Aden and the Persian Gulf, and obtained new ones in IRAQ, Palestine and Transjordan. FRANCE maintained its military base in the MAGHREB and acquired new ones in SYRIA and LEBANON. Britain's military presence was sanctioned in Iraq, Palestine and Transjordan by League of Nations MANDATES; it was approved by the host country in Iraq (treaty of 1930), Transjordan (treaties of 1928, 1946 and 1948), and Egypt (treaty of 1936). However, these treaties, signed by Iraq and Egypt after protracted negotiations, remained controversial, and a struggle for the restriction or abolition of Britain's military presence continued. France's military base was sanctioned in TUNISIA and Morocco by the protectorate treaties, and in Syria/Lebanon by a League of Nations Mandate. A treaty of 1936 containing Syrian and Lebanese approval of France's military presence was never ratified by France, remaining abortive. Spain's Moroccan base was sanctioned by the protectorate.

During World War II Britain's military presence was strengthened. (An Iraqi attempt to expel British troops and occupy their base by military force was defeated in 1941.) France's presence was weakened by its defeat in 1940. Its forces in the Maghreb and Syria/Lebanon collaborated, under the Vichy regime, with the Axis powers being virtually neutralized. Late in 1942, American and allied forces occupied Morocco and Algeria, and Tunisia was taken over by the German army to be conquered in 1943 by British and allied forces. Syria/Lebanon was occupied in 1941 by the British and Free French forces, and a Free French military presence was established. Italy was expelled from Libya, Somalia and Eritrea (as well as Ethiopia). Britain and Free France established a military presence and bases in Libya.

After World War II, the nationalist struggle for the abolition of foreign-imperial military bases intensified, and eventually all foreign military bases in Arab countries were liquidated. France was compelled to withdraw its forces from Syria and Lebanon in 1945–1946 (the UNITED STATES OF AMERICA (US) and particularly Britain supporting the two countries' insistent demand). French bases and forces were evacuated from Morocco and Tunisia in 1961 and 1963—after the failure of an attempt to maintain a privileged relationship and military base, even after the two countries had attained full independence in 1956. The withdrawal of French bases and forces from Algeria (agreed on when Algeria became independent in 1962 was completed in 1968. The handful of troops France kept in the Fezzan area of southern Libya were withdrawn in 1956, at Libya's request. The withdrawal of Spanish bases and troops from Morocco was agreed, as a by-product of France's withdrawal and Morocco's independence, in 1956. It was completed in what had been the northern Spanish Protectorate in 1958. In the southern Protectorate (Tarfaia region), 1961 and in the Ifni enclave, 1969. It did not apply to the "Presidios" on the Mediterranean coast, around Ceuta and Melilla, considered by Spain, though not by Morocco, as being part of its territory.

Britain's military bases were also liquidated one by one. Its presence in Palestine ended in 1948. In Egypt, its military base outside the Suez Canal Zone was handed over in 1947. As to those in the Canal Zone, and the presence of its troops there, it was agreed in 1954, after a long struggle, to evacuate them—while civilian British technicians would maintain the base. The military evacuation was completed in 1956, but the agreement to leave British technicians at the Suez Canal zone was invalidated by

Egypt in 1956–1957 following the Suez crisis and the Anglo-French invasion. The two British military bases in Iraq, Habbaniyya and Shu'eiba, were relinquished in 1955 following an Anglo-Iraqi agreement, to be turned into joint base under the Baghdad Pact. Yet that lapsed when Iraq withdrew from the Baghdad Pact in 1959. In 1956–1957, JORDAN ended its special military links with Britain, including the financing of Jordan's Army, the "Arab Legion", by Britain and the employment of British officers under contract as commanders of that Army. The British base in Aden was abandoned in 1967, when independence was granted to SOUTH YEMEN.

Libya had agreed in 1953 to lease to Britain military bases (mainly at al-Adem and Tobruk). In 1964 it was agreed, at Libya's request, to terminate Britain's military presence, and its troops evacuated Tripolitania in 1966 and Cyrenaica in 1968, but kept the two main bases. Late in 1969, Libya's new revolutionary regime demanded their liquidation, too, and they were handed over in March 1970. In the Persian Gulf, Britain relinquished its protecting presence in KUWAIT in 1961. In 1971 Britain renounced it in the whole Gulf area and liquidated its military base at BAHRAIN and SHARJA (with certain facilities reportedly remaining at its disposal in Bahrain). Britain maintained a special military relationship with OMAN (formerly "Muscat and Oman"), with British officers, on contract, commanding the country's armed forces, and some military base (including one on Masira Island in the Arabian Sea). However, it was agreed in 1976 to close these bases in 1977—though certain "facilities" were to remain at Britain's disposal.

The US had, prior to World War II, no military base in Arab countries. Apart from its operations in Morocco and ALGERIA, it established a military base in Libya and a modest, auxiliary military presence in the Persian Gulf (see also IRAN). During the war, however, several bases were set up in Morocco from 1942–1943 to serve war operations. The US kept these bases after the war, but handed them over, in an agreement with Morocco, in 1963—though certain facilities remained at its disposal. Under a 1954 agreement the US obtained an air base in Lybia ("Wheelus Field"). At Libya's request it was evacuated in 1970. The US also built a base at Dhahran in SAUDI ARABIA, completed in 1946. The lease, formalized in 1951, was terminated in 1961, and the base was returned to Saudi Arabia in 1962, with

certain aviation privileges remaining at US disposal. In 1971, the US obtained certain naval facilities, never called a base, in Bahrain; that country announced their termination in 1973, and in 1977 the base was handed over—again with certain facilities retained. In 1980, when the US was planning to establish a "Rapid Deployment Force" for the defense of the Persian Gulf and the Middle East, Oman and Somalia (as well as Kenya) reportedly agreed to put certain air and naval "facilities"— never officially called bases—at its disposal. These US plans did not fully materialize, but some military installations were constructed on Oman's shores, in its Ras Musandam enclave, and on Masira Island. Egypt also agreed in principle to allow the US to construct "facilities" on the Red Sea coast, mainly at Ras Banas. Major construction was delayed by disagreements over details, but some work seems to have been done. The US was reported to enjoy additional facilities, *inter alia* for electronic surveillance in Egypt and Saudia.

The USSR never confessed to the possession of a military base in the Arab states. It kept, however, a considerable number of military personnel as instructors, advisors and technicians in several Arab countries—Egypt and Syria since the late 1950s, later also Iraq, Algeria, Somalia, Libya and South Yemen—to aid the defense and the armed forces of these countries. In the course of these aid operations, it was frequently reported that Soviet military personnel served the USSR's own strategic and military aims and that military installations of the countries aided—such as the ports of Alexandria and Mersa Matruh in Egypt, Ladhiqiyya in Syria, airfields in both countries, air and naval facilities in South Yemen (Aden and Socotra island) and Libya—were at Russia's disposal, though not amounting to a fully-fledged military base. Egypt terminated the Soviet military presence in 1972, as did Somalia in 1977. Iraq seemed to have moved away, in the 1980s, from its close links with the USSR. A Soviet military presence, officially advisory and defined as technical aid, continues in Syria, Libya and South Yemen today.

al-BASHIR, OMAR HASSAN (b. 1935) Sudanese officer and politician, since July 1989 ruler of SUDAN. During his long years of service in the Sudanese army, rising to the rank of Major-General, Bashir was not involved in political affairs and did

not become prominent. However, as Sudan's civilian, elected government (established in 1985–1986, after the fall of NUMEIRI) deteriorated in continuous crisis, he staged a coup on 30 June 1989, with a group of fellow officers. However, the main force behind the coup was the National Islamic Front (NIF) of Hassan al-TURABI who emerged as the "strong man" of the regime.

Immediately after coming to power, Bashir dismissed the Government, dissolved Parliament, suspended the constitution and banned political parties; he also detained several leaders of the regime he deposed. In July 1989 Bashir formed his own Government. He has ruled Sudan since 1989 as de facto Head of State and Prime Minister. Bashir has not emerged as an inspiring leader and has not seriously tackled any of Sudan's major problems—such as its economic crisis (leading to repeated famines), the continuous civil war with the rebellious African tribes in the South, or the imposition of the punishment code of Islamic Law (the SHARI'A). In an attempt to reshape the regime of Sudan and settle the southern rebellion, he convened several consultative conferences, where a federal system of government was mooted as a solution; but nothing further was done and no serious talks were held with the rebels. In the elections of March 1996, Bashir had a landslide victory.

Several attempts to topple Bashir have been vaguely reported, but his rule has so far not been seriously challenged. However, at the end of 1996 and beginning of 1997, with the deterioration of the economic situation in Sudan, there were some signs of instability that posed a threat to the Bashir-Turabi regime. At the end of 1996, riots erupted in Khartoum following an increase in bread prices. In the first half of 1997, opposition forces initiated a series of attacks in the southern and eastern parts of the country, backed by Eritrea, Uganda, Ethiopia and possibly the US and EGYPT. The aim of the attacks was to bring about the collapse of the regime. So far success has been only partial. Rumors of disagreements between Bashir and Turabi have become more and more persistent but the two appear to understand that the survival of the regime depends on their cooperation.

BASSIJ PARA-MILITARY INSTITUTION see
IRAN.

BA'TH (Arabic: Renaissance) Pan-Arab socialist party. It originated in SYRIA which has remained the area of its main activities and influence. It has ruled Syria since 1963, and IRAQ, by a rival faction, since 1968. The *Ba'th*'s doctrine is radically Pan-Arab; it regards the various Arab states as temporary entities to be replaced by a united all-Arab state—by revolutionary violence or subversion if need be. Accordingly, each of its own branches in the ARAB countries is but a regional leadership (*qiada qutriyya*), subject to a "national", all-Arab (*qiyada qawmiyya*) leadership. In fact, as the *Ba'th* has been deeply split since 1966, with two rival all-Arab leaderships, one Syrian and one Iraqi, the "regional" leaderships in Syria and Iraq were co-opted by the regimes into the state institutional structure. The *Ba'th* slogans are "Unity, Liberty, Socialism" and "One Arab Nation of an Eternal Mission". While the party's Pan-Arab vision is unequivocal and simple, its socialist doctrine is rather vague and avoids clear-cut social, economic and ideological definitions or political programs. It is based on far-reaching nationalizations, a mixed economy of state and private enterprise (with the state as the central element), and a populist semi-totalitarian regime. It claims a single-party monopoly not for itself but for a "national-progressive" front headed by the *Ba'th* and comprising other groups acceptable to the *Ba'th* as "Socialist-Unionist" (usually including the Communists), and bans all other political organizations. The *Ba'th* was originally secularist. In its political practice it has come to terms with the Islamic character of the Arab state, but it opposes and has suppressed extremist-fundamentalist Islamic groups—Sunni in Syria, Shi'i in Iraq. In Syria this issue is aggravated by the fact that the *Ba'th* leadership, from the President down, contains a disproportionally large number of ALAWIS—a sect on the margins of Shi'i ISLAM, considered by most Muslims as heretical and by many as outside Islam.

The *Ba'th* was founded in the mid-1930s as a small group of students and young intellectuals, by two teachers from Syria studying in Paris: Michel AFLAQ, who became its chief ideologist, and Salah-ul-Din Bitar (1912–1980), later Prime Minister of Syria (1963–1964, January–February 1966). The first congress of the "Arab Renaissance Party" (*Hizb al-Ba'th al-Arabi*), still a small group of young men, was held in 1947. Shortly afterwards, it spread also to Palestine, LEBANON and Iraq. In 1947 and 1949 party members stood unsuccessfully in Syrian elections. Secretary-General Aflaq briefly served in 1949 as Minister of Education. In 1953 the party merged with Akram Hourani's "Arab Socialist Party", to become the "Arab Socialist Renaissance Party" (*Hizb al-Ba'th al-Arabi al-Ishtiraki*). It played a role in the overthrow of Adib Shishakli's dictatorship in February 1954. In the Syrian elections that same year, it won fifteen seats, and in the following four years its influence steadily increased in Syria. The party's attraction for young intellectuals and officers was its bold, crisply formulated ideology, its Pan-Arab doctrine, its anti-imperialist, anti-capitalist slogans and its anti-Israel extremism; but the party's real political influence, its transformation from a small group of debating students and young intellectuals into a powerful faction with clout, was due to its ability to recruit among army officers. Whenever the *Ba'th* seized power, it was through coups carried out by army officers and wherever it was able to hold that power, it was the *Ba'th* army officers who wielded it (assisted by the all-pervasive secret police they established). This link with officers' juntas was forged in Syria, Iraq, JORDAN and other Arab states. However, only in Syria and Iraq did the party officers manage to sieze power. While in Jordan, SUDAN, Yemen and TUNISIA the *Ba'th* remained an ineffective group of plotting, subversive intellectuals. Once in power, however, the *Ba'th* officers were guided by state and army interests and the exigencies of power politics rather than by *Ba'th* ideology.

In 1957, the Syrian *Ba'th* officers were a major pressure group pushing Syria towards union with EGYPT in the UNITED ARAB REPUBLIC (UAR), February 1958. The *Ba'th* expected to become the ruling party and the ideological mentor of the new state; but President ABDEL NASSER insisted on the dissolution of all parties other than his single-party "National Union", and of the *Ba'th* in particular. Nasser's doctrine of Arab nationalism, and since the late 1950s Arab socialism, was perhaps influenced by *Ba'th* ideology; but he never acknowledged that debt and remained suspicious of and hostile to the *Ba'th* as a political organization. During the period of the UAR, the *Ba'th* maintained some underground cells, but its leaders were gradually eliminated from positions of power and influence. In the summer of 1959 the

Syrian party leadership, whose activity had been ceased in Syria, renewed its activities in Lebanon. Their growing opposition to Nasser's authoritarian rule of Syria, combined with economic depression due to consecutive years of drought, and state-led radical social reforms, were among the chief reasons for Syria's secession from the Union in the military coup of September 1961.

The *Ba'th* officers were bitterly disappointed with the new secessionist regime in Syria which turned Rightist, did not afford them positions of power and relapsed into constant factional friction and intrigues. In March 1963, they were the principal partners of a new army coup in Syria. The *Ba'th* coup in Syria came a month after a military coup in Iraq led by *Ba'th* officers who joined hands with (non-*Ba'th*) Abdel-Salam Aref, toppled Abdel-Karim QASSEM's military regime and took up key positions in the new government. The *Ba'th* was now in power in both Syria and Iraq, though it had to share that power with other factions.

Despite the trauma of the abortive merger with Egypt, the *Ba'th* had not written off either its general unionist doctrine or its aim to unite, specifically, with Egypt; indeed, it was troubled by the secessionist role it had played in 1961. It now ostensibly advocated a rather looser, federal union—contrary to its own basically centralist, merger brand of nationalism. In fact, however, the main purpose of the newly established *Ba'th* regimes was to win Nasser's recognition as a source of legitimacy in their domestic political arenas. In April 1963 the Syrian and Iraqi *Ba'th* regimes together worked out a new agreement with Egypt for a tripartite federal union, to be called, again, "United Arab Republic", and prepared a detailed draft constitution. This federation plan remained abortive, mainly because within the coalition ruling Syria since the coup of March 1963, a bitter, violent power struggle had erupted between the *Ba'th* and the Nasserists: the latter were purged, and mutual hostility reached a pitch that made reconciliation impossible. In November 1963 the Iraqi *Ba'th* was weakened by bitter factional struggles and was ousted from the government by President Aref.

In Syria, the *Ba'th* has retained power since 1963. But it was split into rival factions that struggled for power and even carried out military coups against each other. One faction, headed (politically and militarily) by General Amin al-Hafez and (ideologically) by Michel Aflaq, was considered "Rightist" and less rigidly doctrinaire. It ruled Syria until February 1966 and controlled the "national", all-Arab leadership and the Iraqi *Ba'th*. A rival, "military" faction, more leftist-militant and doctrinaire, was headed by Generals Salah JADID and Hafez al-ASAD. They gradually gained control of the Syrian "regional" command, and in February 1966 ousted the Hafez-Aflaq group in another military coup. The new rulers removed not only Syria's political and military leaders but also the all-Arab leadership, including the party's founders Aflaq and Bitar, and set up their own rival all-Arab national command. In Iraq the *Ba'th* again came to power, in a coup, in July 1968 (in partnership with non-*Ba'th* officers; these were ousted after two weeks and the *Ba'th* alone assumed total power). The Iraqi *Ba'th* remained linked to the national leadership ousted in Syria, and on its part purged its pro-Syrian faction. Bitter Syrian-Iraqi hostility ensued. The "military" faction in power in Syria since February 1966 soon split, with General Asad heading a new faction that condemned Jadid and his associates (Zu'ayyin, Makhus, Nur al-Din al-ATASSI) as too leftist-revolutionary, denounced Syria's isolation in the inter-Arab arena, and wanted a stronger pan-Arab policy. The rift was obviously motivated by ideological dissension only in part and revolved principally around power. In 1969 Asad gained control in a semi-coup, but agreed to a compromise leaving his rivals in leading positions. In November 1970 he took full control in another semi-coup and ousted and detained the leaders of the defeated faction. In 1971 Asad became President of Syria and Secretary-General of the *Ba'th* (both the Syrian-"regional" and his wing of the "national" all-Arab commands). Since then he has ruled Syria.

The Damascus and Baghdad *Ba'th* parties and governments have remained bitterly hostile (a hostility based only partly on intra-*Ba'th* doctrinaire dissension and rooted in a geopolitically motivated struggle for predominance in the Fertile Crescent). Both wings use the name of the *Ba'th* party and doctrine, but their organizations are completely separate (*Ba'th* branches outside Syria and Iraq, e.g., in Lebanon and Jordan, also split accordingly). Both rule their respective countries with an iron fist—nominally at the head of a "National Progressive Front" but in fact as totalitarian single parties. Both have instituted elected National Assemblies or "People's Coun-

cils"—in Syria since 1973 (replacing appointed councils that preceded the elected body), in Iraq since 1980. In both Syria and Iraq the *Ba'th* party has become a tool serving a ruling group of officers, headed by Asad in Syria and by Saddam HUSSEIN in Iraq. The Iraqi and Syrian *Ba'th* regimes have shown pragmatic flexibility along with hard line and extremity both in international and inter-Arab affairs and particularly *vis-a-vis* ISRAEL. The Iraqi *Ba'th* regime, for instance, first endeavored to solve Iraq's Kurdish problem with a degree of moderation and a readiness to compromise which was unusual in Iraqi politics (see KURDS). However, in the late 1980s, following the IRAN-IRAQ WAR, this moderation changed into an all-out war against the Kurds, including the use of chemical weapons against Kurdish villages. Iraq has also, in the 1980s, mitigated its foreign and inter-Arab policies, despite its *Ba'th* ideology. Needing Arab and Western aid in its war against Iran, since 1980, Iraq has seceded from the "REJECTION FRONT", loosened its ties with the USSR and sought rapprochement with both the West and pro-Western Arab states, including ostracized Egypt.

However, this process was completely reversed after the termination of the Iran-Iraq war, when Iraq brutally deported Arab workers and then invaded another Arab state, KUWAIT, in August 1990—leading to the second GULF WAR, in which other Arab states fought against Iraq along with the Western powers in a multinational coalition. As for the Syrian regime, its hard-line policies in the 1970s and 1980s led to the same isolation in inter-Arab relations from which Asad himself sought to extricate Syria in 1970. (Syria even supported Iran in its war against Iraq, contrary to the position of most Arab states). However, Syria changed its policy in the late 1980s and participated first in the international anti-Iraq coalition and later in the Madrid Conference in 1991 and in the Arab-Israeli peace negotiations that followed. Syria under Asad and the *Ba'th* has also suppressed Muslim-Sunni fundamentalist resistance with unprecedented brutality—a policy aggravated by the fact that its regime is dominated by heretic Alawis. Factional, ideologically motivated (or ideologically coated) struggles within the Syrian *Ba'th* seem to have ceased under Asad. Rivalries and clashes within the ruling group—e.g., over Asad's succession—are hardly connected with *Ba'th* party ideology.

Outside Syria and Iraq, *Ba'th* branches exist in Lebanon, where they are split into (weaker) pro-Iraqi and (stronger) pro-Syrian wings. As Syria operates in Lebanon directly and dominates it, it hardly needs the type of agent a local *Ba'th* branch could provide, and the Lebanese *Ba'th* do not seem to wield much influence. Nevertheless, the *Ba'th* was represented in the National Unity Government formed in December 1990 following the end of the Lebanese Civil War, and its leader, Abdallah al-Amin, a Shi'i-Muslim (like many members of the *Ba'th* party in Lebanon) served as minister. He has served in several Lebanese governments since. Accordingly, the leader of the pro-Iraqi wing, Dr. Abd al-Majid al-Rafi'i (b. 1928), a member of the Lebanese parliament from 1972 to 1992, left Lebanon and is residing in FRANCE, like many Lebanese opposition leaders. In Jordan, a *Ba'th* party was briefly legal in the mid-1950s and until 1957 was represented in most parliaments. After 1957, *Ba'th* figures continued to take part in elections but their party affiliation was blurred. From 1957 the party has been illegal and underground, possessing no political influence apart from joining other radical groups in initiating short upheavals, such as in 1958 and 1963 at the founding of the UAR and the Egypt-Syria-Iraq Unity, respectively. Thus, the party was constantly persecuted by the authorities on grounds of its alleged instigation of internal disturbances. Among the Palestinians in the West Bank and Gaza the *Ba'th* had some influence until 1967, but its power declined after the strengthening of the separate Palestinian national identity. Illegal underground *Ba'th* cells may exist in some other Arab countries—Tunisia, Sudan, Yemen; but they do not seem to wield influence. As an all-Arab political movement or ideological tendency, the *Ba'th*, apart from being in power in Syria and Iraq, seems to have faded over the last decades.

BAYAR, CELAL (1883–1986) Turkish politician; third President of the Republic of Turkey (1950–1960) and first President with no military background since the foundation of the Republic. Born in Umurbey, Gemlik, Bayar attended the French Lyceum in Bursa. He worked for a short time as a bank clerk, but soon entered politics. In 1908, he was executive secretary of the Izmir branch of the Committee of Union and Progress—the dominant political organization of the YOUNG TURKS.

In 1919, he joined the Kemal ATATÜRK-led war of independence against the Greeks (1919–1922), as one of the leaders of the resistance in the Aegean area. He was elected to the "Grand National Assembly" (Parliament) in 1920, and was appointed Minister of the National Economy in 1921. He was acting Minister of Foreign Affairs (1922), a member of the Turkish delegation to the Lausanne Peace Conference in 1923 and, under the Lausanne Treaty, was appointed Minister for the Exchange of Population and Land Settlement. In 1924 he became Minister of Reconstruction and the same year withdrew from the government, establishing a government-backed bank (*Is* Bank), managing it from 1924 to 1932. He rejoined the Government as Minister of the National Economy (1932–1937) and for a short time was acting Prime Minister and from 1937 to 1939, Prime Minister. Throughout the 1920s and 1930s he was largely responsible for Kemalist Turkey's economic policies. In January 1939 he stepped down as Prime Minister.

In 1945 Bayar left the Republican People's Party (RPP) and with Menderes, Koraltan and Koprulu founded the Democratic Party (January 1946). He broke away as significant disputes with President Ismet INÖNÜ developed over land reform laws, and more importantly, over the demise of the monopoly of the ruling RPP and establishment of a multi-party system. Six months later, he and sixty-three other members of his party were elected to Parliament. In May 1950, the Democratic Party won the elections (407 seats, against 69 RPP) and in May 1950 Bayar was elected President.

Loss of a strong man as were his predecessors Atutürk and Inönü, Bayar was nevertheless closely identified with the policies of the ruling Democratic Party and took an active role in shaping them.

Bayar's Presidency ended with the military coup of 27 May 1960. With the other top leaders of the Democratic Party regime of 1950–1960 he was tried by a special tribunal (the Yassiada Trials) and sentenced to death; but his death sentence was commuted to life imprisonment (September 1961). In prison, his health deteriorated and he was hospitalized. He was released in 1964, and in 1974 his full political rights restored.

As a former President he was entitled to be Senator for life, but he refused it. He did not resume an active role in politics, but was regarded as a respected elder statesman. He published six volumes of memoirs.

al-BAZ, USSAMA (b. 1931) Egyptian diplomat and polical adviser to President MUBARAK. Born in Sinbellawin, Dakahliyya district. He graduated from the Faculty of Law, University of Cairo (1954), gaining a Ph.D. in Law from Harvard University. His carreer in the Egyptian Government included appointments as Deputy Attorney General (1953–1956); First Secretary at the Egyptian Foreign Ministry (1959–1967). Later on he was appointed Head of the Foreign Minister's Office (1975). In 1977 he became Head of the Vice-President's Office and in this capacity he participated in the negotiations between EGYPT and ISRAEL which led to the peace treaty between the countries. In 1979–1980 he took part in the Israeli-Egyptian talks on the Palestinian autonomy. From 1981, Albaz has been the Head of President Mubarak's office during which he carried out many missions revolving around Egypt's foreign relations on behalf of the President, particularly to Arab and African states, as well as to Israel.

BAZARGAN, MEHDI (1905–1995) The first Prime Minister of the Islamic revolution in IRAN. Born in Tabriz, the capital of the district of Azerbaijan, to a well known family of tradesmen. Received a degree in engineering, in Thermodynamics from The University of Paris.

From the beginning, Bazargan acted for freedom and human rights. He was Deputy Minister in the cabinet of Mohammad MOSSADDEQ, that served in the years 1951–1953 and took part in the struggle to nationalize the oil industry in Iran. He was active in the NATIONAL FRONT OF IRAN. In 1961 he established the Movement for the Freedom of Iran, whose slogan was "the defense of human rights in the state". He was arrested several times. In 1977 Bazargan was among the founders of the Human Rights Association of Iran. Before the 1979 Islamic revolution he joined the KHOMEINI camp and participated with members of his organization in demonstrations and marches. As a believing Muslim with liberal views, he advocated religious reforms and adaptation of ISLAM to the needs of the modern era. These qualities turned him into a link between the religious leaders of the revolution and the secular intellectuals. Thanks to this, Khomeini appointed him

head of the provisional Government set up in February 1979, right after the revolution. He was also appointed member of the Revolutionary Council (see IRAN). However, the actual executive powers were held by the clergymen. Bazargan protested about this to Khomeini and even tendered his resignation, but it was not accepted. He also protested publicly about the many death sentences issued by the Revolutionary Council at the time. Bazargan criticized the take-over of the US Embassy in Teheran in November 1979 by a group of Khomeini supporters. Eventually he resigned the premiership which enabled the appointment of personalities more committed to Khomeini's course to the post.

In 1980 he was elected to the *Majlis* and continued his criticism of the regime's extremism and the suppression of freedom. Even though his movement was not declared illegal, many limitations were imposed on it, and it was harassed by the HIZBALLAH ("the Party of *Allah*"—a group of thugs acting under the inspiration of the regime). Bazargan occasionally published open letters in the name of his movement, in which he criticized the regime's violations; the suppression of human rights and irregularities in the running of the state. After his death in 1995 he was replaced at the head of the Movement for the Freedom of Iran by Dr. Ibraham Yazdi, who had been Foreign Minister in his provisional Government in 1979.

BEDOUIN, BEDUIN Arab nomads, organized in tribes and live from grazing. The term Bedouin (Arabic: *Badawi, pl. Badu*, denoting an inhabitant of the desert (Arabic: *Badiya*), is used chiefly by the settled population. The Bedouin refer to themselves as "Arab"—a term which originally meant only, or mainly, the nomadic tribes of the Arabian Peninsula. To this day, Bedouin tribes are called "*Arab al-* (name of tribe)", and most tribes claim descent from the early tribes of the Arabian Peninsula. There are some tribes that are not Arab, such as the *Qashqai* in IRAN, the *Tuareg* in the Sahara, or *Turcoman* tribes in northern SYRIA and IRAQ, and quite a few tribes of mixed descent, e.g. with some Negro blood, particularly in SUDAN and North Africa. Pure-blooded Arab tribes look down on those and resent that they are called "Arab."

The classical, fully nomadic Bedouin tribe lived in tents; raised camels and sheep; often raided and looted trade caravans from non-Arabs—collecting payment for protection as well as from other tribes; and clashed over disputed wandering and grazing areas and water rights. It had no fixed, permanent camping place, wandering and grazing areas, firmly established by social and cultural tradition.

Throughout history, Bedouin tribes raided the settled lands in the areas bordering the desert. Whenever the countries concerned were militarily weak, Bedouin incursions gained control and established their domination—often settling in the process. Many villages in Iraq, Syria, JORDAN and Palestine are fully or partly of Bedouin descent. In recent history, with the states of the area growing stronger and more effectively administered, such Bedouin raids and incursions have become rare and virtually impossible. Moreover, in the course of modern development, pasturing on arable land—always a bone of contention between Bedouin and the settled farmers—is being prevented; the settled and cultivated area has extended, farming villages are established, and the Bedouin are increasingly pressured to settle in their familiar areas and abandon their wandering-grazing life.

The Bedouin themselves are in a constant process of transition to sedentary life; a process much accelerated in the last century. The transition usually begins with the raising of sheep and goats in addition to camels; then grazing cattle; gradually, plots of land are sown, shifting and irregular at first, then permanently; dwellings are built—shacks at first, for storage and for occupation during part of the year, when the tribe or family reaches that place in its migrations, and finally, houses for permanent occupation. Most governments of the region encourage and support that process of settlement (though it often raises complex problems of land ownership). Today few fully nomadic, camel-raising tribes remain. Most have become semi-nomadic at various stages of the transition process, and some are fully settled, though in many cases animal husbandry remains their main source of livelihood. All semi-nomadic tribes, and most settled ones, retain their tribal identity and organization long after they have ceased to be fully nomadic Bedouin.

The basic unit of Bedouin social organization is the tribe (ashira). Yet the migrating unit often is the extended family rather than the whole tribe. Frequently, several tribes form a large tribal federation

(qabila). The tribe, usually claiming descent from a legendary common ancestor, is headed by the sheikh, who wields wide authority over his tribesmen, including their personal and family affairs. In tribes settling on the land, the sheikh sometimes secures the formal ownership of the land, changing from a *primus inter pares* into a semi-feudal landlord and large-scale employer and contractor. The sheikh is nominally elected by the heads and elders of all the families of his tribe. In fact his position in most cases is hereditary. Modern governments often reserve for themselves the right to appoint, or at least to confirm, the sheikh.

Bedouin tribes have developed their own customs and lore, such as their renowned hospitality (a social convention strictly necessary in the conditions of the desert). They also have their own tribal law (qanun al-ash''r) based on collective tribal and family responsibility, and the treatment of all conflicts as civil disputes to be settled between man and his fellow, or between the families concerned, rather than criminal matters to be prosecuted by the state or society. Thus, murder or sexual offences are matters to be settled by the family of the transgressor and that of the victim—either by revenge or by a truce (sulfa) based on the payment of compensation. While there are countless cases of blood feuds, deriving from revenge and counter-revenge, inter-tribal or intra-tribal, the general trend is to prefer the compensation-and-truce process, usually with the help of mediating tribal judges and elders. Large parts of this tribal law, particularly customs concerning revenge killings or truce-and-compensation, and killings for sexual offences affecting family honor (such as the murder of women for extra-or premarital relations), have been adopted also by a wide sector of the settled rural population. Tribal law poses a delicate problem to all governments of the region: can they condone murder if committed under rules of tribal custom, thus creating in effect different systems of law for different sectors of the population—or should they treat tribal revenge and honor killings as ordinary murder, thus alienating the Bedouin (and large parts of the rural population)? No government has fully solved this dilemma; most have sought some de facto compromise. While constitutions and laws do not provide for special, different treatment for Bedouin, the courts often show special consideration for their customs, regarding them at least as extenuating circumstances. Western powers in semi-colonial administrations also showed Beduin special consideration. The British were particularly fond of Bedouin customs and were nostalgically eager to preserve them.

The nomadic and semi-nomadic Bedouin have remained a disturbing, anomalous element in the administration of many Middle Eastern countries—though their share in the economy and their role in the social fabric have continuously decreased. Modern communications, particularly air transport, have made irrelevant the Bedouin's control of desert routes and abolished their function as chief suppliers of meat and beasts of burden. Modern administration and enhanced security have rendered raids and the collection of protection payments almost impossible. Semi-desert grazing lands are continuously narrowed down by development, river irrigation schemes and the expansion of cultivated areas. The gradual settlement of the Bedouin breaks up their tribal coherence—the more so as in recent decades as the growing Arabian oil industry has turned many Bedouin into industrial workers and dispersed them. Yet, those Bedouin remaining nomadic and semi-nomadic are not easily integrated into ordinary administration, tax collection, compulsory army service, health and education services. That integration has, in most Arab countrie,s remained partial.

It is difficult to estimate the number of Bedouin. They are not usually included in official statistics, which are rare Middle Eastern countries anyway. Moreover, it cannot be determined with certainty which semi-nomadic Bedouin should still be counted as Bedouin, or at which point of the sedentarization process settled or half-settled tribes cease to be Bedouin. Some estimates put the number of Bedouin tribesmen in Arab country and Israel at approximately 7-8 million. In the Arabian Peninsula there are approximately 4 million—less than twenty percent of the population. In Iraq, estimates range from 2–2.5 million to about one-quarter of the population (which would be approximately 3.5 million in the mid-1980s). In LIBYA, Bedouin form about one-third, i.e. 0.7–1 million. Syria's Bedouin are variously estimated at 250,000–300,000; Jordan's — at 250,000–350,000 or seven to ten percent of the population; Egypt's number approximately 200,000–250,000 (including approximately 60,000 in the SINAI PENINSULA); Israel's approximately 60,000

(40,000 in the Negev Desert, the rest mainly in Galilee; the former are in the process of settlement in townships being built for them, the latter are virtually settled).

In some Arab countries provision is made for Bedouin representation in Parliament (sometimes through nomination by councils of tribal chiefs rather than through general elections); as in Syria's election law of the 1950s. In Jordan two—and lately three—special constituencies, ensure tribal Bedouin representation in Parliament. Specific political influence of Bedouin tribal leaders seems to survive in a few Middle Eastern countries: in Saudi Arabia and the PERSIAN GULF principalities; in Jordan, where Bedouin form a large part of the army—originally created as the "Arab Legion", a specifically tribal force—and dominate its officers' corps, and where they have always been the backbone of the King's conservative regime and his loyal allies in his struggles with Leftist agitation, political ferment and Palestinian guerrillas; in Yemen, where the Zeidi tribal federations were the last support of the royalist regime and continue to wield a restraining conservative influence in the Republic; and perhaps in Libya.

BEGIN, MENAHEM (1913–1992) Leader of the Jewish *Irgun Zvai Leumi* (IZL) underground, statesman, leader of the Herut Movement and the Likud, 1948–1983 and Prime Minister of ISRAEL, 1977–1983. Born in Brest-Litovsk, RUSSIA, as a youth he was a member of *Hashomer Hatza'ir* Zionist socialist movement but at the age of sixteen joined the right-wing *Beitar* movement, joining its national leadership in Poland in 1932. Begin studied at Warsaw University and received a law degree in 1935. In 1937 he was detained for participating in an anti-British demonstration. At the World Conference of *Beitar* in 1938 Begin spoke out against his mentor Ze'ev Jabotinsky, calling for a major change in the movement's policy, which would bring about the "conquest of the homeland" by force of arms. In later years he supported the illegal immigration to Palestine.

On the eve of World War II Begin served as the Commissioner of *Beitar* in Poland. After the outbreak of the War he managed to reach Vilna and was detained by the Soviet authorities in September 1940, allegedly for spying. After his release Begin enlisted in the Polish army, and under the command of General Adreas traveled to Palestine in May 1942. At the end of 1943 he was appointed commander of the IZL. In February 1944 he worded the "proclamation of the revolt" regarding the opening of the campaign against the British mandatory government. In response, the British offered a 10,000 dollar prize for his disclosure. Begin spent the next few years in hiding, but continued to run IZL operations. In June 1948 he was on board the *Altalena* (a ship carrying arms and immigrants) before it was seriously damaged by the *Hagana* (the Jewish defense force that preceded the IDF).

In August 1948, in the midst of Israel's War of Independence (see ARAB-ISRAEL CONFLICT), Begin set up the Herut Movement, as a nationalist political party. He led Herut, and then Gahal (a coalition between Herut and the Liberal Party) in opposition until 1967. In those years he gained a reputation as a brilliant orator. His greatest political rival was David BEN GURION, who refused to recognize the legitimacy of Herut and its ideology. Throughout these years Begin believed that both banks of the Jordan River ought to belong to Israel. In 1952 he was suspended from his membership in the Knesset for three months following disorders against the background of the reparations agreement signed by Israel with the Federal Republic of Germany.

On the eve of the outbreak of the Six-Day War (see ARAB-ISRAEL CONFLICT), as leader of the Gahal Party, Begin joined the National Unity Government headed by Levi ESHKOL as a Minister without Portfolio. In 1970 he left the government headed by Golda MEIR in protest against its acceptance of the Rogers Plan (see ARAB-ISRAEL PEACEMAKING). In 1973 he established the Likud as a coalition of several parties and movements, and led it in opposition until the political upheaval of 1977, when he set up a government under his leadership.

After hosting Egyptian President Anwar al-SADAT in JERUSALEM in November 1977, he negotiated a peace treaty with EGYPT for almost eighteen months, eventually accepting Egypt's insistence on complete Israeli withdrawal from the Sinai and agreeing to the establishment of an autonomy for "the Arabs of Eretz Yisrael" (the term he insisted on using for the Palestinians) in Judea, Samaria and the Gaza area. (see ARAB-ISRAEL PEACEMAKING). Together with Sadat, Begin received the Nobel Prize for Peace in Oslo on 10 December 1979.

Following the resignation of Ezer WEIZMAN from his government in 1980, Begin also assumed the position of Minister of Defense, and decided to bomb the Iraqi nuclear reactor "Osiraq" on the eve of the elections to the tenth Knesset in June 1981. After forming his second government he decided to embark on the Lebanon War. Following the death of his wife Aliza in November 1982 and rapidly losing support as a result of complications in the Lebanon War, Begin resigned from the premiership on 19 September 1983. For the rest of his life he was rarely seen in public.

BEILIN, YOSSI (b. 1948) Israeli academic, politician and main driving force behind the Oslo Talks (see ARAB-ISRAEL PEACEMAKING). Born in Petah Tikva, he worked as a journalist and member of the *Davar* editorial board 1969–1977, while studying Hebrew literature and political science at Tel Aviv University. He taught at Tel Aviv University in the years 1972–1985 and received a Ph.D in political science in 1981. Beilin served as spokesman of the Israel Labor Party in the years 1977–1984, and as Government Secretary when Shimon PERES was Prime Minister, 1984–1986. In the years 1986–1988 he was Political Director General of the Ministry of Foreign Affairs under Peres, in which capacity he was largely responsible for ISRAEL's dissociation from the White apartheid regime in South Africa.

Beilin was elected to the twelfth Knesset on the Labor Party list, and in the years 1988–1990 served as Deputy Minister of Finance under Peres. In the years 1992–1995 he served as Deputy Minister of Foreign Affairs, in which capacity he initiated and secretly supervised the Oslo Talks, before they became official in mid-1993. In July 1995 he was appointed Minister of Economics and Planning, and after the assassination of Prime Minister Yitzhak RABIN, was appointed Minister in the Prime Minister's Office, under Peres. Just before Rabin's assassination, Beilin formulated a plan with MAHMUD ABBAS (Abu Mazen) according to which (within the framework of a permanent Israeli-Palestinian settlement) a Palestinian state would be established but most of the Jewish settlements in the West Bank would remain under Israeli sovereignty. In June 1996, after Labor's electoral defeat, he opened a dialogue with several members of the Likud in an attempt to establish a national consensus toward negotiations with the Palestinians on a permanent settlement. In the primaries for the leadership of the Labor Party in June 1997 Beilin came in second, after Ehud BARAK, with 28.51% of the vote.

BEILIN-ABU MAZEN DOCUMENT see ARAB-ISRAEL PEACEMAKING.

BEN-ʿALI ZEIN al-ABIDIN (b. 1936) Tunisian officer and politician, President of TUNISIA since November 1987. Ben-ʿAli was trained at the French Military Academy, with additional training in the US, mainly in the field of intelligence. He served mostly in Tunisia's intelligence and security apparatus. He was director of military intelligence, 1958–1974, a military attaché in MOROCCO, 1974–1977 and head of secret services, 1977–1980, with the rank of Secretary of State. In 1980 he was removed and sent abroad, as Ambassador to Poland, but in 1984 he returned to his post. With the rise of Islamic fundamentalism and much public discontent in Tunisia, deteriorating economy and weakening of the government due to President BOURGUIBA's declining de facto authoritarian regime, Ben-ʿAli was made Minister of Public Security in late 1985 and Minister of the Interior in April 1986, beginning in fact to control the government. He was also named, in June 1986, Secretary-General of the ruling *Dustour Socialist Party* (formerly *Neo-Destour*). In October 1987 he took over as Prime Minister, keeping also the Ministry of Interior (and Security). After one month, in November 1987, he staged a coup, deposed Bourguiba and proclaimed himself President. In April 1989 he was elected President, as the single candidate, with over ninety-nine percent of the popular vote. At the outset of his tenure, Ben-ʿAli tightened the government and initiated several reforms; he permitted multiparty competition for Parliament, but saw to it that the ruling party (the former *Neo-Destour*, which he renamed *Rassemblent Constitutionnel-Democratique*) continued to win all the seats in the elections of April 1989. His chief opponent—and Tunisia's main problem—was the growing Islamic-fundamentalist movement; he did not permit it to establish a legal organization and suppressed it by various means. Ben-ʿAli was re-elected to a second term as Tunisia's President in elections held in March 1994. As the sole candidate, he again won over ninety-nine percent of the vote. As President,

Ben-ʿAli maintained many of his predecessor's foreign policies, pursuing moderate and pro-Western positions in his relations with Western and Arab countries. Relations with European countries were thus bolstered and nurtured—primarily in the economic sphere—along with attempts to establish North African organizations that would promote regional cooperation. Over the years, Ben-ʿAli expressed his support in creating a more pluralistic political system in Tunisia. However, the suppression of the Islamic movement, as well as steps taken to limit non-Islamic oppostion parties, raised doubts as to Ben-ʿAli's commitment to his stated convictions. Ben-ʿAli managed to stabilize Tunisia's political arena and tighten the government's control of the country. However, the question of establishing political pluralism and a more democratic society is expected to become more acute as Tunisia continues to cement its ties with Europe and other Western countries.

BEN BELLA, AHMAD [or sometimes **Muhammad** (b. 1916? 1918?] Algerian politician and leader of the nationalist revolt. President of ALGERIA 1963–1965. Ben Bella emerged as a nationalist leader after World War II. After serving in the French Army during the war, he joined the *Mouvement pour le Triomphe des Libertés Démocratiques* (MTLD) party led by Messali Hajj, which advocated full independence for Algeria. He soon began advocating armed struggle and set up, with a group of like-minded associates (Belkacem Krim, Muhammad Khidr, Hussein Ait-Ahmad), an underground "Organisation Spéciale" for that purpose, thus breaking with Messali and the MTLD. In 1950 he was arrested and sentenced to seven years imprisonment. He escaped in March 1952 to Cairo and established there the headquarters of the groups preparing an armed revolt. In 1953 his *Organization Speciale* turned into a *Conseil Révolutionnaire pour l'Unité et l'Action*, out of which grew the FRONT DE LIBÉRATION NATIONALE (FLN) in 1954. When the FLN opened the armed revolt in November 1954, Ben Bella was its most prominent leader. In October 1956, when Ben Bella was flying from MOROCCO to Tunis, the French secret services arranged for the pilot to land at Algiers and arrested Ben Bella and four other rebel leaders, including Khidr and Ait-Ahmad. While Ben Bella was in prison in FRANCE and could no longer directly lead the rebellion, his colleagues kept his place in their leadership bodies and apparently managed to consult him; he was named, for instance, Deputy Premier in the FLN's Provisional Governments of 1958 and 1961.

Ben Bella was released in March 1962, with the French-Algerian agreement and cease-fire. He immediately assumed a vigorous leadership—and took bold positions in the factional splits that developed. He advocated leftist-neutralist, anti-Western policies on Nasserist lines and a one-party state socialism, with the party dominant; in the rift between the guerrillas inside Algeria and the rebel army under BOUMÉDIENNE entering Algeria from TUNISIA he backed the latter. In June 1962 he convened the FLN leadership in Tripoli, LIBYA, and imposed his line. He ignored the two rival governments struggling for control—the one set up provisionally by the French-Algerian agreement, and Yussuf Ben-Khedda's FLN government, and imposed his own politbureau's control (with the FLN government acquiescing). In September 1962 the provisional arrangements were ended and Ben Bella formed the government of independent Algeria. He continued imposing his strict, hard-line rule and began suppressing all oppositional trends within and without the FLN. In April 1963 he became Secretary-General of the FLN in addition to the Premiership. In September 1963 Ben Bella was elected President in a referendum, as the only candidate, nominated by the FLN; he kept the Premiership, too, but from 1964 ceased using the title Prime Minister and treated his government as a Presidential one. He made Algeria an ally of the Soviet Bloc (he received the Lenin Peace Prize in 1964) and a mainstay of the Leftist-neutralist camp, aspiring to a position of leadership in that camp.

Ben Bella's harsh policies and his suppression of opposition leaders with a proud fighting FLN record caused much unrest and dissatisfaction. In June 1965 he was overthrown by his associate and protégé Boumédienne, and imprisoned. His confinement was eased from 1979, after Boumédienne's death, and in October 1980 he was released. He refused, however, to associate himself with the regime in power and soon went into voluntary exile in France. Since 1980 he has been linked with various opposition groups in exile—according to some reports with an increasingly Islamic and pro-Libyan line; but these groups, factionally split, do not seem to have much impact on political realities in Algeria. In 1982 he co-founded an "International Islamic Commission for Human Rights."

BEN GURION, DAVID (1886–1973) Israeli statesman, leader of the Mapai Party, and the first Prime Minister of ISRAEL. Born in Plonsk, Poland, Ben Gurion immigrated to Palestine in 1906, spent several years as a farm worker, and was active in the Zionist-Socialist *Po'alei Tzion* ("Workers of Zion") Party. His approach to socialism was pragmatic, maintaining that the realization of political Zionism had precedence over Marxist dialectics. In 1907 he managed to have *Po'alei Tzion* introduce a new article into its platform; that "The Party will strive for an independent state for the Jewish people in this country."

From 1910 Ben Gurion served as editor of the *Po'alei Tzion* organ, *Ahdut*. He studied law in Istanbul and after the YOUNG TURKS revolt in 1908, advocated an Ottoman orientation for the Jews of Eretz Yisrael. He hoped to become a member of the Ottoman parliament and possibly even a minister in the Turkish government, but was expelled from Istanbul at the beginning of World War I. Following the publication of the BALFOUR DECLARATION, on 2 November 1917, Ben Gurion wrote: "A land is only acquired through the pains of labor and creation, through the efforts of building and settling." A few months later he returned to Palestine as a volunteer in the Jewish Legion. Ben Gurion played a central role in the establishment of the *Histadrut* (the Jewish general workers' federation in Palestine) in 1920, and served as its first Secretary General. He also played a central role in the establishment of the Mapai Party—which was to maintain a central role in Jewish and Israeli politics from 1930 to 1968.

In 1933 Ben Gurion became head of the Political Department of the Zionist Executive, and in this capacity held a series of talks with Palestinian-Arab and pan-Arab leaders, which came to naught. 1935 he was elected Chairman of the Zionist Executive and the Jewish Agency.

In 1937, together with Chaim WEIZMANN, he supported the Peel Commission's plan for the establishment of a Jewish state in a small part of Palestine (see ARAB-ISRAEL PEACEMAKING). After the plan was shelved, Ben Gurion participated in the St. James Round Table Conference held in London in February 1939. It was followed by the White Paper of 1939, which

limited Jewish immigration to Palestine and land purchases by Jews there, and aimed at ensuring permanent minority status for the Jews. After the outbreak of World War II Ben Gurion declared "that the Jewish would fight by Britain's side as if there were no White Paper, and fight the White Paper as if there were no war." Ben Gurion was the driving force behind the May 1942 "Biltmore Program", issued by the American Zionist Emergency Committee, on turning Palestine into a Jewish Commonwealth in Palestine. Within the Jewish community in Palestine Ben Gurion fought the dissident groups—the *Irgun Zvai Leumi* (IZL) and *Lehi*, which advocated the use of terrorism against Britain. From 1945 to 1948 Ben Gurion led the political struggle for the opening of Palestine for massive Jewish immigration—especially of Holocaust survivors. Together with Weizmann and the head of the Jewish Agency Political Department, Moshe Shertok (Sharett), he supported a pragmatic solution to the Palestine problem, involving partition.

Upon the establishment of the State of Israel in May 1948, Ben Gurion became its first Prime Minister and Minister of Defense, inviting all the parties, except the Herut Movement and Communist Party, to join his government. Ben Gurion followed a policy of "statism" as opposed to partisan particularism, which *inter alia* involved the disbanding of separate politically oriented organizations within the IDF, and the establishment of a state system of education. He favored a policy of dispersing the population and sending new immigrants to the periphery of the country to "develop the wilderness."

In 1953 Ben Gurion resigned the premiership and joined Kibbutz Sede Boker in the Negev. He returned to active politics in February 1955, against the background of the "Lavon Affair" concerning the uncovering of a Jewish spy and sabotage ring in EGYPT, resumed the post of Defense Minister in Moshe Sharett's government and once again became Prime Minister in June. He was the main architect of the Franco-Israeli military pact which developed in the 1950s, and in face of bitter opposition supported the establishment of relations with the Federal Republic of Germany. He was Prime Minister at the time of the Sinai Campaign, in October 1956, which was the only war fought by Israel in coalition

with other states—FRANCE and Great BRITAIN (see ARAB-ISRAEL CONFLICT). In the years 1955–1963 Ben Gurion made several unsuccessful efforts to establish contacts with Arab leaders.

In June 1963 Ben Gurion once again resigned from the government. Together with a group of younger members of Mapai, including Moshe DAYAN and Shimon PERES, he formed a new party "Rafi", which gained ten seats in the sixth Knesset (1965). Following the Six-Day War (see ARAB-ISRAEL CONFLICT) Rafi joined the Israel Labor Party, without Ben Gurion, who founded a new party, the "State List", which gained four seats in the seventh Knesset (1969). In June 1970, at the age of eighty-four, Ben Gurion resigned from the Knesset and retired to Kibbutz Sede Boker.

Side by side with his political pursuits, Ben Gurion engaged in a wide range of intellectual activities, wrote extensively and corresponded with a large number of world leaders, including foes such as Mahatma Gandhi before the establishment of the state, and Charles de Gaulle in the 1960s. His many books, memoirs and diaries, are a vital source of information on the history of ZIONISM and the first two decades of Israel's existence.

BEN JEDID, CHADLI (al-Shadhili) (b. 1929) Algerian officer and politician, President of ALGERIA since 1979. Born in Eastern Algeria into a peasant family, Ben-Jedid received no higher education. According to French reports, he served in the French Army in the early 1950s. He joined the (FRONT DE LIBÉRATION NATIONALE) (FLN) forces of the armed revolt in 1955, and became Colonel. In 1961 he was appointed to BOUMEDIENNE's General Staff of the rebel army in Tunis, and from 1962 was a member of the Revolutionary Council. In the faction struggles of 1962–1963 he supported Boumédienne (and consequently BEN BELLA). Beginning 1963–1964 he commanded the Oran region for fifteen years and while supporting Boumédienne.

After the death of Boumédienne in December 1978 the struggle for the succession seemed to be deadlocked. This was primarily between Salah Yahyawi (considered leftist-radical and the candidate of the FLN party cadres), and Abdel Aziz Bouteflika, (considered more moderate and a "technocrat"). Ben-Jedid emerged as the Army's candidate and a generally acceptable compromise. In January 1979 he was nominated by the FLN as the single candidate for the Presidency and in February he was elected in a referendum. As President, he kept the Defense Ministry to himself. He appointed a Prime Minister, the first separation of the Premiership from the Presidency since 1962–1963. He was also elected Secretary-General of the FLN. He was re-elected President (being the only candidate) in 1984. He purged the FLN, the Government and the Army of elements which he considered extremist or undesirable.

Since the late 1970s Algeria slipped into an economic crisis due to the mismanagement of the industrialization drive, the decline of oil prices, the stagnation of agriculture, and rapid population growth. Ben-Jedid sought to decentralize the economy, breakdown the large industrial conglomerates into smaller more manageable units, and put greater emphasis on social services and light industries. This was marginally successful. In 1988, mass riots broke out in protest of austere economic measures, which were suppressed by the military with some 500 people killed. Seeking to restore the regime's legitimacy, Ben-Jedid implemented constitutional amendments which broke with Algeria's socialist past, separated the party from the state, and legalized opposition parties. He also toned down Algeria's radical foreign policies, by dissociating it from the inter-Arab REJECTION FRONT. This improved relations with the West, culminating in his support of the US against IRAQ during the 1991 GULF WAR.

Ben Jedid allowed the Islamic movement a free hand to build its power, hoping to use it to break the FLN's grip on the bureaucracy. He failed to realize the extent of popular discontent against the regime manifested in the FIS's victory during the 1990 municipal and regional elections. He changed the electoral law in June 1991 by manipulating electoral districts in order to increase the FLN's representation in the Parliamentary elections. This enabled the military to crack down at the FIS following mass riots in June 1991. Nonetheless, he still allowed the elections to proceed.

Following the FIS victory in the first round of Parliamentary elections in December 1991 (188 seats out of 430), Ben-Jedid was forced by the military to halt the elections process, to dissolve the national assembly, and eventually to resign on 11 January 1992 and retire from politics.

BERBERS   The ancient, pre-Arab inhabitants of north-west Africa (the MAGHREB). Their language belongs to the Hamitic group and is related to Ancient Egyptian. After the Arab-Muslim conquest in the seventh and eighth century the Berbers accepted ISLAM, many of them in the version of the IBADIYYA sect or school, and became the spearhead of its further expansion into Spain and West Africa. They also gradually adopted the Arabic language, but their own Berber language continued to be widely spoken, particularly in remote areas, where the Berbers also maintained their own tribal structure.

The number of Berbers today cannot be reliably established. The majority of the Maghreb population comprises full or part Berber descent; but estimates vary as to the number of those still retaining a degree of Berber distinction, consciousness and the Berber language. Some estimates put their number at more than fifty percent of MOROCCO's population, and twenty to twenty-five percent of ALGERIA's; others estimate it at thirty to forty percent in both countries. In TUNISIA there are very few Berbers, and in Tripolitania (LIBYA)—where an estimate of 1917 still showed them to be a majority—they are today considered to constitute five to ten percent. The unique character of the Berbers was preserved more in the remote mountain areas than in the cities and villages of the lowlands. The French in Morocco, during the period of their domination, fostered Berber particularism, and some conservative local Berber leaders collaborated with them against the nationalists (see MOROCCO).

While Berbers adopted Islam, they resisted the claim that Arabization was an integral part of being Muslims. Consequently, many Berbers showed strong disposition to the left, and have dominated the French language press in Morocco and Algeria. Some conservative political groups in Morocco have Berber characteristics. Some factional struggles in Algeria, particularly in the Kabyle region, in the 1950s and 1960s, also had distinct Berber undertones.

Berber culture and identity experienced a revival in Algeria during the 1980s which manifested in the 1980–1981 "Berber Spring" riots. Following the 1989 political liberalization, a "Berber Cultural Movement" (MCB) emerged and organized massive school boycotts demanding that the Berber language, Tamazight, be recognized as the second official language after Arabic.

Two parties were identified with the Berbers in Algeria. *The Front des Forces Socialiste* (FFS) led by Hussein Ait-Ahmad was founded in 1963. Despite its efforts it failed to attract wide support outside the Berber community. The Rally for Culture and Democracy (RCD), led by Sa'id Sa'di, was established in 1990, combining secularism with a struggle for Berber rights. The military regime agreed to broaden the teaching and usage of Tamazight in schools and the media, in order to gain Berber support against the Islamist opposition, but did not award Tamazight an official status in the 1996 constitutional amendments. Moreover, while the constitution recognized Berber identity (Amazighité) as one of the three components of Algerian identity together with Arabism and Islam, it prohibited its political usage thereby practically banning avowedly Berber parties.

BERNADOTTE, COUNT FOLKE see ARAB-ISRAEL PEACEMAKING

BERRI, NABIH (b. 1938) Lebanese lawyer and politician, political leader of the Shi'i-Muslim community and the AMAL movement and Speaker (President) of the Lebanese parliament since November 1992. Born in Freetown, Sierra Leone, where his father had migrated, Berri returned to the town of his family's origin, Tibnin in South Lebanon, and was brought up there. He later studied law at The Lebanese University and graduated with a law degree. Later he studied at the Sorbonne in Paris, receiving his masters degree from the "Faculte de Droit". He was, in his student days, active in the *Ba'th* party and frequently visited Damascus. Berri started his career as a lawyer in 1963, and for some time was President of the Lebanese Students Movement and the Lebanese Universities Union. Later he lived with his father in Sierra Leone, and then went to the US, married a Lebanese-American, but later divorced her. His divorced wife and some of their seven children remained in the US. (Berri remarried in 1982). Berri returned to Lebanon in 1975 and joined the Shi'i leader Mussa AL-SADR and his recently formed paramilitary organization, AMAL. At the beginning of the Civil War in 1975 the Shi'is of Lebanon were still underdeveloped as a political community and deprived of its fair share in the distribution of political power. However, the civil war expedited the Shi'is

emergence as an assertive group openly claiming the power due to them. Berri gradually became one of their main younger leaders. He soon became a member of the Amal Political Committee, then its Secretary-General (1978) and Chairman (1980). Though his direct control of the organization and its militia remained loose, he has emerged as the chief Shi'i leader.

In the first two years of the Civil War, 1975–1976, the Shi'is did not actively join either of the rival camps and restricted their militias, Amal and local guards, to the protection of their villages and quarters. There were frequent clashes and tension between them and the Palestinian PALESTINE LIBERATION ORGANIZATION (PLO) fighters dominating South Lebanon. In the early 1980s, however, and particularly after the Israeli invasion of Lebanon in 1982 and with the increasing Shi'i resistance to that occupation, Berri allied himself with the "Leftist" anti-government camp, led by the Druze chief Walid JUNBLAT. He did not formally join the several "National Front" coalitions set up by Junblat in 1983 and 1984, but joined their efforts to force on the Christian-led government, a pro-Syrian and anti-Israel policy, and far-reaching changes in Lebanon's political structure. These changes were officially aimed at the abolition of the communal system in Lebanon, but in fact at the enhancement of the Shi'i and Druze share in that system and the creation of Shi'i-and Druze-ruled districts (parallel to the Christian-ruled "canton of Mount Lebanon"). When these efforts succeeded, under Syrian pressure, and a "Government of National Unity" was set up in April 1984, Berri joined it as Minister of Justice. He refused, however, to take his seat until he was given the additional post of Minister of State for South Lebanon, aiming at total control of that region. Even after that he did not fully participate in the work of the government, boycotting most of its sessions—together with Junblat—and sabotaging its efforts to impose a central control. He resided for much of the time in Damascus where he fostered a close alliance with the regime.

In 1984, and after provocative acts carried out by President Amin Jumayyil and the Lebanese Army against the Shi'i population in West Beirut, Amal and the Army's Sixth Brigade (predominantly Shi'i) responded in military operations against both the army and government (of which he was formally a member) and local Sunni "militias" (*al-Murabitun*). They took control of West Beirut and its southern suburbs for the first time in the modern history of LEBANON. After the withdrawal of Israeli troops, Amal took control of the southern coastal plain and most of South Lebanon. These operations were conducted in cooperation with Junblat's Druze forces, and in July 1985 he cemented that alliance in a "National United Front"—but his Shi'is sometimes clashed with those forces too, in the struggle for full control. From May to June 1985 Berri's forces attacked the Palestinian guerrilla camps of Beirut and South Lebanon, aiming at preventing the Palestinians from returning to their pre-war dominant position. The "War of the Camps", as it was called, left thousands dead and lasted until early 1988 when it was stopped as a gesture to the Palestinian uprising, INTIFADA.

Berri became internationally known through his role in the June 1985 hijacking of an American airliner by Shi'i extremists and the detention of its passengers and crew as hostages. He acted partly as mediator, partly as negotiator for the hijackers, adopting their demands. He sent his Amal men to take over partially for the extremist hijackers, and together with Syria, eventually took credit for the release of the hostages. In December 1985 he and Junblat agreed with Elie Hubayka, leader of the Maronite-Christian "Lebanese Forces", on the Damascus Agreement, a plan for a new political structure for Lebanon, in line with Syria's conceptions and demands. The agreement was rejected by the Christian leadership and remained abortive (see LEBANON).

Berri is considered by many as essentially a moderate with limited aims: the enhancement of the Shi'i share in power, and full Shi'i control of South Lebanon and the Biqa'. Towards ISRAEL, too, he may content himself with the achievement of a full Israeli withdrawal from Lebanon and oppose attacks on Israel itself, though he refuses to establish fully fledged contacts with Israel and reach a mutual agreement. With Syria's backing, he opposed any return of an armed PLO presence in South Lebanon and Beirut. But he is under constant pressure from more extremist Shi'i groups (especially HIZBALLAH), inspired by Iran's KHOMEINI and his partisans—groups which clamor for control of the Shi'i community and its military power. Therefore, Berri himself had to adopt more extremist positions so as to maintain

his leadership. However, and despite these challenges, Berri managed to maintain Amal's strong position in the Shi'i community.

The Ta'if Agreement concluded in 1989 enhanced the status of the Shi'i community in Lebanon, giving more power to the community's highest official, the Speaker (President) of the Lebanese Parliament. Together with the Sunni-Muslim Prime Minister, whose power has been greatly strengthened leaving the Christian President without many of his pre-Ta'if powers, the Premier and Speaker of Parliament are truly the leaders of Lebanon, under the auspices of Syria. Berri supported the agreement and is one of the main supporters of the new postwar settlement in Lebanon. Under his leadership, Amal handed over its heavy weapons to the Lebanese Army, and members of the militia took governmental posts. In November 1992 Berri headed the "Liberation List" that competed in the district of South Lebanon. After its victory, he was elected Speaker (President) of the Lebanese Parliament, forming the largest bloc in parliament. Four years later, before the Parliamentary elections of 1996, Berri formed an alliance with Prime Minister Rafiq HARIRI, and both used it and the state apparatus to win them. (Currently, Berri has a bloc of twenty to twenty-five deputies loyal to him while Hariri enjoyed the support of a bloc of thirty to forty deputies). In South Lebanon Amal competed in a list together with *Hizballah*, presumably in an effort to avoid intracommunal clashes, and again emerged victorious.

Despite his official duties, Nabih Berri remains the leader of Amal, which engages in military operations against Israel's declared "Security Zone" in South Lebanon (though, on a much smaller scale than *Hizballah*). Considering Syria's dominant position in Lebanon, Berri maintains close relations with Damascus, earning himself valuable support in the Lebanese political system.

BI-NATIONALISM see ARAB-ISRAEL PEACEMAKING.

BITAR, SALAH al-DIN see BA'TH and SYRIA.

BLACK SEPTEMBER see PALESTINIAN GUERRILLA ORGANIZATIONS.

BOUMÉDIENNE, HOUARI (Hawari; original name: Muhammad Boukharouba) (1925? 1927?

1932?–1978). Algerian officer and politician. Born in the Annaba (Bone) region of eastern ALGERIA as the son of a farm laborer, Boumédienne was later said to have studied Arabic literature at Tunis University and Cairo's al-AZHAR. He stayed on in Cairo, working as a teacher. It was there that he met BEN BELLA and other leaders of the incipient Algerian revolt in 1954. He joined their FRONT DE LIBÉRATION NATIONALE (FLN) and soon became one of the revolt's commanders. In 1955 he landed in Western Algeria with a group of rebels and soon headed the rebel formations in the Oran region. He later returned to FLN headquarters, now in Tunis, became a member of the Revolutionary Council set up in 1956, and in March 1960 was appointed Chief-of-Staff of the rebel army. After the French-Algerian Agreement of 1962 he led that army into Algeria; half-hidden tensions between the guerrillas inside Algeria and the rebel army outside now erupted. Boumédienne firmly insisted on the primacy of the regular rebel army entering Algeria from TUNISIA and soon armed clashes broke out; he also became involved in factional struggles, vigorously backing Ben Bella. In July 1962 he was dismissed by the FLN Prime Minister Ben Khedda, but, firmly backed by Ben Bella, he ignored this order, marched into Algiers and imposed the rule of his army and Ben Bella's faction. When Ben Bella set up the first government of independent Algeria in September 1962, Boumédienne became his Defense Minister and from September 1963 also Deputy Prime Minister and Number Two of the regime (and some thought that he held the real power). But tension developed between him and Ben Bella; Ben Bella did not trust Boumédienne and saw him as a rival, and Boumédienne loathed Ben Bella's factionalism and his treatment of former comrades-in-arms, his allures of grandeur and his aspirations to all-Arab and African leadership.

In June 1965 Boumédienne overthrew Ben Bella in a (coup and imprisoned him. He set up a new Revolutionary Council with himself as chairman. He was now Head-of-State and Prime Minister—without formally assuming these titles—and remained Minister of Defense. For nearly eleven years he ruled Algeria without seeking a formal institutionalization or popular endorsement of his titles and positions. Only in 1976 he convened a FLN leadership conference and had it draw up a new "National Char-

ter", which was endorsed by a plebiscite; a "National Conference" under that charter enacted a new constitution, and under that constitution Boumédienne was elected President, as the only candidate, in a referendum of December 1976.

In his over thirteen years as Head-of-State, Boumédienne made no major changes in Algeria's policies. He put less emphasis on ideology and doctrine and stressed the internal regime and economic rather than foreign and international policy, but his regime remained strict, allowing no deviation from the line he laid down and keeping power within the group of his associates. He purged not only the establishment within Algeria, but during his rule—i.e. probably under his orders—prominent opposition leaders in exile were eliminated by assassination, including Muhammad Khidr and the revolution's most prominent leader after (or with) Ben Bella, Belkacem Krim. His state socialism remained leftist-radical and his alliance with the Soviet Bloc, international leftist neutralism and the inter-Arab REJECTION FRONT was firm. While Boumédienne had not much charisma, his leadership was unquestioned until his death in December 1978.

BOURGUIBA, HABIB (b. 1903) The most prominent leader of Tunisian nationalism, who led Tunisia to independence. President of TUNISIA between 1957 and 1987. Born in Monastir, Bourguiba studied law in FRANCE and began practising as a lawyer. He was active in the nationalist movement represented by the *Destour* (Arabic: Constitution) party. In 1934 he was among a group of younger activists who seceded from the party, dissatisfied with its traditional leadership and lack of vigor, and founded the *Neo-Destour* Party which soon became the chief spokesman of Tunisian nationalism. Bourguiba was imprisoned by Tunisia's French rulers in the later part of the 1930s and early 1940s. He was released in 1942 by the Germans, who occupied Tunisia for a number of years during World War II. After the war, following renewed French surveillance and harassment, Bourguiba fled to Cairo. Bourguiba negotiated Tunisia's independence with France in 1950, but was later arrested after these talks failed. During the final negotiations on Tunisia's independence, Bourguiba was released but kept under surveillence,while exiled to France in 1953 and later returning to Tunisia and mananging to successfully contain extremist elements within his *Neo-Destour* movement.

After Tunisia attained partial independence in 1955 and full independence in March 1956, Bourguiba was elected President of the Constituent Assembly in April, and during the same month formed the first government of independent Tunisia, keeping the Defense and Foreign Minister posts himself. With the abolition of the monarchy in July 1957 he was proclaimed President of Tunisia (though the Constitution was completed and adopted only in 1959). He was re-elected president as the only candidate in 1959, 1964, 1969 and 1974, and in March 1975 was proclaimed president for life. As president he also kept the Premiership until November 1969.

As President, Bourguiba emerged as the supreme leader of Tunisia, determining the character and policies of the state, its organization and its administration. Bourguiba chartered a modernist and moderate, liberal, pro-Western course for Tunisia, abolishing polygamy, restricting the rule of Islamic law and its institutions and making the secular institutions of the state supreme. He intervened personally several times to prevent pogroms or mob excesses against Tunisia's Jews. Despite several sharp conflicts with France, he kept Tunisia close to France and the US, with the French language and French cultural influence nearly dominant. While supporting all-Arab cooperation, he had little sympathy for Pan-Arab rhetoric or for the radical leftist "progressive" regimes and doctrines prevalent in several Arab countries, such as EGYPT or ALGERIA. He frequently clashed with Egypt's ABDEL NASSER, claiming in 1958 that Egypt, and Nasser personally, had assisted in plots to subvert Tunisia and assasinate him. Bourguiba subsequently severed ties with Egypt and the ARAB LEAGUE in the autumn of that year. Relations were renewed in 1961, but remained cool.

Bourguiba did not conform to all-Arab positions on ISRAEL. Although he had no sympathy for Israel, he held that the Arab states did not have the military power to solve the conflict by war and that they should negotiate with Israel and peacefully co-exist with it if it accepted their conditions. As to these conditions and demands, Bourguiba hardly differed from other Arab leaders; but the prospect of peaceful co-existence he held out in public was, in the 1950s and 1960s, unusual and unacceptable to the

Arab states. His dissent reached a peak in the spring of 1965 when he formulated these ideas into a plan. This resulted in a storm of protest, a denunciation by Arab states, who recalled their ambassadors and informed Bourguiba that Tunisia's participation in Arab League sessions was undesirable. Bourguiba dissented also on other issues, such as his 1965 refusal to conform with other Arab states and sever ties with West Germany, following the establishment of diplomatic relations between Germany and Israel, and his sole recognition of MAURITANIA's independence (MOROCCO perceived Mauritania as part of the Greater Moroccan Homeland). During the 1967 crisis and the Six-Day War, Bourguiba returned to the Arab fold and declared his solidarity with Nasser. But after the war, relations reverted to the old pattern: Bourguiba was sharply critical of Nasser's Egypt, boycotted Arab League meetings and severed relations with SYRIA in 1968. After Nasser's death in 1970 relations with Egypt improved. Bourguiba also mended relations with Algeria. Those with LIBYA, on the other hand, sharply deteriorated; the strange episode of the proclamation of a Tunisian-Libyan merger, in January 1974, aggravated Tunisian-Libyan tension when the merger was cancelled soon after.

Bourguiba's internal regime differed from his fostered international liberal image. He installed and maintained a de facto one-party system, limiting opposition and ruling with an iron fist, ousting and purging anyone not wholly conforming to his wishes (see TUNISIA). He became convinced that Islamic fundamentalism posed a serious threat to his regime, and attempts were made to suppress fundamentalist activity. Bourguiba seemed to resent aides and associates whom he considered too strong or independent; thus dismissing Prime Ministers al-Adgham (1970), Nouira (1980, after nearly ten years of premiership) and Mazali (1986, after over six years). Even within his own household, his rule was harsh; in 1986 he divorced his wife Wasila (whom he had married in 1962 after divorcing his first, French-born, wife) amidst rumors of a wide-spread intrigue, and he broke with his son, al-Habib Bourguiba Junior, who had served him in senior posts for many years. In the second half of 1987, Bourguiba's behaviour became increasingly erratic. The Tunisian president had been ailing for years, and appeared to be losing his ability to govern. Poltical appointments were made and revoked shortly afterward. In October 1987, BEN-'ALI ZEIN al-Abdin, who was in fact controlling the government since his appointment as Minister of the Interior in April 1986, was named Prime Minister, with responsiblity for internal affairs and also as Secretary-General of the ruling PSD party. Concern among government ministers about the president's behaviour spread, and an exmination of constitutional provisions allowing the retirement of the President had begun. On 7 November 1987, Bourguiba was declared by seven doctors as unfit to govern, due to senility and ill health, and in accordance with the constitution, Prime Minister Ben-'Ali was sworn in as President. This coup was carried out after having apparently received the advanace approval of other ministers and senior military officers, and was widely welcomed by most segments of the public. Bourguiba was officially retired to his native village of Monastir, and has, by and large, been removed from the public eye. However, he is still regarded within his country as the father of modern Tunisia, who promoted pro-western and secular policies which his successors continue to pursue, at varying degrees, to this day.

BOUTROS-GHALI, BOUTROS (b. 1922)

Egyptian scholar, Minister of State for Foreign Affairs (1977–1991), and Secretary General of the UN (1991–1996). Ghali was born in Cairo to a famous Copt family. Graduate of the Faculty of Law, University of Cairo (1946); and Ph.D. in international law, University of Paris (1949); Professor of International Law and International Relations at the Faculty of Economics and Political Science, University of Cairo (until 1977). Ghali was appointed Minister of State for Foreign Affairs by President AL-SADAT and in this capacity he accompanied the latter in his visit to JERUSALEM in November 1977. Ghali was involved as a senior diplomat and negotiator in the Egypt-Israel peacemaking (1977–1979). Given the opposition of Muslim foreign ministers to Sadat's peacemaking policy, Ghali effectively served as Foreign Minister and was appointed Deputy Prime Minister for Foreign Affairs. In 1991 he was appointed Minister of State for Matters of Immigration and Egyptians Abroad and shortly afterward was elected Secretary General of the United Nations. During those years, he was increasingly criticized by Western states, primarily the US administration for his in-

dependent decisions and views regarding the UN role in world peace in the post-Cold War era. He implemented a number of international mediation missions, especially concerning the civil war in Bosnia.

Ghali served as Professor and lecturer in various universities, *inter alia* the universities of Warsaw, Colombia, Algeria, Belgrad, Rabat, Dar al-Salam and Upsala. He was Head of al-Ahram's Center for Political and Strategic Studies (1975–1977); President of the African Society for International Studies (1980–1991); and member of the Committee for International Law at the UN (since 1978). Ghali is the author of numerous scholarly articles and books on international law and politics, especially concerning Arab and African affairs, as well as on his political memoirs (1997).

BRITAIN, BRITISH INTERESTS AND POLICIES

Great Britain first became involved in the Middle East in the sixteenth century, when the English mercantile system, European power struggles and British imperial dictates prompted the expansion of interests and control to the eastern periphery of the Mediterranean. The resulting commitments, reinforced by strategic considerations, created a string of garrisons and naval bases from Gibraltar (under British control since 1704) to the Indian subcontinent and beyond. As the Middle East was ruled by either the OTTOMAN EMPIRE or the Persian Empire, British traders and statesmen sought to establish amicable relations with both. In 1553, Sultan Suleiman gave English merchants permission to trade within his realm on the same terms as were then enjoyed by the French and Venetians, and in 1578 the first British Ambassador presented his credentials to the Sublime Port. Similarly, in 1566–1568, Shah Tahmasp gave English merchants the right to live and trade in Persia. Subsequent penetration of the Middle East thus came from the two directions of the Mediterranean and the PERSIAN GULF. The India Office was concerned with Persia and the maritime corridors to India, while the Foreign Office involved itself in Turkish affairs.

By the nineteenth century, the Ottoman Empire had declined so much that it became known as "the Sick Man on the Bosphorus" and posed before European diplomacy a sensitive "Eastern Question": what arrangements should replace the Ottoman Empire in the event of its demise? Great Britain was reluctant to see the Turkish domains, and especially Constantinople and the Dardanelles, come under the control of either FRANCE or RUSSIA. As a result, the survival, sovereignty and territorial integrity of the Turkish Empire were cardinal principles of British foreign policy. Britain's commitment to TURKEY often involved it in the external and domestic affairs of the Empire. Through the Treaty of Paris, 1856, the Convention of London, 1871, and the Congress of Berlin, 1878, Britain endeavored to ensure Turkish security, and British interests, by peaceful means. Yet on several occasions Britain used force: against France, 1798; in ending the Egyptian Muhammad Ali's defiance of the Sultan, 1839; and against Russian expansion during the Crimean War, 1854–1856.

French and Russian designs on Turkish territory heightened London's appreciation of the Middle East and actually led to an extension of Britain's control. Napoleon's invasion of EGYPT in 1798 alerted Britain to the vulnerability of its lines of communication to India as well as to Egypt's strategic importance. The Sultan of OMAN and the sheikhs of BAHRAIN and KUWAIT subjected their foreign relations to exclusive British control in 1891, 1892 and 1899 respectively. Britain acquired Malta in 1815 and Aden in 1839. The TRUCIAL COAST, which had been brought under "Trucial Agreements" against piracy in 1820 and 1835, was pacified under a "Perpetual Maritime Truce" in 1853 and became a British Protectorate. Once the dream of a SUEZ CANAL became a reality in 1869, British politicians realized its importance as the primary route between Europe and the Orient. At Disraeli's initiative, Britain acquired a major share in the Canal and obtained a voice in its management. This was reinforced by the British occupation of Egypt in 1882, and transformed into a protectorate in December 1914. In 1878, Britain exploited renewed Russo-Turkish friction by taking over Cyprus.

As European Powers began to compete for oil concessions, one of the first and most important concessions was granted to W. K. D'Arcy in 1901 by Persia. This was acquired in 1909 by the Anglo-Persian Oil Company, in which the British Government possessed a controlling interest from 1914 (see OIL, IRAN). British interests also competed for railway concessions, although few materialized, and endeavored to frustrate rival powers' concessions, such as the German-controlled Baghdad Railway project.

River navigation was also an important British interest, especially on the Nile and Tigris-Euphrates systems. In IRAN, Britain exercised considerable influence, in constant competition with Imperial Russia. An Anglo-Russian Treaty of 1907 divided Iran into British and Russian zones of influence.

Turkey's decision to side with Germany in World War I, 1914, induced Britain to consent to the eventual partition of the Ottoman Empire. Russia was to take possession of Constantinople and the Straits (Secret Agreement of April 1915). According to the SYKES-PICOT AGREEMENT (with France and Russia), 1916, Britain was to obtain possession of southern Mesopotamia with Baghdad, and Haifa and Acre in Palestine. Central IRAQ, the region that later became known as Transjordan, and southern Palestine (the Negev) were to become a British zone of influence; Britain was also to participate in an international administration of the main parts of Palestine. Britain also sought contact with Arab leaders, to activate them against Turkey in the War and to protect British interests in the Arab world. London considered Sharif HUSSEIN of Mecca to be the most appropriate partner (though Britain was since 1915 in local treaty relations also with IBN SAʿUD of Najd, through the government of Britain India). In the MCMAHON-HUSSEIN CORRESPONDENCE, 1915–1916, Britain gave its qualified support for Arab independence, in return for which Hussein sponsored an Arab revolt against the Ottomans. (For later differences as to the extent of Arab independence see MCMAHON-HUSSEIN CORRESPONDENCE.) In November 1917, Britain issued the BALFOUR DECLARATION which extended British support to world Jewry for establishing a national home in Palestine.

The post-war settlement conferred upon British MANDATES to administer Iraq and Palestine (including Transjordan). By 1920, Britain enjoyed an unprecedented primacy in the Middle East. No other great power offered such a challenge. In the wake of the Bolshevik Revolution, Russia's new leaders had renounced traditional territorial claims; the Turkish nationalists under Mustafa Kemal did not wish to restore the Turkish Empire; Germany was defeated; the UNITED STATES OF AMERICA did not want to play any part in the Middle East power game; France was weakened by the war effort and had to use force to assert itsr claim to SYRIA and LEBANON. Local Arab nationalists, however, were unwilling to accept British tutelage, and there were rebellions and unrest in Iraq (1920), Egypt (1919, 1921), and local riots in Palestine (1920, 1921). The several conflicting wartime undertakings—to Hussein, to France and to the Zionist movement—aggravated the problem. Britain remained silent while France forcefully asserted its control over Syria and Lebanon in 1920.

Gradually, national elites in Egypt and Iraq accepted the semi-independence granted them under British guidance. British authority was exercised in Egypt through a protectorate (*de jure* until 1922, de facto until 1936); in Palestine and Iraq through Mandates confirmed by the League of Nations; and in Arabia and along the littoral of the Persian Gulf by direct treaty relationships with local sheikhs.

In an attempt to formulate a coherent policy, Winston Churchill, then Colonial Secretary, summoned British authorities to a conference in Cairo in 1921. Its decisions governed Angora relations during the interwar period. British interests and influence were to be ensured with minimal expenditure. The use of British troops could be avoided, it was hoped, by the efficient employment of air power, local Arab forces and monetary subsidies to various tribal leaders and rulers. Support was extended to Sharif Hussein in HIJAZ and to his soils, FEISAL enthroned by Britain in Iraq, and ABDALLAH made Amir of Transjordan (created in 1921 as a semi-independent principality within the League of Nations Mandate for Palestine). As for Palestine, London was initially confident that the Jewish and Arab communities could eventually be brought to cooperate under British rule; the Zionists considered the British authorities in London to be well-intentioned, but most of the British administrators in Palestine antagonistic. With the passing of time, Britain tended to favor the Arabs, largely for political and strategic reasons. In the Arab countries, British interests were to be fostered by the creation of semi-independent states under indirect British supervision or guidance rather than direct control. Such High Commissioners as General Allenby in Egypt and Sir Percy Cox in Iraq, reflected this spirit. The plan was to guide the Arab state gradually and peacefully to full independence while safeguarding British imperial interests. The transition to independence, and the satisfaction of British interests after its achievement, were to be laid down in treaties between Britain and the countries concerned.

In the period after 1921, British pre-eminence reached its peak. British oil interests increased their involvement in the PERSIAN GULF area, and relations with Iran, Iraq, Kuwait and SAUDI ARABIA grew in importance. Friction developed between Britain and the US, as their oil companies vied with each other for access to the oil-rich countries and concessions, and American companies felt excluded by British imperial rule. By the mid-1920s, Britain had to admit American companies to areas of its concessions and interests, such as Iraq and later Kuwait and in the 1950s Iran. In BAHRAIN and Saudi Arabia, American oil interests won the concessions on their own.

In the Arab countries under British tutelage, the nationalists continued their struggle for more independence, to be codified in new treaties—separate and divergent in each country. (For this process in Egypt—from Britain's 1922 unilateral proclamation of Egypt's independence with reservations, Britain retaining authority for defense, the protection of foreign interests and the governance of SUDAN, to the twenty-year Treaty of 1936—see EGYPT, COLONIALISM. For the similar gradual emancipation of Iraq—from the Treaty of 1922 to the twenty-five-year Treaty of 1930, Iraq's admission to the League of Nations in 1932 and the termination of Britain's mandatory responsibility—see IRAQ, COLONIALISM). Britain continued to exert considerable de facto influence. Its still-privileged position soon caused renewed resentment and agitation in both countries. In Iraq, anti-British resentment played a role in a military coup led by General Bakr Sidqi in 1936, and in the late 1930s, the officers who de facto ruled Iraq were extreme nationalists and bitterly anti-British.

Transjordan provided the least troublesome relationship for Britain. The Amir Abdallah cooperated with Britain upon whom he was dependent financially and militarily. By the treaty of 1946, London recognized Transjordan as an independent Kingdom, but continued to aid it financially and subsidize its Army.

There were persistent rumors of British support for a planned HASHEMITE GREATER SYRIA or Fertile Crescent Union. The French, and anti-Hashemite Syrian and Lebanese politicians, certainly suspected such plans—as part of a secret British scheme to oust France from the Middle East. Indeed there was little British involvement in Syria and Lebanon during the interwar period.

In Arabia, Britain acknowledged Ibn Sa'ud's primacy after 1925, acquiescing in his conquest of Hijaz and the ouster of Britain's Hashemite protégés, Hussein and his son Ali. A treaty with Ibn Sa'ud was signed in 1927. British influence endured in the Persian Gulf sheikhdoms. Efforts to gain influence in Yemen were unsuccessful.

The greatest test of British preponderance in the Middle East occurred in Palestine. (For Arab hostility toward the Mandate, the British and the Jews; the Arab rebellion of 1936; the 1937 partition plan—rejected by the Arabs and soon dropped by Britain; the resumed Arab rebellion, 1937–1939; the Round Table Conference of 1939, including, at Britain's invitation, the Arab states; the White Paper of 1939—see PALESTINE ARABS, ARAB-ISRAEL CONFLICT).

That Britain had not gained the friendship of the Arabs was reflected in the sympathy which Italy and particularly Germany evoked in the region in the late 1930s. During World War II, a group of Egyptian military officers and politicians were in contact with Italian and German officials; and Egypt's government only grudgingly granted Britain the cooperation and facilities agreed to in the Treaty of 1936. The former MUFTI of JERUSALEM and some of his supporters took refuge in Berlin; as did pro-Nazi politicians from various Arab countries. In Iraq, the pro-Axis government of Rashid Ali initiated war with Britain in 1941, when Britain insisted on using the facilities and privileges provided for in the Treaty. Pro-British leaders were reinstated after the suppression of the Rashid Ali regime. In June 1941, Britain and Free French forces took Syria and Lebanon. Anglo-French antagonism soon reappeared—with Britain openly supporting Syrian and Lebanese nationalists against the French. To secure Iran and deny its territory to the enemy, Britain and Russian troops occupied the country in August 1941, and divided it into two zones—with Britain's zone much larger than in 1907. Abdallah of Transjordan was loyal, and the Jews of Palestine, while fighting against Britain's White Paper policy, fully supported its war against Hitler, though Britain was reluctant to form the 26,000 Palestinian-Jewish volunteers into a specifically Jewish Army, as they demanded. (Some of them were permitted to form a Jewish Brigade in 1944.)

The end of the War found Britain exhausted and confronted by new challenges from the Middle East ruling elites as well as from the USSR. Several means were used to maintain influence if not actual power in the region. Britain fostered friendly relations with the ARAB LEAGUE, founded in 1945; joined the US in insisting on a complete and speedy withdrawal of USSR troops from Iran, 1945–1946; put pressure on France to withdraw from Syria and Lebanon by supporting the local nationalists, 1943–1946; tried to retain a degree of influence on the Palestine conflict; endeavored to promote regional security by revising its treaties with Egypt and Iraq (both were suspended shortly after being signed) and organizations such as the abortive MIDDLE EAST DEFENSE ORGANIZATION, 1951, and the ill-fated Baghdad Pact, 1955; and even resorted to military force against Egypt during the Suez crisis of 1956.

Despite these efforts, Britain was unable to arrest the rapid decline of its position in the Middle East. From the late 1940s onwards, Britain encouraged American involvement in the Middle East. Britain was gradually overshadowed by the US, mainly after the Suez affair of 1956. In 1947, it granted India independence, thus removing one of the major justifications for a strong British presence in the Middle East. After final attempts to work out a Palestinian solution acceptable to both Arabs and Jews, Britain admitted failure in 1947, relinquished its Mandate to the UN and withdrew from Palestine in May 1948. In May 1950, it cosponsored (with the US and France) attempts to control arms supplies and vaguely to endorse existing Arab-Israel frontiers (the Tripartite Declaration), underlining the fact that Britain had ceased to be a chief factor. A grave Anglo-Persian crisis, 1951–1953, over the oil concession, ended with a compromise (1954), but Britain lost its exclusive stature in Iran's oil industry when the Anglo-Iranian Oil Company became one of, though not the largest, partner in a newly established consortium, together with a Dutch, a French and five American oil companies (see OIL).

In October 1954—Britain signed a new treaty with Egypt (now under a revolutionary government), in which it agreed to evacuate the Canal Zone bases and renounce any special privileges. Egypt's nationalization of the Suez Canal in 1956 and the abortive Anglo-French Suez War—the last attempt to impose imperial wishes by "gunboat diplomacy"—

highlighted the impotence of the two former imperial powers. Egypt now tore up even the inoffensive Treaty of 1954 and any special treaty relationship with Britain ended. Sudan was granted self-determination in 1955 and assumed full independence without any special concessions for, or treaty with Britain. In 1956–1957, Britain's special position in JORDAN was ended by the dismissal of Brigadier GLUBB, the British commander of Jordan's Army, and the replacement of Britain's subsidy for the army by Syrian-Saudi-Egyptian financial aid (which, however, was not implemented). Britain re-assumed a temporary role in July 1958, when its troops were asked by Jordan to ensure the latter's independence; but its privileged position in Jordan was not restored.

In Iraq, attempts to replace the Treaty of 1930 with a new one, were abortive. That Treaty was terminated, when both Britain and Iraq joined the Bagdad Pact, 1955. The revolution of 1958 ended Britain's privileges in Iraq. Kuwait gained independence in 1961—by peaceful means and in agreement with Britain; Kuwait immediately asked for British protection against Iraq. In 1967, British rule ended in the Crown Colony of Aden and the adjoining Protectorate. In 1970, Britain completed the evacuation of its bases in Libya. Those in the Persian Gulf were liquidated and British protection for the petty rulers of the Trucial Coast ended in 1971. In the course of the 1967 ARAB-ISRAEL CONFLICT, Arab oil producers imposed an oil embargo on Britain on the grounds of supporting its air offensive, but it was a short-lived experience which had hardly any effect on Britain's economy.

British oil companies are no longer as powerful as they once were. Britain's share among the foreign companies decreased from over fifty percent of production at the end of World War II, to less than thirty percent in the 1960s. In any case, all foreign oil companies lost most of their special power when, after a long process of change in the conditions and concessions in favor of the producing countries, the latter began in 1973 unilaterally to determine prices and production terms. Moreover, most oil production has, since the 1970s, been nationalized and the foreign companies continue working only as agents or operators on behalf of the producing countries and their national companies. Britain's primary interest in unimpaired access to the sources of oil in the region still endures, as does a desire to retain influence in the region through normal diplomatic channels. Britain also remains a major supplier of arms, and attempts, sometimes, to use that position as a diplomatic lever.

Britain participates, in some measure, in Western efforts to sponsor a Middle East peace settlement. Hence it was involved in abortive Four-Power talks on the Arab-Israel dispute in 1969–1970, and tried to assist American efforts in the 1970s and 1980s. Since 1973, Britain operated in this respect mainly through the European Community's institutions. On another issue, Britain actively participated in the Western attempts to secure free shipping in the Persian Gulf from 1986, due to the Iranian attacks on Gulf oil producers. Following the Iraqi invasion of Kuwait, Britain was second only to the US in being actively involved in forming the international coalition and in the war against the Iraqi occupation. Britain's own diplomatic relations with the Arab State were disrupted several times. Egypt, Sudan and ALGERIA severed relations in 1965 to protest its Rhodesia policy; Syria, Iraq and Sudan did the same in 1967 in connection with the Six-Day War (Egypt had no relations with Britain at that time). Relations were later resumed. Britain has severed relations with those Arab states it considered to be actively involved in TERRORISM—Libya (1984) and Syria (1986). However, like other European powers, Britain maintains trade relations with Iran, although their relations were interrupted due to the Salman RUSHDI affair (see IRAN).

al-BURAIMI Oasis in the Arabian peninsula, on the border between ABU DHABI and OMAN. Area: 13,490 sq. miles, (34, 948 sq. km.). Population is approximately 25,000 in eight villages of which six belong to Abu Dhabi, two to Oman. In the late 1940s, when it was reported that oil might be found in Buraimi, SAUDI ARABIA claimed the oasis, asserting that it had been ruled in the eighteenth and nineteenth centuries by the Saudi Sultans of Najd. This claim was disputed by BRITAIN, as the power protecting Abu Dhabi and Oman. In the Anglo-Saudi Treaty of Jedda (1927), the boundaries of the Saudi kingdom were drawn. Al-Buraimi had not been defined as Saudi. Behind the dispute, opposing interests of the oil giants were discernible. If Buraimi belonged to Abu Dhabi and/or Oman, its oil would be covered by concessions held by subsidiaries of the largely-British Iraq Petroleum Co. If it was Saudi territory, its oil would belong to the American ARAMCO.

In 1952, after a period of claims and counter-claims, Saudi Arabia sent a military force to occupy al-Buraimi. In 1954, arbitration was agreed upon, but it failed. In 1955 Buraimi was taken by military forces of Abu Dhabi and Oman, under British command. Saudi Arabia protested and after severing relations with Britain in 1956 following the Suez War, declared that relations would not be resumed until the Buraimi issue was settled.

However, Anglo-Saudi relations were renewed in January 1963 with the Buraimi dispute still unresolved. Further diplomatic efforts, including mediation on behalf of the UN Secretary-General, were of no avail. When Britain announced that it would withdraw its protectorate from the PERSIAN GULF sheikhdoms, Saudi Arabia in 1970 reasserted its claim to Buraimi. But when the British indeed withdrew, in 1971, creating a power vacuum, the Saudis resolved to improve their relations with the Gulf principalities and to ignore petty disputes standing in its way. In 1971 it promised the visiting Sultan of Oman that it would renounce its claim to Buraimi. That renunciation was formalized in a Saudi-Abu Dhabi border agreement of July 1974 (against certain concessions by Abu Dhabi in other border sectors).

Oil has in the meantime been found in Buraimi. The oasis has also been linked to Abu Dhabi by a modern highway and is being developed as a tourist resort.

C

CAIRO AGREEMENT, GAZA-JERICHO ACCORD   see ARAB-ISRAEL PEACEMAKING.

CALIPH   (Arabic: *Khalifa*, Successor or Replacement), **Caliphate** (*khilafa*) The Caliph was the head of the Muslim community, succeeding the Prophet Muhammad in his political and social functions (as distinct from his prophetic mission, in which there can be no successor). After the Prophet's death in 632, the Caliphs were his companions—"The Righteous Caliphs" (*al-khulafa' al-rashidun*): Abu Bakr, Othman, Omar, and Ali, then by the Umayyad (661–750) and Abassid (750–1258) dynasties. The succession was frequently disputed and civil wars erupted around it from the early days of ISLAM, attested to by the fact that apart from Abu Bakr, the other three Caliphs were murdered. The significant dispute over the Prophet's succession derived from the intransigent claim of his cousin and son-in-law, the fourth Caliph Ali Ibn Abi Taleb and his sons Hassan and Hussein, that only those in the lineage of the Prophet—namely, of his daughter Fatima and her husband Ali—may legitimately succeed him. All other Caliphs as were regarded usurpators. This dispute left its historic imprint on Islam, causing its split and the emergence of Shi'i Islam (in which both Ali and Hussein were killed). In SUNNI Islam, the office of Caliph remained open to political struggle in which military leaders usually participated, along with repeated wars of succession; the emergence of semi-independent Muslim rulers in various parts of the empire, especially from the tenth century. As a result, the office of the Caliph declined; various Muslim rulers arbitrarily assumed the title of Caliph, and the last Abassid Caliphs were mere figureheads. In 1517, the conquering Ottoman ruler (Sultan) assumed the title Caliph. Yet until the late-eighteenth century this title was of secondary significance compared to others denoting military power, expansion of the Empire and the realm of Islam at the expense of Christiandom, related to the Ottoman Sultanate. From the late eighteenth century, with the weakening stature of the Empire and territorial losses under growing pressure of the European powers, the Ottoman Sultans reasserted the title Caliph as a spiritual authority over all Muslims, including those outside the Empire. Thus the Treaty of Kucuk Kaynarca with RUSSIA, 1774, stipulated that the Sultan retains such spiritual authority over the Muslim Tatars of the Crimea, which was granted independence. A similar provision was applied to LIBYA when, in 1912, TURKEY ceded it to Italy. The Sultan's position as Caliph was further reasserted when, in the late nineteenth century, Sultan ABDEL HAMID II developed PAN-

ISLAMIC policies which were incorporated in the Ottoman constitution of 1876.

During World War I, the Ottoman Sultan used his office as Caliph to arouse sympathy for Turkey among Muslims in the countries allied against it, e.g. in India. Resistance to Britain's war effort emerged with the declaration of Holy War (JIHAD). While there was an element of sympathy, it did not lead to rebellions or resistance. Moreover, loyalty to the Sultan-Caliph, which generally prevailed in the Arab-populated countries of the Fertile Crescent, did not deter the Muslim-Arab Sharif HUSSEIN Ibn Ali of Mecca from declaring Holy War against the Ottoman Caliph, and rebelling against him (see ARAB REVOLT). Yet, after the war, rumors of plans by the Allied Powers to dismember the Ottoman Empire and abolish the office of Caliph led to the formation of a Caliphate (khilafa) movement in India from 1919, to protect it. The institution of Caliph was finally abolished in March 1924 by Turkey's nationalist-secular regime led by Mustafa Kemal (ATATÜRK), forever exiling all members of the Ottoman dynasty, less than two years after the abolition of the Sulatanate and proclamation of Turkey as a republic. These steps ended three years (1920–1923) of fighting against the Peace Treaty of SÈVRES, dictated by the Allied powers and submitted to by the Sultan-Caliph, which would have dismembered the Turkish heartland.

The abolition of the Caliphate, along with Kemal's policy of cutting nationalist Turkey's ties with its Ottoman-Islamic heritage, aroused puzzled hostility among the world's Muslims. Various Muslim rulers now began scheming to have themselves recognized as Caliph, with intensified activity of the Indian Caliphate Committee, led by the brothers Muhammad and Shawkat Ali. Indeed King HUSSEIN of HIJAZ openly staked his claim and proclaimed himself Caliph (1924), while similar plans regarding IBN SA'UD, or Kings Fu'ad and later Farouq of EGYPT, were rumored but never officially confirmed. Anyway, none of them gained much support. In 1926 an Islamic Congress was convened in Cairo to plan the renewal of the Caliphate. However, this was not representative of all Muslims, failed to agree on a candidate, and dispersed with a call for future action. No Muslim consensus was achieved henceforth either, and as nationalism became the dominant trend, calls for the re-establishment of the Caliphate

diminished and were largely disregarded. Even the revival, since the 1960s, of radical Islamic tendencies (see ISLAMIC FUNDAMENTALISM) failed to give rise to any movement for the renewal of the Caliphate.

CAMP DAVID AGREEMENTS see ARAB-ISRAEL PEACEMAKING.

CAPITULATIONS Agreements exempting foreigners from local jurisdiction in various spheres such as personal status, commerce and navigation, as well as their religious, educational and charitable institutions. (The term derives from the chapters or paragraphs—Latin: capitula—of the agreements, not from "capitulation" in the usual sense.) The great medieval merchant powers—Genoa, Venice, Pisa—were first granted the right to exercise jurisdiction over their nationals in the Middle East in the eleventh and twelfth centuries by the Crusader princes, and later also by Byzantium. The OTTOMAN EMPIRE, consolidating and expanding in the fifteenth and sixteenth centuries, and interested in the development of trade with Europe, took over and renegotiated such capitulations and concluded agreements with Genoa 1453, Venice 1454, FRANCE 1535, and England 1583. New Western states (e.g. UNITED STATES OF AMERICA, Belgium, Greece) were accorded similar capitulations rights as late as the nineteenth century. Capitulations' agreements were also concluded by Western states with other Eastern countries, e.g. MOROCCO, Persia, East African rulers, and the Far East. Most capitulations' agreements provided for consular jurisdiction or mixed tribunals.

For centuries, the capitulations were considered necessary to protect foreigners against arbitrariness, corruption, or xenophobia of local rulers. Some autonomy for foreigners also tied in with the Muslim MILLET SYSTEM tradition in the Ottoman Empire which granted the non-Muslim communities jurisdiction in matters of personal status, wide autonomy in religious matters and the maintenance of educational and charitable institutions. The capitulations also encouraged foreign investment, in which the Ottoman Empire and other eastern countries were interested.

The capitulations were abolished, first, in the parts of the Ottoman Empire lost to countries gaining their independence or to the Western powers—e.g. Romania 1877, Bosnia-Herzegovina 1880, Serbia 1882, Tripolitania (taken by Italy) 1913. In Morocco (under a French Protectorate) the capitulations were abolished in 1912. In independent Greece, they were initially maintained, but gradually abolished from 1914. The settlement after World War Iorld War I included the suspension of the capitulations in the Mandated territories of SYRIA and LEBANON, and of Palestine and Transjordan. The Peace Treaty of 1919 imposed the renunciation of capitulations' rights on the defeated Central Powers, too. Soviet RUSSIA voluntarily renounced any capitulations rights in 1921.

Where capitulations still remained, they were now resented, seen as illicit strongholds of Imperialism, and eventually abolished as a result of a nationalist struggle. In TURKEY, the Western powers sought to maintain capitulations rights in the Peace Treaty of SÈVRES they imposed on the Sultan. Yet when the nationalists tore up that document, the West did not insist on capitulations, renouncing them in the new Peace Treaty of LAUSANNE, 1923. In IRAN (1928) and IRAQ (1931) the capitulations were replaced, under juridical reforms, by certain contractual arrangements. In EGYPT they were abolished by international agreement: the Convention of MONTREUX, 1937, provided for a transitional arrangement of mixed courts for a period of twelve years. That arrangement was duly terminated in 1949 and the last remnant of capitulations disappeared. When Syria and Lebanon, JORDAN and ISRAEL became fully independent in the 1940s, no attempt was made to revive capitulations' rights.

CASPIAN SEA

The largest salt water lake in the world, 730 miles long (1,174 km.) and 130-270 miles wide (209-434 km.), with an area of 170,000 square miles (4,408 sq. km.). It is the largest production area in the world for caviar, and contains extensive oil and gas reserves. The total length of the Caspian sea coast in about 4,000 miles (6,432 km.), of which 650 miles (1,045 km.) are on the Iranian side and the rest divided among russia, Azerbeijan, Kazakhstan and Turkemenistan. After the disintegration of the Soviet Union, the coastal states set up an organization called "the Caspian Sea Cooperation Zone", with the goal of cooperating on all issues connected with the lake's environment and the utilization of its natural wealth. However, the organization's member states have not yet reached an agreement as to whether the Caspian sea is a sea or

a lake. If it is agreed to define it as a sea, every state will have the right to act along its own coast as it may see fit, whereas if it is defined as a lake every act will require the agreement of all or most of the coastal states. The importance of this debate grew after Azerbaijan set up an international company to produce oil along its shore in 1995, and under American pressure cancelled a previous decision to sell five percent of the company's shares to Iran.

CATHOLICS

There are about 2 million Catholics in the Middle East. In the *Mashriq*—the eastern part of the Arab world—over eighty-five percent of the Catholics belong to UNIATE churches, i.e. parts of Eastern Christian communities that joined the Greek-Catholic church *en bloc*, accepting the supremacy of the Pope, but maintaining their own Eastern rites and customs, a measure of autonomy concerning liturgy (including its language) and church organization and administration. (Arabic: *Rum-Katholik*, denotes the Uniate GREEK CATHOLIC Church.) Less than fifteen percent belong to the Roman-Catholic church proper (Arabic: LATIN), whose origins lay in the split with the (Eastern) Orthodox Church in 1054. Some are descendants of converts of the Crusader period, but most are more recent converts from the Eastern Church communities. The members of this Church perform the Roman rites, the liturgy used to be said in Latin until the 1960s—following which a greater use of Arabic led to increased participation by the congregation—and follow the practices of the Church in Rome. Proselytizing among the Eastern communities by the Latin Church was banned by the Papal Encyclica *Orientalium Ecclesiarum Dignitas* of 1894, and all such proselytizing was entrusted to the Uniate Churches alone. The 85/15 proportion between Uniate-Catholic and Latin communities does not apply to the Arab countries of North Africa. As SUDAN and the MAGHREB were not within the realm of the Eastern (GREEK ORTHODOX, Byzantine) church and its schismatic offshoots, no Uniate Churches developed there either, and the Catholics there are all Latin. In SUDAN, nearly all Catholics are among the Negro tribes of the South, recent converts (nineteenth and twentieth centuries) of Latin-Catholic missionaries.

The Latin-Catholic church first appeared in the Middle East with the Crusaders and soon embarked on intensive missionary efforts—converting both individuals to the Latin Church and, later, whole groups of Eastern Christians, through the Uniate described. Nearly all converts were Eastern Christians—not Muslims or JEWS. Estimates as to the number of Latin Catholics in the Middle Eastern countries are inprecise due to the absence of official data. The total number, including foreign Catholics, is estimated at approximately 550,000; 230,000 in the Maghreb (mostly in MOROCCO; 200,000 in Sudan; 100,000 in the Fertile Crescent, mostly in LEBANON and JORDAN ; 30,000 in EGYPT; and smaller communities in IRAQ, and IRAN. Administratively, the Latin Patriarch of JERUSALEM is responsible for the Catholics in ISRAEL, the WEST BANK and JORDAN (and also Cyprus), with apostolic delegates (*nuncios*) in Baghdad, Beirut, and Cairo. In other countries of the Middle East, there are apostolic vicarages headed by apostolic administrators. The Latin-Catholic Church maintains several educational, charitable and monastic institutions, particularly in Jerusalem, Bethlehem and Lebanon (including two universities—the University of St. Joseph in Beirut, founded in 1875 out of a Jesuit college established in 1839, and the University of Bethlehem, attaining university status in 1973).

The Eastern Catholic (Uniate) Churches comprise the MARONITES (600,000-700,000—nearly all in Lebanon, or Lebanese migrants in the West); the Greek Catholics, also called Melkites (250-300,000—nearly 200,000 in Lebanon, most of the rest in SYRIA, Israel and the West Bank); the CHALDEANS (about 200,000—almost all in Iraq; more Chaldeans are in India, estimated by some at 200,000—but the distinction between various Eastern churches and their sectarian offshoots has become somewhat blurred in India); the Coptic Catholics in Egypt (about 80,000). The Syrian Catholics (about 60,000) and the ARMENIAN Catholics (about 50,000)—Uniate offshoots from the Coptic, Syrian and Armenian "orthodox" MONOPHYSITIC churches. Each of these six Uniate Churches is led by a patriarch.

CENTO (Central Treaty Organization) New, official name given in August 1959 to the defense alliance between TURKEY, IRAN, Pakistan and BRITAIN (with the USA as associate and chief supporter) established in 1955 by the Baghdad Pact. That former name had become inappropriate with the withdrawal of IRAQ (revolutionary since July 1958) in March 1959. (see also IRAN.)

In 1964 Iran Turkey, and Pakistan established the Regional Cooperation for Development (RCD), the goal of which was twofold: to neutralize the sharp Soviet propaganda over the fact that CENTO was merely a military organization "engaged in inciting war," and to improve the economic situation of the member states. However, the contribution of the organization to economic development of the member states was small. In 1976 it was decided to set up a common market and in March 1977 the establishment of a regional development bank was announced. Steps were also taken to expand the regional cooperation in the spheres of industry, agriculture, transportation, communications and culture. However, the total contribution of the organization to regional development throughout its years of operation remained insignificant. The organization ceased operating in 1978 although it enjoyed a revival by the new Iranian regime, under the name ECO.

CHALDEANS The branch of the Nestorian ASSYRIAN Church that broke away (from it) and joined the Roman Catholic Church in 1552 through the UNIATE, under the leadership of John Sulaka, who had been appointed Patriarch of the Catholic Nestorians by the Pope. They follow East Syriac liturgy and retain administrative autonomy. Originally from Chaldea and Mesopotamia, the Chaldeans live mostly in IRAQ. Some live in IRAN, and there are small groups residing in TURKEY, LEBANON SYRIA, EGYPT and India. The Chaldean community grew considerably after World War I through conversions of Assyrian refugees in Iraq. There are approximately 215,000 Chaldeans in Iraq, residing mostly in Nasseriyya. The Chaldean Church is headed by a the Patriarch of Babylon, who used to reside in Mosul, but transferred his seat to Baghdad.

CHAMOUN, CAMILLE (Sham'un, Kamil) (1900–1987) Lebanese politician. President of Lebanon 1952–1958. One of the primary leaders of the Maronite-Christian community. Born in Deir al-Qamar in southern Mount Lebanon (the Shuf)— a region that remained his home and power base until it was taken over by the DRUZE militias in 1983— Chamoun graduated from the French Law College of Beirut (1925), and has been a member of most Parliaments since 1934. He became Minister in 1938 (Finance) and in 1943 (Interior), playing an important role in the events leading to the "National Pact" that year (see LEBANON, MARONITES). In 1944 he was appointed Minister to Great Britain and in 1946 headed Lebanon's delegation to the UNITED NATIONS. Chamoun belonged to Bishara al-Khouri's "Constitutional Bloc" that stressed Lebanon's Arab character and advocated its integration in all-Arab alignments and the termination of special ties to FRANCE. He was considered anti-French (and pro-British). In 1947–1948 he served again as a Cabinet Minister. But when President Khouri and the government arranged, in May 1948, to have the Constitution amended so that Khouri could be re-elected (as he duly was, in 1949), Chamoun resigned and joined the opposition. As resistance to Khouri during his second term increased and he was accused of corruption and malpractices, Chamoun staged a semi-coup in the summer of 1952 that forced Khouri to resign. In September 1952 Chamoun was elected President, with seventy-four of the parliament's seventy-seven votes.

As President, Chamoun followed a policy of close relations with the West and cautious neutrality towards the other Arab countries. His pro-Western attitudes brought him into growing conflict with the swelling tide of Leftist-Nasserist tendencies inside and outside Lebanon. These forces resented his authoritarian inclinations and accused him of rigging the parliamentary elections of 1957, which left many of his adversaries out of Parliament. When SYRIA and EGYPT merged in 1958, he stoutly opposed the trends pushing Lebanon to join the Syro-Egyptian camp. Clashes developed in May 1958 into a Civil War, which was also fanned by rumors that Chamoun intended, like his predecessor, to seek re-election. Lebanon complained to the UN Security Council against Syro-Egyptian intervention, Chamoun requested the help of the US armed forces, and in July 1958 US marines landed in Beirut. A compromise agreement that ended the civil war in September 1958 included Chamoun's renunciation of any plan to run for a second presidential term, and with the end of his term, the same month, he stepped down. He now founded a political party of his own, the "National Liberal Party", and remained an elder statesman enjoying powerful influence; but he returned to a governmental position, as Minister only for a year, during the Civil War of 1975–1976 and as Finance Minister in the "National Unity Gov-

ernment" since 1984; neither of these governments functioned very well.

In the years since 1958 Chamoun has become a spokesman for the Christian camp, resisting Lebanon's active integration in Pan-Arab alignments and wishing to preserve its pluralistic character under Christian-Maronite leadership and its communal structure protecting that pluralism. In the 1960s Chamoun and his party established a loose "Triple Alliance" with the camp's other factions: Pierre JU-MAYYIL's PHALANGES and Raymond Edde's "National Bloc". During the civil war that erupted in 1975 Chamoun headed a rather loose "Lebanese Front" of various Christian-Maronite-dominated conservative factions that resisted a Muslim-Leftist takeover; but his chairmanship was little more than nominal and the real decisions were taken by the leaders of the factions and their militias. Chamoun and his party set up an armed militia of their own—the "Tigers" ("al-Numur", named after Chamoun's father, Nimer, and headed by his son, Danny)—but in July 1980 the Phalanges forcefully eliminated them as a fighting force. Their remnants were incorporated in the Phalanges-led Lebanese Forces, and Chamoun soon recognized Bashir Jumayyil's leadership over the Christian-Maronite camp. He did not play a dominant role in the post-1982 regime headed by the Jumayyil brothers.

Chamoun was one of the Maronite leaders striving towards cooperation with ISRAEL in the mid-1970s, and at its height, in 1982, delegated his son Danny (b. 1934, assassinated 1990), groomed as his political heir, to maintain contact. In the past, he had never openly advocated cooperation with Israel, although there are reports that in 1958, during the Civil War, he received modest Israeli aid. When President Amin Jumayyil reneged on his brother's policies and annulled the 17 May 1983 agreement with Israel, Chamoun opposed that step and recommended continuing Lebanon-Israel cooperation, but in April 1984 agreed to join the "Government of National Unity". Jumayyil was compelled to form a front dominated by Chamoun's leading adversaries; but he seemed to regard this as a token contribution to national reconciliation and was not very active in the affairs of the government or his ministry.

Chamoun published his memoirs in 1949 (and a revised edition, in 1963), as well as a book on the Lebanese crisis, in 1978.

CHRISTIANS As Christianity spread, from its original home in today's ISRAEL to the Fertile Crescent and EGYPT, this region became the cradle and heartland of the Eastern Christian world, overshadowed by Byzantium. Its main cities—Alexandria and Antioch—were, besides Constantinople, the spiritual and administrative capitals of Eastern Christianity. The main body of Eastern Christianity—later to be called the GREEK ORTHODOX church—was rent from the third century to the fifth, by schisms reflecting the internal differences within the Church on such issues as the natures of Christ (divine, or divine and human) and the relationship of the Holy Spirit to the Father (God) and the Son (Christ). The schismatic churches established the Nestorians, ASSYRIANS, MONOPHYSITES, Monothelites, MARONITES, all had their cradle and center in this region. Ethnic and local opposition to Byzantium—Constantinople's centralistic rule of the church, may well have been linked to the theological issues causing the schisms. At the time of the Muslim-Arab conquest, in the seventh century, the majority of the population was Christian.

Throughout the following centuries, a majority embraced ISLAM and became linguistically and culturally Arabized. Those who remained Christian—most of them also Arab-speaking—became a minority. Some, particularly in remote mountainous areas, retained their Syriac-Aramaic language, at least for liturgical purposes.

The number of Christians probably increased somewhat during the Crusades. From that time on, the Catholic version of Christianity also penetrated the region—through direct conversion (mostly of Eastern Christians, not of Muslims or Jews) to the Catholic-Latin rite, or through the adoption *en bloc* of Catholicism by whole communities of the eastern churches (the UNIATE). Protestant communities were created through the activities of missionaries (from English-speaking, German and Scandinavian countries), from the nineteenth century.

There are approximately 7–8 million Christians in the Middle East comprising two to three percent of the population, with numerically significant communities only in Egypt, LEBANON, SYRIA, Israel and the WEST BANK, and among the Negro tribes of South SUDAN. Demographically, there has been a constant trend, since World War II and the advent of independent Arab-Muslim states, of decreasing numbers of the Christian population in these countries. This is reflective of relatively high proportions of emigration, primarily to the Americas, and low population growth. Although an extreme example, the Christians of Lebanon reflect these trends. They constituted, according to the last census taken in 1932, approximately fifty-three percent of the country's population with the Maronites as the largest single community (thirty percent of the total, nearly fifty-percent of the Christians). They therefore had a predominant influence on the country's informal constitution (the National Pact of 1943), which provided for a communal structure of parliamentary and governmental institutions, with primary status to the Maronites (stipulating for instance, that the President should always be a Maronite Christian, as should the commander of the army, and governor of the central bank). During independence (from 1946), however, the proportion of Christians—and particularly of Maronites— declined. This was apparently due to growing ARAB NATIONALISM which threatened the Maronites' traditional links with Western culture and economy; the rise of Palestinian guerrilla movements and military activities on and from Lebanon's territory, and Israel's retaliations. These events culminated in a long and ruinous Civil War, including a major Israeli invasion and war on the soil of this country. Although no official data is available (for political reasons no official census has been taken since 1932, see LEBANON), the number of Christians in the late 1990s is estimated to form only thirty five to forty percent of Lebanon's population, of whom the Maronites constitute about twenty percent. Egypt's Christians, most of them Monophysite COPTS, constitute about seven percent of the population, over 3 million (the Copts claim a larger percentage). Syria's Christians—about one-third Greek-Orthodox, one-third Armenians, one-third other denominations—form ten to fourteen percent of the population. In JORDAN, Christians constitute five to six percent. Christians comprise about five percent of Sudan's total population, but among the non-Arab, non-Muslim Negro tribes of the south, Christians, mostly Catholics, are estimated at fifteen to twenty percent. In all other Arab countries, Christians are minority groups, less than five percent and in the countries of the Arabian Peninsula and the PERSIAN GULF there are virtually none, except for foreigners. In Israel, there are 90,000–95,000 Arab

Christians (less than two percent of the total population and about twelve percent of the non-Jewish population).

In the OTTOMAN EMPIRE, the MILLET SYSTEM(especially since the nineteenth century) gave most of the Christian communities a large measure of autonomy in their religious life, the administration of community affairs and educational and charitable institutions. Matters of personal status, like marriage, divorce, guardianship etc., were under the jurisdiction of communal-ecclesiastical courts. In some countries—Jordan, Lebanon, Israel—this system still prevails, somewhat adjusted to conditions of modern life. In other countries it has been wholly or partially abolished, representing a drive toward nation building and social integration. Thus Egypt has abolished Christian religious courts, and Syria has restricted their authority. Christian educational autonomy has also been curtailed. Educational institutions, in large part owned and maintained by foreign missionaries, have been subjected to nationalization and expropriation measures and those that were not closed altogether have been placed under strict state supervision. Such restrictive measures derive in part from the growing emphasis on the Islamic character of the Arab countries, and mainly from their nationalist-centralist and in part authoritarian regimes. Their suspicion of Western missionary institutions, seen as a continuation of European colonialism and as serving Imperial interests, plays a significant part.

Arab Christians, mainly from Lebanon and Syria, played a significant role in the formation of Arab nationalism, particularly in its early stages in the early twentieth century, when it was marked by liberal thought, enlightenment and literary revival. Between the two World Wars, however, Arab Nationalism assumed increasingly popular character due to the growing politicization of the masses, and became involved in the struggle for national liberation and political power. Henceforth, Muslims took over the leadership of Arab Nationalism, with the dividing lines between Arab Nationalism and Islamic revival becoming blurred (see ARAB NATIONALISM, PAN-ISLAM), rendering the role of Christians in Arab Nationalist Movements more difficult.

As a minority community in a region where communal-religious allegiances still prevail, the Christian Arabs' attitude to Arab Nationalism has tended to be ambivalent, reflecting concern lest it might impair their communal semi-autonomy or even endanger their very survival. Hence, Arab-Christian communities; largely tended to defend their semi-autonomy and to dissociate themselves from Pan-Arab nationalism, at least in its more extreme manifestations. In Lebanon, the center of Christian political awareness and activity, the Maronites adopted the concept of Christian-based pluralism of their country, and mooted the idea of Lebanon as a "Christian National Home" and a center and refuge for all Christian Arabs. Arab Christians also tend to see themselves closer to the West and its civilization, and socially and educationally more advanced than their Muslim neighbors Christian leaders. Other Christians, however, have displayed a radical Arab nationalism—some of them perhaps out of an age-old minority instinct to over-compensate, to over-stress conformity to the majority's ideals. They assume that the minority's survival is more safely ensured by integrating in the mainstream of the majority's policies than by resisting them. The most conspicuous protagonists of this attitude were GREEK-OR-THODOX intellectuals in Syria and Lebanon who played a leading role in forming some of the most important Arab Nationalist Movements in the contemporary Middle East. Among these figures were Michel AFLAQ, a cofounder of the BA'TH (renaissance) Party and its leader in Syrian politics for two decades; Antoun Sa'adeh, founder of the SYRIAN NATIONALIST SOCIAL PARTY and ideolog of the aspiration for GREATER SYRIA); and Custantine Zuraiq, the spiritual leader of the ARAB NATIONALISTS MOVEMENT.

ÇILLER, TANSU Turkish politician, Prime Minister 1993–1996. Çiller was born in Istanbul in 1946 and graduated from Bogaziçi University in economics. She received a Ph.D. from the University of Connecticut and did post doctoral work at Yale. Returning to Turkey, she taught economics at Bogaziçi, becoming full professor in 1983. In 1990 she joined Süleyman DEMIREL's True Path Party and in 1991 was elected member of the Grand National Assembly from Istanbul. She was appointed state minister in Demirel's cabinet, responsible for the economy. Upon Demirel's election to the Presidency, in June 1993, Çiller was elected leader of the Party and appointed Prime Minister. In September 1995 she was forced to resign after her coalition partner, the Republican People's Party, withdrew from the coalition. Failing to win a vote of confidence for a new government, she formed an interim government with the Republican People's Party until the elections.

In the December elections, the Islamic oriented Welfare Party (led by Necmettin Erbakan) emerged in first place with 158 of the 550 seats, with the True Path Party and Motherland Party winning 135 and 132 seats respectively. Bowing to strong public pressure to keep the Islamists out of power, Çiller in March 1996 formed a coalition government with the Motherland Party and agreed on a rotation system which awarded the premiership first to her bitter rival Mesut YILMAZ. But in May 1996 Çiller pulled her Party out of the coalition after Parliament (with Motherland's support) voted to investigate her on allegations of corruption. In June, Çiller entered into a new coalition government with ERBAKAN's Welfare Party. Another rotation was established in which Erbakan would become Prime Minister for the first two years with Çiller as his deputy and foreign minister. However, growing pressure of the army on Erbakan due to his Islamist policies, resulted in Erbakan's resignation and the fall of the government in June 1997. The new coalition government was formed with the Motherland Party's leader Mesut Yilmaz as Prime Minister. With only two thirds of the True Path Party's members originally elected to the Assembly, Çiller and her Party were driven to the opposition.

The first woman Prime Minister in Turkish history, Çiller basically continued Demirel's line of a strong Western oriented foreign policy, privatization of the public sector and a tough hand against PKK Kurdish rebels. She won wide acclaim for herself in the West, but at home was severly criticized for her toughness, economic failure, and alleged acts of corruption, as yet unsubstantiated. Mutual personal hostility between Çiller and Yilmaz has accounted for weakening the Center Right and its difficulty in forming a "secularists" alliance to block the Islamists from gaining power.

CIRCASSIANS   One of the peoples of the Caucasus. Their region was ceded to RUSSIA by the OTTOMAN EMPIRE in 1829. After rebellions that endured until 1859 and the expansion of Russian control over additional regions in the Caucasus, many Circassians, mostly Muslims, emigrated to the Ottoman Empire. They were willingly accepted and settled there. Some of them reached Thrace, in European TURKEY, while most settled in the Asian, Arab-populated parts of the Empire—SYRIA, IRAQ, Transjordan, Palestine. These had been partially assimilated by the Arabs. They maintained their language for two to three generations, but it later gave way to Arabic. Nonetheless it is still spoken to some degree, and efforts are being made to revive and cultivate it and introduce its teaching in the schools. This tendency has been particularly strengthened with the collapse of the Soviet Union and renewed contact with the Circassians of the Caucasus in the early 1990s. The way of life of the Circassians in their villages and towns is similar to that of the Arabs in whose midst they live. They have, however, maintained their distinctive character and most of them still live in Circassian villages.

The number of Circassians is estimated at 30,000–35,000 in Syria, the same number in JORDAN; 10,000 in Iraq; 3,000 in ISRAEL. In Jordan, many Circassians serve in the army, and the officers' corps contain a disproportionate amount of Circassians. They also have many Civil Service members, and several Circassians have attained high political and governmental office (the more so as they are considered deeply loyal to the royal family and a mainstay of the regime). King HUSSEIN's eldest daughter married a Circassian. The Circassians in Israel usually maintained good relations with their Jewish neighbors and took no part in the Palestine Arabs' struggle against the JEWS. Like Jews and DRUZE they are conscripted for compulsory military service (unlike Israeli Arabs, who may volunteer but are not conscripted).

The migrating Circassians were joined, in the nineteenth century, by a number of Chechens. In the course of time, the differences between these two related peoples disappeared and the Chechens were assimilated by the Circassians.

COLONIALISM   Territories were conquered throughout history by foreign powers, often followed by settlement of the newly acquired lands by the occupiers. The ancient Greeks established "colonies" all over the Mediterranean islands and coasts, as did the Phoenicians and Carthage; the Muslim-Arab conquests and the invasions of Mongol and Turkish peoples entailed, or were followed by, settlement. The term colonialism primarily applies to overseas conquests and settlement since the sixteenth century—by Portugal, Spain, the Netherlands, BRITAIN and FRANCE, Germany, Italy and Belgium in the nineteenth century. The UNITED STATES OF AMERICA never acquired "colonies".—Except for some Pacific islands and the Philippines, never officially a "colony" (for the perception of US economic penetration and influence as indirect colonialism or Neo-colonialism—see below. Russian expansion into Siberia, Central Asia and the Caucasus, in the nineteenth century, can be defined as direct colonialism, and Russia's pressure on and penetration of IRAN and Ottoman territories as indirect colonialism. Yet, as that expansion took place overland, into contiguous, adjacent territories, it was frequently excluded from accounts of great-power colonialism. RUSSIA has never exercised direct control over any Arab territory, which facilitated its breakthrough from the mid-1950s.

Direct colonialism in the narrow sense of the term—i.e. the definition of a territory as a "colony" owned and administered by the foreign power in possession—can be applied to the Middle East in three instances only:Aden colony, which was occupied by the British in 1839, ruled by the Governor of Bombay Province, later (1932–1937) by the Government of British India, and from 1937 as a Crown Colony; ALGERIA, conquered by France in 1830, never termed a "colony", but annexed and considered an integral part of France; and Tripolitania-LIBYA, also not termed a "colony", but annexed in 1911–1912 by Italy and administered, despite some abortive attempts to bestow partial autonomy, as part of Italy (though by a Ministry of Colonial Affairs). One could include SUDAN, ruled since 1899 by a "Condominium" of Great Britain and EGYPT (itself de facto, a British Protectorate). Among the non-Arab countries that joined the ARAB LEAGUE the following should be added: MAURITANIA, a French Protectorate from 1903, defined as a colony in 1920 (renamed "Overseas Territory" in 1946, and a member of the "French Community" 1958–1960); French Somali (DJIBOUTI), a "French territory" or colony from the 1880s; and SOMALIA, acquired by Italy in the late 1880s and administered from 1905 until World War II as a colony. Colonists, settlers, were implanted mainly in Algeria and Libya (and also TUNISIA); all of them left after independence.

All these instances of direct colonial rule have been eliminated: Aden is part of independent SOUTH YEMEN (1967); Algeria has been independent since 1962; Libya (captured from the Italians in World War II)—since 1951; Sudan since 1956; Mauritania since 1960; Djibouti since 1977; and Somalia (also taken from Italy during World War II)—since 1960.

Colonialism in its broader sense, however, may also mean the imposition of a European power's domination by indirect rule, protectorates, or excessive control of economic assets and inequitable concessions (OIL, other raw materials, railways, shipping, canals etc.). It was in that sense that colonialism prevailed for long periods throughout the Middle East. As the OTTOMAN EMPIRE grew weaker in the nineteenth century, the European powers increasingly intervened in its crises—Balkanic and Near-Eastern—imposing a measure of control or supervision and obtaining various concessions. (A similar process affected Persia, which was divided in 1907 into British and Russian spheres of influence.) In 1840 the European powers imposed on the Ottoman Sultan and Muhammad Ali, the semi-autonomous governor of Egypt, who had rebelled against his suzerain and occupied Syria, a settlement officially approving Egypt's semi-independence under Muhammad Ali and his decendants. In the 1840s they began intervening in Lebanon, compelling the Sultan in 1860–1961 to grant autonomy to the Mount Lebanon Christian-majority region. In the 1870s they imposed on Egypt an Anglo-French administration of its foreign debts, i.e., of its finances and economy. In 1882 Britain occupied Egypt and took over its administration—in what it termed a temporary occupation, leaving the ruler (the *Khedive*), in office and recognizing the Ottoman Sultan's suzerainty. This amounted in fact to a semi-colonial protectorate. In 1914 such a protectorate was officially proclaimed. These power interventions were sometimes made in concert, but often in rivalry and dispute—mostly between Britain and France.

In 1881, after increasing intervention and several crises between the powers, France imposed a protectorate on Tunisia, and in 1912, on MOROCCO (neutralizing Italy's objections by allowing it to annex Libya, and agreeing to a Spanish protectorate over parts of Morocco). During the nineteenth century, Britain also imposed its protection, via a series of treaties, on the principalities and sheikhdoms of the PERSIAN GULF—Muscat-and-OMAN, QATAR, BAHRAIN, the TRUCIAL COAST and finally, in 1899, KUWAIT—and those of Southern Arabia (Hadhramaut and the Aden Protectorates), and parts of Somali ("British Somaliland"). Some of these protectorates involved nearly-direct colonial administration. Growing British links with IBN SAʿUD of Najd, formalized in an agreement of 1915, and later, during World War I, with Sharif HUSSEIN of Mecca, led to alliances rather than formal protectorates. Yet in reality they were not equal partnerships and had the flavor of great-power protectorates.

During World War I, the allied "Entente" powers planned to divide the non-Turkish areas of the Ottoman Empire (after victory in the war and the dismemberment of the Empire's Asian territories) into "spheres of influence", or even territorial possessions to be allotted to the various powers (see SYKES-PICOT AGREEMENT, SÈVRES TREATY OF). Yet as the principle of self-determination for all peoples had been proclaimed as one of the war aims, particularly by US President Wilson, and specific promises had been made (e.g. to the Arab Sharif of Mecca) this could no longer be done in the old, straightforward imperial-colonial way. The compromise between the independence promised and imperial plans and interests was the system of the MANDATES, by which a Western power was charged by the LEAGUE OF NATIONS to "guide" to independence "peoples not yet able to stand by themselves". Such Mandates were entrusted to Britain for Palestine (including Transjordan) and IRAQ, and to France for SYRIA and LEBANON. In practice, the regime established by the Mandatory powers was a semi-colonial administration. Under British and French tutelage, semi-independent governments were gradually established in the mandated territories, except for Palestine. Such governments already existed, and continued in Egypt and in the French Protectorates of Tunisia and Morocco, but not in Libya, Sudan and the various parts of Somalia, where the administration was direct and colonial. The principalities of the Persian Gulf, under their British-"protected" sheikhs, had not yet evolved modern structures of administration and government.

The nationalists in the countries under such foreign tutelage regarded that governance—whatever its description—as a form of colonialism or imperial-ism and struggled to abolish it and attain full independence. Although the political elites, including most nationalists, cooperated in the establishment of semi-independent governments under that tutelage, it was the national struggle for its abolition that determined the political climate. The Western tutor countries strove to replace the mandate, or protectorate, with a treaty, according a formally complete independence, while bestowing on the protecting power special privileges that would continue ensuring its imperial political, economic and strategic interests. In the 1930s and 1940s, the local national governments of Iraq, Egypt, Syria, Lebanon, and Jordan looked for such treaty formulae, including most nationalists, though they often opposed the actual terms of the treaty drafted, because this was the only way to reach formal independence. However, in the aftermath of World War II, attempts to revise the existing treaties of Egypt and Iraq failed even though the political leadership was willing to sign the revised version, due to domestic opposition. By 1957 Britain's special position and privileges and the last vestiges of semi-colonialist military British presence had ended in Egypt, and two years later in Iraq as well. In both cases it was mainly as a result of military coups that rejected anything less than full independence, including imposed commitments to the ex-colonial power (see for example EGYPT, IRAQ, JORDAN).

France was always less enthusiastic than Britain with regards to the replacement of semi-colonial control by treaties with independent states. (For its unratified Treaties of 1936 with Syria and Lebanon, its renewed proclamation of their independence in 1941, and the final struggle of 1943–1946—see SYRIA, LEBANON.) By 1945–1946 all French bases and privileges and the last imperial-colonial military presence had been liquidated with no preferential treaty. (For the end of France's Protectorates over Tunisia and Morocco in 1956 and the liquidation of the last French military bases in Morocco in 1961 and in Tunisia in 1963—see TUNISIA, MOROCCO.) Algeria won its independence in 1962, after a seven year rebellion, and the last vestiges of French privileges—military-naval bases and the use of Algerian desert territory for nuclear tests—were liquidated in 1968. Mauritania and French Somali (Djibouti) won their independence in the process of the decolonization of Africa—the former in 1960, the latter in 1977.

Italy's colonial possessions were conquered by allied forces during World War II. A proposal to put Tripolitania (Libya) under an Italian trusteeship failed in 1949 to obtain the necessary two-thirds majority at the UN, and Libya became independent in 1951, after a provisional administration by Britain, and in the South by France, since the end of the war. Certain military bases that remained at the disposal of Britain, the US and France were evacuated—the French one in 1956, and the British and American ones in 1970. Former Italian Somalia was put under a ten year Italian trusteeship by the UN, in 1950, and became independent in 1960, merging with British Somaliland.

The few colonial possessions or semi-colonial protectorates remaining—all British—were liquidated in the 1960s and 1970s. The Aden Protectorates became a semi-independent federation in 1969, and Aden Colony joined that Federation in 1963. In 1967 Britain withdrew and the country became fully independent as "The People's Democratic Republic Yemen" (South Yemen). The British Protectorate of Somaliland became independent in 1960 (and united with former Italian Somalia). Kuwait emerged from the British protectorate in 1961 and became independent. In 1971 Britain withdrew its protection and military forces and bases from the rest of the Persian Gulf sheikhdoms and those became fully independent—Qatar, Bahrain, Oman, as well as the seven sheikhdoms of the Trucial Coast (who federated as the UNITED ARAB EMIRATES). Britain remained directly involved only in Oman, where British officers on contract continued to train and command the armed forces, at Oman's request.

The monopolies and preferential concessions, the economic domination obtained by Western companies (and by Russia in Persia) since the late nineteenth century and particularly between the two world wars have also been regarded as an aspect of colonialism and imperialism. This economic colonialism, too, has been on the decline since the 1950s and has largely been eliminated, particularly with regards to the oil industry. Giant multinational Western oil companies ("The Seven Sisters") dominated most oil extraction in the Middle East, controlled the world market, and were able to determine, through agreements with the producing countries, the terms of their concessions, the oil price and the royalties they paid, making huge profits. In the 1950s most producing countries obtained agreements on an equal, fifty-fifty, sharing of all profits—a process triggered by the bitter struggle of a radical government in Iran, 1951–1952, and the nationalization of the Anglo-Iranian Oil Company. A process of nationalization—by decree, or through the acquisition of a majority of shares in the companies operating in each country by the state (or by national oil companies established by the state)—continued, escalating in the 1970s. In the 1980s most oil companies in the Arab countries were wholly or largely owned by the state, and most foreign companies were operating as local government agents or under modest, greatly reduced concessions no longer conferring a dominating, semi-colonial influence. Since 1973 the local governments were also unilaterally (or in concert, through OPEC—but without the agreement of the purchasing countries or companies), setting the official oil price (escalating it in 1973 and 1979–1980).

Old-type colonialism was thus eliminated in the Middle East. A climate of anti-colonialism, an insistence that further struggle against colonialism is needed, prevails with most nationalists and many governments. It was often argued that "Neo-colonialism" still wields an undue, dominating influence, restricting the real independence of most countries of the "Third World"—through the domination and manipulation of world markets, particularly those for raw materials produced in Third World countries, through the manipulative use of the aid and credits proffered and the military equipment sold by the developed countries, and through their domination of world banking and finance. Such charges are usually levelled against the West (and not, for instance, against the Soviet Bloc—though the acquisition of Soviet influence and power bases in some Arab countries may well be termed indirect colonialism). They are aimed particularly at the USA rather than the former old-type colonial powers. To what extent such claims are just, and whether colonialism or neo-colonialism still exists in the Middle East, is a matter of definition, terminology and political opinion.

COMMUNISM, COMMUNIST PARTIES

Communist parties were founded in the Arab countries in the early 1920s. They peaked in the 1940s and 1950s. These were years of social and political upheaval and escalating struggle for national liberation which gave rise to various popular-nationalist movements. Most of the Communist movements in the Middle East were repressed or coopted by powerful military bureaucracies which had emerged in the Arab states and Iran in the course of the 1960s and 1970s. The majority of the Communist parties practically ceased to exist in the 1980s. Their remnants sustained a death blow with the fall of the Soviet Union in 1991.

Communist parties in the Middle East emerged out of small groups. Most were intellectuals. They failed to make headway into peasant groups. Some dissolved and re-formed. Some were unorthodox Communism or radical groups whose adherence to Russian-line Communism and the Third International was doubtful or wavering. Different dates as to the actual establishment of fully fledged Communist parties are therefore given by different sources. The first were Communist parties in TUNISIA and MOROCCO, in 1920—but these were virtually branches of the French Communist Party and were hardly considered as "Arab" Communist parties. An Egyptian Communist Party was admitted by the Third International in 1921, though its actual foundation is usually put at 1922. The Palestine Communist Party, though containing some Arabs, was mainly Jewish (see below). Syro-Lebanese and Iraqi Communist parties were established later in the 1920s.

These Communist parties were small groups with hardly any influence, and they were soon outlawed and went underground. They recruited their members mainly from the intelligentsia, and largely from minority groups (Arab CHRISTIANS, JEWS, COPTS, Greeks, ARMENIANS, KURDS). This further reduced their influence. They indulged in a great deal of internal and ideological disputes which frequently led to schisms. It was only in the 1940s, after the Soviet Union entered World War II as an ally of Great Britain and Free FRANCE (the powers de facto in control in the Arab countries), that Communist parties were allowed to emerge from underground and becoming semi-legal. As they were considered by public opinion as representing, or at least close to, the Soviet Union—a power in which many nationalists set great hopes as a potential ally and supporter against the Western imperial powers—the Communist parties began attracting some support. This process was set back in 1946–1947 when the USSR retreated

from power positions and activist policies on the fringes of the Middle East (IRAN, TURKEY, Greece), and in 1947–1948 when it supported the partition of Palestine and the emergence of a Jewish state and instructed the Communist parties to do likewise. It gathered new strength when the Soviet Union emerged in the 1950s as the close ally of the radical Arab countries (EGYPT, SYRIA, IRAQ); but it flagged again when it became evident that the Soviet Union was dealing with the non-Communist rulers of these countries and treating them as its allies, while largely ignoring or abandoning the Communist parties. The attitude to be taken toward those radical but non-Communist regimes was much debated inside the Communist parties, causing splits and secessions. Since the mid 1960s the Communist parties (at least in their official mainstream factions, no doubt guided by Soviet advice) accepted the rulers of the radical Arab countries as "progressive" and cooperated with them—for some time in Egypt, and mainly in BA'TH-ruled Syria and Iraq. The Syrian and Iraqi regimes reciprocated by setting up a "National Progressive Front" with the Communist Party and other groups in 1972–1973. Communist party men were appointed as Government ministers. In Iraq this *Ba'th*-Communist cooperation ceased in the late 1970s, and the Communist Party turned against the regime, went underground again and was suppressed. In Syria, cooperation continued and the country had Communist ministers in its governments until 1985.

Because Communists in the Middle East operated by and large clandestinely, details concerning their activities in each country are at best incomplete if not unreliable.

Communism in Egypt Communism in Egypt witnessed a sharp rise in the early 1940s with the dramatic increase of the working class and consequent rising power of trade unions that had resulted by the war. The establishment of the Congress of Workers' Unions—encompassing 115,000 members—was followed by the unification in 1947 of the main Communist groups, creating the Democratic Movement of National Liberation (*al-haraka al-dimuqratiyya lil-tahrir al-watani*). During these years, the Party identified itself with the cause of national liberation, and as of 1951 took part in the guerrilla activities against Britain in the Suez zone. On the eve of the July 1952 revolution the Party had about 5000 members. "The Democratic Movement of National Liberation", at first granted the revolutionary regime its qualified support. The regime, however, did not reciprocate, especially as it suspected the Communist Party was behind violent strikes in August 1952. From 1953 it suppressed its cells and arrested its leaders. Further waves of arrests occurred in 1956 and 1958 (the same year the Communist Party reportedly reunited its various factions). Despite Egypt's increasingly close relations with the USSR, a rift over Egypt's attitude to Communism and the Communists in the Arab world dominated their relations between 1959 and 1962. This was triggered by the role of the Communists in Iraq after 1958 (see below). Egypt's reations with the Soviet Union warmed up again following the UNITED ARAB REPUBLIC (UAR) breakup and formulation of the Egyptian National Charter of Socialist principles. In 1963–1964 all Communists in jail were released, and many joined ABDEL NASSER's administrative and information establishment. In 1965 the Communist Party formally disbanded itself and its members joined the regime's "Arab Socialist Union" as individuals. In 1972, under President al-SADAT, two reported Communists joined the government; but most Communists were assumed to have joined the growing opposition. When political parties were permitted in 1977, many of the Communists probably joined the Leftist "Progressive Unionist Rally". They were suspected to be behind anti-government agitation, which caused the regime to turn against them. In 1975 the Egyptian Communist Party announced in Beirut that it had re-established itself, probably underground. Throughout these years no major Egyptian Communist leader emerged.

In Syria and Lebanon a joint Communist Party was founded in the 1920s. Though the party's legal position under the French Mandate was not quite clear, its spokesmen appeared quite openly, particularly in the freer and more cosmopolitan climate of Beirut. But they had very little influence and took no part in overt political-parliamentary activities, and the party itself remained underground. In 1943, when Syria and Lebanon became independent, the joint Communist party separated into a Syrian Communist Party and a Lebanese one. In Syria the Party was illegal, but after the fall of Shishakli in 1954 it began to wield some influence behind the scenes. Its main leader, Khaled Bakdash, was elected to Parliament as an independent. The Chief of Staff from

1957, Afif al-Bizri, was a sympathizer, if not a card-carrying member. Communist Party cells existed among army officers. Indeed, the fear of growing Communist influence was one of the motives that impelled the officers who were the de facto rulers in 1957–1958 to initiate the union of Syria and Egypt. During the three years of the Syro-Egyptian UAR the Communist Party, along with all other political parties, was suppressed. After Syria seceded from the UAR, in 1961, the Communist Party remained illegal. After the Ba'th coup of 1963, and particularly the second one of the "Leftist military" faction in 1966, it became (without being officially legalized) a partner of the Ba'th regime in a "National Progressive Front" (1972). On the list of that Front it gained representation in the People's Assembly. From 1972 to 1985 there were usually two Communist ministers in the Syrian Government. A faction headed by Riad Turk and Danial Ni'ma opposed that collaboration with the Arab nationalist Ba'th and finally secceded in late 1973. Ni'ma and some of his associates later returned to the Party, but part of the seceding faction, under Turk, stayed out.

The Communist Party in Lebanon gained some influence in the Trade Unions (Mustafa al-Aris) and in intellectual circles. It was officially legalized in 1970. Its leaders were mostly Christian (Antoun Thabet, Farajallah Hilou, Ra'if Khouri, Georges Hawi), but there were also some Muslims (Omar Fakhouri), and by the mid-1970s Shi'i members constituted a significant segment of the party. In 1970 an extremist faction seceded and set up a "Communist Action Organization", with armed squads of its own. In 1972 the Communist Party put up candidates for Parliament, but none were elected. At first it had no "militia" of its own and was therefore not very active in the early stages of the civil war which begun in 1975, though ideologically it supported the radical, "Leftist" camp. A Communist armed militia, however, did take an active part in the later stages of the Civil War, alongside with the leftist-Palestinian coalition though without a significant role. During the civil war the Party lost many of its Shi'i members who joined Shi'i activist movments, such as AMAL and HIZBALLAH. In 1978 the Party hosted a conference of ten Arab Communist Parties in Beirut, which escalated the struggle against ISRAEL. The Party participated in the 1992 general elections for Parliament.

The strongest Communist party in the Arab countries, after World War II, was probably that of Iraq. It was brutally suppressed in the 1940s and 1950s. Some of its leaders were executed. New leaders emerged and the Party—though split into rival factions—was seen to extend its underground activities. After General QASSEM's revolution of July 1958, the Communist Party collaborated with the new republican regime and gained some important positions in the army and administration. In 1959 the Party—and particularly its mostly Kurdish sections in the north—helped Qassem to suppress a Nasserist plot and attempted coup. But when the Communists demanded full and open partnership in the regime and continued penetrating key positions, Qassem tried to restrict their power and tried to balance his regime between the Communists and the Nasserists.

After Qassem's fall in 1963, the Communist Party was again suppressed—by both the *Ba'th* and President Aref's regime. Gradually, however, the *Ba'th* leaders, in power from 1968, sought to gain the cooperation of the Communist Party—at least one or the other of its rival factions. The Communist Party itself was split concerning such cooperation with the *Ba'th* rulers. In 1969–1970 it was reported that of the party's three main factions—the "Central Command" of Aziz al-Haj; the "Central Committee" of Zaki al-Kheiri and Baha' al-Din Nuri; and Salim Fakhri's group—the first cooperated with the authorities, while the second opposed such tactics. From 1969 to 1976 a Communist leader, Aziz Sharif, was a Government minister (but it was doubtful whether he was a card-carrying Party member). The growing *Ba'th*-Communist coalition was formalized in 1973 in a "Progressive and Patriotic National Front". However, conflicting interests, mutual suspicion and old enmity were too strong for that *Ba'th*-Communist Party cooperation to last. By 1978–1979, under the regime's repressive policy the National Front was breaking down. In 1979 most of the leaders went into exile in Europe with the Communist Party going underground. In the 1980s, the clandestine Communist Party was cooperating with Iraq's arch-enemy, Syria, aiding the Kurdish rebels (with guerrillas of its own), joining anti-Government united fronts (in exile or underground), and supporting Iran in the IRAQ-IRAN WAR.

In Palestine in the 1920s the Communist Party (PCP) was a mainly Jewish underground group,

strongly anti-Zionist. In its ideological support for Palestinian-Arab nationalism it sought to cultivate an Arab section and to hand the leading positions to Arab Communists. During the Arab rebellion of 1936–1939, the Communist Party reportedly cooperated with the rebels—mainly its Arab section, with Radwan al-Hilou ("Mussa", died 1975) emerging as its main leader. The Jewish section was thrown into confusion and the two sections were virtually separate—and both declined. When the Communist Party became semi-legal during World War II, stress was laid on trade union activities through the "Arab Workers' Congress", and front organizations, mainly the "League for National Liberation". In 1947–1948, the Communist Party, guided by the Soviet Union, was the only Palestinian-Arab group that did not oppose the partition plan and the creation of the State of Israel. Quite a few of its Arab leaders did not go along with that line. Most of the dissenters, including al-Hilou, were in the Arab part of Palestine or went there as refugees from the areas that became Israel. The Communist Party was the only Arab group in Israel with unbroken continuity, with its accepted leaders (Tawfiq Toubi, Emile Habibi, Emile Touma) and its organ, the weekly *al-Ittihad*.

In 1948 a united "Israel Communist Party" was established. Israel was, at that time, the only country in the Middle East where the Communist Party was legal and took part in elections. In the five elections from 1949 to 1961 it obtained 2.5-4.5% of the total vote, and 3 to 6 seats in the 120-member Knesset. Its anti-Zionist attitude, its struggle against discrimination of Israel's Arab citizens, and support for the establishment of an independent Arab-Palestinian state in accordance with the United Nations partition resolution (1947), made it increasingly popular in Israel's Arab sector. In 1965 the Communist Party split, largely on issues of loyalty to the state and the position on the ARAB-ISRAEL CONFLICT. The "Israel Communist Party", largely Jewish in membership, soon dissolved, merging with other Leftist groups. The "New Communist List," appearing for elections since 1977 as the "Democratic Front for Peace and Equality" (DFPE), became the main Communist Party. Its members and voters were mainly Arab, though it retained several Jews among its leaders and members of Parliament. The New Communist Party's share of the total vote remained at three to five percent, and its Knesset seats three to five. It considerably increased its share of the Arab vote from twenty-three percent in 1965 to thirty-eight percent in 1973 and nearly fifty percent in 1977, then back to thirty-eight percent in 1981, and thirty-four percent in 1984. During the 1980s, the DFPE was more successful in municipal elections. This became the mainstay of political life of Israeli Arabs, controlling the largest Israeli-Arab municipalities (Nazareth, Umm al-Fahm) and several local and village councils. The Communist Party was fully aligned with Soviet policies, and largely espoused Palestinian nationalist positions. Its considerable influence with Israel's Arab population in the late 1970s and the 1980s derived not so much from ideological support for its Communist doctrines, but from focusing on vital matters to the Israeli Arabs on both national and inidividual levels. In addition to supporting the PLO and its claim for an independent Palestinian state in the WEST BANK and GAZA STRIP alongside Israel, the Party also championed the claim for full equality of rights to Arabs in Israel.

In Jordan, the Communist Party remained illegal and lacked any significant influence. In the "West Bank", (annexed in 1948–1950 and held until 1967), the Communists represented the hard core of organized radical opposition to the regime. In this capacity, the party served as a leading militant force which, together with the *Ba'th* Party and the ARAB NATIONALISTS MOVEMENT, maintained a high level of anti-Western agitation, and preventing Jordan from joining the Baghdad Pact in 1955. The Party gained limited representation (two to three delegates) in Parliament through rallying in a "National Front" in the elections of 1954 and 1956, and was represented in the short-lived national-socialist government headed by Suleiman al-Nabulsi (October 1956-April 1957). However, with the repression and banning of all political parties in Jordan in April 1957, the Communists, like other opposition movements, suffered a serious blow and went underground. Remnants of the Jordanian Party, turning after 1967 into a Palestinian Communist Party, was the leading agitator of public protest against Israel after 1967. The main leader of Jordan's Communist Party, Fu'ad Nassar (who had spent many years in prison, exile or hiding), died in 1976 and no prominent new leader emerged. After 1967 the Party formed its own guerrilla group, *al-Ansar*. Their actual operations were

meager and they reportedly ceased in 1971, with the final expulsion of the Palestinian guerrillas from Jordan. With the renewal of political life in Jordan in 1989, the Communist Party obtained a legal status and participated in the 1993 general election but failed to gain representation in Parliament.

After 1967, the Communist Party of the "West Bank" was reportedly separated from the Jordanian one and reconstituted as the Palestine Communist Party, taking a major role in civil disobedience activities agains the Israeli military rule in the West Bank and Gaza Strip. The Communist Party in the West Bank, led first by Bashir Barghuthi and then by Suleiman al-Najjab, remained underground and illegal. It operated among trade unions, professional and front organizations, and its influence increased in the 1970s and 1980s. In the summer of 1973, inspired by the PLO, the Communists were among other Nationalist forces in the West Bank which joined forces to establish the Palestinian National Front, soon to gain major influence in it. However, in late 1973 and early 1974 Israel dissolved the Front and expelled its leaders, including Suleiman al-Najjab and Arabi Awwad. In 1987 Najjab became a member of the PLO Executive. From the mid-1970s the Communist Party accounted for establishing the concept of two-states solution in the Israeli-Palestinian conflict. He returned to the West Bank following the 1993 Oslo Accord. In 1982, Awwad established in Lebanon the short-lived Palestinian Revolutionary Communist Party, as a competitor to the Palestinian Communist Party, which had become identified with the PLO. In 1992, apparently in view of the collapse of the Soviet Union, the Palestinian Communist Party in the West Bank turned into the "People's Party."

Among the Palestinian nationalist organizations operating out of Palestine, leftist-Communist leanings exist in several groups, though they often lean toward Maoist-Trotskyite ideas rather than orthodox, Moscow-oriented Communist. Such tendencies prevail, for instance, in HABASH's "Popular Front for the Liberation of Palestine" and HAWATMA's "Democratic Front". The Orthodox Communist Party also appeared, especially after 1973, among the organizations federated in the PALESTINE LIBERATION ORGANIZATION (PLO) with its expelled leaders taking part in its Palestine National Congresses. In the PLO's factional rivalries it appeared increasingly seeking accommodation with ARAFAT. The Communist Party keeps a low profile within the PLO. A Communist party representative, identified as such, was admitted to the PLO Executive Committee for the first time in April 1987. A significant Communist presence existed in SOUTH YEMEN. There, the ruling Party and the state apparatus until the late 1980s were radical-leftist and Communist-inspired—though, like the Palestinian organizations mentioned, of a Maoist-Castroist rather than an Orthodox Communist Party type. A small regular Communist Party seems to have existed, but it merged with the ruling NATIONAL LIBERATION FRONT (NLF) in 1975, and with the "Yemen Socialist Party", established to unite all factions, in 1978.

Sudanese Communism had its beginnings in cells of Sudanese students in Cairo in the early 1940s. A Sudan Communist Party was founded in 1944—at first as a NFL (Others set the foundation in 1948.) It grew, based on both intellectual circles and the powerful Railway Workers Union in Khartoum and Atbara. Its chief leader was Abdel-Khaleq Mahjub. The Party participated in the overthrow of General Abbud's military dictatorship in 1964 (which it had at first supported but later begun suppressing it) and in the post-coup government. In the elections of April 1965 it won eleven seats in Parliament (which were all seats reserved for college graduates). However, its share in the government caused a bitter dispute which split the regime. government and Parliament banned the Communist Party late in 1965. The Supreme Court invalidated that act, but the regime refused to accept that verdict and to annul the ban. That controversy caused much unrest. Meanwhile the Communists succeeded in establishing strong front organizations of professionals, students, women etc. In May 1969 they took part in NUMEIRI's military coup and remained partners in the new regime, though it was not quite clear whether the four or five Communist Government ministers were card-carrying Communist Party members or belonged to dissident factions or Communist-leaning front organizations. When Numeiri began turning Sudan into a one-Party state, that collaboration soured. Some Communists tended to go along with the regime, but Mahjub and the main Communist Party opposed further collaboration and the self-dissolution of the Party. In 1970, Communist front organizations were outlawed; the Communist min-

isters ousted from the government; Mahjub exiled to Egypt and detained when he returned. In July 1971, Numeiri accused the Communist Party of complicity in an abortive coup, arrested its leaders and executed the most prominent among them, including Mahjub and Shafe'i Ahmad al-Sheikh, and brutally suppressed all Communist organizations. In 1978 some Communist detainees were released, but the Party remained illegal and underground. After the April 1985 coup that toppled Numeiri, Communists were reported to be part of the alliance of professional unions and former parties and to strive for a position of guiding influence within it but there were no indications of Communist gains. In the elections of April 1986, the Communist won three seats.

In Tunisia, the Communist Party became Independent of the French Communist Party in 1934. It took part in the struggle for independence, but was not particularly prominent or influential. In independent Tunisia, from 1956, it at first operated openly, taking part in the elections of 1956 and 1959 without gaining a single seat. In 1963 it was banned—along with other parties—as the country adopted a single-Party system. The ban was lifted in 1981, and Communist Party candidates competed in the elections of the same year but again won no seat; the Communist party boycotted the elections of 1986. None of the Party's leaders achieved great prominence.

The Algerian Communist Party, too, was separated from the French one in 1934 (some sources say 1936). It ideologically supported the struggle for independence, but did not take a very active part in the guerrilla war of 1954–1962. It tried to join with the FRONT DE LIBÉRATION NATIONALE (FLN), the main nationalist fighting organization, in a united front and to obtain representation and influence on the bodies directing the rebellion, but was kept at arm's length by the FLN. In the factional struggle inside the FLN, with the advent of independence, the Communists supported BEN BELLA. But as the new state adopted a strict one-Party regime, the Communist Party was outlawed late in 1962. There have been few reports of underground activities; nor have reports been substantiated of Communist Party support for, or participation in, some of the anti-regime organizations set up in exile, mostly in France. None of the Algerian Communist leaders have achieved great prominence.

In Morocco, as in the two other MAGHREB countries, the Communist Party separated from the French Communist Party in 1934. Its links with the nationalists and its participation in the struggle for the abolition of the French Protectorate were weak and partial. After Morocco became fully independent (1956), the Communist Party was banned in 1959–1960, and its appeal to the courts rejected. As it continued some activities and several of its functionaries stood for elections, as independents, the ban was reiterated in 1964. In 1968, Ali Yata, who had emerged as chief leader of the Communist Parties, tried to get around the ban by founding a "Party of Liberation and Socialism" as a front for the Communist Party. This Party, however, was also banned in 1970. But a new, similar attempt succeeded in 1974. Yata's new front, the "Party of Progress and Socialism", was allowed to operate legally, hold congresses and participate in elections. It did not win any seat in 1976. In 1977 Yata won a by-election, and in the 1984 elections the Party obtained two seats. Yata's tactics of disguising the Communist Party in front organizations resulted in several splits and secessions. One of the seceding splinter groups, the "Organization of Democratic Popular Action", was reported to have won one seat in the 1984 elections.

Communism in Saudi Arabia The Communist Party of Saudi Arabia emerged in the mid-1970s out of the National Liberation Front, established in 1958 by Marxist activists who had led the oilfield strikes of 1953. The Front emerged as a clandestine movement following suppression of the workers' committees by the Saudi government. Operating increasingly outside the Saudi territory due to persecution by the Saudi regime, the Party called for democratic constitution; freedom of political activity and professional organization; the right of trade unions to demonstrate and strike, and state control of the oil industry. With the growing shift of many opposition members to radical Islam from the late 1970s on, the Party effectively ceased to exist.

Islam Communism in Iran: see TUDEH.

CONSTANTINOPLE, CONVENTION OF A

Convention signed in 1888 by the European powers, chiefly BRITAIN and FRANCE, and the OTTOMAN EMPIRE, ensuring free navigation through the SUEZ CANAL. As France objected to a British reservation which in effect suspended certain clauses for the duration of Britain's occupation of EGYPT, the Constantinople Convention became effective only in 1904, following an Anglo-French understanding. Independent Egypt continued to recognize the Constantinople Convention's validity, and frequently cited its clauses concerning the security of the Canal to justify restrictions it imposed on the freedom of passage through the Canal (e.g., with regard to ISRAEL)—see SUEZ CANAL.

The name "Constantinople Agreement" also usually refers to an exchange of diplomatic memoranda, in March –April 1915, between RUSSIA, Britain and France, in which Russia put on record its claim to annex, after victory in the war and the dismemberment of the Ottoman Empire, Constantinople, the Bosphorus and the Dardanelles, certain islands and coastal areas on both the European and the Asian shores. The Western powers agreed in principle, subject to reservations and counter-demands elsewhere. Apart from claims for influence zone in IRAN, British demands included a stipulation that "the Musulman Holy Places and Arabia shall remain under independent Musulman dominion" (implying: under British tutelage). France put on record that it "would like to annex SYRIA together with the region of the Gulf of Alexandretta and Cilicia up to the Taurus range" (with Russia stipulating that "Syria" would not include Palestine—contrary to French notions). This Constantinople Agreement became effective after the Bolshevik revolution.

COPTS The word is derived from *Qibt* which is a distortion of the Greek word *Agyptos*. They were the main inhabitants of EGYPT at the time that the Arabs (led by Amr Ibn al-Aass), conquered Egypt (641-643). The original name was geographical or ethnic. Since most Egyptians at that time were CHRISTIANS, Qibt and Qibties acquired a religious value. The Coptic Church traces its foundation to St. Mark the Evangelist. With the schism at the Council of Chacedon (451), the Coptic Church became MONOPHSITE.

The Copts were a majority in Egypt from the fourth to the seventh century, and in general, supported the Muslims because of the deep animosity between the Orthodox Church in Constantinople and the Catholic Church in Rome. After the Arab-Muslim conquest, many converted to Islam, and Egypt became largely a Muslim country. Under Arab,

Mamluk and Ottoman rule, the Copts were often discriminated against or persecuted. In the nineteenth century, with the growing modernization and Westernization of Egypt, and the increasing influence of the Western powers, the Copts gradually acquired a standard of wealth and education superior to that of the average Egyptian. Some Copts were active in the Egyptian nationalist movement, but none attained top leadership rank. Modern Egyptian nationalism had, at least in some of its streams and factions, strong Islamic currents that erupted from time to time in anti-Copts unrest or pogroms and Muslim-Copts clashes. Independent Egypt professes a strict policy of non-discrimination. Nonetheless Copts frequently complain, being apprehensive toward strong Islamic tendencies which base the Constitution and legal practice more extensively on the Islamic law (SHARI'A). This would relegate the Copts to second-class status. With the revival of radical Islam in Egypt in the mid and late-1970s, Muslim-Copt clashes and anti-Copts outbreaks became increasingly familiar.

Egyptian governments usually include one to three Copt ministers. But this only started when Egypt had a Copt Prime Minister (BUTRUS-GHALI, assassinated in 1910 in a period of anti-Copts agitation). Other members of the same Butrous-Ghali family attained prominent political positions. The most prominent Copt in the nationalist leadership was Makram Ubeid (1889–1961) who occupied high posts, mainly that of Finance Minister. He was one of the prominent leaders of the WAFD Party, but left it in 1942, forming his own "Independent Wafdist Bloc" (until 1953).

According to official statistics the Copts in Egypt form ten percent of the population, at present more than 6 million. Yet some spokesmen of the Copts claim a higher percentage, denouncing these official census figures, while many foreign observers estimate the number of Copts in Egypt at 10 million.

There are small Coptic communities, mainly of Egyptian origin, who live in Arab and Middle Eastern countries, as well as in Europe and the US. The Coptic Church is headed by a Patriarch—also called Pope (al-Baba)—who must be approved by the government. His seat, originally in Alexandria, was later transferred to Cairo. (In September 1981, President AL-SADAT canceled the Government's recognition of Pope Shenouda the third. This unleashed a serious crisis with the Coptic community which still considered Shenouda its spiritual leader. In January 1985 he was reinstated by President MUBARAK.) Small numbers of Copts joined the Catholic Church through a UNIATE in 1741, whilst others converted to Protestantism.

Since the emergence—in the 1970s—of Islamic radical groups, there has been an increase in acts of terror and religious harassment on the part of these groups against the Copts. This has been especially apparent in Upper Egypt, where they constitute a large minority (in Assyout—thirty percent Copts) and where the Islamic Fundamentalists have the upper hand. Members of *al-Jama'a al-Islamiyya* wage assaults against Coptic churches, homes and business. The Government tries—not always successfully—to prevent such assaults, as part of its struggle against Islamic Fundamentalism. Reports about hostilities on the part of Muslim Extremists against Copts are published in part of the Egyptian press, mainly in the Annual Civil Society Report, issued by the Ibn Khaldoun Center, and the Arab Strategic Report published by al-Ahram Center for International Relations.

The Ethiopian (or Abyssinian) Church, which was originally a branch of the Coptic Church, became autonomous to a decree by the Italian authorities after the conquest of Ethiopia in 1936. After World War II, Ethiopia affirmed the independence of the Ethiopian Church, and rejected the Coptic attempts to regain tutelage on it.

D

DAYAN, MOSHE (1915–1981) Israeli military commander, leading politician and amateur archeologist. Dayan was born in Kibbutz Degania and grew up in the cooperative settlement Nahalal. He served in the Jewish police force, in Captain Ord Wingate's Special Night Squads in the years

1937–1939. In 1940 he was tried by the British mandatory authorities for underground activities in the *Hagana* (the pre-state Jewish defense force) and was imprisoned. A year later he lost his left eye in an Allied operation against French Vichy forces in LEBANON. After returning to Palestine he joined the *Palmah* (the *Hagana's* special striking force), and in Israel's War of Independence (see ARAB-ISRAEL CONFLICT) commanded a battalion. In July 1948 Dayan was appointed commander of the Jerusalem District, in which capacity he negotiated with King AB-DALLAH of Jordan and his representatives. In the spring of 1949 he was a member of the Israeli delegation to the armistice talks in Rhodes. In 1953 he was appointed IDF Chief of Staff in which capacity he conducted the Sinai Campaign (see ARAB-IS-RAEL CONFLICT) and became a national hero. In January 1958 Dayan retired from military service and spent a year studying at the Hebrew University in Jerusalem. He was elected to the fourth Knesset (1959) on the Mapai Party list.

In 1959–1964 Dayan served as Minister of Agriculture and in 1965 was one of the founders of the Rafi Party with David BEN GURION. On the eve of the Six-Day War (see ARAB-ISRAEL CONFLICT) Dayan was appointed Minister of Defense. In the aftermath of the war was responsible for the "open bridges" policy across the Jordan River and advocated a functional compromise with Jordan in the West Bank. Dayan, whose image as a national hero strengthened after the Six-Day War, lost much of his popularity as a result of the Yom Kippur War (see ARAB-ISRAEL CONFLICT). He continued to serve as Minister of Defense until after the publication of the Agranat Commission Report in in the wake of the Yom Kippur War.

After the Labor Party's defeat in the elections to the ninth Knesset (1977), Dayan left the party and as an independent Knesset member, joined the government formed by Menahem BEGIN as Minister of Foreign Affairs. As such, he met secretly in MOROC-CO with the representative of Egyptian President Anwar al-SADAT, which preceded the latter's visit to JERUSALEM in November 1977. Dayan also played an active role in the talks preceding the signing of the Camp David Accords and the Egyptian-Israeli Peace Treaty (see ARAB-ISRAEL PEACEMAKING). Dayan was the initiator and main protagonist of an autonomy plan for the Palestinians in the WEST BANK and GAZA STRIP.

When in 1979 Begin entrusted the negotiations with the Egyptians to Minister of the Interior Yosef Burg, with the clear intention of stalling, Dayan resigned from the government.

In 1981 Dayan ran in the elections to the tenth Knesset at the head of a new party, Telem, which won three seats, but soon after the elections he died of cancer.

DECLARATION OF PRINCIPLES (DOP) see ARAB-ISRAEL PEACEMAKING.

DEMIREL, SÜLEYMAN (b. 1924) Turkish politician, Prime Minister (1965–1971; 1975–1977; 1977–1978; 1979–1980; 1991–1993), and President (1993–). Born in a village in the province of Isparta, Demirel studied civil engineering in Istanbul and the USA. He entered the Civil Service of TURKEY and became director of the State Water Board. After the military coup of 1960 he joined the Justice Party (newly formed to replace the ousted and banned Democratic Party) and in 1964 succeeded General Gümüspala as leader of the party. In 1965 Demirel joined Suat Ürgüplü's coalition cabinet as Deputy Premier. Later that year, his Party won the elections and he became Prime Minister.

During his premiership of over five years, Demirel took care not to antagonize the army, restrained the right wing of his party and followed a moderate policy in both external and internal affairs, strongly maintaining strong democratic order. However, social reforms were slow in coming and political pressures on the government lead to continuous disorders. In March 1971 Demirel was forced to resign following an ultimatum presented by the chiefs of the armed forces. During the years of shifting coalition governments that followed, Demirel headed three governments (1975–1977, 1977–1978 and 1979–1980). But as unrest escalated and terrorism spread, the armed forces again intervened in September 1980 ousting Demirel and his government. He was exiled into forced residence for some time, and along with other leaders, was later banned from political activity until 1992. The ban was lifted by a referendum in September 1987, and Demirel took over the chairmanship of the new right-wing True Path Party that had been forming since 1983. The Party won only fifty-nine seats (out of 459) in the elections of 1987, leaving ÖZAL's Motherland Party as the main representative of the right. Demirel from then on devoted his time to strengthening his Party and in the October 1991 elections it emerged in first place, winning 178 seats. Short of an absolute majority in the National Assembly, Demirel formed a coalition government with the Social Democrats and became Prime Minister once more. However, when President Özal died suddenly in April 1993, (he resigned in order to run for Presidency and was elected the following month for a seven year term as President). Demirel no doubt wished to end his long and stormy political career in the capacity of a statesman who was above party politics, and was regarded as such since he became president. He has not refrained, however, from speaking up and actively participating in state affairs and often represents Turkey on foreign delegations.

DERVISH (DARWISH) ORDERS Muslim mystics, Sufis, have since early Islamic days created brotherhoods or orders (*tariqa*, pl. *turuq*—literally "ways", "paths"), which have since the twelfth and thirteenth centuries attracted and organized large groups, mostly city artisans. Local groups of adepts (*dervish* in Persian, *faqir* in Arabic) are led by a *khalifa* (substitute, deputy), who is in practice quite autonomous, while the head of the order, the *sheikh*, usually claiming descent from the founder of the order, is the supreme leader. "Specialists" among the brethren, often wanderers and beggars, reputed to perform miracles, sometimes live in monasteries (*zawiya, takiyya, khankah*). Ordinary members, laymen, usually from the lower classes, visit the tomb of their order's saint or patron (*wali*) and celebrate his anniversary (*mawlid* with processions, dancing etc. The central practice of a Sufi ritual is the *dhikr*, the ever-repeated uttering of God's name or some religious formula, until ecstasy is attained. Some orders, such as the *Rifa'iyya* also take narcotics and add practices like walking on fire, devouring glass, playing with serpents etc.

The official Islamic establishment and the state authorities have always frowned upon such practices, as well as upon certain beliefs seen by them as superstitions, such as the veneration of saints, living or past, and the cult of their tombs. Moreover, orthodox Islam with its intellectual theology and its stress on Muslim Law (the SHARI'A) as the central tenet of Islam, has retained reservations regarding Sufism's emphasis on religious feeling and gnostic

experience—though Sufism has been a legitimate version of Islam since the great medieval theologian al-Ghazzali (d.1111) reconciled Sufism and orthodox Islam. On the other hand, Sufism and Sufi orders have been particularly popular with some non-Arab Muslims, such as Turks and BERBERS (having been originally instrumental in their conversion to Islam).

Some Sufi Dervish orders were particularly strong in Turkey—such as the *Bektashiyya*, the *Mevleviyya* (called the Whirling Dervishes in Europe because of their ecstatic dances) and the *Nakshabandiyya* (popular among the KURDS). All Dervish orders were prohibited in 1925 by the Kemalist republic and their monasteries and mausoleums (*türbe*) were closed down. Despite the orders, the banned sects survived underground to some extent, and since the enforcement of secularization was relaxed, in the 1940s and 1950s, the three orders mentioned came to be accepted, though processions and ecstatic ceremonies remained forbidden. Orders considered to be extreme, such as the North-African *Tijaniyya* and the *Nur* or *Nurju*, remained outlawed.

In Egypt, the Dervish orders were, until the twentieth century, an important social force. The main indigenous orders were the Ahmadiyya (no connection with the AHMADIYYA sect on the fringes of Islam) or *Badawiyya*, named after Sidi Ahmad al-Badawi, whose *mawlid* in Tanta is still a popular feast, and the *Burhaniyya* or *Brahimiyya*, named after Sidi Ibrahim of Dasuq. Also influential were the *Qadiriyya* (of Iraqi origin, and considered to be the earliest order still in existence, and close to orthodoxy), the *Rifa'iyya* (also of Iraqi origin), and the *Shadhiliyya* (an order of North-African origin). Early in the 19th century Viceroy Muhammad Ali established state control over the Dervish orders by creating a high council of the orders and nominating its head. Since then, a government permit must be obtained for the celebration of each *mawlid*. But both the government and the Islamic establishment centered around the al-AZHAR university failed in their efforts to curb those Sufi practices they considered offensive. Despite the changes in social values, the expansion of education, modernist development and westernization, the *mawlids* are still popular and some of the customs considered objectionable are still maintained. According to the head of the Sufi Council, there are now 60 orders in EGYPT, most of them off-shoots of the main ones mentioned. He presents them as a respectable establishment, loyal to the Government and opposed to religious innovation. Since 1958 the Council has published a journal, to which even university professors have contributed. With the exception of one new order, the *Hamidiyya-Shadhiliyya*, which is centralized and cohesive, the orders are but loosely organized, and multiple membership blurs the distinction between them. Generally, however, membership—mostly from the lower classes—seems to be declining.

In the Fertile Crescent, Sufi orders have never enjoyed influence or prestige comparable to their position in Egypt, Sudan or Turkey. There is little information about their present state, but apparently they are rapidly declining. The exception seems to be Iraq, where Sufism may be somewhat more alive. The tomb of Abdel-Qader al-Gilani (d.1166) in Baghdad attracts *Qadiri* pilgrims. The *Rifa'iyya*, the *Nakshabandiyya* and the *Bektashiyya* have followers among both Arabs and Kurds in Iraq.

The SANUSSIYYA in Libya and the MAHDIYYA in Sudan (and similarly the IDRISSIYYA in North Africa and later in Asir), founded in the nineteenth century, were movements similar to, and perhaps originating in, Sufi Dervish orders, and they adopted some of the Dervish orders methods, such as the training of propagandists in monasteries, a central hierarchical organization, the practice of *dhikr* and prayers particular to the order, as well as a general dislike of the orthodox theologians ('*ulama*') and their emphasis on learning. The *Mahdiyya* at first called themselves Dervishes and Europeans continued calling them so. But these orders were not Sufi Dervish orders, but militant fundamentalist and revivalist movements—(see MAHDIYYA, SANUSSIYYA).

Some true Sufi Dervish orders are also active in Sudan—chiefly the *Tijaniyya*, the *Sa'iyya* and the *Ahmadiyya*, all of which came to Sudan from Egypt in the 19th century.

In the *Maghrib*, Northwest Africa, especially MOROCCO, Dervish orders still have considerable influence, although it seems to be declining. The most important orders are the *Shadhiliyya* and its suborders, the *Tijaniyya*, and the *Darqawa*.

DFLP (DEMOCRATIC FRONT FOR THE LIBERATION OF PALESTINE) see PALESTINIAN GUERRILLA ORGANIZATION.

DHIMMIS (Ahl al-Dhimma): This is the special status granted to JEWS, CHRISTIANS, Samaritans and Zoroastrians living under Islamic rule as protected subjects with limited rights compared to Muslims. From the time of the Prophet, ISLAM discerned between those who followed monotheistic religions based on revelation, and those who follow idolatry. The first group, known as *ahl al-kitab* (people of the book), a term commonly used for the Jews but also included other religious communities which recognized scriptures, was allowed to remain under the rule of Islam and continue practicing its religion provided that its believers recognized the superiority of Islam, submitted to the Islamic state, paid the poll tax (*Jizia*), and confirmed other restrictions. The relations between the Muslim state and the non-Muslim subject communities, to which it extended its tolerance and protection, were regulated in Muslim law and practice by a pact called dhimma . (Those benefitting from the pact were known as ahl al-dhimma or dhimmis).

Caliph Omar 2nd (717–720 AD) was the first Muslim ruler to formulate the regulations referring to the tolerated non-Muslim communities (dhimmis). Its guiding line was that a Dhimmi will not be superior to a Muslim. Muslims were not to harm Dhimmis or their property and the Dhimmis were restricted in occupying public posts, special tax rates and even dress codes. The special status of the Dhimmi was by far a compromise of political rationalism of the rulers, especially during the great Islamic conquering period, when they realized that they would not be able to convert all the conquered peoples to Islam. Under the Ottoman Empire the Dhimmi communities became administrative units called MILLET, which were accorded legal and cultural autonomy, headed by the leader of the community (Rabbi or Priest) who was formally appointed by the Muslim ruler and served as the Millet's official representative before the Empire's authorities.

DIMONA NUCLEAR REACTOR see NUCLEAR CAPABILITY.

DISENGAGEMENT AGREEMENTS see ARAB ISRAEL PEACEMAKING.

DJIBOUTI Republic and port town in Northeast Africa (the Horn of Africa), on the Gulf of ADEN, independent since 1977. The majority of its population are Muslims, divided about equally into Issas (of Somali origin) and Afars (part of the Danakil group of tribes). The population is not ARABIC though it includes an Arab minority of a few thousands and Arabic is spoken to some extent as a second language. Djibouti has been officially recognized as an Arab state and joined the Arab league in September 1977, Since then it has maintained a low profile and has followed collective Arab position. Due to its location at the entrance to the Red Sea Djibouti had been a focus of Anglo-French rivalry since the mid-nineteenth century and eventually became a French colony in 1880. Before independence France supported the Afars to promote its own interests in the Horn of Africa but following pressures from the Organization of African Unity, a referendum was reached in May 1977 and the territory became independent in June of that year. Hassan Gouled Aptidon, a senior Issa politician and leader of the *Unified Ligue Populaire Africaine pour l'Indépendance* (LPAI), became president of independent Djibouti. However, the efforts to ensure a harmonious relationship between the two ethnic groups soon reached a deadlock. (In March 1979 replaced the LPAI with a new political party—the *Rassemblement Populaire pour le Progrés* (RPP)—under his leadership, rgarded by the Affars as a political attempt to politically marginalize them, leading to the unification of their main two pre-independence parties into a clandestine opposition movement, the *Front Democratique pour la Liberation de Djibouti* (FDLD).) Since the first elections, held in 1981, Gouled's RPP rejected political pluralism, an attitude that caused clashes with the opposition both on political and ethnic grounds. In April 1991 a new opposition was formed—*Front pour la Rrestauration de l'Unite et de la democratie* (FRUD), comprised of three militant Afar organizations, FRUD took control of many towns and villages in north Djibouti, demanding an equal representation in the government. President Gouled accused them of being agents of Ethiopia's ruler Mengisto and proposed holding a referendum for changing the political system as soon as the "external aggressor" had been expelled. A temporary agreement was achieved with France as mediator but soon many members of FRUD were arrested and as a result FRUD continued militant opposition uprisings fighting throughout the country. In 1992 a referendum to restrict the number

of parties to four was held and approved by 96.79% of the votes. However, France refused to endorse the results because the areas controlled by FRUD boycotted the referendum and there were no independent observers. In fact all parties opposing Gouled, including FRUD were denied party registration. In 1993 the fighting between the government and FRUD was renewed and dozens of people were consequently killed. After being re-elected in 1993 Gouled tried unsuccessfully to negotiate with FRUD. Following his disappointment, he ordered the Djibouti armed forces to raid FRUD's camps. Thousands of Afar civilians then fled to Ethiopia. Under France's economic pressure, Gouled greatly reduced military actions against FRUD but did not cease them entirely. In December 1994 the two parties signed an agreement to establish a coalition government. Gouled granted full amnesty to all FRUD members before the signing of the agreement and FRUD abandoned all militant activity. In 1996 FRUD gained official party status.

International affairs: Djibouti has absorbed a large number of refugees from Somalia and Ethiopia, escaping from their countries due to economic and political hardships, (heavily burdening Djibouti's economy). Since Mengisto's removal from power in 1991, Djibouti has good relations with Ethiopia and had signed several agreements regarding agriculture, industry, border patrols, port facilities, commerce etc. However, the Somalai-Djibouti border remains tense due to Somalia's continuous accusations that Djibouti sympathized with Ethiopia during the Somali-Ethiopian conflict. Another reason for the cold relations is the mutual interference in internal issues by both regimes by supporting the opposition. In 1993 Djibouti became a member in the UN security council. In the same year it strengthened its ties with Egypt and Eritrea which further strengthened in 1996. In 1995 Djibouti signed a defense agreement with Yemen and established its diplomatic relations with several Middle Eastern states, including Israel.

DRUZE Ethno-religious, Arabic-speaking community, in SYRIA, LEBANON, ISRAEL and JORDAN, numbering about 1 million in the 1990s. The sect, an offshoot of the ISMA'ILIYYA, developed in the eleventh century around the figure of the Fatimid Caliph al-Hakim bi-Amr-Illah, regarded by his followers as an incarnation of the divine spirit. The Druze were considered heretics and persecuted by other Muslims, and retreated to remote mountainous areas—Wadi al-Taym on the slopes of Mount Hermon, and later the southern parts of Mount Lebanon. Thoughout their history the Druze acquired a reputation as brave warriors and upholding a strong sense of communal solidarity. Their leaders, Emirs, maintained a de facto autonomous, semi-feudal rule.

Fakhr-ul-Din II (1585–1653), of the Ma'n dynasty, ruled most of Lebanon and parts of Syria and Palestine, under the suzeraignty of the Ottoman Sultan. In 1553 he was executed as a rebel by the Ottomans. This marked the end of the Ma'n dynasty's reign. In the eighteenth century the house of Shihab ascended above rival feudal lords—though their Druze descence and their loyalty to the faith were in doubt because some of the Shihabis converted to Christianity. Under the Shihabi Bashir II (1786–1840) the power of the Druze amirs waned. Tension between the Druze and their MARONITE-Christian neighbors mounted, especially in mixed areas where Druze feudal clans dominated the Maronite peasants. The Maronites—with French support—tried to end that feudal rule and gain control, while the Druze—with British support—strove to maintain or restore their predominance in these areas. This inter-communal strife led to several violent clashes notably in 1840, when intervention by the European Powers—intended mainly to impose a settlement of the conflict between the Ottoman Sultan and his Viceroy in Egypt, and end the Egyptian occupation of the Levant—achieved only a brief respite. Violence continued and in 1860 escalated to a large-scale Druze massacre of Christians; anti-Christian outbreaks also spread to Damascus. These events led to intensified intervention by the European Powers, the dispatch of a French expeditionary force and the creation of a semi-autonomous district (Sanjaq, Mutasarifia) of Mount Lebanon (see LEBANON), where Maronites constituted a majority, though the Druze formed a strong minority (about twelve percent). In the nineteenth century two Druze clans emerged as the chief contenders for leadership: JUN-BALAT (also Jumblat) and ARSALAN (or Yazbaki).

The Druze had been drifting toward the Hawran (Houran) Mountains of southern Syria since the end of the seventeenth century particularly following the battle of Ayn Dara in 1711 between the Qaysi and Yamani rival factions (a primary, pre-Islamic division within Arabia's tribes which sustained well into the twentieth century, cutting across Christians, Muslims, Druze and other religious minorities), when many of the defeated Yamanis emigrated there. In the nineteenth century this migration increased, impelled by the continuing unrest until the Houran region became a major Druze center and came to be called Jabal al-Duruz, (the Druze Mountain.)

Among the Druze leaders in the Houran region, the al-Atrash clan rose to prominence, and some of its sons were appointed by the Ottoman authorities as governors of the district. The French, ruling Syria since 1920, granted the Druze Mountain a degree of autonomy in 1921 and appointed Salim al-Atrash governor, a post he had also filled under the Ottomans since 1914. Incipient friction intensified upon the death of Salim al-Atrash in 1923, and when the Druze notables were unable to agree on a successor, a French officer, Captain Carbillet, was appointed governor. Friction with Carbillet, objection to his administration and his attempts at reform, sparked an uprising at Druze Mountain in 1925, which spread to the Druze populations in the Mount Hermon area. This "Druze Rebellion" soon turned into a national Syrian revolt and heavy fighting took place before the French were able to quell the violence in 1927. The chief rebel leader, Sultan al-Atrash (1881–1982), escaped to Jordan, returning to the Jabal Druze only ten years later; Under the Syro-French agreement of 1936, Jabal Druze became part of the Syrian republic, enjoying a measure of local autonomy. However, with the end of French rule in 1945, Jabal Druze lost that special status and was fully incorporated into the Syrian Republic.

The Druze in Syria constitute between three and four percent of the total population in the mid 1990s, most of them in Jabal Druze, where they represent eighty percent of the population. They participated in Syria's national movement, but apart from triggering the revolt of 1925, their part was not prominent, nor was their participation in the governance of independent Syria. Local autonomy and a traditional hostility to any centralized government (now that of Damascus) remained strong, encouraging the Druze leaders to establish close ties with the Hashemite monarchs (especially ABDALLAH of Transjordan) and the British, which regarded the Druze as disloyal to the Syrian regime. The Druze were indeed reported to have had a hand in several Syrian coups, e.g., that of Colonel Sami Hinnawi in 1949, the overthrow of Shishakli in 1954, rumored pro-Western and pro-Iraqi plots (1956–1957), and a coup attempt led by the Druze Colonel Salim Hatum (1966); (see SYRIA). Several Druze officers reached senior ranks in the armed forces (Muhammad Ubeid, Abd el-Karim Zahr el-Din, Salim Hatum, Fahd Sha'er, Talal Abu-Asali)—but none of them became a first-rank Syrian leaders. Under the BA'TH regime's military faction (since 1966) and the regime of Hafez ASAD (from November 1971) most senior Druze officers were purged from the military.

In LEBANON, in 1920—the Druze formed between seven and eleven percent of the population in the 1990s, most of them in the southern part of Mount Lebanon and south of the Biqa' region, on the slopes of Mount Hermon, around Hasbayya, a town which is also a Druze religious center. A few thousand Druze, on the slopes of Mount Hermon, reside within Israels' self-declared "Security Zone" established in 1985.

Under Lebanon's communal system, modified in the Ta'if Agreement in 1989 (see LEBANON), the Druze are represented in parliament, government, and the civil service, according to their share in the population (under the unwritten "National Pact" of 1943 a Druze served traditionally as the Defense Minister, while another Druze was appointed a Chief of Staff under a Maronite Commander in Chief). The Druze did not benefit much from the post-Civil War settlements in 1989–1990: there are slightly more Druze deputies in the Lebanese Parliament but since the parliament itself was enlarged, the proportional gain for the Druze was meager. Contrary to the Sunni Muslims who hold the post of Prime Minister (a position that was strengthened considerably by the Ta'if Agreement) and to the Shi'i Muslims, holding the post of the Speaker (President) of Parliament, the Druze do not hold any of the top three governmental posts.

The reaffirmation of the Central Governments' control over most of Lebanon's territory, including the areas under Druze control, dealt a blow to their autonomy and exclusive control in their areas, maintained throughout the war. Nevertheless, Lebanese Druze leaders, especially the Junbalat family, have remained a powerful and inportant force in Lebanese political life.

Since the nineteenth century, the Arsalan and Junbalat clans have competed for the community's political leadership (as distinct from the religious leadership)—with shifting factional alliances. Under the French Mandate, the Arsalans were usually considered more militant, allied with the Nationalist faction, while the Junbalats were more pliable and "pro-French". In independent Lebanon, from 1943, the Arsalans maintained their alliance with the main Maronite faction, striving to integrate the Druze into the communal constitutional structure and safeguard their interests and position within that framework. The Junblats gradually became politically alienated and assertive; under Kamal Junblat's charismatic leadership and, after his assassination in 1977, under his son Walid, they turned into opposition, calling for a simple one-man vote democracy to replace Lebabon's communal structure constitution. In fact, they were striving mainly to enhance the Druze position in the power structure and for full Druze control of their power base: the Shuf district of southern Mount Lebanon. In 1949 Kamal Junblat founded the "Progressive Socialist Party" (seePSP). Since the 1950s he became increasingly left-leaning and pro-Nasserist. In the civil wars of 1958 and 1975 (until his death in 1977), his militia was part of the Muslim-dominated pro-Nasserist and anti-*status quo* "Leftist" camp of which Junbalat himself ascended to the position of unchalleged leader. There was near-complete identity between the Druze militias and the PSP, and Junbalat himself appeared as a Socialist leader, although he derived his strength from his position as a Druze chieftain and traditional land ownership. In recent decades the Arsalans' influence has much declined and the Junbalats have become the nearly undisputed leaders of the Lebanese Druze.

In 1983, after the withdrawal of Israeli forces from the Shuf, its Druze population entered a bitter war with the Christian PHALANGES and gained near-complete control. Despite their call for the abolition of the communal structure, the Druze of the Shuf created a virtually autonomous Druze canton. By 1985 the Druze (PSP) militias, in alliance with the Shi'i AMAL movement (though sometimes in rivalry and clashes with them, due to conflicting interests of the Druze "canton" and the Shi'i community), expanded their area of predominance and took control of the coastal strip adjoining the Shuf, the Iqlim al-Kharrub region further south, additional areas of South Lebanon and the hills approaching Beirut from the south-east. They also helped the Shi'i forces to take control of West Beirut and its southern suburbs. The Druze leaders were also able to increase their power because they operated in close alliance with Syria or as Syria's clients—though since the assassination of Kamal Junbalat in 1977 (for which Syria was blamed) Damascus could not rely on their submission to Syria's advice or guidance. In April 1984 Walid Junbalat became a Minister in the Government of National Unity—but in fact he and his Druze forces continued to oppose and sabotage its activity, boycotting most of its meetings. In December 1985 he signed the abortive Damascus tripartite agreement together with the leaders of the Amal Movement and the Maronite Christian "Lebanese Forces". During the campaign for the Presidential elections that were due in summer 1988 he supported the candidacy of former President Suleiman Franjiyeh, a pro-Syrian, and during the conflict between the two rival Lebanese governments, 1988–1990, was a member of Salim al-Huss's Muslim-dominated Government. In the "Government of National Reconciliation," formed in December 1990, Walid Junbalat served as a Minister, but resigned in January 1991 in protest of the dilution of Druze influence in the Government and the government's moves to eliminate the autonomous administration of the Druze in their "canton". However, he rejoined the government in March of that year, and held his post even as it dissolved most of the Lebanese militias, including that of his own PSP. Since 1992 Junbalat served Minister of the Displaced Affairs. Members of the Arsalan clan also held governmental posts since 1990.

In Israel, (mid-1990s) some 94,000 Druze constitute 1.4 percent of the population, about eight percent of the non-Jewish, Arabic-speaking population. Most of them live in one of fifteen villages in Western Galilee and two on Mount Carmel. Some of these villages are purely Druze, some have a mixed population of Druze, Muslims and Christians. Another Druze group (numbering about 15,400) inhabits four villages in the occupied GOLAN, under Israeli occupation since 1967. Most of them have refused Israeli citizenship since 1981.

A long-standing friendship links Jews and Druze in Israel. In Israel's War of Independence (1948)

many Druze aided the Jews against the invading Arab armies. Since 1957, at the community's own request, Druze are subject to compulsory IDF military service (while Arab citizens may volunteer, but are not conscripted); many Druze had volunteered before, and some attained senior ranks in both military and the police force. In 1957 the Druze were given the status of a distinct community with its own recognized communal-judicial institutions (under the British Mandate they had been subject to Muslim communal jurisdiction). First Druze *Qadis* were appointed in the 1960s. Since 1970 Druze matters are no longer handled by departments concerned with affairs of the Arab minority. One or two Druze are regularly elected to Parliament (the Knesset)—either on lists of the general parties or on lists appealing specifically to Arab and Druze voters. Study of Druze religious traditions was introduced in Druze schools in the 1970s, and in 1985 the University of Haifa announced the creation of a chair for Druze heritage.

Measures taken in Israel to treat the Druze as a separate community rather than as Arabs, do not necessarily mean that the Druze regard themselves as non-Arabs. They are Arabic-speaking, their cultural background and traditions are Arab and their brethren in Syria and Lebanon consider themselves Arab (though strong communal-autonomist sentiments persist). The Israeli Druze may register their ethnicity (in the population registry and identity cards) as either Druze or Arab; but they tend to avoid a clear definition or even a frank discussion, as to whether they see themselves as a separate national community—and it is assumed that most of them regard themselves as Arab. Their solidarity with the Druze in Syria and particularly in Lebanon is strong. This was vigorously expressed during the Lebanese Civil War and Israel's invasion of Lebanon, 1982–1985, and even led to Israeli Druze volunteering for service with Lebanese Druze military formations and to a measure of tension between the Druze and the Israeli Government on that account. Since the early 1990s the idyllic Druze-Jewish friendship and the former's integration in Israel have been troubled by increasing Druze complaints of discrimination and insufficient attention to their needs for economic and social development. While a "Druze Zionist Association" continues to foster the full solidarity of the Israeli Druze with the Jewish State, a

"Druze Initiative Committee" represents Druze claims and complaints in an increasingly assertive manner, in addition to a growing resistance to the conscription of Druze men to military service.

The Druze religion, though originally an offshoot of the Shi'i Isma'iliyya, is considered by most as having developed from Islam. It is a secret cult; its tenets are fully known only to the Initiated, the Sages (*Uqqal*), who are the religious heads of the community (notables and leaders may well be uninitiated, commoners—*Juhhal*). The Druze stress moral and social principles rather than ritual. They believe in reincarnation. Their house of prayer, the *khalwa*, is a small, modest structure. Their main holy days are the Feast of Sacrifice (*Id al-'Adha*), like that of the Muslims, and the Day of Pilgrimage (*Ziyara*) to the tomb of their legendary patriarch, the prophet Shu'aib (identified with biblical Jethro) at Hittin near Tiberias. The tombs of other saints, in Lebanon, Israel and the Golan, are also venerated. Due to the persecutions they suffered, and in line with their isolationist tendency, the Druze are permitted by their faith to conceal their religious identity (*taqiyya* "camouflage", as also permitted to Shi'i Muslims). In both Lebanon and Israel religious guidance and leadership are vested in a Supreme Council of religious leaders. The spiritual leader of the Druze community in Israel, Sheikh Amin Tarif, served as a unifying symbol for the Druze community Israel. His death in 1993 initiated a debate over his succession and the religious leadership of the Druze community in Israel. In addition to the three large communities in Syria, Lebanon and Israel, there are 5,000–20,000 Druze in Jordan.

DUBAI One of the seven sheikhdoms on the Trucial Coast of the PERSIAN GULF (TRUCIAL OMAN) which in 1971 formed the federation of the UNITED ARAB EMIRATES. Area: 1,175 sq. miles (3,900 sq. km.) Dubai's population grew rapidly with the development of its port and the discovery of oil—from a few thousand in the 1950s to 65,000 in the 1960s. A 1975 census reported a population of 207,000 and an estimated 675,000 in 1996, majority of them live in the capital, Dubai. Dubai was the most populous of the seven sheikhdoms but was overtaken by ABU DHABI in the late 1970s. The majority of the population is foreign—estimates range from approximately seventy-five percent up to ninety percent.

Even the original, "indigenous" population consists largely of fairly recent immigrants, mainly from IRAN, creating a SHI'A majority.

The rapid increase since the 1960s and 1970s resulted from the influx of foreign laborers—from Iran, Arab countries, such as Yemen, and mainly Pakistan and India. Such a large number of foreign workers without citizenship rights created grave social, and potential political problems—though so far there have been no reports of serious polical unrest.

The Sheikh of Dubai, of the Maktum clan, was, by several nineteenth century treaties (see TRUCIAL OMAN), under British protectorate. Dubai was the seat of the British political officer responsible for the area. This British protectorate was removed in 1971. Dubai, along with neighboring sheikhdoms, formed the independent UAE. The first ruler during independence was Sheikh Rashed ibn Sa'id al-Maktum (1958–1990), who served as Vice-President of the UAE (1971–1990), and Prime Minister (1979–1990). His son, Sheikh Maktum, succeeded him and he is the current Prime Minister of the UAE (1971–1979; 1990-). Since the creation of the UAE there has been constant rivalry between the rulers of Dubai and Abu Dhabi for the primacy of the federation——a rivalry also manifested in constitutional-ideological differences: Abu Dhabi strives for strong federal power, while Dubai is "autonomist", preferring stronger units and a weaker federation. In 1978–1979 this conflict led to a serious crisis (and the addition of the premiership to the positions held by the ruler of Dubai was part of the compromise solution achieved—see UNITED ARAB EMIRATES). Dubai continues to develop economic ties with Iran in spite of the fervent opposition of the US and Abu Dhabi.

Oil concessions for onshore and offshore exploration and production were granted in the 1950s and 1960s to American, British and French companies, after previous concessions had expired or been returned with no results. However, Dubai's rapid development began even before oil production started, with the construction of the largest man-made port and most modern port on the Persian Gulf, Port Rashed, using the deep nine mile (fifteen km.)—wide bay of Dubai and expanding the busy, previously existing harbor. In 1976 it was decided to construct a second large modern port at

Jabal Ali, combined with an industrial estate. With the first phase completed, the port was operating in 1980; ultimately over seventy berths were planned. Dubai also decided to construct a large dry-dock, intended mainly for oil tankers, Although the ORGANIZATION OF ARAB PETROLEUM-EXPORTING COUNTRIES (OAPEC) decided to build its common dry-dock in BAHRAIN rather than in Dubai, the latter refused to renounce its project and proceeded on its own, starting construction in 1973. The Dubai dry-dock, one of the world's largest, was completed in 1979. A compromise had been reached late in 1977 that it would be operated jointly with OAPEC's dock in Bahrain, but it began operating only in 1983—on its own, with a foreign company as operator. A modern international airport was also built.

Oil was struck, offshore, in 1966, and production began in 1969; for production and revenue, and the process of nationalization—see OIL. Nearly all revenues derive from oil; but Dubai is also creating several non-petroleum industrial projects such as an aluminum plant opened in 1979. at Jabal Ali; a refinery and gas liquefaction plant have been operating since 1980.

E

EBAN, ABBA (AUBREY) (1915–) Israeli diplomat and politician. Born in Cape Town, South Africa and educated in Cambridge, England. In 1942 Eban served as Allied Headquarters' Liaison Officer, training Jewish volunteers in JERUSALEM. He joined the Jewish Agency in 1946 and became Liaison Officer with the UN Special Committee on Palestine (UNSCOP) in 1947. Eban was appointed representative of the Provisional Government of Israel to the UN in 1948 and in the years 1949–1959 served as Israel's Permanent Representative to the UN. Concurrently, he was Israel's Ambassador to Washington (1950–1959). During 1958–1966 he was President of the Weizmann Institute for Science in Rehovot.

Eban was first elected to the fourth Knesset (1959) on the Mapai list. He was Minister without Portfolio, 1959–1960; Minister of Education and Culture, 1960–1963; Deputy Prime Minister, 1963–1966; and Minister of Foreign Affairs 1966–1974—through both the Six-Day War and Yom Kippur War (see ARAB-ISRAEL CONFLICT). Eban was not invited to join the government formed by Yitzhak RABIN in 1974. He became a guest professor at Columbia University in the US and continued to be a Knesset member until 1988, serving as chairman of the Knesset Foreign Affairs and Security Committee in the years 1984–1988. Toward the elections to the twelfth Knesset he did not receive a significant place on the Labor Party list, and withdrew from political life. Concentrating on writing and the preparation of television programs on ISRAEL and the Jewish people, he began spending most of his time in the US. Eban is considered one of Israel's most brilliant orators, speaking fluently in many European and Middle Eastern languages.

ECEVIT, BULENT (b. 1925) Turkish journalist and politician. Prime Minister, 1974, 1977, 1978–1979. Born in Istanbul to an upper-class family. He graduated from the prestigious Robert College High School (1944) and studied at the Istanbul University Faculty of Letters. He joined the Government Press Agency in Ankara. From 1946 to 1950 he was an assistant in the London Turkish Embassy Press Office and studied in London University. In 1950 he returned to TURKEY and joined the editorial staff of *Ulus*, the daily paper of the Republican People's Party (RPP). In the mid-1950s he studied in the United States, on a Rockefeller Foundation scholarship. In 1957 Ecevit was elected to Parliament, for the RPP. Due to his close relationship with Party leader Ismet INÖNÜ and his association with a group of reformist intellectuals headed by Turhan Feyzioglu, he gained increasing influence in the Party. After the 1960 coup, he was appointed by his Party to the nominated assembly that drafted the constitution of 1961. That year he was re-elected to the Turkish Parliament and in November 1961 joined Inönü's Government as Minister of Labor, until 1965. He continuously strengthened his position in the RPP leadership and apparatus and was the Party's General Secretary, 1966–1971, moving it further to the left. In March 1971 he resigned in protest against the Party's collaboration with the military intervention or semi-coup. He thus broke with Inönü. In May 1972, backed by a majority at an emergency congress of the party, he forced Inönü to retire and was elected in his place as chairman of the RPP.

The RPP emerged from the elections of 1973 and 1977 as the strongest party, but failed to obtain an absolute majority. Ecevit formed several coalition governments, which were all of short duration. In July 1974 he initiated the invasion of Cyprus, following the coup which ousted President Makarios. This made him a war hero in the eyes of the public. Yet he failed to halt the anarchy, terrorism and inflation that plagued Turkey. When the Army headed by Kenan EVREN intervened in September 1980, the RPP was banned and Ecevit was arrested. Although he was released after a month, he was barred from making any public political statements (and was rearrested several times for violating that ban).

When political parties were legalised in 1983, time was too short for Ecevit's group to organize for the elections in November 1983. Ecevit himself had been banned from political activity until 1992. But in 1985 a Democratic Left Party was formed with Ecevit's wife in the chair and, when the ban on Ecevit was lifted in September 1987, he himself assumed the chairmanship. However, the Party failed to gain a single seat in the Grand National Assembly (with only 8.5 percent of the vote). Ecevit resigned in 1988, only to be re-elected Party Chairman in 1989. Ecevit's position as the major spokesman of the moderate left by then was being successfully challenged by Erdal INÖNÜ's Social Democratic Populist Party which after the 1991 elections entered the government as a member of the coalition formed by Süleyman DEMIREL and his True Path Party. Ecevit's Party succeeded in winning only seven seats, but in the December 1995 elections increased its representation in the National Assembly to seventy-six, ahead of its leftist rivals (by then, Deniz Baykal's Republican People's Party).

Ecevit stayed out of the coalition government formed by the Motherland and True Path Parties and refused to cooperate with the Government led by the Islamist Welfare Party which came to power in July 1996. Following the resignation of Prime Minister ERBAKAN a year later, he joined Motherland's Mesut YILMAZ to form a new coalition government with himself as Deputy Prime Minister.

ECO Acronym for Economic Cooperation Organization, established in the course of the 1980s with the participation of IRAN, TURKEY and Pakistan as a development of the RCD (the Organization for Regional Cooperation and Development—see CENTO). The willingness of the Islamic regime in Iran to revive this institution appeared to contradict its revolutionary slogans, for Turkey and Pakistan had been the Shah's partners in the CENTO military alliance, and continued to maintain close cooperation with the US.

However, at the peak of the war with IRAQ, Iran was in need of commercial and economic relations with its two neighbors, requiring their assistance in various spheres. Even though ECO failed to implement any significant regional projects, in 1992 it was joined by Afghanistan and six Muslim republics from the former Soviet Union: Azerbaijan, Kazakhstan, Krghyzstan, Tajikistan, Turkmenistan and Uzbekistan.

Though in territorial terms the ECO is one of the largest organizations for economic cooperation in the world, its influence is very limited because its member states do not complement each other in the economic sphere. The organization's greatest achievement since its foundation has been the completion of a section of the Iran-Turkmenistan railway. This connects the Muslim republics with the PERSIAN GULF, reviving the historical Silk Road. The member states have also established a shipping line, a regional bank and an insurance company, and have invested heavily in the development of a road network between them.

EGYPT Official name (since 1971): The Arab Republic of Egypt, located at the north-eastern corner of Africa (with the SINAI PENINSULA in Asia), on the southern shore of the Mediterranean, bordering with LIBYA in the west, SUDAN in the south, the Red Sea, ISRAEL, and the Palestinian GAZA STRIP in the east and north-east. The decisive bulk of Egypt's territory is arid desert while the inhabited area—the Nile valley and its delta, and a few oases-is only 3.5–5% of the total territory, 15,000 sq. miles or (38,850 sq. km.), resulting in one of the most densely populated areas in the world approximately 540 sq. miles

(1,400 per sq. km.) The southern border was determined in the Anglo-Egyptian CONDOMINIUM Agreement of 1899. The Sinai border was imposed in 1906 by Britain due to the Ottoman Sultan, who never renounced his claim to Sinai. The western border was agreed upon with Italy, then in possession of Libya, in 1925.

Egypt's population rapidly increased during this century—from 10 million in 1900 to 15 million in the mid-1930s, 30 million in the mid-1960s, 38.2 million in the last census taken (1976); it passed the 50 million mark in 1980, and 60 million in the mid-1990s. Egypt's rapid population growth (in 1996, an annual addition of 1.2 millions) and extremely limited land resources have undermind the government's efforts since the 1960s to reduce population growth by programs of birth control, which scored only limited success (See Table). Nearly all Egyptians are Arabic-speaking and more than eighty-nine percent are SUNNI Muslims. Christian Egyptians, the COPTS, estimated at ten percent—more than 6 million in 1995. Other minorities form less than one percent—descendants of Greeks, Italians and JEWS—poor remnants of a lively and creative community of foreigners from Mediterranean countries, that had played an important role in Egypt's economy and culture until the late 1950s, when the revolutionary regime adopted a policy of far-reaching nationalization of the economy. Egypt's population is largely rural-agricultural. The urban population was estimated at about twenty percent early in the century and at twenty-five percent in the 1930s. This is constantly increasing. More than half of the population is below eighteen (0–14 constitute 37 percent), which means a tremendous economic burden on the government in terms of providing services of education, health and welfare to this mostly non-productive population. It was estimated in the 1980s, at about forty-five percent and migration to the towns continues at relatively high rate. (For Cairo alone, already the residence of about twenty percent of all Egyptians, a rate of 300,000-350,000 per annum is estimated). The percentage of those engaged in agriculture (estimated at about seventy percent in the 1930s and still at more than fifty percent in the 1970s), continues to decrease and was estimated at approximately thirty-eight percent in the mid-1980s. Those working in industry comprise about fifteen percent (some place this figure as high as

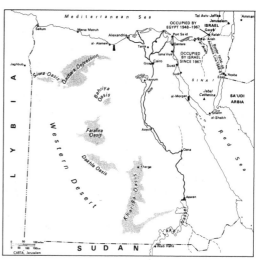

Map of Egypt

thirty percent, depending on the statistical definition of "industry"). More than forty percent of the labor force is engaged in services. An estimated 3 to 3.5 million Egyptians are working and residing abroad, mainly in Arab countries, though their scope seemed to be stagnant since the mid-1980s owing to the plunge of oil prices in the world market and economic recession in the oil countries. The share of agriculture in the national income (approximately forty percent in the early 1950s), is down to less than twenty-five percent, while that of industrial production is up to between fifteen and twenty percent (and according to some data, more than thirty-five percent, again depending on the statistical definition of industry). Egypt's GDP was in the mid-1980s estimated to be 53 billion dollars, the national annual per capita income about 560 dollars.

Constitutional history Egypt has been a Presidential Republic since 1956. It was under Turkish-Ottoman sovereignty from 1517, with local de facto rule exercised until between 1803–1805 by Mamluk governors (interrupted by Napoleon Bonaparte's French occupation, 1798–1801), and from 1803–1805 by a dynasty of Governors (Wali, Pasha) that adopted in 1867 the title of Khedive (Viceroy). From 1882 Egypt was under a "temporary" British occupation—which pro forma recognized Ottoman sovereignty—and since 1914 under a British Protectorate, with the *Khedive* restyled Sultan. In 1922 BRITAIN unilaterally proclaimed Egypt's independence, and the Sultan assumed the title of King. A Constitution of a conservative parliamentary monarchy was adopted in 1923. In 1936, an Anglo-Egypt-ian Treaty affirmed Egypt's formal independence, which allowed Egypt to become a member of the League of Nations in 1937. During World War II Egypt was in fact under British military rule, and used as the Middle East center of civil and military administration. With the end of the war Egypt became a founding member of the UN in 1945. After the July 1952 coup by a group of the "Free Officers," the monarchy was abolished in 1953 (formalized, with a new Constitution, in 1956). Though the Constitution has since been modified several times (including three years of union with Syria, 1958–1961), Egypt remained a Presidential Republic. In 1971 a new constitution was approved by a referendum (and later amended in 1990), defining Egypt as an Arab republic, with a democratic, socialist system. It perceives Islam as the state religion and the Islamic law (SHARI'A) as the primary source of legislation; labels the political system as multiparty and ensures the equality of men and women in accordance with the Shari'a. The constitution protects the public sector and its social and economic manifestations, such as economic societies and trade unions, and guarantees the freedom of the press.

The president has a six-year tenure and must be endorsed by two-thirds of the parliament (*majlis al-umma*: the National Assembly). He possesses all executive powers, including the supreme command of the armed forces, through appointing and dismissing the government.

Political history

1. Pre-Independent Egypt At the turn of the twentieth century, Egypt was ruled by a *Khedive* (Viceroy) of the dynasty of Muhammad Ali, nominally under Turkish-Ottoman sovereignty, and since 1882 occupied by Britain. In fact, the British "Agent and Consul General", Cromer, ruled like a Governor in a semi-colonial, indirect, conservative-paternalistic way. Egypt under the *Khedive* ISMA'ILIS had become insolvent. Anglo-French supervision of its debts and indeed its economy that had been established in 1876 culminated in increasing Anglo-French intervention and control. The *Khedive* was deposed in 1879 and replaced by his son Tawfiq. Unrest led by military officers led in 1882 to semi-coup and the appointment of the officers' leader, Colonel Ahmad Urabi, as Minister of War. As a result of that crisis Britain occupied the country, defeating military resistance by Urabi and the army.

Incipient Egyptian nationalism, which saw its beginnings in the Urabi revolt, was thus directed against the British and their occupation rather than against the Turkish sovereign. Some of the political parties that began organizing from about 1900 had a pro-Turkish flavor which was enhanced by a strong Islamic tendency. Egyptian nationalism was indeed to a large part linked with, and rooted simultaneously in movements of Islamic revival. It had, on the other hand, little connection with Arab nationalism, and regarded itself as Egyptian rather than Arab. Arab nationalists of the time, located mainly in the Fertile Crescent, also did not include Egypt in the region whose independence and unity they envisioned. The main Parties of those years were the "Nationalist Party" (*al-Hizb al-Watani*), formed in 1907 and led by Mustafa Kamel (1874–1908) and after his death by Muhammad Farid (1868–1919). It was particularly anti-British and its main ideology was Nationalism. The "Nation Party" (*Hizb al-Umma*) was founded in 1907 and led by (Ahmad) Lutfi al-Sayyid (1872–1963), with Ahmad Sa'ad Zaghlul, later Egypt's national leader, amongst its junior leaders. The *Umma* Party advocated a more liberal westernized nationalism aspiring to a parliamentary-constitutional regime. It was willing to let Egypt be guided for some time by Britain and was regarded by its adversaries as Lord Cromer's pet or creation. In any case, Egyptian nationalism was intensifying and resulted in several incidents and clashes with a British administration that had little understanding and no sympathy for these national aspirations (for instance, the "Dinshawi Incident" in 1906).

When TURKEY joined Germany and Austria in World War I, Britain in December 1914 severed the formal link between Egypt and the OTTOMAN EMPIRE. It declared Egypt a British Protectorate, under a High Commissioner, promising to guide it to self-rule. At the same time, the British deposed the *Khedive*, Abbas Hilmi. He was considered to be anti-British and involved in political intrigues, and was replaced by his uncle, Hussein Kamel, as "Sultan". The new Sultan in 1917 was succeeded by his brother Ahmad Fu'ad.

During the war years Egyptian resentment against British rule intensified. The war effort imposed on the population economic hardships, soaring prices, martial law, and censorship. Egypt was Britain's main base in the war against Turkey. Britain felt compelled to keep a tight rein and postponed any advancement towards independence, while younger Egyptian leaders were pressing for that independence. Towards the end of the war, a new nationalist group was formed, led by Sa'ad Zaghlul. This group (mainly men of the landed gentry; the commercial middle class and the intelligentsia and free professions), had influence in the villages too. It claimed that it—rather than the Sultan and his government—should represent Egypt in negotiations with Britain, scheduled to be held in London.

In November 1918, a delegation laid the claim before the High Commissioner, Sir Reginald Wingate. That delegation (Arabic: WAFD became the nucleus of the *Wafd* Party. When the British refused to recognize Zaghlul's group as the national leadership representing Egypt, demonstrations and strikes erupted. In March 1919, Zaghlul and some of his leading associates were exiled. But when violent riots followed, the British backed down. Wingate was replaced by General Allenby, who adopted a policy of conciliation.

Early in April, Zaghlul and his colleagues were released and allowed to go to Paris to present the

THE RULING DYNASTY OF EGYPT, 1805–1953

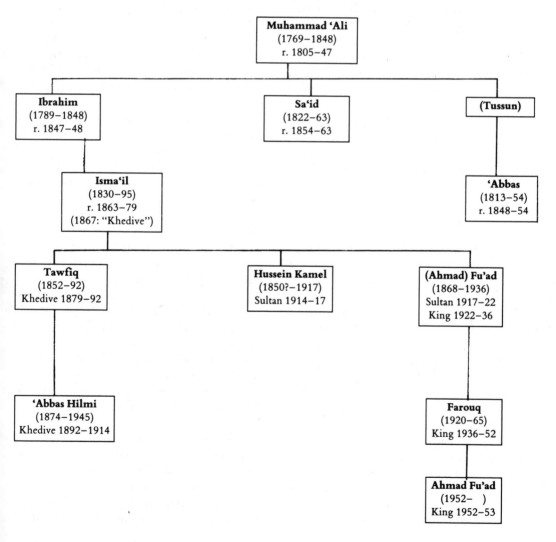

Egyptian demands to the Peace Conference. However, when they arrived, the Conference had already recognized the British Protectorate (May 1919).

In May 1919, the British Government appointed the Secretary for the Colonies (Lord Milner) to investigate the situation and suggest a new regime that would grant Egypt self-government under British guidance whilst safeguarding British and foreign interests. Milner, arriving in Egypt at the end of 1919, was boycotted by the nationalists and most public figures not connected with the palace or the Government. He later contacted Zaghlul in Europe and in June 1920 held talks with him in London, offering Egypt independence on condition that a treaty guaranteeing British interests be signed. But no agreement was reached on the details of such a treaty. Milner presented his report late in 1920; it was published in February 1921. Negotiations with a Government delegation in 1921 failed to reach an agreement on an Anglo-Egyptian treaty, and attempts to recruit leaders who would accept independence on British terms did not succeed. In December 1921, Zaghlul was again exiled; intensified nationalist ferment and renewed violence followed.

As no agreed solution seemed feasible, Britain on 28 February 1922 unilaterally proclaimed Egypt independent. Four matters were reserved to the British government until agreement could be reached upon them: a. the security of British communications in Egypt; b. the defense of Egypt against foreign aggression; c. the protection of foreign interests and minorities; d. the administration of Sudan. Although the Egyptian leaders refused to officially recognize that restricted independence, in effect they accepted it and began establishing their state institutions.

In March 1922, Sultan Fu'ad proclaimed himself King. (The British prevented him from taking the title of King of Egypt and Sudan.) A Constitution was drafted by an appointed committee and promulgated in April 1923. A Parliament was elected (September 1923 to January 1924)—with the *Wafd* winning a decisive majority. The Constitution of 1923 (after a bitter struggle between the nationalist radicals and liberals and the King and his conservative advisers) was a conservative one. The King was to appoint and dismiss the Prime Minister; to dissolve Parliament and postpone its sessions; to appoint the president of the Senate and one-fifth of its members; and had the right to veto all laws. Despite this, the *Wafd* became the defender of the Constitution, whilst the King and his conservative supporters viewed it as restricting their rule.

The thirty years of Egypt's parliamentary monarchy saw a continuous struggle between the *Wafd*, as the main nationalist and radical-liberal party, and conservative anti-Wafdist parties—usually supporting the King, and supported by him. The most important of those was the "Liberal-Constitutional Party", founded in 1922 by Adli Yakan, Abdel-Khaleq Saruat, Abdel Aziz Fahmi, Muhammad Muhammad, and Hassanein HEYKAL. Many of its leaders were seceding Wafdists. In 1937 a new split in the *Wafd* created the second major anti-Wafdist party, the Sa'adist Party (named after Sa'ad Zaghlul). This was led by Dr. Ahmad Maher and Mahmud Fahmi al-Nuqrashi. Usually, whenever a Wafdist or neutral government was in power, the *Wafd* won the elections (1924, 1926, 1929, 1936, 1942, 1950). However, under governments of the anti-Wafdist Parties, it was they who won (1931, 1938 and 1945). But all pre-1936 Wafdist Governments (1924, 1928, 1930) were short-lived, as the King used his prerogative to dismiss them and dissolve Parliament. Several times election laws were changed. For example direct elections were replaced by indirect ones and property, tax or educational restrictions were imposed. This was done in the hope that such measures would reduce the *Wafd's* influence. Most of these changes were later abolished by Wafdist or liberal governments. In 1930, however, ultra-conservative Prime Minister Isma'il Sidqi abrogated the Constitution and enacted a new, much more conservative one. The *Wafd* and the Liberals boycotted the new regime and its elections; their resistance escalated into serious unrest and riots, and in 1935 the King surrendered, reintroducing the Constitution of 1923. The elections of 1936 were overwhelmingly won by the *Wafd*—led by Mustafa Nahhas since Zaghlul's death in 1927.

Whilst the parliamentary-constitutional regime did not operate satisfactorily, nearly all Egyptian parties and the King were united in their desire to replace the semi-independence imposed in 1922 by full independence. They also wanted to abolish Britain's four "reserved matters" by concluding a treaty regulating the issues in question which was also what Britain wanted. Though there were tactical differences between the Parties (and between them and the

King), Egypt's basic "National Demands" were presented by whichever government negotiated for it. Talks on an Anglo-Egyptian treaty failed in 1924, 1927 and 1929–1930. This was mainly due to two principal demands: those concerning defense and the Sudan. Egypt demanded the evacuation of British forces and the handing-over of its defense to the Egyptian army alone. It also demanded the abolition of restrictions on the strength of that army and the transfer of its command (held ex-officio by the British Governor-General of Sudan) to Egyptian hands. With regards to Sudan, Egypt demanded the replacement of the Condominium by the "Unity of the Nile Valley", i.e., Egyptian rule over Sudan (as before the MAHDI's revolt of 1881). Moreover, Egypt complained that it was deprived of it proper share in the joint administration of Sudan as provided under the Condominium Agreement of 1899. Egypt's demands included the freedom for Egyptians to migrate to and settle in Sudan. These complaints were aggravated by a serious crisis in 1924. When the Governor-General, Sir Lee Stack, was assassinated, the British imposed reprisals. These were: the withdrawal of Egyptian troops from Sudan; the conversion of Sudanese units of the Egyptian army into a Sudan Defense Force; the enactment of Sudan's budget without submission to Egypt for approval; the enlargement of irrigated areas in Sudan (implying a threat to reduce the flow to Egypt of the vital Nile flood-waters). Egypt now demanded as a first step, the abrogation of these reprisals. Tension was eased in 1929 when Britain and Egypt reached agreement on the distribution of the Nile waters between Egypt and Sudan. Yet the basic dispute remained unresolved.

A breakthrough came in 1936. Britain was keenly interested in mending its relations with the East Mediterranean in view of two issues. Firstly, Italy's conquest of Ethiopia and general expansionism, and secondly, the growing aggressive strength of Nazi Germany. Egypt had seen how Iraq had attained fuller independence through the Anglo-Iraqi treaty of 1930, proving that an accommodation with Britain—independence in return for certain privileges for Britain—was possible. The restoration of the parliamentary-constitutional regime in Egypt had been encouraged by Britain, and the latter now considered the *Wafd*, though strongly nationalist (or perhaps because of that), as the preferable partner

for a settlement. King Fu'ad died in April 1936, and since his son Farouq was a minor, a Regency Council was established. Elections in May 1936 brought the *Wafd* to power. Even before the elections, an all-party delegation had been formed for resuming negotiations with Britain which excluded the old "Nationalist Party." This group injoyed minimal influence and rejected any agreement with Britain. In August 1936, a Treaty of Preferential Alliance was signed.

A twenty-year Defense Pact allowed Britain to station a defined number of troops (10,000 land forces, 400 pilots, and ancillary personnel) on the SUEZ CANAL. For a limited time, this was also permitted in Cairo and Alexandria. This was the case until the Egyptian Army was deemed by both Parties be able to ensure its defense and the security of navigation. In the event of war or imminent threat of war, Egypt was to aid Britain by furnishing it with "all the facilities and assistance in (its) power, including the use of (its) ports, aerodromes and communications." Sudan would continue to be administered under the Condominium Agreement, without prejudice to the question of sovereignty, and with Egyptian immigration unrestricted. The protection of foreigners and minorities was recognized as Egypt's exclusive responsibility. Britain was to support the abrogation of the CAPITULATIONS (extra-territorial privileges for foreigners; their abolition was agreed in the MONTREUX CONVENTION of 1937). The Treaty of 1936 thus completed Egypt's formal independence. In May 1937, Egypt was admitted to the League of Nations on Britain's recommendation.

2. Independent Egypt (1937–1952)
National Liberation and Regional Policy

Nonetheless, the honeymoon of general satisfaction was brief—both internally and in Anglo-Egyptian relations. Young King Farouq, who came of age and took the reins in July 1937, tended even more than his father to be politically dominant, which brought him into continuous competition over power and prestige with the *Wafd* leader Nahhas. Late in 1937 he dismissed the *Wafd* government. Under its successor the *Wafd*—which had been unable to fulfil popular hopes, and which had split in 1937 (seceding leaders founding the Sa'adist Party)—lost the elections of 1938. Non-Wafdist Governments followed each other. Britain (though her former High Commissioner was now an Ambassador) continued interfering in Egyptian politics. Britian also failed to completely adhere to the military clauses of the Treaty. The number of Britain's troops still exceeded that stipulated, and those outside the Canal Zone were not withdrawn.

World War II further aggravated Anglo-Egyptian discord. As Egypt became Britain's vital Middle East base, military installations were further strengthened and the number of troops increased. Egypt did not declare war on the "Axis" powers, though they violated its territory in the Western Desert, reaching Marsa Matruh in 1940 and al-Alamein in 1942, while the "facilities and assistance" stipulated in the Treaty were supplied, albeit grudgingly. Many Egyptian politicians, including the King and Prime Minister Ali Maher, displayed sympathy for the German-Italian Axis. Some groups displayed openly Fascist tendencies—such as the "Young Egypt" Party (*Misr al-Fatah*), founded in the mid-1930s by Ahmad Hussein (1911–1982).

In 1940 Britain forced the dismissal of Premier Maher and the Chief-of-Staff, Aziz Ali al-Masri, who was (currently) suspected of contacts with the enemy. Al-Masri was thereupon caught trying to escape to the Axis forces and was detained and put on trial (along with some other officers). Britain's intervention policy culminated in February 1942. This was when it forced the King by tanks aimed at his Abdin palace to accept an ultimatum to replace the Government by a Wafdist one, which restored Nahhas to the premiership, but apparently further embittered into his relations with the King.

With the danger of an Axis victory receding, British intervention in Egypt's political affairs lessened. In October 1944 King Farouq dismissed the British-imposed *Wafd* Government. On 24 February 1945 Egypt declared war against Germany and Japan, thus qualifying to be a founding member of the UN. It did not engage in action (Premier Ahmad Maher, who had decided to declare war, was assassinated the same day). In December 1945, Egypt demanded the abrogation or radical amendment of the Treaty of 1936. It wanted to ensure the evacuation of British forces and the "Unity of the Nile Valley", i.e. Egyptian sovereignty over Sudan. Britain was prepared to discuss the replacement of the Treaty (even before its expiry in 1956), by a defense agreement that would satisfy its strategic requirements in the Canal Zone. For Sudan, Britain advocated a gradual development of self-government and eventual self-determination. In 1946, Premier Isma'il Sidqi reached an agreement with Foreign Secretary Bevin. Under this Britain was to withdraw its forces within three years and a joint Anglo-Egyptian defense committee was to be established: Britain and Egypt were to prepare Sudan for self-rule and self-determination "within the framework of the unity between Egypt and the Sudan under the joint Egyptian crown." However, this formula was interpreted by the two parties in contradictory terms: to the British, Sudan had been granted self-determination, while Egyptian-Sudanese unity was no more than a token formula. The Egyptians claimed that the Unity of the Nile Valley and Egyptian sovereignty had been conceded and self-determination was to be a symbolic act. When these contradictory interpretations were voiced in public, the agreement collapsed and Sidqi resigned. Although by 1947 British forces evacuated Egypt's mainland and restricted their presence to the Suez Canal, Egypt's claim for full withdrawal of Britain from Egyptian soil remained the primary issue on Egypt's public and official agendas. In the spring of 1947 the Egyptian government under Prime Minister Nuqrashi submitted to the UN Security Council a complaint against Britain's continued occupation of Egyptian land as well as the Sudan. The Council was unable to reach a decision on the Egyptian complaint and the latter's argument against self-determination for Sudan failed to sway world opinion.

The impasse in relations with Britain along with the growing radicalization of Egyptian politics following the military defeat in the Palestine war of 1948 (see ARAB-ISRAEL CONFLICT), led the *Wafd* government, in October 1951, unilaterally to: declare the abrogation of the Treaty of 1936 and the Condominium of 1899; proclaim King Farouq "King of Egypt and Sudan" (i.e., to declare Egypt's sovereignty over Sudan); and to issue a draft constitution for Sudan envisaging self-government in internal matters while reserving defense and foreign affairs to Egypt. At the same time, Egypt rejected Anglo-American proposals with which FRANCE and Turkey were also associated. Instead, Egypt joined a MIDDLE EASTERN DEFENSE ORGANIZATION. It tried to solve the dispute over British troops and bases in the Suez Canal by placing the bases at the disposal of that organization. Egypt also rejected new British proposals for a settlement of the Sudan issue. Late in 1951 the Government encouraged attempts to force the British out by popular violent resistance. Clashes continued into 1952. In late January 1952 Egyptian and British forces fought in ISMA'ILIYYA, and on 26 January, anti-British riots in Cairo turned against foreigners and minorities ("Black Saturday"). Martial law was declared, and the King held the *Wafd* government responsible.

In the later war years, Egypt became increasingly involved in regional Arab affairs, primarily the quest for Arab regional unity, led until then by the HASHEMITE rulers of IRAQ and Transjordan. Until the late 1930s, Egypt had—despite much sympathy and a measure of emotional-ideological solidarity—taken little part in Arab nationalist struggles outside her borders. The new inclination derived from the growing interest of Egyptian political groups, primarily the MUSLIM BROTHERHOOD Society since the late 1920s, in the cause of Palestine (see ARAB-ISRAEL CONFLICT), and the growing movement of the Egyptian political public to define its political identity in the framework of a unifying Arab-Islamic nation rather than a distinctive—territorial, historical, secular, and cultural—Egyptian identity. This trend assumed a growing official nature as of the late 1930s, especially against the backdrop of the temporary end of the struggle for Egyptian independence and the quest of the rival centers of political power—the King and the *Wafd Party*—for a major mobilizing issue in the domestic arena. Egypt first became officially involved when she responded to a British invitation to attend the London Conference of 1939 on the future of Palestine, which involved inter-Arab consultations as to the joint Arab position, held in Cairo and led by Egypt. During the war Cairo became the venue of much inter-Arab social, economic and intellectual activities due its regional centrality in British civilian and military activities in the region, but also because of the growing influence of the Egyptian press, literature, films and financial resources in the Fertile Crescent. In 1942–1943, the British were actively interested in attaining the Arab "good will" and support in the war, especially in view of the April-May traumatic anti-British nationalist rebellion in Iraq. Britain's wartime declared support of an all-Arab alliance, the expectations for the Allies' victory that would lead to full independence of SYRIA and LEBANON and the solution of the Palestine problem by the end of the war, which underpinned Iraqi Premier Nuri

AL-SA'ID's renewed lobbying of Britain for establishing a Fertile Crescent Federation led by Hashemite Iraq—all triggered Premier Nahhas to enter into competition for leadership of inter-Arab consultations that were to bring about the foundation of the ARAB LEAGUE, 1944–1945, consolidating Egypt's leading role in this regional Arab organization, with Cairo as its headquarters and Egyptians as its general secretaries until 1979.

Egypt's growing involvement in Arab affairs dragged her into the Palestine War of 1948, despite unequivocal proclamations of Nuqrashi's government through 1947–1948 not to intervene with regular forces, and against the official advice of the army commanders (see ARAB-ISRAEL CONFLICT). Within the Arab League, Egypt headed a group of states (with Syria, Lebanon, SAUDI ARABIA and Yemen) which opposed all plans for any regional unity or federation that would involve a revision of the political map of the Arab states, and especially an expansion of the Hashemite dynasty ruling Iraq and Jordan. Under Egypt's leadership, the Arab League was shaped as a loose association of sovereign states, and a watchdog, protecting the inter-Arab balance based on the existing status quo (a policy changed only in the late 1950s).

Domestic Affairs The radicalization of Egyptian politics and the increasing violence reflected a structured malaise, rooted in deep frustration with the social, economic and political order. A constant stream of migration from the villages to the cities created huge slums and a large sub-stratum of society not absorbed in gainful employment; spreading education and the emergence of a new, urban, and highly politicized middle-class, resulted in far-reaching changes in the structure of the Egyptian society, and threatened to wreck the socio-political status of the old Turko-Egyptian elite. The constitutional-parliamentary regime failed to meet the needs of the newly emerging political and social groups and became remote, and increasingly irrelevant. The social and economic frustration led to the growth of militant extra-parliamentary groups (which, in 1945–1950 also included the *Wafd* due to its boycott of the 1945 elections) for whom the street was the primary stage of protest and violence. Among the ex-parliamentary groups were the Communists—though weak, split into factions, with relatively poor appeal to the masses because many of its leaders were of the minorities (Copts, Jews, Greeks)—the ultra-nationalist "Young Egypt," and the largest and most influential of them—the Muslim Brotherhood Society (*al-Ikhwan al-Muslimun*). Founded in 1928 by Hassan AL-BANNA, the movement came to be the most important among several Islamic currents. It tried to teach and spread Islam as a revivalist doctrine and impose it on Egypt's social fabric and state institutions. It also used violence, political assassination and terrorism, such as bombs in film-theaters and other entertainment places. The Muslim Brotherhood was conspicuous in pressing the government to intervene militarily in Palestine following the eruption of hostilities between Arabs and Jews in late 1947. The Brotherhood also sent early in 1948, several hundreds of volunteers to fight with the Palestinian-Arabs against the JEWS, and in May 1948 a larger contingent of about a thousand armed volunteers joined the invading regular Egyptian army: see ARAB-ISRAEL CONFLICT). In December 1948, the Brotherhood was banned by premier Nuqrashi and steps were taken to suppress it. Three weeks later, Nuqrashi was assassinated (the Botherhood's "Supreme Guide" Hassan al-Banna was murdered in retaliation in February 1949).

In its twenty-nine years, until the regime was overthrown in 1952, the regime had seen ten elections and thirty-eight changes of government, and only two parliaments had completed their term (1931–1936, 1945–1950). The rigging of elections, purchases of votes and other corrupt practices had been frequently denounced, and big land-owners and strongmen had imposed their influence and delivered bloc-votes of whole villages. Economic and social problems were even more fundamental. The large increase of the population (from less than 10 million in 1900 to over 22 million in 1952) was not balanced by a parallel expansion of arable land, so that the ratio of cultivated land and food production per inhabitant was in constant decline. Industry did not develop fast enough to catch up with population growth. Standards of life and nourishment were declining and poverty was spreading, while the gap between rich and poor widened. Of the peasants, over fifty percent were landless tenants or agricultural laborers, and of those owning land the majority owned less than 1 *feddan* (acre) i.e. insufficient to feed a family, while some 12,000 big landlord families

owned thirty-seven percent of the land (and the captains of industry, banking and trade mostly came from the same families). The politicians and their parties all spoke of reforms and economic development, and the Wafd had a radical wing which advocated a ceiling of 500 feddan on land ownership (radical Leftists wanted a ceiling of 50 *feddan*). But the political leaders were mostly from the big land-owning and capitalist families, and very little was done in the way of reforms or welfare-oriented development.

3. Egypt Under Nasser (1952-1970)

Domestic Affairs In 1952 the political situation in Egypt was ripe for an overthrow of the regime, which came at the hands of a clandestine group of army officers. These officers were motivated by the humiliating defeat of the 1948 Palestine War, convinced that the debacle had been caused by faulty political leadership and by wide-spread corruption, a generally rotten civil and military administration, sabotaged arms supplies and treacherous intrigues. Their suspicions were confirmed by an investigation (from June 1950) from purges of senior officers (October 1950) and trials (from March 1951). The reinstatement of the most senior dismissed commanders in May 1951 angered them and caused further ferment. The deepening instability of the regime, what they saw as its general corruption, and the King's high life of debauchery exacerbated the situation.

From about 1950 a secret group of "Free Officers" formed. On 23 July 1952, it staged a coup, led by General Muhammad Nagib and Colonel Gamal ABDEL NASSER. (The latter was the real leader, while Nagib, an older and more senior officer, had been invited to join as a figurehead.) There was no resistance, and the officers' twelve-member Revolutionary Council took over. The new rulers established a civilian Government headed by the veteran politician Ali Maher. They forced King Farouq to abdicate and go into exile; transferred the crown to his infant son Ahmad Fu'ad with appointed Regency Council; and suspended the Constitution. The new regime immediately declared its resolve to introduce far-reaching reforms, with land reform at the top of its lists, which, beyond their connotation of social justice, were meant to weaken the old ruling elite. As Maher was reluctant to go along, a new government was formed in September with Nagib as its premier. A

Land Reform Bill was immediately enacted, restricting land ownership to 200 *feddan* (acres), with an additional 100 *feddan* for other members of the family. Another decree made the existence of political parties conditional on the approval of their programs and leaders by the Government. The Parties were ordered to reform and purge themselves. Some who complied, began replacing their leaders. A considerable number of old-regime politicians were arrested, and trials for corruption, maladministration or treason were promised.

Later in 1952, the new regime faced a measure of political resistance. Some of the parties, led by the *Wafd*, demanded the reactivation of the constitution and parliament. The ruling officers thereupon hardened their stance. In December 1952 they abrogated the Constitution of 1923. They set up a special court to try ministers, parliamentarians and civil servants who had "betrayed the trust of the people." Some of the accused, including one ex-Premier, Ibrahim Abdel Hadi and several ex-Ministers and leading politicians were sentenced in 1953 and 1954 to long prison terms and lost their political rights. In January 1953, all political parties were dissolved, property confiscated, and the regime set up a political mass-organization of its own, the "Liberation Organization", with Nagib as President and Nassr as Secretary-General. In June 1953, Egypt became a republic, with a provisional constitution. Nagib was appointed President and Prime Minister and Nasser—Deputy Premier. There were also further arrests and purges—*inter alia* of officers and politicians charged with plotting against the new regime. Moreover, first rifts appeared within the new ruling team. Among the plotters arrested was Colonel Rashad Muhanna who had been close to the Revolutionary Council and a member of the Regency Council, from which he had been dismissed already in October 1952. He was later sentenced to life imprisonment. More significantly, a major rift erupted between Nagib and Nasser over leadership. It was partly a struggle for power, but it also concerned policy. Nagib advocated an early restoration of a constitutional regime and the return of the army to its barracks, while Nasser strove to perpetuate a revolutionary-reformist regime led by army officers. Nagib was also more sympathetic to the Muslim Brotherhood, whom Nasser regarded as a chief adversary to be suppressed. In February 1954, Nagib resigned, in protest, from his positions as President, Prime Minister and Chairman of the Revolutionary Council. Nasser assumed the Premiership, leaving the Presidency vacant. But a semi-coup by groups of officers, (supported by some members of the Revolutionary Council, particularly the Leftist Khalid Muhyi al-Din), restored Nagib to the Presidency and after a few days to the Premiership as well. In March 1954, the Revolutionary Council announced that elections would be held in July for a constituent assembly. The military regime would be lifted before these elections, and after them political parties would be re-permitted and the Revolutionary Council dissolved.

Nagib's victory was short-lived. Nasser and his supporters stirred up opposition within the armed forces, decrying the threat to the revolution and calling for the abrogation of the measures announced. Strikes by transportation workers supported these demands, and in late March 1954 the Revolutionary Council bowed to that pressure and postponed the restoration of a constitutional-political regime to 1956. In April, Nagib was compelled to appoint Nasser Prime Minister, greatly reducing his own authority. In November 1954 he was dismissed and placed under house arrest (he was released only in 1971 by Nasser's successor AL-SADAT). The Presidency remained vacant until 1956. With Nasser now as the main leader, further purges were carried out in the armed forces, regional and municipal councils, the press, and amongst politicians. More "free officers", members of the Revolutionary Council, assumed ministerial positions, a process that had begun in June 1953.

Meanwhile, the contest between the regime and the Muslim Brotherhood intensified. The latter had welcomed the revolution of 1952 and had been treated with sympathy by the Revolutionary Council, some members of which had maintained close links with the Muslim Brotherhood. The decree on the dissolution of parties was not applied to the Brotherhood, as it was not considered a "party." In September 1952 it was even invited to join the government, but refused when the officers rejected two of its three nominees. Differences however, soon became apparent. The Brotherhood demanded that the new regime adopt its principles and base itself on Islam. It also wanted a real share in power (fifty percent of the Revolutionary Council membership), policy-making and full freedom of action and organization. The officers rejected these demands. Tension intensified after the establishment of the "Liberation Organization", as the officers would not allow another popular organization beside their own, while the Brethren—though weakened by internal struggles for the leadership—were not prepared to stop all activities. In January 1954, Brotherhood-inspired student demonstrations led to clashes. The Brotherhood was outlawed and its leaders imprisoned. Nagib released them and relaxed the ban. When Nasser won in April 1954, efforts to eliminate the Brethren's influence resumed and the rift grew. Late in October 1954, an attempt to assassinate Nasser was reported. The Brotherhood was now vigorously suppressed. Its leaders were tried in December and sentenced to death, and though the new "Supreme Guide", Hassan Isma'il al-Hudeibi, was reprieved six of his associates were hanged. The Brotherhood went underground, and in the 1950s and 1960s there were further purges, arrests and executions Nasser continued purges in the army, the civil service, the press and among politicians. He consolidated his position as the uncontested leader, and began dropping members of the Revolutionary Council. In June 1956, a new Constitution was endorsed by a Referendum—a Presidential one, with no Prime Minister. It proclaimed Islam as the state religion, granting women the right to vote. Nasser was elected President, as the only candidate. A new popular mass organization, the "National Union", was entrusted with the nomination of all candidates for election.

Egypt's domestic affairs from the mid-1950s witnessed growing radicalization in both economic and political systems. The constitution of 1956 defined the regime as "democratic-cooperative-socialist", and the main plank of economic policy was the resolve to carry out a far-reaching nationalization of economic assets and build an ever-expanding public sector state economy. This state-centralized policy, explained in terms of necessary rapid industrialization—undertaken since 1957 through five-year programs—was another strategy of building the regime's new social and political basis. The 1956 nationalization applied only to British and French properties, and in some measure to Jewish assets; but that opened the gate. In 1960, banks were nationalized, and so were all newspapers. In July

1961, the land reform of 1952 was further tightened and the ceiling of ownership halved to 100 *feddan*; and a sweeping nationalization was applied to all remaining foreign assets, most industrial and mining enterprises, and all export-import trade. A huge state sector was created which became by far the largest employer and provided in the early 1960s about eighty-five percent of industrial production and thirty-five percent of the GDP. The political regime also took a turn to the left. The break-up of the UAR served as a major impetus for more radical nationalization program, reflected in Nasser's declaration of war against the bourgeoisie which he accused of responsibity for the Syrian secession. In February 1962, a "National Congress" was convened to formulate the country's basic policies and in June endorsed the "National Charter"—the regime's program for re-building Egypt following the break-up of the UAR. That Charter elaborated the concept of "Arab Socialism," now the official doctrine, and initiated the "transitional stage of Socialism." The sole political organization, replacing the "National Union," was henceforth the "Arab Socialist Union" (ASU), to be built on widespread popular democracy, based on about 7,000 "basic units". It was to nominate the candidates for a National or People's Assembly of 350 members, who were elected in March 1964, with workers and farmers constituting over half the representatives, as defined by the National Charter, and eight women. A Provisional Constitution was proclaimed by President Nasser in March 1964, stating that the UAR is part of the Arab nation; its system of government is "democratic Socialist based on the alliance of the working forces of the people." Islam was identified as the state's religion and socialism as the foundation of the economic system. The constitution created a extremely strong presidential form of government, with the president as the supreme executive head of the state. He could initiate and approve laws, appoint and dismiss vice-presidents and ministers. The National Assembly, elected for five year, was to act as a Constituent Assembly charged with drafting a permanent constitution. However, the constitutional process was interrupted by the June 1967 war and remained incomplete until after Nasser's death in September 1970 and entrenchment in power of his successor Anwar al-Sadat in 1971 (for the 1971 Constitution see above).

The implementation of the new measures was entrusted to Nasser's deputy and Commander-in-Chief of the Armed Forces, Abdel Hakim Amer, which he conducted ruthlessly—exploited to arrest and bring to trial the regime's critics and confiscate their property. Amer took advantage of the excessive powers he enjoyed to build a strong personal standing and rehabilitate his tarnished reputation after the disaster of Syria's secession related to him personally in his capacity as the governor of the "Northern Region." Special repressive measures were taken against the remaining wealthy groups in 1964, and the Muslim Brotherhood in 1965. The elaborate constitutional arrangements in fact reinforced the regime's grip over domestic affairs and further consolidated the new, military-bureaucratic ruling elite, after the elimination, since 1952, of the old, pre-revolutionary Turko-Egyptian elite. Though the original "Revolutionary Council" was no longer officially active, the nucleus of the officers' group—shedding some members and gradually admitting new ones—still was the leading group around Nasser, providing, in shifting compositions, the Presidential Council or the Vice-Presidents and the reservoir for top government positions. That group was gradually joined by a growing group of professionals and technocrats, mostly the top managers of the expanding state sector of the economy. Their rule was underpinned—as became publicly evident in the 1970s, when criticism of the Nasserist regime was first permitted—by a dominant police and security apparatus.

The June 1967 defeat triggered another round of purges in the military forces, including trials of senior military officials for conspiring against the regime (see below), restructuring the military command and de-politicizing it, and re-constitution of Nasser's government. Nonetheless, Egypt's social and economic problems intensified, reflected in growing unrest which threatened Nasser's authoritative regime. On 28 September 1970, Gamal Abdel Nasser, the charismatic leader commonly recognized as the inalienable symbol of Arab nationalism—apparently more so throughout the Arab world than in Egypt itself—suddenly died. Although the succession was contested—not in an open, public struggle, but as variously reported—Vice-President Anwar al-Sadat was agreed upon as a compromise candidate, and in October was officially elected President for a six-year term.

In the course of the 1960s Egypt supplemented its High Dam project by further exploitation of its natural resources: petroleum in the Gulf of Suez, western Sinai, and the Western Desert. New projects of land reclamation were planned, with a view to irrigate half a million *feddan* in the New Valley, Fayyum, and Buheira Province for which Egypt counted increasingly on Soviet financial and technical aid. In addition, large reserves of natural gas were discovered in the Delta. By the late 1960s the Aswan Dam enabled the cultivation of 200,000 additional *feddan* (of the projected 1-1.5 million to be irrigated.) However, not only did the Aswan Dam fail to resolve the Egyptian agricultural production-population growth ratio problem, but the huge project turned out to have plagued the Egyptian economy with a high ecological price, due to its prevention of the normal flood of the rich silt, which had ever served as a natural fertilizer for the Egyptian cultivated lands. The great effort to industrialize Egypt also had its weaknesses: surplus labor, low productivity, and short-handed bureaucratic planning, and the centralized state-control led to administrative passivity and discouragement of competition. Above all, the 1967 defeat, with the loss of the Suez Canal and the Sinai oil fields, damaged tourism, reduced industrial production, and brought Egypt to near-bankruptcy due to the serious shortage of foreign currency. Following the war the economy was geared to meet the military needs for the liberation of the occupied Sinai.

Foreign Affairs The new regime displayed, in its first three years, a remarkably moderate attitude. It extracted the Sudan problem from its deadlock by agreeing to Sudanese self-determination and immediate steps towards self-government. This was in an accord between Nagib and Sudanese party leaders (October 1952), endorsed by a formal agreement in January 1953. That agreement (and Egyptian proposals for a three-year transition to self-government) was later endorsed by Britain. In February 1953 they were approved in an Anglo-Egyptian agreement (Sudan became independent on 1 January 1956). With the Sudan dispute solved, the issue of British bases and troops had been tackled. Talks on Egypt's demand for evacuation began in April 1953, and led in October 1954 to a formal agreement. Britain was to hand over the bases and evacuate its troops within twenty months, but was allowed to return troops and use the bases in case of an attack on a member-state of the Arab League or Turkey; British civilian technicians were to maintain the bases. Egypt manifested a certain pragmatism also with regard to the Palestine dispute. The new leaders were not identified with the regime that had entangled Egypt in the war of 1948 and had denounced at least certain aspects of that involvement. Anti-Israel indoctrination, statements and propaganda seemed to diminish considerably—and in Israel there was hope that the new, pragmatic Egypt would accept Israel's existence and make peace. However, several attempts to arrange for Egypt-Israel meetings and talks through a third party as well as low-level secret and direct talks held in Paris, yielded no results.

Egypt's foreign policy began changing in 1955, reflecting a strong shift toward activist NEUTRALISM. Egypt like most newly independent countries of the "Third World" had always inclined to a measure of non-alignment, but this had not been a major tenet of ideology. When Nasser in 1953–1954, in his booklet The Philosophy of the Revolution, formulated the principles of the new regime's policy, he saw Egypt in the center of three overlapping circles: the Arab, the African, and the Muslim ones; a "circle" of neutralist nations was not mentioned. In April 1955, however, Nasser attended the BANDUNG CONFERENCE of Asian and African countries. It was there that he came into contact with leaders of the Afro-Asian world—Nehru, Chou En-lai, Sukarno, Sihanouk, Nkru-mah, Pham Van Dong and other prominent figures. He was accepted as one of them. In the wake of Bandung, when efforts were made to establish a neutralist bloc of nations, Egypt took a leading part and later hosted many conferences of that group. These were official, popular (e.g. the "Afro-Asian Peoples' Solidarity Organization"), and specialized (youth, women, writers). Indeed Nasser along with Nehru and Tito, was regarded as one of the "Big Three" of Neutralism.

Egypt's new neutralist activism caused a growing estrangement between it and the Western powers. While neutralism later became quite respectable, the West, and particularly the US, at that time still vigorously condemned it. Moreover, from 1953 to 1954, the US and its allies resumed efforts to set up a Middle East defense system linked to the West, in which Egypt seemed to be a central member.

However, Egypt remained vigorously opposed to the proposed alliance and to the concept of a defense pact linked to the Western powers. When in late 1954 Iraq and Turkey had reached an agreement on the establishment of an alliance between them, Nasser initiated a meeting of Arab prime ministers in an attempt to prevent the signing of the pact. In February, however, Iraq and Turkey signed a treaty, which came to be known as the Baghdad Pact, sponsored by Britain which, together with Pakistan and Iran, became a member in the Pact. Egypt regarded the Baghdad Pact as a threat to its regional leadership and security and regime; suspected Western-inspired Turkish-Iraqi schemes to bring into the Pact additional Arab states (Syria, Jordan), and began building a counter-alliance of its own, particularly with Syria. Following the Bandung Conference in April, Egypt concluded a large arms deal with Czechoslovakia (with the USSR behind it), the first ever signed between an Arab state and the Soviet Bloc, which represented a break-up of the Western-imposed embargo on arms supplies to the Middle East countries involved in the Arab-Israeli conflict, stipulated by the Tripartite Declaration of the United States, Britain and France of May 1950. The Egypt-Czechoslovakia arms deal lit a red warning light in the West. Talks about large-scale Western aid for Egypt's development, and particularly Egypt's pet project, the ASWAN DAM, ran into difficulties, while the Soviet Union was reportedly offering it aid. In July 1956, the US and Britain withdrew their offer of aid and convinced the World Bank to do likewise. Egypt reacted by nationalizing the Suez Canal in June 1956, a step that created a major international crisis.

As negotiations for settlement of the Suez crisis dragged on and showed little progress, Britain and France late in October 1956 took military action, in collaboration with Israel, bombing and invading Egypt's Canal Zone (see ARAB-ISRAEL CONFLICT). Britain and France, which sought to topple Nasser by their armed action, were motivated by the desire to protect their interests in the Arab world from Nasser's anti-imperialist policies—his vigorous pressures on other Arab states to reduce their links with Britain and his support for the Algerian armed struggle for national liberation from French domination. Israel's joining the two European powers in attacking Egypt reflected a deep sense of siege created by Nasser's intensified pressures on Israel through frequent border raids for sabotage, attacks on civilians, and espionage which she saw as backed and organized by Egypt, and an Egypt—imposed blockade of the Suez Canal, and since 1954–1955 also of the Gulf of Aqaba. As secretly pre-arranged with Britain and France, Israel invaded Egypt's Sinai—giving a pretext for the Anglo-French intervention in the Canal Zone—halting just short of the Suez Canal. However, the Anglo-French invasion failed. Joint US and Soviet pressure compelled the three countries to call it off and withdraw. A UN Emergency Force, UNEF, was set up to supervise the withdrawal and stay on in Sinai. The Sinai Campaign accelerated the Arab-Israeli conflict, approving Israel's image in Arab perception as an aggressive entity and as indivisible part of European imperialism. More specifically, the Sinai Campaign brought an end to the existence of a long-lived Jewish community of about 65,000 of whom only a few dozens remained, mainly in Cairo and Alexandria.

From the crisis of 1956 Egypt emerged victorious and, having defeated an armed assault by imperial great powers, Egypt's prestige was greatly enhanced, particularly in the Arab world. Nasser's stance of "Positive" (i.e. activist) Neutralism hardened and his relations with the Soviet Bloc became closer, while those with the West continued to deteriorate despite the American role in bringing the crisis to its humiliating end for Britain and France. Egypt had severed relations with Britain and France on 1 November 1956 and sequestered the property of their citizens. She had also abrogated, on 1 January 1957, the Anglo-Egyptian Agreement of 1954 concerning the maintenance and reactivation of the British bases in the Suez zone. Relations with Britain were resumed in 1959, and restored to ambassadorial level in 1961 (they were severed again in December 1965 because of the Rhodesia crisis and resumed late in 1967). Relations with France were resumed in 1963, after France had granted independence to ALGERIA and embarked on a pro-Arab policy. Neither Britain nor France was able to recover former positions of political and economic influence in Egypt. Diplomatic relations with West Germany were severed in 1965, along with nine other Arab states, in protest against German recognition of, and aid to, Israel. They were resumed in June 1972. Relations remained cold and hostile also with the USA,

as Egypt suspected American intervention in the Middle East and intrigues to form a pro-Western bloc, resented the EISENHOWER DOCTRINE of 1957, and was irritated by US support for Israel. Soviet aid, on the other hand, both economic, technological, and military grew until Egypt became politically, economically and militarily dependent on the USSR in large measure.

Since the mid-1950s Egypt adopted an activist line in its Arab policies, too, with the aim of deepening its regional Arab leadership by forging inter-Arab alliances guided by its vision of and interests in international affairs. In 1955 it concluded a military pact with Syria and Saudi Arabia, joined by Yemen and Jordan in 1956. With countries not inclined to shape their policies according to Egypt's guidance, pressure was used. Thus, in 1955–1957 Jordan was suppressed to refrain from joining the Baghdad Pact, to dismiss the British command of the Arab Army, and to abrogate the treaty of alliance with Britain. Moreover, in her desire to steer other Arab regimes toward more "progressive" policies, Egypt began intervening in other Arab countries, addressing their peoples directly by the newly established "Voice of the Arabs" (sawt al-Arab) above the head of their governments, inciting the masses by using highly emotional anti-Western slogans and antagonistic language, encouraging "Nasserist" groups and supporting their subversive schemes.

While aiming at imposing conformity of like-minded "progressive" regimes in all Arab states, Nasser did not strive for union of merger with other Arab states. His consent to the Syrian urge for unity of merger and the formation of the UNITED ARAB REPUBLIC (UAR), in February 1958, was a deviation from Egypt's principal policy which had sought hegemony rather than merger and unity even though it had been committed to Arab nationalism, with unity as one of its components. Indeed, Nasser did not initiate that union but was swept along by events in Syria. But he took advantage of the desperate Syrian BA'TH army and party leaders who resorted to that union as a way to maintain their political significance in Syria, by dictating his conditions—including the dissolution of all parties and their replacement with the single, state-run "National Union," with no consideration for Syria's susceptibilities and volatile politics—which in fact meant Egyptian domination over Syria. Once the union was proclaimed, (on 1

February 1958) and endorsed by a plebiscite, Nasser was President and a united Government empowered (with two "regional" subordinate governments administering local affairs in the "Egyptian Region" and in the "Syrian Region" of the UAR); Egypt imposed its rules, policies and its ideologies on Syria.

The establishment of the UAR strongly boosted Nasser's prestige as the unchallengable leader of the Arab world, accelerating the trend of militant nationalism in the Arab world, and placing the conservative regimes under further domestic pressures. Thus, the Iraqi revolution of July 1958, which deposed the Hashemite dynasty in that country, seemed to be another victory for Nasser, nurturing expectations that Iraq would join the UAR. The eruption of euphoria in the Arab states of the Fertile Crescent assumed especially dangerous form in Jordan and Lebanon, which, in view of the Nasserist agitation in the former's case, and armed uprising in the latter, asked Britain and the USA, respectively, to send troops for their protection. The wave of Nasserism, however, was contained mainly by the new revolutionary, Soviet-oriented Iraqi regime, which had no intention to join the UAR, and preferred a rather pluralistic (Iraqi) nationalism to reflect the ethno-religious diversity of the country, which the UAR's propaganda machine denounced as "Shu'ubiyya" (multi-nationalism). Within a few months after the Iraqi revolution relations between Iraq and Egypt fell into a new abyss of hostility, involving mutual propaganda attacks, Egyptian subversion through Nasserist and Ba'thist elements, including attempts on the life of the Iraqi ruler QASSEM, and encouragement of military officers to rebel against the new republican regime, most conspicuous of which was the Shawaf coup attempt in 1959, which caused a breach also between Nasser and the Soviet Union. In his ideological approach to Arab unity, Nasser adopted the slogan of "unity of ranks," denoting a quest for conformity of Arab states' foreign policies, especially in the regional context. However, during the late 1950s and early 1960s Nasserist elements intensified their subversive attempts against political leaders in Jordan and Saudia, which moved toward a new conservative alliance as a counterbalance to the wave of radicalism represented by Nasser. Other Arab states, such as Tunisia, also complained of Egyptian subversion and interference, expelled Egypt-

ian diplomats and military attaches, sometimes even severed relations with Egypt.

Meanwhile, the UAR was confronted by growing difficulties, due to the frustrated expectations of the Ba'thist politicians and military officers who, after leading Syria toward union with Egypt, found themselves gradually stripped of key positions and opportunity to shape the fate of the Syrian region. In fact, Syria became increasingly ruled by Egyptian military officers and bureaucrats headed by Marshal Abdel Hakim Amer, Nasser's deputy, while Syrian officers were transferred to Egypt where they had no political influence. In 1959, the *Ba'thi* ministers in the UAR government resigned en-bloc, and in the summer of that year in Lebanon renewed their party's activity, ostensibly at the all-Arab level, in contrast to their commitment to Nasser. Egyptian social and economic policies imposed on the Syrian region-land reform, nationalization of financial, industrial and trade firms, and prohibition of political activity other than within the ruling "National Union," aggravated by bad years for agriculture and economic crisis, finally accounted for the forces that brought an end to the UAR. Syria's secession from the UAR, in September 1961, after a coup by Syrian officers and politicians, was a heavy blow to Nasser's prestige and indicated a turning point in his Arab policy. Nasser denounced the secession as illegal, refused to recognize Syria's separate independence-though Egypt refrained from rejecting its acceptance as a member in the Arab League. Nasser also insisted on retaining the name "UAR" and its flag as a sign of his commitment to Arab unity and claim for restoration of the union with Syria. A temporary reconciliation took place in March 1963, when the *Ba'th* Party seized power in Syria by military coup; In April, Egypt entered into negotiations with Syria and Iraq (where the *Ba'th* had also seized power, two months earlier), on establishing a tripartite union. In May, the three parties reached an agreement on a federal union, despite their official objection to the principle of federalism, generally considered "rightist" and reactionary. Despite the strong echoes of the new agreement in the Arab world, it soon turned out that the Syrian and Iraqi *Ba'th* regimes had been looking for Nasser's recognition rather than realizing unity with Egypt. Furthermore, unbridgeable differences between the Ba'thists and the Nasserists in Syria, with Egypt backing the latter, culminated in a massacre of Nasserists in Damascus by the *Ba'th* regime, resulting in intensified hostility between Cairo and Damacus, which was to last until 1966, when, at the Soviets' promting, Nasser recognized Syria, resumed diplomatic relations and signed a defense pact.

Syria's traumatic secession from the UAR underlay Nasser's intensified activist interventionist Arab policy, justified by the aim of social revolution as a pre-requisite for Arab unity. Shortly after casting the new slogan of "unity of purpose," which Nasser adopted to legitimize his efforts to get rid of Arab conservative regimes, that policy reached its climax when Egypt intervened in Yemen, in September 1962, by sending an expeditionary force to support the military junta that had deposed the Imam and seized power, but got entangled in civil war with the latter's loyalists. Egypt's military intervention, which was meant to be short and effective, apparently was intended to acquire a foothold in the Arab Peninsula which could be used to encourage the movement of national liberation of South Arabia from British domination, and also serve as a threat against the arch-traditional Saudi regime. The military intervention in Yemen entangled Egypt in a war of attrition with the Yemenite royalists and their Saudi supporters. The war, which soon involved attacks on Saudi targets, tied down considerable Egyptian forces which by the end of the year 1962 encompassed over 50,000 troops. It also deeply involved Egypt in domestic Yemenite politics, arbitrating factional struggles, taking a hand in the nomination and dismissal of Prime Ministers and detaining Yemeni politicians in Egypt. Egypt was bogged down in a the war without ability to control the political or the military affairs.

The near-failure of the Yemeni intervention, coming on the heels of the Syrian debacle, led in the mid-1960s to a toning-down, a mitigation of Egypt's inter-Arab interventionism. That interventionism failed in the long run. Not a single Arab State replaced its "reactionary" regime by a "progressive" or Nasserist one, nor fully accepted Egyptian guidance or predominance. During those years of intense inter-Arab disputes in which Egypt played a leading role, collective Arab action deteriorated to the lowest point since 1948. The Arab League Council, the principal all-Arab forum of deliberation, was weakened and nearly eclipsed. Inter-Arab reconcil-

iation was thus urgently needed in the face of escalating tension on the Arab-Israel front, as a result of Israel's National Water Carrier, which was to become operational in 1964, and growing Syrian, Iraqi, and Palestinian calls to open a guerrilla war against Israel as a means to liberate Palestine. Egypt and Saudi Arabia, since the late 1950s representing the main cleavage between radical and conservative Arab regimes, were deeply divided also by the Yemen Civil War.

At the end of 1963, Nasser's interventionist Arab policy reached a crisis. His relations with most Arab states, including Tunisia and Morocco had been antagonistic (in 1963 Egyptian token force was expedited to Algeria to support its border war with Morocco); he was strongly urged by Syria to lead an Arab war against Israel over the water of River Jordan, which seriously challenged his leadership, while his army-of which some 70,000 still bogged-down in the Yemen war-was unprepared for such military adventure against Israel. In addition, Egypt's involvement in the Yemen war became an increasing source of tension with the United States, threatening the latter's food aid of wheat to Egypt, which constituted a significant proportion of the latter's food needs. In December 1963 Nasser called for an all-ARAB SUMMIT CONFERENCE at the level of heads of state, to discuss the Israeli threat and the Palestine issue. Nasser thus shifted the Arab collective debate from inter-Arab disputes to the rallying issue of Palestine. The first all-Arab summit convened in Cairo in January 1964, resulting in decisions to divert the Jordan tributaries to deny Israel the use of the water, to establish a Joint Arab Command to prepare the Arab states for the anticipated war against Israel, and to examine the tendencies among the Palestinians regarding the establishment of a Palestinian political institution that would represent their cause. Nasser encouraged the creation of such an institution, and apparently persuaded King Hussein of Jordan to acquiesce in the foundation of the PALESTINE LIBERATION ORGANIZATION (PLO), which held its constituent conference in Jerusalem in May 1964, in disregard of the summit's strict recommendation for examination, not foundation of such anorganization. The summit improved Egypt's position in the Arab world, but only temporarily. In October 1964, Egypt agreed with Iraq, under the pro-Egyptian regime of President Abdel Rahman Aref, to establish a near-federal "Unified Political Command"; the plan was not fully implemented and withered, though it was officially abolished only in 1968. Diplomatic relations were also resumed with Jordan. However, the summitry turned to be only a conditional truce, which should have served Nasser's efforts to recover his wounded prestige and ease Egypt's predicament. Nasser and Saudi Arabia's new monarch, Feisal, made serious efforts at reconciliation-mainly to settle the Yemen problem without loss of face for any of them, but to no avail. At the same time, Syria continued its pressure on Nasser by beginning the diversion works, which entangled it in military clashes with Israel, in an attempt to force him to recognize its Ba'th regime. At the same time, Jordan and Lebanon refused to implement their share in the collective diversion plan or for preparing their armies for war.

In 1966 Nasser returned to his policy of "unity of purpose," reviving the ideological war against his Arab conservative rivals. In November 1966, Egypt concluded a military pact with Syria, which entailed a joint military command. The pact signed with the ultra-militant neo-Ba'th Syrian regime (following a coup in February 1966) came against the backdrop of escalating tension along the northern Israeli borders due to increasing Palestinian guerrilla activity, encouraged by Syria, and Soviet urges which meant to dispel the new regime's sense of insecurity. Yet, if the pact was meant to mitigate Syria's fear of being alone in confrontation with Israel, Nasser was to find that it also was to bring on him a disaster. In May 1967, Nasser surprisingly responded to Soviet baseless reports about Israeli military concentrations along the Syrian border by massing most of the Egyptian available forces into Sinai, despite Israeli denials of such military concentrations, which led to the partial mobilization of Israeli reserve forces. Nasser followed up his initial step by removing the UN Emergency Force from the Gaza Strip and the Israel-Egypt border area, and closing the straits of Tiran, thus re-imposing a blockade on the Gulf of Aqaba, which Israel had considered to be casus belli. At the end of May and early June, Jordan and Iraq joined the Egypt-Syria pact, thus completing the Arab siege of Israel. The escalation of the crisis was accompanied by a stream of taunting bellicose speeches, frenzied mass demonstrations, all threatening an imminent attack on Israel (see ARAB-ISRAEL CONFLICT).

When the dimension of military defeat became clear, with Israeli troops on the east bank of the Suez Canal and in possession of the whole Sinai Peninsula, the Egyptian forces in Sinai decimated, and its Arab allies, Syria and Jordan, also defeated, Nasser accepted responsibility and announced his resignation on 9 June. Following mass demonstrations imploring him to stay at the helm, he withdrew his resignation the same day. But Egypt was badly shaken, and Nasser's leadership impaired. He immediately carried out an extensive purge of the officers' corps, reportedly dismissing over 1,000 officers. Amongst those resigning, (or dismissed), were Marshal Abdel-Hakim Amer, Vice President and Commander-in-Chief, considered Nasser's closest aide, as well as the Minister of War and the commanders of the air force and navy; several senior officers, particularly of the air force, were put on trial for dereliction of duty and/or treason and found guilty in 1968. When a later, post-Nasser committee in 1977 investigated the reasons for the defeat of 1967, only a minority went along with that attempt to blame Amer and the military high command, while the majority ascribed the debacle to Nasser's policy and particularly the measures he took in May. Nasser's new government had no Vice President until December 1969, when Anwar Sadat became sole Vice President. In August 1967 a plot against the regime was discovered. The plotters, headed by Marshal Amer, former War Minister Shams al-Din Badran, Intelligence Chief Salah Nasr, were arrested. Amer committed suicide in prison. The others were sentenced in 1968 to long prison terms.

Egyptian policy for the following years was determined by the resolve to recover the territories occupied by Israel. Yet Israeli offers (in the summer of 1967) to withdraw in the context of a peace settlement were rejected. Nasser rejected any direct negotiations with Israel and insisted on unconditional withdrawal of Israel from the occupied Arab territories. Aware of the impossibility of liberating the occupied lands by force, Nasser was willing to accept a settlement supervised by the Powers, with minimal concessions on his part, as was the case with Israel's withdrawal from Sinai and the Gaza Strip in 1957. Nasser's vision of the post-war settlement was reflected in the three "noes" adopted by the Arab summit conference at Khartoum on 1 September 1967: no to recognition of Israel, no to peace and no to negotiation with it until it had withdrawn from all occupied Arab areas. Egypt accepted the UN Security Council Resolution 242, of November 1967, calling for Israel's withdrawal "from occupied areas" in the context of a "just and lasting peace," confirming the right of all states in thregion to live in secure and recognized borders.

However, in Egypt's own interpretation the Israeli withdrawal was to be total, with no need for negotiations, while Israel—which also accepted the resolution—insisted on direct negotiations as a manifestation of recognition, and refused to return to the borders of June 4, 1967. While giving the international peacemaking efforts a chance, Nasser adopted the slogan that "what has been taken by force can be restore only by force," which was meant to complement the international peace-making efforts and recover his legitimacy as an Egyptian and all-Arab leader. Egypt thus turned to rapid rebuilding of its decimated armed forces with Soviet backing, even at the expense of eroding its sovereignty by granting the USSR unprecedented military rights on its soil. At the same time, Egypt escalated border clashes along the cease-fire line of the Suez Canal, amid fruitless efforts to forge an Eastern Command comprised of Syria, Jordan and Iraq. In April 1969, as the international peace efforts based on Resolution 242 had reached a stalemate, Egypt declared a "war of attrition," involving on-going artillery barrages, and commando crossing operations against the Israeli forces on the eastern bank of the closed canal. Israel retaliated by employing its air force, as of July 1969, in growing in-depth bombings which forced Nasser to appeal to Moscow for a strategic ground-to-air defense system, following which two fully equiped Soviet air force brigades and an air defense division became actively involved in the battlefield as of April 1970. The War of Attrition came to an end on August 7, 1970, by a US-mediated cease-fire for three months, with military stand-still, during which a renewed effort was to be made by the international mediator Gunar Jarring.

Just as the cease-fire began, Egypt used the opportunity and in a premeditated operation deployed anti-aircraft missiles along the Suez Canal to gain further depth of air defense, which was to allow a major crossing operation and take-over of a bridgehead on the eastern bank of the canal under its umbrella. A month later, Israel announced its refusal to attend the Jarring talks unless the Egyptian violation of the cease-fire had been rectified, which remained unheeded by Egypt, despite American support of the Israeli demand. On September 28, Nasser passed away and was replaced by his deputy, Anwar al-Sadat.

The 1967 war was a turning point in Nasser's Arab policy. The striking defeat in the war, the strategic losses of the Suez Canal as an essential source of foreign currency and the Sinai Peninsula and its oil fields, and the need to rehabilitate the armed forces, all forced Nasser to control the damage and focus on Egypt's urgent problems. Already during, and in the immediate aftermath of the war, Egypt received financial grants from Kuwait, Algeria and Libya, which by July reached approximately 60 million dollars, a far cry from Nasser's expectations for Arab aid. At the Khartoum summit, Nasser and King Feisal reached an agreement on unconditional withdrawal of the Egyptian forces from Yemen, which was completely implemented before the end of the year. No less significant, at the summit, Nasser agreed to forego his militant ideology of compulsory pan-Arabism and intervention in other Arab states' affairs in the name of social revolution. With Nasser's approval, the oil states agreed to trade off the oil embargo (declared after the end of the war against the United States and Britain), with the allocation of annual financial aid to Egypt (95 million pounds sterling) to compensate for its economic losses in the war (a further 40 million pounds were allocated to Jordan, primarily to support the West Bank Palestinian inhabitants). The Khartoum financial aid was underwritten by the monarchic oil-rich Saudi Arabia, Kuwait, and Libya. This opened a new era in inter-Arab alignment, gradually eliminating the "progressive-reactionary" cleavage to which Nasser had so much contributed. Henceforth, Egypt's strategic priority came to focus on the recovery of the lost territory to Israel for which Egypt badly needed a wide Arab supportive front, both financially and politically. However, the Saudi-led conservative block remained suspicious toward Nasser's real intentions regarding a settlement with Israel or another round of war to liberate Sinai. Hence, in December 1969, at the Arab summit conference held in Rabat, in the midst of the War of Attrition, Nasser's huge requests for Arab financial aid were mostly turned down, reflecting his declining stature in the Arab world and willingness to keep all options open—regarding war or the use of diplomatic means toward Israel.

Nasser's appeasing approach to the oil-rich monarchies was underlined by continued alliance with King Hussein of Jordan regarding Resolution 242 as the main basis for international efforts for the recovery of the territories occupied by Israel in the war. In July 1970, when Nasser accepted the Rogers plan for a three-month cease-fire and standstill of the military situation, King Hussein also endorsed the plan. Similarly, the two leaders had to confront the PLO's objection to the American plan. However, while Nasser contented himself with closing down the "Voice of Palestine" broadcasting from Cairo and expelling a number of Palestinian figures, King Hussein was confronted by a serious menace to his regime, which culminated, in September, in a wide-scale military offensive against Palestinian strongholds in Amman and its environs, triggering Nasser's call for an urgent summit conference in Cairo to discuss ways to put an end to the bloody clashes in Jordan.

At the conference, Nasser finally managed, after King Hussein had had significant success against the Palestinians, to bring the rivals to the armed clash to an agreement on the Palestinian Resistance's position in Jordan. By the end of the last day of the summit, Nasser died.

Following the 1967 war, Nasser gradually distanced himself from the neo-Ba`th regime in Damascus, which remained adamantly opposed to any political concession to the Arab "reaction" and employment of non-military measures in the conflict with Israel. Although Nasser managed to forge an Eastern Command, encompassing Syria, Jordan and Iraq, he failed in activating this command to complement the Egyptian war of attrition along the Suez Canal, mainly due to Syria's antagonistic policy toward Iraq and Jordan.

In June 1967 Egypt severed diplomatic relations with the United States, on the outbreak of the war, accusing Washington of having covertly aided Israel in actual military operations; the US indignantly denied that claim, and Egypt never substantiated and gradually abandoned it, though her resentment of US general support for Israel persisted (relations were resumed in November 1973, shortly after the end of the October 1973 war). Relations with the USSR, on the other hand, became ever closer; Pres-

ident Podgorny and the Soviet Chief-of-Staff, in a symbolic gesture, visited Egypt in June 1967 and undertook to rebuild Egypt's military power, especially the air force and air defense. As of April 1970, Russian SAM missiles, (operated largely by Russian personnel), played a major role. Russian pilots flew Soviet planes, reportedly even on some operational missions. The number of Russian technicians and instructors, most of them military, reached a reported 15,000-20,000. Mutual visits were frequent (including Podgorny attending, in January 1971, the festive opening of the Soviet-financed second stage of the Aswan High Dam), and an increasing number of Egyptian students and officers were trained in Russia and Soviet Bloc countries. Yet, after Nasser's death relations became increasingly uneasy, due to Soviet procrastination over Egyptian demands for large quantities of advanced arms that would enable Egypt to wage a successful war against Israel, apparently because of Egypt's financial shortcomings and the implications on the detente with the the US. The extent and conditions of Soviet aid, and the measure of Soviet influence on Egypt's policy, and the presence of so many Russians, and their behavior, caused frictions at the level of the high and medium Egyptian command. As to relations with Western Europe, there was, after France granted independence to Algeria and virtually ended her alliance with Israel, a remarkable rapprochement between Egypt and France. Relations with West Germany that had been shattered in 1965 against the backdrop of the latter's establishment of diplomatic relations with Israel, were further aggravated by Egypt's recognition of East Germany in July 1969.

4. Egypt Under Sadat (1970-1981) and Mubarak

Domestic affairs Sadat's ascendance to power involved a struggle within the ruling group of veterans of the Free Officers, representing two main rival factions: a right wing tending to a liberalization of the economy and the regime, headed by Zakariyya Muhyi al-Din and Abd-al-Latif Baghdadi and supported by Muhammad Hassanein Haikal, the regime's foremost publicist, editor of *al-Ahram* and since spring 1970, Minister of Information. The left wing faction was headed by Ali SABRI and supported by Nasser's closest aides, the heads of his apparatus, such as Sha'rawi Jum'a and Sami Sharaf. To avoid a bitter struggle, the inner group of leaders chose (as a compromise candidate), Vice-President Anwar AL-SADAT. He was fairly right wing, but nonetheless was considered a man of the center and the core of Nasser's team and capable of mediating between the factions. In October 1970 Sadat was elected President for a six-year term, as well as leader of the ASU. He appointed Ali Sabri and Hussein al-Shafi'i as his Vice-Presidents, and the diplomat-technician Mahmud Fawzi as Prime Minister.

The real contest for Nasser's succession broke out in early1971 when it became clear that Sadat was unwilling to play a titular head of state, and strove to fully exercise the presidential powers legally in his hands. In May 1971 he dismissed Vice-President Ali Sabri. Consequently six ministers and several ASU top functionaries resigned in an attempt to force Sadat to retract his decision, which he perceived as a take-over plot by the leftist faction. Those resigning included the leading leftist Nasserists Jum'a and Sharaf, and Minister of War, Gen. Muhammad Fawzi (who was apparently supported only by a minority of the officers' corps). The leading Nasserist plotters—Sabri, Fawzi, Jum'a, Sharaf and about 100 others—were arrested, and their suspected followers were purged from the Army, the Government services and the ASU. The executive and the central committee of the ASU, seen as center of the plot, were dissolved. May 1971 became a significant date under Sadat's regime, entitled by the regime as "the Correction Revolution." In July, a new ASU congress was elected, nominating a new central committee. The National Assembly expelled 18 members involved in the plot. Sadat, not content with this purge, dissolved the Assembly in September. A month later, a new National Assembly ("People's Council", *Majlis al-Sha'b*) was elected. Sadat also had a new Constitution drafted. It was endorsed, with various ASU amendments and adopted in September 1971 by a referendum. The new Constitution was little different from the provisional one of 1964. It retained a near-presidential system (limiting the President to two six-year terms and permitting him to appoint a Prime Minister—which had become standard since 1961), a 350-member "People's Council," and the ASU as the single party. In addition it reconfirmed Islam as the state religion and enhanced Egypt's Islamic character by laying down that Islamic law (the SHARI'A) should be a main source of legislation. It renamed the republic as "The Arab Republic of Egypt," and restored its original flag (abolishing the name and flag of the UAR). In August, the plotters were sent to trial. Sentences were announced in December 1971: four to death. (commuted to life imprisonment)—including Sabri, Gum'a, and Sharaf; General Fawzi was sentenced to life imprisonment which was commuted to fifteen years; over fifty others were sentenced to prison terms (those still in jail were released starting from 1977, the last ones, including Sabri and Sharaf), in May 1981. No further major upheavals occurred in Sadat's team until 1973—except for the dismissal, in October 1972, of War Minister Muhammad Ahmad Sadeq (who had replaced Fawzi in May 1971 and was a strong contender for the "Number Two" position in the regime). Sadeq was dismissed because of his failure to prepare the armed forces for war as ordered by the president (who proclaimed the Year 1971 to be the "Year of Decision," regarding war or peace in the conflict with Israel).

His power and position assured, Sadat, haunted by the growing social unrest (students riots erupted at the end of 1971), turned first to reshaping Egypt's regime and economic policy. Sadat fostered alignment with the urban bourgeoisie and the new middle class, as well as with the Muslim Brotherhood, to whom pan-Arabism was anathema. He moved cautiously and at first without admitting that he was abandoning the principles of Arab socialism and Nasserism. His measures were officially called a "correction" (of the 1952 Revolution)-a restoration of its true principles. They fully unfolded after 1973, but initial steps were taken from 1971. First measures were intended to alleviate the harsh police-state features of the Nasserist regime. Detainees were released in large numbers; the practice of detention without trial was nearly abolished; and the powers of the secret police and the security apparatus were restricted. More freedom of expression and the press was granted, and gradually the voicing of criticism (e.g., of the excesses of Nasser's security apparatus) was permitted. A certain liberalization applied to the economic regime too. Private capital (both Egyptian and foreign) was encouraged to invest, promising wider freedom of initiative, less state interference, and security against nationalization. Limitations on income, on the use of properties and profits, and of foreign currency earned, were lifted to a certain extent. The stress on and preference for the public, state-owned sector of the economy, and centralized planning was mitigated. A process of de-nationalization, e.g. the restoration of sequestrated properties to their former owners, began.

The policy of "opening" (*Infitah*) Egypt's economic regime was fully adopted in the wake of the 1973 October war, which allowed Sadat to step up the pace of liberalization. The country was opened up to private and foreign enterprise, and undertaking of "de-Nasserization." This led to a certain economic activity upswing , but was unable to solve Egypt's basic economic problems: the limited cultivable land (which, it was assumed, had reached its upper limit, with 6–7 million acres cultivated and, multiple cropping, up to 11 million acres—projects for large-scale reclamation of the Western desert making little progress), as against the constant large increase of the population, with the resulting continuous decline in food production per capita; the slowness of industrial growth was insufficient to absorb the surplus of the rural population and was no longer sustained by agriculture; the growth of an ever-expanding semi-urban population in and around Cairo, with no productive employment, no proper housing, and socially uprooted; an inflated, unproductive bureaucracy. Sadat's policies created a new class of entrepreneurs, displaying their wealth, and an increasing measure of corruption, while the standard of life did not markedly improve for the bulk of the masses despite high expectations, and the gap between rich and poor widened. The resulting social unrest frequently focussed on the problem of government subsidies for the price of basic food and fuel. These subsidies that had to be cut or altogether abolished according to the new policies as well as all foreign and international advisers, even though they were vitally needed by the poorer masses. Attempts to reduce these subsidies and raise the price of basic commodities led to serious disturbances in January 1975 and January 1977, forcing the government to retreat. The disturbances were blamed on Communists and other leftist groups, and steps were taken to suppress them.

The political liberalization that went with the general "opening" of the regime did not apply to the Communists (who in 1975 re-established an Egyptian Communist Party, half underground) and the radical Left. The measures taken against them were endorsed by a referendum in February 1977. Another referendum, in May 1978, specifically restricted all political and media activity of Communists; the old-regime; pre-1952 politicians; and of those linked with the repressive security apparatus of Nasser's time; those who had abused democracy and corrupted political life, as well as atheists and "enemies of religion" - as specified in a law passed by the National Assembly after the referendum.

The liberalization applied to Islamic groups. Sadat tended to favor a growing emphasis on Egypt's Islamic character, which was to appeal to the Saudis and counterbalance the Nasserists in Egypt itself. Sadat thus released their leaders from prisons and permitted them to renew their social and religious activity, including publication of papers and magazines. During the 1970s the Muslim Brotherhood's activity expanded rapidly, with the mushrooming of various radical Islamic groups that gained increasing influence, particularly among the urban lower classes. The Muslim Brotherhood was not formally re-legalized, but it began rebuilding its organization semi-legally. The Brotherhood, however, had become a rather conservative group; a process of radicalization soon generated extremist offshoots which adopted violent strategies against the regime and society in their quest for the re-creation of an authentic Islamic society. These groups preferred to go underground, aiming to impose Islamic rule by force. They repeatedly clashed with the security forces, and with adversaries, and also agitated against Egyptian Copts and tourists, as a source of corruption and immorality. The process was especially salient in Upper Egypt, where growing tension and occasional violent attacks of Islamic extremists against COPTS occurred, including desecration and arson of churches. One group—the "Islamic Liberation Party" (*hizb al-tahrir al-islami*)— in April 1974 attacked a military installation to take over the government. It was suppressed, its leaders tried in 1975, and its main leader, Saleh Suraya, was executed in November 1976. Another group—*al-takfir wal-hijra*—(Discommunication and Migration) which in July 1977 staged bomb attacks and kidnapped and murdered a former minister was also suppressed; trials were swiftly held, and five of its leaders headed by Shukri Mustafa, were executed in March 1978. Islamic extremists also infiltrated the armed forces. Members of the *al-Jihad* Organization, led by Muhammad Abdel Salam Faraj assassinated President Sadat in October 1981. In subsequent riots they gained control of the town of Asyut until dislodged in heavy fighting, and five of their leaders were executed, including Faraj and Khaled al-Islambuli, who had committed the assassination of Sadat (see ISLAMIC FUNDAMENTALISM). The growing return to Islam in Egyptian society came to be reflected in a constitutional amendment endorsed by a referendum in April 1979, establishing Islam and the Shari'a as the (no longer a) main source of legislation. Fundamentalists agitated for the imposition of Islamic law on Egypt's social and legal fabric, and no-one dared openly oppose that proposal in the National Assembly, though many in fact opposed it; it was accepted "in principle" with its implementation deferred for committees and experts to work out the details.

This trend of Islamic radicalization was partly a by-product of Sadat's liberalization, which in its mainstream allowed a diversification of political organization and aggravated the gaps between rich and poor in the Egyptian society. In Sadat's first years, the ASU, although purged of its Nasseist leadership, was still the only political organization permitted. Within it, different trends that had always existed were able in 1975 to organize themselves as "platforms" (minbar, pl. manabir) within the ASU. In March 1976, three such platforms were formally constituted: a right-wing, "Socialist-Liberal" one; a left-wing "National Progessive Unionist Rally" (PUR), led by Khaled Muhyi-al-Din, one of the Free Officers' Revolutionary Council of 1952; and a mainstream, centrist platform led by the Prime Minister and considered the government's faction. These platforms presented themselves to the National Assembly elections of October 1976; the right-wing one got 12 to13 seats, the left-wing 2, the center 270 to 280, and Independents-within-the-ASU about 50. In November 1976, Sadat decreed that the platforms might now organize as fully-fledged parties, and in June 1977 a party law was passed. The new multi-party system was endorsed as an amendment of the Constitution, in a referendum in May 1980. In 1977–1978 the parties constituted themselves. The mainstream center of the ASU at first called itself "Egypt Socialist Party" but in August 1978 Sadat founded a new party, the "National Democratic Party" (al-hizb al-watani al-dimuqrati), with which the former immediately merged (the ASU was formally dissolved in May 1980). To the two other plat-

forms now turned into parties was added a "Socialist Labor Party" (hizb al-amal al-ijtima'i), led by Ibrahim Shukri, whose ideology and policy at its first stage hardly differed from the ruling NDP. The Wafd also reconstituted itself in February 1978, sometimes called the New Wafd; but as the authorities refused their assent to the party's elected leader, Fu'ad Siraj-al-Din, and some of his associates, disqualified as pre-1952 politicians, the Wafd re-dissolved itself in June 1978. It re-emerged in February 1984, when the Government accepted Siraj al-Din (after the courts had so ruled).

In the executive, no major upheavals occurred between 1973 and 1981. During the war of October 1973, Sadat dismissed the Chief-of-Staff, Sa'ad al-Din Shadhili (Shazli). This was kept secret until December-on grounds of the latter's disagreement with Sadat's insistence on holding on to the Egyptian bridgehead on the eastern bank of the Suez Canal. He was replaced by Abdel-Ghani Gamasi, the architect of the Canal crossing operation, who later became Minister of Defense and Deputy Premier, 1975–1978. In 1972 Sadat appointed Prime Minister Mahmud Fawzi as second Vice-President (retired in 1974). Vice-President Shafi'i was dismissed in 1975 and Husni MUBARAK, the the Air Force Commander, became the sole Vice-President. In 1973–1974, Sadat served as his own prime minister, and from 1974 various loyal second-rank associates followed each other in that post. Sadat himself was re-elected as President in September 1976.

Sadat's image as a weak and colorless figure changed gradually throughout the early 1970s once he entrenched himself in power, dismissed the Russian technicians in 1972 (see below), and emerged, in the wake of the October 1973 war as an outstanding statesman and decision-maker; a man of charisma and vision, and yet pragmatic, who cultivated a paternalistic leadership that combined tradition and strong appeal to Western culture and power. However, his popularity was on the decline in his later years. High-pitched, rising popular expectations were frustrated and social and economic problems aggravated. His bold approach to peacemaking with Israel was fiercely attacked by both domestic and regional adversaries, turning into another source of delegitimation of his regime. He was denounced by the extreme Islamists, the Left, the Nasserists, and many intellectuals. While in 1971 he released his rivals (making sure they would not return to positions of power or political influence), and most of those convicted after the 1967 war. In 1980–1981 he began taking harsher measures against his new adversaries. In September 1981 he implemented large-scale purges and arrests of Islamic extremists—and for the sake of "even-handedness"—of Coptic leaders too (including the dismissal and banishment of the patriarch), of Nasserists and Leftists, banning several journals. He had these measures endorsed by another referendum but they remained unpopular. Sadat was assassinated on 6 October 1981—on the reviewing stand of a parade celebrating the anniversary of the October 1973 war—by Islamist extremists led by an army officer. There were few signs of genuine mourning. Vice-President Husni Mubarak took over and after a few days was duly elected President. Mubarak continued Sadat's policies, but endeavored to redress some of their outgrowths seen as harmful. Unlike Sadat or Nasser, Mubarak was first and foremost an executive-technocrat, whose appeal to the public was always marked by pragmatism and absence of long-term vision. He released many of those detained in Sadat's last purge. He tried to restrain excesses of the private sector, to curb corruption, and to re-impose stricter state controls. During his first years in power, he had to concentrate on stabilizing his regime, with an emphasis on internal security and the economy. The trials of the members of the *Jihad* Organization, which was directly responsible for Sadat's assassination, ended in 1984. In February 1986, there was an insurgence among the Central Security Forces in the center of Cairo. The attempted revolt was swiftly suppressed. Islamic militant groups continued to mushroom. The most active was the Islamic Group (al-jama'a al-islamiyya), headed by Sheikh Omar Abdel Rahman. Since Sadat's assassination, this group committed a numerous attacks against the security forces, Copts—especially in Upper Egypt where they constitute a large minority—and against tourists and entertainment centers in Cairo and Alexandria; it also attempted to assassinate prominent politicians (Prime Minister Atif Sidqi in 1994; as well as six ministers or ex-ministers of the interior). In 1990 this group assassinated Dr. Rif'at al-Mahjoub, the Parliament Speaker; and in 1992, the prominent intellectual Dr. Faraj Fuda. In June 1995, the Islamic Group attempted to assassinate President Mubarak

on his arrival in Addis Abeba to take part in the African Summit there. In November 1997 this group perpetrated yet the most detestable attack yet, against foreign tourists in Luxor, killing over sixty of them. In the span of fifteen years, *al-Jama'a al-Islamiyya* was responsible for thousands of casualties among citizens and members of the security forces. The Egyptian authorities are engaged in a constant struggle against this group, especially in its strongholds in Asyut, Minya, Malawi, and other cities in Upper Egypt, as well as in Cairo itself. In the course of 1997 the Egyptian press reported that the heads of *al-Jihad al-Islami* and *al-Jama'a al-Islamiyya* had publicly suggested to the government to halt in the clashes between these groups and the authorities (following the attack in Luxor, there was an announcement of unilateral cease-fire by these groups). The latter were reluctant to give their consent, for fear of losing momentum in the struggle against terrorism.

The Muslim Brothers organization remained the main Islamic opposition element to the Government. This group has no divergences with extremist Islamic groups regarding the need to implement the Shari'a (Islamic Law), but they oppose the use of violence to this end. Yet, the regime realizes the threat they present. Their leaders and activists are often subject to searches and arrests. In 1995, eighty-one amongst them were put on trial, and these trials are considered the largest since those held under Nasser's regime (see ISLAMIC FUNDAMENTALISM).

Multi-party elections to the National Assembly (People's Council) were held in 1979 and 1984. They confirmed the NDP in its overwhelming majority. In 1979, the Socialist Labor Party won twenty-nine seats, and the Socialist Liberals three; the leftist NPUR did not win any seats. In 1984, none of these three groups won any seats and the *Wafd*, now back on the scene, was the only opposition represented; it won fifty-eight seats—including eight from the Muslim Brotherhood which, while not officially recognized, had made an unofficial election alliance with the *Wafd*. New elections in April 1987 confirmed the NDP majority. The Socialist-Liberals, Socialist Labor and Muslim Brotherhood formed a coalition and won sixty seats, the Wafd won thirty-six. In September 1980 an Upper House was recreated; the first of its kind since 1952. It comprised a Consultative Council (*majlis al-shura*) of 210 members, two-thirds elected, one-third appointed by the

President. In the November 1990 elections to the People's Assembly, which had been boycotted by most opposition parties, the NDP won a majority of 86.3% NPUR (383 seats), 1.3%, independents (6 seats), 12.4% (55 seats).

In the early 1980s, Egypt's economic situation constantly deteriorated. Inflation escalated, and economic growth stagnated. Since 1982, three five-year-plans have been implemented, aiming to halt this economic deterioration. The first and second plans focused on strengthening the infrastucture and included building bridges, expanding railways, and establishing a network of underground mass mobile train lines in Cairo, financed by France. It seems that only the third five-year plan (1992–1997) might bring an economic momentum. Egyptian exports began to grow, accompanied by economic growth, and a flow of foreign investments; inflation started to recede. Although half of Egypt's GDP derives from the public sector and most industrial plants are owned by the government, the economy grew rapidly in the post-October 1973 war period until the mid-1980s when the plunge of world oil prices and growing burden of debt sevicing led Egypt to enter into negotiations with the International Monetary Fund for balance-of-payment support and in 1988 signed with it an agreement on economic reforms. In 1993, an agreement was signed with the World Bank on related matters. In 1991–1993 the government achieved progress on liberalizing exchange and interest rates, but refused to implement a major IMF demand, namely, to streamline the public sector. During the early 1990s unemployment grew rapidly, and since 1992 tourism declined due to the attacks of Islamic extremists on tourist groups. In 1995, Mubarak reshuffled his government. Kamal al-Janzuri was appointed Prime Minister, replacing Atif Sidqi. The economic forecast for 1997–1998 shows chances for significant improvements, as the inflation rate is expected not to exceed 6%, while economic growth is estimated to reach 5.5%. External debts are expected to reach less than 50% of the GDP. In July 1997, Yusuf Butrus-Ghali (45) was appointed State Minister for Economic Affairs, and was asked to implement the important process of privatization.

Foreign Affairs Sadat's main preoccupation in the sphere of foreign affairs was with the continuing Israeli occupation of Sinai (and other Arab territo-

ries), and the inefficacy of the international mediation efforts. From early 1971, Sadat attempted to achieve a breakthrough in the efforts to attain a settlement that would enable Egypt to regain Sinai without war. On February 4, 1971, he suggested prolonging the cease-fire with Israel by another month, during which Israel would implement a partial withdrawal of its forces from the Suez Canal (to the al-Arish-Ras Muhammad line), and worked toward reopening of the Suez canal for navigation began. These steps were to be the first steeped in a comprehensive implementation of all the provisions of Resolution 242 according to an agreed-upon timetable. Sadat confided to the UN envoy Jarring, in a detailed memorandum, that Egypt was prepared to enter peace negotiations with Israel and commit herself to some of its requests submitted by Jarring (termination of belligerency; respect for Israel's sovereignty and territorial integrity; freedom of navigation in the Suez Canal and the Straits of Tiran; etc.)— provided Israel committed herself to a total withdrawal to the 4 June 1967 lines and to a "just settlement" of the refugee problem. Yet, although Israel's Prime Minister Golda MEIR responded positively to Sadat's proposals, it would commit itself to a withdrawal only to negotiated "secure, recognized and agreed boundaries," and not to the pre-June 1967 lines, which brought the Egyptian initiative to an end. In March, Sadat announced his refusal to prolong the cease-fire and declared the year 1971 as "the Year of Decision." However, encouraged by Saudi King Feisal, Sadat continued to seek avenues for bringing the American adminstration to play a more active role in a settlement to the Middle East conflict, believing in its ability to force Israel to implement Resolution 242. In April 1972, Sadat began communicating with the White House through secret intelligence and Saudi channels, but Washington's Middle East policy remained unchanged even after Sadat expelled, in July 1972, the Soviet combat personnel and military advisers. Further contacts with the White House, including two secret meetings between Sadat's and President Nixon's advisers for national security, Hafez Isma'il and Henry Kissinger, respectively, in February and May 1973, made it clear to Sadat that Washington perceived the gap between the contending parties too wide for the US to bridge by mediation. On April 5, 1973, Sadat established a war cabinet under his presidency, in which a specific decision on war was made, which became operational as the last contact with Washington in May proved that a diplomatic settlement was not a viable option. The recovery of Sinai—a vital national interest and a matter of national honor, a precondition for Egypt's very future and a matter of survival for any political leader—received under Sadat the highest priority. War was undesirable, but turned out to be an inevitable last resort. Still, Sadat had no illusions that his armed forces could liberate Sinai in its entireties. What he meant was a major military operation that would start a diplomatic process in which Washington be fully involved (for Egypt's road to the October war, see ARAB-ISRAEL CONFLICT). Sadat's policy of *Infitah* inevitably entailed a rapprochement—economic at first, but gradually political, too—with the West, and particularly with the US, to whom Egypt began looking again for investments, equipment, technology and financial aid even while official relations with the US had still been severed. Full relations with the US were restored in November 1973, drawing increasingly closer amidst the American peace diplomacy supervised by Secretary of State Henry Kissinger (see ARAB-ISRAEL PEACEMAKING). From 1974, American financial aid played an important role in encouraging Egypt to proceed in the search of peaceful settlement with Israel. US economic aid was resumed in 1974 and soon reached large proportions, until Egypt became, in the 1980s, the largest recipient of US aid after Israel; from 1976–1977 the US granted Egypt also considerable military aid. In 1974, the American Congress approved an annual aid package of 250 million dollars to Egypt, and later, a limited US arms supplies (6 C-130 transport planes) and a financial grant of 650 million dollars following the signing of the interim agreement between Israel and Egypt in September 1975, mediated by Kissinger. With the signing of the peace treaty with Israel, the American administration promised to give Egypt 1.5 billion dollars in aid over the next three years (which has remained in force). In June 1974, President Nixon visited Cairo, for the first time in the two states' history, and in October 1975, Sadat was the first Egyptian president to visit Washington. Egyptian relations with the US culminated in President Carter's partnership in the Camp David Accords of 1978 that led to the Israel-Egypt Peace Treaty of 1979 (involving Carter's visits to Cairo and Jerusalem

to settle the remaining disagreements and rescue the Camp David accords. Already in February of that year, Sadat and Carter reached a strategic understanding, which substantiated an American willingness to sell Egypt advanced F-15 aircraft. US economic enterprise and investment in Egypt, solicited, did not come up to Egypt's estpectations—largely because of the difficulties posed by Egypt's bureaucracy and its tangled regulations—but assumed a certain role in Egypt's economy. Egypt also became a partner in wider US policy and strategy plans, concerning both the Arab-Israel peace process and US plans for the defense of the Middle East following the Soviet invasion of Afganistan in December 1979. Egypt was one of the states proposed (together with Oman, Somalia and Kenya, to support the US plans for "Rapid Deployment Force" for emergencies, by providing it with "facilities," a euphemistic term for "bases." In August 1980 it was agreed that such facilities be constructed, at US expense, at Ras Banas on the Red Sea. The scheme did not fully materialize, but in the coming years US and Egyptian units conducted joint drills, and it was reported that the US enjoyed certain facilities such as the stationing of surveillance installations.

Egypt's relations with the US remained unchanged under President Mubarak. US economic and military continued, and Egypt's support of a renewed peace process helped maintain the level of coordination and understanding between the two states. Following the Iraqi invasion of Kuwait in early August 1989, Mubarak played a major role in convening an Arab summit conference in Cairo and reaching resolutions that approved the call already made by the Saudis for a US-led international intervention to settle the crisis. Egypt's role in supporting the international war coalition allowed for writing off 14 billion dollars of its national debt, 7 billion dollars by the Gulf oil monarchies and the rest by the US government. In the aftermath of the war, Egypt was instrumental in supporting Washington's efforts to convene the Madrid Peace Conference, by lobbying the PLO and Syria in this regard, and later by taking part itself in the conference and its aftermath multilateral talks (see ARAB-ISRAEL PEACEMAKING)

The USSR remained Egypt's chief ally until the aftermath of the 1973 war, but relations were complex and sometimes troubled. The Russians would probably have preferred Ali Sabri as Egypt's leader, and there seemed to be little sympathy between them and Sadat, who did not accept their guidance, suspecting them of not sincerely supporting his policies. Nevertheless, relations seemed close. President Podgorny came to Egypt twice in 1971, and in May he signed in Cairo a Soviet-Egyptian Treaty of Friendship and Cooperation, the first such alliance signed by the USSR with an Arab state. However, this treaty was in fact an effort to shore up crumbling relationships rather than a sign of firm mutual confidence. Sadat and his top military commanders grew frustrated over the Soviet procrastination and insufficiency toward their required arms supplies. After two visits Sadat paid to Moscow in October 1971 and February 1972, in which he failed to acquire the arms that would enable him to go to war against Israel, he unilaterally terminated the services of some 10,000–15,000 Soviet advisers and combat units in July 1972. Yet, later in 1972 and in the spring of 1973 relations were rectified. In March 1973, a new arms deal, unprecedented in its financial scope and quality of weapons was signed between the Soviets and Egypt, the cost of which was to be covered by the Arab oil states. Although the main part of the deal was not implemented until the October war, it enabled the return of some 1500-2000 Soviet military experts to Egypt and an early supply of ground-to-ground SCUD missiles which enhanced the Egyptian confidence in its military capability. During and after the October War of 1973 the USSR gave Sadat full strategic backing, represented in the air lift it conducted as of the second week of the war. The aftermath of the war witnessed a growing reduction of Egyptian dependence on Soviet technical and arms supplies, cultivating links with European arms producers. As to the strategic sphere, the tightening relations between Sadat and the American administration left little doubt that the Soviet Union was losing its primacy in Egypt to the US. In March 1976 Sadat abrogated the Treaty of Friendship with the Soviets. Later in 1977, Egypt recalled its Ambassador and left its Moscow embassy in the charge of a lower-level diplomat; in 1979 and 1981 it expelled members of the Soviet embassy, charging them with espionage, and in September 1981 requested the withdrawal of the Ambassador himself and closed the Soviet Military Attache's office, simultaneously terminating the contracts of most of the remaining Soviet technicians (some 500-700 re-

portedly departed). Full diplomatic relations were restored in September 1984, but remained cool.

Sadat's Arab policy in fact continued his predecessor's regional policy after 1967, abandoning all attempts to impose Egyptian guidance and domination on other Arab states. Egypt now tended to forge a pragmatic inter-Arab alignment, based on common interests rather than on ideological conformity. Sadat thus continued a scheme for an Egyptian Federation with Libya and Sudan and/or Syria that had been initiated by Libya's QADHAFI late in 1969 and accepted in principle by Nasser. In November 1970, Egypt, Libya and Sudan announced their decision to establish a Federation. Syria later joined, and in April 1971, with Sudan dropping out, Egypt, Libya and Syria established the "Federation of Arab Republics." But the main initiative was Qadhafi's and Sadat seemed to go along half-heartedly—except for a joint Egyptian-Syrian military command that was re-established in October 1971, as Sadat considered it desirable for the imminent confrontation with Israel. The Federation did not get off the ground, though its institutions were formally established by 1972. Despite this, Qadhafi was no longer content with a loose federal association but kept pressing for full merger with Egypt, Sadat, though clearly unwilling, went along with that although he apparently did not take Qadhafi's erratic moves seriously. In August 1972, the two heads-of-state announced the merger of Egypt and Libya, to be endorsed by a referendum and implemented on 1 September 1973. When preparations for that implementation made no progress, Qadhafi resorted to a strategy of appealing to the Egyptian public above the head of Sadat. In June 1973 he appealed, in a barnstorming tour of Egypt, directly to the Egyptian public—with an obscurantist fanaticism that irritated his listeners. In July he had Libya's "People's Committees" mount a mass march into Egypt (30,000–40,000 marchers with 2,000 trucks and cars were forcibly halted and returned to Libya). The merger was shelved by Sadat though Libya provided Egypt a substantive contribution to the war effort in the form of weapons, oil deliveries, and financial aid. Yet, Sadat did not inform Qadhafi about his exact war plan and D-day. The Libya-Egypt relations became particularly bitter following the war and Sadat's decision to enter a diplomatic process under the US supervision. As opposed to his contempt for Qadhafi, Sadat cultivated closer relations with Saudi Arabia, which in the early 1970s emerged as a leading power of the Arab oil-producing states which seemed to gain a dramatic influence in the world's energy market and politics, due to the growing energy crisis in the West. In August 1973 King Feisal informed Sadat that he would be willing to use the oil weapon in the campaign against Israel.

From a military point of view, the October War ended with near disaster for the Egyptian armed forces, when the Third Army was encircled and faced annihilation by the Israeli forces, which were only 101 km from Cairo. But in a wider perspective, and certainly in Egyptian and Arab perception, it was a great achievement: Egyptian (and Syrian) forces had surprised Israel with a bold decision to confront it despite its commonly agreed military eminence, won battles against its army, displayed impressive capabilities of military planning and leadership, and thus wiped off the stain of previous defeats and restored the pride and honor of Egypt's armed forces. Even more important, the deadlock was broken: the unprecedented employment of the oil embargo against the United States and Holland, and the decision to drastically raise prices and adopt a policy of gradual reduction of oil production until Israel had withdrawn from all the occupied territories, was a powerful weapon and forced the US into direct and active involvement in attempts to meet the Arab demands. Israel's occupation dented, Egypt managed to hold on to the east bank of the Suez Canal and use it as a valuable bargaining chip-and Israel had accepted, in the Disengagement of Forces Agreement of January 1974, the presence of Egyptian troops in Sinai, with a UN force manning a buffer zone between the two sides. The Suez Canal was reopened in June 1975 (with Israel-bound cargoes allowed to pass through it on non-Israeli ships).

In the four years following the 1973 October War Sadat kept the inter-Arab arena off balance, due to his repeated efforts to free himself from the Arab restrictions he was committed to namely, to refrain from separate settlements with Israel and remain the leading power in a unified Arab front, even if this meant loss of opportunities for Egypt to recover parts of its occupied land. Apart from fear of delegitimation by his Arab adversaries, Sadat needed the Arab collective to support Egypt's own territorial claims. No less important were Egypt's expec-

tations for a generous financial aid, especially from the oil producing monarchies, whose revenues following the October war tripled and quadrupled themselves within a few months (see OIL). However, the Gulf oil monarchies were unwilling to commit themselves to a comprehensive "Marshall Plan" that would meet Egypt's social and economic needs. In fact, even the financial aid decided in Khartoum in September 1967 was not automatically renewed every year without bitter bickerings that soured Egypt (and Jordan's) relations with the donors. The oil-rich states, though manifesting concern about the stability of Sadat's regime, preferred to direct their financial aid to arms procurements, limited investments in joint projects, such as military production and social development, that would ensure their control over these resources. At times of emergency, Saudi Arabia and Kuwait were also willing to extend Egypt financial grants to cover immediate budgetary needs. This, at a time when Egypt's main problem was the balance of payments, and a huge national debt following six years (1967–1973) of full military mobilization, destruction of the Suez Canal and its cities, and three destructive wars. In the years following the October War, Egyptian public figures and policymakers were increasingly bitter about the stingy oil states that had made fortunes at the expense of Egypt, with growing calls to learn the lesson and wash hands of the conflict with Israel. At the Arab summit conference of Rabat (October 1974), Egypt, Syria and Jordan, renewed their efforts to bring about substantive Arab financial aid to the confrontation states and the Palestinians. The results, however, were disappointing, and much below the Egyptian expectations. Egypt was allocated 575 million dollars, most of which was to be donated by the Gulf oil monarchies (which usually implemented their underwitings, as opposed to Iraq, Libya and Algeria that did not). The annual aid of Rabat ceased in late 1978, in the wake of Sadat's signing of the Camp David accords with Begin, as part of the economic sanctions applied against Egypt by the Arab world. The total Arab financial aid to Egypt, including deposits and investments, was from 1967 to 1978 17 billion dollars (13 billion dollars, since 1973), almost all given by the Gulf oil monarchies.

Sadat was the driving force, together with Saudi Arabia's king, in legitimizing the use of diplomatic means for recovering the occupied Arab lands, by adopting a strategy of phases in the conflict with Israel. The decision, passed at the Algiers summit conference of November 1973 ostensibly confirmed that the Arab strategic goal in the conflict with Israel (i.e., recovery of historic Palestine in its entirety) remained unchanged, enabling a radical regime such as Syria's Ba'th, to go along with the diplomatic process. Sadat continued his pre-1973 war efforts to support the PLO and its claim for the status of sole legitimate representative of the Palestinian people, and for an equal footing in the Middle East peace process. At the same time, Sadat used his influence to convince the PLO's mainstream, led by Arafat, to adopt pragmatic aims in the conflict with Israel and be content with a Palestinian state in the West Bank and Gaza. The promotion of the PLO's status as the representative of the Palestinian people, clearly at the expense of King Hussein of Jordan, which culminated in the Rabat Arab summit conference (1974), led to cooling relations between Egypt and Jordan. In March 1972, Sadat severed diplomatic relations with Jordan in response to the latter's proclamation of the "United Hashemite Kingdom," which suggested a form of Jordanian-Palestinian unity under Husein's crown. In September 1973, shortly before the October war, Sadat and Asad of Syria met with King Hussein in Cairo, apparently to mend fences and encourage him to take action against Israel on his front in case of an all-out Arab-Israeli war, though he was not updated about their coming offensive. Although occsionally supporting Jordanian participation in the peace process when it could serve his interests, Sadat clearly inclined to support the PLO, even though it meant an impasse in the peace efforts due to Israeli and American rejection of the PLO, in order to maintain his all-Arab legitimacy as a peace making seeker in the conflict with Israel. Thus, he made little effort while at Camp David (September 1978) and after, to bring King Hussein to active participation in the Israeli-Egyptian agreement on transitional autonomy for the Palestinians (see ARAB-ISRAEL PEACEMAKING).

In spite of his commitment to Syria and other Arab states to keep in line with a collective form of Arab advancement of the peace process with Israel, he repeatedly surprised his Arab partners with his independent diplomacy, taking advantage of the favorite conditions of Sinai in terms of partial settle-

ments. The US preference of "step by step" diplomacy and Israel's willingness to promote a settlement with Egypt in order to separate it from other Arab states and prevent a discussion of the Palestinian issue, also substantiated Sadat's efforts to promote separate and partial settlements with Israel. Sadat's unwillingness to be restricted by the obstacles that a PLO participation involved, led to his agreeing to take part in the Geneva Conference in December 1973 only with Jordan, without Syria and the PLO, and to sign the Disengagement-of-Forces agreement in January 1974 (see ARAB-ISRAEL PEACE-MAKING). This policy was further implemented in the Interim Agreement of 1 September 1975, reached after intensive mediation efforts by US Secretary of State Henry Kissinger, which also provided for a further Israeli withdrawal and an expansion of Egyptian- and UN-held zones of Sinai (which included the Abu Rudeis oil fields), as well as mutual limitations and a thinning-out of the forces close to the dividing line. It also restored to Egyptian administration part of the oil installations on the western shore of Sinai on the Gulf of Suez. The Interim Agreement (or, Sinai II), included for the first time since the war, essential political elements which amounted to a non-belligerency agreement: it was to remain in force until superseded by a new one; the signatories undertook to refrain from any use of force to resolve their differences. The agreement, which came against the backdrop of deteriorating economic conditions in Egypt, triggered strong Arab criticism from most Arab states, including Saudi Arabia, and was the main cause for a year-long crisis that effectively paralyzed collective Arab action on the peace making process with Israel. Syria and the PLO now led an Arab effort to isolate Egypt and prevent further defections of Arab states from the battlefield with Israel. In response, Egypt shut down the PLO radio station in Cairo and restricted the organization's activity on its soil. It was only in October 1976 that Egypt mended its fences with Syria and the PLO, following the latter's military clashes in Lebanon at the height of the civil war in that country (see LEBANON). At the Arab summit conference held in Cairo that month, Egypt, Syria and Saudi Arabia renewed their coalition, and agreed to work together toward a comprehensive settlement of the conflict with Israel, a concept long demanded by Syria and toward the end of 1976, also by the coming American administration headed by Jimmy Carter. However, despite close Arab cooperation in that respect, the efforts for convening the Geneva Conference (which had not been convened since December 1973), with all the Arab parties concerned, including the PLO, failed. Faced by a deadlock, in the late summer of 1977 Sadat began looking for direct avenues to the newly established Israeli government headed by the right-wing leader Menahem BEGIN.

Sadat's predicament was aggravated by the US-Soviet declaration of 1 October which for the first time since 1973 brought the Soviets back in the Arab-Israeli peace process, denoting additional obstacles on Egypt's way toward full recovery of Sinai. Against this backdrop, in early November Sadat decided to break the deadlock by a dramatic visit to Jerusalem, in the wake of secret diplomatic contacts, though without Israeli assurances as to its willingness to accept his main demands. The visit was a deep shock to the many Arab states though only the radical regimes, led by Syria, Libya and Iraq, and the PLO, rushed to denounce the Egyptian president. In his meetings with Israeli leaders, and his public address to a solemn meeting of the Knesset, Sadat offered a comprehensive peace, though he meant nothing more than the end of the state of war between the two states in return for a total Israeli withdrawal from all occupied territories and a just solution to the Palestinian problem. Sadat's proposals were thus, in substance, not different from previous positions held by Egypt herself and other moderate Arab states. His great achievement was, first, a psychological breakthrough, cutting the vicious circle by meeting the "enemy" face to face and talking to him, and, secondly, spelling out what before had at best been implied: a preparedness to accept Israel and co-exist with it in peace, once it agreed to the concessions he demanded. Sadat made it clear, though, that he would not conclude a separate peace but would consider an eventual agreement as a first step toward a comprehensive Arab-Israel settlement.

The Egypt-Israel peace process soon confronted a deadlock which led both parties to seek US offices of mediation. However, despite the progress attained by Israel's plan for a five-year interim Palestinian self-governing rule in the West Bank and Gaza Strip before the final status of these territories be determined, the difficulties regarding full Israeli withdrawal from Sinai remained unresolved. In Sep-

tember, President Carter convened Begin and Sadat to a summit meeting at his resort in Camp David, in which he threw all his personal weight for concluding an agreement between the sides. The Camp David Accords signed on 17 September 1978 (a "Framework for Peace in the Middle East", and a "Framework for a Peace Treaty between Israel and Egypt"), and the Peace Treaty of 26 March 1979—are described in more detail in ARAB-ISRAEL PEACE-MAKING. Israel completely withdrew from Sinai to the former international Egypt-Palestine border, followed by "completely normal relations... including diplomatic, economic and cultural relations." The "Framework for Middle East Peace" envisaged a Palestinian autonomy, a self-governing authority in the West Bank and Gaza for a transitional period of five years. During this time Egypt, Jordan and elected representatives of the inhabitants would negotiate an agreement with Israel on the area's final status.

The Peace Treaty was ratified by Egypt's National Assembly in April 1979 and endorsed by a referendum that same month. It became effective on 25 April 1979. Its implementation was completed by Israel's total withdrawal from Sinai-after full evacuation of all Israeli settlements-in April 1982 (see ARAB-ISRAEL CONFLICT). Peace now reigned between Egypt and Israel (in 1978, Sadat and Premier Begin of Israel had jointly received the Nobel Peace Prize), but it cooled down under Sadat's successor, MUBARAK, due to Israel's invasion of Lebanon in June 1982. It was a "cold peace," disappointing to both Egypt and Israel. It was dampened by the total hostility of the Arab world (see below); parts of Egyptian public opinion—the Left, Nasserists, Islamic fundamentalists, opposition groups, intellectuals—opposed it. The general Egyptian public, which had at first supported it, (greeting the end of war with joy, and welcoming large streams of Israeli visitors with friendly curiosity), soon cooled off. They were disappointed that peace with Israel did not entail an immediate far-reaching improvement in Egypt's general situation. The implementation of the Framework for Middle East Peace ran into serious obstacles, and several disputes poisoned relations (for details, see ARAB-ISRAEL CONFLICT). Relations improved to some extent in September 1986 when it was agreed to submit one of the disputes over Taba, to arbitration, to an international arbitration tribunal, which resulted in a verdict in favor of Egypt.

Egypt's relations with the Arab states were thus determined mostly by Sadat's divisive peace policy. Identifying the radical Arab regimes and the PLO as a source of trouble for his quest for reaping the fruits of the October War, he maintained close relations with the oil-producing monarchies headed by Saudi Arabia, as well as with Morocco. While he could ignore Iraq and Libya, which established themselves as the REJECTION FRONT, he could hardly do the same with Syria, and thus strove to coordinate policies with Asad, but not at any price, causing repeated periods of tension and the semi-boycott of Egypt by the Syrian regime, such as following the separate agreements signed by Egypt with Israel in January 1974 and September 1975.

Asad was the only Arab leader to whom Sadat revealed his intention to go to Jerusalem and sought to attain his approval. Relations between the two states fell into a deep crisis with Sadat's visit to Jerusalem, which Damascus perceived as detrimental to its national interests and fiercely attacked, calling for deposing Sadat. In December 1977, Sadat announced the severance of diplomatic relations with Syria, Libya, Iraq, Algeria, the PLO and South Yemen, which had just concluded their summit meeting in Tripoli with a decision to suspend their relations with Egypt in the wake of Sadat's visit to Israel. Egypt's relations with Libya were particularly sour after 1973. From 1974, Egypt accused Libya several times of plots, sabotage and terrorism. The tension assumed a military dimension when clashes occurred in July 1977 along their common border, near the Jaghboub oasis.

The Arab world was stunned by Sadat's November 1977 visit to Israel and his decision to embark on negotiations toward a perceived separate peace with Israel and a betrayal of all-Arab solidarity.

Yet the Arab states were hardly in conformity in their reactions. The radical Arab states strongly strived for isolating and punishing Egypt, an effort which began in the Tripoli summit meeting of December 1977 (see above). In November 1978, following the Camp David Accords, an Arab summit conference convened in Baghdad at Iraq's initiative—to discuss those accords, but in fact to replace Egypt as the leading Arab state—concluded, under strong Syrian-Iraqi pressure, that diplomatic and economic sanctions would be applied against Egypt once it signed full peace treaty with Israel. The summit first

offered Egypt a package deal of abrogating the Camp David Accords in return for a 5 billion dollar lump sum of Arab aid to Egypt, but Sadat scornfully rejected the offer as insulting to Egypt's national dignity. The summit's decision was implemented by most Arab states in March 1979, except three (Sudan, Oman and Somalia). Soon afterward, Egypt's membership in the Arab League, as well as in other international organizations was suspended, the Arab League headquarters was transferred to Tunis and the Egyptian Secretary-General Mahmud RIYAD, who had resigned in November 1978, was replaced by the Tunisian Chedli KLIBI (see ARAB LEAGUE).

The punitive measure taken against Egypt by most Arab states in 1979 isolated Egypt, but also paralyzed the ability of the Arab states to work together as a group. In the early 1980s, Egypt's absence from the Arab collective arena was strongly manifested in the fragmentation and weakness which had befallen the Arab world, as indicated by the Iraq-Syria rift since 1980, and Israel's invasion of Lebanon and long siege of Beirut in 1982. The isolation was incomplete, and the boycott far from seriously affecting Egypt's economy. With the exception of the radical states, all others maintained their consular missions in Cairo. The boycott was more effective in trade and the financial flow of aid funds, though its impact had been reduced due to the growing flow of financial aid from non-Arab sources (in 1978, the total Arab financial aid of 750 million dollars, constituted only one-third of the total foreign capital received by Egypt). In banking, tourism, and migration of Egyptian workers to other Arab countries, the effects were only temporary. There was little new investment of official Arab capital from the oil-rich Gulf monarchies, but trade with private firms and institutions—mainly by the oil monarchies—as well as private investments continued, and of the funds invested, very little was withdrawn. Egyptian technicians, experts and workers continued working in Arab countries—estimates of their number varying from 1.5 million to 3 million—and remitting their earnings to Egypt (totalling 1.7 billion dollars in 1978) Communications, particularly air links, were somewhat reduced but continued. Arab tourism declined, but still was approximately forty percent of all foreign tourism, and hundreds of thousands of Arab tourists continued visiting Egypt and frequenting Cairo's night-life.

The remaining effect of the Arab boycott was further diminished by the US government's proposal of a three-year aid program for Egypt worth 1.8 billion dollars annually. On the cultural and political level, the Arab boycott was even less significant. Egypt remained the cultural center of the Arab world, especially in book and film production, though its position as the main center of the Arab press was no longer undisputed. Egypt's exclusion from official and non-official Arab institutions and professional associations was nearly complete. However, Syria, Iraq and Libya failed in their efforts to expel Egypt from UN-based international organizations, the Organization of African Unity or the Organization of Non-Aligned Nations. They scored only limited success in the Islamic Conference Organization, which suspended Egypt's membership (in January 1984 Egypt was invited to attend its meeting).

In the early 1980s ruptures in the anti-Egyptian front became evident, with growing calls for "Egypt's return to the Arab fold," assuming that with the end of Israel's withdrawal from Sinai (scheduled for April 1982), Egypt would be susceptible to renew its membership in the Arab League. However, Egypt adhered to it peace treaty with Israel and refused to trade it off for its re-acceptance to the Arab group of states. Mubarak remained faithful to Sadat's view on this issue, maintaining that it was the Arab world that needed Egypt and hence should adopt its peace strategy in the conflict with Israel. Despite the latter's invasion of Lebanon and siege of Beirut, Mubarak decided to recall the Egyptian ambassador in Tel Aviv only after the massacre of Palestinians in the Beirut refugee camps of Sabra and Shatila, perpetrated by Phalangists with the tacit consent of the Israeli high command in September 1982. During the Lebanon war, Egypt made a clear effort to disassociate itself from Israel and the US policies on Lebanon, and co-sponsored, together with France, a draft proposal to the UN Security Council, calling for an immediate cease-fire throughout Lebanon, a disengagement of forces in the Beirut area under the supervison of a UN force, and simultaneous Israel-PLO mutual recognition. Mubarak further seized the Palestinian issue as a means to pave Egypt's road back to the Arab circle by siding with the PLO in its strife with Syria and calling for full withdrawal of all and foreign forces from Lebanon, including Syria's and Israel's. In the wake of ARAFAT's evacuation of

his last stronghold in Lebanon in the Tripoli area in December 1983, after fierce battles with his Palestinian adversaries supported by Syrian artillery, Mubarak met with Arafat, whose return to Egypt after five years of boycott indicated a renewal of the traditional Egypt-PLO alignment.

Toward the mid-1980s Egypt seemed to be moving out of its isolation, first in practice, and then officially as well. Egypt's interest in breaking its isolation in the Arab arena was reflected in a continuous effort to bring about a resumption of the peace process, with the participation of other Arab states. The Jordan-PLO dialogue, starting in the wake of the Lebanon war, was welcomed by Egypt as a step in the desired direction. In September 1984, Jordan resumed its diplomatic relations with Egypt, breaking up the Baghdad consensus decision of boycotting Egypt, emphasizing the strengthening weight of an Egyptian-led coalition of Egypt, Jordan and the PLO, with Iraqi tacit participation. Iraq, while adhering to its official severed relations with Egypt, in fact collaborated with Egypt by purchasing Egyptian-made ammunition and used Soviet-made weapons, which by late 1982 had reached 1.5 billion dollars worth. The Egypt-Iraq collaboration, also evidenced by the absorbing of Egyptian workers in Iraq, continued to develop until the end of the Iraq-Iran war, counterbalancing the rival Iran-Syria alliance.

The growing concern of the Gulf oil monarchies about the escalating Iraq-Iran war and its implications for their own national security led them in 1987 to renew the financial aid to Egypt (estimated at 1 billion dollars that year), to help it repay its huge external debt. This indicated the Gulf countries appreciation of the significant role Egypt could play in strengthening Arab defense in the war. In November 1987 the Arab summit conference held in Amman resolved that the Arab states were in favor of renewing their diplomatic relations with Egypt, without demanding the abrogation of its peace treaty with Israel. This decision paved the way for immediate resumption of diplomatic relations with Egypt by all Arab states, with the exception of Syria and Libya. However, despite the strong lobbying of Iraq and the Gulf oil monarchies, Egypt's return to the Arab League remained blocked, mainly due to Syrian and Libyan objection. Thus, Egypt was not invited to attend the next summit conference held in Algiers in June 1988. In February 1989, Egypt, together with Iraq, Jordan and Yemen, established the Arab Cooperation Council, which ostensibly meant to promote economic cooperation among its members, but in fact served different interests of its members. For Egypt, this new alignment provided the needed springboard for an invitation to the next summit conference, held in Casablanca in May 1989, during which the return of Egypt to the Arab League was approved. A few months later, the Arab League headquarters returned to Cairo and an Egyptian, Ismat Abdel Majid, was appointed Secretary-General, replacing Chedli Klibi who had resigned his position.

Resuming its leadership position in the Arab world, Egypt came to play a counter-balancing role in the Arab arena in view of the aggressive proclamations made by *Saddam Hussein after ending his war with Iran in 1988. Thus, in view of Saddam's threats to destroy Israel with his gas weapon, Mubarak suggested, at the Baghdad summit conference in May 1990, that the Middle East become a zone free of mass destruction weapons, which will include Israel. In 1994, Egypt brought this issue to the fore, demanding that Israel join the Nuclear Proliferation Treaty (see NON-CONVENTIONAL WEAPONS) and made an effort to enlist the Arab League support for this matter while challenging the US favorite position toward Israel's conceived nuclear capability. In August 1990, Egypt played a leading role in forging support of most Arab states for an international intervention against Iraq. In the aftermath of the war, Egypt attempted, together with Syria and the Gulf oil monarchies led by Saudi Arabia, to create a new framework for maintaining security of the Gulf area, entailing Egyptian and Syrian military presence in the threatened Gulf monarchies. However, although the Damascus Declaration of March 1991 laid the basis for further consultations and meetings of these states, it remained unfulfilled due to the Gulf monarchies' preference to rely on the US for security.

In the context of the Arab-Israeli peace making, Egypt played an important role in convincing the PLO to accept the American initiatives made under the Bush administration, to start an Israeli-Palestinian peace process over the West Bank and Gaza Strip, on the basis of Israel's proposals of May 1989, for elections among the Palestinian inhabitants of these territories and negotiations with their elected delegates (see ARAB-ISRAEL PEACEMAKING). Later on, Egypt acted to smooth Syria's and the PLO's participation in the Madrid peace conference, and took part in it itself, as well as in the following multi lateral talks. Egypt sought to maintain its position as a pivotal state in the Middle East by controlling the Arab-Israeli peace process through playing the ultimate mediator. However, with the signing of the Israel-PLO DOP in September 1993 and the Cairo agreement of May 1994—which Mubarak helped to attain by influencing Arafat—the Israel-Jordan peace treaty, signed in October 1994 without any Egyptian involvement, as well as the establishment of diplomatic relations between Israel and Morocco, Tunisia, Mauritania, Oman and Qatar, was perceived in Cairo as a threat to Egypt's leading role in the Middle East, with Israel looming larger and stronger under the Rabin-Peres government. As a result, Egypt, together with Syria, attempted to call the Arab states to slow down the normalization process with Israel pending progress in the negotiations over the Golan Heights with Syria, and continued progress in the Palestinian track. Apart from its drive to attain regional leadership, Egypt's peace policy with Israel was tightly connected to its domestic politics, namely, the priority given to this issue by the opposition in its criticism of the government. Indeed, the process of democratization in Egypt proved to be another obstacle to the peace process, restricting the regime's freedom of action toward Israel. Egypt's dilemma culminated in the Arab summit conference held in Cairo in June 1996 shortly after the ascendancy of a right-wing government in Israel in the elections of late May 1996, led by Binyamin Netanyahu. At Egypt's behest, the summit resolved that the peace process with Israel was an Arab strategic priority. Yet in order to put pressure on Israel to adhere to its commitments and proceed in the negotiations with Syria, the normalization with Israel was to be conditional on the progress attained in the peace process on both the Palestinian and Syrian-Lebanese fronts.

Education, Culture and the Press Egypt is the most important cultural and educational center of the Arab world. There are over 150 institutions of higher, post-secondary education, including seventeen universities with a student population of over half a million—among them the al-AZHAR Islamic study center (founded 970); the University of Cairo (established 1908, modernized 1925 and called, until

1952, "Fu'ad I University"); that of Alexandria (1942); Ain Shams (1950) and several more in Cairo and provincial towns. There is also an American University, which was founded in 1919 as a secondary school. Several thousand foreign students are also trained at some of these institutions, and thousands of Egyptian teachers work in Arab and Muslim countries. Since 1933, schooling has been compulsory for all children aged six to twelve, although the law has not always been applied. Since the 1960s the Egyptian Government has committed itself to a policy aiming at providing education for all. As a result, almost one quarter of Egyptians are either students or teach in a formal educational institution, compared with a world average of nearly one-fifth. In 1960 there were 2.7 million primary school students, while in 1994 to 1995 this number had risen to 10.7 million. In 1992 the percentage of children enrolled for the first year of primary school was 98.5% for both sexes and 92.3% for girls alone. At secondary school level, enrolment rose from 550,000 in 1960 to 8.1. million in 1994 to 1995. Egypt has thirteen universities, and 125 technical institutes. At university level, enrolment rates rose during the same period from 134,000 to 826,456.

Between 1960 and 1990, the number of schools increased from 13,700 to 24,000. Yet, because of the high population growth rate, the education sector has absorbed most of its resources, and in recent years parents have been requested to cover some of the expenses. The lack of funds has caused a shortage of facilities, double and triple school shifts and overcrowded classrooms. According to UNICEF figures, the average number of students per class in primary schools is 45, and can even reach 100 in densely populated areas. In spite of the efforts to ensure education for all, illiteracy has remained high (according to some estimations, around fifty percent during the period 1985 to 1995. Illiteracy, around sixty percent until the early 1970s, dropped to around fifty percent at the early 1990s, and to thirty-nine percent in 1996.

Egypt is the center of literature, art, books and records, theater and the film industry for the entire Arab world. Its broadcasting stations are the largest and most powerful in the Middle East and transmit in many languages as well as Arabic. Amongst the most well-known Egyptian writers are Nagib Mahfuz, Nobel-prize winner (1988); Tawfik al-Hakim (died in 1987); Yusuf Idris (died in 1991); and Muhammad Mustagab. The young generation of writers and poets includes Edwar Kharrat, Ali Salim, Bahard Tahir, Raja'a al-Nakkash and Nawal al-Sa'adawi. Many of their writings have been translated into foreign languages. Until the nationalization of the press in 1960, Egypt was the center of Arab journalism, the home of a large, rich, and until 1952, comparatively free press—dailies, literary monthlies (al-Katib, al-Hilal, al-Thaqafa), and political weeklies (Akhbar al-Yawm, Akhir Sa'a, al-Mussawwar, Rose al-Yusuf)—which were read in all the Arab countries. There were also dailies and periodicals in English, French, Greek and Armenian. Most of these papers were politically independent, i.e. of shifting orientation and allegiance; political parties also founded organs, but those were never very successful. Since the nationalization of 1960 (which concentrated all publications in several centralized publishing houses, with the NU/ASU as owner and manager), all the press has been controlled. Under the officers' regime since 1952, and culminating with the 1960 nationalization, many papers folded, or were closed down by the Government—including all party organs and well established reputable dailies such as al-Muqattam (since 1886–1889) and al-Misri (1936). In 1975, in the course of Sadat's reforms, it was decided partly to de-nationalize the press, too, and hand forty nine percent of the shares to the editorial staff and the workers of each paper. Political-editorial control was also somewhat relaxed, but the appointment and dismissal of editors remained de facto in the hands of the government. The most important dailies in recent years were al-Ahram (founded 1875, edited from 1957 until his dismissal in 1974 by Muhammad Hassanein HEYKAL) and al-Akhbar (founded 1952); these two papers have a circulation of 1 million each. Al-Gumhuriyya (1953) used to be the daily organ of the regime's party. The government, not always satisfied with the popular weeklies, also established two weeklies that were considered semi-official mouthpieces: October (1976, edited until 1985 by Anis Mansur, and later on by Ibrahim Sa'ada and Rajab al-Banna) and Mayo, the organ of the NDP, established in 1981 and closed down in 1992. Opposition groups also began publishing weekly organs of their own—al-Da'wa and al-Nur, of the Muslim Brotherhood, and other Islamic periodicals; the leftist NPUR's al-Ahali; the

New *Wafd* issued by the *Wafd* Party; the Socialist Labor Party's *al-Sha'b*; a leftist-intellectual monthly, *al-Tali'a* (Vanguard), issued since 1965 with the encouragement of Nasser and the Government by *al-Ahram's* publishing house, with Lutfi al-Khouli as editor, was closed down in 1978 but re-permitted in 1984. These opposition organs do not seem to have much influence.

EGYPTIAN-ISRAEL PEACE TREATY   see ARAB-ISRAEL PEACEMAKING.

EISENHOWER DOCTRINE   US policy statement on the Middle East made by President Eisenhower on 5 January 1957, requesting Congress authorization for US military and economic assistance to Middle East countries asking for such aid, and the use of the US armed forces to protect the independence and territorial integrity of any nation in the region "against overt aggression from any nation controlled by International Communism." Congressional authorization was given on 9 March 1957.

The Eisenhower Doctrine was put to the test by JORDAN in April 1957, when King HUSSEIN accused Communist-controlled forces of attempting to overthrow him. The UNITED STATES OF AMERICA dispatched the Sixth Fleet to the eastern Mediterranean and began extending economic aid to Jordan. Following General QASSEM's coup of July 1958 in IRAQ, both Jordan and LEBANON invoked the Eisenhower Doctrine and requested military aid, including troops. BRITAIN sent paratroops to Jordan, and the US sent 14,000 marines to Lebanon. The Eisenhower Doctrine was also linked to close US co-operation with CENTO (formerly the Baghdad Pact), agreed in March 1959 in bi-lateral accords with TURKEY, IRAN and Pakistan. After 1959, it was not explicitly invoked again. It was strongly denounced by radical-neutralist Arab countries as imperialist interference, and it contributed to the suspicions and charges of US "plots" voiced in 1957–1958. On the other hand, its effectivity was limited, as it applied only to "overt aggression" from outside each country, and not to the danger of internal leftist plots and takeovers.

ENTEBBE OPERATION   see TERRORISM.

ERBAKAN, NECMETTIN (b. 1926)   Turkish politician, Prime Minister 1996–1997. Erbakan was born in the Sinop province and in 1948 graduated from the Istanbul Technical University in mechanical engineering. He received a Ph.D. from Aachen Technical University and began an academic career at the Istanbul Technical University, gaining professorship in 1962. He also established an engine factory and was elected president of the Union of Chambers of Commerce and Industry.

Erbakan entered politics in 1969 when he was elected to the Grand National Assembly as an independent delegate from Konya. In 1970 he formed the National Order Party with a platform combining an Islamist orientation with economic and social reform. In 1971 the Party was banned by the Constitutional Court following the military coup, but Erbakan re-established it in 1973 under the name of National Salvation Party. Gaining support amongst the conservative and small business sections of the population, the Party succeeded in winning forty-eight seats in the 1973 elections and emerged in third place. It entered the coalition government formed by Bülent Ecevit's Republican People's Party in early 1974 with Erbakan as deputy Prime Minister. The partnership fell apart in September when Ecevit resigned, but Erbakan joined Süleyman DEMIREL's coalition government which, under the name National Front, held power until the June 1977 elections. With a reduced representation in the Assembly, amounting to twenty-four seats, the Party rejoined Demirel's coalition for an additional six months until it fell in December. Throughout this period, Erbakan dealt primarily with the economy and actively helped in fostering Turkey's co-operation with Muslim countries.

Erbakan's overt Islamist platform had long been harshly criticized by Turkey's secularist circles, while Erbakan in turn attacked the "anti-Islamic" and Western oriented policies of his rivals. A rally he organized in Konya in September 1980 to protest Israel's annexation of JERUSALEM and Turkey's policy toward Israel and the West was amongst the reasons which led the army (a few days later) to stage its coup and bring down the Government. Erbakan was arrested, brought to trial and found not guilty, but in 1982 he was barred, together with other leaders, from political activity for ten years.

The September 1987 referendum, however, allowed Erbakan to return to politics, and he assumed the chairmanship of the Welfare Party (*Refah Par-*

tisi), already established in 1983 as an incarnation of his former parties. In the following years it became increasingly popular. In 1991 the Party won sixty-two seats in the 450 member National Assembly, gained impressive victories in the March 1994 municipal elections, and in the general elections in 1995 finally emerged as the strongest Party with 158 seats (out of the now expanded 550 member Assembly) and 21.4% of the vote. After a Government formed by the two center right secular parties (the True Path Party and the Motherland Party) failed to hold out for more than a few months, Erbakan in July 1996 entered into partnership with the True Path. He became Prime Minister in a rotation system with Tansu CILLER—the first government headed by an Islamist party in the history of the Republic.

As Prime Minister, Erbakan was extremely cautious. He made significant efforts to appease his critics and sustain his relations with his coalition partner, deviating considerably from his earlier rhetoric. He embarked on tours to a number of Muslim countries, signed a controversial contract with Iran for the supply of natural gas, and made preparations for the establishment of an association of the eight most developed Muslim states. But he took care to declare his loyalty to Turkey's Western allies and even went along with two agreements on military cooperation signed with Israel. At home he desisted from taking any strong legislatory measures designed to reestablish Islam's position in the country. Nonetheless he was sympathetic to the demands (like the wearing of religious scarves by female civil servants) from his supporters and went along with attempts to strengthen their status in Party-held ministries and the religious school system. This "creeping" Islamization was quick to arouse the suspicion of the Army (the bulwark of secularism in the country.) In March 1997 the National Security Council (representing among others the Army's high command) forced Erbakan to agree to a package of eighteen measures designed to curb the influence of ISLAM in the country. Slow in implementing these measures and under continued pressure from the army, his position became untenable forcing him to resign in June 1997. He was replaced by the Motherland Party's leader Mesut YILMAZ.

ERITREA Republic in the Horn of Africa, formally acceded to independence in 1993. Eritrea (which includes the Dahlak islands) borders SUDAN on northeast, Ethiopia on west and south, and Djibouti on south-east. On the east of Eritrea lies a 1,000 km coastline of the Red Sea. Its population is about equally divided between CHRISTIANS and Muslims, with the eastern part predominantly Christian, the western part Muslim. Some Eritrean Muslims consider themselves Arab or semi-Arab, and Arabic is spoken to some extent as a second language, particularly in the coastal towns.

Eritrea was an Italian colony from 1889, under British occupation from 1941 until 1952, and federally united with Ethiopia since 1952, following a resolution of the United Nations General Assembly. In 1958 the Eritrean Liberation Front (ELF) was founded, comprised primarily of Muslims-and began an armed struggle for independence. An internal split in the ELF, resulted in the formation of the Eritrean People's Liberation Front (EPLF), instigated the eruption of Civil War (1972-1974). The semi-autonomous federal regime was reduced to an Ethiopian province in 1962, which intensified the guerrilla war, conducted predominantly by Muslims.

Eritrea's independence movement was politically supported by the Arab states, and its guerrillas were aided and provided with supplies, training and operational bases by some Islamic-conservative Arab countries, primarily SAUDI ARABIA and the Gulf sheikhdoms, as well as by PALESTINIAN GUERRILLA ORGANIZATIONS. The leftist-revolutionary Arab regimes of SYRIA and LIBYA, at first also aided them, reportedly with particular vigor. However, Libya and SOUTH YEMEN changed their stance when Ethiopia became revolutionary and leftist, after 1974. In 1981 these Arab regimes concluded a pact with Ethiopia and stopped all aid to the Eritrean rebels. Arab aid for the Eritrea rebels has put a strain on Arab-Ethiopian relations. The Eritrea problem particularly troubled SUDAN and its relations with Ethiopia, since most arms and supplies for the rebels come from or through Sudan, whom Ethiopia blamed of giving the Eritrean rebels some of their main bases in that country. In the early 1980s Sudan, for the sake of improving its relations with Ethiopia, officially closed down the political and organizational offices which the Eritrean rebels had maintained in Khartoum and liquidated their military bases, forcing thousands of rebels to withdraw from Sudan. But Ethiopia still claimed that these measures were not fully and sincerely enforced and that in fact the Eritrean rebels continued to receive at least some support from Sudan. In 1990, the EPLF managed to take control of the lion's share of Eritrea's territory, including the important port of Massawa and in 1991 they captured Asmara the capital. Following these successes, the EPLF had become the acting government of Eritrea and was recognized by the US government and by Ethiopia. In April 1993 a UN-supervised referendum was held, in which 99.8% of the voters endorsed independence and in the following month Eritrea became a member of the UN. The National Assembly then elected Issaias Afewerky, Secretary General of the EPLF, as President. In February 1994 the EPLF adopted a decision to transform itself from a military front to the People's Front for Democracy and Justice (PFDJ). The EPLF congress also confirmed its support for a plural political system which was to be included in the final draft of a new constitution.

Later that year and in 1995, experts from all over the world were invited to assist in writing the draft of the new constitution (opposition parties were not invited) that was supposed to be adopted in mid-1996, to be followed by elections to the presidency and the parliament in 1997. In 1994 military service in Eritrea became compulsory, with the intention of replacing the liberation fighters with newly recruited, better educated and younger manpower. However, the policy of demobilizing the veterans of the liberation war and general conscription posed social and economic strains for the regime, involving clashes between the government forces and groups refusing to serve in the military.

By mid-1995 the government was obliged to reduce the armed forces by 45% (from 95,000 to 55,000), and planned to further reduce them to some 20,000. Following a visit of President Afewerki to Washington in early 1995, the US government sent thirty military advisers to Eritrea to help in re-organizing its armed forces.

Domestic Affairs: Eritrea is considered one of the poorest countries in Africa. Ninety percent of the population are farmers and fishermen. From 1993 Eritrea has been granted financial support from the International Monetary Fund, the European Union, US, Canada and ORGANIZATION OF PETROLEUM-EXPORTING COUNTRIES (OPEC), as well as from other countries, primarily for the development of economic projects,

industrial and agricultural, as well as of the infra-structure of communication.

Foreign Affairs: In 1993 Eritrea established diplomatic relations with neighboring Sudan and Ethiopia, Israel, Australia and Pakistan, as well as with several international organizations, and this tendency continued in the following years. Relations with several Arab states deteriorated following criticism of Eritrea's President published by an Islamic fundamentalist movement based in Sudan. Relations with Sudan remained strained until Eritrea severed diplomatic relations with Khartoum in December 1994, amid mutual recrimininations of conducting subversive activities against each other. From 1995 border disputes erupted between Eritrea and Yemen and Djibouti.

In 1994, the Eritrean Orthodox Church formally broke with the Ethiopian Church and established itself as an independent church, after having their own bishops inducted by the Shenouda III, the Coptic Orthodox Pope in Cairo.

ESHKOL, LEVI (1895–1969), Israeli statesman, leader of Mapai and the Israel Labor Party and Prime Minister, 1963–1969. Eshkol was born in the Ukraine and as a youth joined *Tze'irei Tzion* ("Youth of Zion"). He immigrated to Palestine in 1913, where he worked in agriculture and as a watchman. He was one of the founders of Kibbutz Degania Beth and was a volunteer in the Jewish Legion in the years 1918–1920. He was active in the labor movement as the initiator and director of several *Histadrut* institutions and companies, serving as Director General of the *"Mekoroth"* water development company in the years 1937–1951. Eshkol served on the High Command of the *Haganah* (the pre-state Jewish defense force) dealing with financial issues. In the years 1944–1948 he served as Secretary of the Tel Aviv Workers' Council.

Eshkol was a member of the Jewish Agency Executive, serving as head of its Settlement Department in the years 1948–1963 and as its Treasurer in the years 1949–1951. Simultaneously, in the years 1948–1949 he helped organize the Ministry of Defense under David BEN GURION.

Eshkol was elected to the second Knesset in 1951. He was Minister of Agriculture and Development, 1951–1952, and Minister of Finance, 1952–1963. In 1963 he was designated by Ben Gurion as his successor as Prime Minister, in which capacity he served until his death in February 1969. In 1964 Eshkol approved the bringing of the remains of Ze'ev Jabotinsky to Israel and thus began the period of rapprochement between the Labor and Herut (led by Menahem BEGIN) movements. As of January 1967, Eshkol's Government abolished the military government over Israel's Arab citizens, starting a new era in the state's relations with its Arab minority. In the years 1963–1967 Eshkol served also as Minister of Defense, but in early June 1967 was obliged to appoint Moshe DAYAN to the job—due to popular pressure and Eshkol's own image of weakness and indecisiveness in the course of the May-June crisis. At the same time Eshkol also expanded his Government to a National Unity Government, by inviting Menahem Begin, at the head of Gahal, to join. In the midst of the Six-Day War (see ARAB-ISRAEL CONFLICT) Eshkol called on the Arab leaders to open peace talks with Israel, and continued in these efforts in the aftermath of the war. In the meantime he succumbed to pressure from within his Government to annex East JERUSALEM and start certain Jewish settlement activities in the WEST BANK (especially the Jordan Rift Valley) and GOLAN HEIGHTS.

EUPHRATES RIVER   see WATER POLITICS.

EUROPEAN COMMUNITY AND THE MIDDLE EAST

Europe is historically connected to the Middle East which it relates to as its backyard. Since colonial times, many of the European states have tried to obtain a foothold and exercise their control in the Middle East in view of its geopolitical importance. Nowadays as well, the proximity of the Middle East to the southern countries bears significant political and socioeconomic implications which inevitably force Europe to seek for an active role in the shaping of events and policy trends in the Middle East. One of the most important concerns for the Europeans is the demographic issue and the fear of population explosion in the Middle East, or an economic crisis, or both. A population increase may spill into Europe, mainly in the form of immigrants. An influx of labor, mainly from North Africa into Western Europe, however, did help in relieving a labor shortage problem experienced during the industrial expansion phase. Euro-Arab relations were always

characterized by changing degrees of interdependence. The equation of specifically Euro-Arab economic cooperation traditionally comprised Arab oil and capital on the one hand, and European industrial goods, technology and economic consultancy on the other. The interdependence was beyond economic considerations, however, as it could not remain isolated from the strategic and political ambitions of both regions.

This inseparable connection between economy and politics was a determining factor in shaping Euro-Middle Eastern relations and may explain why Europe gradually went from maintaining mainly economic cooperation with the Middle East to massive involvement in its political agenda. The first milestone in the complex of Euro-Middle Eastern relations can be traced back to 1973.

European interests in the Middle East and the oil crisis of 1973

In the early 1970s Europe's primal concern regarding the Middle East was oil. The economic growth experienced by Western Europe in the 1950s had been accompanied by a sharp rise in energy consumption. The share of oil in the total energy consumption as well as in industrial inputs showed a marked increase and this aggravated Western Europe's dependency on the import of Arab oil.

Due to the fact that the Middle East was the main oil supplier to

Europe, Europeans were also troubled with issues that reached beyond the immediate concern for the steady supply of oil. They were anxious to ensure the security of the oil facilities in the area against inter-state conflicts and terror attacks and to prevent the danger of possible external interference in the area which may expand to a global conflict or prevent the West from accessing the oil reserves. Europeans were therefore closely following external and internal political developments in the Middle Eastern countries that could potentially bring to power a regime that would set oppressive conditions for consistent and stable oil supplies.

Mu'amar QADHAFI's rise to power in LIBYA in 1969 proved that such European concerns were not groundless. The oil reserves discovered in the 1950s in Libya allowed Qadhafi to declare, at various times, the need to utilize Arab oil as a political weapon against Western nations to force them into altering their pro-Israeli stance. Most other oil producing states were controlled by sheiks, sultans and princes, yet Libya became the great driving force within OPEC. Soon, as the ARAB-ISRAEL CONFLICT deteriorated into another war, European fears turned into reality.

In October 1973, after years of tough negotiations between oil companies and oil producing states represented in OPEC, over control and ownership of the latter's oil resources, OPEC decided not only on a very large increase in price, but more importantly, that future questions of price would be decided upon unilaterally by the producer governments. Subsequently, the Arab producers announced embargoes and production restrictions. Producer government unit revenue almost tripled at the beginning of October 1973, to the end of 1974. The era of oil supply as a political weapon had begun.

Since the oil embargo was governed by political discretions, it was enforced in a discriminating form. BRITAIN and FRANCE, who were perceived more favorably by the Arab states, did not suffer at all. Holland, which appeared to be less understanding of the Arab position was totally denied access to Middle Eastern oil. The rest of the European states suffered in different degrees. In an attempt to relieve the burden, Britain and France pressured other European states to change what seemed to be amicable positions towards Israel to more balanced ones. These differences of attitude proved the limitations of political cooperation between the European states yet also pushed them towards a more common policy which was dictated by political and economic considerations. Inevitably, this policy was based on the demands of the Arab states.

In the wake of the 1973 War, many in the Arab world wished for the formation of some sort of forum to achieve closer Euro-Arab cooperation. In December 1973 ARAB LEAGUE members offered, in a meeting of the foreign ministers of the community held in Copenhagen, to establish the Euro-Arab dialogue. Europe, in response to these appeals and with a desire to improve its relations with the Arab world, accepted the offer. There was no clear definition of the questions and problems that were supposed to be addressed in the framework of the dialogue. The notion of dialogue ignored both the realities of the distinct and competitive relations among the Arab states themselves—which did not form a collective unit—and the fact that European goals in establishing the dialogue were not identical to the

Arab ones. The Europeans hoped for a chance to further various economic issues (mainly the energy question) while the Arabs hoped to promote their political interests by securing European support for the Arab cause in the conflict with Israel. Moreover, the European states were in controversy over the particular issues that should be given priority in the dialogue. The vague concept of the dialogue involved a variety of informal contacts and ad-hoc conferences, as well as embryonic institutions which were created with no follow-up.

The dialogue was frozen in April 1979 after EGYPT was expelled from the Arab League as a consequence of the peace treaty with Israel. The dialogue remained latent without any significant achievements. It is possible to conclude that with regard to Europe as a whole, in economic terms, the oil embargo imposed during the 1973 ARAB-ISRAEL CONFLICT underscored the community's vulnerability, and the subsequent increase in the price of oil entailed a massive transfer of financial resources from the oil consumers to the producers. This was accompanied by a shift of political power in favor of the Arab countries—a shift that was eroding the European Community's ability to maintain the traditional balanced approach between Arabs and Israelis.

Europe's political role in the Middle East and the Arab-Israel conflict

During the period of the first oil crisis, Europe appeared as an economic giant and a political dwarf in matters of a common foreign policy. It had weaknesses which dictated its attitude towards the Middle East throughout the 1970s in the form of declarations, resolutions and missions. These were meant to show the Arab world that the European position is balanced and that the Europeans are sympathetic towards their stance regarding the Palestinian issue. The Arab states, with oil as their weapon, exerted pressures which undoubtedly contributed to the first political resolution of Europe throughout the EPC in November 1973. This resolution, which recognized the Palestinian issue as a political question that could not be handled merely as a refugee problem and called for acknowledgment of their legitimate rights, was the beginning of the change in Europe's position, which had until then related to the issue on the basis of UN resolution 242.

The London Declaration of June 1977 reflected this attitude. It declared, among other things, that a solution to the conflict in the Middle East would only be possible if the legitimate right of the Palestinian people to express effectively their national identity were translated into a situation that would take into account the need for a Palestinian homeland. There were various other declarations in that spirit and in June 1981 the Declaration of Venice was published. This was considered to be the most important declaration of the European Community for many years since it clearly dealt with the Palestinian right for self-determination. The declaration conveyed the message that the Arab-Israel conflict was considered (mainly by Britain and France) the main threat to the oil supply and thus, a fast solution to the conflict is vital in order to sterilize this threat. Europe supported the belief that the Palestinian issue was the heart of the conflict, the solution to which must necessarily be formed along the guiding lines of the formula of land for peace, as stated in UN resolution 242. This declaration was the peak of a unified European stand in relation to the Palestinian question. Notwithstanding this, the Europeans continued to support Israel's right to exist yet became more critical of its policy.

After the Venice Declaration there was a decline which may be explained by various internal and regional factors. Mitterand, who was elected President in France in 1981, dictated a more balanced policy towards Israel. Since France held in a dominant position regarding the shaping of the Community's policy towards the Arab-Israel conflict, it influenced the position of the whole Community. Thatcher's rise to power in Britain in 1979 and Kohl's in Germany in 1980 also influenced this change. In addition, the growing importance of the rich oil exporting states as a source for investments and a market for European export, caused strong competition among the European states and further complicated multilateral cooperation. The members of the European Community were divided over whether the Venice Declaration was the furthest they were prepared to go in foregoing national policies.

Since the 1970s, President al-SADAT of Egypt and other Arab leaders constantly called for a European contribution to the search for a peaceful settlement in the Middle East. Yet the Europeans did not clearly define their preferred role in the conflict beyond relating occasionally to the participation of European states in peace-keeping forces and as guarantors for a peaceful solution. The details, however, remained vague, and there has been great ambiguity concerning the question as to what extent the Europeans have been willing to commit themselves to active involvement.

Throughout the years Europe became involved in a number of endeavors whose aim was to resolve the Arab-Israel conflict in various ways. After the UN and the US post-1967 War diplomacy had failed repeatedly (as in the Jarring Mission and Rogers Plan), Europe attempted to offer an optional diplomacy along the model of an international conference. None of these attempts proved to be successful and the parties in the conflict never adopted the European model. Some European countries participated in two multinational forces which were sent to the Middle East, i.e., to Sinai since 1979, and to LEBANON in 1982–1983. Yet this involvement was perceived as a concern for the particular states involved and not the whole European Community. Nevertheless, the breakthrough in the deadlock was on European soil, in Oslo.

Diplomatically, the Europeans fully supported the renewed ARAB-ISRAEL PEACEMAKING which had begun at Madrid (October 1991). They were participants in the multilateral talks mainly as coordinators of the Regional Economic Development Working Group (REDWG), which appeared at the time to be the most dominant and productive of the five working groups that the multilateral track of the peace process was based upon. Yet, it is in the economic domain that the Europeans, deprived of a political role in the implementation of the peace process, were betting on larger participation, whether collectively within the EC or individually via their bilateral aid.

European financial aid

Europe is a major supplier of aid to the poorer economies of the Middle East in general. The total aid distributed by the EU to countries around the Mediterranean periphery totaled 2.8 billion dollars in 1994. These donations were given both collectively and in bilateral donations by EU members. In regard to the Palestinians in particular, Europe became an important provider of financial aid. There were various ways in which this aid was channeled. From 1971 Europe began donating moneys to the Palestinians, mainly in association with relief organizations such as the UN Relief and Work Agency (UNRWA). In 1986 specific sums were allocated for the Palestinian territories based on the publication of European guidelines. The Strasbourg Declaration in 1989 confirmed the willingness of Europe to be actively involved in the troubled areas of the above territories by contributing for specific purposes, such as the development of economic and industrial sectors. On the eve of the 13 September 1993 signing of the Washington Accords between Israel and the PLO, the EC announced the release of an immediate aid package of 35 million ECUs and pledged an additional 500 million ECUs over five years to the international financial effort for developing Gaza and the WEST BANK. This aid program, half funded from the EC budget and half by government subsidized loans from the European Investment Bank (EIB), made the EC the main lender of funds helping the move towards autonomy starting in Gaza and Jericho. In that sense, Europe's contribution was way ahead of other donors such as the US and Japan. The program also marked the European "return" to the Middle East after its virtual absence following the Madrid Conference.

Europe under the Madrid process was put in charge of "regional economic cooperation" in the multilateral talks. The Europeans were constantly skeptical of the American considerations because the economic cooperation files at times seemed political fiction. The issue of aid coordination and management—a key channel for exerting political influence—has give rise to behind-the-scenes wrangling between the Americans and the Europeans. This situation might have contributed to the fact that the Europeans decided to create a new forum to search for pathways that will lead to a strengthened foothold in the Mediterranean region in general.

Euro-Mediterranean cooperation

European thinking on the economic and security dimensions of relations with the southern Mediterranean littoral evolved in stages. As early as June 1972, representatives of the European Market were asked to propose a global attitude for the economic relations of the European Community with the Mediterranean states. Europe was searching for an inclusive policy for the Mediterranean in view of the ongoing military tensions in the area especially due to the increase in the presence of the Soviet fleet in the Mediterranean.

The Mediterranean states wished mostly to improve their trade with the European market by reducing the damaging effect of Europe's Common Agricultural Policy (CAP). A decision was reached in September 1972 to create an industry-free trade zone with the option of tax-free entrance for Mediterranean industrial products to European markets. In addition, Europe offered some Mediterranean states significant concessions for agricultural export from the Mediterranean and some financial aid. Agreements were signed with MOROCCO, ALGERIA, TUNISIA, Malta, Cyprus, Egypt, Israel, JORDAN Lebanon and Syria. These agreements underwent certain changes in 1981 and 1986 with the addition of new members to the European Market. It is important to mention that these agreements were purely economical and related to the economic power components of the Mediterranean states and to their previous connections with the European Market. Therefore, European trading conditions with the different Mediterranean states were not identical even after the 1972 agreements were signed.

In December 1990 Europe adopted a "New Mediterranean Policy," intended to reinforce existing trade and aid programs with support for economic reforms such as liberalization and structural adjustment. But the process moved beyond this transitory step. Various negotiations with Morocco, Tunisia, Israel and Egypt regarding bilateral free trade with Europe took place until, in October 1994, Europe reinvented a general concept for the Euro-Mediterranean relations. The European Commission, prompted by growing security concerns, particularly in relation to the southern European states, proposed the establishment of a Euro-Mediterranean partnership. The goal was the creation of a free trade area, backed by substantial financial aid. On 27–28 November 1995 European foreign affairs ministers, delegates of Mediterranean countries and the head of the Palestinian Authority, Yasser ARAFAT, came together in Barcelona to pledge a new era of peace and prosperity. This was the first high level meeting of its type, and the Euro-Mediterranean members signed a broad declaration to develop new political and economic links. The most significant part of the declaration was the pledge to work towards the establishment of a free trade zone of industrial goods and services by the year 2010. The EU also pledged 6,000 million dollars of aid towards education and infrastructure projects over the following five years. This was seen as a clear demonstration by the EU of its commitment to forging new partnerships with its southern neighbors.

EVREN, KENAN (b. 1918)   Turkish officer and politician; President 1982–1989. Born in Alasehir in western Turkey, Evren studied at the War College and the Army Staff College (1938–1939). During his long military career he served as Artillery Commander (1947–1957), Chief of Operations and Training Officer of the Turkish Brigade in Korea (1958–1959), Chief of Army Staff schools and Chief of Operations (1959–1961), Deputy Chief of the General Staff (1975–1976), Aegean Army Commander (1976–1977), Land Forces Commander (1977–1978) and Chief of the General Staff (1978–1983).

While Chief of Staff, Evren led the military coup of 12 September 1980, intended to end the wave of political violence and terrorism that had plagued TURKEY for over two years killing 5,000. The ruling military junta appointed Evren Head of State; and Admiral Bülent Ulusu formed a Government. Parliament was dissolved, the constitution suspended and martial law imposed. Approximately 30,000 people suspected of terrorism were arrested and a score hanged.

Harsh emergency measures included restrictions on the press, trade unions and public meetings.

In November 1982, after two years of military rule, which drastically reduced terrorism, decreased the rate of inflation from over 120% to 40% and streamlined the bureaucracy, Evren held a referendum endorsing a new constitution and electing him President for a seven-year term. (He was the only candidate and received more than ninety percent of the vote). The new constitution gave the President wider powers; it also barred many former leaders (such as ex-Prime Ministers Ecevit and DEMIREL) from participating in political life until 1992. (The ban was eased in 1986 and lifted after a referendum in September 1987). The rights of political parties and trade unions and the freedom of the press were also restricted. In November 1983 Evren held general elections, in which only three parties were allowed to run. They were won by the "Motherland Party" led by Turgut ÖZAL. In December 1983 Özal formed a Government. The restoration of the civilian-political rule was largely facilitated by Evren who turned from a military ruler into a constitutional, civilian President. He cooperated with the Government and exerted a moderating stabilizing influence on Turkish politics. He retired in November 1989 and was replaced by Turgut Özal.

F

FADAIYAN-E-ESLAM   see IRAN.

FADAIYAN-E KHALGH   see IRAN.

FAHD IBN ABDEL AZIZ (b. 1921)   King of SAUDI ARABIA since June 1982. Son of Abdel Aziz (Ibn SAʻUD) of a mother from the notable Sudairi tribal clan of Najd. Prince Fahd served as Minister of Education, 1953–1960, during the reign of his half-brother Saʻud. In October 1962, when his half-brother FEISAL became the predominant figure in the court, Fahd became Minister of the Interior, and from 1967 also Second Deputy Prime Minister. When Feisal was assassinated, in March 1975, and another half-brother, Khaled, became King, Fahd was promoted to be heir apparent and First Deputy Prime Minister; he

retained the interior Ministry for half a year only. Upon Khaled's death, in June 1982, Fahd became King and Prime Minister. In 1986 due to some religious revivalist tendencies and the IRAN-IRAQ WAR, Fahd gave himself the additional title of "guardian of the holy places." In the mid-1990s upon a deterioration in his health, Fahd temporarily transferred his powers to his half brother and next for succession, ABDALLAH IBN ABDEL AZIZ. In spite of Fahd's return to the throne later, his authority was somewhat diminished.

Fahd has voiced relatively liberal opinions, becoming an advocate of development and modernization, and supporting strong relations with the Western world. His name is linked to a plan for a comprehensive Middle East peace settlement based on the total withdrawal of ISRAEL from all the territories occupied in 1967. This would include the removal of settlements set up, and the establishment of a Palestinian state. Following this right of "all states of the region...would live in peace". This implies acceptance of, or acquiescence in, the existence of Israel. The "Fahd Plan" was launched in August 1981 and soon became a divisive matter among Arab states, leading to the break-up of the twelfth all-Arab Summit conference held at Fez in November 1981. Although the plan was finally adopted in September 1982, at the second session of the Fez Arab Summit conference, it entailed significant amendments to satisfy SYRIA and other radical states (see ARAB-ISRAEL CONFLICT). It was the first peace plan adopted by the Arab states as a collective, and thus was called "Fez Plan."

FAHD PLAN   see ARAB-ISRAEL PEACEMAKING.

FATAH, FATH   see PALESTINIAN GUERRILLA ORGANIZATIONS.

FATWA (plural: fatawa)   Islamic law ruling, issued by a MUFTI, usually in response to questions, but also on his own initiative.

In the absence of separation of state and religion in Islam, such rulings frequently intend to lay down the proper Islamic response to social and moral problems posed by new and changing circumstances, including public and political matters. The Mufti, who since the medieval Islamic state usually submitted to the ruler and served him, and in most Arab countries is government-appointed, by and large conforms in his fatwa's to the social customary law, or the political line prevailing in public opinion or adopted by the political leadership. Especially in fatwa on public or political affairs, usually based on personal interpretation of the tradition (sunna) of the Prophet Muhammad and his companions, but also of the practices of medieval Islamic rulers. Such interpretation is subjected to other Muftis' criticism and counter-ruling, reflecting the lack of religious hierarchy and supreme ruling or interpretative authority in Islam.

In the contemporary Muslim world, with the deepening concept of nation-states, this means an inclination towards growing diversity of religious opinion, mainly in public and political affairs, reflecting the manipulation of an Islamic value system for political purposes.

Several Fatwa's in the contemporary Middle East, for instance, recommended JIHAD, Holy War, against political enemies, mostly non-Muslim: ISRAEL, COMMUNISM and the Soviet Union, but also against IRAN (issued by an Iraqi Mufti). Another fatwa recognized the Palestinian guerrillas such as Mujahidin, fighters of a Holy War; or legitimized the assassination of the Jordanian Prime Minister Wasfi Tall (1971) as an act of *Jihad*. In the early 1930s, the Mufti of JERUSALEM al-Hajj Amin al-HUSSEIN excommunicated any Arab selling land to JEWS. Another fatwa excommunicated President ASAD of SYRIA. On the other hand, a fatwa by the head of Egypt's AL-AZHAR Islamic college in 1979 ruled that the peace treaty with Israel was not incompatible with the Qur'an and Islamic law. Recent "political" fatwas have dealt with the legitimacy of the Israeli-Palestinian peace process since Oslo.

FEDAIYIN KHALQ GUERRILLA ORGANIZATION   Full name: *Sazman-e Cherik-haye Fadai-ey Khalgh-e Iran* (Iranian People's Fedaiyin Guerrilla Organization). The first communist guerrilla organization of IRAN which carried out its first operation in February 1971. A group of armed students attacked a police station near the town of Syiah-kal in the northern forests. Some members of the group were killed, or imprisoned in this abortive operation. The ideology of the organization, as drafted by two of its founders, Jazni and Ahmad-Zadeh, was based on the writings of Lenin, Mao and Che Guevara. The organization supported urban guerrilla operations in order to bring down the regime and establish a farmers' regime. In its opinion, within Iran's existing social structure, an uprising by the farmers themselves was impossible. Most of those who joined the organization were university students and intellectuals, who underwent intensive ideological education. However, the number of members remained small. Nevertheless, its guerrilla operations, which included the assassination of industrialists and security men as well as the placing of bombs, helped weaken the Shah's regime. Following the 1979 Islamic revolution, KHOMEINI ignored the organization's members who consequently turned against the regime. They renewed their armed activities and boycotted the referendum of March 1979 (see IRAN). In August 1979 they held a mass demonstration in Tehran, with the participation of supporters of democracy against the suppression of freedom. The demonstration was brutally crushed and the authorities started to persecute the organization, which was driven underground. After that its main activities were moved abroad, and it broke up into several peripheral groups.

FEDAI'YYUN   see PALESTINE ARAB GUERRILLA OR-
GANIZATION.

FEDERALISM, FEDERATIONS   see ARAB UNITY.

FEDERATION OF ARAB REPUBLICS (FAR)
see ARAB UNITY.

FEISAL I, IBN HUSSEIN   see HASHEMITES.

FEISAL IBN ABDEL AZIZ (of the House of Sa'ud) (1904/05–1975) King of SAUDI ARABIA 1964–1975. The second son of Abdel Aziz IBN SA'UD (after the death of two elder half-brothers). In 1927 his father appointed him governor, later with the title Viceroy, of the HIJAZ, which had recently been conquered from the Hashemite King HUSSEIN and his son Ali, and entrusted him with its integration into the Saudi kingdom. In 1928 Feisal was also made chairman of the Council of *Ulama* (Islamic savants), acting as an advisory state council. Prince Feisal frequently represented Saudi Arabia in foreign affairs and negotiations and, with Ibn Sa'ud maintaining no formal Council of Ministers in the Western pattern, was considered a kind of foreign minister. In 1953, after the death of Ibn Sa'ud and the succession of Sa'ud to the throne, Feisal's elder half-brother, Feisal was designated Crown Prince, Deputy Prime Minister (the King himself taking the Premiership) and Foreign Minister. A half-concealed fight for power between Sa'ud and flared up in 1958, when Saudi Arabia experienced a severe economic crisis and a deterioration of relations with EGYPT (with ABDEL NASSER and Sa'ud accusing each other of assassination plots). Sa'ud was forced to grant Feisal full powers in fiscal, internal and foreign affairs and to make him Prime Minister in 1962. Feisal instituted financial and administrative reforms, took saving measures and attempted to eliminate waste and corruption. He managed to retrieve the economic sit-

uation and pay all state debts by 1962. The struggle with King Sa'ud continued intermittently, with Feisal the virtual ruler. In 1964, Sa'ud demanded the restoration of his power, but Feisal refused and a new crisis ensued. On 2 November 1964, the Council of *Ulama* deposed Sa'ud (who went into exile) and proclaimed Feisal King.

During his reign, Feisal promoted and accelerated the development and modernization of Saudi Arabia, especially after the October 1973—which triggered the imposition of an oil embargo by the Arab oil producers on the US and Holland, reduced oil production, and sharp rise of oil prices, which brought an unprecedented level of revenues to the producers—led by Saudi Arabia. However, Feisal made few changes in the ultra-conservative system of government. He followed a more active, nationalist inter-Arab policy and became a much-respected all-Arab leader. He endeavored to mend relations with Egypt (which had again deteriorated as the two countries were involved, since 1962, on opposing sides in the Yemen Civil War), but frequently refused to go along with to ABDEL NASSER's policies and emerged as the leader of a bloc of conservative Arab states moderately pro-Western. He also cultivated relations with the Islamic states and was instrumental in the formation of a permanent consultative group of these states from 1969–1970. King Feisal was assassinated in March 1975 by his nephew, Feisal Ibn Musa'id, who was executed for the murder.

Of Feisal's eight sons, several fill senior positions. Prince Sa'ud Ibn Feisal (b. 1941) has served since 1975 as Foreign Minister, Turki (b. 1945) is Director of Foreign Intelligence.

FEISAL-WEIZMANN AGREEMENT   see ARAB-
ISRAEL CONFLICT.

FERTILE CRESCENT   see GREATER SYRIA.

FEZ PLAN   see ARAB-ISRAEL PEACEMAKING.

FLN   see FRONT DE LIBÉRATION NATIONALE.

FLOSY (Front for the Liberation of Occupied South Yemen). Underground nationalist organization in ADEN and South Arabia, founded in 1966 through a merger of several underground groups, reportedly supported, or even sponsored, by EGYPT. FLOSY was mainly an urban movement, based in Aden town, and had strong links with the trade unions. Its aim was to liberate South Arabia (later SOUTH YEMEN) from British rule and unite it with Yemen. FLOSY was at first considered the most radical, and the main nationalist faction; but it failed to develop a popular base in the tribal hinterland of Aden and evolve effective guerrilla formations.

In 1967, on the eve of independence, a more extremist group, the leftist "NATIONAL LIBERATION FRONT" (NLF), got the upper hand and eliminated FLOSY in bloody fighting; FLOSY's leaders were detained or went into exile, mostly to Yemen or Egypt (thus, e.g., Abdel-Qawwi Makkawi). For some years Yemen continued sustaining FLOSY, but the organization, in exile or underground, had no more significant influence on events in South Yemen.

FRANCE, FRENCH INTERESTS AND POLI-CIES
French interests in the Arab countries are complex and of long standing. France was deeply involved in the Middle East during the era of the Crusades (1096–1291), assuming a leading part in eight of them. In 1535, Francois I signed a Treaty of Friendship with the Ottoman Sultan Suleiman I. This gave France certain privileges or CAPITULATIONS, including French jurisdiction over French merchants, and virtually recognized France as the protector of Latin Christianity in the Empire. The capitulations were further extended in 1740, and by Napoleon in 1802.

Apart from direct interests, by the late eighteenth century, France came to perceive the Eastern Mediterranean as an arena of competition with its main European rival, BRITAIN. In 1798, Napoleon invaded EGYPT, to take away Britain's Indian possessions. He conquered Egypt (then ruled by a Mamluk viceroy under Ottoman sovereignty) and advanced into Palestine and SYRIA. However, he failed to conquer Acre and was unable to proceed beyond Sidon on the Lebanese coast. In 1799 he returned to France, and by 1801 the French Army in Egypt was forced to surrender to Britain. Although the expedition was spectacular, its main effects were in the cultural rather than the strategic domain. France played an active role in the diplomatic and military maneuvers of the Great Powers concerning the conflict between Muhammad Ali of Egypt and the Ottoman Sultan in the 1830s, and in protecting the OTTOMAN EMPIRE against RUSSIA—(the Crimean War, 1854–1856).

France granted its special protection to the MARONITES in LEBANON and intervened on their behalf in 1842–1845 and again in 1860. During this time, France pressurized the Sultan to establish Mount Lebanon as an autonomous district (*Mutasarrifiyya*), predominantly Christian. The Sultan had to concede this to France and the other Western Powers that supported it. This led to a considerable extension of French political and cultural influence. French interests were also active in the Ottoman Empire (railways, banking), Persia, and particularly Egypt. The SUEZ CANAL was devised and built by French engineers and predominantly with French capital. France, together with Britain, administered Egypt's foreign debts and was deeply involved in its economy. Even after the British occupation of Egypt (1882), which France bitterly resented, French economic interests and cultural influences in Egypt remained strong.

During the nineteenth century, France built its empire in the MAGHRIB, conquering ALGERIA in 1830 and incorporating it into France as fully French territory. In 1881–1883, France imposed a protectorate on TUNISIA and on MOROCCO in 1912. France's aspirations extended to East Africa, on the margins of the Arab world. It acquired DJIBOUTI in the 1880s. Its attempts to expand its African possessions in the direction of southern Sudan, led to a grave crisis with Britain (culminating in the Fashoda crisis, 1898). This crisis was resolved by France's retreat and the renunciation of any claims to SUDAN, as well as the Anglo-France *entente cordiale* of 1904.

France's claims to the LEVANT were put forward during World War I. Under the SYKES-PICOT AGREEMENT of 1916, France was to obtain possession of the coastal strip of Syria-Lebanon and most of Cilicia in south-east Anatolia. Furthermore, it gained as well as a sphere of influence including the Syrian hinterland and the Mosul province of Mesopotamia, as well as a share in an internationalized administration of Palestine. But in November 1918 the French and British Prime Ministers, Clemenceau and Lloyd George, signed an agreement in which France waived its claim to the Mosul area in favor of Britain, in return for a share in the oil resources of the area (and further compensation in Europe). France also had to acquiesce in a British MANDATE administration for Palestine. Plans for French rule in Cilicia were re-affirmed in the Peace Treaty of SÈVRES with TURKEY, in 1920 but that treaty was torn up by the Turkish nationalists and the partition of Anatolia was abandoned.

In return for its concessions, France was granted a Mandate over the LEVANT, (what is known today as Syria and Lebanon). The distinction between direct administration in the coastlands and guidance-and-influence in the Arab hinterland, stipulated by the Sykes-Picot Agreement, was dropped. In November 1919, French troops under General Gouraud replaced British troops along the Syrian coast. France recognized Amir Feisal's authority in the Syrian hinterland. However, when in the spring of 1920 Feisal accepted the Syrian crown, symbolizing complete independence, this was seen by France as a threat to its "rights" in Syria. General Gouraud's forces entered Damascus on 24 July 1920 and deposed Feisal, asserting French supremacy in Syria (see SYRIA and LEBANON). At first, General Gouraud split the French Mandate territory into four units: Greater Lebanon; the State of Damascus (including the Jabal DRUZE district); the State of Aleppo (including the ALEXANDRETTA district); and the Alawi Territory of Ladhiqiyya. Jabal Druze was granted special status in 1922, and the *Sanjaq* district of Alexandretta gained semi-autonomy in 1924. On 1 January 1925 the states of Aleppo and Damascus were unified as Syria. In 1925–1926 France had to suppress an armed rebellion in Syria.

France's endeavors to establish Western-type parliamentary institutions were more successful in Lebanon than in Syria. In the treaties of 1936, the Lion Blum Government granted Syria and Lebanon independence within three years, in return for a military pact stipulating the presence of French forces and bases and a privileged status for France. However, due to certain developments in France, such as the eclipse of the Socialist-led Popular Front and the preoccupation with the German and Italian danger, France did not ratify the two agreements, reverting on the eve of World War II to unqualified colonial-type rule under the Mandate. The danger of the approaching war also induced France to surrender the district of Alexandretta (Hatay, by the Turks), with its forty percent Turkish minority, to Turkey in June 1939 (see ALEXANDRETTA). At the same time, France and Turkey signed a pact of non-ag-

gression and mutual assistance. This aroused an outcry of the Syrian nationalists who had never acquiesced in the loss of this district.

During World War II, after the capitulation of France in June 1940, French administrators and officers in Syria and Lebanon under General Dentz put their support behind the Vichy authorities. An Italian Armistice Supervision Commission was stationed in the Levant, the presence of German and Italian troops was rumored, and Syria and Lebanon were expected to serve as the bridgehead of a fully fledged invasion of the Middle East. In June 1941, the forces of Britain and unoccupied France moved into Syria and Lebanon in a brief campaign. On the day of the invasion General Catroux declared on behalf of unoccupied France the end of the Mandate and the independence of Syria and Lebanon. Future relations with France were to be determined by a treaty. A British statement endorsed his proclamation, and General Catroux was appointed "Delegate General and plenipotentiary of unoccupied France in the Levant" (rather than the traditional "High Commissioner") and instructed to negotiate treaties with Syria and Lebanon.

However, the Syrian and Lebanese leaders, backed by the US and particularly Britain, were no longer prepared to conclude a treaty conferring upon France's special privileges. Furthermore, France was not willing to grant full independence without such a treaty. A bitter struggle ensued. A grave crisis erupted in November 1943, when the Lebanese government and Parliament formally abolished all articles of the Constitution that limited independence and granted France special privileges. The French arrested the Lebanese leaders, including President Bishara al-Khouri and Premier Riyad al-Sulh, but were compelled, mainly by a British ultimatum, to back down (the British Army being in war-time overall in command of the region). Serious clashes again broke out in Syria early in 1945, as the French refused to withdraw their troops from the Levant and to hand over to Syria the locally recruited "Special Forces". France again had to retreat following a British ultimatum. Early in 1946, the evacuation of French (and British) forces was discussed by the UN Security Council. Although no formal decision was adopted owing to a Soviet veto, France and Britain consented to withdraw their forces from Syria by April 1946 and from Lebanon by December 1946.

This marked the end of French predominance in the Levant.

The evacuation of French forces and the end of France's rule over Syria and Lebanon left France deeply embittered towards Britain, whom it regarded as the chief cause of its dislodgement from the Middle East. France always suspected Britain of scheming for a GREATER SYRIA HASHEMITE-led Federation designed to oust France. Some French economic and cultural influence remained, especially in Lebanon, because of that country's Christian character.

After World War II France took part in the provisional allied military administration of LIBYA. This involved the administration and maintenance of Fezzan Libya's southern province adjacent to its possessions in Algeria, Niger and Chad, and a military base there after Libya's independence in 1951. By agreement with Libya it evacuated that base in 1956, but retained some communication facilities until 1963.

France voted in favor of the partition of Palestine on 29 November 1947. Nonetheless, it delayed its recognition of Israel in order to allay Arab sensitivities. French officers served as UN truce observers in Palestine between 1948–1949, and were elected in December 1948 to the UN PCC(Palestine Conciliation Commission), with the US and Turkey. Although France had given generous assistance to Jewish Holocaust survivors, and had allowed the establishment of transit camps for Jews on their way to ISRAEL and various Zionist activities during the struggle toward independence, its ties with Israel continued to be marked by restraint. France persisted in regarding itself as tightly linked to Arab-Muslim interests, mainly in view of its North African possessions.

In the early and mid-1950s France was engaged in the Western powers' efforts to coordinate their influence in the Middle East by joining Britain and the US in the Tripartite Declaration of May 1950. An arms embargo was impressed on the parties to the Middle East conflict, guaranteeing the territorial status quo. France also participated, albeit in a minor way, in the attempts to establish a regional defense system linked with the West (see MIDDLE EAST DEFENSE ORGANIZATION). At this time France became preoccupied with Tunisia's and Morocco's claim to independence. This contest was resolved in 1955–1956 by the termination of the French Protectorate and both countries' complete independence. France's links with and influence over Tunisia and Morocco remained strong. However, initial French attempts to preserve a position of institutionalized privilege failed. The struggle over Algeria was more violent and protracted. It culminated in a rebellion and fully-fledged war from November 1954 until March 1962, when Algeria, too, became independent. Egypt and most of the Arab countries actively supported the Maghribi nationalists against France. That support, particularly for the Algerian rebels, affected French-Arab relations, inducing France to change its attitude and follow less pro-Arab policies. The Suez crisis of 1955–1956 and Egypt's nationalization of the Suez Canal Company in July 1956, led France to invade Egypt, in the Suez War, together with Britain and in secret coordination with Israel's Sinai War. Britain and France failed to achieve their objective and were compelled to withdraw. Egypt and most of the Arab countries broke off diplomatic relations with France. (Egypt also nationalized all French properties and interests.) France's relations with Israel now became an intimate, semi-secret alliance.

Algeria became independent in 1962 paving the way for the resumption of normal relations between France and the Arab states. Algeria was the last Arab country to restore relations was Egypt in spring 1963. De Gaulle, rejecting Arab pressures, proclaimed a doctrine of "parallelism" to guide France's dealings with both Israel and the Arab states. Gradually, however, the normalization of France's relations with the Arab states and French interests in the Middle East and North Africa and particularly in Algeria, (e.g. the oil resources of the Sahara), caused France to revert to a more pro-Arab policy. This was revealed in a drastic change of attitude on the eve of the Six-Day War in May–June 1967. De Gaulle opposed any act of intervention in the Straits of TIRAN to protect the freedom of navigation. He tried in vain to solve the crisis by Great Powers' diplomacy, and confidentially warned Israel not to start a pre-emptive war. On 3 June, France put a total embargo on the supply of arms and military equipment to the Middle East. Since Israel was the chief buyer of such equipment from France, the embargo was aimed almost exclusively there.

When Israel did open a pre-emptive war, de Gaulle never forgave it for having "fired the first shot"; Israel's protestations that the closing of the Straits of Tiran constituted a *casus belli* and was planned as the beginning of its destruction, left the French President unimpressed. At the UN, France took a distinctly pro-Arab position, demanding a total and unconditional Israeli withdrawal. In 1969 France took the initiative for the abortive talks on the Middle East by the UN Ambassadors of the Four Powers. The reversal in France's attitude was praised by the Arab countries, whereas relations with Israel steadily deteriorated. The embargo mainly affected fifty Mirage-V planes for which Israel had already paid. But following a retaliatory Israeli raid on Beirut airport on 28 December 1968, de Gaulle put a total embargo on arms supplies to Israel. The accession of Georges Pompidou to the Presidency in 1969 did not lead to a substantial change in French Middle Eastern policy. Feelers put out at the end of 1969 with a view to reverting to a selective embargo were withdrawn when five gunboats, built for Israel but kept back by France in accordance with the embargo, were taken smuggled out of Cherbourg harbor by Israeli teams in December 1969.

While maintaining its Middle Eastern arms embargo against Israel (and refunding the amounts Israel had paid), France broke it where Arab countries were concerned. In December 1969, it agreed to supply 110 Mirage jets to Libya (under its new, coup-born, QADHAFI regime), claiming that Libya was not a "front-line" country facing Israel and was therefore not covered by the embargo. From the 1970s France became a major supplier of arms to several Arab states. It also continued taking pro-Arab positions on various aspects of the ARAB-ISRAEL CONFLICT and in October 1975 expressed its official support for the Palestinian people's rights to participation in any negotiations; to self-determination; to "a homeland" or a state (in 1981). It also pushed the other countries of Europe, in the EEC, in the same direction; French influence was discerned, for instance, behind the pro-Arab EEC statement of November 1973; the 1980 Declaration of Venice and the initiative for a European-Arab dialogue. France also supported the admission of the PALESTINE LIBERATION ORGANIZATION (PLO) to various UN bodies (e.g., the conference on the Law of the Sea, 1974 in which other EEC countries abstained). Among Europe's leading statesmen, the French were the first to meet with ARAFAT and other PLO leaders. France was once

of the first European countries to allow the PLO to open an office in its territory (1975). France was unimpressed by, or indifferent to, Egyptian President AL-SADAT's peace moves of 1977, voicing sceptical reservations about the Camp David Agreements, since they provided no general settlement with all Arab states. After the accession of President Mitterrand in 1981, France followed a more balanced policy. It also took a modest part in the multinational force established in Sinai in 1982 under an Egypt-Israel agreement.

The years of France's pronounced pro-Arab policy on the Arab-Israel issue affected several areas. For instance, the French government neutralized a law enacted by the French National Assembly against economic discrimination in 1977, directed against the ARAB BOYCOTT on Israel. Even in the fight against terrorism, which affected France no less than other Western countries, France was not a full partner. Indeed, it was rumored, though never confirmed, that France had concluded, in about 1974, a secret "sanctuary agreement". The PLO granted PLO men free passage through and residence in France in return for a pledge that no terrorist acts would be committed in France. This pledge was not kept. In 1976, after the hijacking of a French airliner en route from Israel to Paris and the Israeli rescue operation of Entebbe (see TERRORISM), France refused to join the US and Britain in a Security Council resolution condemning all air piracy. In 1977 many were aghast when France deported, i.e. let go, a senior PLO terrorist leader, Abu Da'oud, who was accused of planning the 1972 Munich Olympic Games massacre. His extradition had been requested by both West Germany and Israel. Yet, in the 1980s France became the arena of many acts of terrorism.—Palestinian, Lebanese, Iranian and international, which it had to take measures against. Yet even now, many view its steps against terrorism as rather half-hearted.

During the Lebanese Civil War France still manifested a special interest in Lebanon, trying to play a role in mediating the inter-communal conflict. Yet by then much of its traditional influence in that country had faded out. After the Israeli Litani Operation in South Lebanon (1978), it joined UNIFIL, the "UN Interim Force in Lebanon", and in August–September 1982, allotted some 2,000 troops to a multinational force designed to assist and supervise the evacuation of Syrian and PLO forces from Beirut. France also actively assisted the actual transportation of the evacuated PLO forces—both those from Beirut in August–September 1982, and those from Tripoli in December 1983. When the multinational force was withdrawn in February–March 1984, France sent approximately eighty observers to monitor the intra-Lebanese ceasefire. This was a frustrating task, since that cease-fire was never fully operative. These observers were withdrawn early in 1986. Later, in November 1986, France also reduced its UNIFIL contingent from nearly 1,400 to about 500, restricting its task to logistics and maintenance only. This gradual but far-reaching reduction in France's involvement in Lebanon was predominantly due to increasing victimization of French personnel by the Lebanese Civil War and terrorism and its extension to France. Many French officers and men were killed or wounded serving with UNIFIL, the multinational force or as observers. Other Frenchmen were kidnapped and some of them murdered. A French Ambassador was assassinated in September 1981. Eighty-five French soldiers were killed by a terrorist car bomb at their headquarters in October 1983. Furthermore, it was becoming increasingly evident that the presence of French personnel could make no significant contribution to solving Lebanese problems.

French interests were also badly affected by Iran's Islamic Revolution (though it had given asylum to KHOMEINI in the years of his exile) and the IRAN-IRAQ WAR. Iran bitterly resented France being a main supplier of arms to Iraq and granted asylum to leaders and organizations of the regime's foes. Iran refused to reach an agreement on several disputes (outside our scope here) until France changed that policy. In June 1986, France expelled Mas'ud Rajavi, the leader of the Iranian anti-regime Mujahidin-i-Khalq, but this step did not satisfy Iran's demands.

Since the early 1980s, France has been involved in a conflict with Libya over Chad. It refused to take the responsibility for the defense of Chad, and temporarily acquiesced in Libya's de facto domination of northern Chad, but it has sent a small contingent of troops and applied political pressure to halt any further expansion by Libya. An agreement in September 1984 on the withdrawal of both French and Libyan troops was broken by Libya. France reinstated its partial military presence and reconfirmed

a "Red Line" at the sixteenth parallel which Libya would not be permitted to pass (see LIBYA). In 1987 the Libyan forces in Chad were defeated and forced to withdraw from the occupied area, apparently due to French involvement.

France's main interests in the Arab countries have remained centered on the three Maghrib countries—Algeria, Tunisia and Morocco. Since the 1960s (the end of the Algerian rebellion and Algeria's independence, 1962; the French-Tunisian Bizerta crisis, 1962; the agreement with Tunisia on former French properties, 1965; the evacuation of French bases in Algeria, 1967–1968), there have been no major crises in France's relations with the three countries. Nevertheless, those with Algeria were sometimes strained, for instance with the problem of Algerian migrants in France and the fate of former Algerian collaborators. Problems of oil and natural gas development and production also troubled French-Algerian relations. In 1965, an agreement was reached according to French companies (which had been the pioneers of Algeria's oil development) for a major share in the further, large expansion of Algeria's oil and gas economy. But, after several disputes over production and price policies, Algeria nationalized fifty-one percent of the French companies' holdings, and all gas production, in February 1971. As a result, France had to acquiesce. The French companies now became junior partners in Algeria's national oil combine, but Algeria remained a major source of oil and particular, liquefied gas for France. Protracted wrangles over the price of gas were resolved in an agreement of February 1982. Besides various economic enterprises and the supply of arms, oil was indeed a major French interest in the Arab countries. French companies had a 23.75% share in the Iraqi Petroleum Company since its inception, and a 6% share in Iran's oil consortium since 1954. Both these major holdings have since been fully nationalized and France has become a mere buyer of Iraqi and Iranian oil. French companies also operated or had a share in ABU DHABI, DUBAI, OMAN, QATAR, Tunisia and Libya. Some of these concessions have been formally nationalized. The foreign companies turned from concessionaires into operators, on behalf of the respective country's national oil company.

While the Arab countries have remained a major source of oil and gas for France, France (along with the rest of Western Europe) has become somewhat less dependent on Arab oil in the 1980s—*inter alia* due to the vigorous development of nuclear power and the saving of energy. France imported 125 million tons in 1979. More than sixty percent of this came from the Middle East. Four percent came from Algeria (not counting liquefied gas) and three from Libya. Nonetheless, its oil imports in 1985 were down to 73 million tons. Less than twenty percent came from the Middle East; five percent from Algeria and four percent from Libya. (The reduction of France's dependence on Arab oil could well have been one of the reasons for the gradual mitigation of its pro-Arab policies).

French interests in the 1990s focus primarily on economic deals with Iran, in competition with other European countries, primarily Germany, and in defiance of the US "Double Containment" strategy, aimed at pressuring Iraq and Iran to abide by the international rules and restricting their military capabilities. In Lebanon, following the election of Shirak to the Presidency in 1996, France renewed its interest in the Arab-Israeli peace process, particularly with regard to the Syrian and Lebanese fronts, despite Israel's reluctance to allow such a role due to the pro-Arab French perception among Israeli decision makers.

FRONT DE LIBÉRATION NATIONALE (FLN)

Algerian nationalist organization, founded underground in 1954 by a group of younger activists dissatisfied with the leadership of Messali Hajj and other established nationalist leaders and their parties (the MTLD and PPA, see ALGERIA). The younger group held armed struggle to be unavoidable and resolved to prepare for it. They formed an *Organization Secrète* (or *Spéciale*) for that purpose in the early 1950s and later seceded from the MTLD, forming the *Comité Revolutionnaire pour l'Unité et l'Action* (CRUA), which transformed itself in 1954 into the FLN, led by Ahmad BEN BELLA, Belkacem Krim, Hussein Ait-Ahmad, Muhammad Khidr and others, and was headquartered in Cairo and later Tunis. In November 1954 the FLN opened an armed struggle against FRANCE. It established a strong guerrilla force which developed into a fully-fledged army, and also claimed the political leadership. It led an unrelenting armed struggle for over seven years, finally securing Algeria's independence in 1962.

The FLN fought and won an internal (factional) struggle over the formation of independent Algeria's governing institutions. It established itself as the country's single party dominating the government and providing all the leading functionaries. Through this it eliminated all rival groups and also "purged" and ousted all factions within the FLN that opposed Ben Bella's dominant group (see ALGERIA, BEN BELLA). Its leadership officially determined the candidate for the Presidency and all the National Assembly candidates in the elections which were, in reality, well-orchestrated plebiscites sure to endorse the prepared lists. This procedure of selection and appointment was also applied for most other leading positions.

By the 1980s the FLN appeared as a privileged bureaucratic elite which used the socialist system for its own economic advantage, and was responsible for the gross mismanagement of the Algerian economy. Following the 1988 riots, President Ben-Jedid launched political liberalization which legalized opposition parties, broke the FLN's stranglehold on Algerian politics, and enhanced his own power.

During the first round of the parliamentary elections in December 1991, the FLN won 16 seats (twenty-three percent of the votes) compared with the ISLAMIC SALVATION FRONT's 188. The military, which took power in January 1992, blamed the FLN for the country's ills, removing it from the center of power. Under a new general secretary Abdel-Hamid Mehri the FLN joined seven other parties in signing the National Pact in January 1995 calling for the restoration of democracy in Algeria. Mehri was deposed by the party's old guard in February 1996, and was replaced by Boualem Benhamouda, who sought a rapprochement with the military regime. The FLN supported President ZEROUAL's policies and constitutional amendments throughout 1996, but did not regain its position as the ruling party.

FRONT FOR THE LIBERATION OF OCCUPIED SOUTH YEMEN   see FLOSY.

FUDA, FARAJ (1945–1992) Egyptian politician and liberal thinker, born in Dumyat in al-Zarqa district. Attained a doctorate in agricultural economics. He wrote about ten books and many articles in the main journals and magazines in EGYPT and outside, primarily in reaction to religious extremism which he

viewed as an existential danger to Egypt, its future and its culture. He was a member of the New WAFD Party, but quit over political differences in the mid-1980s mainly because of its collaboration with the MUSLIM BROTHERHOOD movement in the general elections. In 1986, Fuda failed to be elected to the Egyptian Council (Parliament). He tried to establish an independent political party called *al-Mustaqbal* (the Future) with the prinicipal aim of economic and social liberalism. He supported peace with ISRAEL providing the solution to the Palestinian problem due to his vehement stand against religious extremism.

Fuda was murdered by members of the Jihadic Islamic Group (*al-Jama'a al-Islamiyya*). In his writings he sharply challenged the zealots' demand to establish an Islamic state ruled by a Caliph to implement the Islamic law (SHARI'A). He was convinced that this demand would lead the country back to the Middle Ages. He stood firmly promoting the separation of religion from state. He called to strengthen Egypt's relations with the West and attempted to integrate Western values such as sciences and technology. He demanded more democracy calling for human rights. His assassination in June 1992 was a turning point in the conciliatory attitude of the government toward the Islamist militants. This has been illustrated in its continuous campaign against Islamic violence, manifested in the publication of books extolling the positive facet of ISLAM and condemning violence of any kind.

al-FUJAIRA   One of the seven sheikhdoms of TRU-CIAL OMAN which, until 1971 a British Protectorate

and in that year formed together with other shikhdoms, the Federation of the UNITED ARAB EMIRATES (UAE). Fujaira is one of the smallest of the seven—with an area of 450 sq. miles (about 1,050 sq. km.). In the 1960s its population was approximately 10,000. In a census of 1975 this had increased to 26,000. According to estimates of the mid-1980s, the figure had increased to approximately 35,000. Situated on the east coast of the Trucial Oman peninsula, Fujaira was in the past part of SHARJA. In 1952 it was recognized by the British protecting power as a separate sheikhdom. It remains closely linked to Sharja, under the 1960 cooperation agreement. Fujaira is ruled by a Sheikh of the al-Shjriqi clan.

In 1966 a concession for the exploloration of oil was granted to a German company. Later the international Shell company took a sixty percent interest. Since no OIL was found, the licence was canceled in 1971. Other companies are prospecting for offshore oil. So far, no oil discovery has been reported.

Thus, while Fujaira benefits from some of the UAE's overall wealth and development, it has not enjoyed the spectacular growth of the richer, oil-producing members of the Federation, such as ABU-DHABI or DUBAI. An oil pipeline from the Abu Dhabi-Dubai area to Fujaira and the development of a major oil port in Fujaira are planned. These would eliminate the need to ship the oil through the straits of HORMUZ.

FUNCTIONAL COMPROMISE   see ARAB-ISRAEL PEACEMAKING.

G

GADDAFI   see QADHAFI.

GAP (GUNEDOGU ANADOLU PROJESI)   see TURKEY.

GAZA STRIP   The only part of historic Palestine left under Egyptian control at the end of the1948 War of Independence, and whose borders were acknowledged in the February 1949 armistice agreement between ISRAEL and EGYPT. The southern coastal

town of Gaza—a biblical town, one of the five cities of the Philistines—was a district capital under the British Mandate and the largest exclusively ARAB town in Palestine. It was primarily Muslim, with a small Christian community (a medieval Jewish community had declined in the eighteenth century, was revived in 1882, but had left after the riots of 1929). In 1948, at the end of the Mandate, the population of Gaza was approximately 40,000. During and after the 1948 War of it grew to over 100,000, due to the influx of REFUGEES from the areas that then became Israel.

The area that came to be known as the Gaza Strip was not, before 1948, an entity or a term in use. It is the area occupied by the invading Egyptian Army in the 1948 War (see ARAB-ISRAEL CONFLICT)— 25 miles (40 km.) long and 4–9 miles (6.5–14.5 km.) wide—an area of about 146 sq. miles (378 sq. km.) The population in 1948—including Gaza town—was 70,000–100,000. During and after the war this grew to 200,000–250,000, due to the influx of refugees. In 1967, when the region was occupied by Israel, there were 380,000 Palestinian residents, which, in the mid-1980s, became over 500,000. Some sixty percent or more were refugees from the 1948 War and their descendants. (Precise figures are in dispute; UNRWA, the UN Relief and Works Agency for Refugees, has over 400,000 on its registers.) In 1997, the area's population was over 900,000, about half of them refugees. One-third of the Gaza Strip population are refugees, residing in eight large refugee camps. Population growth in this area was one of the highest in the world—six percent in 1992—explaining the relatively low average age of the population (in 1996, forty-six percent were under the age of fifteen).

As such, the Gaza Strip is one of the most densely populated areas in the world. In 1986, 667 sq. miles (1730 per sq. km.), compared to 764 sq. miles (198 sq. km), in Israel and 744 sq. miles (193 sq. km.), in the WEST BANK.

The economy of the Gaza Strip itself could not support and employ so large a population, and from 1948 to 1967 a large proportion was unemployed and entirely dependent on the rations distributed by UNRWA, which led to constant emigration to the oil countries and elsewhere. After 1967, the migration tendencies continued, a growing number of Palestinians found employment in Israel (about fifty percent of the labor force) and material conditions as measured in housing conditions and the possession of cars, refrigerators, washing machines and other electrical appliances etc., improved. From 1967, the Gaza Strip economy has been strongly dependent on Israel: ninety percent of the Strip's import comes from Israel and more than eighty percent of Gaza Strip's produce has been marketed in Israel. The economic conditions of the Gaza Strip were seriously affected by the Palestinian uprising (INTIFADA) of 1987–1993. The GDP fell by thirty to fifty percent. In addition, the cease of financial aid from the Gulf oil monarchies in the wake of the Iraqi invasion of KUWAIT in Augutst 1990, diminished the remittances from these countries by fifty percent. Furthermore, since the early 1990s the number of Gaza Strip workers employed in Israel has been constantly shrinking to an average of twenty-five to forty percent, bringing unemployment level in this area to an average of fifty-five percent.

The Israel-Egypt Armistice Agreement of 1949, based on the positions held by the respective forces at the end of the fighting, confirmed Egypt's occupation of the Gaza Strip. In contrast to JORDAN, which annexed the area of Palestine it had occupied in the War, Egypt never annexed the Gaza Strip. Though Egypt claimed special responsibility for the area—even after 1967, when it was no longer in occupation—it never claimed it as part of its national territory, and continued to maintain its Palestinian identity. In September 1948, Egypt supervised the formation in Gaza of the "All Palestine Government" (hukumat umum filastin), claiming control of all of Palestine, including Israel and the Jordan-occupied parts. During the three weeks in which that government existed in Gaza (it moved to Cairo in view of the Israeli offensive of mid-October), however, this government had not been given any self-governing authority over the area under Egyptian control and soon faded out. A formal declaration that it had ceased to operate was issued, by the ARAB LEAGUE, only in 1952 (see PALESTINE ARABS).

From 1949 onwards, the Gaza Strip was administered by a military governor appointed by the Egyptian Minister of War. In 1958, the Governor appointed an Executive Council, including local notables, and a Legislative Council, partly nominated by indirect elections. Little was heard about their activities. In the early 1950s, the Gaza Strip became a constant source of tension between Israel and Egypt due to ongoing infiltration into Israel by its Palestinian residents. This was caused mainly by economic hardships, but increasingly became violent, leading to the murder of civilians. Although Egyptian authorities attempted to prevent such activities, Israel held Egypt responsible for those activities, retaliating by raiding civilian and Egyptian military targets in the Strip.

In February 1955, Israel mounted a large-scale raid against an Egyptian military base in the Strip, later cited by President ABDEL NASSER as a major reason for his conviction that no peaceful settlement with Israel was possible. In 1955–1956 Egypt became actively involved in dispatching "self-sacrificers" (FIDA'IYYUN) for intelligence and sabotage missions inside Israel. The military escalation that had been caused by the incursions from the Gaza Strip and Israeli retaliations, and Egypt's arms deal with Czechoslovakia signed in May 1955, were the main factors leading to the Sinai Campaign of 1956, in the course of which the Gaza Strip was occupied by Israel.

When Israel was compelled to withdraw, early in 1957, the Gaza Strip was returned to Egyptian military administration—contrary to Israel's expectations and assurances it thought it had received; but a UN Emergency Force, UNEF, was stationed there. In the following decade, the border was relatively quiet, on both sides. In June 1967 Israel again occupied the Gaza Strip and placed the region under military government until late 1981, when its title was changed to Civil Administration. During the first years of the Israeli occupation, the Gaza Strip became a center of sabotage and terrorist activity, representing the large concentration of refugees and the social and economic frustration that had accumulated in the Gaza Strip (certainly more than in the West Bank taken from Jordan); the unrest, which peaked in 1970–1971, was brutally suppressed by 1972. One of the ways in which the Israeli administration tried to cope with the growing wave of violence was by "thinning out" the overcrowded refugee camps and re-housing some of the inhabitants, but this was denounced and resisted by most of the population, portrayed as an attempt to wipe out the refugee problem.

During the years of occupation, Israel established nineteen settlements in the Gaza Strip with a population of approximately 4,500, based mostly on agriculture and taking nearly one third of its land, adding further burden on its poor land resources.

Employment in Israel enabled a constant economic growth in the Gaza Strip, parallel to that in Israel, until 1977, when following the ascendancy of Likud-led Government in Israel that growth slowed down due to growing restrictions on entry of agricultural produce from the Strip. The Strip's economic situation was largely affected by political and geographical complications. While West Bank produce was freely exported to Jordan, and through

Jordan to other Arab countries, similar arrangements for the produce of the Gaza Strip, particularly its citrus fruit, frequently met difficulties in Jordan and had to be exported to East European markets which were not always available.

In addition, longtime over-exploitation of aquifer water led to their growing salinity, degrading their quality and imposing another limitation to the possibilities of agricultural economy.

Under Israeli occupation the unbalanced social structure of the Strip deteriorated, deepening the collapse of the already weak indigenous authority based on the original population. Municipal elections, like those held in the West Bank, were not held in Gaza or any other town in the Strip. The Mayor of Gaza was dismissed in January 1971, and the man appointed to replace him, Rashad al-Shawa—of the Gaza Strip's chief clan of notables—was also dismissed in October 1972. He was reappointed in 1975, and dismissed again in 1982. Economic needs, namely, the option of exporting agricultural produce to, and through Jordan, led al-Shawa to foster close relations with the Jordanian regime, but the general leaning among the Gaza Strip population was markedly in favor of the PALESTINE LIBERATION ORGANIZATION (PLO), and particularly of *Fatah* with Fa'iz Abu Rahma as its leading figure, and, to a less extent, with the leftist groups of the PLO, with Shafi HaidarABDEL as the most salient spokesman.

From the mid-1970s, the MUSLIM BROTHERHOOD movement grew steadily as part of the rising trend in Egypt. This led to the proliferation of Islamic welfare and educational associations, construction of mosques, and growing number of followers among the youth, especially in the refugee camps. From the late 1970s, the Islamic Agglomerate (*al-mujamma' al-islami*), was led by Sheikh Ahmad Yassin, former activist in the Muslim Brotherhood Society in Egypt. Israeli authorities looked favorably to that trend, perceiving it as a counterbalance to the PLO's stature in the Gaza Strip. Thus, in the years of 1967–1986, the number of mosques in the Gaza Strip doubled, from 77 to 150, rising to 200 by 1989. Most of the new mosques were private, independent of the existing administration of Islamic endowments (*awqaf*) that was controlled by the Civil Administration.

By the mid-1980s, the Islamic University in Gaza became the center of activity of the Muslim Brotherhood in the Gaza Strip, which by then had manifested discernible measure of penetration into various public institutions, primarily professional associations.

Parallel to this trend, marked by a reformist approach to transform the society into an Islamic one, a national-activist Islamic approach also appeared in the Gaza Strip, conducting a Holy War (JIHAD) against Israel for the liberation of Palestine. This stream, represented by the Islamic *Jihad*, was one of the triggers for the eruption of the Palestinian uprising (INTIFADA) on 9 December 1987 in the Gaza Strip. This then expanded to the West Bank (see also ISLAMIC RADICALISM AND MOVEMENTS).

The *intifada* led to the emergence of HAMAS as a military arm of the Muslim Brotherhood movement, which posed a serious challenge to ARAFAT's PLO by offering an Islamic breed of nationalism and tacitly portraying itself as a moral and political alternative to the PLO's secular nationalism (see HAMAS).

According to the Oslo Declaration of Principles (DOP) signed by Israel and the PLO on 13 September 1993, most of the Gaza Strip (some sixty percent of the territory), with the exception of the Israeli settlements and buffer zones, together with the town of Jericho in the Jordan Valley, was designated for the first phase of establishing the self-governing PALESTINIAN AUTHORITY (PA), that was established in May 1994. Under the DOP and Cairo Agreement, elaborating the transfer of authorities from Israel to the PA, the latter was allowed to build a seaport and an airport, and have a "secure pass" to the West Bank, since the two Palestinian regions had been recognized by the Oslo Agreement as one political, economic and geographical unit.

GCC   see GULF COOPERATION COUNCIL.

GEMAYEL   see JUMAYYIL.

GENEVA PEACE CONFERENCE   see ARAB-ISRAEL PEACEMAKING.

al-GHANOUSHI, RASHED (b. 1941)   A prominent radical Islamic political leader and thinker; currently leader of "*al-Nahda*" movement in TUNISIA; has been in political exile in London since 1989.

Al-Ghanoushi was born in Al-Khama, south-east Tunisia to a peasant family. As a child he received a traditional upbringing. In the early 1960s he studied at Cairo University and continued his studies at Damascus University where in 1968 he received his Masters degree in Philosophy. During that period he was influenced by pan-Arab ideas and was a member of the BA'TH Party. He started a Ph.D. program at the Sorbonne but was forced to leave due to family obligations. He underwent an ideological change and became closer to Islam.

After his return to Tunisia he taught Philosophy at a high school. In the early 1970s he became involved in Islamic activities. At first he was active in a regime-supported group that was intended as a counterweight to the left-wing student bodies. Later on he established an independent group that concentrated on cultural Islamic activities, mainly on campus.

At the end of the 1970s with the growing discontent of the socioeconomic policies of BOURGUIBA's regime (see TUNISIA), his movement became more politically orientated. This was reflected in the broader-based activities that embraced additional realms of society—mainly the working class.

With the liberalization of the Tunisian political system in 1981, Ghaoushi wished to form a party named "The Movement of Islamic Tendency" (*Harakat al-Itijah al-Islami*). He encountered strong disapproval from the regime and the movement was subjected to a series of repressing measures culminating in Ghanoushi's arrest on charges of forming an illegal organization. Ghanoushi was sentenced to eleven years imprisonment. He was released in 1984 as part of the political pardons given by Bourguiba following food riots earlier that year.

Between 1984 and 1987, Ghanoushi's party was active in the political arena despite the restrictions imposed on Ghanoushi himself. During this period the party strengthened its ties with opposition parties, most significantly the Social-Democratic Party of Ahmed Mestiri. In March 1987, Ghanoushi was arrested again on charges of conspiring to overthrow Bourguiba's regime with Iranian aid. He was sentenced to life imprisonment with hard labor.

With the rise to power of BEN-ALI ZEIN AL-ABIDIN (November, 1988), Ghanoushi was released and it seemed that a new era in the relations between the Islamic Movement and the regime had commenced. Ghanoushi and other opposition leaders signed a national pact calling for the right for political Parties to secure political rights. However it soon became apparent that Ben-Ali had no intention of revising the policies of his predecessor regarding Ghanoushi. Indeed, in April 1989, the authorities refused to recognize the right of Ghanoushi's party (that had changed its name to the "Renaissance Party"—*Hizb al-Nahda*) to participate in the elections that took place in May that year. Following that, Ghanoushi moved to London where he still lives today. With the growing repression of his movement by Ben-Ali, Ghanoushi focused mainly on writing and participating in international Islamic forums. Reportedly, Ghanoushi has a good relationship with the Islamic regime in SUDAN and IRAN. Indeed, he possesses a Sudanese diplomatic passport.

Since 1989, disagreements regarding the nature of the Party's policy toward the current regime in Tunisia have resulted in several splits which have weakened the status of *al-Nahda*. For example, a faction headed by Muhammad Ali al-Hourani that advocated a more violent policy toward the regime, broke away and founded a new movement named *La Front Islamique Du Salut*.

Apart from heading the *al-Nahda* movement, Ghanoushi is heralded as one of the more prominent ideologists of Sunni Radical Islam. He has published numerous books and articles on a variety of subjects that are on the agenda of the Islamic Movement such as democracy, human rights and the treatment of minorities and women. Some of his famous works are: "General Liberties in the Islamic State" (*al-Huriyyat al-amma fi al-Dawla al-Islamia*), and "The Rights of Non-Muslims in the Islamic State" (*Huquq al-Muwatana*). In his works Ghanoushi presents a more moderate approach to the issues such as democracy and women's rights etc., than do other radical Islamic ideologists. In most cases, the underlying motive is the prospect of possible political gains rather than an authentic liberal approach.

Since the early 1990s Ghanoushi, alongside with Hassan AL-TURABI, leader of the MUSLIM BROTHERS in Sudan, has become recognized as a leader of a new political trend in radical Islam.

GHASSEMLOU, ABDULRAHMAN see KURDS.

al-GHAZALI, ZAINAB (b.1918) A leading figure among Muslim women activists in Egypt since the 1940s. Born to a prosperous cotton merchant, al-Ghazali attended the Islamic Law College of al-Azhar.

In 1936 she formed the Muslim Women's Society, after becoming disillusioned by the Egyptian Feminist Union, led by Huda Sha'arawi. The society undertook welfare activities, ran an orphanage, assisted poor families and helped Muslim women study Islam. Eventually, it joined forces with the MUSLIM BROTHERS, led by Hasan al-Banna. From 1965 to 1972, under ABDEL NASSER's regime, al-Ghazali was imprisoned for her activism, and the Muslim Women's Society was dissolved. Since her imprisonment, al-Ghazali has continued to promote Islam and women's traditional roles in her lectures and writings. She has written an autobiography, entitled Days From My Life *Ayyam min hayati*.

GLUBB (PASHA), SIR JOHN BAGOT (1897–1986) British officer and commander of the Jordanian Army 1939–1956. Glubb served in IRAQ (1920–1930) and in 1930 he went to Transjordan, where he organized BEDOUIN units within the Arab Legion, the Transjordanian Army. He became the Legion's Second-in-Command and from 1939, its commander (from 1948—Chief of the General Staff), attaining the Jordanian rank of *Fariq*—Lieutenant-General. Although he served JORDAN under contract (not seconded from the British Army), the nationalists in Jordan and other Arab countries regarded him as a symbol of British imperialist domination. They blamed him for the limitation imposed on Jordan's military role in the Palestine War of 1948, its non-adherence to Arab overall Strategic military plans, and specificially the Arab Legion's failure to capture West JERUSLAEM, the loss of Ramle and Lydda, as well as for the Jewish military successes in general (see ARAB-ISRAEL CONFLICT). As the tide of nationalism rose in Jordan after the war, and King HUSSEIN felt compelled to ally himself with EGYPT and SYRIA, the King abruptly dismissed Glubb in March 1956. Glubb retired to BRITAIN and wrote a few books on Arab history and his role in Jordan, and continued expressing strongly pro-Arab views, especially on the Arab-Israeli Conflict

GÖKALP, ZIYA (1875?–1924) Turkish poet and writer. The theorist of Turkish nationalism. Born in Diyarbekir (Eastern Anatolia), Gökalp made contact with the YOUNG TURKS at an early stage, and after the revolution of 1908 he was elected to the council of the "Committee of Union and Progress" in

Salonika. There (and later in Istanbul where he became Professor of Sociology at the University) Gökalp wrote his main nationalist essays and became the spiritual leader of the Young Turks. After the Proclamation of the Republic, 1923, he was elected to the National Assembly. Prior to the dissolution of the OTTOMAN EMPIRE, Gökalp favored the preservation of the supranational state, but called for the revival and promotion of Turkish national culture, the acceptance of European scientific and technical knowledge, and the relegation of Islam to an ethical and personal religion. For some time an advocate of PAN TURKISM, his ideology later identified more with that of ATATÜRK. His social and cultural ideas paved the way for many reforms during the Republican period.

His book, *The History of Turkish Civilization*, was written a short time before he died with only one of its volumes completed.

GOLAN HEIGHTS Part of the Kuneitra and Fiq district in SYRIA, occupied by ISRAEL in the course of the 1967 War (see ARAB-ISRAEL CONFLICT). Overlooking the Jordan Valley and the Sea of Galilee, the area constituted part of the Kingdom of David and Solomon in biblical times. There exists many archeological remains of Jewish settlements from the period of the Second Temple until the fourth century BC. Following World War I the area became part of Mandatory Syria under French rule. However, the border separating the area from Mandatory Palestine, as agreed between FRANCE and BRITAIN in 1923, included the upper part of the Jordan River and the Sea of Galilee within Palestine.

Following the 1948–1949 Arab-Israel War (see ARAB-ISRAEL CONFLICT), Israel and Syria signed an Armistice Agreement. This created demilitarized zones which later became a constant source of friction and military clashes between the two countries. Syria turned the Golan Heights into a stronghold dominating the whole Upper Jordan and Huleh Valleys and their settlements. In the course of the 1960s, Syrian shelling of Israeli settlements—in response to Israeli attempts to cultivate demilitarized zones—increased. The escalation of this was the direct reason for the eruption of the 1967 War. Despite reservations by Israeli Minister of Defense Moshe DAYAN during the Six-Day War, he finally ordered the Israel Defense Forces to occupy the Golan Heights. This caused a flee of most of the Syrian population (about 40,000, mostly in the town of Kuneitra). Only 3,000 DRUZE remained, located in the northern part of the area.

At the beginning of the Yom Kippur War (see ARAB-ISRAEL CONFLICT), the Syrians opened a surprise attack and reoccupied part of the Golan Heights. By the second stage of the battles they were driven back, and Israel expanded the territory under its control by about 8 sq. miles (20 sq. km.). According to the Syrian-Israeli Disengagement Agreement of May 1974 (see ARAB-ISREAL PEACEMAKING) Israel returned to Syria an area which included the ghost-town of Kuneitra. On both sides of the cease-fire line buffer zones and areas with thinned-out forces were created, and a UN observer force was stationed in the area (UNDOF).

On 14 December 1981 the Israeli Knesset (see ISRAEL) adopted the Golan Heights Law. This applied the Israeli law, jurisdiction and administration to the Golan Heights. It was condemned by most states of the world and resulted in a temporary stoppage of arms deliveries from the US to Israel. Following the de facto annexation of the Golan Heights, the Druze population was granted Israeli identity cards, which caused unrest within this population; parts of which continued to regard itself as Syrian.

From the beginning of the 1980s until the beginning of the 1990s, the debate in Israel on the future of the territories occupied during the 1967 War focused on the WEST BANK and GAZA STRIP not the Golan Heights. This was because the chances for a peace agreement with Syria appeared remote, and as the Syrian shelling of Israeli settlements below the Golan Heights were well remembered. However, the Madrid Conference of October/November 1991 (see ARAB-ISRAEL PEACEMAKING) and the opening of bilateral talks between Israel and Syria, raised the issue of the future of the Golan Heights on the Israeli national agenda. The official position of the Likud at the time was that there should be no Israeli withdrawal from the Golan Heights and that the formula for peace making with Syria should be "peace for peace". This was despite the fact that Syria had made its position clear in that it expected the same formula which had been applied in the case of the Sinai Peninsula (i.e. the whole of the Sinai in return for peace) to apply to the Golan Heights. In the Labor Party platform towards the elections to the thirteenth Knesset (1992), it was stated that within the framework of a peace treaty with Syria "the settlement and military presence and control of Israel (on the Golan Heights) would continue" but that the principle of territorial compromise (see ARAB-ISRAEL PEACEMAKING) would be applied on all fronts—including the Golan Heights. Following the establishment of the government by Yitzhak RABINin July 1992, there was some progress in the Syrian-Israeli peace talks, which gave rise to an aggressive propaganda campaign in Israel by those opposed to any Israeli withdrawal. Even though the Rabin government never gave Syria an official undertaking to return the whole of the Golan Heights to Syria in return for peace, Israeli Minister for Foreign Affairs Shimon PERES declared on several occasions that in the past Israel had recognized the fact that the Golan Heights constituted part of Syrian sovereignty. Yet in talks with the Americans, Rabin was reported to have agreed to an Israeli withdrawal to the international boundary with Syria in return for full peace and normalization of relations between the two countries. The position of the Labor Party on the issue toward the elections to the fourteenth Knesset (1996) was that before any Israeli undertaking to withdraw from the Golan Heights either new elections or a referendum on the issue would take place. The government established by Binyamin NETANYAHU in June formally rejected any substantial withdrawal from the Golan Heights.

Since 1967 Israel has established thirty rural settlement on the Golan Heights and one urban center (Katzrin). The total population of the Golan Heights is 30,000, of which over half are Druze.

GREATER ISRAEL A term customarily used as a translation of the Hebrew expression *Eretz Yisrael Hashlemah*, which literally means "the integral Land of Israel." The term, used primarily by the Israeli Right since 1967, rejects any sort of territorial compromise in Eretz Yisrael. It relates to all the territories west of the Jordan River, held by Israel since June 1967, which are to be brought, according to the proponents of Greater Israel, under Israeli sovereignty. Most proponents of the idea reject the notion that the Palestinian population of the WEST BANK and GAZA STRIP should be granted Israeli citizenship. The idea was initially advocated by secular nationalists, but gained growing adherence from the national religious stream, who added to it a religious-Messianic dimension. The religious adherents of the Greater

Israel idea view the transfer of any part of the Land of Israel to the Palestinian Authority as a violation of the *halacha* (the Jewish religious law).

GREATER SYRIA (*Suria al-kubra*), A geographical and political term, corresponding to an area historically identified as "*bilad al-sham*" ("country of the north", that is, north of the Arabian Peninsula) or the Fertile Crescent, encompassing today's SYRIA, IRAQ, LEBANON, JORDAN and historic PALESTINE. As such, it had never been an administrative or political unit. Until the dismemberment of the OTTOMAN EMPIRE in 1918, these countries were divided into a number of provinces (*vilayet*); Basra, Baghdad, Mosul, Aleppo, Damascus and Beirut, the autonomous district (*Sanjaq, Mutasarifia*) of Mount Lebanon and the special district of JERUSALEM. As protagonists of Arab independence and leaders of the ARAB REVOLT during World War I, the HASHEMITE Sharif Hussein of Mecca and his sons, Ali, Feisal and ABDALLAH planned to include the Fertile Crescent in an Arab kingdom. They envisaged a federative structure consisting of three kingdoms: HIJAZ, with Mecca and Medina as its main cities, and two Fertile Crescent kingdoms, Iraq, and Syria at large, including also Lebanon, Palestine and Transjordan with possible autonomy to JEWS in Palestine and CHRISTIANS in Lebanon. Amir Feisal ibn Hussein indeed tried to establish an Arab kingdom of Greater Syria (1918–1920), of which he was proclaimed king in March 1920. However, arrangements by the Great Powers during and after the Paris Peace Conference of 1918–1920, divided the Fertile Crescent into smaller political entities under separate MANDATES, with BRITAIN administering Iraq and Palestine (including Transjordan) and FRANCE administering Syria and Lebanon; these separate entities became firmly established and eventually independent states (Palestine was partitioned twice: in 1922, when Transjordan was separated, and in 1948, when ISRAEL was founded). The concept of the Fertile Crescent as a single political entity, however, persisted, as did the idea of "Greater Syria". In fact, they came to be identified, respectively, with Feisal of Iraq and Abdallah of Transjordan, both of whom aspired to and competed for establishing a regional unity under their leaderships. Aware of the crucial role of Britain in realizing their ambitions, the Hashemite rulers presented their plans as a panacea to the worstening problem of Palestine, by offering autonomy to the Jews in Palestine and continued, but limited, Jewish immigration to that country. Iraqi plans for a Fertile Crescent Federation were presented by King Feisal as early as December 1929, following the Western Wall riots in Palestine four months earlier. After Feisal's death in 1933, his idea remained high on the agenda of his followers, primarily Nuri al SA'ID, until the 1958 military coup in Iraq which deposed this dynasty. Amir (later King) Abdallah's version of Greater Syria was initially fostered by groups of Arab-Syrian Nationalists, but also reflected Abdallah's Revisionist ambitions and dissatisfaction with his small, poor and scarcely populated emirate. Both Hashemite concepts of regional unity were bitterly opposed by France, and as long as the French ruled, Syria had little hope of realization. The French always suspected that the "Greater Syria" notion was a British plot to oust them from the LEVANT, and many Arabs also viewed it as a British scheme; but official British support for a "Greater Syria" plan was never more than partial and half-hearted. After the conquest of Syria by British forces in 1941 from the French Vichy regime, and the scales of the war shifted in the Allies' favor (when the French rule in the Levant seemed to have ended) the Hashemite rulers in Amman and Baghdad reiterated their respective ambitions for Arab unity. In early 1943, Iraqi Prime Mininster Nuri al-Said submitted to the British his "Blue Book" containing a program for the unification of the Fertile Crescent. Abdallah, on his part, revived the Greater Syria idea, launching public overtures to Syrian opposition leaders and political groups, which triggered much tension with the Damascan ruling elite.

The resentment demonstrated by the Syrian ruling National Block to Abdallah's declared plans clearly represented concern for what seemed to be threatening the long-awaited Syrian independence. Until May 1946 Transjordan was still under British Mandate and Abdallah considered the epitome of Britains' stooges in the region, while Syria stood on the verge of independence. In March 1946, after a new treaty with Britain offered Jordan independence and Abdallah became king, he belived that the time was ripe to take bolder steps. In November 1946, at a public session of Parliament, he declared his intention to work toward the union of "the natural Greater Syria", incorporating Syria, Jordan, Lebanon and Palestine, under his crown; he implied that he

would offer the Jews of Palestine an autonomous status within his Greater Syria. (At the same time he was conducting secret talks with the Jewish Agency on a partition of Palestine between them). In 1947 Abdallah published a voluminous "White Paper" on Greater Syria, in which the idea was elaborated and justified by historical and ideological arguments.

Abdallah's scheme had very few open supporters. Among them were a faction of Aleppo politicians from the Syrian People's Party and a small group of Damascas politicians (Hassan al-Hakim, Munir al-Ajlani et al.); some others supported the plan secretly. Publicly, the Greater Syria plan was attacked by the ruling elites in Syria while the Lebanese Christians categorically refused to become part of a Muslim state. The ruling National Bloc in Syria refused to renounce Syria's independence and turn it into a province of a Hashemite-ruled kingdom. The Saudis, who in 1925 took over Hijaz and dismissed King Hussein, became the most ardent antagonist of any Hashemite plan to establish a strong political unity on their northern borders which might threaten their own position in the Arabian Penninsula. Egypt also opposed a Hashemite-led Greater Syria as an undesirable expansion of Hashemite power.

The resumption of Hashemite unity plans during World War II and perceived British encouragement for the idea of Arab unity intensified the inter-Arab competition and ultimately led to the establishment of the ARAB LEAGUE in 1945. The Arab League was dominated by the Egyptian-Saudi-Syrian bloc, which opposed Greater Syria or any other revision of the existing map of the independent Arab states. Britain, Abdallah's ally and main support, did not really back his scheme—fearing both French and Arab hostility. Abdallah's supporters and agents among the Syrian political factions were few, and their schemes and intrigues had little impact. The Palestine Jewish leadership told him that despite their general sympathy for him as the only Arab statesman planning peaceful coexistence with a Jewish state he could not expect any help from them for the Greater Syria scheme. At the same time, and especially since summer 1946, Abdallah and the Jewish Agency had a tacit understanding that in the case of partition of Palestine between Jewish and Arab states, the Jewish Agency would not object to Abdallah's attempt to take over Arab Palestine while the King would not object to the establishment of a Jewish state on the other part. The invasion of Palestine by the Arab armies offered Abdallah the opportunity to conquer—and later annex—the mountainous area from Jenin in the north to Hebron in the south, including East Jerusalem, but not without heavy battles with the newly established Jewish state and bitterness with the Arab allies. Abdallah never stopped aspiring to a Greater Syria throne. However, his assassination in 1951 put an end to the Hashemite Greater Syria plan, as Abdallah's successors had neither the drive nor the means to realize it, focusing on their own kingdom's survival. A partial short-lived realization of the Fertile Crescent idea by the Hashemites came in the Iraqi-Jordanian Arab Federation established in February 1958 in response to the foundation of the UNITED ARAB REPUBLIC of Egypt and Syria. This Hashemite federation was soon abolished in the wake of Iraq's July 1958 Revolution, which eliminated the royal Hashemite family and its supporting oligarchy (see ARAB UNITY).

A different, non-Hashemite scheme for a Greater Syria and a Fertile Crescent union, based on the mystique of a pan-Syrian nationalism, was advocated by a marginal, mainly Lebanese, Fascist-leaning faction—Antoun Sa'adeh's SYRIAN NATIONALIST PARTY. In its erratic shifts, this group, though anti-Hashemite in its ideology, established some clandestine links with Abdallah's agents in the 1940s and 1950s. It was, in any case, without power or influence.

Radical-leftist Syria under the *Ba'th* Party advocated all-Arab Union rather than specifically Fertile Crescent federations; yet, in their search for new patterns of union after the dissolution of the Syro-Egyptian UNITED ARAB REPUBLIC, the *Ba'th* leaders agreed in 1963 to the creation of a federation of Syria, Iraq and Egypt; when that agreement remained abortive they played with the idea of a Syro-Iraqi union. Talks and tentative agreements on that line also remained inconclusive, particularly as Syria and Iraq, ruled by rival *Ba'th* factions, have been in dispute and mutually hostile since the late 1960s.

While a Fertile Crescent union or federation thus seems to have ceased to be a practical political scheme, it has remained a useful myth, a vision which, under some circumstaces might be drawn upon by political leaders for practical political ends. Hence, the idea was resumed by the Asad regime in Syria after the 1973 war and through the mid-1970s, reflecting a claim for patronage over Jordan, Lebanon and

the PALESTINE LIBERATION ORGANIZATION (PLO). Such Syrian hegemony was intended to strengthen Syria's bargaining position in the Middle East peacemaking process, and balance Egypt's magnitude in the Arab world. Although the bitter experience of Arab unity attempts and the more intense process of state formation in the region have diminished the power of any Arab unity scheme, the Greater Syria idea, as well as the Fertile Crescent, have retained their relevance. They define a sphere of influence, an arena in which to struggle for political and strategic control. Both Iraq and Syria aspire to a position of control, influence and predominance in the Fertile Crescent. The notion that Lebanon, Jordan and Palestine (e.g., the Palestinian National Movement) should be dominated by Syria—perhaps as part of a regional power game with Israel—seems to be held by the Syrian leadership under President Hafez al-ASAD. Although Syria apparently does not strive for a straightforward merger with these countries, it seems to envisage a Syrian predominance and a far-reaching adaptation or conformity of these countries' policies to Syrian guidance and prescriptions. As Iraq was absorbed in its war with Iran in 1980–1988 and later severely defeated in the GULF WAR, it is mainly Syria that seems to seek such control. However, the bilateral peace treaties between the PLO and Israel in 1993 and Jordan and Israel in 1994 suggest that Syria's influence remains limited. Besides, other Arab states, such as Egypt and SAUDI ARABIA, have traditionally sought to prevent Syrian or Iraqi domination of the Fertile Crescent.

GREEK CATHOLICS The branch of the GREEK ORTHODOX community that joined the Catholic Church en bloc, through the UNIATE, retaining a certain autonomy regarding both liturgy and its language, and church and community administration. (In ARABIC, Greek Catholics are *Rum-Katholik*, i.e. Roman-Catholic, while those named Roman-Catholic in European languages are called Latin; the Greek Catholics in the Middle East are also called *Melchites* or *Melkites*—from Syriac-Aramaic Meld, King or Emperor, i.e. State Church—a description originally pertaining to the Orthodox church that stuck mainly to the Greek Catholics).

The Uniate parts of the Orthodox with the Catholic Church took place in the eighteenth century—preceded and influenced by Uniates of other eastern communities, such as the MARONITES, and the protection afforded them by FRANCE. There are different versions as to precise dates: 1725, 1730, 1775. The new community was persecuted by the Orthodox Church, backed by the Ottoman authorities; it was not recognized by the latter, and the first Patriarch appointed by the Holy See had to go into exile. It was only in 1837 that Patriarch Maximos III Masloum was recognized as the head of an independent Greek Catholic community (MILLET) and took residence in Damascus. In 1882, a Greek Catholic Seminary was opened by the White Fathers at St. Anne's Church in JERUSALEM and thereafter produced most of the educated Greek Catholic priests; after ISRAEL took East Jerusalem in 1967, it was transferred to Harissa in LEBANON.

The Greek Catholics follow, mainly, the Byzantine rite. Those in the Middle East use Arabic as their liturgical language, with a few Greek parts. The Church is headed by the "Patriarch of Antioch and all the East, Alexandria and Jerusalem", whose seat is in Damascus; the Patriarch, usually an Arab, mostly Lebanese or Syrian, is appointed by the Holy See. The incumbent, since 1967, is Maximos V, Georgios Hakim. There are Greek Catholic communities in Greece, Cyprus, Eastern Europe and the Balkans, and among migrants in America. In the Middle East, they are in Lebanon, approximately 250,000-300,000; SYRIA , 175,000; EGYPT 50,000; JORDAN 30,000; and Israel 45,000.

GREEK ORTHODOX The eastern branch of the official, main body of the Church of early Hellenistic and Byzantine Christianity, separated since 1054 from the Western, Catholic Church centered in Rome. Also called *Melchite* or *Melkite*—from Syriac-Aramaic Melk, King Emperor, i.e., State church—mainly as against the Nestorian and MONOPHYSITE churches that split from it in the fifth century. (The term *Melkite* is mainly used for the GREEK CATHOLICS). The main Greek Orthodox communities are in RUSSIA, Greece, the Balkans and Cyprus, and in the European and American diaspora. Within the Middle East there are no Greek Orthodox in the North-African West, the MAGHRIB, and very few in Egypt, and in IRAQ; in SYRIA, JORDAN and Palestine they are the largest CHRISTIANcommunity and in LEBANON—the second largest, after the MARONITES. In the Middle Eastern countries, they are located mainly in Syria,

400,000; Lebanon, 250,000-300,000; Jordan and the Palestine WEST BANK, 100,000; and approximately 35,000 in ISRAEL.

The Greek Orthodox Church has no overall head, but comprises "*autocephalous*", i.e., autonomous, Patriarchates. In the Middle East there are four: Constantinople, Antioch, Alexandria, and JERUSALEM. The Patriarch of Constantinople used to be considered *primes inter pares*.

Until the end of the nineteenth century, the four Patriarchs and their senior clergy were priests of Greek origin, though the majority of the faithful in the patriarchates of Antioch and Jerusalem were ARABS. Since 1899, however, the hierarchy of the Patriarchate of Antioch, with its center in Damascus, has been entirely Syrian and Lebanese Arabs. (In 1964 and in 1969–1970 serious splits between the bishops of the Syrian and Lebanese parts of the Patriarchate were patched up with difficulty). The language of liturgy, originally Greek, has become mainly Arabic. In the Patriarchate of Jerusalem the Greek character of the senior hierarchy has been maintained, and the Arab Greek Orthodox community, supported by the lower clergy, has been struggling for many years to abolish, or at least reduce, that Greek character of their church.

In general, the Greek Orthodox have been considered the Christian community most firmly integrated and active in the Arab national movement (as opposed to the autonomous, even separatist tendencies in the Maronite community for instance).

GULF COOPERATION COUNCIL (GCC) Sub-regional organization comprised of six SAUDI ARABIA, UNITED ARAB EMIRATES, KUWAIT, QATAR, BAHRAIN AND OMAN, established in May 1981. Abdallah Bishara, a Kuwaiti diplomat was appointed as its first Secretary General, with a Permanent Secretariat in Riyad, Saudi Arabia. The idea of establishing such a body originated from a growing sense of threat experienced by the regimes of these states to their domestic security following the Shi'i revolution in IRAN and subsequent agitation among Shi'i communities in north-eastern Saudi Arabia and other Gulf monarchies; the armed takeover of the *Ka'ba* mosque in Mecca (1979); and the eruption of the IRAN-IRAQ WAR in September 1980.

The objectives of the GCC were to promote cooperation among its members primarily in the sphere of domestic and regional security, including the resolution of border disputes, and to coordinate arms procurement and national economies. Iraq was notified about the intention to establish the organization and its exclusion was explained in terms of the founders' fear of being identified with Iraq in its war with Iran. The GCC holds regular meetings, in alternating capitals, of a "Supreme Council" (of the Heads-of-State) and a "Ministerial Council" (of the Foreign Ministers). The GCC has been much preoccupied with the Iraq-Iran War but its attempt, in June 1982, to end the War failed. In November of that year, the GCC condemned Iran for occupying Iraqi territory. The continuing war between Iran and Iraq drove the GCC members toward further cooperation, especially on common regional concerns. In 1984, the GCC conducted a three-week joint military exercise in the UAE. Shortly afterward, the GCC summit decided to establish a "Rapid Deployment Force" (RDF) of two brigades under the Saudi commander, based in Riyad. With the Iran-Iraq War spilling over and affecting the Gulf monarchies' oil production and sovereignty, a GCC Summit in late 1987 called on the UN Security Council to implement its cease-fire Resolution 598, passed in July of that year. However, though the GCC tried to avoid openly taking a side in that conflict and maintain normal relations with both IRAQ and Iran, the War put the GCC states under constant threat of those warring powers, due to their geographic proximity, strategic eminence, and uninhibited practice of employing subversive and violent means against their neighbors. Thus, the GCC states were pressured to extend staggering amounts of financial aid to Iraq. On the other hand, they were under constant pressure from Iran—exerted pressure through sabotage, political subversion, propaganda warfare, and as of 1986 also by military attacks against oil tankers in the Gulf and Kuwaiti territory. Practically, the GCC accorded its sympathy to Iraq, while individual members, primarily Saudi Arabia and Kuwait, accounted for the massive financial aid to Iraq (see also IRAN-IRAQ WAR). Following the Iraq invasion of Kuwait, the GCC condemned the Iraqi action and sent its RDF to the Saudi-Kuwaiti border. Later on, military units of all the GCC states participated in the international coalition against Iraq.

The GCC also decided to suspend all financial aid to the PALESTINE LIBERATION ORGANIZATION (PLO) because of ARAFAT'S support of Saddam HUSSEIN in the 1990–1991 Gulf crisis. After the Oslo Agreement between Israel and the PLO in September 1993 GCC members renewed their relations with the PLO and later with the PALESTINIAN AUTHORITY established in the GAZA STRIP. The Saudis pledged to contribute 100 million dollars in five years for the development of the Palestinian-governed territories of the Gaza Strip and WEST BANK, though tension and mistrust still prevails in GCC relations with Yasser ARAFAT.

In the wake of the Gulf War the GCC, together with EGYPT and SYRIA'S foreign ministers, in a conference held in Damascus in March 1991, agreed to grant the latter financial aid for the deployment of 35,000 Egyptian and 20,000 Syrian troops to be part of an expanded Gulf defense force that would replace the Western forces ("The Damascus Declaration"). However, this idea was later dropped from the agenda, though the GCC, SYRIA, and Egypt, continued to maintain this forum for collective coordination of regional issues. The GCC states also took part in the post-Madrid conference multi-lateral talks on regional issues, directly meeting the Israeli delegates. In late September 1994 the GCC decided to abolish the indirect boycott on ISRAEL which reflected eagerness on the part of Oman and Qatar to establish official diplomatic links with Israel. However, as the peace making process stalemated in late 1996 and 1997 following the advent of a right-wing government in Israel, the GCC states demonstrated their strategic vulnerability in cooling down their links with Israel. Their meeting in the fall of 1997 ended with urging linkage between normalization of relations with Israel and development of the peace process, including on the Syrian front. The GCC states also manifested reluctance regarding the use of force against Saddam Hussein by the US as a means to enforce the UN Security Council's resolutions regarding inspection and destruction of his non-conventional weapons.

GULF WAR (1991)   The war between IRAQ and the American-led international coalition 16 January to 27 February), was a result of the undecided termination and strategic consequences of the previous War in the region, namely, the 1980–1988 IRAN-IRAQ WAR.

The War stemmed from Iraq's invasion of KUWAIT on 2 August, and its formal annexation to Iraq on 8

August, ignoring the UN Security Council's Resolution 661 passed two days earlier, which imposed mandatory sanctions and a comprehensive blockade on Iraq and occupied Kuwait. (For the background to the Iraqi invasion of Kuwait—Iraqi threats to use chemical weapons against Israel and financial and territorial claims from Kuwait, see IRAQ).

Between August 1990 and January 1991, the American administration led an intensive diplomatic effort to create an international military coalition under titular Saudi command (and effectively American command) to enable the liberation of Kuwait if Iraq had refused to comply to the UN Security Council Resolution 678 of 29 November 1990. This resolution authorized the use of "all necessary means to restore international peace and security in the area," unless Iraq fully implemented the previous UN resolutions, until 15 January 1991.

NATO powers and other European, American and Pacific states, as well as the GULF COOPERATION COUNCIL (GCC) member states, EGYPT, MOROCCO and SYRIA), joined the coalition, sending troops to SAUDI ARABIA to participate in the military effort, bringing the total magnitude of the international force to over 550,000 troops (half of which were Americans) with 2200 tanks, 50 combat helicopters and 1500 war planes.

On 11 January 1991 the Iraqi Parliament decided unanimously to go to War rather than withdraw from Kuwait. A few hours after the expiration of the UN Security Council ultimatum, the American-led coalition started its air and missile offensive which continued for five weeks, aiming at destroying Iraq's infrastructure of roads, bridges, power plants, with little Iraqi effort to fight them, focusing mainly on ground-to-air defense. During this period, Iraq made an effort to entangle Israel in the crisis by launching close to fifty SCUD missiles with conventional warheads against Israel, apparently in an attempt to force it to retaliate and put the Arab members of the international coalition in quandary. In February, Iraq broke its diplomatic relations with the US, BRITAIN, FRANCE, Canada, Italy, Egypt, and Saudi Arabia. Iraq tried to end the War by driving a wedge between the US and the Soviet Union by offering conditional withdrawal from Kuwait (15–23 February). This failed although the Soviets tried to mediate a diplomatic settlement of the conflict to end the War. Ground offensive began on 23 February resulting in

a retreat of the Iraqi forces from Kuwait amid systematic effort to set ablaze the Kuwaiti OIL wells.

Iraq withdrew its forces from Kuwait on 26 February and two days later accepted the truce ordered by US President George Bush. By then, 640 Kuwaiti oil wells were ablaze. Iraq's losses in the War were estimated at roughly 60,000, equally divided between civilians and soldiers. The number of US losses was 376 troops during the seven months of the crisis and they lost 21 warplanes compared to 30 on the Iraqi side. The total cost of the War was estimated at 82 billion dollars, most of which was paid by Kuwait (22 billion dollars) and Saudi Arabia (29 billion dollars), with the rest covered by Japan and the US. The Iraqi losses were claimed to have exceeded 200 billion dollars. The indirect losses are difficult to estimate, especially in terms of the damage to Kuwait's oil wells, environment, and infrastructure. Following the War, the UN Security Council imposed on Iraq a UN-monitored program of total disarmament of its mass-destruction weapons, as well as medium and long-range ground-to-ground missiles, the implementation of which would be a prerequisite to the lifting on the economic sanctions and blockade against it. (For the post-Gulf War developments in Iraq, its struggle to remove the sanctions, and response of the international community, see IRAQ).

GÜRSEL, CEMAL (1895–1966) Turkish army officer and politician, fourth President of the Turkish Republic (1961–1966). Born in Erzurum, Gürsel graduated from the military secondary school in Erzincan and enrolled in the War College in Istanbul. As an officer in World War I, he was a prisoner of war in EGYPT for two years.

After the War he joined the national movement of Mustafa Kemal (ATATÜRK) and commanded a unit in the War of Independence. After slowly rising in rank, he was appointed in 1958 Commander of Land Forces.

He opposed the decision of the Menderes Government (which he viewed as reactionary and repressive) to use the army to suppress the opposition expressing his reservations in a letter to the Minister of Defense. This was ignored. On 27 May 1960, he led a group of thirty-eight military officers in a coup which overthrew the government. He was leader of the ruling National Unity Committee and was Prime

Minister and de facto President. In November 1960, he ejected fourteen radical officers headed by Colonel Türkes, claiming that this group was anti-democratic, nearly causing a second revolution. Shortly later, he suffered a heart attack from which he never fully recovered.

After a new constitution was adopted and a new Parliament elected in 1961, Gürsel was elected President. In early 1966, due to his failing health, he was replaced as President by another former military officer, Cevdet SUNAY; he died the same year.

GUSH EMUNIM Israeli, national religious, extra-parliamentary movement, which advocated the application of Israeli sovereignty to the WEST BANK and GAZA STRIP and considered this a vital goal in the realization of ZIONISM. Gush Emunim argued that it is possible to realize this goal only through a massive Jewish civilian presence in these areas. At the same time it verbally advocated coexistence with the indigenous Arab population. The religious mentor of Gush Emunim was Rabbi Zvi Yehuda Kook. He argued that the essence of the Jewish people is to attain physical and spiritual redemption by means of life in the whole of *Eretz Yisrael* and its upbuilding. The sanctity of *Eretz Yisrael* makes it imperative to continue to hold on to any part of the land which has been liberated from foreign rule. The most prominent figures in Gush Emunim in its early days were Rabbi Moshe Levinger, who settled in Hebron, and Hanan Porath (who was later to become a Knesset member).

Gush Emunim was founded in February 1974. In its early days it was closely connected to the National Religious Party. After a while it cut off the political connection. At first, Gush Emunim concentrated on settlement activities outside the parameters of the Allon Plan (see ARAB-ISRAEL PEACE-MAKING), on which the settlement policy of the first government of Yitzhak RABIN was based. Among Gush Emunim's first settlement targets was Elon Moreh, near the remains of ancient Sebastia in the vicinity of Nablus. It was expelled by the Israel Defense Forces (IDF) from the area by force seven times, but was finally permitted by Minister of Defense Shimon PERES to settle in a nearby military camp.

As time went by, Gush Emunim started to be supported by non-religious groups as well, including the Movement for GREATER ISRAEL. Following the ascendancy of the Likud Party to power in 1977, the settlement policy of the government of Menahem BEGIN was much more to Gush Emunim's liking, though it strongly objected to the autonomy plan as agreed to by the government in the Camp David Accords (see ARAB-ISRAEL PEACEMAKING), and to the Israeli withdrawal from the Sinai, as agreed to in the Egyptian-Israeli Peace Treaty (see ARAB-ISRAEL PEACEMAKING).

Following the establishment of the National Unity Government in 1984 (see ISRAEL), which put an almost complete stop to all Jewish settlement activities in the West Bank and Gaza Strip, the increase in Palestinian acts of armed resistance and terrorism and the outbreak of the INTIFADA in December 1987, Gush Emunim demanded the intensification of the settlement activities, and more effective action in the territories by the IDF. Gush Emunim tried to carry out armed civilian reconnaissance activities in the territories, but was stopped by the IDF.

At the same time, internal difficulties started to emerge in the movement. These developed as a result of the bureaucratization of Gush Emunim; the heterogeneous nature of the settler population (many settlers moved to the territories for economic rather than ideological motives). Above all it was due to the differences of opinion between the more radical and more moderate forces within the movement. The uncovering of the Jewish Underground, was made up of members of Gush Emunim. It was involved in terrorist activities against Palestinians in the years 1980–1984. It had planned to blow up the Mosques on the Temple Mount. The efforts of Daniela Weiss, who had been elected Secretary General of the movement in 1984, to have the members of the Jewish Underground released, brought the crisis to a head. Efforts of the more moderate elements within the movement—including Rabbi Yo'el Bin-Nun, Rabbi Menahem Fruman and Hanan Porath to change the militant leadership, failed. This resulted in a disintegration of Gush Emunim.

In the elections to the thirteenth Knesset (1992), the leaders of Gush Emunim did not manage to run together in a single list. The two lists identified with Gush Emunim—the Tehiya and a list established by Levinger—failed to pass the 1.5% qualifying threshold. An effort by Rabbi Binyamin (Benny) Alon to set up a new movement by the name of "Emunium" following the elections, came to naught. Alon himself entered the fourteenth Knesset as a member of the Moledet Party.

Along the years of its activity, Gush Emunim had obtained a growing influence within the National-Religious Party (*Mafdal*), gradually shaping the latter's political attitude on the territorial aspects of the ARAB-ISRAEL CONFLICT and settlement policy. Since the general elections of 1996, members that had identified with Gush Emunim became a majority in the *Mafdal* Party Knesset members, turned it into the most militant guard of the principles of retaining and settling the whole *Eretz Yisrael* in the government.

HABASH, GEORGE (b. 1924)   Palestinian guerrilla leader, Arab national ideologue and politician. Born in Lod (Lydda) to a Christian Greek-Orthodox family, Habash graduated in medicine from The American University of Beirut. After the ARAB-ISRAEL CONFLICT of 1948 he settled for some years in Amman. In the 1950s, he was one of the founders, and the ideologues of the ARAB NATIONALIST MOVEMENT (*Harakat al-Qawmiyyin al-Arab*). This was a militant pan-Arab nationalist group, largely underground and never endowed with publicly identified leading bodies. The movement upheld slogans of revolutionary Arab nationalism. It called for another round of war with ISRAEL to eradicate the shame of the loss of Palestine. The movement opposed the established Arab governments. Due to Habash's input in the course of the late 1950s and early 1960s, it adopted increasingly Marxist-Leninist doctrines. In December 1967 George Habash, together with Ahmad JIBRIL, Na'if HAWATMA and others, founded the "Popular Front for the Liberation of Palestine" (PFLP). This was a Palestinian guerrilla formation; an offshoot of the Arab Nationalist Movement. Following the split of Jibril's group in 1968 and of Hawatma in 1969, Habash has remained the sole dominant leader of the PFLP. His rigid doctrinaire adherence to the original ideology of the Arab Nationalist Movement left its imprint on the organization's political behavior and attitudes, particularly regarding opposition to Arab conservative regimes and militancy toward Israel. As such, Habash remained a bitter rival of PALESTINE LIBERATION ORGANIZATION (PLO) mainstream politics led by ARAFAT. This explains his conditional and partial participation in the PLO's institutions since 1969.

After the 1973 War, the PFLP suspended its participation in the PLO's Executive Committee, ob-

jected to the political dialogue between JORDAN in the years 1982–1986 and boycotted the Palestinian National Conference (PNC) held in Amman in November 1984. In April 1987 there was a reconciliation between the PFLP and other radical Palestinian movements and *Fatah*. This led to the PFLP rejoining the PLO's PNC and Executive Committee, after Arafat succumbed to their pressure and agreed to abrogate his February 1985 agreement with King HUSSEIN. In the November 1988 PNC, Habash compromised on accepting the UN Partition Resolution of 1947. Nontheless he adhered to his interpretation that it meant no recognition of the State of Israel whatsoever, only legitimizing the Palestinian people's claim for its own state. Habash opposed Arafat's acceptance of Resolution 242 in December 1988 and his dialogue with the US that began thereafter. This included the PLO's participation in the Madrid talks as well as the Declataion of Principles (DOP) and the Oslo process. In 1992, Habash joined the Front of Ten. This was a Syrian-based coalition of militant Palestinian organizations loosely collaborating in rejecting the Oslo Agreement and their results. As a guardian of the old, intransigent Arab attitude to Israel, Habash commands high admiration among many Arabs, and particularly among Palestinians in the diaspora, considered the last guardian of authentic Arab nationalist principles, while being perceived by the more pragmatic as anachronistic and irrelevant.In his relations with Arab states he preserved some freedom of maneuver by cultivating cooperation with several Arab regimes (mostly SYRIA, IRAQ and LIBYA). His overt challenge to Arab conservative regimes, particularly in Jordan and the Arabian Peninsula, rendered Habash a *persona non-grata* in most of the Arab monarchies and EGYPT. Habash's revolutionary fervor led him to cultivate political and military collaboration with other revolutionary and anarchist groups around the globe (such as the Japanese Red Army; Bader-Meinhoff in Germany; the Red Brigades in Italy, and others in Latin America). This laid the foundation for collaboration in international terrorism during the late 1960s and first half of the 1970s; a sphere of action in which the PFLP was the ultimate leading force among Palestinian guerrilla groups.

HAMAS   An abbreviation of *harakat al-mqawama al-ilamiyya*-Islamic Resistance Movement (Arabic:

enthusiam, zeal). Palestinian Islamic movement engaged in social-communal activities as well as in armed struggles against ISRAEL. Officially established in August 1988, *Hamas* emerged from the Palestinian uprising (INTIFADA), as a branch of the MUSLIM BROTHERHOOD Association in the GAZA STRIP and the WEST BANK. From the outset, Hamas set a moral and political challenge to the national secular Palestinian stream embodied by the PALESTINE LIBERATION ORGANIZATION (PLO) and especially its mainstream organization, *Fatah*. It consisted in remaining out of the PLO and soon became its primary opposition in the Palestinian political arena. Since the conclusion of the ISRAEL-PLO Oslo Agreement in September 1993, *Hamas*, through its armed struggle against Israel, has constituted a serious challenge to the Peace Process between Israel and the PALESTINIAN AUTHORITY (PA).

The origins of *Hamas* are rooted in the Muslim Brotherhood (MB) Society, and more specifically, in its main embodiment since the late 1970s, the Islamic Agglomerate (*al-mujamma' al-ilami*) in the Gaza Strip. The first branch of MB in Palestine was established in 1946 in JERUSALEM and various other towns. The movement developed rapidly. On the eve of the 1948 War it had some 10,000 members in thirty-eight branches throughout the country. The movement played no discernible role—communal or military—in the 1948 War and indeed collapsed as a movement.

Under Egyptian military rule (1948–1967), the movement had been constantly repressed, especially after 1954, when the military regime cracked down on the MB and brought about its decline, including even its presence in the Gaza Strip. In the West Bank, the MB were much better off, adopting a line of tacit alignment with the regime against the leftist and nationalist movements identified with NASSERISM.

From 1967 onward, under Israel's military government, the MB in the Gaza Strip slowly resumed their activity, focusing on the classical reformist pattern laid down by the founder of the Brotherhood in EGYPT, Hassan al-Banna. According to this model the main role of the Brotherhood was preaching and teaching ISLAM (*da'wa*) as the primary way to reshape the society into a true Islamic community which would fully submit to the rule of God and Islamic Law (SHARI'A). Throughout the 1970s and early 1980s, the MB stayed out of the armed national action represented by the PALESTINIAN GUERRILLA ORGANIZATIONS that was marked by secularism, revolutionary nationalism, and Marxism-Leninism. During those years, the MB movement grew steadily as part of the rising trend in Egypt and other Middle Eastern countries, leading to the proliferation of Islamic welfare and educational associations, construction of mosques and growing number of followers among the youth, especially in the refugee camps. From the late 1970s, *al-mujamma' al-islami*, led by Sheikh Ahmad Yassin, former activist in the MB in Egypt. Israeli authorities looked favorably to that trend, perceiving it as a counterbalance to the PLO's stature in the Gaza Strip. The expansion of the Islamic movement in that period was illustrated in the rapid growth of the number of mosques—the focal institution of the MB activities—around which a system of welfare, education, health and other communal services was developed based on self-supported charity (*zakah*), direct financial aid from SAUDI ARABIA and funds raised among Palestinians in Europe and the US.

In the years 1967–1986, the number of mosques in the Gaza Strip doubled, from 77 to 150, rising to 200 by 1989. Most of the new mosques were private, independent of the existing administration of Islamic endowments (*awqaf*) controlled by the Civil Administration. By the mid-1980s, the Islamic University in Gaza became the center of activity of the MB in the Gaza Strip, which by then had manifested a discernible measure of penetration into various public institutions, primarily professional associations.

Parallel to this trend, marked by the reformist goal of transforming the society into an Islamic one, a national-activist Islamic approach also appeared in the Gaza Strip, conducting a Holy War (JIHAD) against Israel for the liberation of Palestine. This stream, represented by the Islamic *jihad* (see ISLAMIC RADICALISM AND MOVEMENTS), was one of the triggers for the eruption of the Palestinian uprising (*intifada*) on 9 December 1987 in the Gaza Strip, following which it expanded to the West Bank. The foundation of *Hamas* in the early phase of the *intifada*—marked by a strong enthusiasm for active nationalist participation, especially among the youth—reflected differences within the MB movement regarding the appropriate response and fear lest a continued passivity would cost defection of many youth to the nationalist organizations. Indeed, already before the eruption of the *intifada,* Yassin gave his blessing to the establishment of a security apparatus, whose main role was to enforce social Islamic norms and protect the MB members from harassment by the nationalist elements.

The emergence of *Hamas* as an activist political and military arm of the MB posed a serious challenge to ARAFAT's PLO. *Hamas* offered an Islamic version of Palestinian nationalism. In August 1988, *Hamas* published its own charter, tacitly purporting itself as a moral and political alternative to the PLO. The challenge posed by *Hamas* to the PLO's exclusive standing in the Palestinian society was particularly serious because the new movement adopted most of the principles of the Palestinian National Charter (1968), albeit via an Islamic interpretation. The Islamic Charter defined *Hamas* as an Islamic Palestinian movement, whose final aim was to apply the rule of ISLAM over Palestine as a whole, from the Jordan river to the Mediterranean. The Charter defined this land as an eternal Islamic endowment (*waqf*) which could not be compromised in any way. Holy war (*jihad*) for the liberation of the plundered Islamic land of Palestine was an individual duty (*fard'ein*) of every individual Muslim, and the only way to attain the movement's goals.

Hamas in effect portrayed the current PLO leadership as deviant from its own strategic agenda, which insisted on similar principles (see PLO). By adopting *jihad* against Israel as the only means to liberate Palestine from the hands of Israel, portrayed as the enemy of God (*Allah*) and Islam, *Hamas* revived the Islamic-ARABIC ethos of intransigent resistance to foreign domination, which had always commanded tremendous rallying power among the masses. Moreover, the return to fundamental Palestinian national goals, as opposed to the PLO's political program of "two states solution," was particularly appealing to the refugees, giving them new hope for a return to their original homes in today's Israel.

Within a few months, *Hamas* established itself in the West Bank. From the summer of 1988, it created a unique stature within Palestinian society. While in the early stages of the *intifada Hamas* tended to coordinate its public protest activities and strikes with the Unified National Command (UNC, the PLO-backed local leadership responsible for the day-to-day national activities), it now embarked on an entirely independent course, setting its own strike days, commemoration days and collective conduct. This led to a growing tension with the UNC and eventually with the PLO's mainstream of *Fatah.* *Hamas* was excluded by the secular nationalist groups from the prisoners' committees in the Israeli jails, as its members were often harassed, especially by the PFLP and DFLP members.

Hamas's growing influence among the Palestinian masses brought Arafat's *Fatah* organization to wage, in the course of 1989–1990, a propaganda campaign against it. This was aimed at pressuring the Islamic movement to accept subordination to the PLO, by joining it as one of its components. Unable to reject the idea without being accused of weakening the collective national struggle, *Hamas* leaders expressed a willingness to join the PLO but set conditions for it. These included having have forty percent of the PNC members. However, this was unacceptable to the PLO. Tension between the two factions further mounted against the backdrop of *Hamas's* growing success in gaining primacy in vocational and professional associations, student organizations, and commercial chambers. The *Hamas-Fatah* struggle for setting the *intifada's* agenda, territory and constituency was aggravated by the KUWAIT crisis and the GULF WAR that followed. This turned out to be politically—mainly financially—detrimental to the PLO due to its blunt support of Iraq in the crisis and war. While *Hamas* continued to receive financial aid from both IRAN and Saudi Arabia. The PLO was confronted with growing financial difficulties which forced it to reduce its activities. Furthermore, the image of *Hamas's* leaders was that of clean-handed, decent and dedicated people, compared to the PLO's corrupted establishment.

From the outset, *Hamas* established itself as a separate apparatus from the mainstay of the Islamic movement, and all of its social and communal services, mosques, schools, clinics, hospitals, welfare activities and family centers. This separation was intended to prevent a blow to the civil base of the movement which had been considered the hard core of the MB movement without which it lacked a justification for its very existence. *Hamas's* leadership was initially located in the occupied territories—though this remained secret—and supervised the movement's activities by functional departments of propaganda, security, finance, mobilization and day-to-day activities, with a parallel geographic division to a number of districts in each of the West Bank and the Gaza Strip. However, *Hamas* was seriously affeted in 1989, when Israel cracked down on its activities, arrested many of its leaders and deported others. The movement was thus reorganized, primarily by Mussa Abu Marzuq, to enable it to sustain future repression by Israel.

A Political Bureau was established, located out of Israel's reach. This was put in charge of shaping the movement's international relations, including fund raising and military activities. The district bases were given more freedom of action, including the military apparatuses, organized under the title "Battalions of *'izz al-din al-qassam*" (originally Syrian sheikh and preacher in Haifa in the late 1920s who led a small group of followers in short-lived armed struggle against JEWS and Britons in early 1930s Palestine). The civilian and communal activities of the Islamic movement remained under the local leadership. The new structure gave the movement flexibility and an increased capacity to survive, but also underlined the varying interests of each group. Generally, the outside leadership became identified with a more radical, intransigent position and military activism. On the other hand, the local, inside leadership, became marked by a greater consideration of the local population and the negative implications of the armed struggle of daily life given the harsh Israeli retaliatory measures, such as curfews, closures and prevention of work in Israel. Such measures primarily affected the more devastated population of the refugees.

The PLO's agreement to support the participation of a Palestinian delegation from the West Bank and Gaza Strip in the Madrid Peace Conference in late October 1991, further fuelled the tension between *Fatah* and *Hamas*, which embarked on an intensive campaign against the very idea of a territorial compromise and peacemaking with the Jews, as religiously forbidden and politically inconceivable. The growing *Hamas-Fatah* frictions became increasingly violent in nature in both the Gaza Strip and the West Bank, especially in the summer of 1992. This was repeatedly mediated by Israeli Arab leaders. The lack of progress in the peace process weakened *Fatah's* position which was further confused by Israel's decision, in late December 1992, to deport 425 activists of the Islamic *jihad* and *Hamas* to LEBANON, following the kidnapping and assassination of an Is-

raeli soldier. The mass deportation of Palestinians from the occupied terrtories forced the PLO to suspend the peace talks with Israel in Washington, and reluctantly express solidarity with *Hamas*.

The Israel-PLO Oslo Agreement, was thus a serious blow to *Hamas*, confronting it with entirely new strategic circumstances. Now that *Hamas* had to confront both Israel and the future PA, the movement had to formulate a strategy to prevent public alienation. Most of the public supported the Oslo Agreement, wanting to see the end of Israeli occupation. Yet they simultaneously supported the maintenance of *Hamas's* unique identity and move away from the PA, primarily by continuing the armed struggle against Israel. Hence, resistance to the Israeli-Palestinian peace process was to assume a selective nature and timing, to refrain from a head-on collision with the PA, especially in view of Israel's expected economic retaliations to *Hamas's* TERRORISM, in the form of closures on the Palestinain areas which could be too costly in terms of losing public support. *Hamas's* operations were becoming increasingly suicidal and aimed at Israeli civilians. Hence there were incidents of Israelis murdering Palestinians. For example, there was the massacre of Muslim worshipers in the Cave of the Patriarchs in Hebron in February 1994 and the killing of Yahya Abu Ayyash in Januuary 1996, carried out by state security agencies. There was also response to Israeli actions viewed as hurtful to Palestinian national rights (such as the decision to build a Jewish neighborhood in Jabal Ghneim (Har Khoma), south of Jerusalem, in the spring of 1997).

In October 1997, Israeli Mossad agents failed to assassinate Khaled Mash'al, the head of *Hamas's* Political Bureau in Amman. In view of the internal criticism of the Peace Treaty with Israel, the object and venue of the abortive Israeli operation clearly harmed Israeli-Jordanian relations while Mash'al became a hero.

To retain a more flexible decision-making process regarding the use of the armed struggle and to justify inactivity on ideological issues, from the outset *Hamas* purported that its members follow a clear ideological restriction not to use violence against certain institutions. These included the PLO or any Palestinian organization coalesced in it and the PA, despite their differences over the Peace Process with Israel. Clearly, *Hamas's* decision derived from an awareness of its military inferiority in the face of

Fatah or the PA's security forces, and a fear of being eliminated if it had manifested violent resistance to the PA. Such danger was clearly manifested in the bloody clashes between the PA's police forces and *Hamas's* adherents on 18 November 1994 following a Friday prayer at Filastin Mosque in Gaza. Nonetheless, *Hamas* insisted on maintaining the *jihad* against Israel. In late December 1995, *Hamas* and the PA reached an understanding that *Hamas* would refrain from launching violent attacks against Israel from the PA-controlled areas, so as not to embarrass its relations with Israel. This policy was implemented in the wave of suicide bus bombings and terrorism launched by *Hamas* in February–March 1996 in Jerusalem, Ashkelon and Tel Aviv, and then again in the spring and summer of 1997 in Tel Aviv and Jerusalem, respectively. There is little doubt that *Hamas's* terrorism (together with the Islamic *jihad's* similar operations) following the Oslo Agreement, was the single most important cause for the victory of Binyamin NETANYAHU over Shimon PERES in the direct elections for Prime Minister (and general elections) in May 1996, and the re-emergence of the right-wing parties to power. Given the negative attitude of the newly established Israeli government to the Oslo Agreement and strong objection of Knesset members and parties participating in the coalition, the shift actually fulfilled *Hamas* goals by practically blocking the Oslo process.

Politically, *Hamas* persisted in rejecting the Oslo Agreement, without actively resisting the PA's institutions, but also without fully accepting them or the PA's peacemaking policy. Hence, after a piercing debate within *Hamas*, the outside leadership decided to refrain from participation in the first general elections to the PA's Council held in January 1996. A fledgling Islamic Salvation Party which had been established in Gaza, intending to represent ostensibly independent Islamist candidates, was encouraged not to participate in the elections. Still, a number of unofficially Islamist candidates running independently were elected to the council, reflecting the relative power of the movement in the population (six out of the eighty-nine council members).

HARIRI, RAFIQ (b. 1944) Lebanese politician and businessman, Prime Minister of LEBANON since October 1992. A SUNNI Muslim from the city of Sidon and the son of a poor farmer, Hariri attended the Arab University of Beirut as a business student in 1964, but after two years moved to SAUDI ARABIA where he taught mathematics and business to the Saudi aristocracy's youth and worked as a part-time accountant for a Saudi contracting firm. In 1971 he set up his own company, Sconeast, in 1978 founded Oger-Saudi Arabia, and in 1979 established Oger-International, through the acquisition of a French company. These firms made a fortune from building hotels, palaces and convention centers in the Middle East, including a convention center which Hariri built for the Saudi king in 1977, earning him an excellent reputation in the Saudi throne and paving the way for other projects in other Arab states. In 1983, Hariri expanded his business acquiring the MIG group which included banks in Lebanon and in Saudi Arabia, as well as companies in the fields of insurance, computers, publishing, light industry and real estate. Despite his absence from war-torn Lebanon, Hariri endeavored to help it during the war, especially in the fields of education and social welfare. His company, Oger-Lebanon, rehabilitated major parts of Beirut, and in 1983 he established the Hariri Foundation which financed the education of 30,000 Lebanese students in Europe and the US. Hariri also financed the construction of a large modern health center in his home town, Sidon, and helped build clinics, schools and kindergartens in poor villages. In 1983 and 1984 he had participated in the Geneva and Lausanne Lebanese reconciliation conferences as a special envoy of Saudi King FAHD, and in 1989 he played a role in the reconciliation talks held in Ta'if, Saudi Arabia, between deputies of the Lebanese Parliament, culminating in the Ta'if Accord (see LEBANON).

In October 1992, after the failure of the Omar Karami and Rashid al-Sulh governments to get Lebanon back on track and after the first parliamentary elections held in post-war Lebanon, Hariri was nominated Prime Minister, with both Saudi and Syrian blessings. The Lebanese had high hopes. First, they expected that Hariri's personal success would be repeated on the national level. Next, considering Hariri's enormous wealth it was highly improbable that he would be corrupted. Thus, unlike his predecessors, Hariri was a close ally of both the Syrians and the Saudis. The Hariri government devised an 11 billion dollar plan to rebuild Lebanon and the devastated capital Beirut, in particular, and set out to repair the country's infrastructure, building roads, water and electricity works and clinics in the neglected South. It also endeavored to restore Lebanon's pre-war status as a regional finance and trade center. Hariri's own company, Solidere, was designed to play an important part in this process—a move that raised some public protest. Despite this and despite the unstable situation in South Lebanon, Rafiq Hariri remains the dominant political figure in Lebanon and seems to be the only Lebanese politician both capable and willing to rebuild Lebanon after fifteen years of devastating civil war.

HARAWI, ELIAS (b. 1930) Lebanese politician, President of LEBANON since November 1989. A Maronite Christian, born in a village of the Zahla region in East Lebanon to a land-owning family. Harawi did not pursue the law studies he had started, but took a first degree in business administration and devoted himself to the management of his lands and agricultural interests.

He was elected to Parliament in 1972 (the last Lebanese Parliament elected). From 1980 to 1982 he served as Prime Minister of Public Works. In November 1989 Rene Mu'awwad the President-elect was murdered. Harawi, though not a major leader, was found acceptable to Syria and the Syrian-guided rump Parliament meeting outside Lebanon (in Ta'if, SAUDI ARABIA) to set up a new regime against Michel AWN's government in East Beirut, and was elected President of Lebanon.

As President, Harawi has not given his country inspiring, rallying leadership, but he has succeeded in gradually extending, with the support of Syrian troops, the area his regime controls—including, for the first time in many years, large parts of South Lebanon (1991) and the Biqa (1977)—and in arranging for the dissolution of the various rival militias and their integration into the army and government establishment. Harawi fully "coordinates" his policies with Syria and accepts its "guidance", formalized in a Lebanese-Syrian Treaty of May 1991.

HASHEMITE KINGDOM OF JORDAN see JORDAN HASHEMITE KINGDOM OF.

HASHEMITES, HASHEMIS The ruling dynasty in JORDAN since the establishment of the Emirate in 1921, of the House of Hashem. Banu Hashem are the family or clan of the Qureish tribe to which the Prophet Muhammad belonged. They are descendants of the Prophet Muhammad through his daughter Fatima and his son-in-law Ali, and their son al-Hassan. They thus carry, like all descendants of that line, the title Sharif. In the tenth century, the Hashemites became the ruling family of Mecca and the province of HIJAZ. This lasted until the late nineteenth century when the Ottoman Sultan ABDEL HAMID II exiled Sharif Hussein Ibn Ali (1852–1932) to Istanbul. However, following the YOUNG TURKS revolution in 1908, Sharif Hussein was allowed to return and resume his position as the Sharif of Mecca. In 1916, he staged the ARAB REVOLT against the OTTOMAN EMPIRE and proclaimed himself King of Hijaz. In 1924 he took steps to declare himself CALIPH, but this was not accepted by the Islamic world. In the same year he was defeated by IBN SA'UD and abdicated in order to save his throne for his dynasty. Upon his death in exile (in Cyprus) in 1931, he was laid to rest on the Temple Mount as a tribute to his leadership of the Arab Revolt. His son Ali (1879–1935) succeeded to the throne of Hijaz, but after less than a year he was driven out by Ibn Sa'ud (he died in exile, in Baghdad). Ali's son ABDEL ILAH (1912–1958) was Regent of IRAQ, 1939–1953. Ali's daughter Aliya (d. 1950) married King Ghazi of Iraq.

Two other sons of Hussein founded dynasties. FEISAL (1885–1933) reigned for a short time in Damascus (1919–1920) and was driven out by the French. In 1921, (in an agreement with the British which was endorsed by a sort of referendum), he became King of Iraq and reigned there until his death. His only son, Ghazi (1912–1939), who succeeded him, was killed in an accident. As Ghazi's son, Feisal II (1935–1958), was a small child, his uncle Abdel Ilah acted as regent; when Feisal came of age and was crowned in 1953, Abdel Ilah became Crown Prince. They were both killed in the July 1958 *coup d'état* in Baghdad, and the Iraqi branch of the Hashemites came to an end.

Hussein ibn Ali's second son, ABDALLAH (1882–1951), was appointed by the British in 1921 for the position of Emir of Transjordan—a title they established for him in the framework of their MANDATES for Palestine. In 1946 he obtained independence through an agreement with the British which kept most of the responsibilities in their hands. Following that, he took the title of King, and changed the name of Transjordan to The Hashemite Kingdom of Jordan. Abdallah was assassinated in 1951 at the al-Aqsa Mosque in JERUSALEM. His son TALAL (1909–1972) succeeded him, but was deposed in 1952 on the grounds of mental illness. He was hospitalized in Istanbul where he died. Talal's son HUSSEIN (b. 1935) has ruled Jordan since 1953 and has

THE HASHEMITE DYNASTY

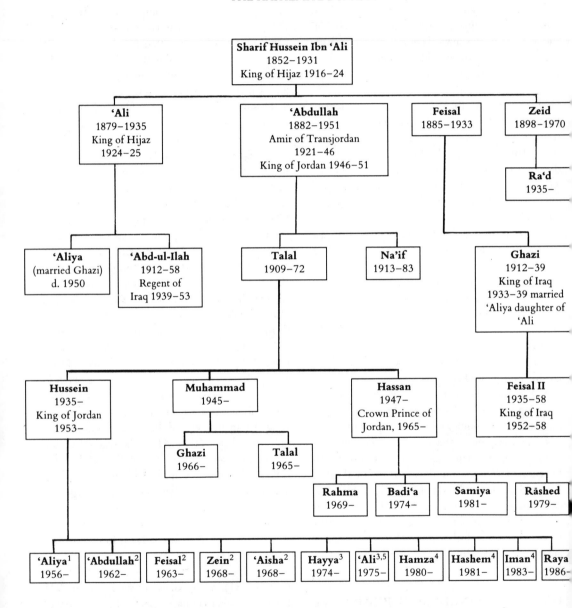

[1] Mother: Dina 'Abd-ul-Hamid al-'Awn, from another H. branch, whom Hussein married in 1955 and divorced in 1957.

[2] Mother: Tony Gardiner (after converted to Islam: Muna), whom Hussein married in 1961 and divorced in 1972.

[3] Mother: 'Aliya Touqan, whom Hussein married in 1972; died in 1977.

[4] Mother: Lisa Halabi (after converted to Islam: Nur-al-Hussein), whom Hussein married in 1978.

[5] Named in 1978 (second) Crown Prince after Hassan.

grown into one of the major statesmen of the Middle East. The Crown Prince is his younger brother Hassan (b. 1947) rather than his brother Muhammad (b. 1945). The eventual succession of Hussein's own sons might pose a problem, since only one of them, Ali (b. 1975), was born from an Arab-Jordanian-Muslim mother—while the mothers of two older and two younger sons were, though converted to Islam, of foreign origin (see table). In 1978 Ali was named (second) Crown Prince, after the King's brother Hassan.

The leadership of the Hashemite Dynasty stood at the cradle of Arab independence in the Fertile Crescent after World War I, with British assistance. However, Hashemite plans to found a single Arab federation of kingdoms failed and the region was divided into separate states under British and French tutelage. After World War I, the Hashemite rulers of Iraq and Transjordan fostered schemes of regional unity—including SYRIA, LEBANON and Palestine—under their separate thrones, and amidst competition between the two political centers of Amman and Iraq. Abdallah was the chief protagonist of the GREATER SYRIA scheme—which sometimes included a claim for Hijaz—while the Iraqi branch under King Feisal advocated a similar plan under the title The Fertile Crescent. Most Arab states opposed both versions of regional unity, particularly EGYPT, Syria, Lebanon and SAUDI ARABIA, and their opposition prevailed. From the late 1930s, the image of the Hashemite family was tarnished in the eyes of Arab nationalists who developed an increasingly suspicious attitude toward the Hashemites for their dependence on, and collaboration with, British imperialism against ARAB NATIONALISM, and their willingness to accommodate the Zionist movement and alleged disrespect of the cause of Palestine (see JORDAN; IRAQ).

HASAN II (b. 1929) King of MOROCCO since 1961, of the Alawi Sharifian Dynasty which has reigned in Morocco since the second half of the seventeenth century. The eldest son of Muhammad V, Ibn Yussuf, Prince Hasan received a French and Arabic-Muslim education at a college founded in 1941 for his and his brother's schooling, and later studied law at Bordeaux University. He became a close collaborator with his father the Sultan, while being reputed to sympathize with the nationalists.

In 1953 Hasan accompanied his father into exile in Madagascar and returned with him to Morocco in November 1955, toward independence. In July 1957 his father appointed him Crown Prince; he also formally headed the armed forces as Chief of Staff. In May 1960, the King, assuming the Premiership himself, entitled Prince Hasan Deputy Prime Minister. In February 1961, Hasan succeeded the throne upon King Muhammad's death. He retained the Premiership until 1963 and resumed it from 1965 to 1967. After the attempted coup of August 1972, he assumed command of the armed forces and appointed himself Defense Minister until 1973. Under the Moroccan constitution, King Hasan held both temporal and spiritual authority as "Amir al-Mu'minin" ("Commander of the Faithful," one of the titles of the Prophet Muhammad). As such, any hint of criticism of him or his family in the Moroccan media was expressly forbidden. He assiduously cultivated his spiritual authority through symbolic rituals, for example: the sacrificing of a ram on Id al-Adha and receiving the bay'a (traditional loyalty pledge) from officials; wearing traditional dress, when appropriate; and engaging in learned Koranic discussions with Moroccan ulama (religious jurists) which were broadcast in the media. Hasan's narrow escapes during the coup attempts of 1971 and 1972 lent him an additional aura of baraka (blessedness, or special attributes), an attribute common to Moroccan holy men throughout Moroccan history. Tangible expression to Hasan's religious status was awarded by the building of the Hasan II Mosque in Casablanca. Completed in 1993, it was one of the largest in the world. When appropriate, however, Hasan also displayed another side of his personage, the urbane cosmopolitan, well-tailored French-educated leader.

Hasan's governing style reflected these various attributes. His public discourse was paternal, educational, scolding and cajoling. Under his rule, the Royal Family and the hundreds of allied elite families, which dominated the Moroccan economy, accumulated enormous sums of wealth. Hasan's involvement in elite affairs also extended to marriage-making and blessing the children of elite families.

Politically, Hasan sought to continue in his father's footsteps. He thus established and then maintained his unchallenged position at the top of

Moroccan society by a complex combination of cooptation, division and repression. Throughout his reign, he sought various stablizing formulas which would sustain a semblance of multi-party pluralism whilst retaining the reins of real power. From the mid-1970s, Hasan's forceful moves to incorporate the Western Sahara into Morocco in the name of the "Great Moroccan Homeland"—an ultra-national revisionist vision—served as important political glue for his regime. But it also over-burdened Morocco's economy, increasing its domestic, social and political strains. In the 1990s, Hasan simultaneously promoted further economic and political liberation, advocating rotation of governmental responsibilities between competing political blocs.

King Hasan's foreign policy was conservative and pro-Western, except for a brief demonstration of radical tendencies in the early 1960s (the "Casablanca Bloc"). He fostered close relations with France and the US. In inter-Arab affairs, he kept Morocco within the moderate-conservative camp. Saudi Arabian financial aid was important for the conduct of the WESTERN SAHARAN CONFLICT in the early 1980s. Hasan's relations with ABDEL NASSER's EGYPT and the rest of the radical camp were sometimes tense. In ALGERIA, where relations were already troubled, radical orientation caused by border disputes and basic conflicts of interest (e.g., over the Western Sahara). Hasan sought to keep communication channels open with Algeria's President Chadli BEN JEDID, who assumed power in 1978, following the death of Houari BOUMÉDIENNE. Algerian-Moroccan relations thawed in the late 1980s but the crisis in Algeria during the 1990s created new tensions. Hasan irritated Algeria's military rulers on several occasions by suggesting that the democratic process should have been allowed to progress in 1992, even at the price of the Islamic fundamentalists' attainment of a measure of power.

During the 1990–1991 Gulf crisis, Hasan tilted toward the Saudis. He sent a symbolic contingent of troops for its defense and refused to formally affiliate them with the Western-Arab coalition or send them into battle. In addition, he tempered his statements regarding Iraq's Saddam HUSSEIN.

On Arab-Israeli issues, King Hasan's self-styled role was that of a supporting actor and mediator to promote the peace process. He secretly hosted Israeli Prime Minister Yitzhak RABIN in 1976 and two years later provided the offices for the secret meeting between Israeli Foreign Minister Moshe DAYAN and Egyptian Minister Tuhami which preceded Anwar al-SADAT's visit to JERUSALEM (see ARAB-ISRAEL PEACE-MAKING). Although he supported President Sadat's peace moves in 1977–1978 he was compelled to join the other Arab states in 1979 in severing relations with Egypt. King Hasan played the role of the ultimate mediator in inter-Arab relations and, as such, hosted more Arab and Islamic summit conferences than any other single Arab state. He also hosted the 1994 Middle East and North African Economic Summit, chaired the Islamic Conference Organization's Jerusalem Committee and, most dramatically, publicly hosted Israeli Prime Minister Shimon PERES for talks in 1986. Hasan's unique orientation to Arab-Jewish issues was based on a combination of *realpolitik* sentiment and the idealization of past Jewish-Arab relations in Morocco. Hasan viewed the Moroccan Jewish community, which had emigrated to ISRAEL, FRANCE and elsewhere, as an important element in the advancement of the peace process and Morocco's political and economic stability. He thus encouraged Moroccan Jews abroad to strengthen their links with Morocco. Hasan hosted Israeli leaders on their way back from the 1993 signing of the Oslo Agreement. Just over a year later, Morocco and Israel officially established low-level diplomatic relations.

HASSAN IBN TALAL (b. 1947) Crown Prince of the Hashemite Kingdom of JORDAN. Born in Amman and educated at Summerfields Preparatory School in England, and later at Harrow. He earned BA and MA degrees from Oxford. In 1965 King HUSSEIN named Hassan Crown Prince, choosing him over the middle brother, Muhammad (b. 1945). Since his appointment, Hassan has served as the closest advisor to the King and his most trusted confidant. Since his designation Hassan has served as the Regent of Jordan upon each absence of the King from the kingdom. He has also represented Jordan at the UN on special occasions.

Though Hassan does not hold any formal title in any governmental field, he is practically in charge of the economic and administrative activities of the kingdom. Prince Hassan played a key role in the peace negotiations between Jordan and ISRAEL and in consolidating their relations after they signed the 1994 peace treaty.

As a result of his hard line positions regarding the Palestinian armed organizations during the 1970 Civil War, Hassan earned the reputation of being "anti-Palestinian". Indeed, Hassan has been a strong opponent of any Palestinian military presence on the East Bank until their final removal in 1971. He advocates less Jordanian involvement in determining the future of the Palestinians in the WEST BANK; a policy which was finally adopted by the King in the 1988 decision to disengage from the West Bank against the backdrop of the Palestinian uprising in the occupied territories.

Hassan is seen by most analysts as a suitable successor to King Hussein, if necessary, in spite of his reputation as an intellectual rather than as a statesman. This image is gradually changing. Hassan has published numerous articles and three books on political and regional issues. His books are: *A study on Jerusalem* (1979), *Palestinian Self-Determination; A Study on the West Bank and the Gaza Strip* (1981) and *Search for Peace* (1984). Hassan is married to Princess Tharwat and has three daughters and a son.

HATAY   see ALEXANDRETTA.

HAWATMA NA'IF (b. 1935)   Palestinian politician and ideologue founder and leader of the Demomcratic Front for the Liberation of Palestine (DFLP, see FIDA'IYYUN), one of the Palestinian resistance organizations comprising the PALESTINE LIBERATION ORGANIZATION (PLO). Born in al-Salt, JORDAN, to a Greek-Orthodox, non-Palestinian family, Hawatma graduated in philosophy and sociology and became a member of the Arab Nationalists Movement (*Harakat al-Qawmiyyin al-Arab*) during the 1950s and 1960s. Based in Lebanon, he was active in the left wing of the movement and helped to expand the movement to IRAQ and SOUTH YEMEN. In December 1967 Hawatma founded, together with George HABASH, the Popular Front for the Liberation of Palestine (PFLP), and headed its left wing. In February 1969, Hawatma established his own organization—the Popular Democratic Front for the Liberation of Palestine (PDFLP, which later became DFLP). Contrary to Habash's organization which preached Arab unity as the first step to a Palestinian national entity, Hawatma, the Marxist-Leninist-Maoist, set the establishment of a popular revolutionary Palestinian state as a means toward the revolutionary ARAB UNITY

that would banish the reactionary Arab regimes. Being an enthusiastic supporter of a world revolution, Hawatma fostered close links with the Soviet Union as well as contacts with various leftist organizations of resistance and national liberation throughout the world including extreme leftist groups in ISRAEL. Nonetheless, the organization refrained from being involved in international TERRORISM and focused on armed struggle against Israel.

The priority Hawatma gave to a Palestinian statehood in part of Palestine following the October 1973 War, enabled him to cooperate with *Fatah*, which adopted the same strategy. Hawatma was also among the first Palestinian leaders who preached the development of contacts with the Israeli non-Zionist Left, as a means of promoting the idea of a Palestinian state in the WEST BANK and GAZA STRIP. During his political career, Hawatma adhered to his principles of social revolution, adopting hostile positions against the American-led peace making process in the 1970s, remaining a sworn enemy of Arab traditional regimes—especially the Hashemite one—which he called to depose. Thus, despite his inclination toward cooperation with *Fatah,* he refused to support the PLO-Jordanian dialog (1983–1986), and joined the opposition to ARAFAT, comprised of the radical fronts and *Fatah's* dissidents. Yet, despite his rapprochement with SYRIA following the evacuation of Beirut in 1982, Hawatma maintained his organization's freedom of maneuver. In 1987 he returned to cooperate with *Fatah*, took part in the PNC sessions of 1987 and 1988 (in which the Palestinian State was proclaimed) and shared its resolutions.

Hawatma objected to the Israel-PLO Oslo Agreement and agreements signed between them since September 1993 (see ARAB-ISRAEL PEACEMAKING). His organization became a member of the "Ten Front"; a Damascus-based coalition of radical Palestinian organizations that oppose the Oslo Agreement and criticise the establishment of the PALESTINIAN AUTHORITY (PA). In 1992, the DFLP split into the Hawatma-led hard-liners and a moderate minority group led by Yasser Abd Rabbo which supported Arafat and the Oslo agreements. Hawatma served as Secretary-General of the DFLP since its foundation and was last re-elected to this position in 1995.

HEBRON AGREEMENT   see ARAB-ISRAEL PEACEMAKING.

HEIKAL, MUHAMMAD HASSANEIN (b.
1923) Egyptian journalist, writer and politician.
Born in Cairo and educated in EGYPT (journalism,
economics and law), he worked as a reporter for
several Egyptian papers (Egyptian Gazette; *Rose al-
Yusuf*), reporting *inter alia* the desert campaign in
World War II. He became prominent reporting on
the Palestine War of 1948 for *Akhbar al-Yawm*. In
the early 1950s he was editor of the weekly *Aakhir Sa'a*
and later co-editor of the daily *al-Akhbar*, becoming
its chief editor in 1956–1957. After the 1952 revolution he became close to ABDEL NASSER, and in 1957
was appointed editor of *al-Ahram*, Egypt's most prestigious daily, in which he wrote a weekly column
Bisaraha ("Frankly"). In this he openly expounded
Nasser's policies, widely quoted throughout the Arab
world as his master's voice. Heikal became Egypt's
most influential journalist, close advisor to and confidant of President Nasser. In 1970 he served briefly
as Minister of Information and National Guidance.
Heikal has been a faithful "Nasserist", though he
cared to demonstrate a certain measure of independent political thinking.

After Nasser's death, in 1970, he continued to
hold his influential position as editor-in-chief of *al-
Ahram* but after the 1973 war he fell out with President al-SADAT—despite their personal friendship.
Remaining a Nasserist, he denounced Sadat's betrayal of Nasser's heritage. He opposed Sadat's growing alliance with the US, and vehemently opposed
peace with ISRAEL.

In 1974 he was dismissed from his position as editor and chairman of *al-Ahram* and barred from publishing his articles in the Egyptian press. In
1977–1978 he was interrogated by the police and the
state attorney, and for some months denied the right
to leave the country. In Sadat's September 1981
purges he was detained, but was released later that
year by Sadat's successor, President MUBARAK. As he
could not publish in Egypt, he began in 1975–1976
publishing articles and regular columns in foreign
newspapers. From 1971 Heikal also published, in
the West, several books on Egyptian and Middle
Eastern politics, becoming well-known in the West.
Heikal, however, never regained his major influence
on Egyptian policy planning and decision making,
or his leading position in the Egyptian press.

He is considered a leftist and ardent pan-Arab nationalist, and wrote numerous books on Egypt's policies under both Nasser and Sadat. Some of his books
sheded light on Egyptian inner circles of policy-
making under Nasser and Sadat, though without departing from his admiration and support of Nasser,
while harshly criticizing Sadat (mainly in his book
Kharif al-Ghadab, (Fall of Wrath) Beirut, 1986.

HERZL, THEODOR (1860–1904) Visionary of
the modern Jewish state, creator of political ZIONISM
and founder of the World Zionist Organization.
Herzl was born in Budapest to a partially assimilated family, and at the age of eighteen moved to Vienna,
where he studied law. Restricted professionally because of his Jewishness, Herzl turned to journalism
and writing. He published hundreds of *feuilletons* and
many plays. In 1892 he suggested that the Jewish
problem might be solved by baptizing all the Jewish children. However, the Dreyfus Affair
(1894–1895) in FRANCE, which he covered for the
Neue Freie Presse, impressed on him the power of
anti-Semitism even in an enlightened democratic
state such as France. He concluded that the only solution was the exodus of the Jews from their dis-
persions and their ingathering in a sovereign state. He
first considered Argentina, where Baron Hirsch had
attempted to settle Jews, but later adopted the Zionist idea, which was already prevalent in Eastern Europe, and favored Palestine. Herzl published his
Judenstaat ("The Jewish State") in 1896 and founded the World Zionist Organization at the first Zionist Congress, which he organized in Basle in 1897.
Until his death in 1904 Herzl attempted to obtain
a charter from the Ottoman Sultan for Jewish settlement in Palestine, and made extensive diplomatic efforts among all sovereigns who might be helpful
in achieving this goal. In 1898 Herzl met with German Kaiser Wilhelm II, in the course of the latter's
visit to Palestine, in an effort to advance his plan to
obtain a charter for Palestine. Herzl was, however,
willing to consider establishing the Jewish state in
Uganda when the possibility was raised in 1903 by
British Colonial Secretary Joseph Chamberlain. The
plan was finally rejected by the Zionist Congress of
1905, a year after Herzl's premature death.

HIJAZ The western region of Arabia, since 1925
part of the Saudi Kingdom. Hijaz extends from the
Gulf of Aqaba and the border of Jordan to Asir, to a
length of over 800 miles (almost 1,300 km.) and a

width of up to 200 miles (320 km.). Area: 120,000–150,000 sq.miles (320,000–390,000 sq. km.). Of the estimated population of 2–3 million more than half were nomads in the past, but in recent times many, perhaps most, have left the nomadic ways. Chief towns: Mecca, Medina, Jidda (Saudi Arabia's chief port on the Red Sea), Ta'if (a summer resort in the mountains), Yanbu' (an ancient small port recently developed and combined with an industrial estate, and the outlet of an oil pipeline from the persian gulf). Hijaz consists of a narrow coastal plain and a mountainous plateau inland, both largely barren—cultivation being possible only where water is available, near springs and wadis.

Since ancient times, a trade and caravan route, the "Frankincense Road" follows an inland line of depressions, with several oases, from South Arabia to the "Fertile Crescent" and Damascus. This road also was the main pilgrimage route to Mecca and Medina, and along it the Ottoman Turks built the Hijaz Railway (in disuse since 1917). In recent years, a network of modern highways connects the main cities.

Hijaz was part of the OTTOMAN EMPIRE from 1517, but effective Turkish rule was maintained chiefly in the holy cities Mecca and Medina, and efforts were made to secure and control the pilgrims' route to there and to the coast. In the interior, authority was in effect in the hands of the tribal chiefs. The local *emir,* the Sharif of Mecca (of the HASHEMITE clan), enjoyed a degree of autonomy, but his authority was limited. For Sharif Hussein Ibn Ali's revolt of 1916; his Kingdom of Hijaz, 1916–1925; his defeat by IBN SA'UD and the incorporation of Hijaz in the Saudi Kingdom see ARAB REVOLT, HUSSEIN IBN ALI, HASHEMITES. After the conquest of Hijaz, Ibn Sa'ud assumed the title King of Hijaz and Sultan of Najd in 1926, changing it in 1927 to King of Hijaz and Najd (until 1932, when the Kingdom was renamed The Saudi Arabian Kingdom). Hijaz was at first administered as one unit and its governor, the King's son FEISAL, was given the title Viceroy. But later Hijaz was divided into several provinces and disappeared as an administrative unit.

HISTADRUT   see ISRAEL.

HIZBALLAH   Shi'ite-Muslim political movement and party in LEBANON. The term Hizballah (the Party

of God) is mentioned twice in the Qur'an (Surat al-Ma'ida, v. 56; Surat al-Mujadila, v. 22). Its main strongholds are the Southern Suburb of Beirut, the Beqa' Valley (especially the town of Ba'albek) and South Lebanon—all poor and underdeveloped areas with an overwhelming Shi'ite majority.

Hizballah is in fact a loose coalition of several Shi'ite radical political groups—mostly cleric unions and militant groups that broke away from the more moderate AMAL movement. It was founded during the 1982 war in Lebanon, inspired by the Iranian Revolution three years earlier and by the presence of approximately 1,500 Iranian Revolutionary Guards (PASDARAN)—troops and clerics sent by Iran to the Beqa'. Its founders, a group of young Shi'ite clerics, were adherents of a Shi'ite high-ranking cleric, Shaykh Muhammad Hussein Fadlallah, who is considered the movement's spiritual leader. They were all educated in the Shi'i religious centers of QOM (in IRAN) and al-Najaf (in IRAQ) and upon returning to Lebanon established Shi'i religious colleges there. Although it portrays itself as a tightly-knit party, Hizballah lacks formal organization and its various subgroups retain their separate existence, relying both on the religious authority of their charismatic leaders as well as on primordial attachments of family and clan. The movement is financed both by donations and outside aid, coming mainly from Iran, and engages both in social and political (including military) activities.

As opposed to Amal, the secular Lebanese Shi'ite movement which persistently tried to gain recognition from the Lebanese state and receive its due share in Lebanese politics, Hizballah offered a complete political alternative to the Lebanese state: the establishment of an Islamic state in Lebanon based on the Iranian model. These contending views, as well as the bitter competition between the two movements over the support of the Shi'i community, led them into violent military clashes between 1988–1990. As Amal moved closer to SYRIA, which became the dominant force in Lebanon since 1983, Hizballah sought aid and guidance from Iran. Iran's proclaimed animosity towards the US and ISRAEL, and Israeli and American military presence in Lebanon, especially in Shi'i-populated areas, added to this hatred. Starting from 1983, Hizballah carried out violent attacks against American and Israeli targets using suicide bombers, abductions (including the kidnapping of over fifty Western diplomats in the 1980s—Hizballah denied responsibility for some of these acts) and airplane hijackings. The movement's radical views and bold methods appealed to young Shi'i militants, who left Amal and joined its ranks, and earned the movement domestic as well as international publication. Syria allowed Hizballah to operate quite freely, using it as a proxy in its struggle against the Israeli forces in South Lebanon and against the Western Multinational Force in Beirut (i.e. the bombings of the American embassy in Beirut, the US Marine headquarters and the French headquarters in 1983, which led to the departure of these forces from Lebanon). However, when the movement's actions stood in conflict with Syrian interests in Lebanon—preserving the Lebanese state and maintaining Syrian hegemony over it—Syria did not hesitate to act vigorously against Hizballah, despite the Syria-Iran alliance. In 1987, for example, when Syrian forces moved into West Beirut, they killed twenty-three Hizballah supporters in what was described as a "massacre" by Shaykh Fadlallah. As the Lebanese Civil War neared its end in the early 1990s, the Lebanese Government did not disarm Hizballah, like it did to all other Lebanese militias, claiming that Hizballah is entitled to keep its weapons and use them for "resistance" against the Israeli occupation in the South. At the same time, Hizballah entered the Lebanese political arena as a political party, and in 1992 and 1996 participated in the Lebanese parliamentary elections and sent deputies to the Lebanese parliament. The main concern of the Hizballah leadership since the start of the Middle East peace process in 1991 and the peace negotiations between Israel and Syria (and Lebanon) has been the future of the movement when peace comes. Lebanese officials have stated that Israeli withdrawal from South Lebanon will lead to the disarmament of Hizballah, and Hizballah leaders expressed concern, bearing in mind the position of similar movements in other Arab states. Meanwhile, Hizballah, acting under the name of "the Lebanese Resistance Movement" is the main force behind the continuous guerrilla war staged against the Israeli Army and its surrogate, the "SOUTH LEBANON ARMY" in South Lebanon, inflicting heavy casualties to both forces.

The current secretary-general of Hizballah is Shaykh Hassan Nasrallah (b. 1953) who was elected in 1992 after the death of his predecessor, Shaykh Abbas Mussawi (b. 1952), in an Israeli air-raid assassination. Nasrallah is considered relatively moderate compared to the more radical former Secretary-General, Subhi Tufaili (b. 1948). Thus, while the former represents willingness to cease the movement's armed struggle against Israel once it has withdrawn to the international border, Tufaili maintains that the war against Israel must continue until the liberation of JERUSALEM from Israel's occupation.

HOLY PLACES The Middle East is the cradle of the three monotheistic religions, Judaism, Christianity and ISLAM, and is extremely important to hundreds of millions of members of these faiths throughout the world.

Islam: Most places sacred to Islam are in the Arab countries and ISRAEL. The city most holy to Muslims is Mecca. This is in HIJAZ which is the birthplace of the Prophet Muhammad and the site of the *Ka'ba* Mosque (with the sacred black rock venerated since pre-Islamic days). One of the five main precepts of Islam is making pilgrimage (*hajj*) to Mecca at least once in a lifetime. The second-holiest city is Medina (*al-madina*), also in Hijaz, where the Prophet took refuge and where he is buried. Third is JERUSALEM (*al-quds*), which was the first direction to which Muslims turn in praying (*uwla l-qiblatain*) before the Prophet shifted it to the *Ka'ba*. More specifically, Jerusalem is the site of two Muslim shrines located on the Temple Mount—the Noble Sanctuary (*al-haram al-sharif*), "The Farthest Mosque" *al-masjid al-aqsa* and the Dome of the Rock (*qubbat al-sakhra*) also incorrectly referred to as the Mosque of Omar. According to Muslim tradition, the Prophet miraculously traveled at midnight to this place, thence to ascend to the seven heavens while his winged horse, *al-Buraq*, remained tied to the Western Wall. This tradition is celebrated annually on 27 of Rajab, as the "Night of Ascension" (*lailat al-mi'raj*), considered by some as post-Qur'anic in its main elements, emphasized the ties of Islam with Judaism and Christianity and created a custom of making a pilgrimage to Jerusalem, too.

The Tomb of the Patriarchs in Hebron (*al-Khalil*) particularly that of Abraham, also called "God's Friend" (*khalil allah*, a mosque, *al-Haram al-Khalili*, built in the seventh century on earlier, ancient foundations, enshrines the burial cave and is also venerated by Muslims.

The Shiʻi branch of Islam also venerates as a holy place the tomb of Hussein, grandson of the Prophet, near where he fell in battle, and its mosque in Karbala in IRAQ. Another Shiʻi holy place is al-Najaf in Iraq—according to Shiʻi tradition this is the site of the tomb of Ali, Muhammad's son-in-law and the fourth CALIPH. Two additional towns in Iraq, al-Kazimain and Samarraʻ, contain the tombs of later heads (IMAM) of the SHIʻA and are places of pilgrimage and centers of Shiʻi-Islamic learning (as are al-Mashhad and Qum in Iran).

Muslim masses in most Middle Eastern countries (but particularly in the MAGHREB), also venerate local tombs of sages, prophets, saints, holy men—many of them reflecting invented traditions—having their memorial days (*mawsim*, pl. *mawasim*), when pilgrimage ceremonies are held. Many of these sites are linked to pre-Islamic traditions (in Palestine, many of the tombs are linked to biblical names), such as seasonal and agricultural feasts. The Islamic establishment has never formally sanctioned this popular veneration of tombs, nor has it ever denounced or banned it.

The DRUZE venerate the tomb of Nabi (the Prophet) Shuʻaib, their legendary ancestor identified with biblical Jethro the Midianite, Moses' father-in-law, at Hittin in Israel. Additional Druze holy places are the tombs of Sheikhs Abdallah al-Tanukhi at Abayya in Lebanon, Ali al-Yaʻfuri in the Golan, Nabi Sablan near Hurfeish and al-Khidr near Kafr Yassif, both in Israel. The BAHAʻIS venerate the tombs of their creed's founders at Haifa and Acre in Israel.

For CHRISTIANS, all of Palestine/Israel is the Holy Land. About 100 sites associated with events related in the Christian scriptures are considered specifically holy places, and churches were built on most of them. The most important holy places are in Jerusalem: the Church of the Holy Sepulchre at the traditional site of the Crucifixion and the Tomb of Jesus; the Via Dolorosa, with its stations; the Cenacle (the Room of the Last Supper), on Mount Zion; the Mount of Olives, with the Tomb of Mary; the Garden of Gethsemane and the Church of Ascension. In Bethlehem, there is the Church of the Nativity and the nearby Shepherds' Field, in Nazareth—the Catholic Basilica of the Annunciation, and the Church of St. Gabriel are held by the GREEK-ORTHODOX to be the site of the Annunciation. Other holy places in the Galilee include the Church of Cana, the place of Christ's first miracle, and Mount Tabor, the site of the Transfiguration. The Lake of Galilee is associated with several miracles performed by Jesus. Churches and chapels near its shore mark scriptural episodes such as the Sermon on the Mount and the multiplication of loaves and fishes. The River Jordan, the site of the baptism of Jesus, is considered sacred.

Several of these holy places, especially the more important ones—such as thus the Church of the Holy Sepulchre, the Church of the Nativity, the Tomb of Mary and the site of the Ascension—are jointly owned by different Christian denominations and have been historically the object of conflicting claims and interdenominational violent disputes. The ownership of and worship at such sites, are thus regulated by the status quo of 1757, as defined in 1852 by a Firman of the Ottoman Sultan. The British Mandatory government, JORDAN from 1948 to 1967, and Israel since 1967, adhered to the status quo except for the Deir al-Sultan monastery adjacent to the Holy Sepulchre—in dispute between the COPTS and the Ethiopians—which was handed to the Ethiopians, by a Jordanian court in 1950, returned to the Copts by King HUSSEIN, overruling the court, then seized by the Ethiopian monks in 1970, with the acquiescence of the Israeli government. The case had been brought before the Israeli Supreme Court which sentenced on principle, in favor of the Copts but left the timing for its implementation to the Israeli government's credence. Israel preferred to maintain the state of affairs intact in concern over the Ethiopian Jewish community (*Falasha*), thus affecting its relations with EGYPT, which has supported the Copts' claims for the restoration of their status).

For Jews, too, the entire Land of Israel is The Holy Land. Especially sacred is the Temple Mount in Jerusalem, barred to Jewish worship. The adjacent Western Wall (part of the Temple Mount Wall) is the only part of the site where Jews pray. Jews also venerate the Tomb of the Patriarchs in Hebron and of Rachel near Bethlehem, the alleged Tomb of King David on Mount Zion (sacred also to Muslims and Christians), as well as several tombs of ancient and medieval sages (such as Rabbi Shimʻon Bar-Yohai in Meron, Maimonides and Rabbi Meʻir Baʻal Hanness in Tiberias etc.).

Holy places to Jews and Muslims in Palestine have been an indivisible part of the ARAB-ISRAEL CONFLICT.

The Western Wall was the cause of serious Jewish-Muslim violent riots in 1929. Since June 1967, all Holy places came under Israeli rule and became, in principle, accessible to all. However, with the unification of East and West Jerusalem by Israel in the wake of the June 1967 War, the Temple Mount became a major concern for the Muslim world and one of the sources of Arab-Israeli tension and dispute. This resulted in intensified political struggle over this place, nourished by the attempts of extremist groups to revive traditions of Jewish worship on the Temple Mount, and competition between both sides over territory and control; attempts of sabotage by Jewish and Christian fanatics (the arson, by an Australian tourist of al-Aqsa Mosque in 1969; the attempt of a messianic Jewish underground to bomb the Temple Mount Mosques in the early 1980s); the opening of the Hashmonean Tunnel along the Temple Mount Wall, in October 1996; Israeli purchases of real estates in the Muslim Quarter of the Old City of Jerusalem; and the construction of new neighborhoods in East Jerusalem, all were interpreted as an attempt to make the city purely Jewish.

Although since 1967 Israel gave access to the Temple Mount to Muslims crossing the Jordan River's "open bridges," very few would make use of this right and visit the Temple Mount. Since 1994 many Muslims from the Far East and Africa started to arrive in Jerusalem for a pilgrimage (following a FATWA—a religious scholarly verdict by the Saudi Mufti al-Baz allowing it while still under Israeli rule). However, Muslims, especially in the Arab countries, still cannot acquiesce in the occupation by Israel of Islam's third holy site (though Israel allows the Temple Mount to be administered by a Muslim institution). This also includes Muslim citizens of countries in a state of peace with Israel, such as Egypt, Jordan, and MOROCCO who make no use of the right to visit as long as the Israeli-Palestinian peace is stalemated.

Since the resettlement of Jews in the city of Hebron in the early 1980s, the Tomb of the Patriarchs also became a permanent site of friction and violence between Jewish messianic settlers and local Muslim residents and worshipers, which culminated in the massacre conducted by a Jewish settler at the Cave of the Patriarchs in February 1994.

HORMUZ, STRAITS OF

HORMUZ, STRAITS OF The straits connecting the PERSIAN GULF with the Gulf of Oman and the Arabian Sea—named after the town and island of Hormuz, close to the Persian shore. It served from 1594 to 1622 as a main center of Portuguese trade and naval control. The Straits are bordered in the north by IRAN, and in the south by "Ras Musandam"; an exclave belonging to OMAN. Their width at the narrowest point is 35 miles (56 km.), or, if measured from the Persian shore islands, 24 miles (37 km.). The Straits are within the territorial waters of either Iran or Oman, as both claim territorial waters of 12 miles (19 km.) The main shipping channel is closer to the Omani shore.

The Straits of Hormuz are the main thoroughfare for most of the Persian Gulf oil. Before the IRAN-IRAQ WAR an oil tanker passed through them every ten to fifteen minutes, with nearly 20 million barrels per day—almost half of the oil consumed by the non-communist world. Estimated oil flow through the Straits in 1995 was approximately 14 million barrels per day. The security and defense of the freedom of shipping through the Straits were therefore vital. (For threats to this security in the 1960s and 1970s and in the Iraq-Iran War since 1980, and the involvement of Iran and the great powers, see PERSIAN GULF.)

A US-Oman Agreement of 1980 (renewed in 1990) on defense cooperation and facilities for the US, does not specifically refer to the Straits, though it includes US aid for the development of defense and naval installations in Oman's Ras Musandam province, strengthening the defense of the Straits. US air crafts flew regularly over the Straits of Hormuz during the Iran-Iraq War from bases in OMAN.

Plans to circumvent the Straits of HORMUZ by the construction of oil pipelines to loading points beyond them, have been thus far only partially realized. The main alternative routes are: the 4.8 billion dollar capacity East-West Crude Oil Pipeline (Petroline), which is used mainly to transport oil to refineries on the Red Sea teminals for direct export to European markets.

HUSSEIN FADLALLAH, MUHAMMAD

HUSSEIN FADLALLAH, MUHAMMAD (b. 1935)   Lebanese Shi'ite cleric and religious authority, considered to be the spiritual leader of the Lebanese Shi'ite Movement HIZBALLAH. Fadlallah was born in Najf, IRAQ, to a family of Shi'i scholars related to the prophet Muhammad. His father came to this Shi'i religious center in 1928 from the South

Lebanese village of Aynata. Fadlallah was a disciple of the Iranian Ayatollah Abu el-Qassem Kho'i, an important Shi'ite scholar and religious authority, and served as his advisor in financial matters. He was also very close to another important, more politicized, Shi'i theologian, Muhammad Baqer al-Sadr (1930–1980), and became acquainted with an Iranian cleric, Ayatollah Rouhullah KHOMEINI. From then Fadlallah adopted not the conservative "quietist" ideas dominating the Shi'i theological circles, including Kho'i, but the more radical views preached by Sadr and Khomeini: a call for social revolution that will replace the existing regimes, paving the way for the establishment of an Islamic Republic led by religious clerics. In 1966 Fadlallah came to LEBANON, settling in the poor Shi'i-populated southern suburb of Beirut, where he found an attentive audience for his preaching. He established charity institutions, schools, clinics and orphanages and encouraged Shi'i religious education. He taught and preached his radical doctrine, emphasizing Shi'i identity and affiliation and active defense of the oppressed, differing in this from his colleague and competitor, the Shi'i leader Mussa al-SADR, who preached taking part in a reformed Lebanese state. After the formation of Hizballah in early 1983, following the Israeli invasion of Lebanon in 1982, Fadlallah became its spiritual leader and religious authority. His status was enhanced in 1986, when during a visit to IRAN, he was acknowledged by Khomeini as a "model to imitate", making him eligible to issue judgments on the application of religious law without consulting any superior authority.

In his books, including *Islam and the Logic of Force* (1976), written after the Lebanese Civil War, Fadlallah dealt with political issues such as the Palestinian problem, the internal Lebanese situation—MARONITE dominance of the Muslims and inter-community violence—as well as religious questions arising from the extreme methods applied by Shi'i radicals in Lebanon—hostage-taking and suicide attacks. Although he insisted on giving primacy to non-violent means, Fadlallah is reported to have authorized the use of more extreme, violent methods, such as the bombing of the Multinational Peace Force in Lebanon in 1983, and the kidnappings of Westerners in Lebanon in the course of the 1980s. This made him a high priority target for his adversaries. In 1980 Iraqi agents tried to as-

sassinate him, as part of their effort to suppress the Shi'i Da'wa movement in Iraq, and in 1985 a car bomb exploded near a mosque where he preached, killing scores of Shi'i people praying. (*Hizballah* blamed the US and Fadlallah himself believed ISRAEL was responsible.)

al-HUSSEINI, FEISAL (b. 1940)   Palestinian politician. Born in Baghdad to Abd al-Qader al-Husseini, the legendary Palestinian-Arab military figure in the history of Arab Palestine (killed in 1948 in the Qastel); nephew of the MUFTI of JERUSALEM, al-Hajj Amin al-HUSSEINI, the most prominent Palestinian national leader of the Palestinian Arabs in Mandatory Palestine. From the late 1980s, Feisal al-Husseini emerged as the most prominent "inside" figure among Palestinians in the WEST BANK and GAZA STRIP (as opposed to the "outside"PALESTINE LIBERATION ORGANIZATION (PLO) leadership). He was educated in Cairo, Beirut, Baghdad and Aleppo and became active in *Fatah* in 1965. After 1967 he was involved in public activities against Israeli occupation of the West Bank and Gaza. Consequently he was arrested, put under house arrest or administrative detention. In 1979, he established the Arab Studies Society; a research and data collecting center in East Jerusalem. The Center was closed down by ISRAEL in 1987 on the grounds of propagation against Israel, but was reopened under international pressure in 1991.

During the INTIFADA, Husseini was secretly among the few representatives of Jerusalem in the "United National Leadership." This gave directions to the population in the Israeli Occupied Territories and kept in touch with the PLO leadership in Tunis. At the same time, however, he remained a prominent speaker of the Palestinians in face of the Israeli authorities, negotiating future solution possibilities with Israeli dovish personalities. As a chief speaker for the "Inside" with the PLO, and due to his family prestige and reputation, he has been in a position that could challenge the Tunis leadership and influence its resolution. Following King HUSSEIN's proclamation of disengagement from the West Bank on 31 July 1988, Husseini was the primary force behind the idea of seizing the opportunity for the proclamation of an independent Palestinian state. This idea was eventually adopted by the Palestinian National Council held in Tunis in November that year. Already before the Madrid Conference (October 1991), Husseini had led a Palestinian delegation to meetings with the American Secretary of State, James Baker, in Jerusalem. This aim was to discuss—in coordination with the PLO—the terms and goals of Palestinian participation in the Madrid Conference. Along with Dr. Haidar Abd al-Shafi and Hanan ASHRAWI, Husseini led the Palestinian delegation to Madrid and Washington from October 1991 until the summer of 1993 which was conducted officially and directly between Israelis and Palestinians.

Still, as an "inside" leader, Husseini had to make his own way up in the Palestinian political heirarchy following the Oslo Agreement and the establishment of the PALESTINIAN AUTHORITY (PA) in June 1994. Already during the Washington Talks, Husseini turned the "Orient House," an old guest house in East Jerusalem, into the "New Orient House." This became the headquarters of the Palestinian delegation to the peace talks. Later, the Orient House was recognized as the center of Palestinian political, social and cultural activities, and indeed, a focal point of Palestinian national activity in Jerusalem. This development aroused much Israeli resentment, particularly from the right-wing parties, due to the overt challenge posed by the Orient House to Israeli sovereignty in the whole unified city of Jerusalem.

In 1996, Husseini was appointed a member in the newly elected PLO Executive Committee in charge of Jerusalem affairs. In this capacity, Husseini exerts himself to gaining moral and financial support for the cause of East Jerusalem among both Western and Arab oil-rich states, in order to meet the city's Palestinian residents' needs in housing, preservation of the holy places for ISLAM and promoting the demand that East Jerusalem should be the capital of the Palestinian state in the final status negotiations with Israel.

HUSSEIN IBN ALI, SHARIF   see HASHEMITES, MCMAHON-HUSSEIN CORRESPONDENCE.

HUSSEIN IBN TALAL (b. 1935)   King of JORDAN. Born in Amman and educated at Victoria College (Alexandria), Harrow, and Sandhurst Military Academy, in BRITAIN, Hussein succeeded his father TALAL in 1952, when the latter was dethroned on the grounds of mental illness. As he was a minor, a Re-

gency Council ruled for him until May 1953, when he came of age and was crowned.

Hussein ascended to the throne at a time of domestic and regional radical ferment. As a ruler of a poor state and politically divided society he had to handle tremendous challenges in which his statesmanship, resilience and pragmatism were repeatedly demonstrated, explaining the survival and entrenchment of his regime. Hussein succeeded in preserving his throne in spite of numerous plots sponsored by enemies from within and outside Jordan. These were led by Palestinians, EGYPT and SYRIA. His success was mostly a result of maintaining a balance between domestic and regional threats and opportunities; shifting alliances; cooptation of domestic enemies to the ruling system and resorting to force against them only as a last resort, as it occurred in 1957 and 1970 (see below).

In the first four years of his reign, he had to make significant concessions to nationalist groups, concerning both internal and foreign affairs. He agreed in 1954 to an amendment of the constitution enabling Parliament to dismiss the government by a simple majority. In December 1955 he had to withdraw a decision to adhere to the Baghdad Pact, bowing to politicians of the opposition and popular demonstrations. In 1956 he dismissed General Glubb Pasha, the British commander of his army, who was viewed by Arab nationalists as a symbol of Jordan's subservience to British imperialism.

Under the leftist-nationalist government led by Prime Minister Suleiman al-Nabulsi, established following the elections of October 1956, Hussein approved Jordan's adherence to an Egyptian-Syrian defense pact and joint command. Early in 1957 the abrogation of the Anglo-Jordanian Treaty and the replacement of British aid, was also approved particularly for his army, by Egyptian, Syrian and Saudi subsidies.

In 1957, however, Hussein halted the integration of Jordan into a leftist-Nasserist bloc. He dismissed the leftist government—a step triggered by the Government's decision to establish diplomatic relations with the USSR. (This was then considered a "leftist" departure from traditional policies. It later became normal, accepted policy.) He averted, by a courageous personal confrontation, a subversive, apparently Egyptian-supported, military plot. He outlawed all parties (party activity was legalized only in

1992). He reinstated conservative governments and army leaders and established a de facto alliance with the US. In February 1958, faced with the merger of Egypt and Syria, Hussein took a determined stand against what he conceived to be a move to expand the power of the leftist-Nasserist Arab states and acquire domination of the Arab world. He created the Jordan-Iraq ARAB UNITY and became its deputy-head. That Federation collapsed in July 1958, due to the republican coup in IRAQ. Jordan felt isolated and threatened by UNITED ARAB REPULIC (UAR) subversion. Hussein then asked Britain to send troops to protect Jordan which remained until October. He also complained to the UN Security Council against the UAR.

In May 1967, in the frenzy of ABDEL NASSER's escalating preparations for war against ISRAEL, Hussein signed a defense treaty with Egypt as a result of heavy domestic pressure. This symbolically placed his Army under Egyptian command. He disregarded Israel's warning and promise not to attack Jordan and entered the Six-Day War. In his memoirs he claims he was misled by Nasser informing him of a victorious Egyptian advance.

Jordan's defeat in that war and the loss of the WEST BANK were a heavy blow to King Hussein. King Hussein became the main protagonist of a negotiated settlement with Israel. This would secure the return of the Arab occupied territories. It was then that he became involved in secret meetings with Israeli leaders—all futile—regarding possible settlement over the West Bank. His alignment with Nasser established on the eve of the war was sustained until the latter's death in September 1970. This was manifested in their joint support of UN Security Council Resolution 242, of November 1967. His position was also undermined by the presence of Palestinian guerrilla organizations on, and operations against Israel from Jordanian soil, and their violation of Jordanian sovereignty. This created a state-within-the-state. For the Jordan-PLO crisis that culminated in 1970, see JORDAN, PALESTINE LIBERATION ORGANIZATION (PLO).

When Hussein completed the elimination of the PLO in spring and summer 1971, he was denounced and reviled in most of the Arab world. Jordan's relations with several Arab states were severed. Syrian troops actually invaded Jordan in September 1970. However these were halted by Jordanian forces which were backed by threats of US and Israeli intervention.

Hussein's status in the Arab world recovered gradually in the 1970s, mainly due to his domestic stability and prosperity, as well as the military support Jordan received from the US in the early 1970s. Despite the gradual erosion of his position *vis-a-vis* the West Bank—a result of the rising political status of the PLO as the representative of the Palestinian residents of this area—the Arab regimes could hardly ignore his vital role in the conflict with Israel or the duties he fulfilled toward the West Bank Palestinian residents. Yet, the king also contributed to his readmission into the Arab fold by adopting a rear guard strategy on the West Bank. He gradually moderated his claim for this territory by offering their Palestinian residents a further role in determining their future within a Jordanian-based political framework. In March 1972 Hussein proposed a united kingdom for the future Jordan-West Bank relationship, to be established after Israel had withdrawn from the territory. The plan was structured after the example of Great Britain, composed of the East and West Banks and granting the Palestinian a large degree of autonomy. However, this idea was widely rejected by the Arab states.

Shortly before the 1973 War (see ARAB-ISRAEL CONFLICT), Presidents al-SADAT of Egypt and ASAD of Syria met with Hussein to mend fences with him and probably probe his willingness to take an active role on his front, in case of war with Israel. Following this summit, Hussein met secretly with Prime Minister Golda MEIR of Israel, warning her of the imminent Arab offensive. Yet he could not specify its exact date. Later he decided to refrain from any hostilities from his borders with Israel, merely sending two armored brigades to help Syria. One of these sustained heavy losses. After the war, US-mediated talks on a disengagement agreement with Israel, similar to those Israel concluded with Egypt and Syria, failed. The gap between what Israel offered in the way of a token withdrawal, or functional sovereignty (over population, not territory) was a far cry from what Hussein regarded as a minimum requirement even for an interim agreement. Moreover, Hussein's failure to attain a foothold in the West Bank through American diplomacy, at the expense of the PLO, triggered the reaction of the PLO-Arab supporters: In October 1974, Hussein had to acquiesce in a decision of the all-Arab summit at Rabat to reaffirm the Palestinian people's right for self-determination and to recognize the PLO as their sole legitimate representative.

Hussein was always considered moderate in Middle Eastern affairs, including the conflict with Israel. While he could do little to educate Arab public opinion and guide it toward coexistence with Israel, he persistently sought to explore the possibility of a settlement with Israel or at least tacit cooperation with it, especially after 1967. He had numerous secret meetings with Israeli leaders from 1963 until the signing of the peace treaty with Israel (1994) but the gap revealed at those meetings was always too wide to bridge. What deterred Hussein from separate peaceful policy toward Israel was the fear of hostile Arab and Palestinian response which would endanger his throne. He insisted on complete Israeli withdrawal from the West Bank, including East JERUSALEM, and even if he was ready to make some territorial concessions, they were far from whatever Israeli leaders demanded or proposed (e.g., the Allon Plan). Nevertheless, he maintained "open bridges" between Jordan and the West Bank for movement of people and goods, fostering political support of the Palestinian residents through financial and administrative support for public institutions and leading figures.

Hussein's rapprochement with the PLO and his February 1985 agreement with ARAFAT represented the king's attempt to exploit the PLO's predicament after the expulsions of its leadership from LEBANON by Israel (1982) and Syria (1983). This was in an attempt to work out an agreed formula of political action in the context of the Middle East peacemaking. Although the agreement tacitly referred to the signatories as equal parties, it recognized the king's seniority as the future head of a confederation of Jordan and the Palestinian political entity. The agreement was abrogated in February 1986 by Hussein, mainly because of the PLO's failure to accept Resolution 242 of the Security Council (see JORDAN and PALESTINE LIBERATION ORGANIZATION). The outbreak of the uprising (INTIFADA) in the territories, expressing strong support of the PLO, and Jordanian concern of a spill-over effect into the East Bank led Hussein to announce on 31 July 1988 his disengagement from the West Bank. He hitherto renounced responsibility to its Palestinian residents, with the ex-

ception of the Muslim establishment in Jerusalem. This step not only finally separated Jordan from Palestine for the first time since 1948, defining them as two distinct nation states, it also paved the way for the PLO's proclamation of the Palestinian independent state less than five months later.

Following the invasion of KUWAIT by Iraq, Hussein adopted a middle-ground position in the inter-Arab arena, apparently due to strong domestic support of Saddam HUSSEIN's action. While rejecting the Iraqi act against Kuwait, he objected to foreign intervention attempting to mediate between Saddam Hussein and his Arab rivals. However, this position identified him as a supporter of Iraq. His traditional alignment with the Gulf conservative regimes, brokeup straining his relations with the US. These relations, however, were improved with the King's early consent to the US proposals for an international peace conference in Madrid.

In home affairs, Hussein succeeded in maintaining a stable, orderly regime and impressive economic development. Even before the era of democratization, beginning in the 1989 general elections, the regime was relatively liberal and formally parliamentary. After a long suspension of Parliament (1974–1984), due to the dilemma of the representation of the West Bank residents, (see JORDAN) Parliamentary elections were held in 1989 and later in 1993. This indicated along with laws granting more political freedom, Hussein's intention of establishing Jordan as a democratic society. At present, Hussein alone leads his country, but he seems to be genuinely popular. Hussein is also internationally highly respected—a standing which, being an excellent speaker, a master of public relations and an attractive media personality, he carefully nourishes.

Hussein married four times and has eleven children. His wives: a. his distant relative Princess Dina Abdel Hamid (1955; one daughter; divorced in 1957); Antoinette Gardiner, daughter of a British army officer, converted to Islam and named Muna al-Hussein (1961; two sons, two daughters; divorced 1972); Aliya Touqan, daughter of the prominent official Baha al-Din Touqan (1972; one daughter, one son; killed 1977 in an accident); and Lisa Halabi, daughter of a prominent American businessman of Lebanese origin, converted to Islam and named Nur al-Hussein (1978; two sons, two daughters). In 1965 Hussein named his younger brother Hassan (b. 1947) as Crown Prince—replacing the middle brother Muhammad (b. 1945). Next in the line of succession is Hussein's third son Ali (b. 1975) as Crown Prince after Hassan.

HUSSEIN-MCMAHON CORRESPONDENCE
see MCMAHON-HUSSEIN CORRESPONDENCE.

HUSSEIN (AL-TIKRITI), SADDAM (b. 1937)
Iraqi President from 1979, and the strong man of IRAQ since 1970–1971. A SUNNI-Muslim born in Auja, a village near the town of Tikrit in north-central Iraq, to a landless peasant who died before he was born. Hussein was raised by his uncle Khairallah Talfa. After arriving in Baghdad for further education in 1955, Hussein joined the BA'TH Party which was then an underground organization. He served in its strong-arm squads. He was involved in plots against the royal HASHEMITE regime and imprisoned in 1956. He continued his subversive activities under the QASSEM regime after his ascendancy to power in 1958. In October 1959, he was involved in an abortive attempt on the life of Qassem, was injured, and escaped, first to SYRIA and then to EGYPT (where he reportedly studied law at Cairo University). He returned to Iraq in 1963, after Qassem was toppled in a coup that brought the Ba'th Party to power, and soon joined the Ba'th leadership. In 1963 he was named a member of its "regional", i.e. Iraqi, command and in 1965 also of the "national", i.e., all-Arab one. In 1966 he became Assistant Secretary-General of the Iraqi Ba'th Party. In 1964, after President Abdel Salam Aref turned against the Ba'th, Hussein was involved in a failed attempt to overthrow him. He was arrested, but escaped in 1966. He was pardoned later the same year.

After the Ba'th coup of 1968, Hussein rose to a top position of power. Although not a member of the Revolutionary Command Council, (RCC), the ruling body of the Iraqi state he was extremely influential due to his blood ties with the RCC Chairman Ahmad Hassan al-Bakr, a cousin of Khairallah Talfa. In November 1969, retaining his post as Assistant Secretary General of the Ba'th Party, Hussein became Deputy Chairman of the RCC, making an alliance between the two figures which secured their dominance at the RCC and outmaneuver their RCC colleagues. Saddam Hussein focused on rebuilding the Ba'th Party and resolving the Kurdish problem (see

KURDS, Iraq). In the factional struggles inside the Iraqi Ba'th, Hussein headed the "civilian" or "party" faction against the "military" one. Having grown within the party apparatus and with no military background, he attained an undisputed primacy of the party. Between 1970–1971 he built an armed party militia and a strong secret service under party control (actually his own). Using this Ba'th apparatus, from 1968 to 1971, Hussein systematically "purged" the state and party establishment, and public and political life, eliminating his rivals and adversaries one after the other—first non-Ba'th elements, "rightists" and "reactionaries" (whom he accused of plots and attempted coups in May 1969 and January 1970), then Ba'th "extremists" (e.g. those opposing the agreement he reached in 1970 with the Kurdish rebels) and finally the Ba'th military faction and other rivals within the party (such as Hardan Abdel Ghaffar, Saleh Mahdi Ammash, Abdel Karim al-Sheikhli and others). In June 1973 he suppressed a coup attempt by Nazem Kazzar, the head of his own security apparatus. Reportedly, he had himself instigated Kazzar to plot against Bakr, but abandoned him when the plot failed.

From about 1971, Hussein ruled Iraq as the chief and primary leader, with Bakr as increasingly a figurehead. In 1975 he signed the Algiers Agreement with the Iranian Shah ending a lengthy dispute over the SHATT AL-ARAB Waterway and putting an end to Iran's support for the Kurdish Rebellion in Iraq. In the late 1970s Saddam challenged Bakr's conciliating policy toward the growing Shi'i agitation inspired by revolutionary IRAN. Hussein completed his takeover of total power in July 1979, allegedly after disclosing a secret message from Bakr to Syrian President al-ASAD to speed up negotiations on unity between the two countries. Bakr was forced to resign and Hussein was named Secretary-General of the Ba'th Party, Chairman of the RCC and President of Iraq. Hussein accompanied the dismissal of Bakr with another bloody purge of the Ba'th command—on the grounds of conspiracy against the state—executing, after a summary trial, twenty-one leading functionaries, including five members of the RCC, and jailing thirty-three more. The purges encompassed also trade unions, student unions and local governments.

As sole leader since 1979, Hussein has been glorified by an incessant personality cult. This political conduct was particularly ruthless and brutal, exceeding all hitherto normative boundaries, even in a society notorious for its violent political culture—which the Iraqi society was. Yet his policies, both internal and external, were pragmatic, with frequent tactical shifts and a capacity to adapt to changing circumstances. Despite his identification with the "party faction", he preserved in the long term, a delicate party-army balance. He followed, sometimes, a remarkably moderate line towards the Kurdish autonomist rebels. It was Hussein who pushed through, in March 1970, an agreement with the rebels conceding many of their demands and granting them a large measure of semi-autonomy. Yet when the Kurds rebelled again, he vigorously suppressed them in 1974–1975 and used his 1975 accord with Iran to crush them. Simultaneously, he continued implementing the Kurdish autonomy as he perceived it. He tried to widen the political base of his regime and in 1973 formed a "Progressive and Patriotic National Front" in which the Communists and a Kurdish faction collaborating with the government joined the Ba'th; but in 1977–1978 he again suppressed the Communists. He suppressed the militant Shi'i movement al-Da'wa, though he was willing to allocate generous funding to Shi'i shrines and community needs, and managed to prevent a general uprising or widespread resistance of the Shi'is (constituting more than half of the population). He held, for the first time since 1958, elections for a National Assembly, in June 1980 and October 1984, with a single list of candidates endorsed by him and his apparatus.

Hussein's foreign policies, too, were rather pragmatic, as evident in Iraq's alliance with the Soviet Union; its *rapprochement* with the West, since the mid-1970s. Its 1975 agreement with Iran; secession from the REJECTION FRONT; and *rapprochement* with the mainstream and pragmatic Arab states—including with Egypt—shortly after the beginning of the war with Iran (see IRAQ).

In September 1980, Hussein declared war against Iran and invaded its territory, originally to ensure Iraqi control of the eastern bank of Shatt al-Arab, which he had conceded to the Shah in the Algiers Agreement of 1975. Yet despite initial Iraqi success, the offensive was soon contained and within two years Iran had made inroads into Iraqi territory. Saddam Hussein became totally immersed in the War for which he had been held responsible and which

he led, assuming the supreme military command. (He made himself a General in 1976). Iran held Hussein personally responsible for the War, demanding his dismissal and trial as a war criminal as a pre-condition for any peace or cease-fire negotiations. Facing an Iranian threat of penetration into Iraq's territory, in 1984 Hussein sought to expand the war in the Gulf to OIL shipping in an attempt to involve the Western world on his side. In 1982 the Western powers and Soviet Union tacitly cooperated in supporting Iraq militarily and economically, perceiving it a bulwark against the Iranian Shi'i revolution. Iraq was also heavily supported financially by the oil Gulf monarchies, particularly SAUDI ARABIA and KUWAIT. By mid-1987, the growing threat to oil shipping in the Gulf brought to the attention of foreign navies, primarily American, in the Gulf, as constituting another threat to Iran. In 1988 Hussein initiated a series of missile attacks on Iranian cities, and made intensive use of chemical weapons in counter attacks aimed at regaining Iraqi territory captured by Iran. This concentrated effort forced Iran to accept unconditionally UN Security Council Resolution 598, and led to a cease-fire in August 1988 (for the war, its history and results, see IRAN-IRAQ WAR).

The Iraqi war machine developed tremendously during the eight-year war—the purchase and development of military, applied technologies, including missiles, chemical and biological weapons, and infrastructure for nuclear capability. While this war machine strengthened Saddam Hussein domestically, it also claimed vast expenses which Iraq could hardly afford following the War with Iran. This, and the fact that the IRAN-IRAQ WAR solved none of the problems in the name of which Saddam had gone to war in 1980, were at the backdrop of his decision to invade Kuwait on 2 August 1990 and annex it to Iraq shortly thereafter.

The American-led international military and economic blockade against Iraq and gathering of forces for a war coalition on Saudi land left Saddam Hussein unmoved, declaring himself a new hero-savior of the ARAB-Muslim world in the face of a new Crusade. When the ultimatum set by the Security Council expired (15 January 1991), the international war coalition began its offensive against Iraq and liberated Kuwait after forty-five days. In April 1991 Hussein accepted the humiliating UN Security Council Resolution 687, which defined the conditions for lifting the sanctions against Iraq: war reparations, destruction of its medium-range missiles and all weapons of mass destruction and their manufacturing facilities (see GULF WAR).

Despite the lengthy War with Iran and the large-scale destruction caused by both that war and the GULF WAR of 1991, the stupendous casualties caused by Hussein's policies and the severe economic conditions in Iraq caused by the international sanctions, his position in power remained by and large, firm and uncontested. Moreover, despite foreign efforts made by the US government to encourage rebellions against his regime by both Kurds and Shi'i opposition groups, and reported attempts to assassinate him, Hussein survived, primarily due to his effective grip on the military and intelligence apparatus. From the end of the Gulf War, Hussein's main effort, apart from repressing any opposition against his regime and rebuilding Iraq's destroyed infrastructure, was aimed at lifting the economic sanctions against Iraq by using a strategy of brinkmanship, initiating repeated calculated crises. Thus, in October 1994 he moved massive force toward the Kuwaiti border, leading to the arrival of American forces in the region and consequent withdrawal of the Iraqi forces. This resulted in RUSSIA lifting the sanctions against Iraq in the spring of 1995. In April 1995, following pressures by Russia, the Security Council opted for Resolution 986 which allowed Iraq to export 2 billion dollars worth of oil over six months. Another tactic Hussein used to create a crisis situation was his repeated restrictions on the UN teams assigned to supervise the disclosure and destruction of mass destruction weapons on Iraqi soil. The defection to JORDAN of his son-in-law and Minister of Industry, Hussein Kamel, in August 1985, and the information he revealed concerning Iraq's chemical and biological arsenal, worsened Saddam's position both domestically and in the international community. In October 1995 Saddam was elected for another seven-year term as President, by 99.96 percent of the vote, demonstrating his public support. On 20 May 1996, Saddam Hussein was forced by economic constraints to sign the "Oil for Food" Agreement with the UN, accepting Security Council Resolution 986, but its implementation was postponed until November. The agreementwas renewed in July 1997.

In January 1998, with UN sanctions still applied, Saddam Hussein initiated a new crisis by preventing access from the UN teams to the presidential palaces, believed to contain mass destruction weapons, primarily biological weapons. The US and BRITAIN were again the leading forces in a diplomatic effort to force Saddam Hussein's unconditional abiding by the UN resolutions, beginning to prepare militarily for a major air strike against Iraq if it failed to fully comply with the UN resolutions. In February, the UN Secretary General visited Baghdad and reached an agreement with Saddam Hussein that would prevent an American military action against Iraq and provide for an uninterrupted work of UNESCOM. The new crisis demonstrated Saddam Hussein's persistence and growing erosion of the US posture in the Arab states, most of which had remained reserved for the use of force against Iraq.

Since the end of the Gulf War Saddam Hussein has ived in quite isolation from his own people and the foreign world. During this period he apparently has become dependent primarily on his Foreign Minister Tareq AZIZ for decision making on foreign policy.

al-HUSSEINI Prominent Arab family in JERUSALEM, claiming descent from the Prophet Muhammad and thus has Sharifian standing (though its members do not use the title *Sharif*). A member of the Husseini clan was MUFTI of Jerusalem in the seventeenth century, and several others bore the title *Naqib al-Ashraf* ("Chief of the Prophets Descendants") of Jerusalem. Since the eighteenth century, some members of the family have held high office, particularly that of Mufti, sometimes succeeded by lineage. In 1921, following the death of the Mufti of Jerusalem Kamel al-Husseini, the British High Commissioner appointed to this prestigious position the latter's stepbrother MUHAMMAD AMIN AL-HUSSEINI, who later became the leading political figure of the Palestinian Arabs under the British Mandate. The Husseini clan accumulated extensive land property from the mid-nineteenth century, mainly in the villages northwest of Jerusalem and Ramallah. Its members held many administrative posts in Ottoman-ruled Palestine, including that of Mayor of Jerusalem several times .

From the 1920s to the 1940s, the name al-Husseini came to denote an influential clan. Also, mainly owing to the dominating influence of al-HAJJ AMIN

AL-HUSSEINI and the Supreme Muslim Council, he headed a political camp. The supporters of Hajj Amin and the Council were called *Majlisiyyun* ("of the Council"), while the opposing camp was called al-*Muaridun* ("The Opposition"); but many simply called the *Majlisiyyun* "Husseinis" (and their opponents "Nashashibis", after the prominent family heading that camp). When the *Majlisiyyun* founded, in 1935, the Arab Palestine Party as their political instrument, it was also often referred to as "The Husseinis".

Under the British Mandate, the Husseinis were identified with intransigent attitudes toward the Zionist movement and the British Mandate, and held the leading positions in the Palestinian-Arab national movement. The most prominent members of the Husseini family in the twentieth century were al-Hajj Amin al-Husseini, the Mufti of Jerusalem (1921–1937), President of the Supreme Muslim Council (SMC) (1922–1937), and Chairman of the Arab Higher Committee (1936–1972); Mussa Kazim al-Husseini, Former Mayor of Jerusalem and President of the Arab Executive Committee (AEC) (1920–1934); Jamal al-Husseini, Secretary of the AEC (1920–1934) and later a member (1936–1948) and Acting Chairman (1946) of the (AHC); and Abd al-Qader al-Husseini, Commander of Rebels Group in the 1936–1939 ARAB REVOLT and commander of the Palestinian-Arab irregular forces in the Jerusalem area during the 1948 War, in which capacity he was killed and became a Palestinian national hero (his son, FEISAL (b. 1940), set up the "Arab Studies Center" in East Jerusalem, considered, as of the late 1980s, the most prominent figure of *Fatah* in the West Bank and Jerusalem). Many other members of the Husseini clan were active in public life during the British Mandate, mostly in nationalist activities, including the Husseini-led Arab Palestinian Party and its organs. Many of the Husseini national activists fled from Palestine to Syria in 1937, with the renewal of the Arab revolt and outlawing the AHC by the British Mandate, and in 1939 joined al-Hajj Amin al-Husseini to his exile in IRAQ. Some of them were captured and detained, or exiled by the British following the repression of the 1941 national revolt which was ostensibly led by Rashid Ali's government but effectively conducted by the Iraqi military, with al-Hajj Amin al-Husseini's inspiration (see IRAQ).

The disintegration and exodus of the Palestinian-Arab leadership in the early months of the 1948

War severely affected the Husseini clan and the political camp it represented (as did the dominating influence of other notable clans among the Palestinians. This was particularly discerned in Jerusalem, the Husseinis' center of power, which had come under divided domination of ISRAEL and JORDAN, sworn enemies of the Palestinian national movement. Some of the Husseinis became political advisors to the rulers in the Arab neighboring states, while others turned to business or migrated out of the Middle East. A leading members of the Husseini clan who still remained in the Jordanian-occupied area was Dr. Mussa Abdallah al-Husseini (1904–1951), a Palestinian Arab national activist who cosponsored the assassination of King ABDALLAH (July 1951), and was tried, found guilty and executed. In spite of the assassination and hostile relations between the Hashemite Jordanian regime and the Husseinis, some of the figures who until early 1951 had been leading opponents of the Jordanian regime, were later co-opted into the political system as members of Parliament and ministers in the Jordanian government. He is considered close to the hard-line wing of the *Fatah* and the PALESTINE LIBERATION ORGANIZATION (PLO).

An exception to the usual ultra-nationalist orientation of the Husseini clan was Fawzi Darwish al-Husseini (1898–1946), who advocated coexistence with the Zionists and in 1946 set up an Arab "New Palestine" association to cooperate with the (Jewish) League for Jewish-Arab Friendship and Cooperation. He was assassinated for this activity in November 1946.

al-HUSSEINI, HAJJ (MUHAMMAD) AMIN
(1897–1974) Palestinian-Arab political and religious leader. Husseini's education included a year at the Jewish-French Alliance school in JERUSALEM, one year at the al-AZHAR Islamic Academy in Cairo under Sheikh Rashid Rida (without graduating) and some time at the Ottoman-Turkish school of administration in Istanbul. During World War I he served as a junior officer in the Turkish Army. After the British and allied forces conquered Palestine, 1917–1918, he served as a recruiting officer for Emir FEISAL's army of the ARAB REVOLT, and later as an official in the provisional British military government in Palestine. At the same time, he became active in nationalist organization and agitation. He was President of

the Arab Club (*al-Nadi al-Arabi*) in Jerusalem, one of the two main associations of nationalist youth—which in 1918-1920 defined Palestine as "Southern Syria"—that is part of historic SYRIA which had been under semi-autonomous Arab administration during those years. He incited and headed anti-Jewish riots in April 1920, was tried in absentia by a military court and sentenced to ten years imprisonment, but escaped. In August 1920 he was pardoned by the High Commissioner who had just begun establishing his administration.

In March 1921, the MUFTI of Jerusalem, Kamel al-Husseini, Amin's stepbrother, died. Husseini offered his candidacy, but was not among the three candidates nominated under Ottoman Law by a small body of voters, one of whom the government was to choose and appoint. However, after considerable pressure by the Husseini family and its supporters, as well as by some senior British officials, one of the three candidates nominated withdrew in Husseini's favor, and in May 1921 the High Commissioner appointed Husseini as Mufti. The British apparently wished to keep a balance between the rival clans: the position of Mufti had long been held by the Husseini family, and that of Mayor of Jerusalem had just been taken from them and given to a notable of the rival Nashashibi family. Husseini had also assured the High Commissioner that he would exercise his prestige and that of his family to keep Jerusalem quiet.

To the position of Mufti, a post carrying much prestige and spiritual and social influence, but no actual power, Husseini soon added another post with greater potential power. The British Mandatory Government deemed it inconvenient and improper to administer the communal and religious affairs of the Muslims, as the Ottoman Sultan, being Muslim, had done, and therefore in December 1921 decreed the creation of a five-member Supreme Muslim Council (SMC), to be indirectly elected following Ottoman procedure. In January 1922, the Council was elected—with Husseini as its President. The chairmanship of the Council, with its considerable financial resources from and control of the WAQF (endowments) and its authority over all appointments of Muslim clerical functionaries and staff, significantly empowered Husseini. He used it to advance his clan's and his faction's influence and to fight his opponents among the PALESTINIAN ARABS,

the Zionists, and the Jewish National Home Policy of the Mandate and the Government. He fostered the Muslim character of Jerusalem and the position of its two great Muslim shrines, and injected a religious character into the struggle against ZIONISM. This was the foundation for his agitation concerning Jewish rights at the Western (Wailing) Wall that led to the bloody riots of August 1929.

The 1929 riots established Husseini's stature as the most prominent political leader of the Palestinian Arabs, though he gave way to his family relative and chairman of the declining Arab Executive, Mussa Kazem al-Husseini, who died in 1934, and entrusted Jamal al-Husseini with the day-to-day leadership of his faction. His politics reflected hard-line national opposition to Zionism, combined with tactical pragmatism toward the British Mandate, of which he had been a civil servant. In April 1936, he formed the Arab Higher Committee (AHC) and became its Chairman. As such, he was the chief organizer of the riots of 1936 and the Rebellion from 1937, as well as of the mounting internal terror against Arab opponents.

In October 1937, Husseini was dismissed by the government from his position as President of the SMC, which was disbanded, and the Arab Higher Committee was outlawed. Husseini escaped to LEBANON and Syria, where he continued to direct the Palestinian-Arab Rebellion. In 1939 he went to IRAQ, where he had fostered close links with the anti-British army officers and assisted them in their revolt in 1941. When that revolt was put down, Husseini escaped to Italy and Nazi Germany, where he was welcomed as a leader of anti-British Arab nationalism, received by Hitler and accorded an honored position. He aided the Nazi war effort as propagandist, mobilizing Muslim public opinion throughout the world, and recruiting Muslim volunteers for the German armed forces from Bosnia and Yugoslavia.

After the War, Husseini was detained by the French Army. He escaped and in June 1946 arrived in EGYPT. He was not allowed to return to Palestine, but was appointed by the ARAB LEAGUE to be chairman of the renewed AHC set up for the Palestinian Arabs (Jamal al-Husseini actually headed the Committee, but its presidency was kept "vacant" for Hajj Amin al-Husseini). He began organizing the Palestinian Arab community for final battle against the Jewish community in Palestine, in an effort to prevent partition of the country and the foundation of a Jewish state.

By now, the Arab states had appropriated the Palestinian issue from its own repositories, and begun to finance, equip and direct that struggle. Husseini saw them only as providers of the help without which the fight could not be mounted, while claiming for himself supreme leadership. But the Arab states were unwilling to grant him that position, and a great deal of half-concealed tension ensued. In the final struggle, before the war of May 1948 and the invasion of Palestine by the regular Arab armies, Husseini exerted some influence on the fighting in the Jerusalem area, where his relative Abdel-Qader al-Husseini commanded the guerillas. However, he was unable to maintain the siege on Jewish Jerusalem long-term and fell in the battle of Qastel in April 1948.

Before the end of 1947 and until after the defeat of 1948, Husseini tried repeatedly to form a provisional Palestinian government, but he was rejected by the Iraqi and Jordanian governments. Toward the end of the war, al-Husseini wholeheartedly supported the foundation of the "All Palestine Government" (September 1948) and attended the Constituent National Assembly convened in Egyptian-occupied GAZA, and was elected President. But that body—welcomed at first by Egypt as an instrument to frustrate Jordan's annexation of the Arab half of Palestine—failed to gain any influence on the course of events and practically ceased to exist after a few months. Attempts to create in Gaza some Palestinian-Arab autonomous entity under Egyptian rule were also not welcomed by Egypt. Husseini, still residing in Cairo, established an alternative residence in Beirut and in 1959 went to live there permanently. He endeavored to keep alive, or revive, the AHC and to continue sabotaging the Jordanian annexation of the Arab part of Palestine, the WEST BANK, but the Committee, and Husseini's own influence, continuously declined, particularly after the foundation of the PALESTINE LIBERATION ORGANIZATION (PLO) in 1964 (which Husseini and his Higher Committee opposed).

Husseini spent the last decade of his life as a respected refugee, hardly involved in public or political affairs and with no influence on them.

I

IBADIYYA, IBADIS Unorthodox Islamic sect which grew out of the *Khawarij* (Kharyite) sect of the seventh century. The Khawarij rebelled against evolving Islamic laws and practices of governance and succession, in both their SUNNI and Shi'i versions, and were suppressed. Their Ibadiyya heirs gradually became a separate sect—principally in the Arabian peninsula and the MAGHREB (North-West Africa). They survived mainly in Oman, where they form the majority of the population and their doctrine is the state religion. In the 1950s, their IMAM rebelled against the Sultan, and was suppressed (see OMAN.) Small groups of Ibadiyya also exist in LIBYA, TUNISIA and ALGERIA, as well as in countries reached by migrants from Oman, such as Tanzania.

IBN SA'UD (1876? 1880?–1953) The name by which Abdel Aziz Ibn Abdel Rahman aal (i.e. of the House of) Sa'ud, King and founder of Sa'udi Arabia, was best known. His ancestors, of the Anaiza tribe, had ruled parts of Najd, but Ibn Sa'ud grew up in exile in KUWAIT (see House of SA'UD). In 1902 he recaptured the town of al-Riyadh and re-established the rule of the Sa'udi dynasty in Najd. In 1913 he conquered the al-Hassa region on the PERSIAN GULF, and his territory thus came within the sphere where Great Britain had negotiated a series of treaties imposing her protection on the rulers of the Arabian coastal sheikhdoms. In a 1913 Anglo-Ottoman draft convention Britain still recognized the Sa'udi Amirate as part of the OTTOMAN EMPIRE; but the outbreak of World War I changed the situation, and in December 1915 Britain concluded a treaty with Ibn Sa'ud recognizing him as ruler of an independent Najd and Hassa (in fact under a veiled British protectorate; later in 1916 Britain agreed to pay him a monthly subsidy of £5,000).

During World War I, BRITAIN encouraged Ibn Sa'ud in his fight against the pro-Turkish Rashidis, but was content with his benevolent neutrality in the war.

After the war, in 1920–1921, Ibn Sa'ud defeated the Rashidis and incorporated their territory into his domain, calling himself, from 1921, Sultan of Najd and its dependencies. For his victory over the HASHEMITE Sharifs of Mecca, in 1924, and the expansion and consolidation of his rule, from January 1926 as "King of Hijaz and Sultan of Najd, al-Hassa, Qatif and Judail and their dependencies", and from 1927 as "King of Hijaz and Najd", and the constitution of his realm as "The Saudi Arabian Kingdom" in 1932, and his war with YEMEN in 1934—see SAUDI ARABIA. Ibn Sa'ud in the 1930s, was, not very active in inter-Arab affairs. In 1936 he was, as arranged by the British, one of the Arab rulers who induced the Arabs of Palestine to end their general strike, promising to aid their struggle, and in 1939 the British government got him officially involved in the Palestine issue, by inviting him to send delegates to the British-Arab Round Table Conference. Unofficial British go-betweens (e.g. H. St.J.B. Philby) also put him, in 1939, in indirect contact with Jewish-Zionist leaders, in search for a solution to the Palestine problem, but nothing came of these contacts. In World War II Ibn Sa'ud kept Saudia Arabia neutral because of his growing ties with the UNITED STATES and US oil interests, and his role in the foundation of the ARAB LEAGUE, 1945, and inter-Arab politics.

Ibn Sa'ud ruled his kingdom as an autocrat, consulting the princes of his dynasty and the tribal sheikhs in the traditional manner, but reserving decisions to himself. He permitted no modern representative political institutions to develop and refrained from formalizing constitutional governance, basing his rule on Islamic laws and traditions. He kept the unruly tribal chiefs—whom he had to suppress in the late 1920s by armed force—under strict control, by paying them subsidies, keeping their sons at his Courts and marrying their daughters to his sons. The tribal unrest was in part linked to a rebellion by Wahhabi "Brethren" (Ikhwan), suppressed in 1929. Ibn Sa'ud continued enforcing strict Wahhabi Islam, but discontinued his initial efforts to establish a nucleus of armed Wahhabi "Brethren" in the colonies. Ibn Sa'ud permitted little economic or social modernization, except for the development of the oil industry by the American "Aramco" company—which began to make the country, and the royal family, immensely rich, and which triggered a process of development and modernization that came to fruition after Ibn Sa'ud's days; he introduced, despite the rule of Wahhabi-Islamic law, increasingly luxurious ways of life which bred a measure of corruption among the dynasty and the ruling class.

Ibn Sa'ud had several wives and over forty sons; thirty-one sons of legitimate full-status wives survive in the mid-1980s, in line for the succession. Ibn Sa'ud strictly controlled the large royal family and determined his succession, appointing his eldest surviving son, Abdallah Ibn Aziz Sa'ud, in 1932, as crown prince and successor, with Feisal next in line.

I.D.F. see ISRAEL.

IDRIS, KING see SANUSSI, AL SAYYID MUHAMMAD IDRIS.

IDRISSI, IDRISSIYYA A dynasty, and an Islamic sect or school. The Idrissi's, are a clan or dynasty of North African origin, claiming descent from the Prophet Muhammad, the fourth CALIPH Ali and the Moroccan Idrissi dynasty (789–974). They gained political power and religious influence in the region of Asir in Arabia (between HIJAZ and YEMEN) in the mid-nineteenth century, under Ahmad al-Idrissi He founded a Muslim school or order (Tariqa), similar to the DERVISH ORDERS in its structure and appearance but traditional and fundamentalist in content and influenced by the WAHHABIS. The Idrissi state in Asir temporarily attained semi-independence early in the twentieth century, and near-complete independence in the 1920s, but was annexed by SAUDI ARABIA in 1933. It was then that the Idrissi dynasty lost its position. The Idrissi School or sect never attaine any real influence in Islam.

IMAM In Sunni ISLAM, the Imam is the head of the mosque; the prayer leader and often also a preacher. (In the larger mosques there is, separately, a preacher—Khatib or, in some cases, a Wa'Úiz).

In Shi'i Islam, the Imam is the head of the Muslim community (Umma) and, in theory, the ruler of its realm. He must be a descendant of the Prophet Muhammad through his daughter Fatima and his son-in-law Ali. Shi'i Islam gradually came to attribute to the Imam mysterious, superhuman qualities. According to the main Shi'i streams, the last revealed Imam disappeared, to become the hidden Imam who will return at the end of time as the Mahdi ("the

Guided One") and Redeemer to institute a reign of justice. For the main body of the SHI'A—the *Ithna-Ashariyya* ("Twelvers"), also called *Ja'fariyya* or *Imamiyya*—the last, and now hidden, Imam was the twelfth, Muhammad Ibn Hassan al-Mahdi or al-Muntazar), in the 870s. The ISMA'ILIYYA (the ("Seveners") consider Isma'il Ibn Ja'far, the son of the sixth Imam, who died before his father, in 760, as the rightful seventh Imam, the hidden one to return. Some Shi'i sects, however, recognize a living Imam. Thus, one branch of the *Isma'iliyya*, regard their leader, the "Aga Khan", as the Imam. The ZEIDIYYA, who seceded in 712 when they inaugarated Zeid Ibn Ali as the rightful fifth Imam, and who survived in Yemen, recognize an unbroken line of revealed, living Imam's. Their Imam, who ruled Yemen until the Civil War of 1962–1967, was elected by the *Sada* (singular *Sayyid*), the descendants of the fourth *Caliph* Hussein Ibn Ali. The Zeidi-Yemeni Imamate lapsed with the end of the Civil War. The Iranian Shi'is, though belong to the Ithna-Ashariyya, (a group regarding the Imam as hidden and not recognizing a living one), in the aftermath of the Islamic revolution of 1979 sometimes called their leader KHOMEINI "Imam." Some esoteric schools of Sunni Islam which have, though orthodox, absorbed certain elements of Muslim mysticism (*Sufism*) and even *Shi'ism*—e.g., the MAHDIYYA in SUDAN—also call the head of their order Imam.

INDEPENDENCE WAR (1948)   see ARAB-ISRAEL CONFLICT.

INÖNÜ ERDAL(b. 1926)   Turkish scientist and politician. Born in Ankara as the second son of Ismet INÖNÜ, he graduated from Ankara University and the California Polytechnic University, with a Ph.D. in theoretical physics. He began teaching at the Middle East Technical University in 1960, later serving as the Dean and President.

In 1983, he founded the Social Democratic Party (SODEP) and was elected chairman at its first convention. Turkey's military rulers (the National Security Council) barred him and his Party from participating in the national elections of November 1983. But SODEP was quite successful in the local elections of March 1984, winning over twenty-three percent of the vote. In 1985 SODEP merged with the Populist Party to form the Social Democratic Populist

Party (SODEPOP). Inönü was chosen to lead the united Party, with ninety-nine seats. In the local elections of 1989 it became, with over twenty-eight percent of the vote, the largest party, but in national politics it remained in the opposition. Inönü fought against Bülent Ecevit of the Democratic Left Party for the status of main opposition leader.

Upon the victory of Süleyman DEMIREL's New Path Party, in the elections of 1991, SODEPOP, with eighty-eight seats, entered the new coalition government and Inönü became deputy Prime Minister. He continued in this position when Tansu ÇILLER in June 1993, succeeded Demirel as Prime Minister, but resigned in September 1994. In March 1995 Inönü was appointed foreign minister by Çiller. In September his party, which had by then merged with the Republican People's Party, left the coalition, leading to Çiller's resignation.

INÖNÜ, ISMET (1884–1973) Turkish military officer and statesman. Second President of the Republic (1938–1950). He served as Prime Minister (1923–1924, 1925–1937, 1961–1965). Born in Izmir, Inönü graduated from the Military Academy of Pangalti in 1906 and served in various military assignments including that of Commander of the Ottoman forces in YEMEN (1910–1913). During World War I he was Commander of the Second Army and fought on the Russian, and later the Syrian and Palestinian fronts. After the War he joined the nationalist struggle led by ATATÜRK against the remnants of the Ottoman regime, the Greek invaders and western plans for the dismemberment of Turkey's Anatolian heartland. In 1920 he was elected to the Grand National Assembly. In 1921 he was appointed Chief of Staff and Commander of the Western Front, winning the two battles of Inönü (from which he derived his family name). He became Foreign Minister in 1922 and led the Turkish delegation at the Lausanne Peace Conference (1922–23).

Upon the proclamation of the Republic in October 1923 he became Prime Minister and served almost continuously until 1937. Upon Atatürk's death in 1938, he was elected President of the Republic and leader of the Republican People's Party (RPP). He implemented Atatürk's policies and kept TURKEY out of World War II. In addition he maintained close relations with the leaders of the Western Alliance, first secretly and from December 1943, openly. After the war he permitted the growth of a multiparty system; his RPP lost the elections of 1950 and he was replaced as President by Celal BAYAR, the leader of the Democratic Party. He led the fight against the Democratic regime in the 1950s, and although he did not take part in the military coup of 1960 which toppled it, he exercised strong influence on the coup's leaders. Inönü and his Party emerged from the elections of 1961 as the strongest party, but without an overall majority. Until 1965 he headed three successive coalition governments.

In 1965 the Justice Party (the successor of the outlawed Democratic Party) won the election and Inönü again became leader of the opposition. In 1971 he gave his blessing reluctantly and reservedly to the ultimatum of the military chiefs that toppled the DEMIREL government and to his party's participation in a new coalition, and he withdrew his participation from the government. From about 1964 Inönü's RPP adopted (under his leadership) a left-of-center ideology (with a right-wing faction seceding) with an increasingly socialist slant. The dominant leftist faction, however, under Bülent Ecevit, gradually adopted a line more radical than Inönü's, disputing his leadership. At a May 1972 RPP Congress it won a majority against Inönü and he resigned as party chairman (in his late eighties). Later in 1972 Inönü seceded from the RPP. He died in December 1973.

INTERIM AGREEMENT see ARAB ISRAEL PEACE-MAKING.

INTIFADA The term refers to the uprising of the Palestinian population in the GAZA STRIP and the WEST BANK against the Israeli occupation that broke out in December 1987, and became for the following few years the predominant cause affecting most aspects of life in these territories. The *intifada* broke out against the backdrop of twenty years of Israeli military occupation, during which the political, economic and social needs of the Palestinian population had been met with frustrating deprivation, particularly since the late 1970s.

Since the early 1980s, Palestinian society in the West Bank and Gaza had been undergoing a rapid process of politicization and institution-building, largely supervised and financially aided by the PALES-

TINE LIBERATION ORGANIZATION (PLO). A new generation with a growing number of university graduates and professionals occupied the center of political action, predominate during the 1980s, by the growing number of spontaneous acts of civil disobedience—stone throwing, riots and demonstrations, the stabbing of Israeli civilians and soldiers—with relatively little use of firearms and explosives.

The uprising, gradually expanded from initial local riots in refugee camps, into full conflagration. The *intifada* was triggered by the death of four Palestinian workers from the Gaza Strip in a car accident on 9 December 1987, believed to have been deliberately planned by the Israeli security services. During the funerals riots erupted especially in the refugee camp of Jebalya. This angered the populace elsewhere in the Gaza Strip as well. Within less than a week, the riots spread out into East JERUSALEM and swept most of the West Bank refugee camps. During the first weeks of the *intifada* the activity was not organized and was characterized by widespread, spontaneous demonstrations, including school and trade strikes throughout the West Bank, the Gaza Strip and East Jerusalem. A new phenomenon of anonymous leadership appeared on the scene, operating by instructing day-to-day behavior of the Palestinian public by the distribution of leaflets and the writing of slogans on the walls, in which the Palestinians were called to resist the Israeli occupation in various ways and parameters.

The Palestinian uprising was a strategic surprise to ISRAEL, the (PLO), and even to its leading figures, in its mass participation—virtually by the community as whole, effectiveness and modes of action by grass-root leadership, and durability. The daily riots and clashes with the Israeli forces soon attracted world media which further fueled the fire, but also underlined the boundaries of legitimate response by the Israeli security forces.

The division of authority between powerless "civil administration" and the military command in charge of security, turned out to be detrimental to the efforts to suppress the uprising. Not only had the IDF not been trained to cope with this type of disobedience and civil strife, but after years of overlooking the Palestinian population and the gradual weakening of the national leadership that emerged in the late 1970s and 1980s, Israel was left with few resources and links to effective leadership capable of ensuring acceptance and obedience on the part of the community. The IDF responded with use of force. During the first two months of the *intifada* fifty-one people were killed and hundreds were wounded. As a result the IDF reduced the use of firearm against the demonstrators and adopted a policy of confronting the rioters with physical beating. It later began using, in addition to tear-gas, rubber and plastic bullets in order to minimize the physical injuries. Because of the blurred boundaries of lawful action in confronting violence, and the massive presence of television crews, the Israeli military soon found itself in moral and legal trouble: soldiers and officers were accused in military courts of using unnecessary force against Palestinians. In addition, massive arrests of Palestinian rioters and deportation of behind-the-scene activists were employed, which were condemned by the UN Security Council and drew favorable international attention to the PLO. Indeed, the Israeli means of suppression not only failed to reestablish law and order, it intensified the world's solidarity with the Palestinian civilian population and their fighting empty-handed against well equipped regular soldiers of a highly reputable army.

On the eve of the uprising the PLO was at one of its lowest points of prestige in the regional arena. It was not only surprised by the magnitude of mass protest in the occupied territories, but also by its perceived independent grass-root leadership, which threatened its exclusive standing as a sole national leadership of the Palestinian people, hence the Tunis-based PLO establishment rushed to ensure full control of the uprising. In January 1988, an anonymous body, self-defined as the "Unified National Command (UNC) of the Uprising," was established inside the occupied territories, encompassing *Fatah*, the PFLP, DFLP and the Communist Party. The new local leadership of the uprising, whose members kept constantly changing, providing the uprising leadership flexibility and continuity despite continuous arrests by Israel. The UNC pleaded full submission to the PLO, which henceforth became the overall authority in guiding the uprising activities and shaping its political goals. The newly formed UNC published a document with fourteen conditions for ending the uprising, most of them dealing with an easing of the Israeli military government. The PLO leadership in Tunis, meanwhile, started to take

action. One of the first initiatives of the PLO was the decision to send a "ship of return" with dozens of Palestinian deportees and reporters on board to Israeli territorial water, but the ship was blown up in February 1988, while docking in the port in Limasol, Cyprus. The Israeli intelligence was accused of carrying out the explosion.

The uprising aroused a deep sense of pride among the Palestinian communities in the diaspora as well as among ARAB masses in the Middle East, praising the "children of the stones", and portraying them as another link in the glorious Arab ethos of confronting foreign domination and oppression. Among the Gaza Strip and West Bank Palestinians there was a growing sense of self-esteem for having finally taken their fate in their own hands. Although the *intifada* was primarily motivated by a strong sense of social and national deprivation, the manifestations of violence and disobedience, especially by the teenagers, also expressed a youth revolt against authority, whether Palestinian or Israeli. Hence, access to villages and urban neighborhoods were often road-blocked and declared "liberated," until the next confrontation with the Israeli security forces.

The popular committees, which had been created during 1980s, especially by *Fatah* in the villages, refugee camps and the urban neighborhoods, initiated organized stone and molotov cocktail throwing at IDF patrols and Jewish settlers' cars among other means of provocative actions which triggered occasional violent reactions of the Jewish settlers. Within less than two months, the uprising became an all-inclusive civil disobedience, encompassing the occupied territories as a whole and all socioeconomic strata and sectors of the population. Under the UNC leadership, the uprising became increasingly organized and politically-oriented, striving to sever the contacts between the local Palestinian population and the Israeli authorities.

The UNC proclaimed a boycott on all Israeli products except the essentials, and encouraged the Palestinian population not to approach the Israeli authorities such as the legal system operated by the civil administration, and avoid going out to work in Israel. Fancy weddings and celebrations were prohibited as well as the purchase of luxury goods. Stores opened for only three hours a day and the population was encouraged to grow vegetables, an nuture rabbits and chickens in their backyards. House owners were requested to refrain from collecting rent from the tenants without means and those considered wealthy were forced to help the needy.

In the spring of 1988 the IDF started to impose prolonged closures and curfews on the refugee camps and villages, as well as economic sanctions the petrol supply to gas stations. The civil administration cut down the services it provided to the population, especially health and welfare, alleging that the income of the administration had fallen due to the reduced number of taxpayers in the Palestinian population. To force the Palestinians to renew their ties with the administration and pay the taxes, those who applied for permits of any sort were required to prove that they paid taxes, and those who did not pay risked confiscation of their property.

On 16 April 1988, ARAFAT's deputy, Khalil al-Wazir (Abu-Jihad), considered by Israeli intelligence as the central operator of the *intifada* from his headquarters in Tunis, was assassinated at his residence in the Tunisian capital, allegedly by an Israeli commando unit, though Israeli officials never admitted responsibility. In any case, the killing of Abu Jihad had no impact whatsoever on the course and means of the uprising. In August 1988 the "Islamic Resistance Movement," (HAMAS), was officially proclaimed, although leaflets carrying its name appeared shortly after the eruption of the uprising. The advent of *Hamas* indicated the joining of the Muslim Brotherhood in the occupied territories to the national struggle under independent leadership which refused to join the PLO, and tacitly challenged its political position both morally and politically. *Hamas* was self-defined as the military arm of the MUSLIM BROTHERHOOD in Palestine, whose main goal was to wage Holy War (JIHAD) against Israel, as the only means to liberate Palestine from the Jordan River to the Mediterranean Sea. While previously *Hamas* had tended to coordinate its public protest activities and strikes with the UNC, it now embarked on an entirely independent course, setting its own days of strike, commemoration and public activities.

In the middle of the school year of 1987–1988, the IDF shut down most of the schools and universities throughout the West Bank and the Gaza Strip because they had been held as foci of subversion and incitement to violence. This policy caused a major malfunction to the educational system in the territories and sent many children and youth to the streets without organized framework and discipline. Furthermore, all the temporary teachers were laid off while others were only half-paid. This policy led the UNC to press the Palestinian employees of the Israeli civil administration to resign, which was responded to by the local police officials, leading to further chaos in the Palestinian areas.

Despite the difficulties and the steadily growing toll, the uprising Palestinians were pleased with their perceived political success. Indeed, not only the Palestinian issue returned to a center stage of world public interest, within its first year the uprising seemed to have reaped tangible achievements on both regional and international levels. These achievements, however, turned out to be mostly temporary and hardly sustainable:

A. In contrast to the joint Jordanian-Syrian attempt to shun the PLO aside in the ARAB SUMMIT CONFERENCE held in Amman in November 1987, within a few weeks the Intifada forced the Arab foreign ministers to convene at the end of January 1988 in an emergency meeting to express their support for the Palestinian cause represented by the PLO, although the latters call for convening a summit conference to provide financial aid to the *intifada* remained unheeded until June 1988.

B. In February 1988 the US administration decided to resume its peacemaking efforts on the Palestinian issue and Secretary of State George Shultz arrived in the Middle East for talks with the Israeli and Jordanian governments as well as with the Palestinian leadership of the West Bank and Gaza Strip. However, the PLO refused to allow the local Palestinian leadership to meet with Shultz, and the latters' plan— a combination of the Camp David agreement on interim Palestinian autonomy, the Reagan Plan, and the idea of an international peace conference which by then had been acceptable to most Arab states and the PLO. However, the plan had little chance of success. King HUSSEIN was cautious and reluctant to play a leading diplomatic role regarding the West Bank at a time when the PLO prestige was at its peak and the *intifada* could spill over to the JORDAN's Palestinian population. Israel was also reluctant to show flexibility under the pressure of violence, and the PLO blocked any possible dialogue between the American administration and the local Palestinian leadership, insisting that the US turn to him in the first place.

C. In June 1988 an Arab summit conference was held in Algiers, dedicated to the Palestinian uprising—to allocate financial aid to the Palestinians to enable them to sustain the Israeli pressure while the uprising continued. The summit's allocation was a far cry from the PLO expectations (immediate sum of 128 million dollars, in addition to 43 million dollars a month promised for the remainder of the year, to be distributed mainly by the PLO). The Arab financial promises, however, were phrased rather vaguely and largely denied by the oil producers, which triggered bitter complaints by PLO leaders.

D. On 31 July 1988, King Hussein announced Jordan's legal disengagement from the West Bank, and that his country had no claims over the West Bank. The announcement was indeed the most significant achievement of the intifada and the PLO leadership in Tunis. It resulted in pressures of the new local leadership in the territories on the PLO, combined with similar effort by Western diplomats, to convince the PLO to adopt a more pragmatic attitude towards Israel, which finally paved the way for the dramatic PLO declaration at the Palestinian National Council (PNC) session held in Algiers in November 1988, of an independent Palestinian state based on the UN resolution 181 on the partition of Palestine and the establishment of Arab and Jewish states. The proclaimed Palestinian state was immediately recognized by all Arab states (save Syria), and most members of the international community.

E. Even more crucial was the new PLO-Jordan close alignment facilitated by the Jordanian disengagement from the West Bank. In December 1988, the US prerequisites for opening a political dialogue with the PLO were finally met by Arafat's declaration in Geneva, in which he renounced the use of terror and unreservedly accepted Resolution 242. However, this dialogue, conducted by the US Ambassador in Tunisia, was shortened. In late June 1989, Washington announced the suspension of the dialogue with the PLO following Arafat's refusal to condemn an abortive terrorist attack against Israel from the sea perpetrated by the Palestine Liberation Front (Abu al-Abbas) a month earlier.

On the main stage of the uprising, cracks began to appear within the Palestinian community during the second year, reflecting the growing discontent at the individual and collective human and economic cost of the uprising with little, if any, discernible benefits for the local population. Indeed, by the end of the first year of the intifada over 300 Palestinians were killed, 20,000 wounded, and almost 12,000 were arrested. During the second year, the hostility and distrust among the various political organizations in the occupied territories led to increasing internal strife, manifested by mutual intimidation, expulsion of one's adversaries from their residence, and executions. Murders of individuals suspected of collaboration with the Israeli authorities were carried out by "striking committees" or "internal security apparatuses". In 1989 over 150 Palestinians were killed by Palestinians and another 300 were killed in clashes with Israeli security forces and Jewish settlers. By the end of its second year, the uprising had gradually lost its popular enthusiasm and became more sporadic and selectively violent, though it continued to be implemented by organized groups. During that year a new kind of terror had appeared, individually initiated terror actions against the Israeli civil population such as the bombing of buses and knifings in broad daylight. Some of these actions were carried out by young Palestinians as an act of revenge for the death of their friends during the intifada.

1990 started with voices among the Palestinians calling to renew the armed struggle against Israel which had been abandoned during the first two years of the intifada. In May 1990, a young Israeli murdered seven Palestinian workers near the city of Rishon Lezion, in a retaliation to acts of TERRORISM against Israelis. A more serious incident was the massacre of twenty-two Palestinians on the Temple Mount (al-haram al-sharif) on 8 October, 1990. This was caused by Muslim worshippers throwing stones on Jewish worshippers at the Western Wall and led to the interference by Israeli security forces. The third year of the intifada was characterized by the continued loss of popular enthusiasm and decreasing occasions of massive demonstrations and civil disobedience, though sporadic violent outbursts continued throughout the West Bank and Gaza Strip and the knifing occasions increased.

In 1990–1991, the number of Palestinians killed by Israeli forces had decreased while the number of those killed by their own people had increased. Indeed by the end of 1992 the total number of Palestinians killed during the intifada reach 1800 people with almost 800 of them killed by Palestinians. (There is a slight discrepency with the exact numbers between the Israeli and Palestinian sources.) The populations' reaction to the internal killings had changed gradually from an initial acceptance of the murders on the grounds of alleged collaboration to a growing uneasiness and anger as the murders became more frequent and were used not only against real collaborators but as a weapon against Palestinians who were accused by Islamic extremists as adopting "the rotten Western culture, " or even as a result of family feuds.

Though it is not possible to define a date to the end of the *intifada* it seems that toward the end of 1991 and the Madrid negotiations it almost totally faded. The then Israeli Defense Minister Yizhak RABIN adopted an iron fist policy toward the uprising leaders and those who participated in the violent demonstrations. Nonetheless, no doubt he realized in the very first months of the *intifada* that even though Israel must suppress the uprisings, the problem would not be solved by military means and Israel must find a way to negotiate with the local Palestinian leaders in the territories. In the wake of King Hussein's announcement of severing relations with the West Bank—which burried the Labor Party's Jordanian Option—Rabin started to develop a plan for holding elections for local leadership with which ISRAEL would eventually negotiate. Rabin strove to drive a wedge between the local leadership and the PLO, and exclude the latter from the diplomatic process he was planning. This plan was reluctantly adopted by the Israeli government in May 1989 as the Shamir-Rabin peace initiative (see ARAB-ISRAEL PEACEMAKING).

The *intifada* did not force Israel withdraw from the occupied territories, but it did show that the Israeli occupation of the West Bank and Gaza Strip was no longer a viable option. Though the two parties were still estranged toward each other, the *intifada* was an important catalyst in making many Israelis refuse military—especially reserve—service in the occupied territories. The Palestinians succeeded in scoring some significant gains, primarily the self-confidence they acquired from the very experience of taking their fate in their own hands for the first time, boosting the sense of pluralist, self-helped political community. The *intifada* also led to more balanced relations between the local leadership and the PLO in Tunis. The Israeli occupation became less popular than ever before throughout the world, while more awareness was shown to the Palestinian cause.

Israeli public opinion became more positive toward the peace process and negotiating with the Palestinians, especially after the Jordanian option no longer existed, as well as the proclamation of the Palestinian state in November 1988. Even though the dialogue between the US and the PLO was short-lived and futile, it created a precedence which paved the way to recognition following the Israel-PLO Declaration of Principles (DOP) signed in September 1993. The Israeli peace plan, which failed to get off the ground in 1989–1990, eventually shaped the dialogue between Israel and the local Palestinian leaders during the *intifada*, and later in the Madrid talks while being aware of the PLO's full behind-the-scene involvement in those talks.

IRAN

Introduction Until 1934 Persia, and since 1979, the Islamic Republic of Iran. An ancient political and cultural center, borders with Azerbaijan and Turkmenistan to the north; TURKEY and IRAQ to the west, and Pakistan and Afghanistan to the east. To the south, Iran is located on the northern shores of the PERSIAN GULF. At the end of 1996 the population of Iran was close to 60 million and the number of households was 12.4 million. About ninety percent of the inhabitants of Iran are Shi's, of the Imami stream (which believes in the twelve IMAMS, who followed the fourth Khalifa Ali and his sons). The official language is Persian, even though there are tribes and ethnic groups that speak Kurdish, Azerian, Pathanian, Arabic, Turkmenian, Armenian and other languages. Iran is a plateau with a dry climate. Thus the cultivable and inhabited areas are limited. A large part of eastern Iran is desert and totally unsettled. Only the area around the CASPIAN SEA is rainy.

Sixty-one percent of the population resides in urban areas. Almost twenty percent (11 million) of this reside in the capital, Tehran. The other large cities are: Abadan, Esfahan, Mashhad, Shiraz and Tabriz. The limited rainfall and small areas worthy of cultivation, as well as old-fashioned agricultural methods, are amongst the main reasons why Iran is obliged to import much of its food (especially rice, wheat and tea). Iran is known for its caviar and fruit products.

Iran has many natural resources, which are not yet fully utilized. It has the second largest gas reserves in the world (after RUSSIA). The copper ore deposits found in the district of Sar-Cheshmeh in the south-east of the state, are considered amongst the largest in the world. Near the city of Kerman there is coal in commercial quantities. Iranian exports are comprised primarily of petroleum—the state's main source of revenue that covers over eighty percent of government expenditure—including crude oil and petrochemical products, in which large investment have been made in recent years. Persian rugs are world famous, constituting the second largest export item after petroleum. Iran also exports pistachio nuts, and artistic craft products.

Despite the great efforts invested in the development of means of transportation since World War I, the road system in Iran is still underdeveloped and the railways outdated. Iran is connected by rail to Turkey, and in 1996 the railways of Iran and Turkmenistan were connected along the route known in the past as the "Silk Road" (see ECO).

The Iranians believe that they are of the white Indo-European race that arrived to the Iranian plateau in the middle of the second century B.C. They refer to themselves as Ary or Airy, and believe that the origin of their state is of the same origin and was in the past "Airyan". However, throughout history, numerous other peoples invaded Iran and mixed with the local population, while nomadic tribes chose to settle in it. The peripheral areas of Iran are populated by ethnic minority groups with unique languages, traditions and cultures.

The KURDS form the largest ethnic minority, whose number is estimated at between 4–5 million. Most of them are SUNNI Muslims. Their language is of Indo-European origin which is similar to Persian, but they speak a mixture of dialects and have no single common language. They live in the west and north-west of Iran and have a long tradition of fighting for autonomy or independence (see also separate entry KURDS). The Arabs in south-west Iran, are the second largest minority, comprising about 2 million. They are Shi'i Muslims, but have a culture and customs of their own. They live in the province of Khuzistan, close to southern Iraq, which is rich in OIL and has fertile soil. Another ethnic minority is the Baluchis who number approximately half a million. They live in the largely uncultivated province of Baluchistan in the south-east of the state, which borders on the great deserts of eastern Iran, Pakistan and Afghanistan. The Baluchis are in close contact

with their brethren in Pakistan and some engage in smuggling drugs and goods across the borders. Iran has always been concerned about their demand to unite with their brethren across the border.

The Turkmenians live in the north-east of the state, close to their brethren in the republic of Turkmenistan. They are engaged primarily in agriculture and number about half a million—most of them being Sunni Muslims. The Azerians live in the north-west of the country and number about 9 million. Despite their different language and unique culture, the Azerians consider themselves an integral part of Iran. The Qajari dynasty (see below) originated from this region. The Azerians were active in the constitutional revolution of 1905 as well as in the Islamic revolution of 1979.

Iran has numerous nomadic tribes, which live primarily in the western part of the state, below the Zagros Mountains. Other tribes live in the Faras district in southern Iran. The main ones are the Bakhtiaries, the Ghashghaies and the Lors. Since the coup in Afghanistan at the beginning of 1979, approximately 2 million Afghanis have moved into Iran. Even though Iran ordered them out in 1996, at least half of them still reside in Iran. In addition, around half a million Iraqi Kurds and Shi's, who escaped Iraq in the course of the IRAN-IRAQ WAR, live in Iran. The number varies according to the situation in Iraq. Iran also contains religious minorities. Sunni Muslims constitute about seven percent of the population and they live in the provinces of Kurdistan (in the west), Baluchistan (in the south-east) and Khurasan (in the north-east—near the border with Turkmenistan).

Iran has four non-Muslim religious minorities, which are recognized by law:

1. The ARMENIANS, who are the largest non-Muslim religious minority, number about 250,000. Most of them belong to the Eastern Church and they have two representatives in the *Majlis*— the Iranian Parliament.

2. The ASSYRIANS number about 30,000—most of them belong to the Eastern Church, and the rest to the Catholic and Protestant churches. There are a further 60,000 Christians, belonging to various churches.

3. The Zoroastrians, who believe in the pagan religion of ancient Iran, number today about 30,000. Most of them live in Tehran and in Yazd, where their

spiritual center operates. They have one member in the *Majlis*.

4. The Jews, who numbered 80,000 before the 1979 Islamic revolution, are today a community of 25,000—30,000, most of whom live in Tehran and about 8,000 in Shiraz. The Jews have one member in the *Majlis*.

Despite the recognized status of these religious minorities, since the Islamic Revolution, tens of thousands of persons belonging to religious minorities have left the country due to religious persecution by the regime. Amongst these religious minorities, the Bahais, about 350,000, have been subjected to the worst persecution because they are considered deserters from Islam, and have no religious rights.

Traditional Persia The ancient Persian empire was established in the sixth century B.C. by King Cyrus II (600–529 B.C.), founder of the Achaemenid dynasty, that ruled until the year 331 B.C. Cyrus united Persia and Media and conquered Babylonia. The religion of ancient Persia was pagan (Zoroastric), and its wars against Hellenism left their mark on human history. After the fall of the Achaemenid dynasty came Persia's Greek era (Alexander the Great). For 500 years, from 250 B.C. the Arsacid-Parthian dynasty ruled Persia. In 242 A.D. the local Sassanid dynasty came to power, ruling for close to 400 years. In 637 and 642 Persia was defeated and conquered by the Muslim Arabs in the battles of Qadisiyya and Nihawand, respectively. It was subsequently divided into provinces and ruled intermittently by local and Arab rulers, as a gradual Islamization of the population took place. In this period Persia ceased to be a separate political entity, despite the fact that it maintained its linguistic and cultural distinction. The Mongolian conquest, which ended the Abbasid Empire in 1258, persisted for about 200 years. From 1502 to 1753 Persia was ruled by the Safavid dynasty, which declared The Shi'a as the official religion of the state. Since then Persia has been the largest Shi'a bastion in the Muslim world. The Safavid era was characterized by a political and cultural renaissance and territorial expansion into Central Asia and Caucasia. In the Qajari era, which followed, Persia started to undergo a process of modernization, establishing contacts with the European powers. However, the Qajari rule was extremely weak, and Persia turned into a pawn in the hands of the European powers—especially Russia and Great Britain, which competed against each other over hegemony in the Middle East. Russia, which strove to expand its borders southwards, had to contend with British resistance, because its ambitions threatened Britain's communications to India through the Persian Gulf. The competition between these two powers at Persia's expense, characterized the international relations of the region in the nineteenth century. It nonetheless had the positive effect of guaranteeing Persia's independence, since Great Britain was interested in preserving a buffer zone between India and Russia, without having to maintain direct rule in it. Nevertheless, Persia's military and economic weakness, and the competition between the powers, led to a deepening of foreign penetration into Persia in the form of special rights in the military and trade spheres, which Persia was forced to grant, in an effort to play one power against the other in order to survive.

As of the beginning of the nineteenth century Persia was obliged to make major territorial concessions to Russia in Caucasia. Some of these were due to military defeats, whilst others were as a result of joint pressure by Great Britain and Russia. In the second half of the nineteenth century, Russia managed to expand its control to the Khanat of Central Asia (Buchara, Khiva, and Kokand), and get a foothold in the South of the Caspain Sea at Persia's expense. It also established a border line with Persia in Turkmenistan, East of the Caspian Sea, which had previously constituted a buffer zone under Persian influence.

While Russia was interested primarily in territorial gains, Britain's main interest was commercial and economic. (Concessions for the construction of railways and roads, and the search for minerals.) In the beginning of the twentieth century, Russia gave Persia two loans in return for the customs duties revenue of the state (except in the Fars province and the Persian Gulf). In 1901 the Englishman William Knox D'Arcy was granted a concession to prospect for oil in Persia for sixty years. In 1908 oil in commercial quantities was discovered in the province of Khuzistan. A year later the Anglo-Persian Oil Company was established.

Persia entered the twentieth century as a weak and poor state, whose leaders had gone bankrupt both economically and politically and had lost their practical and moral authority to rule it. In 1896 the Persian Shah was assassinated; the state's treasury was non-existent and Persia suffered internal difficulties placing its whole future in question. As of 1900 Russia became Persia's sole lender, providing it with additional economic rights at the expense of the Persian treasury. There was a vast gap between the upper classes (the Royal Family, the senior officials, the big traders and the land owners) and the lower classes, which included most of the urban population (artisans and small traders), as well as the rural population, most of whom were landless tenants. Toward the end of the nineteenth century and the beginning of the twentieth century, a thin stratum of intellectuals, who were influenced by European liberalism and ideas of social equality, emerged. The weakness of the regime manifested itself, *inter alia*, in growing criticism in the press and demand for urgent reforms in the regime and for the introduction of a constitution that would limit the powers of the Shah and hand them over to representative bodies. This demand gained popularity following the 1905 Russian revolution. The struggle for the democratization of the regime also became an issue in which the powers intervened: Russia supported the ruler and his conservative approach, while Great Britain supported the "Democratic Party" which demanded liberalization in the political system. In 1906 the crisis peaked with a strike of the traders— the Bazaris—about 5,000 of whom gathered in the yard of the British consulate in Tehran. After they had spent several days there, the Shah agreed to grant a constitution, according to which a national assembly—the *Majlis*—was established on Western lines, and the powers of the Shah were limited. In Russia there were objections to the reforms. Following Russia's *rapprochement* with Great Britain in 1907, the two powers encouraged the Shah, Muhammad Ali, to break free of the constitution and disperse the national assembly, following a military coup, which was performed under his inspiration. However, the Shah's success was temporary. In 1909, the opposition, led by the leaders of the Bakhtiari tribe of the South, entered Tehran, deposing the ruler. The new Shah brought back the constitution and the Democratic Party returned to power. The constitution recognized the civil rights of religious minorities, granting them permanent places in the *Majlis*. However, the realization of this right proved impossible

with regard to the Jews and Armenians, who had been persecuted and suppressed for hundreds of years. As a result, these two communities handed over their representation in the *Majlis* to well known clerics, who were considered supporters of the constitutional revolution.

Germany's growing power, led to a *rapprochement* between Russia and Great Britain. This manifested itself in a Treaty, signed by the two in 1907, which *inter alia* called for the partition of Persia between them into influence zones. The northern area, including Tehran, was in Russia's influence zone, while Britain reserved for itself a dominant status in the south-eastern territories. The South-Western area remained neutral. According to the Treaty, Russia and Great Britain undertook to respect the independence and territorial integrity of Persia, but in fact they continued to intervene directly and indirectly in its internal affairs. Russia conquered the Persian part of Azerbaijan (including its capital, Tabriz), forcing the dismissal of the *Majlis* and the firing of Morgan Shuster—the American advisor on Treasury matters. The Treaty greatly angered Persian elite circles, including the Democratic Party, which turned to Germany in an effort to limit Russia's and Britain's influence. Until the outbreak of World War I, Germany managed to deepen its economic and commercial penetration, while increasing its influence on the Democratic Party. Upon the outbreak of the War in Europe, cooperation between Russia and Great Britain increased against Germany, whilst their intervention in Persian affairs intensified. The Russians maintained a military presence in the north of the country, while the British kept guard over the oil fields of Khuzistan, with the help of Indian forces.

Persia's weakness was also reflected in the state of its armed forces. In fact, Persia lacked a regular army and organized forces that could defend the borders of the state and preserve its internal security. The armed forces that did function in it were all controlled by foreign states. In the north of the country there was a Cossack force at the level of a brigade, which was subject to Russian control and was commanded by Russian officers. At the end of World War I this force developed into a division. In the southern districts of the country there was a force under the command of British officers, called the South Persian Rifles (S.P.R.). The command over the Persian *Gendarmerie* (whose task was to protect the roads and railways) was in the hands of officers from Sweden. There was no coordination or cooperation amongst the three forces and their arms systems were different. At the same time, the strong nomadic tribes in the peripheral districts preserved a significant degree of autonomy from the central administration.

In the course of World War I, Iran remained neutral, though it sympathised with the Central Powers. The War created a new reality for it. Upon the outbreak of the Bolshevik revolution, the Russian pressure over Iran weakened, while Great Britain fortified its hold in the Gulf area through its direct rule in Iraq and greater influence in Persia. In 1919 Britain imposed a treaty on Persia, which was to ensure for BRITAIN a de facto protectorate over Persia, by means of missions on military and financial matters. This was in return for a loan of 2 million pounds sterling to the government of Tehran. However, the *Majlis* strongly objected to the agreement, and since Britain was unwilling to use military force, it gave up the agreement and by 1921 withdrew all its forces from the territory of Persia. On the other hand, in 1918 Bolshevik Russia canceled all the rights of the Czar's regime in northern Iran and in 1921 signed an agreement with the government of Persia in this spirit, as part of its efforts to settle its relations with its Southern neighbors and turn them into buffers between itself and imperialist Britain. The Soviet Union obtained fishing rights in the Caspian Sea, but its most significant gain in the agreement was the recognition of its right to introduce military forces into Persia in the event of intervention by a third party, which would pose a threat to the Soviet Union from the Persian territory. This provision, which was designed to defend the new Bolshevik regime from an invasion by anti-revolutionary forces or foreign powers, constituted for the next decades a regular source of concern in Persia, for fear of Soviet armed intervention. The new situation provided Persia with de facto independence, since the powers either did not want or were unable to intervene in it.

In February 1921, the commander of the Cossack division—an ambitious and energetic officer by the name of Reza Khan—performed a *coup d'état* and established a government, headed by the journalist and statesman Zia ul-Din Tabatabai. Reza Khan appointed himself Minister of Defense, but in fact held in his own hands all the powers of government. In November 1923 Reza Khan appointed himself Prime Minister, forcing the King, Ahmad Shah, to go into exile in Europe. Thus the authority of the Qajari dynasty, that had ruled in Persia for 128 years (since 1795) ended. Reza Khan considered turning Persia into a republic, but this idea was strongly opposed by the religious establishment, to such an extent that republicanism became illegal.

Modern Iran Iran Under Reza Shah (1925–1941)

Domestic Affairs At the end of 1925 the *Majlis* deposed the absent Shah, and several months later crowned Reza Khan as Shah. This began the era of the Pahlavi dynasty.

Despite the fact that he was uneducated and had never left the boundaries of Persia, REZA SHAH strove to liberate Persia from foreign influence and develop it as a modern centralized state, based on the reform model of Kemal ATATÜRK in Turkey. Even though he enjoyed relatively limited freedom of action, compared to that of the nationalists in Turkey, and was required to start from a point of deep backwardness, Iran made an historical jump forward to a modern state during the years of his rule. The construction of a strong army, which would support his reform plan and ensure its implementation, was at the top of his priorities and he invested a great deal of effort into nurturing Iran's armed forces. Following the coup in 1921, Reza Khan ousted all the foreign officers, set up a regular Army with a modern command and unified its weapons systems. He established an academy for officers and announced compulsory military service for men from the age of eighteen. He allocated large sums of money for the armed forces, purchasing large quantities of arms from Czechoslovakia and Germany. With the help of the army units which he commanded, he managed, by 1921, to crush an uprising in the district of Gilan in the north of the country, that had been supported by the Soviets. Over the years several more local uprisings of tribes, which traditionally refused to accept authority, were crushed.

With the help of an American financial advisor, Reza Shah reorganized the state's treasury and managed to increase revenue from taxes. This enabled the financing of a highly important national project: the construction of the trans-Iranian railway, which connected Tehran with the Persian Gulf. The construction of the track began in 1927 and was completed in 1939. The development of internal land and air transportation was perceived as being of major economic importance, but also a tool for the integration and strengthening of the government's control of the peripheral regions. In the economic sphere Reza Shah concentrated on the limitation of foreign influence and industrialization. He cancelled the capitulations and in 1928 established the National Bank of Iran, with exclusive rights to issue money; previously this was in the hands of a bank under British auspices. He passed a law prohibiting foreigners to purchase agricultural land in Iran.

Reza Shah initiated the establishment of consumption industries and developed the infrastructures under state supervision and control. He even invested his own private money in business projects—especially the construction of modern hotels. With the help of Germany, an effort was made to establish an industrial infrastructure and to develop Iran's foreign trade. State-owned factories for textiles, cement and food were established. Reza Khan favored a centralized economy and therefore nurtured national monopolies in the sphere of industry and foreign trade. This damaged the status of the traders and limited private initiative, but nevertheless enabled competition with Russia, whose monopolistic foreign trade created great difficulties for private Iranian trade. Compared to investment in industry, agriculture was neglected and the government encouraged migration to the cities.

Reza Shah also introduced several social and legal reforms. The secularization trend that characterized his rule manifested itself in a systematic effort. This was unprecedented in the history of the state and weakened the religious establishment. It confiscated its traditional power centers: the religious endowments, the SHARI'A courts, the religious schools and the mosques, which were subjected to the state bureaucracy. In 1927 he adopted the French legal system, taking all civilian matters out of the hands of the Shari'a courts. At the same time, the Iranian constitution stated explicitly that ISLAM was the official religion of Iran, and prohibited the passing of legislation contrary to Islam. Nevertheless, discrimination against religious minorities was legally canceled, including the per capita tax previously imposed on non-Muslims. Reza Shah also started to establish a modern primary education system and a higher education law was passed. As of 1930 the duty to study religious

studies in primary and secondary schools was canceled. In 1934 a university was opened in Tehran—the first in Iran—which also included a faculty for religious studies. At the same time all the foreign educational institutions were closed down. In the 1920s and 1930s impressive progress was also made in the sphere of public health. Modern hospitals were established and the public health system was improved. The new education system emphasized values of patriotism and civil nationalism. The means of communication, including the national radio, which was established in 1940, were harnessed to the task of formulating a modern national culture for the younger generation. In 1928 traditional dress was prohibited and was modified to European dress. Legislative action was taken to provide women with rights in the sphere of personal law, and they were permitted to participate in political forums. In 1935 the traditional chador, which covered the whole body and face, was prohibited. Furthermore, the Persian language was "purified" of Arab influences, even though the Arab alphabet remained intact.

The period of Reza Shah's rule was characterized by autarchy, the suppression of political freedoms and manifestations of opposition—occasionally violent—which the social reforms awakened. He deprived the democratic provisions of the constitution of any meaning and turned the national assembly into a rubber stamp for his decisions. He used an iron fist against his critics amongst the intellectuals and suppressed the spirit of liberalism, which had flourished in the first years after the constitutional revolution. He prohibited the activity of the Communist Party in 1931. Under his rule intellectuals and thinkers were thrown into prison, tortured and murdered. During the course of his rule there was a sharp alienation between the state and the religious establishment and with it large sections of traditional society, which remained outside the influence of the reforms. Reza Shah usually preserved the interests of the landlords, but due to his centralized policy in the spheres of mobilization and trade, he failed to secure their support for him.

Foreign Relations The relations between Iran and the Soviet Union were tense, because of the permanent Iranian fear of Soviet expansion at Iran's expense. They were further aggravated by the inclination of the ethnic minorities in the Iranian Azerbaijan region and Khurasan to revolt. The suppression of the Communist Party in Iran also disturbed the relations between Tehran and Moscow. Another cause for tension was the persistent opposition by the Soviet Union to the granting of concessions to British and American companies to prospect for oil in northern Iran, on the basis of the 1921 Treaty between the two countries. The Soviet Union also exerted pressure to attain preferred import conditions for agricultural produce from the northern regions of Iran and fishing rights in the Caspian Sea, and at the same time tried to dump food products into Iran in a way that harmed local production.

Even though the relations with Britain were also not devoid of tension and disputes, Iran drew closer to it, especially due to the activity of the Anglo-Iranian oil company in Khuzistan, whose oil refineries in Abadan were the largest in the world. The British continued to maintain independent relations with tribes and local power centers in the southern part of the state, by means of traders, agents and consuls. Britain's deep involvement in the south of the state led to disputes around the question of the sovereignty in BAHRAIN (1928) and the status of Sheikh Khaz'al, ruler of Muhammara. These problems were resolved in a treaty between the two countries signed in 1928. This canceled the capitulations but granted guarantees to British citizens in Iran. In 1932 the Shah canceled the oil concession of the Anglo-Iranian Oil Company, which had been based on the D'Arcy concession. Britain sent war ships and complained to the League of Nations In 1933 a new Treaty was signed, limiting the area of the concession obliging Britain to pay larger royalties to the Iranian government, At the same time the contract was prolonged to sixty years (see OIL).

Iran strove for friendly relations with its close neighbors, especially Turkey and Afghanistan. In 1926 the three signed a friendship alliance inspired by the Soviet Union, which contributed to the settlement of border disputes between Turkey and Iran in 1932. At the same time, the relations between Turkey and Iran continued to suffer as a result of the Kurdish problem. In 1937 Iran signed the Sa'ad Abad Pact with Turkey, Iraq and Afghanistan. This dealt with non-aggression and cooperation in the prevention of mutual subversion. The alliance was regarded by the Soviet Union as anti-Soviet.

Like many other leaders in the region, Reza Shah strove for close relations with Nazi Germany. In addition to admiration for the symbols of nationalism and power, which Germany exemplified in those days, the decisive consideration on Iran's part was the traditional aspiration to limit the influence of Russia and Britain by means of a third power. Even before the outbreak of World war II, Iran turned into an arena of extensive activity by German intelligence. Several months before the outbreak of the War Iran signed a friendship agreement with Japan and even though it declared neutrality when the War broke out, it continued to tighten its relations with Germany. In 1940 the two countries signed a trade and shipping agreement. A similar agreement was signed in that year between Iran and the Soviet Union.

In August 1941 the Allies invaded Iran in order to establish access by land to the Soviet Union and to put an end to the German activity in the state. Russian units entered Iran from the north and British forces invaded from the south. In 1942 they were joined by American units.

Before the invasion, the Allies sent several memoranda to Iran demanding the expulsion of the Germans. The Iranian Army demonstrated little resistance in the face of invaders, collapsing within forty-eight hours. Reza Shah was forced to surrender the throne in favor of his son MUHAMMAD REZA SHAH, he went into exile in South Africa. He died in exile and in 1950 his remains were returned to Iran. A mausoleum was established for him in the South of Tehran.

Iran under Muhammad Reza Shah (1942–1979)
1942–1963

Domestic Affairs The presence of foreign forces in Iranian territory during World War II weakened the authority of the government, stifling the proper administration of state affairs. The war also brought to Iran foreign investments, which led to certain socioeconomic changes. The transportation network was improved and trade flourished. The increased demand for manpower led to a more rapid migration from the rural to urban areas—especially Tehran. There was a penetration of Western culture and modern management methods. There was also a flourishing of the press and parties. However, this period was relatively short, for once the government recovered and regained control over the life of the state, all the limitations on the press and political activity were reintroduced.

Under the Anglo-Soviet occupation a general amnesty was declared. This led to the release of many political prisoners, most of them communists who formed officially a COMMUNIST PARTY under the name TUDEH ("The Party of the Masses"). This operated primarily in the Russian occupation zone. The Party continued to operate legally also after the departure of the Soviet forces from Iran, but very rapidly began to clash with the government. The *Tudeh* Party reached the peak of its political achievements in the 1946 elections, in which it gained eight seats in the *Majlis*. It was later represented by two ministers in the government of Qavam al-Salaneh, as a gesture of reconciliation towards the Soviet Union, with whom relations were still tense following the withdrawal of the Soviet forces from Iran. However, in February 1949 the party was outlawed, on the grounds of having been responsible for an attempt to assassinate the Shah the previous year, in which he was slightly wounded.

The popular sympathy demonstrated toward the Shah following the attempt on his life led him to play an increasing role in running the state's affairs and take a personal interest in the security of his regime. In 1949 he convened the *Majlis* in order to change the constitution and enable the establishment of a sixty member Senate, half of whose members were to be chosen by the Shah and the rest elected by the citizens. In that year the first elections to the Senate took place. The new constitution laid down that the regime is a constitutional monarchy, and provided, theoretically, for the separation of powers between the government, the *Majlis* (whose members are elected every four years) and the judiciary. In fact, the King was granted extensive powers to control the administration of the state and determine its policy. He was to choose the prime minister (who had to be approved by the parliament) and he was the commander in chief of the armed forces. The establishment of the senate, thirty of whose members were appointed by the Shah, also increased the Shah's political power.

However, the tension in the domestic political arena and terrorist activities against the regime intensified. This represented the growing grievances among Iranian nationalists over the Anglo-Iranian Oil Company's concession and demand to nationalize the oil industry. At the same time the disgruntlement amongst the extreme religious circles

against the secularization process became further aggravated. In 1949 the Court Minister was murdered. In March 1951 the Prime Minister, Ali Razm-Ara was shot dead by a religious fanatic of the *Fadazan-e Eslam*, an underground terrorist group, because of his support for "the foreign infidels."

Prime Minister Razm-Ara indeed argued against nationalization. He purported that Iran was unable to contend alone with the problems of oil production and marketing. The demand for nationalization was led by Muhammad MOSSADDEQ, a *Majlis* member who had managed to unite several political groups into the NATIONAL FRONT OF IRAN. The members of the Front were mostly urban and educated, as well as traders (Bazaaris). Even though the known clerics were not active in the political arena, the Ayatollah Kashani—an influential religious authority—joined the struggle to nationalize the oil industry. Several days after the assassination the *Majlis* passed a bill, proposed by Mossaddeq, to nationalize the Iranian oil industry (see OIL). In April Mossaddeq was appointed Prime Minister, and was swept by popular waves of sympathy for the nationalization policy. The appointment of Mossaddeq constituted a blow to the Shah's posture. Mossaddeq brought Iran into conflict with foreign powers in the name of Iran's sovereignty and national independence. Furthermore he also decided to limit the Shah's powers and to cancel the Senate, which was regarded as a royal instrument to contain the elected *Majlis*. Mossaddeq's slogan was that the Shah should reign—not rule.

In the face of growing support for Mossaddeq by various political groups, including the underground *Tudeh*, the Shah announced, in February 1953, that he intended to leave the state temporarily. This triggered mass demonstrations by supporters of the monarchy, including Ayatollah Kashani who feared the growing strength of the secular groups supporting Mossaddeq, following which the Shah canceled his intention. With the growing economic crisis (caused by the cease of oil sales and the conflict between the Shah and his Prime Minister), the former ordered Mossaddeq's removal on 16 August 1953. He was replaced by General Fazlollah Zahedi. Mossaddeq rejected the order on grounds of its illegality and Zahedi's attempt to impose the order by military force failed, obliging the Shah to leave the state. However, Mossaddeq did not manage to gain the army's confidence. Within three days Zahedi managed to organize a military uprising with the help of the CIA. This put an end to Mossaddeq's rule, enabling the Shah to return to Iran as a victor.

The humiliating experience of the Shah's short exile under nationalist pressure was to underpin his efforts and fortify his position as a ruler and expand the basis of political support for his regime. He prohibited the activity of the parties, started purging the army and government of potential opponents, and intervened intensively in the decisions of the government and the management of the state. After twelve years in power the Shah was determined not to leave the reins of government in the hands of the old politicians, most of whom had risen in his father's period. He gradually turned into an autocrat like his father. However, his active intervention in day-to-day matters did not help solve the socioeconomic problems. The Prime Ministers whom he appointed, were equally unsuccessful in this sphere.

Zahedi, who brought about the deposition of Mossaddeq from the premiership and replaced him, lacked any political or government experience. His rule endured for less than two years. In April 1955 he was replaced by Hassan Ala, who had already served a short term as Prime Minister in 1951. Even though he had been a successful court minister and had fulfilled several governmental and diplomatic posts, he did not excel as an administrator. He was replaced in April 1957 by Dr. Manuchehr Eghbal, who had administrative experience as Chairman of the Iranian Oil Company. He maintained much economic and operational powers; canceled the Martial Law and announced his intention to establish a two party political system in the country. However, due to the absence of a suitable institutional infrastructure, he too failed to resolve the urgent problems. In August 1960 he resigned in favor of Sharif-Emami, who in turn was forced to resign due to a teachers' strike. The next Prime Minister was Dr. Ali Amini. An experienced and brilliant politician, he had served in several previous governments and had dared on occasion to openly criticize the Shah. He prepared extensive plans for administrative reforms, fighting corruption, reducing government expenditure and cutting down the importation of luxury goods. He also strove to introduce political liberalization by dismissing the *Majlis* and holding new free elections. The Shah viewed this as an effort to undermine his

authority and refused to support him. In the meantime the *Tudeh* Party and the conservative clerics, who were opposed to the agrarian reforms and other reforms proposed by Amini, started to gather forces. Against this background there were bloody riots in Tehran in the Spring of 1962 and the economic crisis worsened. Amini, who also failed to present a balanced budget, tendered his resignation in July of that year.

In July 1962 the Shah handed over the premiership to his friend and confidant, Assadollah Alam, who had served in the past as Minister of Court and had set up, under the Shah's instructions, the *Mardom* (People's) Party (see below). He had served as head of the economic giant PAHLAVI Foundation and was deeply involved in the political and economic life of the country. Alam introduced the Shah's reforms, which led to the distribution of land to tenants and the granting of voting rights to women. However, the implementation of these plans led to a wave of bloody riots—an interlude to the religious revolution, which was to take place sixteen years later.

From the early 1950s the Shah repeatedly tried to establish a ruling party under his control. This balanced the influence of the opposition groups that operated illegally—the *Tudeh* and the National Front. In the years 1957–1958 the *Melliyun* (Nationalist) Party was formed, by instruction of the Shah. The party was led by the Prime Minister, and it filled the role of an official opposition. However, this two party system was rejected by the general public and soon disintegrated. In 1963 the Shah once again tried to establish a ruling party and founded the *Iran-e Novin* (New Iran) Party, whose leadership was handed over to the Prime Minister. But this party also failed to fulfill its mission. In the decade following the Mossaddeq crisis, the Shah acted to reconstruct the army on modern lines, with the assistance of American military advisors. This cooperation tightened after Iran joined CENTO, but the Army continued to be viewed primarily as a tool for maintaining domestic order and the regime's security. Its size and current expenditures were hence relatively small.

Iran. The economic gaps widened. The elite group, comprised mainly of landowners who had not only economic wealth but also political power, labeled it as ""the one thousand family regime." The deterioration in the profitability of the agricultural sector, as a result of old fashioned cultivation methods, poor management and an absence of incentives for farmers, led to a mass desertion of the villages and flow into the cities. To counter this situation the Shah started, as early as 1950–1951, to distribute Crown Lands. This was completed at the end of 1963, but due to its limited scope, failed to produce the expected results. In 1958 the Shah established the Pahlavi Foundation which included all the companies, factories and economic and financial institutions owned by the Royal Family. The government took advantage of the fund's profits in order to raise the standards of education, health and life of the masses. In 1961 the Pahlavi Dynasty Trust was established with a registered capital of 40 million pounds sterling for the same purpose. In the 1950s, the Shah called upon the landowners to follow his example and distribute their lands by their own initiative. However, 'this call remained unanswered, and a bill brought to the *Majlis* on this subject was "castrated" by Members of Parliament, many of whom were landlords themselves. When an additional attempt by the Shah to bring this about failed in 1960, he decided to introduce an extensive series of reforms under the slogan "*Anghelab-e Shah va Mardom*" (Revolution of the King and the People). This included not only agrarian reforms but also the advancement of the status of women (including the right of women to vote, first introduced in the elections to the *Majlis* in 1963). The government also opened an extensive campaign to fight illiteracy and improve health services in the rural sector. The reforms, termed "the White Revolution", were confronted with strong opposition of the clerics and land lords, who joined forces with the leftist opposition whose main demands revolved around true democratization and far more radical reforms.

Foreign Affairs During World War II, Iran's foreign affairs were affected by the presence of foreign forces on its soil. Muhammad Reza came to power in January 1942, at a time when the country was in a state of occupation, used by the Allies to transfer strategic assistance to the Soviet Union. In the Tripartite Treaty of Alliance, which they had signed with Iran in 1941, Britain and the Soviet Union undertook to respect the territorial integrity of Iran, its sovereignty and political independence and to defend it against aggression. In return Iran had undertaken to grant the Allies the full use of its transportation systems for the transfer of arms and supplies to the Soviet Union, and other Iranian facilities. The powers undertook to withdraw their forces within six months from the end of the War. Nevertheless, during the course of the War, the Soviet Union exercised pressure on Iran to grant it an oil concession in the north of the country. However, in light of the legislation passed by the *Majlis*, which prohibited negotiations on oil concessions with any foreign factor until the end of the War, the Soviet Union withdrew its demand but continued its subversive activities in Azerbaijan and Kurdistan, while encouraging the demands of local groups for autonomy. During the years of the occupation the Soviet Union stopped the Iranian government from exercising its administrative duties in the Iranian Azerbaijan.

Contrary to the Treaty between them, the Soviet Union continued to maintain a presence in Northern Iran for a year after the end of the War. The government of Tehran complained to the UN Security Council. Under pressure from the Western powers and following a resolution by the Security Council, the Soviets agreed to withdraw. The Iranian Army entered Azerbaijan and Kurdistan. Thus ended the puppet government of the "Republic of Azerbaijan", whose capital was Tabriz, and the "Republic of Kurdistan", whose capital was Mahabad.

The Soviet pressure on Iran, Turkey, and Greece at the end of the War was one of the causes for a new American strategy entitled the "Truman Doctrine". Proclaimed in March 1947, this promised assistance to states under external threat to their security, who sought American support. In the face of weakening traditional influence of the Soviet Union and Great Britain in Iran, the US started to build its stature as Iran's ally. In October 1947 the first military agreement between the US and Iran was concluded. American military experts arrived in Iran to reorganize the army. In the early 1950s the US granted Iran an initial 25 million dollar loan. The US added Iran to the states receiving economic aid within the framework of "Point Four", giving it a grant of half a million dollars. In 1952 US aid was increased within this framework, reflecting greater cooperation between the two states. Following the 1951–1953 oil crisis between Iran and Great Britain, an international consortium was established in 1954 to export Iranian oil. Forty percent of these shares were given to the Anglo-Iranian oil company (which has since become British Petroleum). The remainder was divided amongst several oil companies, including Dutch "Shell" and five American companies (see OIL). Despite being a Muslim state, during the era of Muhammad Reza Shah, Iran maintained close relations with Israel, based on common interests. In 1950 it granted Israel de facto recognition and exchanged resident representatives with it, much to the chagrin of the religious establishment in Iran and of the Arab states. During the period of Muhammad Mossaddeq's government, the Iranian representative was called back from Israel, but the Israeli representation continued to function in Tehran at a low profile.

Following the Mossaddeq crisis (see below) cooperation expanded with the West, in particular, the US. In March 1959 a Defense Agreement was signed between the US and Iran. This granted the Americans the right of military intervention in Iran in the event of external aggression. In the same year Iran joined CENTO. Turkey, Pakistan, Great Britain and the US were also members. Besides military assistance in the form of arms and advisors, the intensifying ties with the US also manifested themselves in financial assistance, which, by 1960, reached the total sum of about 800 million dollars.

British-Iranian relations, which had been cut off during the oil crisis, were renewed in December 1953, after Mossaddeq was deposed. An additional crisis occurred in the relations between the two states in January 1968, when London announced its intention to terminate its presence in the Persian Gulf by 1971 and grant independence to the Arab Emirates along its coast. Iran demanded ownership of Bahrain, but the crisis was resolved after Iran decided to give up its demand.

Relations with the Soviet Union fluctuated. The fall of the Mossaddeq government resulted in temporary tension. However, in December 1954 an agreement was signed between the two states, according to which the Soviet Union agreed to pay its debts to Iran for goods and services it had received from it during World War II. The two states also signed a map of their common border. Despite being a member in a western alliance (CENTO), Iran demonstrated an independent foreign policy. In 1962 it announced, as a gesture of good will to the Soviet Union, that it would not allow the stationing of foreign missiles on its territory. In 1964–1965 a significant improvement in Soviet-Iranian relations occured, when a number of economic and commercial agreements were signed. The Shah visited the Soviet Union three times and was warmly received. In January 1966 an agreement with the Soviet Union for the establishment of a Steel Mill in Isfahan was signed.

Iran's relations with Turkey and Pakistan (Iran's partners in CENTO), improved with the establishment of the Organization for Regional Cooperation and Development (RCD). This was an attempt to formally associate all the members of the alliance, without the US and Great Britain. However, this organization achieved little. Despite their membership, Pakistan and Turkey avoided supporting Iran in its disputes with the Arab states. These disputes emerged from Iraq's territorial demands for full sovereignty over the SHATT AL-ARAB, as well as over the Khuzistan district in south-west Iran; Iran's claim to Bahrain; and a propaganda and subversion campaign by Egyptian President Gamal ABDEL NASSER against the Iranian regime portrayed as an ally of the West. This campaign intensified when Iran joined CENTO and in July 1960 led to the severance of diplomatic relations with EGYPT.

Relations between Iran and SAUDI ARABIA were marked by competition over oil pricing and marketing, as well as by the religious rivalry between the Saudi WAHHABI sect and the Shi's. The Saudis took advantage of the cease of oil exporting by Iran during the latter's nationalization crisis (1951–1953), by increasing their exports and weakening the latter's position in its struggle with Britain. In the early 1960s a basis for cooperation between the two states was created in the face of Nasser's threats to the Saudi regime and involvement of Egyptian troops in Yemen's Civil War (see also EGYPT).

The fall of the monarchy in Iraq in 1958 resulted in a deterioration in its relations with Iran, inter alia due to Iraq's improved relations with the Soviet Union. Immersed in border disputes (Iraqi demand for sovereignty over the waters of the Shatt al-Arab; mutual demands over various land border areas, and the right to pump oil in fields on the common border), and involved in mutual acts of subversion, manifested primarily in the Iranian support of the Kurdish revolt in Iraq, and Iraqi incitement and subversion against Tehran.

1963 to the Islamic Revolution

Domestic Affairs In June 1963 bloody riots erupted in Tehran and other large cities, led by a militant clergyman by the name of Seyyed Rouhollah Moussavi KHOMEINI, who strongly criticized the Shah for his suppression of, and infidelity to, Islam. In the two days of riots, which were suppressed by the Army, hundreds of people were killed and wounded. Following the intervention of senior clergymen, the Shah refrained from executing Khomeini, and instead sent him to exile. In March 1964, Prime Minister Assadollah Alam resigned. The unrest continued and in January 1965 the new Prime Minister, Hassan-Ali Mansour was assassinated by a member of the *Fedaiyin-e Eslam*. (Years later Hojjat-ol-Eslam Ali-Akbar Hashemi RAFSANJANI, President of Iran in the years 1989–1997, admitted that he had provided the gun with which the assassination was performed.) Despite an additional attempt on the Shah's life in April of that year, the policy of reforms continued within the framework of the "White Revolution". Its implementation was assigned to the Minister of Finance, Amir-Abbas Hoveida, who was appointed Prime Minister in place of Mansour. In the 1971 elections the *Iran-e Novin Party*, headed by Hoveida, gained 229 of the 268 seats in the *Majlis* and 27 of the 30 elected seats in the Senate. The *Mardom* (People's) Party (an official opposition party) was severely defeated.

From the end of the 1960s the Shah's domestic policy was characterized by his determination to march Iran toward secular, Western modernism. He acted systematically to weaken the position of the clerics; to move Iran away from the Islamic religious tradition and to renew the symbols of the pre-Islamic Persian culture. In October 1971 the regime celebrated, with great pomp, the 2,500th anniversary of the establishment of the Persian Empire, with the participation of kings, presidents and heads of state from all over the world. The celebrations were designed to present the Shah as the heir of the Great Cyrus; to emphasize Iran's international stature and boast the achievements of the regime's reforms. The celebrations were also the Shah's response to the demands of the left wing opposition and radical clerics that a democratic regime be instituted in Iran and the powers of the Shah reduced. But the wasteful celebrations only intensified the criticism and social fermentation.

From the very beginning the clerics were opposed to the Pahlavi dynasty. Since the rise to power of Reza-Shah, this had conducted a struggle to weaken their social and political status. The clerics took good advantage of the pulpits in the mosques and the Friday sermons to criticize the Shah and the government. This criticism became increasingly pungent and overt in the course of the late 1970s. In these years the religious establishment preached against the reforms in the status of women and their dress; the art festivals and the Western consumer culture; as well as the close ties with the West and ISRAEL. Cassettes, which contained the speeches of Khomeini, were distributed in the country, to enable the illiterate to his speeches, in which he called for the regime to be brought down. The clergymen were directly and indirectly hurt by the reforms initiated by the Shah. Many of them had been landowners and were hurt by the agrarian reform. The granting of social and political rights to women and their integration into senior administrative posts; the establishment of courts for the protection of the family; the enlistment of women to military service and the introduction of a secular calendar (based on the counting of the years since the establishment of the Persian Empire rather than the establishment of Islam)—all undermined the authority of the clerics in the society, constituting a blow to hitherto sacrosanct social norms, which the religious establishment sought to protect.

In the absence of freedom of political organization and expression, many students and intellectuals began supporting the clergy. The mosques and religious clubs (*Hosseiniyeh*) turned into the only gathering venues for the youth to hear lectures and speeches almost undisturbed, since the security forces were wary of acting against these institutions. Thus was created a common basis for the clerics and the younger educated generation. This led to the incubation of revolutionary ideas in religious garb—a combination that manifested itself in the books of Ali Shariati, which gained great popularity amongst the younger generation. The advantage of the religious establishment also stemmed from its control of the network of mosques and charity organizations, with a large number of employees and devoted activists, which was financed from the charity donations (*Zakat*). While the political parties were concentrated primarily in the large cities, the mosques functioned everywhere, giving access to all social groups, irrespective of education and social status. The influence of the clerics was especially decisive amongst the rural population and urban poor.

In an attempt to increase the basis of his regime's legitimization within the public, the Shah established a single ruling party called RASTAKHIZ (Resurgence) instead of the bipartisan system which had failed to fulfill his expectations. Prime Minister Hoveida was appointed Chairman of the new Party, but very soon it became apparent that it did not meet the growing public demand for real political participation. The Communist *Tudeh* Party, the National Front, as well as various Marxist and religious groups continued to operate underground.

In the face of growing weakness in the Shah's position, the Army continued to be a bastion of allegiance to his regime, though even here the Shah's autocratic approach eroded the advantages of the Army's support. Within the framework of his position as Supreme Commander of the armed forces, the Shah appointed not only the Chief of Staff but also the commanders of the various military divisions, actively intervening in other appointments. Fearing a military coup by ambitious and enterprising officers, the Shah suppressed every manifestation of independent thought in the military command, maintaining close supervision over it by means of direct contact with each of the members of the general staff and senior field commanders. In the 1970s the senior command of the army became totally incapable of acting independently of the Shah.

Despite the political unrest, in the second decade of the Shah's rule there was a rise in the standard of living; the middle class expanded and the population growth rate increased. This was a result of the improvement in the public health services. The 1966 census estimated the population in Iran at 25.7 million, of whom only 9.8 percent were urban. The next census, held in 1976, showed an increase of 30 percent in the population, which led the authorities to initiate a birth control campaign. However, the Iranian economy continued to heavily depend on oil exports (which constituted about four percent of its GNP) and the fluctuations in its price on the world market. Thus, Iran enjoyed a substantial increase in its GNP (forty-one percent) in the years 1973–1975, in which there was a boom in oil prices. On the other hand, its GNP fell substantial-ly in the four years of slump in oil prices that preceded the Islamic revolution. In the period of the implementation of the fifth five-year plan (1973–1978) Iran's GNP increased from 17 billion to 55.3 billion dollars in real terms. According to official publications, per capita income stood at 2,500 dollars.

The peak in oil prices in the first half of the 1970s and the slump that followed, as well as the immense growth in government expenditures, boosted inflation and public opposition to the regime. The declining oil prices as of 1975 compelled the government to discontinue many projects, planned in the days of plenty, which had a negative effect on the level of business and trade. This encouraged many tradesmen to join Khomeini's camp. The Shah's efforts to check inflation by punishing those who charged exorbitant prices had no effect on inflation, but did hurt the business sector. The inflation affected the purchasing power of the wage earners, including government officials whose salaries had been eroded and whose advancement had been contained, due to the spread of favoritism and corruption in government institutions. Youngsters, whose number was constantly growing, came across difficulties in finding jobs or being accepted to university. The agrarian reforms proved to be a failure, since inflation disrupted the agricultural production capacity and price control on agricultural products hurt the revenue from it. This encouraged the population flow from the countryside into the cities—especially Tehran. The rapid urbanization caused a major housing shortage, and a collapse of public services. The impoverished migrants became a source of social unrest and rapidly turned into the vanguard of protest activities against the regime and ardent supporters of Khomeini.

Industry entered dire straits, due to excessive government control and a shortage in electricity, government investment in grandiose projects, and the purchase of arms and military equipment, increased the social gaps. Corruption was rampant in government institutions and amongst those close to the Royal Family. The latter took blatant advantage of their position and influence to attain benefits and amass riches from the giant government budgets for public projects and new enterprises. They acted as intermediaries between the government and the business institutions it owned on the one hand, and the foreign companies involved on the other. The ruling elite controlled all the major construction projects, including those for luxury housing, and operated gambling establishments in the outskirts of Tehran. As the protests against the government increased in the second half of 1978, the gambling clubs were shut down, members of the Royal Family were prohibited to engage in business activities, and at the end of the year a commission was established to investigate the amassment of property by those close to the Shah.

The presence in Iran of tens of thousands of foreign military and civilian advisors, most of them Americans, was regarded by the intellectuals and nationalists, as harmful to the independence of the state and its national honor. The massive presence of foreigners from Western countries was also perceived detrimental to cultural and social traditions. In addition to their foreign manners and customs to the average Iranian, the foreigners maintained a standard of living that contributed to the rise in rents in the large cities—especially in Tehran.

In the last years of the Shah's rule, the protest activities of the students increased. At the end of 1977 the students' demonstrations intensified, spreading to all the universities. In addition to the left wingers, students with religious inclinations, who *inter alia* demanded the separation between male and female students in classes, intensified. A central role in the protests against the Shah was filled by the World Confederation of Iranian Students abroad, implementing the struggle outside Iran, especially in Europe and the US, where they gained extensive media coverage.

As internal tension grew, the extreme left wing organizations, encouraged by the Soviet Union, started in August 1976 to engage in guerrilla activities and the murder of American advisors and company representatives, constituting a declaration of war against the Shah and his contacts with the US. Simultaneously, the external subversion against the Shah intensified. From the middle of 1976 the Libyans operated a radio station, which broadcast propaganda in Persian and *inter alia* offered instructions to the opponents of the regime on how to prepare explosives and conduct armed activities. Over the next two years dozens of Iranian diplomats in FRANCE and LEBANON, security men, American military advisors and famous personalities were murdered. Many guerrilla fighters were prosecuted in

military courts and executed. The religious establishment also expanded its protest activities against the Shah. In the summer of 1976 mass demonstrations were held in the religious town of QOM on the anniversary of the bloody riots of 1963. These demonstrations, in which speeches against the Shah were delivered, were organized by Khomeini's supporters. From the end of 1977 a series of cases of arson began against public and government structures: cinemas, theaters, night clubs, the branches of the *Rastakhiz* Party, police stations, department stores etc.

Following twelve consecutive years in which Hoveida served as Prime Minister, with the Shah actually running the state, Iran was on the verge of an economic crisis, hyper inflation, growing social gaps and political fermentation, with increasing subversion by the Soveit Union by means of the *Tudeh* Party and various left-wing organizations. Hoveida was blamed for the situation and in August 1977 forced to resign. He was replaced by a government of technocrats under Dr. Jahangir Amuzgar, Chairman of the *Rastakhiz* Party and a student of western culture. However, the new government failed to improve the situation for the regime, whose prestige kept deteriorating, while the internal unrest developed into a general revolt. In August 1978 Amuzgar was forced to resign. The greater the unrest in the country, so the acts of suppression by the SAVAK intensified, as did Khomeini's incitement. Khomeini's expulsion from Iraq after fourteen years of exile here, and his movement to a location near Paris, after KUWAIT refused to accept him, accelerated the internal crisis in Iran and world interest in the situation. The blatant failure of the reforms, which had been initiated by the Shah, who oversaw their implementation, was a further blow to the prestige of the regime.

Following Amuzgar's resignation, Ja'far Sharif-Emami, a former Prime Minister, who came from a traditional-religious family, was appointed Prime Minister. Sharif-Emami established a government comprised primarily of old time, conservative politicians. He declared a policy of national reconciliation. He promised to respect religious feelings and to hold free elections. He reintroduced the Islamic calendar, closed the gambling establishments and prohibited the appearance of sex magazines. He also freed from prison Khomeini's brother, the Ayatollah Morteza Passendideh. However, none of this helped and his government fell after three months.

The fall of the Sharif-Eamai government marked the failure of the reconciliation policy. In November the Shah appointed a military cabinet headed by General Gholam-Reza Ashari, with the participation of military commanders. Azhari brought back the censorship, intensifying the acts of suppression with the goal of stopping the deterioration in internal security. Khomeini, who had moved from Iraq to Paris in October 1977, now increased his involvement in what was going on in Iran and instructed the workers in the oil industry and in the various public services, to embark on unlimited strikes. This totally paralyzed the economy.

The Ashari government fell in December 1978. The Shah changed direction attempting to reach an agreement with the Liberals and the National Front, but these groups had already decided to support Khomeini. In conversations that the Shah held with the leader of the National Front, Dr. Karim SANJABI in December, the latter conditioned his agreement to join a national coalition government on the participation in it of military men, nationalists and moderate clerics, and on the temporary departure of the Shah from Iran—a condition rejected by the Shah. The Shah finally agreed to leave the state temporarily, after one of the leading activists in the National Front, Dr. Shahpur BAKHTIAR, agreed to establish a government. Bakhtiar, who was strongly condemned by the leaders of the Front for agreeing to form a government and was expelled from the Front's ranks, was a known national figure, who had openly opposed the Shah. He agreed to take the challenge as he opposed religious coercion and considered Khomeini and the clerics a threat to the liberal principles he believed in. The platform of the new government included many of the demands of the Shah's opponents: the disbanding of the Savak and release of political prisoners; the securing of personal freedoms; respect for the Shari'a; the return to Iran of the money transferred abroad by the Shah's relatives and henchmen; the severance of the ties with Israel and recognition of the PALESTINE LIBERATION ORGANIZATION (PLO); and a cease of oil sales to Israel and South Africa. However, Bakhtiar could not bring into his government a single statesman of stature, and remained, in fact, without any support base.

On 13 January 1979, a nine member Regency Council (including the Prime Minister, Chief of Staff and the heads of the two houses of Parliament) was established. Three days later the Shah left the state "for several days", due to fatigue, as he put it. The Shah's departure from Iran came at the end a period of hesitation and inconsistency in his conduct, apparently resulting from his having been secretly treated for cancer, which he managed to keep secret from the public.

The Shah's departure further weakened the government. Bakhtiar tried to reach an agreement with Khomeini. He sent Seyyed Jamaledin Tehrani, who held the position of head of the Regency Council, to him. However, Khomeini, who had in the meantime declared the establishment of the Islamic Revolutionary Council, conditioned the meeting on Tehrani resigning his official position, which he agreed to do. A request by Bakhtiar for a meeting with Khomeini was also met with a demand that he first resign. On 24 January, Bakhtiar ordered that the international airport of Tehran be closed down in order to prevent Khomeini's return from Paris. However, six days later he was forced to reverse his decision and announce that Khomeini could return. Khomeini landed in Tehran on 1 February and was welcomed by masses of admirers. On 11 February the heads of the Army declared their neutrality in the struggle between the legal head of government and the leader of the revolution, thus paving the way for Khomeini's final victory. Several hours later Bakhtiar announced his resignation and went underground. The following day the supporters of Khomeini, the revolutionary guards (the PASDARAN), who were armed with heavy weapons, took control of all the government offices and military bases.

In the absence of the Shah, the army proved unable to defend the regime. Khomeini took advantage of the situation to finalize the split between the Army and the Shah. He instructed his supporters to avoid any direct confrontation with the soldiers and to encourage them to desert from the army. On their part, on numerous occasions soldiers refused to open fire at the demonstrators and many deserted.

The passive position demonstrated by the military command also reflected the pressure exerted on it by the US Administration by means of President Carter's senior emissary, General Robert E. Huyser (Deputy Commander of the American forces in Europe) to avoid a military coup. They feared that this would lead to a communist take-over of Iran.

While there were several army officers who advised the Shah to let them carry out a coup in order to save his regime, the Shah himself demonstrated a lack of determination and in the last months of his rule sacrificed quite a few officers and senior persons in the Savak, in order to please his opponents. This further weakened morale in the military command.

The revolution in Iran reflected the growing hostility to the Shah's regime by wide sections of the public, but there was no consensus on an alternative. In the absence of organizations and interest groups with the ability to act politically, resulting from years of political suppression by the Shah's regime, it was necessary to form a coalition of groups with authority and resources in order to translate public dissatisfaction into protest activities against the regime and violent clashes with it. The central factors in this coalition were the clergy, the tradesmen and the property and business owners. The Bazaaris traditionally supported the religious movements and even financed their activities. This inclination was strengthened by dissatisfaction of the local industrialists and tradesmen with the agrarian reforms and economic policies introduced by the old regime.

The approach of many clergymen and intellectuals at the outset of the struggle against the Shah, manifested a consensus regarding the need to ensure that the regime abide by the provisions of the constitution. From a secular point of view this meant that the Shah should rule but enable the politicians to run the affairs of state, while guaranteeing political freedoms. The clergy, on the other hand, insisted on establishing a five member council, in accordance with the constitution, to supervise the work of the *Majlis* and adapt the laws it passed to the religious principles. The moderate clergymen, like the Ayatollah Shariat Madari, were prepared to make do with such an arrangement, but Khomeini insisted on a fundamental change in the system. He wanted the cancellation of the monarchy and the establishment of a regime based on the Muslim doctrine.

Foreign Affairs The foreign policy of the Shah was, in many respects, a continuation of his father's policy, which had been dictated by geopolitical consideration: the Soviet threat to Iran, and the significance of the Persian Gulf to the US, due to the growing proportion of the Gulf oil supplies in its total oil consumption and that of the West in general. These considerations dictated an effort to establish a tacit alliance with the US, while nurturing commercial relations, including arms supplies, with the Soviet Union, and the construction of an independent defense capacity for Iran, which would ensure its hegemonic status in the Gulf.

From the mid-1960s, the Shah started to construct a large army. This was designed to fulfill national and regional functions, which constituted a change from its traditional role of merely preserving domestic security. In 1977 the growth in the Iranian Army was so significant that it became the fifth largest military force in the world (about 400,000 men), despite the fact that the period of compulsory military service (two years) remained. The military budget, which had stood at 290 million dollars in 1963, increased to 1.9 billion dollars in 1973 and to almost 8 billion dollars in 1977. In the years 1970–1977 Iran purchased arms and military equipment from the US worth 12 billion dollars and its orders until 1980 stood at a similar sum. To a certain extent, the increase in military expenditure reflected the increase in Iran's oil revenue. Behind this policy there were regional security considerations, even though one may assume that prestige considerations were also involved as well as the humiliating memories from Iran's recent past—especially its conquest during both World Wars by foreign forces. The Shah sought to turn Iran into a regional power, capable of defending itself against external aggression. This appeared very tangible in the face of the threat of the irredentist demands by Iran's neighbors (Turkey *vis-a-vis* Iran's Azerbaijan; Iran *vis-a-vis* the oil rich Khuzistan district; Pakistan *vis-a-vis* the Baluchistan district; and the Soviet Union, against the background of its traditional aspirations in Iran). The Shah strove to attain American strategic backing for Iran's hegemonic status in the Gulf area, to guarantee regional stability, in return for a regular flow of Iranian oil to the West, and an alliance with Iran as a strategic asset in the Cold War. At the same time, the expansion of the armed forces contributed to assuring the allegiance and support of the professional officers to the regime and its security.

In the mid 1970s Iran was predominant in the Gulf region due to the size of the air force and navy at its disposal. Most of the arms and military equipment were American, even though in October 1976 the Shah signed a 550 million dollar contract with the

Soviet Union for the purchase of SAM-7 anti-aircraft missiles, half-tracks and tank carriers. A year later he signed a contract for the supply of a million tons of oil to the Soviet Union in return for the supply of more Soviet military equipment. The Shah also made efforts to develop a domestic arms and aircraft industries, cooperating with Israel in the development of medium range missiles. In 1977 Iran's military budget was significantly reduced due to the fall in oil revenue. At the beginning of the year the Shah announced the cancellation of plans to construct new air force and military bases and to purchase destroyers from the US.

The Shah also took steps towards the development of nuclear capability. Iran's ambitious nuclear plans were first made known at the end of 1974. The overall plan advocated the operation of twenty nuclear power stations with a total power of 23,000 megawatts of electricity by 1994. Some of these were to start operating in the 1980s. The effort in the nuclear sphere continued despite the growing internal crisis. In the last three years of the Shah's rule, Iran signed agreements for the construction of six nuclear power stations by France and Germany, and two agreements for nuclear cooperation with Great Britain. Iran also sought to sign contracts for the purchase of eight 1,200 megawatt nuclear reactors from the US; two 900 megawatt nuclear reactors from France, and uranium from Niger, Gabon and foreign companies. However, none of these plans were actually realized.

Iran presented its nuclear plans as an effort to manufacture energy for peaceful purposes, in the face of depletion of Iran's oil reserves. According to forecasts, these were to dry up within twenty-five years, even though new oil and gas reserves were constantly being discovered. Iran was amongst the first to sign the Treaty for the Prevention of the Proliferation of Nuclear Arms (the NPT), and in 1974 called for the de-neutralization of the Indian Ocean and Persian Gulf areas. Nevertheless, the Iranian efforts in this sphere concerned its neighbors as well as the US, which in 1977 ended the negotiations for the supply of nuclear reactors to Iran. What motivated the Shah's nuclear plans were the threats to Iran's national security stemming from the Pakistani and Iraqi efforts in this sphere. The concern lest the US might convince the Western European states to stop assistance in the nuclear sphere, led the Shah to

try to purchase reactors in China and the Soviet Union.

In the years 1957–1967 Iran received about 700 million dollars worth of American economic aid, within the framework of the "EISENHOWER DOCTRINE". In November 1967 the US stopped this aid, as a result of the increase in Iranian oil revenues. It nevertheless continued to grant Iran financial loans for military and civilian purposes and arms supplies, which increased Iranian dependence on it. The huge presence of American military and civilian advisors and experts, created cultural tension with the clerics, who criticized the "Western cultural invasion" and the Shah's secularization policy. On the other hand, the growing military and civilian connection with the US met with opposition from the National Front and the left-wing camp, which was encouraged by the Soviet Union. During the presidency of Jimmy Carter (1977–1980) criticism escalated in US public opinion and government circles regarding breaches of human rights in Iran by the regime, which could interrupt the flow of American financial and military aid. The Shah argued that those condemned to death were not political prisoners but terrorists. Nonetheless he was unable to disregard the pressure exerted on him by the American Administration and by human rights organizations in the West. He released over 5,000 prisoners and gave a public order to stop the torture of prisoners. The Red Cross was permitted to visit twenty prisons in Iran, and the deliberations in military courts were announced open to the public. The attempt to improve the human rights situation was interpreted by opponents of the Shah as a sign of the regime's weakness. This encouraged them to intensify their activities. In an effort to improve the relations with the US, the Shah was also willing to soften his demand to raise the price of oil after 1977, *inter alia* in the hope that the American administration would not place obstacles to the sale of advanced technologies to Iran and would not object to Iran's nuclear plans, which came under criticism in Congress. As a result of this criticism the Shah reduced the military budget and returned the Iranian expeditionary force (about 3,000 soldiers) which had operated in the Sultanate of OMAN to help crush the revolutionaries in the province of Dufar.

As the internal crisis intensified in the Summer of 1977 the Shah opened a diplomatic campaign to gain the support of public opinion and the administration in the US, emphasizing Iran's value to the West. In November the Shah was invited to Washington for a first meeting with President Carter, at which he threatened that if the US would refuse to supply arms to Iran, it would turn to alternative sources. However, Congress continued to oppose the extensive arming of Iran. This opposition grew as the crisis in Iran and the means used by the regime to suppress its opponents, intensified.

At the end of 1978, at the peak of the political crisis in Iran, President Carter visited Tehran. He declared Iran "an island of stability in the stormy seas of the Middle East." Britain too announced its support of the Shah's regime and the importance of Iran to stability in the Middle East. At the same time, both in the US and in the Western European states, the concern of a left-wing takeover in Iran and communist domination in the region. Thus, despite the friendly relations between France and Iran in this period, Paris allowed Khomeini into France, and did not limit his political activities on its territory.

Parallel to the tightening of relations with the US, the Shah tried to improve Iran's relations with the Soviet Union. He did this to show Washington that he was not totally dependent on it, and to end the political subversion by Moscow against his regime while minimizing the threats to Iran's regional security. As far back as the end of the 1960s, Iran attempted to expand its economics ties with the Soviet Union, and in 1967 signed a contract to purchase 40 million dollars worth of ammunition from it. The *rapprochement* between the two countries led to a reduction in Soviet propaganda against the Shah's regime, though Moscow's policy toward him remained basically hostile and was characterized by support for opposition forces.

In the mid-1970s "underground" propaganda broadcasts were operated from the Soviet Union, while the official Soviet media did not stop its criticism of the Iranian regime, even while Prime Minister Houbeida visited Moscow in the middle of 1976. The Soviet threat to Iran intensified as Moscow undertook to supply massive quantities of weapons to Iraq, and its growing military involvement in the Indian Ocean, southern Yemen and the horn of Africa. Nevertheless, in October of that year Iran and the Soviet Union signed a 550 million dollar arms deal (see above) and the latter promised to

stop its anti-Shah propaganda broadcasts. Two months later a new economic cooperation agreement was signed, which included the expansion of the steel mill and the construction of a power station in Esfahan. Agreements were also signed in the spheres of science and agriculture. Despite all this, the Soviet Union continued to support the Shah's enemies both politically and materially, and security sources believed that it was the Soviets who stood behind the attempts on the lives of American advisors in Iran. In the beginning of 1978 the Soviet media openly renewed its attacks against the Shah, supporting the demands of the Iranian opposition.

In 1971 Iran recognized Communist China, shortly after the US had announced the change in its policy towards China. In 1978 Chinese leader Jua Kuo-Feng visited Iran. Nevertheless, Iran was careful not to go too far in its formal relations with China in order to avoid angering the Soviet Union. Close relations and extensive cooperation developed between Iran and Israel in the years 1963–1970—the years of "the White Revolution". Iran sought Israeli assistance to develop an advanced agriculture and accelerated development in other spheres. Groups of Iranian trianees were sent to Israel while Israelis were welcome guests in Iran. The growing tension between Iran and the radical Arab countries also led to military and intelligence cooperation between the two countries. Even though after the Six-Day War (see ARAB-ISRAEL CONFLICT) the Shah joined the Arab demand for a full Israeli withdrawal to the borders of 5 June he supported Security Council Resolution 242 (see ARAB-ISRAEL PEACEMAKING). This purported the right of all the states in the region to exist in security. During the 1970s the military and intelligence cooperation between Iran and Israel intensified, including the joint financing and development of missiles. Despite the official reserve demonstrated by Iran toward Israel, in the mid-1970s the Shah asked Israel to get the Jewish lobby in Washington, to help neutralize the opposition in Congress to his policy. The special relationship with Israel at this time did not prevent the Shah from officially supporting the Arab position in the ARAB-ISRAEL CONFLICT and identifying with the Palestinian demand for self-determination.

Following ABDEL NASSER's death in 1970, an improvement occured in Iran's relations with his successor, Anwar al-SADAT. The Shah became more critical of Israel as he called for negotiations between Israel and the Arabs. Egypt's defeat in the 1967 War removed the threat of Egyptian subversion against Iran. In the face of the growing tension with Iraq around the revolt of the Kurds and problem of Shatt al-Arab, Iran sought now to tighten the relations with it. Following the 1973 War (see ARAB-ISRAEL CONFLICT), relations between Tehran and Cairo tightened. Iran lent Egypt close to one billion dollars and in the years 1977–1978 the Shah and President Sadat exchanged official visits. The Shah supported Egypt's peace initiative (see ARAB-ISRAEL PEACEMAKING), actively exerting his influence with Israel to respond to Egypt's demands and on King HUSSEIN to join the process.

In these years Iraq turned into a haven for the opponents of the Shah and Radio Baghdad boosted the incitement broadcasts against the Iranian regime. Announcements by the Ayatollah Khomeini were frequently broadcast on this radio as were the speeches of other clerics who opposed the regime. In reaction, the Shah increased his support for the Kurdish revolt, while Israel helped by extending military advice and arms supplies. In 1975, due to Soviet pressure, which manifested itself in the stoppage of arms supplies, and the growing Kurdish threat against the oil fields in the North of the country, the government in Baghdad agreed to sign the "Algeria Agreement" with Iran (see IRAQ) in order to settle the border disputes between the two countries. The agreement redrew the land border between them. Iraq recognized Iran's navigation rights in the Shatt al-Arab, whose median was declared the territorial border between the two countries. In return, Iran stopped supporting the Kurds. This led to the collapse of the revolutionaries and the disintegration of their political leadership. The signing of the agreement led to an improvement in relations between Iraq and Iran: the President of Iraq and the Prime Minister of Iran exchanged visits; the propaganda attacks by Radio Baghdad against Iran stopped. In the beginning of 1977 a whole series of cooperation agreements were signed between the two countries. The growing internal crisis in Iran in the summer and autumn of 1978 caused concern in Baghdad, which went so far as to express support for the Shah and limit the freedom of action of Khomeini, who consequently left Iraq for France in October in protest. However, this *rapprochement* was superficial.

The mutual suspicion and hostility between the two regimes remained as it had been and even intensified in face of the Iraqi efforts in the sphere of military procurements and its construction of a nuclear reactor. Above all, the regime in Iraq did not reconcile itself to the compromise at Shatt al-Arab.

In the mid 1960s a *rapprochement* took place between Iran and Saudi Arabia, both against the background of the growing tensions between the monarchies on the one hand and the radical regimes led by the Egyptian President Nasser, and of Iraq's growing military power. In 1968 the Shah paid a state visit to Saudi Arabia. The two states shared joint interests regarding the security of the Gulf region and the containment of Soviet penetration into the region, which they affirmed in an agreement in November 1977, on cooperation in the struggle against subversion and terror. Nevertheless, the competition between the two states continued over leadership of the ORGANIZATION OF PETROLEUM EXPORTING COUNTRIES (OPEC), and the determination of oil production quotas and prices. Saudi Arabia also had reservations regarding Iran's hegemonial efforts in the Gulf region, and its attempts in the mid 1970s to get the Gulf states to set up a regional security alliance, without the involvement of any foreign power. While Oman and the UNITED ARAB EMIRATES, both of which maintained close trade relations with Iran, supported the idea, Iraq, Saudi Arabia and other states rejected it, and the Shah was forced to give it up.

Like its Eastern neighbors, Iran adopted a position of careful support for Pakistan in its war against India in 1971, since Pakistan was regarded part of the pro-Western bloc and thus supportive of Iran's security. At the same time, the Shah feared that in a time of crisis, Pakistan might raise claims over the Iranian Baluchistan district. He was also unable to disregard India, due to its status as one of the leaders of the Third World and its close relations with the Soviet Union. The relations with Afghanistan cooled down after July 1973, when its Prime Minister, Muhammad Daud Khan, started to approach the Soviet Union. Nevertheless, the two countries reached an agreement regarding the distribution of the waters of the Hirmand River along the border between them, which was finally signed in 1977. The growing involvement of the Soviet Union in Afghanistan, following the military coup there in April 1978, increased the Shah's fears of Soviet subversion against him, which he tried to counteract by moving closer to both Pakistan and India.

The Islamic Republic
Iran under Khomeini (1979–1989)

Domestic Affairs Upon the resignation of Bakhtiar, Khomeini appointed a provisional government headed by Mahdi Bazargan, leader of the Movement for Freedom of Iran. Bazargan was considered an intellectual, a fighter for human rights and a believing Muslim, though not a professional clergyman. He was therefore acceptable to almost all the groups opposed to the Shah and able to serve as a bridge between the seculars and the clerics. The members of the provisional government were also seculars, close in their views to the National Front. This reflected Khomeini's careful and gradual approach to the Islamization of Iran.

Side by side with the provisional government, there was also a fifteen member Islamic Revolution Council, which Khomeini established back in Paris. The Council concentrated all the government powers in its own hands and turned the provisional government into an empty vessel. It also functioned as a revolutionary tribunal, engaging in the organization of show trials of the heads of the previous regime, and their execution. Since Khomeini did not trust the army commanders, security issues were placed in the hands of the "revolutionary guards", which were established before Khomeini's return to Iran. The guards operated as local security committees in urban neighborhoods, villages and towns to preserve security and order, the detention of members of the Shah's administration and suppression of the opponents of the revolution. One of the first tasks which the heads of the revolution wanted to implement was the systematic liquidation of the previous ruling elite by revolutionary courts. This had declared and executed hundreds of death sentences against former ministers, heads of the Savak, military commanders and persons who had held key public positions. The appropriation of the powers of government by the Revolutionary Council and the mass executions, aroused protests by Bazargan, but his threats of resignation remained unheeded. Similar protests by the most senior clergyman in the country, Ayatollah Shariat Madari, were also ignored.

Bazargan, who realized that his government was lacking any powers or ability to act, tendered his resignation several times, but Khomeini rejected it because he believed that the time had not yet come for him to take the reins of power into his own hands. At the end of March a referendum was held, asking: "Do you agree to the cancellation of the monarchy and the establishment of an Islamic regime?" The wording of the question led to protests by secular groups, supporting the cancellation of the monarchy but under no circumstances wanting to replace it by a religious regime. However, Khomeini silenced all these protests. According the official figures, 92.5 percent of those entitled to vote, participated in the referendum, and 92.8 percent of whom voted in the affirmative. Many political figures, including Bazargan himself, doubted the credibility of the published results, but on 1 April 1979, the establishment of the Islamic Republic of Iran was officially proclaimed. On 18 June a draft of an Islamic constitution was published. This raised bitter debates, even amongst senior clergymen. After he had promised that a Constituent Assembly would be established, in order to draft and approve a new constitution for the state, Khomeini changed his mind. He announced instead the establishment of an Assembly of Experts, comprised of persons with a legal-religious education, whom he himself would appoint. After a wave of protests and the intervention of the Ayatollah Shariat Madari, Khomeini agreed to hold elections to determine the members of the Council, but laid down strict criteria as to the qualifications of the candidates, in order to ensure that those elected would be fully identified with his approach and goals. In the August 1979 elections, the clergymen who were Khomeini's candidates won an absolute majority (fifty-five out of seventy-three). Senior clergymen with independent attitudes failed in these elections.

The Imami Shi'i Islam was declared the official religion of the state. (This definition had also existed in the 1905 constitution.) The most serious debate regarding the content of the constitution was held over article 5. This stated that in the absence of *Emam-e Zaman* (the hidden Imam, or Messiah), the leadership of the state would be given to a senior clergyman who would hold most of the powers in his hands and make decisions on the basis of the Shi'i doctrine. This article was revolutionary in the approach of Shi'i Islam, initiated by Khomeini. Even though the constitution promised to uphold civil rights and ensure that citizens should enjoy freedom and equality in all spheres. It demanded that these rights be consistent with the Islamic law, which was given predominance over any other law. The draft constitution was presented for a referendum at the beginning of December, and as expected was approved by a decisive majority. The executive powers were handed over to the President, who was to be assisted by the government. The number of members in the *Majlis* was set at 270. Its legislative work was placed under the supervision of "The Council to Watch Over the Constitution." This comprised six Shi'i scholars, appointed by the head of state. In the event of its being impossible to bridge differences of opinion between the Council and the *Majlis* regarding the conformity of a law with the Islamic principles, an institution called "The Forum for Examining the Interest of the Regime" was established. Its membership was made up of the heads of the regime. The representatives of the two bodies was to decide, and its decision was to be final.

The first few months of 1979 witnessed a flourishing of democracy, regarding publications and the expression of opinions by parties and political groups. However, this period was short lived. In June a systematic process of the Islamization of radio and television broadcasts began. This stopped the broadcasting of secular music and programs, which were seen to undermine the new regime. The press was required to serve the Islamic revolution and its political and social goals. The papers that refused to do so were closed down. Strict limitations were also imposed on the continued activity of foreign reporters and most of the foreign news agencies were closed. When the status of Khomeini stabilized in the course of the summer, a drastic suppression of the parties and political movements began. He perceived this as being unsupportive of the revolution. By the end of 1979 most of the political groups, which had stood in Khomeini's way, except for the *Mujahidin Khalq*, were eliminated. The *Mujahidin Khalq* was the only organization that opposed the new trend, and announced an armed revolt against the regime.

1979 was a difficult year economically. Prolonged strikes in the public services and petroleum industry disrupted the life of the state, harming its revenue. Many enterprises were paralyzed due to the escape of the owners, managers, and shortage in raw materials. government institutions did not function properly due to the collapse of the government systems. Many of the workers and farmers were busy participating in daily demonstrations. Khomeini promised the citizens that the revolution would improve the lot of the *mostazafin* (the oppressed people) and would supply them with free electricity and water. However, the economic crisis was too severe to fulfill this promise. In the early months of the revolution tens of thousands of people emigrated from Iran—most of them members of the wealthy, educated urban elite, who feared persecution or were unwilling to live in an extreme religious regime. Their departure from the country aggravated the economic and administrative chaos, but Khomeini belittled the significance of those leaving, demonstrating an attitude of contempt toward them.

Even though the Shari'a became the law of the land in the personal, criminal and property spheres, there were ideological debates and political struggles over socioeconomic issues within the religious establishment, and amongst the group of clergymen who surrounded Khomeini. The radicals demanded a centralized economy, including the nationalization of industry, the preservation of importation as a government monopoly, and the confiscation of large private estates. Opposite them stood a group of *Hojattieh*—conservative clergymen who enjoyed the support of the tradesmen and Baazaris, who defended the right of private property in accordance with the Koran. Khomeini, who had come to power under the slogan of "saving the underdogs" partially supported the radical group. By means of "The Council to Watch Over the Constitution," he rejected those laws which were excessively radical. Khomeini manoeuvered among the various streams and shifted his support from one to the other in order to avoid turmoil in the top echelons of the regime on matters of principle. Debates were also held on issues of civil culture, and above all, human rights, freedom of expression and worship, and the attitude toward foreign investment—especially from Western countries. Such a debate emerged even regarding the acceptance of financial assistance from Western sources after the earthquake in the district of Gilan in the north of the country in June 1990, in which about 50,000 persons were killed. In this particular case those who supported acceptance of the assistance, won. The circumstances in which the regime was forced to operate and establish its authority, rapidly turned it into an autocratic regime based on theocracy. Senior clerics who objected to Khomeini's doctrinal innovations or refused to accept his leadership, were silenced or removed.

The revolution seemed like an opportunity for ethnic minorities, some of whom had contributed to the downfall of the Shah, to demand special rights for themselves. In addition to the Kurds, who demanded autonomy, the Baluchis, Turkmanians, Azerians and those speaking Arabic, also demanded recognition of their language and culture. These minorities—all of them Sunnis except for the Azerians—felt discriminated against by the constitution. This provided the Shi's with a dominant religious and political status and placed in the districts settled by these minorities Shi'i officials and administrators. In May, the Arabic speaking population of Khozistan—the center of the Iranian oil industry—embarked on a series of protest activities against the regime with the encouragement of Iraq. They demanded cultural autonomy and the end of discrimination in the allocation of resources and state investments in development plans in their region. However, the protest was suppressed by force. The Turkemanians, whose number was about half a million, demanded, in addition to autonomy, a redistribution of fertile agricultural lands, which had been confiscated by the Shah's regime. In March–April 1979, bloody battles erupted between them and the Revolutionary Guards. This culminated in the suppression of the protest. Iran accused the Soviet Union and the members of the Marxist *Khalq Fadaiyin-e* of inciting the riots. In July 1979 bloody battles erupted between the Kurds. They were led by the Kurdish Democratic Party, and the Revolutionary Guards. Khomeini responded by outlawing the Kurdish Democratic Party, and established a special revolutionary court to execute Kurdish fighters. The armed conflict with the Kurds enabled Khomeini to strengthen the revolutionary fervor amongst the Shi'i masses and mobilize the public to support the other opponents of the regime. The Sunni Baluchis avoided any social or cultural protest, but participated in many armed clashes with the security forces, who tried to put an end to their smuggling activities, and especially the smuggling of drugs from Pakistan and Afghanistan.

The situation of the non-Muslim minorities—primarily the Jews and Bahais—was especially difficult. Despite earlier declarations made by Khomeini in Paris that the religious minorities would be granted protection and enjoy freedom of worship, in the fanatical Shi'i atmosphere which prevailed upon his arrival in Tehran it became apparent that these minorities would not enjoy equal rights. The Jews were treated with relative tolerance given the fact that more than any other community, the Jews were identified with the Shah's regime and Israel. Their economic prosperity in the 1970s further contributed to the hostile feelings of the poor social groups against them. Even though Khomeini revealed in his book *The Islamic Government*, a clear anti-Jewish position, he met with a delegation of the heads of the Jewish community several weeks after returning to Iran. He then instructed his supporters and heads of the new regime to protect the Jews.

The Bahais were the most persecuted minority, and were considered by the Shi'a as deserters from Islam and condemned to death. In the early months of the revolution, Bahais were massacred in several small towns. By order of the regime the heads of the community were detained, its religious institutions were closed down, and much Bahai property was confiscated. Many Bahais who refused to desert their religious faith and return to Islam, were executed.

The Armenians and Assyrians—the two largest Christian communities in Iran—were promised freedom of worship, but were restricted with regard to dress and joint activities by men and women in public places. They were also prohibited to engage in any missionary work. Christians who were born as Muslims were persecuted by the Islamic regime, which forced most of them to escape Iran. The Zoroastrians, especially those in the town of Yazd, where their temple and center of worship is situated, were also harassed. Some of the Zoroastrians—those who were wealthy and of high social standing—left the country.

The zealot Islamic approach of the regime and its oppressive policy against critics and opponents in total disregard of human rights, resulted in about a million Iranians—most of them of the middle and upper classes—emigrating from Iran,to various countries, especially the US. Several groups amongst these emigrants established opposition organizations in Europe and the United States, which engaged in propaganda activities. However, these groups remained ineffective due to their disagreement on goals and ways of action, and lack of organized support in Iran itself.

In January 1980 the first elections were held for the presidency of the republic. Khomeini selected Ábolhassan Bani-Sadr—one of his close aids during his exile in Paris—as his candidate for president. Bani-Sadr was a former activist in the NATIONAL FRONT, and even though he was not a religious man, he came from a religious family, which had proven its allegiance to Khomeini. Bani-Sadr, who had studied in Paris, was fluent in French and familiar with Western culture. Khomeini's support ensured the election of Bani-Sadr, who received seventy-five percent of the votes.

In the elections to the *Majlis*, the first since the revolution, the Islamic Republic Party, headed by the Ayatollah Mohammad Beheshti, won 130 out of 213 seats which were contested. The regime made it very difficult for secular parties to participate in the elections. Thus only a few representatives, whose allegiance to the regime was not assured, managed to get into the *Majlis*. Following the elections to the *Majlis*, the Revolutionary Council was disbanded in June 1980.

Tension soon prevailed between the President and the newly elected *Majlis*. The latter's members from the Islamic Republic Party were suspicious of Bani-Sadr. This was because he did not belong to the religious establishment and was known for his liberal approach—especially his defense of human rights in face of the process of Islamization. In an effort to weaken the President, the *Majlis* forced him to select Rajai Mohammad Ali as Prime Minister, with whom he did not see eye to eye. Bani-Sadr opposed mass arrests; the torture of prisoners; the holding of summary trials without the defendants having the right to legal defense followed by executions; the suppression of the freedom of expression and the imposition of strict censorship on the press. Bani-Sadr also criticized the way in which the war against Iraq (see IRAN-IRAQ WAR) was being run, and the role filled by the Revolutionary Guards compared to that of the Army. His supporters held a mass demonstration in Tehran, which led to attacks by members of the *Hizballah* (the Party of God), backed by the clergy. The growing tension between the President and the religious establishment, brought Khomeini to dismiss Bani-Sadr from his post as Deputy Supreme Commander of the armed forces (i.e., of Khomei-

ni himself), in June 1981. Several days later Bani-Sadr was also dismissed from the presidency. He went underground and managed to escape to France, together with Mas'ud RAJAVI—the leader of the MOJAHEDIN-E KHALQ-E—where the two were granted political asylum.

Following the dismissal of Bani-Sadr, Khomeini started to liquidate the *Mojahedin-e Khalq*, considered the most dangerous organization to the regime. Despite the Islamic foundations of the *Mojahedin* thinking, its members were considered Marxists. The religious establishment regarded them as deviants from Islam. Efforts to bridge the ideological gap between the clergymen and the *Mojahedin* leaders were futile. After the elections to the *Majlis*, the organization announced an armed revolt against the regime.

In an explosion in the offices of the Islamic Republic Party in the course of a political meeting there in June 1981, seventy-four people were killed, including the Ayatollah Beheshti, four ministers, six deputy ministers and twenty members of the *Majlis*—all central members of the party. Nobody claimed responsibility for the act, but the regime accused the *Mojahedin*, implementing a relentless war against them. Nevertheless, the event did not undermine the foundations of the regime, and even served as a justifiable excuse to increase the suppression of opposition groups. In the elections to the presidency held in July 1981, Rajai Mohammad Ali was elected President, and he appointed Javad-Mohammad Ba-Honar as Prime Minister. Both were killed in a second major explosion in the President's bureau in August of that year, and once again the *Mojahedin* were accused. The armed activities of the *Mojahedin* continued intermittently until the Spring of 1982 when the liquidation of its leader led to a complete termination of the organization's armed activity in the cities. Nevertheless, subversive political activity continued with the assistance of Iraq, which granted the heads of the *Mojahedin* asylum in Baghdad and put at their disposal financial resources to act against the Iranian regime. In March 1988, when Iran was exhausted as a result of eight years of war against Iraq, the *Mojahedin* announced the establishment of the National Liberation Army (NLA) with the help of arms and funds received from Iraq. Guerrilla fighters started to invade Iran, but withdrew following heavy losses. In June the NLA opened a new attack, in the course of which its forces advanced about 93 miles (150 km.) into Iran, but the invasion was repelled, with the help of civilians.

Following the liquidation of the *Mojahedin-e Khalqe* inside Iran, came the turn of the Marxist guerrilla organization *Fadaiyin-e Khalq* and members of the National Front. In 1983 a systematic campaign began to liquidate the *Tudeh* Party. In April the Party was declared illegal, and in a well planned operation about one thousand of the leaders of the Party, including its chairman, Nour-ed-din Kia, and its central activists, were arrested. At the same time eighteen Soviet diplomats, who were accused of operating the Party, were expelled. The regime also limited the activities of "The Movement for the Freedom of Iran" led by Mahdi Bazargan, which preached pragmatism and respect for human rights, and attacked it for preaching Western values. The only party that enjoyed freedom of action and support by the regime was the Islamic Republic Party, under the joint leadership of Hojjat-ol-Eslam Seyyed Ali Hosseini-e KHAMENEI and the chairman of the *Majlis* Hojjat-ol-Eslam Ali Akbar Hashemi-RAFSANJANI. The two personalities cooperated for many years, but once rivalry between them began over the leadership of the party, Khomeini ordered the Party dismantled. He argued that there is one party, which is Islam, and that all party activity is, in fact, divisive. Since then no official party has been allowed to form.

In October 1981 new elections were held for the presidency in which Khamenei was elected by over ninety percent of the voters. In addition to being one of the leaders of the Islamic Republic Party, Khamenei was also the Director and Editor in Chief of the Party's main mouthpiece. Khameini now appointed Mir-Hossein Moussavi as Prime Minister. Moussavi had radical ideas on socioeconomic issues and was a talented administrator. The war economy implemented by the government of Moussavi resulted in a further deterioration in the conditions of the poorer population, which reacted, as of the middle of 1985, with riots in Tehran and other cities. The regime suppressed these riots brutally, detaining many of the demonstrators and executing an unknown number of people. At the end of the first decade of the Islamic regime, not only had the living conditions of the weakest strata of the population failed to improve, but much of the middle class, also became impoverished. In economic terms the

revolution proved to be a continuous crisis, which worsened against the background of the fall in oil prices in the mid-1980s, and the costly eight-year war with Iraq. In addition, the expansion of the bureaucracy which absorbed activists of the revolution, corruption in the government and revolutionary apparatus, the financial aid to Islamic organizations outside Iran and the isolation of Iran in the international arena eroded the chances of the regime to realize an economic improvement.

In September 1985, new elections for the presidency were held, in which the outgoing president was reelected by a majority of eight-five percent. Only candidates loyal to the regime and its religious ideology were allowed to submit their candidacy, and even these had to go through the screening of the "Council for the Preservation of the Constitution", which disqualified many candidates. In May 1988 new elections were held for the *Majlis* and Rafsanjani was elected by a large majority as chairman. Mir-Hossein Moussavi gained the confidence of the parliament with a large majority, and remained Prime Minister.

The Islamic regime totally revised the Shah's strategic goal of turning Iran into a hegemonic power in the Gulf, regarding this goal as serving the West and its oil interests while being detrimental to Iranian poor masses. There was a demand to reduce the size of the army and even sell back to the US seventy-eight advanced F-14 planes, which the Shah had purchased a short time before the revolution. In August 1979 Iran canceled orders for advanced military systems from the US, including F-16 planes, at a total cost of 9 billion dollars. At the same time, Iran went through with agreements to purchase spare parts for F-4 and F-5 planes, which constituted its main air power. The army's structure collapsed, primarily because in addition to the social and cultural gap between them, the Islamic revolutionaries were hostile to the army senior officers due to their previous loyalty to the Pahlavi dynasty and American orientation. Thus, when the Iraqi invasion of Iran began in September 1980, the Iranian Army was in disarray, ill-equipped and unprepared for war. The War ended the debate over the necessary size of the Army and reduction of arms procurements. The degrading defeats suffered by the Iranians in the first stages of the war led to an intensive effort by the government to purchase weapons from anywhere.

In the face of the embargo imposed by the Western states on arms shipments to the area of fighting, Iran was forced to pay exorbitant prices on the black market, for weapons and spare parts for the Western equipment at its disposal. At the time of the revolution the mobilized force of the revolutionary guards, originally designed to defend the revolution, numbered only several tens of thousands of men. However, against the backdrop of the war this force expanded rapidly, turning into a regular army in every way, with hundreds of thousands of enlisted men, military bases, a hierarchical command and multi-arm structures, which included land, air and naval forces. At the same time the guards maintained their religious uniqueness and total loyalty to the clergy, and as such filled a vital function in mobilizing the masses for the Islamic Holy War and crystallizing the legitimacy of the Islamic regime.

When the war with Iraq broke out, the regular Army and the guards were in competition with each other over who would conduct operations and over the allocation of resources. This frequently led to violent clashes and a damaging lack of coordination on the battle field. Following the bitter defeats suffered by Iran in the war at the beginning of 1988, Khomeini appointed Rafsanjani as Acting Supreme Chief of the Armed Forces. He did this with the intention of reorganizing the armed forces and examining the possibility of integrating the guards into the regular army, or at least creating closer coordination between the two forces. Rafsanjani failed to realize these goals due to the Guards' opposition. Following Khomeini's death in 1989 the new spiritual leader, Khamenei, established the General Command Headquarters, combining the two bodies, though without changing the existing structure.

The War which Iraq imposed on Iran gave the Islamic regime an effective rallying instrument, which was used for political mobilization, strict claim of unconditional loyalty of the people, and legitimating suppression of domestic opposition. The mobilization of the youth for the war effort in the name of Islam and the revolution contributed to the deepening of Islamic cognizance and popular support for the regime. This manifested itself in the way men and women dressed and the strict patterns of behavior imposed on the public, frequently by means of threats and use of violence. In April 1982 Ayatollah SHARI-AT-MADARI, who had played a major role in advanc-

ing the revolution but advocated moderation and criticized violations of human rights, was accused of plotting against the regime. The name of Madari was associated with an attempted coup. According to the regime, this had been planned by Sadeq Ghotb-Zadeh—one of Khomeini's close assistants in Paris who, after the revolution, was appointed Head of the Iranian broadcasting service and Minister for Foreign Affairs. While the latter was executed after a summary trial, Shariat-Madari was placed under house arrest and officially stripped of his religious status.

Despite his advanced age and poor health, Khomeini continued to lead the state as the supreme political and spiritual authority, preventing other senior Shi'i scholars from expressing their opinions. In 1988 he chided Khamenei, who in addition to being President, fulfilled the important post of Friday prayer leader of Tehran, for having stated in his weekly sermon that the Islamic government must operate solely within the framework of the Islamic law and the principles of Islam. Khomeini insisted that the preservation of the Islamic state was a supreme command for which one may even temporarily avoid implementing the commands of Islam, including the fast and pilgrimage.

In March 1989 Khomeini published a ruling stating that it was an Islamic duty to murder the British-Muslim writer Salman RUSHDIE. This act strengthened the militants amongst the ruling clergy. In this atmosphere Khomeini publicly condemned the Ayatollah Hossein-Ali MONTAZERI and declared him ineligible to succeed him because of his criticism of the regime, especially in the sphere of human rights. Contrary to Shariat-Madari, Montazeri was not denied his religious status for fear of the spread of protest by his supporters. In April 1989 Khomeini appointed a committee for the purpose of introducing changes in the constitution, which led to the abolition of the post of Prime Minister. All executive powers went to the President. It is possible that Rafsanjani supported this idea, since he had his eyes on the post of President, and was in fact elected to the post in July of that year. In June 1989 Khomeini died after a serious illness, and Khamenei was elected as his heir by the Expert Council.

Foreign Affairs The Islamic revolution led to a drastic change in the foreign relations of Iran, which were now shaped on the basis of totally different considerations than in the Shah's time. The Islamic regime rejected the policy of close cooperation with the West and cordial relations with the East, officially adopting the slogan of "Neither West nor East", which was understood as an expression of intent to establish a radical Islamic bloc led by Iran. The new regime adopted an extreme anti-American policy, which was based on the Islamic system of values.

Khomeini injected new vitality into his view of classical Islam, which divided the world between the believers (the Muslims) and the infidels. He still emphasized that the Shi's are the faithful representatives of Islam, and therefore destined to lead the Muslim world to comprehensive unity and world hegemony. Nevertheless, Khomeini's revolutionary message was directed at the whole Muslim world, not only the Shi's. He claimed that the renaissance of Islam and the resurgence of the Islamic Caliphate, would be realized in stages. He presented the victory of the Islamic revolution in Iran as the first stage. That would be followed by the fall of the existing regimes in the neighboring Arab states, which were described as corrupt and infidel to Islam, and their being replaced by Islamic regimes. On the basis of this approach, Iran became a center of support for Islamic opposition movements throughout the Muslim world and Arab Middle East. This included military assistance in the form of training, finance and the supply of weapons and operational assistance in their various states. Iran also sent religious emissaries and members of the revolutionary guards to other countries, and held gatherings in Tehran in which the anti-Western and anti-Israeli message was spread.

The US, as leader of the Western World and the symbol of Western modernity, the patron of Israel and ally of the Shah, was perceived by the Islamic regime as "the Great Satan," and source of all evil. Thus, although shortly after Khomeini arrived in Tehran President Carter announced that he respected the wishes of the Iranian people and was willing to cooperate with the revolutionary regime, Khomeini immediately embarked on a strong attack against the US. In March 1979 Iran withdrew from CENTO and in June joined the bloc of nonaligned states. Nevertheless, Iran continued to maintain friendly relations with the other members of CENTO in the region—especially Turkey. Despite Turkey's membership in NATO, its strong ties with the US and

commercial ties with Iraq, Iran needed Turkey for the transit of goods that it purchased in Europe.

On November 4, 1979, a group of Khomeini's followers took over the American Embassy building in Tehran, holding all the diplomats and embassy employees present hostage. After several days the women and black diplomats were released, but fifty-three white diplomats were held hostage for fourteen months under degrading conditions. In April 1980 the US tried to release the hostages by means of an airborne military operation, that failed from the beginning. On the day that President Reagan was sworn in, on January 20, 1981, Iran announced that it would release the American hostages, following prolonged mediating efforts by ALGERIA. The issue of Iran held up the release of the hostages and whether this had anything to do with the American election campaign remained ambiguous. The Islamic regime denied its direct involvement in holding the hostages, but took advantage of the tension that this created with the US for domestic political purposes. In the early 1980s US officials of the National Security Council were involved, together with Israel, in delivering arms to Iran (later, known as the Iran-Contras Affair). This manifested the latter's willingness to purchase weapons from every possible source. The relations between Iran and the US continued to deteriorate against the background of subversive and sabotage Iranian activities against the Gulf oil monarchies, and its encouragement of terrorist attacks committed by members of the Lebanese Party of God (*Hizballah*) against the American Embassy and the multinational force in Beirut in the course of 1983. This tension assumed an additional dimension when as of 1986 Iran started attacking oil tankers in the Persian Gulf and placing mines in the Straits of HORMUZ in reaction to Iraq's efforts to paralyze Iranian oil exports. This led to the flagging of the attacked tankers by the US and the presence of Western navies in the Gulf. In April 1988 the US navy destroyed two Iranian oil platforms in the Persian Gulf, sank two frigates and a missile boat in retaliation for the planting of naval mines by Iran in the Gulf, one of which damaged an American frigate. In July the Americans mistakenly brought down an Iranian airliner over the Gulf. All 290 passengers were killed.

The fear of a Western cultural invasion stood at the foundation of the reserved Iranian attitude toward cooperation with the states of Western Europe. Like other revolutionary regimes in the Middle East, revolutionary Iran preferred trade relations and the supply of arms and technology by the Soviet Union and other East European states, despite their inferiority compared to the Western-made ones. The tension between Iran and the Western states further intensified against the background of the embargo imposed by the latter on the supply of arms to Iran, Germany's announcement that it was not going to complete the construction of the Bandar-Khomeini atomic reactor on the Persian Gulf coast, though relations between the two states improved after Iran was allowed to purchase heavy equipment and consumer goods from Germany.

Iran's relations with Britain entered a crisis in March 1989 when Khomeini ruled that the British-Muslim author Salman Rushdie should be executed. Iran reacted to an official British protest by severing its relations with Britain. Relations with France suffered from continuous tension as a result of the massive quantities and quality of arms supplied by France to Iraq during the war with Iran. The holding of French hostages by Shi'i militants in Lebanon; French accusations that the Iranian embassy in Paris had turned into the headquarters of terrorist activities in Europe; a series of terrorist attacks in Paris in 1987, which led to a siege on the Iranian Embassy, and an Iranian retaliatory move against the French embassy in Tehran—all these formed the foundation of the severance of relations between the two states in July of that year. The crisis was settled and relations were renewed after France surrendered its demand to disclose the Iranian embassy's activities and the French hostages in Lebanon were released.

Contrary to the embargo by the West on the supply of armaments to Iran, the communist states were willing to sell it weapons. Nevertheless, tension soon prevailed in Iranian-Soviet relations, when in 1979 the Iranian leaders accused the Soviets of actively encouraging subversion and armed activities of the Kurds and the *Tudeh* Party, and criticized Moscow for its invasion of Afghanistan at the end of 1979. In February 1983, the relations between the two countries reached a crisis as a result of the detention of the *Tudeh* Party leaders and the expulsion of eighteen Soviet diplomats from Tehran.

The relations between revolutionary Iran and the Arab states—especially the Gulf states, were, from the outset, extremely tense due to the Arab fear of popular-Islamic revolutions, despite the fact that Iran was Shi'i while most of the Arab populations were Sunnis. The Shi'i revolution and the declarations of its leaders regarding their intention of saving the "oppressed" throughout the Muslim world, resulted in the outbreak of social protest and political subversion amongst the relatively large Shi'i and Iranian populations in the Gulf Arab states—including Iraq, Saudi Arabia, Kuwait, Bahrain and others. In its efforts to export the Islamic revolution to neighboring countries, the borders were frequently blurred between the universal Islamic revolutionary message and the Iranian national interest. This was the case with regards to the territorial claim raised by Iran on Bahrain, simultaneously with the propaganda and religious incitement campaign carried out against the leaders of the Gulf states in the name of the revolution. Even before he came to power, Khomeini accused the leaders of the Arab states of treason against the principles of Islam and of being servants of the West, demanding that they detach themselves from the US and agree to the principle that regional security be preserved by the states of the region themselves. Bahrain and Kuwait considered themselves especially threatened by Iran's efforts of incitement directed to their relatively large Shi'i minorities which included Iranians.

The Iran-Iraq war caused further deterioration in relations with Kuwait. Iran accused Kuwait of supporting the Iraqi war effort and placing the island of Bubian at the disposal of the Iraqi Army. In December 1981 an attempted coup was uncovered in Bahrain, which apparently took place under Iranian inspiration. At the end of 1983 a series of acts of sabotage took place simultaneously in the capital of Kuwait against Kuwaiti, American and French targets, two months after the suicide attack carried out by members of *Hizballah* in Lebanon against soldiers of the multilateral force in Beirut. In 1986 Iran started attacking Kuwaiti tankers in the Gulf. This forced Kuwait to ask for American protection. In September and November 1987 the Iranians fired surface-to-surface missiles at Kuwait, which had expelled Iranian diplomats from its territory. Iranian-Saudi relations reached a crisis when at the end of July 1987, 400 pilgrim—half of them Iranian—were killed in Mecca while holding a political demonstration in the course of the *Haj* ceremonies. This took place despite the explicit prohibition by the Saudi government on holding demonstrations. The Iranian regime, which described the riots as a "massacre" took advantage of the incident for a propaganda attack against the Saudi regime, the US and Israel. On the morrow of the incident the embassies of Saudi Arabia and Kuwait in Tehran were attacked. Nine months later Saudi Arabia broke off its relations with Iran following an Iranian military attack against Saudi tankers in the Persian Gulf. Relations were renewed in March 1991, after Saudi Arabia agreed to allow 115,000 Iranians to make the pilgrimage to Mecca.

The effect of the Shi'i revolution in Iran was most strongly felt by its immediate neighbor Iraq. About half of the population there is Shi'i-Arab (even though power has traditionally been held by the Sunni-Arab minority). Two of the holy places to Shi'i Islam—Najaf and Karbala—are also there. For these reasons, the revolution in Iran resulted in an increase in subversive and armed activities by the al-Da'wa movement in Iraq, whose leaders maintained close ties with the heads of the religious establishment in revolutionary Iran. The efforts by the Iraqi government to suppress the movement, including the execution of its religious leader, further increased the tension between the two states, and very rapidly border incidents erupted between them. In September 1980 Iraqi President Saddam Hussein announced an all-out war against Iran which endured for eight years (see IRAN-IRAQ WAR). The Iraqi decision to wage the war derived mainly from the regime's fears of the Iranian revolution's repercussions on its domestic security, and estimated that the chaos in Iran's Army and central power constituted an historic opportunity for Iraq to resolve once and for all its conflict with Iran over Shatt al-Arab, and secure a foothold in the oil-rich territory of Khusistan on its north-eastern bank. However, as of 1982, Baghdad started proposing that the War be terminated, after its successes in the first weeks had proved temporary and the Iranian counter-attacks started to constitute a real threat to Iraq itself. Iran was willing to end the war on impossible conditions for Saddam Hussein: exorbitant war reparations and putting Saddam on trial. Only in August 1988, when Iran had been on the verge of moral and economic collapse, following continuous bombings of Iranian cities by Iraqi surface-to-surface missiles, did Khomeini agree to accept the long-delayed cease-fire as suggested by the UN Security Council. However, the official talks held by the two states at ministerial level did not resolve the sharp differences between them over the delineation of boundaries, the exchange of prisoners and the location of those missing in battle. Iran's demand for one thousand billion dollars in war reparations was another reason for the failure of the talks.

The Iran-Iraq War led to a rapid tightening of relations between Iran and Syria. The hostility between the BA'TH regimes of SYRIA and Iraq (which returned after a short period of *rapprochement*—see SYRIA and Iraq now became overt and caustic. In co-operation with LIBYA, Syria fully supported Iran in its war against Iraq, transferring to it Soviet weapons by means of an airlift. In addition to gaining an important regional ally, Iran was granted a foothold in Lebanon. This enabled it to deepen its influence among the local Shi's and encourage armed activity against Israel. In April 1982 Iran and Syria signed an agreement for strategic cooperation, IN which Iran undertook to supply Syria annually one million tons of oil, free of charge, and another 4–5 million tons of oil at a reduced price. In return Syria closed the Iraqi oil pipeline from Kirkuk to the Mediterranean and enabled the arrival of members of Iranian Revolutionary Guards to the Lebanese Valley under its control. The close relations which Syria established with Iran served it as a lever for extorting financial assistance from the traditional oil states in the Gulf, which believed that Syria might be able to constrain the Iranian militancy toward them.

One of the immediate steps taken by revolutionary Iran was to break off Iran's diplomatic relations with Israel. These were replaced by close relations with the PLO. Furthermore, the Islamic states were called upon to join forces for the liquidation of Israel. The Israeli delegation building in Tehran was handed over to the PLO, and Yasser ARAFAT was the first top foreign visitor received by Khomeini in Tehran in February 1979. Henceforth, Iran turned Israel into a major symbol of evil (the "small Satan") which deserved all the Muslims' hostility and relentless effort to eliminate it. The Iranians argued against Israel's control of the places holy to Islam in Jerusalem; its having usurped the rights of the Palestinians; its being the US typical agent in the region; and its past close relations with the Shah's regime and the Savak. However, relations with the PLO were soon shaken, simultaneously with the latter's deteriorating relations with Syria, which reached its nadir in the wake of Israel's invasion of Lebanon in 1982. Iran was not ready to provide the PLO with financial aid. Arafat refused to cooperation with the policy of spreading the Islamic revolution. This threatened the Arab oil monarchies in the Gulf, whose financial aid was of primary importance to the PLO. Arafat participated in the diplomatic efforts to renew the peace process with Israel, while drawing closer to Jordan and Iraq. The advent of the Islamic revolution led to a break-up of diplomatic relations with Egypt and an intense propaganda war against Sadat's regime immediately after the signing of the Israel-Egypt peace treaty in March 1979. Tehran's enmity to the Egyptian regime was also caused by the asylum Sadat granted the Shah shortly after the revolution.

The Post-Khomeini Era (1989–1997)

Domestic Affairs Following Khomeini's death in June 1989, a council of experts elected Khamenei as spiritual leader of the Islamic republic, entitling him Ayatollah. Neither the religious circles nor the general public enthused over this decision, because Khamenei was not considered an authority in the sphere of religious doctrine and lacked the charisma of Khomeini. However, the revolutionary regime expressed confidence in the new leader and did everything to legitimize his election to the lofty position. In July, Rafsanjani, the speaker of the *Majlis*, was elected President by a vast majority replacing Khamenei. In the course of these elections, changes in the constitution, drafted before Khomeini had died, came to force, primarily the abolition of the Prime Minister's position and the handing over of all the executive powers to the President.

The sweeping support of Rafsanjani reflected in particular the hope for an improvement in the economic situation, which had been extremely depressed. Rafsanjani was considered a pragmatist, capable of adapting the principles of the revolution to social and economic realities. Indeed, he established a government of technocrats, with the participation of moderate figures, in an effort to improve relations with the West. The new approach was reflected by the exclusion from Rafsanjani's government of two central (religious) figures who supported the idea of exporting the revolution—-Ali Akbar Mohtashami-Pur and Mohammad Mohammadi-Reyshahri. Despite these changes the struggle between

the pragmatists and revolutionaries regarding both domestic and international policies, remained undecided. Backed by Khamenei, the radicals continued to demonstrate hostility towards the West and supported Islamic revolutionaries and subversion against pro-Western regimes in the neighboring Arab states. On the other hand, the President and his supporters sought to revitalize Iran's economy and rehabilitate the relations with the West European states, though without giving up the goal of spreading a radical version of Shi'i Islam outside of Iran or moderating hostility toward the US.

Rafsanjani's efforts to improve the economic situation were largely unsuccessful. This was reflected in riots and demonstrations against the government. In January 1992 the government doubled the subsidy for basic foodstuffs, in an effort to end the civil protests. However, in April and May new riots erupted in various cities, including Tehran and the religious town of Mashhad, due to economic difficulties and severe housing shortages, resulting in hundreds of detainments and a few dozen executions.

The economic hardships and concern for domestic security led in April 1991 to a merging of the police institutions, the *gendarmerie* and the security committees (offshoot of the Revolutionary Guards), establishing a general staff of "the security and order forces." This further reduced the position of the veterans of the Shah's regime in the internal security services.

The elections to the *Majlis* in April-May 1992 enabled Rafsanjani to bring into parliament more members of the younger generation and educated classes, who would support his policies. At least half of the 270 members of the new *Majlis* were considered supporters of the President, while the radicals were further distanced from key positions. A new speaker of the *Majlis* was elected—the conservative Hojat-ol Eslam Ali-Akbar Nategh-Nouri. The continued slump of oil prices further aggravated the economic situation of Iran, which had difficulties repaying its external debts and entered a state of galloping inflation. The government sought to cancel subsidies on consumer goods or limit them significantly, but came across strong opposition by the radical faction.

In July 1993 Rafsanjani was re-elected President, albeit with a small majority (sixty-three percent of the votes), reflecting the crisis of expectations and a sharp decline in the President's popularity due to the economic deterioration and widespread corruption in the government's apparatuses. Support for Rafsanjani in the *Majlis* also declined, and his government's monetary policy was strongly criticized. An additional attempt to abolish or reduce subsidies in March 1994 once again came across strong opposition in the *Majlis*, even though the cost of subsidies superseded the state's income from oil. The government also failed in its attempt to introduce a single foreign exchange rate and in the first half of 1995 the Iranian currency lost about a third of its value. The weakening of the Iranian currency was partly attributed to the intensifying American economic boycott of Iran (see below).

In 1994–1995 the tension between radicals and pragmatists in the ruling group of clergymen assumed the form of accusing President Rafsanjani by the Islamic press of attempting to westernize economic concepts. The growing criticism of the president forced him to reshuffle his government bringing more hard-liners into key positions. In an effort to regain public popularity, in the summer of 1994, the government announced the establishment of a holding company that would purchase and manage all the major enterprises and assets of the state, which had previously been private. The company's shareholders were to have been the families who had lost their sons in the war, war cripples, released prisoners and all those serving in the institutions of the revolution. This move raised great public dissatisfaction, since it was viewed as overt bribery to the privileged strata, which supported the regime. Despite this, the government was forced to cut its expenditure toward the beginning of the second five year plan. In March 1995 the prices in all petroleum products were doubled. This triggered a rise in the prices of all economic spheres and increased public disgruntlement. The growing economic hardships, and especially the housing shortage, led to several violent outbreaks, which came to a peak in the riots of April 1995 in the poor southern suburbs of Tehran. These riots joined a series of violent events in the course of 1994, which came up against a political-religious and local-administrative background.

Shortly after the end of the war with Iraq, the regime embarked on a systematic policy to liquidate the opposition both within and outside the state for fear of negative public reaction to the bitter failure in the War and its high cost of human lives and material destruction. About 2,000 political prisoners were executed in prisons. Many released prisoners were called in for a renewed investigation and placed before firing squads. At the same time, Iranian agents started liquidating opposition leaders abroad. From the end of the 1980s, over one hundred known opposition activists were assassinated, including Shahpur BAKHTIAR—the last Prime Minister in the Shah's regime—who had established "The National Movement of Iranian Resistance" (NAMIR) in Paris; Dr. Abdol-Rahman Ghassemlou—leader of the Kurdish Democratic Party of Iran; and his successor Dr. Sadeq Sharafkandi, who was assassinated together with three of his friends in Berlin. The investigation of these murders usually revealed the direct involvement of top Iranian leaders. Thus, in the case of the murder in Berlin, Iranian witnesses stated in their evidence that the liquidation had been implemented in accordance with the direct instruction or personal approval of the spiritual leader, the President and Minister of the Intelligence. During Rafsanjani's Presidency, efforts continued to strike at the *Mojahedin Khalq* and its leaders, by means of military attacks on the organization's bases in Iraq. At the same time, all party activities in Iran were prohibited, while the freedom of expression of opposition groups was strictly limited. Mehdi BAZARGAN's Movement for the Freedom of Iran survived, but with minimal political activity.

In the face of growing unrest and public protest over the economic predicament, in mid-1995 the possibility of allowing the activity of political parties was discussed, as a means to ease the pressure on the regime, but the idea was finally rejected for fear of losing control. The subject was once again raised by the Ministry of the Interior toward the elections to the fifth *Majlis* in 1996, but nothing was done to implement such a policy. Not only was party activity prohibited, but near the elections the powers of the Council for the Preservation of the Constitution were expanded to supervise the elections, and it was given the authority to approve or reject the candidacy of any person on the basis of his loyalty to the regime's ideology.

The struggle between the supporters of the rigid Islamic line and the moderate line also manifested itself in the cultural sphere. While the first term of

Rafsanjani's presidency was characterized by limited cultural openness in the media. In his second term of office, freedom of expression was gradually limited. Strict censorship was imposed on the press, even though the government allowed the publication of complaints by citizens regarding the economic and social hardships. Papers were closed down and journalists were tried and punished. The harassment of authors and writers increased, and radio and television programs became much more Islamic in content, resulting in secular protests. Even though Iranian film-making was internationally acclaimed and recognized, most of the films could not be shown in Iran.

The regime's policy on human rights continued to be based on its Islamic philosophy. From this perspective, Iran kept reacting to criticism of its conduct by the UN, the European Community and other international organizations involved in human rights, with contempt, though not with disregard. Nevertheless, from the beginning of the 1990s, the activities of the revolutionary courts—against which much of the international fury was directed—declined, as did the number of executions. In May 1991, Amnesty International was allowed to send a representative to Iran. However, in February 1997, the prize for the head of Salman Rushdie was increased to 2.5 million dollars.

Iran's discriminatory policy toward religious minorities also gave rise to outbursts of violence, especially by the Sunnis (Kurds and Baluchis). The persecution of the Bahais and executions of its leaders and activists continued well into 1997, even though as a result of international pressure on the government there was some improvement in their situation compared to the earlier years of the revolution, and they were given some freedom of worship. At the end of 1996 the government also initiated an international convention of the Zoroastrians in Iran, with the participation of hundreds of representatives.

Despite the erosion in his political power, in 1995 Rafsanjani initiated a change in the constitution. This enabled his election to a third term as President. However, this attempt met with major opposition and Rafsanjani was forced to resign. In May 1997 Hojjat-ol Eslam Seyyed Muhammad KHATAMI, former Minister of Education and member of the Supreme Council of the Cultural Revolution, was elected President. Khatami obtained sixty-nine per-

cent of the votes, even though the spiritual leader of Iran and the regime's institutions supported the conservative candidate NATEK-NOURI. Khatami was the joint candidate of the pragmatists and the nationalists who had been pushed aside in the previous years by the conservative stream. His election, by many youngsters and women, apparently reflected protest against the coercive nature of the regime. Indeed, it deepened the cleavage between pragmatists and radicals in Iran, cutting across the clergy as well.

Foreign Affairs The end of the war with Iraq, which did not resolve any of the outstanding problems between the two states, has been the main cause for the comprehensive effort made by Iran since then to purchase large quantities of advanced weapons, including chemical and biological weapons. The use which Iraq made of chemical weapons in its war against Iran and the uncovering of the advanced state of Iraq's nuclear plans following the GULF WAR, spurred Iran into trying to attain an equivalent non-conventional capability. Iran invested great efforts and vast funds into purchasing middle and long range missiles and the technologies for manufacturing them. Even though the West continued its arms embargo against Iran, and the US implemented an intensive campaign against the Iranian rearmament programs, the Tehran government found what it was looking for in RUSSIA, China and North Korea. Iran's massive arm procurement efforts were further encouraged by the defeat suffered by Iraq in the Gulf War and its additional weakening by international sanctions. The political and military void created in the Gulf region encouraged Iran to nurture its status as a hegemonic power in this sensitive region. The purchase of three Russian submarines and their entry into the Gulf, was viewed by the West as a possible threat to the export of oil through the Gulf, while the purchase of Russian nuclear reactors and technology became a constant source of concern within the region and in Washington. This led to estimates that Iran could have a capability to manufacture a nuclear device within five to ten years.

Iran's relations with the US continued to be marked by hostility, despite secret efforts by both sides to overcome the differences between them. The government of Rafsanjani was apparently interested in renewing the relations, but the conservative-radical faction, led by Khamenei, undermined the *rapprochement* efforts and continued to nurture the image of the US as an enemy, as part of the Islamization policy. As a condition for the renewal of relations, Iran demanded the return of 12 billion dollars. Iran claimed that this had been frozen by President Carter's instruction after the occupation of the US Embassy in Tehran; the end of US support for the Middle East peace process; and an end to Washington's hostile attitude toward the Islamic regime in Tehran. In May 1990 the two states reached an agreement to enable the International Court in the Hague to deal with mutual financial claims, which had resulted from the disruption of relations and the occupation of the US Embassy in Tehran. In 1996, the two states reached an agreement regarding the payment of compensation to the families of 290 passengers killed in an Iranian commercial airline accidentally shot down by the Americans in 1988.

Nevertheless, during the Clinton administration, relations once again deteriorated to an unprecedented level due to the embarkation on a policy of economic pressures on Iran, requiring its European allies to limit and even stop trading with Tehran. The US accused Iran of nurturing Islamic terrorist organizations, acting against the Middle East Peace Process and developing mass destruction weapons, including nuclear capability. In March 1995, the Clinton administration forced the CONOCO oil company to cancel an agreement for the development of new oil fields in the Siri region in the Persian Gulf.

The cancellation of the deal, which had originally been interpreted as a sign of good will by Iran toward the US. This was expected to increase the annual revenue of Iran from oil by a billion dollars and it greatly harmed the prestige of the Iranian regime, deepening its hostility toward the US. In April 1995 the US prohibited American companies and their subsidiaries abroad to maintain trade relations with Iran. The election of Khatami as President of Iran in May 1997, was welcomed by most states and especially Iran's Arab neighbors, since in his election campaign he called for a movement away from adventures in foreign relations. Nevertheless, he refused to call for a renewal of relations with the US, strongly attacking Israel.

Even though the Western European states refused to join the US call for an economic boycott of Iran, the Americans managed to prevent other states from investing in development programs in Iran or engaging in economic deals with it.

In the relations between Iran and the Soviet Union, there was a significant improvement in the face of Gorbachev's *glasnost* policy and the end of the Iran-Iraq war. Extensive trade relations developed between the two states. The Soviet Union turned, together with China and North Korea, into a major arms supplier of Iran. In June 1989, President Rafsanjani visited Moscow and signed a joint Declaration of Principles with Gorbachev, defining the relations between the two states. In January 1990 tension mounted between the two states against the background of Iran's support of the Muslim revolt in the Nehicevan enclave in Armenia. Upon the collapse of the Soviet Union, a new era opened in the relations with Russia, whose economic difficulties and urgent need for foreign currency, made it an interested supplier of arms to Iran, including advanced planes and submarines, worth billions of dollars. Russia also won a contract to complete Iran's nuclear reactor at Bandar Khomeini on the Persian Gulf coast. This agreement met with strong protest by the US and Israel, but the Russians withstood the pressure and Iran announced that in the middle of 1997 it would start operating the reactor for the generation of electricity.

The disintegration of the Soviet Union in August 1991 along with the advent of six Muslim republics, some of which had once been ruled by Persia, opened up new opportunities for Iran to establish political and commercial ties as well as for spreading the Islamic revolution. However, in the economic sphere, Iran came across competition from Turkey and in the religious-cultural sphere, from Saudi Arabia. In February 1992, the Republics of Kyrgyzstan, Tajikistan, Uzbekistan, Turkmenistan and Azerbaijan joined the framework of the Economic Cooperation Organization (eco). Furthermore, a framework for cooperation between the states of the CASPIAN SEA was created with the participation of Iran, Russia, Azerbaijan, Turkmenistan and Kazakhstan. Iran tried to mediate between Azerbaijan and Armenia in their conflict over Ngorno-Karabakh, mediating between the rival groups in Tajikistan. In the summer of 1996, the railways of Iran and Turkmenistan were connected, renewing the traditional "Silk way" which had connected Iran with central Asia. However, the Iranian efforts in the economic sphere enjoyed only limited success, for the Islamic Republics required, first and foremost, technological assistance and capital investments. Iran was unable to provide this, preferring ties with the Western states and Israel. Iran's efforts to introduce an Islamic ideology in the new Islamic republics was met with opposition (their population, except in Azerbaijan, is Sunni) and caused tension with Tehran.

The relations between Iran and the states of the European Union remained ambivalent. On the one hand, these states adopted a critical approach toward Iran, due to its disregard of human rights and its assistance to international terror, implemented on their soil as well. On the other hand, pragmatic considerations have been decisive in the decisions of the Union states in favor of developing economic ties with Iran. The Union states defined their relationship with Iran as one of "critical dialogue", to encourage it to uphold human rights and cancel the FATWA, which had called for Salman Rushdie's execution. However, this dialogue remained futile, serving merely as a convenient cover for some of the European countries to expand their trade relations with Iran. In September 1996 Denmark announced that it was withdrawing from the policy of critical dialogue, due to Iran's refusal to cancel the *fatwa* against Rushdie.

The relations between Iran and each of the Union states varied. The relations with Britain continued to be tense for most of the 1990s. In the middle of 1997 diplomatic relations remained at a level of *charge d'affairs* only. The tension between the two states resulted from the *fatwa* against Rushdie, British claims regarding Iranian intelligence activities in Britain and Iranian assistance to the IRA. The result was the mutual expulsion of diplomats and journalists. In June 1994 Iran was accused of responsibility for placing a bomb near the Israeli Embassy in London. Nonetheless, commercial relations between the two states remained the same. Even the increase of the prize for Rushdie's head to a 2.5 million dollars in February 1997, had no affect, despite official British protests.

Iran's trade relations with Germany were especially extensive. Germany supplied a major part of Iran's requirements in advanced equipment and technologies. However, relations between the two states entered a crisis against the backdrop of the decision of a court in Berlin early in 1997 to convict the government of Iran for direct responsibility for the murder of Dr. Sadeq Sharafkandi—the leader of the Kurdish Democratic Party, and three other opposition activists. When the states of the European Union withdrew their Ambassadors from Tehran in protest, a blockade was placed on the German Embassy in Tehran. The Iranian leaders demanded Germany retract its accusations. However, even this crisis hardly affected the level of business relations between the Union states and Iran.

The prolonged Civil War between Muslims and Serbs in Bosnia-Herzegovina (1992–1996) provided Iran with an opportunity to export the Islamic revolution to Europe. Even before that, Iran complained to the government of Yugoslavia about its persecution of Muslims. After August 1992 the ties between Iran and the Muslims in Bosnia tightened. In April 1995 Iran was accused of breaking the embargo placed by the UN on arms supplies to the warring sides and supplying weapons to the Muslims, allegedly implemented with the knowledge of the US, which sympathized with the plight of the Muslims. Once the war ended, the government of Bosnia established friendly relations with Iran, despite strong US opposition.

The relations between Iran and Turkey were marked by mutual accusations of supporting each other's opposition groups, revolving primarily on Iran's support for Kurdish guerrilla activities and Islamic fundamentalists in Turkey. The advent of an Islamic-led government of Turkey, headed by Mecmettin ERBAKAN in 1996 led to a *rapprochement* between the two states, which included mutual visits at the summit level. In August 1996 the two states signed an agreement for the annual supply of one billion cubic meters of natural gas from Iran to Turkey for twenty-three years, at a total cost of 23 billion dollars. This deal led to a strong American protest. In February 1997 a crisis developed in the relations between the two states due to the support expressed by the Iranian Ambassador to Ankara for terrorist activities against Israel and for the Islamization of Turkey. This crisis led to the mutual expulsion of Ambassadors and Consuls.

Iranian-Iraqi relations remained tense, even though both regimes found themselves in direct confrontation with the US. The suppression of the Shi‘s in Iraq, the refuge that Iraq granted members of the *Mojahedin-e Khalq*; the non-resolution of mutual border disputes and other problems resulting from the long War between the two states; the continued Syrian-Iranian alliance—all these increased the hostility between the two states. In the wake of its invasion of Kuwait, Iraq unilaterally evacuated the Iranian territories which were still under its control. This enabled the exchange of war prisoners and the exchange of ambassadors between the two states in September 1990. Iran responded to the Iraqi invasion of Kuwait by following its national interests rather than those of the Islamic revolution. Hence it remainesd entirely passive during the war. Though it strongly condemned the presence of the anti-Iraq international coalition led by the US, it openly supported the independence and territorial integrity of Kuwait. Nevertheless, while officially Iran implemented the international boycott of Iraq, it allowed an extensive passage of goods into Iraq. However, the suppression of the Shi'i uprising in Southern Iraq in March 1991, following the defeat of Saddam Hussein in the Gulf War, again raised tensions between the two states. In the 1990s, Iran continued to press the Iraqi government to close down the bases of the *Mojahedin-e Khalq* on its territory and carried out several raids into Iraq to liquidate them. The increased involvement of Iran in the autonomous Kurdish area established under international auspices in Northern Iraq following the Gulf War, and the establishment of the Kurdish *Hizballah* (Party of God), added to the tension between the two states. Iran also developed special relations with the patriotic union of Jalal TALABANI in order to increase its status in Northern Iraq. At the same time it tried to establish relations with Talabani's rival: the Kurdish Democratic Party, led by Mas'ud BARAZANI.

The relations between Iran and Saudi Arabia remained tense following the bloody riots in Mecca in July 1987 (see above). While Iran continued to accuse the Saudis of close cooperation with the US and the investment of large funds to prevent the expansion of Shi'i Islam in the Republics of Central Asia and elsewhere. Iran also accused Saudi Arabia of collaborating with the US to bring down world oil prices, in order to stop Iran getting the revenue it required for its revolutionary Islamic activity in other countries. In the beginning of 1997 Iran was allegedly involved in the blowing up of the American base in Daharan, Saudi Arabia. However, the government of RIYAD avoided handing over to the US

the full results of the investigation on the affair, for fear of the Iranian reaction, especially as the US might retaliate.

Iranian-Syrian relations remained close despite Syria's participation in the Madrid Conference (see ARAB-ISRAEL PEACEMAKING), direct negotiations with Israel on a contractual peace, and Syrian support for the demand of the Gulf Emirates to get Iran to return the Tunb and ABU MUSSA Islands. While Syria's Alliance with Iran continued to serve Damascus's interest in influencing the Gulf oil monarchies, especially in the context of slowing down the normalization with Israel until Syria reached an agreement on its terms, Iran's interest in the alliance was linked to *Hizballah's* activities in Lebanon against Israel, believed to serve Syria's interests in Southern Lebanon.

Since the renewal of the Peace Process between Israel and the Arab states at the Madrid Conference, Iran has carried out a campaign of propaganda and subversion against it. In addition to supporting *Hizballah* in Lebanon financially and militarily, Iran has granted financial support to the Palestinian HAMAS and Islamic JIHAD. Several terrorist acts against Israeli and Jewish institutions around the world have been attributed to Iran, including the explosiion of the Israeli Embassy and Jewish center in Buenos Aires, an attack on a Zionist institution in London and an attempt to carry out a similar operation against an Israeli target in Thailand. At the same time, Iran continued to attack Israel in the media and in the central mosques in Iran, presenting it as an illegitimate entity.

IRAN-IRAQ WAR From 1980 to 1988, the Iraq-Iran war was the most salient manifestation of the threat posed by the Iranian Shi'i revolution to the Gulf Arab states' security and indeed to the Middle East as a whole. The length, intensity, and heavy loss of human lives, civilian and war materials, marked this war as the single most important factor shaping the political conduct and preferences of nations in the region. Although the immediate cause of the war was linked to the rise of the Islamic Shi'i revolution in IRAN, it also derived from ancient conflicts revolving around territorial, ethno-religious and political reasons. The modern state of IRAQ inherited the Ottoman-Iranian dispute over the SHATT AL-ARAB-Iraq's sole outlet to the Gulf. This marked the dividing line between SUNNI and Shi'i Muslims, as well as between Arab and Persian languages and cultures. During the 1960s and 1970s, tension between Iraq and Iran was nurtured by the Shah's efforts to build Iran as a regional military power in the Gulf area with clear Western orientation. This did not sit well with Iraq's ideological radicalism and inclination toward the Soviet Union. A traditional indication of the two contenders' relations was the Iranian support of the KURDS of Iraq in their repeated revolts against the Baghdad government. In March 1975, following a growing tension between Tehran and Baghdad, the two regimes signed the Algiers Agreement. In this Iraq succumbed to the Iranian claim to draw their border in the middle of the river along its stream, for all purposes of sovereignty and rights of navigation. Iran's main *quid-pro-quo* was undertaking to cease all support to the Kurdish rebels. Iraq certainly signed the agreement under duress of the Kurdish revolt and Soviet pressure, which included an effective halt of arms supplies.

Before the Iranian revolution Shi'i Islamic radicalism in Iraq was apparent. This was represented primarily by the "*al-da'wa*" movement, which by the late 1970s had commited violent acts against the regime. The Ayatollah KHOMEINI viewed the export of the Muslim revolution as a religious mission of the first order. Following his accession to power in Iran in February 1979, his regime incited the Shi's in Iraq to revolt against the regime there with the goal of replacing it with an Islamic regime. The political radicalization of the SHI'A in Iraq, together with the Iranian incitement, were a source of concern for the Iraqi regime headed by President Saddam HUSSEIN. He wanted very much to build a strong Iraqi nation, unifying its three main ethno-religious groups: the Kurds in the North; the Shi's in the South and the SUNNIS in the center, despite their cultural and religious differences. In 1980 Iraq seemed to have consolidated its position as a leading Arab power following the expulsion of Egypt from the ARAB LEAGUE; closer relations than ever with the Gulf monarchies and a booming economy due to the rise of oil prices following the Iranian revolution. During the first two years of the revolution, Iran's domestic affairs were in a state of chaos; its military weakness reached its ebb due to the Islamic purges of the Army's echelons which paralyzed its functioning capability, and the American embargo on arms supplies. Saddam Hussein's fears of Iran's radical Shi'ism; his aspirations

for Iraqi superiority in the Gulf, and perception of a weak and divided Iran, apparently combined to motivate his decision to open an all-out war against Iran. More specifically, the war was aimed at abolishing the 1975 Agreement; obtaining free and safe passage to the Gulf; bringing down Khomeini's regime and removing his threat to the national integrity of Iraq. Another motive for initiating the war by Saddam Hussein was the desire to gain control over the Khuzistan Province, in South-West Iran, near the Iraqi border. This is rich in oil, and thus would secure full Iraqi control over the Shatt al-Arab. In late October 1979, Saddam Hussein demanded a revision of the Algiers Border Agreement, but his request was unheeded.

The outbreak of full-scale war was preceded by several shooting incidents along the border between the two states. The Iraqis accused the Iranian army of invading a border point in the district of Diali, and demanded its evacuation. The Iranians denied the accusation and rejected the demand. Finally, on 22 September 1980, Iraq invaded Iran without any early warning. In his televised announcement of the war, Saddam tore apart the 1975 Algiers Agreement. Iran, which was caught by total surprise, was forced to withdraw on several fronts. The Iraqis imitated Israel's *blitzkrieg* of June 1967, bombarding the Iranian airports with the goal of paralyzing the Iranian airforce, while simultaneously scoring successes on land. The Iraqi successes in the early months of the war were impressive: the important port of Horramshahr on the WEST BANK of the Shatt-al-Arab was conquered. Iranian border towns such as Dehloran, Mehran, Sar-e Pol-e Zahab and others, fell into Iraqi hands. The Iraqi forces advanced towards Susangerd and Shush, hundreds of kilometers into Iranian territory. However, the huge edge of Iran over Iraq in terms of territorial depth and human resources, as well as its revolutionary situation, made the Iraqi gains temporary and reversible, once the regime decided not to resist the Iraqi offensive, which had become a domestic challenge to the Islamic revolutionary regime.

The war, initially expected to end within weeks with an Iraqi victory, soon became a war of attrition. Within several months, the Iraqi attack was contained. The Iranian forces opened local attacks and managed to regain certain territories that had been occupied by Iraq. Within less than two years, the Iranians had managed to reorganize their forces, waring off the Iraqi forces from most of the occupied territories. In two counter-attacks in March and May 1982, Iran expelled the Iraqi forces from the Shush-Dezful front and liberated the port city of Khorramshahr. In June 1982, Iraq sought to take advantage of the Israeli invasion of LEBANON. This was in an attempt to terminate its war against Iran honorably, once it realized that it was unable to attain the goals of the war, which had become exhausting and dangerous to Iraq itself. Thus, in June 1982, Saddam Hussein exploited the Israeli invasion of Lebanon to announce his willingness to withdraw all the Iraqi forces from the territory of Iran. He wanted to be able to offer assistance in the war against ISRAEL in Lebanon, and proposed a cease-fire and opening of peace talks. However, Khomeini rejected this request and conditioned the end of the war on Iraqi surrender, payment of war indemnations, the overthrowing of the regime of the secular BA'TH Party in Baghdad and putting Saddam Hussein on trial as a war criminal. Iran decided to continue the war. Despite the arms embargo by the Western states on the Islamic regime in Iran and the damage caused to the army as a result of the revolution, the Iraqi threat unified most of the Iranian public around Khomeini's leadership. This constituted an important factor in consolidating the revolutionary regime in Iran. Iraq's early successes in the war, led its rivals in the Arab arena—SYRIA and LIBYA—to implement an air-lift of Soviet arms to Iran, with the knowledge and consent of the Soviet Union.

Khomeini viewed the continuation of the war as a means for exporting the revolution and reinforcing the Islamic ideology inside Iran by encouraging self-sacrifice for the cause of Islam and the homeland. The war also constituted an excuse for a massive suppression of political groups in Iran, that did not identify with Khomeini's course (see IRAN). Khomeini described the operations as "the Islamic war against infidelity"; a stage in the liberation of JERUSALEM (al-quds) and the liquidation of Israel. From February 1983, Iran transferred the fighting into the territory of Iraq. However, while the Iranian soldiers fought bravely to ward off the Iraqi invading army from their land, they did not demonstrate great determination in the fighting within the territory of Iraq. On the other hand, the Iraqi soldier, who had previously preferred to fall prisoner to the Iranian

forces rather than be killed on enemy soil, fought bravely to ward off the Iranian forces from his homeland. Iran, which did not make impressive gains inside Iraq, tried to run a war of attrition with the hope that it would finally gain victory because of its demographic, economic and territorial advantages over Iraq. Iraq responded by escalating its means and targets in order to raise the price Iran had to pay for its strategy and force Tehran to end the war. However, because neither of the warring states could impose a cease-fire on the other, both regimes tried to bring about an end to each other's export of oil by targeting the Iranian oil tankers. In March 1984, Iraq widened the scope of war by attacking Iranian oil tankers, alongside with the use of chemical weapons. A month later Iraq initiated a missile attack against the large cities in Iran. In May, Iran, accusing KUWAIT and SAUDI ARABIA of offering Iraq massive help and providing Baghdad with strategic assistance, responded by hitting Saudi and Kuwaiti tankers in the Gulf. It also embarked on attacks on Iraqi cities, towns and oil installation, especially the oil terminal at the Kharg island. Iraq's blows were stronger because it had enjoyed constant supplies of French arms—of Super-Etendard aircraft and Exocet missiles. These ensured its air superiority and the ability to attack ground targets. The attacks on oil tankers in the Gulf continued despite a UN condemnation of such attacks along with a call to respect free navigation in the Gulf. On several occasions, Iraq used chemical weapons to ward off the Iranian forces that had invaded the marsh-lands in Southern Iraq on the artificial island of Majnoon along the border between the two countries—one of Iraq's important oil reserves. An additional gas attack was performed during the Iranian invasion of the al-Huweizah marshes. Iran conquered these marshes in March 1985 and cut off the Basra-Baghdad road. However, the Iranians were unable to hold on to this territory for very long. That same month Iraq renewed its attacks on the Iranian cities of Ahvaz and Bushar. Iran retaliated by launching surface-to-surface missiles at Baghdad and shelling Iraqi border towns. UN Secretary General Javier Perz de Cuellar, visited Tehran and Baghdad in April 1985, but failed to bring the war to an end. Meanwhile, with the plunge of the oil prices to ten dollars per barrel and less, the economies of the two warring states came under growing pressures although the predicament was more serious on the Iranian side due to the financial aid extended to Iraq by Saudi Arabia and Kuwait.

In 1986 the two states intensified the tanker war. While Iraq attacked Iranian tankers and the oil export installation on the island of Kharg, Iran preferred to hit Kuwaiti and Saudi tankers, in order to instigate Arab and Western pressure on Saddam Hussein. Iran also detained ships carrying goods for Iraq and confiscated them. Iran's last massive attack was carried out in February 1986 under the name Val-Fajr 8. This brought about the occupation of the Faw Peninsula, which cut Iraq off from access to the PERSIAN GULF, paralyzing its only port—Umm-el-Qasr.

Throughout the naval war between the two states, over 100 ships were damaged. In February 1986 the Security Council declared Iraq responsible for the outbreak of the war with the hope that Iran would agree to a cease-fire. However, Khomeini remained adamant in his refusal to end the war. In desperation, Iraq renewed the invasion of Iran in May of that year, and reoccupied the ghost town Mehran which had first been occupied at the beginning of the War. (The Iranians liberated Mehran two months later.) Iraq also renewed the attacks on Tehran and the oil installations. These attacks continued intermittently in the course of 1987 as well. In this year Iran carried out several invasions into Iraqi territory, without any impressive results. The war of the tankers and the Iranian missile attacks on Kuwait in particular, led the latter to request that the US reflag its tankers and ships operating in the Gulf. This led to a presence of Western naval forces in the Gulf. In July 1987 the Security Council approved a ten article resolution (No. 598) stipulating the end of hostilities and the withdrawal of all the forces behind their respective national boundaries. Khomeini rejected this resolution. He argued that it did not declare Iraq responsible for the outbreak of the war nor did it oblige it to pay Iran compensation. Iraq, fearing a collapse as a result of the continuation of the war, once again tried to force the Iranian leadership to end the war by renewing the attacks against the oil installations, tankers and Iranian industry. An additional trip by the UN Secretary General to the region in September 1987 did not convince Iran to agree to a cease-fire. This refusal made the American, British and French position against Iran even more rigid. In November 1987 this led to the approval of decisions against it in the Arab League. The Soviet Union, which was worried by the increase of Western influence in the Persian Gulf area as a result of the continuation of the war, proposed in December 1987, that the arms embargo against Iran be more vigorously imposed. At the same time, Iraq renewed the tanker war in January 1988 as well as the war against the cities. The oil refineries in Tehran were bombarded by the Iraqis in February 1988. Iran bombarded Iraq's petro-chemical industry in Basra in retaliation. The mutual attacks on the economic insfrastructures of the two countries continued for a long while. However, in the first months of 1988 Iran suffered several military defeats and lost its previous gains.

In June 1988 Hashemi RAFSANJANI was appointed Acting Supreme Commander of the Iranian Armed Forces. It was hoped that he would be able to stop Iranian military deterioration and prevent additional defeats. One of his main missions was to examine the possibility of merging the revolutionary guards (PASDARAN) into the regular army in order to end the overlappings and the absence of coordination between them in operations. This had resulted in many losses in life and several painful defeats. Until June 1988 the Iraqi army managed to ward off Iran from the whole area of Iraqi Kurdistan and even reconquered the city of Dehloran in Iranian Kurdistan. On 18 July 1988, Khomeini announced that he was "obliged to drink the poisoned cup" and accept Security Council resolution 598 unconditionally. Despite this, Iraq continued warlike operations for another six days, in order to degrade Iran.

About half a million soldiers were killed on both sides in the course of the war, which lasted for eight years, and a further two million persons were wounded or hurt. The economic damage caused amounted to hundreds of billions of dollars. About 75,000 Iraqi soldiers fell prisoner to the Iranians, and about 50,000 Iranian soldiers fell prisoner to the Iraqis. Iran announced that 50 towns and about 4,000 villages had been badly hit or totally destroyed. In addition, according to Iran, during the eight year war, 14,000 civilians were killed and about 1.25 million inhabitants turned into refugees.

The war was ruinous and sterile. Saddam Hussein failed to realize his goal of bringing down the fundamentalist regime in Iran, "liberating" the district of Khuzistan, and most of all, to secure free access to the Gulf. Khomeini failed in his hope to set up in the neighboring state, with the second largest Shi'i population after Iran; a similar Islamic regime to its own. In the course of the war, Iraq continued demanding that the other Arab states stand by it in its war against Iran, on the basis of the collective security alliance of 1950 (see ARAB LEAGUE), while presenting itself as the defender of the Eastern flank of the Arab homeland. However, this effort did not bear real fruit. Even on the declaratory level, most of the Arab states, and especially the monarchic Gulf states, were careful not to stand publicly against Iran. Only in November 1982 did the Arab summit conference in Fez adopt a resolution which expressed an undertaking "to defend all the Arab lands and to view any act of aggression against all the Arab region anywhere as tantamount to aggression against all the Arab countries."

At the Amman Summit Conference in November 1987—which came a month after the Iranian missile attack on Kuwait and several months after the bloody clashes between Iranian pilgrims to Mecca and Saudi security forces—it was agreed to denounce Iran; to call for the imposition of sanctions against it by the UN for its refusal to accept Security Council resolution 598, and to express solidarity and support for Iraq and Kuwait in face of the Iranian aggression.

From a practical point of view Iraq enjoyed substantial financial help from the Arab oil-producing Gulf states—Saudi Arabia and Kuwait—for whom the Iranian-Islamic danger was very tangible. Other Gulf monarchies, particularly the UAE and Oman, maintained friendly relations with Iran during the entire war. In the course of the war the Saudi-Kuwaiti assistance to Iraq amounted to about 40 billion dollars, mostly in the form of loans, which were never returned. Even though in terms of political resources (territory, population and economic resources), Iran enjoyed a vast advantage over Iraq. Given that it was forced to stand against the Iraqi attack at the peak of the Islamic revolution, as well as the arms embargo on it while Iraq enjoyed a regular supply of Western arms (and from 1987 even American financial aid), all explain the continuation of the war without a final decision at its end. While the US administration adopted a tacit policy of supporting Iraq's war effort, perceiving it as a bullwark against expansion of Shi'i radicalism into the Arab Penninsula which

would threaten the West oil interests, Washington also tried to come to terms with Iran. In January 1986 President Reagan authorized the sale of 4000 anti-tank tow missiles through Israel, as part of a secret deal which came to be known as the Iran-Contra Affair. The total worth of American-made arms sold to Iran through Israeli dealers amounted to 2380 million dollars. However, parallel attempts by the Americans to bring about a *rapprochement* with the Islamic regime in Tehran failed.

The end of the war did not bring the end of the conflict between the two states, or to the settlement of the disputes regarding the prisoners; the delineation of the boundary and the payment of compensation. (On the development of relations between the two countries after the war see IRAN). In fact, the end of the war with effectively no victory to either side, with Iraq's basic political anxieties, deprivation of a secure access to the Gulf, and staggering external debt, were to motivate Iraq's invasion of Kuwait two years later. It was only following the Iraqi invasion of Kuwait that Iraq unilaterally withdrew from the 920 sq. miles (2386 sq. km,) of occupied Iranian territory that it had held since the end of the war and accepted an exchange of prisoners of war. In February 1991 a UN observer force (UNIIMOG) formally announced that the military forces of the two countries had returned to the international borders.

IRAQ   Republic northeast of Arabia, the eastern part and largest state of the Fertile Crescent, ancient Mesopotamia formed by the Euphrates and Tigris Rivers. Iraq borders to the south with KUWAIT and SAUDI ARABIA; to the west with JORDAN and SYRIA; to the north with TURKEY; and to the east with IRAN. It has no direct outlet to the PERSIAN GULF (despite its 26 miles (42 km.) strip of Gulf shore) other than SHATT AL-ARAB, the joint waterway of the Euphrates and Tigris Rivers.

The population in the mid-1980s was estimated at 15–16 million About eighty percent of Iraq's population is ARAB. About twenty-five percent of the population are Arab SUNNI Muslims, residing in the upper Euphrates region northwest of Baghdad to the Syrian border and the upper Tigris region between Samarra and Mosul. They have traditionally been the politically dominant element of the country and the carriers of ARAB NATIONALISM. About fifty

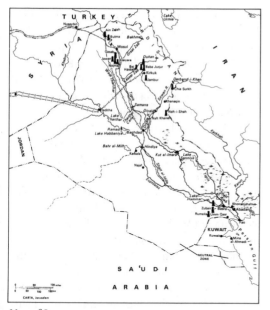

Map of Iraq

to fifty-five percent of the population are Arab Shi'i Muslims, inhabiting the southern and the central Baghdad. KURDS, non-Arab Sunni Muslims, comprise fifteen to twenty percent of the population, living in the mountains of the north and north-east, with large communities in the big cities. CHRISTIANS total at most four percent of the population; nearly all of them belong to Eastern churches. The majority, of them are UNIATE Catholic offshoots. An estimated break-down is: ASSYRIANS-Nestorians 50,000–60,000; Syrian JACOBITES 50,000–60,000; ARMENIANS 20,000; Uniate CHALDEANS 200,000–250,000; Syrian Catholics 75,000–100,000. There are also small groups of GREEK ORTHODOX, GREEK CATHOLICS, Armenian Catholics, Latin Catholics and PROTESTANTS. Other minorities are Turcmen (Sunni Muslims speaking a Turkish dialect), 250,000–300,000 of whom live in Kirkuk and along the border (but larger figures have also been given); YAZIDIS, numbering 25,000–50,000, mainly in Jabal Sinjar west of Mosul; Sabaeans-MANDAEANS, of whom about 25,000–35,000 live along the lower Tigris; and Jews, of whose ancient and large community—100,000–120,000 in the 1940s—a few hundred remain, all in Baghdad. There was, prior to the IRAN-IRAQ WAR of 1980, a Persian-speaking minority group—1.5–2% partly along the eastern border and mainly in the cities holy to Shi'i ISLAM (Najaf, Karbala) and in Baghdad.

Arab nomads (BEDOUIN) comprise approximately five percent of the population; but if semi-nomads at an advanced stage of settlement are taken into account, the percentage is far higher.

Iraq is a predominantly an agricultural country, drawing most of its water from the Tigris and, to a lesser extent, from the Euphrates, particularly from their annual floods, with traditional agriculture and irrigation. Swamps and salt wastes have come to cover large areas of formerly fertile land. However, over the last seventy to eighty years, much land has been reclaimed through a number of spectacular damming and irrigation projects and modern soil preservation methods. The main produce is subsistence crops: barley, wheat, rice and lentils. A vital cash crop is dates, of which Iraq is the largest exporter in the world. Tobacco and fruit are vital in the north, and cotton in the center.

Iraq's main source of wealth is its OIL, produced commercially since 1934. Iraqi oil production doubled between 1958 and 1968, from 731,000 barrels per day to 1.5 million; and more than doubled again by 1979, reaching 3.4 million barrels per day. However average production growth (six percent between 1965 and 1975) lagged far behind other Gulf oil producers (184 percent for Iran and 231 percent for Saudi Arabia). In 1972, the oil industry was nationalized and production began to dramatically increase, exceeding that of other Gulf countries. In 1979, with the decline of oil production in revolutionary Iran, Iraq became the second largest Gulf oil producer after Saudi Arabia (sixteen percent of the total Gulf production compared to forty-five percent by Saudi Arabia), with oil production of over 170 million tons, which in the mid-1980s declined to 50–70 million tons per annum. However, Iraq's oil industry was severely disrupted by its long struggle with Iraq Petroleum C ompany (IPC) in the 1960s, and its dependence on cross-national pipelines due to its lack of access to the open sea, made this industry vulnerable to political instability and disputes, primarily with Syria (see below). By 1980, Iraq had nine refineries with a total capacity of 300,000 barrels per day, which continued to develop. It reached a capacity of 400,000 barrels per day in 1984. By 1980, Iraq was also producing natural gas (11 million cubic meters a day). Oil production is the most important source of foreign currency and investment in social, economic, technological and military development. Mining and industry are still of some importance. Of the labor force, a large majority still live on agriculture, and about eight to ten percent are in government service, including the armed forces.

The country suffers from two main social problems—rapid urbanization without industrialization on a adequate scale, and the presence of an uprooted, under-employed and disgruntled intelligentsia. The Agrarian Reform Act of 1958 (see below) has been the basis for much useful work, and for the distribution of land among some 130,000 peasants; but it has not solved the basic problems of rural poverty, ignorance and exploitation. According to the Provisional Constitution of July 1970, Iraq is a "Sovereign People's Democratic Republic". The supreme body in the state is the Revolutionary Command Council (RCC) of a (maximum) of twelve members who are recruited from among the Regional (i.e., Iraqi) Command of the BAʿTH Party (the sole ruling party). In reality, the RCC sometimes has less than twelve members; in the mid-1980s there were nine. The chairman of the RCC is also President of the Republic and Supreme Commander of the Armed Forces. An elected National Assembly with legislative powers, is provided for by the Provisional Constitution, first established in 1980. In reality legislative powers remained within the RCC.

Political History

1. Pre-Independent Iraq (until 1932) At the beginning of the century, what is today known as Iraq was loosely covered by the three Ottoman provinces (*Vilayet*) of Mosul, Baghdad and Basra. Though "Turkish Arabia" (Mesopotamia) was backward even by Ottoman standards, modernization had by then began in

the shape of improved provincial and municipal administration (brought about by the governorship in Baghdad of Midhat Pasha, 1869–1872), a rudimentary school system based on the Western pattern (e.g., the Baghdad Law School, founded 1908). International competition, particularly with regard to communication projects (outstanding among which was the German-inspired Baghdad railway scheme), and the appropriation of oil rights among British, German and Dutch interests, accelerated that process. There were stirrings of Arab nationalism, which were not easily distinguishable from a striving for greater

local independence, represented, after the YOUNG TURKS' Revolution (1908), by a group of Sunni-Iraq officers in the Ottoman Army, and in Basra, by the Shiʿi Naqib Sayyid Talib ibn al-Sayyid Rajab. These movements, for all their historical significance, affected only a very small sector of even the urban population.

In November 1914 within a week of Turkey's entry into World War I, the British invaded Mesopotamia. The invasion was mounted from India, through the Persian Gulf, owing to the importance attributed to southern Mesopotamia as a vital link to India. Despite a heavy setback (the surrender of the Sixth Division under General Townshend at Kut al-Amara in (April 1916), a powerful army carried its offensive beyond Baghdad by March 1917 and reached the outskirts of Mosul at the time of the armistice. At the same time a civil administration was developed under the forceful direction of Sir Percy Z. Cox and his assistant and deputy, Lieutenant-Colonel (later Sir) Arnold T. Wilson.

In the SYKES-PICOT AGREEMENT, reflected the Allied Powers' interests and plans regarding the future division of the non-Turkish OTTOMAN EMPIRE among them, (see BRITAIN.) This ensured direct control of most of Mesopotamia, with its northern part of Mosul designated to be a zone of French influence. (Following the war FRANCE ceded this area to Britain, but remained until 1926, a disputed area due to Turkey's claim). Similarly, in MCMAHON-HUSSEIN CORRESPONDENCE, the British party emphasized its interest in Iraq in the form of indirect control, suggesting that the Arab rule there would be assisted by British advisors. Declarations made by the British Army and the Allies raised the expectation that Iraq would be granted independence. But Wilson, by then Acting Civil Commissioner of Mesopotamia, with the government of India behind him, believed in the imperial necessity of direct British rule and was convinced that Iraq's population was incapable of full self-government. Discontent grew throughout the country, uniting the Shiʿi religious leaders, resentful of Christian domination, with the Sunni intelligentsia. They were disappointed as they hoped to gain independence quickly. The tribal sheikhs, too, were traditionally hostile to established authority, though Wilson and his collaborators had built better relations with them than they had with other elite groups. In June 1920 a major insurrection broke out in the middle-Euphrates and spread quickly over large parts of the country, shaking the hold of the military occupation. Though hardly a "Great Revolution", this movement clinched the argument in London for a radical departure toward self-government. Wilson left, and with Cox's return as "High Commissioner" Iraq was constituted as a nominally independent country, "guided" by Britain under a MANDATE conferred by the League of Nations (San Remo, 1920, finalized in 1922). Prince FEISAL, son of Sharif HUSSEIN Ibn Ali of Mecca, who in July 1920 had been expelled by the French from Syria, was appointed King of Iraq in August 1921, as a result of British pressure and following a dubious plebiscite.

This arrangement—a Mandate under the League of Nations, and "a sovereign state, independent and free" (the Organic Law of 1925), linked with Britain under the Anglo-Iraqi Treaty of 1922, on the other hand—was resented by the growing Iraqi educated, urban, middle class and marred the political atmosphere. But there were no more violent disturbances, except in the north (see below). A sound administration, guided by British "advisors", a national army (from 1920–1921), a government, a constitution and a Parliament (1925) were set up. Economic progress and the development of education, starved of funds, were comparatively slow. But the newly organized Iraqi Petroleum Company struck oil in large quantities near Kirkuk in 1927. The nationalists continued pressing for a new treaty to give Iraq complete independenence. Negotiations, enhanced by optimism generated by public security, the good will created by Britain's success in retaining the Mosul area for Iraq against Turkish aspirations (1925–1926), and the philosophy of the Labor government in office in Britain since 1929, culmination in the Anglo-Iraq Treaty of 1930 which provided for the termination of the Mandate upon Iraq's admission to the League of Nations. Important strategic, economic and diplomatic privileges were reserved for Britain. (The treaty was therefore opposed by the extreme nationalists). On Britain's strong recommendation, Iraq was admitted to the League and became independent on 3 October 1932.

The new Iraqi administration was shaped by King Feisal and the group of Iraqi officers who had accompanied him through the ARAB REVOLT and the short-lived Arab administration in Syria (1918–1920). From the outset, the HASHEMITE nucleus of power in Baghdad suffered from a deep sense of insecurity on both domestic and regional levels. Being a foreigner to the Sunni-Arab traditional elite, the Hashemite regime endeavored to entrench itself socially and politically in that elite as its main power base, and to co-opt modern Shi'i elements into its ranks. On the regional level, threatened by mighty Iran (Persia) in the east, hostile Saudi dynasty in the south, and strong nationalist Turkish state in the north, claiming the Mosul area (until 1926), strove to incorporate Iraq into the other parts of the Fertile Crescent as a way to secure the promotion of the national security of the newly established state. Given the immense difficulties of forming and consolidating the Iraqi state, the Hashemite administration adopted a concept which portrayed Iraq as Prussia of the Arab world, whose *raison d' tre* was to unify the Arab countries under its leadership. While adopting an anti-British discourse in its approach to the Shi'i tribes of the lower Euphrates as a means to enlisting their support, the Hashemite ruling elite embarked on a long-term strategy of socializing the idea of Arab nationalism into the Iraqi youth through the official system of education. Teachers and scholars from Syria, Palestine and LEBANON were brought in to help implement this mission—most famous of them was the Syrian Sati al-Husri, a leading ideologist of the Pan-Arab nationalist doctrine in the interwar years. In terms of foreign policy, even before independence, Feisal made various efforts to advance his aspiration to lead a regional unity of the Fertile Crescent, to include Iraq and historic Syria, encompassing Lebanon, Palestine and Transjordan. In 1929, in the wake of the Wailing Wall Jewish-Arab riots in Palestine, Feisal proposed to Britain his scheme of establishing such a union, willing to offer autonomy to the Jews of Palestine, which would provide a solution to the British predicament of the Palestine question. Within Iraq, and from the early 1930s increasingly in Palestine, Syria and Lebanon as well, Feisal's Arab nationalist vision and political influence echoed among the new Arab middle class of young urban, professionals. This resulted in the foundation of the Istiqlal Party, with several branches out of Iraq. Although this network of Arab nationalists sustained a blow with the death of Feisal in 1933, their links and acquaintances were instrumental in bringing Iraq into closer interest in the politics of Palestine and Syria.

2. Independent Iraq (1932–)

Domestic Affairs The first decade of Iraqi independence was marked with political instability, military coups, and violent clashes between the government and parts of its population. With British prestige and responsibility removed from the domestic sphere the politicians were unable to rule the country for long without losing credibility. King Feisal was losing control and died in September 1933. His son and successor Ghazi was young, rash and unstable and, though not unpopular, had no real influence in the face of the increased political power of army officers. Shortly after Feisal passed away, the long-standing quarrel between the Baghdad authorities and the Assyrian (Nestorian) community came to a head. Displaced during World War I from their homes to the north of the later Iraq frontier and protected by the British Mandate, in 1933 the government embarked on a premeditated slaughter of hundreds of Assyrian men, women and children at the hands of the Iraq Army. Disturbances throughout the Shi'i south and center, always smoldering and often erupting into uprisings, encouraged or bloodily suppressed by the rival factions in Baghdad, assumed a far greater political importance. By the end of 1936 the first of the many military coup which have since shaken Iraq took place, with General Bakr Sidqi, at first supported by a group of leftist intellectuals (the al-*Ahali* group), was himself overthrown and assassinated in 1937; but he set a pattern of military dictatorship, thinly veiled by civilian governments, with the Organic Law nominally preserved, which lasted until 1941. King Ghazi's death in April 1939 in a car accident and the succession by his infant son Feisal II under the regency of his pale, pro-British uncle ABDEL ILAH only worsened the political weakness of the Hashemite ruling elite. From the late 1930s, growing pro-German sentiment prevailed in the Iraqi military and intelligentsia, combined with intensified agitation against Britain for its role in repressing the Palestinian Arab revolt. The outbreak of World War II and Britain's claim that Iraq declare war against the Axis Powers, increased the tension between the Hashemite oligarchy and the nationalist circles, especially with the then ruling gulf four colonels (called the "Golden Square"). This was the backdrop of secret Iraqi contacts with the German government and attempts to coordinate an anti-British rebellion to be support-ed by Germany, when its forces take over the Balkans and connect to Iraq by air through Syria, then under Vischi France. In the spring of 1941, Iraq slithered into a national rebellion against British influence—represented primarily by its Hashemite proteges and privileged position in Iraq, which, according to the Treaty of 1930, allowed Britain to use two Iraqi airfields and communications at time of war. The MUFTI of JERUSALEM, al-Hajj Amin al-HUSSEINI, then in political exile in Iraq where he became very popular, and in close acquaintance with the leading figure of the "Golden Square," Salah al-Din al-Sabbagh, played a leading role in inspiring the rebellion and determining its timing.

The rebellion—with Prime Minister Rashid Ali al-Kilani as little more than figurehead, threatened Britain from the rear at a most critical time during World War II. It was repressed by Britain in a brief campaign. This ended in May with the routing of the Iraq Army, and the flight abroad of the "Golden Square," Rashid Ali and the Mufti al-Husseini-some of them to Iran and Turkey, and from there to Italy and Germany. During the War, a pogrom (*farhud*) was conducted against the Jewish community in Baghdad, reflecting the growing perception of the Iraqi public, identifying this ancient Jewish community with ZIONISM and British imperialism. After May 1941, Iraq was on the Allied side, with the cooperation of the Regent and senior Hashemite politicians-who had fled from Iraq during the rebellion and could now return to their positions. This was predominated by Nuri al-SA'ID. The Iraqi Rebellion of 1941, in which a small force of Transjordan's Arab Legion took part (as well as elements from the Jewish *Yishuv*), was a turning point in the modern history of the Hashemite dynasty, staining its image irreparably as a stooge of British imperialism and enemy of Arab nationalism. With the repression of the rebellion, Iraq came again under British occupation (until 1946); the Iraqi Army was reorganized and purged of those suspect of having participated in the rebellion; political activity was banned.

In the post-war period, times of political liberalism alternated with strict police rule, comparative quiet with violent disturbances. The weakness of the regime and distance from the populace was repeatedly manifested in the regime' inability to cope with the growing political pressures by radical nationalist and Leftist parties. One way in which the

Hashemite regime tried to cope with the growing radicalization of Iraq's political community, was through adopting extreme positions on the Arab-Jewish conflict over Palestine, which had become increasingly part of the official Iraqi agenda. Thus, when a new draft treaty was signed with Britain at Portsmouth in January 1948, revising the 1930 Treaty, the government was forced to suspend it (and finally abolish it), after fierce demonstrations that brought the country to the verge of chaos.

Although Iraq ended its involvement in the Palestine war of 1948 without being defeated and with no armistice agreement with ISRAEL—as was the case with the Arab states bordering Israel (see below), the establishment of the State of Israel and the prolonged Arab-Israeli War, became a matter of domestic Iraqi politics, directly affecting the Iraqi Jewish community (numbering some 110,000–125,000). In the course of 1948–1949, growing anti-Jewish agitation by Iraqi nationalists and secret Zionist activity within the Jewish community aimed at convincing its members to emigrate to Israel, led to a tacit agreement of the Iraqi government to let the Jews leave the country after giving up their citizenship and property. Domestic—economic and political—considerations motivated the Iraqi decision to allow its Jewish citizens to leave, striving to gain from the abandoned property and mitigation of militant domestic pressures against this community which had put the government in a quandary. During 1950–1951, the decisive majority of the Jewish community left Iraq to Israel-mostly by air—in an organized operation, ending one of the most ancient Jewish communities in the Middle East.

The Palestine War was a blow to the Iraqi economy. It led the closure of the Kirkuk-Haifa pipeline of the Iraqi Petroleum Company, disconnection from the Haifa oil refineries and port, which had served as the main route for Iraqi import and export via railway. Steadily rising oil royalties, especially since the half-and-half profit-sharing principle was adopted in 1952, produced a surplus that was, on the whole, sensibly invested in development projects. Yet, the absence of import and distribution policies, unbridled speculation and an overall lack of social awareness on the part of the authorities more than once brought the masses close to famine.

Feisal II came of age in 1953 and assumed his reign, and Abdel Ilah became Crown Prince. In Sep-

tember 1954 Nuri al-Sa'id was called to lead the government, after the freest elections Iraq was ever to know had returned a sizable opposition to Parliament. Nuri in practice prohibited all party activity and, for the next four years, was the real ruler of Iraq, whether in office or out of it. He determined the state's policy, which meant externally close collaboration with the Britain, while domestically conducting a harsh policy of oppressing the radical leftist opposition, namely the communists, and restricting political opposition and freedom of speech, though in retrospect his rule may look less repressive than it did then. Economic development plans inaugurated in the early 1950s were pursued vigorously, but little thought was given to social progress or the alleviation of immediate miseries. The army, well cared for and considered a bastion of the existing order, was kept strictly away from politics. The regime was unpopular with the politically articulate forces of the kingdom—whether Arab nationalists, liberals, communists, traditionalists or army officers.

Foreign Affairs Iraqi foreign policy during the first decade of independence focused on the regional arena, aiming to promote the Hashemite aspired unity of the Fertile Crescent, particularly Syria. This scheme had been pursued intermittently since the late 1920s, unenthusiastically and ineptly. However, with the eruption of the ARAB REVOLT in Palestine in April 1936, the Iraqi government, under strong influence of the military, unofficially organized and equipped a military force under the command of Fawzi al-Qawuqji, which arrived in June 1936 to Palestine and operated as a volunteer force in the area north of Jerusalem. Qawuqji's attempt to establish himself as the leader of the rebellion was resented by the Higher Arab Committee's President, al-Hajj Amin al-Husseini, and the force was coerced by the British Army to withdraw from Palestine after a few months. Parallel to this effort, Foreign Minister Nuri al-Sa'id arrived in Palestine, apparently with British encouragement, to mediate an end to the Arab revolt and general strike. King Ghazi was one of the signatories on the October 1936 joint call of Arab monarchs to the Arabs of Palestine—inspired by Britain—to put an end to their strike and violence. The Hashemite-Iraqi efforts on behalf of the Palestinian Arabs intensified along with the growing anti-British propaganda in Iraq, and the stirred political atmosphere due to Britain's harsh repression of the Arab revolt in Palestine. Thus, the Hashemite government tried to convince the Mufti al-Hajj Amin al-Husseini, to accept Britain's "White Paper" of May 1939—the most favorable British policy toward the PALESTINE ARABS since the beginning of the Mandate. However, Britain's new policy was rejected, and the Palestine question remained an explosive matter in Iraq's domestic politics, due to its weakening effect on the government, so identified with Britain.

In January 1943 Nuri al-Sa'id submitted his "Blue Paper," to the British government. This proposed the establishment of a regional union of Iraq with Syria, Lebanon, Palestine and Transjordan, with autonomy to the Christians of Lebanon and the Jews of Palestine. The proposal, which followed Britain's favorite proclamations regarding ARAB UNITY, triggered EGYPT's response in the form of opening a series of official consultations with representatives of the semi-independent Arab states over the issue of Arab unity, under the conduct of Prime Minister Nahhas Pasha. These consultations underlined the objection of most Arab states to the Iraqi scheme of Arab Federation, enabling Egypt to establish itself as a leading regional power and shape a loose framework of "Arab Unity" in the form of the League of Arab States, founded in March 1945. The ARAB LEAGUE thus became an organization whose main goals were defined in terms of preserving the political status quo, tacitly defying the Hashemite revisionist aspirations. Yet while Iraq ostensibly acquiesced in the final shape of the Arab League, its regional policies came to be marked by continuous effort to lead the collective Arab policy on Palestine, which, from the outset, topped the League's agenda, by adopting ultra-extremist policies, which were also to serve the regimes domestic needs *vis-a-vis* the militant nationalist opposition. It was in this context that Iraq became involved in separately financing Palestinian ventures—led by Musa al-Alami, a prominent Palestinian Arab, close to the Husseinis—of rescuing Arab land from being sold to Jews, as well as conducting propaganda on the international level on behalf of the Palestinian Arabs, apparently aiming at fostering him as an agent of Iraqi influence. Iraq was the main power behind the secret decisions made by the Arab League's Political Committee in its meeting at Bludan, Syria, in June 1946, to threaten Britain and the UNITED STATES with a reconsider-

ation of the Arab states' relations with them and particularly with taking economic sanction—namely, the use of the oil weapon—against these powers. The Iraqi initiative was nothing but a bluff, deriving from domestic militant pressures, and a desire to confuse Saudi Arabia, knowing that it could not afford such a step, which would exempt Iraq from implementing its own proposal. Bearing in mind the Mufti's role in the 1941 Rebellion, the Hashemite government of Iraq adopted a policy of objecting any attempt by the Arab League to give the Mufti (who, in June 1946 returned to the Middle East from Europe and assumed the official leadership of the Palestinian Arabs) funds, arms or effective authority in Palestine.

When an Arab-Jewish Civil War erupted in Palestine following the UN decision to partition the country and the establishment of Arab and Jewish states, Iraq sent at least two battalions of volunteers—composed mostly of former officers and soldiers who had been dismissed from the army after the 1941 rebellion-as part of the collective Arab effort on behalf of the Palestinian Arabs represented in the "Army of Deliverance" (see ARAB-ISRAEL CONFLICT). Iraq's role in the Palestine War culminated in its official participation in the joint Arab invasion of Palestine on 15 May. Although the Iraqi contingent force failed to cross the River Jordan at Gesher, it later entered through the Jordanian-controlled area into the "Triangle" of Nablus-Jenin-Tulkarm, where it entrenched and played mainly a defensive role. The Iraqi force, which had been initially small, was constantly reinforced until it became the largest Arab force operating in Palestine (over a division, representing an appreciable part of the Iraqi Army. Iraq ended its involvement in the Palestine War in April 1949, refusing to negotiate a cease-fire with Israel, preferring, instead, to cede the territory under its control to Jordan.

In the fall of 1949, Iraq renewed its efforts to establish unity with Syria, following the coup led by Sami Hinnawi, and advent to power of the People's Party, a long-lived advocate of such unity. However, the ongoing instability of Syrian politics, and Egyptian opposition, foiled these attempts. Thus, when Iraq explained its wish to forge unity with Syria on grounds of Syria's security needs in facing the Israeli threat, Egypt began propagating its idea of signing a collective Arab security pact, which would exempt the Iraqi-Syrian scheme of unity. The Iraqi efforts to promote unity with Syria continued throughout the mid-1950s, by playing an intruding role in Syrian domestic politics through Baghdad's loyalists, but in vain. If anything, the Iraqi interference aggravated domestic instability and accelerated the rise of further radicalized forces to power, primarily the *Ba'th* Party and the Communists.

In the mid-1950s, Iraqi-Egyptian relations, marked by competition and mutual loath, deteriorated to a crisis due to their contradictory perceptions regarding the Western schemes of forging a Middle East security alliance that would provide for their cooperation and use of their territories by the Western powers in case of war with the Soviets. Following almost a decade of failures to attain that goal (see MIDDLE EAST DEFENSE ORGANIZATION), in October 1954, Iraq and Turkey announced their intention to sign a treaty of defense. Inspired by Britain, the announcement aroused concern and resistance of Egypt, now led by ABDEL NASSER, in the name of collective Arab security, but effectively representing Egypt's desire to retain its leading role in the Arab region and lead a neutralist line of refraining from formally joining any of the rival global blocks. Iraq, however, rejected all Egyptian misgivings and efforts to dissuade it from the intended pact. In February 1955 Iraq and Turkey signed a Defense Treaty which came to be known as the Baghdad Pact, to which Britain and Pakistan and Iran later joined. The common Anglo-Iraqi membership also provided the basis for a new Anglo-Iraq Treaty, April 1955, which abolished most of Britain's remaining privileges, turning its air bases into joint Anglo-Iraqi bases under the Baghdad Pact. The Pact became a target of fierce Egyptian propaganda attacks and political subversion in an effort to contain it and prevent other Arab states from joining it, primarily Jordan (which announced its wish to join the Pact), and Syria, where it became a central issue in the internal struggle for power. The new Pact was portrayed by its adversaries as a separatist move, harmful to Arab unity and national liberation, facilitating the prolongation of imperialist presence on Arab lands. The Iraqi-Egyptian struggle for regional leadership was the watermark of Arab politics at large in the mid-1950s, encompassing the domestic and regional arenas alike, in which Nasser scored a decisive success by adopting strong anti-Western line of rhetoric, signing a

first arms deal with Czechoslovakia in May 1955, and establishing himself as the hero of Arab nationalism. Nuri al-Sa'id's ambiguous stand during the 1956 Suez crisis exacerbated Egyptian and nationalist antagonism. The Syro-Egyptian merger and the establishment of the UNITED ARAB REPUBLIC (UAR) in February 1958 was seen as a threat to Iraq and a federation with Jordan was hastily set up that same month, as a counter move; but it remained unpopular and its implementation was cut short by the fall of the monarchy, in July 1958.

3. Revolutionary Iraq (1958–1979)

Domestic Affairs The Revolution of 14 July 1958 was prepared by a conspiratorial group of "Free Officers" who had come together during the previous four or five years. The leaders of the coup were Brigadier General Abdel Karim QASSEM, a Baghdad-born Sunni of lower middle class origin, and Colonel Abdel Salam Aref. The takeover was quick, full of bloodshed, and extremely brutal toward the Hashemite family and the ruling oligarchy. Aref commanded the units which occupied the capital and executed King Feisal II and Crown Prince Abdel Ilah at their residence. Nuri Said was killed by the mob the following day while trying to escape abroad.

Qassem proclaimed a "Popular Republic". He was Commander-in-Chief, Prime Minister and Acting Minister of Defense. Aref became his deputy. No officers' council was established, as the "Free Officers" had planned. The Presidency of the Republic was vested in a "Sovereignty Council" of three respected but powerless individuals. The Cabinet appointed included leading personalities representing all the shades of opposition to the defunct regime—a near-communist, liberal socialists, Arab nationalists of various hues and Kurds (though not members of the rebellious KDP—see below). However, Qassem and the officers close to him were the real rulers.

The Revolution was received throughout Iraq enthusiastically The UAR and its Arab allies, as well as the Communist Block, recognized the new regime with alacrity. The West followed within less than a month; its acceptance was made easier by soothing statements from Qassem which included promises not to harm their rights with existing oil concessions. Iraq even refrained for the time being from leaving the Baghdad Pact, though its membership was henceforth a mere formality (it was formally abrogated in March 1959). But the atmosphere of general rejoicing and harmony did not last. Nasserists and adherents of the *Ba'th* group soon discovered that Qassem was determined to guard Iraq's full independence *vis-a-vis* Nasser and trend of Pan-Arab unity, and started undermining his position, with Qassem's deputy, Aref, as the leader of the ensuing opposition to the new regime. Qassem's refusal to join the UAR challenged Nasser's leadership also because the new Iraqi regime represented no less revolutionary approach to the ancient regime, with the shifting policies it entailed both domestically and in foreign affairs, shattering the commonly accepted premise among Arab nationalists, that mere elimination of the "Reaction" by the "Progressive" forces would necessarily augment the Pan-Arab trend. The growing alienation with *Ba'th* and Nasserists Arab nationalists, on the one hand, and Nasserist propaganda campaign and subversive attempts, on the other, pushed Qassem into an alliance with the Communists who, taught by the Syrian example, bitterly opposed Iraq falling under Nasser's domination. The unprecedented participation of Communists and Kurds in the new regime, accorded Qassem the derogative term—from an Arab nationalist viewpoint—*shu'ubi* (cosmopolitan). An atmosphere of intrigue and violence speedily spread. In September 1958 Aref was stripped of his offices and forced into exile as Ambassador at Bonn (a post he never took up). When he returned from Europe against Qassem's order, he was arrested on charges of attempting to assassinate Qassem, and in February 1959, was sentenced to death in a "People's Court" presided over by Qassem's cousin Mahdawi, but reprieved by Qassem.

As Communist influence and self-assurance developed, various nationalist bodies took to conspiracies—including a plot by a group around Rashid Ali (who had returned to Iraq in September 1958, hoping to join or take over the leadership of the new regime) in December 1958. There was an uprising of Arab nationalist and anti communist officers led by Colonel Shawaf, chiefly in the Mosul area, in March 1959, and a *Ba'thist* attempt on Qassem's life in October 1959. The Iraqi regime blamed Nasser's UAR for all these foiled conspiracies, especially for the Mosul uprising, which had been repressed with heavy bloodshed and Communist help. By the spring of 1959 all Arab-nationalist activity was vir-

tually paralyzed, and a Communist take-over appeared possible. However, Qassem outdid the Communists, threatening them with suppression by the army after a Communist-led massacre at Kirkuk in July 1959, and at the same time promising the legalization of political parties, including theirs, due in the beginning of 1960. The Communists shied away from an open contest with Qassem, apparently at the behest of the USSR which cultivated close relations with the Iraqi revolutionary regime, and also in the belief that restraint would bring them easy victory through their superior clandestine and hierarchic organization. From then on their fortunes waned. The authorities increasingly harassed them and street terror started to turn against them. In January 1960 Qassem issued a decree legalizing political parties but it was hedged with safeguards enabling the regime to interfere with their activities whenever it so chose. The Communists in particular were cheated of their expectations when Qassem licensed a dissident Communist with virtually no following as chairman of a legal "Iraq Communist Party". The Communists, though very bitter, acquiesced. The licensed parties quickly withered away under the unfriendliness and obstruction of the regime. During this, Qassem made enemies of the liberal-socialist National Democratic Party, hitherto generally supportive to him. By 1961 the Cabinet had lost practically all its political members, who had been replaced by technicians or proteges of Qassem. Measures of social reform that were passed immediately after the revolution (the most important being the Agrarian Reform Law of September 1958) ended as the political atmosphere darkened. There was no internal political activity during the last two years of the Qassem period. These years are noteworthy for the Kurdish rising, Qassem's claim to Kuwait and his quarrels with the oil companies (see below).

The Kurdish north had remained largely unassimilated to the Iraqi state throughout its existence. Since World War I, the British occupation authorities had promised administrative decentralization and cultural self-expression, and when these promises were not fulfilled, the Kurds resisted, led in the 1920s by the eccentric personality of Sheikh Mahmud Barzenchi (Barzinji) and from the early 1930s by the heads of the BARZANI tribe, Sheikh Ahmad and his younger brother Mulla Mustafa. For this resistance, the Kurdish republic of MAHABAD, on the Iranian side of the border, Barzani's return in 1958, the Kurds' disappointment and their rebellion from September 1961—see KURDS.

On 8–9 February 1963, Qassem was overthrown by a coup of the clandestine *Ba'th* group and sympathizers from among army officers. For nine months civilian leaders of the *Ba'th* tried to rule Iraq, with Abdel Salam Aref as nominal President of the Republic. Their failures were conspicuous, attesting to administrative inexperience and factional disputes, the failure of negotiations with the Kurds and defeats in battles against them in the north, the antagonism aroused by the unbridled violence of the *Ba'th* militia, and the jealousy of the military, as well as the hostility of Nasser (apart from the short period following the agreement on a federal union of Egypt, Syria and Iraq, concluded in April 1963). On 18 November 1963 the officers around Aref brushed the *Ba'th* government aside, forcibly broke up its militia, and established Aref and themselves as rulers (for nearly five years). When Aref was killed in an air crash in April 1966, he was followed as President by his elder brother, General Abdel Rahman Aref.

The post-Qassem period under the Aref brothers was one of domestic restlessness and unresolved difficulties. For some months in 1965–1966 an attempt was made to reintroduce a semblance of civilian government with Abdel Rahman al-Bazzaz as Prime Minister, but he was forced out of office by the jealous military. A settlement with the Kurds which he had reached in 1966 was tacitly abandoned and the Kurdish Rebellion flared up again in 1968. The Tripartite Union Agreement signed with Syria and Egypt in April 1963, ended an Iraq-Egyptian "Union" agreement of 1964 was never implemented, except for some partial measures (it was formally abrogated in 1968, after the change of regime). Far-reaching nationalization decrees were published but not implemented. An ARAB SOCIALIST UNION on the Egyptian pattern was founded as a single party, but never became firmly established. An end to the constitutional "transition period", a term for the resumption of some form of representative government, was fixed, and put off. In 1966 the Nasserist Brigadier General Aref Abdel Razzaq staged an abortive coup attempt. An agreement with the oil company was initialled, but remained unratified in view of nationalist and "progressive" objection.

In July 1968 the regime was toppled by a new coup staged by a coalition of the *Ba'th* and a group of army officers led by Colonel Abdel Razzaq Na'if. The latter was made Prime Minister, and the *Ba'th* leader General Ahmad Hassan al-Bakr became President. However, within two weeks the *Ba'th* ousted its non-*Ba'th* allies and established an exclusively *Ba'th* regime (Colonel Na'if was assassinated in exile, in 1978.) Another alleged coup attempt by General Aref Abdel Razzaq failed in October. The new *Ba'th* regime, headed by a "Revolutionary Council", systematically purged the army and all political and administrative bodies, brutally eliminating all rival groups—except for "Socialist-Unionist" factions prepared to accept the unquestioned leadership of the *Ba'th*; with such factions it established a united "Progressive and Patriotic National Front" in 1973. This Front included Kurdish factions prepared to collaborate, and the Communists (who were already de facto represented in the government from 1972). But the collaboration between the *Ba'th* and the Communists, always split into rival factions, did not last. In 1978–1979 the Communists withdrew from the United Front and went underground, sustaining brutal repression by the regime.

Shortly after taking over, the *Ba'th* regime was confronted with intensified Kurdish rebellion, increasingly supported by Iran—including direct involvement of Iranian units in the fighting-and secret ties with Israel. In 1969 the rebellion turned into a full-scale war with the government, threatening to paralyze Iraq's oil production. In March 1970, the government reluctantly concluded an agreement with Barazani. The agreement, which was negotiated by Saddam HUSSEIN, provided—for the first time-for Kurdish autonomy in the northern region; proportional representation in the government and equitable sharing of the national oil revenues, recognition of the Kurdish language as equal to Arabic; and the appointment of a Kurdish Vice President. The implementation of the agreement was to be delayed for four years. From the viewpoint of the government the agreement-disputed on both Kurdish and ruling *Ba'th* Party was meant to gain time for stabilizing the new regime, especially in view of the reopening of the Shatt al-Arab dispute with Iran. To make Kurdish autonomy more acceptable to Iraqi public opinion, it was described as part of a general decentralization for all provinces, and a measure of cultural autonomy was proclaimed for the Chaldeans, the Assyrians and the Turcmen. Within the next two years relations between the government and Barazani's KDP deteriorated again: Baghdad attempted to isolate the Kurds by forging closer links with Moscow and pressuring the Communists to join the National Front, and to assassinate Barazani. In 1974, the rebellion was renewed in full scale. (For the breakdown of the agreement, Iraq's unilateral inauguration of a semi-autonomous Kurdish Region in 1974, the resumption of the Kurdish rebellion, its defeat in 1975, and its re-eruption in the late 1970s— see KURDS).

The post-1968 Ba'th regime, not content with eliminating all rival groups and establishing the complete domination of its party apparatus, was embroiled for over ten years in a near-constant intra-Ba'th factional and personal wrangle and incessant purges. A "leftist", pro-Syrian faction headed by Ali Saleh al-Sa'adi, had been purged and expelled in 1963. After 1968, Saddam Hussein (al-Tikriti) gradually emerged as the strong man, dominating the party's militia and secret services. From November 1969 he became Deputy Chairman of the Revolutionary Council. In this capacity he systematically eliminated all his rivals. In January 1969, Abdel Karim Nasrat of the leftist faction, a leader of the Ba'th coup of 1963, was murdered. In 1970 Saddam Hussein ousted Vice-President Hardan Abdel Ghaffar (al-Tikriti) —later assassinated in 1971, and in that year he got rid of Vice President Saleh Mahdi Ammash and Foreign Minister Abdel Karim Sheikhli (assassinated in 1980). In 1973 he suppressed a coup by Nazem al-Kazzar, the head of the security services, and had him executed (though he was widely reported to have instigated the coup himself. During the coup Defense Minister Hammad Shihab was killed. With President Bakr ailing, during the early 1970s Saddam Hussein became the de facto ruler of Iraq. An agreement was negotiated with the KDP and bringing the Kurdish rebellion to an end. The 1975 Algeirs' agreement with the Shah of Iran was signed, ending a long dispute over the Shatt al-Arab and putting an end to the latter's support of the Kurdish rebellion, causing its collapse. Al-Bakr's strategy of conciliating SHI'A dissidents inspired by the Islamic Revolution in neighboring Iran was overruled. Saddam Hussein completed his take-over in July 1979 by compelling Bakr to resign, after discovering that the latter had sent Syria's President Asad a secret message insti-

gating him to enter unity negotiations with Iraq resigned (or compelled to resign) and Saddam Hussein became President, Prime Minister, Chairman of the Revolutionary Council and Secretary-General of the Ba'th Party.

Foreign Affairs The Qassem regime's domestic isolation was matched in foreign affairs. On the regional level, the dispute and rivalry with Nasser overshadowed Iraq's stature in the Arab arena, while Iraq's withdrawal from the Baghdad Pact and shift toward the Soviet Union as a strategic ally alienated neighboring Turkey and Iran, leading to a declining cooperation of these states with Iraq regarding the Kurds.

On the inter-Arab level, the Nasser-Qassem mutual propaganda attacks, which by early 1959 had assumed strict ad-hominem abuses, and continuous subversion by Nasserist agents, determined a state of constant crisis between the two states, focusing on regional Arab issues of ideological significance, such as Pan-Arab unity and the Palestinian cause. In March 1959, Nasser called for the establishment of a "Palestinian Entity," namely, a political expression of the Palestinian national rights and cause of usurped land. This aggravated the Nasser-Qassem competition, turning it into a propaganda race for championing the Palestinian Entity idea increasingly as a matter of national liberation and no more as a mere refugee problem. Yet, while Nasser adhered to his idea of a political expression of Palestinian identity, Qassem, with no common border with Israel or any significant Palestinian population, called to turn the WEST BANK and GAZA STRIP into a "Palestinian Republic" to serve as a basis for an armed struggle against Israel. Iraq also followed the Egyptian example (1957) of establishing the Ein Jalout Brigade based on Palestinian refugees from the Gaza Strip, as a nucleus of the "Palestine Liberation Army," and in 1960 created the "Qadesiyya" brigade-within the Iraqi army.

Under Qassem, relations with Iran deteriorated rapidly. In September 1959 Iran questioned the validity of the 1937 Agreement on Shatt al-Arab, which had drawn the border at the low-water mark on the Iranian side and given Iraq control of the shipping channel. Qassem reacted by nullifying the agreement altogether, in December of that year, and claiming further sovereignty over the anchorage area around Abadan, the main Iranian harbor on the waterway. Iran responded by demanding the border be placed in the center of the waterway along the entire channel. The renewed dispute led to some violent incidents in early 1961, and the cease of shipping until April, when the two governments agreed to negotiate a settlement. Parallel to the Shatt al-Arab issue, Iraq aggravated Iran's concerns by undertaking to represent Arab interests in the Gulf, raising claims over the Arab-inhabited area of Khusistan (termed Arabistan by Iraq), and renaming the Persian Gulf the Arab Gulf.

The KUWAIT crisis erupted when Qassem publicly claimed the principality as a former district of the Basra province (*vilayet*) under Ottoman rule, after Britain had granted it independence in June 1961. Although Iraqi politicians had been claiming this since the mid-1930s, Qassem's move met with strong opposition from all other Arab states, primarily the UAR. Responding to the Iraqi claim, Britain rushed to return some of its forces to Kuwait to protect its independence, and the Arab League created an all-Arab force which was dispatched to Kuwait to defend it (see KUWAIT). Qassem, however, made no move to enforce his claim, and a stalemate ensued which caused him much ridicule at home and abroad. His successors recognized Kuwait's independence in 1963, but in 1990, Iraq renewed its claim for Kuwait, this time after taking it through force.

Relations with the Soviet Union under Qassem developed slowly. Immediately after the revolution, the Soviet Union was allowed to reopen its embassy in Baghdad. Qassem's alignment with the Communists led to the latter's pressure toward closer ties with the Soviet Union. In March 1959 Qassem announced Iraq's withdrawal from the Baghdad Pact, signing an extensive economic agreement with the Soviets. This provided Iraq with a loan—worth 48 million Iraqi Dinars—for the development of industrial projects, which was augmented by another 15.8 million Iraqi Dinars a year later, as well as with technicians to help the Iraqi effort of industrialization. This was followed by cultural and tourism exchanges and massive arms supplies which led to the modernization of the Iraqi armed forces, effectively linking the Iraqi army to the Soviet Union.

Relations with the Soviet Union continued to strengthen under the *Ba'th* regime. Agreements on economic cooperation, arms supplies, and technical aid, included the accords of 1969 which provided for Soviet aid and participation in the development of Iraq's oil. In April 1972 Iraq signed a Treaty of Friendship and Cooperation with the USSR; several visits were exchanged between the heads of the two states, and though relations were not completely free of crises and dissent, Iraq became one of the Soviet Union's two major allies in the Middle East. In 1975 Iraq also joined COMECON, the Soviet Bloc's economic alliance, as an associate member.

Qassem's dispute with the oil companies, the IPC and its subsidiaries, broke out in 1960 over the demand for new contracts assuring Iraq of significantly increased benefits. It led in December 1961 to "Law No. 80" which limited the companies' concession to about one percent of their former area (areas which were actually producing were not affected), resulting in alienated relations between Iraq and the Western powers. Relations with the US and Britain were severed in 1967, along with a collective Arab decision to this effect (relations with the US were resumed only in 1984.) Relations with Britain were more precarious; severed in 1961, against the backdrop of the Kuwait crisis, they were resumed in 1968, broken again in 1971 (due to Britain's inability to prevent the seizure by Iran of the Persian Gulf islands of the UAE), and resumed in 1974. They were also exacerbated by Iraq's final disputes with the British-dominated IPC. In 1972 Iraq nationalized the IPC, and in 1973 an agreement was reached on compensation and details of the takeover; the nationalization of the IPC subsidiaries, the Basra PC and the Mosul PC, were completed in 1975 (see OIL).

From 1963, onwards the *Ba'th* regime put Iraq firmly into the leftist-radical camp in inter-Arab and international affairs—at least until 1980. Relations with Egypt were improved in 1964 despite the fiasco of the Tripartite Union Agreement signed in April by Iraq, Syria and Egypt. In 1965 Egypt and Iraq conducted negotiations on unity, which became futile. Relations with Syria, remained generally tense and irritant. There was a fundamental antagonism, which had come mainly from rivalry for the position of the dominant country of the Fertile Crescent. The *Ba'th* split into two bitterly hostile factions since the 1966 coup in Syria, which deposed the old guard of the Party's leadership, between the radically doctrinaire *Ba'th* regime in Syria, and the rival "Right" in Iraq (identified with the founding fathers of the *Ba'th*, who took refuge in Iraq). In December

1966 Syria sealed off for three months the IPC oil pipeline running from Kirkuk to Banias on the Mediterranean, on which the Iraqis depended for half of their oil exports, in an attempt to force the Western-owned company to pay higher royalties for oil piped across Syrian territory. Hostility between the two Ba'th regimes deteriorated in the spring of 1975 to a crisis over sharing the Euphrates waters, when Syria inaugurated the Tabaqa Dam on the river, which led the two regimes to mass military forces along the common border. The relations between Baghdad and Damascus were aggravated by the Syrian invasion of Lebanon in the summer of 1976, due to their colliding interests in this country (namely, protection of rival Lebanese factions of the Ba'th Party, and shifting support for the PLO in its struggle against Syria). That same year Iraq closed the oil pipeline through Syria that had been operating since 1952—a closure that damaged its own oil exports, (The IPC pipeline to Haifa had been inoperative since 1948 and that to Tripoli since 1976.) This induced it to step up the construction of an alternative pipeline through Turkey to the Gulf of Alexandretta-Hatay which was opened in 1977. In 1976–1977 Iraq's borders with Syria were closed altogether. There was a reconciliation in 1978–1979; borders were reopened late in 1978 and the pipeline in February 1979. Syrian President Asad paid two state visits—and it was agreed to unite or merge the two countries. However, negotiations on that merger plan collapsed in June 1979, the union was called off and relations once again became bitterly hostile, with Syria supporting Iraqi subversives and rebels.

Iraq's part in the Six-Day War was limited. It sent a strong force to the north of Jordan, but it took no major part in the War and was withdrawn in 1971, after much tension with Jordan due to its sympathy for the Palestinian guerrillas, although its armed forces remained idle during their battle with Jordan in September 1970. In the 1973 War, Iraq sent two armored mechanized divisions to the Syrian front, in addition to four squadrons, and another squadron to the Egyptian front, the largest Arab expeditionary force in that war (see ARAB-ISRAEL CONFLICT). Following the War, Iraq adopted a radical line, rejecting any political settlement with Israel, which was to give Baghdad a convenient position to attack its arch Arab rival for joining this trend. Iraq thus joined LIBYA in forming the loose alignment of the REJEC-

TION FRONT,and began a terrorist campaign against both Syrian and PALESTINE LIBERATION ORGANIZATION (PLO) figures, executed by ABU NIDAL. In 1977 it was in the forefront of the Arab states denouncing al-SADAT's peace moves and ostracizing Egypt. Iraq refused to join, in December 1977, "The Steadfastness Front," established in Tripoli and combining Libya, SYRIA, ALGEIRIA, SOUTH YEMEN and the PLO, ostensibly on the grounds of the absence of a determined rejection line toward the principle of a political settlement with Israel. Nonetheless, following the Camp David Accords of September 1978, Iraq initiated an emergency ARAB SUMMIT CONFERENCE to discuss the collective Arab response, combined with a quick *rapprochement* with Syria which effectively turned Iraq into the new leading force in Arab regional politics. However, the Iraqi-Syrian alignment was short-lived, and with the Iraqi entanglement in war with Iran in September 1980, Iraq lost its influence on the Arab arena.

4. Iraq Under Saddam Hussein (1979)

A. The Iran-Iraq War (1980–1988) The takeover by Saddam Hussein in July 1979 was accompanied by another bloody purge. Twenty-one leading officers and functionaries were executed including five members of the Revolutionary Council. Saddam Hussein's rule since 1979 has been marked by an excessive use of terror as a means of establishing his unchallenged authority. Despite his brutality, after all potential nuclei of opposition had been eliminated, Saddam implemented the provision for an elected National Assembly, laid down in the Constitution of 1970. However, this was not implemented for ten years. In June 1980 elections were held—the first since 1958—*albeit* as a referendum on a single list of Ba'th-approved candidates of the United Front; and in September 1984 new elections were held.

Iraq's most crucial problem under Saddam Hussein's reign has been its relations—and in 1980–1988 its War—with Iran. Always beset by difficulties—over border disputes, particularly in the Shatt al-Arab; Iranian aid to Kurdish rebels; political and international orientation; the status of Iranians in Iraq—relations became increasingly tense in the late 1960s. In 1969 the Shah denounced the Agreement of 1937 setting the Shatt al-Arab border at its eastern shore rather than along its median line or thalweg (except for a stretch opposite Abadan). He announced that he would enforce a regime on the waterway conforming to Iranian claims. Tension and clashes ensued, relations were severed from late 1971 to October 1973, and scores of thousands of Iranians were deported. But with Iran's power much enhanced, Iraq was not strong enough to enforce its position on the Shatt al-Arab. In March 1975, it had to accept a new agreement with Iran legitimizing Iran's position and establishing the thalweg of the Shatt al-Arab as the border. In return, the Shah stopped supporting for the Kurdish rebels, causing the Rebellion to break down. But Iraq chafed under the Agreement imposed on it by a neighbor too strong to resist.

The situation changed in 1979 with the Shah deposed, Iran in turmoil and militarily weakened, and its Army in disarray. After increasing tension and border clashes accompanied by intensified Shi'i opposition led by al-Da'wa movement committed to overthrow the government, Iraq announced in September 1980 the abrogation of the 1975 Agreement, reasserting its sovereignty over the Shatt al-Arab. On 22 September she opened an all-out war by a major offensive across the Shatt al-Arab. (Iraq considers the beginning of the war from 4 September when, she claims, Khanaqin was shelled by Iran). Iraq's official war aims were the enforcement of its sovereignty over the Shatt al-Arab; minor territorial claims, mainly in the Qasr-i-Shirin area and several small islands in the Gulf; and an end to Iranian subversion and Shi'i-revolutionary, anti-Iraqi instigation. Yet in repeated statements, mainly for home consumption, it also claimed the whole of Khuzistan, Iran's oil-bearing southwest. Iraq's initial offensive achieved certain territorial gains, especially in Khuzistan (Khorramshahr destroyed and taken, Abadan cut off and besieged), but it did not lead to a major victory and Iranian resistance rallied. Iraq had a significantly superior air force (whose performance, however, was seen by experts as mediocre or sub-standard), while Iran disposed of much larger man-power which it used in massed attacks of "human waves", sacrificing many thousands. From 1981–1982 Iranian counter-offensives regained most of the territory taken by Iraq; Khorramshahr was reconquered in May 1982, and from 1985–1986 Iranian forces made inroads on Iraqi territory (in February 1986, they reached, for instance, the Fao peninsula on Iraq's Gulf coast) and kept Basra and its surroundings under near-constant shelling and threat of conquest. Iraq used chemical weapon and launched massive air and missile attacks on economic targets, mainly the centers of oil production and terminals, as well as on major urban centers in Iran. Casualties were estimated at hundreds of thousands. Both countries' oil exports, vital for the financing of their war effort, were gravely damaged: Iraq's facilities for oil loading and shipping on the Gulf were paralyzed and largely destroyed and could no longer be used, while Iraq incessantly bombed Kharg Island, Iran's main loading center, and its shuttle tankers to loading points farther down the Gulf. Iraq's only means of direct oil exports were the pipeline through Turkey and a new feeder linking with the Saudi pipeline from the Gulf to the Red Sea at Yanbu. Iran maintained the bulk of its oil shipping despite Iraqi attacks and great losses. From early 1984 both countries attacked oil tankers, mostly of neutral third parties, in the Gulf, and Iran extended its missile and air raids to shipping not directly linked to Iraq, such as tankers *en route* to and from the Arab Gulf oil ports; Iran also claimed the right to intercept and search neutral shipping en route to Iraq and confiscate supplies. And while the great powers tried to protect their own shipping, little action was taken to insure the freedom of shipping for all (see IRAN-IRAQ WAR).

The War, though continuing with furious tenacity, was seen, as of 1982–1983, as stalemated— from the mid-1980s perhaps with a slight edge in Iran's favor. From 1982, Iraq was offering a cease-fire based on the withdrawal to its borders and negotiations for peace. Iran refused all such offers and insisted on a list of harsh preconditions, including Iraq's denunciation as the aggressor and admission of guilt, the payment of huge compensation, the dismissal of Saddam Hussein and his regime and his trial as a war criminal. Mediation efforts—by Arab states and the UN; the non-aligned group of states; the Islamic states group; and individual statesmen— have all failed.

The rise of Saddam Hussein as Iraq's sole leader brought the recent *rapprochement* with Syria to a dead end. In August 1980 Iraq expelled the Syrian Ambassador and when Syria and Libya supported Iran in the War that Iraq opened in September 1980, Iraq severed relations with both of them. In April 1982, the pipeline was again closed down, this time by Syria—to deprive Iraq of its economic benefits.

Syria persisted in supporting Iran against Iraq, despite several attempts to mediate and reconcile the two countries, mainly by Jordan and Saudi Arabia, and Syrian-Iraqi mutual hostility remained unabated.

In February 1986, the Security Council declared Iraq responsible for the outbreak of the war in hope that Iran would agree to a cease-fire. However, KHOMEINI remained adamant in his refusal to end the war, and Iraq renewed the invasion of Iran and the missile attacks on Tehran and the oil installations. In 1987 Iran invaded Iraqi territory, on several occasions without much success. The war of the tankers and the Iranian missile attacks on Kuwait in particular, led the latter to request an American reflagging of its tankers and ships operating in the Gulf, which led to a presence of Western naval forces in the Gulf. In July 1987, Security Council resolution 598 stipulated the end of hostilities and withdrawal of all the forces behind their respective national boundaries. Khomeini rejected this resolution, arguing that it did not declare Iraq responsible for the outbreak of the War and did not oblige it to pay reparations to Iran. Iraq, fearing collapse as a result of the continuation of the war, once again tried to force the Iranian leadership to put an end to the War by renewing the attacks against the oil installations, tankers, industrial plants and, as of January 1988, intensified its missile attacks on Iranian cities. The mutual attacks on each other's economic insfrastructure, particularly against oil refineries and petrochemical industries affected Iran more seriously. Moreover by June 1988 the Iraqi Army managed to ward off Iran from the whole area of Iraqi Kurdistan and even conquered back the city of Dehloran in Iranian Kurdistan. On 18 July 1988, Khomeini reluctantly announced the end of the War and the acceptance of Security Council resolution 598 unconditionally. Despite this, Iraq continued warlike operations for another six days, in order to degrade Iran. (For the war's course, and evaluation of its results, see IRAN-IRAQ WAR).

Iraqi foreign relations in the 1980s were marked by a search of a pragmatic course, which in retrospect, turned out to be sheerly tactical, motivated by war necessities. From the mid-1970s, it sought a *rapprochement* with the West—mainly economic relations, investments, arms supplies—with France as a main Western partner, but also with the US, resuming official diplomatic relations with it in 1984, and accordingly toned down its links with the Soviet Bloc. This trend gained further momentum after 1980, due to the Iran-Iraq War. The Superpowers were officially neutral—and caught on the horns of a dilemma. As far as arms supplies, vital to both Iraq and Iran, were concerned, both the Western powers and the USSR supported Iraq, within limits (though the USSR's defense pact with Iraq could not be seen as fully operative), while Iran got its arms initially from Syria and Libya (transferring Soviet arms, apparently with Moscow's approval), as well as from China, North Korea and Vietnam; but, as revealed in the American "Irangate" affair, American, Israeli and other military supplies continued reaching Iran, too. The Arab states, except for Syria, Libya and South Yemen, supported Iraq—politically and morally. Egypt supplied Iraq with arms, though their diplomatic relations were resumed only in late 1987. Jordan put its port of Aqaba and its communications at Iraq's disposal; and most significantly, Saudi Arabia and Kuwait provided massive financial and strategic aid without which Iraq could not have survived. They exported oil on Iraq's account; Saudi Arabia allowed Iraq to ship oil through the Saudi pipeline to the Red Sea; and their aid credits and grants were estimated at over 40 billion dollars. Iran bitterly resented Arab aid and repeatedly warned the Gulf Arab states that it would regard them as Iraq's allies in the War and accordingly act against them—a threat that caused much concern, particularly in Kuwait. During the War Iraq kept demanding the other Arab states to stand by it in its War against Iran, on the basis of the Collective Arab Security Pact of 1950 (see ARAB LEAGUE), while presenting itself as the defender of the Eastern flank of the Arab homeland.

However, this effort did not bear real fruit. Even on the declarative level most of the Arab states, and especially the monarchic Gulf states, were careful not to stand publicly against Iran. Only at the Amman summit conference in November 1987—which came a month after an Iranian missile attack on Kuwait and several months after the bloody clashes between Iranian pilgrims to Mecca and Saudi security forces—was it agreed to denounce Iran; to call for the imposition of sanctions against it by the UN for its refusal to accept Security Council resolution 598, and express solidarity and support for Iraq and Kuwait in face of Iranian aggression.

Iraq's dependence, from 1980, on the West and the mainstream Arab states, and particularly on Saudi Arabia, caused it further to mitigate its radical policies and adopt a pragmatic orientation—though there was no change in its internal regime or in Saddam Hussein's brutal rule in domestic affairs. It even somewhat toned down its anti-Israel stance and was rumored to support Egyptian-Jordanian moves for negotiations on a Middle East peace settlement, though it has not conformed such rumors or taken any official steps to join these moves for a settlement.

In the final analysis, Saddam Hussein failed to realize his goal of bringing down the fundamentalist regime in Iran, "liberating" the district of Khuzistan, and most of all, to securing free access to the Gulf. Indeed, the end of the War did not end the conflict between the two states, nor the settlement of the disputes regarding the prisoners, the delineation of the boundary and the payment of compensation (see also IRAN). In fact, the end of the War with effectively no victory to either side, with Iraq's basic political anxieties, deprivation of a secure access to the Gulf, and staggering external debt, were to motivate Iraq's invasion of Kuwait two years later. It was only following the Iraqi invasion of Kuwait that Iraq unilaterally withdrew from the 920 sq. miles (2,195 sq. km.) of occupied Iranian territory it had held since the end of the war and accepted an exchange of prisoners of war. In February 1991 a UN observer force (UNIIMOG) formally announced that the military forces of the two countries had returned to the international borders.

B. The Kuwait Crisis and the Gulf War Iraq ended the eight-year War with Iran with no tangible achievements. Contrary to its official line of claiming victory over Iran, none of the problems which might have driven Iraq to war in 1980—primarily the Shatt al-Arab dispute—were resolved, leaving the conflict essentially unfinished. In addition to the human and material losses, and the overwhelming external debt, Iraq was now under constant threat of renewed war against a potent power with decisive strategic edge over Iraq, and a regime which had meanwhile been entrenched deeply in Iranian society.

With its only outlet to the Gulf still blocked, Iraq's strategic situation was intolerably disadvantageous. Thus, despite its heavy debt and continuing fall of oil

prices, which threatened Iraq with financial suffocation, the regime continued to spend a significant portion of its budget on purchasing military-oriented technologies and development of missiles as well as chemical and biological weapons. Moreover, now that the war with Iran was over, Saddam Hussein made it understood that Iraq aspired to return to an active and leading role in regional politics-seeking to punish Syria for its alliance with Iran and escalating his rhetoric of war against Israel. Saddam's post-war Arab policy led to the establishing of the ARAB COOPERATION COUNCIL (ACC) in February 1989 (with Egypt, Jordan and Yemen), to secure wide Arab support for Iraq's strategic needs and isolate Syria, although the proclaimed purposes of the new alignment was primarily economic. At the same time, Iraq turned to intensive involvement in the renewed crisis in Lebanon, following the constitutional crisis that erupted in August-September 1988 and the emergence of two Lebanese governments, each claiming exclusive legitimacy: a Syrian-backed one, headed by the Sunni Muslim Salim al-Huss, and a Maronite-based one led by General Michel AWN, who declared War of Liberation to rid Lebanon of Syrian occupation. The new cycle of violence in Lebanon provided Iraq with an opportunity to tighten the pressure on Syria by supplying Awn with heavy weapons, which reportedly included short-range FROG missiles. Egypt and Jordan facilitated the arms deliveries through Aqaba and the SUEZ CANAL. The intensifying Syria-Iraq crisis and fears lest it escalate into a fully-fledged war between the two states underlay the convening of an Arab summit conference in Casablanca in May 1989, which affected some mitigation of the Lebanese crisis but left it essentially unresolved.

Parallel to Iraq's involvement in Lebanon and continued armament race, Saddam Hussein sought to alleviate its financial burden and obtain reliable and secure access to the Gulf. This caused him to exert growing pressures on the Gulf monarchies, especially Kuwait, to write off Iraq's debt (12–14 billion dollars) and extract additional substantive financial aid. Kuwait was apparently willing to write off the Iraqi debt in return for Iraq's recognition of its borders, but not while facing further Iraqi claims over its territory. In early 1990 Saddam Hussein raised claims over the Bubian and Warba Kuwaiti islands near the northern shores of the Gulf and also over territory at their common border that Kuwait had allegedly taken over during the war with Iran.

Meanwhile, Saddam had embarked on an aggressive propaganda campaign against the US and Israel, in an attempt to establish himself as the hero-savior of the Arab world from Israel's threats—particularly in view of the collapse of the Soviet block and Arab loss of its strategic friendship—thus justifying his financial and territorial claims from Kuwait. He lobbied his partners in the ACC to use their offices to bring the Gulf monarchies to meet his financial needs, but to no avail.

On 2 April, after a period of escalating attacks against the US policy toward Iraq's projects of NON-CONVENTIONAL WEAPONS, Saddam revealed that his country possessed a binary chemical weapon and threatened to attack and burn "half of Israel" if it dared to attack Iraq. Saddam's aggressive rhetoric, openly calling for a Holy War (JIHAD) against Israel, apparently reflected fears lest Israel might launch another premature attack on its installations of non-conventional weapons, as it had done in the attack against the Iraqi nuclear reactor in 1981. In May 1990 Saddam Hussein hosted the Arab summit conference in Baghdad in which he continued to present his fierce aggressive line against Israel and the US, calling for rallying around Iraq with its advanced technological development.

In July, following the resumption of diplomatic relations between Kuwait and Iran, Saddam Hussein shifted his attacks from Israel to Kuwait, accusing it of stealing billions of dollars worth of oil from the Rumeila oilfield at their common border. Saddam also accused Kuwait and the UAE of having caused Iraq ongoing financial losses due to the former's cheating on their ORGANIZATION OF PETROLE-UM-EXPORTING COUNTRIES (OPEC) oil production quotas and pressing down prices in the world oil market, claiming 14 billion dollars of compensation for Iraq's losses. Iraq's vehement claims led to mediation attempts by Egypt's and Jordan's heads of state as well as by Yasser ARAFAT, in which Saddam Hussein had reportedly promised not to employ force against Kuwait. At the OPEC emergency meeting in Vienna on 26 July 1990 Kuwait agreed to reduce its production but Iraq's demand to raise the oil price was refused. On 1 August, while Iraqi troops had already been massed on the Kuwaiti border, Iraq and Kuwait made another attempt to resolve

their differences in a high-level meeting in Jedda. Its collapse that same day removed the last Iraqi inhibition, and on 2 August Iraqi forces invaded Kuwait. The next day, an emergency meeting of the Arab ministers of foreign affairs met in Cairo and agreed with a decisive majority to condemn Iraq and call for its immediate withdrawal from Kuwait, although due to the abstaining representatives the decision refrained from mentioning the name of the aggressor, arguing that it would hamper future mediation efforts.

Chances for such meditation, led mainly by King Hussein, rapidly faded out. Iraq took immediate actions which indicated that the conquest was by no means temporary, while Saudi Arabia requested from the US to bolster its defense. The UN Security Council resolution 661 passed on 6 August, imposed mandatory sanctions and an embargo on Iraq and occupied Kuwait. On 8 August, Saddam Hussein effectively buried the hopes for an "Arab solution" by announcing the formal annexation of Kuwait to Iraq, reminding that it had always been part of the Iraqi "mother state." That same day the first American contingent force arrived in Saudi Arabia, operating till the end of the war in February 1991 under titular Saudi command. Meanwhile, an international military and economic blockade was imposed on Iraq by the UN. When the Arab summit convened in Cairo on 10 August, Saddam had been left with no room for conciliation. By now, Arab public discourse shifted from a debate on Iraq's aggression to one on the legitimacy of foreign military intervention in an Arab-Arab dispute. In the summit, Iraq and a minority group of supporters—the PLO, Libya, Algeria, SUDAN, and Jordan—pressed for an Arab solution of the crisis but were opposed by an Egyptian-led coalition which included the Gulf monarchies, Syria and MOROCCO. The latter brought to the conclusion of decisions which adopted the UN Security Council resolutions regarding sanctions on Iraq, agreeing to dispatch Arab forces to support the Gulf states in defense of their territories "against any Arab aggression." On 4 December, Saddam Hussein hosted a mini-summit of his Arab supporters, which also included King Hussein, Arafat, and Yemen's President, which underlined Iraq's relative isolation.

With the invasion of Kuwait, the Iraqi propaganda machine embarked on an offensive against the

West and those Arab regimes that had condemned it, increasingly using Islamic rhetoric and symbols, which ostensibly matched the prevailing Islamic discourse in the Arab states. Iraq denounced the American-led international coalition as a "new Crusade," and "American neo-colonialism" desecrating the soil of Islam's holy shrines of Mecca and Medina. Saddam's strategy along the crisis indeed focused on an effort to incite the masses in those Arab states collaborating with the US (Saudi Arabia, Egypt, Syria and Morocco) against their rulers in an effort to exclude these states from the international coalition and bring to its collapse. Although the crisis was purely Arab, on August 12, 1990 Saddam Hussein linked the Iraqi withdrawal from Kuwait to Israel's withdrawal from the territories it had occupied in 1967, which had a particularly strong echo in the Arab world. However, on the whole, the Iraqi efforts to incite the Arab masses scored little success, as manifested by the low-key responses of Islamic movements.

Iraq's occupation of Kuwait was marked by brutal acts of mass arrests and executions without a trial by the Iraqi military forces. As a result, Egyptian and Palestinian migrant workers in Kuwait fled from occupied Kuwait. Saddam Hussein's proposal to open talks with the US and Saudi Arabia remained unheeded. During November, American President Bush ordered the doubling of the American force in the Gulf area, while Iraq mobilized an additional 250,000 soldiers, a large segment of them sent to Kuwait. On 29 November the UN Security Council resolution 678 authorized the use of "all necessary means ... to restore international peace and security in the area," unless Iraq fully implemented the previous UN resolutions, until 15 January 1991. The ultimatum came after the economic sanctions proved to be ineffective as a means to force Iraq to withdraw from Kuwait. On January 9, Iraq Foreign Minister Tareq AZIZ and Secretary of State James Baker met in Geneva in a last ditch attempt to resolve the crisis, but to no avail. Over the next few days, both sides clearly proceeded toward an armed showdown: the US Congress authorized President Bush to employ American troops in order to implement UN Resolution 678, and two days later the Iraqi Parliament decided unanimously to go to war rather than withdraw from Kuwait. A few hours after the expiration of the ultimatum, the American-led coali-

tion started its air and missile offensive which continued for five weeks. During this period, Iraq made an effort to entangle Israel in the crisis by launching close to fifty SCUD missiles with conventional warheads against Israel, apparently in an effort to force it to retaliate and put the Arab members of the international coalition in a quandary. Iraq withdrew its forces from Kuwait by 26 February and two days later accepted the truce ordered by Bush. (For the war, losses and cost, see GULF WAR.)

C. Iraq Since the Gulf War (1991–)

Domestic Affairs With the end of the Gulf War, and following President Bush's call to overthrow the Iraqi regime, battles broke out in northern and southern Iraq. The Kurdish rebellion, which united disputed factions, took advantage of the Iraqi army's preoccupation with fighting the Shi'i rebels in southern Iraq, taking over strategic towns in northern Iraq (such as Zakhu, Dahuk, Suleimaniya, and Erbil). At the end of March 1991, the Kurdish rebels even conquered the strategically important town of Kirkuk with the important oil-rigs located to the west. The leadership of the Kurdistan Iraqi Front, (established in 1988, uniting eight Kurdish factions), claimed that the goal of the uprising had been to bring about the implementation of the autonomy agreement that had been signed between the Iraqi government and the Kurds in March 1970 (see above, and KURDS). However, both the Kurdish and Shi'i uprisings failed due to the government's military superiority, while the US-led international coalition forces remained idle. The passive position demonstrated by the international coalition derived from fears—and strong objection of Turkey—lest an overthrow of Saddam's regime lead to the dissolution of Iraq; increased Iranian influence; and serious threat to existing territorial order in the region, particularly regarding Turkey and Syria due to Kurdish irredentist claims on areas in these countries. In early April, 1991, Iraqi military forces recovered its domination over Kirkuk, Erbil, Dahuk and Zakhu, with a staggering number of Kurds reported to have been killed in the battles (up to 50,000).

The Iraqi takeover and the fear of Iraqi massacres as an act of revenge brought about a mass wave of Kurdish refugees (estimated at 1 million), approaching the Iran-Iraq border and the Iraq-Turkey border. Turkish interest to prevent those refugees from entering its territory, fearing that these refugees would worsen its already acute Kurdish problem, and pressure applied by Western public opinion and human-rights organizations, brought about international intervention to prevent an Iraqi takeover of the North. In April 1991, based on UN Security Council resolution 688, and the European Union's decision, an autonomous Kurdish region in northern Iraq was proclaimed, to be protected by UN forces and open to relief organizations aiming to offer aid to the civilian population. The US added its tacit support by declaring the formation of a no-fly zone for Iraqi airplanes and helicopters north of latitude 36, in order to create "safe skies" for the Kurdish forces and to ensure the return of the refugees to the area. An international supervision team that included the US, Britain, France and Turkey was formed in order to safeguard the autonomous Kurdish region with surveillance flights departing from the Turkish air-base of Inchirlik.

Following these steps, Kurdish refugees began returning to the area in large numbers, and Kurdish-Iraqi negotiations began in Baghdad on the status of the Kurds in Iraq. At the end of April 1991, Jalal TALABANI, leader of the Patriotic Union (PU), announced that the Iraqi government had agreed in principle to implement the autonomy agreement of March 1970, but at the end of 1991 the talks seemed to be deadlocked. The main reason was disagreement over the issue of the borders of the Kurdish autonomous area (the Iraqi government opposed the Kurdish demand to include Kirkuk or to share Kirkuk oil revenues with the Kurds), and the Kurds' refusal to disband their military militias and to completely abandon their ties with Western states.

The failure of the talks brought an "economic siege" on the northern region by the government in October 1991. Kurdish factions started to conduct talks aimed at establishing a semi-independent Kurdish regime in Northern Iraq. (For the results of these talks, elections, in May 1992, the formation of a Kurdish government and its collapse due to factional disputes, and international mediation efforts, see KURDS.) By mid-1997, talks between the two factions had come to standstill, and the status-quo by which the Kurdish autonomous area was divided into two areas remained valid. From July 1997, intense cooperation between Barazani and the Turkish government commenced in fighting the (PKK) Partyia Karkeran Kurdistan.

The ongoing intra-Kurdish fighting enabled the Iraqi government from 1994, and especially after the takeover of Erbil (August 1996), to gradually return to the northern area in the form of renewed presence of Iraqi intelligence personnel in the Kurdish cities, and the lifting of the economic embargo from the Kurdish region by Iraq that brought about increased trade activity with the rest of the country. Furthermore, the disagreements among the international coalition members on the use of force against Iraq after the signing of the "Oil for Food" agreement in May 1996 (culminating in France's withdrawal from the International Supervision Force in December 1996), hastened the return of Baghdad to the northern part of Iraq. Turkey, who had suffered heavy financial damages due to the international sanctions imposed on Iraq , turned increasingly against the mandate of "provice comfort," fearing it could lead to the establishment of a Kurdish state in northern Iraq and reflect on the internal situation in Turkey. Indeed, in January 1997 the Mandate's character was changed, with the presence of ground forces canceled and the headquarters of the supervision force moved from Zakhu in Iraq to Silufi in Turkey.

With the quelling of the Shi'i and Kudish revolts in March–April 1991, the major threat to the regime, caused directly by the Gulf War, was lifted. Despite the harsh effects of the sanctions on the Iraqi economy and quality of life of the ordinary citizens, no significant threat had arisen to Saddam's regime. A number of coups were reportedly planned or attempted (January and March 1995, July 1996, mainly by air force personnel), yet neither of these attempts nor the defections of senior army officers—among whom General Wafiq al-Samarra'i, former Chief of the Military Intelligence who, in 1994, escaped to Damascus, and Gen. Nizar al-Khazraji , former Iraqi Chief of Staff who, in 1996, fled from Iraq to join the Jordan-backed Iraqi National Accord—seriously threatened Saddam's regime.

Indeed, the relative stability and survivability of Saddam Hussein was largely maintained due to the persistent loyalty of the main services and forces in charge of Saddam's personal and regime security, primarily the Republican Guard, the Presidential Guard, the *Fida'ii Saddam*, and others. Another factor was the weakness of the Iraqi opposition, and the ambivalent position on the regional powers regarding the overthrow of Saddam Hussein by means of subversion and encouragement of Iraqi opposition forces. This position could well indicate the fear of neighboring regimes lest toppling Saddam's regime might cause political chaos in Iraq that would affect all surrounding countries.

The most severe threats to the regime during this period stemmed from the intensifying battles between members of the ruling elite and mainly in Saddam's own family, in which his eldest son, Udday, the leading candidate for inheritance played a major role. Though his official titles have not been directly connected with power-owning, the most influential Iraqi newspaper *Babel*, and the television station *al-Shabab*—Udday's main source of power, stemmed from commanding the Fidda II Saddam (a semimilitary force in charge of the protection of the regime). Since the mid-1990s, Saddam has increasingly bestowed more authority onto his other son, Kussay who was commander of the Special Republic Guard and in charge of Saddam's personal security. Kussay was always seen as a more responsible person than his brother. Udday arose as a prominent figure in the Iraqi regime in the early 1990s, employing his powers to force other members of the family, especially Saddam's step-brothers, out of their senior posts, putting them under house-arrest, such as Watban Ibrahim, who was dismissed from his post as Minister of Interior Affairs and later shot by Udday, sustaining a severe leg injury. Saba'awi was dismissed from his post as Chief of the General Security; and Barzan al-Tikriti, former father-in-law of Udday, who remained in self-imposed exile while officially serving as Iraq's delegate to the UN in Geneva. Udday's brutal drive to power was a major reason for the defection to Jordan of two of Saddam Hussein's sons-in-law, Hussein Kamel, Minister of Industry, in charge of the Iraqi Army armaments, and his brother Saddam Kamel, in August 1995. The defection appeared to be a serious blow to Saddam's regime due to the valuable information Hussein Kamel revealed regarding the regimes' projects of non-conventional weapons. But Kamel's attempts to be recognized as the leader of the Iraqi opposition failed, mainly due to his role in the brutal suppression policy committed by the regime, which made it unthinkable for the Iraqi exiled opposition to support him. In February 1996, Kamel returned abashed to Baghdad, having been promised full pardon for him and his brother by Saddam. Upon their return to Iraq they were forced to divorce their wives and were later executed by other members of the family, including Saddam's sons. The Kamel incident left its mark on the ruling Tikriti clan. In December 1996, as Udday Hussein was seriously injured in an attempt on his life-most probably by Kamel's family members—for which a number of parties claimed responsibility, including the Shi'i opposition movement "al-Da'wa," identified with Iran.

Saddam's success in maintaining his regime also stemmed from the deep fragmentation of the Iraqi opposition, which remained devoid of any significant power, immersed in ideological and personal squabbles, and dependent on patrons with differing interests, such as Syria, Iran and Jordan. The Kurdish groups and other opposition groups disputed over the status of northern Iraq in a post-Saddam era, with the Shi'i and Sunni parties opposing the Kurdish claim for autonomy in the northern part of the country. Disagreement also marked the opposition's attitude on lifting of the sanctions imposed on Iraq. The most prominent Shi'i group has been the Supreme Council of Islamic Revolution in Iraq (SCIRI), led by Ayatollah Muhammad Baqir al-Haqim, backed by Iran and possessing armed force (The Bader Force). The Iraqi National Congress, a London-based umbrella organization of the Iraqi opposition groups, established in 1992, in which all Iraqi ethnic groups (Kurds, Sunnis and Shi'is) were initially represented and headed by Dr. Ahmad Shalabi, a Shi'i, had manifested from the start great diversity which prevented it from gathering any significant influence. Another relatively important organization, the Iraqi National Accord, led by Dr. Iyad al-Alawi, a former *Ba'th* member and allegedly funded by the US, Jordan and Saudi Arabia, was involved in the failed coup attempt in July 1996, following which it lost much of its appeal. The opposition efforts to overthrow Saddam's regime were severely frustrated by the Iraqi invasion of the north at the invitation of Barazani (August 1996), because the autonomous Kurdish area had served as the main basis of anti-government activity. During that invasion, Iraqi forces wiped out a sizeable proportion of the opposition's infrastructure in the area.

A salient trend in domestic Iraqi politics in the 1990s was the growing alliance between the regime and tribal chieftains, whose loyalty was secured by economic rewards, such as bequeathing lands and funds to tribal leaders, granting them judicial autonomy in maintaining the tribal law, and exemption from military service. This trend discernibly weakened the *Ba'th* Party and, to a certain extent, central institutions of the state, allowing the re-emergence of traditional communal forces. Thus, the first national conference of the *Ba'th* Party since 1982, which was held after the Gulf War in 1991, indicated that the Party remained nothing more than a rubber stamp. Indeed, the process of stripping the party of its powers, centralizing key power positions in the hands of Saddam's sons, and widening the local authority of the tribes, constituted a reversion from the regimes previous effort to dissolve the tribal identity and to create a new Iraqi national identity.

Despite the regimes ensuing alliance with tribal chieftains, Sunni tribes that had been the mainstay of the regime rebelled against the regime in response to harm done to their senior representatives in the ruling institutions. In January 1990, a plot against Saddam by officers from the *Jubayr* tribe was exposed, leading to a major purge of many officers of this tribal confederation. In May-June 1995, a group of the *Dulaym* tribal confederation started an uprising against the regime that lasted three weeks in retaliation against the murder of an officer of their tribe.

A few months after the Gulf War, Saddam Hussein took a number of steps aimed at displaying some openness in internal affairs, such as permitting the activity of political parties (October 1991), and gave up the role of Prime Minister that he had held since his rise to power in 1979, in favor of the Shi'i Sa'dun Hammadi a step that was aimed at winning the support of the Shi'i community) and more.

However, in May 1994 Saddam reclaimed the post of Prime Minister, reflecting his efforts to concentrate power in his family, mainly in the hands of his sons, Qusay and Udday. Later, however, certain measures were taken to display liberalization and democratization toward the Iraqi public: the referendum of October 1995 on the extension of Saddam's Presidency; the elections for the "Iraqi National Council " (Parliament) that has been stripped of any authority since the Gulf War; in March 1996, and the holding of elections for the local councils in May 1996.

Foreign Affairs Immediately after managing to suppress internal revolts that had erupted in the Kurdish and Southern regions following the Gulf War (March–April 1991), the Iraqi regime concentrated its efforts on the struggle to lift the sanctions imposed on Iraq following its invasion of Kuwait. This struggle topped the Iraqi political agenda, with all other issues being set aside or subordinated to the lifting of the sanctions. The significance of this effort has been attested to by the total absence of, or low-key Iraqi role in regional inter-Arab affairs, and regional affairs in general. The Iraqi effort in this regard was multi-facetted: propagating the humanitarian effect of the sanctions, primarily on health services for the civilian population; attempts at highlighting the differences between coalition members whilst emphasizing the economic advantages awarded to its supporters; and initiating occasional crises with the UN inspection team, by blocking its access to certain installations suspected to possess non-conventional weapons.

The Iraqi regime initially refused to negotiate with the UN over granting permission for limited Iraqi oil exports with the revenues going to war victim compensation and the purchase of food and medicines for Iraqi civilians. Instead, the Iraqi regime opted for a total lifting of sanctions by implementing Clause 22 of UN Security Resolution 687.

Negotiations between Iraq and the UN over limited Iraqi oil sales with revenues earmarked for war victim compensation, and food and medicines had started in 1991, following Security Council Resolution 712, that called for the establishment of a special fund for the Gulf war victims. However the talks did not achieve any progress, because of Iraq's refusal to accept UN terms. Iraq even withdrew from the talks (February 1992), but later agreed to their renewal. Talks between Iraq and the UN continued with ups and downs, and in April 1995, following pressures from RUSSIA, the Security Council opted for resolution 986 which allowed Iraq to export 2 billion dollars worth of oil over six months. Chances for lifting the sanctions seemed promising in view of a relatively positive semi-annual report written by Rolf Ekhaus, the Chairman of the UN-ESCOM. However, the defection of Hussein Kamel and his disclosing of the Iraqi biological and chemical capabilities increased Ekhaus' suspicions and during the following two years no progress was made on the sanctions issue. Ekhaus claimed that Iraq was continuing to hold six to eighteen medium and long range scud missiles and was continuing to develop biological and chemical weapons. According to American Defense Secretary William Cohen, Iraq had produced over two million tons of VX gas.

Initially, Iraq refused to accept the decision claiming that it contained paragraphs contradicting Iraq's sovereignty, such as the one holding the UN as the responsible authority for food distribution in Northern Iraq. However, Iraq acquiesced, following the worsening economic situation in Iraq during 1995 and Saddam Hussein's understanding that the lifting of sanctions had not yet been feasible, especially after the information revealed by his son-in-law Hussein Kamel about Iraq's mass-destruction weapons industry. Following further talks, on 20 May 1996, the "Oil for Food" agreement was signed by Iraq and the UN, accepting resolution 986, but its implementation was postponed until November. Initially this was due to the British and American insistence that Iraq fully abide by the terms of the Agreement including the deployment of UN representatives at their posts in Iraq. The Iraqi invasion of the Kurdish area (September 1996) caused another delay in implementing the Agreement. On 27 November 1996, the Agreement was finally brought into motion and was renewed once again in July 1997.

The signing of the "Oil for Food" agreement somewhat eased Iraqi economic hardships, which were visible in the exchange rate of Iraqi Dinar 400 to the dollar compared to Iraqi Dinar 1100 to the dollar as had previously been the case. The most significant change was the end of Iraqi isolation in the international arena. The signing of contracts for the purchase of food and drugs in return for oil with many countries led to a change in Iraq's status with some European countries such as Italy, Spain, Portugal, Greece, Latvia, and Bylorussia, which led to renewal of diplomatic ties or upgrading existing ties. Especially prominent were Russia, China and France. These countries signed contracts for the development of oil fields in Iraq after the lifting of the sanctions. They were also opposed to taking military action against Iraq following the invasion of Northern Iraq (August 1996) and the serious crisis with UNESCOM. Iraq's relations with most Arab countries also improved considerably. However, the continued obstacles which confronted the UN effort to finalize the elimination of Iraq's mass-destruction infrastructure and weapon poured cold water over any prospects of lifting the sanctions. Relations between Iraq and UNESCOM had remained rocky ever since the supervision had started. Iraq accused Ekhaus of being a CIA agent, and from time to time initiated a new crisis so as to force a lifting of the sanctions, e.g., by moving forces to the Kuwait border in October 1994, forbidding UN teams to enter Iraqi presidential sites (March 1996), and the expulsion of American supervisers from the UNESCOM team, accusing them of being US intelligence agents who had been deliberately preventing a positive report on Iraq's mass destruction weapons so as to prolong the sanctions. Iraq demanded that the team also include representatives of the five Security Council permanent members, to be deputies to the Chairman of the UN Committee and that a timetable be set for the lifting of sanctions. The US and Britain responded firmly to the Iraqi demands but refrained from taking military measures because of the objection of other members of the Western coalition. This objection marked the Arab states' position regarding such action, and Russia whose mediation helped to settle the differences and renew Iraq's cooperation with the UNESCOM team. Thus, by early 1998 the sanctions were still valid, primarily due to the American and British firm insistence that the sanctions could not be lifted until Iraq had fully complied with the UN resolutions regarding its mass-destruction weapons.

By the end of the Gulf War, Iraq's economy and infrastructure were heavily damaged by the war, regionally isolated and deeply preoccupied with existential problems, primarily to rid itself of the international sanctions. Iraq had lost its ability to play a leading role in either the Gulf area or the Arab world. The determined stand of Saudi Arabia and Kuwait against the return of Iraq to all-Arab forums until it had met all the security council resolutions, combined with convenience at Saddam Hussein's isolation on the part of Egypt and Syria, contributed to Iraq's isolation from the Arab world. Hence, Iraq did not participate in the first Arab summit conference convened in Cairo in June 1996, to discuss the implications of the rise to power of Binyamin NE-TANYAHU as Israel's Prime Minister. Another indication of this isolation was Iraq's almost complete absence from the Arab-Israeli arena not even as an opposition to the peacemaking.

The imposed isolation of Iraq started changing following the signing of an Agreement on military cooperation between Israel and Turkey (February 1996), and furthermore after the signing of the "Oil for Food" Agreement (May 1996), and the stalemate in the Arab-Israeli peace process following Netanyahu's rise to power in Israel. For some Gulf states such as the UAE, QATAR and OMAN, the wish to contain the Iranian threat and to create a balance of power in the Gulf area was the main motive for changing the policy. However, the firm anti-Iraqi stand of Saudi Arabia had prevented any major change in Iraq's isolation in the Arab world. Hence, the refusal of Lebanon to receive an Iraqi sports delegation to the Inter-Arab Games that were held in Beirut in July 1997.

On the bilateral level, Iraq continued to heavily count on Jordan as its sole route for the import and export of goods. However, the signing of the Jordan-Israel Peace Treaty in 1994 and Jordan's eagerness to restore its friendly relations with the Gulf states (severely damaged during the Gulf War), relations between the two states cooled down, culminating in the political asylum given by King Hussein to Saddam Hussein's son-in-law, Hussein Kamel and his brother in August 1995 (see above). King Hussein also allowed Iraqi opposition organizations such as the "Iraqi National Accord" to operate from within Jordan. Nonetheless, both countries chose to maintain their economic links due to their mutual benefit and Iraqi dependence on Jordan as a transit area. This cooperation continued after the signing of the "Oil for Food" agreement in May 1996 though it somewhat diminished Iraq's dependency on Jordan. In view of Jordan's failure to become a recipient of substantive financial Saudi support, Jordan stopped supporting Iraqi opposition groups, opting to maintain its economic links with Iraq, which provides it with all its oil consumption.

No significant development occurred in relations with Iran. The traditional dispute between the two states over Shatt al-Arab, their support to each others Kurdish opposition groups, and the Iranian links to Shi'i opposition groups in Iraq, prevented any substantive improvement. The signing of the Agreement on military cooperation between Israel and Turkey in February 1996, perceived to be directed

mainly against them brought Iran and Iraq closer. However, despite the sporadic exchange of prisoners and corps between the two states and talks at a ministerial level, both regimes continued to exchange mutual accusations of subversion. While Iraq blamed Iran for interfering in its northern region, Iran pointed to Iraq's support of the *Mujahidin Khalk*, the main Iranian armed opposition.

Despite the Turkish participation in the Gulf War as a member of the anti-Iraqi coalition and Turkey's continued military presence in northern Iraq and military operations against the PKK, economic cooperation between the two countries tightened. This cooperation accelerated after the signing of the "Oil for Food" Agreement, when they signed contracts, mainly concerning Iraqi oil supply to Turkey. As in the case of Jordan, Iraq's dependence on Turkey as a main outlet for Iraqi oil exports and imports forced Iraq to maintain a functional relationship with Ankara and to keep a low profile response toward both Turkey's Military Agreement with Israel and the deepening military activity in northern Iraq. Despite hopes for a change in Turkey's policy toward the northern area following the ascendancy of ERBAKAN to premiership, the Turkish Army continued to conduct large scale military operations in Iraq's northern territory against PKK bases (March 1995 and summer 1997), effectively retaining a "security zone" in that area. Baghdad was forced to come to terms with Ankara's role in conducting the peace talks between the Kurdish factions following the takeover of Erbil by the Iraqi Army and the KDP forces in August 1996. Iraq also viewed with suspicion the growing Turkish agitation within the Turkmani minority in northern Iraq which was, perceived as an attempt to renew Turkey's irredentist claims over the province of Mosul.

Iraqi relations with Syria remained strained though the two regimes tended to work out tactical coordination *vis-a-vis* Turkey on the distribution of the Euphrates waters. Toward the end of 1995 and especially after the signature of the military agreement with Israel (February 1996) and the "Oil for Food" Agreement, a certain *rapprochement* was observed and during 1997 the border pass at Tenaf was opened; some limited trade deals were signed, within the framework of the "Oil for Food" agreements; and for the first time since the early 1980s a senior Iraqi official, Deputy Prime Minister Tareq paid an official visit to Damascus. Syria, however, has shown no interest in improving relations beyond the existing economic ties, using the Iraqi card as a means of pressure on its neighbors (Jordan, Turkey) as well as on the US and Israel, displaying its other options in case of deadlock in the peace process.

Iraq's relations with the Gulf monarchies, though still overshadowed by the 1990–1991 experience, witnessed some change of attitude on the latters part since 1996, especially Saudi Arabia and Kuwait, which had to tone down their hard line approach. When Iraq invaded the Kurdish territories in August 1997 the two countries did not support US airforce bombing missions in Iraq, and repeated this position in view of the crisis initiated by Iraq toward the UNESCOM in November 1997. Other Gulf monarchies manifested an even more conciliatory attitude toward Iraq, especially the UAE, whose leader, Zeid Bin Sultan, had been calling from late 1995 for a reconciliation and full return of Iraq to the Arab fold. This trend has apparently been motivated by the need to counterbalance Iran's growing power in the Gulf region, which concerns the UAE's dispute with Iran over islands in the Gulf.

IRAQ PETROLEUM COMPANY (IPC)   see IRAQ.

ISLAMIC CONFERENCE ORGANIZATION
An official international institution, encompassing (from 1994) forty Islamic states and the PALESTINE LIBERATION ORGANIZATION, (PLO) concerned with promoting Islamic solidarity and coordinating the efforts to safeguard Islamic HOLY PLACES, especially those under Israeli domination. The organization was established in 1969, following the arson of al-Aqsa mosque in JERUSALEM, the third holiest shrine of ISLAM, by an Australian fundamentalist Christian, Michael Rohan, in August of that year. At the behest of Saudi Arabia's King, FEISAL IBN ABDEL AZIZ, a conference of Islamic Heads of State was held in Rabat, MOROCCO, the following month, which led to the institutionalization of this forum entitled "The Islamic Conference Organization" (ICO). From the outset, the initiative at convening the Conference was meant to give SAUDI ARABIA a leverage to promote its regional and international stature by manipulating Islamic commonality to strengthen traditionalism at the expense of declining NASSERISM. From 1971 the ICO has

been based in Jedda, Saudi Arabia, and funded primarily by the Saudi government. In 1975 the Saudis established al-Quds (Arabic name of Jerusalem) Committee to monitor the situation in Jerusalem, and implementation of the ICO resolutions concerning the city at large. The organization proved to be of limited effectiveness in its mediation efforts between two Muslim member states—IRAQ and IRAN—in 1981, nor was it able or willing to mitigate the Lebanese predicament caused by the presence of the PALESTINIAN GUERRILLA ORGANIZATIONS on its soil. The dominant position of Saudi Arabia in the organization and tacit support of Iraq in its war with Iran led the latter to twice boycott the ICO summit conference: in 1984, at Casablanca, and in 1987, at KUWAIT city, when the IRAN-IRAQ WAR had already spilled over to the Gulf as a whole. The summit in Kuwait urged a cease-fire in the War. The ICO helped EGYPT's return to the Islamic and ARAB fold by inviting President MUBARAK to its summit conferences in 1984 and 1987. It is noteworthy that Morocco's King HASAN II has played a central role in the organization, in coordination with the Saudi monarchs, particularly as the Head of the Jerusalem Committee.

ISLAM, MUSLIMS   The most prevalent monotheistic faith in the world, estimated, by the late 1990s at over a 1.2 billion. Islam is a faith of over ninety-seven percent of the Middle Eastern population and it has been the dominant religion since it swept the region in the seventh century with the Arab conquests. Apart from the Middle East, Muslims constitute a majority in the former Soviet Central Asia—Kazakhstan, Kirghizistan, Tadzhikistan, Turkmenistan, Uzbekistan, and Azerbaijan-as well as Afghanistan, Pakistan, Bangladesh, Malaysia, Brunei, Indonesia, and northern Cyprus, several African countries—MAURITANIA, SOMALIA and DJIBOUTI, as well as Gambia, Guinea, Mali, Niger, Chad and Senegal. It is the official faith of all Middle Eastern states, except LEBANON (though of Muslim majority), ISRAEL (a Jewish state) and TURKEY (Muslim by faith but officially secular.) In addition the constitutions of all Middle Eastern states—except of those three—define Islam as the source of legislation.) A detailed description of its beliefs and practices would be outside the scope of this volume (however, see entries SUNNIS, SHI'A, SHARI'A, IMAM, MUFTI, DERVISH ORDERS, as well as those on various sects and Islamic schools such as DRUZE, ALAWIS, ISMA'ILIYYA, MAHDIYYA, SANUSSIYYA, WAHHABIYYA).

Islam is an over-arching system of beliefs encompassing the individual and the society as a whole, based on the unity of religion and state (*din wa-dawla*). It shapes public as well as private social patterns, political thought and state behavior. Muslims form significant minorities in India and several southern and East-Asian countries, in RUSSIA and former Yugoslavia, and in a number of Black African countries. In Israel, Muslims form thirteen to fourteen percent of the population (without the Druze). Considerable non-Muslim minorities exist in the following Middle East countries: Lebanon (forty to forty-five percent), SYRIA (about thirty percent if the Druze and Alwais are considered non-Muslim, fifteen percent if they are counted as Muslim), EGYPT (seven to ten percent), SUDAN (twenty-five to thirty five percent concentrated mainly in the south, where non-Muslim African tribes form a large majority).

The Muslims of the world are divided into two major streams: SUNNIS, comprising the majority, and Shi'is. Sunnis constitute the majority in all Middle Eastern states except IRAN (mostly Shi'i), IRAQ YEMEN, BAHRAIN, DUBAI (with Shi'i majority), and OMAN (if the IBADIYYA is considered non-Sunni). Within Sunni Islam, there are four major schools (*madhhab*, plural *madhahib*): a. *Hanafi*—mainly in Turkey, Syria, Iraq and among urban Palestinian Muslims, predominant in official Islamic institutions in the countries formerly of the OTTOMAN EMPIRE; SHAFE'I—widespread in lower Egypt, among rural Palestinians, the KURDS, and in the Saudi provinces of HIJAZ and Asir, Yemen and SOUTH YEMEN; c. *Malek*—in Upper Egypt, Sudan, LIBYA, Bahrain and KUWAIT; d. *Hanbali*—in SAUDI ARABIA. The distinction between the four *madhahib* concerns principally the interpretation and application of Islamic Law—the SHARI'A—and centers on the question how far the early Islamic scholars (*ulama*) of the eighth and ninth centuries (and initially the first place the founders of the four schools [*mujtahidun*]) were entitled to apply Analogy (*qiyas*), Consensus (*ijma*), and Independent Reasoning (*ijtihad*), and how much they had to restrict themselves to the strict application of the Tradition (*hadith*). The *Hanafi* School of Thought is considered the most flexible or innovative in that respect, and the *Hanbali* the most conservative or restictive.

However, all four *madhahib* are considered equally orthodox and the difference between them mainly concerns fine points of the Shari'a, and the *Ulama*. Little affects the beliefs and practices of the general Muslim population—except for the stricter fundamentalism imposed by the *Hanbali* School (which also gave birth to the fundamentalist-puritan movement of the Wahhabiyya).

Within Sunni Islam, several reforming revivalist or fundamentalist movements emerged in the eighteenth and nineteenth centuries. One of these was the Wahhabiyya in the Arabian Peninsula, whose tenets were adopted and spread by the Saudi clan of tribal leaders in Najd and later became the ruling creed of Saudi Arabia. Other movements were influenced to a greater or lesser extent by the Wahhabiyya, such as the MAHDIYYA and *Khatmiyya* (or *Mirghaniyya*) in Sudan, the Sanussiyya in Cyrenaica (Libya), and the IDRISSIYYA in Asir. These movements, though orthodox and opposed to Islamic mysticism (*Sufiyya, Sufism*) and its Dervish Orders, adopted some *Sufi* practices and methods of organization, establishing orders of their own. *Sufism* and its orders, are frowned upon by the Islamic establishment, but remain within recognized, legitimate Sunni Islam.

Shi'i Islam is divided into several trends or sects (see SHI'A). The principal trend—the *Imamiyya*, or the "Twelvers" (*ithna-'ashariyya*), or *Ja'fariyya* dominates Iran, constituting a majority in Iraq and DUBAI. About half the population of BAHRAIN, a strong minority in Lebanon (estimates varying from approximately thirty percent to thirty-five percent of the population), and smaller minorities in Saudi Arabia and several PERSIAN GULF sheikhdoms. ZEIDI Shi'is dominate Yemen, comprising approximately fifty-five percent of the population. The Isma'iliyya are a sect on the fringe of Shi'i Islam, and considered by many as outside Islam. Though they ruled Egypt, large parts of north Africa and parts of other Arab countries from the tenth to the twelfth century, few of them have survived in these countries—in Syria (less than one percent of the population), Yemen and the eastern al-Hasa province of Saudi Arabia. Two sects that emerged from the Isma'iliyya or were greatly influenced by it, are the Druze (in Syria, Lebanon and Israel) and the Alawis or Nusseiris (in Syria, in Turkey's Hatay district, and some in Lebanon). These two sects are considered by many Muslims as outside the pale of Islam (though the Alawis in Syria, are in official practice, treated as Muslims. The President, who must be a Muslim, is an Alawi).

Islam is the state religion in Iran and all Arab states except Lebanon, where there is no state religion. Saudi Arabia and Oman have no written constitution, and the provisional constitutions of Kuwait, Bahrain, QATAR, and UNITED ARAB EMIRATES (UAE) do not deal with basic principles, though their Islamic character is evident. The links between Islam and the state are particularly strong in Saudi Arabia whose growth and conquests also spread the Wahhabi concept of Islam, and in MOROCCO, where the royal dynasty is also endowed with the status of Islamic religious leadership (the king is entitled "The Commander of the Faithful" (amir al-mu'minin). Similar links existed in the past in Yemen (where the Zeidi-Shi'i Imam was king) and Libya (where the king was also head of the Sanussi order), but these special links were severed by the revolutions of 1962 in Yemen and of 1969 in Libya. Most Arab states recognized Islam in their constitution, while still under Western tutelage and before complete independence was achieved, either formally as the state religion (Egypt 1923; Iraq 1925; JORDAN 1928), or by the stipulation that the Head-of-State must be a Muslim (Syria 1930). New constitutions adopted after full independence have continued that practice (Libya 1951; Jordan 1952; TUNISIA 1959; Morocco 1972). Islamic law is state law in Saudi Arabia, the Persian Gulf principalities, Yemen, Iran (since the revolution of 1979), and Sudan (since 1989). The military coups of the 1950s and 1960s and the revolutionary, sometimes socialist or leftist character of the regimes established have effected no basic change in this context: Islam is the state religion in the constitutions— most of them provisional—of these regimes (Egypt 1956, 1964, 1971; Iraq 1958, 1970; ALGERIA 1963 and 1976; Libya 1969; Yemen 1970; Sudan 1971–1973—reinforced in 1983 by the imposition of the Shari'a laws and punishments, and since 1989, Islam has been the state Law). Syria does not explicitly name Islam as its state religion, but its Constitutions of 1950 and 1973 state that the President must be a Muslim and that Islamic Llaw is the principal source of legislation. (For attempts to adapt the Islamic code of law to the needs of modern states, see SHARI'A.)

Radical Islamic groups, however, have not been content with that official and constitutional recognition of Islam. They reject the law codes based in all Arab states (save Saudi Arabia and several other countries of the Arabian Peninsula and the PERISAN GULF) on Western models and the fact that constitutional-political life in most Arab states is structured on modern rather than Islamic principles, demanding the imposition of the Shari'a and its codes of punishment as the law of the state and the social code of behavior. Many Islamic scholars have always advocated similar views or demands. During recent decades organized militant movements sprang up to propagate and enforce them (for the history of these trends, see MUSLIM BROTHERHOOD and ISLAMIC RADICALISM AND MOVEMENTS).

ISLAMIC ACTION FRONT   see MUSLIM BROTHERHOOD, ISLAMIC RADICALISM AND MOVEMENTS.

ISLAMIC JIHAD   see ISLAMIC RADICALISM AND MOVEMENTS.

ISLAMIC LIBERATION PARTY   see ISLAMIC RADICALISM AND MOVEMENTS.

ISLAMIC RADICALISM AND MOVEMENTS
From the late 1960s onwards, the Muslim world has encounted an intensifying wave of religious awakening, along with the emergence of Islamic movements with a radical cultural, social and political agenda. By the early 1990s, this phenomenon of political ISLAM, or Islamism, became socially and culturally dominant in all ARAB and Muslim countries of the Middle East. It was reflected in the primacy of the Islamic discourse in a political manner of these countries and the powerful appeal it gained to their populations.

Much of the attention given to this by the West came from the violent nature of this trend of religious fervor and the fanaticism marking some Islamic groups and regimes , raising fears of "a clash of civilizations" and "threat" to Western liberal, democratic values and social order. Indeed, the Shi'i revolutionary fervor of IRAN remained confined to the Shi'i comunities in the PERSIAN GULF and LEBANON, and has been gradually diminished since the late 1980s. Indeed, SUDAN has been the only state in the Muslim SUNNI-world to be dominated by an Islamic radical regime (since 1989). Nonetheless, the international dimension of the Islamic radical trend had an important impact on Islamic movements in the Middle East. Veterans of the Afganistan War against Soviet occupation formed the hard core of armed Islamic groups in EGYPT, ALGERIA and YEMEN. The civil war between the government and some Islamist incomparably murderous groups in Algeria since 1992, along with the armed attacks of Islamist groups against tourists, public figures and CHRISTIAN sites and peoples in Egypt have have been at the forefront of the concerns of an Islamist takeover of other states' power with detrimental implications for Western economic and security interests. Adding to these manifestations of internal war, the violent nature of the Islamist wave has also been nurtured by the suicidal attacks by the Shi'i Lebanese Islamist HIZBALLAH against the multi-national force in Lebanon in 1983 and its continued armed struggle against Israeli military presence in south Lebanon; and the attacks conducted by the Palestinian HAMAS movement against Israeli civilians—mainly in the form of mass-killing suicidal bombings—since the signing of the Oslo Agreement between ISRAEL and the PALESTINE LIBERATION ORGANIZATION (PLO) in September 1993. Moreover, from the early 1990s international TERRORISM has been increasingly identified with Islamic regimes (mainly Iran and Sudan) and movements, adding an urgent and immediate dimension to the "Islamic threat" to the West. The internal violence and international terrorism perpetrated by Islamic JIHAD-groups in the 1980s and 1990s has increased to disturbing levels, presenting governments with a grave domestic challenge. Hence they are desperate to maintain consultations and examine ways to curb this threat through coordination and mutual consultation.

Indeed, despite the horrifying scope of Islamic violence in Algeria (the toll of the civil war in late 1997, estimated at between at 60,000–80,000), violence has been relatively minimal compared to the mainstream Islamic trend whose activities and interests focus on religious guidance and education, communal services, and increasingly on political participation. The continuous repression of political activity in most Muslim Middle Eastern states rendered the Islamic "party" the only viable option. The Islamic trend has been the main driving force claiming political participation in some Arab states, reflecting the desire of the mainstream groups of the Islamist tide to enter the political process with

the aim of sharing, if not seizing, power for the sake of applying the Islamic Law and (SHARI'A) make it the sole source of legislation. All the militant Islamic groups believe that the only solution to their social problems is the establishment of an Islamic Shari'a state. The question that divides them is the method of changing the government.

Overall, radical Islamic movements tended to adopt violence in response to violent repression, while in those states that tolerated Islamic political movements the latter has been willing to accept the rules of the political game and refrain from violence, such as in the case of the MUSLIM BROTHERHOOD (MB) in JORDAN and Sudan. Participating in the political system—even when dominated by non-Islamist regimes—is apparent across the Middle East, from Algeria and Sudan through TURKEY, Yemen, Lebanon and Jordan. Even in Israel, defined as a Jewish state, a group of the Islamic movement—at the cost of a split—took part in the 1996 general elections, winning a seat in the Knesset. This inclination reflects first and foremost the new opportunities for political participation opened by some Arab regimes. The very willingness of Islamic movements to participate in varying levels of state-controlled and limited democratic systems, demonstrates the Islamists' belief that they can attain influence and promote their goals by operating within the existing political process. In the case of Algeria, some Islamist groups used violence—but not the mainstream of FIS—after their electoral victory in 1991 had been denied, and Lebanon's Hizballah remained committed to armed struggle against Israel even after taking part in two elections (1992, 1996). The issue of political participation also confronted the Palestinian Islamic Resistance Movement HAMAS, when elections to a legislative council within the PALESTINIAN AUTHORITY (PA) were held in January 1996 in theGAZA STRIP and the WEST BANK. Though HAMAS eventually passively boycotted the elections, the movement established a loosely affiliated Islamic Salvation Party to serve as a political arm and participate in future contests without staining HAMAS's reputation as an ardent opponent of the Oslo Agreement under which the PA had emerged.

The most conspicuous advocates of this increasingly dominant trend in the Arab world have been Hassan al-TURABI (leader of the Islamic National Front in Sudan) and Rashed GHANUSHI (leader of the al-Nahda movement of TUNISIA). This trend adheres to active participation of the Islamic movements in the political process, including involvement in tactical coalitions with non-Islamist movements, with the aim of exploiting the opportunity of political participation to seize power and impose Islamization "from above." They call for adopting modern strategies of mass mobilization rather than elitist seclusion embedded in al-SAYYID QUTB's philosophy, although both of them underline the importance of ideological guidance as a necessary stage for creating a wide base of cadres for the Islamic movement. According to this approach, though the use of violence is not illegitimate under circumstances of repression on the part of the regime, it is not recommended due to the overwhelming power of the state and danger of giving the ruling elite a pretext to wage an all-out war against the Islamic movement. Hence Turabi's reference to the option of gradual penetration into the armed forces and bureaucratic apparatuses, parallel to participation in the political process (reflecting Turabi's experience and road to power in Sudan).

The Islamic trend has been termed revivalism (nahda, ihya'); renewal (tajdid); awakening (yaqza); fundamentalism (usuliyyav); protest (ihtijaj); and resurgence (inbi'ath jadid). Some of the movements were identified with the idea of liberation (tahrirv); salvation (inqazv); fanaticism; radicalism; militancy (asabiyya) or political violence (unf siyasi). These references reflect the vast variety of the phenomenon. Indeed, the Islamic movements are highly diversified in their socio-political background and motives, both individually and collectively, their goals, and means of action. They tend to assume an autonomous nature, overall, lacking strong horizontal ties, intra-state or across national borders, except their reference to the same Islamic sources—though giving it different interpretations and meanings in accordance with the defined goals, opportunities and constraints of action. This variety also underlines the integral nature of Islam and its deep roots in the social and political culture of these societies.

Islam is perceived by faithful Muslims as the supreme and final faith, as well as a way of life and culture capable and worthy of organizing human society. The Qur'an and the Hadith (the oral tradition of the Prophet) comprise a kind of constitutional order according to which the faithful must behave and which is appropriate to all people in all places in all periods of time.

For almost three decades, slogans such as "Islamic Fundamentalism"—literally, the roots of Islam—(al-usuliyya al-islamiyya), "The Ancestral Heritage" (al-salafiyya), "The Islamic Awakening" (al-sahwa al-islamiyya), "The Islamic Alternative" (al-badil al-islami), and "Islam is the Solution" (islam huwa al-hall) have attracted millions of young Muslims in the Middle East into the mosques and to religious practices, but mainly brought them back to traditional behavior in their dress, inter-personal relations and observance of religious duties. Those who preach an Islamic resurgence claim that Islam is the only type of regime which has not been tried yet, and which, in their opinion, will cure the maladies of the Muslims in the current era.

Attempts to explain the causes for the resurgence of Islam on its various manifestations—driven especially by the 1979 Islamic revolution in Iran—raised the main following theories regarding the rise of this trend:

The first and most dominant theory maintains that the Islamic trend originated primarily from a fervent cultural and ideological crisis, reflecting frustrated hopes from, and rejection of the Western-based ideologies experienced in by the Muslim peoples in the modern era-liberalism, nationalism, socialism-but particularly of the liberal, permissive social culture, material consumarism, and the destructive impact of the electronic media on established traditional values. embedded in modernity. This sense of cultural crisis has been nurtured by recurrent political failures such as the attempts to attain Arab unity—once defined as the cure to all malaise and a recipe for Arab renaissance—military defeats in wars with Israel; the frustration caused by the rise and fall of OIL prices in 1973–1982 and the manifestation of waste and corruption it entailed; the crisis of legitimacy of the military-bureaucratic regimes in the Muslim states, mainly due to their failure to live up to their proclaimed goals and to cure the inherent social and economic problems of their societies. This theory underlined the crisis of the encounter of the tradition with modernity, especially among the modernizing educated groups of students and professionals, whose crisis of expectations drove them forcefully to adopt the "Islamic solution" as a refuge and relief from this crisis, on both individual and collective levels. This was particularly salient in view of the social disintegration and collapse of traditional supporting formations in the increasingly urbanizing masses whose poverty and crisis of orientation motivated their quest for spiritual guidance no less than material welfare. Under these circumstances, the impact of Islamist charismatic preachers on frustrated young Muslims could have been one of absolute submission and willingness to follow all his mentor's instructions.

It is in this context that the mainstream Islamic political movements—especially the MB society. met necessary social needs, boosting their prestige along with the failure of the modern state to realize the expectations of its masses. These movements were politically unique in combining communal work and political mission. The social and cultural activity of *da'wa* (literally, preaching) which includes a comprehensive system of social services—education to all age groups, welfare, health care—all submitted in the framework of familiar context of Islamic values and institutions, with the mosque central to these activities, that made these movements so attractive and capable of mobilizing the masses.

The second theory interpreted the rise of political Islam as a result of the success scored by the Muslims, such as in the War of October 1973 (in Arabic: *harb ramadan*, after the name of the month of fasting during which it took place, see ARAB-ISRAEL CONFLICT); the legendary wealth accumulated by some Gulf states, mainly SAUDI ARABIA, and the use it made of this wealth to amplify Islamic activities throughout the world. Above all, it was the *Shi'i* revolution in Iran (1979) which brought home to the Islamists from MOROCCO to Indonesia that it was not only possible but inevitable, and that the Islamization of the state can be attained through popular revolution and violence.

The third theory maintained that the current tide of Islamic resurgence is a cyclical phenomenon, that appeared in the history of Islam from its very advent, under conditions of decay, fear of marginalization, and waves of change. According to this theory, the current rise of Islamism is evolutionary, namely, a conservative response to the forces of reform in Islam. During the last two centuries such responses characterized the reaction of the Islamic world to the modernizing trends in Islam which represented the impact of the West.

Such crises, have been affected by the repeated emergence of conservative interpretations of Islam by religious scholars, and preaching encouraging Muslims to adhere to the original Islamic rules defined by the Qur'an and Hadith. Most salient of those scholars were Ibn Hanbal (Abu Abdallah Ahmad Ibn Ahmad—780--855), the founding father of the Puritan School of Sunni Islam (see ISLAM; Sunnis), considered by the current Islamic resurgent groups as their spiritual leader, and Ibn Taymiyya (Taqi al-Din Ahmad—1263–1328) who called for a *Jihad* against the Mongols (who had adopted Islam after conquering Baghdad in 1258), claiming that they were only paying lip service to Islam as a way of consolidating their conquest.

The writings of Ibn Hanbal and Ibn Taymiyya were of great influence on the leaders of the Islamic revivalist movements, especially on the WAHHABIYYA movement (1703–1878), named after the founder and leader of this movement, Muhammad Abdel Wahhab,who denounced the religious practices of the Ottoman Empire, and succeeded in strengthening his exegesis of the *Qu'ran* and the *Hadith*. Like Ibn Hanbal and Ibn Taymiyya, Abdel Wahhab called for a return to the original sources of Islam and, combined with the political power of IBN SA'UD, brought large parts of the Arabian Peninsula, including Mecca and Medina, under the domination of the Wahhabi concept of Islam. Considered a threat to the *Ottoman Empire*, the Saudi-Wahhabi state was finally defeated by the governor of Egypt, Muhammad Ali (1818).

The declining power and shrinking territory of the Ottoman Empire under pressure of the European powers since the late eighteenth century, brought to the return of Islam as a rallying force by the Ottoman Sultan ABDEL HAMID II. The conquest of Tunisia by FRANCE in 1881, and especially the conquest of Egypt by BRITAIN in 1882, led to increasing opposition to Western penetration and an effort to take Islam up as a primary political ideology in shaping the Muslim response to Western domination. The response to the impact of the West was articulated by a group of Islamic scholars in Egypt, primarily Jamal al-Din al-Afghani (1839–1897) and his disciple, Muhammad Abduh (1845–1905), whose approach was marked by defense of Islam as a valid doctrine of life and faith, and yet called for reforms that would provide for renewal of its glory. In 1884, they went to Paris, and formed a clandestine group that worked for Islamic unity and the introduction of reforms into Islamic societies. They also founded a journal called *al-Urwa al-Wuthqa* (the strong bond), which preached a return to the values of Islam as interpreted by Ibn Taymiyya.

Muhammad Abduh was prominent in shaping and disseminating Afghani's vision of a new Islam and his conception of PAN-ISLAM. Abduh claimed that there was no inherent contradiction between reforms based on Western values and the spirit of Islam, stressing that Muslims should take from the West—as a matter of interest—what is right for them as long as it was not in conflict with basic tenets of Islam. This approach between Western culture and Islam, known as conciliation (*al-tawfiqiyya*), was to become essential in the current Islamist political discourse.

Rashid Rida (1865–1935), another Egyptian religious scholar and Abduh's disciple, preached ion his Islamic journal *al-Manar* (lighthouse), for the purification of Islam from later accretions, the reform of higher education, and the defense of Islam from external attacks. Unlike his mentor, Rida went as far as to disqualify Western culture as a source of inspiration, supporting social and institutional reforms necessary for Islam. Instead he also stressed the need for renewal of the Caliphate (abolished by the Turkish republic in 1924). Hisfundamental premise was the superiority of Islamic rule, as it derived from divine inspiration. In his view, the Caliphate was important for warding off the assault of national secular ideology—inspired by the Turkish nationalist example and concept of territorial nationalism—which he regarded as a threat to Islam's universal ideology.

For over a decade after its abolition in 1924, the issue of the Islamic Caliphate was high on the agenda of Islamic scholars, primarily those centered around the most prominent Islamic academy of al-AZHĀR. The significance of the debate derived from the contention between the mainstream, adhering to the renewal of the Caliphate as a symbol of the universal community of Muslims (*umma*), and the minority group led by Sheikh Ali Abdel Razeq (1888–1966), who called for the abolition of the Caliphate, on the grounds of the separate functional nature of the state from the spiritual nature of the Islamic community. He contended that the Prophet's

Umma had no meaning or essence of government and that the current community of Muslim believers does not have to be united politically, and indeed it cannot be. Abdel Raziq was fiercely critized by many of al-Azhar's Council of Ulama who blamed him for weakening Islam and dividing it.

The liberal ideological approach represented by Abduh and Abdel Razek—integrating local Egyptian nationalism and Westernized cultural life of the Turko-Egyptian elite—flourished in the 1920s, indicated by the development of modern literature, the press, and secular political and social thought. A movement for the liberation of women, calling to caste off the veil and traditional garb, emerged but was short-lived. By the late 1920s Egypt witnessed a strong shift toward religious radicalization in the form of the advent of the MB. The new movement, was founded in ISMA'ILIYYA in March 1928 by Hasan al-Banna (1906–1949), who warned the Muslims of the dangers of Westernization, and especially the liberation of women, as a grave danger to the moral character of the Islamic society. The MB opposed women in political and social life; the reform of *Shari'a* (Islamic Law) courts, and the battle of liberals against polygamy. They saw, Westernization as anarchy and corruption, and they struggled for the return to the ancestral (*salafi*) Islam. Although the objectives established by the members of this movement did not initially indicate that they had political intentions—stressing a process of reforming the society from below, through preaching and education—the movement had to define its ideological position concerning the Islamic and political problems on the public agenda. Thus, it gradually developed a comprehensive ideology, fundamentally different from the one with which it started.

The basic tenets of the MB can be summarized as follows:

a. The inclusiveness of Islam: Islam is religion and state, prayer and holy war (or effort) (*jihad*), obedience and rule, book (*mushaf*) and sword (*seif*).

b. Islam must be restored to its early and original teachings.

c. Pan-Islam: all Muslims are one nation, and the Islamic homeland is one homeland, thus the defense of any part of the Muslim land is a religious duty of any Muslim.

d. The caliphate is the symbol of Islamic unity and must be restored.

e. Islamic government—based solely on the Islamic Law, is the only legitimate government.

Moreover, with their strengthening power, the MB tacitly developed a political approach to the issue of Islamization of the society, of taking power over and changing society from the top to bottom. Between 1934 and 1937, the movement of the Muslim Brothers turned to become a paramilitary organization. In 1938, al-Banna entered political life and, also reorganized the paramilitary units. During World War II, the paramilitary organization was officially registered as part of the scouts movement. By the end of the war, there units numbered 45,000, and on the eve of the 1948 Palestine War they were 75,000 members, rendereing a major showdown with the government inevitable (see ARAB-ISRAEL CONFLICT; MUSLIM BROTHERHOOD; and EGYPT).

Indeed, from the mid-1940s, the MB became a constant threat to Egyptian governments which tended to restrict the movement's activity or implement Western interests, with political assassination becoming increasingly employed by the movement against Egyptian politicians. The role played by the MB in the Palestine War of 1948, and actions against British and Jewish property in Egypt itself during and after the war, helped the movement strengthening its military power and popular prestige, but also brought it to a head-on collision with the government. In December 1948, Prime Minister Nuqrashi Pasha was assassinated by the MB for attempting to disband the movement, leading three months later to the assassination of al-Banna himself, and the consequent MB attempt on the life of Prime Minister Abdel Hadi.

In May1948, the Constitution of the MB was finalized, combining social and political principles in accordance with the nature of the movement as "an inclusive Islamic body acting to attain the objectives for which Islam came into being". The eight sections of this Constitution include, *inter alia*: interpreting the Qur'an according to the original covenant; the inclusiveness of the Qur'an and its compatibility with the spirit of the times; social justice and social insurance for every citizen; war against illiteracy, disease, poverty and corruption; the liberation of every Arab country and all parts of the Islamic homeland from foreign domination; and the establishment of an integral state that will function according to the precepts of Islam, to protect Islam from within, and to universally spread the precepts of Islam.

By the late 1940s, the MB movement expanded its activities to other Arab countries, primarily Sudan, Syria, Jordan and Mandatory Palestine. Although these movements continue to share the same sources of inspirations and religious principles, there is no supra-national Islamic movement, leadership, or "international" organization that supervises or inspires these movements. In fact, over the years, each of these has movements developed its own leadership and style of action in accordance with local conditions and specific national allegiance, explicitly recognizing the existing international order based on mutual respect of each Muslim state's independence and sovereignty, maintaining that even after Islamization is achieved, such states might cooperate on the basis of Islamic solidarity but would remain politically separate. Indeed, apart from extreme marginal Islamist groups, the mainstream Islamist movements in the Middle East have been marked by a strong national identity which has superceded their common Islamic solidarity.

Another important stream of Islamic radicalism has been represented by the Islamic Liberation Party (*hizb al-tahrir al-islami*). The Party was established in Jordan by Sheikh Taki al-Din al-Nabhani, a Palestinian Muslim judge and former member of the Muslim Brotherhood, who yearned for the establishment of the Islamic Caliphate, but dissented from the Muslim Brotherhood's concept of "reform from below", that is Islamization merely by education and preaching. Nabhani took an activist position toward Western political influence, especially in Jordan, and adhered to a revolutionary pattern of action, withouth abandoning the elements of education and preparation of society for a take over by the Islamists. In the course of the 1970s the Party spread out to Egypt and the MAGHREB (especially in TUNISIA, in 1982–1988), and activist members endeavored to initiate military coups in the Arab states and forceful transfer of power to the hands of Islam. The Party thus developed as a tiny subversive group, attempting to penetrate the ruling circles in the Arab states, while the Muslim Brotherhood remained a popular movement.

Islamic Radicalism in Egypt was, and still is, of primary significance in terms of its ideological impact on other Sunni Muslim societies in the Arab world, manifested primarily through the Islamic Brotherhood movement, but also by the justification of the use of violence against non-Islamist regimes and other deviant Muslims. The temporary alliance between the MB and leading figures of the military coup of July 1952 in Egypt soon ended when the ruling junta refused to let the MB affect the process of legislation. Their relations reached a crisis following a decision by the Revolutionary Council in early 1954 to disband the MB, which was followed by massive arrests of the movement's members; an attempt on the life of ABDEL NASSER in October of that year, and further arrests of MB members, especially among members of the underground. Among those arrested was al-Sayyid Qutb (1906–1966), former supporter of the coup, who spent a few years in prison, where he continued to write, trying to organize the Muslim Brothers, many of whom were in prison. In 1965, following a short period of release from prison, Qutb was arrested again, sentenced to death, and executed with other MB members on the grounds of plotting against the regime.

Qutb, who spent two years studying in the UNITED STATES (1948–1950), was the main MB ideologue in the years of repression by the Egyptian regimes. His early writings, combining a humanitarian approach of social justice; limiting property; the redistribution of wealth, and a minimum wage—all frequented in the writings of liberals, leftists, and communists—affected some of the "Free Officers" who became in 1952 the rulers of Egypt. Qutb's most important book—*Ma'alim fi al-Tariq* (Milestones)—is considered a constitutional framework for Islamic groups whose goal is to take control of the government by any means, and turn it into a *Shari'a*-dominated Islamic state. The philosophy of al-Sayyid Qutb can be summarized as follows:

1. Two conceptions are in absolute opposition: Islam and Ignorance (*jahiliyya*-the term used for the pre-Islamic period), faith and apostasy. There can be no compromise between them, other than the eliminition of one, and clearly jahiliyya should be eliminated for true Islam to prevail in the world.

2. The entire world is one of *jahiliyya* and apostasy, including the Islamic states and their current regimes.

3. Only Islam is the religion of truth. All other religions—philosophies, theories and ideologies—are futile and misguided.

4. Change will emerge via action and fundamental revolution.

5. *Jihad* is an ongoing precept to liberate the entire world so that only Islam will prevail.

6. JEWS and Christians are infidels and none of their interpretations or studies of Islam should be used.

7. Islam does not despise materiality, which is part of the universe in which we live, and theories and training for development should not be rejected out of a true belief in Islam.

The building of a true society of Muslim believers according to Qutb, was to be made in isolation and disconnection from the rest of the society and especially from the regime and its powerful impact attained through its domination of the media, education, and economy. al-Sayyid Qutb's later writings were significantly influenced by Abu al-A'la al-Mawdudi from Pakistan who was apparently the first to raise the concept of "The New *Jahiliyya*." Mawdudi's concept of *Hakimiyyat Allah*-the rule of the Kingdom of Heaven, and the *jahiliyya* of society in general was a revolutionary concept which meant that all human society is composed of infidels and therefore it is permissible and even obligatory to struggle against it by force. There is no obligation of obedience except to the IMAM. Qutb's legitimization of the use of violence in order to realize the goal of true Islamic community must be seen against the backdrop of the harsh repressive measures taken against the MB in Egypt under Nasser.

The first organization in the spirit of Qutb's ideology—The Society of Muslims (*jama'at al-muslimin*)—was founded by Ali Abduh Isma'il, a young Egyptian graduate of al-Azhar, during his years of imprisonment. Its members, still in prison, began to isolate themselves from society, and aimed to create the nucleus of a new Islamic society, which would declare a *Jihad*, in accordance with the preaching of al-Sayyid Qutb.

In the late 1960s and the early 1970s, a number of militant Islamic organizations began to plot and to take violent action against the government. One of them, The Islamic Liberation Party (*hizb al-tahrir al-islami*)—also known as Youth of Muhammad (*shabab muhammad*)—was led by Dr. Saleh Abdullah Siriyya. This organization was exposed as a result of its abortive attempt to take over the building of the Technical College near Cairo in April 1974, when

Anwar AL-SADAT was riding the tide of leading the October 1973 war. Siriyya, confident of initial success, had prepared a proclamation to be broadcast over radio and televison, as he was planning to announce a curfew and his own appointment as Amir of Egypt.

Another militant Islamic organization which was exposed in the 1970's, was the one founded by Shukri Ahmad Mustafa, which became known as the Society of Excommunication and Migration (jama'at al-takfir wal-hijra). Mustafa was imprisoned for distributing MB's leaflets. In prison, he became an ardent supporter of Ali Isma'il joining his Jama'at al-Muslimin. In 1971, with the entrenchment in power by Sadat a change in the regime's relations with the MB and other Islamic groups occured. Faced with Nasser's legacy of PAN-ARABISM and radical socialism, Sadat opted for the MB as allies to widen his basis of legitimacy. In 1971 thousands of MB members and other Islamists were released from prison. From 1972, Sadat cultivated close relations with the MB, allowing them to renew their publications. However, after the October War (1973) growing friction between Sadat and the Islamic groups that had been determined to continue their struggle against the regime emerged. Shukri Mustafa, the leader of Jama'at al-Muslimin returned to intensive activity while completing his studies in agronomy in Asyut. He drew much of his ideas of Islam from al-Sayyid Qutb, but went further to advocate the notion that of the need to abandon existing society in order to form the nucleus of the desired Islamic society through migration (hijra) to the mountains and caves. A true Muslim must distance himself from acts forbidden by commandment, otherwise he will be considered an infidel (fulfilling the five elements of Islam is not sufficient). The only sources for the laws and commandments are the Qur'an and the Hadith. The principles of Islamic action were defined as creating the organizational structure of the group and electing Shukri Mustafa as Amir (commander of the faithful); rental of flats to be used as the local underground headquarters in Cairo, Alexandria, and other districts; migration of the group members to the caves and cliffs of the mountain region in order to implement the ideology; recruitment of as many military men as posible to play a role in operations and for training members of the organization to use weapons.

Mustafa and his companions sought refuge in the mountains of the al-Minya region in September 1973. They were soon caught, with their weapons, and imprisoned. In April 1974, they were released, and they renewed their underground activity. In July 1977, Mustafa and his senior comrades kidnapped Shaikh Muhammad Hasan al-Dahabi, a former minister of the WAQF. When their demands were rejected, they killed him. By the end of July, most of the group had been captured. Mustafa and another four were condemned to death, and many were sentenced to various prison terms. Consequently, serious attention was given to the gravity of the activities of the militant Islamic groups, as Jama'at al-Islamiyyin was estimated to have between 3000–5000 members.

Despite the harsh measures taken by the Egyptian authorities against the extremist Islamic groups in Egypt, they were not weakened. On the contrary, there was a proliferation of competing Islamic orgaizations which aspired to bring down the regime of Sadat, to introduce Islamic rule through Jihad and to return to the Caliphate as the integral principle of the Islamic state. The most widespread and dangerous group that appeared in the late 1970s was the Jihad organization, consisting of three militant groups. These groups first formed a coalition, and in June 1981, merged into one organization, based on the ideas of Muhammad Abdel Salam Faraj, and under his leadership. Faraj (born in1952) initially joined the Jihad organization in Alexandria, and later on moved to Cairo where he began setting up a Jihad organization. He recruited for his organization young students, as well as young people he met in the mosques of Cairo. A young man drafted into the organization would immediately begin his ideological education and military training. It was one of the members of this group, Khalid al Islambuli, a lieutenant in the artillery who assassinated Sadat on 6 October 1981. It should be noted that Sheikh Omar ABDEL RAHMAN, a blind sheikh and central spiritual figure in the Jihad organization, issued in the late 1970s, a FATWA (an Islamic scholarly opinion), which was interpreted as legitimizing the assassination of Sadat

In his book published in 1980, Faraj advocated an Islamic state headed by a CALIPH as an alternative to the Egyptian regime. Such a state, Faraj contended, cannot materialize except by Jihad, which was currently the missing commandment. He compared the current rules of Egypt with those during the Tatar conquests at the time of Ibn Taymiyya, concluding that there was no choice but to wage *Jihad* to rectify the distortions. Asserting that the Qur'an and *Hadith* legitimize war against all those preventing the realization of Islam, he permitted attacks on shops belonging to COPTS. In general, the *Jihad* organization abhorred Jews, considering them to be criminal enemies of the Islamic *Umma*, going so far as to dissociate them from the 'people of the book' in the Qur'an. As for the Christians, they were seen as the continuation of the Crusaders who fought Islam. In his book, Faraj criticized the other Islamic movements, especially the Muslim Brotherhood, as opportunitst, seeking integration with non-Islamic political parties, but also the organization of al-Takfir wal-Hijra, for preaching migration and withdrawal instead of *Jihad*.

Following the arrest of most of the *Jihad* organization's leaders after Sadat's assassination, and after the security forces took over the militant groups' strongholds in Asyut, these groups suffered a serious setback. But, as from the mid-1980s, *al-Jama'a al-Islamiyya*, headed by Sheikh Abdel Rahman, succeeded in reorganizing its members and began launching terroristic attacks against the security forces in Upper Egypt, as well as in Egypt's main cities and especially Cairo.

Between 1985 and 1997, thousands of Egyptian citizens and members of the security forces were killed. *Al-Jama'a al-Islamiyya* proved to be the most cruel Islamic organization acting in Egypt, claiming responsibility for the assassination of ministers, intellectuals, Copts and police officers. Members of *al-Jama'a* attempted to assassinate Egypt's Prime Minister, Atif Sidqi (1992), as well as President MUBARAK (1994). The Egyptian authorities expanded their struggle against this group, and by the middle of 1997, their efforts had weakened the organization. Consequently, its main leaders, who were serving long-term imprisonment, proposed an armistice to the authorities. The Interior Minister, Hasan al-Alfi, rejected this proposal, accusing the organization of trying to cheat the government in order to gain time. In September 1997, members of But *al-Jama'a* attacked a group of German tourists who were coming out of Cairo's Museum, killing ten of them. It seems that the battle today remains far from ended.

In summary, the question of violent methods was discussed by Shaikh Hasan al-Banna, the founder and Supreme Guide of the Muslim Brothers. He left behind a complete legacy of organized codes which were disseminated in the Muslim Brothers' publications and are followed to this day. They are codified under the title *Aqidatuna* [our faith] emphasising "Islam is the complete constitution of the world, and it should order life in this world and in the world to come". Hasan al-Banna says that "The Muslim Brothers must be strong and must attain power. Power will come gradually. First there will be the power of faith, then the spirit of unity and solidarity among members of the movement, and later the power of force and arms."

The Muslim Brotherhood's ideology is widespread in most parts of the Islamic world. Sayyid Qutb, Shukri Mustafa, Salih Sariyya, Abd al-Salam Faraj and the vast majority of the *Jihad* activists were all "graduates" of the Muslim Brotherhood movement, and drew their preaching from this source. Their violent action reflects impatience toward the evolutionary strategy of building the Islamic society from below, and probably an awareness that such an evolution would never reach the desirable goal given the decisive eminence of the state and modernizing forces. Hence, they opted to wage violent revolution to take over the government at once and apply the *Shari'a* from above.

The Islamic Jihad (Palestine) The idea of Islamic Jihad against the infidels was boosted by the Shi'i revolution in Iran, but even more so by the Soviet invasion of Afganistan and the Islamist nature of resistance developed, *inter alia*, by Saudi and American support to the holy war combatants (*mujahidin*) who were joined over years by many volunteers from the Middle Eastern Muslim states. These two major events in Iran and Afganistan had an important impact on the rise of an Islamic *Jihadist* tendencies among Palestinians, both in Israel and the occupied West Bank and Gaza Strip. In Israel, "The Family of Jihad" (*usrat al-jihad*) was exposed in 1981, following which the group members shifted their activity to sheer social and political endeavor. A similar group appeared in the early 1980s in the Gaza Strip, which stressed a combined Palestinian identity and strive for national liberation through an armed struggle against Israel, articulated in universal Islamic principles and beliefs, coined as an Islamic Holy War and defined as a religious duty for every individual Muslim. The group, led by Sheikh As'ad Bayudi al-Tamimi, Abdel Fattah 'Awda and Fathi Shiqaqi, drew on the militant activist approach of the Islamic Liberation Party—the call for the defense of Islamic land anywhere from being taken by the enemies of Islam.

The Islamic *Jihad* established from the mid-1980s has close links with Iran and began armed attacks against Israeli soldiers in the Gaza Strip at a time of discernible decline of the armed struggle by the secular organizations of the Palestinian national movement embodied by the groups coalesced in the PLO. The Islamic *Jihad* group played a crucial role in triggering the Palestinian uprising (INTIFADA) in the Gaza Strip and the West Bank, and apparently on the establishment of *Hamas* as an offshoot of the local Muslim Brotherhood movement shortly afterward. (For details, see HAMAS.) Although it remained a small group without a strong social basis among the Palestinians in the Israeli-occupied territories, it had an active role during the Intifada. Following the Israel-PLO Oslo Agreement and the establishment of the (PA) in May 1994, the group initiated a number of suicidal attacks against Israeli civilians and soldiers within Israel, out of objection to the Oslo process, sustaining repressive measures by the PA. In the summer of 1995, Fathi Shiqaqi was assassinated in Malta, apparently by Israeli agents and replaced by Ramdan (?) Shalah. The leading figure in the Gaza Strip is Sheikh Abdallah al-Shami.

The Islamic Front (Syria) A Muslim Brotherhood branch has been active in Syria since the mid-1940s. A contingent of MB volunteers particpated in the 1948 Arab-Israeli war in Palestine. The mainstay of the movement was always in the Sunni cities of the north, primarily Hamah, Homs and Aleppo. During the late 1970s, growing violent activity, primarily attempts on the life of leading figures of the ASAD regime and ruling BA'TH Party, dominated by the ALAWIS, were implemented by Islamist underground groups. In 1980 the MB faction combined with the Islamic Liberation Party and other groups forming the Islamic Front of Syria, led by Muhammad Bayyuni, Adnan Sa'ad al-Din and Sa'id Hawa, the leading ideologue of the new coalition. The Front enjoyed Iraqi support, which increased throughout the 1980s in response to similar Syrian subversion and support of Iran in its war with IRAQ. In February 1982 the Front initiated a rebellion in Hamah, and ap-

pealed to the Syrians to join in civil mutiny against the Asad regime. The Rebellion was forcefully repressed, at the cost of tens of thousands of casualties, and the destruction of the old city of Hamah. The mass-repression of the Front led to its going underground, and a split between the MB who opted for continued links with Iraq, and a more purist group led by Adnan Uqla, which loathed Saddam HUSSEIN on the grounds that he had invaded an Islamic country. That same year the MB faction forged and led an alliance of seventeen other opposition groups to form the "National Alliance for the Liberation of Syria" under the exiled Syrian leader Amin al-Hafiz in Baghdad. The coalition's main demands were the introduction of constitutional parliamentary regime, Islam as the state religion, and the *Shari'a* as the main source of legislation. The split within the Front caused a decline in the radical Islamic activity in Syria.

Islamic Jihad (Lebanon) An Iran-backed *Shi'i* Lebanese organization, formed in the spring of 1982. The group became known mainly for its numerous kidnappings of Western diplomats, scholars and clergy in Lebanon, taking them as hostages or assassinating them, mostly in the service of Iran's revolutionary regime. In April 1983 the organization set a truck-bomb at the US Embassy in Beirut, killing sixty-three people, seventeen of whom were Americans. In October of that year, similar operations were conducted against the US Marines headquarters in Beirut (part of the multi-national force stationed on Lebanese soil since August 1982), killing 241 troops, and against the French force, killing 59 troops. A similar operation was made against the Israeli headquarters in Tyre, killing 60, half of whom were Israeli troops.

In 1991, following a series of diplomatic contacts with Iran and Syria that led to the release of some Western hostages, UN Secretary General Javier Perez de Cuellar became personally involved in a diplomatic mission aimed at releasing the remaining Western hostages held by the Islamic *Jihad* in return for the release of some 450 Lebanese and Palestinian prisoners held by Israel without charge. The mission bore fruits in late 1991, including the return of seven dead or captured Israeli servicemen. The Islamic Jihad ceased its activity with some of its activists joining *Hizballah*, another Iranian-backed *Shi'i* faction.

For further details on Islamic radical movements, see TURKEY, for the Islamic Welfare (*Refah*) Party; the Lebanon's HIZBALLAH and AMAL; IRAN; ALGERIA's FIS; HAMAS; and MUSLIM BROTHERHOOD.

ISLAMIC SALVATION FRONT (*Front Islamique du Salut*)

The major Islamist movement in ALGERIA, wages both a political and military struggle against the military-backed regime in order to turn Algeria into an Islamic state. Opposition Islamic groupings grew in Algeria from the mid-1970s in response to the regime's efforts to monopolize Islam and also due to growing popular disillusionment with Algeria's failed socialism. While they advocated an Islamic state ruled by the SHARI'A a radical trend led by Mustafa Bouyali (an ex-FLN fighter) attempted an armed insurrection in the countryside during 1984–1987, but was crushed by the regime.

The October 1988 mass riots, together with the brutal suppression by the military, prompted President BEN-JEDID to implement political reforms. He legalized opposition parties in order to restore the regime's legitimacy, and enhance his own authority. The Islamists took advantage of this liberalization to unite forces, and, on 18 February 1989, founded the Islamic Salvation Front (FIS). This was led by Dr. Abbasi Madani (b. 1931), a graduate of the Sorbonne, and teacher at the University of Algiers. His more radical Deputy, Ali Ben Haj (b. 1956) who represented the younger impoverished generation, lacked formal education, but was known as a charismatic orator. A five-level organization was established headed by a five-member National Executive Bureau also known as the Consultative Council (*Majlis al-Shura*).

The FIS was dominated by the younger more politicized and pragmatic "Algerians" (*Jaza'ra*) branch which advocated an independent Islamic Algeria, and supported Madani in his campaign to replace the regime, even through confrontation. While denouncing democracy as a system, they demanded Parliamentary elections as the vehicle to gain power. The more theologically-orientated*Salafi* trend (see ISLAM RADICALISM), led by older leaders adopted a more gradualist approach in an attempt to achieve a supra-national Islamic state. The FIS spread rapidly throughout Algeria, using its networks of 8,000 mosques and social welfare institutions. It took control of fifty-five percent of the local councils and two-thirds of the regional *wilayas*, during the June 1990 local and regional (*wilaya*) elections. In June 1991, Madani initiated a confrontation with the regime following an amendment of election law, which led to his arrest and that of thousands of other activists. Whilst he was in prison, his supporter Abdel-Qadir Hashani convened a national conference in Batna on 25–26 June 1991, during which he removed many of Madani's opponents from the leadership, further radicalizing the movement.

In the first round of the general elections held on 26 December 1991, the FIS won 188 out of 430 parliamentary seats, even though it lost a million votes compared to the 1990 elections. With the FIS poised for victory in the second round, the army took power, deposed Ben-Jedid, dissolved the National Assembly and banned the FIS.

The military takeover pushed the FIS to a fully-fledged armed resistance. Veterans of the *Bouyali* movement, led by Abdel-Qadir Shabuti (killed in 1994), organized a guerrilla force called Armed Islamic Movement (MIA). In July 1994 the MIA and several other smaller Islamic armed groups formed the AIS (*Armee Islamique du Salut*), as the FIS military arm. Madani Merzaq, a veteran of the Afghan war was appointed as its national commander (Amir) in March 1995.

The FIS leadership was divided between the imprisoned Madani and Ben Haj as supreme leaders; five "sheikhs" who were released from prison; an executive committee in exile led by Rabah Kebir, and Anwar Haddam, head of its parliamentary delegation stationed in the US. Since 1993 the FIS has adopted a dual position of pursuing armed struggle against the military regime, while calling for a dialogue with the military in order to end the violence, and restore the legal political process. It failed to thwart the 1995 Presidential elections, and the 1996 referendum on constitutional amendments, and was engaged in growing conflict with the more radical Islamist movement *al-Jama'a al-Islamiyya al-Musallaha* (Group Islamique Armee—GIA) Yet it still remained a key factor for solving the Algerian domestic crisis.

ISMA'ILIYYA, ISMA'ILIS

A sect that split off Shi'i ISLAM in the mid-eighth century over the identity of the seventh IMAM, recognizing Isma'il, the son of the sixth Imam Ja'far al-Sadeq, who died before his father (against Mussa al-Kazim accepted by the mainstream Shi'a). The Isma'iliyya later developed doctrines based on esoteric interpretations of the Qur'an and adaptations from Neoplatonic teachings. Some Isma'iliyya groups also propagated radical social and political ideas, such as the Qarmatians (*al-Qaramita*) of eastern Arabia in the nineth and tenth centuries. The Isma'iliyya Fatimids founded a dynasty in North Africa in the tenth to twelfth centuries, and ruled EGYPT, SYRIA and both shores of the Red Sea, including Hijaz with the holy cities of Mecca and Medina, and Yemen. An eleventh-century offshoot of the Isma'iliyya was the DRUZE sect. The ALAWI sect also grew out of the Isma'iliyya.

Salah-ul-Din conquered Cairo in 1171 and defeated the Fatimids, and the Isma'iliyya were suppressed and gradually disappeared from Egypt and the MAGHRIB. Isma'iliyya groups survived mainly in Syria, PERSIA and Yemen. They split into two main branches—the *Musta'lis* or Western Isma'iliyya, and the *Nizaris* or Eastern Isma'iliyya. The former, believing in a hidden Imam were centered mainly in Yemen; but in the seventeenth century their center was moved to Gujarat in India and has remained there. These Isma'iliyya have survived in India and are today called *Bohras* or *Boharas*, or *Tayyibis*. Some *Bohra* communities exist in East Africa and Burma, mainly among Indian migrants, but none in the Arab countries.

The *Nizaris*, who recognize a revealed, apparent Imam, ruled several regions in Persia and Syria from fortresses they built, and became known as *Hashshashiyyun* ("Assassins" in Western languages, with their legendary leader the "Old Man of the Mountain"). They developed a doctrine of holy terror, executed by "self-sacrificing" bands, *Fida'yyun*—a term that has come in modern times to denote guerrillas or terrorists. The rule of the Isma'iliyya Assassins was destroyed by the Mongols in the fourteenth century. They survived underground and within certain *Sufi* (mystic) orders and gradually lost their violent character. In the nineteenth century, the Shah of Persia conferred on the forty-fifth imam of the *Nizaris* the title of Aga Khan; but as he developed ambitions to the throne of Persia or some territorial rule, he had to flee in 1840, to India, where the British, while firmly discouraging his territorial

ambitions, accepted him as the spiritual leader and *imam of the Nizaris* Isma'iliyya, called in India *Khojas*. The title "His Highness the Aga Khan" has passed to his descendants. The Aga Khan, claiming descent from the Caliph Ali and the Fatimid Caliphs, is considered an incarnation of the Divinity and his word is law among the *Khoja* Isma'iliyya, who number an estimated 15–20 million, mostly in India and among Indian migrants in East and South Africa. The *Khoja* Isma'iliyya under the Aga Khan are a tightly knit community; they have developed an elaborate network of welfare, health and educational institutions, and the Aga Khan himself is immensely rich. (The third Aga Khan, Sir Sultan Muhammad Shah, 1877–1957, was the most widely known.)

Few Isma'iliyya have survived in the Arab countries—some 100,000, mainly in Syria and also in the al-Hassa province of SAUDI ARABIA and in Yemen. Their links with the *Khoja* community and the Aga Khan seem to be weak. In Syria, where they are concentrated in the Salamiyyah region, some Isma'iliyya were active in the BA'TH-led *coups* and the régime they established. Most prominent was the al-Jundi clan (Sami al-Jundi— Cabinet Minister and Ambassador; Colonel Abdel-Karim al-Jundi—chief of the secret service; Khaled al-Jundi—head of the trade unions)—but they were dismissed in the late 1960s (Abdel-Karim committed suicide or was murdered in 1969, and Sami went into exile).

ISRAEL

Introduction Independent republic at the eastern end of the Mediterranean, bordering with LEBANON in the north, SYRIA and JORDAN in the east and southeast, the Red Sea in the south and EGYPT in the southwest. JERUSALEM is the capital, even though it has not been narrowly recognized as such, internationally (see below). Israel emerged following the end of the British Mandate on Palestine. This was on the basis of the UN resolution 181 of 29 November 1947 on partition of Mandatory Palestine into two states, one for Arabs and one for Jews. According to the UN partition plan the area allotted to the Jewish state should have covered approximately 6,170 sq. miles (16,000 sq. km.), out of the total of 10,217 sq. miles (26,493 sq. km.) of Mandatory Palestine west of the river Jordan. However, the end of the Mandate and proclamation of the Jewish state resulted, respectively, in a Civil War with the indigenous Arab population and invasion of four regular armies from the Arab neighboring states into Palestine (War of Independence—see ARAB-ISRAEL CONFLICT), at the end of which Israel had expanded the territory under its control beyond the UN boundaries to 8,010 sq. miles (20,770 sq. km.) Following the 1967 war, Israel annexed East Jerusalem and in 1981 applied the Israeli law on the GOLAN HEIGHTS), albeit without officially annexing this territory. At the end of the War of Independence (see ARAB-ISRAEL CONFLICT), Israel's borders with Egypt, Lebanon, Jordan and Syria were drawn in UN-sponsored negotiations. These led to separate armistice agreements (February–July 1949) between Israel and each of its immediate neighbors. The border with Egypt corresponded to the Mandatory one concluded by BRITAIN in 1906, with the OTTOMAN EMPIRE (except for the GAZA STRIP, which remained under military Egyptian rule), which was reaffirmed in the Israel-Egypt Peace Treaty of 1979. With Lebanon, the border corresponded to that signed by Britain and FRANCE in 1923. It has remained recognized as such by Israel regardless of its military presence in southern Lebanon since the late 1970s. The armistice border with Syria was slightly west of the international border between Mandatory Palestine and Mandatory Syria. It included demilitarized zones the sovereignty which has remained disputed between the two states. The current border between the two countries is that laid down in the Disengagement Agreement signed by the two countries in May 1974, (see ARAB-ISRAEL PEACEMAKING) which left much of the Golan Heights, conquered by Israel in the 1967 war (see ARAB-ISRAEL CONFLICT), in Israeli hands. The armistice border between Israel and Jordan (the Green Line) divided the area that came under Jordanian sovereignty—the WEST BANK—from the rest of Mandatory Palestine. In 1967 Israel occupied this territory but never officially annexed it. Israel and Jordan finally settled their disputes over their mutual border in the Peace Treaty of October 1994, accepting the international line dividing independent Jordan from Mandatory Palestine (1946) which runs along the Jordan River, the Dead Sea and the Arava valley. Israel's national borders remained unsettled on two fronts: with Syria, which claims Israeli withdrawal to the pre-1967 border (a matter discussed by Syria and Israel in their peace negotiations (1991–1996)); and with the PALESTINE LIB-

POPULATION OF ISRAEL IN THOUSANDS

Year	Total	Jews	(% of total)	Muslims	Christians	Druse and others
1944*	1,697.9	509.2	(30%)	1,042.1	132.8	13.8
1949**	1,173.9	1,013.9	(86%)	111.5	34.0	14.5
1954	1,717.8	1,526.0	(89%)	131.8	42.0	18.0
1959	2,088.7	1,858.8	(89%)	159.2	48.3	22.3
1964	2,525.6	2,239.2	(89%)	202.3	55.5	28.6
1969	2,929.5***	2,506.8	(86%)	314.5	73.5***	34.6
1974	3,421.6	2,906.9	(85%)	395.2	78.7	40.8
1979	3,836.2	3,218.4	(84%)	481.2	87.6	49.0
1984	4,199.7****	3,471.7	(83%)	559.7	98.2	70.0****
1989	4,559.6	3,717.1	(82%)	655.2	107.0	80.3
1994	5,671.5	4,441.1	(78%)	781.5	157.3*****	91.7
1997	5,759.0	4,637.0	(80%)	842.5	183.2	96.3

* Mandatory Palestine
** The State of Israel at the end of the War of Independence
*** Including the population of East Jerusalem, with its large Christian population
**** Including the Druze population of the Golan Heights
***** The new immigrants from the former Soviet Union including many non-Jews
The figures since 1967 do not include the non-Jewish population of the West Bank and Gaza Strip, and of the Golan Heights until 1981. They do include the Jewish population of these areas******

ERATION ORGANIZATION (PLO) and the Palestinian Authority (PA), over the West Bank and Gaza Strip.

Israel's population is mainly Jewish (seventy-nine percent); Christians, mostly from the former Soviet Union (two percent), and a large Arabic-speaking minority—mostly Muslims, with a small minority of Christians, DRUZE, and Circassians—(nineteen percent), made up of an indigenous population which lived in the country long before the beginning of Zionist immigration into Palestine, and which did not flee or expelled from it in the course of Israel's War of Independence (see ARAB-ISRAEL CONFLICT and PALESTINE ARABS in Israel). The major part of Israel's population occupies the central coastal plain, between Netanya and Ashdod, despite the official policy of even distribution of the population and efforts to settle the Galilee in the north and the Negev in the South. About half the population of the Galilee is Arab. Unified Jerusalem and its environs is Israel's largest city, with a population of over half a million.

The State of Israel was proclaimed on 14 May 1948, and was recognized de-facto by the United States and the Soviet Union that same day. The proclamation of the State of Israel was the realization of ZIONISM. It is unique amongst the independent states of the post-colonial era in that it was founded as a Jewish state while the overwhelming majority of the Jewish people was—and still is—out of its territorial boundaries. The Jewish population in the fledgling state was just over 600,000. This facilitated the immigration of many other Jews into the country, mostly of the remaining European Jewry after the Holocaust, and the Middle East countries, who had come under growing pressure of the local Muslim societies and governments. Although JEWS everywhere always yearned to be in the land of Zion and Jerusalem, the immediate reasons of migration to Israel of Jewish communities from Yemen, IRAQ, and North Africa, were mostly political, resulting from the deepening conflict between Jews and Arabs in the Muslim world. In 1948 this culminated in a comprehensive, regional Arab-Israeli conflict. Israel, which was proclaimed a Jewish State, is the only state in the world which grants a particular national-religious group—the Jews—the right to settle in it and gain automatic citizenship. This is based on the Law of Return of 1952.

Despite its definition as a Jewish state, Israel is not Jewish in terms of its laws. In other words, the law of the land is not the *Halacha*, or Jewish religious law, but the secular law made by its parliament—the Knesset (see below). While the religious parties, representing less than twenty percent of the population, strive to turn the religious law into a state law, the majority of the Jewish Israeli population perceives Jewishness as a national and cultural identity, with basic attributes of belonging to the Jewish community through Jewish marriage and divorce, circumcision, burial ceremony, and observance of the Sabbath as the official day of rest, as well as most of the state's official holidays, dictated by the Jewish calendar.

The first official language in Israel is Hebrew, with Arabic officially recognized as the second official language (even though in practice it is hardly applied).

Israel is generally considered to be Western in its cultural orientation. In its formative years the official policy was that of the "melting pot", turning all the newcomers, irrespective of their country of origin, into Israelis, more or less in the image of the original secular socialist settlers. Israel has since developed into a pluralistic society, in which the various cultures—secular-religious, western-eastern, modern-traditional—claim formal acceptance and equality. If a *kulturkampf* does exist within the Israeli society, it is most evident on the religious-secular level.

Political History The territory on which the State of Israel was formed had constituted part of the Ottoman Empire until 1917. From 1917 to 1947 it was under British rule, which in 1922 was officially mandated to Britain by the League of Nations. The Mandate document included the BALFOUR DECLARATION in its terms of reference. During the years of British rule the Jewish community of Palestine—which grew from approximately 50,000 in 1917 to approximately 600,000 in 1948 primarily through immigration—developed a modern political community with autonomous and modern systems of education, health, and welfare, trade unions, clandestine military capability, economy, and central political institutions acceptable to most of the *Yishuv* (the Jewish community during the Mandate.

Thus, when Israel was officially proclaimed on 14 May 1948, most of the apparatuses of state had already been functioning. Upon gaining independence, Israel had been led by David BEN GURION, leader of the dominant *Mapai* (Palestine Workers' Party).

Apart from a short interval (1953-1954) Ben Gurion remained Prime Minister until 1963, while *Mapai*, and later on the Israel Labor Party, remained in power without interruption until 1977.

Immediately after its proclamation the Arab armies of Egypt, Syria, Jordan and Iraq invaded the new state, in addition to the "Army of Deliverance," comprised of Arab volunteers from most Arab countries. After the initial phase of containment of the Arab offensive, which endured for three weeks, and under pressure of the UN Security Council's resolutions— orchestrated by Great Britain—on cease-fire, embargo on arms supplies to the warring parties and UN-sponsored mediation, a month-long truce was reached upon during which Israel managed to reinforce its military capabilities through arms procurements—despite the embargo—as well as new immigrants. When the fighting resumed on 9 July, for ten days of fighting, Israel moved to the offensive which meant to obtain strategic goals, primarily to link Jewish Jerusalem to the Jewish populated coastal plain, widening of the "narrow waist" of the state according to the UN Partition Resolution, and the expulsion of the invading armies from the areas allotted to the Jewish state by the UN. A new truce imposed by the UN prevailed until Israel launched its second offensive, with the main effort directed against the Egyptian Army which sustained a serious blow and was expelled from the Negev save a small enclave. After two weeks of fighting, another truce was imposed by the UN. Within less than two months, Israel launched another offensive against Egypt, penetrating into Sinai, in order to force Egypt to enter negotiations on ending the war. Although the Arab Armies also grew in scope and arms, on the whole, they suffered more from the international embargo than Israel. Furthermore they lacked coordination which allowed Israel to wage decisive attacks against each of the Arab armies separately (see ARAB-ISRAEL CONFLICT). From June 1948 until his assassination in September that year, the UN mediator Folke Bernadotte shuttled between Tel Aviv and the Arab capitals to resolve the conflict on the basis of Arab recognition of a "small and compact" Jewish state, repatriation of the Arab-Palestinian refugees, and the annexation of Jerusalem to Jordan (later replaced by the internationalization of the city). Although these proposals had been rejected by Israelis and Arabs alike, its main components were adopt-

ed by the UN General Assembly's decision 194 of 11 December 1948. The fighting ended in the second week of January 1949 and was followed by separate Armistice agreements between Israel and each of the four Arab states bordering with it—Egypt, Lebanon, Jordan and Syria. Although the role of the Lebanese Army in the war was meager, it served as a territorial and logistic rear for the Army of Deliverance which operated in the Galilee during the war. This led to Israeli penetration into the Lebanese territory in late October 1948 (see ARAB-ISRAEL PEACE-MAKING). Israel was left with a territory significantly larger than that allocated to it by the UN partition plan. The elections to a Constituent Assembly, which was to have drawn up a constitution for the new state, were held on 25 January 1949, and soon the Assembly declared itself the first Knesset of the State of Israel. On 5 December 1949, Ben Gurion declared Jewish Jerusalem the capital of Israel, despite its internationally disputed status. This decision caused world wide discontent which remains unresolved to this day.

Though the Jewish community had developed a high level of cultural, administrative and political autonomy during the British Mandate in Palestine (1917–1948), the first few years of the State necessitated a great deal of groundwork in terms of forming the machinery of government; developing an economy (see below); adapting the laws and legal system to the new reality, and organizing the Israel Defense Forces (IDF) in a way that would meet the security needs in the face of continued Arab hostility (see below). Although the Jewish Agency had maintained foreign links with Western governments already during the Mandate, Israel had to shape its own foreign policy in a divided international system according to its needs and limitations.

Domestic Affairs The first years of the state witnessed a mass influx of Jewish immigrants from Europe and from the Arab world. This increased the Jewish population of the country from approximately 600,000 in 1948 to 1,013,900 in 1949 and 1,526,000 five years later. The mass immigration from the Muslim countries resulted in changing the nature of the Jewish pre-independent community. This was predominantly European by origin. It soon became a multi-cultural society, with an increasing amount of newcomers. The mass immigration also caused an acute shortage of housing. This led to the establishment of transition camps whereby the living accommodations were tents and shacks. There was large scale unemployment, resulting in government initiated public works. There was a tremendous amount of sickness and disease brought in by the immigrants or caused by the poor housing conditions and malnutrition.

In its absorption of the mass immigration, the government and the Jewish Agency tried to turn all the new arrivals as rapidly as possible into Israelis. This neglected their traditions and customs. This erupted years later in the form of social and political protest against the Labor movement in general. On 9 May 1959, there was a first inkling of this anger and frustration in an outbreak of violence against an ethnic background, in the neighborhood of Wadi Salib in Haifa. Most of the immigrants from the Muslim countries were subjected to the difficulties of absorption and mistakes committed by the authorities in treating them as communities and individuals. Nonetheless, it was mainly the Moroccan Jews who expressed their sense of humiliation through political protest against the Labor-Ashkenazi elites. They increasingly supported the rival *Herut* (and later, the *Likud*) Party. In the early 1970s violent demonstrations erupted in Jerusalem, organized by a group calling itself the Black Panthers. This was made up primarily of North African youths, protesting against the poor social and economic conditions resulted by discrimination of those Jews of Middle Eastern origin. The government and police were utterly insensitive to this very real social problem, and tended to relate to it as a manifestation of violating law and order. In the 1977 general elections the second generation of these immigrants was instrumental in de-electing the Labor Party for the first time since the state came into being.

For over a decade after its foundation, the process of state formation and nation-building continued to draw on the Zionist ethos and visions of gathering Israel's peoples from the diaspora in the State of Israel, settling the land, and defending its sovereign territory. The service in the IDF and external threats to the survival of the state—embodied by intensive tension on the borders due to infiltration of Arab-Palestinians into the Israeli territory for grazing their flocks, thefts, sabotage, and terror. This triggered Israeli military retaliations against the neighboring Arab states.(This culminated in the Suez war of 1956,

see below) and served as major themes in creating the Israeli collective identity and sense of common fate and goals. Furthermore, the commemoration of the Holocaust and the historic lessons drawn from it were turned into a powerful instrument of nation building, namely, that Jews could rely only on themselves and that the State of Israel was to be the main guarantee that such a disaster would never again befall the Jewish people anywhere. It was in this context that in May 1960 the Mossad caught Adolf Eichmann. He was the main figure in charge of implementing the Nazi "Final Solution" of systematic extermination of European Jewry during WORLD WAR II, in Argentina and kidnapped him to Israel to stand for trial. Eichmann's trial opened before the District Court in Jerusalem eleven months later, ending with a death sentence which was implemented shortly afterwards. He was the first and so far the only person to be officially executed in Israel.

The economy had to cope with the almost total absence of natural resources; monumental development requirements; a rapidly growing population, largely without the skills required in a modern economy; the burden of defense expenditures due to the continued state of war with the Arab neighboring states, and the reality of the ARAB BOYCOTT of Israel, all resulted in the need to impose a strict policy of economic austerity and rationing and in a chronic shortage in "hard currency." Israel's decision in 1952 to negotiate the Restitution Agreement with the Federal Republic of GERMANY. This was finally signed on 10 September 1952, despite strong moral opposition from large circles in the country (especially the *Herut* Movement led by Menahem BEGIN). This was almost exclusively the result of the difficult economic situation. Against this backdrop, the Kastzner Affair burst into the open in 1953 when Dr. Israel Kastzner, a Jew of Hungarian origins and a member of *Mapai*, was publicly accused by certain personalities in Israel of collaborating with the Nazis during the World War II, in order to save a group of Jewish Hungarian dignitaries. In 1957, Kastzner was murdered. The question of whether he had been a devil or saint continues to raise strong emotions in Israel to the present day.

Elections to the second Knesset were held on 30 July 1951. In the course of its term, four governments served—two under Ben Gurion and two under Moshe Sharett—who from 1933 to 1948 had served as the head of the Jewish Agency Political Department and Foreign Minister in Ben Gurion's first four governments. This was a stormy period within the predominant Labor movement. A split on ideological grounds occurred within the Kibbutz *Hame'uhad* kibbutz movement in 1951. This resulted in many kibbutzim, and families within them, splitting in two. A violent strike amongst seamen in Israel's shipping company Zim, organized in 1951 by radical elements within the *Mapam* Socialist Party, was crushed with force. Not long afterwards *Mapam* split also on ideological grounds. However, none of this affected the predominance of the various workers' parties in the Israeli political system for another two and a half decades.

In this period Israel experienced its first spy scandal, involving the Mossad, with far-reaching implications for the dominant *Mapai* Party. Toward the end of 1954 an Israeli spy ring, involving thirteen Egyptian Jews, was uncovered. Two members of the ring were executed on 31 January 1955. This affair came to be known as *essek habish* (the bad business), and bedeviled the ruling *Mapai* Party until 1963 Ben Gurion insisted on those he felt to have been responsible—especially Pinhas Lavon who was Minister of Defense when the spy ring was put into operation being implicated.

In 1963, the growing dispute within *Mapai* drove Ben Gurion to split from the party which he had led since the early 1920s. With this, the Ben Gurion era came to a close, even though he went on to establish a new party in 1965, with the participation of Moshe DAYAN and Shimon PERES. This ran in the elections to the sixth Knesset, gaining ten seats. Following Ben Gurion's split from *Mapai*, Levi ESHKOL became Prime Minister. The Eshkol era saw a change in the official attitude of the regime towards Menahem Begin and his right-wing *Herut* Movement, which Ben Gurion had continuously ostracized for political reasons. Symbolically, Eshkol decided to allow the bringing to Israel of the remains of the Revisionist leader Ze'ev Jabotinsky. It was also Eshkol who for the first time since the establishment of the state, invited Begin and his Party to join his government on the eve of the 1967 War (see ARAB-ISRAEL CONFLICT. Eshkol also finally cancelled the special Military Administration under which Israel's Arab citizens had lived until 1966 (the DRUZE population was freed from it in 1962). Although Eshkol con-

tinued Ben Gurion's practice of holding the security portfolio in addition to his premiership, he remained in the shadow of Ben Gurion. His young protegées identified with the military and security concerns of Israel, primarily Dayan and PERES. The shaky position of Eshkol came to the forefront during the May–June 1967 crisis on the Egyptian front (see ARAB-ISRAEL CONFLICT), when he was forced to reshuffle his cabinet, submit the Ministry of Defense to Dayan, and establish a national coalition government. This included, in addition to Dayan from Rafi, also Menahem Begin and Yosef Sappir from *Gahal* (this national unity came to an end in August 1970 when Gahal—the predecessor of the *Likud*, made up of the *Herut* Movement and the Liberal Party)— left the government on grounds of objection to its decision to accept the Rogers Plan (see ARAB-ISRAEL PEACEMAKING).

Israel encountered its first grave economic recession in the two years which preceded the Six-Day War. In an attempt to contain inflation and reduce the budgetary deficit, the government adopted a policy of reducing investments, and slowing down private construction. This soon eroded economic growth, causing high rates of unemployment. The economic recession was cut short by 1967 War due to the massive expenditures on security, transportation and settlements invested in the occupied SINAI PENINSULA, the West Bank and Gaza Strip and the Golan Heights.

The quick and sweeping victory of Israel in the war triggered a wave of messianic and national excitement among Jews worldwide, bringing a new wave of immigration to Israel. In the early 1970s, a temporary opening of the gates for Jewish emigration in the Soviet Union brought another wave of immigrants to Israel. A direct result of the war and occupation of all the territory west of River Jordan was the rise—in the course of the years—of a tacit alliance between secular national right-wing, and the National-Religious Party (NRP, in Hebrew: *Mafdal*). For decades, this had been an ally of the labor movement. This shifting alliances reflected the transformation undergone by this party, from a moderate religious-Zionist movement to a messianic militant-nationalist movement. Its primary goal became defined in terms of redemption of the "Land of Israel" in its entirety (*Eretz Israel Hashlema*). This had always been a leading principle of the secular nationalist *Herut* Movement. The new alliance reflected the growing significance of religiosity in the Israeli identity. The quest for retaining the West Bank and Gaza Strip took on the argument that these territories are indivisible parts of the Promised Land and hence, of the very identity of the Jewish state. While the secular right explained the idea mainly in terms of strategic needs of security, the religious-nationalists has seen the redemption, through settlement of, the West Bank and Gaza Strip as an essential part of Judaism.

The occupation of Arab territories by Israel also resulted in the intensification of the use of violence in the conflict between Israel and its Arab neighbors. This reflected the rising active role and prestige of the Palestinian guerrilla organizations. The War of Attrition (see ARAB-ISRAEL CONFLICT) along the SUEZ CANAL resulted for the first time in Israel's history in slight fructures in the national consensus on the price of security and the government's decision on security. At the same time, the ongoing violence on the part of the Palestinian guerrilla organizations, generated a wave of hijackings of (beginning with hijacking an "El-Al" plane to ALGERIA in October 1968), and attacks on Israeli and Israel-bound commercial airlines. Especially after 1970, when *Fatah* joined the Popular Front for the Liberation of Palestine (PFLP: see PALESTINE ARAB GUERRILLA ORGANIZATIONS) in conducting international guerrilla warfare, strikes at Israel's air communications became more frequent and effective. Among the acts of terror that followed was the attack at Lod Airport. In 1972 twenty-six people, most of them pilgrims from Puerto Rico, were killed there. Eleven Israeli sportsmen at the Munich Olympics, were slayed in the same year. These activities triggered a growing international interest and sympathy to the Palestinian national cause, which began to echo among leftist Israeli groups, but primarily among ISRAEL ARAB CITIZENS, for whom the 1967 war was a watershed in their political history. Reunited with the West Bank and Gaza from where they had been disconnected for nineteen years, the Israeli Arabs began exploring their political identity and links with the rest of the Palestinians within and outside historic Palestine.

Since the end of the 1948 War, Israel's Arab minority was tolerated as a passive non-Jewish group. Not only they had been put under military government until 1966, they also became subject to insti-

tutional and legal discriminations, manifested in land appropriation, perpetuation of underdevelopment, and marginalization and dependency on the Jewish majority in all spheres of life: financial allocations, access to national and public economies and participation in power of the Arab Knesset members. Several days before the outbreak of the Sinai Campaign, on 29 October 1956, forty-nine inhabitants of the Israeli Arab village of Kafr Qassem were shot dead by a unit of border police, for being in breach of a curfew of which they had known nothing. The massacre was above all a reflection of the Israeli perception of its Arab citizens, namely, a fifth column. The event is still traumatic for the Arab citizens of Israel, who until 1966 lived under a special military government, with limited rights of movement in the country.

In the late 1960s and early 1970s, Israeli Arabs became increasingly aware of their political rights as citizens of Israel. They protested against their discrimination, insisting on equality with the Jewish majority. On 30 March 1976 an event occurred which left a deep mark on the relations between Jews and Arabs within Israel. Six Israeli Arabs were killed by security forces in the course of violent demonstration to protest the confiscation of Arab lands. Since then the Israeli Arabs, and since the *intifada* the Palestinian population in the occupied territories as well, have commemorated "Land Day", in the form of protests and demonstrations.

From its very advent, the Israeli political system has been divided over the basic premises and principles that should shape the state's individual and public law. This is primarily due to the dispute between a minority of Jewish orthodoxy and the liberal-secular majority. The founding fathers led by Ben Gurion refrained from deciding these differences by a majority vote in the Knesset, even though it seemed to be politically attainable. With the proclamation of the state, it was preferred to continue the "status quo" that had consolidated during the pre-state period under the Mandate. This gave the (orthodox) Chief Rabbinate an exclusive standing on personal law and observation of propriety (*kashruth*) in the public sector; with no separation of state and religion. The ultra-orthodox groups were allowed to enjoy a limited number of exemptions from army service. It is primarily this secular-religious cleavage that made it impossible to codify a constitution. There are a number of basic laws, of constitutional status which were formatted in the early and mid-1990s. It is also due to this constitutional vacuum that especially in the 1990s, the High Court of Justice turned increasingly into a guiding authority on basic legislation through decisions which have often drawn on liberal and secular philosophies. This has intensified the tension between orthodox and seculars in the Israeli society and political system. In the beginning of 1970 a major debate connected with the Jewish identity, as manifested in the Law of Return, was partially resolved when the Knesset passed amendment No. 2 to the Law. This defined a Jew, for the purpose of the application of the law, as "anyone born to a Jewish mother or has converted, and is not a member of another faith." However, twenty-seven years later there was still a major fight in Israel as to what constituted a conversion, since the Orthodox religious establishment in Israel does not recognize conversions performed by Reform or Conservative rabbis.

The 1973 War was a watershed in terms of Israel's internal political situation. Though the Israel Labor Party still won the elections to the eighth Knesset held on 31 December 1973, there were signs of growing discontent, primarily in view of the strategic surprise of the coordinated Egyptian-Syrian offensive. This inflicted on Israel over 3,500 casualties— more than any previous war except the 1948 war. The next two years were marked by gloomy national mood, deriving from deep sense of collective crisis and vulnerability. The American-mediated negotiations between Israel and its neighbors, mainly Egypt, was accompanied by a wave of Palestinian terrorist attacks against Israel-meant to assert the claim to include the PLO in the diplomatic Middle East process. This intensified the public sense of insecurity. Most conspicuous among those attacks, waged in 1974–1975, were on Maalot (where twenty-six people were killed—of whom twenty-one were school children), Kiryat Shmona, Beit She'an, Nahariya, Shamir, the Savoy hotel in Tel Aviv, and Jerusalem. In July 1976 an "Air France" plane, bound for Israel, was hijacked to Uganda. This episode ended with a daring operation by the IDF to release the Jewish and Israeli hostages from Entebbe.

The failure of the political and military leadership to cope with the early warnings of war brought to rise grass-root protest movement, demanding the establishment of a State Commission of Inquiry. Part of the protest vote went to the new Ratz Party formed by Shulamit Aloni—a fighter for human and civil rights and former Labor MK who fell out with Prime Minister Golda MEIR—and the *Likud*, which was formed shortly before the war. As a result of the interim report of the Agranat State Commission, which was appointed to examine the decision-making process toward the outbreak of the war and published its report on 1 April 1974, Golda Meir resigned. The new government formed by Yitzhak RABIN in June, did not include well known figures such as Moshe Dayan, and Abba EBAN. However, the inexperienced Rabin seemed to be weak, with Defense Minister Peres challenging his leadership, both in the Party and the government. In the face of right-wing protests against his peacemaking diplomacy with Egypt, and persistent efforts by a newly emerging national-religious group (GUSH EMUNIM) to settle the West Bank and Gaza, regardless—and despite—of the government's policy, to preclude any territorial compromise on these areas between Israel and Jordan. To the Labor Party's deteriorating status were added scandals involving financial irregularities on the part of several senior party members, including a minister in the government.

The elections to the ninth Knesset, held in May 1977, saw the first electoral defeat since the establishment of the state, of the parties belonging to the Labor Movement. Following the "political upheaval"", Menahem Begin became Prime Minister. Labor's defeat was so great that Begin was able to form a right-of-center government even without the support of a totally new centrist party— the Democratic Movement for Change, headed by former Chief of Staff Yigael Yadin, which won fifteen Knesset seats, though the DMC did eventually join the government. Moshe Dayan, who deserted the Labor Party, joined the new government as Minister for Foreign Affairs, while Ezer WEIZMAN was appointed Minister of Defense.

Prime Minister Yitzhak Rabin resigned his post temporarily at the beginning of 1977, following the revelation of a bank account held by his wife in the US. The alliance between the NRP and the Labor Party survived until 1976, when the latter broke up on the pretext of the desecration of the Sabbath resulting from an official ceremony held upon the arrival in Israel of newly purchased F-15 fighter planes from the US on a Friday afternoon.

The first Likud-led government in Israel accelerated the establishment of Jewish settlements in the West Bank and Gaza Strip, including the entrance of the first Jewish settlers into the old city of Hebron. This brought the number of Jewish settlers in the occupied territories to approximately 8,300. The new settlement policy, forcefully implemented by Minister of Agriculture Ariel SHARON, clearly wanted to prevent any future possibility of a territorial compromise in the West Bank, and with a view to retain the whole territory, regardless of the demographic implications of de-facto inclusion of a large Palestinian population in the area under Israeli government. The Begin government thus differed from the "frontier settlement" policy of the Labor Party, designed along the lines of the Allon Plan, whose logic was based on security, rather than sentimental, considerations. The priority given by the Begin government to Israeli settlements and settlers was combined with deteriorating economic and political conditions for the Palestinian population under the Israeli military government.

The new Israeli pioneer was represented in the figure of a religious-nationalist, a student or graduate of a religious seminary (*yeshiva*), elevating the settlement of the West Bank to a religious duty with a mission of redemption, ostensibly based on the *Halachic* foundations. In 1980 the "Jewish Underground", made up of extremists from amongst these settlers, started to operate in the territories. The members of the underground, which was uncovered only in 1984, were responsible for an attempt to assassinate several mayors of Arab towns in the territories, known for their affiliation with the PLO. Extremists, also the religious-nationalist movement planned to bomb the Muslim shrines of al-Aqsa and Dome of the Rock Mosques on the Temple Mount, as part of a plan to hasten the coming of the Messiah. The settlement policy of the Begin government caused growing frictions between Jewish settlers and the Palestinian inhabitants, reflected in its part by political agitation and discontent within the Palestinian political community.

The intensifying national debate over the political future of the occupied territories, which was aggravated due to the peace agreement with Egypt and the beginning of the autonomy talks between Israel and Egypt generated an official policy of entrenchment with an eye toward the domestic arena. It was in this context that on 13 December 1980 the Knesset passed the basic law: Jerusalem the Capital of Israel, as a result of which most of the foreign embassies, that had functioned in the city until that time, moved down to Tel Aviv. In December 1981, almost six months after the formation of the second Begin government, the Knesset adopted the Golan Heights Law, that applied the Israeli law to this area. The Act was condemned by most countries, resulting in a temporary cancellation of all arms deliveries from the US to Israel. Following the annexation of the Golan, Israel provided all the Druze inhabitants living there with Israeli identity cards. This was fiercely resisted by the Golan Druze who adopted strikes and a boycott of Israeli services, demonstrating their objection to the Israeli citizenship imposed on them. At the beginning of 1982, the Israeli military government in the West Bank and Gaza Strip was replaced by a "Civil Administration," subordinated to the respective military sector command. The change had little if any implications on the administration of the occupied territories which remained in the hands of the military, but it meant to maintain Israel's status as the óverall source of authority in the territories toward possible establishment of autonomy according to the Camp David Accords (see ARAB-ISRAEL PEACEMAKING). The establishment of the civil administration caused uproar among the Palestinian residents, intensifying the international voices criticizing Israel's policy in the occupied territories. As a result, the internal debate within Israel regarding the future of the occupied territories intensified, polarizing the Israeli society and political system between left and right. On the left end of the political spectrum, the "Peace Now" movement, established during the stalemated Israeli-Egyptian peace process in 1978, turned into a primary mass grass-root movement increasingly adopting the Palestinian issue in opposition to the government policy of land confiscation, settlement and violation of human rights in the occupied territories.

By mid-1980 the Begin government lost two of its senior ministers who had been deeply involved in the peacemaking process with Egypt—Dayan and Weizman who resigned due to differences with Begin over the peacemaking policy. Moreover, following the general elections of 1981, a hawkish leadership emerged headed by Begin, with Yitzhak SHAMIR as Foreign Minister; Ariel Sharon as Defense Minister and Raphael Eitan as Chief of Staff. Hence, in the early 1980s the official policy on Arab affairs manifested rigidity and excessive use of military means against the Palestinian guerrilla movements. This culminated in the Israeli invasion of LEBANON on 6 June 1982, ostensibly to eradicate the Palestinian military presence in South Lebanon at 25 miles (40 km.) depth within the Lebanese territory (see ARAB-ISRAEL CONFLICT). The war, which at first enjoyed a broad consensus in Israel, rapidly turned into the focus of controversy. This intensified when the IDF reached Beirut and placed the Lebanese capital under siege for nine weeks, maintaining constant pressure through air and land bombings and shelling in order to force the armed Palestinian personnel and leadership to retreat from Lebanon altogether. The controversial war, which came to be named "war by choice," shattered the Israeli consensus on national security, placing in growing doubts over decisions of security and national defense. The controversy regarding the prolonging War peaked in September following the massacre of Palestinian refugees in the camps of Sabra and Shatilla in Beirut by Phalange militias, with the tacit agreement of the IDF high command. Under unprecedented public pressure expressed in mass demonstration, combined by President Yitzhak Navon's call for the appointment of a state commission of inquiry to investigate the massacre the Begin government succumbed. In October, such commission was indeed appointed, headed by Judge Kahan.

The commission's report, published in February 1983, found that while Israeli political and military authorities had not instigated the massacre, they had borne effective responsibility by allowing the Phalange to enter the refugee camps, and understanding that such a massacre was highly probable. The report resulted in the dismissal of Defense Minister Sharon, the removal of a general from his position, and the end of the Chief of Staff's term. The report intensified the tension between right and left, culminating in the killing of a leftist activist during a demonstration held by "Peace Now" in Jerusalem by a grenade thrown by a right wing fanatic. By that time Israel was bogged-down in the Lebanese march, sustaining increasing losses on the hands of Islamist Lebanese guerrillas.

In the economic sphere the first term of Begin's government witnessed the implementation of a policy of foreign currency liberalization, which led to growing inflation. At the same time, the previous policy of favoring the public social and economic foundations, historically identified with the labor movement, namely, the *Histadrut* (the workers federation) economic sector and the *kibbutzim* (the collective settlements) was changed. However, the *Likud* was unable to formulate a coherent economic policy during these years, and three ministers of finance served in Begin's first government. In October 1983 the shares of the major Israeli banks collapsed, following several years in which the banks themselves manipulated the trade in their own shares. In order to prevent a financial disaster, the state practically nationalized all the shares of the five banks involved, promising the shareholders a fixed interest after a number of years. The total cost of the rescue program by the government was close to 7 billion dollars. A national commission of inquiry—the Bejski Commission— investigated the whole affair throughout 1985 and part of 1986, recommending the removal by resignation or dismissal, of the managing directors and general managers of the five banks. Legal action against these personalities was completed only in the course of 1996. The rate of inflation continued to rise, reaching extremely high levels of three digit figures in the years 1983–1984.

At this juncture of economic and political impasse, the elections to the eleventh Knesset held in July 1984 resulted in almost parity between the two major political blocks, Labor and *Likud* Parties. Hence they were both prevented from forming a government without the other. It was during these elections that *Shas*—a new ultra-orthodox Sephardic party—first entered the Knesset with four MKs, becoming the tip of the Israeli political scale. This almost balanced weight of Labor and *Likud* paved the way to a national unity government for the term of the eleventh Knesset, with Labor leader Shimon Peres and *Likud* leader Yitzhak Shamir serving as Prime Ministers in rotation, each for two years. This government, especially the Labor part of it, was responsible both for the decision to withdraw the IDF from Lebanon, and to recover the economy by adopting "Economic Stabilization Plan," designed to combat inflation.

From mid-1985, Israeli politics became increasingly haunted by the Palestinian issue, indicating a rising attention to the problem, yet further polarization regarding its possible resolution. While the PLO seemed to have largely lost the ability to wage an armed struggle against Israel through its borders due to the loss of the Palestinian autonomous territorial base in Lebanon and expulsion of the PLO's headquarters from Beirut, by 1985 the center of gravity of Palestinian activism had clearly moved into the West Bank and Gaza Strip. The increasing number of individual violent attacks of Palestinians against Israeli Jews, the growing politicization and mobilization of the Palestinian public through grass-root movements and PLO-based institution, and the rise of new young local leadership which had matured in the Israeli jails, all gradually changed the nature of the Palestinians in the occupied territories from acquiescent to rebellious.

At this juncture the Israeli public was forcefully exposed to the demographic-democratic problem facing the Jewish state. Due to economic recession in the Arab oil-producing countries since 1982, labor migration of Palestinians to these countries almost totally ceased with many coming back into the West Bank and Gaza Strip. The demographic proportion of thirty eight per cent to sixty-two percent of Palestinian Arabs and Jews, respectively, in the whole area under Israeli domination (the Land of Israel, or historic Palestine) brought up an estimate that due to the Arab high rates of population growth it would be only a question of time until parity and even an Arab majority could be attained. This would confront Israel with either of two hard options: losing its democratic nature—by maintaining the occupation and preventing political rights from the Palestinian residents of the West Bank and Gaza Strip—or its Jewish identity—if the occupied territories were to be annexed to the State of Israel. The election to the Knesset in 1984 of the extreme right-wing-militant-orthodox Rabbi Meir Kahane—upholding the idea of expulsion of Arabs from the Land of Israel—thus indicated a sort of response to this problem, constituting, together with Shas, another indication of the growing fragmentation and polarization of the Israeli political spectrum over the political identity and moral values of the state. The scandalous, provocative and violent phenomenon introduced by Kahane to Israel's public life led to the amendment of several laws. The intention here was to turn incitement to racism into a felony and to

prevent candidates and political movements found guilty of such incitement, being elected to the Knesset. However, the price which the Labor Party paid for enlisting the Likud to support it and enable the passage of this law was the acceptance of an amendment of the Order for the Prevention of Terror in August 1986. This prohibited all unauthorized contacts with the PLO and other terrorist organizations. This amendment was canceled only in January 1993.

In 1986 Israel's security establishment was shaken by the General Security Service (GSS) scandal. This derived from the latter's secret murder of two Palestinians who were involved in highjacking a bus in southern Israel in April 1984, after they had been captured alive in the course of the rescue operation. Having failed to cover the fact that the prisoners had been actually murdered, they tried to blame Brigadier General Mordechai, the military commander involved in the rescue operation. However, the GSS members responsible for the murder and cover collusion were never brought to trial, though a major reshuffle took place in the organization, including the resignation of the GSS head. With the backing of Prime Minister Yitzhak Shamir they were pardoned by President Haim Herzog, ostensibly to prevent irreparable damage to the service.

The Palestinian uprising (INTIFADA) that erupted in December 1987 became the dominant issue on Israel's public agenda. The elections to the twelfth Knesset in November 1988, however, left the political balance between right and left almost intact. This led to another National Unity government, even though the Likud could have formed a right-wing—religious government without the Labor Party. Differences between Labor and Likud components of the government surfaced with the former increasing its pressure to renew the Arab-Israeli peace process. Following King HUSSEIN's announcement of disengagement from the West Bank, the only practical option for breaking the diplomatic stalemate, was on the Palestinian front. On 14 May 1989, the government adopted Defense Minister Rabin's proposal for holding elections among the Palestinian residents of the West Bank and Gaza Strip and negotiations with their elected leadership on implementation of the Camp David autonomy plan. The adoption of the proposal by the Likud was motivated by the desire to preserve the coalition's unity and, similarly to the Labor, to drive a wedge between the Palestinian "inside" leadership and the "outside" PLO leadership which had remained an anathema to the Israeli government. Nonetheless, the significance of the government initiative lay in the unprecedented recognition in Zionist and Israeli history, of the Palestinian residents of the occupied territories as the main partners to a negotiated settlement, after a hundred years of mostly denial of the Arab-Palestinians as the major party to a settlement of the Arab-Jewish conflict on Palestine, preferring instead, negotiations with neighboring Arab rulers (see ARAB-ISRAEL PEACEMAKING).

However, the initiative was futile due to the *Likud's* reservations and conditions regarding the Palestinian delegates—who had to be not associated with the PLO and yet approved by the latter—with whom Israel would be willing to negotiate. This led to a diplomatic deadlock, and finally to a split in the government.

On 15 March 1990, several days after the Labor Party left the government, it was brought down in a vote on a motion of no-confidence. This was the only time in the history of Israel that a government was ousted like this. Although the chances of the Labor Party to form a new government under Peres's leadership, with the support of the ultra-religious Parties, seemed stable, Peres failed and Shamir managed to form a narrow right-wing government together with the ultra-orthodox Parties. The period of government crisis witnessed some of the ugliest political horse-trading in Israel's history. This resulted in an accelerated political and public effort to limit the impact of individual Knesset members on the stability of governments. On March 18, 1992, the old basic law: the government was replaced by a new law which introduced the system of the direct election of the Prime Minister (see below).

The collapse of the Communist bloc, and then of the Soviet Union itself, resulted in a huge wave of immigration to Israel from these countries. Indeed, in 1989–1996 over 600,000 new immigrants arrived in Israel. On 24 May 1991, 15,000 Ethiopian Jews were airlifted from Addis Ababa. Although Ethiopian Jews had come earlier to Israel, the later wave of immigrants confronted the society and absorption institutions with new cultural and social problems. Despite initial difficulties, a new absorption strategy of letting the immigrants settle anywhere they pleased, sems to have worked better in the longer run, especially with the immigrants from the former Soviet Union. Moreover, by the mid-1990s, the wave of immigration from the former Soviet Union turned out to be a blessing for Israel's economy which reached in those years six to seven percent a year. In order to help with the absorption, Israel requested that the US government grant it 10 billion dollars worth of loan guarantees. However, the US conditioned the guarantees on Israel's stopping all Jewish settlement activities in the territories—which the Shamir government refused to do. The requested guarantees were eventually granted to the Rabin government toward the end of President Bush administration.

Early elections were finally called for June 1992. By this time, the government faced growing difficulties maintaining coalition discipline, and after three small right-wing parties—*Tsomet*, the *Tehiya* and *Moledet*—left the government. In the meantime, the Labor Party held primaries for the party leadership. After fifteen years, Yitzhak Rabin was once again elected Chairman of the Party. Under Rabin's leadership, the Labor Party won its first electoral victory since 1973, forming a narrow government with the participation of the left-wing *Meretz* and ultra-religious Sephardi party *Shas*. For the first time in Israel's history the Arab Parties were enlisted to support the government informally, and without effective participation power, to strengthen its narrow basis. This was reflected in unprecedented financial allocations to the Arab sector in Israel, and uncertain influence of the Arab parties on the changing government peace policy toward the PLO, which led finally to the signing of the Oslo Accord. (see ARAB-ISRAEL PEACEMAKING).

The signing of the Document of Principles (DOP) in Washington on 13 November 1993, initially supported by the majority of the Israeli public, turned increasingly controversial due to a series of suicidal bombings against Israeli civilians and soldiers, beginning in mid-1994. That the perpetrators were of the Palestinian Islamic movements rejecting the Oslo process (HAMAS and the Islamic JIHAD) and located in the Gaza Strip and West Bank, caused many to doubt the benefit of the Oslo Agreement. The right-wing opposition intensified its demand that the Oslo process be stopped, or at least put on hold until the Palestinian Authority (PA) headed by ARAFAT , which had been established in June 1994 in the Gaza Strip and Jericho, implement its commitment to fight TERRORISM. However, the Rabin government refused to condition the peacemaking process with cease of atrocities by Palestinians, contenting with tightening security measures, primarily closures on the Palestinian areas, thus practically separating them from Israel. The Taba Agreement, signed in September 1995 between Israel and the PA stipulating a timetable for gradual redeployment of the Israeli forces in the West Bank, the first phase of which was to transfer full self-governing authority to the PA in the major urban centers of this region and holding general elections among all the Palestinians, including East Jerusalem. The new agreement, shuttering the ideal of wholeness of the Land of Israel, led to violent demonstrations by various extreme right-wing extraparliamentary groups, as well as by the opposition parties, which made little if any effort to contain the extremists. There was also increased personal incitement against the Prime Minister and the government's peace policy, including *Halachic* rulings by some extreme rabbis, implying Rabin was expendable. It was against this background that on 4 November 1995, Yitzhak Rabin was assassinated by a Jewish assassin, following a mass rally in Tel Aviv supporting the Peace Process. The event caused deep shock to the country, and indeed the world. In Israel it was regarded by the depth of political differences, but, even more acutely, the unbridgeable gap between the secular-democratic logic and the *Halachic* national-orthodox, many of whom rejected the democratic decision on such an issue as giving away any part of the Land of Israel.

Under Shimon Peres, who replaced Rabin as Prime Minister, the implementation of the Taba Agreement continued. Nonetheless, Peres decided, especially under another wave of suicidal bus bombings in February–March 1996 in Jerusalem, Ashkelon and Tel Aviv, to postpone the redeployment in Hebron to the aftermath of the elections to the Knesset, which he advanced to May of that year. These elections were the first in which the new law of direct election of the prime minister, voting separately to a list of candidates or a party, came into effect. This ended with the victory of the *Likud* leader since 1992, Binyamin NETANYAHU, whose slogan "secure peace" appealed to voters in the Jewish sector. Netanyahu's victory over Peres was by less than 30,000 votes. On the parliamentary level the results of the elections

were of great surprise, apparently due to the splitting voting (one for the premiership and one for a political party). This indicated further fragmentation of the political spectrum and clear cultural and identity cleavages represented by political parties. Netanyahu, Israel's first Prime Minister to be born after the establishment of the State of Israel, had been elected mainly due to the fact that he had the almost complete support of the religious voters—both amongst the nationalists and the ultra-orthodox. The direct election of the Prime Minister (see below), which brought Netanyahu to power as Israel's first directly elected premier, weakened the Knesset. It also undermined the two large parties—the Labor Party and the *Likud*—in the fourteenth Knesset. Several sectorial parties were strengthened, such as the ultra-orthodox Sephardi *Shas* (which increased its six seats in the thirteenth Knesset to ten in the fourteenth), the NRP (up from six to nine seats), the new Russian Party for new immigrants, *Yisrael Be'aliya* (which gained seven seats), the new Third Way Party (which gained four seats) and the two Arab parties *Hadash* and the United Arab List (up from five to nine seats). The net result was thus increasing dependency of the government on the smaller parties.

In June 1996, a right-wing coalition government headed by Netanyahu came to office, based on the *Likud, Shas*, the NRP, the Third Way and the small ultra-orthodox parties. Although the coalition included a strong element of rejectionists of the Oslo Agreement and its results, the government was confronted with strong regional and international pressures to continue the peacemaking process with the Palestinians. The first major decision that the Netayahu government had to make was whether and how to implement the redeployment in Hebron. Finally it demanded amendments to the already signed agreement. Although Netanyahu eventually agreed to meet with Arafat, and a new agreement was signed between Israel and the Palestinian Arabs on the IDF redeployment in Hebron, the Oslo process virtually came to a halt.

The Netanyahu government disappointed the ideological right, which had hoped it would reverse the Oslo process. At the same time, it was marked from the beginning by tense relations between Netanyahu and some of his *Likud* ministers, leading to the resignation of two of them. Furthermore, the occurrence of repeated harmful decisions by the prime minister's office on both domestic and foreign policies, reflecting disordered or lack of appropriate procedures of government, gradually eroded Netanyahu's prestige and credibility. The new Prime Minister was heavily criticized for failing to bring "secured peace" as he had promised in his election campaign. He failed to stabilize the economy without the cost of stagnation following the huge budgetary deficit left by the Labor government. On the level of foreign affairs, Netanyahu lost his credibility among regional Arab leaders, such as MUBARAK and King Hussein, even before the disgraceful Mossad's failed attempt on the life of a political Hamas leader in Amman (October 1997). Simultaneously, US President Clinton and his Secretary of State made no secret of their growing reservation from his peacemaking policy. On the domestic level too, Netanyahu's position weakened during his first year and a half in office due to the decision to open the Hasmonean Tunnel in the Old City of Jerusalem (September 1996). This led to bloody armed clashes between Palestinian policemen and Israeli soldiers. Netanyahu was personally involved in the attempt to appoint to the powerful position of an unqualified lawyer to Attorney General. It was suspected that this was, a conspiracy aimed at exempting a former Interior Minister from a trial on charges of felony (January 1997). His misleading position on the abolition of the primary elections system in the *Likud* (November 1997), resulted in mutiny against him by many of the *Likud* Knesset members and some ministers as well. The malfunctioning of the Netanyahu government aroused doubts as to the wisdom of the new basic law of direct election of Prime Minister in Israel.

In 1994 an upheaval occurred in the *Histadrut*—a huge conglomerate of trade unions, industry, banking, health and other social services, combining hundreds of thousands of members. Once a major center of political and economic power and main pillar of the Labor movement in Israel, by the early 1990s it had come close to bankruptcy due to years of financial mismanagement, which frequently bordered on corruption, failure to adapt to new social and economic realities and a long lack of excess to power during the terms of *Likud* governments. Against this backdrop, a young Labor leader and ex-Minister of Health in Rabin's second government—Haim Ramon, who was elected Secretary General of the *His-*

tadrut, introduced major changes in the organization. He did this primarily by reducing its activities to the available human and financial resources and encouraging privatization. Although many accused him of focusing on images and destroying the mythical organization, by 1997, the new *Histadrut*—no longer in control of an economic empire (see below)—was well on its way to turning into little more than a trade union federation. It offered a variety of social and legal services to its members and remained powerful when dealing with labor conditions with the public sector.

Foreign Affairs After the 1948 war and the armistice agreements signed with Lebanon and Jordan, Israel's major foreign policy issues were stabilizing its relations with the Arab neighbors and securing international economic and military support to enable the absorption of the mass immigration, and to withstand the possible Arab effort to resolve the conflict by force, respectively. Israel was accepted as a member of the UN in May 1949, in the midst of international mediation efforts to settle the conflict between Israel and its Arab adversaries, conducted by the Palestine Conciliation Commission (PCC) comprised of representatives from the United States (chair), France and TURKEY. Yet the Lausanne Conference, convened by the PCC in April with Israel, Egypt, Jordan and Lebanon, as well as informal Arab-Palestinian delegates of the refugees, soon reached a stalemate, despite the signing, in May 1949, of the Lausanne Protocol by Israel and the Arab states, in which the two sides recognized both the UN map of the 1947 partition resolution, and the resolution of 11 December 1948, reflecting the Bernadotte proposals (see ARAB-ISRAEL PEACEMAKING). Relations with the Arab states soon deteriorated due to the unresolved refugee problem and growing social and political upheavals in the Arab neighboring states. Even with Hashemite Jordan, where King Abdallah himself championed the efforts to reach a settlement with Israel and a five-year non-belligerency accord had been initialled between the two states in February 1950, no progress in the peacemaking was ever made.

Initially, Israel tried to maintain cordial relations with both Western and Eastern blocs. However, despite the support they had extended to Israel before and during the 1948 war, by 1949 the Soviet Union and its satellites became increasingly hostile toward it and their own Jewish populations. This led to Israel's growing reliance on the United States, which became its main source of economic aid, mainly in the form of loans, and the West as a whole. Israel's hopes of joining the non-aligned-mostly decolonized-nations were finally dashed in 1955, when due to the senior position of Egypt and its leader Gamal ABDEL NASSER amongst the non-aligned states, Israel was not even invited to participate in the BANDUNG CONFERENCE.

In the early 1950s Israel's security and defense were challenged mainly by the daily infiltrations of Arab-Palestinians through its borders demonstrating its permeability and vulnerability. One of the worst terrorist attacks in this period was that on an Israeli bus at Ma'aleh Ha'akrabim in the Negev on 18 March 1954, resulting in ten Israeli civilian casualties. Israel's response to this threat assumed the form of forceful, and at times, exaggerated retaliations, against the neighboring states from which the perpetrators arrived in order to force the latter to seal their borders with Israel on their side. The Arab attacks and Israeli retaliations escalated and intensified the search of both sides for arms for possible deterioration to full scale war. A major retaliatory operation implemented by the IDF in late February 1955 against the Egyptians in Gaza was apparently a major trigger for Egypt's president to look for an alternative source of arms out of the Western world. This culminated in a major arms deal signed between Egypt and Czechoslovakia in April, with the blessing of the Soviet Union. The Egypt-Czech arms deal seemed by Israel to be a major shift to the Arab benefit in the balance of power between them, hence the quest for a preemptive war, or return to the previous Israeli military edge. The strategic status quo in the Middle East was ostensibly guaranteed by the Tripartite declaration of May 1950, by the US, Britain and France. This also included an embargo on offensive arms to the states involved in the conflict. Israel, in practical terms, had a quality edge over the Arabs. Nonetheless, Israel's security was self-perceived as being constantly threatened by possible alliance of two Arab states or more. While Britain and the US refused to provide Israel with arms, Israeli-French *rapprochement* from 1954 on began to bear fruits in terms of arms supplies in 1956. The Arab states in general and Egypt in particular, also intensified the application of their boycott against Israel

in these years. Britain was still formally in control of the Suez Canal. Numerous UN Security Council resolutions reiterated the right of passage of Israeli ships and cargoes through the canal. Nonetheless, on 28 September 1954, the Israeli ship "Bat-Galim" was denied passage and its crew detained temporarily by the Egyptian authorities. In 1955 Egypt closed the Straits of Tiran, preventing Israeli navigation to the port of Eilat.

Following secret negotiations with France and Great Britain, Israel embarked on the Sinai Campaign, on 29 October 1956. (see ARAB-ISRAEL CONFLICT). Apart from the need to preempt a shift in the balance of power in the region to the Arabs' favor following the Egyptian-Czech arms deal, Israel went to war in order to put an end to the persistent acts of terror committed within Israeli territory by infiltrators coming from the Gaza Strip, and to break the blockade on navigation to Eilat. This was the first and only war fought by Israel in alliance with other states. It did, however, also teach Israel a lesson, that without American support it could not enjoy long term gains from any military venture. The combination of American pressure and Soviet threats finally forced Israel to withdraw from the Sinai Peninsula for the second time (the first time having been in early 1949) the following year.

The withdrawal from Sinai involved international guarantees arrangements for securing Israel's free navigation in the Gulf of Aqaba to Eilat and the presence of UN Emergency Force along its border with Egypt. Egyptian forces in the Sinai Peninsula were significantly reduced. This gave Israel more security and time for early warning in case of Egyptian military intentions against it. Egypt, however, refused to make any direct contact or commitment to Israel, preferring to handle the issue through the United States and the Soviet Union. The decade following the withdrawal from Sinai was relatively quiet on the Israeli-Egyptian border, save Egypt's surprising decision to mass forces into the Peninsula in 1960. Although the crisis caused by this act was short, it was an early demonstration of the fragility of the security arrangements between the two states. (The same Egyptian act was repeated in May 1967.) However, while Egypt maintained a relatively quiet border with Israel, it deepened its activity on the regional Arab level toward establishing its hegemony in the Arab world, primarily on the grounds of growing antagonism toward the West and hostility toward Israel. This was embodied by Nasser's growing commitment to the ideal of pan-Arab unity, which necessitated the elimination of Israel. The proclamation of the UAR in February 1958, unifying Egypt and Syria in one political unit, the revolution in Iraq, and the upheavals in Lebanon and Jordan in the summer of 1958, indicating a wave of success for Nasser's ultranationalist concept, were perceived with great concern by Israel, as an unprecedented threat to its national security. It was against this backdrop that Ben Gurion sought to reach an alliance with NATO or American commitment to Israel's security, but to no avail. However, with the beginning of President Kennedy's administration in 1960, the US was more willing to meet Israel's needs for defensive weapons. This triggered an arms race in the region, with the Arab states, primarily the UAR and revolutionary Iraq, increasing their procurements from the Soviet Union.

Despite the Arab states' efforts to isolate Israel in the world arena, as a young state with impressive achievements in various economic and social spheres, Israel started to court the newly independent states of black Africa, in the late 1950s, with a substantial measure of success. Israel offered technical guidance and training, primarily in agricultural settlements and military training. (see also AFRO-ARAB RELATIONS).

By force of circumstances and necessity, Israel started to come to terms with the Federal Republic of Germany, with which it established diplomatic relations in 1965. This came after the affair of Geman scientists working on the development of missiles in Egypt was cleared up, and the Nazi war criminal Adolf Eichmann was brought to trial in Israel. However, the Holocaust memories prevented a true normalization of relations between the two countries, in addition to affecting Israel's attitude to the world and the personal lives of hundreds of thousands of Holocaust survivors and their children.

The relatively tranquil period following the Suez Campaign of 1956 ended in the early and mid-1960s, when in January 1964 a summit conference (see ARAB SUMMIT CONFERENCES) of the Arab heads of state was initiated by Nasser in Cairo. This discussed the Arab response to the Israeli national water carrier project (from the sea of Galilee to the Negev). The summit came, for the first time since 1948,

with a plan for collective Arab action against Israel. It was aimed at preventing Israel from utilizing the River Jordan waters by diverting its tributaries, starting in Syrian and Lebanese territories, from their natural flow. To protect the Arab project from possible Israeli retaliation, the summit decided to establish a Joint Arab Command to supervise and coordinate Arab military preparations for a possible war with Israel. At the same summit, Nasser laid the foundations for the establishment of a "Palestinian Entity". This was embodied by the Palestine Liberation Organization (PLO) established in May 1964 in Jerusalem. Although Nasser's initiative was meant to prevent the possibility of an untimely war with Israel which had been strongly advocated by Syria, he soon found himself in an unbearable dilemma, between his interest to preserve his position as the Arab world leader and his refusal to be entangled in war with Israel for which he had not been ready (also because of his military involvement in Yemen since late 1962), both militarily and internationally. Nasser's dilemma derived primarily from Syria's continuing efforts to impose its priorities on Nasser by effectively starting (Spring 1965) diversion works. This forced Israel into military action against the attempt to undermine its project which had just become operational. The growing Israeli-Syrian border clashes, which soon developed into air battles, were combined by sabotage activities of Palestinian guerrilla organizations, primarily Fatah, instigated and military supported by the Syrian BA'TH regime. The growing tension on the Israel-Syria border due to these acts were the immediate cause for Nasser's decision on 15 May 1967 to mass forces into Sinai as a counter-balance act to alleged Soviet information that Israel had been concentrating forces on its northern border to attack Syria (for the development of the crisis, see ARAB-ISRAEL CONFLICT).

Israel enjoyed wide scale international sympathy during the three-week crisis before the war. Its policies of restraint and willingness to exhaust all reasonable diplomatic avenues to remove the tightening siege around it triggered by Nasser's acts in Sinai, when Israel decided to strike first, gave it a positive image. Nevertheless, France-Israel's main supplier of arms until that time declared an arms embargo on it. Soon after the fighting ended all the countries of the Eastern Block, except Romania, broke off their diplomatic relations with it. Nevertheless, Israel was in a state of euphoria, and shortly after the war it officially annexed the formerly Jordanian Jerusalem, including the Old City (East Jerusalem), declaring the unification of Jerusalem under its sovereignty. The swift and overwhelming victory in six days of war at first raised major hopes regarding the prospects of peace between Israel and its neighbors, since now Israel had some trump cards it could play. However, despite Israeli suggestions delivered through the United States to Egypt and Jordan less than two weeks after the war for direct talks on permanent peace in return for its full withdrawal to the international borders except for modifications needed for security considerations (Jerusalem and Gaza Strip were not included in the proposal). Yet, not only Israel's earlier annexation of East Jerusalem had already created an obstacle, the Arab leaders could not meet the Israeli demands under the humiliating effect of the military defeat and urgent need to recover their legitimacy within their own constituencies. Hence, the September 1967 Khartoum Arab Summit Conference (see ARAB SUMMIT CONFERENCES), came out with three strict "nays" regarding any future settlement which may give them back the occupied territories: No to negotiations and peace with Israel, or to recognition of it. Nonetheless, Israel, as well as Egypt and Jordan, accepted Security Council resolution 242 of November 1967. This called for Israeli withdrawal from territories occupied by it in the June 1967 war, paving the road to the Gunar Jarring's mission of international mediation between Israel and its Arab neighbors (see ARAB-ISRAEL PEACEMAKING). This mission, however, failed to take off the ground due to the unbridgeable gap between Israel and its Arab neighbors, as well as fundamental inter-Arab differences regarding the very idea of negotiating even an indirect settlement with Israel. The process triggered an ongoing public debate, which in a sense has not yet been completely resolved to the present day, over whether Israel should accept the principle of full withdrawal from the occupied territories, and on the price Israel should or should not be willing to pay for peace.

The aftermath of the war witnessed a sharp rise in the use of violence between the Arabs and Israel compared to the period that preceded the war. The Palestinian guerrilla organizations came to the fore as a substitute for the defeated and largely destructed Arab regular armies. Furthermore, the growing

skirmishes along the Suez Canal between Israel and Egypt soon escalated into a War of Attrition (March 1969-August 1970). The War of Attrition came to its end as a result of the Rogers Plan, of July 1970, calling for three-month cease-fire and renewal of the Jarring mediation efforts. While the cease-fire was indeed applied and tacitly prolonged, Israel refused to renew the diplomatic efforts under the Jarring umbrella due to the Egyptian breach of the cease-fire agreement by advancing ground-to-air missiles to the Canal on the night before it came into power.

In February 1971, Israel was challenged by Egyptian President Anwar al-SADAT's proposal for a gradual process by which all the provisions of Security Council Resolution 242 would be implemented. It proposed that as a first step Israel withdraw from the Canal to the al-Arish-Ras Muhammad line, to be followed by work toward reopening the Suez Canal to navigation. Yet despite Prime Minister Golda Meir's public response in favor of the approach, the Egyptian initiative turned to be insufficient for bridging the gap between the two sides. Al-Sadat perceived his proposal as an indivisible part of the a comprehensive Arab-Israeli settlement, to be implemented according to an agreed upon and committal timetable. It was doubtful that he would accept Israel's condition for direct negotiations. Israel, on its part, refused to return to the 1967 borders even in return for peace with Egypt, and was willing to accept an interim agreement which would guarantee it a free passage in the Suez Canal and indefinite cease-fire. Following the 1973 war, Gold Meir came under criticism for losing an opportunity to reach peace with Egypt, which could prevent the war.

With the failure of both the Rogers Plan and the Jarring mission (see ARAB-ISRAEL PEACEMAKING) a no-war, no-peace mode prevailed along the Israeli-Egyptian front. Sadat's unfulfilled declaration that 1991 was the "year of decision," and the relative tranquility along the state's other borders, underpinned the perception that such mode could continue indefinitely. On 6 October, the Jewish Day of Atonement, Israel was caught in a strategic surprise by a coordinated offensive on both the Suez Canal and Golan Heights fronts (see ARAB-ISRAEL CONFLICT). The surprise offensive determined the length and cost of this war in human lives, which where greater than any other war since 1948. It took Israel a few days to repulse the Syrians and turn to counter offensive. This enabled it to expand the pre-1973 occupied Syrian territory. Shortly afterwards, a counter offensive against Egypt was waged by crossing the canal and penetrating into Egypt's heartland in a crescent movement southward to Suez city. This put the Egyptian Third Army under siege and danger of elimination by air attacks. Before the war was over, most of the African states broke off their diplomatic relations with Israel as a gesture of solidarity with Egypt as an African state. For the first time in the history of the ARAB-ISRAELI CONFLICT the Arab oil weapon was effectively employed, as of 16 October applying an embargo on oil shipments to the United States and Holland was proclaimed by the ORGANIZATION OF ARAB PETROLEUM-EXPORTING COUNTRIES (OAPEC) states. Furthermore, the Arab oil producers decided that the embargo, as well as a cut of their oil supplies by five percent a month would be implemented until Israel withdrew from the territories occupied in 1967 and the rights of the Palestinians were guaranteed. These measures, accompanied by consecutive drastic rises of oil prices which quadrupled themselves within less than three months (see OIL), heralded a new era of growing Arab economic power in the international arena, particularly among developing states that had constituted the majority of the UN's members. It resulted in Israel's growing isolation in the international arena and increased sympathy worldwide for the Arab point of view in the conflict with Israel. This was most conspicuously expressed by the sweeping support for the Palestinian national cause and the PLO as its legitimate representative. This was clearly reflected in the UN General Assembly's debate on the Palestinian issue in the Fall of 1974, culminating in Arafat's speech on 13 November, and ending with resolution 3236 recognizing the Palestinians' rights for self-determination; national independence and a return to their homes. One of the lowest points in Israel's international status was the passage, the next year, of UN General Assembly resolution 3379, equating Zionism and racism.

Israel's weakened position in the international arena underlined its growing dependence on the United States, whose air-lifted arms supplies during the war enabled the IDF to continue fighting and reverse the military situation. Yet the main manifestation of Israel's tarnished invincibility after the

war was its willingness to cooperate with Secretary of State Henry Kissinger. It was Kissinger who championed the American diplomatic efforts to stabilize the region by bringing Israel and its Arab neighbors to the negotiating table. His shuttle diplomacy reflected a new era in the Arab-Israeli conflict, in which the leading Arab Parties competed against each other in their attempt to exploit the favorite regional and international conditions for the Arabs to extract territorial gains from Israel. However, the attempt to bring all the parties concerned under the same roof and auspices of the two superpowers once again proved to be highly problematic. The Geneva Peace Conference, convened towards the end of December 1973 (see ARAB-ISRAEL PEACEMAKING), was not only boycotted by Syria for ignoring the PLO, but was ultimately little more than a ceremonial, legitimating mechanism for bilateral military agreements negotiated indirectly through Kissinger. In January and May 1974, Israel signed agreements with Egypt and Syria, respectively, which included military disengagement, Israeli withdrawal to new lines; areas of limited armament and forces, and stationing international observer forces. While Israel's ability to negotiate a settlement on its Jordanian front remained limited due by party politics and coalition considerations, Egypt's willingness to enter negotiations over another agreement in Sinai in March 1975 was welcomed by the Rabin government as an opportunity to reinforce the peace process with the leading Arab state. Despite a breakdown of the negotiations and a short period of US "reassessment" of its policy toward Israel, the reopening of the Suez Canal for navigation in June of that year was a clear message of Egypt's constructive purposes. In September, another agreement between Israel and Egypt on Sinai was signed. For the first time this included clear political provisions: that the Middle East conflict shall not be resolved by military force but by peaceful means; that the signatories were determined to reach a final and just peace settlement by means of negotiations; and refrain from resorting to the threat or use of force or military blockade against each other. Israel was willing to sign the agreement after receiving secret commitments from US President Ford for massive financial and military support, as well as a commitment not to engage in a dialoguee with the PLO unless it had recognized Israel, accepted UN resolution 242, and renounced terrorism (see ARAB-ISRAEL PEACE-MAKING).

Five months after a new government in Israel was formed by Menahem Begin, Egyptian President Anwar Sadat paid a historical visit to Jerusalem, addressing the Knesset on 20 November. Sadat's initiative was decided independently of the US government. He wanted to circumvent the American-Soviet declaration of 1 October regarding the resumption of the Geneva conference. However, the deadlocked negotiations that began soon after Sadat's visit to Jerusalem, underlined the necessity of the American mediation. This represented two major problems: Sadat's need for a framework of comprehensive settlement, to legitimate a bilateral Egyptian final settlement with Israel, and Israel's insistence on retaining its settlements in Sinai. Israel's proposal for an interim autonomy for the Palestinians in the West Bank and Gaza Strip submitted to Egypt, was a major contribution to the peace-making efforts. However, it needed the active mediation of US President Jimmy Carter to bring about the signing of the Camp David Accords on 17 September 1978. These included two frameworks of principles: one for peace in the Arab-Israeli conflict, including the Palestinian autonomy, and a bilateral Israeli-Egyptian peace agreement. The latter was still to be translated into a fully-fledged and elaborated peace treaty. This was realized six months later, again, with the active involvement of President Carter, and signed in the White House in Washington (see ARAB-ISRAEL PEACEMAKING). However, the Israel-Egypt Peace Treaty was collectively rejected by most of the Arab states, adopting a diplomatic and economic boycott against Egypt and preventing any Arab leader from following Sadat's strategy. Furthermore, the talks between Israel and Egypt on the implementation of an autonomy plan in the West Bank and Gaza Strip failed to arrive at any results due to the Israeli effort to retain maximum control of these territories and secure its claim for sovereignty over them in the aftermath of the five-year interim autonomy period. The assassination of President Sadat on 6 October 1981, further diminished the chances for any advancement at this stage. Nonetheless, Israel and Egypt adhered to their commitments regarding the beginning of normalization of relations between the two states (early 1980) and the full evacuation of Sinai (April 1982) according to the timetable agreed

upon in the Treaty. Nevertheless, a disagreement on the border demarcation of a minor area called Taba, just south of Eilat, was only resolved in March 1989, following a ruling by an international arbitration tribunal.

Despite the signing of the Peace Treaty with Egypt, Israeli security continued to be threatened by a possible Syrian-Iraqi coalition, which seemed to become effective in late 1978-1979. With the eruption of the IRAQ-IRAN WAR, Israeli security was significantly enhanced, leaving Syria alone in the face of Israel. Furthermore, the plunge of oil prices in 1982 significantly weakened the power of the Arab oil weapon in the international arena. The fragmentation and strategic weakness of the Arab world apparently encouraged the Israeli decision makers to adopt a far-reaching plan regarding the Lebanon war. Despite Iraq's involvement in a war with IRAN, its nuclear project-constructing, with French assistance, a nuclear reactor—Osiraq—had become a security concern to Israel, believed to be military-oriented. In June 1981, shortly before the elections to the tenth Knesset the Israel Air Force bombed and destroyed the Iraqi reactor.

The eruption of Civil War in Lebanon in April 1975, brought deepened involvement of Israel in Southern Lebanon, which had been marked by occasional raids against Palestinian guerrilla bases in retaliation for their attacks against Israel's northern towns and settlements. In 1975–1976, Israel began to provide humanitarian services to the border Lebanese population, which had been cut off from the embattled capital and major cities, under the title "the Good Fence." This involvement soon developed into growing military support to the MA-RONITE MILITIAS, in return for intelligence cooperation and coordination of a southern Lebanese militia, led by Maronite officers and backed by Israel, to serve as a buffer zone between the Palestinian guerrillas and Israel's territory. In March 1978, in the midst of the Israeli-Egyptian peace process, Israel launched a massive operation ("Litani") against the Palestinian guerrillas in south Lebanon, occupying and clearing the area up to the Litani river, after a *Fatah* squad infiltrating through the sea, hijacked a bus with Israelis. While driving it along the coastal road it was confronted by the police force, resulting in thirty-two Israelis being killed. Israel withdrew its forces from most of the occupied area after a few months, following resolutions by the UN Security Council to call upon Israel to withdraw from Lebanon (Resolution 425), and to establish a special peace-keeping force for south Lebanon (UNIFIL). However, Israel remained active in south Lebanon, both directly and through sponsoring the south Lebanese militia. At the same time, Israeli links with the Maronite militias tightened, especially after the 1981 elections to the Knesset following which a hawkish-led government was established, with Ariel Sharon as Defense Minister. There were growing violent confrontations between the Lebanese Forces headed by Bashir JUMAYYIL Syrian forces were deployed in Lebanon since 1976. This gradually dragged Israel into the Lebanon march, culminating in the invasion of Lebanon on 6 June, 1982. Israel's invasion of Lebanon was officially meant to secure "peace for the Galilee", by eradicating the Palestinian military infrastructure in a territory of twenty-five miles (forty km.) depth that would prevent artillery shelling and rockest launching against Israel. Unofficially, however, the plan designed by Sharon and confided to the Lebanese Forces, intended to link with the latter in the Beirut area, and help the establishment of a favorite Lebanese government which would see to expell the Syrian forces and the Palestinians from Lebanon, and liquidate the PLO both militarily and politically (see ARAB-ISRAEL CONFLICT).

The Lebanon War formally ended with the withdrawal of the IDF from Lebanon in May 1985, after failing to obtain any of its strategic goals. The Israel-Lebanon agreement of 17 May 1983, turned out to be inapplicable due to the Syrian and non-Maronite communities' objection. This lead to its abolition in less than a year. The PLO indeed lost its autonomous territorial base. However, its leadership remained intact. While operating from Tunis, it managed to adjust itself to its newly restricted capabilities, accepting the Egyptian track of peace making with Israel. Furthermore, Israel withdrew from most of the territory it occupied in Lebanon under the pressure of the guerrilla warfare waged mainly by the Shi'i militias of AMAL and HIZBALLAH, sustaining painful casualties. Yet Israel retained a self-defined "security zone" along the border of six to nine miles (ten to fifteen km.) wide. This was to be defended and maintained by the SOUTH LEBANON ARMY (SLA), with Israeli military and moral support. However, it soon became clear that the SLA was unable to withstand the attacks by the Shi'i militias, particularly *Hizballah*, which forced Israel to deploy its own forces in the security zone and sustain a constant, though relatively low, cost in casualties, mainly within the security zone. Israel's invasion of Lebanon, while at first accepted with understanding as a necessary measure of self-defense, both domestically and internationally, became a source of world-wide criticism. It turned out that its intentions were far more ambitious and brutal, manifested in the nine-week siege of Beirut. During this time, the city was heavily shelled and bombed in an attempt to force withdrawal of the Palestinian guerrilla personnel that had massed into the city. The wave of rage against Israel's military action in Lebanon peaked when in September, a Phalange force perpetrated a massacre in the Sabra and Shatila refugee camps in Beirut, following the IDF's entrance into its Western part. The massacre was a major turning point in the Israeli public opinion toward the war. This weakened Israel's position in the international arena. More specifically, it led to a temporary withdrawal of the Egyptian Ambassador from Tel Aviv (an Egyptian Ambassador was reappointed after Israel, (under Shimon Peres's premiership), agreed in 1984 to an international arbitration of the Taba dispute).

The first national coalition government (1984–1988) witnessed the widening gap between Labor and *Likud* regarding the resumption of the peace process, especially on the Jordanian-Palestinian front. From 1985 on, Prime Minister Peres made efforts to enlist American, Arab, and Israeli support for the idea of convening an international peace conference. This idea had become acceptable by Jordan, the PLO, Egypt and other Arab states. It was a mechanism in which to break the stalemated peace process. Peres conceived the conference as a ceremonial opening to bilateral negotiations that would follow between Israel and a Jordanian-Palestinian delegation. However, the *Likud* leader Shamir viewed the conference as an instrument for imposing a settlement that would be detrimental to Israel. In July 1986, Peres's efforts were highlighted by a dramatic visit to KING HASAN II in Ifran, MOROCCO, culminating a decade of secret links and mutual interests between the two states. In April 1987, as a Foreign Minister, Peres met with King Hussein in London where they reached an agreement on attending an international conference that would serve as an umbrella for direct negotiations between Israel and a Jordanian-Palestinian delegation. The agreement, however, encountered strong opposition from Prime Minister Shamir, even though he also met the King secretly shortly afterwards.

The *intifada* broke out on 9 December 1987. This brought the debate in Israel about the future of the occupied territories and relations between Israel and the Palestinians to a head, forcing the Israel Defense Forces into playing a policing role for which it was ill equipped and poorly trained. Although the eruption of the *intifada* was spontaneous, in January 1988, the PLO took control of the *intifada* activities sponsored by the secular-nationalist groups, establishing the Unified National Command, which combined *Fatah*, the PFLP, DFLP, and the Communist Party. The *intifada* witnessed the emergence of the Islamic Resistance Movement (*Hamas*) in the Gaza Strip, constituting a transformation of the MUSLIM BROTHERHOOD MOVEMENT into a national combatant movement. The *intifada*, which at first took the form of mass demonstrations, stone-throwing at Israeli soldiers and cars traveling through the West Bank and Gaza Strip, and civil disobdenience on the part of the Palestinian population, shifted after the first twenty months to less popular and more violent methods, both within the Palestinian society and against Israel. The Islamist movements—*Hamas* and the *Islamic Jihad*—leading in both spheres. The Islamic violence turned terror into a constant reality for every individual in Israeli society. This came at a time when the collective threat to the existence of Israel had faded. The issue of security once again became more real and immediate for Israelis. Thus, in 20 May 1990, a young Israeli shot seven Palestinian workers dead in Rishon Letzion. This was in retaliation for the death of fourteen Israelis in a bus from Tel Aviv to Jerusalem, which had been swerved from the road into a ravine by an Islamist fanatic. In October 1990, during the Jewish Feast of Tabernacles, riots erupted on the Temple Mount, when Palestinian worshipers started throwing stones at Jewish worshipers at the Wailing Wall. The intervention of the Israeli Police resulted in twenty Palestinians being killed and a further fifty-three wounded.

The *intifada* was a major turning point in Israel's quest for a peaceful settlement on its Jordanian-Palestinian front. The American efforts to revive the peace process, which were renewed shortly after the breakout of the *intifada* by Secretary of State George Schultz, combining the Reagan Plan with the Camp David framework on Palestinian interim autonomy in the West Bank and Gaza Strip, were futile due to the objection of the PLO and Israel. However, these efforts sharpened the differences of opinion within the Israeli government. The announcement of King Hussein of Jordan on disengagement from the West Bank on July 31, 1988 paved the way for the PLO's proclamation of the Palestinian independent state at the PNC session in Algiers in November of that year, denying the Labor movement's long-lived "Jordanian option" for a settlement with Hashemite Jordan over the West Bank. Thus, the government initiative of May 1989, proposing to hold negotiations with an elected Palestinian delegation from the West Bank and Gaza Strip on a settlement based on the Camp David parameters of interim self-government, was an essential shift from past policy. This had always attempted to circumvent confrontation with Palestinian nationalism and preferred to negotiate a settlement with neighboring Arab regimes. In retrospect, it was a step toward accepting the new reality that the *intifada* had shaped. Despite its perceived pitfalls—mainly the exclusion of the PLO—President MUBARAK of Egypt, as well as the US administration, were actively involved in trying to promote the plan by arranging a meeting in Cairo between Israeli representatives and Palestinians from the occupied territories, who were not associated with the PLO, yet approved by it. However, growing opposition within the *Likud* to the government initiative, along with PLO objection to its exclusion, finally resulted in deadlock.

The GULF WAR, which errupted in January 1991, was the first Middle East war experienced by Israel, in which it remained totally passive, despite the fact that at least forty Iraqi scud missiles fell in its territory, and its civilian population spent many long hours in sealed rooms wearing gas masks. Although the war was the result of a purely inter-Arab dispute, Israel became involved by virtue of its link to the Palestinian issue. Iraq endeavored to emphasize this in order to delegitimate the international coalition forged by the United States against it, with active cooperation of the Gulf Arab states and Egypt. It is against this backdrop that the United States and Soviet Union made a commitment to the Arab states solicited to participate in the coalition against Iraq, to see to the resumption of the Middle East Peace process after the KUWAIT crisis is resolved. Thus, despite the pro-Iraqi position adopted by the PLO during the Kuwait crisis and the Gulf War that followed, the aftermath of the war and liberation of Kuwait witnessed an intensive effort by the US Secretary of State James Baker, to forge an agreed upon formula for the convening of an international peace conference on the Middle East. An assertive US diplomacy and use of Israel's request for American guarantees for ten billion dollar loans to enable the absorption of the mass immigration from the former Soviet Union, brought Israel to accept Baker's formula, although Shamir's right-wing government was able to dictate most of its demands regarding the identity and modalities of participation of the Palestinian delegation to the international conference. The peace conference convened in Madrid at the end of October 1991. It was followed by separate bilateral talks between Israeli and Syrian, Lebanese, and Jordanian-Palestinian delegations. Multilateral talks on various issues connected with the Middle East Peace Process began shortly after the opening of the Madrid Conference. Israel, most of the Arab countries and other states, including European and North-American states, as well as Japan all participated. Though only limited progress was made in the various talks while the *Likud* was in power, Israel's international status improved significantly. This trend began in the late 1980s. It manifested itself, in particular, in a major increase in the number of states maintaining diplomatic relations with it, and the less rigorous application of the Arab boycott of Israel (see ARAB-ISRAEL PEACEMAKING).

The change of government following the June 1992 elections did not have an immediate impact on the peace making process, despite Prime Minister Rabin's announcement during the election campaign that he would sign an agreement on Palestinian self-government within six to nine months. Little progress occurred in the bilateral talks in Washington. On 17 December 1992, 415 *Hamas* and Islamic *Jihad* leaders were expelled by Israel to Lebanon, due to their increased terrorist attacks. Another outbreak of terrorism in March 1993 led to prolonged closures on the territories. This in turn resulted in great economic hardships for the Palestinian residents of the West Bank and Gaza Strip and the beginning of an inflow of both legal and illegal workers from abroad. In the beginning of 1993, secret negotiations between Israel and the PLO began in Norway, after a phase of informal talks between Israeli and Palestinian academics. The talks finally led to the signing of the Declaration of Principles (DOP) between Israel and the PLO in Washington D.C. on 13 September 1993. This agreement involved mutual recognition between Israel and the PLO, Israel's withdrawal from Gaza and Jericho and the establishment of a Palestinian authority (see ARAB-ISRAEL PEAECMAKING). The agreement raised significant controversy in Israel, but was approved in the Knesset on 23 September, 1993. A vote on a motion of no-confidence, brought by the opposition, was defeated by sixty-one MKs who voted against the motion. Fifty MKs voted in favor, eight abstaining and one absent. The agreement with the PLO—an organization which for years was demonized and came to be regarded by Jews in Israel as their most vicious enemy; the incarnation of everything that is evil—was accepted by the Israeli public with an amazing degree of resignation. However, there were some extreme manifestations of opposition to the peace making process, represented primarily by Israeli zealots from the religious-national movement, to whom the Oslo accord seemed to threaten their vision of redeeming the whole Land of Israel. The murder of twenty-nine Palestinians during a Muslim prayer in the Cave of the Patriarchs in Hebron by a Jewish settler on 25 February 1994, and the wide support and admiration manifested for the perpetrator and the massacre by other settlers, particularly in Hebron, attested to the sense of disaster that the Oslo agreement caused to many of them.

The Oslo Accord clearly led King Hussein to seek an agreement for his country as well. However, it took another year until an Israel-Jordan Peace Treaty was signed, on 26 October 1994, primarily because the King preferred to have Syria coming to an agreement with Israel before he followed Sadat's and Arafat's separate agreements with Israel. It was only after the Israel-Syria negotiations remained futile, that the King was willing to take the risk and sign the Peace Treaty with Israel, negotiated bilaterally and without a need for American, or Egyptian mediation. The Treaty with Jordan enjoyed massive support in the Knesset, representing the absence of substantive differences, especially territorial ones, between the two states.

On the Isreli-Syrian track, negotiations entered a substantive stage under Rabin. Unlike his predecessor, Rabin was willing to negotiate peace with Syria on the basis of "as the depth of withdrawal (from the Golan Heights) as the depth of peace." This implied that Israel was in fact willing to retreat from the occupied Golan area to the international border in return for Syrian acceptance of full normalization of relations with Israel, and appropriate security arrangements. Whether Rabin had confided to the Syrians that he was willing to trade off full withdrawal to the international, armistice, or the pre-1967 war, remained unclear. However, despite a number of visits to Damascus by Secretary of State Christopher in the years 1992–1996, and repeated suggestions by Rabin (and Peres, after November 1995) for raising the level of negotiations or holding a summit meeting with Asad, the negotiations reached no tangible results.

An additional agreement, the Taba Agreement, was signed between Israel and the Palestinians on 27 September 1995. Under these terms, Israel was to withdraw from the cities in the West Bank and some additional areas, and elections were to be held for a Palestinian Authority. The agreement was implemented despite Rabin's assassination five weeks later, save the redeployment in Hebron which was implemented by the new government led by Netanyahu. The renewed talks with Syria under US auspices in early 1996, now with Peres as Prime Minister, apparently led to progress regarding the meaning of normalization by the Syrians. However, this round was cut off by the wave of suicide bombings perpetrated by *Hamas* in late February and early March 1996. Asad failed to denounce these and hence was isolated by not being invited to the Sharm al-Sheikh international summit against terrorism held shortly afterwards. With the election of Binyamin Netanyahu as Israel's new Prime Minister in May 1996, the stalemate remained unchanged due to his refusal to adopt the positions of his Labor predecessors, returning to the attitude that Israel was willing to make no more than cosmetic changes in the border in return for peace. Syria on its part insisted that the negotiations should continue from the point they had been stopped. Though the opinion polls indicated that Shimon Peres would win in the elections which were to be held later in 1996, Peres felt that the time was not opportune for any further Is-

raeli concession to the Arabs before the elections. Hence he postponed the implementation of redeployment in Hebron till after the elections. In addition, in response to intensified attacks by the *Hizballah* against the Israeli forces in Southern Lebanon and on settlements in Northern Israel, Peres decided to embark on a major military operation-restricted to artillery shelling and air raids against *Hizballah* targets—in April 1996. These were supposed to operate with surgical accuracy, but ended up with a disastrous killing of close to a hundred of Lebanese civilians at Kana village in Southern Lebanon.

The first eighteen months of the Netanyahu government witnessed a gradual erosion in the achievements of the previous government in the international arena, attained primarily due to Oslo. Under Netanyahu, the government failed to implement the agreements signed by the Rabin-Peres government, as well as the Hebron agreement, in which Netanyahu gave further assurances regarding the agreed phases and timetable of Israel's redeployment in the West Bank. During this period, the government lost much of its credibility in the Arab world as well as in the American administration. The Arab-Israeli process of normalization came under strong criticism of the Palestinian Authority as well as of Syria, due to the stalemated peace process.

Economic Affairs Israel is poor in natural resources. Like most of the other countries in the Middle East its water resources are scarce. The construction of the National Water Carrier was completed in 1964 with a capacity to divert 320 million cubic meters of water annually from the Sea of Galilee to the coastal plain and the Negev. Nonetheless, before long Israel will either have to start desalinating sea water, or importing fresh water. The only minerals Israel has in commercial quantities are potash and magnesium in the Dead Sea area, and cement in various mountainous areas. Very small quantities of copper and oil were found in the Negev. It is frequently stated that Israel's main economic resource is its brain power.

Even before the State of Israel was established, the ARAB LEAGUE declared an economic boycott of the Jewish economy, which went into effect in the beginning of 1946 (see ARAB BOYCOTT). The Israeli economy was thus forced to develop in complete regional isolation, while having to contend with the effects of the secondary and tertiary boycotts. This had a major effect on the economic relations between Israel and companies in third countries that surrendered to the boycott. It was only after the Madrid Conference, toward the end of 1991 (see ARAB-ISRAEL PEACEMAKING), that the boycott, whose full economic effect on the Israeli economy is difficult to calculate, started to disintegrate. This broadened Israel's trade opportunities, and increased the willingness of foreign companies to invest in Israel and cooperate with it.

During the early years of the State's existence, marked by mass immigration, the government introduced a national austerity policy and rationing. On September 10, 1952, against the background of an extreme shortage in foreign currency, a Restitution Agreement was signed with the Federal Republic of Germany. Under this agreement Germany undertook to pay DM three billion in goods and services to the State of Israel for Jewish property robbed during the Nazi period, and in order to help resettle "destitute Jewish refugees uprooted from Germany and from territories formerly under German rule", in Nazi times. In addition to helping Israel pay its oil bill, the controversial restitution payments helped Israel construct a merchant and passenger fleet, infrastructures and numerous factories. Israel also received large sums of US aid, which for the first few decades of its existence helped it pay for part of its balance of trade deficit.

One of Israel's major economic successes was in the sphere of agriculture, where from a net importer of foodstuffs in mandatory times, it turned into a net exporter, due to modern technologies, such as drip irrigation, and sophisticated marketing techniques. Cut diamonds have constituted an important component of Israel's exports. Israeli textiles enjoyed major successes in European markets until the 1980s. Especially as of the 1970s, Israel developed a highly sophisticated arms industry, soon becoming one of the world leaders in the sphere of computer software. In the mid-1990s, hi-tech export of hardware and software reached a third of Israel's total export. The main economic problems continuously faced by the Israeli economy, despite extremely high rates of economic growth in the 1950s, 1960s and the first half of the 1990s, have been inflation. Toward the mid-1980s this reached three digit figures, and chronic balance of trade

deficits. Following the Yom Kippur War in 1973 an additional problem was that a very large part of the Israeli national budget had to be directed to debt repayment and servicing.

In the first thirty years of Israel's existence, a major part of its economy was socialist, in the sense that a large part of its industrial sector was developed and owned either by the government or by the *Histadrut*. The kibbutzim (collective settlements) and *moshavim* (cooperative settlements) were responsible for most of the agricultural production. However, by the late 1980s the government slowly began privatizing its corporations. (This policy supported both by the *Likud* and the Israel Labor party). "Koor"— the Histadrut's industrial conglomerate, which in its heyday ran twenty percent of Israel's industry, including many unprofitable companies that were kept open for social reasons—was in dire straits; while the kibbutzim and *moshavim* were also in deep debt and started a slow process of adaptation to free market conditions, not only in their relations with the external world, but also internally. By 1997 the government was not only well advanced in its privatization efforts, but was also in the process of selling off the bank shares, of which it became the owner at the end of 1983, when the shares of five of Israel's major banks collapsed on the stock market. "Koor"—still the flagship of Israeli industry, but in control of a much reduced sector—was now totally privatized and traded on Wall Street and the Israeli stock market, while rapidly turning into a multinational. The kibbutzim and *moshvim*, still struggling with the debts of the past, were in the process of major changes both in their economic and social structures.

Israel has a dense system of roads; three international sea ports at Haifa and Ashdod on the Mediterranean Sea and Eilat on the Red Sea; one major international airport near Tel Aviv (Ben Gurion airport) and two small international airports in Jerusalem (Attarot) and Eilat, and a railway network partially dating back to Turkish (before 1917) and British mandatory times, and the rest (mostly suburban lines) recently constructed. Since 1982 Israelis have been able to drive to Egypt, and since 1995, to Jordan.

Government and Institutions Israel is a parliamentary democracy, in which, since 1996, the Prime Minister has been directly elected. Israel does not yet have a constitution, only some basic laws, and once the enactment of the basic laws have been completed, these together will make up its constitution. Israel has a President, who is elected by the 120 members of the Knesset—the Israeli Parliament—and has primarily ceremonial functions.

The law in Israel is that enacted by the Knesset, however in all matters relating to personal status (marriage, divorce and burial), the religious laws of the various religious denominations prevail. In the sphere of basic human rights—one of the spheres in which the enactment of basic laws has not yet been completed—the reality in Israel is problematic, though the rule of law prevails. Among the main causes for this situation is the fact that Israel is defined as a Jewish state, with no separation between state and religion, which discriminates its large Arab minority. The Knesset is unicameral and is elected approximately once every four years, though early elections can shorten the Knesset's term, and there have been Knessets which have served for over four years.

For the purpose of the elections, Israel is a single voting area. The elections are universal, secret and based on proportional representation, with a qualifying threshold of 1.5. Once elected to the Knesset, parties are funded by the government budget, according to their number of Knesset members.

The Knesset's main functions are to legislate, to prepare the state's constitution and to supervise the government. It also elects the President of the State and the State Comptroller.

Until 1996 one of the few real powers of the President was to decide who should form the next government. This ended with the law of direct election of the prime minister that was enforced that year. All the governments in Israel have been coalition governments, since no party ever had an absolute majority in the Knesset.

Under Israel's system of parliamentary democracy, the government (today the Prime Minister) requires the support of at least 61 out of the 120 Knesset Members to survive. Only two governments—that of Yitzhak Rabin from August 1993 to November 1995 and that of Shimon Peres from November 1995 to June 1996—managed to survive as minority governments. This was because they were supported in the Knesset by two predominantly Arab parties that were not members of the coalition—*Hadash*—and the Arab Democratic Party. Until 1996, the prime minister was considered "first

among equals". At least theoretically there was to have been "collective responsibility". However the level of discipline in the government had usually been low and the dependence of the Prime Minister on the good will of his coalition partners enabled slack discipline on their part. The Prime Minister had the right to remove his ministers, but this only rarely happened. From the late 1980s, a movement committed to changing the system to direct election of the prime minister started to gather momentum against the backdrop of the government crisis of March 1990, when Peres failed to form a government after the National Unity government formed by Yitzhak Shamir was brought down by a vote on a motion of no-confidence, revealing ugly political horse trading. In order to change the system, a new version of the basic law emerged: the government was tabled before the Knesset by members representing four different parties, with the aim of strengthening the prime minister's status, and preventing, as far as possible, the political horse-trading and defection from one party to another. The law was passed in March 1992 and came into effect toward the elections of the fourteenth Knesset (1996). It lays down the rules and conditions for the direct election of the PM. The PM must be elected by at least fifty percent of the voters, and if there are more than two contenders in the first round and none of them gains an absolute majority, a second round will take place. The elected PM has forty-five days to form a government. The government does not require the confidence of the Knesset, but the appointment of ministers—whose number may not exceed eighteen—requires the approval of the Knesset. In addition, sixty-one MKs can bring about the resignation of the PM in a vote on a motion of no-confidence in him, and the calling of new elections for the PM and the Knesset. The following will also lead to the same result: a decision by the PM to dissolve the Knesset; a decision by the Knesset to dissolve itself before its term is out and the failure of the Knesset to pass the state budget within three months of the beginning of the new financial year (in Israel that being 31 March). Special elections for the PM only, will be held: if the elected PM does not manage to form a government within forty-five days; if the PM resigns of his own initiative; if the Knesset decides to impeach the PM because he has been convicted of a felony; a decision by eighty MKs to impeach the PM for some other reason; or because of the inability of the PM to fulfill his duties or due to his death.

The Parties The Party Law, passed in 1992, rules that a party must be registered with the Party Registrar; must have rules of procedure, by which it functions, and certain institutions which ensure its well ordered functioning. Under the law, a party cannot be registered if its goals or activities state, explicitly or implicitly, one of the following: 1) the denial of the existence of the State of Israel as a Jewish democratic state; 2) incite to racism; 3) a reasonable basis to believe that the party will serve as a front for illegal activities. According to amendment 19 to the Basic Law the Knesset of 1996, only a party can participate in elections to the Knesset.

The parties in Israel are an extremely heterogeneous group of political bodies, whose large number is a result primarily of the electoral system in the country, but also of the historical background of the state and its complex social structure. Some of the parties and political blocs in Israel have roots in the pre-state Jewish community, or in the World Zionist Organization. (see ZIONISM) These include the social-democratic Israel Labor Party with roots in the historical *Mapai*; the liberal-rightist *Likud* with roots in the Revisionist Movement and General Zionists; the National Religious Party with roots in the *Mizrahi* Movement; and the ultra Orthodox *Agudat Yisrael*, which emerged from a movement with the same name. The origins of these parties are reflected in their ideological platforms and their historical frames of reference.

On the other hand, new parties have constantly appeared on the scene, merged with others, or run in a joint list for elections, or disappeared. Some of these parties have represented ethnic groups (e.g., the predominantly *Moroccan Tami*, which was first elected to the tenth Knesset (1981) and then vanished after the eleventh). Others represented more radical political positions than the existing parties (e.g. the *Tehiya* on the right, which was represented in the tenth to twelfth Knessets (1981–1992), or *Sheli* on the left, which was elected only to the ninth Knesset (1977)). Several parties developed around charismatic leaders [e.g. *Rafi*, in the elections to the sixth Knesset (1965) around David Ben Gurion; *Shlomzion*, in the elections to the ninth Knesset (1977), around Ariel Sharon; *Telem*, in the elections to the tenth Knesset (1981) around Moshe Dayan; *Yahad*, in the

elections to the eleventh Knesset (1984) around Ezer Weizmann; or *Tsomet*, which was represented as a separate Party in the eleventh, twelfth and thirteenth Knessets (1987–1996), around Rafael Eitan]. Eleven lists entered the fourteenth Knesset, elected in May 1996, of which five represented more than one party or political group: the *Likud-Gesher-Tsomet; Meretz*—representing *Ratz, Mapam* and *Shinui*; the predominantly Arab *Hadash-Balad* Party; the ultra Orthodox United Torah Judaism—representing *Agudat Yisrael* and *Degel Hatorah*; and the United Arab List—representing the Arab Democratic Party and parts of the Islamic Movement.

The Israeli party system has been marked by relative fragmentation, with no single party possessing a majority of the Knessest members. This has necessitated a coalition of a number of parties, led by either of the two largest parties—the Labor and *Likud*. Although these Parties are still the largest, their representation was significantly reduced in the 1996 elections, to thirty-four and thirty-two MK, respectively. The third largest Party since 1996 is *Shas*—an ultra-Orthodox Sephardi Party, founded in 1984, with ten seats in the fourteenth Knesset. Like the Ashkenazi ultra-orthodox parties (*Agudat Israel* and *Degel Hatorah*), it is led by a council of rabbis, headed by the charismatic religious authority, Rabbi Ovadia Yosef. *Shas* had been a member of Rabin's government from July 1992 to August 1993, but left it on the eve of the signing of the DOP with the Palestinians. In 1996 it joined Netanyahu's government.

Next is the National Religious Party, with nine seats. The NRP has been represented in all Israeli governments except the Labor government of 1992–1996. The fifth parliamentary group is *Meretz*, with nine seats, which in the elections to the thirteenth and fourteenth Knessets was a list comprising three separate parties—*Ratz, Mapam* and *Shinui* was founded by Shulamit Aloni towards the elections to the eighth Knesset (1973). It is left wing, placing strong emphasis on the peace process, human and civil rights, separation of religion and state, and social welfare. *Mapam* was founded in 1948, and in its early years was Marxist and pro-Soviet in its orientation. After 1954 it dropped its pro-orientation, gradually shifting to social-democratic positions and joining the Socialist International in 1983. From 1969 to 1984 it ran in all the elections within the

Alignment (*Ma'arakh*) together with the Israel Labor Party, but it left the Alignment because of its opposition to the National Unity government formed in 1984. Much of its support came from the *kibbutzim* of the *Shomer Hatza'ir* movement.

Shinui is a dovish liberal party, with a *laissez faire* economic orientation, first formed in 1976. Its members joined the new Democratic Movement for Change in that year, and within its framework joined the first *Likud*-led government formed by Menahem Begin in 1977. In 1978 they left the DMC to form an independent parliamentary group, and ran as a separate Party in the elections to the tenth, eleventh and twelfth Knessets (1981, 1984, 1988). It was represented in the National Unity government in the years 1984–1990. In February 1997 *Ratz, Mapam* and a group of members from *Shinui* united into a single party. The rump of *Shinui* remained an independent group within *Meretz*.

The sixth Party is *Yisrael Be'aliya*, representing new immigrants, primarily from the former Soviet Union, which is headed by former Prisoner of Zion Nathan Sharansky. It gained seven seats and joined the Netanyahu government. The seventh parliamentary group is *Hadash-Balad*, with five seats. This is an alliance between the Israel Communist Party and various Israeli Arab nationalist groups. The United Torah Judaism, which is a member of the coalition, is an ultra-Orthodox parliamentary group made up of two parties—*Agudat Yisrael* (which has been in all the Knessets since 1949) and *Degel Hatorah* (founded in 1988)—which was first formed in 1992. The ninth Party is the Third Way. This was established toward the elections to the fourteenth Knesset. Most of its founders were formerly members of the Labor Party, and two of its four Knesset members were formerly Labor Knesset members, who left Labor because of their objection to an Israeli withdrawal from the Golan Heights. The tenth parliamentary group is the United Arab List, made up by the Arab Democratic Party formed in 1988 and Abdel Wahhab Darawsha, an Arab Knesset member who left the Labor Party against the background of the outbreak of the *intifada*. The ADP was joined by a group of members from the Islamic Movement, which until 1996 had boycotted all the Israeli national elections on nationalist grounds, and the joint list gained four Knesset seats. Finally, there is *Moledet*—an ultra-right wing party headed by Rehav'am Ze'evi—which

first entered the Knesset in the elections to the twelfth Knesset in 1988, and is currently represented in the Knesset by two MKs.

ISRAELI-ARAB CITIZENS The ARABS in ISRAEL are a national, ethnic and religious minority, who emerged from the establishment of the State and the departure of most of the Palestinian Arab population that had lived in the areas which became the State of Israel during 1948–1949 Arab-Israeli War (see ARAB-ISRAEL CONFLICT). At the end of the War, the Arab population in Israel numbered about 160,000 (approximately eighteen percent of the total population)—most of it in villages in the Galilee and the Triangle in the Western slopes of Samaria, and a minority of BEDUINS in the Negev.

Becoming a minority in the new state was of deep national, social and economic significance to the Arabs in Israel. They were part of a people, whose political leadership had fallen apart, whose territory had been conquered by others, and whose social structure had been undermined. The Arabs, who remained in the territory that became the State of Israel, were badly hurt economically. Many families lost their main bread-winners and/or lands and assets. The state limited their ability to cultivate their agricultural lands by denying them water, closing certain areas and confiscating extensive lands soon after the establishment of the State. The Military Administration, imposed on the Arab population, stopped them from becoming hired laborers outside their places of abode. In addition, amongst the Arab minority there were at least 23,000 "internal" REFUGEES—persons whose villages had been destroyed and who were absorbed in existing villages (the so called "present absentees"). The Arab minority was, to a large extent, rural, with no educated or "white collar" middle class, and lacking any sort of active political or social experience outside the boundaries of the village. Under these conditions, the quality of the Israeli policy toward the Arab minority in its territory was of vital importance. This policy reflected the Zionist goal of settling JEWS in the country and strengthened the new political entity. Furthermore, it was designed to leave the Arab minority weak and economically and socially divided, while subjecting it to the rule of the majority in every possible way. The State of Israel granted the Arab minority Israeli citizenship, but at the same time imposed tight supervision over it and limited all of its activities in all spheres. This not only preserved but also deepened the gaps in the quality of life and standards of living between the Jewish and Arab populations. In general, the Jewish national interest was given priority—usually within the framework of security excuses—over universal principles such as justice and equality, which received legal validity in various rulings of the High Court of Justice.

The arrangements introduced to deal with the Arab citizens were based on the assumption that they constituted a security risk to the state that had just emerged from a bloody war with the neighboring Arab states, which had come to the assistance of the Palestinian Arabs. Therefore, their affairs were left in the hands of the various security apparatuses: the Military Administration and security services, which were coordinated by the office of the Prime Minister's Advisor on Arab Affairs. The Military Administration drew its authority from the Emergency Regulations, promulgated by the British MANDATE in 1945, and which remained in force in the State of Israel. However, the Military Administration diverged from the powers granted it in the regulations, intervening in all spheres of life of the Arabs, groups and individuals. First, it divided the Arab population by taking advantage of family, tribal and communal allegiances and encouraging internal cleavages and conflicts. Second, it deepened the isolation of the Arab population and kept it separated from the Arab world by limiting their freedom of movement, and imposing strict control over those traveling abroad. Third, it confiscated economic resources owned by the Arab population and the refugees and present absentees. Fourth, it prevented the growth of independent political organizations, which could represent the Arab population. Finally, it mobilized Arab votes for the ruling party (*Mapai*). In 1966 the Military Administration was finally abolished, and in the following year the 1967 War broke out, which drastically changed the living conditions of the Arabs.

Demography and Geography From the establishment of the state until the mid-1990s, the total population of Israel grew more than six-fold, but the numerical ratio between Jews and Arabs, which changed from time to time as a result of waves of immigration, remained more or less stable. In 1995 there were 881,000 Arabs in Israel (not including East JERUSALEM). However, while the increase of the Jewish population resulted from immigration and natural growth, the Arab population grew only due to natural growth, which was especially high during the years 1960–1964 (40.9 per thousand) and decreased to 30.6% in the years 1980–1984.

Today the annual growth amongst Jews is 3.7% while that amongst Arabs is 4.1%. The main explanation for the rise in the natural growth of the Arabs has been the drastic fall in the rate of infant mortality, which used to be much higher than amongst the Jewish population. In addition, life expectancy amongst the Arabs has risen much more rapidly than amongst the Jews.

When the State was established, there were 104 recognized Arab towns and villages in it, of which four had municipal status—two municipalities (Nazareth and Shfar'am) and two local councils (Kfar Yassif and Rameh). By the end of the 1980s, an additional 60 local governments were established. This trend continued throughout the 1990s to include the Beduin settlements in the Negev. Today seventy percent of the Arab population lives in localities which are run by Arab governments. The rest live in mixed towns and another 70,000 live in "unrecognized settlements". In 1961 thirty-six percent of the Arabs lived in localities defined as rural compared to only nine percent toward the end of the 1990s. Urbanization was not the result of population movements, but the growth in the number of inhabitants in the villages, which resulted in the status of many of them being changed, and the settlement of the Beduins in newly established towns. The Arab population lives in some fifty localities whose population is over 5,000, in addition to the population living in mixed towns (Acre, Haifa, Jaffa, Lod, Ramleh, and Upper Nazareth). sixty-two of the Arab population lives in the northern districts and Haifa, twenty-nine percent in the Jerusalem district and the center, and nine percent in the southern district. The distribution according to districts has hardly changed since 1948, except for the change caused by the addition of the Palestinian population of East Jerusalem. The Arab population is concentrated and remains in the periphery of the country, in areas comprising blocks of Arab localities, with a low level, of geographical mobility. However, due to housing shortages amongst the Arabs and a migration of Jews to the center of the country, in the 1980s a migration of Arabs into Jewish towns in the periphery began. (This has been especially marked in the case of the settlement of Arabs in Upper Nazareth, in which the Arab inhabitants constitute today close to fourteen percent of the population.) The concentration of the Arab population in the periphery has plumetted in terms of employment opportunities, and the level of services and welfare. Also noteworthy is the fact that the rate of Arab emigration from the country is lower than that amongst the Jewish population.

Economy and Services The level of economic development in the Arab sector is determined by the policy of the central government over which it has almost no influence. The government's policy of discrimination and denial *vis-a-vis* the Arab sector, has manifested itself in different ways, of which the following have been the main ones: 1) the confiscation of lands, or their transfer to the jurisdiction of Jewish authorities, resulting in the diminution of agricultural areas and major limitations on the opportunities for construction and development; 2) discrimination in budgets and grants to local authorities; 3) red tape in the validation of contour plans; 4) the exclusion of the Arab settlements from preferred development areas and thus of Arab businessmen and entrepreneurs from the ability to receive direct and indirect grants; 5) the absence of any encouragement for the development of Arab agriculture; 6) the refusal to recognize dozens of Arab villages, built without the approval of the authorities, and the withholding of budgets from these villages.

This policy resulted in a great regression in Arab agriculture, which today formally employs 26,000 persons, of whom only nine percent are independent and employers. Alternative economic branches developed very slowly, due to bureaucratic barriers placed on the way of Arab entrepreneurs and a shortage of vital resources. As a result, most of the industrial enterprises in the Arab sector have remained small and labor intensive, employing unsophisticated technologies.

The survival of the Arab entrepreneur depends on his ability to supply exclusive products, which Jewish enterprises do not produce, or to act as a sub-contractor for Jewish enterprises engaged in the production of labor intensive products, such as textiles. Nevertheless, in recent years changes have started to occur. There has been an increase in the level of investment by Arab entrepreneurs in their enterprises. Arab manufacturers have been making great efforts to break into new markets and compete in Jewish markets. Several relatively large factories have emerged in the wood, textile and construction materials industries, which have managed to break into local, regional and even overseas markets. At the same time, for many Arab entrepreneurs it has been difficult to break away from their status as sub-contractors of large Jewish enterprises and moving on to independent marketing.

The economic underdevelopment of the Arab sector has kept the Arab population heavily dependent on the Jewish majority, significantly reducing the bargaining capacity of the Arab workforce. Unofficial discrimination and security excuses continue to limit the full integration of Arabs into the civil service, the apparatuses of the *Histadrut* and most types of public institutions and private businesses. (The percentage of the Arabs in the government apparatus is less than two percent.) This discrimination affects the Arab professionals most severely, since they suffer more than any other group from lack of career opportunities. Consequently the majority of Arab university graduates (fifty-seven percent) are employed as teachers in the Arab school system.

Despite the improvement that has taken place in the work conditions of the Arab workers, they are still significantly inferior to their Jewish counterparts. Arab workers have also been adversely affected in recent years due to the opening of the Israeli market to foreign workers and the movement by Israeli entrepreneurs of sewing facilities in the textile industry to JORDAN and EGYPT.

The status of the Arabs in the Israeli economy has preserved the gaps between them and the Jewish population in terms of income and standards of living. Thus, 77.1% of the Arab families are to be found in the four lowest levels of a ten level scale, showing the distribution of the total Israeli population, according to net average total income. 18.2% are in the fifth to seventh level and only 4.7% in the three highest levels. Poverty in the Arab sector is much more prevalent than in the Jewish sector; and the incomes of the Arab poor being on an average much lower than those of the poor in the Jewish sector. Whereas in 1994 the percentage of families living below the poverty line amongst the total population was eighteen percent, in the Arab sector the figure was forty-two percent. Nevertheless, it is noteworthy that the Arab population has managed to improve its standard of living many times since the establishment of the State, and the gaps between itself and the Jewish population have diminished in terms of ownership of electrical appliances and various types of durable goods. Nonetheless, the gaps are still wide with regards to ownership of cars, computers, videos, air-conditioners and heating.

Education Following the establishment of the State, the Arab education system remained intact as separate from the Hebrew system,. However, it remained accountable to it and almost totally dependent on it in terms of infrastructure development, supply of services; determination of curriculae and management. In the early years, the Arab education system was controlled by the General Security Services (GSS or *Shabak*) and the Military Administration. Thus, the Arabs had no control over the goals of education, its standards and structure. In addition, much fewer resources were invested in the Arab system, and in 1992 the average budget per Arab pupil was 37.5% of that for a Jewish pupil, while the investment per pupil in the school system by Arab local authorities was only 16.7% of the average investment by the Jewish authorities. The great gaps in budgeting are especially noticeable with regards to infrastructures: the shortage in school rooms, laboratories, service rooms, sports fields and gymnasiums. Many Arab schools lack basic services such as water, electricity and bathrooms, and are unfit to serve as schools. However, the gravest problems of the system concerns the quality of the teaching staff; the teaching methods; the curriculae and extra-curricula activities, as well as the shortage in technological vocational education frameworks. The level of dropouts in the Arab education system is high, especially at high-school level. Only forty-five percent of those in the system complete a high-school education, compared to eighty-two percent of the Jews. The gaps in the budgets and quality of the two education systems are clearly reflected in the achievements of the pupils. Only thirty-three percent of those graduating from Arab high schools sit for the matriculation exams as compared to fifty-eight percent in the Hebrew schools, and only thirteen percent of all the Arabs of graduation age receive a matriculation certificate compared to thirty-six percent amongst the Jews. While a large part of the Arab students with a matriculation certificate apply to universities, the majority (over fifty percent) are not accepted due to low marks, while about eighty percent of the Jewish applicants are accepted.

In the last decade there has been a certain regression in terms of the number and proportion of Arab students in the universities. Thus, in the academic year 1992–1993 they constituted 6.2% of the first degree students compared to 7.9% in the year 1984–1985, and a similar drop took place also in the studies for a second and third degrees.

Despite the weaknesses of the Arab education system, in comparison to the Jewish one, it should be noted that in the last fifty years there has been a rapid expansion of the system, especially in secondary education, which led to an impressive increase in the number of Arab students in institutions of higher learning and graduates. There has also been a general rise in the level of education, including amongst women, and the level of illiteracy has declined significantly. The improvement in education has increased both social and economic mobility within the Arab society. New political and social elites have been formed from amongst those who have received a secondary and higher education, and since the 1970s they have stood at the forefront of the political struggle for civil and political rights for the Arab population in Israel, and greater control over the determination of the policies concerning this population—including those concerning the education system. The improvement in education has also led to a rise in the professional standards of the Arab labor force and to general sociocultural changes. Despite the improvement both in the economic and education spheres, the Arab population in Israel is still unable to meet its own requirements for social and welfare services and to offer solutions for its social distresses by means of voluntary and communal institutions, beyond those offered by the central government and its various agencies. Hence, there is a shortage in all types of services and there is a good deal of poverty accompanied by poor health conditions.

The difficulties of the Arab population are not only the result of a shortage in voluntary and communal institutions able to operate in the sphere of social services. They are also due to inequality in social security allocations, caused by the military service criterion for certain rights. In 1995 the Labor government decided to gradually start equating the allocations. The distress in the Arab sector is especially marked with regards to the aged, retarded persons, cripples, and juvenile delinquents (comprising twenty-six percent of juvenile delinquents in the country).

In the health sector the Arab population suffers from the absence of adequate water and sewage systems in its towns and villages. (Only nineteen percent of the water consumed in the Arab sector is conveyed by means of the water system compared to eighty-four percent in the Jewish settlements.) Furthermore, a shortage in basic health services such as clinics, pharmacies and hospitals—especially in settlements lacking any local authority (in which about thirty percent of the Arabs live today) has resulted-from neglect by the Ministry of Health. Poor environmental conditions and an inadequate health service are responsible for the gap in the quality of life between the two populations: the life expectancy is higher within the Jewish population (by 2.1 years for men and 2.6 years for women); the level of infant mortality amongst Arab babies is almost double that of the Jewish population (14.1 per thousand compared to 7.1); and the rate of deaths due to infectious diseases is much higher in the Arab sector.

The Arab minority suffers from inferior conditions also in the sphere of housing, once again, due to the use of the military service criterion as a key for determining entitlement to government mortgages. (A Jewish family is entitled to a loan which is fifty-two percent higher and a grant which is two hundred and ten percent higher than an Arab family.)

Furthermore, most of the Arab families are unable to use their mortgage rights due to difficulties in obtaining building permits, and in many cases because these rights are conditioned on the size of the apartment. In the Arab sector the apartments built privately are usually large due to the size of the family. As a result, the Arab sector relies on its own resources to finance construction for living, and this fact is reflected in the quality of the living conditions of the Arab population compared to that of the Jewish population. The number of inhabitants per room is almost double while water and electricity supply systems—especially in mixed towns, in unrecognized villages and in the Negev—are of much lower quality.

There is no doubt that the main source of Arab social distresses is from its marginal status within Israeli society. As their problems intensify, its feelings of marginality and helplessness deepen, its dependence on the government and official institutions grows and its ability to become organized and contend with the existing situation decreases.

The gaps between the Arab and Jewish populations, and the objective differences in culture, religion, nationality, social structure, *weltanschaungs* and traditional patterns of organization and activity, emphasize the fact that in Israel there are two societies which are essentially different. Nevertheless, certain similarities between the two societies have developed over time, due to life together in a single political system, the growing use of means of transportation and communications and the rising standards of living and socioeconomic changes.

The June 1967 War (see ARAB-ISRAEL CONFLICT) and its aftermath were, without a doubt, an important turning point for the Arab population. Until that time the contacts between the Arabs in Israel and the rest of Israeli society were extremely limited, and their political organization and activity were limited and confined to the local level. The abolition of the Military Administration in 1966 and developments within Israel, in the region and the world, led to the beginning of a change, which was so deep and dramatic, both on the individual and the collective level that it is difficult to speak of the same society. The rural-farming society which had existed throughout the 1950s and 1960s ceased to exist. The village underwent a process of rapid and comprehensive modernization, in addition to the major growth in its population. The village inhabitants are today comprised of businessmen, contractors, professionals and scholars. All types of products and goods, as well as public and personal services, are available and various workshops and factories may be found in village. Lifestyles have changed and the standard of living has risen. As the level of education has risen, the distribution of roles has changed, especially in the integration of women in all spheres of life. Consumption patterns have undergone drastic change, both in quantitative and qualitative terms, and traditions, behavioral norms, organizational patterns and types of activity have been transformed. Modern institutions have been established: local authorities, public and personal services, education and welfare institutions—even if not in sufficient quantity. Public libraries, clubs, various students, professional and sports associations, theaters, publishing houses, voluntary associations, newspapers and magazines, have been all opened.

These developments have been accompanied by changes in the patterns of social organization and structure. The most significant change has been the way in which the *hamulah* (tribe) and extended family function. These frameworks used to constitute the basis for social and political organization. The extended family has lost much of its socioeconomic role and as a unit of living and housing. Youngsters have increased their power and influence at the expense of the older generation, and by the end of the 1970s most of the old *hamulah* leaders disappeared from the political scene. The younger generation has taken over leadership positions both on local and national levels, and has created new political alliances on the regional and national levels.

Far reaching changes have also taken place in the national identity of the Arab population, and in its relations with the Israeli society, on the one hand, and the Palestinian society, on the other. Arab citizens of Israel have crystallized into a special group, with marked similarities to and differences from each of the two societies. The Arabs increased their knowledge and familiarity with the Israeli society, absorbed the effects of the contacts with it on the personal, social, economic and political levels, and hence increased their involvement in its life. Growing sections of the Arab community became integrated into the economic life of the country, tying their interests to those of the Israeli market. Arab living patterns and personal behavior—affecting consumption and leisure, and even from patterns of thinking and values—were influenced by those prevalent in the Israeli society, as have patterns of social and political organization. Arabs were also integrated into the country's political life and various joint Jewish-Arab frameworks including many of the Jewish parties, entering institutes of higher learning in growing numbers. The increased knowledge and use of the Hebrew language, and the intensive use of the Israeli means of communication, further deepened the knowledge and familiarity with the Israeli society. Simultaneously with the greater integration into the society and frameworks, and the accumulation of material resources and enrichment of personal

ability which followed, there also developed a greater consciousness regarding the large gaps in the realization of civil rights and the distribution of the society's resources, which in turn contributed to the crystallization of the national identity of the Arabs in Israel.

Along with the changes in the relations with the Jewish Israeli society, changes took place in the relations with the Palestinians outside Israel. Following the 1967 War, the Arabs in Israel renewed their ties with the Palestinians in the occupied territories, and with relatives and former neighbors, now living in Arab states. Cultural ties were renewed by means of various joint activities, symposia, festivities and national events. Political ties were established and tightened between organizations, movements and leaders on both sides of the border. The Arabs of Israel became increasingly involved in the political struggle, and especially in protests against the Israeli occupation of the territories, while their national identity became linked to the development of the Palestinian national movement in neighboring states.

However, this process, which emphasized the common interests with the Palestinians outside Israel, also highlighted the differences which had emerged between the two communities, resulting from the growing integration of the Arabs in Israel in the life of the State and growing similarity to the Jewish Israelis. The tightening of relations between the local Arab leadership and the Palestinian leadership, especially after 1982, and the growing familiarity with the various political streams within the PALESTINE LIBERATION ORGANIZATION (PLO), on the one hand, and the tightening of relations between the Arab leaders (especially the activists in the Israel Labor Party) with the Israeli authorities, on the other, strengthened the realization amongst the Arabs in Israel that their political fate was different to that of their brethren outside the State, and that their basic interest was to seek ways to accommodate themselves to the Israeli reality. At the same time they were also convinced that their integration in Israel served the Palestinian interest, because it would enable them to influence the decision making within the Israeli political system. This, in turn, encouraged them to take greater responsibility for, and play a more active role in defining their own identity and goals; in determining their specific interests and in shaping their living conditions and future. In other words, one is dealing here with a new society in terms of its socioeconomic-political structure, patterns of organization and activity.

Political Organization 1967–1992 The socioeconomic conditions within the Arab society and its dependence on the Jewish majority society, has had a decisive effect on the political orientations of the Arabs, their attitude to the state and their political organization, which after 1967 started to undergo far reaching changes, both onlocal and national levels. Until 1966 the Arabs could not take advantage of the right of political participation, that was granted to them by force of their being citizens, due to the Military Administration. The only independent, non-Zionist Arab party which was allowed to operate was the COMMUNIST PARTY (*Maki*), but its members' activities were limited. Thus, the choice the Arabs had was either to vote for this Party or for Jewish parties. Many of the Jewish parties made alliances with the leaders of the *hamulahs*, who engaged in mobilizing votes in return for benefits. As a result of the patronage system, the percentage of voters amongst the Arabs eligible to vote, was high, and most of the votes were either given directly to the ruling Party (*Mapai*) or to Arab lists connected to it. Nevertheless, before 1967, two significant efforts were made at independent political organization.

"The Popular Front", was founded in May 1958, following the use of force by the police in dispersing a May Day demonstration, and the detention of some of the movement's future leaders on the pretext that the demonstration was illegal. The Front did not survive for long, splitting as a result of a conflict between the supporters of *Maki* and youngsters with nationalist tendencies. The latter founded the "*al-Ardv*" (Land) movement, which had a Pan-Arab philosophy and supported the Egyptian leader Gamal ABDEL NASSER. In 1964 the movement was declared illegal and dismantled. After that the authorities managed to prevent the establishment of any new Arab political movement until the early 1970s. Nevertheless, during the period until the abolition of the Military Administration, there was extensive cultural activity amongst the Arab minority, which expressed its national and political aspirations. Especially prominent were the writers and poets whose works were known as "opposition literature" (*Adab al-muqawama*). Thus, the leadership of *Maki* (technically a mixed Jewish-Arab Party) remained the only

leadership on the national level, in addition to the traditional leadership connected with the Jewish parties. The activities of Maki focused on safeguarding the rights of the Arab minority and protesting against the policy of the regime toward them. In 1965 *Maki* split due to conflicts between the Arab majority and the Jewish minority in its ranks, regarding the attitude toward the Arab national movement. The majority established the New Community List (*Rakah*), while a small minority, which remained in *Maki*, vanished from the political arena after a short while.

From the early 1970s, a new political awakening, which bore an institutional character, was discernible. On the national level, Arab students committees were established at the universities, which were associated in the Arab Students' Union. Other organizations that emerged included the high school Students' Union, the DRUZE Initiative Committee, the Committee for the Protection of Lands and, most important of all, the Committee of Heads of Local Authorities. In addition, new political frameworks were established, such as "the Democratic Front for Peace and Equality" (DFPE), with *Rakah* (which later changed its name again to *Maki*) at its center, and extra-parliamentary movements such as "the Village Sons."

The common denominator of all the new organizations was an expression of a separate Arab identity, and the demand for the realization of civil equality. In practical terms this translated into an aspiration for the integration into Israeli society. The only organization that was different was the "Village Sons" movement, representing national aspirations. This movement rejected Arab integration into the Israeli society, calling instead for the preservation of the separate national identity and linking the fate of the Arabs in Israel to that of the Palestinian people as a whole, within the framework of a general solution of the Palestinian problem.

The political organization of the 1970s gave rise to new patterns of mobilization, reflecting the tightening relations and cooperation amongst different localities and regions. The new associations were democratic by nature and the relations amongst them became more open and tolerant.

The political protest reached a climax in the events of the strike declared on "Land Day," 30 March, 1976. This strike (during which bloody clashes with the police took place) signified a sharp change on the level of organization and political activity in the direction of emphasis on national identity. This led to an intensification of the demand by the Arabs in Israel to be recognized as a national minority. The appearance of the "Progressive National Movement" (PNM) in 1983 contributed significantly to this change. The PNM defined itself as a Palestinian, national political movement, constituting a stream within the Palestinian national movement outside the borders of the State. At the same time, it was the first political movement that expressed the wish to integrate into Israel on a collective basis. The issue was even more outstanding due to the fundamental clash between how the movement defined itself, on the one hand, and its aspirations and the opposition by the Zionist parties to allow its participation in the elections, on the other.

As a result of the movement's success in attaining representation in the eleventh Knesset, which was elected in 1984, within the framework of the Progressive List for Peace, the "Basic Law: the Knesset" was amended, to the effect that a list that rejects Israel as being the state of the Jewish people, cannot run in the elections.

At the same time the "Village Sons" movement underwent important changes, which manifested themselves in a greater emphasis on national affiliation and a willingness to accept a political solution based on stages, rather than a comprehensive solution to the Palestinian problem. These changes led to the crystallization of a consensus within the Arab population in Israel. While emphasizing the Palestinian identity of the Israeli Arabs this consents to a solution of the Palestinian problem which will exclude them, but constitutes a basic condition for the improvement of their living conditions and their receiving full rights Israeli citizens.

Whilst national awareness was developing, the sense of identity with ISLAM also strengthened. Toward the end of the 1970s this emerged as a religious-political organization. Even though this appeared to indicate a strengthening of the religious identity in its radical form and a moving away from the Israeli society, the young Islamic movement did not exclude itself from the framework of the Palestinian political consensus. From 1983 onwards the movement made significant achievements in local elections and its weight in the adoption of decision in the national organizations increased.

In these developments, the role of the Arab local authorities, that turned into the central axis in the "Supreme Follow-Up Committee" of the Arabs in Israel (a body comprising the heads of the Arab authorities and the Arab Members of Knesset), established in 1982 as the supreme representative institutions of the Arab population in Israel, became significant.

These trends peaked during the strike on "Equality Day," 24 June, 1987. This was the result of intensive political activity, and raised both the national demand for a solution of the Palestinian problem, and the demand for the realization of civil rights for the Arab population in Israel under the slogan "Peace and Equality".

The political activity of the Arab public in this period was characterized by growing self-confidence and the ability to organize and react quickly to events in Israel and in the region, as opposed to the silence and waiting that had characterized it in previous decades. These characteristics reflected the change which the Arab population underwent in the course of two decades, and were entwined with a change the political atmosphere and behavior. The most important expression of this behavior was voting for the Knesset and local authorities. Following the elections to the seventh Knesset in 1969, the Jewish parties began losing support in the Arab sector, so that in 1977 the DFPE alone won a majority of the Arab votes. Four years later, the Arab lists connected with the Labor Alignment, disappeared. Upon the appearance of the "Progressive List for Peace" (the PLP—a mixed Arab-Jewish Party) in the elections to the eleventh Knesset in 1984, the Jewish parties further weakened in the Arab sector. This trend continued until the 1992 elections. Furthermore the direct election of mayors and heads of local councils, as of the 1978 municipal elections, strengthened the status of the Arab political leadership imbuing it with much self-confidence.

The INTIFADA, that erupted at the end of 1987 in the occupied territories, marked the beginning of a new stage in the political activity. It emphasized the difference between the Arabs in Israel and the rest of the Palestinian groups, especially in the territories. The involvement of the Arab population did not usually diverge from the limits of material and medical assistance to the Palestinians, and protest against the Israeli policy within the framework of Israeli law. The Israeli reaction to this involvement included threats; the establishment of a special police unit to deal with the Arab sector; use of force and an increase in the media effort to isolate the Arabs from the Jewish population. At the same time, the authorities increased their efforts to coopt the Arab elites. These efforts succeeded in attaining their goals to a large extent. The coopting policy and the new political conditions created a new situation , which led to important results on the level of political values and behavioral norms. However, the most marked change was a rethinking on the issue of the integration of the Arabs in the life of the State and the feeling, which kept deepening, that they constitute a marginal group within the Palestinian people.

As a result of the *intifada* and its influence, changes took place in the patterns of the political organization and activity, reflected in the following phenomena. First of all, the resignation of Knesset member Abdel Wahab Darawshe from the Labor Party in January 1988 and the establishment of the "Arab Democratic Party"—the first independent, totally Arab Party since the establishment of the State. It represents a new direction in terms of political thinking, at the core of which was the withdrawal to the national origin group, and the mobilization of political power to be used in order to advance individual integration in the political system and Israeli society. Second, the withdrawal of the "Progressive List for Peace" from the idea of Jewish-Arab cooperation and its turning into an Arab list. Third, the emergence of new political thought in the Communist Party and the DFPE combined with caustic criticism regarding the ideology, positions and conduct of the "eternal and non-democratic" leadership of the party. Finally, the rapid rise of the Islamic Movement, which started to distinguish itself as a socio-political force, with great influence on local and national levels.

These developments pointed to a temporary mood of isolationism in the Arab population, standing in contrast to the new inclinations, which were crystallizing in the PLO, in the direction of openness to the Israeli society and a search for ways to influence public opinion in the elections for the Labor Party and the Left. The Palestinian leadership started to cooperate with Arab activists in the Jewish left-wing parties, and at the same time to encourage the participation in the voting, while secretly acting to weaken the "Village Sons" and the "Progressive Movement". The new orientation was of important and deep significance in the long run, in terms of removing the delegitimization from ZIONISM, and consequently the main barrier to the integration of the Arabs in Israeli society.

The inclinations that crystallized in the Palestinian leadership corresponded with the inclination amongst large parts of the Arab population, that did not feel comfortable with the existing contradictions in their lives. Therefore, they welcomed the decision of the PLO, of November 1988, to declare independence in the WEST BANK and GAZA STRIP. This declaration was interpreted by them as a recognition of the fact that their political fate was different from that of the rest of the Palestinians, and that their future is connected with the extent of their integration in the State of Israel. These trends further strengthened in face of the Gulf crisis and the collapse of the Soviet Union and the Communist bloc, which actually did away with all the ideological and political alternatives open to the Arabs in Israel. The changes which the Arabs underwent manifested themselves in the elections to the thirteenth Knesset in 1992, in the following ways: First membership in the Jewish parties, including right-wing parties, turned into a significant phenomenon in the Arab population, which was not necessarily condemned. Second, the movement from one political position to its antithesis and the changing of allegiances, turned into an inseparable part of the political scene, and an accepted expression of the supremacy of personal interest. Third, the internal struggles within the political elites greatly sharpened, to the point of inability to organize joint activities of a national nature. Finally, the Jewish parties gained fifty-three percent of the Arab votes—a result which had not been encountered since 1973. The most significant figure was that part of the right-wing parties (*Likud*, National Religious Party and *shas*) received twenty-two percent of the Arab vote, while the PLP—which emphasized national motifs in its propaganda—did not even pass the qualifying threshold.

The election campaign was accompanied by an unprecedented phenomenon: First of all, direct and overt involvement by the PLO and Egypt in putting together the Arab lists, support of certain lists and attempts to influence the Arab voters. Second, the decline in the importance and influence of national slogans in the mobilization of voters for personal and family interests. Third, the strengthening of the consensus amongst the various political organizations regarding the integration of the Arabs in Israel and the abandonment of the national solution—as if to say that it relates exclusively to the Palestinians beyond the Green Line.

Thus, the 1992 elections were a sharp turning point in the history of the Arabs in Israel, both in terms of their course and content and in terms of their results. They revealed unequivocally the desire of the Arab public to integrate in the Israeli society, landing a serious blow to those groups that continued to oppose such integration. The significance of the 1992 election results was especially marked following the signing of the Declaration of Principles (DoP) between Israel and the PLO on 13 September, 1993 (see ARAB-ISRAEL CONFLICT). The Agreement served as an injection of encouragement to the political stream, which was encouraged by the Labor government led by Yitzhak RABIN, that accepted the reality and supported the integration in the Israeli society. However, the DOP also led to the recognition of the fact that there is no direct link between the living conditions of the Arabs in Israel and progress in the peace process, and that in the short term the improvement in their situation and status is a function of their relations with the State of Israel.

Political Organization 1992–1996

This period has been of special importance in the history of the Arabs of Israel in several respects: First of all, despite the results of the 1992 elections, their representatives in the Knesset turned into a decisive factor for the existence of the Center-Left government, led by the Labor Party, giving them an unprecedented bargaining position, without their joining the coalition. However, they were unable to take advantage of this position, since they could hardly threaten to bring down a government, engaged in the signing of historical agreements with the Palestinian leadership and Jordan. Second, only toward the end of the term of the Labor government, did it become apparent that the position of the Arabs on the political map remained as marginal as it had been, except for an increase in the financial allocations for their local authorities and public institutions, and that the peace did not open up new horizons for them. Nevertheless, the general at-

mosphere in the country became more comfortable due to manifestations of greater openness and tolerance on the part of the Jewish majority, and the feeling was that the relations between the two groups are progressively improving. Third, the developments in this period greatly accelerated the process of integration of the Arabs in the life of the State. Even though they remained outside the central decision making body, their presence in the life of the State became more significant and noticeable, with their affairs becoming part of the agenda of the media.

These developments had great influence on the political alignment of the Arab population toward the elections to the fourteenth Knesset, which were held on 29 May, 1996, in which new lists appeared and several old ones vanished. There were also discernible changes in the manner of operation and content: the use of means of mass communication became the main tool in the elections propaganda; emphasis was placed on the character of the candidates and their characteristics; the local affairs of the Arab population took a much greater and more prominent place in the political platforms. Toward the elections at least nine political organizations appeared, but finally there remained only four parties and movements, organized into two Arab lists, in addition to the political activists in the Jewish parties.

1) The DFPE suffered more than any other political organization in the Arab sector from the collapse of the Soviet Union and the Communist regimes in Eastern Europe. As a result, the Front lost its main source of financial support, its ability to mobilize new forces by channeling generous scholarships from socialist countries to students, and ideological support. From now on the PLO became the main source of inspiration for the formulation of the political positions of *Rakah* and the Front, especially with regards to the solution to the Palestinian problem and the status of the Arabs in Israel. The Front turned to seeking solutions to the domestic problems of the Arab citizens of Israel, by means of mediation with the authorities or by exerting political pressure, while limiting its involvement in problems affecting the Arab public as a whole. The Front remains the largest political force in the Arab sector, supported by a certain strata in the population and families that made alliances with it on the basis of mutual support in the elections to the Knesset and local au-

thorities. However, the crisis in *Maki* and the Front caused certain prominent intellectuals and organizers to leave. Furthermore, the Front got into a leadership crisis as a result of the death of Tawfiq Ziad, who had great personal charisma. On the other hand, there were great pressures on the Front from within, for renewal and democratization, especially in the election of candidates for the Knesset list. The alliance between the Front and the "Democratic National Alliance" (see below) in 1996 gave back to the Front something of its political uniqueness.

2) The Arab Democratic Party was characterized by continuity with regards to its position on the national-Palestinian issue and the issue of the integration in the State of Israel on an individual basis, while solving local problems. The ADP was based from the start on family alliances, receiving much support from the Nazareth area and from the Beduins in the Negev. In the course of the preparations toward the last election campaign in 1996, there was a deterioration in the status of the Party, due to the fact that the PALESTINIAN AUTHORITY (PA) lifted its support from it, preferring instead to support other candidates. The ADP consequently tried to obtain material and moral support from other Arab regimes. The Party suffered from competition coming from the Labor Party and *Meretz*, as well as from new Arab lists, whose political platforms were similar to its own. Finally it registered an important tactical victory over its rivals entering an alliance with the Islamic List, with which it ran in a single list in the elections.

3) The PLP: The political changes in the country and the region led the PLP to a state of disintegration. The PLO preferred to support other political movements which had contacts with Jewish parties, precisely at a time when the PLP became a purely Arab list. It also suffered from an ideological crisis as a result of the Gulf War and its consequences, and failed to pass the qualifying threshold in the 1992 elections, suffering an additional shake-up following the signing of the Oslo Agreement. As a result of these developments, as well as personal clashes within the movement, the PLP disintegrated and no longer exists as an independent political force, even though some of its former leaders participated in consultations with other political groups to put together a list toward the 1996 elections.

4) The Islamic Movement proved its ability to mobilize votes on the local level, becoming a leading force in the Arab political arena in the country. Until the elections to the thirteenth Knesset in 1992, the members of the Movement and its supporters avoided voting. In 1992, the leaders of the Movement decided not to call upon its supporters to boycott the elections, and did not play an active role in them. On the eve of the 1996 elections, the leadership of the Movement once again decided not to participate in the elections in an independent list. However, Sheikh Abdallah Nimr Darwish, who led a pragmatic stream in the Movement, accepted the Oslo Agreement, and tried to bring about a change in this decision. The Movement and its leaders were under great pressure by the authorities and left-wing parties, as well as by the Palestinian Authority, not to boycott the elections, especially after the suicide attacks in Israel by supporters of the HAMAS and Islamic JIHAD in the beginning of 1996, eroded the support for the peace process and the Labor candidate for the premiership, Shimon PERES. The struggle in the Islamic Movement finally led to a split, and a decision by the members of the pragmatic stream to participate in the elections to the Knesset in a list together with the ADP.

5) The Village Sons: The movement continued to oppose participation in the Knesset elections for about twenty years, as an expression of its opposition to the integration of the Arabs in the state. Its platform regarding a solution to the Palestinian problem was considered more radical than that of the other political movements in the Arab sector. The Gulf War and the Oslo Agreement constituted a harsh blow to its rigid political line that resulted in a deep crisis, emphasizing its isolation in the Arab public in Israel and amongst the Palestinians in general. The Movement lost many of its members, its power in the local elections weakened and its influence over the public on the issue of boycotting the Knesset elections eroded. Following some serious soul searching and out of concern for its mere existence, it finally decided, towards the elections to the fourteenth Knesset in 1996, to join the Democratic National Alliance, and run within the framework of the DFPE.

6) The Democratic National Alliance (DNA) emerged as a coalition between three political forces in the Arab sector: the "Village Sons" movement, the "Equality Alliance Movement" and a splinter of the "Progressive Movement". In the 1996 elections

it joined the list of the DFPE gaining representation in the Knesset. Even though it does not have a clear political platform and its components represent different approaches on various issues, it supports the principle of equality for the Arab population, turning the State de facto into a state of all its citizens, granting administrative autonomy to the Arab sector in the spheres of culture and education. The Alliance has remained independent of the DFPE, even competing against it in various forums, such as the Arab students committees in the universities.

There are today four main streams regarding the status of the Arabs in Israel:

The dominant stream is convinced that Israel as a Jewish state is a tangible reality, which cannot be changed. This stream emphasizes the separation between the Arabs' national and cultural identity and their civil identity, and does not consider there to be a clash between them. It tries to attain equality by means of integration in party and political activities, whilst demanding a realization of the Arabs' civil rights and preserving their unique cultural and national characteristics. Most of those who belong of this stream are activists in the Jewish-Zionist parties, such as the Labor Party and *Meretz*, but there is also an unknown number of activists, supporting right-wing parties. One may learn about the power of this stream from the 1996 elections in which the Arab district was the largest in the Labor Party, while in the 1997 Labor Party Conference it was the second largest district after the Kibbutz district.

Despite this the Arab members in the Labor Party have very little, if any, influence over the decision making process in the party, especially in the political sphere.

The second stream recognizes the State of Israel, but without accepting its Jewish-Zionist character, demanding to turn it into the state of all its citizens. This steam tries to further this goal by means of participation in all types of activities and in all spheres and events. It is represented by the DFPE and the ADP, as well as by a small group of intellectuals, who are not organized in a political body and whose positions do not manifest themselves in any political platforms, even though they are reflected in the media.

The third stream emphasizes more than the previous two the issue of national or religious (Islamic) identity, demanding autonomy in the running of its education and culture. It also calls for equality and turning the state into the state of all its citizens. In other words, it demands both integration into the life of the state and the preservation of the collective identity and the realization of collective and not only individual rights. It is represented by groups that are in a struggle amongst themselves: the Islamic Movement, on the one hand, and the DNA, on the other.

The fourth stream is relatively weak and not organized. Its members do not appear publicly. It does not recognize the State of Israel from a nationalist or religious position. It comprises academics and some members of the Islamic Movement, who reject the participation in activities and events of an official character, and do not participate in the elections to the Knesset. It is under heavy pressure from all sides, and is in a state of ideological and political distress, which grew as a result of the split in the ISLAMIC MOVEMENT toward the 1996 elections.

IZZ al-DIN al-QASSAM   see HAMAS.

J

JACOBITES   Alternative name, used mainly in the West, for the Syrian-Orthodox MONOPHYSITE Christians. The name derives from Jacob Baradaeus who reorganized the Syrian Church in the sixth century, after its beginnings in the secession of the Monophysites from the main body of the Church at the Council of Chalcedon (451). The language of the Jacobite liturgy is Syriac-Aramaic, and a few Jaco-

bites still use that language as their spoken tongue. The head of the Church, called the Mar Ignatius, is based in Damascus. One of the eleven dioceses of the Jacobite Church is headed by the Archbishop of Jerusalem; the Jacobites have certain rights in the Church of the Holy Sepulchre in Jerusalem and in the Church of the Nativity in Bethlehem. There are today an estimated 150,000–200,000 Jacobites in the

Middle East—about half of them in SYRIA and the rest in IRAQ, LEBANON, TURKEY, and a very few in Jerusalem; about 50,000 live in the Americas, and there is an ancient Jacobite community numbering more than 1 million in South India (the "Malabar Christians").

JADID, SALAH (1926–1993) Syrian officer and politician. An ALAWI born in Ladhiqiyya, Jadid became a professional officer. In the 1950s he joined a clandestine cell of the leftist pan-Arab BA'TH Party and soon played a leading role. He was among those who prepared and staged the coup of March 1963 that brought the *Ba'th* to power in coalition with the Nasserists. After the *Ba'th* won in a bitter factional struggle with the Nasserists, Jadid became, in 1963, Chief of Staff of the Syrian army. In October 1964 he was also made a member of the Presidential Council and of both the national (i.e., all-Arab) and the regional, Syrian high command of the *Ba'th* Party. In the intra-*Ba'th* factional struggle that erupted in 1964–1965, Jadid headed the military faction that was also more extreme-leftist and doctrinaire in its political orientation (besides having a more pronounced Alawi profile). When the civilian and more moderate wing, led by Michel AFLAQ, Bitar and Amin Hafez, won out, Jadid was dismissed in September 1965 both from the Presidential Council and as Chief of Staff. However, in February 1966 Jadid ousted the ruling Aflaq-Hafez faction in a coup and installed his military faction both in the Syrian state and army and in the Syrian regional *Ba'th* command. As the Aflaq faction, now in exile, retained its leadership of the all-Arab *Ba'th* command, Jadid and his associates set up a rival all-Arab command in SYRIA.

In the new regime that he established in 1966 Jadid took no formal post in either the government or the army but contented himself with the position of Deputy Secretary General of the *Ba'th* Party, leaving the Secretary Generalship to Nur al-Din al-ATASSI. Jadid was the strong man of Syria for over four years. His rule was characterized by revolutionary and doctrinaire ideology and antagonistic policies both inside Syria and in foreign relations (see SYRIA). The increasing isolation of Syria within the Arab world caused by Jadid's policies was one of the reasons for a widening split within the *Ba'th*. Parts of Jadid's own military faction, led by Defense Minister Hafez al-ASAD, coalesced in a nationalist

faction and turned against Jadid. This conflict also had an intra-communal nature: while Jadid was a member of the Haddadin, the largest Alawi tribe, Asad was a member of a small tribe, the Kalbiyya. In February 1969 Asad, in a bloodless semi-coup, gained control of the government and the party command. He accepted as a compromise a coalition in which the Jadid group kept some important posts (including the posts of President and the Prime Minister).

However, In November 1970 Asad, in a second semi-coup, seized full control. Jadid and his associates were dismissed and detained. Jadid died in a Damascus prison in August 1993, after the Syrian regime refused to release him despite pressure from international groups and the Syrian opposition in exile.

A brother of Jadid, Major Ghassan Jadid, also a professional officer, had been politically active in the formation of the SYRIAN NATIONALIST PARTY which was opposed to Jadid's *Ba'th*. He was murdered in February 1957, while in exile in LEBANON. Another brother, Major Fu'ad Jadid, was jailed in connection with the murder of Syria's leftist and pro-Egyptian Deputy Chief of Staff Adnan al-Maleki by the same Syrian Nationalist Party in 1955; Jadid released him from prison in 1964.

JALLUD, ABDEL SALAM (b. 1943) Libyan officer and politician. Seized power together with Mu'ammar QADHAFI on 1 September 1968 and served until his removal from the center of political power in the early 1990s as Qadhafi's second in command.

In March 1978, with the completion of the system of "People's Power"—a Libyan "revolutionary" form of participatory democracy—Qadhafi divested himself and his closest aid Jallud of any formal vestiges of power.

Later in the 1980s, Jallud's major arena of activity was in foreign affairs. He was particularly involved in handling relations with the Soviet Union, the MAGHREB and IRAN. These aspects led to the widely held belief that Jallud had close ties to the radical Islamic movement.

Domestically, Jallud was responsible for the oil sector and the Revolutionary Committees, the regime's watch dog groups formed in 1977. Qadhafi appeared apprehensive of Jallud's close interactions with the powerful Revolutionary Committees and of their prosperity and acted to reduce their power as well as Jallud's authority.

In May 1986, Jallud allegedly escaped an attempt on his life at his home in Tripoli. No official details were available regarding the incident, and the perpetrators remained unidentified. Nevertheless, the event fueled rumors on the existence of a fierce power struggle between Qadhafi and Jallud. These rumors were further nourished by Jallud's long absence from Tripoli, from late 1986 until early spring of 1987. He spent this time in Damascus, officially to mediate between the two warring factions in the Lebanese "camps war" between the SHI'A, AMAL militia and the PLO. His long stay abroad for a mission in LEBANON, where his influence was relatively negligible, and the fact that his family was with him all the time created speculations that he was in a voluntary or forced exile, though the Libyan official media ignored the rumors.

Nevertheless, various sources persistently claimed that differences between the two leaders revolved around a broad set of issues, among them Jallud's cool attitude toward Libya's military intervention in Chad (1980–1987) and his disagreement with changes in the banking and oil sectors. Allegedly, Qadhafi blamed Jallud for the disorganization among the Revolutionary Committees.

Nonetheless, Jallud's return to Libya, albeit maintaining a relatively low-key public presence, implied that the two leaders had reached some sort of *modus vivendi*, whatever their differences. But it did not take long until tension erupted anew between Qadhafi and Jallud, with the latter criticising the economic policy advocated by Qadhafi, including his promise to distribute oil revenues to the people. Jallud also criticized the Libyan pilgrims' visit to JERUSALEM in May 1993; as well as some aspects of foreign policy identified with his leader. The political gap between Qadhafi and Jallud grew wider, leading to the latter's removal from the center of political power. In the summer of 1993 Jallud was sent to what seemed to be an imposed exile in Greece.

Jallud was finally removed from politics in 1994. Since then, the state's controlled media has systematically ignored him, while foreign sources claimed he was put under house arrest, and that the authorities banned him from traveling abroad.

JARRING MISSION see ARAB-ISRAEL PEACEMAKING.

JERUSALEM Capital of the state of ISRAEL, though it is not recognized as such by most of the states in the world, which maintain their embassies in Tel Aviv. Population in 1995 was 591,400. A city holy to the three monotheistic religions. According to a list prepared by the UN, there are fifteen places holy to Christianity, five holy to Islam and ten holy to Judaism. During the years of the British Mandate for Palestine (1922–1948), Jerusalem was the capital of Palestine. In the course of the 1948–1949 Arab-Israeli War (see ARAB-ISRAEL CONFLICT) the Old City of Jerusalem and the Eastern part of the city, except for Mount Scopus, were conquered by the Jordanian Arab Legion. The Western half of the city was held by the Israel Defence Force. Since the 1967 war (see ARAB-ISRAEL CONFLICT) the whole of Jerusalem has been in Israeli hands.

Jerusalem is built on the mountains of Judea, about 700 meters above sea level. It was first mentioned in Egyptian sources between the seventeenth and eighteenth centuries BC, and was a Jewish city from the period of King David (1037–969 BC) until the destruction of the Second Temple by the Romans (70 AD). It once again turned into a Jewish city during the Jewish revolt against the Romans in 135 AD. After the revolt it was crushed and its name changed to Aelia Capitolina and Jews were forbidden to live there. In the years 614–629, when the Persians ruled the city, Jews were once again allowed to settle in Jerusalem. After the Islamic conquest of Palestine (638) an Arabic-speaking Muslim community lived in the city, side by side with the Jewish community. Jews were once again excluded from the city during the Crusader period between 1099–1187 and 1229–1244.

YEAR	POPULATION	% OF JEWS
1860	12,000	50.0%
1892	42,000	61.9%
1922	63,000	53.9%
1942	140,000	61.4%
1948	165,000	60.5%
1967 (July)	266,000	75.2%
1994	567,100	71.7%
1995	591,400 ·	70.5%

The history of West Jerusalem begins in 1860, when the first Jewish neighborhoods outside the walls of the Old City were constructed. Since that time, Jews have constituted a majority of the population of the city. The presence of Jews in the Old City ended on 28 May 1948, when the Jewish quarter (1,700 inhabitants) surrendered to the Jordanian Arab Legion. UN General Assembly Resolution 181 of 29 November 1947, regarding the partition of Mandatory Palestine into a Jewish state and an Arab state, recommended that Jerusalem remain under an international regime. This would remain separate from the two states, and under the supervision of a UN Trustee Council. The internationalization plan for Jerusalem, which was presented by the UN mediator Count Folke Bernadotte (see ARAB-ISRAEL PEACEMAKING), was rejected both by the Arabs and the Jews and was not approved by the UN. However, on 11 December 1948, the General Assembly approved a resolution to the effect that the city must remain "under effective UN control." The UN Palestine Conciliation Commission prepared a "detailed proposal for a permanent international regime" for Jerusalem, while the Security Council was to ensure the demilitarization of the city (but in fact did nothing). In December 1949 the General Assembly "restated its intention" to establish an "international regime" which would provide adequate protection for the holy places, and charged the Trusteeship Council with preparing the "Statute of Jerusalem." JORDAN stated during the debate in the General Assembly that it would not discuss any plan to internationalize Jerusalem.

Upon the UN Resolution on partition of Palestine (29 November 1947), Jerusalem became a theater of violence from which Arab-Jewish hostilities spread to other parts of the country. The war ended with the conquest by the Jews of several Arab areas in Western Jerusalem, while the Old City and East Jerusalem came under Jordanian occupation. On 1 December Jordan established its administration there. On 24 April 1950, it formally annexed the WEST BANK, including the eastern part of Jerusalem, and this despite the strong objection of all the other Arab states. In fact, Israel and Jordan tacitly agreed to divide Jerusalem between them and thus defy the UN decision of internationalization.

In a report published by the Trusteeship Council in June 1950, it was proposed again that Jerusalem would constitute a separate entity under international administration. But in light of Israeli and Jor-

danian opposition, the Soviet Union withdrew its support for the idea of the internationalization of the city and on January 1952 the General Assembly adopted a resolution which placed on the governments concerned the responsibility for reaching an agreement between them on all the disputed issues, in accordance with the previous UN resolutions. This resolution, which recognized the *status quo*, de facto was the last resolution adopted by the UN on the issue until 1967.

The Israeli-Jordanian Armistice Agreement of 3 April 1949 (see ARAB-ISRAEL PEACEMAKING) completed the partition of Jerusalem. The agreement proposed the establishment of a joint committee that would ensure Israel's free access to the holy places; Jewish cultural institutions (the University) on Mount Scopus and the Jewish cemetery on the Mount of Olives, and determined the quantities of arms which could be held in Jerusalem. This joint committee never convened and the Jordanians disregarded their undertaking to allow Jews access to the holy places, while the Jewish cemetery on the Mount of Olives was desecrated. Access to Mount Scopus was granted to a limited number of policemen only.

On 23 January 1950 the Knesset (see ISRAEL) decided that upon the establishment of the State of Israel, Jerusalem once again became the capital of the Jewish people. However, most of the foreign diplomatic representations were established in Tel Aviv, since most of the countries that maintained relations with Israel never recognized Israeli rule over any part of Jerusalem. The reasons for this were: (1) the status of a *corpus separatum* assigned to Jerusalem under the UN partition plan; (2) the fear of angering the Arab states; (3) the refusal on the part of some states to accept Jewish control over the Christian holy places. Twenty embassies were nevertheless established in West Jerusalem at the time of the outbreak of the 1967 war. Only two of them—those of the Netherlands and Yugoslavia—represented European states. Under Jordanian annexation, the municipal status and allocation of resources had undergone a deliberate reduction in an attempt to weaken the sense of Palestinian identity and allegiance to Jerusalem and foster instead, Amman as the capital of the two banks of River Jordan.

In June 1967, after the conquest of the city by Israeli forces, Israeli law, jurisdiction and administration were applied to Jerusalem. On 30 July 1980 the Knesset passed "the Basic Law: Jerusalem the Capital of Israel" (see ISRAEL), which declared united Jerusalem to be the capital of Israel and the seat of the President of the State, the government and the Supreme Court. The State ensures the sanctity of all the holy places.

Following the annexation of the city, the Arab inhabitants of the Jerusalem were given Israeli identity cards and the right to apply for Israeli citizenship. Most of them refused, maintaining Jordanian citizenship and refusing to recognize the city's annexation by Israel. Only a few have since made use of their right to vote in municipal elections, and no inhabitant of East Jerusalem has ever contended for a place in the city council. In 1989, however, Christian pharmacist and newspaper editor Hana Seniora considered running.

For close to thirty years, Jerusalem's mayor was Teddy Kollek. Kollek, who was born in Vienna in 1911, was elected Mayor in 1965 on behalf of David BEN GURION's Rafi Party. He was later associated with the Israeli Labor Party, though he always ran as an independent. He remained Mayor until the 1993 municipal elections when he was defeated by the Likud's Ehud Olmert, who had the support of the religious parties.

Teddy Kollek tried to turn Jerusalem into a truly united city. He wanted to adapt the city's bylaws to the special needs of the Arab inhabitants of the city and to provide adequate municipal services in the Eastern part of the city. However, Jerusalem remains a divided city. There have also been occasional outbursts of tension between Jews and Arabs following Arab terrorist attacks against Jews in the city; various incidents in and around the Temple Mount and provocations by Jewish extremists against Arabs. Even though the INTIFADA, which broke out in December 1987, was not accompanied by as much violence in Jerusalem as in the West Bank and GAZA STRIP, the commercial strikes, the avoidance of any public celebrations and entertainment on the side of the Palestinians and the closure of schools by the Israeli authorities were felt in Jerusalem as well. On 22 January 1988, a curfew was imposed by Israel on the Arab neighborhoods of Jerusalem for the first time since the 1967 war. Following the disturbances on the Temple Mount on 8 October 1990, in the course of which seventeen Palestinian worshippers were killed by Israeli police forces, there was a rise

in the cases of Jews in Jerusalem being stabbed by Palestinians. However, the most serious terrorist attacks to hit the city were the repeated bus bombings by Islamic fundamentalist suicide bombers which peaked in February and March 1996.

After 1967 the Jewish quarter of the Old City, which had been destroyed during the 1948–1949 war, was reconstructed and reinhabited by Jews. The Hebrew University campus and Hadassah Hospital on Mount Scopus were also reopened and expanded. All around the city new Jewish neighborhoods were constructed, in a manner that would make the repartition of the city almost impossible. Following the 1967 war the Israeli government also moved most of the government ministries that had remained in Tel Aviv to Jerusalem, except for the Ministries of Defense and Agriculture.

Toward the 1980s, and until the formation of the Labor led government by Yitzhak RABIN in July 1992 (see ISRAEL), there were efforts by various right wing groups and individuals, such as *Atteret Cohanim*, to purchase houses and land, and settle in Arab neighborhoods, despite opposition from Mayor Teddy Kollek.

Since 1967, Israel has made great efforts to preserve the security of all the holy places; the freedom of access for worship by all; and the rights of the various religious communities to their holy places. Nevertheless, the annexation of East Jerusalem raised continuous cries of protest, both amongst the Arab states and in the General Assembly of the UN. The General Assembly resolved on 4 and 14 July, 1967, that the unilateral measures taken by Israel to change the status of Jerusalem are invalid, and called upon it to end all such activities. For over twenty years, the General Assembly continued to regularly denounce Israel's control over Jerusalem. In two sharply worded resolutions, of 21 May 1968 and 3 July 1969, the General Assembly called on Israel to cancel all the measures it had taken to annex East Jerusalem. UNESCO also started sending supervisory groups to observe Israel's archeological activities in the city, and denounced it for "changing the character of Jerusalem by means of archeological digs." The passage of the "Basic Law: Jerusalem the Capital of Israel," raised harsh international reaction. On 20 August 1980, Security Council Resolution 478 called on all states to remove their diplomatic representatives from Jerusalem. Thirteen states that had left their embassies in West Jerusalem following the Yom Kippur War, now moved them to Tel Aviv. Only Costa Rica and El Salvador did not move their embassies. On 24 October 1995, the Unites States Senate passed a law instructing the administration to move the US Embassy to Jerusalem no later than May 1999, even though the option was left to delay the transfer. More than ten states continue to maintain consulates in Jerusalem. Their official status remains unclear, since most of them are independent of the embassies in Tel Aviv, and deal primarily with matters connected with the occupied territories and the PALESTINIAN AUTHORITY.

Following the 1967 war, several Arab leaders announced that they would be willing to accept the internationalization of Jerusalem, even though most of the Arab spokesmen demanded that the eastern half of the city be returned to Arab hands. Jerusalem became a rallying cry for Arabs and Muslims following the July 1969 fire at the *al-Aqsa* mosque of the *Haram al-Sharif* (the third most sacred place in the Muslim world). It led to the convening of an Islamic summit conference led by SAUDI ARABIA, and later enabled the gathering of Arab heads of state at Rabat in December 1969. Following the 1973 war (see ARAB-ISRAEL CONFLICT) there was a growing movement to establish an independent Palestinian state, with East Jerusalem as its capital.

After the war of October 1973 pan-Arab and pan-Islamic sentiments in the Arab world reached their peak, and Islamic states throughout the world called for East Jerusalem to return to Arab sovereignty. Saudi King FEISAL was the most outspoken Islamic leader to defend the Islamic character of Jerusalem. At its February 1974 meeting in Pakistan, the IS-LAMIC CONFERENCE ORGANISATION (ICO) established the Al-Quds (Jerusalem) committee, headed by Prince HASAN of MOROCCO.

In recent years, Jerusalem has again been a source of tension between Israel and the Arab states. One of the understandings that led to the 1993 Declaration of Principles (DOP) between Israel and the PALESTINE LIBERATION ORGANIZATION is that neither side would discuss the issue of Jerusalem before negotiations began on a permanent settlement. However, in the Israeli-Jordanian Peace Treaty of 1994 (see ARAB-ISRAEL PEACEMAKING) Israel recognized Jordan's special status regarding Islamic holy places in Jerusalem.

Following the 1967 War, the government of Israel prohibited Jews from praying on the Temple Mount, in order to prevent tension with the Muslims. Most of the Jewish religious authorities approved this order, for religious reasons, but many, including Chief Rabbi Shlomo Goren, objected and several groups, such as the "Temple Mount Faithful" continue to make efforts to pray on the Temple Mount. Some groups also have plans to rebuild the Jewish Temple (the Third Temple).

In order to facilitate Jewish prayers at the Western ("Wailing") Wall—the holiest site for the Jews in the world, which is supposed to have constituted part of the retaining wall of the Second Temple—after the 1967 war the buildings close to the wall were torn down and their inhabitants moved elsewhere. Archaeological digs around the wall have revealed the continuation of the Western Wall northwards, and digs toward the South revealed the city of David. Archaeological digs in Jerusalem continue to cause periodic disturbances, and in September 1996 the opening of the so called "Hasmonean tunnel," which *inter alia* connects the Western Wall with the *Via Dolorosa*, was the background to violent clashes between Israelis and Palestinians.

Within the Jewish part of the city, the numerical balance between the ultra-orthodox (*haredim*) and secular population is constantly shifting in favor of the former. The ultra-orthodox have been successful in ensuring that roads in or bordering on their neighborhoods will remain closed over the Sabbath. Although the *haredim* have been successful at keeping these roads closed on the Jewish Sabbath, they have not been as successful in other areas. In the 1950s they failed to prevent the construction of public swimming pools in the city, and in the late 1980s restaurants and places of amusement were permitted to open on the Sabbath and Jewish holidays, despite strong *haredi* opposition. In political terms, the Jewish part of the city is predominantly right-wing—religious, even though from 1965 to 1993 the Mayor of Jerusalem, Teddy Kollek, was liberal. In 1993 Ehud Olmert of the Likud party was elected Mayor of Jerusalem with the support of all the religious parties.

JEWISH AGENCY see ISRAEL.

JEWS Until the mid-twentieth century, ancient, deeply rooted Jewish communities existed in most Middle Eastern countries. Ancient kingdoms and tribes in the Arabian peninsula that had been converted to Judaism, such as the Kingdom of *Himyar* in YEMEN (in the sixth century), or the *Khaibar* tribes in north-western Arabia, disappeared after the victory of ISLAM. But Jews continued living in Yemen as a minority group, tolerated as DHIMMIS (*Ahl al-Dhimma*) and as *Ahl al-Kitab* (People of the Book). They were forced to pay a poll tax (*jizya*) and encountered grave restrictions and many forms of institutionalized humiliation. Some Jewish tribes survived in the *Hadramaut*. In the Fertile Crescent countries and North Africa Jewish communities preceded the Arab conquest and the advent of Islam, remaining in these countries throughout medieval and modern times. They were Dhimmis until the constitutional modernization of the nineteenth century. The Middle Ages were a time of great prosperity for many Jewish communities. In such places as Spain, EGYPT, and MAGHREB Jews were influential in philopsophy, science, literature, and poetry, in a Hebrew–Arabic symbiosis. Following their expulsion from Spain in 1492 Jews were permitted to settle in the OTTOMAN EMPIRE.

DISTRIBUTION OF JEWS IN THE MIDDLE EAST
Estimates (in thousands)

	Pre-World War I	1947-48	1952	1980s
Iraq	85	125	6	(A)
Egypt	60	65	40	(A)
Yemen	45	50	3	1.5
Syria	32	19	5	4-5
Lebanon	3	6	5	(A)
Libya	25	35	3	(A)
Tunisia	80	100	90	4-5
Algeria	100	120	100	1
Morocco	180	200	200	15-20
Arab States (Total)	610	725	450	25-35
Iran			60-70	25-30
Turkey			50	25

(A) Less than 1000

At the beginning of the twentieth century, the number of Jews in the Middle East countries (including Palestine) was estimated at approximately 650,000–700,000 (see table). On the eve of the 1948 Arab-Israel War they numbered approximately 800,000 (excluding Palestine). That war along with the ARAB-ISRAEL CONFLICT led to the persecution of Jews in the Arab countries, and Israel's willingness to absorb them in unrestricted numbers. Thus, during that crisis and the first two decades of the State of ISRAEL, most of the Middle East Jews——up to 600,000——immigrated to Israel. Only 25,000–35,000 Jews remained in Arab countries, most of them in MOROCCO (15,000–20,000), and small, decaying communities in Baghdad; Damascus, Beirut, Tunis, and Yemen. In Iran until the Islamic Revolution of 1979, the Jewish community (80,000) continued to enjoy stability and prosperity. Under the Shi'i revolutionary regime, only 25,000–30,000 Jews remained, most of them in Tehran. In the mid-1990s there was also a large Jewish community in Turkey, estimated at approximately 25,000.

Most of the Jews in the contemporary Middle East were small craftsmen and traders. Some climbed the social ladder into the middle class; and a few wealthy families moved in the upper class governing elite of their respective country. Like many minority groups in the Ottoman Empire, many Jews acquired foreign citizenship to obtain better security and consular protection. Those who were not foreign citizens were considered citizens of the respective Middle East countries but some degree of discrimination persisted along with the Islamic tradition that tolerated the Jews as second class citizens.

The Arab-Jewish conflict over Palestine increasingly added elements of Arab antagonism and hostility (see ANTISEMITISM). Sporadic acts of violence and discrimination against Jews in IRAQ, SYRIA and Egypt escalated. In June 1941 a large-scale pogrom (*farhud*) was organized in Baghdad; and as the Palestine crisis came to a head, pogroms occurred also in Aleppo, ADEN and BAHRAIN (December 1947), in LIBYA (November 1945, June 1948, June 1967), Algiers (August 1934, May 1956, December 1960), and in Cairo (June 1948). Zionist, Jewish-nationalist organizations were banned, and though Arab governments officially distinguished between "Zionists" and Jews, their actions during the Palestine war amounted in fact to a harsh oppression of their Jewish subjects—hundreds of Jews in Iraq, Syria and Egypt were detained and sent to concentration camps and many were sentenced to prison on charges of ZIONISM and/or COMMUNISM. Similar steps were taken again whenever the Arab-Israel conflict erupted in a new crisis. Thus in Egypt thousands of Jews were expelled during the 1956 Suez-Sinai war and the 1967 war. In 1968-1969 Iraq executed several Jews (and some Arab Iraqis) following show trials in which they were convicted of being "Zionist and Western spies." The governments prevented or quelled anti-Jewish outbreaks in LEBANON, Tunisia and Morocco. In times of tension, such as May–June 1948, the Lebanese government even posted guards to protect the Jewish quarter of Beirut (as did the paramilitary PHALANGES organization). The freedom and relative safety of Beirut (until the civil war that began in 1975) also attracted many Syrian Jews to seek a haven there (although officially Syria banned their emigration).

Before 1948, there was a trickle of Jewish emigration from the Arab countries—mainly to Europe (FRANCE, Italy) and the Americas. Though Zionist activities were permitted in Egypt and not officially banned in Iraq (until the 1930s), Syria and Lebanon, and in the French-ruled Maghreb, few went to Palestine. The exception was Yemen; its Jews had begun migrating to Palestine, for national-religious reasons and in search of a better life, in the nineteenth century. Between the World Wars an estimated 17,000 of them reached Palestine. After 1948–1949, however, Jews left the Arab countries in a mass exodus, many of them to Europe (particularly, those from the Maghreb went to France). The majority went to ISRAEL, with the help of that country and of Western Jewish organizations. Indeed, the number of Jews from the Arab countries that came to Israel—some of them expelled, most compelled to leave their property behind—was nearly 600,000. While some of these migrants were motivated by Zionist, nationalist-religious reasons, the principal motive of the exodus was the deterioration of the economic, social and political security for them in the Arab states, and in some cases—the oppressive measures taken by the latter, or actual expulsion. About 45,000 Yemeni Jews were airlifted to Israel in 1949–1950; these included most of the Jews of *Hadramaut* and most of the approximately 4,000 Jews of Aden (most

of them of Yemeni origin). Some 35,000 were brought from Libya. Iraq permitted its Jews to be airlifted to Israel (officially camouflaged as destined for other countries) in March 1950, and within a year almost the whole community had disappeared, nearly 140,000 to Israel. Some 30,000 came from Egypt. Morocco virtually permitted the semi-clandestine organization of emigration to Israel, and more than 140,000 of its Jews came to Israel (over 50,000 went to France, 25,000 to North America). About 40,000 came to Israel from Tunisia. Most of the Jews of ALGERIA went to France, and only approximately 15,000 to Israel.

By 1952, the Jewish communities of the *Mashriq* (the Arab countries in the East) had already dwindled to insignificant numbers. Those in the Maghreb were not yet affected by the mass exodus: some 40,000 were still in Egypt; approximately 6,000 in Iraq; 5,000 in Syria; 5,000 in Lebanon. By the 1980s, the Jews had nearly disappeared from the Arab countries—a total of 25,000–35,000 remained, comprising small numbers of Jews mainly in Syria and a significant community only in Morocco (see table). See also REFUGEES AND MIGRANTS.

JIBRIL, AHMAD (b. 1929) Palestinian founder and leader of the Popular Front for the Liberation of Palestine—General Command (PFLP-GC) (Arabic: *al-Jabha al-Sha'biyya li-Tahrir Filastin—al-Qiyada al-Aamma*) since 1968. Born in Yazur near Ramla, Jibril left his home with his family in 1948, as a refugee. He grew up in JORDAN and SYRIA. Until 1958 he served in the Syrian Army as a military engineer, reaching the rank of major. In 1958, he was dismissed by the Syrian Army and moved to Cairo where he established a secret cell called the National Palestinian Front. In the mid-1960s he began organizing a guerrilla group to operate against ISRAEL, called the *Jabhat Tahrir Filastin* (Palestine Liberation Front).

In 1967 his group joined the Popular Front for the Liberation of Palestine (PFLP) led by George HABASH. In 1968, however, Jibril seceded, forming his own organization called the "PFLP General Command." The split derived from personal and group disputes rather than ideological reasons. Jibril was also responsible for a controversial prisoner exchange in which Israel released 1150 detainees and convicted prisoners in exchange for three kidnapped Israeli soldiers.

Ideologically it remained strictly militant pan-Arab like the PFLP, with a special connection to Syria. Nonetheless, from the outset the PFLP-GC excelled in sophistication and perfection in its operations against Israel. Its methods, selection of targets and highly technical devices used in terrorist attacks against Israeli targets both inside Israel and out of the Middle East was an indication of its specialization in operations rather than on the political-ideological sphere. Among the more famous terrorist attacks perpetrated by the organization was the bombing of the Swissair airliner from Lod to Zurich in February 1970; the ambush against a children's bus from Avivim near the Lebanese border in May 1970; the suicidal bombing of children and civilians in the town of Kiryat Shmona; and the attack on an Israeli military base near that town in November 1987 by a fighter flown in on hang gliders.

In intra-PLO politics, Jibril and his group formed the fourth largest group, represented both in the Palestinian National Council and the Executive Committee. However, due to objection to Yasser ARAFAT and the PLO mainstream attitude on the peace process after 1974, there were consecutive periods of boycott of the Executive Committee. In 1983 he joined a Syrian supported armed rebellion of dissident PLO-*Fatah* squads against Arafat and his men in LEBANON and Tripoli. From 1985 he adhered to a "National Alliance" and a "National Salvation Front" of anti-Arafat groups inside and outside the PLO. In 1987 Jibril and his groups were suspended, and expelled from the PLO. Though Jibril did not fully accept Syrian "guidance and discipline," most of the time he was hosted and tolerated in Syria. In the late 1980s, he allegedly developed strong links with IRAN as well. Since 1992 Jibril has been a member of the Syrian-based Ten Front, combining ten Palestinian organizations opposing the Israel-PLO Oslo agreement and the establishment of the PALESTINIAN AUTHORITY under its terms.

JIHAD (Arabic: Holy War or, literally, great effort.) One of the fundamental tenets of ISLAM and an obligation on every Muslim. Its original goal was to impose on non-Muslim peoples the acceptance of Islam or the status of protected subjects (*ahl al-dhimma*, DHIMMIS) under Islamic rule—the latter choice being open only to the "People of the Book," i.e., JEWS, CHRISTIANS and Sabaeans-MANDAEANS. Muslims view the world as divided into *Dar al-Islam* (the "House of Islam")—the countries under Muslim rule—and *dar al-harb* (the "House of War")—countries to be conquered. Some traditions mention a third realm, *dar al-ahd* (the "House of Truce")—countries paying tribute to the Muslims.

Since the eighth century, when wars involving major conquests were no longer possible, some theologians have held that the obligation of *Jihad* has changed. Conceived in the particular situation of the Arabian Peninsula at the birth of Islam in the seventh century, it had clearly lapsed with the advent of changing circumstances.

Orthodox Islam, however, argues that *Jihad* is obligatory in all generations and circumstances. Theologians have tried to find answers as to how such a duty was to be fulfilled. For example, does *Jihad* mean constant Holy War (which historically had not happened), or should it occur only when circumstances are favorable, as some theologians argue? Furthermore, who was to proclaim *Jihad* in the absence of a CALIPH, with no recognized head of Islam? Who proclaims *Jihad* for Shi'i Muslims whose recognized leader, the IMAM, remains hidden until the Day of Judgment? Or is Shi'i *Jihad* altogether impossible in the absence of the *Imam*? Must *Jihad* be an offensive, Muslim-initiated Holy War? Or is it, as many modern theologians hold, principally the defense of Islam? Must all Muslims engage in *Jihad*, or can selected fighters (*Mujahidun*) fulfill the injunction on behalf of the entire community? Must *Jihad* be actual warfare, or can it be interpreted as a "Great Effort," which is not necessarily military? The latter view is supported by many theologians.

In the absence of an all-encompassing theological authority, there are no generally accepted answers to these questions. This results in various individual and group interpretations according to current political needs.

Any war by a Muslim country against a non-Muslim one may be termed *Jihad*, but Muslim tradition requires *Jihad* to be officially proclaimed. Many Muslim rulers did over the centuries declare *Jihad*, but such a declaration generally did not affect Muslims in other countries. In modern times, too, Muslim countries or movements engaged in fighting non-Muslim powers have tried to obtain the support and sympathy of Muslims worldwide by proclaiming *Jihad*.

The MAHDI in SUDAN, in the 1880s, used the term *Jihad*, and so did the SANUSSIS in LIBYA in their fight against the Italian conquerors, from 1911–1912. The Ottoman Sultan and Caliph proclaimed a *Jihad* upon TURKEY's entry into World War I, in November 1914. His call aroused pro-Turkish sentiment among the Muslims of the world, e.g., in India, but it did not generate active military help for Turkey or serious rebellions in the countries of its enemies—except for some Libyan Sanussis, who described their fight against Italy as part of the Caliph's *Jihad*, and a local Sultan in West Sudan, Ali Dinar. Nor did it stop the Muslim ruler of HIJAZ—the HASHEMITE Sharif of Mecca—from rising against the Caliph in the 1916 ARAB REVOLT and a number of Muslim-Arab officers in the Ottoman Army from joining the rebels.

Muslim fighters in more recent times have continued to use the term *Jihad* and describe themselves as *Mujahiuin*—mostly without formally proclaiming *Jihad* (which only a Muslim state or government can do).This was what, for instance, the Algerian rebels did against French rule, 1954–1962, and so did the Afghan rebels and other Muslims who volunteered to fight in this war after 1980. The term *Jihad* also appeared, sporadically and marginally, in the struggle of India's Muslims against Hindu rule and for the creation of Pakistan. During the IRAN-IRAQ WAR (1980–1988) these two Muslim states often used the term *Jihad* to substantiate their battle. Militias and underground organizations fostered or inspired by IRAN, call themselves *Jihad* or *Mujahidun*—e.g., in LEBANON or in terrorist operations in Europe; but those who fought against the revolutionary Shi'i regime in Iran also invoke the image of the Holy War by calling themselves *Mujahidin-i-Khalq* (Fighters of the People's *Jihad*). Muslim governments have also used the term Jihad for various purposes, e.g. their struggle for economic development or against illiteracy. Hence the *ulama*, the Muslim sages, in TUNISIA permitted the easing of the Ramadan Fast as the country was waging an "economic *Jihad*."

The Islamic radicalization in the Middle East led to the advent of militant *Jihad* groups actively promoting violence against their respective governments, defined as "infidels," and purification of their societies after having been polluted by modernity. In the ARAB-ISRAEL CONFLICT, too, Arab leaders have tried to increase their strength and popular support by speaking of a *Jihad*. While no Arab government ever

formally proclaimed a *Jihad*, the sages of al-AZHAR—the main Islamic center of learning—did, in 1948. Several *ulama* and *Muftis* repeated that proclamation in sermons, religious rulings (FATWA) or speeches. Even without a formal governmental declaration of *Jihad*, some governments allegedly established *Jihad* funds (e.g. Libya) or collected a *Jihad* tax (SAUDI ARABIA). The Palestinian Arab guerrillas prefer to call themselves *fida'iyyun*—those who sacrifice themselves (also a term from the traditional Islamic terminology)—rather than *Mujahidun*; but the latter term is also used. According to some reports *fida'iyyun* groups applied for formal recognition as *mujahidin*, so that contributions to their funds would qualify as the fulfillment of a religious duty or even as part of the charity payments (*Zakat*) obligatory for Muslims. The Arab governments and the secular PALESTINIAN GUERRILLA ORGANIZATIONS linked to the PALESTINE LIBERATION ORGANIZATION (PLO) have avoided defining their war against ISRAEL unequivocally and officially as a Holy War. However, the Islamic radicalization of the Palestinian society resulted in the creation of two movements since the late 1980s, that adopted the *Jihad* as an interpreting myth to substantiate their armed struggle against Israel—namely, the Islamic *Jihad* and HAMAS. Both movements define *Jihad* as strictly individual, rather than collective, duty (*fard'ain*), which legitimizes the initiation of the armed struggle against Israel regardless of the PLO's decision making, or current political conditions (see also ISLAMIC RADICALISM AND MOVEMENTS).

JORDAN Hashemite Kingdom, a kingdom bordered in the north by SYRIA; in the north-east by IRAQ; in the east and south by SAUDI ARABIA and in the west by ISRAEL. Jordan was founded by Great Britain in 1921 as the semi-autonomous Emirate of Transjordan, headed by Hashemite ABDALLAH IBN HUSSEIN, under the Palestine Mandate and its terms as stipulated by the League of Nations. In 1946 the Emirate became independent. Already before its independence, the Emirate was one of the founding members of the ARAB LEAGUE in 1945, and given UN membership in 1955. The borders of Transjordan were largely defined in 1921–1923, and some parts of the desert borders with the HIJAZ in 1925. In the same year, Aqaba and Ma'an, also claimed by Hijaz, were annexed. Saudi Arabia acquiesced in the Anglo-Saudi Treaty of Jidda, 1927, and formally consent-

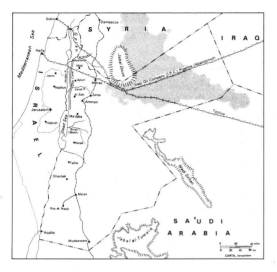

Map of Jordan

ed in 1965—when an exchange of territory also took place and Jordan acquired a coastal strip south of Aqaba in return for an inland area. In 1948, Jordan occupied—and in 1950 formally annexed—the central mountainous part of Arab Palestine (namely, the WEST BANK), including East JERUSALEM. In the June 1967 war, it lost this territory to Israel, practically reverting to its pre-1948 area of the East Bank. Jordan's pre-June 1967 area was 37,000 sq. miles (95941 sq. km.)—including the West Bank, an area of approximately 2,165 sq. miles (5.614 sq. km).

The population on both banks of the Jordan River was estimated in 1967 at approximately 2 million, most of it in the East Bank. The population of the East Bank, that had been approximately 450,000 in 1948, reached more than 1.2 million by 1967 mainly because of the influx of Palestinian-Arab refugees in the course of the 1948 war (some 200,000) and continuing migration from the West Bank 1948–1967 (estimates range from 250,000–500,000, with about 400,000 as a reasonable estimate). Until the take-over of the West Bank in 1948, Jordan's economy was based mainly on primitive agriculture and stock-breeding. Only about five percent of the total East Bank area was cultivated, with wheat, barley, vegetables, grapes and olives as the main products.

During and immediately after the 1967 war another wave of refugees arrived from the West Bank. Estimates range from 200,000–350,000, with about

215,000 as an accurate estimate (the Israelis found a population of approximately 650,000 on the West Bank).

Until August 1988 Palestinian residents of the West Bank and East Jerusalem (over 1 million) had maintained their Jordanian citizenship. This came officially—though not immediately—to an end when King HUSSEIN proclaimed Jordan's disengagement from the West Bank. In 1990–1991 Jordan absorbed another wave of immigrants (200,000–300,000). These were mostly Palestinians from the Gulf oil states, resulted by the Kuwaiti crisis and war, and mass expulsion of Palestinians from Kuwait and the Gulf states, setting the net migration rate (1996) at 6.2/1000. Estimates valid to 1996 put Jordan's population (i.e., in the East Bank alone) at over 4.2 million. Most of Jordan's inhabitants are SUNNI Muslims (ninety-eight percent); Christians comprise less than two percent, mostly GREEK CATHOLIC (30,000), and small numbers of GREEK ORTHODOX. Arabs constitute the largest ethnic group (nineteight percent) with the CIRCASSIANS and Chechens (Muslims originating in the Caucasus), and Armenians at one percent each. Post-1988, Jordan's population includes a large proportion of Palestinians. Estimates vary, though it is commonly accepted that they make up a majority—perhaps up to sixty to sixty-five percent. About half of them still have the status of refugees, though they enjoy full citizenship. These figures, however, ignore the question "Who is a Palestinian?" It was not only Palestinian families which had resided in East Jordan since the early nineteenth century. It is questionable what rate of the current Palestinian population in Jordan defines itself as such, and for what purposes. Most of the Jordanians living abroad are of Palestinian origin.

Two oil pipelines traverse Jordan—the Iraq petroleum company's Kirkuk-Haifa line, and ARAMCO's "Tapline" from Dhahran, Saudi Arabia, to Sidon, LEBANON; they stopped operating in 1948 and 1975, respectively. Oil has reportedly been struck in Jordan but so far no production has been possible in commercial quantities. Rock phosphates have been mined since 1951–1952 and constitute Jordan's chief export. Deposits of potash and bromine in the Dead Sea have been exploited since 1982–1983, and several Arab states participate in the "Arab Mining Company." The oil industry includes: oil refining, cement, and light manufacturing.

Poor communications are a major obstacle to Jordan's economic development. The only railway is the single-track narrow-gauge HIJAZ line, the southern parts of which have been out of order since World War I (its joint reconstruction by Syria, Jordan and Saudi Arabia, planned for years, has not materialized). A railroad operates inside Jordan, with extensions to the phosphate mines and to Aqaba which were opened in 1975. The rail link to Syria has also been reopened. Aqaba is the country's only port, linked to Amman by a 200 mile long road (322 km.) opened in 1960. The port has been much improved and developed *inter alia* so as not to be dependent on Beirut and transit through Syria. A new, expanded port was opened in 1972, which prospered during the eight-year long IRAN-IRAQ WAR during which it served as the main commercial link for Iraq. Tourism is an important contributor to Jordan's economy. One of Jordan's main motivations for supporting the Middle East peace process has been the hope of attracting more of the tourists visiting Israel, hoping for 2 million visitors annually.

Jordan's lack of natural resources and overwhelming economic and security burdens, especially after 1948, underscored its dependency on foreign aid. Until 1956–1957, Jordan's public finances were heavily subsidized by BRITAIN. Budgetary deficits were covered by Britain, which also paid the cost of the Jordanian Army, called the Arab Legion. Since 1957, Jordan has been a recipient of US economic aid but Britain continues to assist on a modest scale. Following decisions of the Arab summits of Khartoum (September 1967), Rabat (October 1974), and Baghdad (November 1978), the Arab oil countries, undertook to pay Jordan an annual subsidy of 112 million dollars; 300 million; and 1,250 million, respectively. In addition, Jordan and the PALESTINE LIBERATION ORGANIZATION (PLO) were allotted as of 1979 150 million dollars a year to be distributed among the Palestinian residents of the West Bank and GAZA STRIP. But the amounts pledged have not always been fully or timely paid. Jordan's economy suffered in the late 1980s and the early 1990s. Oil prices and revenues of the producing states after 1982 plunged, affecting Jordan's economy through both reduction of the direct Arab financial aid and decrease of workers' remittances. Transit services provided by Jordan to Iraq via Aqaba port during the war with IRAN (1980–1988), added approximately 750 million dollars annually to Jordan's econmy, and helped alleviate Jordan's financial difficulties. However, the end of the war led to diminished income from transit, and the Palestinian uprising (INTIFADA) in the West Bank and Gaza Strip, followed by the plunge of the Dinar's exchange rate in late 1988, doubled Jordan's financial difficulties. In 1989, Jordan was forced to ask its creditors for the re-scheduling of its debts, introducing reforms in government expenditures along with the International Monetary Fund's (IMF) conditional assistance. The reforms (namely cutbacks of subsidies and raising prices of basic commodities) caused popular discontent. In April this was expressed with demonstrations and riots, most notably, from the Bedouins in the south—the backbone of the Hashemite regime. This ominous reaction, along with the KUWAIT crisis, the mass flight of Palestinian workers from the Gulf countries to Jordan and the pressing needs, caused Jordan in late 1990 to abandon the recovery plan.

Political History Contemporary Jordanian history has been shaped by Amir (later, King) Abdallah, King ABDALLAH, and the current king, King Hussein. Their lengthy reigns and overarching personalities were crucial to Jordan's formation and political conduct in regional and international affairs. The Emirate of Transjordan was created by Britain in 1921, with Amir Abdallah Ibn Hussein as its semi-autonomous ruler. Unlike other political units created in the post-Ottoman period by the Western powers in the Fertile Crescent, which had their roots in ancient history and revolved around a traditional political center, Transjordan was, from the outset, shaped by Britain's strategic needs as a buffer zone for the SUEZ CANAL, with no distinguished political center, bureaucracy, or history as a distinctive political unit. It is against this backdrop, and long-lived dependence on Western aid, that Jordan has been perceived as the most artificial Arab political entity. Yet this artificiality also made it possible for the Hashemite monarchs to lay the foundations for the new state and form particular political traditions and instruments of power.

Although it was part of the Palestine Mandate, the territory was excluded from the clause by the provision of a Jewish National Home. By appointing Abdallah as the ruler of Transjordan, Britain accommodated a loyal ally, preventing him from making trouble with the French, given his threat to march on Damascus after the expulsion of his brother FEISAL. The British even tried to create the impression that they were making good on a war-time pledge to his father Hussein to recognize this area as Arab and independent (under British tutelage).

Initially, Transjordan comprised approximately 300,000 inhabitants; half of whom were nomads or semi-nomads. Most of the population was Arab Muslims, with about 25,000 Christians and 10,000 Circassians. The Emirate was dependent on British economic aid, since most of its area was desert and lacked economic resources. Assisted by a small number of British advisers, at the head of which was a Resident (representing the High Commissioner in Jerusalem), Amir Abdallah ruled his country in autocratic and patriarchal fashion. The British helped Abdallah create an administration and a military force, which started as a desert police unit and later developed into full-fledged professional army. The Arab Legion, called the Arab Army after Jordan gained independence (al-jaish al-arabi), was commanded until 1956 by a British officer (F.G. Peake, 1921–1939; J.B. GLUBB, 1939–1956), with other Britons in senior command posts. From World War II until the termination of the British Mandate, Arab Legion units became employed as security forces in Palestine, guarding military bases and strategic installations.

In 1928 Transjordan signed a treaty with Britain widening its autonomy but leaving financial and foreign affairs to be handled by the British Resident. In 1928, a constitution provided for a Legislative Council, in part indirectly elected. In 1934 Transjordan was authorized to establish consular ties with EGYPT, Syria and Iraq. In 1939, the powers of the British Resident were reduced. A Cabinet of departmental heads, responsible to the ruler, was reconstituted and an elected Legislative Assembly of twenty members was established. During World War II, Abdallah remained loyal to his British allies. In 1941 he dispatched a contingent of the Arab Legion to help British troops fight the Iraqi nationalist, anti-British rebellion and restore the Hashemite regime (see HASHEMITES).

In May 1946 a new Anglo-Transjordanian Treaty came into effect. This granted Jordan formal, but very limited, independence, while providing for a political and military alliance and for British aid. Britain was authorized to maintain troops and bases

in Transjordan. This treaty seemed to be a façade of independence and brought upon Jordan the contempt of political rivals and Arab nationalist circles. It was modified in March 1948. The new treaty stressed Transjordan's independence and the equal status of the two contracting parties. Abdallah assumed the title of King in 1946, and re-named the country The Hashemite Kingdom of Jordan. This was used from 1948–1949.

From the outset, Abdallah fostered ambitions to create and rule a GREATER SYRIA, i.e., a union of Transjordan, Palestine, Syria and Lebanon (and, after 1925, also Hijaz), to be followed by the unification of the Fertile Crescent through the federation of Iraq with Greater Syria. Britain demonstrated no commitment to Abdallah's scheme. The French suspected this, that it was mainly to oust them from the LEVANT. Local British representatives tended to support Abdallah's aspirations. From the late-1930s, the British Colonial Office toyed with the idea of establishing a Jewish state in part of Palestine and incorporation of the rest of the country with Transjordan under Abdallah's throne. In 1937 the Royal (Peel) Commission that was appointed to assess the 1936 Palestinian-Arab revolt, also recommended the establishment of a Jewish state, but the plan was aborted as a result of widespread Arab objection. Abdallah also received some support from opposition elements in Syria and Palestine. He was opposed by the French, the ruling parties in both Egypt and Saudi Arabia, most Syrians and mainstream Palestinian nationalists, led by the Mufti of Jerusalem, al-Hajj Amin al-HUSSEINI.

To advance his scheme, Abdallah's main efforts were focused until World War II on Palestine. For this goal, he maintained close contacts with the Palestinian-Arab opposition led by the NASHASHIBI and Touqan clans. He also endeavored to reach an agreement with the Zionist Movement which would ensure continued—albeit limited—Jewish immigration into Palestine and autonomous status to the Jewish community under his throne. In 1930 he agreed to, and encouraged, Jewish settlement in Transjordan. This plan had to be shelved because of Palestinian-Arab nationalist outcry and British opposition. In 1933 a law forbidding the sale of lands to foreigners was enacted. The conquest of Syria and Lebanon by British troops in 1941 and a shift of the scales in World War II in favor of the Allies in late 1942 triggered a renewed effort on Abdallah's part to promote his scheme. This agitated opposition minority groups in Syria (DRUZE and ALAWIS), urging Britain to support the plan and include it in the post-war settlements. These efforts grew vigorous with the acquisition of independence, bringing about much tension with the Syrian and Lebanese governments.

Since 1946, at the peak of Britain's efforts to reach an agreed solution to the Palestine problem, Abdallah and the Jewish Agency held secret talks. These talks resulted in a tacit agreement on the partition of Palestine and the establishment of a Jewish state in part of the country. Abdallah favored Jewish autonomy in part of Palestine under his crown, but acquiesced in the Zionist solution of partition of the country and the establishment of a Jewish state in one part. Abdallah undertook to refrain from interfering in the Jewish state's affairs while the Jewish Agency would not interfere with his plan to take over the Arab part. In view of the UN resolution on the partition of Palestine and the establishment of separate Jewish and Arab states (November 29, 1947), in early 1948 Abdallah's plan to take over the Arab part of Palestine was secretly endorsed by Britain as a possible way to prevent full-scale war in Palestine. However, the eruption of the Civil War in Palestine in early December 1947 and the growing unofficial involvement of Arab states in that war eventually compelled Abdallah to pursue his plan in cooperation with the collective Arab assault on nascent Israel. Practically, however, Abdallah's military and political efforts attempted to achieve his limited goals in Palestine's decisions—mostly because of limited capabilities and strict British constraints.

In the war (see ARAB-ISRAEL CONFLICT), Abdallah avoided attacking the areas allotted to the Jewish state. The fighting centered on Jerusalem, designated as an international enclave, and its approaches from the coastal plain. Abdallah's Arab Army took over the Old City of Jerusalem and the eastern Arab part of the new city. This ensured control of the mountainous area stretching from Jenin to Hebron. Once his territorial goals had been reached, Abdallah demonstrated a willingness to end the war. This exposed him to harsh criticism from his Arab rivals.

Abdallah's early measures in the territory occupied by his army reflected his intention to annex them to his kingdom. This added frustration to the Arab failure to prevent the proclamation of the Jewish state and its international recognition. It was against this backdrop, and the international mediator Count Polke Bernadotte's proposals for an Arab-Israeli peace settlement (recommending the incorporation of the Arab part of Palestine into Jordan and recognition of the Jewish state) that Adballah's Arab adversaries, led by Egypt, initiated the establishment in September 1948 of the "All-Palestine Government," in Gaza, marked by strong Husseini influence. Although this government was short-lived and had no practical purpose other than to challenge the Hashemite King's intentions of regarding the areas occupied by his Army, he responded by accelerating his campaign against the Palestinian-Arab residents. He held mass gatherings of notables (most significantly in Amman, 1 October, and Jericho, 1 December), according legitimacy to his plans by proclaiming him sovereign of Palestine. The Jordan-Israel Armistice Agreement, signed in early April 1949 in Rhodes, was negotiated in secret meetings between the two parties under the king's supervision in his winter resort at Shuneh, in the Jordan Valley. The agreement tacitly confirmed Jordan's authority over the Jenin-Hebron area (the West Bank), including East Jerusalem. In March 1949 the military Government in the occupied West Bank was replaced by a civil administration. In May, Palestinian ministers were included for the first time in the Jordanian Cabinet. In June 1949 the country's new name of "The Hashemite Kingdom of Jordan" was officially gazetted. This illustrated that Jordan was no longer confined to one side of the Jordan River.

In April 1950 the Palestinians participated for the first time in parliamentary elections. Later the same month the new Parliament decreed the formal annexation of the West Bank, under the slogan "unity of the two banks" (wahdat al-daffatain). With annexation, all Palestinian residents of the two banks, including the refugees, became Jordanian citizens. While only Britain and PAKISTAN formally recognized the annexation (Britain refrained from recognizing the annexation of Arab Jerusalem), most countries accepted it de facto. This annexation coincided with the secret Israeli-Jordanian peace negotiations. These talks culminated in February 1950 with a draft agreement of non-belligerency and economic cooperation that would last for five years. However, the agreement never materialized because of the Jordanian government's strict opposition. This was reflected by three consecutive resignations of prime ministers, all of whom were loyal Hashemites, to avoid responsibility for ratification of the agreement. The act of annexation was vehemently opposed by the Arab League, which threatened to expel Jordan. In particular, Egypt, Syria and Saudi Arabia objected to any territorial aggrandizement of the Hashemite dynasty. A compromise formula was devised by the Prime Minister of Iraq: the West Bank would be held by Jordan temporarily and in trust, until its restoration to its owners would be possible. In fact a "deal" was made; the League accepted the annexation of the West Bank under this face-saving formula—in return for Abdallah's renunciation of his plan to sign a separate treaty with Israel.

The influx of Palestinian refugees to the East Bank during the 1948 War of Independence and the annexation of the West Bank increased the kingdom's population by nearly three times. The populace grew from approximately 450,000 to some 1.2 million. Nearly 400,000 Palestinians were refugees; half of them located in the West Bank. The war thus led to a significant change in the socio-political character of the kingdom. Not only were Palestinians a majority of the population, but a large segment of them were modernized town dwellers with high levels of education and a tradition of active political protest (though not of political responsibility). The early 1950s thus witnessed the activity of many ideological parties (COMMUNIST, BA'TH, Arab Nationalists, MUSLIM BROTHERHOOD, and the Islamic Liberation Party). These were mostly nationalist and leftist, advocating panacean visions agitating the public against the ruling oligarchy.

The population of the East Bank had as a whole been loyal to Abdallah. Nonetheless pockets of opposition had existed even before the war, mainly among the tribes in the north, connected by blood to their brethren in Syria, and in the towns of al-Salt and Irbid. This opposition was considerably reinforced by the Palestinians, many of whom supported Abdallah's foe, al-Hajj Amin al-Husseini. The West-Bank urban elite, which occupied half the seats in Parliament, soon made their presence felt. While they voiced no demand for secession and separate Palestinian-Arab independence, they did demand that the monarch's powers be curtailed; that the Cabinet be made responsible to Parliament; and political life

in Jordan democratized. Opposition to the King increased as rumors of his secret negotiations with Israel spread. Jordan was obliged to develop its resources in order to absorb the additional population. Preference was given to the East Bank in terms of investments in both agricultural and industrial projects in order to strengthen its economic base as well as the indigenous elements of this area traditionally supporting the regime, especially the Bedouins. The development project using the waters of the Yarmuk River for the irrigation of the Jordan Valley (al-Ghor)—see WATER POLITICS—considerably expanded and modernized cultivation.

On 20 July 1951, King Abdallah was assassinated by a Palestinian, while entering al-Aqsa Mosque in Jerusalem. (Among those tried and executed for the murder was a prominent member of the Husseini clan.) Abdallah's eldest son TALAL succeeded to the throne. In January 1952 Talal assented to a new constitution which made the Cabinet responsible to Parliament; a majority of two-thirds was required to dismiss the Cabinet. This was amended in 1954 to a simple majority. The King also pursued a new foreign policy. He strove for a *rapprochement* with Egypt and Syria and ratified the Arab Collective Security Pact of 1950. But in August 1952 Talal was found to be mentally ill. Parliament declared him unfit to rule and deposed him. His son Hussein was crowned in May 1953 (after a council of regents had briefly ruled for him until he reached the age of 18).

Jordan under King Hussein Jordan continued to encounter active opposition eager to democratize the political system; rid the state of its financial (and political) dependence on Britain; and to improve ties with Egypt and Syria. Foreign policy difficulties increased as the Cold War between the world powers intensified and Britain's efforts to create a regional defense system linked to the Western alliance. In December 1955, violent demonstrations erupted during the visit of the Chief of the British Imperial General Staff, General Robertson. Robertson's visit was allegedly to discuss Jordan's joining the Baghdad Pact that had been concluded in February 1955 between TURKEY and Iraq as the nucleus of a regional British-based treaty. The widespread objection to the treaty, encouraged by Egypt and Syria, forced the resignation of the Cabinet, which had been headed by Hazza al-Majali. The new government announced that Jordan would not join the Pact. In

March 1956 the King dismissed the British Chief-of-Staff of the Arab Legion, Lieutenant-General Glubb, regarded by Arab nationalists as the symbol of British domination.

The parliamentary elections of October 1956 resulted in the establishment of the first nationalist-leftist coalition government in Jordan's history, with Suleiman al-Nabulsi, the leader of the "National Socialist Party," as the Prime Minister. Shortly afterwards, Jordan joined the military alliance of Egypt, Syria and Saudi Arabia, and the Egyptian-Syrian Joint Military Command. During Israel's Sinai Campaign of October-November 1956, Jordan allowed Saudi, Iraqi and Syrian troops to take up positions on its territory (they were withdrawn when the crisis had passed). In January 1957, Egypt, Syria and Saudi Arabia agreed to grant Jordan an annual subsidy of 12.5 million dollars over the next ten years to finance its Army and defense expenditures, thus enabling it to abrogate its treaty with Britain. The Anglo-Jordanian Treaty of 1948 was annulled in March 1957. All British troops were evacuated by July. In March-April 1957 the government decided to establish diplomatic relations with the USSR and to accept Soviet aid—a step still considered revolutionary.

In April 1957 King Hussein, after having prepared for confrontation with the leftist and nationalist parties, decided to halt this accelerating movement toward the Nasserist line of regional and international affairs. He announced the discovery of a Syrian-Egyptian plot against him and dismissed the Cabinet. This led to riots and demonstrations. All political parties were outlawed and many of their leaders arrested or compelled to flee the country. A plot of army officers supported by Egypt was averted when the King himself appeared in the Zarqa Camp and persuaded the officers to support him. The Chief-of-Staff, General Ali Abu Nuwar, was dismissed and fled the country. Purges in the army and the civil service followed.

The UNITED STATES emphasized its support of the King by sending units of the Sixth Fleet to the eastern Mediterranean, in line with the EISENHOWER DOCTRINE, and began supplying economic and military aid.

In the following years more unrest and attempted plots in the officers' corps were suppressed. However in general, the King had re-established a stable regime. An extremist-Islamic plot by the "Islamic Liberation Party" was suppressed later, in the 1960s.

The King's reassertion of his leadership worsened relations with Egypt and Syria. The two countries did not pay the subsidy agreed upon in the agreement of January 1957. (Only Saudi Arabia paid one installment of 5 million dollars.) A violent campaign of defamation against Jordan was launched and subversion against its regime encouraged. The February 1958 merger of Syria and Egypt into the UNITED ARAB REPUBLIC (UAR) was seen to be a grave threat by Jordan, inducing it to form a (Hashemite) Iraqi-Jordanian "Arab Union" (14 February 1958). King Feisal II of Iraq became the Head of the Union with King Hussein as his deputy. A federal Parliament with equal representation for both countries was formed and a joint government was to handle foreign affairs, defense and monetary policy. Each country continued to preserve its Parliament, cabinet and civil service. The Union was perceived as a hollow Hashemite response to the "real" union of the UAR and the unpopular fact came to an end with the Iraqi *coup d'etat* of 14 July 1958 which eliminated the Hashemite regime there. Several top Jordanian leaders, acting on behalf of the union, were murdered in Baghdad with those of Iraq. King Hussein now proclaimed himself Head of the Union; called the Iraqi people to quell the revolution, and asked for US and British aid. The UAR closed its airspace and roads to Jordanian traffic. There were reports of active UAR subversion within Jordan. Hussein expected immediate UAR-Iraqi hostilities (possibly co-ordinated with a coup). Britain responded to Hussein's urgent request and a contingent of British paratroopers arrived in Jordan in July 1958 via Israeli air-space. Jordan severed diplomatic relations with the UAR, lodging a complaint against it to the UN Security Council for interference and the dispatch of armed infiltrators. US proposals to replace British troops in Jordan (and American troops in Lebanon) with a UN force were vetoed by the USSR and the issue was transferred to a special session of the UN General Assembly. In August, the Assembly unanimously adopted a compromise resolution, drafted by the Arab states. This reported that these states had agreed in the Arab League Pact to respect each other's sovereign independence, welcoming their renewed assurances to observe that commitment. Furthermore, it requested arrangements to be made that would "facilitate the early withdrawal of the foreign troops." British troops were withdrawn by October.

King Hussein abrogated the Jordan-Iraq Union on 1 August 1958. As it became clear that the new regime in Iraq was no satellite of the UAR, relations between Amman and Baghdad improved. Diplomatic ties were renewed in December 1960, despite the blood-feud the 1958 coup had created. Relations with Saudi Arabia also improved, along with the deepening rift between Gamal ABDEL NASSER and the Saudi dynasty. King Hussein and the Saudi rulers cast aside the old enmity between their respective dynasties which had driven King Hussein's great-grandfather from Hijaz. The Saudi ruler realized that his conservative monarchy was threatened by Egypt, abandoning their alliance. Jordan's diplomatic relations with the UAR were renewed in August 1959, but the latter continued to support subversion. This culminated in the assassination of Prime Minister Hazza al-Majali in August 1960.

Relations between Jordan and the UAR were again severed in September 1961 when Egypt denounced Jordan's recognition of Syria (which had just seceded from the UAR), accusing it of conspiring with the secessionists. After the April 1963 declaration of a new Arab union (Egypt, Syria and Iraq), riots broke out in the (Jordanian held) West Bank emanating from Palestinian desire to incorporate Jordan in that union. The April–May 1963 domestic crisis which ensued signaled a major internal threat to the existence of the kingdom. Jordan saw Egypt as mainly responsible for this crisis. Relations with Egypt were restored in January 1964, during the first ARAB SUMMIT CONFERENCE held in Cairo. At the conference, Jordan reluctantly agreed to cooperate with other Arab states to prevent Israel from diverting the waters of the Jordan River, and also to recognize the Republican regime in Yemen. With even greater reluctance Jordan acquiesced in the creation of a PALESTINE LIBERATION ORGANIZATION (PLO) to which a military component—to be under Arab command—was added later that year. Any recognition of a Palestinian national entity was likely to cast doubts on Jordan's annexation of Arab Palestine.

However, Hussein's consent to Nasser's urges to allow for the establishment of the organization, was apparently perceived instrumental for improved control of current nationalist trends among the Palestinians in Jordan. Hussein thus halfheartedly allowed Ahmad al-Shuqairi (Palestine's representative in the Arab League and founder of the PLO), to hold the founding convention in Jerusalem (May 1964) and to have a permanent representation in Jordan. However, relations between the Hashemite regime and the PLO's leader soon deteriorated due to the latter's excessive activities among Palestinians in Jordan and repeated attacks on Amman's refusal to allow mobilization and military training of Palestinians in the kingdom. However, the deteriorating relations between Jordan and the PLO reflected the deepening mistrust and hostility between Hussein and Nasser over other issues, primarily Jordan's failure to abide by the collective Arab military plan against Israel, refusing to allow stationing of Iraqi and Saudi expeditionary forces on its territory. In July 1966 the Jordanians closed down the PLO office, claiming that PLO Chairman AL-SHUQEIRI was engaging in pro-Communist activities.

Israeli raids on Jordanian territory escalated in response to intensified Palestinian guerrilla attacks from Jordan, which had been carried out despite the objection of the Jordanian government. This resulted in a crisis in November 1966, when Israeli troops attacked the village of Samu' in the Hebron district. King Hussein was accused of neglecting the defense of his people, mainly by Syria and the PLO who called on the Jordanians to revolt against the King. Egyptian broadcasts escalated their ad-hoc attacks on the King. They described him as an "imperialist stooge" with whom no cooperation was possible. This led Jordan to sever its diplomatic relations with Egypt.

Nonetheless, the evolving crisis between Egypt and Israel in May 1967 led Jordan to re-establish relations with Egypt. As it looked certain that Egypt and Israel were headed for war there was hysteria among the Arab masses, particularly among Jordanian Palestinians. Under intense pressure Hussein agreed to join Nasser, and on 30 May 1967, King Hussein flew to Cairo and signed a defense agreement with Egypt. This placed his troops under Egyptian command. When the 1967 war broke out, on 5 June 1967, the Israeli government advised King Hussein via the UN to stay out of the war with the assurance that Israel would not attack Jordan. However, due to either lack of control or a willingness to confront a mass revolt against his authority, King

Hussein ignored this advice. On 5 June clashes in the Jerusalem area began, leading to Israel's conquest of the West Bank and the destruction of Jordan's air force and part of its armored units. A new influx of refugees, estimated at 200,000–250,000 people, crossed the Jordan River eastward, increasing the burden on Jordan's economy which had already been hard hit by the loss of the West Bank. However, Israel's "open bridges" policy enabled commercial exchange and mutual visits between Jordan and the West Bank to continue. Jordanian authorities also maintained ties with West Bank leadership and continued to pay salaries to former government employees.

Post-1967 Jordan The results of the 1967 war underpinned Jordan's foreign and domestic affairs over the next two decades, focusing on the king's efforts to recover his authority over the West Bank, or at least maintain his legitimacy as the primary claimant of that territory. Despite the Israeli occupation, the two banks of the Jordan River remained linked economically, monetarily, and demographically. Hence, the King's insistence on representing the Palestinian residents of this area was motivated by strict national security considerations though at times it seemed merely a matter of prestige. Maintaining such policy and claim on the Palestinian issue indeed ensured Jordan's role in shaping the relations with the West Bank, and preserved its status as a "confrontation state" eligible to receive Arab financial aid. These were crucial for the regime's survival. Thus, regardless of the real prospects of recovering the West Bank from Israel, the King was compelled to maintain his claim for the West Bank and representation of the Palestinians. Following the war, King Hussein campaigned vigorously, in both the Arab and international arenas, to gain legitimacy and sympathy for his predicament, namely, the loss of the West Bank. He participated as the leading Arab figure in the UN General Assembly which was convened shortly after the war. He visited several countries, including the USSR (with whom diplomatic ties had been established in 1963), and initiated closer economic relations with the countries of the Soviet bloc. However, the King rejected Soviet proposals for military assistance (with a brief exception in the early 1980s).

In this context, King Hussein maintained close alignment with Nasser who was also interested in a diplomatic solution to the loss of Arab territories to Israel. Both leaders thus accepted the UN Security Council Resolution 242 (22 November 1967). This called for Israel's withdrawal to the 1967 borders and recognition for all states in the region to live within secure and recognized boundaries. The King had reportedly received Nassser's consent to explore all possible avenues to recover the West Bank, including direct contacts with Israel. However, his mission met immovable obstacles created by Israel's decision to annex East Jerusalem shortly after the war had ended.

Hussein's Arab policy until Nasser's death in 1970 was marked by its acceptance of Resolution 242 and the priority it had given to the recovery of the occupied territories. In March 1969, Jordan joined the "Eastern Command" initiated by Egypt to coordinate military activities against Israel. The Command failed before it even got off the ground, and disbanded in 1970. With Jordan's agreement, Iraqi and Saudi troops were stationed on its territory with the declared aim of helping to defend against Israel, but also with a view to looking after their own interests. There was also a large Pakistani training mission in Jordan. The Iraqi troops were evacuated in 1970–1971.

Jordan's main political problem in the post-1967 years, affecting the very root of its existence and shaping its relations with other Arab regimes, was its conflict with the Palestinian guerrilla organizations (FIDA'IYYUN). The *fida'iyyun* grew after the 1967 Arab military defeat into a large establishment, well financed and generously equipped by Arab governments that strove to attain legitimacy and power by sponsoring Palestinian guerrilla groups. These armed groups gradually assumed control of the refugee camps; moved their headquarters to Amman and took effective control of wide areas along the border. Their stepped-up operations against Israel from Jordanian territory brought about Israeli retaliations, and in March 1968 Israel launched a major raid on a central guerrilla base near the town and refugee camp of Karame in the Jordan Valley. The Israeli losses in the war, in terms of both men and armored vehicles, were exploited to propagate the "battle of Karame" as a victory for the Palestinian *fida'iyyun* over the formidable Israeli Army. From a historical perspective, the battle was a turning point in the history of the PALESTINIAN GUERRILLA ORGANIZATIONS boosting their prestige and political growth. It also forced them to move inland into towns and cities at a safe distance from the Jordan river. This process led gradually to the creation of a "state within the state," constituting a double challenge to the Hashemite regime. Not only had the Palestinian guerrilla groups exempted themselves from abiding by Jordanian law and order—the more radical groups called openly to topple the Hashemite regime—the PLO in fact appealed to the large Palestinian population as an alternative authority to the Hashemite regime. The mounting tension between the state and the revolution eventually erupted in a full-scale confrontation in which the Jordanian regime demonstrated its viability in the conflict with both domestic and regional adversaries.

From November 1968, violent clashes recurred between the Jordanian Army and the guerrillas. This resulted in a diminished capacity of the Jordanian security forces to enforce law and order on the armed Palestinian groups. This trend resulted primarily from King Hussein's vacillation between his military hard-liners and the pro-Palestinian circles, and efforts to avoid a full-scale civil war for both domestic and regional (maintaining the alignment with Nasser) reasons. Rather, the Jordanian government attempted to reach an agreement with the guerrilla organizations which would restrict their modes of operations within and from Jordanian territory so as to avoid Israeli retaliations. Thus, the Palestinian guerrilla groups undertook not to shell Israeli targets from Jordanian territory; attack only targets deep in the Israeli-controlled area, and operate in coordination with the Jordanian forces. However, these agreements were never fully implemented and failed to prevent continued deterioration of the Jordanian authority and relations with the Palestinian armed groups.

The fragmentation of the Palestinian guerrilla camp and competition among their elements further interrupted possible compromise with the Jordanian regime. New agreements that followed failed too, while the Palestinian organizations attained increasing freedom of movement and exemption from Jordanian control. They absorbed deserters from the Jordanian army or men liable for conscription. The late 1960s witnessed frequent government reshuffles (invariably interpreted as either pro- or anti-guerrilla).

After a new round of violent clashes in early 1970, King Hussein confirmed the November 1968 accord confirming the equality of all parties. These clashes had been in response to the Army's attempt to impose strict regulations. In June, a renewed attempt by the Army Commander in Chief, Nasser Ibn Jamil, a hard-liner and uncle of the King, to control the Palestinian guerrillas, led to widespread clashes in Amman with hundreds of casualties. The Army bombed refugee camps near Amman held by the guerrillas, but the *fida'iyyun* gained control of several districts in Amman, including hotels in which foreign guests were held as hostages by the PFLP. Following mediation efforts by several Arab states, especially Egypt, Iraq and LIBYA, the King again backed down. On 10 June an agreement to cease hostilities was reached, but it was implemented only after the King yielded to the guerrillas' demand to dismiss Nasser Ibn Jamil (the King himself becoming Commander-in-Chief of the Army) and Zeid Ibn Shaker, the Commander of the armored divisions. The agreement provided, *inter alia*, for an exchange of prisoners and the creation of mixed commissions to devise measures to prevent future clashes; enquire into the causes of the riots, and supervise the implementation of this and previous agreements. An unofficial summit conference in Tripoli (Libya) in June, established a committee composed of representatives of Egypt, Libya, Algeria and Sudan to tackle disputes between Jordan and the guerrilla organizations "in a manner that both the sovereignty of Jordan and *fida'iyyun* action be preserved." By agreeing to the creation of this committee, King Hussein in fact accepted a sort of inter-Arab guardianship, while the guerrilla organizations obtained a status equal to that of the Hashemite regime.

The increasing importance of the Palestinians in Jordan's public life was reflected in the composition of the new government. Of the seventeen ministers, nine were Palestinians, some of them sympathetic to the guerrillas. The King also suspended conscription, thus enabling Jordanian youth to join the guerrillas. The King's retreat of June 1970 seriously undermined his position and the Army's prestige, creating a permanent state of crisis. In August, King Hussein endorsed the American proposals (see ARAB–ISRAEL PEACEMAKING) for a three-month cease-fire and renewal of the international mediation by Ambassador Jarring, along with president Nasser. The Jordanian decision further strained the King's relations with the Palestinian leadership, which had vehemently opposed any such initiative. Yet the King could draw comfort from the rift that erupted between the PLO and Nasser as a result of its criticism of his willingness to accept the American proposals. Pressed by his senior Army officers to take a strict action against the guerrillas, the King could feel safer taking such action with the possible backing of Nasser. He re-appointed General Zeid Ibn Shaker to a senior army post and went to Cairo for talks with Nasser (20–23 August). In the meeting, Nasser reportedly warned him against a confrontation with the Palestinian guerrillas. However, the eruption of heavy battle between the Jordanian forces and the guerrillas shortly after the Nasser-Hussein meeting, created an impression that the Egyptian president had given a "green light" to a military action against the Palestinian armed organizations. On 6 September, PFLP guerrillas brought two hijacked foreign airplanes to an airstrip near Zarqa and a third plane a few days later, and prevented the army from approaching the planes or rescuing their passengers by threats to blow them up. Ten days later, following an alleged abortive attempt on his life, Hussein proclaimed martial law and named Brigadier Muhammad Dawud, a Palestinian, to form a military government aimed to crush the guerrillas. Despite more abortive cease-fire agreements, a full-scale military offensive by the Army against guerrilla concentrations began, mainly in Amman and refugee camps—claiming the lives of many civilians (casualties were variously estimated at between 700 and 20,000 killed). The *fida'iyyun* now called openly for the overthrow of the King and his regime.

The Arab states were deeply shocked by the Jordanian operation (soon referred to as "Black September"). King Hussein was denounced as a butcher and a "Nero." Kuwait and Libya suspended financial aid to Jordan. Libya severed diplomatic relations; Tunisia recalled its envoy. Iraq and Syria promised aid to the *fida'iyyun* and threatened military intervention. On 19 September, Syrian armored units, disguised as forces of the "Palestine Liberation Army," invaded Jordan and occupied a strip in its north, including the town of Irbid. However, failure to obtain air cover to the Syrian land column enabled the Jordanian air and armored forces to repulse the Syrian

offensive and inflict on its force heavy losses. Deterred by Israeli threats of intervention along with an American request (and perhaps also Soviet and Arab advice), the Syrian force retreated four days later. The Iraqi expeditionary force in Jordan did not intervene. The USSR, on its part, warned the USA against intervention.

Meanwhile, an Arab Summit Conference convened in Cairo by President Nasser (Syria and Iraq absented), succeeded in imposing a cease-fire on the warring parties, after the Jordanian Prime Minister Dawud, sent to Cairo to gain time, had resigned and defected. With increasing Arab pressure on Hussein, he arrived at the summit where an agreement to end the dispute was signed under Nasser's supervision, on 27 September, by the Arab representatives attending the summit, including King Hussein and PLO leader Yasser ARAFAT. A "Supreme Arab Committee," chaired by the Prime Minister of TUNISIA, was to supervise and enforce the normalization of relations between the Jordanian authorities and the *fida'iyyun*. Both the army and the guerrillas were to withdraw from Amman. Government administration was to be restored everywhere, including the guerrilla-held Irbid area in the north. Commando operations against Israel were to continue with Jordan's full support. The guerrillas were to respect Jordanian sovereignty and operate "within the law, except where necessary for commando action." The Arab cosignatories of the agreement undertook to intervene against whichever side broke it. Further, detailed agreements were added in October and December 1970 and January 1971.

Nonetheless, King Hussein continued strengthening his position. In September he named a new Commander-in-Chief, Habes al-Majali, and in October established a strong government under Wasfi al-'Tall. During 1971, he used PLO provocations and renewed clashes to launch further military operations and suppress whatever remained of effective *fida'iyyun* formations—despite all-Arab supervision and new Egyptian and Saudi mediation attempts.

By July 1971, the PLO's military and organizational establishment in Jordan had been liquidated and the Hashemite regime restored its sovereignty over all Jordanian territory. The leading Palestinian guerrilla organization, Fatah, operating under the name "Black September," responded by adopting acts of personal terrorism against the Jordanian regime: in November 1971, Prime Minister Wasfi al-Tall was assassinated in Cairo. In March 1973 an attempt to topple the regime was suppressed. However the PLO's state-within-the-state with its strong military arm no longer existed. Most of the PLO headquarters and manpower moved to Lebanon.

The following years witnessed Jordan's growing domestic security and economic rehabilitation, with an intensified debate at the elite level regarding Jordan's future relations with the West Bank, indicating the rise of an attitude in favor of abandoning the West Bank and focusing on the East Bank alone. On the regional level, however, Nasser's death and the King's determined action against Palestinian resistance led most of the Arab states to condemn and isolate Jordan. ALGERIA and Syria severed relations. Iraq withdrew its Ambassador, and new Syrian-Jordanian clashes erupted. In March 1972, Egypt also severed relations with Jordan following the King's announcement of his Jordanian-Palestinian federation under his throne. Gradually, however, relations with the Arab states were restored. In September 1973, official relations with Egypt and Syria were resumed following a tripartite summit of Anwar al-SADAT and Hafez al-ASAD and Hussein in Cairo. The summit was apparently intended to probe the prospects for a Jordanian participation in the imminent war that Egypt and Syria had been preparing to open against Israel on 5 October (see ARAB-ISRAEL CONFLICT).

During the October War, Jordan, torn between the desire to show Arab solidarity and the fear of another defeat, did not join the war officially and rejected demands to initiate guerrilla or conventional military action from its own territory. Jordan, however, dispatched two armored brigades to help Syria—a line of action that was welcomed by Egypt and Syria, the first of which arrived on the front on 12 October when the tide had already turned, sustaining heavy losses in battle against Israeli forces advancing inside Syria.

The American-brokered diplomatic process between Israel and its neighbors that started following the October War, brought up the bitter dispute between Hashemite Jordan and the PLO over the representation of the Palestinians. The centrality of the Palestinian issue in regional Arab politics and the conflict with Israel, determined that it be decided by the Arab states as a collective. Jordan's passive front during the war diminished its legitimacy in

Arab eyes as a confrontational state, and diminished its claim for a separate military agreement with Israel, similar to those signed with Egypt and Syria shortly after the war (see below). At the same time, despite the defeat and expulsion sustained by the Palestinian Resistance Movement in Jordan, and the PLO's minor role in the October War, its political cause had gained continuous momentum in the international arena, with growing willingness of the Eastern Bloc states to recognize the organization as a national liberation movement and as a representative of the Palestinian people. Already in 1971, Sadat's drive toward a political settlement with Israel underpinned his idea of establishing a "mini Palestinian state" in the West Bank and Gaza Strip led by the PLO. The combination of these trends with Palestinian international TERRORISM in the early 1970s, contributed to enhance the PLO's political status as a symbol of Palestinian nationalism.

Jordan's strategy on the issue of representing the West Bank had also undergone a process of adaptation in accordance with the changing political conditions. While initially its interest was in re-gaining sovereignty over the West Bank, by March 1972 it was proposing a federal structure of relations with the West Bank. This would grant a fair measure of autonomy under the Hashemite crown—following Israel's withdrawal from this territory. Although the generally negative response in the Arab world to Hussein's plan demonstrated the King's loss of legitimacy regarding the West Bank, the King adhered to it. (A few years later, the federal principle would become a basis for a Jordan-PLO political dialogue.) The Arab Summit Conference convened in Algiers in November 1973, resolved to recognize the PLO as "the sole representative of the Palestinian people," on which Jordan alone disagreed. During the summer of 1974, King Hussein made intensive diplomatic efforts with the United States, Israel, and Egypt, to promote an agreement with Israel on the River Jordan front, along with the parameters of the agreements on military disengagement that Israel had signed with Egypt and Syria in January and May 1974, respectively. However, Israel's new government headed by Yitzhak RABIN was strictly paralyzed in terms of making any territorial concession in the West Bank due to coalition considerations.

Furthermore, the Sadat-Hussein joint declaration of Alexandria (18 July 1974), which had vaguely legitimized Jordan's status as a representative of the Palestinians in the West Bank, raised a general Arab protest at what seemed to be a violation of the Algiers summit's resolution on this matter. The strong outcry soon led Sadat to backtrack on his declaration with Hussein and return to reinforced support of the PLO's primary status regarding the West Bank. In October 1974, the Arab Summit Conference at Rabat approved "the right of the Palestinian people to establish a national independent authority led by the PLO, the sole legitimate representative of the Palestinian people, on any Palestinian soil to be liberated." Jordan acquiesced under duress in the resolution, undertaking to continue its responsibilities toward the West Bank's Palestinian residents. This undertaking was congruent with the PLO's interest given its practical limitations, primarily its lack of access to the West Bank.

King Hussein's frustrated hope to play an active role in the Middle East peacemaking did not diminish the value of his regime in the tense and fragmented regional Arab system. Since the 1973 war, the wartime coalition of Egypt, Saudi Arabi and Syria had undergone a series of shocks due to Sadat's inconsistent peacemaking diplomacy, moving back and forth from independent, separate diplomacy to commitment, to the collective advancement of the Arab parties' interests in recovering their occupied territories from Israel. It was against this backdrop that an unprecedented *rapprochement* began between Syria and Jordan in the spring of 1975, shortly after the failure of separate Israeli-Egyptian talks on a second Israeli withdrawal from Sinai (eventually concluded in September). Hussein and Asad exchanged visits and the two regimes were soon discussing plans of close military, political and economic cooperation, under slogans of "one homeland" and "one people." The new alignment with Syria was of a tactical nature as Jordan preserved its diplomatic and military freedom of maneuver. Apart from restoring Jordan's role as a central confrontational state, it would be instrumental in taming the PLO, given Syria's leverage on the Palestinian armed groups. Syria's growing involvement in the Lebanese Civil War, which erupted in April 1975, and its entanglement in armed confrontation with the Palestinian-Lebanese Left coalition in June 1976, further strengthened the tactical alliance between Syria and Jordan. Despite some progress in the fields of trade

and exchange of military visits and limited coordination, by 1980 relations with Syria relapsed into a state of tension and hostility until 1986. The renewed conflict evolved around a number of issues, primarily, resulting from shifting alliances of the Arab actors in the Fertile Crescent. First, Syria accused Jordan of supporting the Islamic opposition which had escalated its subversive activity against the *Ba'th* regime and threatened its domestic stability. Syria was also frustrated by the close alliance that had emerged between Jordan and Iraq, especially in view of the growing Syria-Iraq hostility, which culminated in Asad's full backing of Iran in its war with Iraq. A third reason for the Syria-Jordan tension was the latter's political dialogue with the PLO from late 1982 to early 1986, at a time when Syria's relations with the PLO had plunged into an abyss of enmity following the 1982 Lebanon war. On its part, Jordan complained that Syria was responsible for a campaign of subversion-sabotage and political assassinations against its institutions and delegates abroad through terrorist groups. The tension between the two regimes came to a head during the Arab Summit Conference held in Amman in November 1980, when Syria, together with other radical states, boycotted the summit. This forced Lebanon and the PLO to follow suit and massed two divisions along its border with Jordan, forcing summit participants to refrain from decisions that disagreed with Syrian policy. This legitimized Jordan's role in the peace process. In 1986, following the suspension of the Jordan-PLO dialogue in February, a successful conciliation effort by an Arab League delegation enabled a new normalization between Amman and Damascus.

Particularly against the backdrop of inter-Arab fragmentation and proliferated conflicts that had resulted from the Egypt-Israel peacemaking efforts of 1977–1979, the Hashemite Kingdom of Jordan, frequently referred to as the most artificial Arab state and as a weak link in Middle Eastern politics, seemed to have gained more stability and international respect. This had little to do with the Hashemite ruler's statesmanship, resilience and deep consciousness of Jordan's domestic and regional constraints and vulnerabilities. His ability to cope with Jordan's opportunities and constraints was clearly manifested by shifting alliances with regional actors to maximize his capabilities and minimize threats to domestic stability. Throughout the 1980s and early 1990s, the King successfully endeavored to develop a respectful international and inter-Arab position. Identifying himself as both part of the Iraq-Gulf monarchies' alignment and an ardent supporter of the Middle East peace process, the King enjoyed a special status as a link and go-between on both inter-Arab and Arab-American relations. He often visited foreign capitals, especially in Europe, received many foreign statesmen in Amman. In September 1984, shortly after the establishment of a national coalition government in Israel headed by Shimon PERES, and with a view to possible renewal of the peace process, he resumed official relations with Egypt and exchanged ambassadors. His connection with President MUBARAK personally, as well as Jordan-Egyptian links in all fields, was remarkably improved. This breach of the all-Arab resolution of boycott against Egypt, taken in 1979, did not adversely affect Jordan's relations with the Arab states.

The Egypt-Israel peacemaking, starting with Sadat's visit to Jerusalem in November 1977 and culminating in the Camp David Accords, left King Hussein further behind in terms of the prospects of advancing his own interests in the West Bank. Although the Camp David Accords meant to include Jordan as a partner to the Palestinian Interim Autonomy Plan, and he was contacted during and after Camp David regarding his active participation in the negotiations on this matter, the King made no promises. More significantly, however, was the collective hostile Arab response to the Camp David Accords, interpreted as separate Egyptian-Israeli peace, which the King could not ignore. Jordan thus endorsed the resolutions concluded in the Arab Summit Conference in Baghdad (November 1978) regarding application of diplomatic and economic sanctions against Egypt once its had signed a fully-fledged peace treaty with Israel. Jordan indeed implemented these sanctions, severing its diplomatic relations with Egypt shortly after the Israel-Egypt Peace Treaty had been formalized, preempting misunderstanding of his position and possible Arab criticism and domestic troubles.

Sadat's visit to Israel and his drive toward a peace agreement paved the way to improved relations between Jordan and the PLO. An unexpected meeting of Hussein and Arafat was mediated by Libya's Mu'ammar QADHAFI, obviously in order to tie the king's hands and prevent him from joining the Camp David Accords. The Jordan-PLO *rapprochement* was further motivated by the Baghdad summit's resolution to allocate the Palestinians of the West Bank and Gaza Strip an annual financial aid of 150 million dollars for the next ten years, to be distributed by a joint Palestinian-Jordanian committee. (Until 1987, the committee distributed less than 500 million dollars due to failure of most of the oil states to fully implement their commitments.) The establishment of the joint committee created a constant channel of consultations and coordination between the two parties, who could not ignore their particular benefit of such cooperation despite their traditional rivalry. Following a series of visits to Jordan by PLO delegations, in March-April 1979 Arafat himself came to Amman for talks with the King. In the following months, Jordan again permitted PLO delegates and departments to establish offices in Amman, but strictly banned—though not always effectively—any Palestinian military activity on Jordanian soil. Talks with Arafat reportedly centered around two main issues: the possibility of establishing a Palestinian political entity in the West Bank and Gaza Strip, which would become part of a future Jordanian-Palestinian confederation; and the advancement of peace negotiations on a settlement with Israel, possibly by a joint Jordanian-Palestinian delegation. PLO-Jordan relations continued to develop, leading to the increased presence of PLO institutions in Jordan. However, the two parties could jointly move forward in the context of peacemaking with Israel only after the PLO's expulsion from Lebanon and the loss of its territorial base there as a result of Israel's invasion of Lebanon, as well as the Reagan Plan (September 1982). This accorded Jordan a primary role in negotiating a peaceful settlement with Israel over the West Bank and Gaza Strip. Another motivation which drove both parties to political cooperation was their shared fear of Israel's intensified policy of settlement in the West Bank, which threatened to empty the area of its Palestinian inhabitants and push them eastward, undermining Jordan's domestic stability.

In November 1982, Jordan and the PLO began official talks regarding a formula of joint political action regarding a possible settlement on the occupied territories. In April 1983 a draft agreement between Arafat and Hussein failed to gain the support of Fatah's Central Committee, leading to a break in the talks. In November 1984, the seventeenth Palestine National Council (PNC) session—boycotted by the extremist and anti-Arafat wing of the PLO—was held in Amman, indicating the PLO's political weakness after the expulsion of Arafat from Tripoli in December 1983, this time by the Syrians and their Palestinian subservient groups. Another incentive to the Jordan-PLO accelerated efforts to reach an agreement on joint action was the ascendancy in August 1984 of a national coalition government in Israel, led by Shimon Peres of the Labor Party.

The PNC resolutions facilitated the conclusion of an agreement between Hussein and Arafat in February 1985. When exercising, after Israel's withdrawal, their right of self-determination, the Palestinians would establish an entity in confederation with Jordan. The PLO and Jordan would jointly negotiate a Middle East peace settlement, based on UN resolutions and the principle of "land for peace," in the framework of an international conference. The agreement was heavily criticized by Fatah's leading members. Consequently Arafat's position was stiffened and the agreement was short-lived. The idea of a confederation—vague as it was—aroused controversy over whether or not the Palestinian entity would be established *ab initio* in confederation with Jordan, as the King desired. Alternatively an independent Palestinian state would first be established which would then join the confederation, as Arafat had insisted. But the joint Jordanian-Palestinian negotiations did not materialize. One of the obstacles was Arafat's refusal to accept UN Security Council Resolution 242 (mainly because the Palestinian issue had not been addressed). This was seen by the US administration and King Hussein as a precondition for the PLO's participation in the peace negotiations. Arafat also preferred the PLO to be represented by an independent PLO delegation or as part of an all-Arab one rather than as part of the Jordanian delegation, as he had agreed. Arafat was, in any case, unable to obtain an endorsement of the agreement by the PLO: not only did all the radical and anti-Arafat factions oppose it altogether, but even within his own Fatah wing there were doubts and objections. Ultimately, the PLO inner struggles led to major differences of interpretation with the PLO. In July the King closed Fatah's offces and institutions (though not all PLO departments) in Jordan, expelling several leading Fatah functionaries. Furthermore Jordan made new low-key efforts to enhance its influence in the West Bank through coordination with Israel, *inter alia* by announcing a billion dollar five-year development plan for the West Bank. This remained strictly theoretical in the absence of Jordanian financial capabilities. In April 1987, the PNC formally abrogated the February 1985 Amman Accord (though reconfirming the "special relationship" with Jordan and implicitly endorsing the principle of a future confederation). King Hussein himself moved rather strictly toward weakening the PLO's position regarding future negotiations on the West Bank. In April 1987 he reached a secret agreement with Israeli Foreign Minister Peres in London. In this he supported the convening of an international peace conference to serve as a ceremonial opening, with no coercive power over the participants. Following this negotiations would be conducted bilaterally between Israel and each of its neighbors. The King undertook to negotiate a settlement on the West Bank regardless of the PLO's position. At the November 1987 Arab Summit Conference held in Amman, the King made an overt effort to deprive the PLO of its status as the sole representative of the Palestinian people and retreat from the all-Arab commitment to the establishment of a Palestinian state.

With the Palestinian uprising (*Intifada*) in the occupied territories (1987–1992), Jordanian interests changed altogether with regard to both Israel and the PLO. From the start, the Jordanian regime was concerned about a spill-over effect of the *Intifada* on its own Palestinian population, taking strict security measures to prevent similar eruption in his domain while publicly praising the uprising. The ongoing demonstrations and civil disobedience deterred the King from full endorsement of the American Secretary of State Shultz's proposals for a renewed peace process. This incorporated elements from both the Reagan Plan of 1982 and the Amman Accord of Hussein and Arafat. At the Algiers summit conference (dedicated to the *Intifada*) held in June 1988, the King failed to ensure for Jordan any share of the Arab financial aid allocated to support the Palestinian uprising. Struck by the sweeping public support for the PLO in the occupied territories as well as in the Arab and international arenas, Jordan reacted

after eight months of widespread uprising by renouncing all links with the West Bank. A royal speech
to that effect (July 31, 1988) concluded that Jordan's efforts to regain the West Bank had transferred
all responsibilities for the future of the West Bank to
Palestinian hands through the PLO. By its disengagement from the West Bank, Jordan ceased paying salaries to government officials, except for the
Islamic establishment in Jerusalem, and also abrogated
the Jordanian citizenship of the West Bank Palestinians, though they could maintain their Jordanian
passports for another two years.

Jordan's disengagement from the West Bank was
a turning point in the kingdom's history. For the
first time since 1967, Jordan redefined its political
borders on the basis of reality; that is, within the
boundaries of the East Bank. The regime made it
strictly clear that those choosing to remain in the
Hashemite Kingdom must adopt its identity and
abide by its laws. The disengagement from the West
Bank allowed for the first time since 1967 the holding of general elections to Parliament, resolving the
constitutional problem created by the loss of the
West Bank to Israel and stalemated international
peacemaking efforts. The Senate, appointed by the
King, was not affected by the suspension of Parliament and the King has regularly named new members (from 1988 on, they had all been East Bank
residents). Because elections could obviously not be
held in the West Bank under Israeli occupation, the
Parliament's term, which expired in 1971, was extended for two years. In November 1973 Parliament was dissolved but later the dissolution was
considered as merely suspended, and the Parliament
reconvened in 1976 and 1984; from 1984 it held
regular sessions. In the interim period, it was replaced by a King-appointed Consultative Council
(1978–1984). Only following the announcement
of disengagement from the West Bank, were the
first elections since 1967 held (November 1989).
The general elections came at a time of economic recession, six months after the riots and protest against
the deteriorating economy. This enhanced the demand for political participation. The elections resulted in a victory for the Islamic block whose
candidates (21 Muslim Brothers and 13 independent Islamists) now constituted forty-three percent
of the Parliamentary members. The remainder of
the seats were divided among the leftist-nationalist

group (13), conservatives (22), and independents
(11). The low participation rate (forty percent) apparently helped the Muslim Brotherhood candidates
who enjoyed incomparable organization and a permanent public presence, an advantage none of the
other political currents enjoyed. The results of the
elections were an unpleasant surprise to the regime,
which coped with them rather than resisting them.
This allowed the Muslim Brothers to participate in
the Parliament and the government of "national
unity" established in early January 1991. However,
in view of the Islamist achievement, the regime
adopted a number of measures with the aim of tightening its control over the political system, primarily the Islamist movements. In 1991, the regime
published "the National Charter." This was a set of
principles and rules of political participation, which
defined the limits and opportunities of the democratic game, as an indivisible part of the allegiance to
the Jordanian homeland and responsibility for its
wellbeing. The Charter stressed the principles of
pluralism, negotiation, sharing power, rejection of violence and ideological monopoly, and illegality of
maintaining international links. Loyalty to the Charter's principles was presented as a prerequisite for political participation in Jordan. In August 1993 the
regime amended the election law, introducing the
principle of "one man, one vote." This enabled each
eligible voter to elect only one candidate. This abolished the possibility—according to the previous
law—of combining primordial (familial or tribal)
and ideological considerations in his election. The new
law triggered calls from Islamic leaders to boycott
the coming elections, toward a confrontation with the
regime, although the Islamic movement—acting
under the umbrella of "The Islamic Action Front"
(jabhat al-amal al-islami)—eventually did participate
in the November 1993 elections. These elections
proved the primacy of primordial considerations in
the voting pattern. This resulted in a significant drop
of the Islamists' power in Parliament. Only eighteen
Islamist candidates were elected. Nonetheless the
Islamic block remained the largest one in the Parliament. In the summer of 1997, during a recess in
the Parliament's sessions, the regime introduced restrictive amendments to the press law, triggering
strong protests from various political parties. Shortly afterwards, nine nationalist factions of the center
political spectrum announced unification under "the

National Constitutional Party," (al-hizb al-watani al-dusturi). This was seen by the Islamist opposition to be a product of the regime's efforts to block the Islamists in the approaching elections. Consequently, the Islamic Action Front decided to boycott the 1997 elections, in protest of the government's non-democratic conduct which in effect stripped the Parliament of its powers, and attempted to decide the results of the coming elections.

The process of controlled democratization supervised by the King brought to the surface new threats to Jordan's domestic stability. The economic difficulties confronted by the regime since the late 1980s strengthened the Muslim Brotherhood in Jordan, which were apparent in the results of the 1989 general elections. Despite their drive to participate in the political process and power, the Islamists were able to gain more prestige by providing social and economic services to the public than by participating in the government, which labeled the movement with responsibility to the economic and social predicament. However, if democratization was intended to mitigate opposition to the regime, it had the opposite result, especially against the backdrop of continued socio-economic difficulties and the Jordanian-Israeli peacemaking. The Islamic movement overtly opposed the 1991 Madrid peace conference and the bilateral negotiations that followed, culminating in the peace agreement with Israel signed in October 1994. The Islamic movement in Jordan, maintaining close alliance with HAMAS in the West Bank and Gaza Strip, became the leading opposition to peace relations with Israel, placing this issue on top of their political agenda.

The 1990 Kuwait crisis came at a time of economic crisis in Jordan, continued Palestinian uprising, and fear that the growing wave of Jews from the Soviet Union would be settled in the West Bank. These events caused a mass exodus of its population to Jordan. The King's repeated appeals—together with the PLO—to increase the financial support to Jordan and the Palestinian population in the occupied territories were all rejected. This might explain the increased bitterness between the Jordanian and Saudi regimes. This strengthened Hussein's obligation to adhere to an "Arab solution" which he attempted to forge through intensive mediation, in vain, and to refrain from joining the Saudi-Egyptian-Syrian line of supporting an international intervention. This position cost Jordan the cease of oil supplies from the Saudis and a blockade imposed on Aqaba port by the United Nations. The Jordanian passivity during the Kuwait crisis and the Gulf war was clearly shaped by domestic considerations, not by consent to Saddam Hussein's aggressive regional conduct. His decision to include the Islamists in the government during the crisis reflected the regime's internal constraints. When the GULF WAR ended and the US administration launched its initiative of convening an international peace conference in Madrid, the King manifested no reservations in shifting policies. He dismissed the current government and accepted the American proposals.

Despite ups and downs, Jordan's relations with Israel since 1967 have been largely marked by common interests and secret cooperation. This was very much in line with old-lived geostrategic Hashemite-Israeli tacit alliance. As a result of the April 1963 showdown with the Palestinians and the increased Arab republican threat, the King opened a direct and secret top level channel of negotiations with Israel. Immediately following the 1967 War and conquest of the West Bank by Israel, King Hussein maintained secret negotiations with Israeli leaders of the Labor governments regarding a peaceful settlement by which Israel would withdraw from the occupied territory and East Jerusalem. However, hundreds of hours of talks never resulted in even a bridging of the gap between the two proponents. While the King would not concede with less than withdrawal to the pre-1967 war borders, including East Jerusalem (albeit with some necessary rectifications), Israel was unwilling to even consider such a sweeping withdrawal, and particularly not from East Jerusalem. While the Labor governments (1967–1977) were willing to negotiate a territorial compromise, the Likud governments (1977–1984; 1990–1992) refused to even consider a such compromise. Following the Rabat resolutions of 1974, King Hussein tried to maintain his primacy around the negotiating table by a joint Jordanian-Palestinian representation under his leadership. While such a combination in principle would have been acceptable to Israel, the latter insisted on approving each Palestinian delegate, to ensure no PLO participation. The Reagan Plan (September 1982) and the establishment of a national coalition government in Israel (August 1984), headed by Shimon Peres (in ro-

tation with Yitzak SHAMIR), underpinned Hussein's renewed effort to reach political coordination with
the PLO, aimed at forging a formula on joint representation which would be acceptable to both Israel
and the United States. These efforts also failed. And
yet, during most of these years, Israel and Jordan
maintained high-level contacts and constant channels
of communication. King Hussein himself met with
most Israeli Prime Ministers of the Labor Party, including Golda MEIR, Yitzhak Rabin, and Shimon
Peres, as well as with Likud's Yitzak Shamir. The
two states collaborated in the fields of intelligence and
anti-terrorism, particularly during and after the years
Jordan had had to cope with the Palestinian guerrilla
presence on its soil. That secret cooperation between Israel and Jordan continued despite the deadlocked peace process. This represented their common
interest in a careful and agreed upon administration
of the West Bank's affairs in which they both had
high stakes. Jordan and Israel also shared regional
security interest. They wanted to prevent nationalist militancy and employment of subversion and violence by neighboring Arab states and the Palestinians.
Fundamentally, however, it was the rise—and
threat—of Palestinian nationalism after 1967 and
its repercussions for both Israel and Jordan in terms
of their territorial and security concerns, that brought
the two states together.

The wave of Jewish migration to Israel, starting
in 1989, aggravated the tension between Jordan and
Israel, at a time of growing PLO presence and Islamist activity in Jordan. The tension grew stronger
due to Jordan's perceived support of the Iraqi invasion of Kuwait and objection to the US-led international military action against Iraq. Due to Israel's
refusal to negotiate with the PLO, and in accordance
with its conditions, the beginning of the Madrid
process saw a joint Jordanian-Palestinian delegation.
(The Palestinians were West Bank and Gaza Strip
residents, with none from East Jerusalem.) During
the Washington talks that followed the Madrid Peace
Conference it became clear that Jordan had been
dependent on collective Arab decision making, which
included Syria and the PLO. Thus, despite the fact
that after the 1988 Jordanian proclamation of disengagement from the West Bank Israel and Jordan
had not engaged in any significant disagreements,
substantial negotiations between the two governments had to wait until progress was achieved on

the more complicated Israeli-Arab fronts—the Palestinian and the Syria-Lebanese fronts. Thus, a day
after the signing on 13 September 1993 in Washington, of the Israel-PLO DECLARATION OF PRINCIPLES
(DOP), Israel and Jordan signed a memorandum of
principles to serve as a basis for their respective negotiations. Still, the King remained cautious not to
move ahead alone before a visible progress was
reached with the Israel-Syria track of negotiations.
It was only in July 1994, following American encouragement, that King Hussein—after a joint appearance with Israeli Prime Minister Rabin in the
US Congress—that the king decided to begin official bilateral negotiations with Israel. These culminated in a fully-fledged peace treaty signed in October
1994. The agreement resolved the minor territorial disputes between the two states along the River Jordan, as well as the issue of water sharing and
development of new sources to help Jordan overcome its shortage of water. The Agreement included two unprecedented undertakings: a) an
arrangement by which Israel leased a sovereign Jordanian land in the Arava valley, which had been cultivated by Israeli farmers, and b) a joint commitment
to coordinate issues of common national security.
The Israel-Jordan Peace Agreement triggered harsh
Syrian attack, joining similar domestic criticism.
Nevertheless, relations between Israel and Jordan
experienced growing intimacy and normalization
during the Rabin-Peres government (1992–1996),
in conjunction with the continued Israeli-Palestinian peacemaking, which remained a major Hashemite
concern. This intimacy stagnated following the ascendancy of a Likud-led government headed by
Binyamin NETANYAHU, primarily due to the side-ef-
fect of the blocked peacemaking process with the
PALESTINIAN AUTHORITY.

The Hashemite alliance with the United States
remained a cornerstone in Jordanian foreign affairs
after 1967. Particularly after the confrontation with
the Palestinian guerrillas in September 1970, the
United States was willing to provide Jordan with
unprecedented arms supplies and economic support to enable its rehabilitation. Despite the generally stable alliance with the United States, three main
complexes had a straining impact on their relations.
One was the sale of advanced US arms to Jordan,
considered by Jordan to be vital. Sales were frequently held up or foiled altogether by US Con-

gressional opposition. Thus a sale of Hawk missiles ran into difficulties. These were resolved by a compromise—that the Hawks should be in fixed positions, not mobile—but the financing and the actual supply had to overcome further obstacles. A June 1980 sale of tanks was confirmed after a wrangle. In these circumstances, King Hussein increasingly relied on alternative sources of military supplies (Britain, FRANCE). For the first time these included some Soviet arms. King Hussein visited the USSR in 1976 and 1981, and the purchase of SAM missiles was reportedly finalized in 1981. The second complexity concerned the Middle East peacemaking in which Hussein seemed to be hesitant and probably too cautious. Hussein was the only Arab leader outside Egypt who did not reject President Reagan's plan announced in September 1982. But, put out by all-Arab resolutions and his inconclusive negotiations with Arafat and the latter's own constraints regarding political collaboration with Jordan, the King was unable to be a surrogate to the PLO, or to bring Arafat into the negotiating table—as he had repeatedly assured the US government he would do. In March 1984 he told Washington that he would not be able to join any peace negotiations without the PLO and outside the framework of an international conference on the Middle East (in which the USSR and China would participate)—i.e., on conditions unacceptable to the United States and Israel. Hussein remained a key-figure in the US-envisaged peace process, and the possibility of Palestinian representation by independents approved by the PLO, rather than the PLO itself, continued to be examined. However these efforts remained deadlocked. Although the US capability proved limited in terms of advancing an Israeli Arab peace settlement, it regarded King Hussein as a key figure in that context, fostering close relations with him. The US administration continued, until the Israel-PLO Oslo Agreement, to accord Hashemite Jordan the primary role in any settlement with Israel on the West Bank and Gaza. Yet the United States could not overcome the Arab reservations—and the king's inhibitions thereabout—of such role. The third complexity had to do with the neutral-pro-Iraqi position adopted by Jordan during the Kuwait crisis and the Gulf War (1990–1991), during which the United States led an international coalition in war against Iraq. Despite some American criticism of the Jordanian position,

Washington basically viewed it with understanding due to the King's domestic constraints, especially since the Jordanian policy contented itself with verbal support for Iraq. However, shortly after the end of the Gulf war, King Hussein was the first Arab leader to announce his unreserved support for the US proposals for convening an international peace conference. The new American administration led by Bill Clinton fully encouraged an Israeli-Jordanian peace agreement, offering to write off a Jordanian debt to the United Sates and provide Jordan with financial support.

JORDAN RIVER   see WATER POLITICS.

JORDAN-ISRAEL PEACE TREATY   see ARAB-ISRAEL PEACEMAKING.

JUMAYYIL   A Lebanese Maronite-Christian family from Bikfayya that played an important role in the history of LEBANON from the mid 1930s.

Pierre Jumayyil (1905–1984) Lebanese politician; founder and leader of the paramilitary Lebanese PHALANGES organization; father of President-elect Bashir Jumayyil and President Amin Jumayyil (see below). A pharmacist, educated in Beirut and FRANCE, Jumayyil was active in sports and youth organizations. After being much impressed by Fascist and German brands of nationalism and political organization, he founded the paramilitary *Phalanges Libanaises (al-Kata'ib)* in 1936. Designed to protect the MARONITES (though this was never explicitly spelled out), that organization soon took a political stance, stressing Lebanon's independence and Christian character and opposing its integration in pan-Arab schemes. It gradually became more of a political party, making Jumayyil one of the leaders of the pro-Western camp.

In the 1930s and 1940s, Jumayyil cultivated the Phalanges as a youth and paramilitary organization and was not active in politics. He took no prominent part in the struggle of those years between pro-French and anti-French factions (The "National Bloc" and the "Constitutional Bloc") and in the crisis of 1943 (see LEBANON). In the civil war of 1958 he was one of the leaders of the Christian-led resistance to the Nasserist, Muslim-led rebels, and when that dispute was being settled, in September 1958, he and others prevented, by threatening a coup, the formation of a government dominated by the Nasserist rebels and insisted on a more balanced team. In October Jumayyil became one of the four members forming the neutral government. He supported President Shihab and was a Cabinet Minister during most of Shihab's Presidency (to 1964). During the Presidency of Shihab's successor, Hilou, Jumayyil was Minister of Finance (1960–1961), Minister of the Interior (1966 and 1968–1969), and most of the time he served as Minister of Public Works and/or Health. Since 1960 he was also a member of Parliament—elected as an independent, but gradually appearing as a representative of the Phalanges (along with a handful of other Phalangists in Parliament). Jumayyil did not take a strong stand on the basic Christian-Muslim issue, though his general attitude was well known. (In 1962, for example, he proposed the neutralization of Lebanon along the Swiss and Austrian models.) He did not join other Christian factions to form a strong, united Christian bloc, but formed, in the 1960s, a loose "Triple Alliance" with Camille CHAMOUN's "National Liberal Party" and Raymond Edde's "National Bloc." In 1970 Jumayyil presented, with their support, his candidacy for the Presidency, but withdrew in favor of a more "neutral" candidate, Suleiman Franjiyyeh.

Jumayyil supported, since the later 1960s, a strong position against the use of Lebanon by the Palestinian guerrillas as a base for their operations and the growth of their separate and dominant establishment in South Lebanon. He did not follow the official Arab line of total hostility toward ISRAEL, but neither did he associate himself with the willingness to coexist in peace and cooperation evinced by some other Christian politicians (such as Emile Edde), some leaders of the Maronite Church and his own Phalanges, who maintained some ties with Israel. He certainly was aware of Israel's low-profile aid to, and cooperation with, the Phalanges since the 1950s, but he was not directly involved in it, and took no part in the intensification of that cooperation in the 1970s and its culmination in June 1982. Of his two sons, he seemed closer to the positions taken by the cautious and balanced Amin than to those of the extreme, brash and militant Bashir.

Since the early 1970s, Jumayyil was not very active in Lebanon's public and political life. He did not play a prominent role in the marshalling of the Christian-conservative camp in the civil war of 1975, though he was, of course, identified with the Phalanges and his sons. Later, in April 1984, he agreed to serve in the Syrian-backed government of National Unity established by Rashid KARAMEH imposed on his son and President Amin. In July 1984, he retired from the chairmanship of the Phalanges, appointing as his successor Elie Karameh (who was duly elected in September 1984, soon after Jumayyil's death).

Amin Jumayyil (b. 1942) Lebanese politician, President of Lebanon, 1982–1988. Amin Jumayyil is the elder son of Pierre Jumayyil, the founder and leader of the Phalanges, and the brother of Bashir Jumayyil, who was elected President in August 1982 and killed before assuming office. Jumayyil studied jurisprudence and worked as a lawyer and businessman with widespread economic interests and activities. He was not very active in politics and barely involved in the military activities and organization of the Phalanges; but as the son of the founder-leader and the brother of the emerging younger military commander he remained identified with them. Jumayyil entered Parliament in 1970, in a by-election. He was generally considered less determined, less hard-line, than his father in the defense of the Christian-Maronite predominance in Lebanese politics, and was more inclined to seek accommodation with the non-Christian communities, with the radicals striving for constitutional reforms that would abolish the communal structure of Parliament and government, with SYRIA and with the Palestinian guerrilla presence and operations in Lebanon. He did not share his brother's inclination to cooperate with Israel. Jumayyil therefore played no important part in the organization and defense of the Christian-conservative camp in the civil war of 1975 and in the late 1970s maintained some contact with Syria and the PLO leadership. Jumayyil was the victim of several assassination and kidnap attempts in the late 1970s.

Amin Jumayyil was propelled into the Presidency when his brother and President-elect Bashir, was killed in the bombing of the Phalanges headquarters in September 1982. Parliament elected Amin with a majority (and an attendance) larger than his brother's a month before, as he was considered less identified with the Maronite camp in the civil war, and as Syria did not oppose him. (The only rival candidate, Camille Chamoun, withdrew before the vote.) He had pledged to continue the policies of his late brother, and the first pressing point on his agenda was the conclusion of an agreement with Israel, to provide Israel's withdrawal from the large parts of Lebanon that it occupied. Though Jumayyil was not enthusiastic, and the agreement was whittled down in protracted negotiations to much less than Israel desired and had hoped for, it was signed on 17 May 1983. However, Syria and its Lebanese supporters, the rivals of Jumayyil and the Christian camps, with whom Jumayyil strove to achieve accommodation, were pressing to abrogate that agreement altogether as a pre-condition to any reconciliation. Jumayyil therefore procrastinated, delaying his final signature. He was at any rate incapable of assuring a coordinated withdrawal and transfer, as Israel requested, as he, and his government and army had but little effective control. (Jumayyil's power was also hurt on the eve of his election by the massacre perpetrated by the Phalanges in the Palestinian camps of Sabra and Shatila. If, as he insisted, he bore no responsibility at all for that operation, it showed that he had no control over the Phalanges.) When Israeli forces began unilaterally withdrawing, in September 1983, bitter fighting broke out between Christians and Druze in the Shuf region, spreading to Beirut, where Shi'i militias took over the Muslim western part and Druze the southeastern suburbs and approaches, and the power and control of President Jumayyil and his government were further reduced. These moves were largely the consequence of Jumayyil's own actions. By refusing to take into consideration the Shi'i (or Druze) interests and needs and relying solely on the Sunni notables (Zu'ama) and American aid, he alienated the Shi'ite and Druze leaders, Nabih BERRI and Walid JUNBLAT, who eventually turned against him. The newly reorganized Lebanese army again disintegrated in 1984 into separate Christian, Shi'i, Sunni and Druze parts. Repeated changes in the command of the Phalanges and the "Lebanese Forces"—changes over which Jumayyil had no control—were at least in part directed against his policies and deprived him, in effect, of any military support.

Efforts for a general pacification led to a National Reconciliation Conference in Geneva in October 1983 and Lausanne in March 1984, in the course of which Jumayyil had to accept a large part of his rivals' and Syria's demands. He formally abrogated the agreement with Israel in March 1984, before, and as the price for, the second Reconciliation Conference. He accepted far-reaching policy coordination with Syria. He agreed to the need for basic reforms in Lebanon's constitutional and political structure—giving more weight to Muslims, particularly Shi'i Muslims, and Druze, toward an eventual abolition of the communal system, with details and procedures to be worked out. Jumayyil set up a "Government of National Reconciliation" headed by his adversaries (Rashid Karameh as Premier, the Shi'i leader Nabih Berri and the Druze chief Walid Junblat among the Ministers). However, the hope for a cease-fire and the initiation of reforms and reconciliation proved illusive. A bloody, nearly incessant battle continued between a coalition of Druze and Shi'i militias and Christian ones; the divided army was ineffective. Berri and Junblat boycotted the government, of which they were members, and in effect sabotaged it and called for Jumayyil's resignation or dismissal. Syria, now in effective military and political control, was pressing for a general agreement on lines that it would deem acceptable. However, Syria was unable to attain such an agreement. In December 1985, Elie Hobeika, commander of the Maronite-Christian Lebanese Forces, signed in Damascus an agreement with the Shi'i and Druze militia leaders on radical political reforms, as well as total "coordination" of Syria's and Lebanon's defense, foreign and inter-Arab policies and security services. Hobeika's rival, Samir Ja'ja', now rebelled, rallied with Jumayyil and those Phalange formations that had remained loyal to Jumayyil, and defeated Hobeika's forces. Jumayyil himself did not reject the December 1985 Agreement openly and totally, but clearly indicated that while accepting the cease-fire and the military provisions, he had grave reservations concerning the political reforms dictated, the abolition of the Christian-dominated confessional government and the reduction of the President's powers. He insisted that any reform plan should be adopted through constitutional channels and not imposed by the militias; and he implied that the total subservience to Syria envisaged in the agreement was not acceptable. Jumayyil accepted the military alliance and support offered by Ja'ja', who was much more radical in his rejection of the agreement, and supported him in the ensuing military clash with

Hobeika and his allies. Syria did not officially join Berri and Junblat in demanding Jumayyil's dismissal and maintained minimal relations with him. However, Syria's forces backed the Shi'i and Druze militias, as well as Hobeika and Jumayyil's Maronite rival, former President Suleiman Franjiyyeh; Jumayyil's position in 1986–1987 was precarious. In autumn 1988 as Jumayyil's Presidential term was nearing its end, the various groups involved in Lebanon tried to influence the outcome of the Presidential elections, always a "window of opportunity" to local and foreign actors to attain influence on Lebanese politics. However, the required number of deputies could not be assembled and no President was elected. Jumayyil was appointed Commander of the Lebanese Army, General Michel AWN, a Maronite-Christian, as Prime Minister of an interim military government designed to rule Lebanon until the next President is elected, thereby contributing to the major crisis that followed (see LEBANON). Jumayyil himself left Lebanon for France, becoming one of the leaders of the Lebanese opposition in exile.

Bashir Jumayyil (1947–1982) Lebanese militia leader and politician. Elected President of Lebanon in August 1982, he was assasinated before assuming office. A Maronite-Christian born in Beirut, Jumayyil was the younger son of Pierre Jumayyil who founded and led the Christian Phalanges, and the brother of Amin Jumayyil (who succeeded him as President). Jumayyil studied law and political science at the Jesuit St. Joseph University of Beirut, but did not complete his studies. From his early youth he was active in the Phalanges, and in the late 1960s organized student agitation against the military presence and activities of the Palestinians in Lebanon. Considered ruthless and endowed with charismatic leadership, he rose rapidly in the organization's military command during the civil war from 1975 onward—stressing a youthful activism and a measure of disdain for the leaders of the older generation and their political deals and intrigues. In 1976, Jumayyil became the chief military commander of the Phalanges, and shortly afterward also of the "Lebanese Forces" (an umbrella formation of the Phalanges and other Christian-Maronite militias) that gradually became an independent actor. He is credited with the bloody conquest, in August 1976, of the Palestinian refugee camp and stronghold of Tel al-Za'tar in an East Beirut.

From 1976–1977, Jumayyil strove to impose on the Christian "Lebanese Forces" the complete primacy of his Phalanges, in effect the merger of all other Christian formations in the Phalanges—by force if necessary. He was held chiefly responsible for bitter intra-Maronite fighting—with Franjiyyeh's North Lebanese militias that had seceded from the "Lebanese Forces" and with Chamoun's National Liberal Party "Tigers" (which Jumayyil eliminated as a fighting force in 1980, absorbing their remnants in his Phalange-Lebanese Forces). Jumayyil thus became involved in bitter blood feuds and, while adored by his supporters, was hated by many, even within his own Maronite community. He and his relatives were also targets for terrorist attacks during the civil war; in one such attempt, in February 1980, his baby daughter was killed. Jumayyil's political line was radical. No longer content with the elder Christian leaders' struggle to maintain the inter-communal equilibrium with a measure of Christian-Maronite primacy, he aspired to a Christian, Maronite-dominated Lebanon. In the first place he wanted to defend and strengthen Maronite control of the heartland of Mount Lebanon. He was apparently not averse to the thought of Lebanon as a federation of semi-independent communal cantons dominated by the Maronite canton and he seemed willing to consider even the cession of the Muslim-majority north, south and east that had been added in 1920 to create "Greater Lebanon," and the recreation of a smaller, Christian Lebanon (a "Maronistan"). He vigorously opposed Syrian intervention and the presence of Syrian troops in Lebanon, even if disguised as an all-Arab peace or deterrence force. He objected to Pan-Arab interference and the integration of Lebanon in pan-Arab power blocs. He fought the Palestinian organizations' use of Lebanon as a base for their operations, did not believe in coordination agreements with them and wanted them out of Lebanon altogether. Beginning in about 1976, Jumayyil strengthened the clandestine links with Israel that the Phalanges had maintained, albeit on and off, for many years. He received Israeli aid in arms, training and advice, and met Israeli leaders and intelligence officers both in Israel and in Lebanon. The invading Israeli forces in June 1982 made it possible for Jumayyil and his Phalanges to take control of Beirut and the key levers of government, but Jumayyil understood that he could not become an accepted leader of all Lebanon, being borne to power on the coat-tails of an Israeli invasion and as Israel's collaborator; he therefore began, though clearly seen as cooperating with Israel, to shun visible collaboration. Thus, he refused to be actively involved in the nine-week Israeli siege of Beirut intended to force the PLO military evacuation of Lebanon.

When President Elias Sarkis's term expired, in September 1982, Jumayyil was, under the political circumstances created by the Israeli invasion and the predominance achieved by the Phalanges, the only candidate for the Presidency. It proved difficult to convene Parliament, particularly as Syria did not permit the attendance of members from the areas it occupied. But eventually, sixty-two of the ninety-two members surviving were drummed together and on 23 August 1982 they elected Jumayyil President, with fifty-seven votes, on the second ballot.

On 14 September, before he was sworn in, Jumayyil was killed in the bombing of the Phalanges headquarters (a bombing avenged by the Phalanges, three days later, in the massacre in the Palestinian camps of Sabra and Shatila). Jumayyil was succeeded by his brother Amin Jumayyil, who was elected President one week after Bashir's death.

JUNBLAT, KAMAL (1917–1977) Lebanese-DRUZE politician. The son of Fu'ad Junblat (assassinated in the 1920s), and Nazira Junblat (d. 1951), leaders of the Junblat clan centered in the Shuf mountains; one of the two strong Druze clans in LEBANON in the nineteenth and twentieth centuries (the other is the ARSALAN clan). Junblat studied law and sociology in Beirut at St. Joseph University and Paris at the *Sorbonne*. He became head of the Junblat clan in the later 1940s. He was considered a widely cultivated man with much original thought. Junblat was a skilled politician who had, in the complex community-party-clan politics of Lebanon, no permanent allegiance but played a power game of shifting factional alliances. A supporter of Emile Edde and his "National Bloc" in his youth, he switched his support to Bishara al-Khouri after 1943. He soon turned against him and joined Camille CHAMOUN to bring about Khouri's fall in 1952. Junblat first joined the youth as Minister (Economic Affairs) in December 1945 and was a member of Parliament since 1947—except for the period between 1957–1964.

Junblat drew his political strength from being recognized as the leader of the Druze community, and later, of its armed militias. Although he was not recognized by his political-ideological views, he began turning Left in the late 1940s adopting increasingly radical Socialist, and gradually also Nasserist and pan-Arab, views. In 1949 he founded a party of his own, the "Progressive Socialist Party" and began appearing as a Socialist leader, while keeping his position as a great landlord and semi-feudal chieftain with various financial and business interests (though he did distribute some of his land to his tenants). His Party was mainly Druze, but claimed to be above communal interests. It advocated far-reaching social reforms and the abolition of the Lebanese system of communal representation and government. (This system deprived the Druze, including the ambitious Junblat himself, from holding the three top governmental posts.)

In 1958, Junblat turned against President Chamoun's intention to be elected for a second term. Together with others, he began organizing extra-parliamentary, Nasserist-inspired opposition that led to a violent insurrection and civil war. The ending of that crisis along with American military intervention strengthened his anti-western, leftist-Nasserist views.

Under the post-1958 regimes of Presidents Shihab and Hilou, Junblat held several ministerial posts: Education 1960–1961; Public Works 1961 and 1966; Interior 1961–1953 and 1969–1970. In 1969 he formed the "Lebanese National Front," combining the many leftist organizations in Lebanon, fostering a strong alliance with the Palestinian organizations. He was prominent, and as Home Minister instrumental, in his support for the Palestinian military operations and their establishment in Lebanon. As clashes erupted between the PALESTINE LIBERATION ORGANIZATION (PLO) men and Lebanese army units, mainly Christian, from 1970, he was involved in several crises on that issue. This alliance with the Palestinian resistance movement enabled Junblat to ensure that the latter refrained from any military presence or activity in the dominantly Druze Shuf region. In 1970, as Minister of Interior, he legalized several outlawed parties, such as the BA'TH Party, the Communist Party and the SYRIAN SOCIAL NATIONALIST PARTY (SSNP). He also fostered relations with the USSR (in 1972 he was awarded the

Lenin Peace Prize). He applied for membership for his Party in the Socialist International; obtained observer status and was welcomed as a participant in several meetings of the International.

In the civil war of 1975, Junblat soon became the leading figure of the leftist-Muslim-Palestinian camp. His Druze (or "Progressive-Socialist") militias became one of the main military formations of that coalition. Although he had cultivated close relations with Syria (including during the early months of the civil war), their relations soon deteriorated to hostility. This began in February 1976 due to Junblat's adamant objection to the Syrian proposals for a comprehensive settlement and reforms of the political crisis. He established close relationships with the PLO and the military successes of their joint forces in March–May 1976 against the Christian militias and Syrian-backed groups. This was an important trigger for Syria's invasion of Lebanon in early June 1976 and its consequent confrontation with the Lebanese left-PLO alliance. The full-fledged Syrian involvement in Lebanon aggravated the rift with Junblat who continued to oppose Damascus' reform plan. In his view this did not go far enough and made too many concessions to the Christian conservatives. Junblat became Syria's most vocal opponent. Junblat was assassinated in March 1977, it was generally assumed by Syrian agents, though this has never been proven.

Junblat, who also taught for some years History of Economic Thought at Beirut University, wrote several books on Lebanese political issues (*The Truth about the Lebanese Revolution*, 1959; *Pour le Liban*— recorded by a French associate, 1978; *I Speak for Lebanon*, 1982).

JUNBLAT, WALID (b. 1947)

Lebanese DRUZE politician and party and militia leader, Lebanese minister from the mid-1980s. The son of Kamal JUNBLAT (his mother was of the ARSALAN clan; the daughter of the Arab nationalist leader Shakib Arslan), Junblat studied at the American University of Beirut and for some time in FRANCE. He was not very active in politics in his youth, and though he belonged to his father's militia, was considered a playboy. However, when Kamal Junblat was assassinated in March 1977, Walid had to succeed him. Reluctantly, he did succeed his father, and he became leader of the PROGRESSIVE SOCIALIST PARTY (PSP); its militias (in effect Druze militias), and of the Druze community.

At first it was thought that the community, and particularly its religious leaders, would not accept him (mostly because he broke sacred Druze customs by marrying a non-Druze, a Jordanian of Circassian origin); but he soon asserted his leadership. In the beginning he was seen to be moderate, but he soon took his father's line of anti-Western leftism by forging a close alliance with the leftist-Muslim camp in the civil war. His statements were bold and somewhat erratic. He had significant media exposure. Like his father, he advocated the abolition of the Lebanese system of communal representation and government, in effect asserting the power position of the Druze community. He had to enhance that power to unprecedented strength after September 1983. During the first months of the Israeli occupation, from June 1982, he stayed in his home at Mukhtara maintaining a low profile. Notwithstanding his extremist politics, he had, as leader of the Druze in the Israel-occupied Shuf region, some contacts with the Israelis, who hoped for cooperation with him in the pacification of the area, security arrangements, and the coordination of their withdrawal. However, Israel's overt alliance with the Lebanese Forces, enabling them to establish strongpoints in the Shuf area, made such cooperation impossible. Junblat thus preferred to leave his occupied home and spent some time in SYRIA. He returned to reassert his leadership and organize resistance to ISRAEL and to the JU-MAYYIL's Christian-dominated regime established under Israeli auspices.

In August-September 1983 he foiled efforts to arrange a peaceful Israeli withdrawal from the Shuf and a coordinated takeover of the area vacated. When Israeli forces withdrew without such coordination, he organized an immediate Druze onslaught on Christian forces in the Shuf and on Christian villages. (These had coexisted with the Druze for centuries—though clashes and massacres had occurred before.) The Druze won that bloody battle for the Shuf, and in 1984–1985 extended their control farther south and west, to Iqlim al-Kharrub, reaching the coast, and to the hills dominating Beirut and its south-eastern suburbs. They also helped the SHI'A militias occupy West Beirut and kept Christian east Beirut besieged and under constant threat, with frequent battles in the hills to its east. In this way, Junblat brought the Druze to a position of unprecedented strength.

In a move toward national reconciliation, 1984–1985, Junblat took a hard, extremist line. He insisted on speedy far-reaching reforms toward a non-communal constitution, and an immediate redistribution of power, with a larger share for the Druze (and Muslims) and a reduction of the powers of the Maronite president. He also repeatedly demanded the dismissal or resignation of President Amin Jumayyil. He tightened his alliance with Syria, in effect becoming its client depending on its support in arms supplies etc. He sometimes agreed to compromise formulas worked out under Syrian guidance, but he frequently reneged, shifted his tactical positions, and burst out in new extreme pronouncements. He accepted the compromise formula of March 1984 and joined Rashid KARAMEH's "Government of National Unity" (as Minister of Tourism, Public Works and Transportation), but boycotted. This in effect sabotaged the government of which he was a member.

Junblat cultivated his alliance with the Shi'a AMAL militias and their leader Nabih BERRI—though that alliance, too, was unstable and punctured by crises and armed clashes.

In the bitter fighting between Amal and Palestinian guerrillas since 1985, he took, despite his alliance with Amal, a rather neutral or even pro-Palestinian position, sometimes attempting to mediate. Junblat was instrumental in the foundation of several coalitions (a "National Salvation Front" in July 1983—nine factions and militias of the civil war leftist camp; a "National Democratic Front" in October 1984—six parties, including the Communists and the pro-Syrian BA'TH). In December 1985

Junblat signed the failed Damascus tripartite agreement together with the leaders of Amal and the Maronite-Christian Lebanese Forces. During the campaign for the Presidential elections that were due to take place in the summer of 1988, he supported the candidacy of former President Suleiman Franjiyyeh, a pro-Syrian Maronite leader. He remained a member of Salim al-Huss's pro-Syrian Muslim-led government (Minister of Public Works) during the conflict in 1988–1990 between the two rival Lebanese governments. In the "Government of National Reconciliation" formed in December 1990 after the defeat of General AWN's anti-Syrian Maronite-dominated military government, he served as Minister of State. He resigned in January 1991 in protest of the dilution of Druze influence in the government and its moves to eliminate the separate administration of the Druze in their "canton." He resumed his post in March remaining a government member even as it dissolved most of the Lebanese militias, including that of his own PSP, in the same month. Junblat was Minister of State in Rashid al-Sulh's government (May 1992–October 1992), serving as Minister for the displaced in Rafiq Hariri's government (since October 1992). He is also a member of the Lebanese Parliament since June 1991.

Following the disbanding of most Lebanese militias, including that of his PSP, and the strengthening of the central government in Lebanon, Junblat's autonomy and power declined. Nonetheless he remains one of Lebanon's most prominent politicians, maintaining political control over his area (as reflected in his victories in the Parliamentary elections of 1992 and 1996).

KARAMEH, RASHID (1921–1987) Lebanese politician, many times Prime Minister. Scion of a SUNNI-Muslim family of notables from Tripoli, whose sons held the office of MUFTI of Tripoli. For a long time Karameh's father, Abdel-Hamid Karameh (1895–1950), served as Mufti and was the political and religious leader of the Muslims of Tripoli. In 1920 he opposed the creation of Greater Lebanon. Following the "National Pact" in 1943 (see LEBANON)

he became the Tripoli Muslims' chief representative in Parliament. He also served briefly, in 1945, as Prime Minister.

Rashid Karameh studied Law in Cairo. When he graduated in 1947 he opened a law practice. Upon the death of his father, he succeeded him as leader of the Muslims of Tripoli, and was elected to every Parliament from 1951. He joined the government in 1951, as Minister of Justice. He served as Minister of Economy and Social Affairs, 1953–1955, becoming Prime Minister for the first time in 1955. In line with the tradition of the Sunni-Muslim leadership in Lebanon, Karameh joined shifting parliamentary factions. On occasions he formed such groups himself, but never stabilized a permanent party organization (or, later, a militia). He belonged, like most Sunni leaders, to the mainstream faction of Lebanese politics. Yet he was on its "leftist" fringe—for far-reaching reforms; the abolition of the Lebanese system of communal representation, against Christian predominance; strongly nationalist and for a pan-Arab Nasserist orientation; radically anti-Israeli and supportive of Palestinian guerrilla activities. Thus he differed from most traditional, conservative Sunni leaders in Beirut (Yafi, Salam, al-Sulh); his rivals for the top position at the head of the Sunni community. His Nasserist tendencies came to the fore in 1958, when he was one of the leaders of the resistance to President CHAMOUN, leading to civil war. When that crisis ended with a compromise and the election of General Shihab to the Presidency, Karameh headed a "Government of National Salvation" in September 1958, remaining Premier until May 1960. He was Prime Minister again in 1961–1964, 1965–1966, 1966–1968 and 1969–1970. His Premierships were controversial. He was involved in many crises, sometimes resigning and withdrawing his resignation. In April 1969, for instance, no other Prime Minister was appointed after his resignation. The country was without a government for over six months until he resumed the Premiership. During the 1967 war, he reportedly ordered the army to enter the war. This was refused by the Army's Maronite commander. From the late 1960s, Karameh supported the Palestinian military establishment in Lebanon and its operations. As Prime Minister he tried to reach agreements with them on a measure of coordination, while foiling efforts to curb them by armed action.

In the civil war that erupted in 1975, Karameh initially kept his image as a mainstream man who could hold the country together and mediate. Therefore, after five years out of power, he was again made Prime Minister in June 1975. He was, however, unable to maintain a functional controlled administration. The government and the army disintegrated. In December 1976 he resigned. He now identified himself with the "leftist"-Muslim camp, but played no prominent role in its organization and leadership. He was handicapped, like the conservative Beirut Sunni leaders, by having no militia at his disposal. Moreover, as Tripoli, his own bailiwick, was torn in battle between the fundamentalist al-Tawhid al-Islami and the pro-Syrian, ALAWI-dominated BA'TH militias, his leadership there became ineffective.

After the Israeli invasion of 1982, Karameh took an uncompromising anti-Israel line. He rejected all security agreements with ISRAEL. He opposed the JUMAYYIL administration that seemed prepared to sign such an agreement and collaborate with Israel. He strengthened his links with Syria and fostered an alliance with Syria's other clients in Lebanon—JUNBLAT's DRUZE, BERRI's SHI'A, AMAL, and Maronite ex-President Suleiman Franjiyyeh. In July 1983 he established, with Junblat and Franjiyyeh, a "National Salvation Front," in which he played a leading role in the negotiations toward a national reconciliation and reforms (the Geneva and Lausanne conferences of 1983–1984). These represented, under Syrian guidance, the more moderate forces within the leftist-Muslim camp. In April 1984 he formed a "Government of National Unity," with both camps represented. However, it was dysfunctional, being composed of forces diametrically opposed to each other. It was mostly boycotted by some of its key ministers (Junblat, Berri). It was supposed to work with a President who had been compelled to appoint it and whom some of its own members strove to dismiss. It failed to convene for many months. It had no means to impose its will and administer and control the country, divided in effect into separate "cantons" at the mercy of rival, battling militias.

Karameh, frequently threatening to resign, was Prime Minister pro forma only. From early 1986 he boycotted President Jumayyil, refusing to convene the government. In May 1987 he finally resigned in frustration, but his resignation was not accepted by the President. On 1 June 1987, Karameh was assassinated when his helicopter was blown up by a bomb. The identity of his assassins remains unknown, although Maronite extremists were suspected. His brother, Omar Karameh (b. 1935), served as Prime Minister of Lebanon's first post-war government (December 1990–May 1992) and has been a member of the Lebanese Parliament since 1991.

KATA'IB   see PHALANGES.

KHADDAM, ABDEL HALIM

KHADDAM, ABDEL HALIM (b. 1932) Syrian, SUNNI-Muslim politician from the town of Banyas in the Ladhiqiyya area. Vice-President of SYRIA since March 1989. While in high school, Khaddam joined the BA'TH Party and befriended another member, Hafez al-ASAD. After studying Law, Khaddam became a lawyer and teacher in Damascus, 1951–1964. From 1963, after the *Ba'th* assumed power, he engaged in politics full time and was Governor of Hamah during the anti-*Ba'th* uprising in 1964.

In the 1967 war he served as Governor of Quneitra, a Syrian town in the Golan occupied by the Israeli Army. He was later appointed Governor of Damascus. In May 1969 he joined the government as Minister of Economy and Foreign Trade. In the intra-*Ba'th* factional struggle he was a follower of General Hafez al-Asad. When the latter assumed power, in November 1970, Khaddam became Foreign Minister and Deputy Premier, and a member of the *Ba'th* high command. Considered knowledgeable, even brilliant, he has directed Syria's foreign relations ever since, interpreting President Asad's policies with suave, professional firmness. During the Lebanese Civil War (1975-1990), Khaddam was chief arbitrator in the inter-communal dispute. Yet he was primarily responsible for Syria's policies and operations in Lebanon. As such, he expended great efforts in the Lebanese arena, welcoming Lebanese leaders in Damascus for countless consultations and briefings, trying to guide and instruct Syria's many allies and clients.

In 1983–1984 he represented Syria as an observer at the Lebanese reconciliation conferences held in Geneva and Lausanne. After the end of the Civil War in 1990 and the agreements signed by Syria and LEBANON in 1991 (that established close cooperation and coordination between the two countries), he remained in charge of Lebanese affairs. He met regularly with Lebanese officials during this period. In the struggle for Asad's succession, Khaddam has been viewed as one of the potential contestants, possibly favored by Asad himself. In 1983, when Asad suffered a severe heart attack, Khaddam was one of the members of the committee called by Asad to run everyday matters (together with two other Sunni military officers—Chief of Staff Hikmat SHIHABI and Deputy Prime Minister and Minister of Defence Mustafa TALAS). He supported him during the challenge posed by Asad's younger brother, Rif'at. As First Vice President (one of three Vice Presidents), he has at least formal ground for such claim but he lacks the military backing without which succession would be impossible. Being a Sunni, he perhaps does not belong to the inner leadership core dominated by ALAWIS (although he is married to an Alawi). He might be an acceptable compromise candidate, enjoying considerable support in the *Ba'th* Party and the governmental Bureaucracy.

KHALIFA, AL

KHALIFA, AL ("House of") The ruling dynasty of sheikh (or emirs) BAHRAIN. The Al-Khalifa arrived in the islands in the mid-eighteenth century. They came from KUWAIT where they had helped their relatives, the AL-SABAH, to establish their rule. The beginning of their own rule over Bahrain began in 1782–1783 (or 1816), when the Bahrain Islands were taken from Persia by raiding Arab tribes from the mainland. From the 1820s until 1971, the sheikhs were under a British Protectorate. The rulers in the twentieth century were Sheikh Issa ibn (bin) Ali Al-Khalifa (1869–1923) who was deposed in 1923 by his son, with British encouragement; Sheikh Hamad ibn Issa (1923–1942); Sheikh Salman ibn Hamad (1942–1961); and Sheikh Issa ibn Salman—since 1961. Other sons of the House of Khalifa have usually served in key positions of government and administration, and as ministers since the establishment of a Council of Ministers in 1970.

KHAMENEI, AYATOLLAH SEYYED ALI HOSSEINI-E

KHAMENEI, AYATOLLAH SEYYED ALI HOS-SEINI-E (b. 1939) The spiritual leader of IRAN since June 1990 and President of Iran in the years 1981–1989. Khamenei was born in the religious town of Mashhad to a family of clergymen. He studied at the Shi'ite theological center in the town of QOM in 1964, where he was one of the students of Ayatollah Ruhullah KHOMENEI, and continued his religious studies in his home town. In 1963 he was one of the activists in Khomeini's protest movement (see IRAN). In the years 1964–1978 he was arrested several times and was also exiled in the distant Baluchistan-Sistan province (1975–1977) due to his activities against the Shah's regime. In 1964 he returned to Mashad where he taught theology. In 1978, when Khomeini ran the revolution from Paris, Khamenei was appointed by him a member in the Revolutionary Council. After the victory of the revolution he filled many positions, among them: as Khomeini's representative in the armed forces, head of revolutionary affairs in the Ministry of Defense, commander of the revolutionary guards (PASDARAN) and of the *Emem-Jome'* (the Leader of Friday Prayer) in Tehran, an extremely powerful religious-political post.

In 1980 Khamenei was elected as a member of the Majlis, and in 1981 demanded, in a strong speech, that Abul-Hassan bani-sadr be removed from the position of President. In the same year he was wounded in an attempt on his life (apparently by the mojahedin) and his right arm became paralyzed. In 1981 he was elected President by a majority of ninety-five percent and in 1985 elected for a second term. In these years he was also head of the Supreme Defense Council and the Supreme Council for the Cultural Revolution. He was greatly trusted by Khomeini, even though he had differences of opinion with him on tactical matters (such as the implementation of the Islamic laws or the cancellation of the fatwa ordering the killing of Salman rushdie). In June 1989, one day after the death of Khomeini, Khamenei was elected by the Experts Assembly as his heir and was raised from the title of Hojatt-ol Eslam to that of Ayatolla. However, this election came across criticism by senior clergymen who doubted his religious education and spiritual experience to fill the post. Since the beginning of 1994 he increased his involvement in the matters of the state and started to erode the powers of Ali-Akbar Hashemi rafsanjani as President.

Even though during his years in office as President he used to express relatively moderate declarations, since being elected as spiritual leader he has gradually become more militant in his declarations on matters of foreign policy, especially against the US and ISRAEL. He expresses support for "the Islamic Revolutionary Organizations" throughout the world and declares a relentless campaign against the "Western cultural invasion." He frequently argues that "the enemies of ISLAM" and "the godless" declared war against the Islamic regime in Iran and "the pure Islam of Mohammed." He tries in these declarations to justify the title "the Spiritual Leader of the Islamic World" and to present himself as "the only defender of the Muslims through the world." His religious opponents argue that he has not yet published a collection of religious law decisions and therefore he is not worthy of the title *Ayatollah Ozma*

(Grand Ayatullah), which is necessary to reach the status of spiritual leader.

KHATAMI, SEYYED MOHAMMAD (b. 1943)

Clergyman at the level of Hojjat-ol Eslam and statesman, who was elected President of IRAN in the elections of May 1997. Khatami was born to an Orthodox religious family in the town of Yazd in the center of Iran. He received his elementary education from his father and completed his matriculation in his home town. He left in 1961 for the religious town of QOM to study theology. He then studied Philosophy at the University of Esfahan, whilst continuing with his religious studies in the theological institute of the city. Khatami completed his religious studies in Qom and received the rank of *Mojtahid*. In 1970 he was accepted for a second degree in Education at the University of Tehran. Later, he received a scholarship to complete a doctorate abroad. He served for several years as head of the Islamic Center of Iran in Hamburg, where he also studied German, which added to his knowledge of English and Arabic.

After the revolution Khatami was elected to the *Majlisas* as representative of his native region. In 1980 he was appointed by KHOMEINI to be responsible for the important evening paper *Kayhan* and other publications. In 1982 he was appointed Minister of Education and Islamic Instruction in the government of Mir-Hossein Moussavi. During the ten years that he served in this capacity, he contributed to the advancement of culture, literature and art. However, he was forced to resign in 1992 under pressure of conservative clerics. He was appointed by the pragmatic President RAFSANJANI as his advisor and chairman of the national library. He continued to teach political theory at the University of Tehran. After 1996 he also served as a member of the Supreme Council of the Cultural Revolution, whose task was to adapt the educational institutions in Iran to the regime's religious-ideological stance.

In the elections to the Presidency in 1997, Khatami obtained sixty-nine percent of the votes, even though the spiritual leader of Iran and the institutions of the regime supported the conservative candidate NATEK-NOURI. Khatami was the joint candidate of the pragmatists and the nationalists who had been pushed aside in the previous years by the conservative stream, and many youngsters and women voted for him.

Commentators viewed this as a protest vote against the coercive methods of the regime.

Khatami's victory was welcomed by most states and especially Iran's Arab neighbors. In his election campaign he had called for a move away from adventures in foreign relations. Nevertheless, he refused to call for a renewal of relations with the US and strongly attacked ISRAEL.

KHOMEINI, AYATULLAH SAYYID RUHULLAH MUSSAVI (1912–1989)

Iranian Shi'i spiritual and political leader of the Islamic Revolution, 1979, founder of the Islamic Republic of Iran. Born in Khomein in the Isfahan region to a clergyman (who was murdered when Khomeini was five months old). At the age of six, he knew the Qur'an by heart. In 1917 he began studying theology with his eldest brother, Ayatullah Murteza Pasandideh, and from 1921 he studied in QOM. He completed his studies in 1926 and began his career as an Islamic cleric. He soon gained a reputation as a brilliant teacher of theology.

In the early 1940s, he published his first political book, *The Key to Secrets*, and continued to teach at the Greater Fayzieh Seminary. Khomeini was drawn into Islamic political activities, e.g., campaigns against a law allowing non-Muslims to run for local councils. That law was canceled, but the Shah's reforms, known as the "White Revolution," caused further protests from the clerical leadership, escalating, from about March 1963 and after harsh measures to suppress it, into a violent anti-Shah movement. After the death of the top Shi'i leader Ayatullah Borujerdi in 1962, Khomeini became the main leader of this movement. He was arrested and in 1964 was exiled. He went to TURKEY and then to IRAQ, directing the struggle against the Shah from his exile.

Late in 1977, Khomeini began calling himself IMAM—the highest, sacred appellation for Shi'i ISLAM which had not been applied to anyone for many centuries, and he ordered an escalation of the Islamic revolution. The Iraqis considered his activities dangerous and expelled him. In 1978 he was given refuge in FRANCE and set up headquarters near Paris. The Shah's regime collapsed in early 1979 and Khomeini triumphantly returned to Tehran in February 1979 and took over the supreme leadership of Iran. At first he set up a provision government headed by Mehdi BAZARGAN. The following month, Khomeini proclaimed the foundation of the Islamic Republic. It would be based on the ideology of pure Islam, as interpreted by him and his followers, and would provide remedies to all of society's ills. The Republic would be led by a selected master of Islamic religious law and jurisprudence (*Wilayat al-Faqih*); according to Khomeini's book *Islamic Governance* (*Hokamat-e Eslami*, 1970), the clerical leaders, whom he saw as the legitimate rulers, should guide the affairs of state (e.g., lay down guidelines in their Friday sermons). A new Constitution reflecting their principles was drafted under Khomeini's guidance and endorsed by plebiscite in December 1979. Khomeini himself was the undisputed "Savant Guide" (*Wali Faqih*) or "Revolutionary Leader" (*Rahbar*), above the institutions of state and government.

Khomeini and his regime ruthlessly and bloodily suppressed any opposition—actual or potential. Khomeini himself was the ultimate arbiter of all issues in doubt or dispute (e.g., the constant factional wrangle between hard-liners and "moderates" within the new political and religious establishment; the division of powers between the various government institutions and Councils of "Guardians" and "Experts;" and the problem of determining his successor). In June 1981 he dismissed President Bani SADR (he formally "guided" Parliament to vote him unfit) and saw to it that the new Head of State would be a man fully loyal to him (KHAMENEI). Khomeini also decided on matters of foreign policy—Iran's hard aggressive line against the US ("the Big Satan"), its refusal to yield to Iraq's demands and invasion, even at the price of a cruel eight-year war in his quest for building the Islamic regime in Iran. He viewed nationalism as an "imperialist plot" to divide the Muslim world. He also advocated and initiated the export of his Islamic revolution, his model of an Islamic society to other countries. Even by force or subversion, Khomeini never challenged the very idea of nation states or the existing regional order of separate Islamic states. Khomeini's ten-year rule immersed Iran in a grave international crisis—internal and external. However, the country stood firm and until his death in June 1989 no one, except for some revolutionary guerrillas and exiles, dared question the supreme guidance and leadership of the Imam.

al-KHULI LUTFI, AHMAD (b. 1929)

Egyptian writer, thinker and politician; born in Kalyubiyya district. He graduated from the Faculty of Law, University of Cairo (1949), practicing as a lawyer for sixteen years. Khuli edited the well-known leftist journal *al-Tali'a* (1965–1977). Since 1988, he has served as Chairman of the Asian and African Writers' Union and has been a member of the Board of Directors of the Mediterranean Studies Center. Previously, he was a leading voice expressing enmity to ISRAEL and critical of Egyptian peace relations with Israel. In the 1990s Khuli became an overt supporter of peace between Israel and its Arab neighbors. He took part in the Egyptian delegation to the Madrid Conference for Peace in the Middle East (1991), and became a co-founder of the Copenhagen Forum of the International Arab-Israel Peace Pact (January 1997). In this framework he visited Israel, and was subsequently dismissed from the *Tajammu'* left-wing party. Al Khuli is one of the prominent columnists in the semi-official *al-Ahram* daily, and in other Arab and international journals. He has also written a number of plays, novels and short stories, as well as books on Middle Eastern politics.

KLIBI, CHEDLI (al-Shadhily al-Qulaibi) (b. 1925) Former Tunisian minister and Secretary-General of the ARAB LEAGUE (1979–1990). A graduate of the Sorbonne in Arabic Literature, Klibi worked in the mid-1950s as a journalist and academician. In independent TUNISIA he served as Director General of Tunisian radio and television (1958–1961); Director of the Tunisian Ministry of Culture and Information (1971–1973); Minister of Cultural Affairs (1976–1978); and Minister of Information (1978–1979).

Klibi was appointed Secretary-General of the League of Arab states in June 1979, and served in this position until September 1990. His appointment followed Egypt's expulsion from the Arab League (after the signing of the 1979 Egyptian-Israeli peace treaty) and transfer of the oganization's secretariat general to Tunis, reflecting Tunisia's growing involvement in its work (see TUNISIA). Klibi's tenure marked the weakening of the Arab League and collective Arab action as a whole due to the absence of EGYPT and prolonged inter-Arab disputes (IRAQ-SYRIA, Syria-PLO, the Sahara conflict), the IRAN-IRAQ WAR, and Israel's war in LEBANON. As Secretary General, Klibi sought to preserve the Arab League's stature and prestige by offering his own (and other Arab

leading figures') services of conciliation and mediation within the framework of the Arab League. This was an attempt to mitigate and resolve inter-Arab conflicts and improve collective Arab action. He often referred to the need for the Arab League to play a more vital and effective role in contemporary issues, which would need amendments in the all-Arab organization's Charter and institutional structure.

Klibi resigned from his post in September 1990, following the Arab League's decision in March 1990 to transfer the League's secretariat back to Cairo. He denied being pressured by the Tunisian government to do so. Other reports tied his resignation to his stand *vis a vis* the August 1990 Iraqi invasion of KUWAIT, which he allegedly did not unequivocally denounce. This was reported to have angered other Arab states, in particular the Gulf monarchies at the time. Klibi is the author of several books on Islam and Arab culture.

KNESSET   see ISRAEL.

KOLLEK, TEDDY   see JERUSALEM.

KOMORO ISLANDS   see QAMARAN ISLAND.

KORUTÜRK, FAHRI (1903-1987) Turkish officer and politician, President of TURKEY 1973–1980. Born in Istanbul to an aristocratic family from eastern Anatolia, Korutürk graduated from the Naval Academy in 1923 and was sent to Germany for further study. Upon his return to Turkey, he graduated from the War College (1933) and served in the Navy, *inter alia* as naval attache in Germany (1937, and again in 1943), Greece, Italy, and Sweden. He became Commander of the Navy in 1959 with the rank of Admiral. After the military coup d'etat of 1960, he resigned from the armed forces to serve the new regime in political and diplomatic posts. He was ambassador to the USSR, 1960–1964, and to Spain, 1965–1966 (resigning due to poor health). In 1968 he was appointed to the Senate as an independent. In December 1971 he agreed (after much pressure) to become Prime Minister, but on condition that parliamentary elections be postponed for several years and the Prime Minister's authority be increased. These conditions were unacceptable to the Parties.

When in March 1973 the election of a new President ran into an impasse, Korutürk as a highly respected independent emerged as a compromise candidate and was elected President. After serving his seven-year term, he retired in 1980.

KURDISTAN DEMOCRATIC PARTY OF IRAN
see IRAN.

KURDS A nation inhabiting north-west IRAN, north-east IRAQ and east TURKEY—with some members also in north-east SYRIA and Soviet Transcaucasia (mainly Armenia). The Kurds have a long history; some identify their ancestors as the *Kuti* mentioned in Sumerian inscriptions of the third millennium B.C. and the Modes in ancient Iran. They speak an Indo-European tongue closely akin to Persian (and divided into several dialects). Most of the Kurds are SUNNI Muslims. They are divided into tribes, frequently engaged in internecine rivalry and violent struggles. Although they have never assumed territorial sovereignty, the Kurds have played leading roles in the history of the Middle East, (most notably Salah al-Din and his Ayyubid dynasty). After World War I the Kurdish claim for self-determination was ignored, then repressed, in the course of the competition over the dismantled OTTOMAN EMPIRE by BRITAIN, FRANCE and Turkey.

Kurdistan, the domicile of a population predominantly Kurdish in speech and consciousness, has never been defined precisely or formed a political unit. The predominantly Kurdish area covers about 135,000 sq. miles (350,000 sq. km.). However, many non-Kurds live within this area, and many Kurds outside it. There are large and long-established urban Kurdish communities in several cities outside Kurdistan, e.g., Baghdad, Basra, Aleppo and Damascus. (Some Iranian Shi'i tribes, e.g., the *Lurs* and *Bakhtiaris*, are thought by some to be of Kurdish origin, but are not usually considered Kurds; the non-Muslim YAZIDIS of *Jabal Sinjar* in Iraq speak Kurdish, but do not consider themselves Kurds and are not usually counted among them.)

Estimates of the total number of Kurds and their distribution among the states they inhabit differ significantly. However, a realistic estimate of the total number of the Kurds would be 24 million: 13 million in Turkey, 5 to 6 million in Iran, 3.5 million in Iraq, 800,000 in Syria and 150,000 in Armenia.

Kurdish sources tend to maintain higher estimates, totaling more than 26 million. The discrepancy between these two estimates results primarily from the lack of official statistics of the states concerned, which do not usually refer to Kurds as such. Particularly in Turkey, the term Kurds was until the early 1990s unused and unacceptable and the Kurds of eastern Turkey were often referred to as "Mountain Turks."

The tribal structure of the Kurdish people was until the mid-nineteenth century, organized in several local principalities under the nominal sovereignty of the Ottoman Sultan or the Shah of Iran. The mountainous nature of Kurdistan, divided into isolated valleys, meant that a modern Kurdish nationalist movement was late in coming. Toward the end of the nineteenth and the beginning of the twentieth centuries, Kurdish intelligentsia in Constantinople and later in Europe began working for a national revival, at first culturally and later politically too. Traditionally leading families, like the Badr Khan and Baban, who had recently lost their positions as local rulers, formed the nucleus and leadership of this national intelligentsia, founding the first Kurdish political societies and later parties. They had little or no effect in Kurdistan but gained a hearing in political circles in Europe. It was partly in response to their pleading that the victorious allied Entente powers, dismembering the Turkish-Ottoman Empire after World War I, envisaged an autonomous region of Kurdistan in eastern Anatolia and the Mosul province of what was to become Iraq, with an option for later independence. They included a provision for such a Kurdish entity in the abortive peace treaty of SÈVRES which they imposed on Turkey in 1920. But when Turkish nationalist resistance replaced that treaty with the new peace treaty of LAUSANNE, 1923, the provision for Kurdish autonomy or independence was dropped (no Kurdish representatives had been allowed to participate in the negotiations). In the Turko-British wrangle over the province of Mosul (following the establishment of Iraq by Britain in 1921), the problem of the Kurds and claim of autonomy was manipulated by the latter so as to keep the oil-rich region an integral part of Iraq. Thus, when the League of Nations Council finally awarded the province to Iraq in December 1925, it did so with the understanding that Kurdish national "distinctiveness and consciousness" would be recognized, that Kurds would play a leading role in the region's administration and that Kurdish would be a second official language there. The provision concerning Kurdish as an official language was formally reiterated by Iraq in the obligations it took upon itself in May 1932 before the League of Nations agreed to end the British Mandate and recognize Iraq's independence. Iraq did not fulfill these commitments to Kurdish satisfaction. In Turkey and Iran, no commitments were made for any kind of Kurdish semi-autonomy or the recognition of Kurdish national rights.

The fragmentation of Kurdistan, and the very different circumstances prevailing in Iraq, Iran and Turkey, caused a parallel fragmentation in the Kurdish nationalist movement. Most of the Kurdish associations and "parties" were formed in exile and remained unrepresented in, and unrepresentative of, the homeland. The first and main organization akin to a modern political party was *Khoibun* ("Independence"), founded in 1927 in Beirut. Its chief leaders were of the old princely Badr (Bedir) Khan clan, particularly Kamuran Aali Bedir-Khan. *Khoibun* remained essentially an organization of exiles, mostly in Europe; it was pro-Western and non-Socialist. *Khoibun* lost influence and waned when nationalist organizations began to grow in Kurdistan itself—such as the right-wing *Heva* ("Hope"; which claimed to have been founded before World War I) and the Marxist *Rizgari* ("Salvation") in Iraq, and the left-wing *Komala i-Zhian i-Kurdistan* ("Committee of Kurdish Resurrection") in Iran. Late in 1945 the Komala reconstituted itself in Mahabad as the "Kurdish Democratic Party" (KDP), which gradually emerged as the link between the sophisticated diaspora, the urbanized, de-tribalized Kurds with their educated, intellectual elements, and the incipient nationalist consciousness of the main part of the Kurdish nation, the tribes. The KDP, active in both Iran and Iraq, became the focus of Kurdish nationalism both institutionally and ideologically, with Mulla Mustafa BARZANI (or Barazani) as its main leader.

In Kemalist-nationalist Turkey, Kurdish distinctiveness and nationalist organizations remained underground, with little impact on the Kurdish tribal-rural rebellions of 1925, 1930 and 1937 that were ruthlessly suppressed. A measure of Kurdish unrest continued, and since the mid-1980s has intensified, growing into a near-constant semi-uprising that had resulted in the death of 22,000 people by mid-1997. In the early 1990s, President ÖZAL initiated a plan for a solution of the conflict based mainly on granting the Kurds cultural autonomy, but his untimely death brought about the scrapping of the plan (see PKK and TURKEY).

The Kurds are largest ethnic minority in Iran (5.6 million). The language they speak is similar to Persian, but they speak many dialects such as Guarani, Kermanshahi and Leki, and do not have a single central language. While about ninety percent of the population of Iran are Shi'is, most of the Kurds are SUNNIS. They live mainly in the mountainous areas of Iranian Kurdistan to the west of the state in the towns of Baneh, Sardasht, Saqqiz, Mahabad and Sanandaj, as well as in Kermanshah.

One of the first accomplishments of Reza Shah Pahlavi after his coup in 1921, was the suppression of Isma'il (Simko) Shikak, who had established for himself since 1919 an independent feudal regime in the Kurdish region, with the encouragement of the Soviet Union. Simko suffered a defeat in August 1921 and his tribal principality fell apart. Reza Shah fiercely suppressed the heads of the tribes, most of whom he exiled to Tehran, prohibiting the dissemination of the Kurdish language and culture. The Kurdish "autonomy" was totally defeated at the end of the 1930s and the population submitted to the Shah's control. In the following years, many of the tribal chiefs took advantage of the situation and registered the lands of the villages on their names, became rich and entered the political arena of Iran.

During the Second World War, when the Soviet Union conquered the district of Azerbaijan and the British operated in Southern Iran and in the Kermanshah district, the tribal chiefs started to return to their homes. The two powers competed to dominate the Kurds. A group of Kurdish leftists, consisting of young teachers, officials and *petit-bourgeois* in the town of Mahabad, took advantage of the situation, and in 1942 established a party called the *Komala-i Jiyanawi Kurdistan*, which engraved on its banner the slogan of struggle against both the central government and the tribal system. They established contacts with a Kurdish movement with a similar approach in Iraq called *Hiwa*. With encouragement from the Soviets, the movement's leadership was handed over to Qazi Muhammad, who in 1945 established in Iran the Kurdish Democratic

Party (KDPI) and the Komala ceased to operate. Qazi Muhammad announced in January 1946 the establishment of the independent Kurdish republic in Mahabad, which included the towns of Bukan, Naghdeh and Oshnavieh. Some of the tribal chiefs expressed support for this move. However, the leader of the Iraqi Kurds, Mulla Mustafa Barazani, joined the movement with 3,000 fighters. Even though the leaders of the Mahabad demanded autonomy only, the government of Tehran was convinced that the real intention was to establish an independent entity, and therefore vehemently objected to it. In May 1946, when the Soviet forces were forced to leave Iran under international pressure, the Iranian army entered Mahabad with the help of Kurdish fighters from other tribes. Qazi Muhammad was caught and executed and the short existence of the independent Kurdish republic came to an end. Mulla Mustafa refused to surrender and declined to return to Iraq, where he would have been hanged. He opened guerrilla warfare in the mountainous area in order to break through an escape route to the Soviet Union, where he arrived in June 1946.

The KDPI ceased its activities for many years. Mohammad Reza Shah continued the military administration in the whole of Kurdistan. However, in the 1960s, when the relations between Iran and Iraq became a serious crisis (see IRAN and IRAQ) and the movement of Mulla Mustafa urgently required external assistance, the Shah provided him with full assistance in return for his help in Iran to suppress the internal Kurdish movement.

In the years 1967–1968, when guerrilla activities inside Iran began by the Kurds, Mulla Mustafa detained and delivered the fighters who had escaped to Northern Iraq while fighting against the Iranian army.

During the Shah's White Revolution (see IRAN), which included the distribution of the lands of the landowners amongst the farmers, the social and political influence of the tribal chiefs, who had taken over lands in the region, declined and the urban population amongst the Kurds grew. These changes to a large extent broke up the traditional structure of the tribal society. However, from an economic point of view there was no significant improvement amongst the Kurds. Following the growth that swept Iran in the 1970s the Kurdish district was markedly deprived.

Due to the fact of the political suppression and economic discrimination by the Shah's regime, the Kurds were amongst the first groups that joined the movement of KHOMEINI to defeat the regime. Despite the fact that most of the Kurds were Sunnis, it was clear to them that Khomeini's goal was to establish an Islamic Shi'i regime in Iran. Before the revolution Khomeini repeatedly emphasized that there was no difference between the Shi'is and Sunnis, and created the impression that he would listen to the desires of the Kurds in Iran. Even though he never explicitly undertook to grant Kurdistan autonomy, the Kurdish leaders expected this in return for their contribution to the revolution. For a short period they enjoyed a certain degree of self-rule due to the disorder which existed during the first few months of the revolution. They were exceedingly disappointed when the declaration of a referendum regarding a new constitution declared that Shi'i ISLAM was the official religion of Iran.

When quiet protest activities and negotiations with the authorities failed, the Kurds once again prepared for battle. Their spiritual leader Sheikh Ezzeddin Hosseini continued to emphasize the fraternity amongst all the sections of Islam and their political leader Dr. Abdolrahman Ghassemlou announced that the demand was for autonomy—not independence. The government forces opened a massive attack. In August 1979 Khomeini took the supreme command over the armed forces into his hands, placed the Kurdish Democratic Party outside the law and sent Hojjat-ol Eslam Sadeq Khalkhali (known as "the Butcher") to Kurdistan, where he executed hundreds of Kurdish fighters.

Even though the revolt was fiercely suppressed, the guerrilla acts continued. The Kurds received help from the Iraqi government, which at the time was at war with Iran. After the IRAN-IRAQ WAR, the Iranian regime intensified the struggle against the Kurds, extending it outside the borders of Iran; carrying out raids against KDPI bases on Iraqi soil; liquidating the movement's leaders abroad and using the Kurds in Iraq against their brethren in Iran. Several times the Iranian forces carried out raids into the border areas with Iraq to liquidate KDPI camps. These raids intensified after the announcement of the Kurdish district in northern Iraq semi-autonomous areas following the GULF WAR. In addition, Iran received help to liquidate the Iranian Kurds from the Patriotic Union of Kurdistan of Iraq led by Jalal Talabani, in return for logistic and economic support which it had granted him in his struggle against the Kurdish Democratic Party of Iraq, led by Mass'oud BARAZANI. In 1969, while negotiating with the official emissary of Iran to settle the dispute, Ghassemlou, (the leader of the KDPI), was murdered in a terrorist attack in Vienna. Three years later, in September 1992, his heir Dr. Sadeq Sharafkandi was also murdered with three colleagues, during a conversation with a group of opposition activists in Berlin. Following an investigation, in 1997 the German government officially blamed leading Iranian figures for the assassination, causing a crisis in the relations between the two states (see IRAN).

In Iraq, nearly constant unrest marked the Kurdish region since the end of Turkish rule in 1918. At first, this unrest was linked to Turkish and British agitation among Kurdish tribes in their competition over the province of Mosul; but the unrest remained endemic even after the province had been officially recognized as part of Iraq (1925–1926) and Turkish agitation ceased. In its early years in Iraq, the British administration simultaneously encouraged a degree of de facto semi-autonomy whilst suppressing the rebellious tribes. In the 1920s and 1930s, several Kurdish uprisings occurred, although some Kurdish leaders collaborated with the HASHEMITE Iraqi government. In fact, the latter always contained one or several Kurdish Ministers—mainly from the urbanized Kurds, but sometimes also tribal leaders. (The urbanized elite was in any case of tribal origin and had tribal links.) The Kurds also received, during those years, several promises toward a degree of local autonomy (e.g., the Iraqi declaration of May 1932 referred to above); but these (hardly satisfactory steps in the first place) were never implemented. The main leader of the tribal unrest and rebellions in the 1920s and the early 1930s, was Sheikh Mahmud (al-Barzinji). In the 1930s the Barzanis became the chief leaders—first Sheikh Ahmad and then Mulla Mustafa. The struggle, entirely tribal at first, became increasingly "national," as the de-tribalized urban intelligentsia became more deeply involved. This synthesis of traditional-tribal and modern nationalist elements found its expression in Mulla Mustafa Barzani's assumption of the Presidency of the KDP in the 1940s. The association of the Iraqi KDP with the Kurdish Republic of Mahabad (1946) gave

further impetus to the nationalist struggle, triggering a new rebellion among the Iraqi Kurds, which was repressed by the Iraqi army.

Barzani was permitted to return to Iraq after the QASSEM coup of 1958. He and his men helped Qassem against both Nasserist and Communist attempts to overturn him, although Barzani was kept under surveillance in Baghdad. But Kurdish hopes for a settlement that would satisfy their national aspirations were frustrated by the Qassem regime, and unrest spread again. In 1960 Barzani escaped to his mountains, and in 1961 the Kurdish unrest turned into a full-fledged rebellion, which the Iraqi armed forces were unable to liquidate, partly because of the help it received from Iran, as described. Barzani reportedly also received aid from Israel. The Iraqis established irregular units from among Kurdish tribes hostile to the Barzanis and encouraged rival factions, e.g., one set up by Jalal Talabani, a former lieutenant of Mulla Mustafa. The impact of these rival groups on the struggle was insignificant.

During the years of the rebellion, negotiations were intermittently conducted, aiming to end the revolt and achieve Kurdish-Iraqi reconciliation on the basis of an agreed autonomy for the Kurds. In June 1966, an agreement was reached with Prime Minister al-Bazzaz. It envisaged a partial de facto autonomy for the Kurdish provinces, to be based on a general de-centralization of Iraq's administration; the use of the Kurdish language in local government and education; a fair, proportional share for the Kurds in government, army, civil service, and national revenues; and freedom of Kurdish political organization (with a secret clause reportedly permitting the Kurdish rebel forces, the *Pesh Merga*, to remain intact as a militia). The agreement, however, was never implemented due to strong opposition within the Iraqi ruling elite, entangling Bazzaz in trouble over it. The cease-fire it entailed was never completed, and in 1968 a full-fledged rebellion resumed.

This pattern repeated itself in the 1970s. In March 1970, full agreement was reached with the government, now of the BA'TH Party with Saddam HUSSEIN as the "strong man" of the regime. The new agreement went even further than that of 1966. It formally recognized the existence of a Kurdish nation as one of the two nations forming Iraq. The local autonomy granted, and the use of the Kurdish language envisaged, were wider than in the previous agreement. A Kurdish Region was to be formed by the primarily Kurdish areas, i.e., the three districts of Suleimaniyya, Arbil and Dohuk (the last one newly created in 1969–1970 out of the Kurdish northern parts of Mosul province). A "High Committee" was to supervise the implementation of these measures. The leading officials in the Kurdish areas were to be Kurds; a Kurd was to be named Vice-President of Iraq, and Kurds were to be appointed to the Revolutionary Command Council; Kurds were to be represented proportionally in parliament, government—and reportedly (informally) also in the army and the civil service. Kurdish military forces were to be dissolved (but a secret clause allegedly permitted the retention of some 10,000 to12,000 *Pesh Merga* as border guards or militias). The agreement was to be fully implemented within four years.

The recognition of the Kurdish nation as one of Iraq's two nations was incorporated (as agreed) in Iraq's new provisional Constitution of July 1970. Five KDP-nominated ministers joined the government of Iraq. A Kurdish University in Suleimaniyya commenced its first courses; the preparation of Kurdish-language instruction in the Kurdish-majority areas and of Kurdish textbooks started; Kurdish broadcasts and Kurdish publications were taken in hand. The leader proposed by the KDP as Vice-President of Iraq was rejected. No Kurds were nominated to the Revolutionary Council and there was no progress in the installation of a Kurdish semi-autonomous administration in the Kurdish districts and in the Kurdish Region envisaged to embrace them. Moreover, there was persistent disagreement on the delimitation of that Kurdish Region, especially concerning its western and southern boundaries in the Mosul and Kirkuk areas. For Kirkuk, it had been informally agreed that a census would be taken to determine which parts of the district had a Kurdish majority. This census was delayed, and the Kurds claimed that the government was deporting Kurds from the disputed area and replacing them with Arabs. The share of the Kurdish Region in Iraq's revenue (mainly the oil revenue derived in large part from the region) was also in dispute. Additionally, the cease-fire was not fully maintained. Barzani and his associates were convinced that all this derived from ill will of the government and its deliberate sabotage of the agreement. Tension mounted again with

the government encouraging Kurdish anti-Barzani factions to re-emerge.

When in March 1974 the deadline came for full implementation of the autonomy agreement, the government unilaterally began implementing the measures it had designated. The KDP neither approved, nor co-operated with this and the districts of Mosul and Kirkuk were excluded. The five KDP Ministers, and the Kurdish Governors of Arbil, Dohuk and Suleimaniyya, resigned and went to the mountains. The rebellion re-erupted. Iraq's new Kurdish Region was established with collaborators and anti-Barzani factions only. In April 1974 a Kurdish Vice-President was appointed (Taha Muhyi al-Din Ma'ruf), and in September-October an Executive Council, headed by Hashem al-Aqrawi. In addition, a sixty-member Regional Council (at first with nine seats left vacant for KDP representatives) was appointed for the semi-autonomous Kurdish Region proclaimed. In the 1980 and 1984 elections for the Iraqi National Assembly, the Kurds of that region—no longer called "Kurdish" in official parlance—elected twenty-six members of that assembly (which would be much less than its proportional share) and, simultaneously, also elected their Regional Council. There were Kurdish ministers in the government, and a pro-government section of the KDP was part of the *Ba'th*-led ruling National Front. At the same time, the rebellious parts of the tribes and the KDP were ruthlessly suppressed. These operations were, so Kurdish spokesmen claimed, not confined to actual rebels, but amounted to a comprehensive suppression of the Kurds in general, including the forcible transfer of Kurdish population from the Kurdish areas and their replacement by Arabs, large-scale arrests and executions.

The Kurdish rebellion that was renewed in 1974 again had shifting military fortunes, but it managed to tie down considerable Iraqi forces without being fully suppressed. The rebellion collapsed only when the Shah of Iran (following his March 1975 agreement with Iraq) stopped his aid to the rebels and denied them the use of Iranian territory as a supply base and staging ground. The *Pesh Merga* disintegrated, its leaders fled (including Mulla Mustafa Barzani who died in 1979 in the USA where he had lived as a refugee). Most of its fighters sought refuge in Iran. The number of Kurdish refugees to Iran was reportedly 200,000. When they began drifting back (under an amnesty) they were allegedly not permitted to go back to the Kurdish region but transferred to Arab areas in the South.

In the late 1970s Mulla Mustafa's sons (Mas'ud and Idris Barzani) tried to rekindle the rebellion and rebuild the Pesh Merga. But the movement was split and in confusion. Parts of the KDP (including another Barzani brother, Ubaid-ullah) collaborated with the government. Talabani revived his rival faction, now calling it "Patriotic Union" (PUK); and Idris and Mas'ud themselves were at loggerheads. Syria, in conflict with Iraq, apparently supported the rebels, especially the Talabani faction, but kept a low profile. However, after the Iran-Iraq Warr broke out in September 1980, Khomeini's Iran resumed a degree of aid to the rebels in Iraq. The Barzani-KDP collaboration with Khomeini alienated the Iranian KDP branch led by Abd-ul-Rahman Qassemlou, then in a state of rebellion against the Khomeini regime. The Iraqi KDP rebels also joined in a "National Front" of several anti-government organizations underground and in exile. The Iraqis (who could ill afford to divert parts of their army for the fight against the rebels) tried to win Talabani and his PUK as collaborators and partners. Yet talks, from 1982 broke down in 1984–1985, and from early 1985 Talabani and his group rejoined the rebellion, though not in co-operation with the Barzanis' KDP. Some of Iraq's Kurdish collaborators also defected and joined the rebel camp.

Following the failure of the Iraqi-PUK negotiations, a *rapprochement* began between the PUK and the KDP, which resulted in an understanding in July 1987 on the creation of the Iraqi-Kurdistan front. The front included (besides the KDP and the PUK) some other, smaller Kurdish groups such as the Socialist Party of Kurdistan in Iraq and the Kurdistan Popular Democratic Party (KPDP). The front declared its main goals to be the temination of the Ba'th regime, the formation of a genuinely democratic government in Iraq, and the development of a federal status for the Kurds in Iraq.

However, during this period, the Iraqi regime transferred significant forces from southern Iraq to Kurdistan, engaging in massive, indiscriminate attacks against the Kurdish population. These attacks included the use of chemical warfare resulting (in the case of Halabje, March 1988) in the death of as many as 5,000 people. Following an additional chem-

ical attack in August 1988, large numbers of Kurds escaped to Turkey and Iran. The cease-fire between Iran and Iraq in 1988 that ended the war between the two countries effectively dampened any Kurdish hopes of independence.

The Iraqi invasion of Kuwait in August 1990, and the GULF WAR that followed, raised the hopes of the Kurds. Cautious at first, the Kurds followed President Bush's call to overthrow Saddam Hussein's regime and together with the Shi'ites in the south, rebelled in March 1991. In early and mid-March, most of the major cities in Kurdistan such as Arbil, Sulaymaniya, Zakho and Kirkuk fell into Kurdish hands. The success, however, was short-lived. After repressing the Shi'ite rebellion in the south, Saddam turned his modern army northward. The US chose not to interfere at first, apparently against the backdrop of proclaimed Turkish objection to the division of Iraq. By April 1991, Saddam had succeeded in reconquering the lost territories. The Iraqi invasion caused another wave of Kurdish refugees (about 500,000) to flow to areas near the Turkish border. Turkey (fearing that the entrance of half a million Kurds to Turkey might cause domestic instability) initiated a plan for the creation of "safe enclaves" in Northern Iraq. Later modified to "safe havens" the proposal established a "non-fly zone" beyond the thirty-sixth parallel, prohibiting Iraqi aircraft from flying beyond that line. The plan was supported by Britain, the US and France which established (along with Turkey), a force named "Provide Comfort" to supervise the program's implementation. Concomitantly, the Kurds conducted negotiations with the regime in Baghdad on the establishment of an autonomy. The negotiations were a failure because the Iraqis presented severe demands to the Kurds that included the disbandment of all Kurdish military militias, handover of radio stations to the central regime, and additional issues such as the status of Kirkuk.

Following the failure of the negotiations with Baghdad, elections were held in the Kurdish region. A regional Kurdish government with the participation of both parties was established in northern Iraq in 1992. However, the traditional squabbles over territories and political influence brought about a renewal of the battles between the PUK and the KDP in May 1994. While Talabani was supported by Iran and Syria, Barzani maintained secret ties with the Iraqi regime, and a more overt alliance with the Turkish government.

A number of cease-fires were achieved by international mediators but they were short-lived. In August 1996 a new outburst of the conflict between the two erupted. Barzani (who feared a change in the balance of power in the region following the extensive Iranian military aid to the PUK) together with Saddam Hussein and the help of the Iraqi army, conquered Arbil, capital of the Kurdish region, which had been under PUK rule since December 1994. He also captured most of the areas which had been traditionally under PUK influence, including Sulimaniya, the PUK center. After a while, Talabani managed to retrieve most of the territories that had been lost, except Arbil. In October 1996, US pressure led to a cease-fire and the two warring parties sat down at the negotiating table under the auspices of Turkey, the US and Britain. Despite certain progress achieved, some central issues such as the status of Arbil and the sharing of revenues from the Khabour border-pass, still remained serious obstacles to the conclusion of a comprehensive political agreement between the Parties that would enable a functioning autonomous Kurdish administration.

KUWAIT Emirate at the northwestern corner of the PERSIAN GULF, bordering IRAQ in the north and SAUDI ARABIA in the east. Kuwait also owns two islands—Bubian and Warba—in the northern part of the Gulf. These were for many years a matter of contention with Iraq (see below).

The emirate's population grew rapidly along with the development of oil resources since the first estimates of population (1910) which mentioned about 35,000 residents. Official census has been held at regular intervals since 1957. The first official figure was 206,000, reflecting the transformation of Kuwait into a major oil producing country. In 1985 the population increased to over 1.7 million. The 1990 figure was 2.1 million, of which seventy-three percent were non-Kuwaiti residents. Post-war estimates (1996) estimated the total number at less than 2 million reflecting the departure of many foreigners.

Until World War II and the beginning of oil production, Kuwait was a small, poor settlement of BEDOUIN, fishermen, pearl divers and boat builders, with a negligible population. But, situated on the Bay of Kuwait, the only deep-water bay in the Gulf,

it had a natural port. It thus acquired an important strategic role as a potential gateway to Iraq and the Arabian peninsula. For this reason, Germany intended, at the end of the nineteenth century, to extend the planned Baghdad Railway to the Bay of Kuwait. BRITAIN saw these plans as a threat to its domination of the Persian Gulf and its route to India. Beyond foiling the railway extension scheme, in 1899 it agreed with the Sheikh of Kuwait to place his realm under British protection—though the Ottoman Sultan's nominal sovereignty was not formally abolished. Under this Protectorate, Britain conducted Kuwait's foreign affairs, supervising its administration, law and order. After the OTTOMAN EMPIRE entered World War I, in November 1914, Britain recognized Kuwait as independent under British protection. The Protectorate remained in effect until 1961, when Kuwait became fully independent, under its Sheikh of the House of SABAH, now styling himself Emir.

The discovery of oil changed Kuwait's fortunes; caused rapid development and made it immensely rich. An oil concession was granted in 1934 to the "Kuwait Oil Co.," a 50:50 partnership of the Anglo-Iranian Oil Co. and the (American) Gulf Oil Co. Oil was discovered on the eve of World War II, but production began only after the war, in 1946. Production rose rapidly, as did oil revenues (see OIL). The concessionaire company was taken over, in stages, and by 1975 was fully nationalized. By the mid-1990s Kuwait's proved crude oil reserves stood at about ten percent of world reserves. Most of Kuwait's oil is processed locally and exported as refined products.

Kuwait's economy is almost exclusively dependent on oil revenues. During the 1970s, oil revenues led to tremendous economic development. Kuwait City and its suburbs, where nearly ninety percent of the population live, have become a richly developed modern urban conglomeration. An extensive network of modern roads was built, along with a large international airport. Kuwait has become an international finance and banking center (a development intensified by the decline of Beirut since the late 1970s, but not without problems—such as the growth of an "unofficial," shady stock exchange, whose billion-dollar collapse in 1982 shook Kuwait's economy). Extensive deposits and investments abroad were estimated in the 1980s at over 70 billion dollars and by some at 100 billion dollars. This included various business activities in international banking and finance; participation in foreign industrial and commercial enterprises; real estate; hotels etc. These yielded revenues of several billion dollars per annum. The relative failure of diversification efforts worsened Kuwaitian economic conditions in the 1980s. The 1990 invasion added to Kuwaitian troubles. Extensive damage was inflicted on the oil industry. This was eventually repaired by 1994 with Kuwait returning to pre-war production. The combined effect of the slow-down in world oil markets caused continuous deficits in the Kuwaitian balance of payments. The large investment needed to reconstruct Kuwait's infrastructure left the state in need of economic reforms.

Another change in Kuwait's socioeconomic status was the issue of foreign labor. With its economic development, oil riches, and a high national income per capita, Kuwait has become in the 1970s a top-rate welfare state providing a variety of services to its residents free of charge or at a symbolic fee. As Kuwait's economy developed and expanded, it increasingly needed labor, and the population grew rapidly. This was primarily by migrant laborers from abroad: Palestinians, Jordanians, Egyptians, Iraqis, Yemenis, Iranians, Indians and Pakistanis. The share of foreigners in the total population grew steadily: from thirty-five to forty percent in 1957; to fifty-three percent in 1970 and fifty-nine percent in 1980. The largest foreign group were Palestinians—nearly twenty percent of the population. Foreigners were not only a majority of the labor force, but they occupied key positions. In the 1960s, nearly fifty percent of the civil service, and eighty percent of the teachers, were foreign Arabs, mainly Palestinians and Egyptians. This vast presence of foreigners resulted in growing tension with the autocratic regime which objected to granting any civic or voting rights. Their grievances escalated during the recession of the 1980s. Moreover, foreign Arabs, and particularly Palestinians, were presumed to be the main reservoir for radical and subversive groups, as was manifested by the overwhelming support Iraq was given by this population during the 1990 invasion. Another source of concern for the regime was the SHI'A Iranian presence, especially after the 1979 Iranian revolution. The indigenous and Iranian Shi'ites combined constituted in the late 1980s approxi-

mately twenty-five to thirty percent of the population. The deportation of illegal or undesirable foreigners that had begun in 1979–1980 was stepped up during the 1980s, and no effort was made to call back the workers leaving in 1990–1991. On the contrary, the Kuwaitian regime conducted a systematic policy of expulsion of most of the 400,000 Palestinians who resided in Kuwait until the Iraqi invasion—and of whom only 15,000–20,000, remained. This allegedly was on the grounds of collaboration with the Iraqi occupation. In fact, the Kuwaitian regime evicted the state of a foreign, destabilizing element, regardless of its Arab identity.

Kuwait's emergence into independence proceeded along with its growing economic viability in the course of the 1950s. In 1960, the Sheikh's government began taking over departments that had been in British hands (Finance, Justice). In April 1961 Kuwait established its own currency, the Kuwaiti Dinar, to replace the Indian Rupee. In June 1961 the British Protectorate was abrogated. Kuwait was proclaimed fully independent, arousing Iraq's claim that it rightfully owned Kuwait. The Iraqi claim was based, *inter alia*, on an Anglo-Ottoman draft agreement of 1913, which was never ratified. This described Kuwait as part of the Ottoman vilayet (province) of Basra, i.e., the land that later became Iraq. Similar claims had been made several times in the 1930s, but had not been pressed as long as Kuwait was under British protectorate. Iraq's declaration in 1961 included an implied threat of occupation by force. Kuwait immediately requested Britain to return its military forces and lodged a complaint with the UN Security Council. The renewed presence of British forces caused the Soviet Bloc and leftist-neutralist countries to take a position against Kuwait. Iraq complained to the Security Council that British military intervention threatened it and violated Kuwait's alleged independence, while it, Iraq, had no intention of using force. The Security Council was deadlocked when a resolution recognizing Kuwait's independence was vetoed by the USSR in July 1961 and an appeal for the withdrawal of British troops, sponsored by the UNITED ARAB REPUBLIC (UAR), failed to secure a majority. However, that same month, the ARAB LEAGUE entitled Kuwait to membership, thus recognizing its independence (Iraq walked out in protest and boycotted the League until 1963). It also set up a joint Arab force to defend Kuwait. Recognized by the Arab states and symbolically defended by an Arab peace force, Kuwait's independence seemed assured. In September, the Amir asked Britain to withdraw its troops. Britain responded immediately and the withdrawal was completed by October 1961. In November, however, Kuwait's application for UN membership was vetoed by the USSR.

With the immediate Iraqi threat removed, and following contacts with Iraq, Kuwait asked the Arab League in 1962 to reduce the Arab peace force to a token contingent and then to withdraw it altogether. It was dissolved and withdrawn early in 1963. In October 1963 (following the overthrow of the QASSEM regime in February), Iraq recognized Kuwait's independence. At the same time it received a grant of 84 million dollars from Kuwait. Iraqi objections to Kuwait's UN membership, and the Soviet veto, had been withdrawn even before. In May 1963 Kuwait was admitted to the UN. It had agreed in March 1963 to establish full diplomatic relations with the USSR—the first Persian Gulf country to do so.

There remained an unresolved border dispute between Kuwait and Iraq, both on the mainland and, particularly, over various branching western outlets of the SHATT al-Arab and the islands created by them. Iraq was especially interested in securing control of the islands of Bubiyan and Warba—either by full possession or, at least, by a lease and agreed occupation. Though this was not agreed upon, the presence of Iraqi troops on Bubiyan and elsewhere on Kuwaiti territory was reported several times. The border dispute led to several armed confrontations, and even clashes—in 1973 and 1976. In 1977, a provisional standstill agreement was achieved, and in November 1984 a fuller border accord was reported. In retrospect this agreement resulted from Iraqi dependence on Kuwaiti subsidies during the war with IRAN. Nonetheless, Kuwait's fortunes, along with Iraq's strategic predicament at terminating the war with Iran in 1988, motivated Baghdad's decision to invade Kuwait in early August 1990. All international efforts, including UN resolutions, failed to convince Iraq to retreat from Kuwait. In January 1991 a multi-national military coalition of foreign powers under US command, including some Arab states, launched an offensive against Iraqi forces in Kuwait and Iraq. By late February 1991 Kuwait was liberated from Iraq's occupation and, shortly after,

its rulers returned and resumed their sovereign power. The war came to a formal end in November 1994 by the Iraqi acceptance of UN Security Council Resolutions 687 (1991), 773 (1993), and 883 (1993) defining the permanent border between the two countries. With that, Iraq formally surrendered its claim to the Bubiyan and Warbah islands as well.

Kuwait's foreign policy was shaped by its complex national security dilemmas. This came from both domestic—large foreign migrant population, mostly Arab—and regional threats from powers, primarily Iraq and Iran. Kuwait's ruling elite, fully aware of those threats, manoeuvered through vast use of its financial resources. Thus, despite its conservative character and interests, Kuwait was, since its independence, emphatically neutralist. Kuwait's need to balance Iraq's threat to its independent existence made it necessary to foster close relations with Baghdad's Arab rivals, especially Egypt (in the 1960s) and Syria (in the 1980s). In the ARAB-ISRAEL CONFLICT Kuwait usually adhered to a militant line which would meet Palestinian and Arab confrontation states' expectations.

It was the disintegration of the USSR and the formation of the war-coalition by the US that eventually made Kuwait fully identify with the US in its foreign affairs. This change in Kuwaiti policies brought to an end an uneasy era between the two countries. Getting no full satisfaction from the US and the West for what it considered its needs for arms and military equipment, it contracted, from the late 1970s, for the supply of sophisticated arms systems from the USSR.

Kuwait also had to manoeuver a complex neutral policy between Iraq and Iran—an exercise that became increasingly difficult in the context of the Iran-Iraq War. Its sympathies were no doubt with Iraq and it afforded that country large-scale financial aid in the form of grants and credits; the assurance of supplies, and help in channeling Iraqi oil imports and exports (since Iraq's facilities on the Gulf were paralyzed and largely destroyed). Despite its official neutral stance in the IRAN-IRAQ WAR (1980–1988), Kuwait's geographic proximity to Iran and its oil-based economy made it extremely vulnerable to both Shi'a subversive activity and external threats, aggravated by the GULF WAR, to its national security as well as to its oil production and export. Kuwait was first alarmed when in December 1983 a series of car bombs, mainly against American targets, revealed the presence of terrorist cells— apparently linked to the Iranian-inspired Lebanese HIZBALLAH, radical Shi'a organization whose actions in Kuwait corresponded to its suicidal bombings against the multi-national forces (Americans and French) in Beirut. More terrorist attacks occurred in 1985, apparently Iranian-inspired. The stalemate that had prevailed in the Iran-Iraq War in 1986 resulted in the widening of hostilities between the two countries, including indiscriminate attacks on oil tankers in the Gulf. This led Kuwait to appeal to the United States and other European countries for flagging its tankers to protect them and then to be escorted by Western naval forces. In 1987 Kuwait became a target of missile attacks from Iran, on grounds of extending support to Iraq, exacerbating Kuwait's resort to Western protection.

Kuwait took a neutral position in inter-Arab politics, too, sometimes offering itself as a mediator. Yet, despite its concern about external interference in its domestic affairs by radical Arabs—Nasserists, Palestinians, or others—and subversive elements inside Kuwait, it usually took a rather radical line in its verbal, declarational postures. Kuwait also used its financial resources to buy off the potential threat of radical Arab countries or organizations. A "Kuwaiti Fund for Arab Economic Development," established in 1962 with capital that was constantly increased (authorized capital, since 1980, 2,000 million dollars working capital—over 3,500 million dollars), disbursed easy credits to most Arab states to the tune of hundreds of millions each year. Kuwait also used its reserves for direct governmental aid in large sums. It contributed over 150 million dollars per annum to Egypt and Jordan after 1967, following the Khartoum Arab Summit's decision to aid the countries confronting Israel; 400 million dollars per annum after 1973–1974, to the confrontation states and Palestinian organizations; 550 million dollars per annum (other reports speak of 340 million dollars per annum) after 1978 (Egypt now excluded). Large additional sums, with no details published, were given until 1990 directly to Palestinian institutions in the West Bank and Gaza Strip as well as to the PLO. Kuwait also paid a large share in other aid funds, such as that set up by the Arab oil producers—the Arab Fund for Economic and Social Development; the Arab-African Development Bank

and Fund, and various international funds and organizations. Sometimes it used its aid for political pressure. It suspended its aid to Jordan in 1970 out of solidarity with the Palestinian guerrillas. Its National Assembly several times resolved to withhold aid to Syria which had never materialized. Following the plunge of oil prices after 1982, Kuwait was reportedly withholding parts of the collective support to the confrontation states and the Palestinians decided upon by the summit conference of Baghdad in 1978.

The regime and government of Kuwait remained by and large conservative in its practices of government. However, in some respects Kuwait represented a unique case among the Gulf monarchies. In 1961, first elections were held (men only) for a Constituent Assembly. A Constitution was promulgated in 1962. This provided for a constitutional monarchy, with a single-house fifty-member Parliament (with Ministers added ex-officio). It was elected for a four-year term by the male suffrage (a restriction that has remained in force, since the National Assembly rejected several attempts to grant voting rights to women). As only citizens could vote, the electorate has remained very small—57,000 or 3.5% of the population in 1985. The First National Assembly was elected in 1963, and elections were duly held in 1967, 1971 and 1975. Those elected were in the majority conservative supporters of the Amir and his government, with left-inclined radicals and Nasserists winning a few seats. Yet, the Assembly gradually became assertive and independent, pressing the government for more radical policies (e.g. concerning the nationalization of foreign oil interests and inter-Arab positions). By 1975–1976, about one third of its members were considered "uncooperative" and oppositional. In August 1976, the Assembly was dissolved, parts of the Constitution being suspended. In 1981 the Constitution was reactivated. National Assembly elections were held that year and in 1985. Political parties were not permitted, and the composition of the Assembly remained basically unchanged. Most of the fifty elected members were conservative and pro-government, with a few nationalist "radicals" and a few Islamic fundamentalists. The Assembly as a whole tended to assert its independence. In July 1986 this assertiveness and a dispute with the government again led to the dissolution of the Assembly, with no date set for new elections. The Emir ended this suspension by holding new elections in 1992. This demonstrated his gratitude for US efforts during the war and commitment to resume democratic practices. Nevertheless, US human rights reports state that political parties and private associations are still banned and that limitations on women's rights remain in place. Even after the war, reports regarding opposition activity in Kuwait surface at times. The Kuwaiti Party of God (*Hizballah*), an underground Shi'a organization linked to Iran, has been active in post-Iraq-occupation Kuwait. With the coalition victory, executive powers were returned to the hands of the ruling AL-SABAH dynasty, whose members continue to hold key ministerial posts and most of the major executive positions.

The dynasty itself is divided into two branches, the Jaber al-Sabah and the Salem al-Sabah branches, who have since 1915 alternated in power, with a certain rivalry. The Jaber branch ruled 1915–1916, 1921–1950, and since 1978; the Salem branch—1916–1921 and 1950–1977.

Since 1965 the head of the branch not holding the Amirate has served as Crown Prince and Prime Minister.

L

LAHAD, ANTUAN   see SOUTH LEBANON ARMY.

LATIN   CHRISTIANS of what in European languages is called the Roman Catholic rite are in ARABIC called Latin, while the term "Roman Catholic," (*Rum Katholik* in Arabic), designates the GREEK CATHOLICS.

LAUSANNE CONFERENCE   see ARAB-ISRAEL PEACEMAKING.

LAUSANNE, TREATY OF   A Peace Treaty signed on 24 July 1923 after eight months of negotiations between TURKEY and its World War I enemies: BRITAIN, FRANCE, Italy, Japan, Greece, Yugoslavia and Rumania. The Treaty replaced the SÈVRES TREATY signed in 1920 by the Ottoman government and invalidated after the Turkish nationalists' successful military struggle against the dismemberment of their homeland and the restriction of its sovereignty. In the Treaty, Turkey renounced all claims over the non-Turkish provinces of the former OTTOMAN EMPIRE, but its full sovereignty in Anatolia was reconfirmed. The clauses in the Treaty of Sèvres concerning Greek administration in Izmir, Armenian independence in eastern Anatolia and Kurdish autonomy, were all dropped. Turkey undertook to safeguard minority rights and arranged (in a separate agreement with Greece) a Greek-Turkish exchange of populations. Turkey retained control of eastern Thrace and the Aegean Islands of Imbros and Tenedos. The capitulations (privileges to European citizens in the Empire) were abolished, as were the Ottoman Public Debt Administration and some pre-war foreign concessions and contracts.

The new Convention of the Straits, in the formulation of which the USSR also played a part (though did not sign it), was added to the Treaty. This stipulated freedom of navigation for all merchant vessels and warships with certain limitations in the event of Turkey being at war, and made restrictions on the forces of non-riparian states allowed into the Black Sea. Although the Straits were under full Turkish sovereignty, Turkey agreed to their demilitarization and supervision by an international Straits Commission. The rival claims of Turkey and Britain (acting as the mandatory power on IRAQ) to the Province of Mosul were not resolved in Lausanne but left for future negotiations and arbitration (settled in 1926 in favor of Britain). The Treaty represented a great victory for the Turkish nationalists—nearly all of whose demands were met. Additionally, it allowed Turkey to devote its subsequent years to internal reform and modernization.

There was another less famous Treaty of Lausanne signed in October 1912 after the war between the Ottoman Empire and Italy. This followed the Italian invasion of Tripolitania (LIBYA), in which the empire agreed to withdraw its forces and in fact renounced its possession of Libya (though it never did so *de jure*). The Ottoman Sultan was, however, to be represented in Tripoli in his capacity of *Khalifa* (CALIPH) of all Muslims.

LEAGUE OF ARAB STATES see ARAB LEAGUE.

LEBANON   Republic on the eastern coast of the
Mediterranean ("the LEVANT"), bordering on SYRIA
in the east and north, ISRAEL in the south, and the
Mediterranean in the west. Its official name is the Republic of Lebanon and its population numbers approximately 3.1 million (1996 limited census),
excluding 350,000 Palestinian refugees and about
the same number of foreign migrant workers, mainly Syrians. The population is overwhelmingly Arab,
i.e., Arabic-speaking (ninety-five percent—four percent ARMENIANS and one percent other), but composed of many ethno-religious communities, none
of which constitutes a majority. Although some districts have traditionally been the mainstay of a specific ethno-religious community, they are far from
being homogeneous, presenting a constant source
of intercommunal conflict. Lebanon's capital city of
Beirut is an extreme reflection of the mixed population that inhabits a large part of the country's villages and towns. The MARONITES are concentrated in
the Mount Lebanon districts and in the eastern part
of Beirut; Sunni Muslims in the Tripoli district of
the north, in the southern coastal area and the western part of Beirut; Shi'i Muslims in the south ("Jabal
Amel"), in al-Biqa' (Coele Syria in European languages, the plain lying between the Lebanon and
Anti-Lebanon mountain ranges) and in the southern
suburbs of Beirut; the Druze in southern Mount
Lebanon ("al-Shuf") and the south-eastern district
of Hasbayya and Rashayya. Several millions of
Lebanese emigrants reside abroad, mainly in the
Americas, and some 150,000–200,000 retain their
Lebanese citizenship; most of these are Christians.

Until 1989, the political-constitutional structure
of the country was based on the census of 1932, according to which all Christian groups together formed
about fifty-one percent of the population: MARONITES
thirty percent; GREEK ORTHODOX ten percent; GREEK
CATHOLIC six percent; Armenian Orthodox (Gregorians), Armenian Catholics, PROTESTANTS, Syrian Orthodox and others approximately six percent. All
non-Christian communities constituted forty-nine
percent: SUNNI Muslims twenty-two percent; SHI'A
Muslims twenty percent; DRUZE seven percent. For
political reasons no census was taken between 1932
and 1996, and then the people's religious affiliations were not requested. As such, the figures of

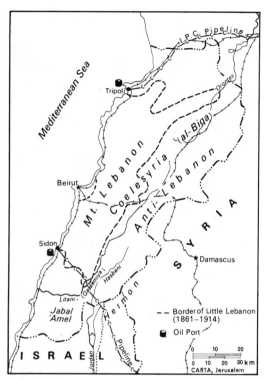

Map of Lebanon

1932 no longer conform to recent and present-day
demographic realities. Due to a low birthrate and
high emigration rates the Christians lost their overall majority and the Maronites lost their status as
the single largest community. Estimates of present
percentages of the various communities vary widely. The following may be a realistic estimate: all-
Christians—thirty   to   forty   percent
(Maronites—twenty percent); all non-Christians—
sixty to seventy percent (Sunni Muslims—twenty-
one   to   twenty-seven   percent;   Shi'i
Muslims—thirty-three to thirty-five percent;
Druze—seven percent). In the Ta'if Agreement of
1989 (see below) it was decided that the political-
constitutional structure would be based on a 50:50
ratio between Christians and Muslims, replacing a 6:5
ratio in favor of the Christians adopted in 1943.

Less than half of Lebanon's largely mountainous
area is considered cultivable. The population is over
sixty percent urban. About twenty-five to thirty percent engage in agriculture (12.6% of the GDP),
twenty to twenty-five percent in industry, transport
and construction (industry and construction amount
to 28.5% of the GDP), and over one-third in services

(25.5% of the GDP). Fruit is exported, but staple foods must be imported.

Lebanon's economy is more modern than that of most Arab states and supports a higher national income. Tourism, shipping, banking and finance used to play an important role, and Beirut was a major world center for the gold trade and banking. This vital economic sector was gravely damaged by the Civil War (1975–1990). The nature of Lebanon's economy, and political system (i.e., the power held by the semi-autonomous local chiefs, the mutual suspicion between Lebanon's seventeen officially-recognized religious communities and the inherent weakness of the state's institutions) induced Lebanon to maintain a system of free enterprise and eschew controls and state planning. The Customs and Currency Union with Syria, inherited from the period of French rule, was dissolved in the 1950s soon after full independence was attained, as Syria favored a protectionist and controlled economy. Some sections of the infrastructure previously leased to concessionaires were nationalized—e.g., the railways, the port of Beirut, the Iraq Petroleum Company (IPC) oil pipeline and Tripoli refinery—otherwise, Lebanon has avoided any nationalization of its economy. River development for irrigation and power, reserved to the state, has not been very enthusiastically promoted. The Orontes River, flowing north into Syria, is still untapped, and a project for the development of the Litani River, which began in the early 1950s, has been only partly implemented.

Lebanon is a communications and transport center. Its railways, however, are underdeveloped. A narrow gauge line runs to Damascus (opened in 1895), a standard-gauge line from Aleppo (built 1903–1904) enters Lebanon and ends at Rayak on the Damascus line, and a coastal line runs from Beirut to Tripoli, where it joins the pre-World War I Syrian Aleppo-Tripoli railway (its southern connection to Haifa and EGYPT was cut in 1948). Beirut has a major port that used to serve the land transportation of goods to Syria, JORDAN, IRAQ and the PERSIAN GULF, and a large international airport. Lebanon's "Middle East Airlines" (largely owned by private shareholders) is the largest in the Middle East; all these services have been badly damaged and frequently paralyzed by the Civil War. Oil pipelines from Iraq (built by the IPC in 1934, expanded in 1949, and nationalized in 1973) and SAUDI ARABIA

(the "Tapline," laid by ARAMCO in 1950) terminate at the Mediterranean in Tripoli and near Sidon respectively; the Tapline stopped operating in 1975, the Iraqi line in 1976.

Political History What is now Lebanon was part of the OTTOMAN EMPIRE until the end of World War I. Parts of it formed the semi-autonomous district (*Sanjaq, Mutasarifiyya*) of Mount Lebanon established in 1860–1861 after anti-Christian riots and massacres. This arrangement was imposed on the Empire by the Great Powers and maintained a degree of supervision over it.

Maronite Christians formed nearly sixty percent of the population in this district; the Christian communities as a whole amounted to eighty percent; the Druze were more than eleven percent, while Sunni and Shiʻi Muslims represented less than ten percent. The governor of the semi-autonomous district was a Christian (but non-Lebanese, therefore non-Maronite) and a twelve-member council was formed, in which the six religious communities (Maronites, Greek Orthodox, Greek Catholic, Sunni, Shiʻi and Druze) were represented proportionally, laying an important precedent to be followed in the future. The rest of what is now Lebanon formed part of the Ottoman provinces (*Vilayet*) of Beirut and Damascus. When Ottoman Turkey entered World War I, it abrogated the semi-autonomous status of Mount Lebanon.

Beirut had been, before the war, one of the centers for Arab and Syrian-Lebanese societies, some clandestine, striving for independence, autonomy or at least a decentralization of the Ottoman Empire (see ARAB NATIONALISM). Some of these societies also advocated a wider autonomy for Lebanon, possibly with an enlarged territory. Several Lebanese Arab leaders were in contact with the Western powers, particularly FRANCE. Thirty-three Arab notables, including several Lebanese, were tried and executed as rebels by the Turks in 1915–1916 on the basis of suspicion and their previous contacts with foreign diplomats, though in fact there was no nationalist insurrection in Lebanon or the other Arab regions of the Fertile Crescent. The country was occupied in 1918 by Allied Forces under General Allenby and placed under a temporary Allied (de facto French) military administration. Attempts to establish a nationalist Arab government, as was done in Damascus under British supervision, were foiled.

In accordance with the decisions of the Paris Peace Conference, Lebanon and Syria were placed under a French Mandate on behalf of the League of Nations in July 1922. On 1 September 1920, before the Mandate was formally confirmed, and following great lobbying efforts by the Maronite leadership, a French decree created "Greater Lebanon" (Grand Liban) by annexing the overwhelmingly Muslim districts of Tripoli in the north, the Biqa' in the east, Jabal Amel and the Tyre and Sidon coastland in the south, and the city of Beirut, to the predominantly Christian district of Mount Lebanon. This move created an economically viable political entity with a major city and port. It fulfilled the political dream of the Maronite-Christians, but replaced the predominantly Maronite-Christian character of the former semi-autonomous district with a Lebanese society consisting of many communities, each a minority, with about half of the population composed of non-Christian groups, Muslim and Druze.

The populations of the annexed districts had not been consulted before the annexation and most of the Muslim inhabitants opposed and resented it. Some of them advocated the absorption of all Lebanon into Syria (as did Syrian nationalists), while others favored that course at least for the newly annexed Muslim districts. In general, the Christian communities, particularly the Maronites, supported the new independent Greater Lebanon and developed a separate Lebanese, as opposed to Syrian or Arab, nationalism. This fundamental Muslim-Christian dichotomy found little open expression in the political parties which were mainly formed by coalitions of pressure groups and networks of prominent semifeudal families and their retainers. But it was a very real and profound ideological division which ultimately determined Lebanon's fate. The struggle against foreign tutelage and the Mandate, although fundamentally similar in most of the Arab Countries, could not be waged with the same extreme intensity in Lebanon because of its unique conditions: France had created Lebanon's enlarged boundaries and French support guaranteed its existence. Protagonists of Greater Lebanon's independence tended, therefore, to be pro-French, while the radical anti-French Arab nationalists had less regard for Lebanon's independence and integrity.

At first, France ruled with an appointed administrative commission. The Representative Council, including directly elected by the various communities, was established in 1922. This Council participated in the drafting of Lebanon's constitution, enacted by French decree in 1926. This constitution, with several amendments, remains the basic law of the land. Its provisions included—until the amendments of 1990 (see below)—an equitable communal representation in Parliament, government and public administration as a "transitory measure." From 1926, Lebanon was ruled by a president elected for a six-year term by Parliament, and a government appointed by the President. The four-year term Chamber of Deputies was two-thirds elected, one-third appointed by the President (until 1943, when it became fully elected), with the communal proportion pre-determined to each constituency. An appointed Senate was also provided for but was abolished in 1927. Since implementation of the constitution was made "subject to the rights and obligations of the Mandatory Power," France retained de facto authority.

The new constitution did not work successfully and was suspended in 1932 by the French High Commissioner and the President. The French ruled thereafter without Parliamentary sanction. A struggle to restore constitutional government ensued. The faction which most consistently fought for its restoration, and refused to cooperate with the government, was consolidated in 1934 as the "Constitutional Bloc" under the Maronite leader Bishara al-Khouri (1890–1964); it was considered anti-French and advocated Lebanon's integration in the Arab world as a separate entity. Its chief rival, the "National Bloc," led by the Maronite leader Emile Edde (1866–1949), also advocated a speedy return to constitutional government, but was prepared in the meantime to cooperate with France; this faction emphasized Lebanon's special Christian-dominated character, and preferred reliance on France over association with pan-Arab nationalism. Edde maintained contacts with Zionist leaders, and accepted the general idea of cooperation between Maronite-led Lebanon and a Jewish state. Authority to elect the President was restored to Parliament in 1936. Edde narrowly defeated Khouri for the Presidency, and the constitution was fully restored in 1937. The struggle for constitutional government had temporarily overshadowed the issue of complete independence with a treaty of alliance between equals to replace French tutelage.

After protracted negotiations, such a treaty was signed (parallel to a Franco-Syrian treaty) in November 1936. Lebanon was to become fully independent, and France was to defend Lebanon in return for military bases and the right to station French troops on Lebanese soil. Signed by the Popular Front government of Léon Blum, the treaty was not ratified by its successors and never took effect.

While French rule remained colonial, and Lebanon's independence was postponed, the draft-treaty had a far-reaching impact. It meant recognition for the country's independence and territorial integrity not only vis-a-vis France but Syria also. Indeed, the parallel Franco-Syrian draft-treaty included Syria's recognition of Lebanon's independence. Those elements in Lebanon (mostly Muslim) still objecting to Lebanon's separation from Syria, or at least to the inclusion of the "new" Muslim-dominated districts within its borders, now resumed their agitation.

Although the resulting tension was over a basically political problem, it had distinct communal, Muslim-Christian, undertones. A young Maronite activist, Pierre JUMAYYIL, founded the paramilitary organization of the PHALANGES (al Kata'ib) for the defense of the Maronite community. Other communities established similar groups (e.g., the Muslim Najjada). The proliferation of paramilitary formations was also encouraged by the growing influence of Fascist Italy and Nazi Germany. A clearly Fascist, Pan-Syrian organization, the SYRIAN SOCIAL NATIONALIST PARTY (Parti Populaire Syrien—PPS), founded by Antoun Sa'adeh, was outlawed in 1936.

Partial self-government in Lebanon was further restricted with the approach of World War II. Parliament was dissolved and the constitution suspended in 1939; President Edde resigned in 1941. French administrators and officers in Lebanon remained loyal to the Vichy government after the fall of France in 1940. Under the armistice concluded with France, a German and Italian base was gradually built in Lebanon and Syria and full-scale German-Italian penetration into the Middle East seemed imminent, particularly when German assistance was requested by the nationalist revolutionary regime in Iraq in 1941.

British and Free-French forces invaded and occupied Syria and Lebanon in a brief campaign in June 1941.

General Catroux now proclaimed, in the name of Free France and strong British advocacy, the termination of the French Mandate and the independence of Lebanon and Syria. But France intended to retain a predominant position in Lebanon and Syria by concluding new treaties of alliance, granting it privileges. Lebanese nationalists found this unacceptable. The elections of 1943 brought the "Constitutional Bloc" to power and Bishara al-Khouri became President. Khouri nominated Riyad al-Sulh (1894–1951), an Arab Nationalist leader and a son of an influential Sunni-Muslim family, as Prime Minister. In October 1943, the new government and Parliament enacted the abolition of all articles of the constitution giving precedence to France's rights and obligations thus restricting Lebanon's independence. The French immediately arrested the President and members of his government, declared the measures taken unlawful, and appointed Emile Edde President. Some ministers, however, escaped to organize demonstrations and resistance. Invoking the needs of security and the war effort, the British Commander of the Middle East supported the Lebanese nationalists and, threatening armed intervention, demanded the restoration of Parliamentary rule and the legitimate government. France had to yield, the national government was reinstated, Edde was discredited and his political career was over. The finale of French domination came in 1945–1946, when France evacuated its military forces and handed authority over locally recruited troops to the Lebanese government, to become the nucleus of its national army—but not before the withdrawing French forces bombarded Damascus and a complaint was filed by Syria's independent government to the UN Security Council against France.

In December 1946, with the withdrawal of the French forces, Lebanon became fully independent. On the eve of the crisis of 1943 an unwritten "National Pact" was concluded between Christian (mainly Maronite) and Muslim (mainly Sunni) leaders, represented principally by Khouri and al-Sulh, on the political and institutional character of Lebanon. The Muslims accepted the country's separate independence and territorial integrity within its post-1920 frontiers, while the Christians abandoned their dependence upon French protection and accepted independent Lebanon's integration into the Arab family of nations as well as its Arab identity. The

Pact also reconfirmed the communal structure of Lebanon's government and fixed a Christian-Muslim quota of 6:5 for the composition of Parliament (so that the House would always number a multiple of eleven). It also ruled that the President would always be a Maronite, the Prime Minister a Sunni Muslim and the Speaker of Parliament a Shi'i Muslim. The Commander of the armed forces and the Head of the Security Services were also to be Maronites (the Minister of Defense was usually a Druze and the Foreign Minister was Greek Orthodox, but this was not stated in the Pact). Other government ministers were appointed according to the above quota; later, a Druze Chief of Staff was appointed under the Maronite Army Commander. For traditional and political reasons, the bulk of the army's officers were Maronites and they commanded most combat units and manned key posts. In past decades, the Maronites advocated keeping a small, volunteer army that would guarantee Lebanon's internal stability.

The National Pact also formed the basis for the state's joining in the foundation of the ARAB LEAGUE. Lebanese apprehensions compelled the Arab states to add to the Alexandria Protocol (which laid the foundation for the League) an appendix solemnly recognizing Lebanon's independence. Only when the League proved to favor cooperation among separate, sovereign states, rather than a policy of pan-Arab unification, Lebanon agreed to sign its charter and become an active member and ardent supporter.

In its nation-building and internal politics, Lebanon was less successful. The unity of 1943 proved unstable—though the National Pact's rules for the distribution of power were not seriously questioned until the 1970s.

Permanent and responsible parties did not develop. governments rose and fell in quick succession, and accusations of nepotism and corruption were frequent. The elections of 1947, returning the Constitutional Bloc of Khouri and al-Sulh to power, were denounced as rigged. Louder protests were heard when an acquiescent Parliament amended the constitution in 1948 to permit the re-election of President Khouri for a second term. A right-wing coup by the SSNP was reported to have been attempted and suppressed in 1949; Antoun Sa'adeh was summarily tried and executed (Premier al-Sulh was assassinated in revenge, in 1951). A bloodless coup stage-managed by Camille CHAMOUN (Sham'un), compelled President Khouri to resign in 1952 and Chamoun was elected President.

A grave crisis occurred in 1958. The traditional Christian-Muslim antagonism now focused upon Lebanon's inter-Arab orientation. The leftist parties and many Muslims favored integration with an Egyptian-led Nasserist revolutionary union or bloc, strengthened by the February 1958 merger of Egypt and Syria as the UNITED ARAB REPUBLIC (UAR). Most Christians (especially the Maronites), and the Chamoun regime, opposed such an integration, insisting on Lebanon's separate independence, and favored a rightist, pro-Western policy and neutrality in inter-Arab affairs. An opposition National Front was formed in 1957 under the predominantly Sunni-Muslim leadership of Sa'eb Salam, Abdallah al-Yafi, Rashid KARAMEH and the Druze Kamal JUNBLAT. Officially, the aim of the Front was to prevent a constitutional amendment permitting President Chamoun's election for a second term, but the real, fundamental issue was the question of Lebanon's inter-Arab integration. Violence flared up in 1957, turning into a general rebellion in May 1958. The government and its supporters insisted that the rebellion was a Nasserist attempt to seize power, organized and supported chiefly by Syria. The rebels consistently denied these accusations. The government submitted a complaint to the UN Security Council in May 1958, charging the UAR with interference in Lebanon's internal affairs. In June the Security Council dispatched an international military observers group (UNOGIL) to Lebanon. The group failed to detect the infiltration or presence of foreign forces or arms (though such an infiltration was generally assumed). A leftist revolution in Iraq (July 1958) aggravated the crisis. Claiming that Lebanon's independence was being threatened by external power, President Chamoun appealed to the US for assistance, to which President Eisenhower responded by dispatching troops to the country. US proposals to replace the troops (and the British contingents sent to Jordan during the crisis) with UN forces were vetoed by the USSR. In view of this deadlock, the issue was transferred to a special session of the UN General Assembly. An Arab draft resolution was adopted by the Assembly in August, noting that the Arab states were committed to respect each other's independence, welcoming their renewed undertaking to "observe" that commitment, and requesting arrangements that would "adequately help in upholding the principles of the Charter, and facilitate the early withdrawal of the foreign troops." US troops were evacuated in October.

The Civil War of 1958 was conducted with restraint. The Lebanese Army under the command of General Fu'ad Shihab (1902–1973), a Maronite-Christian professional officer who commanded the Army since it was established, in 1945, refused to intervene, thus avoiding a confrontation that might have destroyed the army's apolitical and non-communal character. President Chamoun let it be known that he did not intend to run for a second term. At the end of Chamoun's term, General Shihab was elected President in 1958. Under his paternalistic administration, which enhanced the powers of the Presidency and central government, the army command and the Secret Services, efforts were made to stabilize the political system and introduce reforms in the administration, but these could not succeed mainly due to the power of his rivals: the traditional politicians who refused to give up their privileges. Modernization efforts and projects proved to be double-edged, leading to massive immigration to the capital of Beirut, mainly of poor Shi'is from the south, and weakening the traditional leaders (the Zua'ma). The pro-Nasserist rebels of 1958 were appeased and returned to play a leading role in the government; their leaders (Karameh, Yafi and Salam) headed virtually all governments after 1958, while Chamoun and his associates went into temporary political eclipse. An approximate balance in Parliament was later achieved between the pro-Nasserist, pan-Arab Left and a "Triple Alliance" of the right-wing, moderate, Christian-led factions of Chamoun, Pierre Jumayyil and Raymond Edde. When Shihab declined Parliament's offer to amend the constitution so as to enable his re-election for a second term in 1964, this balance was preserved, and politically neutral Charles Hilou (b. 1912) became President. Shihab retained considerable influence behind the scenes and a loose "Shihabist" faction was strong in Parliament.

However, despite the economic and financial prosperity which marked the years of Shihab's presidency, the atmosphere of crisis and uncertainty with regard to Lebanon's future, created by the events of 1958, did not disappear entirely. Some violence became endemic, with occasional clashes, kidnappings and political assassinations. In December 1961 a coup attempt by the Syrian Nationalist Party was suppressed. Some Christian leaders returned to the concept of a smaller, more homogeneous Christian Lebanon that would relinquish the Muslim-dominated districts, while others called for Lebanon's neutrality, an idea seen by pan-Arabists as an attempt to pull Lebanon out of the inter-Arab system and abandon its common political issues and goals. The country was also affected by the Arab-Israeli crisis mounting in the mid-1960s: Arab plans to prevent Israel's use of the Jordan River included the diversion of its Lebanese tributaries westward into the Litani and eastward into Syria's Baniyas and Yarmuk. Such schemes called for military protection. As Lebanon could not provide such protection, it declined to implement its share in the project or to invite Arab forces into its territory to defend the diversion works against possible Israeli attack. While formally participating in the war of June 1967, Lebanon escaped defeat by refraining from military action. However, it could not escape involvement in inter-Arab and ARAB-ISRAEL CONFLICTS which took place on its soil since the mid-1960s.

The political equilibrium was critically endangered from 1968–1969. Palestinian military organizations (Fida'iyyun), based in Lebanon or infiltrating across the Syrian border, stepped up their military operations against Israel, leading to painful Israeli retaliations. Lebanon held several important advantages for these Palestinian organizations during Israel's War of Independence (see ARAB-ISRAEL CONFLICT) some 100,000 Palestinians took refuge in Lebanon (currently estimated at about 350,000). These Palestinian refugees, who had not been granted citizenship and resided mainly in refugee camps in or near the main cities, turned into a mainstay for the Palestinian armed organizations, offering them a constant source of mobilization and extra-territorial space. The pluralistic environment in Lebanon, and particularly in Beirut, enabled the organization to publish newspapers and mouthpieces and to mobilze both political and military support. The Lebanese leftist and pan-Arab movements gave them political support and regarded them as potential allies against the powerful, conservative Maronite-based establishment. From the late 1960s, The Palestinian organizations, led by the *Fatah*, demanded freedom of action tantamount to a state-within-a-state. The conservative Maronite-led "Triple Alliance" opposed *Fida'iyuun* presence in, or operations from, Lebanon (although their objections were not always openly expressed), while the Nasserist Left encouraged them. President Hilou and the army favored the right-wing position and was opposed to commando operations from Lebanese soil, but failed to take strong action, fearing a new Left/Right or Muslim/Christian confrontation. Several compromise formulas (such as commando operations controlled by the army, use of Lebanon's territory for transit only, etc.) were suggested and rejected. Following a grave crisis late in 1968—aggravated by an Israeli military raid on Beirut's airport that had resulted in destruction of airplanes and emphasized the weakness and impotence of the Lebanese army, a new crisis in April 1969 left the country with only a caretaker government for seven months, with the constant threat of an army takeover or a non-parliamentary Presidential government. (General Shihab was often mentioned both as the potential author of a coup and as a candidate for the Presidency in 1970.) In November 1969, an agreement with the *Fida'iyyun* was reached thank to President Nasser's mediation. The agreement laid down a *modus operandi* for the Palestinian commando groups, prescribing their bases and location (in the south-eastern corner only), limiting their raids and imposing some army control. But the *Fida'iyyun* never abided by the Cairo Agreement fully and in good faith; clashes continued with both the Phalanges and the army, and new "coordination" agreements brought no solution. Lebanon's south-eastern corner, the Arqoub, remained outside government control and soon came to be called "Fatahland," and the country was continuously exposed to Israeli counter-blows against operations conducted from Lebanese territory.

In 1970 Shihab refused to present his presidential candidacy since he was not guaranteed a decisive majority. The candidate he sponsored, Elias Sarkis, lost by one vote to Suleiman Franjiyyeh (1910–1992), a Maronite-Christian leader from the northern town of Zagharta considered to be "neutral," in somewhat questionable elections. President Franjiyyeh chose Sa'eb Salam as Prime Minister, with the leftist Nasserist Druze leader Kamal Junblat in the key position of Minister of the Interior.

PLO operations in and from Lebanon, Israeli reprisals, and the resulting confrontation between the PLO and the Lebanese army and the Phalanges, remained Lebanon's chief problem. Clashes continued, and new agreements in 1970, 1972 and 1973 were not implemented. In May and September 1973 the army conducted serious military operations against the *Fida'iyyun*, but failed to break them (a fact that hardened the resolve of the Phalanges that Lebanon, or at least its Christian heartland, could be saved only by their military efforts, perhaps with outside support). The PLO expanded its de facto control of south-eastern Lebanon to include also large parts of the south-west, the Shi'i-majority Jabal Amel. The PLO's heavy hand on the local population and its operations against Israel and Israel's reprisals, caused an increasing flight of Lebanese from the south—many of them to Beirut, where large suburban quarters of Shi'i refugees sprang up in the south-west and led to an increase in intercommunal tensions.

The intensifying Lebanon-PLO confrontation and attempts to restrict Palestinian armed presence and activity on Lebanon's soil led to grave repercussions in terms of Syrian and other Arab states' interference on behalf of the Palestinians, matched by growing intra-Lebanese strife over power. Selfish domestic and inter-Arab political interests motivated the Arab states' support for the PLO, imposing on Lebanon (and Jordan) a costly burden of paying the price of Israeli military reprisals—which they themselves avoided by prohibiting a Palestinian use of their territories to attack Israel. After the expulsion of the Palestinian guerrilla organizations from Jordan in 1970–1971, Lebanon became their main territorial base, which further aggravated the tension within the Lebanese political system. Thus, following the Israeli raid on Palestinian headquarters in the heart of Beirut in April 1973, Lebanese Army units and Maronite militias, in yet another attempt to restrict armed Palestinian activity, entered an armed clash with the Palestinian guerrilla groups. Syria responded by extending military support to the Palestinians, closing its border with Lebanon and exerting pressures on the Lebanese government to cease all violent activities against the Palestinians. In July 1974 an all-Arab Defense Council discussed proposals to dispatch Arab troops to Lebanon to separate the forces and enforce the agreed arrangements. Though the idea of inviting Arab troops or UN peace-keeping forces had already been discussed in Lebanon for some years, Lebanon declined the offer and demanded an end to Arab arms supplies to the *Fida'iyyun*. The Arab states were, in any case, not in a position to take effective united action. Syria, by then more politically stable and stronger militarily, had its own interests in Lebanon and regarded the country as part of its strategic sphere of defense. Syria was backing the *Fida'iyyun* in Lebanon, and it was believed that Syrian troops, disguised as *Fida'iyyun* and especially as fighters of the PLA (regular Palestinian troops forming part of the Syrian army), had been operating in Lebanon since 1970. Early in 1975 Lebanon and Syria were reportedly discussing the entry of regular Syrian troops to Lebanon but no agreement was reached.

It was, however, the internal Lebanese affairs that were most gravely affected. The question of how to deal with the *Fida'iyyun* deeply divided Lebanon's political community: the Maronite-dominated groups (sometimes referred to as the "Right") pressed for determined action against the *Fida'iyyun* state-within-a-state and terror operations, while the Muslim-dominated groups (the "Left") opposed such action and sympathized with the *Fida'iyyun*; and the Lebanese army, torn by these conflicting tendencies, strained for action but did not dare take decisive steps. Interior Minister Junblat was reported to be in acute conflict with the army, denouncing its operations against the PLO and claiming that it acted as an instrument of the Maronites; and Premier Salam, though more moderate, partly concurred with him.

In April 1973 Salam and his government resigned, and several ineffective governments, formed by second-rank leaders, followed each other until 1975. Behind the split over the *Fida'iyyun* issue loomed the danger of invalidating the national consensus on Lebanon's intercommunal structure, based on the "National Pact" of 1943, and the polarization of Lebanon's body politic into a conservative camp determined to preserve the status quo—namely, the existing communal structure—and a radical camp anxious to change that structure—its moderates content with a change in favor of the Muslims within the communal structure, and its extremists bent on the abolition of that structure altogether.

Eventually, it was this polarization that led to a total confrontation of Christians versus Muslims, with the Palestinians being dragged unavoidably into the fray.

The dreaded eruption of Lebanon's civil war took place in April 1975. Preceded by a violent confrontation over a local issue in Sidon in February, a bloody clash between the Phalanges and members of a Palestinian organization in Beirut on 13 April is usually seen as the beginning of that civil war. The Muslim-dominated radical camp joined the *Fida'iyyun* against the Phalanges, and soon Beirut was engulfed in incessant fighting and terror. There were innumerable attempts and agreements to reach a cease-fire, but none of them were effective; they were also marred by a constant wrangle over what should come first: a political agreement, to remove the causes of violence, or an end to the violence, to make possible a quiet, reasoned discussion of the political issues. The government—after an attempt to form a military rule that collapsed within days, headed from June 1975 by Rashid Karameh—was paralyzed. The President and government shied away from ordering the army into action, fearing that it might split if it became involved in the civil war. And indeed, the army soon disintegrated; many officers and whole units deserted to join "their" camps and communities. In January 1976 a junior officer, Lieutenant Ahmad al-Khatib, broke away and formed an "Arab Lebanese Army" that joined the radical camp. In March 1976 a senior officer, Brigadier Abdel Aziz al-Ahdab, tried to stage a military coup, which fizzled out but further disrupted the army. Actual power was increasingly exercised by "militias," some of them communal-political and others bands of toughs recruited by local bosses.

The conservative, Maronite-led camp was politically represented by the Phalanges, Chamoun's National Liberals (Chamoun was also Minister of the Interior in 1975–1976 and as such ordered the army to act against the "Left") and, to a lesser degree, Franjiyyeh's faction. However, the Maronite camp was divided by long-maintained traditional rivalries between these three leaders and their militias. As President, Franjiyyeh could not identify himself fully with any of the camps, and he was not on friendly terms with the Phalanges. He did, however, have an old acquaintance with the al-Asad family in Syria. Raymond Edde's National Bloc had no militia. It was backed—and encouraged—by communal Maronite organizations, such as the Maronite League and the extremist Guardians of the Cedar, who emphasized Lebanon's separate, Phoenician, identity and later called openly for annihilation of the Palestinians. The Maronite Patriarch backed that camp, but cautiously tried to stay out of the political struggle. The Maronite commanders of the army also sympathized with it. Late in 1975 efforts were made to create a joint roof organization; they materialized only later, in September 1976, in a Lebanese Front chaired by Chamoun—but the Front was not efficacious. Militarily, the Phalanges were the mainstay of the conservative camp, with Chamoun's "Tigers," to a lesser degree Franjiyyeh's *Marada* militia (which controlled the Zagharta-Batroun region in the north, but did not intervene much in Beirut and other areas of fighting) and deserting army units, mostly Maronite. Most of the members of the other Christian communities—the Greek Catholic, Greek Orthodox and Armenians—tried to stay out of the fighting, though some of them defended their quarters with local ad hoc militias and others allied with the warring parties—e.g., Greek Orthodox, who dominated both the "Syrian Social Nationalist Party" (SSNP, formerly PPS) and the Communist Party, were part of the radical camp, while Greek Catholics tended to side with the conservative, pro-status quo camp. The Maronite President, Elias Sarkis (1976–1982) failed to bring the parties together, was pressured by the Syrians and in fact did not control much more than his own palace. He did, however, manage to keep the state institutions and bureaucracy from totally falling apart.

The Muslim-dominated camp was far less homogeneous. The traditional Sunni-Muslim leaders—conservatives in the social sense, despite their adhesion to the leftist pro-Nasserist camp—had their factions and parliamentary blocs, but none of them had grown into a stable, permanent party. Some Sunni leaders did not fully join the radical camp but tried to maintain a center faction, supporting President Franjiyyeh. The radical, leftist camp included Junblat's PROGRESSIVE SOCIALIST PARTY, (PSP) based on Druze communal allegiance rather than ideological principles, the Communist Party and various small pro-Nasserist factions that did not accept the traditional Sunni leadership. The *Ba'th* Party in Lebanon was split into mutually hostile pro-Syrian and pro-Iraqi wings, but both elements belonged to the camp. The SSNP, formerly pro-Fascist right-wing, now belonged to the radical camp, but had little influence. The old Sunni-Muslim *Najjada* militia now appeared as a party, but it was small and had little impact. The Shi'i leadership wanted a basic change in Lebanon's structure, but it was antagonistic to the Sunni leaders and the Druzes and was only now beginning to set up a strong organization; it began defending Shi'i villages and quarters, but kept out of the civil war in its first few years. The Muslim and/or radical groups were allied with the Palestinian organizations, but attempts to set up a joint leadership were made only later, from 1976.

The military set-up of the radical camp was at first rather haphazard and disorganized. The traditional Sunni leaders had no militia, and therefore increasingly lost influence. The *Ba'th*, the Communists, the *Najjada* and the SSNP had small fighter squads. So had various Nasserist factions, e.g., the Union of the Working People's Forces, led by Kamal Shatila and Najah Wakim; Ibrahim Quleilat's "Independent Nasserists," whose militia, *al-Murabitun*, became the main Sunni fighting group in Beirut; Mustafa Saa'd's People's Liberation Army in Sidon; and Farouq Muqaddam's non-Nasserist 24th of October Movement in Tripoli. These militias were local groups, confined to their town or quarter—and were not much different from non-ideological bands of toughs in town quarters led by local leaders. In Tripoli, a Muslim-fundamentalist militia, also came into being *al-Tawhid al-Islami*, led by Sheikh Sa'id Sha'ban, which later clashed with pro-Syrian *Ba'th* fighters reinforced by a growing ALAWI population, and lost to them. Gradually, the main military effort of the radical camp was taken on by the Druze-PSP militia and the Shi'i communal organization, which grew in the mid-1970s and was renamed AMAL, turned into a militia and gradually became involved in the civil war.

The Palestinian mainstream faction, *al-Fatah*, tried at first to stay out of the Lebanese imbroglio (radical Palestinian groups such as the PFLP General Command, the PFLP, and DFLP had some responsibility in triggering the eruption and early acceleration of the civil war), but it did supply arms to the radical camp, especially because the Syrian-based Palestinian units of the al-Sa'iqa, as well as the radical PLO organizations, took part in the fighting. In January, *Fatah* itself joined the battle in response to the Phalanges' policy of ethnic cleansing, manifested in the efforts to capture Palestinian refugee camps in East Beirut and massacre or expell their residents. Thus, the fall of Dbayya, and siege of other refugee camps (Jisr al-Basha and Tal al-Za'tar) pushed *Fatah* into the battle. *Fatah's* participation in the fighting, and Syrian-controlled PLA units sent to Lebanon in January 1976, soon shifted the balance between the disputing radical and conservative camps in favor of the former, which came to define itself as the National Movement, or the Progressive Front. The National Movement set up a joint command though it remained rudimentary. By March, the National Movement's forces had captured large parts of Lebanon, threatening a final collapse of the Maronite coalition.

The civil war, accompanied by brutal acts of violence and terror against civilians, soon turned into a territorial fight, with each camp trying to consolidate its rule in the parts of Lebanon it dominated. Territorial control was as follows: the Maronites in Mount Lebanon, the coastal region north of Beirut and East Beirut; the Sunni Muslims in Tripoli, West Beirut and Sidon; the Druze in southern Mount Lebanon; the Shi'is in South Lebanon and the Biqa'. The brunt of the fighting concerned (a) the liquidation of enclaves of the rival camp (such as the Palestinian camps in East Beirut, and Christian villages in the Druze-dominated Shuf and Matn parts of Mount Lebanon and in parts of Shi'i-dominated South Lebanon); and (b) mixed and border areas (such as and mainly, Beirut, which eventually was divided by a "green line" into Muslim West and Christian East Beirut, its port and airport, the slopes of Mount Lebanon southeast of Beirut, the coastal region south of Beirut, Mount Lebanon's eastern slopes towards the Biqa' around Zahla and its northern borders toward Tripoli). The consolidation of regions dominated by one community gradually reinforced the idea of the establishment of cantons as a permanent solution and the transformation of Lebanon into a federation of such cantons. This idea came to dominate much Maronite-Christian thinking, but was anathema to the anti-status quo camp (though de facto the Druze and the Shi'is adamantly enforced their rule in their cantons). The government was paralyzed, the army was at first kept out of the war and later disintegrated, and central, united administration of Lebanon became impossible. The civil war also destroyed the main base of

Lebanon's economy—Beirut's role as an international banking and finance center (though the full effects of that process became apparent only later)—and paralyzed Beirut's port and airport as world crossroads. It also gravely affected Lebanon's prestigious higher education centers and its lively and diversified press (see end of entry). Parliamentary life was also crippled; no new elections could be held and the existing House could meet only rarely and with great difficulty, in no-man's-land. In early 1976, Parliament extended its term by two years (a measure repeated later several times until the nomination of forty new deputies in 1991 and the Parliamentary elections of 1992).

The Lebanon civil war attracted external Arab interference motivated by self-interest which further entangled the situation, adding an inter-Arab dimension to the crisis. In 1975–1976 the Arab League and a number of Arab states made repeated attempts to mediate, but these attempts were half-hearted and to no avail. Syria, however, had a greater stake in Lebanon both historically, politically and economically. Since the rise of Hafez al-ASAD to power in 1970–1971, Syria enjoyed unprecedented stability that enabled it to become the predominant actor in the now less stable Lebanon. From the early 1970s, Asad's regime pushed to secure Syria's traditional interests there, namely, to preserve a weak Lebanese state that would not endanger Syria as a *place d'armes* for other forces hostile to Syria and its regime, to reach a predominant position in Lebanon that would compel it to coordinate its foreign policy with Syria and to secure Syria's economic interests in Lebanon. To achieve these ends, Syria systematically stepped up its intervention. At first Syria backed the radical camp, trying at the same time to mediate and devise a political formula that would end the civil war and preserve the Lebanese state. In January 1976 Syria stepped up both its military intervention and its search for a political solution and offered a settlement plan. That plan was adopted by President Franjiyyeh and publicly presented by him, in February 1976, as his proposal. It provided for a new distribution of power, stipulating an equal representation ratio between Christians and Muslims for Parliament and senior administration posts (against the 6:5 ratio established by the 1943 National Pact). By doing so, it accepted the principle of a continued communal structure and postponed its abolition to an undetermined future. It also proposed to reduce the powers of the (Maronite) President and increase those of the (Sunni-Muslim) Premier. The reform plan was accompanied by Syrian security guarantees (and implied a degree of Syrian involvement and supervision).

Franjiyyeh's Syrian-backed reform plan caused a major change in the situation. The pro-status quo camp accepted the plan, while the radical camp rejected it as not going far enough toward the abolition of the communal division of power; the Palestinian organizations also rejected it—mainly because it seemed to imply a restriction of their independent action and the imposition of Syrian supervision. The situation was further complicated by a serious onslaught on Franjiyyeh's position as President: he was suspected of planning to extend his term beyond its September 1976 expiry, and refused to heed requests to resign earlier, the constitution was amended to permit the election of the new President six months in advance and in May Elias Sarkis was elected for September with Syrian support—and after reported strong Syrian pressure—with no votes against him. Franjiyyeh had fled the presidential palace in March to Maronite-controlled Jounieh, north of Beirut, threatened by civil war and terror attacks.

Given the growing power of the radical camp, now led by the PLO and Junblat's Druze militia, in the spring of 1976 Syria decided to enforce its reform plan, to prevent the radicals' victory and a partition of Lebanon that might have followed. Syria thus turned against its allies and clients and allied itself, de facto, with its foes. In April 1976 Syrian regular troops entered Lebanon, gradually establishing de facto control of some of northern, eastern and south-eastern Lebanon areas strategically important to Syria. Syria preferred a remote control policy rather than a direct involvement in Lebanon. However, the overt rift that developed between Damascus and the radical camp, which in May led to the elimination of the Syrian-based (and prominent member of the PLO) Sa'iqa organization, left Asad little choice. On 1 June after securing—through Jordanian and American diplomatic services—Israel's consent (setting an agreed "red line" which the Syrians would not exceed) Syrian forces opened an offensive against radical and Palestinian positions, unmoved by Soviet pressure. This offensive did not make much headway. The Syrians obviously wished to avoid a full-fledged battle and did not use their full strength. A new offensive in September was more successful, but was not pursued to complete victory and the liquidation of the radical and Palestinian camp's military strength. The Syrians did, however, allow their new Maronite allies to intensify their military offensive. The Phalanges laid siege, for instance, to the Palestinian camp of Tel al-Za'tar in East Beirut from January 1976, later they attacked it and in August stormed it, with bloody massacres reported thereafter (the Palestinians held Syria responsible for that debacle).

Inter-Arab involvement in the Lebanese crisis was intensified in 1976. Syria's intervention caused a crisis in its relations with several Arab states, particularly Egypt and Iraq. Mediatory efforts, *inter alia* by Libya's Prime Minister JALLUD, remained unsuccessful. In June, following the Syrian invasion of Lebanon, however, it was decided to send all-Arab troops to Lebanon; the plans provided for a force of 4,500–5,000, and the first contingents, mainly Saudi, Sudanese and Libyan, entered Lebanon that month. This force, however, had little impact. It was instructed not to become involved in actual fighting, and despite continued cease-fires, all abortive, there were no accords (or cease-fires) which it could have observed and enforced. In October 1976, an informal mini-summit in Riyad (Egypt, Syria, Saudi Arabia, Kuwait, Lebanon and the PLO) decided to set up a larger and more effective Arab Deterrence Force (ADF) of some 30,000 men, and later that month a full summit in Cairo endorsed that decision. In addition, the summit worked out a plan for the disarmament of all militias, including the Palestinians, of the heavy weapons—save those areas designed for Palestinian armed deployment according to the 1969 Cairo Agreement. An Arab League Committe was established to supervise the implementation of these resolutions. The bulk of the ADF was to be Syrian troops already present in Lebanon. In effect, the all-Arab summit acknowledged Syria's dominant military presence in Lebanon and lent its troops an all-Arab legitimate role, supported financially by the Arab oil-rich states. Together with other Arab security forces already in Lebanon, the ADF was nominally subordinated to the Lebanese President, but in fact gave Syria almost a free hand in

Lebanon. The PLO's and Iraq's objections were dismissed by the strong Arab coalition of Egypt, Saudia Arabia, Kuwait and Syria, whose consolidation was essential in the Arab realignment toward the resumed peacemaking efforts by the newly elected American president.

By early 1979, the Syrian forces comprised exclusively the ADF. The Libyan contingent was withdrawn shortly after the Cairo Summit, and the rest of the non-Syrian forces withdrew in the course of 1977 and 1978. Syria continued to present its troops in Lebanon as an all-Arab force, mandated by an all-Arab decision. At first, the ADF was nominally commanded by a Lebanese officer, but over the years this fiction faded away.

In October 1976, with the entry of the ADF and the proclamation of a general cease-fire, the civil war officially ended. Syria concentrated its troops mainly in the Biqa' and the north, taking over complete de facto control of these regions; but smaller ADF contingents also entered Mount Lebanon, Beirut, Sidon and parts of South Lebanon, stopping about ten miles short of the Israeli border, in accordance with the "red line" understanding with Israel. In December 1976, a new government under Salim al-Huss (b. 1929) was installed, and gradually re-established a measure of control; it also began rebuilding the army. But the army was, in reality, divided into brigades loyal to the different communal leaders; the camps remained mutually hostile. The pro-status quo camp, since September 1976 operating under an umbrella of the Lebanese Front, jealously guarded its de facto control of its canton, while the Druze maintained their own control and the Shi'is gradually asserted a more effective control of their area as well. The radical National Movement still maintained its resentment toward Syria's intervention and position against the Left, which peaked with Kamal Junblat's assassination in March 1977 (largely related to Syria). Nonetheless, Syria managed to restore its old alliance with this camp. Syria and the ADF were also party to several new agreements with the Palestinian organizations, trying to regulate their presence in and operations from Lebanon—culminating in the Shtura Agreement of July 1977. But this new accord, like the preceding ones of 1969 and 1973, provided no solution to the problems and dangers raised by the PLO's operations from South Lebanon.

It was, indeed, the PLO's presence and operations in South Lebanon, that triggered Israeli response and resumed fighting in 1977. Syria, from late 1977 at loggerheads with Egypt over Anwar al-SADAT's divisive visit to JERUSALEM that November, was paralyzed regarding the enforcement of the Cairo Agreement's provisions on the PLO. Not only was the Palestinian armed activity concentrated in the border area where Syria had no easy access, but Syria needed the PLO now as an essential partner in the anti-Egyptian coalition. The Shi'i population of South Lebanon began resisting the PLO's domination of the region and its exposure to Israeli reprisals; but the main resistance came from the Christian-controlled enclaves in South Lebanon, aided by Christian militia men from the main areas further north and, more important, by army personnel who returned to the south to protect their homes. The Christians of the south, and the Phalanges in general, had been secretly collaborating with Israel for some years; this cooperation became more open and publicly known from 1976. Christian South Lebanese militias endeavored to establish, with Israeli assistance, a cordon sanitaire between the PLO concentrations and the Israeli border, and Israel opened that border to assist the Lebanese border region, cut off from the rest of Lebanon, and to enable its inhabitants to find work, medical treatment, etc., in Israel (the "Good Fence" policy). In March 1978, following a Fatah raid on Israel from the sea and bus hijack, resulting in thirty two casualties, Israeli forces invaded Lebanon and occupied the border zone, up to the Litani River (see ARAB-ISRAEL CONFLICT). When Israel withdrew, in June 1978, under UN and Great Power pressure, it left the border zone under the control of a mainly Christian Lebanese militia, later called the SOUTH LEBANON ARMY, under Major Sa'ad Haddad, that was trained, financed and equipped by Israel. In March 1978, under a UN Security Council decision, an UN Interim Force in Lebanon (UNIFIL) was sent to South Lebanon, composed of some 4,000—later nearly 6,000 soldiers from different nations. However, since UNIFIL's mandate barred it from actually fighting, it was not in effect able to prevent intra-Lebanese clashes in the area it had came to deploy nor PLO raids and intrusions into Israel on the resulting PLO-Israel confrontation. Since the late 1960s, the ongoing violence and armed activity across the border with Israel, among Lebanese Forces, Lebanese-PLO and PLO-Israeli skirmishes and Israeli reprisals, forced thousands of South Lebanon's inhabitants to flee the area; their number was variously estimated at over 200,000—about one-third of the region's population.

In the rest of Lebanon too, clashes soon resumed. While Syria gradually effected a reconciliation with the radical camp and the Palestinians, its de facto alliance with the Maronite-dominated camp revealed itself as a passing episode and soon crumbled. However, and considering some shared interests of the two parties, Syria maintained close relations with some members in this camp, primarily with Franjiyyeh's family and other pro-Syrian elements. The Syria-Franjiyyeh reform plan of 1976 remained unimplemented. All attempts to devise a formula for a national reconciliation failed and Syria was left consolidating its de facto dominance without being able to impose its formula for a settlement. Syrian attempts to formalize its presence with a Syro-Lebanese defense treaty also failed. The Christian camp resisted Syrian inroads into the canton it controlled, and in December 1977 clashes erupted between Christian militias and Syrian troops. During 1978 the clashes intensified, the Muslim-Palestinian camp joined the fight and resumed attacks on, and the shelling of, East Beirut. Haddad's militia also resisted and prevented the dispatch of Syrian-controlled units of the Lebanese army to South Lebanon (see SOUTH LEBANON ARMY).

During the late 1970s, the Phalanges' leader, Bashir Jumayyil, strove to unify the entire Maronite camp under their leadership and to take over at least its military command—a campaign that caused grave intracommunal clashes. From 1976, an umbrella formation, the Lebanese Forces (LF), tried to unite all Christian militias; in fact, in this stage of the war, the LF were still dominated by the Phalanges. In May 1978 Franjiyyeh dissociated himself from the Lebanese Front, strengthening his relations with Syria and effecting a rapprochement with the radical camp; his Marada militia (controlling his northern fief, but not active in Beirut and the rest of Lebanon) thus became unreliable for the Phalanges and the LF. In June 1978 the Phalanges attacked Franjiyyeh's centers, and a unit led by Samir Ja'ja' killed his son Tony (b. 1942) (Parliament member from 1970, government minister 1973–1975, and leader of the Marada) with his wife and small daughter. Franjiyyeh's militia was eliminated. The Phalanges repeated and completed the process of unifying the Maronite militias. In July 1980 they also liquidated, in bloody clashes, the National Liberal Party's militia, the Tigers, as an independent formation and forcibly incorporated its remnants in the LF. The Phalanges now dominated the more or less united formations of the Maronite camp, but a bitter vendetta was added to the existing feud between Jumayyil's Phalanges and the Franjiyyeh clan. Camille Chamoun, on the other hand, admitted defeat and remained a member of the Lebanese Front, by then weakened considerably compared to the more militant LF under Bashir Jumayyil.

On the political side too, the Maronites' resolve to keep control of their canton hardened, and tendencies to turn Lebanon into a federation of cantons came to the fore. A charter issued by the Lebanese Front in December 1980 seemed to point in that direction; its reference to precise constitutional proposals was vague but it stressed the autonomy of Lebanon's various communities. A demand for the withdrawal of the ADF (i.e., the Syrian Army) was voiced with increasing frequency (by Prime Minister Shafiq al-Wazzan too,) though it did not crystallize into a formal government demand. Syria did not heed such requests but claimed that only an all-Arab decision could terminate the all-Arab mandate conferred upon it. However, Syria withdrew the bulk of its forces from Beirut in March 1980; on the other hand, Syria further consolidated its control of East and North Lebanon. In April–May 1981, the Syrians besieged the Christian-majority town of Zahlah in the Biqa', demanding the withdrawal of the Lebanese Forces from it. The siege, which resulted in Israel's air force intervention and Syrian deployment of ground-to-air missile batteries, soon brought the two states to the verge of a direct showdown, leading to intensive American efforts to diffuse the tension led by Deputy Secretary of State Philip Habib. Eventually, the Syrian missiles remained in place and the Lebanese Forces were compelled to withdraw from Zahlah and leave its control to Syria.

In July, attention was drawn from the missile crisis to wide scale artillery battles in South Lebanon between Israel and the PLO, which led to another American mediation effort to effect a cease-fire between Israel and the PLO, with Syria and Saudi Arabia as informal partners. Although the tacit cease-fire agreement was respected by the PLO's mainstream, the radical Palestinian organizations deliberately violated it. The Israeli government, now led by a group of military and civil militant figures, also looked for a pretext that would enable it to end the restricting agreement. At the same time, it was planning a large-scale operation against the Palestinians and practically tightening military cooperation with the Lebanese Forces. In June 1982 Israeli forces invaded Lebanon in a massive operation (see ARAB-ISRAEL CONFLICT). Originally proclaimed to achieve only the liquidation of the PLO's military establishment and to halt at a line about 25 miles (40 km.) from the border, the operation continued beyond that line and soon Israeli forces occupied all of South Lebanon and its coast up to the south-western suburbs of Beirut, the southern Biqa', the Shuf region and southern Mount Lebanon, reaching and cutting the Beirut–Damascus road at several points. Israel did not occupy Beirut but, linking up with Phalanges forces in and around that city, was free to move in East Beirut and up to the coast north-east of Beirut and to besiege and shell West Beirut. The Israeli forces also attacked the Syrians in the Biqa'. The Phalanges collaborated with the invading army to some degree (though not in the siege of Beirut, for example, and much less than expected by the Israeli General Staff), yet they insisted on establishing their almost complete domination under the umbrella of the Israeli occupation. Israel seemed to aim at the establishment of a Maronite-dominated Lebanon under a Phalange leadership that would make peace with Israel and be its ally.

While the older conservative Christian leaders, especially Pierre Jumayyil, were cautiously reserved, the younger, more radical commanders of the LF led by Bashir Jumayyil, went along with Israel's design. The Israelis endeavored to foster relations also with the Shi'i and Druze leaders in the occupied area (and beyond); but relations with the Maronites were given priority, and while the Shi'is of South Lebanon had at first welcomed Israel's forces as liberators from the arbitrary domination of the PLO, and while both Shi'i and Druze local leaders had made arrangements with the occupying army, resentment to Israel's presence grew as the occupation continued. Israel's overt support of the Lebanese Forces further aggravated the the relations with the

Shi'i and Druze leaders, driving them to identify with the Muslim-dominated camp.

The first aim of both Israel and the Phalanges, which had the cooperation of the Lebanese President was the eviction of the PLO's military formations and headquarters not only from South Lebanon (achieved, in the main, by the Israeli army operations) but also from West Beirut. The US again dispatched Philip Habib to mediate, while Israel accelerated its pressure on the besieged Palestinians in West Beirut by heavy shelling and air bombing. The nine-week siege of Beirut and Israel's insistence on eviction of the Palestinian armed forces from Beirut led to inter-Arab consultations, headed by Saudi Arabia's king Fahd, who served as the main link to the American mediation. These consultations resulted in collective Arab acquiescence in the Israeli demand, practically collaborating with its government in expelling the PLO from Lebanon.Yet the long siege of Beirut also eroded Israel's international position, and underlined the acuteness of the Palestine problem. The PLO made a tenacious effort to gain international recognition before giving its consent to the Israeli-American-Arab demand to evict Beirut. A Multi-National Force of US, French and Italian troops was sent in August to supervise that evacuation. It began on 21 August and was completed on 1 September. About 11,000 PLO men were evacuated (though other estimates cite higher figures), mostly by sea, with about 3,000 Syrian troops who withdrew back to Syria. The Multi-National Force was withdrawn by mid-September, only to return two weeks later, after the Sabra and Shatila massacre, but had no significant impact on the situation. They were withdrawn again in February–March 1984, with only France leaving some fifty observers—who had even less impact and were withdrawn by April 1986.

In August 1982, with the expiry of President Sarkis' term nearing, Bashir Jumayyil was elected President of Lebanon; there was no rival candidate, but of the ninety-two surviving members of the ninety-nine-member Parliament, only sixty-two attended (including only five Sunni and twelve Shi'i Muslims). Three weeks later, on 14 September, Jumayyil was killed when the Phalanges' headquarters were blown up by a member of the pro-Syrian SSNP. Israeli forces immediately entered West Beirut to keep law and order and prevent an eruption of violence. However, while they took charge in West Beirut, Phalange commandos stormed the Palestinian camps of Sabra and Shatila—killing blindly—about 460 bodies were found, including 15 women and 20 children (an Israeli commission of inquiry later maintained in its report, published in February 1983, that Israeli commanders bore a share of the responsibility for the massacre, since they should have prevented it; a Lebanese inquiry produced no significant results). The Multi-National Force returned, and Israeli troops withdrew from Beirut in late September.

On 21 September 1982, Bashir Jumayyil's elder brother Amin Jumayyil was elected President; again there was no rival candidate, but the number of Deputies attending (eighty) and of votes cast in favor (seventy-seven) was higher than that achieved by Bashir. Amin Jumayyil, though a member of the Phalanges leadership (who had not played an important role in its military arm), was much less militant than his late brother. He was inclined to seek a compromise with the radical camp and Syria, and a formula for a political settlement (such as the Syria-Franjiyeh plan). He was also much less committed to cooperation with Israel. An agreement with Israel on the withdrawal of its forces was the first urgent point on the agenda of the new President and the new government of Shafiq al-Wazzan appointed in October. Israel was eager to withdraw from Lebanon—on condition that a formula for co-existence could be agreed upon, optimally a peace accord (and an alliance) but at least security arrangements that would prevent clashes in the border region and the recurrence of raids on Israel from Lebanese territory. Negotiations began in December 1982 and proved to be difficult, since the Lebanese side no longer shared the basic conception of Lebanon-Israel peace and could offer only security arrangements that fell far short of what Israel expected and demanded. After a protracted wrangle, with the help of US mediation, an agreement was signed on 17 May 1983 which satisfied Israel's minimum requirements: the state of war was terminated; Lebanon was to prevent the existence, entry or passage of irregular forces and their incursions into Israel (and previous Lebanon-PLO agreements permitting such activities were declared null and void); a security zone in South Lebanon would be policed by an Army Territorial Brigade, to incorporate "existing local units"

(viz). Haddad's Israeli-sustained South Lebanon Army, was not named); mutual liaison offices would be set up; UNIFIL would be moved from the border region to a second-line security zone further north; Israeli forces were to withdraw from Lebanon within three months from the ratification of the agreement (simultaneously with the remaining PLO and Syrian forces—a provision not spelled out but informally understood, and confirmed in an Israeli-US exchange of letters).

The May 1983 agreement was vehemently opposed by the Muslim-dominated radical camp and by Syria, who saw it as a violation of the terms according to which it accepted Lebanon's separate existence in the 1930s, i.e., that Lebanon will not defy its Arab character and ally itself with foreign forces hostile to Syria. Since President Jumayyil sought an accommodation with the radical camp, he hesitated to ratify an agreement and finally annulled it on 5 March 1984 (the Lebanese Parliament cancelled it formally and finally on 21 May 1987, although it never actually voted on it). Since the summer of 1983, Israel was unwilling to wait for the constantly delayed ratification and prepared to evacuate Lebanon, in stages and unilaterally—if possible, in coordination with the Lebanese army and militias. Israel was not prepared to bear the responsibility, as an occupying power, for the complex intracommunal problems and confrontations, particularly between the Druze and Christians in the Shuf region. Growing resistance—at first mainly Palestinians reinfiltrating from the Syrian-held regions, but increasingly Shi'i militants—also imposed a burden of casualties and security problems which Israel deemed senseless to bear. In addition to small-scale raids, suicide car-bomb attacks inflicted heavy losses—the first in November 1982, another in November 1983, both on Israeli headquarters in Tyre (Shi'i terrorists also blew up the US Embassy in April 1983, and the headquarters of US and French troops in October 1983, leaving more than 400 dead, mostly Americans). Israel's attempts to coordinate its withdrawal with the government, the Lebanese army or the militias failed (the government and army were, in any case, not in control of the region concerned), and Israeli forces withdrew, in September 1983, unilaterally from the Shuf area and the adjacent coastal Iqlim al-Kharrub to a line beginning on the Awali River, north of Sidon. US mediation efforts to arrange talks on the coordination of further withdrawals met with persistent obstacles and failure. When Israel-Lebanon talks finally resumed, in November 1984, and Israel re-proposed security arrangements for the southern border zone similar to those provided for in the annulled agreement of May 1983, no accord was reached. The Lebanese insisted on unconditional withdrawal with no security arrangements and "no gains derived from the invasion." In January 1985, the newly established Israeli National Coalition Government decided to withdraw unilaterally from South Lebanon. The withdrawal was completed in April 1985, with Israel retaining de facto control of a self declared "Security Zone" along the border inside Lebanon, 3–6 miles (5–10 km.) wide and with a population of approximately 150,000, mostly Shi'i, policed by the-South Lebanon Army and by occasional Israeli patrols, which were later reinforced and became increasingly stationary. Lebanon protested and continued demanding the total evacuation of all its territory according to UN Security Council Resolution 425 from 1978. Attacks on the South Lebanese Army, on Israeli patrols and sometimes on border villages in Israel (mainly sporadic Katyusha shells) continued; these were mounted mainly by Shi'i groups—HIZBAL-LAH or, to a lesser extent, Amal,—from the region north of the Security Zone. Other radical Lebanese and Palestinian organizations also took part in this effort in the late 1980s and early 1990s. The result was a constant expansion of Israel's preventive or punitive activity within the Security Zone and beyond.

Within Lebanon, the resumed civil war was again escalating. In late 1982 Christian-Druze clashes erupted in the Shuf, with the Druze resisting LF efforts to extend Christian domination to that area (allowed, or encouraged, by the Israeli occupying forces) and trying to reinforce Druze primacy and expel Christian strongpoints. This battle escalated after the September 1983 Israeli withdrawal from the region. The Druze were gaining the upper hand, expelling not only LF military centers but large parts of the Christian village population; they were also reaching the coastal plain west of the Shuf. In July 1983, Walid Junblat set up an alliance with Karameh and Franjiyyeh, the National Salvation Front, and endeavored to attract the Shi'is—among whom Nabih BERRI was emerging as the chief leader—to

join. In Beirut and on the hills south-east of it, almost constant clashes were continuing. The PLO was re-infiltrating fighters into South Lebanon and Beirut and re-establishing its domination of the Palestinian camps. In the Syrian-occupied Biqa' region, on the other hand, Syria took action against Arafat's wing of the PLO which refused to accept Syria's guidance; in May 1983 Syria allowed and aided anti-Arafat Fatah rebel formations led by ABU MUSSA, formerly a high ranking Fatah officer, to attack Arafat's forces and expel them from the Biqa'. In the autumn of that year, when Yasser ARAFAT concentrated his forces in Tripoli, in a last attempt to reassert his autonomous presence in Lebanon, Syrian-based Palestinian factions supported by the Syrian army attacked Arafat's strongholds in the city and neighboring refugee camps (Nahr al-Bared and Badawi). In December 1983 Arafat was forced to admit defeat after a bloody battle (despite the support of the Sunni fundamentalist al-Tawhid al-Islami group), and was expelled from Tripoli in December 1983; Arafat's forces were evacuated by sea with the help of foreign and international bodies.

From the summer of 1983, mediation efforts were intensified, e.g. by the US and SAUDI ARABIA, aiming at a cease-fire and security arrangements, and at a political reconciliation conference to be held by the government, the leaders of the two rival camps (with President Jumayyil considered as part of the Christian camp rather than as a neutral head of state and Syria. In September 1983 agreement was reached on a cease-fire and a security plan (which collapsed) and on a reconciliation conference. That conference convened in Geneva on 31 October for five days, but could reach no agreement on either the conflicting plans for a reform of Lebanon's constitution and structure or the ratification or abrogation of the agreement with Israel; several committees were set up to discuss the various proposals, but did not make progress. The conference's only accomplishment was the definition of Lebanon as an independent and sovereign Arab state (the National Pact from 1943 spoke only of Lebanon's "Arab face" or "Arab character").

The need to resume and intensify the conciliation process was urgent as the civil war continued to escalate, but President Jumayyil continued to act as a Christian leader and not as Lebanese President: American aid given to Lebanon to rebuild the

Lebanese army did not induce the President to broaden his base of support, and the Shi'is, by now a powerful political and military force, were treated harshly. In February 1984, Christian formations of the army entered West Beirut to impose their control, and buildings in the Shi'i neighborhoods were destroyed to make way for reconstruction. Shi'i militias, which had become a dominant element in Beirut's southwestern suburbs and approaches, resisted the impostion and, aided by the army's Sixth Brigade, whose majority of men were Shi'is, succeeded in seizing control of West Beirut. Some Shi'i officers defected. A Shi'i-Druze alliance was finally formed and the militias of the two groups joined forces to seize the coastal region south of Beirut and most of the hills to its east. The LF forces in South Lebanon, cut off by these Shi'i-Druze advances, left their positions, exposing the Christians of the south and the coast to a process of harassment and expulsion. The President's reconstruction efforts, including plans to rebuild the army, were shattered.

In February 1984, Saudi mediators resumed their efforts. President Jumayyil traveled to Damascus on 29 February and gave in to Syria's demands: he annulled the agreement with Israel on 5 March, as the pre-conditioned price for the resumption of the reconciliation process, and Syria guaranteed internal security in Lebanon. In March 1984 another reconciliation conference was convened, this time in Lausanne. The two rival camps again presented diametrically opposed plans: Junblat and Berri demanded the abolition of the communal key in Lebanon's structure and constitution (while in reality they were reinforcing their communal control of their respective cantons); Chamoun and Pierre Jumayyil emphasized the emergence of cantons and envisaged the transformation of Lebanon into a federation of cantons; Franjiyyeh mediated and sought compromise as did the Saudi observers (including Rafiq al-HARIRI, who had participated both in the Geneva and Lausanne Lebanese reconciliation conferences as a special envoy of Saudi King FAHD) and Syria (represented by Abdel Halim KHADDAM). The latter sympathized with the anti-communal proposals of Junblat and Berri, but envisaged their realization in the distant future only, while retaining for the present the traditional communal key, at least for the top posts (and an intensified linkage and coordination of Lebanon's policies and security with Syria). Compromise plans that seemed to crystallize were akin to the 1976 Syria-Franjiyyeh plan, i.e., a change in the communal proportion in Parliament and administration from 6:5 to 50:50. The Prime Minister was to be elected by Parliament rather than appointed by the President. The President's powers were to be reduced and those of the Premier expanded. It was also proposed to institute a senate, and to have the President elected by a majority of at least fifty-five percent of the deputies instead of the simple majority needed before.

The final declaration of the Conciliation Conference, however, did not contain an agreement on these proposals, but instituted a committee of experts to prepare the reformed future constitution of Lebanon (a committee that did not get off the ground). The declaration concerned mainly a new cease-fire and detailed security arrangements and their supervision (arrangements that were not fully implemented). It did not even mention the Government of National Unity that was the main outcome of the conference. The conference declared itself ready to continue its deliberations if reconvened by the President (but was not reconvened).

The Government of National Unity was formed on 30 April 1984 by Rashid Karameh after talks in Damascus. It comprised the leaders of the rival camps—Chamoun and Pierre Jumayyil on one side, and Premier Karameh, Junblat and Berri on the other (Berri, not content with being Minister of Justice, had extracted an additional appointment as Minister in Charge of South Lebanon); but it was strongly weighted in favor of the Muslim-dominated camp despite the equal distribution of seats between Christians and Muslims. The Government of National Unity never became fully operative. Junblat and Berri boycotted its meetings, mounted an opposition campaign calling, in particular, for the resignation or dismissal of President Jumayyil and continued operating their militias in disregard of government orders and security agreements. Both saw Damascus as their center of operations and spent much of their time there. Syria did not go along with its clients; it demanded not only Jumayyil's dismissal, but his cooperation in and acceptance of Syria's plans for Lebanon (and for a greatly enhanced Syrian role in Lebanon). It frequently summoned him to Damascus for pressing consultations. Jumayyil, however, while seeking accommodation with Syria, did not give in and withheld his approval. The government was also boycotted by Franjiyyeh and his supporters.

The horrors of the civil war were mitigated for some time after the Conciliation Conference. In June 1984, a Syrian-devised security plan was agreed upon, and in July, and again in November, the army announced that it was taking over West Beirut (mainly with its Shi'i Sixth Brigade), that Beirut was reunited and that the "green line" dividing it was abolished. The cease-fire and the improvements did not, however, hold for long. Muslim-Christian clashes and mutual shelling soon re-erupted in Beirut, in the hills to the south-east, and in South Lebanon. In the spring of 1985, the Druze PSP militias completed their take-over of the coastal region west of the Shuf and south of it, Iqlim al-Kharrub. Most of the Christian population of those areas and the northern part of South Lebanon was expelled, but succeeded in holding the town of Jezzin and its area (thanks to protection of the Israeli-sponsored South Lebanon Army—which extended its area to include Jezzin). In July 1985, the semi-alliance of the Druze and the Shi'is was formalized in a "United Front" by Junblat—who came to speak in the name of a "National Democratic Front," comprising his PSP and several other left-wing groups (the Communists, the pro-Syrian Ba'th, the SSNP and other groups)—and Berri (who had not been a member of the "National Democratic Front"). This was preceded by a joint Druze-Shi'i operation against the Sunni pro-Nasserist militia, al-Murabitun in West Beirut in April 1985, iquidating it as the last significant competing power in West Beirut. The Druze-Shi'i alliance of July 1985 included a Syrian-sponsored agreement on a security plan to be implemented first in West Beirut and then in the rest of the capital, as well as the resumption of the inter-communal dialogue concerning political and constitutional reform; some Sunni religious and secular leaders also adhered.

The liquidation of al-Murabitun was not the only instance of internal fighting in the Muslim-dominated camp. In September 1985, the fundamentalist al-Tawhid al-Islami in Tripoli was liquidated in bloody battles by its adversary, the Arab Democratic Party, largely Alawi, pro-Syrian and supported by Syrian forces. This move was designed to take control of the city and the port, used to deliver weapons and supplies to pro-Arafat Fatah units in Lebanon. (al-

Murabitun in West Beirut was also an ally of pro-Arafat Fatah, and its liquidation was also interpreted as a move against the pro-Palestinian forces.)

Amal refused to acquiesce in the re-establishment of PLO control in the Palestinian refugee camps of South Lebanon, and later also in Beirut, and entered a long battle with the Palestinian organizations. Clashes, and a Shi'i siege of Palestinian camps, erupted in May 1985; there were several cease-fires, including one concluded in June 1985 in Damascus, (with Syrian and Druze assistance),with the Syrian-dominated Palestinian Salvation Front—which had little effect, since the Fida'yyun in South Lebanon and Beirut were mostly of the Arafat wing (it is noteworthy, however, that the Salvation Front allied with the pro-Arafat units against the Shi'is during the fighting). Fighting erupted again in September and December 1985, and escalated in September 1986, with an almost complete siege of the main camps in South Lebanon (Ayn al-Hilweh and Miyeh-Miyeh near Sidon and Rashidiyya near Tyre) and in Beirut (Sabra, Shatila and, the largest, Burj al-Barajneh). Syria tried to mediate through its own Palestinian organizations of the Salvation Front, but seemed to encourage and support Amal in its fight against the camps controlled by Arafat. Amal's battle with the Palestinians put a strain on its alliance with the Druze,—an alliance that was brittle in any case and was several times disrupted by armed clashes between the allies—since the Druze tried to stay neutral and sometimes even helped the Palestinians (e.g., by letting arms supplies pass through Druze-controlled territory).

The fight with the Palestinians involved also intra-Shi'i problems. As early as late 1982 extremist Shi'i elements, influenced and supported by KHOMEINI and the revolution in IRAN and considering Berri and the mainstream leadership to be far too moderate, were active inside Amal—and outside, in radical groups that appeared under different names (Amal al-Islami, Islamic JIHAD) but generally became known as Hizballah. They regarded a relentless guerrilla fight against Israel as a main, sacred, task; and their men were behind many of the suicidal bombings of Western targets such as the Multi-National Security Force, as well as of Israeli targets in both South Lebanon and Israel's northern border zone. In the course of the 1980s, these ultra-radical Shi'i factions also became involved in the kidnapping of foreigners. They took no part in *Amal's* battle against the Palestinians; on the contrary, they regarded the Palestinians as allies, while they suspected Berri and the mainstream *Amal* of wishing to restrain or halt Shi'i attacks on Israel's sovereign territory and to reach some de facto accommodation with Israel in response to the interest of the South Lebanon Shi'is to avoid renewed involvement in the Palestinian-Israeli cycle of raids and reprisals (the Palestinian fighters, who began returning to South Lebanon, particularly after Israel's pull-out in 1985, resumed Katyusha attacks against Israel in 1986). Observers saw the influence of the Islamic radicals increasing both within *Amal* and through their separate organizations; some also thought that radical pressure was inducing Berri and his associates to take more extreme positions in order to keep their leadership. The two Shi'i organizations, *Amal* and *Hizballah*, finally clashed directly with each other in March 1988 (see below).

The Maronite camp, the Phalanges and the Lebanese Forces also experienced sharp internal crises. Pierre Jumayyil, the founder and leader of the Phalanges, died in August 1984; he was succeeded as chairman by Elie Karameh (designated by Jumayyil), who was replaced in 1986 by Georges Sa'adeh. But the civilian-political leadership of the Phalanges was losing influence, as the center of the stage was taken by its military leaders and their Lebanese Forces. In 1984 the long-time military leader Fadi Fram was eased out and replaced by Fu'ad Abu Nader. But in March 1985, a more militant group under Samir Ja'Ja', incensed by what it regarded as the overly conciliatory, pro-Syrian policy of Abu Nader (and, behind him, President Amin Jumayyil), staged an internal rebellion and took over the command. While Abu Nader, the civilian Phalange leaders and the President tried to achieve reconciliation and devise a compromise, Elie Hubeika—in the past considered a hard-line militant (and the organizer of the Sabra and Shatila massacre of 1982), but by now pro-Syrian and seeking accommodation with the Muslim-dominated camp—emerged as Ja'ja''s chief rival and secured the top movement's position in May 1985. In December 1985 Hubeika went to Damascus and signed a Syrian-sponsored tripartite agreement with the Druze and Shi'i militia leaders Junblat and Berri. The Damascus Accord went far beyond anything any Maronite leader had ever consented to. Hubeika accepted the old reform plan of 1976 that had been discussed again at the 1984 Conciliation Conference but had not been finalized—a reconstitution of Parliament on a 50:50 basis of equality between Christians and non-Christians, to be implemented by new elections for an expanded Parliament within three years; a reduction in the powers of the (Maronite) President; the establishment of an Upper House (probably with a Druze chairman)—and agreed to a re-escalation of the fight against Israel and its presence in its self-declared security zone. Hubeika also agreed to the complete abolition of the communal structure after a transition period of a maximum of ten years that could be shortened by Parliament, to the disbandment of all militias (including his own military force that kept the Christian canton intact and protected), and to the complete coordination of Lebanon's international and inter-Arab policies, Lebanon's army, security and secret services with Syria. The "potentialities and capabilities" of Lebanon and Syria were to become complementary (i.e., in reality, the acceptance of a Syrian protectorate). Lebanon was declared of "Arab affiliation and identity." When this agreement (which had not been authorized by the leadership institutions of the Phalanges or the Lebanese Forcesâ was reported, Ja'ja' and the militants violently denounced it and deposed Hubeika as a traitor whose signature did not commit the movement. And this time, Ja'ja', who took over as commander, had the support of President Jumayyil and most of the Phalange leaders. In January 1986, Ja'ja' and the formations of the Phalange and Lebanese Forces loyal to him defeated Hubeika in battle. Hubeika fled, via Europe, to Syria and Syrian-dominated East Lebanon; there he continued to organize formations of the Lebanese Forces loyal to him. The victorious Ja'ja' called for re-negotiation of the Damascus Accord. In August 1986, and again in September, new clashes erupted, but Hubeika and his forces were defeated again, and the tripartite accord remained a dead letter.

The civil war was continuing and re-escalating—Muslim-dominated West Beirut versus Christian East Beirut; *Amal* versus the Palestinians; Ja'ja's LF against Hubeika's supporters. It also had mounting international repercussions. For some years a spate of kidnappings and assassinations had been extended to foreigners; the kidnappers belonged to various terrorist groups and were frequently traced to

Iranian-guided Islamic extremists. Efforts by Western governments to obtain the release of their citizens, *inter alia*, through contacts with Syria and/or Iran, had little success until 1991 (see below). Lebanese terrorists also operated in foreign countries, particularly France. Lebanon's government was paralyzed, unable even to convene particularly since early in 1986 all Muslim ministers boycotted President Jumayyil.

After the failure of the Damascus Accord, Syria stepped up its intervention in Lebanon, which became more and more direct and encompassing. In July 1986 a small force of a few hundred Syrian commandos entered West Beirut to enforce pacification. The move had apparently not been fully endorsed by President Jumayyil and the Christian leadership, and some of the latter protested, but acquiesced. As the small Syrian contingent failed to enforce a cease-fire, a larger Syrian force—an estimated 4,000 which quickly increased to 7,500 troops— entered West Beirut on 22 February 1987 and took full control, again without the full endorsement of the President and the Christian leadership but with the agreement of Prime Minister Karameh, Berri and Junblat. The Syrian troops met no significant resistance, except for a bloody clash with Shi'i *Hizballah* men which left twenty-three dead. They succeeded, by enforcing strict controls with a heavy hand, in calming the situation to a large extent, particularly on the *Amal*-Palestinian front, but their success was not complete. Shelling across the "green line" and acts of violence continued sporadically, albeit on a smaller scale than before (the Syrians avoided entering the southern Suburbs of the capital controlled by *Hizballah* in order to prevent alienation of its Iranian ally). President Jumayyil, while initially opposing the Syrian deployment, welcomed several clauses in a Syrian-sponsored agreement on political reform, which would reduce the powers of the Maronite President and increase the role of the Muslim communities, but no significant progress has been made in the political arena and since Lebanon's constitutional-political problem has remained unresolved.

On 4 May 1987 Prime Minister Rashid Karameh finally resigned in frustration, but his resignation was not accepted by the President (they had no mutual dealings since early 1986 and therefore Karameh's move had only declarative significance). In a session on 21 May, Parliament annulled the Cairo Agreement of 1969, a move inspired by Syria that was aimed to prevent the redeployment of Arafat's PLO in Lebanon. The 17 May 1983 agreement with Israel was also annulled. On 1 June 1987 Premier Karameh was assassinated when his helicopter was blown up. The identity of his assassins remains unknown, although it was suspected at the time that they were Maronite extremists. Minister Salim el-Huss was nominated acting Prime Minister, and the Muslim leadership demanded a full investigation of the assassination. Speaker of Parliament, Hussein al-Husseini, resigned on 5 June claiming President Jumayyil was trying to conceal the truth about the assassination. The political crisis contributed to the worsening economic situation in Lebanon, and a major crisis broke out in the summer of 1987 which resulted in multi-communal demonstrations and strikes against the decline in living standards. Under Syrian auspices, a "Unification and Liberation Front" was formed in July, including *Amal*, the PSP and other leftist organizations. In September an agreement was reached between Amal and the PLO, ending the "war of the camps" which left more than 2,500 dead. Fighting continued in Sidon, but in January 1988 the siege was lifted from the refugee camps in Beirut and Tyre, and Syrian troops replaced *Amal* fighters and soldiers from the army's Shi'i Sixth Brigade around the camps in Beirut. Amal now turned to deal with militant *Hizballah*, and had initial success in the south, while Arafat's PLO failed to eliminate Abu Mussa's men from the Palestinian camps in Beirut, following a partial reconciliation between the PLO and Damascus inspired by the IN-TIFADAthat broke out in December 1987. Fighting between Amal and *Hizballah* in the Shi'i-dominated southern suburb of Beirut began in May 1988, leading to Syrian intervention: in 27 May Syrian troops entered this area for the first time, while Arafat's PLO units were evacuated from Beirut to Sidon in June and July. Syria now controlled most of Lebanon's territory, including West Beirut and PSP-controlled Iqlim al-Tuffah, and *Amal* and the PSP were reported to have reduced their military activity there. Attention was now given to the upcoming Presidential elections, a traditional occasion for internal tensions and dealings as well as for foreign interest and intervention. The ending of the IRAN-IRAQ WAR in August 1988 added to this tension as Iraq, now free from Iran's grip, turned to settle scores with Syria, its regional rival and Iran's only Arab ally. From then until the Gulf Crisis in August 1990 (see GULF WAR), Lebanon served as a battleground between the two states. President Jumayyil's term was due to expire on 22 September 1988, and a successor was due to be elected by Parliament before that date. Initial American-Syrian talks did not yield an agreed candidate, and the three main candidates were General Michel AWN, commander of the Lebanese army from May 1984, Deputy Raymond Edde, the leader of the National Bloc who had left Lebanon in 1976 and resided in France ever since, and former President Suleiman Franjiyyeh. In response to Franjiyyeh's candidacy, regarded as a Syrian-inspired move to install a pro-Syrian President that will help Syria achieve its goals (it was Franjiyyeh who as President, requested, Syrian intervention in 1976), the Maronite leaderships—Jumayyil, Ja'ja' and Awn—united against him, and were able to prevent his election. Parliament did convene twice, on 18 August and 22 September 1988, but without securing the needed quorum (fifty-one members, two-thirds of the seventy-six members left of the Parliament elected in 1972). A new President was therefore not elected—neither Franjiyyeh nor Michael al-Daher, whose candidacy was announced in September following more talks between the US and Syria. Last-minute efforts to establish an interim-government led by a Maronite failed, and so, in the last minutes before his term expired, President Jumayyil nominated a six-member military interim-government led by General Michel Awn, which included three Christian officers and three Muslim officers (who refused to join it). This move came after a period of unprecedented involvement of the Maronite Army Command in Lebanese politics. Earlier, on 2 September, Premier Salim al-Huss withdrew his government's resignation. After Awn's nomination as Prime Minister, the Maronite-Christian members in al-Huss' government resigned, and for the first time since the end of the civil war, two of the most important institutions in Lebanon were paralyzed. There was a vacancy in the Presidency and two rival governments existed, each claiming it was the only "legitimate" government. This situation had grave effects on other state institutions, such as the army, which split into a strong Christian army and a weak Muslim one; the Lebanese diplomatic missions abroad

and the Central Bank, which kept financing both governments and therefore placed itself in quite a delicate situation. In the political arena, in the Muslim-dominated government, a Greek-Orthodox, Abdallah Rasi, was named Deputy Prime Minister in order to give it intercommunal legitimacy. It enjoyed support from Syria, while the Christian government received support from Iraq (and the PLO). From September 1988 until the defeat of Awn's government two years later, the main question was which of the two Lebanese governments would gain the upper hand in terms of domestic, regional and international legitimacy and support.

As the political crisis reached its peak, military clashes broke out in the Shi'i community—between *Amal* and *Hizballah* in early 1989, and in the Maronite-dominated camp, between Awn's forces and the LF in February 1989, following an attempt by Awn to take over the unlawful, militia-run ports. But hopes of reassertion of Awn's government's authority—after an agreement between Awn and the LF reached in 22 February—vanished on 14 March, when he declared a "war of liberation" against the Syrian forces, who by then controlled some sixty percent of Lebanon's territory. A violent confrontation between the Maronite units of the army and the Syrian army ensued, leaving about 300 dead in April only. Twenty-three Christian deputies called for an immediate cease-fire and appealed for intervention by the Arab League, the UN and the EEC, undermining Awn's position. However, all efforts by the Arab League, including those made by a six-member commission of foreign ministers formed in January, to reach a cease-fire and bring the two sides together were abortive. In late May 1989, an emergency summit of Arab leaders convened in Casablanca and appointed a Tripartite Arab High Commission consisting of King HASAN II of MOROCCO, King Fahd of Saudi Arabia and President Chadli BEN JEDID of ALGERIA. The Commission aimed at the implementation of a cease-fire in Lebanon in six months, the deployment of a group of Arab observers to monitor the cease-fire and mediation between the warring parties in order to facilitate an agreement concerning the question of political reforms and the election of a new President. Iraq, by now the chief supplier of arms to Awn's Lebanese army, demanded the withdrawal of the Syrian forces and called for the deployment of Arab Security Forces in greater Beirut in their place. Egypt, Iraq, Jordan and the PLO supported the call for evacuation of the Syrian forces and their replacement by Arab Peacekeeping Forces, but Syria thwarted this plan, and the Casablanca Conference called only for the re-assertion of the Lebanese state's sovereignty over all its territory by a future "National Reconciliation Government." On 28 June 1989 the Tripartite Arab High Commission called for a cease-fire and a peace plan for Lebanon that included the ending of the siege on the Muslim and Christian ports and the opening of roads linking West and East Beirut. toward convening the Lebanese Parliament in a foreign country. Awn rejected this last point and fighting continued. On 30 July the Commission suspended its work and blamed Syria for the lack of progress after Syria refused to discuss the withdrawal of its forces before the establishment of a National Reconciliation Government. Syria claimed that the Commission was not objective and insisted that Iraq continue to supply Awn with weapons. An attempt by France to mediate in August 1989 and efforts by the UN security council did not yield substantive results. Meanwhile, Syria acted both militarily and politically. Syrian troops attacked Christian-controlled Souq al-Gharb on 13 August, and two days later a sixteen-member "National Lebanese Front" was formed, including Lebanese and anti-Arafat Palestinian organizations, supported by Syria and Iran. By early September 1989 it was becoming clear that the al-Huss government was gaining the upper hand both in terms of international support and military power. The US moved its embassy from Lebanon after receiving threats from Awn's supporters, and Awn was deprived of American support. In addition, Awn was not able to broaden his base of support to include members of the other communities, while support in his own community was declining. Syria, using both military and political means, was getting its own way: internationalization of the crisis—bound to help the weaker, Maronite side—was prevented; the pro-Syrian camp was organized, and Syrian troops remained stationed throughout Lebanon despite Arab criticism. The Tripartite Arab High Commission resumed its work in September and high-level meetings were held in Beirut and Damascus. On 16 September, a seven-point plan was announced. It called for a comprehensive and total cease-fire and a stop to weapon supplies to both sides by sea. Both

aspects were supervised by an Arab League Security Committee; for the lifting of the Syrian siege on the Christian enclave; for the re-opening of the Beirut Airport, and, after implementation of all these steps, for convening the Lebanese Parliament on 30 September to discuss a "National Reconciliation Pact" in a location to be announced in the future.

Syria welcomed the plan, which did not call for demobilization of its troops from Lebanon, while Awn rejected it. On 18 September 1989 the cease-fire came into effect, and on 30 September, sixty-two of the seventy-three deputies who survived from the Parliament elected in 1972—thirty-one Muslims and thirty-one Christians—convened in Ta'if, Saudi Arabia, and in a session held on 22 October 1989, fifty-eight of them endorsed a "Document of National Understanding," known as the Ta'if Document the outline of which was reached with the Tripartite Arab High Commission's mediation. The Ta'if Document is considered a turning point in the civil war, and maybe even in the political history of Lebanon. It was a formal agreement endorsed by a formal Lebanese institution—the only remaining institution enjoying legitimacy from the majority of Lebanon's population—not a tacit and unofficial understanding like the National Pact of 1943 or an agreement by militia leaders, like the Damascus Accord of 1985. In its declarative part, the document stated that Lebanon is a "final homeland for all its sons," thus giving the once-illegitimate Lebanese entity decisive wall-to-wall recognition. It stated that Lebanon is "Arab in its affiliation and identity," in contrast to this the more vague expression, "an Arab face" used in 1943 and similar to that used in 1985. It stated that any "authority which contradicts the pact of communal coexistence" is illegitimate, emphasizing by this that the communal coexistence, i.e., the agreement of the various communities to live together and the sharing of power by them, is the source of legitimacy for authority in Lebanon, and implying that any authority that might challenge this agreement will be removed by force. On the political-institutional level, executive power was transferred from the President (a Maronite) to the government and the Premier (a Sunni-Muslim), and to a lesser extent, to the Speaker (a Shi'i). Instead of the informal 6:5 ratio in favor of the Christians in effect since 1943, a ratio of 50:50 was adopted for the distribution of parliamentary seats and high-level posts in all state institutions, while other posts were to be manned according to ability and talents, thereby eliminating the principle of representation according to one's community. A national body was to be set up for this last purpose. Important reforms were also introduced in the field of national security, where an effort had been made to put an end to the prevailing ambiguity that had such a grave effect in the past. It was decided that the Armed Forces are subordinate to the government, and that the government is responsible for declaring an emergency, war, peace and mobilization, as well as for the supervision of all governmental agencies, including security and military bodies. The Lebanese National Reconciliation government was to devise a security plan that would expand its control over all of its territory, and the militias, both Lebanese and non-Lebanese (i.e., including the Palestinian organizations), were to be dismantled. The concluding part of the agreement emphasized the special relations between Lebanon and Syria and called for agreements between the two states in all fields. Lebanon was prohibited from becoming "a source of threat on Syria's security" and from becoming a passageway or *place d'armes* for any force, state or organization that might endanger Syria's security. It is noteworthy that this concluding part was a result of a prior agreement between the Tripartite Arab High Commission and Syria, and the Lebanese deputies were unable to change it. Responses to the Ta'if Agreement were of mixed nature. Michel Awn condemned the Document of National Understanding as a betrayal of Lebanon's sovereignty, claiming that the Christian deputies promised him that concessions would be made only in return for full withdrawal of the Syrian army. However, the Maronite camp was not united in backing him. Some Maronite leaders, including George Sa'adeh, the leader of the Phalanges, took part in the formulation of the Ta'if Agreement and others supported it. In early November 1989, Parliament convened in the northern town of Klei'at, in the area controlled by the Syrians, and elected Rene Mu'awwad, a deputy from Zagharta and former minister, as President by a majority of fifty-two out of the fifty-eight deputies present. Parliament also ratified the Ta'if Agreement unanimously and elected Hussein al-Husseini as Speaker. Before this session, General Awn called all deputies to consult him, and after the Muslim deputies departed to Klei'at without

doing so, declared the dismissal of Parliament and Mu'awwad's election null and void. On 13 November 1989 President-elect Mu'awwad invited Salim al-Huss to form a "Government of National Conciliation," but Maronite leaders were reluctant to join it and openly opposed Awn. Nine days later, President Mu'awwad was assassinated and on 24 November Elias al-Harawi, a deputy from Zahla, was elected President in his place and Parliament's term was extended until the end of 1994. A new government was formed the next day, and George Sa'adeh participated in it as minister. The new government declared the dismissal of General Awn from his post as Commander of the Lebanese Army and appointed General Emile Lahoud to the post. In the face of an attempt to depose Awn by force, Ja'ja' stated that he would side with Awn. Meanwhile the Central Bank halted money transfers to the areas controlled by Awn and the Ministry of Defence stopped paying salaries to his men. Awn, on his part, did not take advantage of the widening gaps in the pro-Ta'if camp, and from late January 1990 tried again to curb the LF in bloody battles, which left hundreds dead and pushed the LF to recognize al-Huss's government and the Ta'if Agreement. On 21 August Parliament convened again, and amended the Lebanese constitution to include all the reforms decided upon in Ta'if. Forty new deputies were to be appointed (and not elected, due to the "extraordinary situation" prevailing in the country) so that Parliament would include 108 members, divided equally between Christians and Muslims (these were appointed later, in June 1991). Areas controlled by Awn were put under siege in late September, and on 13 October Syrian forces and Muslim units of the Lebanese army stormed the Christian enclave and defeated his forces with little resistance. In fact, Syria took advantage of the American efforts to maintain the International Coalition formed against Iraq after its invasion of Kuwait in August, receiving a "green light" from the US (as well as tacit agreement from Israel) (see AWN).

A new thirty-member Government of National Reconciliation was formed on 24 December 1990 by Omar Karameh, brother of the deceased Rashid and an ally of the Syrians. Among the ministers were leaders of most Lebanese militias, except for *Hizballah*, the Communist Party and the National Liberal Party. These included Ja'ja' and Sa'adeh, who found themselves outnumbered by pro-Syrian militia leaders, Berri, Junblat and Hubeika. The inclusion of militia members in the government was intended to facilitate the upcoming task: the peaceful disbanding of all militias with the consent of their leaders. On 28 March 1991 the government decided that all militias were to be disbanded by 30 April and a ministerial committee was formed to facilitate the disbanding and the collection of all heavy weapons. It held talks with Palestinian leaders and made it clear that the days of the Cairo Agreement were over and that Lebanon would not permit special military arrangements with Palestinians, despite the Palestinian claims that their weapons are "regional" and not "local," i.e., not under the jurisdiction of the Lebanese government. The militias were disbanded duly (with the exception of *Hizballah*) and the now united Lebanese army was strengthened as it received the militias' heavy weapons and underwent a process of reorganization that included the shuffling of its units and commanders in order to prevent the formation of sectarian units that might lead to disintegration (like in 1975–1976). For this reason, the army command opposed the enrollment of the militia personnel in it, and preferred conscription of fresh soldiers instead. It also grew in size, from about 20,000 in 1975 and about 35,000 in 1988 to approximately 45,000 in 1995. With Syrian backing, it now became the strongest military force in the country and from February 1991 began deploying in areas formerly controlled by the militias, including the semi-autonomous Druze canton, the areas around the Palestinian refugee camps and parts of South Lebanon. The only remaining militias were were *Hizballah*, engaged in resistance to the Israeli occupation in South Lebanon and enjoying an Iranian support, and the Israel's surrogate militia, the South Lebanon army active in Israel's self-declared Security Zone. It is noteworthy that in February 1996, following demonstrations by the labor unions, the Lebanese army demonstrated its ability in imposing a country-wide curfew.

The "special relations" with Syria, mentioned in the abrogated Damascus Accord in 1985 and in the Ta'if Agreement in 1989, were formalized in the signing of the Treaty of Brotherhood, Cooperation and Coordination between Syria and Lebanon in May 1991. This agreement called for cooperation and coordination between the two states on all po-

litical, economic and security issues and established a formal structure—five joint councils that were to meet regularly—to develop and execute policies affecting Lebanon. It also reiterated the Syrian-inspired clauses which appeared in the Ta'if Agreement (see above). Considering the imbalance in the political and military power of the two states, as well as the presence of 35,000 Syrian troops in Lebanon, the Treaty's opponents, mainly from the Maronite camp, claimed that it had in fact turned Lebanon into a Syrian "protectorate" and established a situation "constituting a violation of Lebanon's sovereignty." Suspicions deepened as Syria, despite the far-reaching Treaty, sustained its refusal since the independence to establish full diplomatic relations with Lebanon, and opposition leaders feared another step had been made toward full annexation of Lebanon by Syria. Indeed, Syria has controlled Lebanon's foreign policy since 1991, thwarting, at times, moves concerning Lebanon inconsistent with its own interests (e.g., Israeli moves to reach an agreement with Lebanon that would enable the former to pull its forces out of South Lebanon). The treaty's supporters, on the other hand, denied that Lebanese freedoms were hurt and argued that close relations with Syria were vital for Lebanon's stability and prosperity after the devastating civil war, as well as in negotiations with Israel, where Israeli pressures could be balanced by Syria.

Since August 1991, foreign hostages kidnapped in Lebanon from the mid-1980s were gradually released, and by June 1992 all Western hostages in Lebanon were free. This process helped Lebanon restore its international status and reputation on the one hand, and receive international aid necessary to rebuild it on the other. As many countries renewed their dealings with Lebanon, foreign leaders, e.g., French President Jacques Chirac, visited Lebanon (Chirac's two visits in 1996 were the first visits by a French President in Lebanon since 1943).

Following the formation of the government, the disbanding of most militias, the deployment of the army and the formalization of relations with Syria, political life in Lebanon slowly began to return to normal. The Lebanese Parliament adopted a General Amnesty Law for war crimes, except political murder and killings of diplomats and clergymen, and Preparations for first post-civil war Parliamentary elections began in summer 1992. Election laws were discussed in Parliament in June–July, and the new law was approved on 16 July; it increased the number of deputies from 108 to 128, equally divided between Christians and Muslims. Maronite groups threatened to boycott the upcoming elections, since the Syrian army did not re-deploy and might affect the outcome of the elections. The majority of the Maronite community did boycott the elections, which were held in three stages in August–September 1992, and pro-Syrian candidates were elected in all areas. On 31 October, a thirty-member government, including many technocrats, was formed by Rafiq al-HARIRI and hopes were that Lebanon was finally on the right track, after two years of weak, unstable governments, and with Hariri's promising background. Since the end of the war, and particularly after Hariri's nomination as Premier, Lebanon began a process of reconstruction, received loans from the World Bank and was given promises for aid from the Arab League. Meanwhile, Lebanon's GDP was rising steadily. The Hariri government devised a 11 billion dollar plan to rebuild Lebanon and the devastated Beirut in particular, and set out to repair the country's infrastructure, building roads, water and electricity works and clinics in South Lebanon. It also endeavored to restore Lebanon's pre-war status as a regional finance and trade center.

On the regional level, Lebanon participated in the Madrid Conference (see ARAB-ISRAEL PEACEMAKING) in 1991 and held negotiations with Israel in the bilateral Lebanese-Israeli track. Lebanon's participation in the Conference was criticized by some politicians, who claimed that since the terms of reference of the Conference were UN Security Council Resolutions 242 and 338 only, Lebanon would gain nothing from it since relations with the two countries were regulated by the 1949 Armistice Agreement, while Resolution 425, calling for the withdrawal of Israeli forces from Lebanon, would be linked to the implementation of the other resolutions. After Madrid, and under the Treaty of Brotherhood, Cooperation and Coordination of May 1991, Lebanon's regional policy was closely linked to that of Syria, and progress on the Lebanese-Israeli track was conditioned on the progress of the Syrian-Israeli track, thus frustrating any attempt by Israel to reach a bilateral agreement with Lebanon that would permit the former to withdraw its forces. South Lebanon remained a source of tension and violence as Israel

kept its Security Zone, while *Hizballah*, acting under the slogan of "resistance," and supported and armed by Iran with Syria facilitating its activities, escalated its attacks on Israel's forces and those of the South Lebanon Army, and sometimes bombarded Israel's northern towns. Major escalations in this area took place in July 1993 and April 1996, causing massive devastation to homes and services and forcing hundreds of thousands of civilians to leave South Lebanon and flee north.

In October 1995, the six-year term of President Elias Harawi was extended exceptionally for a period of three years, presumably to prevent arenewed embroilment in Presidential elections. Parliamentary elections, however, were held duly in August–September 1996, after the election law had been changed. According to the new law, the elections were held in four of Lebanon's five areas (*Muhafazat*): the North, South, Beirut and the Biqaʻ, whereas in the fifth region, Mount Lebanon (largely Christian), elections were held separately in each of the subdistricts (*Qadas*). The purpose was to block the election of Maronite opposition leaders, as well as prevent the Maronites from ousting leading governmental leaders, such as Walid Junblat. After much opposition and an appeal to the Lebanese Constitutional Court, the new law was declared unconstitutional, but the government added a clause to it making it valid for one time only and the elections proceeded duly. Before these elections, Nabih Berri, the Speaker of Parliament from 1992, formed an alliance with Prime Minister Hariri, and both used the state apparatus to win them. (Currently, Berri has a bloc of twenty to twenty-five deputies loyal to him while Hariri enjoys the support of a bloc of thirty to fourty deputies.) This alliance allowed the two leaders to have their supporters elected in areas other than which they were candidates themselves. As for the Maronite-Christian opposition, a few of its leaders were elected, while most of its leaders lost to governmental candidates. Other Maronite opposition leaders, such as Edde, Jumayyil and Awn, still reside in France while Samir Jaʻjaʻ was sentenced to prison after the LF was involved in unlawful activities after it was disbanded in 1991 and became a political party.

Education, Press The level of literacy in Lebanon and the percentage of children attending schools are, from the nineteenth century, higher than the other Arab countries (and later, the Arab states). Until the eruption of the civil war in 1975, Beirut was an important educational and intellectual center with significant influence in the Arab world. Some of its most prestigious academic institutions were founded by foreign missionaries: the French-Catholic University of St. Joseph, established in 1875 by the Jesuits, and the American University of Beirut (AUB), founded in 1866 as the Syrian Protestant College, a university since 1920. The University of Lebanon was founded in 1951, and the Arab University in 1960. The American University attracted students from all the Arab Countries and was an important training ground for the modern nationalist Arab elite. All these institutions were gravely affected by the civil war; some were paralyzed, if they did not close altogether, .

Lebanon was also a center of Arab literature and cultural activity—though Cairo has always come foremost in this field. Beirut had an active and highly diversified press, a plethora of daily, weekly and monthly journals, most of them with small circulation. From the nationalization of Egyptian newspapers in 1960 until the mid-1970s, Beirut was the principal source of free, uncontrolled political information in and about the Arab states. Some of Beirut's newspapers were propaganda organs of, and financed by, foreign countries, international movements and political factions. There were several foreign-language publications—e.g., *L'Orient* and *Le Jour* (merged in 1971), *Daily Star*, and *Monday Morning*. Among the more important Arabic-language daily newspapers were *al-Hayat* and *al-Nahar* (Western-oriented; *al-Hayat* moved to London during the civil war and was bought by Saudi businessmen, but it still publishes news from Lebanon on its front pages), *al-Anwar*, *al-Safir* and *al-Ahrar* (leftist). Several weeklies were mouthpieces of leftist, Marxist factions and Palestinian guerrilla groups, which moved out after 1982–1983. Though many of the more important organs have survived even though the difficult conditions of the civil war, their influence and standing in the Arab world have considerably diminished.

The post-civil war governments in Lebanon also discussed laws and decrees that would restrict the media, such a broadcasting law in 1994 which enabled the state to restrict radio and television broadcasts. Such laws were met with opposition both from

Maronite figures, who feared Lebanon was becoming "another Arab state" with restrictions and limitations on the press, and from radical forces, such as *Hizballah*, who feared restriction of its media organs as a first measure toward its repression altogether. It is yet to be seen what kind of arrangements will be adopted in this field, although it is apparent that post-civil war governments will not allow a repetition of the pre-war anarchic situation in Lebanon.

LEBANON WAR (1982)   see ARAB-ISRAEL CONFLICT.

LEVANT   "Lands of the Rising Sun". Originally designated the entire East, as seen from southern Europe, but particularly the eastern coast of the Mediterranean, from Greece to EGYPT. The concept and use of the term gradually changed to mean only the Asia Minor, SYRIA-LEBANON and Palestine. Recent usage limits the term Levant to Syria and Lebanon. Since the late nineteenth century the term came to be increasingly used by Europeans in the adjective (Levantine), referring pejoratively to a set of behavioral and character traits of the Levant modernizing coastal population, such as an inlination toward superficial imitation of Western ideas, manners and clothing, empty rhetoric and lack of integrity.

LIBYA   A Republic in the north African MAGHREB region, gained independence on 24 December 1951, under the aegis of the UN. It borders EGYPT and SUDAN in the east, thus is geographically separated from the Mashriq and the heart of the Middle East. In the south, Libya borders the black sub-Saharan countries of Chad and Niger . In the west, it borders ALGERIA and TUNISIA. In the north Libya borders the Mediterranean Sea, the outlet for the country's export of oil—the country's major oxygen lifeline. Libya's main towns are located on the Mediterranean coast: Tripoli, the capital city, with a population of 2 million, Benjhazi, Misurata, Tuwara and al-Khums.

Demographically, about eighty percent of the Libyan population is concentrated in the north of the country, where population density is over 19 per sq. miles (50 per sq. km.), whereas elsewhere population density is less than 0.4 per sq. miles (1 per sq. km.). Population is estimated at 5 million and its growth rate is one of the highest in the world (3.9–4.2%). Almost fifty percent of the population was estimated to be under fifteen years of age in the mid-1990s.

Most Libyans are Arab SUNNI-Muslims. The official language is ARABIC sometimes with Berber dialects. The number of foreign residents fluctuates according to the state's needs for foreign workforce, exceeding 2 million at prosperous economic times.

Libya's official name as declared in March 1977, is The Great Socialist Libyan Arab Peoples's *Jamahiriyya* (state of the masses) and in Arabic: *Al-Jamahiriyya al Arabiyya al-Libiyya al-Sha'biyya al Ishtirakiyya al-Uzma*. The last adjective, the "Great" (*al Uzma*) was added, however, nine years later in the aftermath of the American air raid on Libya in April 1986 (see below). By this, QADHAFI wished to mark the Libyans' victory as he claimed, over the US.

Political History before Independence Libya was conquered by the Ottomans in the middle of the sixteenth century. The area had a degree of autonomy between 1711 and 1835, after a Tripolitanian notable, Ahmad Qaramanli, defeated the Pasha sent from Istanbul and secured recognition for himself as Pasha by Sultan Ahmad III.

His descendants, the Qaramanli dynasty, continued ruling under nominal Ottoman sovereignty and engaged in piracy in the Mediterranean. Concerted action by the European powers brought an end to their exploits, causing the ruin of Yussuf, the last of the Qaramanlis. In 1835 the Ottomans reoccupied the territory to counter expanding French influence in North Africa.

In the mid-nineteenth century, there emerged a movement of religious reform, the SANUSSI order. This was popular among the local tribes, especially those in Cyrenaica and in the desert hinterland where neither the Qaramanlis nor the Ottomans had ever exerted effective control. The Sanussi movement gave the nomads of Cyrenaica, Fezzan and southern Tripolitania the rudiments of a social structure and a sense of a political community, and emerged into a political and military force.

In the late nineteenth century, when colonialism was at its zenith, Italy began to covet Libya, aspiring to acquire "its share" of North Africa, where other powers, especially FRANCE, were expanding their influence. By a series of separate agreements signed with Austria in 1887, BRITAIN in 1890, France in 1900 and RUSSIA in 1909, Italy secured the backing of the major European powers for the conquest of

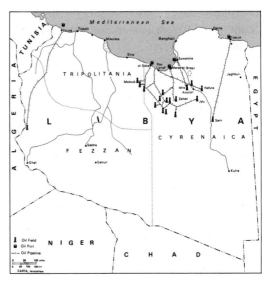

Map of Libya

the Turkish provinces of Tripoli and Cyrenaica. In September 1911 Italy declared war on TURKEY and Italian troops landed at Tripoli. They encountered unexpected resistance on the part of local tribesmen and Sanussis, who fought together with the Turks under the command of Turkish officers, such as Enver Pasha (from 1913, the leading figure in power of the Ottoman Empire) and Mustafa Kemal (later known as ATATÜRK). However, owing to increased difficulties on other fronts, the Ottomans were compelled to pacify Italy in October 1912, relinquishing their sovereignty over Libya in the LAUSANNE TREATY.

Libyan tribesmen, however, continued a guerrilla war against the Italians. In April 1915 after defeating an Italian force at Qasr bu Hadi, in the desert of Sirte, the Sanussis under Sari al-Din tried to unite the whole of Tripolitania under the Sanussi flag. But they were thwarted by the traditional feud between the Sanussi nomads of Cyrenaica and the interior and the Tripolitanian urban and coastal nationalists headed by Ramadan al-Suweihili. Safi al-Din was defeated by Ramadan in 1916.

Thereafter resistance against the Italians, mainly in Cyrenaica, was led by the Sanussi chief, Sayyid Ahmad al-Sharif. He was aided by a number of Ottoman troops who had remained in the country despite the treaty of 1912.

After Italy's entry into World War I in 1915, Sanussi resistance became part of the general war

LIBYA

operations. The Ottomans encouraged Ahmad al-Sharif to attack EGYPT so as to ease British pressure on them.

The Sanussis first overcame the small British garrison at al-Sallum and advanced as far as Sidi al-Barrani. A British counter-offensive forced them to retreat in 1916. Ahmad al-Sharif then left the country aboard a German submarine for Istanbul, relinquishing political and military control in Cyrenaica to his cousin and rival, Sayyid Idris al-Sanussi. He had all along opposed any action against the British and had even cooperated with them.

Early in 1917, negotiations took place at Ikrima between Britain, Italy and Sayyid Idris, who was recognized as "The Grand Sanussi". Britain and the Sanussi leader agreed on mutual cooperation.

Negotiations with Italy were more difficult, as the Italians could not agree to Libyan or Cyrenaican-Sanussi independence, but they eventually did lead to a precarious agreement on a cessation of hostilities.

After World War I the Socialist government of Italy, pursuing a more liberal colonial policy, took steps towards granting civil and political rights to the people of Cyrenaica and Tripolitania. Separate statutes for the two provinces provided for a parliament and a government council for each province and local council. In a new accord, signed at al-Rajma in October 1920, Idris al-Sanussi was recognized by Italy as Emir (Prince) at the head of a self-governing Sanussi regime in the interior of Cyrenaica, comprising the oases of Jaghbub, Ajila, Jalu and Kufra, with the right to use Ajdabiyya as the seat of his administration, which was to be subsidized by Italy. The Emir, for his part, was to ensure the disbandment and suppression of any armed Sanussi formations.

The Emir was unable to fulfill this obligation, and so, a year later, the Bu Maryam Accord provided that, until the establishment of full Italian control, Sanussi formations still existing would be maintained jointly by Sanussis and Italians in "mixed camps".

In view of the favorable terms obtained by Idris al-Sanussi at al-Rajma, the Tripolitanians—who had established a semi-independent regime of their own before the Italians had been able to exert full control—decided to make him their leader and invested him formally with the Emirate of Tripolitania on 28 July 1922. When the Italians took steps to prevent this extension of Sanussi self-government to Tripolitania, Idris al-Sanussi broke with them and reopened a bitter conflict. However, he was not strong enough to fight and left the country for Egypt in December 1922; his exile was to last more than twenty years.

After 1922 fascist Italy increased operations to subjugate the rebellious tribes and gain complete control of the country. In 1923 it declared null and void all previous Italo-Sanussi accords; seized the "mixed camps" in a surprise action, and attacked the rebels.

The renewed guerrilla war was to last nine years. It was led by a Sanussi follower, Omar al-Mukhtar, and based on small, mobile bands usually comprised of members of the same tribe. Gradually, the Italians took the Sanussi strongholds. Jaghbub fell in 1926, Kufra—the last—in 1931. The Sanussi rebel leader, Sheikh Rida (Idris' brother) surrendered in 1928. The Italians erected a barbed wire barrier along the Egyptian frontier, to bar the rebels' arms supply routes. Omar al-Mukhtar, continuing a desperate fight, was wounded and captured in September 1931. Tried and publicly hanged the same month, his name became a symbol of the fight for freedom in Libya and the Arab-Muslim world. With al-Mukhtar's death, resistance broke down. In 1934 Italy nominally united Cyrenaica and Tripolitania, added Fezzan and named the combined area Libya

The colonization of the territory by Italian settlers started in 1920, but was hindered by the guerrilla war. In 1933 settlement was given a new impetus by the Italian administration, and agencies were created to help and finance it. By 1940, the number of Italian settlers had reached approximately 90,000 in Tripolitania as well as some 60,000 in Cyrenaica. The Italians extended the cultivated areas, enlarged cities, set up public buildings and established a network of roads. However they did little to raise the standard of living and the cultural level of the local population.

When Italy entered World War II, Sayyid Idris al-Sanussi, in his Cairo exile, endeavored (at Britain's suggestion), to recruit a Sanussi force which would help the Allied forces to liberate Libya. A meeting of Cyrenaican and Tripolitanian leaders, in August 1940, endorsed his plans—despite the opposition of a number of Tripolitanian leaders, asking him to negotiate Libya's future independence with Britain.

The Sanussi force of five battalions took part in the campaign in the Western Desert. In return, the British Foreign Secretary, Anthony Eden, expressed in January 1942 his government's appreciation of the Sanussis' cooperation and pledged that "the Sanussis in Cyrenaica will in no circumstances again fall under Italian domination."

During the war, Libya became a battlefield, on which Rommel's Afrika Korps and the British Eighth Army fought for control of the Western Desert. After changing hands three times, Cyrenaica was taken by the Allied forces in November 1942, and Tripoli in January 1943. Fezzan fell to the Free French forces advancing from Chad. By February 1943 the last of the Axis forces were evicted and Italy's rule of Libya came to an end.

After the war, disagreement between the Powers delayed a settlement of Libya's future and from 1943 to 1951 the country was ruled by a Provisional Military Administration; British in Cyrenaica and Tripoli, French in Fezzan.

The question of Libya's future, linked with the fate of other Italian colonies in Africa, formed part of long-drawn peace negotiations with Italy. For Libya, a temporary UN trusteeship was agreed upon, but there were conflicting views as to its form and the identity of the trustee country or countries. Finally, in the Italian peace treaty of 1947, the disposal of the Italian colonies was deferred for a year. Should no agreement be reached by the end of that time, the matter would be referred to the UN General Assembly. No agreement was reached, and the issue was discussed at the UN General Assembly in April 1949.

Meanwhile, Britain and Italy had agreed to place Libya under three UN trusteeships for ten years: Tripolitania was to go to Italy; Cyrenaica to Britain and Fezzan to France. After ten years, Libya would be granted independence upon a recommendation by the General Assembly.

The plan caused strong protests and disturbances in Libya. It was adopted in the UN Political Committee, in May 1949. Nonetheless, in the General Assembly it fell short by one vote, of the required two-thirds majority, and was thus rejected.

Instead, on 21 November 1949, the Assembly ruled, by forty-eight votes to one (with nine abstentions) that "Libya, comprising Cyrenaica, Tripolitania and Fezzan" should become independent by 1 January 1952 at the latest. A UN Commissioner was to advise and assist in the establishment of an independent government and the formulation of a constitution, in cooperation with an Advisory Council comprising one representative from each of the three provinces of Libya; one from its minorities and one each from Egypt, France, Italy, Pakistan, Britain and the US.

In December 1949 Adrian Pelt of the Netherlands was appointed Commissioner. With the assistance of the Advisory Council, he established a twenty-one member committee to prepare the establishment of a Constituent Assembly. The Assembly convened in November 1950. The main difficulty in the drafting of a constitution lay in the rivalries between the three provinces, and Cyrenaica's and Fezzan's insistence on status and representation equal to that of Tripolitania, despite the great difference of population and area.

Cyrenaica was made independent on 31 May 1949 by Idris al-Sanussi, with himself as Emir, with British support and for the time being under the supervision of the British military administration. Elections for a Cyrenaican Parliament were held in June 1950. Provisional representative assemblies for Tripolitania and Fezzan were also formed in 1950. Provincial Executive Councils were set up in 1950 and a provisional government of Libya in March 1951. The constitutional problem was solved by the establishment of Libya as a federation, giving wide internal autonomy to each of its three component parts. The constitution was adopted in October 1951; the throne of Libya was offered to Emir Idris al-Sanussi. On 24 December 1951 Libya was declared independent under King Idris.

Independent Libya: Domestic Affairs: Friction between Tripolitania and Cyrenaica bedevilled Libya's internal affairs. Tripolitania strongly favored a unitarian state, whereas Cyrenaica and Fezzan advocated federalism. Prior to the first elections of February 1952, an (opposition) National Congress of Tripolitania campaigned against the federal constitution. The elections were won by moderate pro-government candidates, except in the city of Tripoli, where riots occurred. These were suppressed, the National Congress leader, Bashir Sa'dawi (holder of a Saudi passport), was expelled and the National Congress ceased to exist. Rivalries between Tripolitania and Cyrenaica frequently turned into conflicts between provincial and federal authorities. Yet the King and his government remained in firm control. Subsequent elections were held without major trouble.

Nationalist elements, mainly in Tripolitania, also disagreed with the King's conservative regime and his pro-Western policy. With the rising tide of anti-Western nationalism in the Middle East and North Africa their influence grew.

In 1963, as a result of their pressure, the King abolished the federation and a new unitary constitution was adopted by Parliament. The traditional division of Libya into its three provinces was replaced by ten administrative districts. Libya's economic boom, following the exploitation of its oil resources since 1960, made the country independent of Western financial assistance and strengthened the nationalists. They were also increasingly under Nasserist influence and favored Libya's integration in an Egyptian-led Arab alliance based on Socialism at home and neutralism in foreign relations.

King Idris, (1951–1969) followed a pro-Western foreign policy. Treaties signed with Britain, in July 1953, and the United States in September 1954, allowed these powers to maintain military bases and forces in Libya, in exchange for military and economic aid (then still needed). An agreement with France, in August 1955, provided for the liquidation of its military base in Fezzan by November 1956, but gave it forces communication facilities in that desert region (which were curtailed late in 1963). Close ties were also maintained with Turkey and Greece.

Within the ARAB LEAGUE, which it joined in March 1953, Libya supported the conservative bloc, despite insistent demands by the urban intelligentsia for a pro-Egyptian and neutralist policy. Nasserist Egypt, for its part, encouraged subversive activities in Libya, and Egyptian diplomats and military attaches were expelled on several occasions. However, after Egypt's defeat in the 1967 war, and along with the conclusions of the Arab summit in Khartoum, Libya—together with SAUDI ARABIA and KUWAIT—began extending financial aid to Egypt (and JORDAN) in view of their economic and military losses in the war.

Libya advocated closer cooperation among the Maghreb states and talks were held with Tunisia, Algeria and MOROCCO, but no progress was made. Under the combined internal and external pressure for the liquidation of foreign bases, the government felt compelled publicly to favor their early evacuation. It nonetheless took few practical steps. In February 1964, for instance, President Nasser publicly called for the liquidation of the American and British bases in Libya; a day later, the Libyan government declared that the military agreements with the US and the UK would not be renewed upon their expiry (i.e. in 1971), to which the US and Britain responded in acceptance.

In June 1967, the government officially requested Britain and the US to liquidate their bases "as soon as possible". The evacuation of some bases and posts was agreed upon. However, the matter was taken up with determination only under the post-1969 revolutionary regime.

On 1 September 1969, a bloodless military coup d'etat occurred. A Revolutionary Command Council proclaimed a "Libyan Arab Republic" that would strive for a revolutionary, socialist and progressive Libya and fight against imperialism. The constitution was abolished; the King deposed, and the government dismissed. All nationalist prisoners were released. There was no resistance, either by the police, thought to be loyal to the King, or the tribes of the interior, traditionally linked to the Sanussi dynasty. The King (visiting Turkey at the time) made a feeble attempt to ask for British help (which was rejected), but gave up without further resistance and renounced his throne.

Libya Under Qadhafi The strong man of the new regime was Colonel Mu'ammar al-Qadhafi, aged twenty-eight. He was appointed Commander-in-Chief of the Armed Forces and emerged as chairman of the twelve-member Revolutionary Command Council, the supreme body of the new republic. In January 1970, he became Prime Minister as well. His chief aide was Abdel Salam JALLUD.

Since the early 1970s, Libya increasingly radicalized its policies, in both domestic and international spheres. In December 1969 agreements were reached with Britain and the US on the evacuation of all their military bases (al-Adem and Tobruk bases, and Weelus airfield, respectively) which was completed by mid-1970. Libya turned to purchase massive arms and military quipment from France and Italy, but increasingly from the Soviet Union.

The new regime followed a policy of diminishing foreign influence and presence in Libya in the economic and cultural realms as well, by which the power of old social and political elites would be also curtailed— although the new regime declared that it would not nationalize the oil industry and would honor contracts with the oil companies. However, most foreign companies soon submitted to pressure to increase tax and royalty payments to the government and follow strict government instructions as to production and development.

In November 1969 foreign banks were nationalized by a decree that fifty-one percent of capital and full contrul must be in Libyan hands. In April 1970 the state took over the heavy industry and mining. The use of foreign languages in public places was banned as was the employment of foreigners, except in the case of necessary experts and by special dispensation. The properties of Italian settlers and Jews were confiscated in July 1970, and most of the remaining Italians left.

At the same time, the new regime encouraged new investments in fields it chose, particularly in oil. In spring 1971 Libya obtained, after tough negotiations, new and still more favorable terms from foreign oil companies. The Libyan example soon became a role model for other oil-producing states, leading to major structural changes in the global oil economy (see OIL).

In the early 1970s, the Qadhafi regime, under the strong influence of Nasserist Egypt, formed the state's single political party—the ARAB SOCIALIST UNION (ASU), similar to the Egyptian pattern. But this Party failed to advance Qadhafi's political aims, most important among them was the rallying of the Libyans around his leadership. Alternatively, he gradually incorporated into the Libyan public attention a new political system, to which he referred to as a "Popular Revolution". This ideology had eventually crystallized into the "People's Power" (sultat al-Sha'b) system with a network of local and national bodies: Basic Congresses, People's Committees, and a General People's Congress. Formally charged with decision-making, in practice these institutions mainly approved decisions made by Qadhafl, who continued to maintain a tough centralized rule.

The new system reflected Qadhafi's revolutionary vision, his "Third Universal Theory," as formulated in the first part of his "Green Book," published

in 1976. (Two more parts of the "Green Book" were published in 1978 and 1979). The new system became formally effective since March 1977. The Qur'an was declared to be the code of society. Direct "people's power" was proclaimed. Since the country's defense was the duty of all citizens, general military training was decreed. The state's institutions were renamed. The government became the "General People's Committee," the Revolutionary Command Council—the "General Secretariat". Embassies throughout the world were renamed "People's Bureaus," run by "People's Committees".

This system, a kind of direct popular rule, was aimed, according to Qadhafi's ideology, at avoiding the need of political middlemen and bureaucratic systems and enabling the Libyans to have a true democracy.

March 1979 saw the completion of the system of "People's Power" founded in 1977. Qadhafi and the four other surviving members of the original Revolutionary Command Council relinquished their formal posts on the "Secretariat"—officially to devote themselves to promoting the revolution.

In practice, however, there was no basic change in Libya's political system which remained a military regime completely dominated by Qadhafi. Nevertheless Qadhafi increasingly relied on, and used, the "People's Committees" or "Revolutionary Committees" formed since the late 1970s under the "People's Power" system. By the early 1980s they had become powerful instruments of the revolution. They served primarily as the regime's "watchdogs". Controlled directly by Qadhafi, they were charged with inculcating revolutionary consciousness in the masses and eradicating any deviation from or resistance to his revolutionary ideas. They did so, inter alia, by physically liquidating the revolution's enemies and potential nuclei of opposition within the country and abroad.

The Opposition to Qadhafi. Opposition to the regime—underground and in exile—appeared to grow since the late 1970s. One of the peaks of this opposition activities was the serious attack on Qadhafi's residence and headquarters in the Bab al-Aziziyya barracks in Tripoli in May 1984 by men sent across the Tunisian border by the National Front for the Salvation of Libya (NFSL), then the most significant of the opposition groups. Later in the 1980s—throughout the 1990s, threats to Qadhafi's regime steadily grew. The continuing drop in world oil prices, combined with the authorities' mismanagement and the military defeat in Chad, resulted in more and more socio-political dissatisfaction. The economic recession had also negatively affected the military—considered by many as the most serious potential threat to Qadhafi's power.

As a result of the rigid, repressive measures, the main opposition acted abroad. About fifteen expatriate opposition groupings acted in various European, and Middle East countries, as well as in the US at the beginning of the 1990s. Yet they were played by political and personal divisions, with no collaboration among them.

In any case, the effect of the expatriate opposition was increasingly eclipsed by the growing challenge of Islamic fundamentalist dissidence at home. Although Qadhafi struck mercilessly at the Islamists, they continued to gather momentum, becoming the major threat to Qadhafi's hold on power from the mid-1990s. The Libyan regime reinforced its battle against religious Islamic extremism. Qadhafi's anxiety was nurtured by the spread of Islamic extremism in Libya's immediate region—Algeria, Sudan and Egypt. Qadhafi did his utmost to block this influence, but in vain. In 1996–1997, Islamic extremists repeatedly clashed violently with the regime. This constituted an alarming security threat to Qadhafi by virtue of the combination of their aim to overthrow the regime and impose the application of the Islamic law as well as their venue of operation—the Banghazi area in the northeast, where most of the country's oil industry is situated.

Economy Since the early 1960s oil production and export was the backbone of Libya's economy, a major source of financing the government's activities, as well as its economic and technological development. The stakes involving this economic source explain why the regime took care not to disturb the oil sector regardless of its militant ideology, and assured that the oil industry be kept away from possible intervention of the revolutionalry People's Committees. The extreme dependency on oil revenues affected Libya's economy and domestic stablity. While the oil boom of the post-1973 war enabled Qadhafi to expand Libya's economic investments and purchase of advanced technological systems (including arms) and deepen its interventionist policies in the neighboring countries, the decline in the country's oil ex-

ports from a peak of 22 billon dollars in 1980 to 10 billion dollars in 1985 and 7.3 billion dollars in 1994, severely hit the Libyan economy.

The enormous scale of economic hardship troubled Qadhafi, since it was increasingly felt at both the national and local levels. The economic difficulties were further exacerbated due to the UN Security Council sanctions which had been imposed on Libya in 1992 and still were in effect in 1997. While the sanctions did not restict oil or gas exports, they covered spare parts and overseas financial assets—crucial elements in fostering the oil industry, which was the backbone of the Libyan economy.

The squeeze on finances, combined with the UN sanctions effect, led to a reduction in the volumes of economic activity, affecting most of the government's development schemes, excluding the development of the oil fields and the construction of the largest man-made river project. This started in 1983 and was aimed at transferring water from aquifers under the Sahara in southern Libya to the country's coastal areas.

The economic difficulties caused a growing rate of unemployment, estimated at thirty percent in mid-1990s. Qadhafi feared that this would induce a popular unrest. Wishing to ease domestic dissatisfaction, he repeatedly ordered mass expulsion of illegal foreign workers, whose number was estimated early in the 1990s at 2 million, including 1 million Egyptians.

Foreign Affairs Libya's foreign policy in general, except that concerning oil, must be viewed against the backdrop of Libya's geographic location. This was marked by marginality in both the core area of the Arab states system as well as of the Maghreb subsystem—state capabilities deriving from oil revenues, the regime's domestic insecurity and Qadhafi's personal aspirations. His ideological doctrine and political conduct reflect his frame of mind and interpretation of the regional and political realities. His Third Universal Theory is presented as an alternative to communism and capitalism, applicable specifically to Islamic countries but also to non-Islamic Third World states, even as a world panacea.

Qadhafi's extremely activist, unconventional and often belligerent foreign policy is both a reflection of his revolutionary idealism and a calculated attempt to advance his country's political, strategic and economic interests. Support for Islamic causes and worldwide "liberation movements"—often indistinguishable by Qadhafi from political terrorism—is one of the cornerstone of his concept.

The list of foreign liberation movements aided by Libya was headed by the Palestinian organizations—primarily the extremist factions. It included the West-Saharan POLISARIO; Muslim rebels in the Philippines and Thailand; anti-government underground cells in Egypt, Sudan, Morocco, Tunisia, Chad, Niger, Mali, and Senegal; extremist Muslim groups in Malaysia and Indonesia; Ceylon Tamil rebels; separatist movements in Spain (the Basque ETA, Canary Islands and Andalusian autonomists, and Italy) (Sardinian and Sicilian secessionists); Latin-American leftists, particularly in Central America (Nicaragua, El Salvador); the Irish Republican Army (IRA), and American "Black Muslims". Libya's support of these groups was sometimes political, often financial, and in many cases military, turning Libya into a major sponsor of international terrorism.

Nevertheless, since 1986 onwards, after Libya was accused of being responsible for international TERRORISM, it was therefore air bombed by the US airforce. In 1992 again it was toughly punished by the imposition of UN sanctions. Due to terrorist involvement, Libya largely lowered its profile of activities in foreign arenas.

Relations with the West have been for long strongly problematic. The dispute with the US and Britain over the suspicion of Libya's responsibility for the explosion of a Pan-American aircraft over Lockerbie, Scotland in 1988, dominated Tripoli's relations with the West, casting a pall over Qadhafi's standing at home and abroad. The Lockerbie bombing, notwithstanding Libya's denial of any connection with it, urged the West to impose, in 1992, sanctions on Libya through the UN Security Council.

Even more worrisome to Qadhafi was the fear that the US was determined to topple his regime, and was using the extraditing demand of the two Libyans suspected of the bombing merely as a pretext for the sanctions in order to undermine his hold of power. In 1997, the Lockerbie dispute continued to be deadlocked for its fifth successive year, causing both regional and international isolation of Libya.

The Arab arena, where Qadhafi was persistently involved emotionally and ideologically, remained a major source of discontent to him. His aggressiveness and antagonism on the one hand, and marginality within the inter-Arab states system, led to growing alienation and disgust toward Qadhafi's regime by most Arab states, culminating in the avoidance of all of them, excluding Egypt (only in 1996–1997) from backing Libya against Western sanctions.

Much of the reserved, if not hostile, attitude that most Arab states developed toward Qadhafi derived from his subversion, agitation and intervention in other Arab states' domestic and foreign affairs. These were all in the name of his revolutionary concepts and fervent adherence to all-Arab solidarity and unity. As first steps toward such wider unity, he has consistently sponsored mergers of Libya and other Arab countries, neighboring or even remote. None of these mergers has been successful.

They began in 1971 with the federation proclaimed with Egypt and SYRIA—the Federation of Arab Republics (FAR). But Qadhafi pressed for full union with Egypt and in August 1972 pressed Anwar al-SADAT to agree to a merger by September 1973. As Sadat obviously had no intention of implementing that agreement, Qadhafi in June–July 1973 made a barnstorming tour of Egypt, harrangued the Egyptian public and organized Libya's mass march into Egypt. In August 1973, the merger was re-decided, but it has never taken off. As a result, Libya-Egypt relations deteriorated, turning into hostility in the aftermath of the 1973 October War. Qadhafi, who supported Egypt's preparations for the war by extending financial and military support—including a number of Miraj-3 squadrons—was particulary frustrated for not being informed about the timing of opening the war, and due to Sadat's decision to stop the fighting and accept American mediation in what turned out to be a long march toward peacemaking with Israel.

In January 1974 Qadhafi persuaded President BOURGUIBA of Tunisia to proclaim an immediate merger of Libya and Tunisia. This proclamation had to be scrapped by Tunisia with a great deal of embarrassment. In September 1980, Libya and Syria announced the merger of the two countries—but the merger has not really been implemented. In August 1984, Libya and Morocco (a conservative country heretofore vilified by Qadhafi and the target of Libyan subversion) proclaimed a "union" of the two countries. That union was planned as a loose confederation only. It was abrogated by Morocco in August 1986 when the Moroccan Monarch hosted Israel's Prime Minister Shimon PERES in Ifran, Morocco.

Libyan efforts to interest Algeria in moves toward a union, reported for instance in 1975–1976 and again in 1981, were always cautiously rejected by Algeria. Qadhafi went as far as proposing a union even to non-Arab countries such as Chad (1981) and Malta (1971); both of which represented a strive to promote Libyan regional domination.

Qadhafi's fervent unionist zeal tended to be erratic and at times compulsive, which ridiculed his merger proposals. Moreover, despite Qadhafi's incomparable hostility to Israel and proclaimed willingness to support an Arab war effort aimed to defeat the Zionist state, after the 1973 war, Libya was the least of all Arab oil-producers to contribute to such effort. In fact, Libya's relations with the Arab countries, whether targeted for merger or considered recipients of Libyan financial aid, were determined by sheer selfish interests. Qadhafi severed relations with Jordan (resumed only in 1976) following the elimination of Palestinian armed presence in most of its territory in September 1970, including the financial aid decided in Khartoum. Despite Qadhafi's championing of the Palestinian cause, his support for the PALESTINE LIBERATION ORGANIZATION (PLO) was subordinated to the latter's acceptance of Libyan inter-Arab policies, and as of the late 1970s, also with Libyan hostility to any peacemaking process with Israel.

Relations with Egypt in the post-1973 war were greatly affected by Libya's participation in the REJECTION FRONT and its hostility toward Arab-Israeli peace diplomacy led by Sadat. It was against this backdrop and continuous Libyan subversion against Sadat's regime, that the tension with Egypt resulted in armed clashes between their armies in the Western Desert in July 1977. Libya was, in 1977–1978, in the forefront of the radical coalition of Arab states established in Tripoli in December 1977 under the title Front of Steadfastness and Confrontation, to ostracize Egypt and deter other Arab states from following its line by pushing toward a total boycott of Egypt.

Tunisia also repeatedly complained of plots and hostile action by Libya, including an armed intrusion and attack on Gafsa in January 1980, and the expulsion of Tunisian workers in 1985. Relations were severed that same year.

Libya's relations with Saudi Arabia were antagonistic. It resented their royal conservatism and this was reciprocated by the Saudi suspicion of Qadhafi's revolutionary doctrines, including his revolutionary Islam. Relations with Lebanon were clouded by Libya's reported involvement in Lebanon's civil war and support for some of the rival militias (and by the disappearance—possibly assassination—in Libya of the Lebanese SHI'A leader Mussa al-SADR in August 1978).

Relations with Iraq were troubled by Libya's friendship with Syria and since 1980 in particular, by its open support of Iran in the IRAN-IRAQ WAR. Official relations were severed in 1980. Libya's relations with Sudan were erratic and shifting. Until NUMEIRI's fall in April 1985, they were disturbed by its hosting and supporting anti-government factions (such as the "Democratic Unionists" and Sadeq al-MAHDI's Ansar—see SUDAN), its reported aid, for some time, to the South-Sudanese rebels and incessant reports of Libyan plotting.

Libya's relations with its African neighbors and other African countries were also frequently troubled. Mali, Niger, Senegal, Gambia (all Muslim-majority countries), Benin, Ivory Coast and others often complained of Libyan interference and subversion, and official relations were cut several times.

A special case occured with Chad int which Libya maintained a long policy of intervention and occupation. Libya strove for influence in Chad, an approach based on considerations of security and territorial claim for the Aouzou strip region of northern Chad (an area variously estimated at 27–44 sq. miles (70–115,000 sq. km.). This became part of Chad according to a French-Italian colonial deal of 1935. (The Strip was important to Libya also because it was reputedly rich in uranium).

Even though this policy was already maintained by the monarchic regime, under Qadhafi it assumed the form of direct military presence in Chad. In addition, the semi-Muslim and semi-Arab nature of that country provided him with ample argument to justify his interventionist policy. Libya supported rebelling factions in Chad from the mid-1960s and hosted the then rebel leader, providing him with a base for his operations. Libya occupied the Aouzou

Strip in May-June 1973, formally annexing it in 1975. The Chad government was too weak to resist. Libya claimed it accepted its possession of the Strip. But no Chad government ever recognized Libya's annexation—not even the rebel governments formed by Libya's clients.

By 1980, Libya's support for a Chad rebel faction turned into a long military intervention. After mediation efforts by the Organization of African Unity (OAU) and others, Libya announced the withdrawal of its troops in 1981. Its actual withdrawal remained in doubt. In any case it resumed its full military intervention in 1983. Renewed mediation efforts by the OAU, the UN Security Council, and particularly France (itself semi-committed to the defense of Chad), led to a French-Libyan agreement in September 1984. This provided for the withdrawal of Libyan troops and bases. However, Libya did not implement that agreement and its troops continued controlling northern Chad, far beyond the annexed Aouzou Strip. France had to acquiesce, as it did not wish to enter a fully fledged military conflict with Libya. Yet it set the sixteenth degree as a red line whose crossing by Libya's troops would cause France to take military action.

In 1987, Libya's forces in Aouzou were defeated and driven out of Chad's territory by an alignment of the Chadian rebels led by Libya's chief client, Goukouni Wada'i (Ouedei), and the Chad government.

Libya's relations with the Western powers were troubled mainly due to its involvement in terrorist operations in the West (including the assassination of Libyan exiles and dissidents who had taken refuge there). Some half-hearted counter measures have been taken against Libya since the mid-1980s. Relations deteriorated even with those Western countries that endeavored to maintain them due to strong economic links—such as Italy, Germany, Spain and France (embarrassed also by Libya's operations in Chad, having supplied arms to Libya for years).

Relations with the United States have been tense since the early 1970s. They reached the point of confrontation in 1976 when the US banned the export of military or potentially military equipment to Libya. The US had recalled its Ambassador in 1972 and reduced the staff of its embassy. When the embassy was sacked by demonstrators in December 1979, it closed it altogether.

In May 1981 the US expelled all Libyan diplomats and severed relations. In August 1981 a military dimension was added when two Libyan war planes were shot down by US aircrafts in exercises over the Mediterranean Gulf of Sirte. This seemed to be a disciplinary action against Qadhafi due to his involvement in international terrorism and subversion against his neighboring countries. Following that incident the US imposed economic sanctions, banning the import of Libyan oil from March 1982. It further tightened these sanctions in January 1986, after Libya was reportedly involved in a terrorist attack on Rome and Vienna airports. The 1981 confrontation over the Gulf of Sirte escalated, as the US Mediterranean fleet-and-air-arm insisted on their right to sail what they considered international waters, though they actually asserted that right in infrequent test cases only. Threatening confrontations and near-clashes occurred several times in 1983 and an actual battle, followed by US retaliatory bombing raids, in March 1986. In April 1986 the US mounted another air raid on the Tripoli and Benghazi military bases and installations. The threat of further raids and a kind of psychological warmongering remained.

The only power with apparently firm and stable relations with Libya was the Soviet Block. This was somewhat surprising, as Qadhafi and his colleagues were (despite their revolutionary zeal and anti-Western orientation), strongly anticommunist. The Soviet Union, on its part, was aware of Qadhafi's erratic extremism and his questionable doctrines and could not possibly regard him as a reliable ally. Yet Moscow and its allies supplied Libya with large quantities of advanced arms and other aid (e.g., East German security expertise) and frequently proclaimed Soviet support for Libyan positions in its disputes with the West.

Throughout the late 1980s, and 1990s, Libya (which became a pariah state not only in the West but also in the Arab and African worlds), was not in a position to offer anymore any unity framework with its Arab sister countries.

Libya joined the ARAB MAGHREB UNION established in 1989. This regional framework never took off the ground.

Throughout the 1990s, Libya continued to activate its anachronistic self-image as a devoted guardian of the Palestinian cause. Tripoli's media featured ardent rhetoric advocating "liberating the sacred land of Palestine" and condemning "the occupying Zionist enemy".

In the same breath, Libya virulently denounced the "treacherous" Palestinian Authority, headed by Yaser ARAFAT. Unilaterally rejecting the PLO-Israeli peace accord, as well as any other political agreement with the Israeli "enemy," the Libyan ardently called to liquidate "the artificial Jewish state". The only solution to the conflict over Palestine, as Qadhafi saw it, could be achieved by the return of the Palestinians "to their country" and the return of the JEWS who arrived from abroad to their countries of origin.

MADRID CONFERENCE see ARAB ISRAEL PEACE-MAKING.

MAGHREB (Arabic: the West) Originally, the Arabic-speaking countries of Northwest Africa—MOROCCO, ALGERIA and TUNISIA. After the 1970s for political reasons it extended to MAURITANIA as well as LIBYA, or at least Tripolitania, its western part. There are significant differences—ethnic, in dialect and customs—between the Arabs of the Maghreb and those of the other Arab countries, particularly those of its eastern part (the *Mashriq*). A large part of the Maghreb population is of BERBER descent.

Until the mid-twentieth century, during the decades of the growth of ARAB NATIONALISM and the struggle for independence, there were no close connections between the Maghreb and the eastern part of the Arab world—though there has always been a measure of emotional solidarity and mutual support. Furthermore the Maghreb was excluded from the political plans of ARAB UNITY in its formative period on the eve of, during and after World War II. As the Arab countries of the *Mashriq* attained independence before those of the Maghreb, they—particularly EGYPT—provided the nationalists of the Maghreb, during the decisive years of their struggle for independence in the 1950s, much aid, hosting the headquarters and command centers of their national liberation movements.

After attaining independence—Libya 1951, Tunisia and Morocco 1956, Mauritania 1960, Algeria 1962—the Maghreb countries joined the ARAB LEAGUE, becoming an integral part of the Arab family of nations, though in general they were reluctant to be too involved in *Mashriq* issues. The exception was Libya, which became, in the wake of the 1969 Revolution headed by QADHAFI, very active in inter-Arab affairs and the ARAB-ISRAEL CONFLICT, taking ultra-militant positions as the mainstay of the REJECTION FRONT. Algeria, too, belonged to that Front and followed militant-radical inter-Arab policies, but has moderated its position since the late 1980s. Tunisia and Morocco primarily belong to the moderate-conservative camp.

From the late 1960s, under King HASAN II, Morocco has been relatively active in inter-Arab and all-Islamic matters, hosted numerous ARAB SUMMIT CONFERENCES and mediated in inter-Arab disputes. Due to his close links with the Moroccan-Jewish community and Israeli politicians of Moroccan origin, the King established secret links with ISRAEL as early as the mid-1970s, later offered his mediating offices in the Israel-Egypt contacts that preceded President al-SADAT's visit to JERUSALEM in 1977. In the course of the 1980s he gradually opened his country to Israelis of Moroccan origin, and from the early 1990s, it was open practically to all Israeli visitors.

Maghrebi Arab leaders have fostered, since before independence and particularly after attaining it, the idea of an all-Maghreb union or at least close cooperation in terms of economy, development and other spheres. Committees have been established and inter-governmental meetings and discussions held from time to time, but the idea never materialized.

Attempts have been made to forge partial unions between individual Maghreb countries, which were short-lived and declarative rather than practical. A sudden merger of Libya and Tunisia was proclaimed in January 1974. This was a surprise move manipulated by Libya's Qadhafi and was swiftly abrogated by

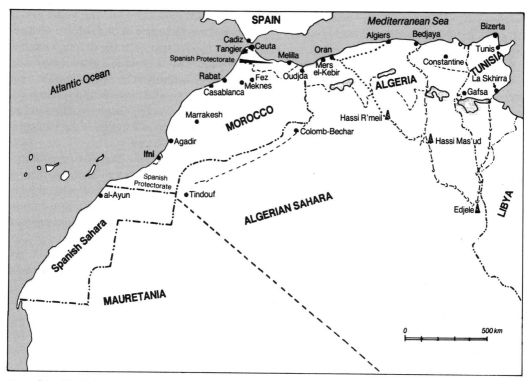

Map of the Maghreb

Tunisia. Apart from contributing to the deterioration of Tunisia-Libya relations, it was ineffective. In August 1984, Morocco and Libya announced an agreement to form a union. This was effectively a plan for a loose confederation. While its provisions were implemented only slowly and partially, it caused grave misgivings in Algeria and Tunisia. The Union was abrogated in late August 1986 by Morocco (after Libya denounced King Hasan for inviting Premier Shimon PERES of Israel to meet him in Morocco). The last major attempt was made in 1989, when Morocco, Algeria, Tunisia, Mauritania and Libya joined in the ARAB MAGHREB UNION (AMU), which turned out to be another abortive attempt to substantiate the Maghreb unity idea or to affect closer economic or political cooperation between the countries.

These efforts failed primarily due to conflicting interests and competition for the Maghreb leadership (especially between Morocco and Algeria); mutual distrust; divergent policies and ideologies of the regimes concerned; as well as a lack of economic incentives, such as the limited scope of possible complementary economic integration. Revolutionary, socialist and radical Algeria, Islamic-socialist, extremist and erratic Libya, and conservative Western-oriented Morocco and Tunisia maintain fundamentally divergent basic political philosophy and foreign policy.

Algeria and Morocco were enmeshed in a permanent dispute over borders, political orientation and the problem of Western Sahara. Clashes have occurred between Libya and Tunisia, due to Libyan subversion and tensions over Tunisian labor migrants in Libya. Much of these contradictions were aggravated by, and surfaced, in the context of the WESTERN SAHARA CONFLICT, which from 1975 to the late 1980s was pivotal in shaping inter-Maghreb conflicting relations. Triggered by the Moroccan claim— and take-over—of this previously Spanish ruled region, the consequent guerrilla war waged against Moroccan rule by the POLISARIO, the Western Sahara conflict enabled Algeria and Libya to fulfill their radical, anti-colonialist and libertarian ideologies in supporting the guerrilla warfare against Morocco. Domestic instability and tendencies among the regimes of these states to offer political asylum to dissidents and opposition leaders of, and conduct subversive activities in neighboring Maghreb states as bargaining chips in their conflicts, was another obstacle on the way to closer relations and cooperation.

Thus, the on-going civil war between the government and violent Islamic groups in Algeria since 1992 was another discouraging reason for closer cooperation among the Maghreb states, deepening the fear of spill-over effect of the Islamic violence to Algeria's neighbors.

MAHABAD Autonomous, break-away Kurdish republic established in 1946 in north-western IRAN, with Soviet encouragement, in an attempt to acquire a foothold in that part of Iran which had been under Soviet occupation during World War II. Iraqi Kurdish rebel groups participated in the venture, with Mulla Mustafa BARAZANI as its military leader. The Republic of Mahabad was crushed by Iranian forces at the end of 1946 when Soviet forces had to withdraw from northern Iran. (see kurds, iran).

MAHDI, MAHDIYYA The Mahdi (Arabic: the Guided One) is part of Islamic theology referring to being chosen by God at the end of time to fill the earth with justice and equity (and sanctioned to overthrow the regime of evil).

In 1881, in SUDAN (then under Egyptian occupation), Muhammad Ahmad Ibn Abdallah (1840–1885) claimed to be the Mahdi and IMAM (the head of the Muslim community). His followers established a religious order, the Mahdiyya with a body of activists called *al-Ansar* (Arabic: the Helpers; the original *Ansar* were the "Helpers" of the Prophet Muhammad in Medina). The Mahdi movement was also supported by some tribal groups.

The Mahdi called for a Holy War (JIHAD) against the infidels, including Muslims who did not acknowledge his mission. His fanatic followers, whom Europeans incorrectly called "Dervishes" (a term usually applied to members of the mystic (*Sufi*) orders, strongly opposed to and by the Mahdi), defeated the Egyptian troops sent against them, conquering the provinces of Kordofan, Darfur and Bahr al-Ghazal. The British advised the Egyptians to evacuate these territories, sending General Gordon, former Governor-General of Sudan, to organize the evacuation. But the Mahdi besieged Gordon in Khartoum, and took the town in January 1885, after having killed Gordon, and established his rule over Khartoum and most of Sudan. The Mahdi died in 1885 and was succeeded by Abdallah Ibn Muhammad, the *Khalifa* (successor). The order lost much of its vigor and failed to establish a well-ordered state. In 1896, the British sent an Anglo-Egyptian force commanded by General Kitchener that re-conquered Sudan, 1896–1898. The *Khalifa* was killed in battle. Continuing resistance was quelled at the beginning of the twentieth century.

The Mahdiyya gradually changed from a fanatic-military revolutionary force into an ordinary sect or order which, in time, gained great political influence. It later became generally pro-British, anti-Egyptian, was in favor of Sudanese independence (as opposed to union with EGYPT) and sponsored the *Umma* Party which represented that trend in the political arena. Its main rival was the fundamentalist *khatmiyya* or MIRHANIYYA order.

The Mahdiyya is strongest in central and western Sudan. From the 1950s it was a focus of opposition to the military-revolutionary regimes controlling Sudan. In March 1970 the order was accused of mounting a rebellion which was suppressed; its last *Imam*, al-Hadi al-Mahdi, was killed, and no successor was proclaimed.

The Mahdiyya, and the *Umma* Party it sponsored (which was, during the 1970s semi-illegal and half-underground), were partners in a "National Front" that continued opposing NUMEIRI and his regime (see SUDAN). The Mahdiyya played an important role in the overthrow of NUMEIRI, April 1985, and in the new regime established after the elections of April 1986.

The Mahdiyya order (*al-Ansar*) was led by Sir Abdel Rahman al-Mahdi (1885–1959), the posthumous son of the Mahdi (al-Mahdi gradually was used as the family name). During World War I he helped the British combat the Pan-Islamic propaganda of the Ottomans. He gradually took a pro-British line and was knighted in 1926. In the 1940s he became Patron of the *Umma* Party. Efforts to elect him President of independent Sudan failed.

Sir Abdel Rahman's son, Siddiq al-Mahdi (1911–1961), succeeded him in 1959 as head of the order. Under him, the Mahdiyya became the spearhead of resistance to General Abbud's military rule (1958–1964).

Siddiq was succeeded as leader of the order, in 1961, by his brother al-Hadi al-Mahdi (1915–1970).

He caused a schism in the *Umma* Party, 1966, by patronizing its conservative right wing. He was a strong candidate for the Presidency but his ambitions were thwarted by the Numeiri coup of May 1969. After the coup he retired to the Nile island of Aba. He was considered to be a leader of the opposition to the new regime, and in March 1970 was accused of igniting a rebellion. When the rebellion was crushed, the *Imam* al-Hadi was killed, allegedly while trying to escape to Ethiopia. Since al-Hadi's death, another brother, Ahmad al-Mahdi, was considered leader of the order, though not formally proclaimed *Imam*.

al-MAHDI, AL-SADEQ (b. 1936) Sudanese

politician, a member of the MAHDIYYA sect and the son of Imam Siddiq al-Mahdi; grandson of the Imam Sir Abdel-Rahman al-Mahdi, and great-grandson of the Mahdi himself.

Mahdi, an Oxford graduate, held no position in the religious establishment of the Mahdiyya order (see SUDAN), but became a leader of its political wing, the Umma Party. The Umma Party advocated independence rather than union with EGYPT and was considered anti-Egyptian. He became Prime Minister in July 1966, heading a coalition government, but was ousted in May 1967 due to a division in his party. His uncle (the Imam Hadi al-MAHDI) sponsored the semi-secession of a more conservative faction.

NUMEIRI's coup of May 1969 put an end to Mahdi's legal political activities, and he was in and out of prison or house arrest. After the alleged Mahdiyya rebellion of March 1970 he was deported to Egypt. He returned in 1972, was arrested again, and in May 1973 went into exile in England, SAUDI ARABIA and LIBYA. He was one of the leaders of a semi-clandestine "National Front" in Sudan and mainly in exile, increasingly with Libya as a base of operation, and led the fight against Numeiri culminating in July 1976 in an attempt to overthrow him. After a reconciliation with Numeiri, Mahdi returned to Sudan in August 1977 and cooperated with the regime for some time. However, he soon fell out with Numeiri and resigned his position on the ruling single party's politbureau (*inter alia* because he objected to Numeiri's approval of Egyptian President al-SADAT's peace moves toward ISRAEL). In September 1983, he publicly denounced Numeiri's decrees imposing the

Islamic law (SHARI'A) code of punishments. He was again arrested and detained until January 1985.

In April 1985 Mahdi was among the leaders of the coup that overthrew Numeiri. A year later he led his Umma Party to victory in the April 1986 elections and formed a coalition government. He served as Prime Minister until the military coup of General BASHIR in June 1989.

Intense political pressure that came mainly from the direction of the NIF (Hassan al-TURABI's party), caused political instability that led Sadek to adopt non-decisive policies. Sadek refrained from abolishing the *Shari'a* laws that were implemented by Numeiri in 1983 despite his harsh criticism of them in the past.

After the ascent of the Bashir-Turabi regime in June 1989, Sadek did not leave Sudan, unlike other opposition leaders. He opted to remain there running his opposition front from within.

Sadek's operations were closely monitored by the authorities and he was arrested on several occasions. Sadek advocated peaceful protest against the regime and hoped that that would lead to popular upheaval as in the uprisings of 1964 and 1985. In addition, he conducted discussions with various elements within the regime, hoping to bring about a change of policy or to join the country leadership. All this was to no avail. In December 1996 he fled to ERITREA, somewhat surprisingly, claiming that the authorities were planning to hold him hostage following the military operations of the opposition in the southern and eastern parts of the country. Sadek conducted negotiations with Sudanese opposition leaders in exile, in particular with the National Democratic Alliance (NDA: the major Sudanese opposition body) in an attempt to formulate a strategy to bring about an end to the regime. He also met with regional leaders such as the leaders of Uganda, Eritrea and a number of Arab statesmen to advance the cause.

Although he had preferred using peaceful means to overthrow the regime, following his flee from Sudan, he appeared to have withdrawn his objection to violent action against the regime instructing his supporters to join the military struggle of the NDA in the south and the east. Nonetheless, there are differences between him and other opposition leaders as to the future of the regime in the post-Bashir-Turabi era mainly on issues related to the character of the regime and the solution for the civil war in the south.

al-MAKTUM The clan or dynasty of sheikhs ruling the small sheikhdom of DUBAI, in the TRUCIAL OMAN and since 1971 the UNITED ARAB EMIRATES (UAE). The first ruler during independence was Sheikh Rashed ibn Sa'id al-Maktum (1914–1990; ruled 1958–1990). He succeeded his father, Sheikh Sa'id, in 1958, upon the latter's death. He served as Vice President of the UAE (1971–1990), and Prime Minister (1979–1990). His son, Sheikh Maktum, succeeded him and has been the Prime Minister of the UAE (1971–1979; and since 1990). Sheikh Rashed and his son also held the position of the Vice President of the UAE since its creation in 1971.

Of the younger brothers of the incumbent ruler, Muhammad Rashed al-Maktum has been Defense Minister of the UAE since its creation, and Hamdan Rashed al-Maktum Minister of Finance and Economy. Reports speak of rivalry and friction among them.

The al-Maktum clan, as rulers of Dubai, have been in constant rivalry with the rulers of ABU DHABI, of the al-NUHAYAN clan—both over leadership of the UAE, and over its shape and constitutional structure. The Maktums insist on the retention of stronger and wider powers by the individual sheikhdoms (mainly Dubai), opposing the creation of too powerful federal institutions (with the Sheikh of Abu Dhabi as President of the UAE). The positions held by the al-Maktum clan in the Federal government are the result of a careful balance worked out in nearly constant struggle.

MANDAEANS (also Sabaeans or Sabians, in Arabic: *Subba*). A small community in southern IRAQ, estimated at between 15,000–30,000, living mostly in towns, as artisans (mainly silversmiths). The Mandaeans' faith comprises elements of Christian and Islam, as well as traces of other religions. The Mandaeans speak Arabic, but in their religious rites they use an ancient Chaldean-Aramaic language. Ritual immersion in a river is an important part of their religion, and they are sometimes referred to as "Christians of John the Baptist." The Mandaeans have not played a prominent part in Iraq's national movement or in public-political life outside their own community.

MANDATES After World War I the victorious allies devised, as part of the peace settlement, a new system of governance for the former German colonies and the Asian areas that had been severed from the OTTOMAN EMPIRE. The system was a compromise between the principle of self-determination for all nations (generally accepted and proclaimed in particular by US President Wilson), and secret war-time agreements to divide the non-Turkish parts of the Ottoman Empire into imperial zones of influence (the SYKES-PICOT AGREEMENT).

Article 22 of the Covenant of the League of Nations instituted the system of the mandate. It speaks of "peoples not yet able to stand by themselves," whose "well being and development. . . form a sacred trust of civilization"; "tutelage of such peoples should be entrusted to advanced nations ... as Mandatories on behalf of the League."

Three types of mandates were created. The B and C mandate, with wider powers for the Mandatories, comprised the former German possessions in Africa and Oceania. The A mandate included Palestine (with Transjordan), Mesopotamia (IRAQ), SYRIA and LEBANON. The Mandatory powers were to give administrative assistance and advice and—in the case of Iraq, Syria and Lebanon, "to facilitate the progressive development" of these territories "as independent states." Constitutions were to be drawn up within three years. The Mandatories were to submit annual reports to the Permanent Mandate Commission of the League of Nations (see below). However, since the UNITED STATES had not joined the League of Nations, the Mandate Commission was stripped of any effective influence on British and French policies, retaining, in the best case, some moral power.

The distribution of the mandate was agreed upon at the San Remo Conference of the principal allies, April 1920, and finalized by the League of Nations Council on 24 July 1922 (except for Iraq). The mandate for Palestine that was conferred upon Great Britain, effectively included the main provisions of the BALFOUR DECLARATION (see ZIONISM) in the Mandate Document. This recognized the "historical connection of the Jewish people with Palestine," and obliged the Mandatory to assist in the establishment of a Jewish National Home.

Under Article 25 of the Palestine Mandate, added in August 1921, the Mandatory was entitled, with the consent of the League Council, to "postpone or withhold application of such provisions ... as he may consider inapplicable" (meaning those concerning the Jewish National Home) from "the territories lying between the JORDAN and the eastern boundary of Palestine as ultimately determined."

In September 1922, Britain requested, and obtained, the consent of the Council to make the Jewish National Home provisions inapplicable to Transjordan and to create there, under the Palestine Mandate, a separate, semi-independent administration.

The Palestine Mandate did not include a clause concerning independence and a constitution, but the Mandatory was made "responsible for the development of self-governing institutions, and also for safeguarding the civil and religious rights of all the inhabitants of Palestine, irrespective of race and religion." For the history of the Palestine Mandate and its termination in 1948, see ARAB-ISRAEL CONFLICT.)

The Mandate over Transjordan was terminated in March 1946, when BRITAIN recognized Transjordan's independence, signing a treaty of alliance with it. Full international recognition of that independence by the admission of Transjordan to the UN was held up by a Soviet veto and took place only in December 1955.

Iraq was also an A mandate conferred upon Britain. However, firstly, the territory concerned was not finally defined in 1922 with the establishment of the mandate. The fate of the oil-rich Mosul province, held by Britain but claimed by TURKEY, was ostensibly left open for further negotiations and arbitration by the League of Nations though de facto it was already incorporated in Iraq.

The inclusion of the province in Iraq was finally approved in 1926. Secondly, as Iraq's nationalists opposed the imposition of any form of mandate, demanding full independence, Britain and Iraq reached, after two years of struggle, a compromise in the shape of the Anglo-Iraqi Treaty of Alliance of October 1922. This included most of the provisions of the mandate, so that Britain could present it to the League of Nations as merely an instrument to implement the mandate, while telling the Iraqis that relations were governed by a freely agreed treaty and not by an imposed mandate. An Iraqi Constitution came into effect in 1925.

The League of Nations watched Iraq's progress toward independence with some misgivings. It made the award of Mosul to Iraq conditional on the extension of twenty-five years of the Anglo-Iraqi Treaty, i.e., a measure of British tutelage. (This was complied with in a new treaty of January 1926.) When Britain agreed in the Anglo-Iraqi Treaty of June 1930 to terminate the mandate and grant Iraq full independence, the League made its approval and the admission of Iraq to the League, conditional on a solemn declaration by Iraq on the protection of minorities. (This was made in May 1932.) In October 1932, the mandate was terminated. Iraq was admitted to the League of Nations, being the first Arab country to attain such a status.

The mandate for Syria-Lebanon was granted to France (The draft treaties of 1936 envisioned its termination, but not ratified: the declaration of its termination in 1941; the crisis of 1943–1946; and the mandate's termination by the admission of Syria and Lebanon to the UN in 1945 see SYRIA, LEBANON).

The League of Nations' Permanent Mandate Commission was constituted in February 1921. It studied the annual reports of the governments of the mandated territories and advised the League Council as to whether the provisions of each mandate were strictly observed. It summoned governors and other high officials for questioning and accepted representation from inhabitants of the territories concerned.

The Commission was often critical of the Palestine Mandatory administration, particularly in response to Jewish representations on the implementation of the clauses concerning the Jewish National Home. In 1930 it sent a commission to investigate Jewish and Arab claims concerning the Wailing Wall. In 1937 it expressed a preference for the cantonization of Palestine rather than its partition as recommended by the Peel Report. In 1939 it declared the White Paper on Palestine then issued by the British, to be contrary to the spirit of the mandate. For its misgivings over the termination of the mandate for Iraq—see above.

With the decline of the League of Nations in the late 1930s, its supervision of the administration of the mandates became much less effective. Indeed it lapsed entirely when the war broke out in 1939. Upon establishing the United Nations in 1945, it was resolved that the mandate territories should be granted full independence or put under UN Trusteeship.

MARONITES An Eastern Christian Church centered in LEBANON, Catholic through a UNIATE. According to Maronite tradition, the Church was founded in the fifth century by a monk called Maroun in the Orontes River valley. In the seventh century the Maronites adhered to Monotheism—a doctrine that emphasized the One Will of Christ. This was used by Emperor Heraclius of Byzantium in a futile effort to reconcile in the schism between the MONOPHYSITE and Orthodox churches concerning the divine-and-human nature of Christ. It was subsequently turned into a schismatic doctrine of its own.

The Monothelites-Maronites sought contact with the Catholic Church during the Crusades and eventually adhered to it through the Uniate, i.e., retaining a certain autonomy in the administration of the Church and the community, headed by a Patriarch, and in its liturgy, the language of which remained Syriac-Aramaic. There are different versions as to the date of the Uniate—from a first union in 1182–1184 (re-confirmed in 1438–1445), to a definite, formal Uniate in 1736.

Since the seventeenth century, the Maronites enjoyed a certain degree of special relations with, and protection by, FRANCE. They were concentrated mainly in the northern and central part of Mount Lebanon. Since the late eighteenth century they began moving southwards, into a region mostly inhabited, and dominated, by DRUZE. The close cohabitation of Maronites and Druze in Mount Lebanon soon led to trouble between Maronite tenant farmers and Druze landlords. The Maronite Church began to agitate against the Druze. This was boosted by the conversion to the Maronite faith of the Druze Amirs of Mount Lebanon. Relations were further aggravated when the Egyptians occupied Lebanon in the 1830s and sided with the Maronites against the Druze. Serious clashes occurred in 1840–1841, when the Egyptians withdrew, and again in 1860 culminating in a Druze massacre of CHRISTIANS.

These developments led to a growing intervention by the great powers. In 1861 they induced the Ottoman Sultan to establish an autonomous District of Mount Lebanon (*mutasarifiyya*). This comprised approximately eighty percent Christians and more than sixty percent Maronites. In 1920, at the behest of Maronite leaders, France created, under its MANDATE, a "Greater Lebanon," by joining with the previously autonomous Mount Lebanon the Muslim-majority regions of Beirut, the South, Tripoli and the North, and the Biqa' valley in the East. The Maronites lost their majority; but remained the largest single community; approximately thirty percent of the total population and some fifty-seven percent of the Christians. They wielded a decisive influence in the new state. They determined its character as a pluralistic society based on a communal structure—with the Christians, and particularly the Maronites, as the dominant group.

The Maronites were the staunchest defenders of greater Lebanon's independence and territorial integrity—against Sunni-Muslim and Syrian demands to sever the Muslim areas added in 1920 and annex them to SYRIA. Syrian schemes of cooperation or integration with Lebanon, were viewed as a ploy for taking over Lebanon as a whole and the abolition of its unique communal structure of the parliament and governance. Especially before independence, Maronite leaders tended to stress Lebanon's predominantly Christian and non-Arab character.

The Maronite community, however, was never uniform in its political inclinations, divided along clan and family traditional rivalries and power politics as to relations with the Lebanese Muslim communities and future identity of independent Lebanon. One camp took a strong, assertive stance, which led it to rely on "special relations" with France, and also predestined some of its leaders to favor friendly relations with the Jews of Palestine and later ISRAEL. The other camp favored close cooperation with the Muslims inside Lebanon, with a stronger emphasis on the Arab character of the country and a larger measure of integration in all-Arab political structures (although objecting to all plans for an Arab Union). It was this latter current that prevailed after years of struggle during the French Mandate. This culminated in the "National Pact" of 1943 that, based on the census of 1932, ensured Christian and Maronite predominance with a 6:5 Christian/non-Christian ratio in representation (for its breakdown in the 1970s and consequent Civil War—1975–1990—and the post-Civil War settlements, see LEBANON).

In 1936, the leader of the first camp, Emile Edde, won the Presidency against Bishara al-Khouri, leading the rival faction. Some Christian-assertive Maronite activists created, in 1936, a paramilitary organization, the PHALANGES (al-Kata'ib), for the protection of the community. Other, more radical Maronites, adhered to the recreation of a truly Christian Lebanon, advocating the cession of the Muslim-majority areas and the re-creation of a smaller, Christian-majority Lebanon.

The demographic basis for the predominance of the Christians, and particularly the Maronites, had indeed become invalidated over the years due to the Maronites' emigration and low birth rate. The distribution of representation and power, meant that the 6:5 ratio in Parliament thus became increasingly challenged by the less priviledged groups, as well as by radical social and political movements which advocated the abolition of the communal system as a whole. For obvious reasons the Christian-Maronite leadership prevented a new official census. It was unable to prevent wide acquienscence with the existing system for a long time as the Civil War showed. It is generally assumed that the share of the Christians declined to forty–forty-five percent and that of the Maronites to twenty-two–twenty-five percent. Some even estimated this to be as low as 20 percent (600,000–700,000), while the Shi'is have become the largest community, 35–40 percent. (These figures do not account for Lebanese emigrants, which number at an estimated 2.5–3 million Christians or even more, especially in the Americas, among whom the Maronites are a majority. It has always been in dispute whether those emigrants retaining their Lebanese citizenship should be reckoned in the calculations of Lebanon's communal structure).

Efforts to end the Civil War after 1975 and devise a political solution were based on three alternative schemes:

a) The retention of the communal structure, with the 6:5 ratio replaced by a 50:50 ratio (with the Maronites retaining the Presidency. Perhaps there would be a reduction of powers in favor of senior officials from other communities). This was the scheme that was adopted in the Ta'if agreement in 1989, under strong Syrian pressure.

b) The abolition of communal representation altogether and the establishment of a non-communal, one-man-one-vote democracy. This would take effect immediately or after a period of transition

during which the powers of the Maronite President and his community would be much reduced.

c) The division of Lebanon into cantons, each dominated by one of the communities, accepting the de facto division of the war period (for further details see LEBANON). This was fiercely rejected by Syria.

During the Civil War, The Maronites were deeply divided concerning their political conceptions and leadership. This prevented them from realizing their objectives. The problem of how to preserve the survival of the Maronites and their primacy—manifested in the past by the division between assertive-Christian, pro-French (Edde) vs. Arab-integrationist (Khouri) became more critical. This was caused by the demographic decline of this community and the increasing political demands of the Shi's and Druze since the 1970s.

Marginal, radical groups in the Maronite community, dissatisfied with the established leadership, also sought new solutions to the growing threat of the Muslim-Left-Palestinian alignment to Maronite domination. These were mainly the "Guardians of the Cedars" organization led by Etienne Saqr (Abu Arz); the Maronite Monks Association under Boulos Nu'man and other small, radical organizations (such as the "Tanzim," the first organization to contact Israel). They, together with former President Camille CHAMOUN's militia (al-Numur), and the largest military organization, the Phalanges, constituted the mainstay of the Maronite military power.

By 1980, the Phalanges' leader Bashir JUMAYYIL had forcefully integrated—or liquidated—all Maronite factions under his Lebanese Forces. The joint Maronite militia with the former Phalanges was its nucleus and main component. These were the Chamoun family's "Tigers," and the Franjiyyeh family's "Marada" militia. They operated mainly in the Zgharta region in northern Mount Lebanon. While the Tigers succumbed to pressures and accepted Bashir Jemayyil's leadership, the latter broke away from the Maronite camp and sought revenge for the sheded blood of their members by joining the Syrians. Other Maronite leaders, such as deputy Raymond Edde, did not form a militia and thus could not assume leadership (eventually, Edde left Lebanon for France).

The new unified Maronite militia continued to develop the relations with Israel, previously cultivated separately by each of the factions constituting the Lebanese Forces. The weight of the joint Maronite militias soon became a matter of concern for Syria. Yet in 1976–1978 it sided with the Christian camp against the left-PALESTINE LIBERATION ORGANIZATION (PLO) camp. Clashes soon erupted between the two sides, culminating in the siege of Zahla in April–May 1981 which entangled Israel into a direct military involvement against the Syrians in an effort to support the Lebanese Forces. The Phalanges maintained links with the Syrians even as their relations with Israel peaked.

The top political leadership of the Maronites from the late 1970s through most of the 1980s by the Jumayyil family (Pierre, Bashir and Amin successively). Under Bashir Jumayyil, the Lebanese Forces obtained hegemony within the Maronite community and, due to the disintegration of the Lebanese army, and fragmented leftist camp, the main non-Maronite Lebanese militia.

Following the assassination of President-elect Bashir Jumayyil in September 1982 and the turn of his brother, Amin Jumayyil (President 1982–1988), toward Damascus in 1983, a struggle broke out over the Lebanese Forces leadership in the mid-1980s. This occurred mainly between Samir Ja'ja' and Elie Hubeika. The former was strongly anti-Syrian whilst the latter was pro-Syrian. As the militias' leader, Hubeika signed the Damascus tripartite agreement in December 1985, only to be deposed by Ja'ja' a month later.

In Summer–Autumn 1988, as President Amin Jumayyil's term was nearly completed, the Maronite leadership of the Lebanese army, until then refraining from direct involvement in politics (although some of the Maronite soldiers had joined the Maronite militias), began to be involved politically, eventually taking control after a new President had not been elected. In February 1989 and again in early 1990, fierce fighting broke out in the Christian enclave between Maronite-dominated units of the Lebanese army. This was commanded by General Michel AWN, the Lebanese army's commander, nominated in September 1988 as Prime Minister, and the Lebanese Forces militia, led by Ja'ja'. Another Maronite leader, the Phalanges' leader Georges Sa'adeh, played an active role in the Ta'if Lebanese Reconciliation Conference in autumn 1989. He later joined the Lebanese government. In 1990, Ja'ja' too

accepted the Ta'if Agreement. This paved the way to Awn's isolation and later, to his defeat by the Syrian army and its Lebanese allies on 13 October, 1990.

The end of the Civil War in 1990 left the Maronite community divided and weakened both by lingering inter-communal conflicts and by the new, Syrian-sponsored, political order. There were several consequences:

a) The Maronite President, traditionally Lebanon's most powerful official, was significantly weakened following the Ta'if Agreement. He became a semi-symbolic figure with much of his authorities transferred to the Sunni-Muslim Prime Minister;

b) The 6:5 ratio in favor of the Christians was replaced by a 50/50 ratio, depriving them of their dominance in the government;

c) The Maronites were left with a weak, divided, leadership as the veteran politicians (Chamoun, Jumayyil, Franjiyyeh), who dominated Lebanon since the 1940s, passed away. They left behind them rash, mostly irresponsible heirs who were either assassinated or left Lebanon altogether;

d) Since the end of the war, the Maronite opposition leaders have been residing in France. The boycotting of the parliamentary elections in 1992 by their followers proved counter-productive. This caused, in 1996, a further split over this issue;

e) The Maronite leadership of the army was defeated and Awn himself left Lebanon for France;

f) The Lebanese army, once a power base of the Maronites, turned into a multi-confessional and pro-Syrian force, increasingly manned by Shi'is;

g) The Lebanese Forces, the most powerful Maronite militia, was forced to disband and become a political party in 1991. (In 1994 it was dissolved, following an attempt to blow up a church. Samir Ja'ja' was tried and imprisoned);

h) The Phalanges became an ordinary political party with its pro-Syrian tendency strengthened;

i) Other Maronite leaders, especially those from the Biqa' and the north, adopted increasingly pro-Syrian positions. This enabled them to occupy the post of president as well as senior governmental posts;

j) the Maronites were left with no backing of a foreign power, especially after the US and Israel gave up their schemes for Lebanon and pulled out their troops from it's soil (with the exception of Israel's self-declared "Security Zone." This had little effect on the Maronites' position);

k) the Maronite Patriarch, who in the past held the community together and wielded considerable political influence.

However, Elias Howeik, until 1932; Antoun Arida, 1932–1955; Boulos Ma'ouchi, 1955–1975—lost much of his influence, although Nasrallah Butrous Sfeir, the Maronite Patriarch since 1986, is currently one of the only Maronite leaders in Lebanon voicing opposition to the new political order.

MAURITANIA An Islamic republic in northwest Africa, independent since 1960. Mauritania lies on the western fringes of the Sahara desert and forms a geographical link between the Arab MAGHREB and Black Africa. It is mostly desert, bordering in the north on formerly Spanish Sahara SADR (or MOROCCO, if its annexation of that territory is considered valid) and ALGERIA; in the east on Mali; in the south on Senegal; and in the west on the Atlantic Ocean.

Although Mauritania is officially Arab and a member of the ARAB LEAGUE since November 1973, only a minority of its largely tribal population is Arab-speaking. The scarce population includes two thirds of Moors, tribes of Arab-BERBERS, and therefore it considers itself Arab or semi-Arab. (The remaining third are Black Africans.) There is no national language (except the various tribal tongues). Of these Arabic has long served as an auxiliary language or *lingua franca*, and since 1966 has been proclaimed the national language and the main language of instruction. In 1991 Arabic became the sole official language, while French is used mainly in the commercial sector.

When Mauritania, formerly a French possession, became independent (in 1958 semi-independent within the French Community and in November 1960 fully independent) the Arab states—with the exception of TUNISIA—refused to recognize it. This was due to its mainly solidarity with Morocco's claim that Mauritania was a part of its historic, pre-colonial, territory (Morocco severed its diplomatic relations with Tunisia following its recognition of Mauritania.) Nor did many other states, especially those of the Communist bloc, that considered it an artificial creation of French COLONIALISM.

In the early years of independence, Mauritania relied on FRANCE and Black African states' diplomatic support. Mairotania's request for admission to the UN was blocked by a Soviet veto, while Arab and Third World states' proposals to submit its independence to a plebiscite or negotiations, failed to receive majority support In 1961, the Soviet veto was withdrawn and Mauritania was admitted to the UN, with ten Arab states (of the thirteen then UN members) voting against and many Third World countries abstaining. However, during the 1960s, the Arab states accepted Mauritania's independence and established diplomatic relations with it.

Morocco even gradually relented with some French mediation—and in January 1970 also recognized the state's independance establishing diplomatic relations with it. Relations have nevertheless remained cool, especially since they were disturbed by conflicting attitudes toward WESTERN SAHARA CONFLICT. Mauritania frequently suspects Moroccan interferences in its internal factional struggles and upheavals. Official relations were in the 1980s twice severed, and later resumed.

The fate of Spain's Western Sahara territories entangled Mauritania in a protracted dispute. A gradual handing-over by Spain to the local population, with the prospect of eventual independence, had been discussed and called for by the UN. But in November 1975 Spain agreed with Mauritania and Morocco to hand over the territory to them, which was done in February 1976. In April 1976 the two countries agreed to divide the territory; Morocco also agreed to let Mauritania have a share in the territory's rich phosphate mines, its main resource, which is located in Morocco's part. Morocco immediately annexed its part of Western Sahara; Mauritania did not.

Demands for independence crystallized in 1975 though the guerrilla organization, POLISARIO, and led in February 1976 to the proclamation of SADR. While Morocco was prepared to fight POLISARIO and its Republic (and clash with Algeria which supported and assisted it), Mauritania was neither able nor willing to do the same, mainly because large sections of its Moorish population had ties of kinship with Western Sahara groups. In 1978 Ould Daddah, Mauritania's president since independence, was overthrown by a military coup and two days later the POLISARIO announced a cease-fire.

In August 1979, following pressures from the Organization of African Unity and an announcement of POLISARIO on ending the cease-fire, Mauritania renounced, in agreement with POLISARIO, its part in the territory. Morocco immediately annexed that part, too. Mauritania's abrogation of its agreement with Morocco in accord with POLISARIO was bitterly resented in Morocco, further underming the relations between the two countries. Their relations continued to deteriorate because of the Western Saharan conflict: in December 1983 Mauritania adhered to an Algerian-Tunisian Treaty of Friendship and Cooperation of March 1983—a Treaty with an apparent anti-Moroccan edge—and in February 1984 Mauritania recognized SADR.

Domestic Affairs: After attaining independence in 1960 Moktar Ould Daddah, whose *Parti du regroupement mauritanien* (PRM) won all the Parliaments' seats in the elections, became the head of the state. In 1964 he merged all parties into the *Parti du peuple mauritanien* (PPM) and Mauritania was declared a one-party state. In 1975 a PPM Congress adopted a charter of Islamic, national, central and socialist democracy. In 1978 Ould Daddah was deposed in a military coup and replaced by the Chief of Staff Lieutenant Colonol Moustafa Ould Muhamed Salek, as leader of the Military Committee for National Recovery (MCNR). This suspended the constitution and disolved the national assembly and the PPM. In March 1979 Salek assumed absolute power and shortly afterward disolved the MCNR, replacing it with a Military Committee for National Salvation (MCNS). He resigned in June and was replaced by Mohamed Ould Ahmed Louli, but following Mauritania's withdrawal from the Sahara War, later that year, Defense Minister Muhammad Ould Haidallah displaced Louli as President in early 1980.

The new shift of power and dismissal of several MCNS members resulted in the formation of a nucleus of exiled opposition movements, most salient of which was the Paris-based *Alliance pour une Mauritanie democratique*, (Mauritania Democratic Alliance) led by Ould Daddah. A draft constitution was published in late 1980, with provision for a multi-party system, but was abandoned in April 1981, following a coup attempt in March—believed to have been tacitly supported by Morocco—which was repressed by Haidallah and brought to reshuffle in the government top positions, with Lieutenant Colonel Maawiya Ould Sid Ahmed Taya as the new Prime Minister. Haidallah remained in power until the coup led by Taya in December 1984, following general discontent with the regime. Under his regime,

diplomatic relations with Morocco were resumed in April 1985.

During the 1980s, ethnic tensions arose mainly as the Black Africans resented what they perceived as the increasing Arabicization of Mauritania by the Moorish majority, which discriminated against the former group. The government reacted by arresting many leaders of the Black community and the provocateurs of the ongoing unrest and riots that had erupted in that community in late 1986, with some of them sentenced to death. As a result, the government stressed the Islamic—rather than the Arab—identity of the Mauritanian people and accelerated the process of applying Islamic Law (SHARI'A). The regime also promised to democratize political life through direct legislation and presidential elections. In 1991 Mauritania incorporated a constitution into a referendum, despite strong opposition. This gave the President of the Republic vast authorities.

In January 1992 presidential elections took place, with four prominent figures competing for the office, including Taya who won the majority of the votes cast. In March of that year general elections were held, after six opposition parties announced their withdrawal, claiming that the election law favored the government-backed Democratic and Social Republican Party. Nonetheless, the elections led to a multi-party system. However, Mauritania's politics continued to be marked by ethnic tensions and economic difficulties, which grew severed following the general elections.

In 1994 the first multi-party municipal elections were held. Together with democratization processes during the 1980s and 1990s protests against the government on civil rights issues erupted—most of them culminating in the mass arrest of the demonstrators. Another problematic issues on the Mauritania internal agenda has been the Islamic radical groups. In 1995 Mauritania, Morocco, Tunisia, EGYPT and ISRAEL participated in talks with NATO on tackling the rising tide of Islamism in the Middle East and North Africa. In the second legislative elections held in October 1996, the ruling DSRP increased its representation to over two-thirds of the seats in the national assembly with the opposition parties mostly staying out, leading to strong accusations regarding the dishonesty of the elections and involvement of the authorities in determining their results.

Foreign Affairs In 1991 Mauritania resumed its relations with Senegal though the main disputed issue between the two states—the status of Mauritanian refugees in Senegal and refusal of Mauritania to recognize their rights. These issues remained unsettled, but it was agreed they would be discussed. Mali also renewed its relations with Mauritania after solving the problem of Mauritanian refugees crossing its borders and vice versa. In 1996 the three countries agreed to co-operate on this matter, using military measures on their mutual borders.

Though France remained an important source for Mauritania, financially and politically, the Taya regime considered itself part of the Arab Maghreb and strove for links with the Arab world as a whole. In February 1989 Mauritania became a founding member of the new regional economic unity—the ARAB MAGHREB UNION (AMU) together with Algeria, LIBYA, Morocco and Tunisia.

Although the AMU never took off the ground it made it possible for Mauritania to cultivate closer links with the Maghreb states. In the course of the KUWAIT crisis and the GULF WAR (1990–1991), Mauritania supported Iraq for economic reasons—the end of financial aid from the Gulf monarchies. In 1994 Mauritania renewed its relations with Kuwait and in the following year it followed Morocco and Tunisia and established low diplomatic relations with Israel, which led to the closing of the Libyan embassy in Nouakchott. However, the two states renewed their relations in 1997.

MCMAHON-HUSSEIN CORRESPONDENCE

Ten letters exchanged between 14 July 1915 and 30 March 1916 by Hussein Ibn Ali Sharif of Mecca and Sir Henry-McMahon (1862–1949), the British High Commissioner in Egypt, 1914–1916. The letters discussed the terms under which the Sharif would ally himself with BRITAIN in World War I and revolt against Turkish rule. Hussein asked Britain to recognize, and assure, the independence of the Arab countries—meaning all of the Arabian Peninsula except ADEN, and the entire Fertile Crescent—after the war, and to support the re-establishment of an Arab Caliphate. Britain accepted these principles, but could not agree with Hussein's definition of the area claimed.

In his second note, of 24 October 1915, McMahon-Hussein's correspondence excluded certain areas: "The districts of Mersin and ALEXANDRETTA and portions of SYRIA lying to the west of the districts of Damascus, Homs, Hama and Aleppo, cannot be claimed as purely Arab. Hence it must be excepted from the proposed delimitation." The interpretation of that sentence later gave rise to a long argument between Britain and the Arabs as to whether Palestine was part of the area excluded (as it was west of the province of Damascus, which covered all of Transjordan, but not geographically west of the four towns mentioned). Britain always maintained that it had never intended to include Palestine in the area of Arab independence. This was confirmed in the McMahon-Hussein correspondence in his letter to the Colonial Office of 12 March 1922. However, several British spokesmen admitted that the wording was not clear, as did the government when publishing the hitherto secret correspondence, in 1939 (". . . the language in which this exclusion was expressed was not so specific and unmistakable as it was thought to be at the time"). The Arabs claimed that Palestine was included in the area they considered promised to them and that both the SYKES-PICOT AGREEMENT of 1916 and the BALFOUR DECLARATION of 1917 contradicted the McMahon-Hussein correspondence's promises to Hussein, revealing Britain's bad faith.

The McMahon-Hussein correspondence also claimed a special position for Britain in the provinces of Baghdad and Basra, a claim that Hussein implicitly accepted. As to the coastal lands of western Syria and LEBANON, Hussein did not accept their being granted to FRANCE, indicating that he would claim them after the war. The degree of great power (British and French) tutelage envisaged also remained rather vague, later generating much controversy.

No complete agreement was reached in the McMahon-Hussein correspondence and it did not constitute a formal treaty or a firm commitment. But regardless of the limited scope of the ARAB REVOLT and its contribution to the British war effort, an Anglo-Arab alliance was established.

The Arab Revolt began in 1916, on the assumption that Britain would generally support Arab independence. The SYKES-PICOT AGREEMENT and the post-war settlement were regarded by Arab leaders, beyond the Palestine question and specific territorial claims, as a betrayal, since they substituted zones of imperial influence and tutelage, or even direct imperial control, for the full independence which, the Arabs insisted, had been promised.

MEIR (MEYERSON), GOLDA (1898–1978) Is-
raeli politician, leader of the Israel Labor Party and Prime Minister, 1969–1974. She was born in Russia and educated in the US, where she was trained as a teacher. She immigrated to Palestine in 1921 and lived in Kibbutz Merhavia in the years 1921–1924. Golda Meir was active in the *Histadrut* Labor Federation, becoming Secretary of its Council for Women Workers in 1928, a member of its Executive Committee in 1934 and head of its Political Department in 1936. Meir played an active role in the *Mapai* Party, and in 1946, when Moshe Sharett was arrested by the British, Golda Meir replaced him as Head of the Political Department of the Jewish Agency (see ZIONISM).

Before the outbreak of Israel's War of Independence (see ARAB-ISRAEL CONFLICT) she held secret meetings with King ABDALLAH of JORDAN in an effort to come to an agreement on the partition of Palestine and the establishment of a Jewish state in part of it. Following the establishment of the State of IS-RAEL she was appointed Israel's first diplomatic representative to Moscow.

Meir was a member of Knesset from 1949 to 1974, first on the *Mapai* list and later on the Labor-*Mapam* list of the *Ma'arach* (Alignment). She was Minister of Labor, 1949–1956, and Minister of Foreign Affairs 1956–1966. In the latter position she initiated Israel's policy of active cooperation with the newly independent states of Black Africa. (see AFRO-ARAB RELATIONS). In 1965 Meir was appointed Secretary-General of *Mapai*. In this capacity she played an active role in reuniting Mapai with *Ahdut Ha'avodah-Po'alei Zion* and with *Rafi*, which together formed the Israel Labor Party in 1968. When Levi ESHKOL passed away in March 1969 Meir became Prime Minister.

She was Prime Minister during the Yom Kippur War (see ARAB-ISRAEL CONFLICT), and following the elections to the eighth Knesset (December 1973) formed another government. She conducted and concluded disengagement agreements with EGYPT and SYRIA (see ARAB-ISRAEL PEACEMAKING). However, after the publication of the interim report of the Agranat Commission of Inquiry on the background to outbreak of the war, she resigned.

Meir's views on the ARAB-ISRAEL CONFLICT and Israel's social problems were generally considered to be simplistic and conservative. Nevertheless, she was highly regarded and held in awe both in Israel and abroad. In 1972 she was elected Deputy President of the Socialist International.

MENDERES, ADNAN (1899–1961) Turkish
politician, Prime Minister 1950–1960; executed in 1961. Born in Aydin to a landowning family, Menderes studied law at Ankara University. In 1930 he was active in the Liberal Republican Party, an opposition group permitted to function for a short time. When it was dissolved the same year, he returned to the ruling Republican People's Party (RPP) and was elected to its National Assembly. In 1945 he resigned together with BAYAR, Köprülü and Koraltan. He demanded far-reaching liberalization, including a multi-party system. When competing parties were permitted, Menderes and his group in 1946 formed the Democratic Party. They lost the first elections they contested in 1946, but won those of 1950 and Menderes became Prime Minister.

During the ten years of his premiership he greatly strengthened Turkey's Western alignment by sending a Turkish brigade to Korea in 1950, joining Nato in 1951–1952 and the Western-sponsored Baghdad Pact in 1955. During this time economic, technical and military cooperation with the US were fostered.

He also embarked on an ambitious program of economic development, and adopted a permissive attitude towards Islamic education and organization, contrary to Kemalist secularism. These policies earned him the trust of Turkey's peasant majority; but he was rejected by the intellectuals, and later by the army, because of his allegedly irresponsible economic policy, his repression of the opposition, and his deviation from Kemalist principles. He was ousted by an army coup in May 1960.

Menderes was tried with other leaders of the Democratic Party and the government on Yassiada Island; they were accused of violating the constitution and corruption. He was sentenced to death and hanged.

MERNISSI, FATIMA (b.1940) A well known
Moroccan feminist scholar. Mernissi studied political science and sociology at Brandeis University,

the Sorbonne, and at Mohammed V University in Rabat. She then taught at Mohammed V University, from 1974 until 1981. Mernissi was then appointed a position at the Institute Universitaire de Recherche Scientifique.

She has written extensively about Islam as a religious and historical text which determines gender roles and women's rights. Specifically, Mernissi has argued that Islam regards women's sexuality as dangerous, and capable of disturbing the social order. Her more recent works have focused on women in Islamic history. Mernissi has been active in forming research groups and conducting workshops on women's issues. In 1989 she received a grant from the United Nations to market multimedia works about women. Among her works translated into English are *Beyond the Veil, Doing Daily Battle, The Forgotten Queens of Islam, Islam and Democracy* and the autobiographical *Dreams of Trespass*.

MIDDLE EAST DEFENSE ORGANIZATION

From the end of World War II, with the emergence of the Arab states into full independence, the approaching end of the existing treaties of alliance between BRITAIN, IRAQ and EGYPT, and in view of the Soviet strategic threat, Britain sought to revise those treaties in order to preserve its strategic privileges in the Arab countries. It did this by establishing a regional defense system in which it would play a focal role. Strong domestic opposition frustrated these attempts in the late 1940s with Egypt and Iraq. In the early 1950s, Britain renewed its efforts, and together with the UNITED STATES, suggested a multilateral defense pact, or command, for the Middle East states to be linked to and guided by the Western allies. These plans were clearly directed against military and political penetration of the region by the USSR, and were stepped up with the intensification of the Cold War. It was also hoped that such multilateral arrangements would solve bilateral problems that had remained unresolved—e.g., the future of British military bases and privileges in Egypt and Iraq.

Britain and the US were the most active in the search for such a Middle East Defense Organization, while TURKEY and for some time FRANCE associated themselves with their efforts.

In October 1951, Britain, the US, France and Turkey presented to Egypt a plan for a Middle East Defense Organization. This was also termed the Supreme Allied Command for the Middle East (SACME). They invited Egypt to join as an original signatory. Other states in the region were kept informed, on the understanding that they could later adhere to the treaty. Egypt rejected the concept outright, having no desire to join a Western alliance and did not see Soviet policies as a threat. Its position remained intact even when the plan was re-submitted in November 1951 in a revised version thought to be more palatable to it. Other Middle Eastern states were not receptive either and negotiations were suspended.

Overtures were renewed in 1954–1955, with the US Secretary of State, John Foster Dulles, as the prime mover. There was an added emphasis on the creation of a "Northern Tier" (Turkey-IRAN-PAKISTAN) as the first and main line of defense. This time, Iraq was persuaded to join and the BAGHDAD PACT was concluded between Turkey and Iraq; it was later joined by Britain and Pakistan. But this Pact did not turn into a true Middle East Defense Organization and it harmed the Arab states' relations with the West.

MIDEASTERNISM (or New Middle East): (Arabic: *sharqawsatiyya*) A new concept of the Middle East identity, or rather, approach to its regional order, debated by ARAB intellectuals, primarily in EGYPT, and identifying new possibilities of political and economic alignments in the Middle East.

The recognition of this new regional stream, or identity, reflects a break with the contemporary Arab perception of the Middle East as an Arab-Muslim region, in which ISRAEL was—and largely still is—regarded as alien and one that is in, but not of the region. Based on pragmatic considerations of the Middle East nations the new approach to intra-regional state relations in the Middle East seems to have begun a shift toward one based on mutual needs and benefits—through which Israel is acknowledged as an active regional partner in alliances with Arab-Muslim states in the region, rather than on Arab national, or Islamic identities.

The debated concept of *Sharqawsatiyya* emerged alongside the ARAB-ISRAEL PEACEMAKING represented by the convening of the international peace conference in Madrid (October 1991), the Oslo Agreement between Israel and the PALESTINE LIBERATION

ORGANIZATION (PLO) in September 1993, and the Israel-JORDAN peace treaty of October 1994. No less important were the global and regional changes shaped by the end of the Cold War and the GULF WAR.

Assuming that the peacemaking process will attain its goals and result in a final settlement on all Israeli-Arab disputes, Mideasternism maintains that the changing trends in the world and the Middle East have already paved the way for new patterns of inter-state relations between Israel and its Arab and Muslim neighbors. These future relations have been identified mainly with the breakdown of the Arab paradigm as a decisive determinant of Arab state behavior. Observing the growing diversity of national Arab economic and strategic interests, Arab thinkers tend to diminish the acuteness of Arab national identity in shaping the policies and foreign alignments of Arab states, and to give further weight to pressing needs and selfish interests of these states.

The debate on Mideasternism has not been conducted without concerns over possible repercussions on issues such as Arab identity, culture, and collective security, as well as Islamic values and tradition, and regional political hegemony. Thus, for example, the peaceful relations built between Israel, the PALESTINIAN AUTHORITY (PA) and Jordan, seemed to have created a strong economic block through which Israel would be able to penetrate economically into the Arab world. Combined with the fears of Israeli economic domination, the discourse of Mideasternism also referred to fears of Israel's technological eminence (assuming the possession of nuclear weapons). Typically, these fears were aroused by opponents of the Arab-Israel peacemaking process, primarily Islamist and Pan-Arab spokesmen.

By mid-1995, an offshoot of this concept, namely Mediterraneanism (*sharq mut awassatiyya*), had appeared, maintaining a new regional identity centered on the Mediterranean basin.

An equivalent term to Mideasternism, "The New Middle East," was coined under the same circumstances by Israel's Foreign Minister Shimon PERES, the architect and main driving force in the RABIN government (1992–1996), and Prime Minister after the latter's assassination. Peres envisions a Middle East of economic cooperation as a necessity and a way in which to reinforce links of coexistence and mutual security, instead of the current balance of de-

terrence and military power. Peres' vision culminated in the international conferences for economic cooperation and development, sponsored by the Russian and American Presidents, that had been held annually since October 1994 (in Casablanca, Amman, Cairo, and Doha, respectively). These were attended by private and official economic leaders from most Arab states, Israel, European and Asian countries. However, they lost much of their momentum due to the deadlocked peacemaking process in 1996–1997. Nonetheles, they scored some modest successes and beginnings of joint Israeli-Arab (sometimes with third party) economic ventures, especially between Israel and Jordan and the Gulf emirates.

Peres' idea of a New Middle East, focusing on the economic sphere, however, were viewed with suspicion in Israel, particularly in view of the terrorist attacks by Palestinian Islamists, and the deadlocked peace process. On the Arab side too, the discourse on *Sharqawsatiyya* lost its incentives though is still discussed in various ways, reflecting a consciousness to the deep changes of orientations, needs and ways to fulfill them in the region.

MILITARY IN POLITICS   see ARMED FORCES.

MILLET, MILLET SYSTEM   The Turkish term "millet," derived from the Arabic *Milla*, meant any one of the religious communities within the OTTOMAN EMPIRE. The Millet System was the organization of the non-Muslim population into religious communities. It established their rights and obligations under their ecclesiastical leaders.

Based on the Islamic tradition and administrative concept, the Ottomans granted the CHRISTIAN and Jewish religious communities wide autonomy in matters of personal status, community affairs, legal procedure and education, giving their heads jurisdiction over their members. These leaders were responsible for the maintenance of order within their communities, and the payment of the *jizya*, the poll tax, and other taxes required of non-Muslims.

Until the nineteenth century there were only three such officially recognized Millets: the GREEK ORTHODOX, the Armenian Gregorian, and the Jewish. Millet status was given in response to pressures from European powers, to various other denominations and sects, so that by 1914 the number of Millets had risen to fourteen, representing the broadening of the system to include many ethnic and religious groups.

The proliferation of Millets in the mid-nineteenth century, combined with the Capitulations (privileged status, originally granted to foreign residents in the sixteenth century to facilitate trade granted the European powers further economic and cultural influence in the Ottoman Empire). The Millet system also encouraged the development of nationalism among Christian communities, further undermining the bases of the Ottoman Empire. Although Ottoman reforms in the 1850s and 1860s included legislation which improved the non-Christians' civil status, it also sought to undermine the system for the sake of Ottoman sovereignty and integrity. One way was the introduction of the Millet constitutions in the 1860s, seeking to increase lay participation in the affairs of the community. Owing to foreign pressure and the Millet's insistence of self-preservation, the Millet System was maintained until after the final dissolution of the Empire, when the new Turkish constitution established the principle of national unity and equality. The rights of minorities became a major issue in the Lausanne Peace Conference (1923) and the Western powers secured an undertaking by the Turkish government to uphold some of the traditional religious, judicial and educational rights of the non-Muslims, to be guaranteed by the League of Nations. These rights were voluntarily renounced by the Jewish, Armenian and Greek communities in 1925–1926, following the steps taken by the Turkish government to secularize the state.

MINORITIES The main socio-political source of identity and allegiance in the Middle East was, for many centuries, the primordial ethno-religious community. Although this structure has been somewhat undermined by the advent of nationalism since the late nineteenth century, and more forcefully by the state—especially since independence—communal entities and allegiances, quasi-national in many cases, still play a crucial role in defining group identity and political behavior. One major reason for that is the link between a community and its traditional area of living. Large ethno-religious-mostly Muslim—communities, which preserved their significant majority or even pure homogeneity in specific areas which they had inhabited for many centuries, to the extent that some of these areas carry the name of its community. Such is the case of the DRUZE in SYRIA (with their center in Jabal Druze), LEBANON and ISRAEL, the KURDS in east Anatolia, northern IRAQ, north-western IRAN and north-east Syria (Kurdistan); the ALAWIS, in north-western Syria; Maronite-Christians in Mount Lebanon; and Shi'is in the Biqa' and south Lebanon; Baluchies in eastern Iran (Baluchistan); Arabs in south-western Iran (named Arabistan, by Arabs); BERBERS in the MAGHREB countries, etc.

Another reason is the social, cultural, and often political autonomy enjoyed by those communities throughout Islamic history—granted or acquired by rebellion—as well as under foreign rule. This effectively encouraged separate tendencies of some minorities: Druze and Alawis under the French Mandate on Syria were granted local autonomy. The Kurds of northern Iraq were meant to receive some autonomy when the League of Nations decided in 1925–1926 to award the Mosul province to Iraq. The promise was not implemented by either the British administration or post-1932 independent Iraq. Southern Sudan with its African tribal population was deemed by the British-Sudanese Administration not ready for fully-fledged autonomy, but it was kept separate as a closed, protected area. Independent Sudan abolished these precautions and tried to extend its administration to the South.

The architects of modern Lebanon, before and after its independence, sought to protect the various minority communities by building a system of government based on a predetermined representation of the communities and an agreed distribution of power among them. In all these cases, the rooted sense of communal or proto-national distinctive identity, led to a clash with the state once it became independent.

In the Arab states, the dominating majority is Arab in language and culture and SUNNI-Muslim in religion. Minorities are therefore all groups that differ from that majority in either their linguistic-ethnic or their religious character. Exceptions to the majority status of the Sunni-Muslim community are Lebanon (where no single community constitutes a majority. All Christian groups together comprised about fifty-five percent of the population in the 1930s, which is now forty to forty-five percent); Iraq (where the majority is Shi'i-Muslim—but the Sunni-Muslim minority is in fact the ruling group); Yemen (almost evenly divided between ZEIDIS Shi'is and SHAFE'I Sunnis, with a slight majority for the former); OMAN (where the Muslim-IBADI majority is not usually counted as Sunni); and DUBAI and BAHRAIN (whose indigenous population, excluding foreign workers, is about evenly divided between Sunnis and Shi'is, with a slight Shi'i majority).

Some minority groups differ from the dominant group in both culture and religion. In the Arab states, the black African animist tribes of southern SUDAN, ARMENIANS and Kurdish-speaking YAZIDIS in Iraq. Except for South Sudan's African tribes, and the Armenian communities in Syria, Lebanon and Israel, these are all small groups.

Border-line cases consist of a few ancient communities, mostly Christian, who preserve some measure of almost-national group consciousness that goes beyond the religious-communal identity: Nestorian-ASSYRIANS and Syrian JACOBITES in Iraq and Syria, Sabaeans-MANDAEANS in Iraq, MARONITES in Lebanon (all with Syriac-Aramaic dialects as their ancient tongue—surviving in most cases only as the language of liturgy); and Egypt's COPTS (preserving remnants of ancient Egyptian). Of these, only the Maronites and the Copts are significantly large population groups. In Iran, such minorities are mainly the Azeris, KURDS, Arab, and Turkmenian; in TURKEY, Kurds and ARMENIANS, and Arabs in Israel (see ISRAELI ARAB CITIZENS).

Minority groups differing in religion only are the Christian communities of the Arab countries. The degree to which they regard themselves as separate, quasi-national entities or unreservedly as part of the majority nation, varies. From the strongest sense of cultural and historical group distinction of the borderline groups mentioned, a greater solidarity with the Arab majority nationalism in the GREEK CATHOLIC, and the greatest in the GREEK ORTHODOX communities.

In the same category of differing in religion, but not in linguistic-ethnic nationality are the Shi'i Muslims in some Arab countries (especially Iraq, Yemen, Lebanon and Bahrain), and the heretic communities on the fringes of Islam—ISMA'ILIYYA, Alawis, Druze in Syria and Lebanon.

Differing in their ethnic-linguistic nationality only, but belonging to the Muslim-Sunni mainstream in their religion, are the Kurds in Iraq, Iran, Turkey and Syria; Arabs, Azeris, and Turkemenians in Iran; and some Turks and Turcemenian tribes in Iraq and Syria. The Berbers of the Magrib also belong to this category—indeed even their ethnic-linguistic distinctiveness survives. So do the remnants of several ancient peoples in Sudan (Beja, Nubians, Nuba who are Muslims but non-Arab).

Arabic-speaking or ethnically Arab minorities are found in the southern border regions of Turkey and the ALEXANDRETTA-Hatay District; in south-western Iran (Khuzistan-"Arabistan"); in some countries of Northwest Africa bordering on the Arab Maghrib (Chad, Niger, Mali) and the three semi-Arab African countries that have joined the ARAB LEAGUE: MAURITANIA, SOMALIA and DJIBOUTI; and in Israel (where they form over eighteen percent of the population see ISRAELI ARAB CITIZENS).

Minorities comprise a considerable part of the population, and therefore pose a political problem, actual or potential, to processes of national integration and political development. All minorities wish to enjoy equal rights whilst preserving their distinctive character, whether ethnic-linguistic or religious-communal. This has led to repeated violent disputes between the state—sometimes dominated by a minority group, such as in the case of Iraq and Syria—and minority groups, representing social and political grievances. Most of the Middle Eastern states have suffered, in varying degrees, from this problem:

Lebanon, a mosaic of ethno-religious groups, none of which constitute a majority, which had undergone a long and costly civil war (1975–1990); Iraq, whose Arab majority is struck by Sunni-Sh'i cleavage, in addition to the Kurdish-Arab cleavage which has been the source of repeated rebellions and claims for self-rule; Yemen, divided almost equally between Shi'i Zeidis and Sunni Shafe'is, nurturing internal disputes and civil war); Turkey, where the government has been engaged in war against the rebellious PKK since the late 1980s; Bahrain and Dubai, almost equally divided between Shi'is and Sunnis); Sudan, with twenty-five to thirty percent non-Arab non-Muslims, constituting almost the entire population of the three southern provinces, engaged in war with the Muslim-Arab government since 1983; the surviving distinctiveness of the Berbers, who make up at least thirty percent of the population in ALGERIA and MOROCCO and claim to be recognized as a distinct cultural group.

Some of the minority communities struggled for a greater measure of autonomy. The Assyrians in Iraq failed. The Kurds rebelled for decades. Since 1974 Iraq has granted them a degree of local autonomy, but as they are not content with that very partial autonomy and accuse Iraq of breaking agreements and promises in that respect, a rebellion continues (see KURDS for details).

The African tribes of South Sudan rebelled from 1962–1963 and eventually in 1972 obtained an agreement on a far-reaching autonomy. Since the agreement was broken, they resumed their rebellion in 1983. Berber resentment and complaints create a measure of tension, and sometimes clashes, in Algeria (where Berbers were in the forefront of the nationalist struggle against France). In both Algeria and Morocco, there is an emergence of movements for Berber cultural rights.

MIRGHANIYYA An Islamic political-religious order in SUDAN, named after its founder, Muhammad al-Amir Ghani al-Mirghani (1793–1853), and mainly refered to as *al-Khatimiyya*. The *Mirhaniyya*, rivalled the MAHDIYYA order. However, both supported a revival and purification of orthodox Islam using (although not belonging to Sufi Islamic mysticism and its "DERVISH ORDERS") some Dervish rituals, customs and organizational methods.

Unlike the *Mirhaniyya* (which advocated the overthrow of existing regimes that had deviated from pure Islamic traditions), the *Mirhaniyya* recommended co-operation with the regime. Generally, the *Mirhaniyya* appeared, despite its basic fundamentalism, as more moderate than both the *Mirhaniyya* and militant Muslim organizations like the MUSLIM BROTHERHOOD. Similar to the *Mirhaniyya*, though not as publicly and vigorously as the latter, it objected to the imposition, in 1983, of the harsh SHARI'A code of punishments.

The *Mirhaniyya* has always been considered pro-Egyptian. In the years of the struggle between the advocates of separate independence and those of union with EGYPT, it supported the pro-Egyptian *al-Ashiqqa* Party (becoming, in 1952, the "National Unionist Party"); from 1956 it backed the "People's Democratic Party"; and since 1967, the "Democratic Union Party" (DUP), which constituted the merger of the two latter groups. The order also accommodated itself more readily than the *Mahdiyya*

to Sudan's revolutionary regimes—those of Abbud (1958–1964) and NUMEIRI (1969–1985). Its basic orientation remains unchanged, and it continues advocating close co-operation with Egypt, resisting Libyan blandishments more firmly than the *Mahdiyya*. It has maintained its involvement in politics, though low-profile, through the DUP.

The leadership of the *Mirhaniyya* order has always been maintained by the descendants of its founder. The leaders during this century were al-Sa'id Ali al-Mirghani (1870–1968) and his son, al-Sa'id Muhammad Uthman al-Mirghani (b. approximately 1942), since 1968. The leaders of the order refrained, in general, from directly participating in political affairs and party organizations—though their support for the "National Unionists" and later the DUP was well known. In May 1986 Ahmad al-Mirghani, the younger brother of the Mirghani leader, was elected chairman of the new Supreme Council of Sudan, i.e., Head-of-State (but a post with little actual power).

MISSIONS, MISSIONARIES The propagation of the Christian faith through missionary activities in the Arab countries and the Middle East has been directed at proselytizing adherents of the Eastern Christian churches as well as Muslims and Jews. The conversion of Muslims was certainly difficult, nearly impossible, since it was illegal under Islamic law. Indeed, a Muslim converting to another faith was considered an apostate and subjected to harsh punishment—until the nineteenth century: the death penalty. Most converts made by Catholic and Protestant missionaries were therefore Eastern Christians. Missionaries have also established many educational and charitable institutions open to members of all communities and not engaging in direct, immediate propagation of conversion.

Catholic religious orders have been engaged in missionary activities in the Middle East since the Crusades, assisted since the seventeenth century by a Vatican Congregation for the Propagation of the Faith. They and have built hundreds of educational and charitable institutions. The "Latin" (in Western terms: Roman-Catholic) communities in the Arab countries, as distinct from UNIATE-Catholic ones, are mainly the result of such missionary activities. By a papal decree of 1894, however, all proselytizing in the Middle East, where Uniate Churches existed (i.e. not including SUDAN and the MAGHREB) have been entrusted exclusively to the Uniate churches.

Protestant and Anglican missions were active from the eighteenh, and mainly the nineteenth centuries, with the first American missionary arriving in Syria in 1819. Presbyterians worked mainly in SYRIA and LEBANON, Congregationalists in Armenia, German and Swiss Lutherans in Palestine and Lebanon, Anglicans-Episcopalians in Palestine, EGYPT, Sudan and LIBYA. Baptists, Methodists, and Pentecostals joined later. As a result of this activity, Protestant communities, practically non-existent before, grew to about 250,000 in the Arab countries and Palestine. In 1927, a Near Eastern Christian Council was formed as a meeting ground for the Protestant Missionary Societies. In 1958 it became a regional component of the World Council of Churches. From the nineteenth century, the Russian Orthodox Church also engaged in missionary activities, establishing its own institutions.

Prominent missionaries that established Catholic educational institutions such the University of St. Joseph in Beirut, founded in 1875 by the Jesuits, the Coptic-Catholic Seminary of Ma'adi in EGYPT was also founded by the Jesuits. A Syro-Chaldean Seminary in Mosul was founded by the Dominicans. The Greek-Catholic Seminary of St. Anne was established by the White Fathers in JERUSALEM (transferred to Lebanon in 1967). The Dominican-founded Ecole Biblique in Jerusalem; the University of Bethlehem—previously a college, was granted university status in 1973.

The most important educational institutions established by Protestant missionaries are the American Universities of Beirut (founded in 1866 as a college, becoming a university in 1920) and Cairo (1919). The Protestant-established institutions of the YMCA became important social-educational centers. The various religious orders and congregations have also founded numerous hospitals and clinics, greatly contributing to the development of public health in the region.

Missionary-established educational institutions have, since the nineteenth century, trained generations of a modern elite, an intelligentsia that became the growing ground of nationalism and its leaders. Missionary-founded printing shops were the birth place of an Arabic press, pamphlets and modern books, thus contributing to the same process. But later, most of the emerging independent, national Arab states have tended to regard missionaries and their activities with a measure of suspicion and resentment, as an outgrowth of imperialism and foreign rule (added to the traditional Islamic condemnation of the conversion of Muslims).

Even educational and charitable institutions established by missionaries have been suspected to be a way of attracting converts by the material benefits offered. Missionary activities by foreigners (and most missionaries indeed were foreigners) have been banned or restricted by several Arab states. Most Arab states have also restricted the independence of missionary-established educational institutions, compelling them to conform to national curricula and imposing a degree of supervision by the state educational authorities.

Islamic missionary activity has always been directed only to countries outside the Arab world and the Middle East, i.e., to countries not considered Islamic—e.g., in Africa, Asia and the West. But Islamic institutions in the Arab states, such as, chiefly, the al-Azhar University in Cairo, have served as missionary centers and training grounds.

MOJAHEDIN-E KHALQ-E IRAN ORGANIZATION (MKO)

An Iranian guerrilla movement, established in 1965 on an ideological basis combining Marxist and Muslim principles. It is the strongest Iranian opposition organization since the Islamic revolution (1979), both inside and outside the country. The founders of the movement were Sa'id Mohsen and Mohammad Hanifnezhad, who had operated previously within the framework of the Liberation Movement of IRAN, but concluded that only by means of armed struggle would it be possible to realize a socio-political revolution in Iran.

The choice of the name "Mojahedin" (fighters of Islam's holy war) pointed to an orientation, which was both religious and warlike at the same time. The movement's emblem, adopted in later years, portrayed a verse from the Qur'an, side by side with a map of Iran, a hammer and submachine gun. The movement mobilized its members from amongst students and youngsters, who underwent a process consolidation and indoctrination.

In 1969 the movement crystallized its political platform, stating that victory could only be attained by means of a popular uprising and a "liberation army," carrying out guerrilla activities. In 1969, the movement sent some of its members to Lebanon to train in guerrilla tactics in *Fatah* camps and established contacts with QADHAFI in LIBYA. Guerrilla operations inside Iran began in 1971. Many of the movement's activists were detained by the authorities in Iran and some were executed. Against the background of differences of opinion on the issue of the balance between ISLAM and Socialism, there was a split in the movement in 1975. In May the Marxists established an independent movement of their own.

The movement played an important role in the success of the Islamic revolution in 1979, and in the early months of the new regime, gained popularity among the younger generation. However, KHOMEINI viewed its ideology as a deviation from true Islam, and held extensive ideological debates with its leaders. However, when this dialogue did not lead to a change in their position, Khomeini decided to liquidate them.

In 1980 all the branches of the movement were closed and many of its leaders detained. In June 1981 the movement opened an armed struggle against the regime which led to street fights in Tehran. In February 1982, the leader of the movement, Moussa Khiabani, who had gone underground, was located and assassinated.

On its part, the movement killed dozens of leaders of the Islamic regime by laying bombs in a branch of the ruling party and the President's offices. The new leader of the movement, Mas'ud Rajavi, escaped from Iran together with the deposed President Abul-Hassan BANI-SADR, and set up his headquarters near Paris. However, when the French government pressed him to stop his activities on French soil, he accepted an offer by President Saddam HUSSEIN of IRAQ and transferred his staff to Baghdad.

Throughout these years the movement was constantly persecuted by the Iranian regime. Several of its marked leaders abroad were liquidated and there were numerous raids by commando units of the Iranian revolutionary guards on its military camp inside Iraq as well as attacks against its headquarters in Baghdad.

The movement maintains an organized force of about 10,000 men in Iraq, which is financed by Saddam Hussein. However, due to the cooperation with Iraq and the terrorist methods used by it, the movement lost much of the sympathy it had enjoyed inside Iran.

In 1981 the movement established the National Council of Resistance of Iran, together with Bani-Sadr, the Kurdish Democratic Party of Iran, and the Liberation Army of Iran, as a loose coalition of opposition movements. However, this coalition broke up in 1984 due to the movement's desire to control the Council's leadership. Later on, small left-wing groups, which agreed in principle to Rajavi's course, joined "the Council."

Since 1995 the movement has tried to become more moderate and strengthen the nationalist elements in its ideology. It also tried to rid itself of the image of a guerrilla movement. However, these efforts did not improve its status significantly. Many Iranians still have their reservations while the US continues to consider it a terrorist organization which was responsible for killing several American military personnel in Tehran (see IRAN).

MONOPHYSITES Christian Churches that split from the main body of the Eastern (GREEK ORTHODOX) Church following the Council of Chalcedon in 451 A.D. The schism concerned the nature of Christ, the monophysites holding that there is only one (*monos*) nature (*physis*)—divine—in the person of the Incarnate Christ. The Orthodox believed that Christ has a double nature, divine and human. However, the schism was also political-national, as it expressed the traditional hostility of the provinces of EGYPT and SYRIA to Byzantium and their unwillingness to accept Orthodox doctrine as laid down by Byzantium. Indeed, the monophysites organized themselves in four separate, "national" churches: the Ethiopian ("Orthodox") Church (over 20 million); the Armenian ("Orthodox," or Gregorian) Church (7–8 million—(of whom there are about 1 million in Arab countries); the COPTS in Egypt (5–6 million); and the Syrian ("Orthodox," or JACOBITE) Church (0.5 million in the Middle East, about half of whom are in Syria).

Since the seventeenth century (for the ARMENIANS even earlier), parts of the four churches seceded to join the Catholic Church through "UNIATES," while retaining also a measure of autonomy ("Syrian-Catholics" etc.)

MONTAZERI, GRAND AYATOLLAH HOS-SEIN-ALI (b. 1922) Senior Iranian cleric and the-

ologian, and one of the noted personalities of the Islamic revolution in IRAN. Montazeri was born in the town of Najaf-Abad near Isfahan in central Iran. He studied Islamic theology and jurisprudence in QOM, *inter alia* under KHOMEINI and Borujerdi. By the age of thirty, he was accorded the rank and title of *Hojjat-ol-Eslam*.

In the early 1960s he joined the Islamic resistance and particpated in demonstrations against the arrest of Khomeini. In 1964 he visited Khomeini in his exile in Najaf, IRAQ. He was arrested in 1966, along with other clergymen, and sentenced to nineteen months in prison. After his release he secretly left for Iraq and resumed contacts with Khomeini. Upon his return to Iran he was arrested and exiled.

In 1975, he was once against arrested and sentenced to ten years imprisonment for conspiring against the Shah. He was released in November 1978 when the escalating Islamic resistance started rioting.

Before the Islamic revolution, Montazeri concentrated on teaching philosophy, theology and science in the Islamic Seminary in Qom. He also wrote several books on ISLAM. He was considered Khomeini's representative in Iran and Khomeini appointed him to the Council of the Islamic Revolution before the revolution began. In the summer of 1979, after the victory of the revolution, he was considered the natural successor to Khomeini as spiritual leader, though he lacked Khomeini's personal charisma and political sophistication. When in November 1985 Khomeini appointed Montazeri as his deputy, this was viewed as an appointment to succeed him.

However, Montazeri gradually adopted moderate positions, which clashed with those of the regime's leadership. He criticized the regime's harsh attitude toward political prisoners and advocated the return of exiles, especially professionals, without calling them to account for their past opinions and actions. He was willing to allow a measure of opposition and recommended the adoption of a more liberal economy .

Differences between Montazeri and Khomeini deepened in 1988–1989, as Montazeri developed contacts with semi-liberal critics of the government and called on the government to confess and redress the mistakes committed during the ten years of the revolution.

In March 1989 Montazeri resigned from his public posts in response to a letter from Khomeini advising him to stay out of politics and to concentrate on religious issues. Since then he has kept a low profile and has refrained from intervening in political and governmental affairs. When Khomeini died in June 1990, Montazeri's candidacy as his successor and the new spiritual leaders was no longer mentioned. In recent years he has been teaching at religious seminaries in Qom but is not allowed to make political statements.

Nevertheless, from time to time "open letters" are published in his name, in which he criticizes the acts of repression by the regime and questions the fitness of the Aytollah KHAMENEI to be a spiritual leader and publish religious rulings.

MONTREUX CONVENTION

1. An agreement of July 1936 concerning the Straits of the Bosphorus and the Dardanelles, signed by TURKEY and the signatories of the Treaty of LAUSANNE (1923) save Italy, which restored the jurisdiction to the Turkish government and confirmed its right to re-militarize the straits. With this agreement Turkey regained control of this strategic waterway, strengthening its position in the Black Sea-Mediterranean area. The main provisions contained in the convention were:

a. Merchant ships: In peacetime, the principle of free passage was reaffirmed without a time limit. In wartime, if Turkey was neutral, the principle of free passage remained valid. If Turkey was a belligerent, or threatened by war, freedom of passage still prevailed, but ships would have to enter the straits in day time and follow the route designated by the Turkish authorities.

b. Warships: In peacetime, the tonnage of all foreign warships, whether riparian or non-riparian, in transit through the straits was to be limited to 15,000 tons. Black Sea powers were allowed to send capital ships with more tonnage, provided they passed in single file and were escorted by no more than two destroyers. Warships of non-riparian states were not to stay longer than twenty-one days in the Black Sea. In wartime, if Turkey was neutral or nonbelligerent, freedom of passage as in peacetime was to apply to nonbelligerents only. Should Turkey become a belligerent, or threatened by a war, it would acquire complete discretion as to the passage of warships through the straits.

The convention was much to the dislike of the Soviet Union, which tried, in vain, to reduce Turkey's sovereignty on the straits area even before World War I.

After the War, the Soviet Union exerted pressures on Turkey in an attempt to revise the convention. The Soviets demanded that other Black Sea countries share with Turkey the control of the straits, and that their defense should be jointly organized by Turkey and the Soviet Union. Turkey persisted in refusing the Soviet demands which were part of a wider Communist pressure on Turkey and Greece. In March 1947, US President Truman announced his policy of extending support to those countries facing Soviet threats. In 1950, Turkey officially and finally rejected the Soviet demands for joint control of the straits.

2. An agreement of May 1937 between EGYPT and the twelve powers enjoying privileges of CAPITULATIONS, i.e., extra-territorial jurisdiction over their citizens. The Montreux Convention provided for the abolition of the Capitulations after a twelve-year transition period, and was duly implemented (see CAPITULATIONS).

MOROCCO (Arabic: al-Maghrib—the West) Kingdom on the north-western corner of Africa, on both the Mediterranean and Atlantic shores, bordering on ALGERIA in the east and south-east, and MAURITANIA in the south-west; exercises de facto control over eighty percent of the Western (formerly Spanish) Sahara. Approximately 1.5 million Moroccans lived abroad, mostly in Western Europe. Casablanca is the largest city, with a population of over 3 million. In the mid-1990s, approximately fifty-two percent of all Moroccans lived in urban areas. Most Moroccans are SUNNI Muslims and ISLAM is the state religion. ARABIC is the official language, with French serving also as a de facto official language, especially of the urban, educated elite. In addition, there is wide knowledge and usage in the home (particularly in the mountainous regions), of at least one of Morocco's three main Berber dialects (Tashelhit, Tamazight, Tariffit).

BERBERS constituted the indigenous population of the country before the waves of Arab invasion and migration in the seventh to eighth and eleventh to twelfth centuries.

An estimated thirty-five to forty percent of Moroccans today are Berber-speaking. The foreign European (mostly French, Spanish and Italian) population numbers around 60,000.

Traditional Morocco Since the middle of the seventeenth century, the core of what today constitutes Morocco (bilad al-makhzan, lit. "lands of the treasury") has been under the rule of a Sharifian dynasty, the house of al-ALAWI. There were areas beyond the effective control of the Sultan known as bilad al-siba' (lands of dissidence), whereby the tribes usually recognized the sultan's religious standing but refused to pay taxes, and were frequently in conflict with him.

FRANCE started to show interest in Morocco in the nineteenth century, especially after its occupation of Algeria in 1830. From the late nineteenth century, and particularly from about 1900, France penetrated Morocco and increasingly gained control of large sectors of its economic and political life. This control was generally imposed on Morocco in the form of agreements on guidance and expert advice. France also fully occupied certain areas of Morocco—beginning with oases on the Moroccan-Algerian border, 1900–1903, and later adding to vital and central points: Casablanca and Oudjda, 1907; Fez, 1911. France accompanied that penetration by a series of agreements with other Western powers granting it a free hand in Morocco: with Italy, 1900; BRITAIN, 1904; Spain, 1904 (an agreement in which France had to grant Spain similar rights of penetration and control in a Spanish zone of interest in northern Morocco and in the far south); Germany, 1909 and 1911. (Germany itself had ambitions of penetrating Morocco, so such agreements were achieved only after sharp Franco-German crises in 1905 and 1911.) In 1906 an international conference at Algeciras reaffirmed Morocco's independence and equal economic opportunities for all powers in Morocco, but endorsed the predominant position of France and Spain in their respective zones, and particularly their control of police and security matters.

On 30 March 1912, in the Treaty of Fez, the Sultan of Morocco accepted a French protectorate over his country. A French Resident-General became responsible for foreign affairs and defense and was empowered to introduce reforms. The Sultan remained formally responsible for internal affairs, but French influence in this sphere was also significant. Later that year a Franco-Spanish convention defined Spain's status and its zones of influence in southern Morocco and on the northern shore, and a special international status for TANGIER. The status of Spain's zones thus derived from France, the protecting power, and not from the Sultan of Morocco.

As France's actual control of Morocco spread gradually over the country, both France and Spain faced resistance by local tribesmen in the Rif mountains in the north. The most important resistance leader, Muhammad Abd al-Karim (al-Khattabi), a tribal leader in the Spanish Rif, in 1921 declared himself Emir over an independent state, the "Republic of the Rif." The Spanish, and later the French too, tried both to co-opt him and to fight him. He was finally defeated by the French in May 1926 and exiled from Morocco. (In 1947, while the ship transporting him from the island of Reunion to France passed the SUEZ CANAL, he escaped and sought asylum in EGYPT. He died in Cairo in 1963.) By the mid-1930s the subjugation of Moroccan resistance was completed.

Colonial Morocco French policy in Morocco was shaped mainly by the first Resident-General, General L.G.H. Lyautey (1912–1925). The Sultan himself had little power even in internal affairs. Most of the urban population and the emerging modern economy were under direct French control, including transportation, industry, mines, modern agriculture by French settlers, taxation, finance, the judiciary, security and foreign affairs. Thus the Sultan's government, the *Makhzen*, controlled only restricted sectors of public life. Moreover, in the mountainous regions, the French preferred decentralized, indirect rule, based on the traditional tribal chiefs, mostly Berber, whom the French supported, not intervening much in their activities and leaving the secluded small mountain villages in their undeveloped state. Lyautey's support of Berber tribal leaders in time developed into a general policy of cultivating the Berbers against the Sultan and his government, and against Moroccan and Arab nationalism. Agriculture and industry were actively encouraged in the modern sector, which greatly expanded between the two World Wars. European immigration was encouraged as well, its population reaching some 200,000 in the 1930s.

The French introduced a limited system of representation, with most of the power and advantages reserved to French settlers. In 1919 a wholly French advisory council was established, and a few years later some Moroccans were included. In 1926 the council was divided into four "colleges": three of them French (for agriculture industry and commerce) and one indigenous Moroccan; French representatives were elected, Moroccans appointed.

In 1930 the French forced the Sultan to issue the "Berber *Dhahir*" (decree) which provided for the Berbers to be under the jurisdiction of their tribal chiefs and customary courts according to their own customs and traditions, and not under that of the Islamic SHARI'A courts. Both traditional-religious Muslim leaders and educated, modernized urban nationalists strongly opposed the "Berber *Dhahir*," and their joint resistance paved the way to a common national movement. In 1934 a *Comite d'Action Marocaine* was set up and demanded a limitation of the powers of the Protectorate, and an extension of self-rule. When the French and the Sultan rejected its demands, it organized demonstrations resulting in clashes. In 1937 the Committee was dissolved by the authorities only to take the form of several other organizations, which the French also dissolved. Amongst the important national leaders who emerged in this period was Allal al-Fassi. In 1937 all nationalist activity was forbidden. The nationalist leaders were arrested or exiled, but some were given refuge in Spanish Morocco.

The national struggle was renewed during and following World War II, after the allied invasion of November 1942. In 1943 the nationalists founded the *Istiqlal* (Independence) Party, headed by Ahmad Balafrej and the exiled al-Fassi. The *Istiqlal*, backed mainly by the urban intelligentsia, soon became the main national party. It demanded complete independence, with a constitutional government nominally under the Sultan. Other nationalist groups in French and Spanish Morocco seemed to have lesser support. Concurrently, Sultan Muhammad bin Yussuf (MUHAMMAD V), began making veiled declarations of support for the national movement. His aim was to assuage the nationalists' opposition to his actual rule and focus their resistance against the French.

France introduced gradual reforms in Morocco in 1946–1947, but did not intend them to result in Moroccan self-rule. These reforms provided for the establishment of elected local and provincial councils, a reorganization of the Sultan's government and closer cooperation between the Sultan's government and the French directors and advisers. They also envisaged economic development, the expansion and modernization of the education network, and the foundation of trade unions. The *Istiqlal* Party rejected these reforms as insufficient. The Sultan indicated that he took the same position and in late 1950 demanded radical changes in the French Protectorate. When the French dismissed eleven Moroccan elected members of the Council who had criticized the French administration and budget, the Sultan declared a personal protest strike and refused to sign any orders or laws. In early 1951 he was compelled to end his strike, but the relations between Sultan Muhammad and the French had deteriorated. The national struggle now became more violent, marked by demonstrations, clashes and arrests. In 1951–1952 the Moroccan issue was brought before the UN several times, but no decisive result was reached.

In 1953 the tension between France and the Sultan reached a crisis. Backed by the French, the Pasha of Marrakesh, Tihami al-Glawi, supported by numerous other district governors and tribal chiefs—all among the traditional Berber chiefs cultivated by the French against the modernized, urban nationalists—demanded the removal of the Sultan, claiming that his cooperation with the nationalist, secular modernists was a deviation from Islam. On 20 August 1953, Sultan Muhammad V agreed to go into exile and another member of the Alawi family, Muhammad Ben Arafa, became Sultan. The nationalists considered Ben Arafa a French puppet, and though Muhammad V had not been a leader of the national movement, his removal made him a symbol of nationalism, and the demand for his return to the throne became dominant among the nationalists. Their demands also became more radical. They now refused to accept gradual transition to independence or to consider French economic and security interests, increasing violent activities.

French policy changed in 1954 when Pierre Mendes-France came into power with a Socialist government. It became evident that the end of French rule was inevitable. At first it was decided that Ben Arafa would vacate his seat, and Muhammad V would move from his exile in Madagascar to France, but

would not return to the throne. Instead, a Regency Council would be established, as well as a representative government. On 1 October 1955 Ben Arafa stepped down without formally abdicating and moved to Tangier, and a four-member Regency Council was sworn in. But a few days later, Tihami al-Glawi changed his mind and demanded the return of Muhammad V to the throne, having sensed the dominant political trend and the need to join it at the last moment rather than remain in the losing camp. Muhammad V returned to France in late October and on 5 November was recognized once more as the legitimate Sultan. On 16 November 1955 he returned to Morocco. Early in December the first representative Moroccan government was established, including members of the *Istiqlal* Party, the *Parti Democratique pour l'Independence* (PDI) headed by Muhammad Hassan al-Wazzani, and independents. The transition to independence was completed on 2 March 1956 with a Moroccan-French agreement abrogating the 1912 Protectorate and a French recognition of Morocco's independence. However, the agreement also spoke of French-Moroccan "interdependence" and cooperation in defense and foreign affairs, to be defined in new agreements. It granted France the right to keep military forces and bases in Morocco for a transitional period. On 7 April 1956 a similar agreement was signed between Morocco and Spain. The latter's Protectorate in Spanish Morocco was canceled; but Ceuta, Melilla and the other small *Presidios* remained fully Spanish territory, and Ifni, the Spanish Sahara and several small islands remained under Spanish authority. In October 1956, an international conference agreed to the abolition of Tangier's special international status and its integration in Morocco (it became a free port in January 1962).

Independent Morocco Domestic Affairs: Morocco reached independence with little experience in self-government. The Sultan's authority under the French had been limited and both foreign affairs and most internal matters had been handled by the French. Morocco had to develop its system of government and legislature, and their relationship with the monarchy. The division between the urban, more modern and rural conservative population continued to affect politics. The state also had difficulties between 1956 and 1959 in overcoming irregular military forces, generally known as the "Liberation

Army," before finally subduing them. Each of the three political powers—the monarchy, urban nationalists and rural conservatives—tried to gain as much authority as possible. Neither of the two latter groups were homogeneous.

In Autumn 1956 the Sultan appointed a seventy-six-member Consultative Assembly including representatives of the parties as well as professional, social and religious organizations. This assembly had extremely limited power, ceasing to exist in 1959. In July 1957 the Sultan proclaimed his son, Moulay Hassan, heir to the throne. (Previously the succession was not decided during the monarch's life, and any member of the Alawi house could succeed.) In August 1957, Sultan Muhammad assumed the title of King.

A central part of the monarchy's successful strategy to consolidate its hegemony over Moroccan political life was to encourage and exploit divisions within the political parties. In 1957 Berber rural notables and tribesmen (some of whom belonged to the army of Liberation) and small landholders established the *Mouvement Populaire* (MP) headed by Mahjoub Ahardan, and supported by the King. In 1958–1959, a left-wing faction split from the *Istiqlal* and founded the *Union Nationale des Forces Populaires* (UNFP) headed by Mehdi Ben Barka and Abd-ul-Rahim Bou'abid; at that time, Morocco's sole labor and trade union confederation, the *Union Marocaine du Travail* (UMT), represented the majority of the UNFP's followers. The following year, the *Istiqlal* formed a rival trade union, the *Union Generale des Travailleurs* (UGTM). Though the UNFP supported the government of Abdallah Ibrahim, of the left wing of the *Istiqlal*, 1959–1960, it soon became the object of repressive measures by the King's security forces which were under the direct control of Crown Prince Hassan. Relations between the King and the parties worsened in 1960 and many *Istiqlal* and UNFP leaders were arrested. In May the King dismissed the government and led a new one, with the Crown Prince as his deputy. He appointed right-wing members of the *Istiqlal*, the MP and the UGTM for his ministers. The same month, country-wide municipal elections were held which marked the first general elections in Morocco. Contests in rural areas were held without much reference to political parties. This was not the case in the urban areas. Nationally, the *Istiqlal* won approximately forty per-

cent of all seats, the UNFP twenty-three percent; and the MP seven percent.

In February 1961 King Muhammad V died suddenly following routine surgery and was succeeded by his son as King HASAN II, who also assumed the Premiership. He tried to consolidate his control by establishing a political party loyal to him. Following several attempts, the *Front pour la Defense des Institutions Constitutionelles* (FDIC) was founded in 1963, headed by Ahmad Rida Gudeira, a close confidant of the King, including the MP. In 1964 it split into the *Parti Socialiste Democratique* (PSD) and the MP. They both served the King in his endeavor to appear as supporting democracy and a representative regime. They favored socioeconomic modernization whilst avoiding far-reaching political liberalization and democratization. A provisional Fundamental Law of June 1961 and a first formal constitution (approved by referendum on 7 December 1962), represented such conservative conceptions; the King retained wide authority to establish and dismiss governments and parliaments, and held both supreme temporal and spiritual status, the latter as *"Amir al-Mu'minin"* ("Commander of the Faithful"). Parliament was to consist of a House of Representatives (elected by universal, direct suffrage) and an Upper House indirectly elected by a council of electors. Islam was declared the state religion.

The first elections under the new constitution were held in May 1963. The *Istiqlal* competed as an opposition party, since its ministers had resigned, or been dismissed, in December 1962. The newly formed FDIC was pro-palace. The elections failed to produce the expected clear majority for the government party: of 144 seats, the FDIC attained sixty-nine, *Istiqlal* forty-one, the UNFP twenty-eight, and Independents six. In the indirect elections to the Upper House in October 1963, however, the FDIC and other government supporters attained the majority of the seats. The King did not continue as Prime Minister, but the government, composed of his appointees and Parliament, had little influence. In the second half of 1963, repressive action was taken against the opposition parties. Most of the UNFP leaders were arrested in July 1963, in connection with an alleged coup attempt, and several of them were later sentenced to death, including Ben Barka, who had fled to Paris, *in absentia*. The King commuted the death sentences in 1964, with the exception of Ben Barka, for whom the King was only willing to suggest a possible pardon were he to return to Morocco. Tension increased, especially amongst the educated urban youth, and student riots erupted several times, which were harshly crushed. The FDIC, with no adequate majority in Parliament, tried in vain to attract the opposition parties into forming a coalition government. In the face of a weak government, unemployment, rising prices and general discontent among the urban population, riots erupted in March 1965. The King proclaimed a state of emergency in June and, re-instated as Prime Minister, assumed full executive and legislative power. Parliament was dissolved and the opposition was treated harshly. In October 1965 the UNFP leader Mehdi Ben Barka disappeared in France. Moroccan prominent figures (amongst them General Muhammad Oufkir, the Minister of the Interior and head of the secret services) were found guilty (*in absentia*). In France, of being an accomplice to his abduction and murder. Years later, it became known that Israeli Mossad agents had assisted Oufkir, causing a crisis both within the Israeli government and security establishment and in Israeli-French relations.

In July 1967 Hasan II relinquished the Premiership. The following years witnessed repeated reshuffles of cabinets composed mainly of the King's men and technocrats. As the King apparently felt the need to increase public support in the face of further student and worker unrest, there was, from 1969, a gradual return to political activity, but under strict royal control. In October 1969 local elections were held, but were boycotted by the opposition. An experiment in "directed democracy" was made by a new constitution approved by referendum in July 1970. It provided for a 240-member House of Representatives. Ninety were elected by direct suffrage, ninety by local councils, and sixty, (representing the professions and economic bodies), by an electoral college. Elections in August 1970—boycotted by the opposition—returned 158 Independents, most of them supporting the King, 60 MP candidates, and only 22 from opposition parties.

The King-controlled government and Parliament were unable to resolve the continuing tension amongst students, intellectuals and workers. The revolutionary fervor infiltrated even the army and led in July, 1971, to a coup attempt by senior officers and numerous cadets who denounced the corruption in

the royal administration and its ineptitude in dealing with the Left-instigated ferment. It wanted to abolish the monarchy and establish a republic. Several senior officers were killed during the coup and others were later sentenced to death. Following this crisis, one of the King's closest aides, Home Minister Muhammad Oufkir, was transferred to the Defense Ministry, to purge the army of revolutionary elements.

While fighting the opposition and suppressing subversion, the King again tried to assuage dissent by a measure of political liberalization. A third constitution was prepared, and approved by referendum on 1 March 1972. It provided for a 240-member House of Representatives. Two-thirds were elected by direct general suffrage and one-third by trade unions, chambers of handicrafts, commerce, industry and agriculture, and communal councils. While the King was empowered to dissolve Parliament, the government was to be accountable to both the King and Parliament—which was, for the first time, given the right to topple the government by a vote of no-confidence or censure. But the opposition was not assuaged. A "National Front" of *Istiqlal* and the UNFP boycotted the March 1972 referendum. Parliament was suspended by the King. That same year, the left-wing opposition, the (UNFP) was split into a "Rabat section," headed by Abd al-Rahim Bou'abid—regarded as more leftist, and a "Casablanca section," headed by Abdullah Ibrahim, and supported by the trade unions. The latter was considered more pragmatic and ready to cooperate with the royal administration. The Left's "National Front" of the *Istiqlal* and the UNFP was now a dead letter.

More serious coup attempt, engineered by the King's strongman Muhammad Oufkir and the Air Force, and including an air attack on the King's plane and on his palace, was suppressed in August 1972. Oufkir was executed following the failed coup, more than 200 officers were arrested and several were sentenced to death or imprisonment. Hasan II himself assumed the command of the army, and became Minister of Defense until March 1973. The coup attempt, and Hasan's narrow escape, pointed to the precariousness of his position: at a time of rampant political opposition and popular dissent, the army had revealed itself as unreliable.

To consolidate his position, Hasan II acted on two fronts: large-scale purges of centers of dissent, coupled with nationalist policies. The attempted 1972 coup along with new attacks on government buildings throughout Morocco in 1973 were seen as a new plot to overthrow the regime by the UNFP and leftist activists. Together with Libyan backing, this served as a pretext for continuous trials and harsh sentences. Concurrently, in March 1973, Hasan II announced plans for the Moroccanization of the economy and the nationalization of foreign-owned (mainly French) lands and their distribution among the peasantry. Other expressions of a stronger nationalist stance were the extension of territorial waters from 12 to 70 miles (19 to 112 km.); a more active part in the ARAB-ISRAEL CONFLICT; and shortly after, the conflict over Spanish Sahara.

In 1974 the split within the UNFP became final and the "Rabat Section," which had been outlawed in 1973, established an independent party, the *Union Socialiste des Forces Populaires* (USFP). In May 1974 the veteran *Istiqlal* leader Allal al-Fassi died, leaving the Party without a prominent leadership. The Left was further split in 1974 by the foundation of the *Parti du Progres et du Socialisme* (PPS), headed by the veteran Communist leader Ali Yata. This was in contrast to the suppression of previous similar attempts to legalize the Communist Party that the PPS was allowed to organize. The King, whose position was being strengthened by his Saharan policy, continued harassing and half-suppressing the leftist opposition, while partially responding to its political pressure. In the summer of 1976 the King announced local and parliamentary elections for the coming months, and, with the exception of the UNFP, the opposition parties agreed to participate. Municipal elections were held in November 1976, provincial ones in January 1977, and elections for professional and vocational chambers in March 1977. More than sixty percent of the seats were won by Independents, most of them conservative supporters of the King. Hoping to ensure fair general elections, Muhammad Boucetta, the new leader of the *Istiqlal*, and the USFP's Bou'abid joined the government as Ministers of State on 1 March. Elections for a 264-seat Parliament were held in June 1977 (176 directly elected, 88 indirectly). Independents won 141 seats, *Istiqlal* 49, MP 44, USFP 16 and PPS one seat (the UNFP boycotted the elections). The new government, formed in October, included 8 *Istiqlal* members, with Boucetta as Foreign Minister, MP leaders,

and Ma'ati Bou'abid of the UNFP, whose party disowned him. The USFP took no ministerial posts except for its leader's symbolic Minister of State position. Thus, the King succeeded in winning over an important part of the leftist opposition without conceding much of his authority. In 1978 the pro-government Independents' group in Parliament established a *Rassemblement National des Independents* (RNI) headed by Prime Minister Ahmad Osman, the King's brother-in-law. Osman resigned from the Premiership in March 1979 to devote himself to organizing of his Party; Ma'ati Bou'abid replaced him. In 1981 a faction based on rural areas split from the RNI, forming a *Parti des Independants Democrates* (later renamed *Parti National Democratique*; PND) but stayed in the government.

Socio-economic issues continued troubling Morocco. Bou'abid, himself a former trade union leader, negotiated with the unions and agreed to wage rises. This provided a temporary, partial answer to social unrest, but added to the burden on the state budget and the economy. In order to cut government spending, the student grants were cut and university admission was restricted. Consequently, student strikes broke out, and unrest continued from 1981 to 1983. The unrest increased in June 1981 following price hikes of subsidized food, and culminated in a general strike and riots in Casablanca in which some seventy people were killed (opposition sources quoted much higher figures). The USFP and its affiliated trade union (since 1978 reorganized as the *Confederation Democratique du Travail* (CDT) and headed by Noubir al-Amaoui), were accused of creating this unrest. All CDT offices were closed and its leaders were arrested. When the USFP subsequently denounced the government's Saharan policy as too "soft," its senior leaders, including Abd al-Rahim Bou'abid, were arrested and put on trial, and its newspapers suspended. Dissent increased in October 1981 following constitutional changes, mainly the extension of the term of Parliament from four to six years. The opposition claimed that the 1977 elections had not been fairly conducted and that the majority parties' deputies were not fulfilling their parliamentary duties, and all fourteen USFP deputies boycotted Parliament. A government reshuffle in November 1981 eliminated all RNI ministers—to create, as the King and the outgoing Premier announced, a loyal opposition.

In March 1982, in an effort to improve relations with the opposition, USFP leader Bou'abid was pardoned and USFP and CDT offices were allowed to reopen in April. Many union leaders, however, remained in prison, and the ban on USFP newspapers continued until 1983. In 1982, Prime Minister Ma'ati Bou'abid established a new party, the *Union Constitutionelle* (UC). In June 1983 municipal elections took place, with the UC and other pro-government center-right candidates gaining a majority. General elections, however, were delayed several times beyond the expiration of Parliament's six-year mandate. In November 1983 the government was replaced by a caretaker government of National Unity headed by Karim Lamrani, in which representatives of the six major parties took part, including the *Istiqlal* and the USFP. It was to organize general elections and formulate an economic program. But when the government announced price hikes of basic foodstuffs and education fees in January 1984, riots broke out in the urban centers. They were quelled by the army, with more than 110 killed and some 2,000 arrested. The rioting ended only after the King announced the price increase reversal. While Communists and the Left were blamed for these disturbances, Islamic fundamentalists were also accused of plotting to overthrow the monarchy during these riots. Some of their leaders were tried in 1985 and several were sentenced to death or imprisonment.

Parliamentary elections were held in September 1984. The seats—including the 104 chosen by indirect election were distributed as: UC 83 seats; RNI 61; MP 47; *Istiqlal* 43; USFP 39; and PND 24. Lamrani formed a new government in April 1985, which was updated in similar style by Izz al-din Laraki in September 1986. Nonetheless, political life remained in a state of suspended animation for the remainder of the decade.

By the beginning of the 1990s, Hasan had firmly consolidated his rule, co-opting major segments of the political opposition and successfully engineering Morocco's de facto incorporation of most of the Western Sahara. He turned to a policy of incremental, "homeopathic" measures of political liberalization. This was designed to complement economic liberalization and privatization measures in order to further integrate Morocco fully into the developing global economy. Hasan's underlying purpose was to maintain political stability and demonstrate to Western governments and financial bodies his commitment to political and economic liberalization. This was done to safely tackle Morocco's endemic structural problems that had emerged due to decades of rapid population growth, urbanization, economic stagnation and consequential unemployment. The dangers of ignoring these problems was highlighted by the outbreak of violent riots in Fez and other Moroccan cities in December 1990. This followed a general strike initiated by opposition labor unions and the emergence of various Islamist opposition groups, most notably the "Justice and Charity" movement of Abd al-Salam Yassin, which implicitly questioned the Moroccan monarch's Islamic credentials as "Amir al-Mu'minin" and challenged the existing socio-political order.

In August 1992, Hasan re-appointed Prime Minister Lamrani for his third caretaker term. In the meantime, the opposition parties—the *Istiqlal*, the USFP, the PPS, the left-wing splinter organizations *pour l'Action Democratique et Populaire* (OADP), and the rump UNFP— had established a "democratic bloc" (*al-kutla al-dimuqratiyya*) to coordinate their efforts. Cosmetic constitutional reform was ratified that same year. Although, the *kutla* (apart from the PPS) boycotted the constitutional referendum, it was eager to participate in the long-delayed national Parliamentary elections. In response, three of the "loyalist" parties, the UC, the PND (headed by Muhammad Arslan Jadidi and the MP now headed by Mohand Laensar), formed their own electoral bloc, the *Entente National*.

These were held in two stages. The first, on 25 June, in which 222 seats were chosen directly by the electorate, was probably the fairest election ever held in Morocco. The *kutla* parties won 99 seats (44.6% of the vote), up from 58 seats in 1984, with most going to the USFP (48) and *Istiqlal* (43). The *Entente* won only 74 seats (33% of the vote): the UC, won 27 seats, a decline of 50%. Together with the RNI and Ahardan's *Mouvement National Populaire* MNP—founded in 1991, the "loyalist" parties won 116 seats (52.16%). Smaller parties won the remaining 7 seats. The second, indirect stage of the elections was held on 17 September, for the remaining 111 seats. As expected the loyalists did significantly better, winning 71% of the seats. Thus, the *Entente* group, the RNI and the MNP together controlled 58.5% of the seats in Parliament. The *kutla* parties gained 115 seats (34.5%) and its affiliated trade unions an additional 7 seats. One particularly noteworthy feature of the elections was that two women were elected to Parliament for the first time, one each from the USFP and *Istiqlal*.

For the next four years, King Hasan tried periodically to promote "political bilateralism" by "*l'alternance*" of government, in which the *kutla* parties would assume the bulk of the Cabinet positions. However, he also insisted on reserving key positions for his close confidants, particularly the all-powerful Interior Ministry headed by Driss Basri, as well as the Prime Ministership, and foreign and justice ministries. The *Istiqlal* and the USFP balked, even after Hasan offered the Prime Mministership during late 1994 to the *Istiqlal*'s Boucetta. For the *kutla* parties (excluding the PPS) Basri's removal was a *sine qua non* for their assumption of governing responsibilties. Hasan was just as adamant about Basri's retention of his post. This caused him to fail to achieve his goal of rotation of power.

Initially, in early November 1993, Hasan appointed a caretaker Cabinet headed again by Lamrani which included mostly non-party technocrats, hoping that the *kutla* parties would eventually agree to assume governmental positions. The appointment of Serge Berdugo (the head of the Casablanca Jewish Community) to the post of Tourism Minister, marked the first time since 1957 that a Jew had been appointed to a Cabinet post. Also of interest was the appointment of Umar Azziman (the co-founder of an independent human rights organization) to the newly created post of minister delegate in charge of human rights affairs. Hasan dissolved the government on 25 May 1994, replacing Lamrani with Abd al-Latif Filali, who retained his post as Foreign Minister. Most of the other ministers, including Basri, were reappointed, but not Berdugo. Hasan's dialogues with the political parties continued but without results. Thus, after more than a year of this unsatisfactory, blatantly unrepresentative situation, Hasan appointed in February 1995 a government drawing mainly on the "loyalist" parties, again headed by Filali.

The new government consisted of fifteen technocrats, (thirteen of whom had been in the previous government), and twenty representatives from the core of the loyalist parties. Nine came from the UC, eight from the MP, and three from the PND. The other two centrist parties, the RNI and MNP, stayed out of the government but pledged to support it in Parliament. Morocco thus had a government based on the 1993 elections. Nonetheless, it was clear that the parties whose leaders were actually serving as ministers did not command a parliamentary majority. This situation did not please the the King who considered it unhealthy for the promotion of greater democracy in the country. In addition, most of the key ministries were left in the hands of the technocrats and "king's men," to the disappointment of the parties. Apart from the interior and foreign ministries, the list included trade and industry, energy and mines, privatization and education. Moreover, two key portfolios, finance and foreign investment, and agriculture, were conferred on individuals, Muhammad Kabbaj (UC) and Hasan Abouyoub (MP), respectively, whose party affiliations were seen as only nominal.

At least one feature of the new Cabinet was encouraging to the advocates of greater democratization. The *Kutla's* campaign against the excessive concentration of power in the interior ministry led to the removal of information and environment portfolios from the hands of the Interior Minister. Of greater concern amongst the opposition and in the Western press was the appointment of former government prosecutor Muhammad Ziane as the new minister delegate for human rights, replacing Umar Azziman.

In 1996, voters approved constitutional reform measures to create a second parliamentary chamber. Beginning with the 1997 general elections, Morocco's lower house of Parliament would be determined entirely by direct election. Representatives of the new upper house would be appointed indirectly.

Accompanying Morocco's tentative moves in the 1990s toward greater political pluralism was the increasing significance of "civil society" elements: labor unions, human rights groups and women's organizations. The latter spearheaded a campaign in 1992–1993 to reform Morocco's Personal Status Law (the *mudwanna*) with regards to women's rights in marriage, divorce and child custody. The campaign was partially legitimized by the King, although the actual changes made were largely cosmetic. International human rights groups and European political bodies subjected Morocco's human rights record to frequent scrutiny and criticism, strengthening Morocco's own human rights groups. The regime responded in part to international pressure during the first half of the 1990s, closing the notorious Tazmamart prison, releasing long-held political prisoners and providing amnesties for exiles. They were then allowed to return to Morocco. This more liberal policy was highlighted by the release in July 1994 of 424 persons, of whom the longest-held had been incarcerated in 1972. At the same time, hundreds of alleged "disappeared" Sahrawis opposing Moroccan rule of Western Sahara remained unaccounted for, even after the release of more than 200 such persons in 1991, and new arrests continued to be made. Labor union activists (increasingly engaged in job actions) were also kept off balance by numerous harsh applications of the penal code.

The King's inherent religious standing and assiduous cultivation of that status helped insulate Morocco, to a large degree, from the challenges of radical Islamist movements manifesting themselves elsewhere in the Middle East. At the same time, the authorities also subjected Islamist activists and groups to arbitrary and often harsh treatment. These groups were not monolithic; some, less political ones, were even encouraged by the regime. During the 1970s and early 1980s, a small group advocating a violent overthrow of the regime, *al-Shabiba al-Islamiyya*, (led by Abd al-Karim Muti), was broken by the authorities. The most prominent of Morocco's Islamic personages, Abd al-Salam Yasin, of the banned "Justice and Charity" movement, had been detained under different forms of arrest since 1983. Tentative moves to ease his detention were made in December 1995. However, the authorities quickly reimposed the house arrest following Yassin's unauthorized sermons in a neighboring mosque. Political Islamic parties remained officially banned. Nonetheless, hundreds of Islamic-oriented groups and associations emerged up during the 1980s and 1990s. By 1996, student associations in most Moroccan universities were controlled by Islamists, and campuses periodically witnessed bouts of violence between Islamist and left-wing groups.

Relatedly, the raging civil war in neighboring Algeria (beginning in 1992) between the military regime and Islamist groups, was watched closely by Morocco. Islamist guerrillas in Western Algeria apparently used the adjacent Moroccan countryside as a sanctuary. The Moroccan authorities made a number of arrests of arms traffickers to Algerian Islamists, although the Algerian regime was not fully satisfied. With one exception, the violence in Algeria did not spill over into Morocco. That came in August 1994, with the shooting of two Spanish tourists in a Marrakesh hotel. The alleged perpetrators, a group of four French-Algerian and French-Moroccan Islamists, (some of whom had received weapons training in Pakistan near the Afghan border), were arrested within two weeks. Hundreds of additional suspects were rounded up in autumn 1994. In January 1995, the group of four, plus fourteen others, were put on trial for the shooting and other crimes. Three received death sentences, the others, varying prison terms. The Marrakesh shooting also precipitated a crisis in Moroccan-Algerian relations (see below).

Morocco's economy in the mid-1990s was relatively diversified. Eighteen percent of the GDP came from manufacturing, fifteen to twenty percent from agriculture (which employed forty percent of the workforce); and over thirty percent from a large commercial and service sector. It also had a significant mining and refining sector, based on phosphates. Including Western Sahara, Morocco possessed forty percent of the world's phosphate reserves. An informal sector, underpinned by the manufacture and export of cannabis (*kif*) from the northern Rif region to Europe, constituted a considerable portion of the GDP, perhaps as much as thirty percent. Poverty was widespread and the gap between the rich and poor intensified. The average per capita income was approximately $1,000, with urban unemployment running between twenty and thirty percent. Annual economic growth remained heavily dependent on the results of the rainy season, with the severe droughts of 1992–1993 causing the GDP to contract. Morocco's economy was dominated by an estimated 300 families, many of whom had links to the royal family. The most notable case in point was the leading privately-owned consortium, Omnium Nord Africain, headed by the King's brother-in-law, former Prime Minister and RNI party head, Ahmad Osman. The chief executive-designate of its subsidiary French trading house Optorg was Robert Assaraf, one of the coterie of Moroccan-born Jews on intimate terms with the King.

Since the mid-1980s, Morocco adopted an IMF-sponsored restructuring program, involving: debt rescheduling cuts in subsidies, liberalization of capital movements, and a plan to privatize state firms. In early 1996, a new association agreement with the European Union was signed (replacing a more limited 1976 agreement), in order to improve access of Moroccan goods to European markets, and to encourage free trade between Morocco and the EU over a twelve-year period. Despite Morocco's commitment to free-market policies, excessive bureaucracy and taxes, together with weakness in technological and human resources (with illiteracy at around fifty percent, and seventy percent for women), significantly hindered efforts to promote competitive development as an "emerging market."

Foreign Affairs Morocco became a member of the UN in 1956 upon achieving independence, and of the ARAB LEAGUE in 1958. In the first years of independence, Morocco was driven by its differences with France and Spain (see below) and the concurrent militant regional atmosphere accompanying Algeria's war for independence, to seek closer cooperation with leftist-radical Arab and African countries, despite its own internal conservatism. Thus, Morocco hosted a conference of radical states in Casablanca in 1961. Its dispatch in 1961 of a contingent of troops to a UN Peace Force for the Congo (later Zaire) was perceived in the UN as being part of the radical camp's contribution. However, the improvement of relations with France and Spain, coupled with the radical states' support of Algeria and POLISARIO in their dispute with Morocco over Western Sahara, moved Morocco closer to the West. The dispatch of another contingent of Moroccan troops to Zaire in 1977–1978, was in defense of a pro-Western, right-wing regime assailed by leftist radicals from Angola.

Belying its initial radical image, Morocco's relations with the US were friendly from the start. Initially, it allowed the US to maintain several military bases in Morocco. These were evacuated and handed over by 1963, but certain "facilities" remained at the disposal of the US, Morocco receiving American aid. During the 1980s, France and the US, along with SAUDI ARABIA's financial aid, heavily supported Morocco's Western Saharan efforts. At the same time, Morocco also fostered normal relations with the USSR, a major clients for phosphate exports. Thus, the WESTERN SAHARAN CONFLICT did not, as had been feared, take on an East-West dimension.

Relations with France and Spain have always been central components of Morocco's foreign policy agenda. The consolidation of authority in all regions it considered part of its territory was Morocco's top priority after achieving independence. The French-Moroccan Agreement of March 1956 provided for protocols on French military and economic interests in, and cooperation with, Morocco. But no such accord was ever signed, as Morocco was not willing to establish the special relations with France that had been envisaged. In addition, France realized that its formal position in Morocco was similar to that of other foreign states. In 1960, France agreed to liquidate its bases and evacuate its troops. All French military left Morocco by 1961. Most French agricultural property was nationalized (significantly in 1963 and 1973) a final agreement on compensation was reached in 1974. Morocco continued to benefit from French technical expertise, but the number of French citizens in Morocco decreased gradually. French-Moroccan relations worsened due to the Ben Barka affair in 1965, and were repaired only in 1969.

In addition to France's military and economic support for Morocco on the Western Sahara question, it also backed Morocco's efforts to forge closer ties with the EU. France was the single largest destination of Moroccan exports in 1995 (29.7%), and origin of the largest percentage of Moroccan imports (21.8%). France's concern over rising Islamist sentiment in North Africa and among its own North African immigrant population meant it was particularly interested during the 1990s in fostering closer ties with the Moroccan regime and promoting economic development there, in order to avoid the kind of breakdown of order which occurred in Algeria, and the triggering of a worst-case scenario—a mass flight of emigrants across the Mediterranean to its shores.

Agreements with Spain concerning the termination of the Spanish Protectorate were reached in 1956, but relations worsened due to a conflict over several enclaves in the southern Spanish zone which Spain was reluctant to hand over. Agreement was reached only in 1958, and the area was handed over, with the withdrawal of Spanish troops in 1961. However, Spain still retained an enclave at Ifni; the struggle over that issue was resolved only in 1969, when Ifni was handed over. These agreements did not include the towns of Ceuta and Melilla (*Presidios*) and several tiny islands on Morocco's Mediterranean coast, which Spain regarded as fully Spanish territory and which Morocco continues to claim. Spain's agreement in 1975–1976 to withdraw from Spanish Sahara and hand it over to Morocco and Mauritania removed a major bone of contention between them (see below).

Spanish-Moroccan relations during the first half of the 1990s were heavily shaped by a dispute over fishing rights in Moroccan waters. A four-year agreement defining them was tortuously concluded in 1992. In 1994, Morocco surprised Spain by invoking a mid-term revision clause. The stakes were high: Morocco's own fishing industry accounted for 400,000 jobs, direct and indirect. Up to 40,000 Spaniards (including those from the Canary Islands) were dependent on catches in Moroccan waters. According to the Moroccans, Spain was exceeding its quotas and depleting fish stocks. After much acrimony, a banning of Spanish (and Portuguese) ships from Moroccan waters in April 1995, high level diplomacy, and public demonstrations in both countries, a new four-year agreement was concluded in mid-November. Morocco was generally satisfied with the terms, which reduced Spain's overall allowed catches by nearly forty percent. It also obligated greater participation of Moroccan crew members on Spanish boats and more use of Moroccan processing facilities. The EU agreed to provide funds to modernize Morocco's own fisheries industry. The fisheries agreement cleared the way for the initialing and subsequent signing of the new Moroccan-EU Association Agreement. As the Morocco's closest European neighbor and host to tens of thousands of both legal and illegal immigrants, Spain shared France's concerns in the mid-1990s over political and economic trends in Morocco, and the need to forestall instability.

From the mid-1960s, a dispute arose over Spanish Sahara, claimed by Morocco (for details see WESTERN SAHARA CONFLICT). From the early 1970s, Morocco increased pressure and agitation. This culminated in October 1975 in a peaceful mass procession, a "Green March" by an estimated 350,000 Moroccans into Spanish Sahara, which was stage-managed by the King. In November 1975, Spain surrendered, and agreed to hand the territory over to Morocco and Mauritania. It did so in February 1976, and the

two recipient countries divided it between themselves in April 1976. But a movement among the Sahrawi population demanding independence emerged in the early 1970s to challenge Moroccan and Mauritanian ambitions. Beginning in 1973–1974, it established a guerrilla force, "POLISARIO." This was supported, armed and maintained by Algeria and centered on Algerian soil. In February 1976, POLISARIO proclaimed a "*Sahara Arab Democratic Republic*" (SADR). Morocco and Mauritania thus became involved in a protracted, costly guerrilla war. In August 1979, Mauritania renounced its part of Western Sahara. Morocco immediately occupied and annexed the Mauritanian part, and then had to fight for the whole of the territory. Throughout the 1980s, Morocco gradually built a network of earthen walls and military strongpoints to encompass approximately eighty percent of the territory and effectively hinder guerrilla raids. Upon its completion, it was over 1,244 miles (2,000 km.) long, running parallel to the Algerian and Mauritanian borders. Morocco also invested hundreds of millions of dollars in the territory, building roads, housing, hospitals, schools and telecommunications facilities. Moroccan professionals were given incentives to work in the region, while some 35,000 persons were dispatched to the region to live in tent-camps to help bolster Morocco's claims there.

The Sahara conflict also clouded Morocco's international (in particularly, African) relations. By the end of the 1980s, over seventy countries had recognized SADR. The UN continued recommending a referendum under international supervision, and so did the Organization of African Unity (OAU). In 1981, Morocco agreed in principle to such a referendum. However, protracted negotiations with OAU envoys and committees brought no agreement on its actual terms and modalities. The issue of SADR's membership and participation in OAU meetings caused much bad blood between Morocco and many African countries, paralyzing the OAU between 1982 and 1984. In November 1984, Morocco suspended all further involvement in the OAU in protest against the seating of a SADR delegation at the twentieth OAU Summit.

More sustained UN involvement in the disput (beginning with the sponsoring of indirect talks between Moroccan and Polisario officials) began in 1986. Five years later, in September 1991, a UN-broken cease-fire took effect. However, the accompanying agreement to implement a referendum to determine the area's future (independence or union with Morocco) remained unimplemented as of early 1997. While Morocco continued to proclaim its commitment to the UN-sponsored referendum process, it also fought vigorously to ensure terms of the referendum (most importantly, on the question of voter eligibility) which would guarantee a victory. In the meantime, the "Moroccan Saharan" provinces were included in national and local elections.

The "Greater Arab Maghreb" concept first emerged early in the twentieth century, and was a proclaimed goal of all Maghrib states following their achievement of independence. However, their social and political diversities, as well as competing interests, rendered its realization difficult.

The primary difficulty lay in Morocco's relations with Algeria, which were characterized mainly by mutual suspicions, rivalry and geopolitical competition, interspersed with occasional thaws. Beginning in 1975, the Western Saharan conflict was the central focal point of that rivalry. In the late 1980s, Algeria partially decoupled its relations with Morocco from the Saharan issue, which was now in the hands of the UN, and, together with Morocco, engineered the creation of the five-state ARAB MAGHREB UNION (AMU) in 1989. However, Algeria's internal crisis and civil war, beginning in 1992, impeded the functioning of the AMU; together with the continuing diplomatic stalemate over Western Sahara, Moroccan-Algerian relations again deteriorated.

Following Algeria's achievement of independence in 1962, territorial disputes arose between Rabat and Algiers over border regions left by France with Algeria and claimed by Morocco. These regions were rich in coal and iron ores, especially the Colomb-Bechar and Tindouf areas. The conflict caused several armed clashes and erupted in fully fledged military confrontation in 1963. Morocco claimed that Egypt had been supporting Algeria militarily in this confrontation, and severed relations with Egypt (until 1964). It also refused the Arab League's mediation due to Egypt's dominant influence in the League. Following the mediation of Ethiopia and Mali on behalf of the OAU, an interim agreement was reached, based on the status quo—i.e., the territories were left under Algerian sovereignty. But Morocco did not regard this settlement as final, and its rela-

tions with Algeria remained tense and unfriendly. Beginning in 1975, the confrontation over Western Sahara added bitterness, with Algerian and Moroccan troops clashing on at least one occasion in 1976, and Morocco continually threatening to invoke the right of "hot pursuit" of POLISARIO units into Algerian territory. The mediation of Saudi Arabia's King Fahd brought about a summit in 1983 between Hasan and Algeria's President Ben-Jedid. As the Saharan stalemate continued and the UN became more directly involved, Algerian-Moroccan relations thawed. Formal diplomatic relations were restored in 1988, setting the stage for the AMU's founding. A 1972 agreement demarcating their common border was finally ratified in 1989 as well.

Algeria's increasing internal crisis, and continued unwillingness to cut its support entirely for POLISARIO, made it impossible to achieve a lasting Moroccan-Algerian rapprochement. King Hasan's occasional asides that the Islamists should have been allowed to assume power (following their electoral victory in 1991) irked the Algerians considerably. The Moroccans remained irritated with Algeria's support for POLISARIO. Each country suspected the other of supporting their domestic Islamist opposition movements. The height of tension came in the aftermath of the Marrakesh hotel shootings in August 1994. Morocco's re-imposition of visa requirements for Algerian nationals following the incident created havoc for thousands of Algerians returning to Europe from summer visits via Morocco. In retaliation, Algeria closed its land frontier, and imposed identical visa requirements for Moroccan travelers. In mid-September, the Moroccan Interior Ministry openly blamed the Algerian security services for instigating the attack. Various Arab mediators (including the Egyptian and Tunisian Presidents) sought to defuse Algerian-Moroccan tensions, and a certain level of dialogue was slowly renewed. In addition, work continued unabated on the Euro-Maghreb pipeline carrying Algerian natural gas via Morocco to Spain. This was completed in 1996.

Morocco claimed Mauritania's territory and bitterly opposed the full independence granted to it in 1960. Most of the Arab states at first supported Morocco in its rejection of Mauritania's independence, except Tunisia, whose support of Mauritania angered Morocco and caused it to sever relations with

Tunisia (until 1964). However, as most Arab states gradually accepted Mauritania, Morocco reluctantly did so too, officially establishing diplomatic relations in 1970. Together with Spain, the two countries agreed in February 1976 to partition Western Sahara, following the Spanish withdrawal. Morocco received the northern two-thirds, and Mauritania the southern third. However, Mauritania could not withstand POLISARIO pressure and withdrew entirely from the territory in 1979. To block POLISARIO's takeover of the region, Morocco dispatched its own forces to occupy the area. The entire episode added to already existing suspicions between the two countries. From then on, Mauritania struggled to maintain a position of neutrality on the Western Sahara issue. This was no easy task in the face of POLIS-ARIO's usage of Mauritanian territory to stage attacks, along with Morocco's military responses, and both Moroccan and POLISARIOo efforts to influence the composition and policies of the Mauritanian regime. The emerging stalemate on the ground in the late 1980s and UN-sponsored referendum process, brought the Mauritanians some relief, and Moroccan-Mauritanian relations slowly normalized.

Relations with LIBYA were also far from friendly. Morocco suspected post-1969 Libyan subversive intrigues behind many of its internal troubles. In addition, Libya served as POLISARIO's chief arms supplier until 1983. In July 1971 official relations were severed, and resumed only in January 1975; in 1980 Morocco again withdrew its Ambassador. Yet, in August 1984, Morocco and Libya joined together in the "Arab-African Union," based on a *quid pro quo* of Qadhafi's cessation of all aid to POLISARIO in return for Hasan's tacit support for Libya's ambitions in Chad. The new alliance came one year after a Tunisian-Algerian-Mauritanian friendship treaty, and thus confirmed the temporary polarization of the MAGHREB in two competing blocs. However, the few steps taken toward the very partial implementation of the Moroccan-Libyan agreement (e.g., a joint Secretariat) indicated that the real aim was not the much-heralded "union," rather a political alliance and a degree of coordination. Two years later, it broke up as Libya violently denounced King Hasan for inviting Israel's Prime Minister Shimon PERES and meeting him in Morocco, and called for all-Arab action against Morocco. In response, the King denounced and abrogated the 1984 agree-

ment. During the 1990s, Morocco's compliance with UN-sanctions against fellow AMU member Libya (together with the rest of the AMU states), was a source of additional tension between the two states.

Iraq's invasion of KUWAIT in August 1990 created the worst inter-Arab crisis in the forty-five-year history of the Arab League. Morocco's stance toward the crisis was unique among Arab states, guided, as it were, by competing forces: the regime's conservative, pro-Saudi and pro-Western orientation, and the considerable support among the Moroccan public for Iraq against the West's military actions. Thus, at the emergency Cairo All-Arab Summit Conference on 10 August, Morocco voted with the small majority of Arab states to condemn Iraq's invasion of Kuwait; support Saudi Arabia's right to defend itself by inviting in foreign forces; and to comply with the Saudi request to dispatch Arab forces to assist in its defense. Morocco quickly dispatched a symbolic contingent of 1,000–1,200 troops to Saudi Arabia. However, unlike the other Arab contingents, they were not placed under a common command, and took no part in the subsequent fighting. Cognizant of public opinion, King Hasan sanctioned one of the largest mass demonstrations in Moroccan history, on 3 February 1991, in support of Iraq and against the American-led war. More than 200,000 persons took part in the Rabat rally, from all walks of Moroccan political life, including the Islamist "Justice and Charity" movement.

During the 1960s, Morocco's emphasis on nationalist policies—motivated by domestic considerations—drove it to demonstrate in Arab and Islamic affairs, and in the Arab-Israel conflict. It identified with the Arab states involved in the Six-Day War of 1967, sending troops to Syria to participate in the October War of 1973. At the same time, it sided with the moderate Arab states, and King Hasan II was repeatedly active in efforts to mediate between the rival camps within the Arab world and renew inter-Arab co-operation. Morocco's involvement in Arab affairs was epitomized by its repeated hosting of all-Arab summit conferences, more than any other Arab State (September 1965, Casablanca; December 1969, Rabat; October 1974, Rabat; November 1981 and September 1982, Fez; August 1985, Casablanca; May 1989, Casablanca). Morocco also hosted the Islamic Conference Organization (ICO) ministerial and summit meetings (e.g., the first ICO summit of September 1969, Rabat; and the December 1994 summit in Casablanca).

Calculations based on realpolitik (common pro-Western and anti-radical Arab nationalist orientations) and a less tangible intertwining of sentiment, personal connections, and an idealized version of historical Muslim-Jewish relations, had always made Morocco's relationship with Israel unique among Arab countries. As early as the mid-1970s, the Moroccan regime had maintained secret links with the Israeli Mossad, and in 1976, King Hasan secretly hosted Israel's Prime Minister RABIN. As the Arab-Israeli peace process gathered momentum, (from the late 1970s), Moroccan involvement became more pronounced and above board. King Hasan II supported SADAT's peace initiative of 1977, and played a role in hosting the secret Egyptian-Israeli talks that preceded Sadat's visit to JERUSALEM. However, Morocco went along, in 1979, with the all-Arab decision to sever official relations with Egypt, while maintaining lower-level links and restoring full relations in November 1987.

In July 1986 King Hasan became the second Arab leader (after Sadat) to establish a measure of open and public relations with Israel, by inviting Israel's Prime Minister Shimon Peres to visit Morocco and meet him. The talks were not, the King insisted, "negotiations." In substance he did not deviate from positions taken by other Arab states of the more moderate wing. But the invitation and the meeting were seen, symbolically, as morally significant and were bitterly denounced by radical Arab leaders, mainly QADHAFI and ASAD.

Following the September 1993 Oslo agreement between Israel and the PLO, Israeli Prime Minister Yitzhak Rabin and Foreign Minister Peres stopped in Casablanca on their way home from Washington, where they received Hasan's endorsement of the agreement. One year later, Morocco and Israel agreed on the opening of low-level diplomatic liaison offices in each other's country. At the end of October 1994, Morocco hosted the first Middle East and North African Economic Summit, a framework designed to promote the economic dimension of the peace process. Prime Minister Fillali's presence at Rabin's funeral in November 1995 again underscored the uniqueness of the Moroccan-Israeli relationship, although official bilateral economic and political links remained minimal, as Morocco carefully measured its actions according to developments in the peace process itself.

Morocco's Jewish community in the late 1940s numbered almost 250,000 persons. Since then, it has been steadily reduced by emigration, to ISRAEL (more than 150,000), France and North America, dwindling today to no more than 5,000–8,000 persons, residing mostly in Casablanca. From the mid-1970s onward, Morocco has steadily cultivated relations with the former Moroccan Jews abroad, including the Moroccan Israeli community. These ties constitute part of today's unique Moroccan-Israeli relationship.

MOSLEM   see ISLAM.

MOSSADDEQ, MUHAMMAD (1881–1967) Iranian politician, Prime Minister 1951–1953. Mossaddeq was educated in Paris (Ecole des Sciences Politiques) and Switzerland (Neuchatel University).

Elected to the *Majlis* (Parliament) Mossaddeq served as Minister of Justice, Foreign Minister, and was the governor of a province. In 1949, he became the leader of a national front of opposition parties, which gained power in 1951, and in May 1951 he became Prime Minister. The same month he nationalized the Iranian oil fields, which led to a grave crisis and an international embargo by oil importers. The effectiveness of the embargo resulted in decreased public support for Mossaddeq and the loss of his majority in Parliament.

As he was determined to continue his nationalist policies and rid Iran of the conservative Shah, he dissolved the *Majlis* in July 1953. But his Islamic allies deserted him and popular unrest erupted. The following month the Shah ordered Mossaddeq's removal from his post, and appointed General Fazlullah Zahedi Prime Minister. Mossaddeq refused to accept his dismissal and rebelled, and the Shah left Iran. The revolt failed, however, when the army continued to support the Shah. General Zahedi arrested Mossaddeq, suppressed the unrest and enabled the Shah to return to Iran (supported by the American CIA, which feared the turn to the left under Mossaddeq).

Accused of treason, Mossaddeq was jailed (1953–1956) and banned from participation in political activities. However, he enjoyed widespread popularity and government attempts to silence him actually increased his political status.

Mossaddeq died while under house arrest in Ahmadabad.

MOUSSA, AMR (b. 1936) Egypt's Foreign Minister since 1991. Born in Cairo. He graduated from the Faculty of Law, Cairo University (1957), where he later earned his Ph.D. In 1958, Moussa began his career as a diplomat at the Egyptian Foreign Ministry. In 1981, he was appointed member of the Egyptian delegation to the UN., the following year Ambassador to India. Between 1990–1991, he served as Egypt's Ambassador to the UN. Moussa represented his country in various Arab, Islamic and international conferences. He also participated in the talks which led to the Declaration of Principles (DOP) between ISRAEL and the PALESTINE LIBERATION ORGANIZATION (PLO) (1993), and later on in the peace talks between Israel and the PALESTINIAN AUTHORITY.

MUBARAK, (MUHAMMAD) HUSNI (b. 1928) Egyptian officer and politician. Vice President of EGYPT 1975-1981; President from October 1981. Born in Kafr al-Musaliha village in the Manufiyya district north-east of Cairo (the son of a petty official of peasant stock), Mubarak graduated from the Military College in 1949 and the Air Force Academy in 1950. After serving as a fighter pilot, between 1954 to 1961 he became an instructor at the Air Force Academy. He attended several training courses in the USSR, including a full year (1961–1962) at the Soviet General Staff Academy. In 1967 he became Commander of the Air Academy, with the rank of Colonel. In 1969 he was Chief of Staff of the Air Force, with the rank of General (Air Vice Marshal). In 1971–1974 he was Commander in Chief of the Air Force. In that capacity, Mubarak played a key role in the preparations for, and the conduct of, the October War of 1973. Additionally, the successful manner in which the Air Force fulfilled its task in that war is usually seen as Mubarak's personal achievement. In 1974 he was promoted to the rank of Air Marshal.

In April 1975 President al-SADAT appointed Mubarak as sole Vice President. Until then, Mubarak had never been active or politicized and was seen as a professional officer. Sadat's motivations for elevating Mubarak from political obscurity to a position of top leadership may had been linked to the politically colorlessness of Mubarak and his being a successful representative of the Egyptian armed forces whose support has always been prominent to any regime in Egypt. As Vice President, Mubarak fully followed Sadat's lead and policies, without much independent action or attitudes. He served as the President's envoy on many missions to the Arab states and around the world, including the USSR and China. Observers thought that even as Vice-President Mubarak did not create a political base for himself. Nonetheless some saw his hand in the dismissal of several potential rivals (such as War Minister and Deputy Premier Gamasy in October 1978, or Mansur Hasan, Minister for Presidential Affairs and Information, in September 1981). Mubarak was fully associated with Sadat's moves towards peace with ISRAEL, from November 1977 to the Camp David Agreements of September 1978, to the peace treaty of March 1979 although he himself did not participate in the actual negotiations.

When President Sadat was assassinated in October 1981, Mubarak immediately took over as President. Within a week he was nominated by the "National Democratic Party" and confirmed by a referendum (with no rival candidates). For some months he also held the role of Premiership. However in January 1982 he appointed a new government headed by Fuad Muhyi al-Din, with Fikri Makram Ubaid, a Copt, as Deputy Prime Minister. Mubarak himself became Chairman of the ruling National Democratic Party, speaking to many of the need for an economic austerity policy. He demonstrated an even-handed policy in domestic affairs. While releasing more detainees, he remained firm with regard to the punishment of Sadat's assassins approving death sentences on five of them.

Having been officially elected for presidency, he promised the continuation of Sadat's policies which he basically did. Yet, his Presidency was different from Sadat's in style, mode of operation, and eventually in some of its policies.

Mubarak's presidency was marked by secular and pragmatic policies both on domestic and foreign affairs. Unlike his predecessors, his political speech has been absent of emotional or ideological inputs. He appeared as a solid hard-working administrator, who was honest and cautious, rather than a brilliant tribune. He also emphasized, in contrast to his predecessors, an unusual modesty in his personal life style. Mubarak's philosophy somewhat diluted the liberalization, open-door and free enterprise culture of Sadat's regime. He re-imposed stricter state control, and in particular tried to eliminate the excesses, negative side-effects and the measure of corruption that had grown under Sadat.

In the face of growing Islamic fundamentalist movements, he continued Sadat's policy of forcibly suppressing their extremist excesses, whilst emphasizing Egypt's Islamic character and strengthening orthodox Islamic elements in public manifestations of his own regime. Yet, he adopted a general policy of denying religious groups a political status and in this context he continued to refuse the MUSLIM BROTHERHOOD's demand to be recognized as an independent political party.

In October 1987, Mubarak was re-elected for a second term of Presidency. Mubarak also departed from Sadat's inter-Arab policy which, since the late 1970s, was antagonistic costly to Egypt's position in the region. Mubarak strove to restore Egypt's status in the Arab world by adopting a conciliatory tone and ceasing the propaganda, but primarily by championing the Palestinian issue. Thus, Mubarak was the most active Arab leader in the international political arena during Israel's war in LEBANON and siege of Beirut (see ARAB-ISRAEL CONFLICT) on behalf of PALESTINE LIBERATION ORGANIZATION the PLO and the Palestinians in general. His first significant success in this regard was ARAFAT's visit to Cairo in November 1983 directly from Tripoli from which he had been expelled by his fellow Palestinian rivals with Syria's military backing. In 1981–1982 Egypt became increasingly aligned with IRAQ—*albeit*—unofficial—supplying the latter growing quantities of arms and ammunition of Egyptian production. The fragmented and weakened Arab world, especially due to the IRAN-IRAQ WAR and Shi'i threat to the Gulf oil monarchies helped Mubarak to become gradually involved in regional Arab and Islamic meetings. This paved the road to resumption of diplomatic relations between most Arab states and Egypt by late 1987 and full return of Egypt to the ARAB LEAGUE in 1989. As a result, Ismat ABDEL MAJID was elected Secretary General of the Arab League, and the Headquarters of the organization were reestablished in Cairo (after being in Tunis since 1979). The return of Egypt to the Arab League allowed Mubarak to resume the traditional position of Arab leadership, which came into effect in two main respects: accelerated effort to develop the peace process between Israel and other Arab states, as well as with the Palestinians; and leading the Arab world into clear a collective decision that opposed to the Iraqi invasion of Kuwait and supporting an international military action.

Mubarak indeed remained an ardent solicitor of the peace process, endeavoring to bring the PLO, SYRIA and JORDAN into peacemaking with Israel, while doing the same effort in trying to convince Israel to accept the PLO as a partner in this process. Mubarak was instrumental in convincing his Arab colleagues to accept the American formula for the Madrid peace conference, and later in promoting the Israel-PLO Oslo process through offering his personal and regime's services of mediation and auspices for the negotiating parties. Mubarak, however, demonstrated alienation to the Israel-Jordan peace treaty signed in October 1994, for not being brought in or involved in the negotiations that had led to it. Despite his deep self-interested involvement in the peacemaking between Israel and its Arab neighbors, Mubarak has never lost sight with Egypt's interest in preserving its leading position in the region. It is in this context that Mubarak showed, already during the Rabin-Peres term (1992–1996) reservations at its expanding diplomatic relations and influence in the Arab world.

At the same time, Mubarak strengthened Egypt's relations with the West, especially with the US culminating in the Kuwait crisis and the GULF WAR (August 1990–January 1991).

In the domestic field, he had to face two main challenges: to fight against the growing threat of extremist Islamic terror (see EGYPT); and to take drastic steps to improve the economic situation. To implement his economic policy, he appointed Atif Sidqi, a well known economic expert, as Prime Minister (1986), and launched his second five-year economic plan in 1987.

The militant Islamic groups, especially the Jama'a al-Islamiyya, insisted on the immediate implementation of the SHARI'A and doubled their attacks against politicians, high-ranking officials and liberal intellectuals. Realizing the size of such a threat, the regime launched a massive campaign in the mass-media trying to explain the dangers of such ideologies. They tried to gain the support of the Islamic religious institutions (and of the public in general), in the struggle against these groups. This campaign had very limited—if any—success, and the authorities turned to taking harsh oppressive measures against the militant groups, including large-scale arrests and trials. Nevertheless, the militants did not lose strength. They even attempted to assassinate Prime Minister Atif Sidqi (1992), and even President Mubarak himself (1995). As a result, the authorities launched relentless counter-attacks, hunting down the leaders and activists of these groups everywhere they could reach them. In particular they attempted to surprise them in their strongholds in Cairo and in the main cities of Upper Egypt. It seems that these harsh measures were efficient to a certain degree, but it was only in July 1997 that the leaders of *al-Jihad* and *al-Jama'a al-Islamiyya* (see ISLAMIC FUNDAMENTALISM) asked for a truce. The authorities were reluctant to respond, harboring suspicions over the true intentions of the proposal.

During his third term of presidency (beginning October 1993), Mubarak persisted in his efforts to rehabilitate the Egyptian economy. He implemented an anti-inflation policy with fairly satisfactory results. He also took steps to encourage foreign investments, and to develop tourism, which was badly damaged in the 1980s, due to terrorist actions against tourists. Tourism indeed developed into Egypt's second largest source of revenue which in 1996 was estimated at 3 billion dollars with the number of tourists exceeding 4 million people. In 1996–1997 Egypt seemed to be steadily heading towards economic recovery. Annual economic growth reached close to five percent, inflation was curtailed, and the budget brought almost to balance. The main economic target set by the regime was the implementation of privatization. To achieve this goal, Mubarak appointed Kamal al-Ganzuri as Prime Minister (January 1996). In a cabinet reshuffle (July 1997), Yusuf Butrus-Ghali was appointed State Minister for Economic Affairs.

MUFTI A Muslim religious official who issues rulings (FATWA, plural *fatawi*), based on Islamic Law (SHARI'A), generally in response to questions. In most Islamic countries the Mufti is government-appointed, usually for life.

The Mufti has a highly respected status and spiritual and social influence, but plays no executive or political role. However, his rulings frequently concern issues of political significance and in many such cases conform to the wishes and conceptions of the government in power (see FATWA). A salient exception to the basically non-political character of the office of the Mufti was the Mufti of JERUSALEM, Hajj Amin al-HUSSEINI who exploited his position to consolidate his political leadership (see PALESTINE ARABS).

MUHAMMAD, ALI NASSER (b. 1939) South Yemenite politician, Prime Minister 1971–1985, President 1980–1986. From a tribal background, Muhammad was trained as a teacher in ADEN. He graduated in 1959, and became a school principal in his Dathina tribal area. In the 1960s he was one of the founders and leaders of the NATIONAL LIBERATION FRONT (NLF), specializing in its fighting squads. During the decisive struggle of 1967, he commanded the NLF's guerrilla formations in the Beihan area. When SOUTH YEMEN became independent under the NLF, late in 1967, he was appointed governor of several provinces successively. In 1969, when President Qahtan al-Sha'bi was ousted by a more leftist-extremist faction, he joined Muhammad Haitham's government, first as Minister for Local government and later the same year as Minister of Defense. Though active in the victorious leftist faction, Muhammad was not yet a member of the five-men Presidential Council. However some observers already viewed him as one of an emerging ruling "triumvirate" (with Salem Rubai Ali and Abdel-Fattah Isma'il). In August 1971 that triumvirate ousted Haitham and took over as a new Presidential Council. Muhammad also became Prime Minister, retaining the Defense Ministry for some time.

In June 1978, Salem Rubai Ali was overthrown by Abdel-Fattah Isma'il and Muhammad, and was killed. Muhammad became President, but ceded the Presidency to Isma'il after a few months. He was content with the Premiership and membership of the Presidential Council. Within the ruling leftist faction and the triuvirate at its head an unrelenting struggle now began escalating. It appears to have been generated by personal rivalry between Muhammad and Isma'il, by each one's desire to wield full power, tribal-factional interests, and some political differences. Isma'il was a doctrinaire extremist, guided by a strict Moscow-loyal partyline, which led South Yemen into a near-complete isolation within the Arab world, while Muhammad gradually tended to more pragmatic policies, a measure of reintegration in the Arab mainstream and an improvement in South Yemen's relations with its Arab neighbors, particularly SAUDI ARABIA. In April 1980 Muhammad won. Isma'il was ousted and went into exile to Moscow.

As President and in full power, Muhammad gradually implemented his more pragmatic line, achieving some improvement of South Yemen's inter-Arab standing and relations. The factional struggle, however, continued even in Isma'il's absence, as other members of the ruling junta turned against Muhammad (particularly Defense Minister Ali Antar, made Vice President in 1981, and Deputy Premier Ali Salem al-Beid). After several attempts at mediation and reconciliation, and apparently some Soviet pressure, Isma'il was allowed to return in 1985. His return reintensified the factional struggle. The course of the final showdown in January 1986 has remained confused, reported in conflicting versions, with each side claiming that the other had attempted to stage a coup and assassinate its rivals. In the fighting, Isma'il, Antar and several others were killed. But Muhammad was defeated and ousted. He escaped death and went into exile in Yemen and/or ETHIOPIA. He continued speaking of rallying his supporters and resuming the fight. In December 1986 he was put on trial, *in absentia*, with approximately 140 others. Muhammad has not been active in Yemeni politics since.

MUHMAMMAD REZA SHAH   see PAHLAVI, MOHAMAD REZA SHAH.

MUHAMMAD V, BEN YUSSUF (1909? 1911?–1961)   Sultan of Morocco, 1927–1957, King, 1957–1961, member of the ALAWI sharifian dynasty which reigned in Morocco since the latter part of the seventeenth century. Sultan Muhammad, addressed (according to Moroccan custom) also as "Sidi Muhammad" or "Moulay Muhammad," succeeded his father, Sultan Yussuf, in 1927. Under the French Protectorate, his authority was very restricted. In fact, his administration, the *Makhzen*, was limited to the "native" sector of life and economy. Even in that restricted sphere he was repeat-

edly forced to take measures or sign decrees he disapproved of, such as the "Berber Decree" of 1930 (see MOROCCO), and sometimes he resisted the French dictate. In general, Sultan Muhammad was considered an instrument of the French, and the incipient national movement turned in some measure against him too. During World War II, under France's Vichy regime, he protected his Jewish subjects to some extent (the degree is in dispute). As the nationalist movement intensified, from the late 1940s, Sultan Muhammad's identification with it increased; thus, growing conflict developed with the French, while the nationalists and popular opinion began to view Sultan Muhammad more favorably.

In August 1953 the French exiled him to Madagascar and his relative Moulay Muhammad Ben Arafa replaced him (although he did not abdicate or renounce his claim). But mounting unrest (virtually a nationalist uprising) transformed him into a unifying national symbol and thus compelled FRANCE to reinstate Sultan Muhammad. In November 1955 he returned to Morocco and his throne, and it was during his reign that Morocco became independent in 1956. In August 1957 Sultan Muhammad assumed the title of King. In May 1960, in one of the crises of Morocco's governance, he assumed the Premiership himself, and held it until his death. He died unexpectedly in February 1961 following routine surgery and was succeeded by his eldest son, Moulay Hasan.

MUSLIM BROTHERS, BROTHERHOOD
(*Jama'at al-Ikhwan al-Muslimin*—"Brotherhood Association of Muslims")   An ultra-orthodox Islamic and political organization founded in EGYPT in 1928 by Sheikh Hassan al-Banna, as a youth club which aimed to introduce moral and social reform through Islamic preaching and teaching. Al-Banna became the "Supreme Guide" (*al-Murshid al-Aam*), a title taken from the vocabulary of the Muslim mystics (*Sufis*) and the DERVISH ORDERS, along with some organizational and missionary techniques.

The Muslim Brotherhood (MB) was strictly orthodox and its teachings had no *Sufi* or Dervish tendencies. Its aim has been to apply the Islamic Law (SHARI'A) to the social, political and constitutional life of the Muslim population. Though it displayed certain conservative-reformist tendencies, its understanding of ISLAM is orthodox-revivalist, with Pan-

Islamic aspirations and strong xenophobic, anti-Christian and anti-Jewish sentiments.

During the late 1930s the Muslim Brotherhood became increasingly involved in politics, capitalizing on the popular resentment of the Anglo-Egyptian Treaty of 1936, and strong sense of solidarity with the 1936–1939 ARAB REVOLT in Palestine. The transformation that the Muslim Brotherhood movement underwent turned it into a major force in shaping Egypt's growing tendency to identify itself as an Arab-Muslim entity. Consequently it became a natural leading power of the Arab world. The rapid rise of the Muslim Brotherhood in Egypt and expansion to other Arab countries in the course of the 1930s and 1940s illustrated a social, political and cultural response of the Westernization of the Muslim societies. From a conservative Islamic viewpoint, the main threat of Westernization lay in its impact on the Arab-Muslim society, manifested in the growing secularization and abandonment of social traditional values.

The Muslim Brotherhood was one of the movements that emerged from the *salafi* (Islam's ancestral way of life) doctrine. This developed in the late nineteenth century, particularly in Egypt. It pointed to the normative example set by Islam's pious ancestors (the Prophet Muhammad and his companions) as the only authentic Islam. Adhering to this would enable the Muslim world to salvage itself from the state of continued decline and subordination to Westernised culture, and to revive the glorious past of Islam. From the outset, the movement's potential depended in the lower social classes, the newly urbanized and educated generation, whose sociocultural origins were deeply rooted in the traditional Islamic rural provinces. A dominant characteristic of the movement was its empasis on reshaping the society and creating an Islamic space, focusing on the local community level (with the mosque, Islamic education, and other social services) as the nucleus of the future Islamic society.

The Muslim Brotherhood movement became, over the years, a strong, semi-clandestine popular organization. Its growing involvement in political issues, increased primarily the struggle for national liberation, combining the religious ethos of Holy War (JIHAD) with popular anti-Western sentiments, a sense of deprivation and resentment toward the ruling elite, especially among the low middle class.

Indeed, the Muslim Brotherhood's concept of restoring the primacy of Islam identified the Muslim society itself as the main arena of activity, with the agents of secularization and social liberalization (mostly the ruling elites themselves) as its sworn enemies.

In the late 1940s the Muslim Brotherhood's strength was estimated at between 100,000 and 500,000 members, comprised of 75,000 fully active members (*Mujahidun*)—the hard core of the movement known as the "Special Organization"" (*al-tanzim al-khas*)—and a few hundreds of thousands of less active sympathizers, organized in over five thousand branches. It also maintained a paramilitary youth organization and underground striking squads. The Muslim Brotherhood has generally been in extreme opposition to all Egyptian governments; its power and influence were extra-Parliamentary (al-Banna stood for election to Parliament only once, in 1945, and was defeated) and were manifested through agitation, demonstrations, and riots. The movement attracted young military officers from a low social background, which helped in providing military training to Muslim Brothers. Its striking squads were held responsible for the wave of political assassinations that engulfed Egypt in 1945–1948, the most famous victims of which were former Finance Minister and WAFD leader, Amin Uthman (January 1946); and Prime Minister Nuqrashi (December 1948).

In 1948 the Muslim Brotherhood was most active in propagating popular support for the cause of Palestine, delegating the largest number of volunteers sent by a single political movement in the Arab world to fight the Jews. The Muslim Brotherhood's volunteers—"The Light Forces"—deployed mainly in the Bethlehem-Hebron area as well as on the outskirts of Jerusalem and in the northern Negev, implementing Egypt's secondary military effort.

The impact of the Muslim Brotherhood on the Arab-Jewish war in Palestine was indeed unique. Not only did it force the Egyptian government to allow its volunteers to receive military training and penetrate Palestine prior to the end of the British Mandate (15 May), but it also accounted (more than any other political movement) for Egypt's decision to officially enter (with its regular army) the war in Palestine. Holding the Egyptian government responsible for the debacle in Palestine, the Muslim Brotherhood renewed its terrorist activity, resulting in the banning of the movement's activity by the government in December 1948. The Muslim Brotherhood had to go underground, and shortly afterward, Premier Nuqrashi was murdered by a Muslim Brotherhood member. The government retaliated by assassinating al-Banna himself in February 1949.

In 1950 the Muslim Brotherhood, (now with Sheikh Hassan Isma'il al-Hudeibi as the Supreme Guide) was allowed to resume activity on condition that it would limit its functions to spiritual, cultural and social matters, and not engage in political activities (which, its spokesmen claimed, it did not do anyway), nor maintain any paramilitary formations. However, the government's abrogation of the 1936 Anglo-Egyptian Treaty and intensified popular agitation against Britain's military presence in the SUEZ CANAL, tacitly legitimized the Muslim Brotherhood's return to politics.

The Muslim Brotherhood failed to regain its previous strength and impact. The "Free Officers" coup of 23 July 1952, which banned all political parties in 1953, initially overlooked the Muslim Brotherhood, which maintained close relations with some members of the new military junta. The Muslim Brotherhood resumed its criticism of the regime as the social and political agenda of the latter which turned out to be entirely secular-liberal. The regime, on its part, suspected the Muslim Brotherhood of subversion and banned it in January 1954. The power struggle of 1954 between General Muhammad Nagib and Colonel Gamal ABDEL NASSER was exacerbated by Nagib's attempt to soften the regime's attitude toward the Muslim Brotherhood, which reportedly tended to support him. When Nasser won, measures to suppress the organization were further tightened. In October 1954, shortly after Nasser signed an agreement with Britian that would end their dispute over the SUDAN and Suez Canal, an attempt to assassinate him by a Muslim Brother led to severe measures of repression against the movement. Thousands of Muslim Brothers were arrested, and many others fled to the neighboring Arab countries. The movement's top leaders were put on trial. Seven were sentenced to death—including al-Hudeibi —and nine to imprisonment; Hudeibi was given life imprisonment, but six were executed.

The Muslim Brotherhood—now reportedly under a collective leadership without a Supreme Guide— was not completely broken and continued operating underground. The regime, on its part, continued to denounce the Brotherhood's plots, holding it responsible for various political difficulties. A revival of its activities was reported (especially in the mid-1960s), including a plot on Nasser's life, and in 1965 and 1966 thousands were again arrested and hundreds were put to trial. Sentences, in August–September 1966, included several death verdicts and three were executed (including the Muslim Brothers' most prominent idealist and writer, Sayyid Qutb); Hudeibi, who had been released in 1956 on compassionate and health grounds, was re-arrested and sentenced to imprisonment, with two of his sons. He was released in 1970 and died in 1973.

Although in retrospect the Arab debacle of June 1967 illustrated a starting point in the emergence of Islamic fundamentalism, its immediate impact on the movement remained unclear. However, the intellectual self-searching debate that engulfed the Arab world (following the political and military defeat of whatever Nasser symbolized to the Arab world) also included analyses by Islamic-oriented thinkers. Affected by the manifestations of piety and religious symbols by Israelis following their victory, the diagnosis and prognosis suggested by these Islamic-oriented thinkers called on the Arabs to adopt the Muslim value system rejecting secular pan-Arabism in order to cure their political predicament. The Muslim Brotherhood remained Nasser's sworn enemies until his death in 1970. Student unrest in 1968 was again ascribed to the Muslim Brotherhood.

Under al-SADAT from 1970, and since 1981 under MUBARAK, the Muslim Brotherhood was treated more leniently. In mid-1971, shortly after Sadat established himself in power, He released thousands of the imprisoned Muslim Brothers as part of his departure from Nasserist ideology and political practices. Some observers find a certain affinity between this and the new leadership (Sadat himself had reportedly been close to it in the 1940s and 1950s). As the Muslim Brothers were thought to have considerably moderated their stance—under the leadership of Umar Tilmissani (without the title of "Supreme Guide"; he died in May 1986)—there was even talk of a sort of alliance between them and the regime— against the Left, and against more extreme Islamic groups. In any case, they were permitted official press organs and could acquire an increasing influence, even a large measure of control, in lower-class quarters of the cities and especially at the universities. It is not clear how much of that control was wielded by the Muslim Brotherhood and how much by other, more extreme groups. But the Muslim Brotherhood was not permitted to establish a political organization or openly put candidates up for public office, such as the National Assembly. Thus, in 1979 Sadat refused the Muslim Brotherhood's request to join the newly established "stages" (in fact parties), which indicated the beginning of democratization of Egypt's political system.

Relations between Sadat's regime and the Muslim Brotherhood soon deteriorated against the backdrop of his separate peace agreement with Israel and the growing rift with SAUDI ARABIA and other Arab regimes. This encouraged the rise of extreme Islamic groups whose connections to the Brotherhood was not always clear. The movement's main press organ, al-Da'wa, was sometimes banned and in 1981 Sadat clashed with the Muslim Brotherhood head-on, arresting thousands, a few hundreds of them member of the Muslim Brotherhood. This collision (during the Summer–Autumn of 1981) created the atmosphere and justification for his assassination in October of that year by a group of Islamic extremists.

The continued democratization under Mubarak was an incentive for the Muslim Brotherhood to participate in the political system, despite the legal restrains on the establishment of a religious party. In the National Assembly elections of 1984, the Muslim Brotherhood made an informal alliance with the WAFD Party and ten Muslim Brothers entered the Assembly on the *Wafd* ticket. In the 1987 elections they were in coalition with the Socialist Labor and Socialist Liberal parties, and among that list's sixty elected, some thirty-five were reportedly Muslim Brothers.

Under the leadership of Hamed Abu al-Nasr (named Supreme Guide in 1986), the Muslim Brothers continued presenting a moderate line attempting to be incorporated into Egyptian politics. However, the regime remained adamant in its refusal to allow the Muslim Brotherhood to form a political party slated to participate in parliamentarian elections. As a result, they boycotted the elections of 1990 along with other opposition parties. This, however, did not prevent the Muslim Broth-

erhood from strengthening its political role in the society through various social and economic activities. Apart from fostering an "Islamic economy" with financial organs, these activities focused on penetration and take-over of professional and worker's unions where the Brotherhood won almost complete control, despite legal and political measures taken by the regime to curb its power in this sphere.

In the Parliamentary elections of November 1995, the regime again forbade the Muslim Brotherhood to compete as a party. A number of Muslim Brotherhood representatives participated as independent candidates. They attained minimal success; only a small number were actually elected. Prior to the elections, the regime arrested eighty-one of the Muslim Brotherhood, accusing them of attempting to overthrow the regime by penetration into government institutes. This step was intended to de-legitimize the Muslim Brotherhood and prevent its participation in the elections.

In early 1996, Supreme Guide Hamed Abu al-Nasr died and was replaced by Mustafa Mashhour, who belonged to the founding generation of the Muslim Brotherhood. His appointment and the almost complete monopoly of the old guard in the movement leadership resulted in a split in its ranks shortly after. A number of young leaders, headed by Abu al-Ala al-Madi, head of the engineers union, established a break-away party named "al-Wasat" (The Center). This move, together with the increasing measures taken by the regime, caused a weakening of the Party's position.

The Muslim Brotherhood had never been the sole Islamic organization in Egypt, but as a mass movement, it was significantly larger than any other Islamic group. Since its foundation it constantly excelled in its political radicalism and opposition to the regime. Other groups, such as *Shabab Muhammad* (Muhammad's Youth) of Shukri Mustafa active in the 1960s, or Saleh Harb's *Jam'iyyat al-Shubban al-Muslimin* (Young Men Muslim Association), had remained part of the establishment. Since the 1970s, however, the Muslim Brotherhood was outflanked by more extremist underground Islamic organizations, using violent and terrorist means (which the Muslim Brotherhood had gradually abandoned)—such as the *al-Tahrir al-Islami* (Islamic Liberation), *al-Takfir wa'l-Hijra* (Excommunication and Migration) and *al-Jihad* (Holy War) groups (see EGYPT). But the Muslim Brotherhood has its own extremist wing, there are underground links, and there may be clandestine double membership.

The home and center of the Muslim Brotherhood is Egypt. Attempts to create branches in other Arab countries have been only partially successful. However, no all-Arab or all-Islamic Muslim Brotherhood association has been founded. Apart from Islamic organizations under other names, groups adopting the name Muslim Brotherhood and its slogans were established, from about 1945, in Palestine, JORDAN, SYRIA, LEBANON, and later in Sudan. Some of them were short-lived, and the links between those surviving associations with the Egyptian movement was rather loose.

The Muslim Brotherhood in Sudan (established in the 1940s) became in the 1970s (under Hassan al-Turabi's leadership) a major force in Sudanese politics. The Muslim Brotherhood in Sudan, unlike its Egyptian counterpart, has remained mostly within the establishment as a political party. Even during periods of military regime in Sudan, the Muslim Brotherhood managed to steer clear of major confrontations with the regime. Its most significant leap forward came in 1977 when it joined NUMEIRI's government. The Muslim Brotherhood succeeded in acquiring key positions in all realms including the armed forces. This enabled the movement's rise to power in 1989 through a military coup led by officers with an Islamic orientation headed by General BASHIR. The Muslim Brotherhood in Sudan was the first radical Islamic movement that rose to power in the Sunni Islamic world. Since 1989 the Muslim Brotherhood has been the major political force behind Bashir's regime. In Sudan and Egypt the two groups are vying with each other over the leadership of the Sunni radical Islamic movement (see also SUDAN).

The Muslim Brotherhood in Jordan was established in 1946 by a number of people led by Sheikh Abd al-Latif Abu-Qura and Qassem al-Amri. Its first Supreme Guide was Muhammad Abd al-Rahman al-Khalifa (1953–1994) who was replaced by Abd al-Majid al-Zneibat.

The Muslim Brotherhood—led by Abd al-Rahman al-Khalifa—was for most of the time tolerated as a quasi-legal organization within the establishment. Though often in opposition it contested elections (though its candidates usually appeared, formally, as "Independents") and several times won seats in

Parliament. In the 1950s and 1960s, the Muslim Brotherhood aligned with the HASHEMITE regime as a lesser political evil compared with the revolutionary Arab regimes. The Hashemite regime, on its part, needed the Muslim Brotherhood as a counterbalance to the pan-Arab left-wing parties. From 1967 till the late 1980s (during which parties and political organizations had been banned), the Muslim Brotherhood focused on educational activity in the society, and penetrated the universities and professional associations in a similar way to its Egyptian sister-movement.

In 1989, the regime initiated democratization measures following the bread riots that had taken place earlier that year. These measures included the right to form political parties. The Muslim Brotherhood participated in the elections that took place that year, winning twenty-two out of eighty parliamentary seats. It collaborated with independent Islamic Parliament members and with pan-Arab movements, such as the BA'TH, constituting a major opposition block. The Muslim Brotherhood even participated in Badran's government for a short time (1990–1991). It resigned with the GULF WAR and the King's shifting policy toward co-operation with the UNITED STATES and willingness to take part in the Madrid Peace Conference. The regime that so feared the rise of the Muslim Brotherhood, changed the election law before the 1993 elections. This resulted in the weakening of the Muslim Brotherhood's representation in Parliament.

The Muslim Brotherhood usually refrained from major confrontations with the regime. For example it did not participate in the bread riots of 1996. However, in the 1990s, the Muslim Brotherhood became the most serious challenge to the Hashemite regime, turning the October 1994 peace agreement with Israel, into the main target for criticism of the regime. The signing of the peace treaty between Israel and Jordan was harshly condemned by the Muslim Brotherhood, worsening its relationship. Since 1996, there has been heated discussion in the party as to the appropriate tactic that it should adopt in view of its declining affect on politics. The more pragmatic stream supports strong political activity, including participation in the government to strengthen its power and oppose the normalization with Israel. The more hawkish stream objects strongly to government participation, emphasizing educational activity. Further measures taken by the government in the first half of 1997 to restrict opposition activity led the Muslim Brotherhood's leadership decision (in July) to boycott the general elections for Parliament due in November of that year.

A more extreme Islamic group, *Hizb al-Tahrir* (The Islamic Liberation Party), split in 1952 from the Muslim Brotherhood under Taqi al-Din al-Nabhani. It appealed to the same public and was later accused of subversion and plotting against the regime. It was outlawed in 1969.

The country outside Egypt where the Muslim Brotherhood had the strongest impact was Syria. The Syrian Muslim Brotherhood was founded in the late 1930s and became significantly active from 1945 to 1946. Its mainstay has always been the predominantly Sunni northern provinces of Aleppo, Homs and Hamah. Its founder-leader was Mustafa al-Siba'i, Professor of Islamic Law at Damascus University (died in 1964). Until the early 1960s, the Syrian Muslim Brotherhood, though often dissenting from the mainstream (and linked to, or even clandestinely founding, more extreme groups of different names, such as the "Islamic Liberation Party"), was a legal part of the establishment. It participated in elections for Parliament, usually as Independents. In 1961, for instance, seven to twelve deputies (according to different versions), were considered Muslim Brotherhood members. It was even represented in the government (e.g., in Khaled al-Azm's government in 1962). Its leader Siba'i was for some time Deputy President of Parliament.

But after the *Ba'th* Party came to power, in the coup of 1963, the antagonism between the Muslim Brotherhood and the ruling leftist-revolutionary nationalist trends erupted into open mutual hostility. This was further aggravated by the ever-increasing role played in the ruling establishment by the Muslim Brotherhood of the ALAWI sect, whom the Sunni-fundamentalist Muslim Brotherhood could not but consider heretics or non-believers. Led by Issam al-Attar (who soon went into exile), the Muslim Brotherhood was outlawed in 1963 and went underground. In the 1970s it began increasing acts of sabotage and violence, which escalated particularly from 1978 to

1979. In June 1979 it attacked officer-cadets, most of them Alawis, in Aleppo, culminating in a massacre.

Counteraction by the regime and its efforts to suppress the Muslim Brotherhood were equally brutal, resulting (in June 1980) to a massacre of Muslim Brotherhood detainees in Palmyra prison. In February 1982 a veritable insurrection in Hamah and fully-fledged army and special forces action against it left the old city of Hamah nearly destroyed by artillery shelling and reportedly tens of thousands deaths (in the official version about 1,200, in other reports 10,000–30,000).

After these battles, Muslim Brotherhood violence and sabotage seemed to have abated. However, during the 1990s the trend of return to Islam among Sunni Muslims seems to be on the rise, though without political or violent means.

The Muslim Brotherhood was weakened considerably following the Hamah massacre. During the 1980s and early 1990s little has been reported of its activity. Most of its leaders were in political exile in Jordan or in Europe.

From early 1996 and onward, attempts at negotiations between the Muslim Brotherhood and the regime have been conducted by the Jordanian Muslim Brotherhood and some of the Syrian Muslim Brotherhood leaders (such as Amin Yakan and Abu-Ghada). The motives of each side are unclear. A number of reports have mentioned the possibility of the regime granting pardons to the Syrian Muslim Brotherhood members but, for now, no significant progress has been made.

MUSLIM, MUSLIMS see ISLAM.

MUTAWALI, MUTAWALIS (In Arabic, the plural is *matawila*). The Shi'i Muslims of LEBANON, of the mainstream *Imami* (or, *Ithna-Ashariyya, the Twelvers*), trend of the SHI'A, believing in the Twelve IMAMS.

The term Mutawali refers principally to those in southern Lebanon (Jabal Amel), but also to those in the northern Biqa, the Baalbek region. For data about the mutawalis see LEBANON, ISLAM, SHI'A, MINORITIES.

N

AL NAHAYAN see ṆUHAYAN, AL.

NASSER see ABDEL NASSER, GAMAL.

NASSERISM An ideological trend in the Arab world, prevalent particularly in the Fertile Crescent countries and EGYPT from the mid-1950s to the late 1960s, containing radical social and Arab nationalist attitude, identified with Egypt's Gamal ABDEL NASSER. Nasserism represented a sentimental adherence of and identification with Nasser as a symbol, regarding him as a hero and charismatic leader of the Arab nation, with Egypt under his leadership as the prototype of an Arab nation progressing toward national freedom and social justice. The term Nasserism is primarily a foreign, Western creation and seldom used in Arabic. Indeed, Arabs usually term this ideology ARAB SOCIALISM or "Arab Socialist Unionism". Nasserism is neither a well-defined doctrine, nor an organized movement, but rather a general socio-political outlook, marked by substantial protest against the ancient Arab regimes and Western influence in the Middle East, and ISRAEL as symbol of that influence. These are elements that turned Nasserism for some years into the most popular ideological-political trend in the Arab world, developing against the background of disillusionment with the West and its protected conservative regimes, and the quest for power and self-esteem as a nation.

Incipient Nasserism was a strongly nationalist reformism, emphasizing vigorous economic and social development with an expanding state sector, enlarged by a process of nationalization, based on a single-party near-totalitarian populism. (In fact, though not in doctrine, led by an activist core of the officers' corps.) It professed a strident neutralism—with strong anti-Western undertones determined by anti-colonialist memories and the urge to eliminate positions of privilege still held by Western powers. In the early 1960s, Nasser and his regime—and therefore Nasserism—became increasingly Socialist, adopting a populist-totalitarian version of state socialism. A Pan-Arab element, the wish to unite all Arab countries under similar "Socialist-Unionist" regimes, also received a stronger emphasis.

Ideologically, Nasserism had to compete with several similar "Socialist-Unionist" trends— e.g. the clandestine "Arab Nationalist Movement" (*Harakat al-Qawmiyyun al-Arab*, see ARAB NATIONALISM) and the Syrain-centered BA'TH group—although it would be difficult to define precisely the doctrinal differences. Nasserism was less doctrinaire and rather more pragmatic, and with Egypt's power and prestige behind it, it seemed to have a stronger impact on all-Arab opinion, while the *Qawmiyyun*, initially considered somewhat younger, more extreme Nasserists, were drifting into an increasingly leftist-Maoist position.

However, Nasser and his associates were not content with the gradual growth of their influence, but tried to expand the power of Nasserism as a doctrine, as a political regime, and as a tool of Egyptian predominance, by means unacceptable to the other Arab states, including underground intrigues, plots, political assassination and subversion (see EGYPT, ABDEL NASSER, ARAB NATIONALISM). Because of these strong-arm or subversive tactics, Nasserism lost much of its attraction. Those Arab states that were the target or scene of Nasserist attempts to gain control resisted and denounced them, and even pro-Nasserist Arab countries or groups did not fully accept Nasserist guidance, at least not in its Egyptian version. In IRAQ and SYRIA, particularly the latter, Nasserist factions were locked in combat with the dominating *Ba'th* stream, and their claim for co-equal leadership was defeated.

As Nasserism failed to impose itself on Arab countries outside Egypt, doubts were cast as to its success even in its Egyptian home and base. As Egypt got bogged down in its military intervention in Yemen (1962–1967), and especially after the 1967 defeat, Nasser and his associates in the later 1960s tuned down their efforts to "export" Nasserism to other Arab countries. With Nasser's death in 1970, Nasserism lost much of what remained of its magic. Even in Egypt Nasser's successor, Anwar al-SADAT, changed policies that amounted to de facto departure from and destructing Nasserism as a guiding line of Egypt's governance and society.

In Egypt, the officers' regime's single party—the "Liberation Rally" 1953–1958; the "National

Union," 1957–1962; and the "Arab Socialist Union" 1962–1977 (formally dissolved in 1980)—may be regarded as the organizational instrument of Nasserism. For the three years of the abortive Egyptian-Syrian union (the UNITED ARAB REPUBLIC, (UAR), 1958–1961, the "National Union" operated in Syria, too, as the only legal political party. But even at its peak, Nasserism had no organized, unified instruments outside Egypt, no all-Arab roof organization uniting the small groups or factions that could be seen as inclining to, or being guided by, Nasserism. Such groups, usually calling themselves "Socialist-Unionist" in different versions and splitting into competing factions, existed mainly in Syria and LEBANON (after Nasserism was eliminated in Iraq as a serious organized force in 1959). In Syria, they were liquidated or driven into exile after 1963, except for splinter factions prepared to submit to Ba'th primacy and to join a united front led by the Ba'th. In Lebanon, various small groups that could be described as Nasserist continued operating—such as the Muslim-SUNNI "militia" of the Murabitun in Beirut, or a similar formation maintained by the Muslim-Sunni leaders of Sidon.

Traces or elements of Nasserism, in a measure that cannot be precisely pinned down, may be seen in various leaders and organizations in Arab countries—such as the Lebanese DRUZE leader JUNBLAT and his "Progressive Socialist Party"; Iraqi President Aref, 1963–1966; Sudan's NUMEIRI, 1969–1985; the Algerian FRONT DE LIBÉRATION NATIONALE (FLN), especially in its first stages under BEN BELLA; radical independent opposition members of the National Assembly in KUWAIT. Even LIBYA's QADHAFI, whose doctrine is quite different from Nasserism, was a fervent admirer of Nasser and would probably describe himself as his disciple. Nasserism is still said to exert some influence, despite its general decline in the Arab world, mainly in Egypt itself—where it is imbued with a certain nostalgia and absorbs feelings of discontent with the post-Nasserist regime and present conditions.

NATEK-NOURI, HOJJAT-OL-ESLAM ALI AKBAR (b. 1943) An Iranian clergyman and politician, Speaker of the Majlis (the Iranian Parliament) and the main contendant for the post of President of the state in the elections of May 1979. Natek-Nouri was born in the town of Nour in the district

of Mazanderan near the CASPIAN SEA. At the age of fifteen he moved to the town of QOM to complete his religious studies. In 1963 he made a speech against the Shah's regime, and after that was arrested several times. In 1978 he escaped to SYRIA and LEBANON. After the Islamic revolution of 1979 he was appointed representative of KHOMEINI to a development fund. In 1979 he was elected to the Majlis. In 1981 he was appointed Minister of the Interior for four years. In 1993 he was once again elected to the Majlis and tried to strengthen his position as one of the most noted clerics in the conservative camp. He is considered close to KHAMENEI, and was viewed as his candidate for President in the May 1997 elections. However, despite the wide support which he received from the clergy, Natek-Nouri won only twenty-five percent of the votes.

NATIONAL FRONT OF IRAN (Jebhe-ye Melli-e Iran) A coalition of parties established in October 1949, when for the first time a group of Iranian politicians and intellectuals marched towards the King's palace and demanded respect for civil rights and the Shah's obedience by the instructions of the Constitution. The group was headed by Dr. Muhammad MOSSADDEQ, a nationalist statesman, known for his opposition of Reza Shah, founder of the Pahlavi dynasty. The Front was comprised at first of a coalition, which included the Hezb-e Iran (The Iran Party), Hezb-e Mellat-e Iran (The Iranian Nation Party), Jame'e-ye Mojahedin-e Eslam (Society of Islamic Combatants) and Hezb-e Zahmatkeshan-e Iran (The Toilers' Party). This Front, which represented a moderate nationalist ideology, was the only competitor of the revolutionary-Communist TUDEH PARTY. Upon the appointment of Mossaddeq as Prime Minister in 1951, the Front's popularity reached its peak. However, the fall of Mossaddeq was a severe blow to the Front, from which it was unable to recover until the eve of the Islamic revolution. The Front renewed its semi-overt activity in 1978, but it was not a crystallized body and did not have an energetic leadership acceptable to all its sections. Upon the renewal of its activities, the Front demanded the implementation of political reforms; an undertaking by the Shah not to diverge from the limitations of the constitution; respect for civil rights and the running of an independent and nationalist foreign policy. However, very rapidly the Front became a follower

of KHOMEINI and lost the arena to the extremist clergymen. Prominent personalities in the Front refused the Shah's invitation to accept the premiership. The leader of the Front, Karim SANJABI gave in to Khomenei's demands to bring down the regime, and Dr. Shahpur BAKHTIAR, who had accepted the invitation of the Shah to establish a government, was excluded from the Front and boycotted.

In the beginning, the revolutionary regime took steps to weaken the Front and blur Mossaddeq's contribution to the nationalization of the oil industry in Iran and the struggle against the Shah. Sanjabi was deposed after several months from the post of Foreign Minister of the provisional government of the revolution, and later on was forced to leave Iran. Other leaders of the movement died or were forced to leave Iran. The only one who still operates in Iran in a semi-overt manner is Dariush Foruhar, leader of the Iranian Nation Party. He too operates under strict limitations. In the Iranian dispersion the Front broke up into several sections and no longer carries out any significant activities.

NATIONAL LIBERATION FRONT (NLF) FOR OCCUPIED SOUTH YEMEN

Militant nationalist underground and guerrilla organization in ADEN and South Arabia (later SOUTH YEMEN). Based mainly on the tribal hinterland of Aden, the NLF was founded in 1963, with Qahtan al-Sha'bi as its main leader. It was considered the strongest group in the nationalist rebellion that errupted in October 1963 and intermittently continuing until independence was gained in 1967. In 1966 the NLF joined a roof-organization, FLOSY, but it seceded the same year, re-establishing itself as a separate organization. In 1967 it gained increased authority of the South Arabian principalities, defeating both FLOSY and the sheikhs' and princes' armed forces. This forced the British to transfer authority to the NLF (and not to the princes, as planned, or to FLOSY).

In November 1967 the NLF formed the ruling group, single party and government of the new People's Republic of South Yemen, with Qahtan al-Sha'bi as President. Although at first sometimes supported by EGYPT (which in general preferred FLOSY), the NLF had been closely associated with, and influenced by, the Arab Nationalist Movement (*Harakat al-Qawmiyyin al-Arab*, seeARAB NATIONALISM) and its increasingly Leninist-Maoist ideas. From

1967 it veered further to the left, gradually becoming a Moscow-guided Communist Party (though for some years there was a struggle between RUSSIA-oriented and CHINA-oriented factions). In October 1978 the NLF, still the ruling single party, renamed itself "Yemen Socialist Party" (for the factional struggles within the NLF/YSP and the coups they engendered, see SOUTH YEMEN).

NESTORIANS see ASSYRIANS.

NETANYAHU, BINYAMIN (b. 1949–) Israeli politician, leader of the *Likud* Party since 1993, Israel's ninth Prime Minister; the first Prime Minister to be born after the establishment of the state and the first to be directly elected. Netanyahu was born to a Revisionist family in Tel Aviv. As a child and youth he lived with his family in the US (1956–1958 and 1963–1967). He returned to ISRAEL to serve in the Israel Defence Force (IDF) in the years 1967–1972, and reached the rank of captain in an elite unit. After concluding his military service Netanyahu returned to the US. There he received a first degree in Architecture and a second degree in Business Administration at Massachusetts Institute of Technology, and started working for the Boston Consultant Group. At the same time, he engaged in propaganda activities in the US on behalf of the State of Israel. After his brother Jonathan (Yonni) was killed in the course of the "Operation Entebbe," in which Israeli hostages were released (1976). Netanyahu returned to Israel and began to advocate international cooperation in fighting terrorism. In 1980 he set up and headed the Jonathan Institute for the Study of Terrorism, and started working as marketing manager in a JERUSALEM based furniture company. In 1982–1984 he served in the Israeli Embassy in Washington under Ambassador Moshe Arens, and later as Israeli Ambassador to the UN. In this capacity he, *inter alia* insisted on the opening of files on Nazi war criminals held in the UN archives, and frequently appeared in the American media to explain Israeli positions.

In 1988 Netanyahu was elected to the twelfth Knesset on the *Likud* list, and served as Deputy Minister of Foreign Affairs under Moshe Arens. During this period he expressed support for the idea of "Jordan is Palestine". Following the fall of the National Unity Government in March 1990 he was appointed Deputy Minister in the Prime Minister's Office and in this capacity participated in the Madrid Conference (see ARAB-ISRAEL PEACEMAKING), where he was Israel's main spokesman.

Netanyahu was one of the few staunch supporters in the *Likud* of instituting the system of direct elections for the Premiership in Israel (see ISRAEL) and after the Labor victory in the elections to the thirteenth Knesset in 1992, supported the institution of primaries for the election of the *Likud* chairman and candidate for the Premiership. In the *Likud* primaries for the leadership, which were held in March 1993, Netanyahu was elected by a majority of 52.1%. In this period he expressed hawkish views, and spoke in favor of massive privatization of government-owned companies and state lands. Netanyahu ran in the elections for the Premiership in May 1996 under the slogan of "Peace with Security" against Labor's Shimon PERES, and received 50.49% of the votes. Within two weeks of the elections he formed a government with all the religious parties, the new immigrants party *Yisrael Be'aliya* and the Third Way. Despite his reservations on recognition of the PALESTINE LIBERATION ORGANIZATION (PLO) and the Oslo Process, Netanyahu met with Yasser ARAFAT in September 1996 and his government signed the Hebron Agreement in January 1997 (see ARAB-ISRAEL PEACEMAKING). Netanyahu was involved in the unfortunate short lived appointment of Ronnie Bar-On as Attorney General in January 1997, and though it was decided not to indict Netanyahu, he was severely criticized for his decision making. Netanyahu's leadership remains controvertial both within the coalition and in the opposition.

NEUTRALISM Neutrality in time of war— an accepted and well-defined concept of International Law—was practised in World War II by the Arab states that were independent at the time: EGYPT, IRAQ, SAUDI ARABIA and Yemen. However, as an allied victory became certain, three of them joined the Allies. Iraq declared war in January 1943, Egypt in February 1945, and Saudi Arabia proclaimed its "adhesion" to the Allies in March 1945. None of them participated in actual war operations against the "Axis" powers.

Neutralism—as a concept or a general inclination (which would not automatically prescribe actual neutrality in time of war)—is quite a different issue. The desire to avoid involvement in the struggle of

great powers and power blocs is natural for small states and was indeed practiced by many countries throughout history, long before the term Neutralism became widespread. Neutralism as a concept—for which soon the term "non-alignment" was preferred—was born after World War II, as a growing number of Asian and African countries became independent. Several statesmen stood at its cradle. The man who gave the notion currency was India's Jawaharlal Nehru, in close alliance with Tito of Yugoslavia and Egypt's ABDEL NASSER. In 1949–1950, ISRAEL, too, inclined to Neutralism—but was rebuffed by the nascent non-aligned camp and anyway switched to a more pronounced pro-Western attitude from about 1950.

The new Neutralism added several new dimensions to the natural desire to avoid involvement in power blocs. Its sponsors argued that Neutralism was a particularly appropriate stance for the newly independent states of Asia and Africa, and gave it a sharp edge against COLONIALISM—i.e., against the former Western rulers, now seen by many as aspiring to "neo-colonialist" control (while most of them ignored the colonialist aspects of RUSSIA's acquisition of and rule in its Asian parts). Neutralism thus acquired a distinct anti-Western hue and the countries professing it were closer to the Soviet bloc than to the American-led Western one. This tendency was enhanced by the attitude of the West. Both power blocs at first disdained Neutralism; but the Soviet bloc soon came around to favor and support it. Nonetheless the UNITED STATES OF AMERICA in the 1950s condemned Neutralism and thought it immoral (e.g., J.F. Duller), changing its views much later. The fathers of Neutralism, and particularly Nehru, also endowed their Neutralism with a moral dimension. They considered it the proper, the "right," doctrine for Third World countries and were highly critical of countries linked to the great powers, and especially to the US.

The leftist-"progressive" Arab states were among the first to adopt the new Neutralism. Egypt's Nasser was among its sponsors and its main protagonist among the Arab state, naming his version "Positive Neutralism," i.e., emphasizing active policies and doctrines of his own rather than passive-negative neutrality in relation to the powers. The other leftist Arab states—in the 1950s mainly SYRIA and Iraq, later also ALGERIA, Yemen, SUDAN, LIBYA—soon joined the Neutralism camp. (The rift between them and the conservative, Western-linked Arab states split the ARAB LEAGUE into rival camps.)

The Neutralism camp soon expanded to include more and more Asian and African countries—even states allied to the Soviet bloc or the West which would not fit into the original definition of Neutralism. Gradually, almost all Asian and African countries joined the Neutralist or non-aligned group, until membership of the group had grown from an original twenty-five to ninety-nine countries (plus two "Liberation Organizations"). The conservative Arab states were in the forefront of that quasi-neutralist stampede. Indeed, Saudi Arabia, MOROCCO and TUNISIA joined the neutralist camp right at its first fully-fledged Congress in 1961. JORDAN joined a little later, and by the mid-1960s all Arab states were members.

The neutralist group had no common policy on most world issues, except for its anti-colonial stance. In fact, Neutralism did not prescribe common policies, as it determined general attitudes only, leaving it to each country to interpret the principles of Neutralism in the light of its own circumstances and interests. However, as membership expanded until it included fully-fledged members of the Soviet bloc like North Vietnam and North Korea (since 1975) and allies of the US, both South Vietnam and its Communist Vietcong rebels (since 1972–1973), the group became less and less cohesive and its members took different and conflicting positions on most controversial international problems, such as Korea, Vietnam, the Congo, Cambodia, and Afghanistan. In fact, within the Neutralist bloc there emerged a leftist, pro-Soviet camp, a Western-inclined one, and a "neutral" one in the center. Yet, as to rhetoric and verbal declarations and resolutions, the left-inclined camp retained the upper hand. Concerning the ARAB-ISRAEL CONFLICT, the neutralist group fully supported the Arab side (including countries that maintained friendly relations with Israel).

No neutralist country takes a favorable view of Neutralism or non-alignment when its own interests are concerned. India, for example, the leading proponent of Neutralism, bitterly resents neutralist positions taken even by friendly countries with regard to its border dispute with China or the problem of Kashmir. Nor do neutralist IRAN and Iraq accept a neutralist position in the war between them.

In its first years the non-aligned group of nations was content with informal meetings of its leaders or envoys, mainly at the UN during its General Assembly. Nor did it establish a formal organization in later years either. But the BANDUNG CONFERENCE of Asian and African states (1955) was to a certain extent a meeting of neutralist countries. Since then, the non-aligned group has institutionalized, in an increasingly formal way, with regular meetings—both at the "summit" level of Heads of States and at the working level of Foreign Ministers. It has also established a permanent co-ordination bureau of a number of Foreign Ministers. Its first summit conference was held at Belgrade in September 1961, with twenty-five countries participating; similar meetings followed from time to time: Cairo 1964 (forty-six countries plus eleven observers), Lusaka 1970 (fifty-four countries, eight observers), Algiers 1973 (seventy-six countries), Colombo 1976 (eighty-five countries), Havana 1979 (ninety-six countries), Delhi 1983 (ninety-nine countries, and two organizations), Harare 1986 (same attendance). Various Afro-Asian organizations, such as the Afro-Asian Peoples' Solidarity Organization and similar bodies are also, in spirit and function, if not by definition, neutralist or non-aligned bodies.

NEUTRAL ZONES In British-led negotiations over the northern frontiers of Najd (later SAUDI ARABIA), in the early 1920s, large areas on the borders with IRAQ and KUWAIT remained in dispute. They were the domain of nomadic BEDUIN tribes who ignored boundaries and resisted centralized government control. It was therefore agreed, at a December 1922 meeting in Uqair between Sultan (later King) IBN SA'UD and Sir Percy Box, the British High Commissioner for Iraq, to set up two zones of neutral and common ground—one on the Najd-Iraq frontier and the other on Najd and Kuwait. In the latter, OIL was later discovered and exploitation rights were given separately by Saudi Arabia and Kuwait to different companies. However, since no borders between the two concessions were delineated, the companies on the two sides had to cooperate. In 1964–1965 Saudi Arabia and Kuwait agreed to divide the neutral zones between them. An agreement on the border demarcation was finalized in December 1969, except for two offshore islands that remained in dispute. It was, however, agreed to let the oil companies continue their operations, and for the two countries to share the oil revenues. However, in some statistical and other data the neutral zone is still separately listed. Saudi Arabia and Iraq also agreed, in July 1975, to split the neutral zone between them with a straight line which would divide it into equal parts. Some border rectifications were agreed in 1981.

NILE see WATER POLITICS.

NON-ALIGNMENT see NEUTRALISM.

NON-CONVENTIONAL WEAPONS Weapons of mass destruction or non-conventional weapons refer to three types of weapons—nuclear, chemical and biological.

In some contexts the term is widened to cover not only the materials but also their means of delivery—usually referring to ballistic missiles. Despite the differences between these categories of weapons, their nature as "more deadly" than "conventional" is manifested by the growing tendency of the global community to ban or limit their use and proliferation by conventions, treaties and other forms of international regimes.

In the course of the 1980s, countries in the region have given non-conventional weapons (mainly chemical weapons and ballistic missiles) an important role in their strategic thought and practice due to domestic and external threats. These weapons are designed, acquired and stockpiled primarily for the purpose of terrorizing a civilian population. Without diminishing their possible offensive use, the proliferation of these weapons in the Middle East represents mainly a defensive application.

Nuclear and chemical weapons have played an important role in Middle East conflicts since the 1960s. Israel's alleged nuclear capability is said to have demonstrated its technological preponderance over its Arab neighbors. At the same time, IRAQ (before the GULF WAR) and SYRIA perceived their chemical capability as a major deterrent against Israeli attack. This suggests that these weapons might proliferate even more than they already have in the region. The other side of this grim prospect is that strategic thinking, in terms of deterrence and balance of terror, was responsible for the relative stability of the Cold War.

Chemical weapons were used extensively in Europe in World War I. Since then they have been used occasionally, mostly in the Middle East and mostly against civilian populations (in Spanish MOROCCO in the 1920s, Yemen in the 1960s, Iraq in the 1980s), though also in the battlefields (during the IRAN-IRAQ WAR).

The development of chemical weapons in the Middle East is due to the escalation and intensity of regional conflicts, and the availability of production means. The production of chemical weapons in substantial quantities requires a good chemical industry, but is not very different in its methods and equipment, from what is needed to manufacture other organo-phosphorous compounds, like insecticides. Although chemical weapons are considered more deadly than conventional weapons, their lethality is comparable to that of conventional weapons. The lethal ability of chemical weapons is limited by various methods of defense and protection against them.

Chemical Weapons EGYPT was the first country in the Middle East to acquire and use chemical warfare capability. Between 1963 and 1967 Egyptian forces there conducted numerous attacks on the royalist rebels there, using mustard and phosgene. Egypt did not employ chemical weapons however, during the 1967 War—not even in an attempt to avoid its defeat. Formally, Egypt renounced using chemical weapons, but it is believed that Egypt retained and even improved its chemical weapon production capabilities.

Syria acquired its first chemical munitions from Egypt after 1967. Although Syria did not use them during the 1973 Arab-Israeli War, it began to consider them a major element of its strategic capabilities. Thus, Syria invested significant resources in acquiring the capabilities to produce various types of chemical agents and munitions. Currently Syria produces and stockpiles sarin nerve gas, and possibly VX nerve agent. Syria can produce air bombs, and has chemical warheads for its Scud-B and Scud-C missiles (ballistic missiles with ranges of 300 and 500 km).

On the eve of the 1991 Gulf War, Iraq had the largest military stockpile of chemical weapons. During its war with Iran (1980–1988) Iraq employed mustard and sarin in several battles. It also used nerve agents against the KURDS in northern Iraq (in the village Halabja hundreds of villagers were killed).

Iraq's chemical infrastructure was destroyed by the United Nations'

Special Committee (UNSCOM) following the Gulf War, under UN Security Council Resolution 687. UNSCOM's inspectors found tens of thousands of munitions (rockets, bombs, artillery shells and some thirty warheads for Scud missiles), and hundreds of tons of chemical agents in bulk.

Currently Iraq is under strict UN supervision, but it is widely believed that Iraq could resume its capability within months, once the sanction regime is lifted.

Other countries in the region are alleged to have chemical weapons as well: Iran is believed to have substantial capability to produce them, due to its advanced chemical industry. LIBYA is also believed to have chemical capability; it has made at least two attempts to build large chemical weapons production facilities—first in Rabita (in the late 1980s) and later in Tarhuna.

Nuclear Weapons Production of nuclear weapons has always been an enormous undertaking for a state. It is probably impossible to "construct a bomb in the basement." The only state in the Middle East which is alleged to have nuclear weapons is Israel. Its nuclear program began in the 1950s, with essential assistance from FRANCE. Following the SUEZ CANAL crisis in 1956 France agreed to sell Israel a nuclear reactor, and allegedly a plutonium extraction plant. Israel probably crossed "the nuclear line" in the late 1960s, and at present is believed to have up to 100 nuclear devices. Israel never acknowledged its nuclear status, and maintains a policy of "nuclear opacity".

The second nuclear aspirant was Iraq. Its first attempt to acquire nuclear capability was frustrated in 1981, when Israel destroyed Osiraq—its French made nuclear reactor. Apparently Iraq launched a large, clandestine program, and erected several plants for the enrichment of uranium, using different methods. Following the second Gulf War in 1991 the UN Security Council imposed a tough regime of sanctions on Iraq. All its installations were demolished. In 1997 Iraq was still under constant supervision of UNSCOM and the International Atomic Energy Agency (IAEA) which prevent any further development. It is believed that once these sanctions are raised, Iraq could resume its program, using its existing expertise.

Iran is the third country that is believed to pursue an offensive nuclear plan. In the early 1990s it launched an ambitious nuclear energy program meant, it was widely believed, to establish a firm technological infrastructure for nuclear weapon development. The program was scaled down, probably due to financial difficulties and currently only one power reactor is under construction, under supervision of the IAEA, which gave Iran a clear "card of conduct". It is also believed that the actual nuclear weapon program follows the "uranium enrichment track," and that for that purpose Iran has established clandestine uranium enrichment plants. Western intelligence agencies believe this could equip Iran with a nuclear device within five to ten years.

During the past twenty years some other countries in the region were considered "nuclear aspirants": ALGERIA, Libya and Syria, but none has the technological capability.

Biological Weapons Biological weapons are often considered to be more lethal than chemical weapons. This is true if one measures the lethality of various agents in the laboratory. Their actual efficacy would be influenced with scores of different factors (such as the method of dispersal, weather conditions and measures of defense) which would make the actual outcome highly indeterminate.

There are no proven instances of the use of biological weapons in warfare. Production of some types of biological weapons is very similar to the production of vaccines in the pharmaceutical industry.

Iraq is the only country in the region that has proven biological warfare capability. For five years Iraq denied all allegations about its pre-1991 capabilities. UNSCOM inspectors, in spite of their heavy suspicions, were unable to find any evidence. Then, in August 1995, following the defection of two Iraqi generals, it admitted to having a large biological weapons program. The program included the development of various micro-organisms, like Anthrax, several types of toxins (Butolinum, Aflatoxin, Mycotoxins) and viruses. The program includes studies of mass production of the agents, various delivery and dispersion methods and the development of various types of delivery systems, including bombs and warheads for ballistic missiles.

Other countries in the region have been suspected of holding a biological weapon capability. Among these are Syria, Egypt and Iran.

NUCLEAR WEAPONS see NON-CONVENTIONAL WEAPONS.

NUHAYAN, AL The ruling clan of ABU DHABI in TRUCIAL OMAN; since 1971 the UNITED ARAB EMIRATES (UAE). The ruler and head of the clan during recent decades is Sheikh Zayed ibn Sultan al-Nuhayan (1918). Sheikh Zayed was for twenty years, 1946–1966, Governor of the sheikhdom's al-Ain district, with the oasis of al-BURAIMI at its center. In 1966, still under BRITAIN's Protectorate, he overthrew—reportedly with the encouragement of the British (then still the protecting power)—his brother Sheikh Shakhbut ibn Sultan. (He had ruled the sheikhdom since 1928 and was considered an obstacle to development and progress.) He then became the ruler of Abu Dhabi. He played a major role in the negotiations toward the federation of the Trucial Coast sheikhdoms as the UAE and in efforts to overcome the rivalries and disputes between the various sheikhs (chief among which was his own clan's near-permanent rivalry with the sheikhs al-MAKTUM; the rulers of DUBAI). With the foundation of the UAE in 1971, Sheikh Zayed became President of the Federation, remaining also ruler of Abu Dhabi. He was re-elected since for successive five-year terms. Sheikh Zayed has been pressing, with gradual, slow success, for stronger federal institutions—with the main resistance coming from the ruler of Dubai.

NUMEIRI, (MUHAMMAD) JA'FAR (b. 1930) Sudanese officer and politician, ruler of SUDAN 1969–1985. After graduation from the pre-independence Military College of Khartoum in 1952, Numeiri served in the infantry and armor units. He was suspected of being involved in anti-government agitation and heading a subversive group of Free Officers. He was suspended for this in 1963, and arrested several times (1957, 1959, 1965), but reinstated each time. After his rehabilitation of 1966 he completed a course at an American military college and was later made Brigadier-General.

In May 1969 Numeiri seized power in a military coup. He dismissed the Presidential Council and the government; dissolved Parliament and banned all political parties. He formed a Revolutionary Council as the supreme state organ, which he headed. He also appointed himself Commander-in-Chief and Defense Minister, and then in October 1969, Prime Minister. Numeiri had to balance between conservative groups (such as the two great orders, the MAHDIYYA and the Khatmiyya—both of which had little sympathy for his regime); the Army (on which he relied), and the Communists (whose main faction he half-suppressed, while letting other factions participate in his government). In March 1970 he suppressed *al-Ansar*, the militant organization of the Mahdiyya. In July 1971 he was overthrown in a coup headed by leftist officers whom he had purged in 1970; but a counter-coup returned him to power three days later (allegedly with Egyptian and Libyan help). He then brutally suppressed the Communists.

In September 1971 Numeiri was elected President, the only candidate in a plebiscite. He was re-elected in 1977 and 1983. As President he also retained the Premiership. In 1972 he founded a single party on the Egyptian pattern, the Sudan Socialist Union, heading its political bureau. From 1972 he also convened a People's Council, or National Assembly. In March 1972 he reached an agreement with the South Sudan African rebels by conceding a wide local-regional autonomy—his major domestic achievement. However, his regime did not attain real stability. The single party did not take roots. He frequently changed his Vice-President and the heads of the Defense establishment. A National Front, comprising both the Mahdiyya with its Umma Party and its adversary, the National Unionists, supported by the Khatmiyya, harassed his regime. They did this from bases in LIBYA. The settlement with the South Sudanese rebels turned sour and he began reneging on it. The economic situation deteriorated continuously (for these developments see SUDAN). Numeiri's foreign policy was also somewhat erratic. In 1969–1970 he planned to join a Federation with EGYPT and Libya; but in 1971 he opted out. However he did foster close relations with Egypt, signing a Defense Agreement in 1977; an accord on gradual integration in 1982 and instituting a joint Nile Valley Parliament.

In the early years of his regime he established close relations with the Soviet Union. In the mid-1970s he formed close relations with SAUDI ARABIA, and the USA. The West came to regard him, in his later years, with sympathy. Numeiri gradually cultivated an alliance with fundamentalist Islamic groups, chiefly the MUSLIM BROTHERHOOD. In September 1983 he decreed the full implementation of the code of punishments of Islamic law, the SHARI'A—a measure that aroused strong opposition.

A new rebellion of the South Sudanese Africans also erupted. It may be reasonably assumed that these two developments hastened Numeiri's fall. He was overthrown in April 1985 in a coup mounted by the army in collaboration with his civilian political foes.

Numeiri escaped to Egypt and received political asylum there, despite his successors' repeated demands for his extradition.

A decision to try him in *absentia* was reported, but not implemented.

NUSSEIRIS, NOSSAIRIS see ALAWIS.

OAPEC see ORGANIZATION OF ARAB PETROLEUM-EXPORTING COUNTRIES.

ORGANIZATION OF ARAB PETROLEUM EXPORTING-COUNTRIES OAPEC Established in January 1968, OAPEC soon included ALGERIA, BAHRAIN, EGYPT, IRAQ, KUWAIT, LIBYA, QATAR, SAUDI ARABIA, SYRIA, the UNITED ARAB EMIRATES (UAE) and TUNISIA—i.e., all oil-producing Arab countries except OMAN and MOROCCO; four of these countries were not members of OPEC (Bahrain, Egypt, Syria and Tunisia).

Egypt's membership was suspended in 1979 and restored in 1989; Tunisia seceded in 1986. For the circumstances and aims of OAPEC's creation and its policies—especially during the crisis of 1973—see OIL.

Apart from its mainly political aims, OAPEC has not been very active. It has been instrumental mainly in two specific projects: the foundation of an Arab tanker fleet in 1973 (established, eventually, by several Arab countries, not by OAPEC and not as an all-Arab venture); and the construction of a large dry dock in Bahrain, inaugurated in December 1977 (bitterly opposed by DUBAI who was building its own dry dock and wanted all-Arab support to be focused on its project).

OCTOBER WAR (1973) see ARAB-ISRAEL CONFLICT.

OIL The Middle East and North Africa has approximately 700,000 million barrels of oil reserves, equal to about seventy percent of the world total. Half of the global reserves are concentrated in four countries in the Gulf (SAUDI ARABIA, IRAQ, KUWAIT and IRAN), with Saudi Arabia possessing one-qaurter of the world's oil reserves, more than any other country in the world. With such oil reserves Gulf states enjoy (at the early 1990s' rates) a long production expectancy: Saudi Arabia and Iran—65–70 years; Iraq and Kuwait145–150 years;

EGYPT—25 years; ALGERIA—30 years; and LIBYA—40 years. The size and production expectancy of oil (and gas) deposits, especially in the Gulf, imply that the region will continue to be critical to the world oil market.

The development of the oil industry in the Middle East, which began in 1901, was based on concessions granted to foreign companies—a pattern that was terminated by 1976. There were mainly eight multinational oil companies: Anglo-Iranian (British Petroleum), Royal Dutch-Shell, Compagnie Française des Pétroles and five American companies. These companies dominated the oil industry, determined production rates and set prices. The period was characterized by three major, and at times parallel, struggles. The first was between the powers, through their companies, to obtain concessions. The main struggle, between Great Britain and the US, came to an end in 1954 when the US obtained a forty percent share in what was then the exclusively British oil concession in Iran, giving the US the lion's share in Middle East oil. The second rivalry was among major oil companies. This ended in 1928 with the "Red Line Agreement," which admitted American companies to the British-led Iraq Petroleum Company, obliging them not to seek concessions on their own in the former Ottoman territory. This created an international cartel which virtually controlled the free world oil supplies and set their prices. The third contention—the longest and most complex one—was between the oil producing countries and their foreign concessionary companies. This came to an end in 1976 when practically all the region's oil industry was nationalized. At first, the Middle Eastern countries did not develop their oil resources themselves due to a lack of technological knowledge and financial resources and because of international political conditions. Due to Western domination, or influence, the terms of the concessions they granted were set by the foreign companies in their own favor.

As the oil producing countries began to realize the enormous value of their oil, they started a long battle with the foreign companies to obtain basic modifications in the concession terms, which originally granted the companies, in addition to the right of exploiting the oil, extraordinary privileges. The main targets of this campaign were higher royalty payments and a reduction of the concession areas. But the oil producing countries made slow progress. The first major breakthrough occurred in 1950–1954 when royalties were raised to fifty percent. To guarantee stability of income the two sides agreed on a

posted price for stated periods of time. The various companies also agreed to relinquish, at set periods, considerable parts of the original concession areas.

The early 1950s were perhaps the golden age of relations between the producing countries and the concessionary companies. Demand for oil was high and the revenues of both the countries and the companies were steadily mounting. However, at the end of the decade a recession set in and demand for oil dropped. The companies reduced the price of oil by ten percent early in 1959 and by approximately another ten percent late in 1960. This twenty percent cut in the countries' revenue caused serious difficulties in their development programs. But acting alone, none of them were powerful enough to force the companies to restore the price cuts.

In 1948 the Venezuelan government introduced an income tax law giving the state fifty percent of oil companies' profits. In 1950 and 1951, Saudi Arabia, Iraq and Kuwait introduced similar tax regimes. As a result, the producing countries' revenue per barrel increased from an average of twenty-two US cents to eighty cents. This arrangement did not,

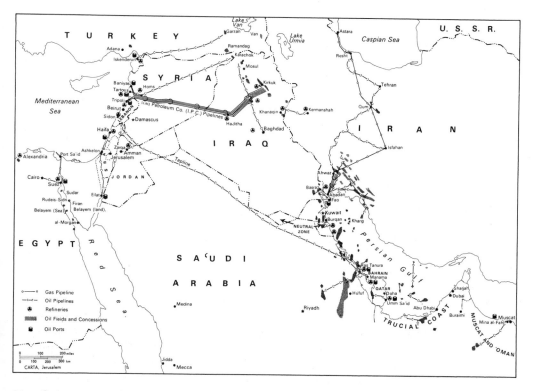

Map of oil resources in the Middle East

however, apply in Iran. In 1941, following the German invasion of the USSR, the British and Soviets invaded Iran and deposed Reza Shah PAHLAVI who had expressed sympathy for the Germans. He was replaced by his son Muhammad Reza PAHLAVI. The subordination of the country to foreign powers intensified Iranian national feelings, which soon after the end of the war manifested themselves in claims for higher revenues of Iran's produced oil. In 1949 the Anglo-Iranian Oil Company and the Iranian government reached an agreement which gave the latter royalties and profit sharing terms as good as those that applied in neighboring Arab states. The Iranian National Assembly rejected the agreement and the chairman of the Parliamentary Oil Committee, Dr. Muhammad MOSSADDEQ, discredited the government on this issue. In December 1950, the Iranian government was forced to renounce the deal signed with the Anglo-Iranian Oil Company. The company suggested a 50/50 deal, but in February 1951 Mossaddeq called for nationalization of the company. Iran was lurching toward chaos and on 1 May 1951, the Shah was forced to give his assent to nationalization and to the appointment of Mossaddeq as Prime Minister. Over the next two years, Mossaddeq rejected compromises offered by the oil company and Iranian oil exports were embargoed on international markets. The Iranian economy, denied its main source of foreign exchange, faced collapse. In July 1953, having failed to dismiss Mossaddeq, the Shah was forced to flee to Rome. Mossaddeq was overthrown in a coup, which was backed by the US and the Shah returned (see IRAN). Nationalization remained in place but the National Iranian Oil Corporation, as it became, granted a lease, or concession to a consortium of foreign oil companies. This represented the reassertion by the multinational oil companies of their dominance in international oil markets, which sustained for twenty more years.

OPEC. On 14 September 1960, the Middle East producers and Venezuela established the Organization of Petroleum Exporting Countries (OPEC), believing that by uniting they could force the companies to restore the price cuts and grant them other concessions. During the 1960s the companies continued to determine both production ratios and price levels, and OPEC gained only minor concessions. OPEC could not force the companies to grant its

price demands because the demand for oil was low during the 1960s and because the greatest share of the Middle East concessions was in the hands of the major American oil companies which also produced US oil and thus had alternative oil sources and continued to dominate the international oil markets.

In 1970 prosperity returned to Europe and the US and the demand for oil rose rapidly. Yet for the first time US oil production began to drop and US reserves declined swiftly. As a result, the power of the companies began to dwindle and that of the producing countries was dawning. In 1971 a five-year agreement was signed in Tehran between the PERSIAN GULF oil producers and twenty-two oil companies, providing for an immediate price increase of thirty-eight cents a barrel, a tax increase bringing the tax up to fifty-five percent and an additional price increase of 2.5% per annum to compensate for inflation and devaluation. The revenue for the Gulf countries in 1971 was estimated at 1,400 million dollars more than in 1970, and the total additional income for the five-year period at 1,700 million dollars.

The producing countries formed two groups: the Persian Gulf group, and the Mediterranean group under the leadership of Libya. Each group negotiated separately with the respective companies. This developed into a "leapfrogging" technique as the gains achieved by one group became the minimum demand of the other. Being a late-comer to oil exploitation, Libya's concessionary pattern was the grant of small areas to many companies, among them small independent ones with no other oil sources. Thus, Libya could play the small companies against the multinationals, to whom Libyan oil was of little importance, and obtain better terms than the Gulf producers even before 1971.

The results of the agreements signed in Tehran and Tripoli opened a new era in the relations between the producing countries and the companies. The companies appeared weak, almost helpless, and submitted to all the demands of the producer governments, while the governments displayed growing power, self-confidence and inflexibility, and were prepared to continue the struggle. When the US devalued the dollar late in 1971 by about ten percent, OPEC asked for an equivalent increase in price—in spite of the five-year term of the agreements and the 2.5% compensation for inflation and devaluation. An agreement was signed on 20 January 1972 for an immediate increase of 8.49% in posted prices. This agreement became known as Geneva I.

The producers also demanded participation in the foreign companies. This was to be the first step toward the ultimate takeover of the industry. Some of the early concessions enabled the producing country to acquire up to twenty percent of the shares of the foreign companies, but until 1969 the producers did not take advantage of these provisions. However, at the June 1968 OPEC conference the Saudi Oil Minister Ahmad Zaki Yamani raised the issue, and negotiations began.

After many conferences and warnings by the Saudi Oil Minister that the only alternative to participation was nationalization, an agreement was reached with Saudi Arabia, Kuwait, QATAR, BAHRAIN and the UNITED ARAB EMIRATES (UAE) at the end of 1972 that provided for an immediate acquisition by producers of twenty-five percent of the companies in January 1973, with five percent more each year from 1979 to 1982, and six percent in 1983, which would give the governments fifty-one percent control of the companies.

OPEC's demands continued. In February 1973 the US devalued the dollar again by 11.11%. The oil companies promptly raised the posted prices in accordance with the January 1972 formula, but the producers refused to accept the companies' offer. A new agreement of 1 June 1973—the Geneva II Agreement—provided for an 11.9% increase in price with a new formula for future contingencies. The Tehran and Tripoli agreements, although contracted for five years, were no longer valid, and the technique applied was "leapfrogging" between the Gulf group under the leadership of Saudi Arabia through its Oil Minister, Ahmad Zaki Yamani, and the Mediterranean group under the leadership of Libya's Colonel QADHAFI.

The next objective for the producing countries was to set the price and the production rates unilaterally, and fully nationalize the industry. In August 1973, Libya nationalized fifty-one percent of the concessions of the American companies. In October 1973 OPEC asked for a fifty percent increase in the posted price. The companies refused and the meeting was closed. Eight days later the Gulf OPEC unilaterally increased posted prices by seventy percent. This was a great triumph over the companies,

and the beginning of a grave crisis which coincided with the ARAB-ISRAEL CONFLICT of October 1973.

Political Aspects The leaders of the Arab states, realizing the political potential of Arab oil resources, soon attempted to involve Arab oil in the political struggle. But the major oil producers, Saudi Arabia, Kuwait and Iraq, resisted these attempts to turn their chief economic asset into a football in the political game. However, when the June 1967 Six-Day War swept the Arab world, the Arab oil producers and transporters proclaimed, on 5 June, a boycott to stop the flow of oil to any country that supported ISRAEL. The negative economic consequences for the Arab oil countries were soon apparent, and by late June the major oil producing countries virtually revoked their boycott on oil exports, except for the United States and Britain. However, a struggle erupted between the main oil producers and the radical Arab states, especially Egypt, over their official revocation. Only after Saudi Arabia, Kuwait and Libya undertook to extend an annual payment of 135 million dollars to Egypt and Jordan—the victims of the war—did the ARAB SUMMIT CONFERENCE of September 1967 resolve to resume the pumping of oil, regardless of Iraqi and Algerian objections (that later legitimized their rejection to share the burden of payments to the confrontation states). Thus the three major Arab producers were doubly hurt by the boycott as they lost revenue and had to pay those who had lost the war. However, these payments—the Khartoum Financial Aid—also served the oil producers' interest in securing legitimacy and prestige in the regional Arab system, giving them a leverage on Egypt they had never enjoyed before.

To prevent a recurrence of such contingencies, Saudi Arabia, Kuwait and Libya established the Organization of Arab Petroleum Exporting Countries (OAPEC) in January 1968. Its' stated objective was the protection of the economic character of oil policies, and the protection of foreign investments in oil development. They intended to restrict membership to insure the preservation of OAPEC' s aims. However, after the Qadhafi revolution in Libya (1969) its nature changed. Membership requirements were modified and the radical Arab states became members. Instigated by radical Libya and Algeria, by March 1972 OAPEC was transformed into the antithesis of its original aims. It became an instrument for the use of Arab oil resources as a political weapon in the

CRUDE OIL PRODUCTION
(millions of tons p.a.)

	1950	1960	1970	1980	1985	1995
United Arab Emirates		-	37.6	82.5	54.5	112.8
Algeria	-	8.6	46.4	48	50	56.8
Bahrain	1.51	2.3	3.8	2.5	2.5	-
Egypt	2.2	3.1	19.0	30	45	46.0
Iran	-	53.4	191.4	83.1	112.5	182.2
Iraq	7.0	47.6	76.4	138	71.5	26.4
Kuwait	17.2	81.9	137.3	85	53.5	104.4
Libya	-	-	159.6	86	55.5	67.9
Oman	-	-	16.4	14	25	43.2
Qatar	1.7	8.2	17.0	23	15	21.3
Saudi Arabia	27.3	62.1	175.7	495	170	426.5
Syria	-	-	4.5	8.5	8.5	31.7
Tunisia	-	0.2	4.1	5.5	5.5	4.3
Total	57	267	893	1,102	669	1123.5

ARAB-ISRAEL CONFLICT, by escalating threats to cease oil supply to the Western world due to its support of Israel. Qadhafi, and as of late 1972 Saudi King FEISAL- were particularly active in exerting pressures on Black African states to sever diplomatic relations with Israel.

On 17 October 1973 OAPEC proclaimed an Arab oil embargo with an immediate five percent production cutback, and a guarantee to cut the same percentage each month until Israel had withdrawn completely from all the Arab territories occupied in June 1967 and the legal rights of the Palestinian people were restored. At first the embargo was imposed on virtually all consuming countries. Later they were classified into three groups: friendly countries would get their regular supplies; neutral countries would be subject to the monthly cuts; and to the hostile countries, the US and the Netherlands a total embargo would be applied. However, the embargo was not implemented as planned due to sharp divisions and economic competition among the members. The level of its percentage cuts and the classification of countries changed each time OAPEC met. Above all, following the Israeli-Egyptian disengagement of forces in January 1974 the Arab oil block, represented by Saudi Arabia, came under heavy American pressure to lift the embargo as a prerequisite for Washington's continued mediation of a parallel settlement on the Israeli-Syrian front. Finally, the embargo was lifted on 18 March 1974.

In October 1973, the Gulf countries raised the posted prices of crude oil by an average of fifty percent and in December 1973 by a further fifty percent. The price rose as a result from an average of three dollars a barrel at the beginning of October to twelve dollars a barrel at the end of December. The producers also pressed the companies concerning participation percentages, royalty levels, and taxation rates. By 1974 the participation percentage was raised to sixty percent, first by Kuwait—royalties were raised from 12.5% to 20%— and the tax rate was increased to 85%. By 1976, practically all the producing countries had gained full control of their oil resources. Some producers dismissed the foreign companies and operated the industries themselves, others retained the companies to operate the industries on a fee basis. In spite of conflicting interests and orientations, the producing countries now dictated, through OPEC, oil prices which they constantly raised, almost at will. As a result, wealth from the consumer countries was transferred to the producing countries. The latter, wielding the oil weapon, also seemed to have acquired the financial weapon by accumulating imaginary surpluses of "petrodollars" and there seemed to be no limit to their power. Each OPEC conference was anxiously watched to

CRUDE OIL PRODUCTION
(daily average in thousand barrels)

	1950	1960	1970	1980	1985	1995
United Arab Emirates		-	757	1,737	1,090	2,485
Algeria	-	183	980	960	1,000	1,325
Bahrain	30	45	76	55	50	105
Egypt	45	62	361	600	900	185
Iran	-	1,068	3,829	1,662	2,250	3,643
Iraq	140	972	1,560	2,645	1,430	545
Kuwait	344	1,692	2,372	1,700	1,070	2,015
Libya	-	-	3,32	1,750	1,110	1,415
Oman	-	-	323	285	500	870
Qatar	34	175	359	480	300	460
Saudi Arabia	547	1,314	3,548	9,900	3,400	8,885
Syria	-	-	90	165	170	610
Tunisia	-	3	87	110	120	90
Total	1,140	5,514	18,032	22,047	12,390	21,918

see how much the price would be raised. The consuming countries attempted to adopt measures to protect themselves. The US initiated a conference of the major consuming countries in February 1974, which set up the International Energy Agency (IEA).

To counteract the steady outflow of ever greater financial resources from the consuming to the producing countries (see Crude Oil ProductionTable), several recycling measures were developed: 1) the producing countries invested their surpluses in the consuming countries; 2) consumers increased exports to the producers, including sales of sophisticated technologies, arms and ammunition; 3) contracts from the producing countries for the implementation of gigantic development projects were obtained (Saudi Arabia allocated 144 billion dollars for its 1975–1980 development program). These recycling devices worked well. In 1977–1979 the financial flow from the Middle East oil countries to the US balanced the cash outflow from the US for oil imports. The high prices also seriously reduced demand for oil. A substantial drop in production first showed in 1975, after the price jumps in 1973–1974, and again in 1978. In both cases prices stabilized.

In 1979 a second oil crisis erupted. The Iranian revolution eliminated, at first, about 5 million barrels a day from the market. A new wave of panic buying engulfed the market, resulting in enormous price jumps. By March 1979 the price of Arabian Light oil went up to 14.55 dollars a barrel, against 12.70 dollars in 1978, and from then until October 1981 OPEC had no uniform price. Above an official bottom price every producing country set its own price, some reaching as high as 46 dollars a barrel. Saudi Arabia for reasons of its own interests, tried to stick to the official price of 14.59 dollars. However, in an effort to persuade the others to re-establish the uniform price, Saudi Arabia increased its price to 18 dollars, then 24 dollars 28 dollars and finally to 32 dollars. But each time Saudi Arabia raised its price, the others added the differential to their prices.

The consequences of this mad rush for higher prices were soon felt. The demand for oil began to fall rapidly in 1981 and by October the drop reached such proportions that the other OPEC members agreed to re-establish a uniform price at 34 dollars a barrel, provided Saudi Arabia also raised its price to 34 dollars. Saudi Arabia agreed and the uniform price was re-established. But the compromise failed; the demand continued to drop. OPEC's high prices also created a rival in the non-OPEC producers. While oil prices were low, the oil resources of several North Sea countries and others were not developed. However, when prices skyrocketed, a number of new producers entered the oil market and competed with the OPEC producers. For the same reason a number of alternatives to oil were activated, at first on a small scale.

With a glut forming in the world oil market the third oil crisis was setting in. OPEC's base was still limited to price control but when it was formed, Venezuela advocated production control as the second element of a cartel.

The Middle East producers however, refused to submit, as sovereigns, to the control of production. Now, with the growing supply and declining demand, OPEC was ready to attempt rationing production for its members. In March 1982 OPEC decided, for the first time, to control production and set a production ceiling of 18 million barrels a day, to defend the price at 34 dollars a barrel. But the glut continued. OPEC leaders blamed it on the increased production, which exceeded the set limit.

OPEC members produced more than their quotas, a tendency that resulted from the lengthy and costly IRAN-IRAQ WAR which involved not only the main disputing parties but the Gulf area as a whole. By the end of 1982 it became clear that production ceilings alone would not increase the demand for oil. Non-OPEC producers, especially Great Britain, lowered their prices by five dollars to about thirty dollars, while the OPEC price for Arabian Light was still thirty-four dollars. Consequently, in March 1983 OPEC decided to lower the price of Arabian Light to twenty-nine dollars a barrel. Yet demand continued to fall and the glut kept growing. Henceforth OPEC battled on two fronts: the non-OPEC producers must curtail production and maintain OPEC prices; and OPEC members must abide by OPEC's production quotas and prices. But OPEC lost out on both fronts. Cheating on both price and production rate was widely practiced, and members tried to overcome the restrictions of price and production levels. In desperation, OPEC reluctantly abandoned the uniform price in October 1985 and attempted to concentrate on production control.

Saudi Arabia was a victim of the situation. In 1982 it assumed the role of swing producer, agreeing to produce the quantity remaining after the fulfillment of all the other states' quotas. As a result, the Saudi share fell from about 8 million barrels a day in 1982 to about 2 million in August 1985. In mid-September 1985, Saudi Arabia's Oil Minister threatened both OPEC and non-OPEC producers with a price war which would bring down all producers.

At the same time Saudi Arabia gave up the role of swing producer and accepted a quota of about 4.35 million barrels a day. This created new difficulties in OPEC, for no member was prepared to reduce its quota.

OPEC's turning point came in December 1985. OPEC abandoned its position as the determiner of oil prices. While deciding to secure and defend for the orgainzation a fair share of the world oil market consistent with the necessary income for member countries' development, and maintaining a production quota, OPEC began, de facto, acting as the world swing producer, and its share of the world market dropped from about forty-five percent in 1970 and nearly two-thirds in 1979–1980, to thirty-two to thirty-five percent in the early and mid-1980s. OPEC's abandonment of price control and the threat of a price war caused oil prices throughout the world to tumble from about twenty-eight to twelve dollars a barrel. In spite of Saudi Arabia's threats and dire predictions in case the price of oil dropped to twenty dollars a barrel, the consuming world welcomed the reduced oil prices. No economic depressions set in, and the world's financial institutions did not collapse. During 1986 OPEC was bickering about quotas and ways of raising prices and by how much. Its members could not agree on any of the issues. Saudi Arabia's threat of a price war backfired, and King Fahd dismissed his Oil Minister Yamani, since 1962 a chief architect of OPEC.

During the first half of 1986, the oil price fell to below ten dollars a barrel. Some non-OPEC countries agreed to cooperate with the majority of OPEC members in reducing output, but disagreements within and outside the cartel prevented an agreement in the spring. In August OPEC members, with the exception of Iraq, agreed on a cut in production. Iraq insisted on parity with Iran, an issue that was to bedevil OPEC until late in 1988. As a result, oil prices rose to fifteen dollars a barrel and in December 1986, OPEC agreed on a fixed pricing system with a reference price of 18 dollars a barrel, and OPEC production for the first half of 1987 was set at 15.8 million barrels a day. During 1987 OPEC exceeded its production targets, thus undermining the relative stable oil price which prevailed in the first half of the year. In June 1987 a production ceiling of 16.6 million barrels a day was set, including Iraqi production, and intensive efforts were made to have OPEC member states comply with the organization's target. During the second half of the year however, production was still between 1 and 2 million barrels a day above the ceiling. By the second quarter of 1988, prices had fallen below fifteen dollars a barrel. Saudi Arabia and Iran had a total of 800,000 barrels a day in storage on tankers or overseas. Non-OPEC members once again offered to reduce promotion if OPEC would cooperate but Saudi Arabia refused and demanded that existing OPEC quotas should be more strictly enforced. In June, the previous production limit was rolled over for six months with the expectation that higher demand would result in an increase in prices. With the end of the Iran-Iraq War, in October 1988 the oil price fell to twelve dollars a barrel. OPEC member states, excluding Iraq, agreed to reduce output to 18.5 million barrels a day, including Iraqi production, from 1 January 1989. This compared with an estimated actual production level of 21 million dollars a day in the eight-year long Iran-Iraq War. In June 1989, with prices at eighteen dollars a barrel, OPEC ministers agreed to increase the production ceiling to 19.5 million barrels a day for the second half of the year. Kuwait and the UAE rejected the quotas implied in this ceiling and by September the ceiling was increased to 20.5 million barrels a day. In November a production level of 22 million barrels a day was agreed on for the first half of 1990. Production during the first half of 1990 was, once again, so high that prices declined. Although some production costs were implemented, the oil price was only fourteen dollars a barrel in June 1990. In July Iraq threatened to take military action against Kuwait unless it reduced input. OPEC agreed to raise prices to twenty-one dollars a barrel and to limit production to a total of 22.5 million barrels a day.

On 1 August 1990, Iraq invaded Kuwait. An international embargo was placed on Iraqi and Kuwaiti exports which had totaled 5 million barrels a day before the invasion. The oil price jumped to twenty-three dollars a barrel, but later in the month OPEC agreed on an increase in production, mainly implemented by Saudi Arabia, the UAE and Venezuela. Oil prices reached forty dollars a barrel in early October 1990 but fell to twenty-five dollars a barrel at the end of that month. OPEC revenues rose by up to forty percent in 1990 as a result of the price rise and panic buying by some consumers. Most of this accrued to Saudi Arabia which used the increase in revenues to fund the US-led military build-up and offensive on Iraqi forces in Kuwait early in 1991.

In the first quarter of 1991, OPEC produced about 23 million barrels a day and the average price was 19 dollars a barrel. The oil price fell to 17.5 dollars a barrel in the second quarter and to 16 dollars a barrel a year later. The world economy had gone into recession and the demand for oil was weak. OPEC members' revenues rose as a result of the reallocation of Iraq's and Kuwait's quotas.

By 1992, Kuwaiti production was being restored and Iran was opposing the high overall production level in OPEC which it saw as the main cause of low prices. In February 1992 a production ceiling of 22.98 million barrels a day was agreed on for the second quarter and in September a level of 24.2 million barrels a day was agreed on for the final quarter.

During 1993, OPEC continued to accommodate Kuwait's return to full production. OPEC was also preoccupied with the United States' and European Union's proposals for increased taxation on petroleum, designed to reduce pollution. By the middle of the year, the oil price was further disrupted by discussions between Iraq and the United Nations on possible oil sales by the former. Iran demanded that Saudi Arabia accommodate increased Kuwaiti production. By October a compromise agreement was reached under which Saudi Arabia froze production at current levels. This did not prevent the price from falling to a low level of 12.87 dollars a barrel at the end of the year.

In March 1994, OPEC ministers agreed to maintain quotas set in September 1993 until the end of the year. The oil price rose to 15.60 dollars during the summer as a result of lower Nigerian production. The average oil price in 1994 was 15.36 dollars a barrel.

In 1995 the average price rose to 16.73 dollars as a result of increased demand and in 1996 it was estimated to have averaged just over 20 dollars a barrel, reaching a peak of 24 dollars in May. The increase in the price was due to stronger demand and constraints in North Sea and other non-OPEC production.

Thus the period since 1985 brought dramatic changes in OPEC's fate. The market price system was abandoned. Most significantly, Saudi Arabia stated that it would not adjust its production downward to compensate for other OPEC members' overproduction. This resulted in a fall in the the oil price and it remained weak until recovery in the world economy in 1989. Saudi Arabia opposed attempts by more radical OPEC members to raise prices because it felt that only stability of prices and quantities would guarantee a place for oil in the international energy market. The events of 1973–1974 and 1980–1981 had resulted in massive attempts to reduce oil use and increase energy efficiency in Western economies. This lessened the demand for oil, weakened oil prices and OPEC's revenues. Unlike previous political crises, the Iraqi invasion of Kuwait caused only a temporary jump in prices and virtually no disruption in international oil trade. Following the GULF WAR Iraqi output was replaced with Saudi and other OPEC production and then Kuwaiti production was resumed. OPEC members once again were unwilling to restrain production in order to support prices and so the oil price remained weak from 1991 until 1995. The recovery in 1996 was temporary, once again resulting mainly from increased demands.

The Oil Producing Countries *Iran*, the first Middle Eastern country to produce oil—since 1908—following a concession granted to William Knox D'Arcy, an Englishman, in May 1901 and with the establishment of the Anglo Persian (later Anglo-Iranian) Oil Company in 1909, with the British government as the major and controlling partner since May 1914. Events concerning Iran's oil industry and their political repercussions, had a strong influence on oil developments in the region. In 1932 the first conflict between the producing country and the concessionaire company (and the imperial power behind it), took place in Iran. The Anglo-Persian Oil Company, with the backing of the British government, rejected the demands of the Persian government for increased payments in return for its concession. In November 1932 the Persian government cancelled the D'Arcy concession but the British government intervened on behalf of the Company. In December 1932, Britain took the matter to the League of Nations. The Persian government argued that the concession had been granted by an unconstitutional regime as a result of foreign influence. In April 1933 a new concession was offered and in May 1933 a settlement was reached. This specified a more precise method for calculating royalty

payments, including cash amounts to be paid. The new concession was granted for a period of sixty years.

However, the struggle between the Iranian government and Anglo-Iranian Oil Company resumed in the aftermath of World War II, culminating in the May 1951 nationalization of Iran's oil industry and the ascendancy of a nationalist government headed by Muhammad Mossaddeq. The two-year crisis came to its end in the October 1954 agreement in which a new International Iranian Oil Consortium recognized the National Iranian Oil Company (NIOC) as the owner of the former Company's properties. The Consortium's production and refining operations were now based on a lease and reduced the share of the Anglo-Iranian (renamed British Petroleum, BP) to forty percent, while five major American companies held forty percent, Royal Dutch-Shell fourteen percent, and the Compagnie Française des Pétroles six percent.

The Consortium operated from 1954 until it was dissolved in March 1979. In 1973, however, NIOC took over formal ownership and control of the petroleum industry in the area leased to the Consortium. The latter set up a new operating company, Standard Oil Company of California, (SOCAL) which became the production contractor for NIOC. In return, each of the members of the Consortium was granted a twenty-year supply of petroleum as a privileged buyer, in proportion to the share in the Consortium. In 1981 a subsidiary of NIOC took over the operating functions.

The Revolution of 1979 and the turmoil that followed it resulted in a lack of maintenance and some damage to the oilfields and to oil installations. In 1979, Iran increased its oil prices to a maximum of 37 dollars a barrel, compared with 17.17 dollars a barrel a year earlier. However, Western companies stopped buying Iranian oil and attempts were made to increase sales to East Bloc countries, to Turkey and India. In September 1980 Iraq attacked Iran and destroyed the Abadan oil refinery. The ensuing war wrought heavy damage on refining and transportation facilities and production, which was just recovering from the paralysis caused by the Islamic Revolution of 1979. Apart from the destruction of the giant refinery at Abadan, Iran's export and loading installations on the Gulf-Kharge Island, and later loading stations further down the Gulf, like Sirri Island, were attacked as were Iranian tankers in the Gulf. These attacks provided the rationale for Iran's frequent attacks on Arab and foreign tankers and other vessels in the Gulf: In 1983–1984, Iran, desperate for foreign currency, broke OPEC quotas and offered discounts on its oil prices. In 1986, falling oil prices on international markets and lower export revenues resulted in another policy reversal: Iran offered a suspension of exports in order to push prices up, on condition that other OPEC members did the same. This apparent willingness to be self-sacrificing, was based on the fact that Iran was finding it extremely hard to export oil as a result of the war with Iraq.

From 1989 Iran made major efforts to repair war damage. The international boycott of Iraqi oil from 1991 enabled it to increase its volume of exports and revenues. From 1991, as the economy began to recover from the war, domestic demand for oil rose and major plans were announced for expanding production capacity. These could only be carried out with foreign capital and technology, which was not available on a sufficient scale. In 1994, a 9.5 billion-barrel oil discovery was announced worth forty-one billion dollars. In May 1995, the US announced an embargo on Iran which restricted trade and investment there. In 1993 petroleum accounted for ninety-seven percent of Iran's exports and in 1994, oil revenues accounted for sixty-four percent of government revenues in the budget approved by Parliament. Iran has the world's second largest natural gas reserves: 20 trillion cubic meters.

Iraq. Since the beginning of the century, German, Dutch, British and American companies were seeking oil concessions in the Mosul and Baghdad vilayets of the Ottoman Empire. An American concession of 1909 for the construction of three railway lines (one of them through Mosul and Baghdad) included the right to exploit mineral resources 20 km. on either side of the lines; but it was never ratified.

In 1912 a British company, the Turkish Petroleum Company (TPC) was formed. The three European groups united in March 1914 in an effort to prevent the US from entering the race: the British were to have fifty percent of TPC, the Dutch twenty-five percent, the Germans twenty-five percent; a five percent share was to be proportionally deducted for Colouste S. Gulbenkian for his mediation;

and the partners would seek concessions in Ottoman territories, excluding Egypt and Kuwait, only through the TPC. The Ottoman government consented in principle to grant a concession, but reserved the right of Turkish participation. However, World War I halted further action.

During the War Britain and France agreed on the division of Turkish territories after victory. Mosul was assigned to France, but Britain wanted it to be included in the rest of Iraq which was its assigned territory. In April 1920, at the SAN REMO CONFERENCE, France ceded Mosul to British Iraq, in return for the German twenty-five percent in the TPC; it also agreed to let the TPC lay pipelines and build railroads across SYRIA to bring out the oil.

The US accused its two allies of depriving it of a fair share in the Mesopotamian oil and a bitter struggle ensued. After a long wrangle between the US and British governments, and between American oil companies and the Anglo-Persian Oil Company, it was agreed in 1925 (finalized in July 1928) to grant an American company half of the British share, i.e., 23.75% of the TPC. The concession was revalidated by a new Iraq government concession in March 1925 (the company was renamed in 1929 Iraq Petroleum Company, IPC). In July 1928 the Near East Development Co. (Standard Oil of New Jersey and Standard Oil of New York, the only two companies left of the American group) became part of the IPC, with 23.75 percent.

The US group had to undertake, not to seek separate concessions in the Asian territories of the defunct OTTOMAN EMPIRE, except Kuwait. This was the Red Line Agreement of 1928, an undertaking the US group broke in 1946, when they joined another American group that obtained concessions in Saudi Arabia.

Iraq's territory was divided into three separate concessions: the IPC east of the Tigris River for seventy-five years (1931); the Mosul Petroleum Co. (1932) west of the Tigris River; and the Basrah Petroleum Company (1938) in all other lands. Royalties were to be four shillings (gold) per ton. Internal pipelines were constructed and production began in 1927. In that first year production was 45,000 tons, in the late 1930s it passed 4 million tons and in 1951 it rose to 8.35 million tons. The oil produced in the Basra region in the south was transported to world markets by tankers. From Mosul and Kirkuk in the north a pipeline was constructed in 1934, branching out to Tripoli (Lebanon) and Haifa (Palestine), where refineries were built. After World War II, the line to Tripoli was expanded several times and a new branch to Baniyas (Syria) was added in 1950. By 1965 these pipelines conveyed 40 million tons per annum, sixty-four percent of Iraq's oil output; by 1970 a capacity of over 50 million tons was reported. In the 1970s, however, the lines were closed down for long periods because of the Lebanese Civil War and Syro-Iraqi disputes. The branch to Haifa has been inoperative since 1948, when Iraq stopped the flow of oil in protest of the foundation of the State of Israel and following the eruption of the Arab-Israel War.

In November 1950 Iraq obtained a fifty percent royalty increase, from four to six shillings per ton, and in 1951 after the nationalization of the oil industry in Iran and the 50/50 profit sharing arrangement in Saudi Arabia—a 50/50 sharing of profits. Production grew steadily from 33.5 million tons in 1955 to 84 million tons in 1971. Oil revenue, 214 million dollars in 1955, rose to 840 million dollars in 1971. But the Iraqis became more and more discontented with the terms of the concessions, their pressure mounted and relations between government and Company deteriorated. In December 1961, Abdel Karim QASSEM (ruling Iraq since a coup of July 1958) enacted a law which deprived the three companies of their concession areas except the parts under actual exploitation, 740 sq. miles, (1,919 sq. km.) less than one to two percent of the original concession. Even areas already developed by the company but not yet in actual operation, such as the North Rumaila field in the south, were confiscated. An Iraqi National Oil Company was set up in February 1964, to operate the expropriated area.

Abortive efforts were made to reach agreement with the Iraqi regimes after Qassem was toppled in 1963. On 1 June 1972 President Bakr announced the nationalization of the Iraq concession. At first neither the Mosul Petroleum Company nor the Basrah Petroleum Company were nationalized. In the area nationalized, France with its 23.75% interest, was allowed to continue to lift its share for the next ten years. The small Mosul company voluntarily surrendered its concession. With the Basrah PC the government agreed in Februray 1973 to increase production considerably. But during the Arab-Is-

rael War of October 1973, Iraq nationalized the share of the two American companies, Exxon and Mobil, in the Basrah PC; two weeks later, that of Royal Dutch-Shell; and in December, that of the Lisbon located Partex Foundation (Gulbenkian). This was officially meant to punish the US, the Netherlands and Portugal. Early in 1975, Iraq took a sixty percent participation, in agreement with the remaining British and French partners in the Basrah PC. In December, it nationalized the remaining foreign interests in the company.

Iraq opposed OAPEC's October 1973 oil embargo, explaining that the cutback unjustly harmed friendly countries and that it was preferable to nationalize and expel the foreign oil companies. The real reason for Iraq's opposition was its desperate need for markets for its nationalized oil. Iraq now took advantage of the shortage of supply and increased its oil sales. In 1975, when other OPEC countries experienced an average drop of nineteen percent in production, Iraq increased production by 21.5%. Algeria and Saudi Arabia accused Iraq of having cut one dollar a barrel off the OPEC price. Production rose to 138 million tons in 1980, and revenue to 26 billion dollars.

Iraq's oil industry has been historically affected by its problematic access to the sea. It has a very short coastline in the Persian Gulf, and its only outlet to the sea is through the Shatt-al-Arab waterway, the sovereignty over which was disputed between the riparian states since Ottoman times. Iraq's dependence on Shatt al-Arab has restricted its ability to export oil by sea and has given its neighbor and rival, Iran, a strategic asset. If Iran seized, or blocked, the Shatt al-Arab it could disrupt Iraq's oil exports and much of its imports. In addition to its vulnerability to developments in Iran, Iraq also faced difficulties with its pipelines to the Mediterranean. The line running through Syria was often sabotaged or closed. Periodically the Syrians would impose higher transit fees.

In December 1966 Syria impounded all IPC assets until claims for back royalties and higher transit fees had been satisfied, and stopped the flow of Iraqi oil to Baniyas in Syria and Tripoli in Lebanon; in March 1967 the producing company agreed to increase the transit fees by fifty percent. A similar episode occurred in 1970. When Iraq nationalized the IPC and Syria nationalized the pipeline in its territory (1972), Syria demanded a 100% increase, and after long negotiations a 50% increase was agreed upon.

In the face of these transit fees and other demands, possible sabotage and frequent interruptions, Iraq constructed a pipeline connecting the southern oil fields and their Persian Gulf ports with the oil fields in the north, completed in 1976. It also agreed with Turkey, in August 1973, to build a pipeline from the Kirkuk fields to a Turkish port on the Mediterranean, in Hatay-ALEXANDRETTA; each country was to build its part. In January 1977 the 700 mi. Kirkuk-Dortyol (Ceyhan) pipeline was opened, with a capacity of 25 million tons a year; in 1980 Turkey and Iraq agreed to increase the capacity to 45–50 million tons a year (900,000 billion barrels a day).

From April 1976 to February 1979 Iraq stopped pumping oil through the Syrian pipeline. In April 1982, as part of its alliance with Iran, then at war with Iraq, Syria closed its lines to the flow of Iraqi oil. As loading facilities on the Gulf were paralyzed by the War, Iraq's export capacity was reduced to 700,000 barrels a day through the Turkish line. Iraq, therefore, planned an expansion of the line through Turkey, and an outlet through Saudi Arabia. In April 1985, it agreed with Turkey to construct a second, parallel pipeline, to add 500,000–600,000 billion barrels a day. A two stage pipeline was planned through Saudi Arabian facilities: first, a line from Basra to the Saudi Ghawar-to-Yanbu Petroline, which would then carry Iraqi oil to the Red Sea; later, Iraq would build a line of 1 million barrels a day capacity parallel to the Saudi one and a terminal at Yanbu. In October 1981 Saudi Arabia consented, and in January 1984 a formal agreement was concluded. In March 1986, stage I was completed and Iraq demanded a 500,000 billion barrels a day increase in its OPEC quota.

Over the years, Iraq developed new oil fields, built and expanded refineries, widened the internal pipeline network, increased the utilization of natural gas and built up a petrochemical industry. It engaged in direct marketing, mobilizing oil tanker companies. During the war against Iran, Iraq insisted on parity with Iran in OPEC quotas and this was agreed at the end of the War in 1988. The urgent need of funds to rebuild its war-damaged economy led Iraq to demand that Arab Gulf states cease producing above their OPEC quotas. In July 1990, Iraq threatened action against Kuwait and the UAE and in August 1990 it invaded Iraq. This led to an international boycott of Iraq and its oil sales virtually ceased. Air attacks during the Gulf War of 1991 led to massive damage to the oil industry. Experts estimated that production could be restarted rapidly under suitable conditions, though it would take up to three years to reach an export capacity of 3.2 million barrels a day, and the cost would equal 6,000 million dollars. At the end of 1993, the UN proposed an emergency export quota which would permit Iraq to export 1,600 million dollars worth of oil a year. The first sales were made in December 1996.

Saudi Arabia. The oil industry had its most dramatic revolutionary impact in Saudi Arabia. Nowhere in the Middle East has oil development produced such striking contrasts between the indigenous nomadic mode of life and the Western technological innovations introduced by the oil companies, and nowhere has the change been so radical.

In the 1915 treaty with Britain, Abdel-Aziz Ibn SA'UD, Sultan of Najd, undertook not to grant concessions without the consent of the British government. In August 1923, he granted an oil concession in the al-Hasa area to Major Frank Holmes, representing Eastern and General Syndicate, a British group that acquired the concession not to work it, but to sell it. But the groups efforts to sell it in Britain and the US failed, and its concession lapsed. After Ibn Sa'ud's conquest of the HIJAZ in 1925, Britain recognized the Saudi Kingdom's independence and in the Treaty of Jidda (1927) removed the restrictive provisions of the old treaty. After preliminary studies by an American engineer, K. S. Twitchell, and negotiations with other candidates, among them IPC, Saudi Arabia awarded a concession in 1933 to Standard Oil of California (SOCAL), which set up the California Arabian Standard Oil Company and began exploration.

Three years later SOCAL sold half of the company to the Texas Oil Company. In March 1938 oil was discovered in Dammam. One year later a supplemental agreement extended the concession area to 440,000 sq. miles (1,140,920 sq. km.) By that year production in Dammam reached 30,000 barrels a day. At first the oil from Dammam was shipped on barges to Bahrain, where the company had a refinery. In 1939 Ras Tanura was selected as the terminal and connected with Dammam by a thirty-nine-mile pipeline.

During World War II, oil production was curtailed. As the Saudi King needed and demanded revenue, the Company advanced him loans on future royalties; but his demands persistently increased and the Company asked the US government for aid to protect their concession, presenting it as vital to US national interests and security. After a number of moves the US decided in February 1943 to grant Saudi Arabia lend-lease aid. US government plans to acquire the concession were successfully resisted by SOCAL. In January 1944, the name of the company SOCAL was changed to the Arabian-American Oil Company (ARAMCO). In December 1946, ARAMCO agreed to sell thirty percent of its shares to Standard Oil of New Jersey and ten percent to Socony-Vacuum (finalized late in 1948); both these groups, partners in the IPC, broke the Red Line Agreement by joining ARAMCO.

ARAMCO planned to construct a pipeline to bring the oil to a Mediterranean port. Attempts to have the US government build it were opposed by other US oil companies, and were dropped. In July 1945 ARAMCO set up the Trans-Arabian Pipeline (Tapline) Company. Plans to build the line through Jordan and Palestine to Haifa were dropped, and it was constructed through Jordan, Syria and Lebanon, with its terminal at Sidon. The Tapline—1,040 miles long, and with a capacity of 310,000 barrels a day (about 15 million tons per annum), later expanded to 400,000 barrels a day—was opened in November 1950. Syria soon asked for increased transit royalties, and there were frequent negotiations and increases. In May 1970 Tapline was sabotaged in the GOLAN HEIGHTS and Syria permitted its repair only in January 1971, against additional payments. Since 1975 Tapline has not been used, because of the cheaper tanker rates and the instability in Lebanon.

With the termination of the War, production increased rapidly—from 645,860 tons in 1943 to 26.2 million tons in 1950, and, after the completion of Tapline, 36.6 million tons in 1951, 46.2 million tons in 1954. In 1950, ARAMCO agreed to pay Saudi Arabia fifty percent of the Company's net operating profit (the per ton royalty to be part of that profit share). Saudi revenues rose from 1.5 million dollars in 1940 to 260 million dollars in 1954 (with total profits of 520 million dollars; of 1.75 dollars a barrel sold by the company 1.40 dollars was profit). Saudi Arabia also had a share in the Saudi-Kuwait

NEUTRAL ZONE. In February 1949 it granted a concession to the American Western Pacific Oil Corporation (later Getty) for onshore oil exploitation on terms considerably better than those of ARAMCO. Early in 1957, Saudi Arabia granted a concession to the Arabian Oil Company (Japanese) for the offshore area of the zone, on even more favorable terms, including a fifty-six percent government share of the profits. Getty produced 0.6 million tons in 1955 in 1972 produced 3.9 million tons Arabian Oil produced in 1961, its first year, 0.5 million tons and in 1972 10 million. Saudi Arabia's revenue amounted to 2.6 million dollars in 1955, and 97 million dollars in 1972.

Saudi Arabia's oil reserves were constantly rising in spite of the ever increasing production rate; the Saudi concession obviously covered the greatest oil producing fields in the Middle East. Production was steadily and constantly growing and reached 375 million tons in 1973, nearing the 500 million-ton mark in 1979 and 1980–1981. Revenue was nearly 53 billion dollars in 1973, passed 30 billion dollars in 1976–1977 and 100 billion dollars in 1980. ARAMCO also discovered new oil fields, onshore and offshore; expanded the internal pipeline system; enlarged tank farms, loading and port facilities; and built a sea-island for the accommodation of very large tankers. (For the impact of the oil industry on Saudi Arabia and its development and modernization see SAUDI ARABIA.

Relations between ARAMCO and the Saudi government were generally good and the Company complied in most cases with the government's requests. After Iraq's 1961 confiscation of more than ninety-nine percent of the IPC concession areas, ARAMCO in March 1963 agreed to relinquish about seventy-five percent of its concession area, all but 125,000 sq. miles, with six additional relinquishments at five-year intervals. In November 1962 Saudi Arabia established the General Petroleum and Mineral Organization (Petromin) to supervise all oil affairs, and empowered it to enter any phase of oil and mineral operations.

Saudi Arabia also aspired to enter downstream operations. It set up the Saudi Arabia Refining Company (SARCO), which built and operated refineries, and a tanker company. It increased the utilization of natural gas resources aided by ARAMCO, and developed a large scale petrochemical industry, partly in joint ventures with foreign oil companies and other enterprises.

SARCO began building two gigantic industrial cities based on the oil and gas industries: Jubail in the Gulf and Yanbu on the Red Sea, each estimated to cost 15–20 billion dollars. In 1976 it set up the Basic Industries Corporation (SABIC) to hold the government's share in the equities of the various joint venture refineries, petrochemical complexes and industrial undertakings. From 1977 a 750-mile 48-inch oil pipeline from the Ghawar-Abqaiq oil fields in the eastern province to the port of Yanbu on the Red Sea was constructed, with a capacity of 1.85 million barrels a day (to be expanded to 2.35 million barrels a day) at a cost of about 51,550 million dollars. The line went into operation in 1980.

Saudi Arabia's takeover of ARAMCO began in 1972 with twenty-five percent and culminated in a total takeover settled in 1976 and fully implemented in 1980. This is described above, in the general part of this entry. While its judicial status and financial arrangements have changed, ARAMCO has continued operating on behalf of the Saudi government. Also described earlier in this entry are Saudi Arabia's role as a main leader of OPEC, its maneuvers and manipulations concerning prices and production quotas; its attempts to keep price increases to a level that would not endanger the oil economy or antagonize the US its role as a swing producer (1982–1984) and its reintroduction of a higher production quota from 1985. During the oil recession of the mid-1980s, Saudi Arabia's production declined to less than 250 million tons in 1983 and 1984, sinking to about 2 million barrels a day in August 1985. Its oil revenues dropped to 40 billion dollars in 1984 and 28 billion dollars in 1985. Since 1985, Saudi Arabia has increased its production rate again, basing itself on an OPEC quota of 4.35 million barrels a day (about 220 million tons per annum) and hoping that with the stabilization of the oil market the drop in price and revenues would be halted.

Between 1985 and 1990, Saudi Arabia refused to act as a swing producer and ceased to reduce its production in response to production above OPEC quotas by other members of the cartel. Following the Iraqi invasion of Kuwait in 1990, Saudi Arabia agreed with other OPEC members that they would compensate for the loss of Iraq's and Kuwait's production as a result of the international boycott of Iraq.

Saudi Arabia was the major beneficiary of this policy. Its production rose by about 3 million barrels a day in response to the crisis and in 1991 its oil export revenues reached 43 billion dollars—an increase of thirty-eight percent over 1990. In 1989 the Saudi Arabian Oil Company (Saudi Aramco) took over the nationalized ARAMCO assets. In 1993 Saudi Aramco took over the operations of the Saudi Arabian Marketing and Refining Company (SAMAREC) and the government owned General Petroleum and Mineral Organization. A Supreme Oil Council was formed to oversee the industry's development and to encourage the involvement of the private sector. Since 1991 major investment has raised production capacity to about 10 million barrels a day with an emphasis on the production of light grades of crude oil.

Bahrain. The Sheikhdom of Bahrain, a British protectorate, undertook since 1880 not to grant any concession without British approval. A concession was granted in 1925 to Major Frank Holmes, representing the Eastern and General Syndicate. In 1927 a subsidiary of the American Gulf Oil Corporation took as an option to purchase the Syndicate rights; in 1928 Gulf transferred its rights to Standard Oil of California. After long negotiations the concession was granted in 1930 to the Bahrain Petroleum Company (BAPCO), a subsidiary of Standard Oil of California, registered in Canada. In 1935 that company sold one half of the concession to Texas Oil, forming a joint new company, California-Texas (Caltex). The concession was extended in 1940, to cover all of Bahrain, 1.64 million acres, for fifty-five years from June 1944.

Production started in 1932. BAPCO built a refinery to serve Bahrain and mainly Saudi Arabia; it went into operation in July 1935. Production reached 20,000 barrels a day (1 million tons per annum) in 1939. During World War II it was reduced, but in 1946 it again attained 1.1 million tons, in 1958 2 million, and in 1967 it passed the 3.5 million ton mark. Since the mid-1970s it has declined to 2–2.5 million tons. Revenue, based since 1953 on a fifty percent share of profits, was 1 million dollars in 1940, passed the 8 million dollar mark in 1954, and reached 30 million dollars in 1970 and nearly 400 million dollars in the mid-1970s. Thus, production and oil income, as well as reserves, were modest if compared with other Arab oil countries and the Middle East in general. Since Bahrain exported refined oil products, not crude oil, it did not join OPEC; it did not become, however, a member of OAPEC in May 1970.

Oil revenue was divided into three parts: one third to the Sheikh, one third for current expenses and socioeconomic development, and one third was invested abroad, mainly in England.

Relations with BAPCO were generally good. In 1965 Bahrain granted offshore concessions to other companies. In 1971 it set up the Bahrain National Oil Company. In October 1972, Bahrain agreed with BAPCO to take a twenty-five percent participation share, to reach fifty-one percent in 1983. It did not implement that agreement, but in September 1974 it acquired a sixty percent participation (not including the refinery). In December 1975 all the oil fields, but not the refinery, were transferred to the Bahrain National Oil Company. In July 1980 the government acquired sixty percent in the refinery. Bahrain exports petroleum productions and no crude oil. Output levels are determined by the volume of crude oil imported from Saudi Arabia.

Kuwait. As in Bahrain, the Sheikh of Kuwait, under British protection since 1899, was committed to grant an oil concession only with British approval. In the early 1920s Major Frank Holmes, representing the Eastern and General Syndicate, obtained a concession and, after the Anglo-Persian Oil Co. declined to acquire it, offered it to the American Gulf Oil Corporation. Here, as in Bahrain, the British government insisted on compliance with the British Nationality clause and from late 1931 a long British-US wrangle ensued. But the British were determined not to lose again to the Americans (Saudi Arabia and Bahrain) and a compromise was reached in December 1933: Anglo-Persian and Gulf were to form a joint Kuwait Oil Company (KOC) in equal partnership. In December 1934 KOC obtained a seventy-five year concession covering the entire sheikhdom. World War II interrupted operations, but production began in 1946 and grew rapidly and from 800,000 tons in 1946 it reached 17.3 million tons in 1950, 37.6 million in 1952, 106 million in 1964, and rose to 152 million tons in 1972. Estimates of reserves were also constantly rising. In 1948 Kuwait granted another concession to the American Independent Oil Co. (AMINOIL) for its one-half share in the Kuwait-Saudi Neutral Zone. Production in

that zone reached over 1 million tons in 1955, 19 million in 1965 and nearly 28 million tons in 1972—of which one half was Kuwait's. Despite the 1964 and 1970 agreements to divide the Neutral Zone, the sharing arrangements remained in force.

A 1.25 million ton per annum refinery at Mina al-Ahmadi was completed in November 1949. Its capacity was expanded to 190,000 barrels a day, over 9 million tons per annum by 1959, and 250,000 barrels a day, 12.5 million tons, in 1970. Each of the three companies operating in the Neutral Zone (one on Kuwait's share, two on Saudi Arabia's) also built a refinery.

Royalty payments, at first nine cents per barrel, were turned in December 1951 into a 50/50 profit sharing (and in return the Sheikh extended the concession for an additional seventeen years, i.e. ninety-two years from 1934). Oil revenue was 800,000 dollars in 1946, 139 million dollars in 1952, 464 million dollars in 1960 and climbed to over 1.5 billion dollars in 1972; it reached 8–9 billion dollars in the mid-1970s and peaked in 1979–1980 at over 20 billion dollars. Of these revenues, one-third went to the Sheikh, one-third to social and economic development, and one third was deposited abroad for future contingencies and interest income. The rapid growth of oil production and revenues brought radical changes to Kuwait's economic and social structure, turning it into into a total welfare state (see KUWAIT).

In 1961 Kuwait established the state-owned Kuwait National Petroleum Company (KNPC). The government also set up petrochemical and transportation companies, and assigned new foreign companies to exploit the areas relinquished by KOC and offshore oil. Kuwait was the first Middle Easteren country to reduce production for conservation reasons.

As a member of OPEC and OAPEC, Kuwait was in the forefront of the struggle with the foreign companies. It was active in the achievement of the Tehran Agreement of Februrary 1971, and subsequently demanded participation in the foreign companies. In 1972 Kuwait accepted a twenty-five percent share, but its National Assembly rejected that share as insufficient, and the government demanded full nationalization. In 1974 Kuwait was the first to obtain a sixty percent participation. But late in 1975 Gulf Oil and British Petroleum surrendered their remaining forty percent equity. In July 1977 Kuwait also nationalized its share in the Neutral Zone. Through the crises since 1973 Kuwait mostly followed the policies of Saudi Arabia. In the recession of the mid-1980s, its production declined to 45–55 million tons per annum and its revenue reverted to about 9 billion dollars.

By the late 1980s Kuwait and the UAE exceeded their OPEC quotas. This was a major factor behind the low price of oil and in July 1990 Iraq threatened action against the two Gulf states. In August 1990 Iraq invaded and occupied Kuwait. Oil production ceased and the occupation and subsequent war in 1991 caused massive damage. Retreating Iraqi troops set alight 600 wells and another 200 were damaged out of a total 950. The rehabilitation of the oil industry became the government's main priority after the country was liberated and by the end of 1991, production reached 500,000 barrels a day. By 1994 Kuwait's oil industry had recovered from the Gulf War and OPEC accommodated its return to the international oil market.

Qatar. After Standard Oil of California obtained the oil concession in Bahrain (1930), the IPC authorized the Anglo-Persian Oil Co. to negotiate for a concession with the Sheikh of Qatar. In May 1935 Anglo-Persian was granted a seventy-five-year concession covering all of Qatar, and in 1937 an IPC subsidiary, Petroleum Development, took it over (it changed its name in 1953 to Qatar Petroleum Co.) Oil in commercial quantities was struck in 1939. Production was interrupted because of World War II and resumed in 1947, with first exports in December 1949. Production was 1.6 million tons in 1950, passed the 5 million mark in 1955, reached 10 million in 1964–1965, rose to 24 million tons in 1973; it dropped to 20 million tons in 1975, rose again, and declined since 1981 from 12 to 19 million tons per annum.

In June 1952 Qatar granted an offshore concession to Royal Dutch-Shell, and in 1969–1970 to a group of Japanese companies. From the 1960s, production was about sixty percent onshore and forty percent offshore; from the mid-1970s it was about 50/50, sometimes with a higher offshore production. Qatar also obtained half of the revenue of an offshore concession granted by Abu Dhabi in the al-Bunduq area. Qatar had claimed that area its own territory while a demarcation commission ruled in 1969 that al-Bunduq was on the median line be-

tween the two countries, and they agreed to share the revenue.

From September 1952 payments to the government were based on a 50/50 sharing of profits. Payments rose from 1 million dollars in 1950 to 54 million dollars in 1960, 198 million dollars. in 1971, reaching over 2 billion dollars from the mid 1970s, and peaking at over 5 billion dollars in 1980–1981. Of that revenue, twenty-five percent went to the Sheikh, thirty-five percent to public utilities, welfare services and development, and forty percent to the reserve fund. The oil revenue made possible an impressive development of Qatar's economy and its transformation into a wealthy welfare state (see QATAR).

Relations between the oil companies and the government conformed with the pattern usual in the region. The companies extended production and loading facilities, built refineries (for internal needs), and developed natural gas resources. They relinquished portions of the concession areas, and had to comply with OPEC decisions. In 1968 the government of Qatar took over the refining and distribution facilities. In April 1972 Qatar established the Qatar National Petroleum Co., replaced in July 1974 by the Qatar General Petroleum Corporation. In 1972 the government took a twenty-five percent participation, to reach fifty-one percent in 1983. In February 1974 it raised its share to sixty percent and in October 1976 it nationalized the remaining forty percent. Since February 1977 the fully nationalized company was named Qatar Petroleum Company. Qatar's proven oil resources on 1 January 1995 totaled 3,700 million barrels, equal to 20 years production at the 1994 level.

United Arab Emirates (UAE). The TRUCIAL COAST was covered by a concession of an IPC subsidiary; but this was relinquished or lapsed in most cases. In the Federation of the UAE, formed in 1971 with the abolition of the British Protectorate, oil production and revenues are not a federal matter but belong to the individual sheikhdoms.

Abu Dhabi granted Petroleum Development (Trucial Coast), an IPC affiliate, a seventy-five-year concession in 1939. A 65-year offshore concession was granted to Abu Dhabi Marine Areas (ADMA)—two-thirds Anglo-Iranian, renamed British Petroleum (BP), and one-third Compagnie Française des Pétroles (CFP)—in 1953. ADMA discovered oil in 1958 and exports began in 1962 when a terminal was built at Das Island. Petroleum Development (Trucial Coast)—renamed Abu Dhabi Petroleum Co. (ADPC) in 1962—discovered oil onshore in 1960 and began exporting in December 1963. Production advanced rapidly both onshore and offshore from 800,000 tons in 1962 to over 50 million tons in 1972 peaking at nearly 80 million tons in 1977. In the early 1980s it declined to 36–38 million tons.

The government's share was twenty percent of the profits for both ADMA and ADPC concessions. In 1965 ADPC raised the profit share to fifty percent and agreed to relinquish unexploited areas; ADMA did the same in 1966. As the companies relinquished sections of their concessions, the Sheikh granted them to new companies, including a Japanese consortium in the late 1960s. Revenue rose from 3 million dollars in 1962 to 105 million dollars in 1967, passed the 1 billion dollar mark in 1973 and peaked at over 10 billion dollars in 1979–1980.

In 1971 the government established the AD National Petroleum Company, and in 1972 it acquired a twenty-five percent participation in all foreign companies to rise to fifty-one percent in 1983. In 1974 the Company increased state participation to sixty percent. However, Abu Dhabi did not follow the other producing countries in total nationalization. The government also entered joint ventures with foreign companies on a 60/40 basis in the expansion of the oil industry. The only enterprise totally state-owned was the exploitation of natural gas, of which Abu Dhabi took control in April 1976 after foreign companies declined to participate. Abu Dhabi also built new refineries and established a tanker company. A large 500 million dollar refinery with a capacity of 120,000 barrels a day (6 million tons per annum) was opened late in 1981 in the Ruweis Industrial Center. Refining capacity reached 226,000 barrels a day in 1994 and plans exist for further expansion. For Abu Dhabi's general development, (which gave it the highest per capita income in the world) see ABU DHABI.

Dubai granted the first oil concession, offshore, in 1952 to Dubai Marine Areas (DUMA)—two thirds BP and one third CFP. In 1963, Dubai Petroleum Company (DPC), a subsidiary of the American Continental Oil Co., obtained a concession covering the mainland and territorial waters; in August 1963, it also bought a fifty percent interest in

DUMA. In 1968 DPC discovered oil and production began in September 1969. It reached 4.3 million tons in 1970, 13 million in 1975, and passed the 18 million mark in 1978–1979; in the 1980s it declined to 16–17 million tons per annum.

In January 1971 Dubai raised the companies rate of payment to fifty-five percent. Its revenues reached 1 billion per annum in the 1970s and peaked at over 3 billion dollars in 1980. In July 1975 Dubai acquired 100% ownership of all the operating oil and gas companies—which were to continue managing the operations. The decline of Dubai's oil exports in the 1980s was not as steep as in other countries, since it reportedly did not fully conform to OPEC policies and sold on the "spot market." In 1992 the Dubai government announced plans to build a major new oil refinery at Jebel Ali, the third in the UAE, with a capacity of 150,000 barrels a day but no timetable was issued.

Abu Dhabi and Dubai are the UAE's main oil producers, but there are beginnings in other UAE sheikhdom, as well.

Sharja granted oil concessions to a number of companies, onshore and offshore, in the late 1960s and early 1970s. Production began, offshore, in 1972–1975 and reached in the mid 1980s 2.5 million tons. In 1976 Sharja established a sixty percent participation in all the companies. RAS AL-KHAIMA, another sheikhdom of the UAE, granted concessions to several companies from the late 1960s. In the mid-1970s a consortium—with the National Oil Company taking a fifty percent interest—struck oil and commercial production was reportedly beginning in the 1980s. UMM AL-QAIWAN also granted concessions to several companies from the late 1960s, mainly offshore, later also onshore. So did al-FUJAIRA in the 1970s. No major oil finds have yet been reported.

Taking the UAE as a whole, oil production was about 53 million tons in 1971, exceeded 80 million in the mid-1970s, and peaked at over 100 million tons in 1977–1978 (84.8% Abu Dhabi, 13.3% Dubai, and 1.9% Sharja). In the 1980s production dropped to less than 50 million tons, with Sharja's share rising. Total revenue was over 1 billion dollars in 1974 and 12–13 billion dollars since 1979. Production levels averaged 65,000 barrels a day in the period 1987–1990 but in 1991–1992 output fell sharply.

Oman. In 1937 Petroleum Development (Oman), an affiliate of the IPC group, obtained a seventy-five year oil concession covering the Sultanate except the province of Dhofar and in 1953 two American companies, Cities Service and Richfield, were granted a concession in Dhofar for twenty-five years after commercial oil discovery. As no oil was struck all the IPC members withdrew except two: Shell retained eighty-five percent, and Partex (Gulbenkian) fifteen percent. When oil was discovered in 1966, CFP bought back ten percent from Partex. In March 1966 the Sultan's share was raised to fifty percent of the profits. In 1968 PDO acquired exploitation rights in the Dhofar province too, and early in 1970 it relinquished one third of its concession area, and agreed to two further relinquishments. In the relinquished areas new and offshore concessions were granted. Oman was not a member of OPEC, but complied with most of the changes OPEC introduced. In February 1974, the government acquired twenty-five percent participation in PDO and in July 1974 raised its share to sixty percent.

Production began in 1967 (after a pipeline was laid to the coast) and reached 11.75 million tons in 1968, 18 million in 1976, 14–16 million in the later 1970s and early 1980s, 20 million in 1984 and 25 million tons in 1985. Oil revenue was 115 million dollars in 1971 and reached 4 billion dollars in 1984. In the mid-1980s it declined somewhat. A 50,000 barrels a day (2.5 million tons per annum) refinery was opened in November 1982. Oil revenues reached almost 4 billion dollars. Proven petroleum reserves were estimated at 5,200 million barrels in 1994, when production equaled 800,000 barrels a day.

Syria. Syria benefited from the Middle Eastern oil industry as a transit land for pipelines from Iraq and Saudi Arabia (see above). Many exploration concessions were granted in Syria (including one to an IPC subsidiary), but no oil was found. The American Menhall Drilling Company reported in October 1956 that it had struck oil at Karachok, in the northeast, close to the Iraqi border. In October 1958 the government (now the UAR) canceled the Menhall concession and took it over. In August 1959 a German company struck oil in the same area, but later in 1959 it was agreed that the Soviet Union would aid Syria's oil exploration. More oil fields were discovered in the northeast, and commercial production began in the 1960s.

Production reached 1 million tons in 1968, 5–6 million in the early 1970s and 10 million in 1978; it stands at 8–9 million tons per annum in the 1980s. In the mid-1980s, oil revenue was estimated at over 2 billion dollars.

A refinery in Homs—intended mainly to refine Iraqi oil from the pipeline—was completed in June 1959 by a Czechoslovak company; its capacity was expanded several times. A second refinery, near Baniyas, with an annual capacity of 6 million tons, was opened in August 1979. By the mid-1980s annual refining capacity reached 11.5 million tons.

In 1994 oil exports of between 300,000 barrels a day and 360,000 barrels a day were worth about 2 billion dollars. Despite the government's desire to develop the oil sector, the fiscal climate was unattractive for many oil companies.

Egypt. Prospecting for oil in Egypt began in the late nineteenth century, and oil was first produced in 1908–1909 at Gemsa, on the African side of the Red Sea, at the mouth of the Gulf of Suez. In 1912–1913 Anglo-Egyptian Oilfields (AEOF), a Shell subsidiary, obtained a concession from the Egyptian government. A second field, Hurghada, discovered in 1913, south of Gemsa, was for twenty-five years Egypt's major producing field. A third field, Ras Gharib, between Gemsa, Hurghada and Suez, discovered in 1937–1938, was Egypt's most prolific and accounted for about half of its production. Royalty payments, 5% of production until 1923, then 12.5%, were raised in 1938 to 14%. From 1946 oil was discovered on the Asian side of the Gulf of Suez at Ras Sudr and other locations in Sinai, exploited by AEOF in partnership with Socony-Vacuum. Egypt's production passed the 2 million ton mark in 1949 and remained 1.8–2.3 million tons per annum until 1957.

From 1947 Egypt enacted several laws limiting new oil mining licenses to Egyptians, restricting directorship of foreign companies and their share in enterprises (no more than forty-nine percent) and imposed higher royalties. The foreign oil companies operating in Egypt refused to accept the new conditions. Standard Oil of New Jersey withdrew in 1949; Socony-Vacuum and AEOF suspended exploration.

After the Officers coup of 1952, the new regime modified these laws to permit foreigners to continue with oil exploration and exploitation. Royalty payment was set at fifteen percent of oil produced for a number of years, then to rise to twenty-five percent. A number of foreign companies obtained new concessions and the old foreign companies returned to continue their operations (AEOF's assets were sequestrated following the Suez crisis of 1956, and though the sequestration was lifted in 1959, the government took over the major share of the company in 1964). Soon the eastern and western deserts and the Gulf of Suez coasts were dotted with oil exploration and exploitation units. (Most Egyptian oil wells have a short life span, and to keep up production levels Egypt must continuously seek new sources of oil.) Offshore exploration also yielded large oil supplies, especially in the Gulf of Suez. Production rose to over 6 million tons from 1963, over 10 million from 1968, 20 million in 1970, over 15 million tons in 1971–1972 (the last three figures exclude the oil produced in Israel-occupied Sinai), and, after a decline, over 20 million from 1977, over 30 million from 1980, and over 40 million tons in 1984 and 1985—with much fluctuation. (The al-Murgan offshore field in the Gulf of Suez, for example, produced 15 million tons in 1970 but in 1973 production dropped to 7 million and continued to drop at the rate of 0.5 million tons a year.)

In 1913 AEOF erected a small refinery at Suez and enlarged it in 1919. The Egyptian government built its own refinery at Suez in 1922, to refine the oil it received as royalty, and doubled its capacity in 1938. By 1954 the two refineries had a capacity of 3.3 million tons per annum.

Later the Egyptian government took over the AEOF refinery and built a new one in Alexandria. By 1963 Egypt's three refineries had an annual capacity of 6.6 million tons. With additional refineries built, it reached 15 million tons in the 1970s. (In the 1969–1970 Egypt-Israel War of Attrition the Suez refineries were heavily damaged, but by 1972 they were repaired and enlarged.)

In 1973 Egypt, still vitally interested in extensive and steady exploration by foreign companies, introduced a new system of small area concessions and production-sharing. Companies were to invest minimal stated amounts in exploration over a stated period of years and to pay a bonus at signature. Their concession was to run for twenty to thirty years after the discovery of oil in commercial quantities. They were entitled to forty percent of production to recover their investment; of the balance, the government was to receive eighty to eighty-seven percent and the companies thirteen to twenty percent. After a stated period the companies were to relinquish the non-exploited areas. The new system was very successful, and by late 1979 companies from the US, Europe, South America and Japan had signed some sixty production-sharing agreements and committed themselves to invest over 1 billion dollars in exploration, paying hundreds of millions of dollars in bonuses at signature. By 1984 the number of agreements had reached eighty-nine. However, the resulting rise in production was matched by a fast-increasing home consumption of oil, and exports that were still about two-thirds of production in the late 1970s declined to one-third in the mid-1980s. Revenue increased accordingly until the impact of the third oil crisis reduced production and forced Egypt to cut prices.

The later price drop of 1985–1986 caused a serious financial crisis in Egypt. Egypt is not a member of OPEC; its OAPEC membership was suspended in 1979, in the wake of its signing a peace treaty with Israel, and was restored in 1989, with its return to the ARAB LEAGUE.

Egypt was also a major oil transporter. Until 1967 the bulk of the oil coming from the Persian Gulf area passed through the Suez Canal and Egypt derived much revenue from the transit tolls (see SUEZ CANAL). After the closure of the Suez Canal in 1967, Egypt proposed to compete with Israel's Eilat-Ashkelon pipline and, as an answer to the giant tankers which carried the oil around the Cape of Good Hope, to build a pipeline parallel to the Suez Canal further inland, which was endorsed by the Economic Council of the Arab League. The scheme presented a complex of problems: financing, commitment of the international oil companies to ship sufficient quantities of oil through the pipeline, and competition with the large tanker rates. Plans were changed several times; a tentative July 1969 contract with a European consortium for a 175 million dollar pipeline to Alexandria was modified in July 1971: SUMED (Suez-Mediterranean) pipeline would consist of two parallel forty-two inch lines from Ain Sukhna, twenty-five miles south of Suez, to Sidi Krer west of Alexandria; cost increased to 300 million dollars. In October 1971 the American Bechtel corporation was awarded the contract. Because of financing difficulties, however, an Arab stock company was set up late in 1973 to finance the scheme. Egypt canceled the contract with Bechtel and awarded a new one to an Italian company.

In August 1976 the pipeline was completed and it was officially opened in February 1977. Shipping commitments through SUMED presented a major difficulty. Its capacity of 80 million tons was never fully utilized. In 1977 it had commitments of 20 million tons and in 1978 its throughput reached 40 million As tanker rates came down, shipping through the pipeline was no longer economical, and in 1978 SUMED had to reduce its charge by nearly fifty percent. Yet throughput reached only 66 million tons in 1981 and in 1984 it fell to 45 million tons. The reopening of the Suez Canal in 1975 might have also reduced the pipline's usability.

In July 1976 Egypt's National Production Council recommended dropping the plan for a second parallel line, to increase SUMED's capacity to 120 million tons; instead, it opted to widen and deepen the Suez Canal so it could handle 250,000–300,000 ton tankers by 1982. The Suez Canal had its own problem of keeping transit charges competitive with the giant tankers around Africa. Although Egypt envisaged SUMED as complementary to the Suez Canal, not competing with it, many Egyptian leaders doubted whether their country could economically maintain both the Suez Canal and the SUMED pipeline.

In the 1990s Egypt made serious efforts to reduce domestic oil consumption and thus release more oil for exports. This was done by increasing domestic prices and by developing the gas production and distribution systems. In 1993 crude petroleum exports equaled 1.3 billion dollars while refined and other oil product exports equaled 1.7 billion dollars. In 1994, the annual output of refined products was 25.4 million tons.

Plans for an Israeli/Swiss/Egyptian private sector refinery (with sixty percent ownership in the hands of the public sector General Petroleum Company) at Sidi Krer have been announced. The refinery will have a capacity of 100,000 barrels a day and will cost 1 billion dollars.

Libya. First oil exploration and exploitation concessions in Libya were granted in 1954–1955 to several foreign companies; by 1957–1958, eleven companies were prospecting, and in the 1960s about forty companies were operating—twenty-four of them American (including some of the giants), with major British, French, Italian and German groups among the others. Oil was struck in the later 1950s and commercial production began in 1960–1961, increasing rapidly. In the 1970s eighty-five to ninety percent of the oil was produced by American companies. Production reached 55 million tons in 1965, 160 million in 1970 and declined in the 1970s to about 100 million tons; in the crisis of the 1980s production further decreased to 50–55 million tons. Oil revenue passed 500 million dollars in 1967 and 1 billion dollars in 1968; it reached 10 billion dollars in the mid-1970s and passed 20 billion dollars in 1980; in the early 1980s it declined to 10 billion dollars with a further substantial decrease expected for 1986–1987. (Data about Libya's oil revenue are not officially published and estimates are frequently conflicting.) Of the revenues, seventy percent were to be spent on development and fifteen percent to go to reserve funds.

As the oil fields were all inland, in the desert, an extensive pipeline system to the coast, with terminals and oil ports, had to be constructed. One such system, terminating at Marsa al-Brega (Bureika) was completed late in 1961; others, with terminals at Ras Lanuf, al-Sidr and Zuweitina, followed; and a network based on the longest trunk pipeline, 320 miles to Tobruk was completed in 1966–1967. A first refinery, at Marsa al-Brega, was opened in 1974; two more, at Zawiya and Tobruk, were built in the late 1970s. An Esso-built gas liquefaction plant, also at Marsa al-Brega, was opened in 1970.

Although Libya's remarkable oil economy was by and large the product of foreign, chiefly American, companies, with Qadhafi's revolution in 1969 Libya's relations with these companies embarked on a trajectory of collision. Under Qadhafi, Libya drove a hard bargain and constantly tightened the screws concerning production quantities, prices and royalties and taxes, frequently playing one company against the other. In 1971 it imposed on all companies a fifty-one percent state participation, and in 1973–1974 it wholly nationalized six of the companies; additional companies withdrew subsequently and in the early 1980s, including some of the major groups. The four or five American companies still operating in Libya were ordered by the US to withdraw in 1986, in the context of the deterioration of US-Libya relations.

Libya has proven reserves of 22,800 million barrels, enough to maintain 1991–1992 production rates for 38 years. In 1994 oil production was about 1.38 million barrels a day. For Libya's general oil policies in the context of OPEC see above.

Algeria. Concessions in Algeria were granted in the early and mid-1950s while Algeria was still French-ruled, mainly during the Algerian rebellion of 1954–1962. The concessionaires were four major groups of French oil companies, government and private, with the participation of international companies, mainly Shell. Production began in 1956 at Edjele, in the Sahara Desert near the Tunisian border; it reached 1.25 million tons in 1959, 8 million in 1960, 20 million in 1962, 40 million in 1968, 50 million in 1971, 45–50 million tons in the 1970s, peaking in 1978–1979 with nearly 60 million tons; in the 1980s it declined to around 30 million tons per annum (though conflicting data give higher figures, up to 50 million tons). Algeria also produced natural gas in large quantities. Independent Algeria's oil revenue, since 1962, rapidly increased: it amounted to 50 million dollars in 1963, 325 million dollars in 1970, over 3.5 billion dollars in 1974, nearly 6 billion dollars in 1978, and peaked with 11 billion dollars in 1980; in the 1980s it declined to 8–10 billion dollars per annum.

As the oil and gas fields were all in the Sahara Desert in Algeria's far south, a large network of pipelines had to be constructed to the Mediterranean. The first, from the Hassi Mas'ud-Hawd al-Hamra fields to Bedjaya (formerly Bougie) was completed in 1959, one from Edjele to a Tunisian terminal at La Skhirra in 1960, a third one from Hassi Rmeil to Arzew near Oran, with a branch to Algiers, in 1964; this was extended south-eastward to Hassi Mas'ud in 1966, and both these fields were connected with Skikda (formerly Philippeville) by new lines in 1970. A liquid gas pipeline to Italy, through Tunisia, was agreed upon in 1973, but its construction was delayed for four years by Tunisian demands concerning the ownership of the Tunisian part of the line; when the line was completed in 1981, its operation was delayed by an Algerian-Italian dispute over payments; it was opened in May 1983.

Refineries were also constructed—the first, in Algiers, was opened in 1969, one in Arzew in 1973, and one in Skikda in 1977. Several gas liquefaction plants were built in Arzew, from 1964, and one in Skikda was opened in 1972.

Independent Algeria's relations with the foreign companies, first and foremost the major French groups, were highly complex and beset by frequent disputes concerning production, prices, and Algeria's participation. In July 1965, Algeria imposed new arrangements of equal partnership and a 50/50 participation. In 1971 it unilaterally took a majority share in all the French companies; some of those agreed to the new conditions and accepted compensation terms—after a long wrangle—and some withdrew. Other foreign companies were nationalized and taken over entirely: five American companies in 1967, and five others in 1969 and 1970. Inland marketing was nationalized in 1968, and the takeover steps of 1971 included a complete nationalization of all pipelines and all gas production and processing. Algeria's state oil company, SONATRACH, became a major empire and the primary power in Algeria's economy (in 1982 it was decided to split it up into several smaller state companies). New agreements with foreign companies in the 1970s and 1980s were based on new principles, SONATRACH keeping full control and the foreign companies acting as operators only. Even after the nationalization process, Algeria's relations with the major buyers remained troubled. Oil sales to France were regulated by long-term agreements, but large-scale long-term agreements on the sale of liquefied gas caused protracted disputes. One agreement, with the American El Paso group (1969), was canceled in 1980 by the company, while others, with France (1970), Italy (1973) and Belgium (1975), were amended and reconfirmed in 1982.

Despite the state of near civil war which has prevailed in Algeria in the 1990s, oil, oil products and gas production has been unaffected. In 1992, crude oil and petroleum product exports totaled 7.1 billion dollars.

Algeria has 4.5 trillion cubic meters of natural gas reserves or 36 billion dollars barrels of oil equivalent. In November 1996 the Maghreb-Europe Gas Pipeline (GME), which runs from Algeria to Europe via Morocco, was completed. It was designed to transport 10 billion cubic meters of gas a year to Europe. The Transmed Gas Pipeline (TME), running from Algeria to Italy, has been expanded to 25 billion cubic meters per annum. There are plans to expand its capacity to 75 billion cubic meters at the beginning of the next century.

Tunisia. Oil concessions were granted in Tunisia from 1949, still under the French Protectorate, to various foreign companies: French, US, Italian and others. Tunisia, independent since 1956, issued further concessions until about 15 companies were operating in Tunisia. From 1964 this included concessions for offshore prospecting. Oil was struck in 1964 in the al-Borma region in the Sahara Desert in southern Tunisia, on the Algerian border. Commercial production began in 1966, reached 3.3 million tons in 1967 and passed the 4 million mark in 1971; it stood at 5 million tons in 1979 and fluctuated between 5 million and 6 million tons in the 1980s. About half of Tunisia's production was used for home consumption. Oil revenue reached about 600 million dollars in 1980 and 800 million dollars in 1985. By 1993 oil revenues had fallen to 430 million dollars. Relations with the foreign companies were generally smooth. Tunisia did not join OPEC; it joined OAPEC, but seceded in 1986.

A pipeline from the far-away production area to the Mediterranean at La Skhirra was completed in 1966, using for most of its length the line which Tunisia had allowed Algeria to lay from Edjele to La Skhirra in 1960. Tunisia also agreed to the passage through its territory of a gas pipeline from Algeria to Italy though it held up the final agreement from 1973 to 1977, until Algeria was recognized as the owner of the pipeline on its territory, and its demands for transit fees were met (the pipeline was opened in May 1983). Tunisia became involved in a dispute with Libya over the offshore borderline; the matter was raised before the International Court which ruled, in February 1982, against Tunisia's petition, in favor of the status quo, and rejected a second Tunisian appeal in February 1985. In 1994 petroleum reserves were estimated at 1,700 million barrels, enough to maintain production at 1993 rates for forty-four years.

Morocco has produced oil since the 1930s, with various companies holding concessions. However, production has so far remained very small, in the 20,000–40,000 tons per annum range. Morocco has not joined either OPEC or OAPEC.

OMAN (UMAN)

Formerly Muscat and Oman. Sultanate in the south-eastern corner of the Arabi-an peninsula, on the coast of the Gulf of Oman and the Arabian Sea, bordering in the north and northwest on the UNITED ARAB EMIRATES (UAE, formerly TRUCIAL OMAN), in the west on SAUDI ARABIA, and in the southwest on Yemen. The borders, mostly in desert areas, are largely undemarcated. The main, central part of Oman has a narrow littoral. Behind this, to the north and west, are mountains reaching heights of over 3,000 meters (al-Jabal al-Akhdar—the "Green Mountain"). Behind them stretches a plateau which merges into the Great Arabian Desert. The southwest of Oman is called Dhofar. This was fully incorporated into the Sultanate only since the 1970s. Oman also owns—as an exclave, separated from Oman by the UAE—the tip of the Trucial Oman peninsula, jutting into the Straits of HORMUZ and is called Ras al-Jabal or Ras Musandam. It also owns several islands in the Arabian Sea, chiefly Masira and the Kuria Muria islands. Furthermore it ruled the small Gwadar Peninsula on the Pakistan coast across the Gulf of Oman. In 1958 it sold it to Pakistan.

The population, estimated in 1970 at 650,000, rose to over 2 million in the mid-1990s. This reflected the country's rapid economic development. Of this figure a little over half a million are foreigners (workers from India constitute sixty percent, others are Pakistani, Bangladeshi etc.,). The majority speak ARABIC in the dialects current in the Arabian peninsula and the PERSIAN GULF area. The ancient South-Semitic dialect spoken in Dhofar is defined by some linguists as a non-Arabic tongue. The population is Muslim—seventy-five percent belong to the IBADIYYA sect usually classified as non-Sunni. Ibadiyya ISLAM is the state religion. Over one-third of the work force is employed in agriculture, though it cultivates only about two percent of the total area of Oman mostly in the mountains. Farther inland, nomadic tribes graze their animals. The inhabitants of the coast were in the past mostly fishermen, pearl-divers, boat-builders and traders. Since the late 1960s, the growing oil economy has provided an increasing share of employment.

Oman, or at least strong points on its coast, was held by Portugal from 1508 to the mid-seventeenth century, and subsequently by Persia. From the mid-eighteenth century, it has been ruled by an Arab dynasty, the Aal (House) of Abu Sa'id (for rival "Imams" inland see below). The Abu Sa'id Sultans expanded their rule to parts of eastern Africa, especially on the island of Zanzibar, where many Omanis traded and settled. But Zanzibar and Oman were divided, in 1856, between the two sons of Sultan Sa'id ibn Sultan (ruled 1804–1856), with Britain mediating the division. In 1877, Dhofar was annexed (but not yet firmly controlled).

Oman (then "Muscat and Oman") was the first country in the Persian Gulf area to sign a protectorate treaty with BRITAIN—in 1798, at first: with the British East India Company; the first British Governor arrived in 1800. Anglo-Omani protectorate treaties were amended and redrawn several times. The most recent re-formulations, in 1951 and 1958, played down the protectorate, emphasizing Oman's independence. Yet Britons, mostly under contract rather than seconded from the British government, still headed the Army directing wide sectors of the administration. As Britain withdrew its protecting presence from the Persian Gulf area—announced 1968, implemented 1971— Oman became fully independent in 1971. It was admitted to the ARAB LEAGUE in September of that year, and to the UN in October. Friendly relations with Britain continued after independence.

Oman's economy was extremely poor and backward until the late 1960s. Marine activities had declined, and little agriculture was practised. There were no modern roads, no airfield, no urban development, no health and education services. Sultan Sa'id ibn Taimur, ruling since 1932, kept Oman isolated from the outside world and did not introduce any economic or social reforms.

The change came with the discovery of oil and the inevitable growth of a modern oil economy. Oil revenues made possible the initiation of far-reaching modernization and development—not as rapid and ambitiuous as in other Gulf countries, but revolutionary in terms of Oman's past. (For data on oil production, from 1967, and oil revenues, see OIL.)

As Sultan Sa'id ibn Taimur continued resisting pressures for modernization and reforms that mounted in the late 1960s (and that were joined by British advisers and the British government), his son QABUS, strongly encouraged by the British, mounted a coup d'etat in July 1970. He deposed his father (who went into exile and died in London in 1972). The new Sultan, who had been kept inactive and confined to the palace for many years, now stepped up development and modernization—including the

construction of ports, airfields, roads; some industrialization (mainly oil-linked: fertilizers, gas liquefaction); and a network of health and education services. Sultan Qabus endeavored to direct these economic and social changes in a conservative manner and to go slow on the introduction of representative government. However, he took first steps in that direction, too, by creating, in October 1981, an appointed Consultative Assembly, with no legislative powers. It was replaced by a Consultative Council (1991) with one member from each of the fifty-nine administrative regions. No political parties exist in Oman.

Oman was disturbed for many years by two separate rebellions, both with international repercussions. One concerned the emergence, among the inland tribes, of an IMAM of the Ibadiyya sect. They claimed not only religious authority but political autonomy or even independence for the mountainous, inner regions. Though traditionally the Sultan had also been the Imam, the separation of the spiritual-religious Imamate from the secular-political Sultanate was an old issue and latter-day Sultans were willing to concede such a separation. But in 1913 the Imam rebelled and established himself as ruler of inner Oman. An agreement was signed in 1920 in Sib which, the Imam claimed, legitimized his rule. The Sultan, however, later contested the validity of that agreement. He maintained that, even if valid, it granted only limited local autonomy. While Muhammad ibn Abdallah al-Khalili was Imam, 1920–1953, the dispute was simmering. In 1954 a new Imam, Ghaleb ibn Ali, rekindled an armed rebellion, supported by several tribes. He was defeated in 1955 and 1957 by the Sultan's Army, with the help of British forces. The Imam, usually living in exile in EGYPT or IRAQ, insisted on his claims and kept his rebellion going.

The Arab states supported the Imam, presenting his revolt as a national and anti-colonial struggle. Saudi Arabia also joined the campaign against the Sultan and the British and aided the Imam, for geopolitical reasons and interests of its own. From the late 1950s, the Arab states with the support of the anti-colonialist Afro-Asian group, endeavored to involve the UN in the issue. In 1963, the UN sent a Swedish diplomat to investigate the problem. In 1964–1965 it set up a sub-committee for the same purpose. Neither reached clear conclusions as to the Imam's and the Sultan's claims and the guerrilla war the Sultan was denying. However, the sub-committee ruled that the issue was an "international," not a domestic problem. The UN De-colonization Committee was invited to examine it. The latter, and in its wake the UN General Assembly, adopted, each year from 1965 to 1970, resolutions affirming Oman's right to full independence and calling on Britain to withdraw its troops. The Sultan's government, together with Britain, rejected these resolutions as unwarranted and illegal UN interference (a) in the internal affairs of Oman (the rebellion), and (b) in the relations between independent Oman and Britain.

After the takeover by Sultan Qabus and the withdrawal of the British Protectorate, "decolonizing" UN intervention ceased, Third World pressure relented. Some Arab states began supporting Oman and its Sultan in large part in connection with the other rebellion in Dhofar (see below), and under the influence of Saudi Arabia. The rebellion was defused, in 1971–1972, with Saudi Arabia and some Gulf sheikhdoms mediating in informal talks with the Imam. The rebellion has not been an issue since.

Another revolt erupted in Dhofar in the mid-1960s. A "Front for the Liberation of Dhofar" was established there in 1965. This "Front" aimed not only to overthrow the government of Oman, and perhaps the secession of a revolutionary Dhofar, but at the destabilization of the conservative (and in the 1960s still British-protected and dominated) Gulf principalities in general. It renamed itself "Popular Front for the Liberation of the Occupied Arab Gulf" (PFLOAG). It was closely connected to the leftist-revolutionary wing of the Palestinian guerrilla groups, the "Popular Front for the Liberation of Palestine" and the ARAB NATIONALIST MOVEMENT (*Harakat al-Qawmiyyin al-Arab*, see ARAB NATIONALISM). It was supported by radical Arab regimes such as SOUTH YEMEN but also Iraq, SYRIA and perhaps Egypt. While it claimed to control Dhofar and to have underground cells in the Gulf area, it was obviously based in South Yemen. It got its arms, finance and supplies from there (reportedly with Soviet, and perhaps Chinese, support). This rebellion engaged Oman forces in sporadic, sometimes heavy, fighting in Dhofar during the later 1960s and early 1970s.

In the fight against that PFLOAG, however, Oman was supported not only by the British. Conservative Arab states and Iran, then still under the Shah, dread-ed by the leftist-revolutionary character of that rebellion and aimed to dis-establish the Gulf region as a whole, gradually rallied to Oman's side. Of the Arab states, only JORDAN actually sent a military contingent (volunteers, commandos, aircraft). Saudi Arabia helped financially, paying for military equipment etc., and began exerting pressure on South Yemen. IRAN maintained, from late 1972, a substantial expeditionary force in Oman (3,000–6,000 men, aircraft and naval equipment; an Iranian force of approximately 3,000 men was actually fighting, and defeating, the rebels). In 1974, Iran's military aid was regulated in an Oman-Iran Agreement on the joint defense of the Straits of Hormuz.

Political pressure on South Yemen grew heavier. Several Gulf sheikhdoms tried to mediate. The Arab League also tried (unsuccessfully, as the rebels refused to accept its mediation). But the decisive element was Saudi pressure. In 1975, South Yemen surrendered and ceased supporting the rebels. This was reaffirmed in March 1976 in a Saudi-mediated Oman-South Yemen Agreement. The Dhofar rebellion, deprived of its bases and supplies, faded out. However the Front itself maintained an organization, held congresses etc. In 1982, after further mediation, Oman and South Yemen established full, normal relations.

In return for the conciliation with South Yemen and the end of the rebellion, Oman undertook to liquidate British bases and end the British military presence. Oman announced, in 1976, that the British naval base at Masira island was being closed. British air force units were withdrawn from Salala. Actually, "facilities" remained at Britain's disposal. British officers continued serving in Oman's armed forces, heading several of their branches (the British commander-in-chief was replaced by an Omani Officer in November 1984). Iran's involvement in the defense of Oman was also gradually phased out. By 1977, the bulk of the Iranian forces were withdrawn. Plans for the institutionalization of a joint defense of the Gulf were shelved. With the fall of the Shah and the emergence of KHOMEINI's revolutionary Islamic regime in 1979, Iran turned from a close ally into a potential threat and enemy—both to Oman itself and, particularly during the the IRAN-IRAQ WAR, (1980–1988), to the security of, and free navigation in, the Gulf. While Oman remained strictly neutral in the Iran-Iraq War (at least outwardly and formally), it was in the context of this new, sharpened concern for the defense of the Gulf that Oman granted the US air and naval facilities. It agreed in 1980, to serve as one of the potential staging and supply bases for a planned US "Rapid Deployment Force." It also expanded (with US aid) its own defense installations, particularly in the Ras Musandam exclave in the Straits of Hormuz. US military support of Oman paid off during the war with Iraq, when Oman served as a major supply station for US and British troops arriving in the Gulf on their way to the front.

In international relations Sultan Qabus kept a rather low profile, fostering active cooperation with Saudi Arabia and the other Gulf states within the GULF COOPERATION COUNCIL he co-founded in 1981, but otherwise refraining from too active a foreign policy. Oman did not join either ORGANIZATION OF PETROLUEM EXPORTING COUNTRIES(OPEC) nor ORGA-NIZATION OF ARAB PETROLUEM EXPORTING COUNTRIES (OAPEC). The Sultan set a cautious pro-Western course, cultivating his alliance with Britain and the US. Despite that , he joined the group of non-aligned nations. In September 1985 Oman established official relations with the USSR, but did not actually exchange ambassadors. In inter-Arab politics, Oman evidently belonged to the conservative-moderate camp, without much activity.

During the Israeli-Egyptian peace process of the 1970s, Oman adopted a conciliatory line towards Egypt and ISRAEL. It became one of the three Arab League members not to sever diplomatic relations with Egypt after the signing of the peace treaty. In 1994 Oman established low-level diplomatic relations with Israel. The two countries opened commercial offices and an Israeli diplomat now serves in Oman. Prime Minister RABIN visited Oman in 1994. The environmental forum of the multinational talks for peace in the Middle East met in Oman. This reflected its ability to be accepted by all parties to the negotiations.

Oman foreign policies in the late 1990s demonstrates the Arab states acceptance of its low-profile, conservative and moderate positions.

OPEC   see ORGANIZATION OF PETROLEUM-EXPORTING COUNTRIES, OIL.

ORGANIZATION OF PETROLEUM-EX-PORTING COUNTRIES OPEC Formed in Sep-

tember 1960, OPEC had from the 1970s thirteen members, including all the major oil-producing countries of the Middle East and five non-Middle Eastern countries (Venezuela, Indonesia, Nigeria, Gabon, Ecuador). Gabon left the organization in 1995. The Middle East members were IRAN and seven Arab countries: SAUDI ARABIA, IRAQ, LIBYA, AL-GERIA, KUWAIT, QATAR and the UNITED ARAB EMIRATES (UAE); before its establishment of the UAE in 1971, ABU DHABI and DUBAI. Six Arab oil-producing countries were not members: EGYPT, SYRIA, BAHRAIN, OMAN, TUNISIA and MOROCCO. For OPEC's aims and policies and its impact on the world's oil economy see OIL.

OSLO AGREEMENT   see ARAB-ISRAEL PEACE MAKING.

OTTOMAN EMPIRE   The Ottoman Empire arose from a small Turkish principality founded in the second half of the thirteenth century in north-western Anatolia, on the Byzantine border. Originally a vassal of the Seljuks, Osman I asserted his independence around 1300 and gave his name to a dynasty which ruled for over 600 years.

By the late fourteenth century, the Ottoman rulers (Sultans) managed to expand their domain west of the straits into Europe. This aided the new empire in terms of diplomatic contacts with the European powers, the availability of manpower sources for conscription to their armed forces, and for the system of government. The Ottomans' increased strength enabled them to conquer what had been left of the Byzantine Empire and take Constantinople at 1453 as their new capital, Istanbul. After continued expansion the Ottoman Empire under Süleyman the Magnificent (1520–1566) stretched from Hungary to Yemen and the Abyssinian coast, and from the Moroccan border to the PERSIAN GULF. The Black Sea was virtually an Ottoman lake. After Süleyman, Ottoman progression was halted by the powerful enemies in the East (Persia) and the West (the Habsburg Empire.) Nonetheless, various territorial gains were still made occasionally.

The Ottoman Empire's decline was indicated by the failure of the siege of Vienna in 1683, and the Treaty of Karlowitz, 1699. During these it lost control over a large part of its domain in central Europe. The Ottomans suffered further defeats during the eighteenth century mainly at the hands of Austria and RUSSIA, while the rise of powerful autonomous local rulers and chiefs demonstrated the limits of the Empire's power. This futher weakened the Sultan's authority within his own domains. By the first decades of the nineteenth century the fate of the declining Empire ("The Sick Man on the Bosphorus") had become a major European concern ("The Eastern Question") because a gain to one power at the expense of the Ottoman Empire would mean the undermining of the European balance of power and increase the threat of war. British opposition to Russian designs to advance southwards was largely responsible for the Empire's survival. The Great Powers' efforts to acquire territorial gains, extend privileged rights for their protegés (see CAPITULATIONS) and obtain economic concessions, contributed to the emergence of nationalist movements. This could be seen primarily amongst Christian communities, aiming at self-rule and independence of the Ottoman Empire. The Ottoman Empire's repeated defeats and sense of political weakness generated an ever-increasing effort to introduce a series of reforms (the *Tanzimat*). These were initially aimed at strengthening the Empire's military capabilities, but later—largely encouraged by the European powers—expanded to include economic, administrative, legal, and educational reforms. This culminated in the granting of a constitution in 1876. The Ottoman government also adopted a policy of Ottomanism, designed to induce loyalty to the dynasty and the state amongst the various ethnic and religious communities. However, the reforms proved inefficient and too late to arrest the process of disintegration of the Empire. The modernizing rulers faced Islamic and traditional objections and were unable to finance the growing duties they had undertaken by their self-imposed reforms. The Ottoman government was aslo weakened by nationalist insurrections and Great Power encroachments. During the nineteenth and early twentieth centuries the Ottoman lost all their Balkan and African provinces, and at the outset of World War I they were left with only Anatolia, part of Thrace and the Arab provinces in Asia. The entry of the Ottoman Empire into World War I on the side of the Central Powers hastened its final dissolution, and by the time of the Armistice of Mudros it had also lost its Arab provinces. The Ottoman government was discredited by failure, defeat, and the Sultan's approval of the humiliating terms imposed by the Allies (see SÈVRES TREATY, 1920). These events undermined his prestige and legitimacy and the Turkish nationalists under Mustafa Kemal ATATÜRK were able to challenge Istanbul, create an alternative national center and wage a successful War of Independence. This turned over the terms dictated by the Treaty of Sèvres, and they were thus able (in November 1922 and March 1924) to abolish the Ottoman sultanate and caliphate respectively. The dynasty was then permanently exiled from TURKEY.

ÖZAL, TURGUT (1927–1993) Turkish politician, Prime Minister (1983–1989) and President (1989–1992). Born in Malatya in eastern TURKEY. Özal graduated from Istanbul Technical University in 1960 as an electrical engineer; he also studied economics and engineering in the US. After working in power station and electrification projects, and on the Scientific Committee of the Defense Ministry, from 1965 to 1967, he became technical adviser to Prime Minister DEMIREL. From 1967 to 1971 he was the manager of the State Planning Organization. He was an adviser to the World Bank (1972–1973) and after returning to Turkey, he joined the private sector.

Özal was appointed by Prime Minister Demirel as his chief economic adviser and in January 1980 launched a stabilization program aimed at pulling the country out of its severe economic crisis. He was allowed to maintain this capacity even after the September 1980 military intervention. A typical professional, Özal fitted well into the goverment of technocrats that was established after the coup and became Deputy Prime Minister in Bülent Ulusu's cabinet. Özal was largely successful in reducing inflation and the balance of payments deficit. He liberalized the Turkish economy bringing it more in line with market forces resulting in a significant rise in production and exports.

When in 1983 the military regime again permitted political and party activity, Özal founded the Motherland Party (MP). In the elections of November 1983, the MP won a majority of 211 seats, (out of 400) defeating the Nationalist Democracy Party which was favored by the military, as well as the left. Hence Özal formed the government.

In the elections of November 1987, the Party's representation in the Grand National Assembly grew to 292, granting Özal a further term in office. As Prime Minister, Özal continued the pursuit of his liberal economic policies, although they suffered some setbacks in the later 1980s. In 1987 he formally applied for Turkey's membership in the European Union and in the following year was the first Turkish statesman to visit Athens in a quarter of a century. He also expressed his support in granting the KURDS a measure of cultural rights.

In October 1989, Özal was elected President to succeed Kenan EVREN whose term had ended. Özal's candidacy had been strongly opposed by the opposition which argued that he would be unable to rise above party politics. He was elected on the third ballot only, with the opposition boycotting the session. Özal's term as president, the second civilian (after Celal BAYAR) to hold the office, can be divided into two. With his old party (from which he had to constitutionally resign) continuing to hold the majority in the National Assembly, he remained politically active and exercised great influence on his successor as Prime Minister, Yildirim Akbulut. He was largely responsible for shaping Turkey's stance during the Gulf crisis following Iraq's invasion of KUWAIT,

firmly placing Turkey on the side of the coalition fighting Saddam HUSSEIN. In this he followed his long time policy of promoting Turkey's relations with Europe and the United States.

When Süleyman Demirel's True Path Party (TPP) won the elections of October 1991 and formed the government, Özal could no longer influence government decisions. But Demirel and Özal, although bitter rivals, succeeded in forming a working relationship and Özal continued to actively participate in state affairs. By contrast his relations with the new leader of his former party, Mesut YILMAZ, deteriorated.

Suffering in his later years from heart trouble, Özal died in April 1993, succeeded by Demirel. Özal had been greatly criticized at home for his stance during the Gulf crisis but his strong Western oriented policies gained him many admirers in the West. In Turkey, too, while many did not like his personal authoritarian style of politics, there were those who commended him for displaying rare qualities of creative leadership despite the country's pressing problems. He is particularly remembered for his economic accomplishments.

P

PAHLAVI, MOHAMMAD REZA SHAH
(1919—1980)   King or Emperor (Shah) of IRAN from 1941–1979.

As Crown Prince he was sent to Switzerland for a modern education. Later he studied at the Army Officers Academy of Tehran. Mohammad Reza ascended the throne in September 1941, after his father, REZA SHAH, was forced to abdicate by the Allies after they had occupied Iran as a supply route to the USSR, due to the sympathy he had demonstrated for Nazi Germany.

Mohammad Reza's first wife was Princess Fawzia, sister of King Farouq of EGYPT, whom he divorced both for personal and political reasons, namely, a rift between Iran and Egypt. His second wife was Soraya Esfandyari of Bakhtiari origin. He divorced her after she failed to bear children. In 1959 Mohammad Reza married Farah Diba, an Iranian student of art in Paris, who bore him a son.

In an effort to contend with the problem of growing poverty and to prevent social unrest, Mohammad Reza began taking measures toward a multi-staged land reform. This involved the distribution of lands to farmers in over 2,000 villages. These lands had been confiscated by his father and turned into Crown estates. This plan was stopped under the pressure of the landlords, who were in fact the ruling class ("the thousand families"). In August 1953 Mohammad Reza was forced to leave Iran after Prime Minister Mohammad MOSSADDEQ, leading a national coalition, refused to obey him. However, several days later Mohammad Reza returned from exile, after Mossaddeq was ousted by a military coup led by General Zahedi. After that, Mohammad Reza did everything in his power to consolidate his position. After 1959 he put into effect far reaching land reforms, which were further extended in 1962. In 1963, under US pressure, resulting from American fears that the TUDEH Communist Party might overthrow the government, Mohammad Reza declared extensive social and economic reforms. These were called *enghlab-e Sefid* (the White Revolution), and described as *enghlab-e Shah va mardom* (the Revolution for the King and People). However, they were were not accompanied by political freedom, and Mohammad Reza maintained his tight control over the government and parliament, with the help of a large conservative majority, and strong personal involvement in daily affairs.

In the last year of his rule Mohammad Reza increasingly distanced himself from the people and engaged in glorifying his own name and immortalizing the Pahlavi dynasty. He implemented grandiose plans for the rapid development of the country—with the help of oil revenue, which had grown significantly in the 1970s—and turned Iran into a regional power, while becoming increasingly dependent on the UNITED STATES. He invested vast sums into strengthening and modernizing the armed forces in Iran (see IRAN). It became urgent to implement these plans as he had contracted lymphatic cancer in 1974. His illness was kept a strict secret. In the last years of his life Mohammad Reza frequently acted with impatience and haughtiness towards those surrounding him (perhaps because of the chemotherapy which he was secretly receiving). In the summer of 1978 the first signs that his self-confidence was weakening became visible. In the 1978 riots he instructed the army to avoid using an iron first for fear of bloodshed. This restraint was interpreted as a weakness by his opponents and was taken advantage of to intensify the acts of protest.

In January 1979, when he left the country with a small number of followers, many states avoided giving him permission to enter, due to KOHMEINI's threats. When it became known that the US had granted him an entrance permit for medical care, the American Embassy in Tehran was occupied with the goal of attaining information about his whereabouts. The Shah escaped to Panama but even there he did not feel safe. He thus chose to go to Egypt, where President Anwar al-SADAT invited him to settle. He was hospitalized in the military hospital and died on 27 July 1980 at the age of sixty-one. He was buried in the Al-Rifai mosque in Cairo. His supporters viewed him as an enlightened King who symbolized the national unity and aspiration to return Iran

to the era of historical glory. His enemies described him as a cruel ruler who robbed his people of their freedom and loyally served the interests of the West, especially the US.

PAHLAVI, REZA SHAH (1878–1944) Shah of IRAN 1925–1941. Soldier, statesman and founder of the Pahlavi dynasty. Born to a poor family in the town of Savad-Kuh in the Mazanderan district, along the southern shores of the CASPIAN SEA—a third generation in a family of military men. As a youngster, he joined the Cossak Brigade, attaining a high rank of command due to his qualifications and ambition. In February 1921 he took advantage of the confusion that prevailed in Iran and enacted a military coup along with the journalist and politician Z. Tabatabai (see IRAN). In November 1925 he announced the dismissal of the Shah of the Qajar dynasty. One month later he declared himself Shah. Despite lack of formal education and never having left the borders of Iran, his goal was to unite the country; end the rule of local rulers and the power of the tribes; establish a modern army equipped with modern weapons and march Iran in the direction of modernization, emulating Mustafa Kemal ATATÜRK in TURKEY.

He renovated the Iranian army, introduced a modern education system, fought against the excessive influence of the clergy, disbanded the Islamic dress and established a railway system and several factories. Reza Shah ran the state in an extremely centralized manner, cruelly suppressing the intellectuals and writers. In foreign affairs he fought against the influence of RUSSIA and BRITAIN, which from the beginning of the twentieth century had divided Iran into areas of influence, and in the hope of countering their power, approached Nazi Germany for support. In August 1941 the Allies invaded Iran, in order to put an end to Reza Shah's cooperation with Germany and to create a land bridge in order to transfer military supplies to the Soviet Union. Reza Shah was forced to vacate the throne in favor of his son Mohammad Reza PAHLAVI and went into exile in South Africa, where he died. His heir returned his remains to Iran and built for him a grand mausoleum in the South of Tehran, which was demolished in 1979 by the revolutionary regime.

PALESTINE ARABS (This entry reviews the political history of the Arabs of Palestine under British rule 1918–1948) Palestine was not a political-administrative unit during Ottoman-Turkish rule until 1918 (though as a general geographic term the name Palestine had been in use). The identity of its ARAB population—nearly 600,000 by the end of World War I, mostly Muslims, with a minority of CHRISTIANS—was comprised primarily of allegiance to their religious community, local and primordial links (the village and clan), except for a small urban elite which had begun to acquire some attributes of Palestinian-Arab identity. The Arab population was marked by diversity in accordance with the areas of living, which shaped their social structures and economic resources. In the mountainous areas of the Galilee, Judea and Samaria, the population, mostly rural, preserved its traditional social structure, although since the mid-nineteenth century there has been a growing migration to the coastal plain, a weakening of the rural leadership, and an emergence of the urban elite families due to the accumulation of land property. In addition, this society suffered from a built-in cleavage, deriving from an ancient tribal division into Qays and Yaman, that split the Arab villages of these regions. The Negev was scarcely inhabited by nomadic tribes, whose seasonal wondering northward had created tension with the rural and urban populations. In the coastal plain, growing financial flow from foreign sources and economic development of its towns, mainly Haifa and Jaffa, since the mid-nineteenth century, attracted migrants from the inner parts of the country, further weakening the rural leadership and creating a new cleavage— between traditionalism and modernism.

From the outset, the Zionist enterprise, beginning in the late nineteenth century, expedited the development of a specific Palestinian identity, which was increasingly salient among urban notables. Already before World War I, there were manifestations of political opposition to the Zionist settlement in the form of petitions, announcements and articles in the Christian-owned newspapers published in Haifa and Jaffa. The publication of the BALFOUR DECLARATION of November 1917, in which BRITAIN, now the ruler of Palestine, committed itself to help creating a Jewish National Home in the country, and the autonomous Arab administration established in Damascus by Emir FEISAL IBN HUSSEIN in 1918, rendered most Palestine Arab leaders to adhere to the idea of "Southern Syria," reflecting their opposition to the separation of Palestine from SYRIA at large. Two rival groups then speaking for incipient nationalism—the "Cultural/Literary Association" (al-Muntada al-Adabi) and the "Arab Club" (al-Nadi al-Arabi)—were more-or-less united on that point, and several leading activists were in Damascus with the group accompanying Feisal, endeavoring to establish an Arab administration for GREATER SYRIA. However, in July 1920 the HASHEMITE vision of a greater Syrian Arab kingdom was shattered by the French occupation of the country and the dismissal of Feisal from Damascus, as part of the division of the region into separate entities under French and British tutelage. The Palestinian Arabs had thus been forced to conduct their communal and political activities within the boundaries of Mandatory Palestine, and the new geographic-political realities led to the emergence of the Palestinian Arabs as a political community. The struggle against the British MANDATE, and even more so against the Jewish-Zionist National Home, greatly enhanced the development of a particular Palestinian Arab national consciousness.

Unlike the process that marked the neighboring Mandate regimes, the Palestinian Arabs remained until the end of the British Mandate with no representative institutions or national government. However, from the late 1920s, they explicitly demanded the creation of such institutions. The main reason for this exception of the Palestinian Arabs was the inclusion, within the Mandate document, of the Balfour Declaration, which postulated any Arab participation in such institutions under the Mandate auspices as a tacit acceptance of the Jewish National Home. Thus, the Palestinian Arab leadership rejected the initial British proposal, in 1922, for the establishment of a Legislative Council, boycotting the elections to this body in the following year. Later attempts to bring the British Mandate to implement the idea were confronted with a strong Zionist objection, and with the eruption of the revolt in 1936, the idea was practically shelved. Neither did the Palestinian Arabs establish effective national institutions of their own like the Jewish-Zionist community (Yishuv) did (knesset yisrael with its elected Assembly and the National Council—va'ad le'umi—nominated by that Assembly). The Mandatory government suggested the establishment of an "Arab Agency" parallel to the "Jewish Agency for Palestine" provided for in the Mandate, officially to represent and lead the Palestinian Arabs; but this proposal was rejected.

The Palestinian Arabs had communal-religious representative bodies. The Christian communities had their own church hierarchies with administrative and judicial organization. (Local leaders struggled, in some cases, against the largely foreign hierarchy for the "Arabization" of that organization and a stronger lay representation—particularly in the GREEK-ORTHODOX community.) As for the Muslim community, whose affairs had been managed in the OTTOMAN EMPIRE by the state, the Mandatory government ordered a "Supreme Muslim Council" (SMC) (al-majlis al-islami al-a'la) to be created (1922) to administer the religious affairs (Muslim Courts, schools, endowments and worship sites), which soon became the most important institutions in the Palestinian Arab community due to their control of financial resources, jobs, and effective apparatus. Their political-representative organization, however, remained rather sporadic and fragmented.

The two associations or clubs mentioned withered after 1920. From 1919–1920, political efforts were led by the "Muslim-Christian Associations," so named to stress, against the government's official classification according to communities, an Arab national, supra-communal unity. These committees, composed of small numbers of notables, convened several congresses. The first one, in Jaffa, January 1919, still saw Palestine as "Southern Syria" not to be separated from Syria. The third congress, Haifa, December 1920, centering now on the struggle in Palestine (with "Southern Syria" no longer mentioned), established an "Arab Executive" that became a permanent body, with Mussa Kazem al-Husseini as Chairman.

These congresses, and the Executive, also sent several delegations to Europe, mainly to London and Geneva, for talks, contacts and to propagate the Palestinian-Arab cause. The first such delegation went out in August 1921; in Geneva it co-operated with the permanent "Syrian-Palestine Office" maintained there for some years by a group of Pan-Arab exiled leaders, participating in a conference convened by that group. Similar delegations were sent in 1922 and 1923. But the Executive, its congresses and its delegations had no tangible success in their lobbying efforts and showed little active leadership. Hence the Executive gradually waned. The political cleavage between the Husseinis, represented by the SMC and the Executive Committee, and the opponent faction led by the Nashashibi clan (see below) deepened and prevented the convening of further national congresses after 1923, except for one in 1928 when a joint attempt was made to revive the Executive without much success.

When Mussa Kazem al-Husseini died in 1934, the Executive ceased to exist. At the same time, the SMC and its President, al-Hajj Amin al-HUSSEINI continued to gather power and reputation, which culminated in the wake of the 1929 Western Wall riots, in which this institution and its leader played a central role.

Behind the united front of the Arab Executive of the early 1920s, the real political leadership was increasingly wielded by Hajj Amin al-Husseini, MUFTI of JERUSALEM since 1921, and his faction. They used the SMC as an instrument of political and factional power, and a fierce struggle of rival camps over this issue largely shaped political life among the Palestinian Arabs during the most of the 1920s and 1930s. Neither the supporters of the Council—al-Majlisiyyun, also often called, after the clan leading them, "Husseinis"—nor their adversaries, "the Opposition,"al-Mu'aridun, also called "Nashashibis,"since that clan led them—organized themselves in the 1920s as formal political parties. Both camps derived their main strength from an informal network of urban clans supporting them, each with a network of client clans in the villages around their town, where they were frequently land-owners holding positions of economic power and patronage. While both camps had such networks, the Majlisiyyun-Husseinis were generally stronger among the urban intelligentsia and the Islamic establishment, especially in Jerusalem and Hebron, while the Mu'a ridun-Nashashibis and the clans supporting them (such as the Dajani in Jerusalem, the Touqan [Tawqan] and Masri in Nablus, Irsheid in Jenin, Bitar and Abu Khadra in Jaffa, Kheiri and al-Taji al-Farouqi in Ramla) had a stronger base of client clans in the rural areas and centered themselves around local and municipal interests. There were also influential clans, with their rural networks, whose allegiance was fluctuating or who tried to keep their independence of the two main camps (such as the Shawa in Gaza or the Abdel Hadi in Nablus), and there were individuals who did not follow their clan's orientation.

In general, the Husseinis were considered more militant or extremist than the Nashashibis—more moderate and prepared to collaborate with the government and the JEWS. However, this found scant expression in their public statements. Publicly, both camps were strongly nationalist, rejected the Mandate and the Balfour Declaration, opposed the government and the Jews and their National Home aspirations. Neither came up with any plans for an Arab-Jewish settlement or a compromise solution to the conflict. During the 1920s there were several attempts to establish political parties, based in the main on local, municipal or rural-agricultural interests, some of them half-supported by the opposition Nashashibi camp, and some with clandestine government or Jewish support. None of them had much impact and most soon withered. The dominating influence among the Palestinian Arabs remained that of the two main camps, with the "Husseini" camp setting the pace and fanning the violence that erupted again in the riots of 1929, and dragging the "Nashashibi" camp along.

The political weakness of the Palestinian Arabs—represented in their fragmentation and weak institutions—was manifested in the sporadic eruptions of violence (1920, 1921, 1929). These were spontaneous, short-lived, uncontrolled, and politically ineffective due to the lack of agreed upon realistic goals. The level of political mobilization and use of violence among Palestinian Arabs was, by and large, determined by the level of fear of the Zionist enterprise, but also by political rivalries and social tensions within the Arab community. Thus, the decline of Jewish immigration in the mid-1920s led to compliance on the part of Palestinian Arabs; fears of possible establishment of a Legislative Council (with the agreement of the leading political figures of the two rival factions—Mussa Kazem al-Husseini and Ragheb al-Nashashibi, led the *Mufti* al-Hajj Amin to amplify the dispute over the Western Wall, triggering the riots of August 1929. The wave of Jewish immigration after the ascendancy of the Nazis in Germany in 1933 was the main reason for the eruption of violence and political protest in April 1936.

With the demise of the Arab Executive and the intensification of the political pace in the early 1930s, several parties were founded in 1934–1935, primarily representing clan and local interests. The two main ones were the "National Defense Party" headed by Ragheb al-Nashashibi and rallying the *Mu'aridun*, and the "Palestine Arab Party" organizing the *Majlisiyyun*-Husseini camp and headed formally by Jamal al-Husseini (effectively by the *Mufti* Hajj Amin al-Husseini, who did not wish to compromise his powerful official position, or his ostensible above-party leadership position, by formally chairing the party). A third party, the *Istiqlal* ("Independence"), was founded by Awni Abdel Hadi in 1932. This was a militantly nationalist, Pan-Arab Party, ideologically rooted in the pre-World War I nationalist formations and the *Istiqlal* group they had tried to establish after the war, and with connections to the remnants of that group (though, by now, without the links to the Hashemites and the British that the group had in 1918–1919). In Palestine, the party comprised younger, militant intellectuals, but had little impact or influence. Three other parties seemed to have even less influence: the "Youth Congress," which emerged from a congress held in 1932 and was led by Ya'qub Ghussein; the "Reform Party" founded in 1935 by Dr. Hussein al-Khalidi, Mayor of Jerusalem 1934–1937; and the "National Bloc" of Abdel Latif Salah of Nablus. The leaders of these six parties became members of the new leadership of the Palestinian Arabs established in 1936: the Arab Higher Committee.

When in April 1936 an Arab general strike was declared, beginning with acts of violence against Jews and soon turning into a rebellion (then called "Disturbances"), an "Arab Higher Committee" (AHC) was formed to assume the overall leadership of the Arab community. The ten-member Arab Higher Committee, chaired by the *Mufti* Hajj Amin al-Husseini, comprised the heads of the six political parties, two additional representatives of the "Husseini" Party, and two other representatives, one from the Nashashibi party and the other close to the *Istiqlal* party. Among the ten, there were two Christians, one from the Nashashibi and one from the Husseini Parties. For the next few months the AHC provided an ostensibly united leadership. In effect, the political bases of this body soon became too weak to sustain the inherent differences that divided the rival factions and paralyzed the AHC's capability to function as a national leadership long before its official collapse in the fall of 1937. Thus, the AHC could not put an end to the prolonged strike of the Palestinian Arabs from April 1936, and needed the joint intervention of the Arab monarchs (of IRAQ, YEMEN, SAUDI ARABIA, and Transjordan) to finalize the strike. When in July 1937 the Rebellion was resumed, after having been suspended since October 1936 (see ARAB-ISRAEL CONFLICT), that unity finally broke down: the two Nashashibi party members of the AHC resigned and the leadership remained with the militant Husseini faction alone.

In October 1937 the AHC was outlawed by the Mandate government, now determined to suppress the renewed rebellion by force. Three of its members (Khalidi, Hilmi, Ghussein) were arrested, deported and kept in detention in the Seychelles; the *Mufti* and his close aid and relative Jamal al-Husseini escaped to Syria/LEBANON; Abdel Hadi had gone into exile even before, after being briefly detained. The AHC thus ceased to be an operative body, but the *Mufti*, Jamal al-Husseini and their associates tried to maintain the Rebellion from their Syrian-Lebanese exile, through a clandestine, non-institutionalized high command, aided by Arab nationalist circles in Syria and Iraq. Inside Palestine, municipal and village affairs were managed by the local notables, many of them close to the Nashashibi camp, but no alternative political leadership emerged. One chief reason for that was the brutal campaign of terror mounted by the rebel squads and the exiled leaders against the rival camp and its leadership. This induced the Nashashibi camp to form, from 1937–1938, counter-terror squads, so-called "peace gangs," but it still managed to paralyze and stifle any attempt to form a political leadership in the absence of the exiled extreme faction.

The actual rebellion—mainly guerrilla attacks on Jewish settlements and urban quarters and road communications—were conducted by small guerrilla-type squads ("gangs," *isabat*), most of them village-based. The AHC, and later the clandestine high command in exile, tried to establish a centralized military command, but never succeeded in imposing on the "gangs" a disciplined military command structure. In August 1936 the Syro-Lebanese Fawzi al-Qawuqji led a volunteer force into Palestine and assumed the supreme command of the Palestine Arab rebellion. He never succeeded in integrating the guerrilla squads into his force—which was in any case a brief episode that ended when the strike-and-rebellion was suspended in October 1936 (see ARAB-ISRAEL CONFLICT). In the resumed Rebellion,

1937, the head of the "gangs" in the *Tulkarm* region, Abdel Rahim al-Hajj Muhammad from Dhannaba village, declared himself commander in chief and was supported by the exiled leadership. His command was contested by several rivals and in any case never extended to the south, where the guerrillas were controlled by Hassan Salama from the Ramla area southwards and by Abdel Qader al-Husseini in the Jerusalem area. Abdel Rahim was killed in 1939 by the "Peace gangs"; the absent high command appointed Ahmad Abu Bakr from Burqa village to replace him. His command was never effective, and the rebellion was waning at that time under an intense British repressive effort.

The Rebellion of 1936–1939 had a far-reaching effect on the Palestinian-Arabs in several respects:

(a) The internal terror decimated the elite deeply affecting a large stratum of Palestinian Arab society in both towns and villages. There are no reliable figures, but the number of victims was variously estimated at 4,000–8,000, and there was hardly a family of notables not hit. Beyond the bitter, fearful memories of those years, the climate of internal violence and strife persisted for decades afterwards, and was of significant impact on the ability of this society to cope with the Zionist challenge during the 1947–1948 Civil War.

b) Political life was paralyzed (not the least due to the government's martial law during World War II). A vacuum, a near-total lack of leadership existed for almost ten decisive years, by the combination of internal terror with the absence (abroad or in detention) of many first-rank leaders of the militant, extremist camp.

c) The leadership of the Palestinian Arab struggle was in fact gradually taken over by the Arab states—a take-over encouraged by the British from the intervention of the Arab rulers in finishing the strike in October 1936 through the Anglo-Arab conferences on Palestine in 1939 and 1946–1947, and up to the involvement of the Arab states in the 1948 War of Independence. Yet, while waging the Palestine struggle, the Arab states did not impose their views and policies, but allowed, from about 1946, the militant Husseini faction of the Palestinian Arabs to call the tune.

d) The domination of the Palestinian Arabs, in 1937–1939, by "gang" commanders and internal terror, accelerated a growing disintegration of the traditional structure of Palestinian Arab society. The dominating influence of the leading families of notables with their network of client clans in the villages, declined—as did the decisive position of the extended family, the clan (*hamula*), in social life in general.

From 1939 to 1941, the *Mufti* al-Hajj Amin remained in Iraq, where he became involved in internal Iraqi politics through his influence on the ruling junta of military officers and his reputation as a combatant against British domination and ZIONISM and as a symbol of ARAB NATIONALISM. He played a central role in provoking the Iraqi nationalist Rebellion of April 1941 against Britain and the ruling Hashemite oligarchy, in secret collusion with Nazi Germany. In the wake of the failure of that Rebellion and reconquest of Iraq by Britain, the restored Hashemite elite were left with bitter hostility against the *Mufti*, whose repercussions were to be manifested in the preparations for the 1948 war.

During the first years of World War II, the Palestinian Arabs were numbed into political inactivity. When in 1943–1944 some notables wished to resume political action, toward the decisive years of the postwar settlement, the Husseini faction opposed any such resumption, and particularly the creation of a new representative body, in the absence of its leaders (many of whom had drifted in 1940–1941 from Syria-Lebanon to Iraq. From there the *Mufti* and some associates had gone to Nazi Germany, while Jamal al-Husseini and others had been arrested and deported). The Nashashibi camp, still paralyzed by the years of terror and disappointed that the government had not encouraged it to form an alternative leadership, was inactive. Thus, activities had to be led by marginal, minor groups, non-party individuals such as Mussa al-Alami, and non-political associations such as the Chamber of Commerce or the Trade Unions. But even they accepted the Husseini ruling that activities should not extend to the major political issues and that no representative body should be formed, and focused their energy on the prevention of the sale of Arab land to Jews, and information/propaganda efforts (see ARAB-ISRAEL CONFLICT).

The basic questions concerning the country's future, and the re-establishment of a leadership body that would deal with them, could no longer be postponed. During 1944, several of the minor parties (but not the Nashashibis) tried to re-establish their party organizations. Though they had little success, the Husseini faction felt compelled to do the same—taking care to appoint only provisional, acting officers and to leave the top posts vacant for the absent leaders. When the Palestinian Arabs were asked, in September 1944, to send a delegation of observers to the Alexandria Conference, called to prepare the foundation of Arab unity-which culminated in the establishment of the ARAB LEAGUE, they could not agree on the composition of such a delegation and the Husseini faction prevented its formation. With difficulty, it was agreed to send the respected non-partisan Mussa al-Alami as a single observer. But Alami was involved in controversy (over rival land salvation schemes) and his position was soon contested. In November 1945, the Arab League sent a mission headed by the Syrian Jamil Mardam to mediate the land salvation controversy and help establish an agreed upon leadership body. As Mardam brought a British promise that Jamal al-Husseini would soon be released, and helped the Husseinis obtain a dominating position, the latter agreed to re-establish a twelve-member Arab Higher Committee, consisting of the same six party leaders as in 1936 (with Jamal Husseini provisionally replaced by another Husseini), four more representatives of the Husseini faction, one Nashashibi (Ragheb) and two independents (pro-Husseini Alami, and pro-Istiqlal Ahmad Hilmi), with the chairmanship left vacant—meaning for the *Mufti*. But the new Arab Higher Committee did not operate smoothly and soon new controversies erupted. When Jamal al-Husseini was released and returned to Palestine early in 1946, he vigorously assumed the leadership. In March 1946 he expanded the AHC to consist of seven Husseini-based men, twelve "neutrals" (many of them in fact pro-Husseini), and ten for the other parties, two each.

The non-Husseini groups refused to accept this coup, boycotting the new AHC. Talks on a compromise (including the addition of ten pro-opposition "neutrals") failed in May, and in June the non-Husseini groups set up a rival leadership body, the "Arab Higher Front." Faced with this open split, the Arab League again intervened: it dissolved both of the rival committees and appointed a new, five-member Arab Higher Committiee, with the *Mufti* Hajj Amin al-Husseini as chairman (still in exile—

since June 1946 in Egypt), Jamal al-Husseini as deputy chairman, one more Husseini man and two pro-opposition neutrals (Hilmi and Dr. Hussein al-Khalidi). Thus the League, though it knew that the Husseinis did not accept the policies adopted by most Arab states and took a more militant line, handed the dominating influence to the Husseini faction.

The new AHC took an uncompromising line in the decisive phase of the diplomatic struggle for Palestine (1946–1947). It declined all British compromise proposals, such as cantonization and semi-autonomy, rejected the UN partition plan, and called for war to prevent its implementation. But the split had not been healed and the new AHC was not really in control. Even the military instrument it tried to forge toward the inevitable Arab-Jewish showdown, blunt and ineffective, was split into the Husseini-founded *Futuwwa* and the opposition-leaning *Najjada*, and the decision to merge them was not realized. The Palestinian Arabs opened violent action on the morning of the UN decision of 29 November 1947. While poorly and effectively prepared, they launched a strong, united leadership.

The events of 1947–1948—the guerrilla war from December to May; Qawuqji's volunteer "Army of Deliverance"; the invasion of the regular armies of the Arab states and the Arab-Israel war; the flight of the refugees; the occupation of the Arab parts of Palestine by Jordan and Egypt—are described in the entry ARAB-ISRAEL CONFLICT. The end of the war found the Palestinian Arabs divided and their body politic shattered. In 1947–1948, the Palestinian Arabs numbered 1.3 million—double their number at the end of World War II and the inception of the Mandate. That remarkable growth, larger in the mixed cities and the coastal regions of Jewish settlement than in the purely Arab districts, included a number of immigrants from neighboring Arab countries who were illegal and mostly unregistered. It is impossible to accurately establish their number, but the usual estimate is 60,000–100,000. Of these 1.3 million Palestinian Arabs, approximately 650,000 remained in their homes—over 400,000 in the Jordan-occupied WEST BANK and East Jerusalem, 70,000–100,000 in the GAZA STRIP and 160,000 in ISRAEL (see ISRAEL ARAB CITIZENS). 650,000–700,000 left their domicile as refugees—some 300,000–350,000 remaining within Palestine (200,000 in the West Bank and 120,000–160,000

in the Gaza Strip), 150,000-2000,000 going to JORDAN, and about 150,000 to other Middle East countries primarily to Syria and Lebanon (and a very few to other countries). Those in Jordan and the Jordan-occupied part of Palestine received Jordanian citizenship—approximately 800,000 (400,000 original inhabitants of the West Bank, 200,000 refugees in the West Bank, 100,000 refugees in Jordan). The 160,000 in Israel became Israeli citizens including the internal refugees (23,000). Those in the Gaza Strip, Lebanon and Syria had no citizenship.

In Ottoman times, Palestine was a backwater and the Palestinian Arabs were hardly different from the Arab population of the surrounding regions in their social and educational level. However, during the twenty-eight years of the Mandate, under the impact of the general development of Palestine and its Jewish sector, and the political struggle with the Zionist enterprise, the Palestinian Arabs greatly advanced in their health and educational standards; their social institutions; their political awareness and activity. Indeed it may be estimated that their average educational level was by 1948 more highly developed than that of the Arab countries (with the exception of Lebanon). While in the arts and literature very few of them attained all-Arab acknowledgement, they had a lively press. (Two main dailies regularly published for most of those years: *Filastin*—founded 1911, a daily from 1929, published by an Arab-Christian family—and *al-Difa'*, founded 1934, several other dailies published for some time. There was also a highly developed educational network (mostly governmental, some private, and some missionary), and rising average educational standards. This development continued, and was enhanced, despite the adverse general and political situation of the Palestinian Arabs, after 1948. In fact, among the Palestinian refugees educational standards rose most conspicuously, owing to the intensive schooling provided by UNRWA, the UN agency caring for the refugees. A large number of young Palestinians studied at universities in the Arab countries and in Europe and America, and the Palestinians are estimated to have a higher ratio of academically trained citizens than any other Middle East population.

From 1948 to the mid-1980s the number of Palestinian Arabs, divided and partly dispersed as they were, has greatly increased; in fact, they have quadrupled to about 5–6 million, as detailed below. In some of their divisions, this was the result of their high natural birth-rate, with no major other demographic changes. Thus, for instance, in Israel though some 40,000–50,000 refugees were allowed to return through a scheme of family reunion, and some may have drifted back undetected, most of the more than four-fold growth to over 900,000 in the late 1990s was due to natural increase. The same is true of the Palestinian Arabs in Syria and the Gaza Strip with its massive concentration of Palestinian Arab refugees. In Lebanon there was some additional influx of Palestinian Arabs from Jordan after the latter expelled the Palestinian guerrillas in 1970–1971—but that influx concerned mainly PALESTINE LIBERATION ORGANIZATION (PLO) activists and officials and "regular" fighters, not a population movement of any size. (The same, in reverse, goes for the evacuation of 11,000–14,000 PLO men from Beirut in August 1982—and the re-infiltration of a few thousands after 1984: these movements of PLO professionals meant no demographic change for the bulk of the Palestinian Arabs in Lebanon).

Significant demographic change concerned the Palestinian Arabs in the Jordan-occupied West Bank, Jordan and the PERSIAN GULF. In the latter area, many Palestinian Arabs found employment and settled, especially in KUWAIT, from the early 1950s onwards. In Kuwait alone, their number was estimated by 1990 at 350,000–400,000, and in the Gulf region as a whole at nearly 1 million. But the permanence of their settlement was in doubt. As Jordanian citizens they could return—or be made to return—to Jordan or the West Bank. Indeed, when the OIL boom and its labor market began shrinking in the 1980s, a movement in that direction did set in. During the nineteen years of Jordanian rule in the West Bank (1948–1967) a considerable migration of Palestinian Arabs from the West Bank to the East Bank was reported. Figures cited are unreliable and vary greatly—from 250,000 to 500,000, with approximately 400,000 as possibly the most accurate estimate. A further wave of migration occurred during and immediately after the 1967 War (most of the West Bankers fleeing to the East Bank were in the West Bank since 1948, as refugees). Figures vary again—from 200,000 to 300,000, approximately 250,000 being a likely estimate. In any case, precise figures could not be given: the West Bank Palestinian Arabs were Jordanian citizens and there was

no way of telling whether movements from the West Bank to the East Bank or the Gulf were meant as permanent emigration. The Israelis occupying the West Bank in 1967 found a population of some 650,000 (or 585,000 without East Jerusalem, soon separated and incorporated into Israel). Some movement—to Jordan, and to the Gulf—continued after 1967, and again, there was no indication as to those going for temporary labor purpose, or for permanent migration; it is estimated, from 1967 to the mid-1980s, at about 185,000, but some cite figures up to 300,000. By the late 1990s the Palestinian population of the West Bank, excluding East Jerusalem, was approximately over 1.2 million.

In Jordan (the East Bank), constant migration of Palestinian Arabs from the West Bank, transformed the Palestinian Arabs into a majority after 1967 even without counting the pre-1948 population of Palestinian origin. Detailed figures again vary, but the fact of a Palestinian majority—put by some at over fifty-five percent—is generally accepted since the mid-1970s. Indeed Jordan counts its Palestinian-Arab inhabitants, informally, at less than forty percent. Following the Iraqi invasion of Kuwait and GULF WAR most of the Palestinians in Kuwait were expelled, leaving behind no more than 20,000, as was the case regarding other Gulf monarchies. Thus, in 1990–1991, close to one million migrants from the Gulf region (mostly Palestinians) migrated to Jordan, and for the most part settled there.

The total number of Palestinian Arabs is in the mid 1990s is estimated at 5–6 million—about 2.2 million in Jordan; 1.2 million in the West Bank; 900,000 in the Gaza Strip; 0.9 million in Israel; 0.4 million in Lebanon; 0.3 million in Syria; 0.2 million in the Gulf countries, 0.2–0.4 million in other Arab countries and in Europe or the Americas. Of these 5–6 million, approximately 2.5–3 million are refugees and their descendants. Of the refugees, some 800,000–900,000 live in refugee camps in the West Bank, Gaza Strip, Jordan and Syria—in fact fully grown refugee towns.

The post-1948 political activities of the Palestinian Arabs (see also ARAB-ISRAEL CONFLICT) were initially final convulsions and after-throes of the war of 1948. Several rallies of notables, late in 1948, had urged King ABDALLAH of Jordan to save and take over the Arab part of Palestine. Since the Palestinian Arabs on the West Bank welcomed, or acquiesced in, the

Jordanian occupation, there was little specific Palestinian political activity in those regions. In the Egyptian-occupied Gaza Strip, however, efforts were made—and indeed even encouraged by Egypt—to keep the Palestinian Arab entity alive and foil its erosion by Jordan's annexation of the West Bank. In July 1948, the Arab League resolved to establish an "Administrative Council for Palestine," but with a follow-up to implement this decision. In September, again at the Arab League's behest, a "Government of all Palestine," was established in Gaza claiming authority over the whole territory of Mandatory Palestine. This was established by the remnants of the AHC, and dominated by the *Mufti*, al-Hajj Amin al-Husseini, whose position superceded that of the Prime Minister. This "government" was headed by Ahmad Hilmi and included Jamal Husseini as Foreign Minister and, at first, the non-Husseinis Awni Abdel Hadi and Hussein al-Khalidi. It was recognized by all the Arab states except Jordan. An eighty-six-member "Constituent Assembly" was also convened shortly afterward, presided over by Hajj Amin al-Husseini. However, the All-Palestine government was bound to fail since it had no independent resources, nor was it given authority over any part of Palestine or its people. The Arab governments, even supporters such as Egypt, did not allow it to exercise power, perceiving its role mainly as an instrument to frustrate King Abdallah's scheme of incorporating parts of Palestine into his Kingdom. The Palestinian Assembly met only once, in October 1948, and was never reconvened.

By mid-October, Israel had waged its largest military offensive ever since the War had begun, in order to expel the Egyptian forces from Palestine. Although a narrow strip from Rafah to the north of the city of Gaza remained in Egypt's hands, the All-Palestine Government members left for Cairo, and after a short time the organization disintegrated. The non-Husseini members drifted away and joined the service of Jordan, and the government did not function. In September 1952, the Arab League announced officially that the All-Palestine Government had ceased to operate and that Palestine would be represented in the League by the Arab state. (Hilmi continued to function as low-ranking "Representatives of the Palestinian Arabs" in the League.) As Egypt did not annex the Gaza Strip, some rudiments of local self-government were established in the late

1950s and a Gaza-Palestine Arab entity was maintained. In 1958, a "Palestinian National Union" was founded —parallel to, and part of, the "National Union" that was the single political organization of Egypt and the UAR of 1958–1961; but it did not take root or develop into a nucleus of a revived Palestinian Arab entity.

The Hashemite King vigorously opposed the Egyptian-based overture of a Palestinian government. He responded to this by encouraging gatherings of Palestinian Arab notables and political leaders in Amman and the occupied part of Palestine, proclaiming their unconditional support for the King as the sovereign of Palestine. This culminated in the Jericho Conference held on 1 December 1948, which proclaimed King Abdallah "King of Palestine," urging him to liberate the rest of Palestine. Administrative measures of the practical annexation of the occupied area of Palestine to Jordan had been taken as early as summer 1948, and the Palestinian Arabs were appointed, from 1949, also as Jordan Cabinet Ministers, civil servants, and diplomats. In March 1949 the use of the term "Palestine" in official documents was banned, substituted by the term "West Bank." A new election law of December 1949 gave the inhabitants of the West Bank the right to vote (with equal, 50:50 representation to the two parts of the Kingdom).

In April 1950, elections were held, and the formal incorporation of the occupied West Bank in the Kingdom was solemnly proclaimed, upholding the slogan "Unity of the Two Banks" (*wahdat al-daffatein*) as the main principle shaping the relationship between the two parts of the Kingdom. This annexation caused a serious inter-Arab crisis, since the Arab states bitterly opposed it and threatened to expel Jordan from the Arab League. The crisis was resolved in April 1950 by a double formula: first, the Arab states acquiesced in their annexation of the West Bank, officially termed "temporary," until the liberation of Palestine in its entirety; second, in return, Abdallah secretly consented to scrap a non-aggression pact with Israel which he had negotiated and initialled in February of that year.

The Palestinian Arabs, as new citizens of the Hashemite Kingdom, educationally more advanced and accustomed to vigorous, volatile political activity and factionalism, fermented conflict in the Kingdom. While many of them were prominent in public positions at all levels, many others were active in opposition agitation. Apart from the remnants of the Husseini faction in Jerusalem (some of whom were actively involved in the assassination of King Abdallah in July 1951 at the al-Aqsa Mosque in Jerusalem), the Jordanian regime was confronted by militant Palestinian opposition whose main effort was aimed at derailing the Hashemite Kingdom from the Western orbit and incorporating it into the Arab nationalist one. Palestinians tended to identify themselves with radical Pan-Arab nationalist and anti-Western political streams, and from the mid-1950s, increasingly with NASSERISM—avoiding the idea of a separate Palestinian identity or entity—as the shortest and most effective strategy to bring about the recovery of Palestine from the hands of Israel (see also JORDAN).

The idea of a Palestinian entity was reopened in the late 1950s and early 1960s by both Palestinian Arabs outside the West Bank and some of the Arab regimes, primarily Egypt, in the context of, and as an instrument in, disputed relations inter-Arab. The idea reflected the rise of a new Palestinian Arab generation with a new political consciousness and demands. Yet, the Arab states hesitated to adopt unequivocally the slogan of a Palestinian Arab state, realizing that that very slogan threatened the existence of the Hashemite Kingdom of Jordan and legitimacy of its regime, since a distinct Palestinian state would necessarily invalidate Jordan's rule over the West Bank. (For the inter-Arab circumstances that led to the foundation of the PLO in 1964, its Charter, and political development, see PALESTINE LIBERATION ORGANIZATION and PALESTINIAN GUERRILLA ORGANIZATIONS.)

The takeover of the West Bank and Gaza Strip by Israel in the 1967 War, along with the rise of PALESTINIAN GUERRILLA ORGANIZATIONS and their takeover of the PLO in 1969, boosted the demand for an independent Palestinian state by both the Palestinian national movement and the Arab governments apart from Jordan. Now that historic Palestine came under Israeli occupation and the anti-Jordanian implications of the demand for an independent Palestinian state were blurred, the Arab states gradually came to adopt this idea. From 1972, King HUSSEIN advocated a federation or confederation between the future liberated Palestinian territory and Jordan, but in 1974 Jordan was forced to acquiesce in the ARAB SUMMIT CONFERFENCE's decision to recognize the PLO

as the sole legitimate representative of the Palestine people. However, ups and downs in the PLO's politcal situation, together with Israel's vehement opposition to its participation in the peacemaking process, preserved Jordan's role as a relevant partner to any settlement of the Palestine conflict. The idea of confederated Jordanian-Palestinian relations indeed remained theoretically optional, though on the Palestinian side it was a tactic and not a strategy. Hence, in the mid-1980s the PLO under Yasser ARAFAT accepted it in principle, enabling the signing of the Amman Agreement between Arafat and King Hussein in February 1985. This Agreement, however, was abrogated by the PLO in 1987, and in November 1988, following King Hussein's announcement of disengagement from the West Bank and abrogation of the Unity of the Two Banks, the PLO proclaimed the Independent Palestinian State (see INTIFADA and ARAB-ISRAEL PEACEMAKING).

PALESTINIAN AUTHORITY (PA—the Palestinian term is: Palestinian National Authority) Semi-official, self-governing Palestinian authority, established in May 1994 under the auspices of the PALESTINE LIBERATION ORGANIZATION (PLO) exists in most of the GAZA STRIP, and the town of Jericho in the Jordan Valley. The PNA, the first government to be formally established inside historic Palestine, came out of the mutual Declaration Of Principles (DOP), signed by PLO Chairman Yasser ARAFAT, and Israel's Prime Minister Yizhak RABIN in Washington, on the White House lawn on 13 September 1993 (Oslo I). In this declaration, (reached followed secret negotiations in Oslo, Norway), the signatories expressed mutual recognition between ISRAEL and the PLO. This set forward a process of interim arrangements of Israeli withdrawal ("redeployment") from territories in the WEST BANK and Gaza Strip, which were to culminate in "permanent status talks" to begin in May 1996, on all major issues in dispute between the two parties (settlements, JERUSALEM, Palestinian refugees, and final status of the PA). Israel's withdrawal from Gaza Strip and Jericho ("Gaza and Jericho first") and the establishment of a Palestinian self-governing authority over those territories, were to be the first phases in the process. The Oslo I agreement stipulated that transferring of responsibilities to the PA would be completed within five years, and would include education and culture, health, social welfare, direct taxation and tourism. It was also agreed that a Palestinian police force would be established in order to maintain the internal security and prevention of hostile acts of terror against Israel by the Palestinian population under its authority. Israel would retain the overall authority for security and defense regarding all external threats, and particularly the safety of the Israeli settlers.

The foundation of the PA emerged from King HUSSEIN's proclamation, on 31 July 1988, which had formally relinquished Jordanian legal and administrative control over the Palestinian territories. After this the Palestinian National Council (PNC) declared unilaterally the establishment of an independent Palestinian state, based on the UN partition resolution of November 1947.

On 17 May 1994, Israel and the PLO signed the Cairo Agreement. This elaborated on the transferring of authorities to the Palestinians, as well as the security arrangements between the two sides. Soon after, the PLO officially established the PA. It was a nucleus of government apparatus which assumed control of the Gaza Strip (save the Israeli settlements) and Jericho. Before the end of June, Yasser Arafat arrived in Gaza to head the PA. The interim agreement signed on 28 September 1995 (Oslo II) between Israel and the PA, set the timetable and modalities for the later stages of the process. According to this agreement (Oslo II), by December 1995 the IDF would withdraw from five major towns in the West Bank (out of the six stipulated in the agreement) in preparation for elections to both the Palestinian Council, and for the office of the PA's Chairman. The withdrawal from the city of Hebron was postponed by Shimon PERES's government due to the strong public resentment of the Oslo process and the Rabin assassination.

The interim agreement divided the West Bank into three jurisdictional zones as follows: Zone A, including the urban aras, under full Palestinian authority; Zone B, including a large part of the rural areas, under Palestinian authority on public order issues and Israeli authority on security issues; and Zone C, the larger part of the West Bank, including the settlements, the IDF bases, the Jordan Valley, and the desert area—under full IDF authority, except for personal law.

In February 1995 the Higher State Security Court was established in Gaza. One of its first decisions was the abolition of the Israeli legal system (military and civilian) that had existed since the occupation of these territories in 1967. Instead, the previous legal system was applied—the Jordanian law in the West Bank, and the British Mandatory law in the Gaza Strip. According to the interim agreement, both legal systems are valid in criminal and civilian affairs only. The agreement, however, left in power the Israeli law in all three zones of the West Bank.

The PNA held its first meeting on 26 May 1994 with twenty members of the temporary nominated forum, headed by Yasser Arafat. The lion's share of the PA's bureaucracy came from the PLO headquarters in Tunis, complemented by local active members of *Fatah*, the mainstream organization, many of whom had spent varying periods in Israeli prisons. This PA new bureaucracy doubled the already existing apparatus of teachers and officials (about 20,000), who had been employed by the Israeli civil administration in the West Bank and Gaza. Furthermore, the PA created a huge body of various security and police forces, encompassing 25,000–30,000 men, mostly from previous Palestinian security apparatuses and military units. The PA thus became the largest employer in the territory under its control, indicating its strategy of centralized economy.

On 20 January, 1996, the first elections to the Palestine [Legislative] Council (PLC) and PA's Presidency took place under international supervison. Many participated, with approximately eighty-eight percent of eligible voters in Gaza and seventy percenet of voters in the West Bank. Palestinian residents of East Jerusalem also participated in the elections, though with a much lower participation level. The elections were officially boycotted by the Islamic Resistance Movement (HAMAS), although some of the council-elect members, who ran independently, were identified with the movement.

As expected, the *Fatah* list—shaped and backed by Yasser Arafat—won forty-nine of the total eighty-eight seats in the PLC (more than fifty-five percent). In addition to other *Fatah* independent candidates, this constituted some seventy-five percent of the Council's seats.

Political opposition to the PA remained in disarray, having minimal impact except for HAMAS. This opposition, whose leaders and sources of political support are in the diaspora, is comprised of three main forms: a) The Ten Front, a Syrian-based loose alignment of militant Palestinian groups, including: the Popular Front for the liberation of Palestine (PFLP), the Democratic Front for the Liberation of Palestine (DFLP), the Palestine Liberation Front, Palestine Popular Struggle Front (PPSF), Popular Front for Liberation of Palestine—General Command (PFLP-GC), Palestine Revolutionary Communist Party, *Fatah* the Uprising, SA'IQA, *Hamas*, and the Islamic Jihad.

b) Individual personalities, such as Shafi Haidar ABDEL (who resigned his membership of the PLC) and other Council members.

c) PLO mainstream figures in the diaspora, such as Faruk QADDOUMI, head of the PLO political department who placed his objection to the Oslo Agreement and its implementation by Arafat.

The main criticism of the militant opposition organizations against the PA leadership has revolved around the perceived excessive concessions made by Arafat in the Oslo agreements. Criticism against the PA within the Palestinian community, primarily in the West Bank, has hinged on the decisive role played by the PLO's apparatuses arriving from Tunis and other Arab countries in manning key positions, in preference of local inhabitants. This criticism was strengthened by Arafat's authoritarian rule, the PA's centralized decision making process, especially on financial allocations, and growing manifestations of corruption and abuse of power by the security agencies and senior officials of the PA. This led to a report submitted to the elected PA's Council in the fall of 1997, resulting in an ultimatum to Arafat to reshuffle his ministers. In principle he agreed to this after much pressure.

The foundation of the PA, along with the elections to its council, finally shifted the center of gravity of Palestinian politics from the diaspora into the Gaza Strip and West Bank. This centrality came to the fore with Arafat's dual roles as both Chairman of the PLO Executive Committee and the PA's Chairman. This drew the criticism of many Palestinians, especially among the West Bank intellectual elite.

From the outset, the PA's existence was marked by dependency on external financial sources, due to the need for urgent infrastructural and economic development. To secure the implementation of the Oslo agreement, in October 1993, economically powerful nations (particularly the US, Canada, the European Community and Japan) met under the auspices of the World Bank to set up plans for financial aid to the PA. Pledges made in late 1993 reached 2.4 billion dollars for four years. (By late 1997 the total amount of pledges had reached 3.68 billion dollars), of which a total of 1.8 billion dollars was given in two main ways: long-term projects of infrastructural, industrial and other development purposes; and short-term, stop-gap projects, such as creating new jobs to curtail unemployment and covering budgetary deficit.) The World Bank founded the Holst Fund (named after the late Norwegian Foreign Minister Jorgen Holst) to marshal the short-term aid. (This was originally intended to operate until late 1997, but was prolonged to 1998.) An Ad Hoc Liaison Committee was set up to monitor the disbursement process, while the PLO established PECDAR (the Palestine Economic Council for Development and Reconstruction) as the main vehicle for economic policy. To the first three projects of World Bank's Emergency Assistance Program (EAP) that were approved in May 1994, donors pledged immediately 42 million dollars. However, problems arose soon after the funds started flowing to the PA. There were discrepancies with the PA's accountability (who managed the aid with the donor community) and transparency of the ways and goals for which this financial aid was spent. A number of PA ministries claimed this role, including the PLO political department headed by Faruk Qaddoumi. Other problems were caused by external economic factors like the Israeli closure that was imposed due to terrorist acts committed by the Islamic opposition movements. The closure had an immediate impact on the Palestinian population's ability to pay their taxes to the PA. Moreover, the PA-Israel economic agreement signed in 1994 in Paris, remained mostly unimplemented. All this came against the backdrop of years of uprising (INTIFADA) and a huge expulsion of Palestinians from the Gulf countries since 1990, reducing the remittance from these Arab countries. Thus, much of the aid flowing to the PNA has been spent on plugging the PLO's deficit. In response, the donor nations tended to hold back on granting new sums. In August 1994, the UN appointed Terje Larsen, who took part in the Oslo negotiations, as the envoy in charge of the disbursement of funds in Gaza. Larsen's plan included a new mechanism of controlling the funds through committees composed by representatives from both the PNA and the donor countries. All the committees are devoted to key issues such as the creation of jobs; education; infrastructure etc. Another source of investment in the PNA is the Palestinian private investors. They come mainly from Jordan, but there are also some from elsewhere in the diaspora. In 1993, Padico (Palestinian Development and Investment Company) was founded with a capital of 200 million dollars. This initiative helped build factories and some tourist projects with the financial aid from Palestinians, Jordanian banks and US and Egyptian companies. However, prospects for larger scope of private investments by Palestinians faded out due to the PA's centralized economy, and the sense of insecurity caused by terrorist attacks and closures, culminating in the virtual halt of the Oslo process after the advent of a right-wing government in Israel, headed by Binyamin NETANYAHU (May 1996).

Following the interim agreement of September 1995, US Secretary of State Warren Christopher, hosted an Ad Hoc Liaison Committee (AHLC) on Palestinian assistance. This is to support projects that address infrastructure needs and create employment opportunities for Palestinians. Furthermore it created a framework for increased assistance by the European countries and the US.

PALESTINE CONCILIATION COMMISSION (PCC)   see ARAB-ISRAEL PEACEMAKING.

PALESTINIAN GUERRILLA ORGANIZA-TIONS   Representing a claim for the national liberation of historic Palestine in its entirety as the inalienable right of the Palestinian ARAB nation, from the late-1950s onwards groups of Palestinians began clandestinely organizing themselves for armed struggle against ISRAEL. Palestinian Arabs conducted guerrilla warfare against Israel throughout the 1950s. They infiltrated from the neighboring Arab states for sabotage, intelligence, and murder—during 1955–1956 at the behest of EGYPT, carrying the name "self-sacrificers" (*fida'iyyun*). However, those activities lacked the national-libertarian revolutionary ideology and institutionalized characteristics of the popular armed struggle adopted by Palestinian organizations in the 1960s following disillusionment of Pan-Arabism and of the Arab states' declarative commitment to the liberation of Palestine.

The catastrophe (*nakba*) sustained by the Palestinian Arab people in the 1948 War, was manifested, among other ways, by their disappearance from the Middle East political and military scene for over a decade. The ARAB-ISRAEL CONFLICT was on an international level a conflict between Israel and the Arab neighboring states. Meanwhile the Palestinian Arab national cause was shunned aside, degenerating into a refugee problem. The PALESTINE ARABS, whether refugees or non-refugees, were still shocked by the mass exodus from their homes and dispersion in the Arab countries; the division of Mandatory Palestine by Israel, JORDAN and Egypt, and the disintegration of their political leadership. The new trend amongst the young, educated, professional Palestinian refugees in the Arab states (LEBANON, SYRIA, Egypt, KUWAIT) established the concept of popular armed struggle as the essential element of Palestinian national liberation, and as a way of resuming Arab action in support of the Palestinian problem. The awakening of self-reliant Palestinian activism derived from the poor socio-economic conditions of the Palestinian refugees in the Arab states; the sense of alienation by the hosting Arab societies and the security restrictions imposed on them by the Arab regimes; the intense inter-Arab disputes and absence of any collective Arab effort to prepare for a "second round" against Israel. Furthermore, the late 1950s and early 1960s were marked by a growing process of de-colonization and the rise of national revolutionary guerrilla movements (ALGERIA, Cuba). Their success over established regimes and foreign domination served as a role model for similar effort envisioned on the part of the Palestinians.

This trend of Palestinian national activism coincided with, and was part of, the rise of the Palestinian Entity idea in the late 1950s. This had initially been created by Palestinians. In 1959 it was adopted by ABDEL NASSER and QASSEM, in their intense propaganda duels. The indications of political awakening, along with the radicalization of Palestinians in the GAZA STRIP and the WEST BANK, apparently prompted Nasser's support—confirmed reluctantly by King HUSSEIN of Jordan—for the establishment of the PALESTINE LIBERATION ORGANIZATION (PLO) in May 1964. In any event, the establishment of the PLO cast its image as an empty political vessel dominated by conservative Arab inaction, a typically Nasserist instrument rather than a revolutionary, combatant organization. The establishment of the PLO led to *Fatah*'s decision to use armed action from January 1965, taking advantage of the Syrian-Egyptian animosity and Syria's adherence to the idea of popular armed struggle in 1963. Algeria also supported this type of activity, and provided *Fatah* with political representation, arms supplies and military training. *Fatah* was followed by other guerrilla organizations, which mushroomed after the June 1967 War, representing the same pattern of activity, though not the same ideology or political allegiance.

Historically, the Palestinian guerrilla organizations have represented three major ideological and political concepts. (Indeed, the main guerrilla groups also viewed themselves as political formations.)

a) National activism and social pragmatism—the mainstream represented by *Fatah*. This adhered to the concept of Palestinian nationalism, striving to establish an independent Palestinian state on the liberated territory of historic Palestine, instead of Israel. This stream persisted in maintaining its freedom of decision making from Arab states' pressures.

b) The Pan-Arab revolutionary trend, represented by the ARAB NATIONALIST MOVEMENT (*harakat al-qawmiyyun al-arab*), which in 1967 led to the formation of the Popular Front for the Liberation of Palestine (PFLP). Later splits formed the Popular Front for the Liberation of Palestine General Command (PFLP-GC), and the Democratic Front for the Liberation of Palestine (DFLP). While the original PFLP and the PFLP-GC remained markedly Pan-Arab in their ideology, the DFLP adopted as of the October 1973 war increasingly national attitude, close to that of *Fatah*, but remained deeply committed to social revolution, similarly to the PFLP.

c) The Arab-based organizations—established by Arab regimes to serve their national interests and provide them a foothold in the Palestinian political arena, namely, the Sa'iqa of Syria and the Palestine Liberation Front (PLF) of IRAQ. While their ideology derived from the Pan-Arab BA'TH doctrine, they in effect represented first and foremost Syrian and Iraqi interests, respectively.

The Arab regimes responded to the new trend of Palestinian national and military activism somewhat ambivalently. Ideologically, they expressed their commitment and unswerving support, but in practice, they imposed strict prohibitions on any autonomous Palestinian political or military activity on their sovereign soils, except when such activity served the interests of a specific Arab regime. Initially, the Palestinian guerrilla organizations strove to clandestinely establish themselves within the Arab states bordering with Israel. This was especially in the case of Lebanon, Syria and Jordan, whose proximity to the Israeli population could facilitate their access to Israel's territory and protect them from Israeli retaliations. These states were perfect for the guerrilla organizations, also due to their large Palestinian refugee populations that served as an available reservoir of manpower a live shield for the guerrilla elements entrenched within its camps, and a fertile arena for reshaping the Palestinian refugees as a national community and exercising exclusive authority over the Palestinian people. The Israeli occupation of the West Bank and Gaza Strip in the 1967 War created, for the first time, ostensibly ideal conditions for classical guerrilla warfare based on the purely Palestinian population in these occupied areas. However, attempts to establish such guerrilla infrastructure immediately after the War soon collapsed. Though it never ceased, it remained marginal. The armed struggle took mostly the form of cross-border raids, shelling, and infiltration for sabotage and in-depth military operations. The necessity of a territorial base for the Palestinian guerrilla organizations on the one hand, and Israel's painful retaliations against the neighboring Arab states to force them to block such operations from their territories, led inevitably to collision between the *raison d'etat* and the *raison de la revolution*. The guerrilla organizations managed to entrench in Lebanon and Jordan, whose domestic and regional constraints made it difficult for them to repress the Palestinian guerrillas. Yet, while Jordan successfully fought the Palestinian guerrillas entrenched in its soil (1970–1971), Lebanon—with its fragmented political arena and weak army—became the ultimate territorial base for the Palestinian guerrilla organizations until Israel invaded Lebanon in 1982. (For the political history of Palestinian-Arab relations, particularly Jordan and Lebanon, see PLO.

The June 1967 War was a watershed in the process of rising Palestinian nationalism and guerrilla warfare. The number of guerrilla groups multiplied, and though they were unified by the Palestinian National Charter and increasingly incorporated into the PLO, Many of them were small groups divided by political conceptions, political allegiance to Arab patrons, and conflicting methods of operations. Several groups repeatedly split. Some were ephemeral, and some "fronts" were no more than covers for secret operations of existing groups. The more important ones are listed below.

During the course of 1968–1969 the guerrilla groups, led by *Fatah*, took over the PLO and *Fatah's* leader Yasser ARAFAT was appointed chairman of its executive committee. The shifting leadership to the younger activist generation also transformed the PLO from a purely political body into a Palestinian national umbrella organization within which all Palestinian institutionalized sectors and groups—both in the homeland and the diaspora—would be represented. Still, the armed Palestinian organizations remained the backbone and decisive element in shaping the PLO's institutional structure and policies. Notwithstanding their alignment within the PLO, these Palestinian guerrilla groups strove to maintain their independence, separate financial resources, and military operations, which led to occasional collision between the mainstream Fatah and Arab patrons of certain Palestinian groups.

The military development at the disposal of *Fatah* and other organizations supporting Arafat became the backbone of the Palestinian police forces under the PALESTINIAN AUTHORITY (PA), stipulated by the Camp David and Oslo accords. Follwing the foundation of the PNA and following the elections to its Legislative Council in 1996, the organizations which participated in the PA are: *Fatah*, DFLP (*Hawatmeh* faction), FIDA (DFLP—the Yasser Abd Rabbo faction), ALF, PLF, PPF. Those opposing the PNA are members of the "Ten Front," a loose Syrian-backed alignment of Palestinian groups opposed to the Israel-Palestine Peace Process: PFLP, DFLP (anti-*Hawatmeh* faction), PLF (Abdel Fattah Ghanem faction), PPSF, PFLP-GC, al-Sa'iqa, Fatah al-Intifada (ABU MUSSA), HAMAS, the Islamic JIHAD, and the Palestinian Revolutionary Communist Party.

Fatah (Arabic: *fateh*—victory, conquest. H-T-F is the abbreviation of an acronym in reverse: *Harakat al-Tahrir,* or *al-watani al-Filastini*—Palestinian National Liberation Movement). Founded in the late 1950s and commemorating January 1965 as the beginning of its actual guerrilla operations, *Fatah* was always recognized as the largest and most dominating constituent group of the PLO, and while its del-

egates do not have a majority in the PLO Executive Committee or the National Council, they usually control these bodies and command the support of their majority by nominating "independent delegates" and representatives of professional and geographical sectors identified with *Fatah*. Since 1969, *Fatah's* leadership has largely overlapped, becoming almost identical to that of the PLO. *Fatah's* top leaders (including the five founding fathers of the organization since 1959) were Yasser Arafat, Khalil al-Wazir (Abu Jihad), killed in 1988; Salah Khalaf (Abu Iyad), killed in 1991; Faruq al-Qaddumi (Abu al-Lutuf); and Khaled al-Hassan, Yusuf al-Najjar (killed in 1973); Mahmud ABBAS (Abu Mazen); Hani al-Hassan; and Salim al-Za'nun, former representative in Kuwait, and since 1994 the Chairman of the Palestinian National Council.

The origins of *Fatah* were rooted in the Palestinian Student Association in Cairo. In 1952 Arafat headed this with Khalaf as his deputy. In 1956, Khalaf succeeded Arafat, who had graduated from the University. The founding fathers of *Fatah* represented a revolutionary shift from the traditional type of notable families that had comprised the Palestinian national leadership until 1948. Furthermore, like many other Palestinian organization leaders, they represented the rising middle class and new *bourgeoisie* in the Palestinian society, whose mobility and escalation to national leadership had been made possible due to the collapse of the Palestinian social structure by expulsion and uprooting from the land and social resources.

Beginning its consolidation in 1959 in Kuwait, the group of founders set forward—through a forum named "Our Palestine" (*filastinuna*)—the concept of a popular armed struggle as the only way to break the deadlock created by Arab indifference to the Palestine problem and pave the way for the liberation of Palestine. Their basic assumption was that in view of the regional Arab situation and low priority given to the liberation of Palestine, the Palestinians must themselves move to the vanguard in that mission. Furthermore they must use their limited capabilities in guerrilla warfare against Israel. The Arab masses would then gradually join this until a critical mass would emerge that would force the active cooperation of the Arab regimes in the liberation war. The Arab regimes were to be entangled in the war of liberation against their own will. Thus, while *Fatah* called for self-sustained national struggle, it effectively underlined the concept that only a common Arab effort could defeat Israel.

From the outset, *Fatah* occupied the core of the Palestinian national liberation effort due to its simple and focused concept of popular armed struggle, which had no restrictive ideological color and hence strongly appealed to the Palestinian youth. The armed struggle idea was thus a useful mechanism of nation building. *Fatah* also benefited from its strictly pragmatic and political approach to Arab regimes and potential Palestinian recruits to its ranks, and absence of social ideology. *Fatah*'s nationalism has been pragmatic, rejecting both Marxist and Leninist leanings of other Palestinian guerrilla groups, with strong traditional and Islamic tendencies. *Fatah* maintained that discussion of divisive social and political-ideological issues should be avoided until it is victorious. It strove to establish itself as the nucleus of the Palestinian state in the making by undertaking a variety of military, social, economic and cultural responsibilities toward the Palestinian refugee population. Its scope and penetration into Palestinian communities in the Middle East and Europe exceeded all other guerrilla organizations. To control the mass movement envisioned by *Fatah*'s leaders, a rigid hierarchic institutional structure was created, reflecting nominal democratic process from bottom to top—The General Conference (300–500 members); The Revolutionary Council (75 members), and the Central Committee (15–21 members). Yet the domination of the hard core leadership was preserved. Thus, until 1989, the General Conference has only been convened five times and rarely based on elections. Members of the Revolutionary Council were mainly appointed, not elected. The Central Committee members were appointed by Arafat.

Fatah remained clandestine until its first communique, announcing in the name of its military arm "Thunderstorm" (*al-'assifa*), the first military operation on 1 January 1965. This was apparently aimed at the Israeli National Water Carrier. Henceforth, the organization operated mainly from Lebanon and the West Bank of Jordan, enacting punitive measures on the part of these two Arab states, but partly supported by Syria. Although the number of all guerrilla operations conducted by Palestinians against Israel until the 1967 War was only slightly over sixty, they had considerably affected the growing tension between Israel and Syria, especially in 1966–1967, the escalation of which ended with the full scale war of June 1967. Notwithstanding the failure of *Fatah*'s efforts to establish a secret guerrilla infrastructure within the West Bank in the course of the summer of 1967, its prestige skyrocketed following the retaliatory operation of Israel in March 1968 against their bases in Karameh, a village in the Jordan Valley. Regardless of the high number of Palestinian casualties, and the Jordanian army's involvement in the battle, the Israeli forces, still viewed as indestructible, sustained thirty-three casualties in the operation and left armored vehicles on the battlefield, all of which boosted the image of the Palestinian guerrilla forces as the only real Arab force actually fighting Israel.

Fatah's military buildup, evolved throughout the late 1960s through the 1970s. It took on two main forms:

a) clandestine apparatuses—under the "Western Sector" (*al-qita' al-gharbi*)—aimed at building secret cells in the occupied territories, Israel, and the Arab countries, and conducting guerrilla warfare against Israeli military and civilian targets alike.

b) In the wake of the expulsion from Jordan in 1970–1971, *Fatah* established semi-regular formations organized in three brigades (Qastel, Yarmuc, and Karameh), deployed in Lebanon.

There is no reliable way to determine the scope of *Fatah*'s military power, i.e., how many of its full-time mobilized fighters received regular payment at any given time. Varying estimates attest that, at its peak in the mid- and late-1970s it ranged from 6,000–10,000 (though considerably higher figures were also mentioned) while other guerrilla groups were estimated at no more than a few hundred full-time fighters, except, perhaps, for Syria's *al-Sa'iqa*.

Throughout its military history, *Fatah* was supported in various ways by the Arab states. (Until 1976 primarily by Syria, Algeria, USSR, and China.) From the early 1970s *Fatah* acquired growing quantities of Katyusha rockets. It later developed its artillery capability, deployed in south Lebanon, which came into full manifestation in the summer of 1981. During the 1970s, *Fatah* developed a small maritime force, equipped with rubber boats to enable access to Israel through the sea, culminating in a number of such operations. The most famous was the takeover of an Israeli bus north of Hadera which was taken toward Tel Aviv, resulting in thirty-two Israeli casualties. After this Israel initiated "Operation Litani," in which the whole area of south Lebanon up to the Litani River was occupied and purged of Palestinian guerrilla forces.

In the wake of the expulsion from Jordan in 1970–1971, *Fatah* embarked on a new area of military operations, which had not been employed before—international TERRORISM—under the ironic title "Black September" (*eilul al-aswad*), taking its name from the Jordan-PLO war that climaxed in September 1970. The operations of Black September were conducted by the security apparatus headed by Salah Khalaf. The first victim of this kind of operation was Jordanian Prime Minister Wasfi al-TALL, with many other deadly raids on Jordanian, Israeli, and American targets, in the Middle East and Europe. These spectacular operations included the hijacking of planes and attacks on planes and terminals in airports. The most famous operation perpetrated by Black September was the takeover and massacre of eleven Israeli athletes in the Olympic Games of Munich in 1972. Throughout the early 1970s *Fatah's* international terrorist apparatus developed links with other guerrilla movements in Latin America and Europe. In 1974, *Fatah* ceased to conduct international guerrilla operations, apparently under strict Arab and American pressure along with an awareness that such operations would not serve the PLO's political cause.

Although initially *Fatah* rejected any settlement with the "Zionist entity," defining the armed struggle as a "strategy and not tactics," its leadership was fairly flexible in conducting the national Palestinian struggle. *Fatah's* role as the PLO's essential element and pragmatic approach enabled it to adjust itself to the changing conditions in the Arab arena and the conflict with Israel, by adopting the necessary changes in the PLO's attitudes that would ensure the organization's survival and legitimacy. Hence, the negative impact of the rephrased National Charter (1968) caused *Fatah* to adopt the concept of a secular, democratic Palestinian state in which Muslims, CHRISTIANS and JEWS would live in harmony, instead of Israel. The idea aroused fierce debates within the Palestinian resistance movement and, though presented by Arafat in his address to the UN General Assembly in November 1974, it had effectively been dropped in the wake of the 1973 war. In June 1974, again inspired by *Fatah*, the PLO adopted the idea of

establishing a national fighting authority on any liberated part of Palestine, implying the acceptance of a transitional process of recovering the national territory of Palestine, while the State of Israel still existed on most of that territory. This trend of adjustment and pragmatization continued in the course of the 1970s, when Arafat-backed *Fatah* spokesmen expressed increasing willingness on the part of the PLO to accept a Palestinian state in the West Bank and Gaza Strip, followed by meetings with Israelis, eventually leading to the Israel-PLO Oslo accord. (see PLO, ARAB-ISRAEL PEACEMAKING).

As the largest group within the Palestinian national movement, *Fatah* was frequently struck by internal struggles for power, ideological debates and even splits. However, until the late 1980s—early 1990s *Fatah* was led by a strong collective leadership, represented by Arafat, Khalil al-Wazir, Salah Khalaf (and, to a lesser extent, also Faruq QADDUMI). Al-Wazir was killed by Israel in 1988; Khalf's assassination by a member of Abu NIDAL's terrorist group left Arafat alone at the helm, which, in the wake of the 1991 GULF WAR resulted in open criticism from the Palestinians. The most serious split within *Fatah's* ranks was in May 1983, when a *Fatah* military force in the Biqa' (Lebanon), led by Colonel Sa'id Mussa Maragha (Abu Mussa), rebelled against Arafat's leadership and proclaimed the name *Fatah al-'Assifa* for its secessionist group. Supported by two leading political members of *Fatah's* Central Committee—Samih Abdel Qader (Abu Kuwaik) and Nimr Saleh (Abu Saleh)—the rebellion was apparently inspired by Syria, whose animosity to Arafat had been no secret in the wake of the Israeli siege of Beirut and the expulsion of the armed Palestinian personnel from the Lebanese capital. For this rebellion and the expulsion of Arafat's forces from eastern and northern Lebanon, see PLO. Another split, led by Colonel Atallah Atallah (Abu Za'im), took place in the wake of the collapse of the Jordan-PLO dialogue (see JORDAN) in 1986, apparently inspired by Jordan. However, these splinter groups failed to attain legitimate stature out of the borders of the states supporting them.

The Popular Front for the Liberation of Palestine (PFLP): The most important among the Palestinian guerrilla groups in opposition to *Fatah's* conduct of the PLO, especially on issues linked to Israel and the peacemaking process. Led by Dr. George

HABASH (one of the few Christians among the leaders of the Palestinian organizations), the PFLP emerged in December 1967 from several small groups—"Heroes of the Return," the "Palestine Liberation Front," and the "Youth of Vengeance," a radical, clandestine element in the "Arab Nationalist Movement" (*Harakat al-Qawmiyyun al-Arab*) to which it also remained closely linked. The PFLP, like the Arab Nationalist Movement, combined ultramilitant nationalism and unrestrained violence, explained and justified in neo-Marxist-Maoist terminology. The PFLP remained rigid in its rejection of any political solution to the Arab-Israeli conflict. During its history the PFLP moved back and forth between Marxist-Leninist Pan-Arabism and Palestinian nationalism, remaining faithful to its creed and refusing to adjust to the changing realities. In April 1968, a group of the PFLP members led by Ahmad JIBRIL—former leader of the PLF—split and established the PFLP-GC. In February 1969 the PFLP was struck by another split, this time by the leftist group headed by Na'if HAWATMA.

From the outset, the PFLP had been in conflict with *Fatah* over issues of principle, power and representation in the PLO's institutions. Habash, an extreme doctrinaire, elitist and uncompromising revolutionary, refused to join the PLO in 1968, remaining adamant about this until 1972. Following the September 1970 bloody showdown in Jordan, the PFLP agreed to take part in the PNC and other PLO institutions. However, this participation remained conditional, and the PFLP occasionally boycotted the PLO's institutions and political decisions. Thus, despite its acceptance of the PNC Resolutions of June 1974 (see PLO), it later boycotted the Executive and Central Council from 1974 to 1981(with the exception of the 1978 PLO Executive Committee meeting after the signing of the Camp David Accords) and did it again from 1983 to 1987. In the late 1970s PFLP cooperated with Lebanese left parties in the Lebanon Civil War. It sided with the rebels in the 1983 PLO split, but it did not join the Rebellion nor its military operations and agreed to negotiate with Arafat and seek a formula for reunification. Like other Palestinian leftist factions, the PFLP rejected the Jordan-PLO dialogue (1983–1986). In 1984 it formed an anti-Arafat "Democratic Alliance" within the PLO. In 1985 the Alliance joined forces with the pro-Syrian "National Alliance" in a "National Salvation Front." In 1987 it effected a reconciliation with Arafat's camp, following the collapse of the dialogue with Jordan, the Shi'i siege of the Palestinian refugee camps in Lebanon, and Arafat's *rapprochement* with Iraq. The PFLP returned to full participation in the PLO and its Executive Committee, and cooperated with Arafat's mainstream during the early years of the INTIFADA. In 1988 the PFLP supported the PNC declaration of the Palestinian state, based on UN resolution 181 (Palestine partition of 1947). The PFLP returned to opposition following the PLO's decision to join the Madrid conference in late 1991, and more so in the wake of the Israel-PLO Oslo Accord of September 1993, aligned with other Syrian-backed opposition groups in the "Ten Front."

Because of its doctrinaire revolutionary approach to any manifestation of conservatism in the Arab world, the PFLP has no permanent ties of allegiance to any Arab state. While the conservative regimes conceived it with horror, it occasionally found support in Iraq, LIBYA, SOUTH YEMEN, and Syria, but refused to become dependent on any of them. The extreme Leninist concept adopted by Habash in 1969, in an attempt to emulate Fidel Castro's example, strictly limited the organization's capacity to attract many members into its ranks and determined its nature as a small, highly educated and ideologically motivated organization. Considering its restrictions, and in order to maximize these characteristics, the PFLP turned to international terrorism, especially against air traffic vehicles, as its main battlefield. Habash and his close aid Wadi Haddad headed international operations. They conceived the goal to be to awaken world public opinion to the Palestinian issue. This could be best attained by extreme atrocities and spectacular operations, capable of attracting the attention of the media. Beginning with the hijacking of an El Al Israeli airliner to Algiers in July 1968, the PFLP gradually escalated its operations, scoring international acclaim, and serving as a role model for other Palestinian guerrilla organizations, most notably *Fatah*. The PFLP was also prominent in establishing links with other revolutionary movements involved in international terrorism, such as the Badder Meinhoff and the Japanese Red Army. Among its most conspicuous operations were the hijackings of four European and American airliners at the same time (6–9 September 1970), one of which was forced to land in Cairo and the other three in Zarqa, Jordan. All four were exploded after its passengers had deplaned. The PFLP hijacking operation legitimized the Jordanian regime in its decision to finally eliminate the Palestinian guerrilla bases in Jordan by force, which began a few days later ("Black September").

In 1971–1972, a schism became apparent between Habash and Haddad regarding the benefit of international guerrilla operations, especially after the massacre of passengers at Tel Aviv Airport in May 1972. In 1974 the PFLP followed *Fatah* in ceasing international guerrilla operations, but this decision was rejected by Wadi Haddad, who continued to operate as before, accounting for the attack on ORGANIZATION OF PETROLEUM EXPORTING COUNTRIES (OPEC) headquarters in Vienna (December 1975), and the hijacking of an Air France plane to Entebbe, Uganda. Only his death in 1978 finally put an end to these operations. The terrorist operations of the PFLP repeatedly embarassed the PLO as it used its name in these activities, delaying the latter's attempt to secure an image of moderation. Its main strength remained rooted in its uncompromising attitude toward Israel, the West, and the Arab regimes, which still appeals to deprived Palestinian groups, especially the refugees.

The (Popular) Democratic Front for the Liberation of Palestine (DFLP): A small group headed by Na'if Hawatma, a Jordanian Christian, which seceded from the PFLP in February 1969 due to problems of doctrine and leadership. Its ideology does not compare to that of *Fatah*. The latter supported it from the beginning since it opposed Habash's PFLP, paving the way for it to be represented in the PLO, including the Executive Committee. As a splinter group of the PFLP, it endeavored to portray itself as the real representative of the mother group, emphasizing that its Marxism-Leninism was more doctrinaire and attempting to implement the Communist concept by establishing in 1970 Soviet and cooperative farms in northern Jordan (hence, it added the word "democratic" to its name, and in the mid-1970s dropped the word "popular"). Like other revolutionary leftist factions, the DFLP was extremely hostile to all conservative Arab regimes, such as Jordan, calling for a continued struggle against them. Since 1969, it viewed Israel as a cultural element in the Middle East, supporting the establishment of a popular democratic Palestinian state in which the Jews will have the right to develop their own culture (not as a nationality). Following this attitude, the DFLP initiated contacts with Marxist elements in Israel. Some of them cooperated with Hawatma and the Syrian intelligence in 1972 in terror actions against Israeli targets. They conducted rural guerrilla operations but opposed the hijacking of foreign civilian aircrafts and terrorist operations in foreign countries. In August 1973, the DFLP proposed for the first time the establishment of a Palestinian state on both banks of the Jordan River with the exclusion of the Israeli borders of 1948 as a first step in a transitory (phased) plan. This idea was rejected by the PLO.

In the wake of the 1973 War, the DFLP led the shift of the PLO position from rejection of any political settlement that would not provide the recovery of the full territory of historic Palestine to a transitory concept of proceeding in stages, much under Soviet influence. The DFLP cooperated in this respect with *Fatah*, and helped the affirmation of that approach—establishing a Palestinian national authority in part of Palestine—in the twelfth PNC of June 1974 (see PLO). It was this shift toward a more concrete goal in the DFLP ideology that encouraged the organization to initiate suicidal attacks on Israeli civilians near the Lebanese and Jordanian borders, as well as in JERUSALEM, in 1974–1975, in an attempt to force Israel to acknowledge Palestinian rights. Relations with *Fatah* deteriorated following the siege of Beirut, Arafat's rift with Syria and the beginning of the Jordanian-PLO political dialogue in 1983. Though the DFLP fervently opposed Arafat's policy, it did not join the 1983 rebellion. It allied in 1984 with the PFLP in the "Democratic Front," but did not join the "National Salvation Front," formed in 1985 by the PFLP and the pro-Syrian groups. In 1987 it returned to full participation in the PLO. In 1988 it supported the PLO's recognition of UN resolutions 181, 242 and 338. This cooperation continued during the first three years of the *intifada*, but later began to weaken due to Arafat's willingness to join the American-led peace process. From the late 1980s there was an internal split within the organization between Hawatma and his supporters, adhering to an uncompromising and continued armed struggle against Israel, and an opposition faction, headed by Yasser Abd Rabbo, which supported Arafat's policy of participation in the Madrid peace process. With the establishment of the Palestinian Authority, this group turned into a political party and was incorporated into the PA's institutions. Hawatma's DFLP split into a group opposed to the peace process and establishment of the PA, while Hawatma himself, with a group of supporters, came to play an opposition role within the PA.

al-Sa'iqa (Arabic: Lightning and Thunder) Full name: Vanguards of the People's War of Liberation. The Sa'iqa Forces were established in 1968 by the ruling *Ba'th* Party of Syria, to represent the Palestinian sector in the all-Arab *Ba'th* Party. In fact, the Sa'iqa was meant to be another apparatus in the Party-military struggle for power. Sa'iqa derived its manpower fundamentally from Palestinian refugee camps in the Damascus area, but Syrians also served in the organization. By 1969 the organization had 1,500–2,000 armed men, organized in a few battalions, and was considered the second largest Palestinian organization, with twelve delegates to the Fifth Palestinian National Council (PNC) held in February 1969 (compared to thirty-three *Fatah* delegates). With the ascendancy of al-ASAD to power in November 1970, the organization, under its newly appointed Secretary General Zuheir Muhsin, was intended strictly to promote Syria's national interests by affecting the PLO's decision making process. Al-Sa'iqa maintained military bases in Syria and Lebanon, but like all other Palestinian organizations was not allowed to wage guerrilla raids from Syria's territory.

Over the years the organization waged many operations against Israel as well as against Jewish targets abroad. The most famous of these was the seige in Vienna, in September 1973, of a train carrying migrant Jews from the Soviet Union. This resulted in the closing down of the Jewish migrant transition camp. As long as Syria and the PLO (namely, *Fatah*) were in agreement regarding political and military policies, al-Sa'iqa could easily tackle its divided loyalty between Palestinian and Syrian interests. However, the growing tension between Syria and the PLO in Spring 1976—which culminated in fierce military clashes in June of that year—put al-Sa'iqa on the horns of the dilemma. A group of Sa'iqa members split and turned to support *Fatah*, which in late May initiated an offensive against the Syrian-backed organization and effectively eliminated its base in Beirut.

Over the next few years the Syrians tried to rehabilitate the destroyed organization, but the next crisis of allegiance was to repeat itself in the course of the 1982 Lebanon war, when al-Sa'iqa operated as a Syrian organization, causing much friction with *Fatah*. During the siege of Beirut by Israel, al-Sa'iqa spoke out against the PLO's political overtures regarding a political settlement with Israel. Al-Sa'iqa preferred to evacuate its members to Syrian-dominated territory and not, like most Palestinian military personnel, to Tunis.

In the aftermath of the war, al-Sa'iqa supported the *Fatah* rebellion against Arafat's leadership. In October-November 1983 he fought against Arafat's last stronghold on Lebanese territory, in the vicinity of Tripoli (see PLO). Reflecting Syria's policy, al-Sa'iqa rejected the Jordan-PLO dialogue, boycotting the seventeenth PNC held in Amman. This resulted in the suspension of its membership in the PLO. In 1979, Muhsin was murdered and was succeeded by Issam al-Qadi. Other leading figures in the organization were Sami al-Attari, Farhan Abul Hija (spokesman), Muhammad al-Ma'aita and Dafi Jumai'ani. The organization remained a Syrian political instrument and had no role in the process that led to the PLO's moderation resulted by the *intifada*. Al-Sa'iqa was condemned to marginality and full subordination to Syria's needs. Thus, it was available for criticizing the PLO, and particularly Arafat's policies following the 1991 Gulf war and the Madrid peace process. Since 1993, al-Sa'iqa has participated in the Syrian-based "Ten Front" of Palestinian organizations opposing the Oslo process.

The Popular Front for the Liberation of Palestine—General Command: A small splinter group of a few hundred armed men that seceded from the PFLP in April 1968, soon after its formation. Since then it has been led by Ahmad Jibril, a former Engineering Officer in the Syrian army, who had previously been active in the pre-1967 guerrilla group "Palestine Liberation Front." The organization gave exclusive priority to the armed struggle against Israel, though it also maintained radical leftist attitudes toward "reactionary" Arab regimes. It operates in tightly organized clandestine cells which underlay the mystery about its composition and internal processes. Its military operations are usually daring, highly professional, even inventive, especially in the use of new devices and military methods, including the hijacking and air bombing of foreign aircrafts, and taking hostages by suicidal perpetrators which led to mass killing. The PFLP-GC's ideology remains obscure, though its political leanings have been marked by close political and military links with Syria since its establishment, and followed the Syrian line. It has always been based primarily in Syria in addition to its bases in Lebanon. It also enjoyed Libyan support. Despite differences over timing and type of guerrilla attacks against Israeli in 1981–1982, the PFLP-GC collaborated with the PLO's mainstream until the Israeli invasion of Lebanon. This cooperation came to its end following the PLO-Syria rift after the evacuation of Beirut. In 1983 it joined the Syrian-backed anti-Arafat coalition and fought his forces in the Tripoli area of northern Lebanon. In 1985 it attained unprecedented prestige due to its success in releasing 1150 Palestinian prisoners from the Israeli prisons in returned for three Israeli soldiers captured in Lebanon in 1982. It did not participate in the reconciliation of 1987. Since the Oslo Accords, the PFLP-GC has been part of the alignment of Palestinian Syrian-backed opposition groups, the "Ten Front."

The Palestine Liberation Front: A small organization that broke away from the PFLP-GC in 1977 on the grounds of a severe dispute between pro-Syrian leader Jibril and pro-Iraqi leader Muhmad Abbas. In the late 1970s and early 1980s the group conducted a series of terrorist acts along Israel's northern border and from the sea. Since 1983 it allegedly split into three factions hostile to one another—one, radically anti-Arafat, headed by Tal'at Ya'qub, which operated in Lebanon until Ya'qub's death in 1988. The second, pro-Syrian faction is led by Abd Al-Fattah Ghanem and located in Damascus. The third, and main faction is pro-Arafat, led by Muhammad Abbas (Abu al-Abbas). It was located in Tunis until the foundation of the PNA. Since 1984 the Abu al-'Abbas faction has been represented in the PLO, considered to be compensation for Arafat in view of the long periods of boycott of the PLO adopted by the radical leftist PFLP and DFLP from the PLO. In 1989 the first and third factions reunited in Tunis and initiated a joint attack on Israel from the sea that was thwarted by Israel. Yet this became an obstacle to the PLO-American dialogue when Arafat refused to denounce the operation. The PLF is a member of the PA.

The Arab Liberation Front (ALF) : A small organization founded in 1969 by the Iraqi previously *Ba'th* Party in order to serve Iraq's interest on the Palestinian issue and affect the PLO decision making, counterbalancing the Syrian involvement through al-Sa'iqa. The organization was accepted to the PLO since its foundation and had representation in the Executive Committee. It has been led, since the assassination of its leader Abdel Wahhab al-Kayyali in 1981, by Abdel Rahim Ahmad, who also replaced Kayyali in the Executive Committee. The ALF remained marginal, strictly under the direct command of Iraq's *Ba'th* Party and army, and hardly conducted guerrilla operations against Israel. (Given the scarcity of Palestinian refugees in Iraq, there is a very small potential to recruit members to the organization's ranks.) Following a shift in Iraq's policy toward the PLO in the aftermath of the 1982 Lebanon war, and the split within *Fatah* and between Arafat and the radical groups, the ALF was the only faction other than Fatah and its "independent" supporters to remain loyal to Arafat. In the past, the ALF rejected the idea of an independent Palestinian state and considered the liberation of Palestine as an interim goal in the struggle against imperialism, reactionary regimes and ZIONISM and for ARAB UNITY, preferably under Iraq. However, the growing collaboration between Arafat and the Iraqi regime since the mid 1980s, but particularly during the 1991 Gulf War, brought the ALF to tight cooperation with the PLO mainstream under Arafat's leadership. In 1988, the ALF participated in the PNC session in Algiers and supported the declaration of the Palestinian state, and remained in coalition with *Fatah* following the Oslo accord. It has also been incorporated into the Palestinian Authority.

The Palestine Popular Struggle Front (PPSF): A small group that seceded in 1967 from *Fatah*, representing leftist views. It rejoined *Fatah* in 1971, though it retained its independence. In 1974 it joined the REJECTION FRONT led by George Habash's PFLP. In the same year, Bahjat Abu Gharbiyya retired from leading the organization and since then it has been led by Samir Ghoshah, supported by Iraq but also by Syria and Libya. It joined the "National Alliance" formed in 1984 by the anti-Arafat, Syrian-guided factioins, and the "National Salvation Front" of 1985.

From 1988, the PPSF shifted toward support of the PLO mainstream, and since then has been an ally to Arafat in supporting the peace process and developing the Palestinian Authority. Ghosha is a member of the PA.

The Palestine Liberation Army (PLA): When the PLO was established in 1964, it was meant to have a regular military arm—the Palestine Liberation Army. In the second ARAB SUMMIT CONFERENCE of September 1964, it was decided to endorse the establishment of such an army, with nominal link to the PLO, while in fact its units would remain under the respective Arab armies' command. In late 1957 Egypt had established the Ein Jalut Brigade, ostensibly as a contribution to the Liberation War of Palestine, which in 1966 conducted large scale exercises in Sinai. Iraq followed suit in 1960 establishing the Qadisiyya Brigade. Other Palestinian units were established in Syria (the Hittin Brigade), and in Jordan (two battalions: *al-Badr and Zaid Ibn Haritha*). Their combined strength was variously estimated at 8,000–12,000 men. The overall command of this PLA changed several times—*Uthman Haddad; Abdel Razzaq al-Yahya; Misbah al-Budeiri et al*—sometimes in the context of intra-PLO and PLO-Arab controversies and struggles for power. In any case, the notion of an overall PLO command of the PLA units incorporated in the various Arab armies, and of PLO control of these forces, turned out to be illusory, as the Arab regimes perceived these forces as political tools in their Arab and Palestinian policies. The only PLA force that has come under the PLO command was the Ein Jalut Brigade—which after having participated in the 1973 War in the Egyptian front—was transferred from Egypt to Lebanon in 1976, where it continued to operate until the evacuation of the Palestinian armed personnel from Beirut in September 1982.

The PLA, as a regular force in the framework of Arab armies, was not meant to engage in guerrilla/terrorist operations, though in several cases it backed such operations. The Syrian brigades were also used in the Lebanese Civil War—on Syria's behalf and under its commands.

PALESTINE LIBERATION ORGANIZATION

(PLO) Founded in May 1964 at a Palestinian congress held in East JERUSALEM (then under Jordanian rule) following the intensive efforts of Ahmad al-SHUQEIRI, the representative of the PALESTINE ARABS in the ARAB LEAGUE. The PLO adopted at this congress, the "Palestinian [Pan] National Charter" (*al-mithaq al-qawmi al-filastini*) and an organic law, giving decisive powers to its Chairman Shuqeiri, including the appointment of the Executive Committee members. The foundation of the PLO, which was fully supported by Egyptian President Gamal ABDEL NASSER, and reluctantly acquiesced to by JORDAN, was a result of inter-Arab and Palestinian circumstances. In 1959, Nasser suggested the establishment of a "Palestinian Entity"—a political organization that would represent the Palestinian national cause internationally. Nasser's initiative, which was part of the political struggle he had been waging against Abdel Karim QASSEM of IRAQ, had been discussed by the Arab League Council but not advanced, primarily because Jordan opposed it. The Jordanian position reflected concern lest any expression of Palestinian nationalism arouse separatist tendencies among the Palestinians in the kingdom (constituting more than half of the population, which could threaten the very existence of the HASHEMITE regime).

In 1963, inter-Arab relations were turbulent, representing the bankruptcy of Nasser's aggressive and interventionist policies in the Arab arena, particularly his proclaimed war against the conservative ("Reactionary") regimes. Under this banner he had entangled EGYPT in a costly and hopeless war by intervening in the Civil War of YEMEN. By the end of the year Nasser came under threat by SYRIA's urges to go to war against Israel over the ensuing inauguration of its National Water Carrier, exploiting the Jordan River's water to irrigate new areas in the northern Negev. Against this backdrop, Nasser initiated the first ARAB SUMMIT CONFERENCE in Cairo, held in January 1964, in which he shifted the focus of Egypt's regional policies from the inter-Arab arena to the ARAB-ISRAEL CONFLICT, in view of establishing the Palestinian Entity as part of this shift. Resistance on the part of Jordan and reservation toward the proposed organization on the part of others (Syria wanted a combatant organization that would wage an armed struggle, as did some newly established Palestinian guerrilla groups, including *Fatah*; the Saudis feared it would be merely an Egyptian political instrument). The "Arab Higher Committee" (AHC), by now a body representing mainly its historical leader al-Hajj (Muhammad) Amin al-HUSSEINI, bitterly objected to the foundation of a new political representation for the Palestinians, declaring itself to be the sole representative of the Palestinian Arabs. Nonetheless its claims were disregarded. Hence, the first Arab summit conference refrained from officially approving the establishment of such an entity, instructing Shuqeiri to examine the attitudes among the Palestinians in the Arab world regarding such idea, without even mentioning the word "entity" in its decisions. The *rapprochement* struck between Nasser and King HUSSEIN at the summit paved the way for the latter's reluctant consent to hold the constituent Palestinian congress on its soil, which enabled him to decide the composition of the congress. (Most of the representatives were considered pro-Hashemite.)

Although the second Arab summit conference held in Alexandria in September 1964 approved the establishment of the PLO, the organization remained highly controversial, criticized by Palestinian and Arab regimes alike. In the coming three years, the PLO, headed by Shuqeiri, was the subject of much discontent and bitter attacks by almost all the Arab states. Representing Nasser's Arab policies, the PLO could not remove its image as an Egyptian instrument which had come to the world to legitimize Nasser's attempts to avoid war against ISRAEL. Shuqeiri was indeed aware of that image and, while rejecting the claim of Palestinian guerrilla groups to be represented in the PLO, he repeatedly tried to acquire military attributes as well. Such attributes became particularly necessary when *Fatah* began in January 1965 operating as a guerrilla organization, with other groups also taking part in such warfare. Thus, the second Arab summit conference approved Shuqeiri's proposal to establish a Palestinian Liberation Army (PLA), but only as units attached to the regular armies of the various Arab states. The PLA was officially subjected to the PLO Executive Committee and put under the titular command of a Palestinian officer, but with no effective significance. Palestinian Brigades had already been formed by Egypt (named *Ein Jalut*) and Iraq (*Qadessiyya*). Syria also followed suit, forming its own Palestinian brigade (*Hittin*). It was only in 1968 that Jordan also established its own PLA unit (see PALESTINIAN GUERRILLA ORGANIZATIONS). Shuqeiri's repeated efforts to acquire freedom of action in mobilizing and training Palestinians in Jordan and LEBANON in preparation

for the "War of Liberation" caused hostility with these two governments and soon came to negatively affect their relations with Egypt. By late 1965, Shuqeiri became anathema to the Jordanian authorities, leading to arrests of PLO activists there. With the return of Nasser to his aggressive policies in the inter-Arab arena in 1966, Shuqeiri and his PLO were increasingly marginalized, even by Nasser himself.

Until the June 1967 War, the Palestinian National Council (PNC—a sort of "parliament" of the Palestinian people) convened twice more in Gaza. This represented the deteriorating relations with the Jordanian regime, but with no significant development since late 1964 other than the beginning of quasi-autonomous broadcastings from Cairo, further aggravating the Arab antagonism toward the PLO. The Arab defeat in the 1967 War worsened Shuqeiri's quandary, illustrated by his isolation at the Arab summit conference held in Khartoum (August–September 1967) to discuss the results of the War and implications on the collective Arab policies. Not only was Nasser now forced to give priority to the liberation of Egypt's own national territory over that of Palestine, the defeat of the Arab regular armies in the war; but *Fatah*'s role in entangling them in that war, and the speedy rise of the Palestinian guerrilla ideal in late 1967, all forced Shuqeiri to resign in December 1967. He was replaced by Yahya Hamuda, another veteran Palestinian politician who did not represent the guerrilla groups. The fourth session of the PNC, held in Cairo in July 1968, which approved Shuqeiri's resignation, manifested the scope of success scored by the guerrilla organizations by including them for the first time, and electing their leaders to key positions in the organization. (*Fatah*'s leader ARAFAT became the PLO's spokesman.) The increasing representation of the PNC and the PLO Executive obtained by the guerrilla groups led, in February 1969, at the fifth council session, to their seizure of full control of the PLO, gaining the majority on the Executive (four *Fatah*, two *Sa'iqa*, one pro-PDFLP, one kept for the PFLP, which refused to take its seat, and four to five "Independents" of whom at least three were close to *Fatah*).Yasser Arafat was elected Chairman.

The guerrilla groups took over the PLO. This represented the core claim of the new Palestinian generation to play an active role in determining their people's fate rather than leave it to the Arab states. The fourth PNC session was a watershed in PLO history. It went from being a merely political representation of the Palestinians (reflecting Nasser's interests and constraints), to an umbrella organization for various Palestinian groups, military and civilian alike, with the guerrilla groups as its core, as well as for Palestinian communities all over the world. Its leadership and bureaucracy, dominated by *Fatah*, did not attain complete control over the various rival organizations—all retaining operational and ideological independence. Some of them, such as the PFLP, were in near-constant opposition and unwilling to submit to the discipline of the PLO Executive and its decisions. A major result of the changing nature of the PLO was a persistent and uncompromising claim for exclusive authority to speak in the name of the Palestinian people, sometimes imposed by violence on Palestinian figures under Israeli occupation in the WEST BANK and GAZA STRIP who dared raise ideas such as "Palestinian Entity" in the occupied territories only, or those conducting talks with the Israeli authorities over the political future of these areas.

The new nature of the PLO now manifested itself in introducing radical modifications in the PLO's Charter. The new Charter assumed a clear Palestinian national nature, carrying the title "The Palestinian National Charter" (*al-mithaq al-watani al-filastini*), stating that "the Palestinian Arab people" (being an "inseparable part of the Arab nation") "possesses the legal right to its homeland"; that "The Palestinians are the Arab citizens who were living permanently in Palestine until 1947" and their descendants. "Jews who are of Palestinian origin" (1964)—or "who were living permanently in Palestine until the beginning of the invasion" (1968), dated in another resolution of the Council at 1917—"will be considered Palestinians" in the future Palestinian state to be established on the whole territory of Mandatory Palestine. The Charter stipulated that the BALFOUR DECLARATION, the MANDATE, the partition of Palestine, and the establishment of the "Zionist entity" are "null and void"; "the claim of a historical or spiritual tie between JEWS and Palestine" is denied, "Judaism... is not a nationality ...the Jews are not one people." "The liberation of Palestine... is a national duty to repulse the Zionist, imperialist invasion... and to purge the Zionist presence from

Palestine." "The Palestinian people... through the armed Palestinian revolution, reject any solution that would be a substitute for the complete liberation of Palestine." "Armed struggle is the only way to liberate Palestine," defined as "a strategy and not a tactic," and "*Fida'iyyun* [i.e., guerrilla] action forms the nucleus of the popular Palestinian war of Liberation." (A postscript to the Charter of 1964 stated that the PLO had no sovereignty over the parts of Palestine occupied by Jordan and Egypt; this was dropped in the Charter of 1968.)

The new Charter served as a rallying cry among the various factions coalesced in the PLO under *Fatah*'s leadership, but also subjected the PLO to much criticism in the Western world, due to its extreme language and determination to eliminate the state of Israel and force most of its citizens to leave historic Palestine. It is against this backdrop that since the Charter was adopted, the thinking of the PLO gradually changed, in several respects, but without actually changing anything in the Charter until May 1996 (see below). Thus, in 1969 the PLO adopted the idea of a Secular Democratic Palestinian state in which Muslims, CHRISTIANS and Jews would be living in harmony. However, this idea met with objection on the part of some factions, mainly the PFLP, and failed to attract world public support. In the early 1970s as the Palestinian national cause had begun penetrating the world's public cognizance—primarily due to Palestinian international TERRORISM—the PLO leadership also came under growing pressure of the inter-Arab arena to modify its practical political positions. Hence, following the defeat and expulsion of the Palestinian guerrilla groups from Jordan in 1970–1971 (see JORDAN and PALESTINIAN GUERRILLA ORGANIZATIONS) President Anwar al-SADAT of Egypt repeatedly urged the PLO leadership to accept a realistic solution based on the West Bank and Gaza Strip, but to no avail.

Following the October 1973 War, confronted with Egyptian and Syrian determination to employ diplomacy as a legitimate means to recover their territories occupied by Israel, and induced by the Soviet Union to adopt a strategy of phases, the PLO resolved, in its twelfth PNC session held in Cairo in June 1974, to establish a "combatant Palestinian National Authority on any liberated part of Palestine." The decision also reflected the PLO's intensifying competition with Hashemite Jordan over attaining exclusive representation of the occupied West Bank in the internationally-supervised diplomatic process (see ARAB-ISRAEL PEACEMAKING). Indeed, in November 1973, the Arab summit conference held in Algiers recognized the PLO as the legitimate representative of the Palestinian people at the expense of Jordan. Furthermore, in October of the following year the Arab summit conference held in Rabat resolved that the PLO was the "sole legitimate representative of the Palestinian people," effectively excluding Jordan from the Middle East peace process. From an Israeli and American viewpoint, however, the PLO remained disqualified to be a partner in the peace process due to its extreme ideology, terrorist attacks on Israeli civilian targets, and an unwillingness to recognize Israel or UN resolution 242, which established the parameters of a peace settlement of the Middle East crisis.

In retrospect, the decision of June 1974, accepted by the PFLP (which joined the PLO fully in 1972) is seen as the beginning of the PLO's shift toward acceptance of a mini-Palestinian state in the West Bank and Gaza Strip only, alongside Israel. This tendency became clearer in the following years. Thus, in March 1977, the PLO adopted the resolution adopted by the Arab summit conference in Cairo (October 1976) affirming the PLO's right to establish its independent state on its own national soil. Moreover, in the course of the middle and late-1970s, *Fatah* delegates in Europe such as Issam Sirtawi, Sa'id Hamami, and others, repeatedly proclaimed that the PLO intended to establish such a state alongside and in harmony with Israel. (However, statements were often denied and those particular spokesmen and others were assassinated by Palestinian extremists—see ABU NIDAL.) In the late 1970s, PLO leaders were willing to meet Israelis—first, non-Zionist, and then leftist-Zionist—under the auspices of Communist European governments such as Rumania and Hungary. Although the PLO itself had no specific apparatuses for military raids, it was often identified with terrorist activities, mainly because of the direct responsibility of *Fatah* leaders, including Arafat, for such actions and their dominant position within the PLO. By mid-1974 international TERRORISM against foreign airliners, hijacking and the capture of hostages, waged by PLO member organizations, intensified, especially since the end of 1970. This was due to a political decision based on

the PLO's desire to be incorporated into the Middle East peace process, though such actions continued by a dissident group of the PFLP headed by Wadi Haddad, and other dissident factions such as Abu NIDAL.

Relations between the PLO and the Arab states remained ambivalent. While the latter praised the Palestinian Resistance (guerrilla) Movement and its armed struggle against Israel, the PLO's attempts to impose on them its own agenda and priorities often seemed to threaten their own sovereignty. This culminated in repeated collisions between the Palestinian "revolution" and Arab states. Egypt, which prevented Palestinian armed activity on its soil, but allowed limited political activity and broadcastings from Cairo, had to retaliate in response to the PLO's attacks against its policymaking on war and peace with Israel, by closing down the PLO Radio Station and blocking political activity of PLO personnel. Syria also prevented—with rare exceptions after 1967—Palestinian penetrations into Israeli territory through its own border, attempting to subjugate the Palestinian establishment to its own political needs, especially after the ascendancy of Asad in the late 1970s. Syria constantly supported the PLO politically, encouraging its activity against Israel from South Lebanon until 1976, when its forces invading Lebanon clashed with *Fatah* and its Lebanese allies. Henceforth, Syrian-PLO relations deteriorated, reaching their nadir in the aftermath of the Israeli war in Lebanon when the Syrians became hostile to Arafat for his independent policymaking, his *Fatah* organization, and Palestinian followers. The worst clashes between the Palestinian revolution and Arab states took place on the soil of Lebanon and Jordan, whose large Palestinian population and relative political weakness made them attractive for political and military entrenchment, creating a situation of "a state within a state" apart from the guerrilla attacks launched against Israel, causing painful Israeli retaliaitions against the "hosting" Arab state.

In Lebanon, a governmental crisis in the course of 1969 due to clashes between predominantly MARONITE units and the Palestinians led to Nasser's intervention in striking an agreement (the Cairo Agreement) in November 1969. This legitimized Palestinian armed activity on Lebanese soil, and set regulations for launching attacks on Israel from Lebanese soil. This settlement only aggravated the internal Lebanese situation, culminating in the eruption of the Lebanese Civil War of 1975. In Jordan, the growing power accumulated by the Palestinian organizations and violation of the state's sovereignty eventually led to the use of the regular Jordanian army against the Palestinian guerrillas in September 1970, and again in the following year, resulting in the expulsion of the Palestinian guerrillas from Jordan and the full recovery of the Hashemite sovereignty over the Jordanian territory (see JORDAN, LEBANON).

From the outset, the PLO managed to extract funds from the OIL monarchies in the Gulf as well as from the Palestinians working in those countries. These Arab funds enabled the PLO to build a growing establishment with large offices, economic and financial enterprises, social, health and educational institutions, a press, research centers and the publication of books and periodicals, diplomatic representation in many world capitals, and an intensive information/propaganda campaign as well as a large and well-paid body of functionaries to maintain all these activities. PLO chairman Arafat was constantly traveling around the Arab and world capitals for consultations and conferences (including a November 1974 appearance at the UN General Assembly, at the invitation of the Assembly). Visits—"official" or unofficial—were treated in many capitals as visits from a foreign head of state. From 1974, the PLO became a recipient of "steadfastness" (sumud) funds which allowed the organization to distribute them among its followers in the West Bank and Gaza Strip. The Baghdad Arab summit conference of November 1978 allocated an annual sum of 100 million dollars a year for ten years. This was designated for the Palestinian residents of the West Bank and Gaza Strip. A "Jordan-PLO Joint Committee for the Occupied Territories" was established to distribute these funds, enabling Fatah to deepen its penetration within the Palestinian population in the occupied territories and build an institutional political infrastructure to support the organization from within. Indeed, from the late 1970s, a certain rapprochement took place between Jordan and the PLO. A limited presence of PLO offices and representatives was again permitted, and from late 1982 King Hussein negotiated with Arafat a formula for joint Jordanian-Palestinian political action in the context of the Middle East peace negotiations and future Jordanian-Palestinian confederation. (For these nego-

tiations, the Hussein-Arafat Agreement of February 1985, Arafat's difficulties in having the agreement endorsed by the PLO, and its abrogation by the PLO in 1987—see ISRAEL-ARAB PEACEMAKING, JORDAN)

The problem of PLO participation in the peace process was indeed a major procedural obstacle for moving from the military Israel-Egypt and Israel-Syria disengagement agreements signed in early 1974 to a comprehensive settlement said to be discussed within the framework of the Geneva conference. The problem was caused by the PLO's status as the "sole legitimate representative of the Palestinian people," as recognized by the Rabat summit conference in October 1974. However, knowing the Israeli attitude toward the PLO, the Arab regimes had been well aware of the implications of such a decision on the peace process. Moreover, in 1975, following the signing of the Israel-Egypt Interim Agreement in Sinai, Israel received an American commitment that the UNITED STATES government would not hold contact with the PLO as long as the organization had not renounced terror, accepted resolution 242 and recognized Israel's right to exist. The PLO, however, adamantly objected to making such compromises before being practically recognized as an equal party in the Arab-Israeli peace making process.

It was the deadlock regarding the Palestinian participation in the Geneva conference that led Sadat to his decision to take the initiative and visit JERUSAELEM. This, however, did not render the PLO decision making any easier. The Israel-Egypt peace negotiations forced the PLO leaders to close ranks with the radical Arab regimes, in order to survive politically. Thus, the PLO joined the "Steadfastness and Confrontation Front" established in Tripoli, Libya, in December 1977 in response to Sadat's visit to Jerusalem. Hussein's pressure for the PLO to accept resolution 242 in the course of their negotiations in 1983–1986 failed, as did that of Egypt's President MUBARAK, with whom Arafat resumed political relations in late 1983 after six years of boycotting Egypt. The real issue was a formal acceptance by the PLO of Israel's right to exist and a clear commitment to peaceful co-existence with it—evidently in part of Palestine (which may be seen as implied in the PLO's desire to take part in peace negotiations, but which the PLO refused to make explicit). In the diplomatic code this was formulated as "accepting Resolution 242" (see ARAB-ISRAEL PEACEMAK-ING).

On the PLO's part, there was an additional reason for rejecting resolution 242: the resolution speaks of Palestinian refugees only, not of the Palestinian people and its national rights. Formulae suggested by the US—such as accepting the principles of the resolution while registering a reservation concerning that objection—proved unacceptable to the PLO. Evasive, open-ended remarks, like accepting "all" UN resolutions—as mentioned in the Hussein-Arafat agreement of February 1985—were unacceptable to the US and Israel, as were PLO pre-conditions like a prearranged recognition of the PLO once it endorses resolution 242, or the pre-guaranteed acceptance of its demands for Palestinian statehood or self-determination. This vital issue therefore remained, through most of the 1980s, unresolved. In any case, beyond Arafat's apparent inability to take bold decisions, since the early 1980s, he has been unable to commit even his own *Fatah* organization, let alone the PLO as a whole.

Israel's invasion of Lebanon in June 1982 and siege of Beirut ended in late August, after nine weeks of fighting, with the expulsion of the Palestinian armed forces and bureaucracy. The evacuation of 11,000–14,000 PLO personnel—mostly *Fatah*'s three semi-regular brigades and PLA Brigade Ein Jalut-from Beirut was internationally supervised, and tacitly supported, by most Arab states, including SAUDI ARABIA, Syria, and Lebanon. The PLO headquarters and some military units moved to TUNISIA, while others were accepted in SUDAN, Yemen, and SOUTH YEMEN. With its headquarters in Tunis and military forces dispersed far from the borders of Israel, the PLO was stripped of its military option, politically weakened and under threat of demise. This threat came to the fore with the rebellion of *Fatah*'s dissidents in the Biqa' (the eastern part of Lebanon, dominated by Syria) in May 1983, and the humiliating expulsion of Arafat from Damascus in June of that year. Arafat's effort to rehabilitate his position and widen the margins of his political freedom by entrenching in Tripoli's refugee camps of Badawi and Nahr al-Bared in the fall of 1983 was vehemently opposed to Syria and its Palestinian allies, who collaborated in expelling Arafat once again from Lebanon. In December 1983 Arafat and 4,000 of his men were evacuated from Tripoli—again with

international supervision and support. Between 1983–1986, Arafat succeeded in re-infiltrating some of his men and renewing the military infrastructure by smuggling weapons into the Palestinian camps in south Lebanon and Beirut.

These attempts to reestablish a military presence in Lebanon were one of the chief reasons for the continuous clashes between Palestinian gunmen in the camps and the Shi'i AMAL militia, and the imposition of siege on these camps, with Syria's full backing.

Of the various anti-Arafat groups within the PLO, the Syrian-controlled Sa'iqa and the PFLP-GC collaborated with the *Fatah* rebels in battles against Arafat's loyalists. The PFLP, DFLP, PSF, PLF (see PALESTINIAN GUERRILLA ORGANIZATIONS) did not join the actual fighting, but they stepped up their political struggle against Arafat and the mainstream. The anti-Arafat factions boycotted the seventeenth National Council held in Amman in November 1984, due to their ideological hostility to the Hashemite regime. They organized themselves in anti-Arafat fronts (split in themselves): a "Democratic Alliance," founded in May 1984 by the PFLP, the DFLP, the Communist Party and the PLF; also a "National Alliance," founded at the same time by the Sa'iqa, the *Fatah* rebels, the PFLP-GC, the PSF and some smaller groups. The "Democratic Alliance" was prepared to negotiate with Arafat's mainstream—demanding more hard-line policies and reforms in the structure of the PLO. This amounted to a paring-down of Arafat's powers and the formation of a "collective leadership." Yet the National Alliance opposed any deal with Arafat, insisting that he be deposed and that the PLO as a whole accept its hard-line policies and a new (Syrian-guided) leadership. In March 1985 the two anti-Arafat groupings formed a joint "Palestinian National Salvation Front." This was closer to the hard-line Sa'iqa and *Fatah* rebels than to the more flexible and independent PFLFP and DFLP; but the DFLP and the Communists refused to join the new Front. Arafat's mainstream was itself not fully united behind him: a hard-line faction, headed by Salah Khalaf (Abu Iyad) and Farouq QAD-DUMI, greatly constrained his freedom of action.

Reconciliation efforts continued from 1984, and in the fight against the Shi'i assaults on the camps in Beirut and south Lebanon the rival formations even cooperated to some degree. More than a year after King Hussein had suspended the Amman Agreement—which was one of the major causes of intra-Palestinian frictions—a reconciliation was achieved, reflected in the eighteenth PNC session held in April 1987 in Algiers, and its resolutions to abrogate the 1985 Accord with King Hussein, to sever the PLO's "offical" relations with Egypt, and the reaffirmation of the rejection of resolution 242. The PFLP and DFLP participated in the session and the Executive Committee, with the Communist Party also admitted for the first time to the latter body. However, the extreme pro-Syrian groups, and indeed Syria, took no part in this reconciliation.

The INTIFADA in the West Bank and Gaza Strip, which erupted in late 1987, came as a surprise to the PLO, sending a message of threat to undermine the PLO dominant authority over the Palestinian people "inside" the homeland. At the nineteenth PNC session, in November 1988, the PLO proclaimed the establishment of an independent Palestinian state on the basis of UN resolutions 181 (of November 1947, on the partition of Palestine). A month later, Arafat publicly renounced terrorism and accepted resolutions 242 and 338. The decision was taken under pressure from the Palestinian "inside" leadership following a year of uprising, and American pressure conditioning the opening of a political dialogue with the PLO on such steps.

However, the dilemma within the PLO still existed as to whether to abandon the armed struggle and cling to the political process or to keep both on the agenda. This dilemma was manifested on several occasions such as the terror action attempt near Israel's coastline in May 1990 by the PLF (see PALESTINIAN GUERRILLA ORGANIZATIONS), which Arafat refused to renounce, causing the cease of the diplomatic dialogue with the US. Another example is the supportive attitude shown by Arafat himself toward Iraq during the Gulf crisis in 1991, which brought upon Arafat and the PLO the wrath of the Gulf oil monarchies, and the decision to cease all financial funding by these states to the PLO and the Palestinians in the occupied territories. This led to a financial crisis within the PLO's mainstream Fatah, which had been forced to strictly reduce its activities such as the publication of newspapers, welfare services, and funding of its supporters in Arab states and the occupied territories. Furthermore, the growing power of HAMAS in the occupied territories and

refusal to join in the PLO as one of its factions according to Arafat's conditions, all determined the PLO's reluctant acceptance of the American formula for the Madrid conference in late 1991. The PLO had to acquiesce in Israel's conditions for the participation of Palestinian delegates from the occupied territories (and not from the PLO, see ARAB-ISRAEL PEACEMAKING) within the framework of a joint Jordanian-Palestinian delegation. However, during the talk, the Palestinian delegates were constantly and overtly instructed by the PLO.

During the winter-spring of 1993, the PLO and Israeli unofficial delegates began exploring ways to overcome the deadlocked Israeli-Palestinian talks in Washington.

The secret talks held in Oslo, Norway, soon amounted to full-fledged official negotiations, representing the PLO's attempt to regain control of the diplomatic process with Israel and keep the American hosts at bay. In August, Arafat informed Israeli Prime Minister Yizhak RABIN that the PLO was committed to the peace process in the Middle East, reaffirming its recognition of resolutions 242 and 338. A few weeks later the DOP between Israel and the PLO was signed on the White House lawn, the most conspicuous part of which was the parties' mutual recognition. The PLO was officially recognized by Israel and the US government as the legal representative of the Palestinian people in the peace process and in implementing its resolutions until elections to the PALESTINIAN AUTHORITY (PA) were to be held.

The elections to the PA's council and of its chairperson were held in January 1996, reaffirming Arafat's unchallenged position, with Fatah members winning a dominant position in the Council. Arafat remained the PLO Chairman and at the same time the President of the PA. Following the elections, the PLO underwent a reshuffle to adjust it to the new needs, primarily in the diaspora. Nonetheless, the PLO came under much criticism for neglecting its duties while representing both the Palestinians of the PA and the diaspora.

PALESTINIAN REFUGEES   see REFUGEES.

PAN-ARABISM   A supra-national ideological trend that emerged after World War I, its main aim being the comprehensive unity of all Arabic-speaking peoples. ARAB NATIONALISM—the doctrine from which

Pan-Arabism grew—derives its rationale from common language and civilization. It embodies a history of joint confrontation of, and resistance to, foreign domination, symbolized by cultural and political penetration of the West—with ISRAEL perceived as its spearhead—and a strong emotional-ideological consciousness of collective Arab-Islamic identity. While the formative years of ARAB NATIONALISM were most prominent during the inter-war years, the concept of Pan-Arabism as a sweeping popular force gathered momentum mainly in the aftermath of the Arab-Israel war of 1948, as a result of the socio-political turmoil that swept the Fertile Crescent countries (IRAQ, JORDAN, SYRIA, Palestine) and EGYPT, and led to the rise of new elites, primarily from the military. By then most of these countries had become independent states and had desperately tried to strengthen their separate sovereignty and sense of territorial nationalism (*Wataniyya*). Hence the claim of Pan-Arabism (*Qawmiyya*) that aspired to blur the boundaries among Arab states and merge them into a single unified state, or even unify their foreign policies, effectively clashed with the principle of sovereignty and independence of each individual state.

The issue of all-ARAB UNITY became highly popular and intensively articulated by politicians hungry for legitimacy, on the one hand, and a constant threat to regional inter-Arab stability, on the other. The vision of Arab Unity thus clashed head-on with the emergence of local patriotism and separate authoritative institutions; different geographic, economic, social conditions and interests; a history that had been largely divergent; spoken dialects of Arabic very different from, and to some extent incomprehensible to, each other; political and dynastic rivalries, conflicting ideological orientations, and the vested interests of incumbent ruling elites. The existence, in some Arab countries, of non-Arab minority groups—such as the KURDS in Iraq, the African tribes in southern SUDAN, the BERBERS in North-West Africa (see MAGHREB, MINORITIES)—tends to operate against all-Arab unity, as do manifestations of non-Arab, pre-Islamic allegiances (derogatively termed in Arabic *Shu'ubiyya*—internationalism), such as PHARANISM in Egypt or Phoenicianism in LEBANON—though these have never been a serious threat to ARABISM.

Pan-Arabism is primarily a mood, marked by a bitter protest against abstract or real enemies to progress and a better future (usually defined in the triangle:

the West, Israel, and Arab "Reaction"); a quest for a revolutionary transformation, assuming a general feeling of unity among the Arab masses and an aspiration to emphasize and cultivate the components of Arab commonality and translate them into power and prestige. The goal is to institute and develop as close as possible cooperation between the all Arab states.

Pan-Arab sentiments and its ideology tend to be stronger in the Fertile Crescent than in the Arab Peninsula and North Africa, although the Pan-Arab vision had been cultivated by Egyptian elites from the 1930s, and especially since the reign of ABDEL NASSER (1954–1970), albeit mainly in the context of regional Egyptian hegemony. Especially in Egypt and the Maghreb countries marked by strong national identity, and linked to other regional systems (the Nile Valley for Egypt, the Sub-Sahara for the Maghreb states), the Pan-Arab sentiment has been relatively weak. Arab Unity plans began during World War I. In the 1950s, they were nurtured mainly by the HASHEMITE dynasty and small groups of activists affiliated to the *Istiqlal* Party with adherents in Iraq, Syria, Lebanon and Palestine. In addition, it was primarily focused on the Fertile Crescent rather than the whole Arab world. From the 1950s, Pan-Arab aspirations were cultivated mainly through cross-national ideological movements that exercised powerful attraction to the youth and newly emerging middle class, especially in the Fertile Crescent, such as the Arab Nationalist Movement (*harakat al-qawmiyyin al-arab*); the BA'TH Party; Nasserist Egypt (though Nasser aspired to a closely knit Egyptian-dominated Arab bloc rather than to full all-Arab union); and LIBYA's QADHAFI. However, with the growing entrenchment of elites in power and strengthening state machinery, Pan-Arab fervor declined as a result of successful containment and co-optation of those popular movements by Arab regimes. Thus, despite its Pan-Arab vision and institutions, the *Ba'th* party branches in Syria and Iraq (finally split between them in 1968, with each of them claiming to represent the "true" *Ba'th*) became effectively subordinate to the state, serving as an ideological anchor in the process of state formation.

Pan-Arabism was marked by the aggressive behavior of Arab rulers and political movements to establish their own legitimacy and power, rather than mutual respect and willingness for equitable sharing of power and risks. In this context, Pan-Arabism, represented by the ability of an Arab leader or state to incite the citizens of another Arab state to denounce this state's leaders and delegitimize them in the name of the lofty ideal of Arab unity (introduced into regional Arab politics primarily by Nasser), paradoxically played a role in the formation of Arab states, as a defensive need, but also as a source of legitimacy. Nothing was more detrimental to the idea of Pan-Arab unity than the traumatic secession of Syria in 1961 from the UNITED ARAB REPUBLIC established in 1958 between Egypt and Syria. (For attempts of creating all-Arab unions, complete or partial, see ARAB NATIONALISM; ARAB UNITY; BA'TH NASSERISM.

Pan-Arabism has declined since the end of the 1967 War, which represented the defeat of Nasserism and Arab social revolution, giving way to conservatism and growing Islamic identity. Pan-Arabism underlay the outcry for inter-state Arab conformity on two interrelated issues: the attitudes toward the West and Israel. On these issues, Pan-Arabism proved to be highly effective, especially when backed by strong, assertive Arab regimes, such as Nasser's Egypt, Ba'th Iraq (since 1968), Syria and Qadhafi's Libya. Yet, even in this context, Pan-Arabism was an obstacle rather than a blessing, despite impressive successes it scored, especially in deterring Arab conservative regimes from linking themselves in alliances with the West (see MIDDLE EAST DEFENSE ORGANIZATION; CENTO); and preventing separate peaceful policies toward Israel by individual Arab states (especially JORDAN). Indeed, when Pan-Arabism became less used by Arab regimes from the late 1960s and early 1970s, a higher level of inter-Arab cooperation seemed to be on the rise in the spheres of financial aid and political consultation and coordination of foreign policies toward Israel (see for example ARAB-ISRAEL PEACEMAKING, ARAB-ISRAEL CONFLICT).

PAN-ISLAM The idea and doctrine of the unity of the Islamic world-community (*umma*) and the movement to realize and foster that unity. While a sentiment of Islamic unity has always been part of the consciousness of the world's Muslims, a modern Pan-Islamic movement emerged at the end of the nineteenth century. Its principal thinker and propagator was the Persian or Afghan Jamal al-Din al-Afghani (1837–1897). Several other prominent

Islamic scholars—Muhammad Abduh, Abdel Rahman al-Kawakibi (1849–1903), Muhammad Rashid Rida—also propounded Pan-Islamic ideas; most of them combined these ideas with those of reform and the revival of ISLAM.

The Turkish-Ottoman Sultan ABDEL HAMID II encouraged the Pan-Islamic movement and, emphasizing his position as Khalifa (CALIPH) of all Muslims—a position that the Ottoman Sultans had not officially upheld for a long time—tried to use it to establish his own political authority. While he did not call for an all-Islamic empire or the extension of his rule over non-Ottoman Muslim areas, he did hope to foster some allegiance from all Muslims that would ward off European pressure and penetration into his empire; cultivate pro-Ottoman sentiment among the Muslim subjects of the European powers (RUSSIA; FRANCE in North Africa; BRITAIN in India); strengthen his empire internally and avert the disaffection of its non-Turkish Muslim subjects. Abdel Hamid and his successors were only partially successful concerning these aims. When, on the outbreak of World War I in 1914, the Sultan-Caliph declared a JIHAD (Holy War), to get the Muslim subjects of his enemies to rise against their European rulers, his call was ignored by most Muslims—at least in its political and operational implications, though it may have created a degree of sympathy for TURKEY as a Muslim country. Turkish efforts to foster Pan-Islam also failed to prevent the emergence of an Arab nationalist movement within the Empire. Yet, Islamic feelings and loyalty to the Sultan induced the SANUSSI Muslims of Cyrenaica, after the Italian conquest of LIBYA, 1911–1912, to mount a continuous resistance to the conqueror.

When Sharif HUSSEIN Ibn Ali of Mecca (see ARAB REVOLT), Muslim-Arab governor of Hijaz, staged in 1916 a British-aided revolt against the Sultan, with a few Arab officers who deserted the Ottoman army to join and lead the Rebellion, most of the Arab population of the Empire remained loyal to the Sultan throughout the War and did not rebel. This was arguably because the Islamic allegiance to the Sultan-Caliph apparently played an important role in that loyalty.

Following the abolition of the Caliphate in 1924 by Republican Turkey, a new element was added to Pan-Islamic aspirations: the desire to restore the Caliphate. Various Muslim rulers or former rulers aspired to the position of Caliph and some even took actual steps to achieve it (the HASHEMITE King Hussein Ibn Ali of Hijaz proclaimed himself Khalifa), but none of them won significant support in the Muslim world. Several conferences were held in the 1920s to discuss the renewal of the Caliphate, but no consensus was reached. Several societies propounded the idea of Pan-Islam, but it created no effective political organization. In the course of the 1920s and early 1930s, the Palestinian Arab national movement led by Hajj Amin al-HUSSEINI tried to exploit Pan-Islamic sentiments for the political and financial mobilization of Muslims everywhere on behalf of the PALESTINE ARAB cause and struggle against ZIONISM. These efforts, manifested in the funds raised for the benefit of restoring the Muslim shrines in JERUSALEM, and defending these shrines from falling into the hands of the Zionists in the 1929 riots over the Western Wall, led to the holding of congresses and establishing committees and collective resolutions. However, these activities did not produce any organized Pan-Islamic movement, though they certainly played an important role in turning the Palestine issue into an all-Islamic problem, and affected the growing sense of ARAB NATIONALISM and the creation of inter-Arab institutions, primarily the ARAB LEAGUE.

After World War II, several newly independent countries had Muslim majorities. These included Pakistan, Indonesia, Malaya (later Malaysia), from 1971 also Bangladesh, and several African countries (Senegal, Gambia, Mali, Niger, Guinea, the semi-Arab countries of MAURITANIA, SOMALIA and DJIBOUTI), and the Arab independent states: JORDAN, SYRIA, MOROCCO, TUNISIA, ALGERIA, LIBYA, SUDAN, and later SOUTH YEMEN and the PERSIAN GULF sheikhdoms. Strongly Islamic SAUDI ARABIA, became, owing to its OIL production and economic strength, increasingly influential from the mid-1960s in attempts to consolidate and lead an Islamic block as an alternative to the radical revolutionary trend represented by NASSERISM (see below). During the following years, growing Saudi financial contributions to Arab and non-Arab Muslims, whether in the Middle East or outside the region, became a permanent phenomenon of promoting communal and religious Islamic activities, encouraging conservatism and religiosity rather than political Islamism. These developments gave new impetus to the pan-Islamic trend toward stronger cooperation between Muslim countries and the cre-

ation of all-Islamic institutions that would foster such cooperation.

Since 1949 several all-Islamic organizations have been established, with Pakistani activists and functionaries in the forefront; none of these associations, loosely organized and to some extent overlapping, had significant impact or influence. They included a "Muslim World Congress" which held several sessions until the late 1960s (and presented itself as the continuation of a previous World Muslim Congress organization, electing as its President the ex-MUFTI of Jerusalem, Hajj Amin al-Husseini, who had organized and chaired a similar Congress in Jerusalem in 1931); a "World Congress of Muslim" *ulama* (religious scholars), since 1952; a Muslim Youth Congress, 1955; an "Islamic Conference of Jerusalem" (sponsored by the MUSLIM BROTHERHOOD), 1953 and 1960; a "Conference of Islamic Liberation Organizations," Cairo, 1953; a "World Muslim League" (*Rabita*)—Saudi-sponsored—since the early 1960s; an "Afro-Asian Islamic Conference,"centered in Indonesia, since 1965; and others. Most of these congresses and associations were non-governmental, but government leaders and functionaries frequently participated in them. Some of them were unofficially sponsored by governments.

The creation of an association of Islamic states or governments was of course more difficult, since most Islamic states were understandably cautious and hesitated to add an Islamic dimension to their international commitments—and political interests and orientations were divergent and often conflicting. Despite these obstacles attempts were made. Pakistan's first Premier Liaqat Ali Khan (assassinated in October 1951) tried to arrange a conference of Islamic governments, which failed. So did the Malayan Premier Tungku Abdel Rahman in 1961. EGYPT's ABDEL NASSER, King SA'UD, and Pakistan's Governor-General Ghulam Muhammad in 1954 spoke of the creation of a Congress of Islamic states, but nothing came of this. In the mid-1960s, King FEISAL of Saudi Arabia tried to establish an alliance of Islamic states (in effect: the conservative ones, against Egypt's revolutionary-subversive Nasserism)—but he did not persevere. Late in 1980, President SADAT of Egypt announced the formation of a "League of Arab and Islamic Peoples" (a move against the Arab League that had suspended Egypt's membership); but this Islamic League did not get off the ground and was formally dissolved in 1983 by Sadat's successor MUBARAK. A loose association of Islamic states was finally formed after the Islamic Summit of Rabat of September 1969 (convened after a demented foreign visitor had set fire to al-Aqsa Mosque in Jerusalem. This was misinterpreted in the Arab and Islamic world as an "Israeli plot" and caused great excitement and a resolve of Islamic Heads of States to consult about possible action). That summit instituted regular meetings of the Islamic states' Foreign Ministers—meetings formalized since the early 1970s as an ISLAMIC CONFERENCE ORGANIZATION (ICO) with a permanent secretariat (the First Secretary-General, until 1973, was the Malayan ex-Premier Tungku Abdel-Rahman, followed by the Egyptian Hassan Tihami, the Senegalese Abdel-Karim Gaye, from 1979 the Tunisian Habib Chatty, and since 1984 the Pakistani Sharif-ul-Din Pirzada). While at the first meetings twenty-three to twenty-five countries attended, the ICO membership has in recent years been approximately forty-one (not including the PLO).

The Islamic countries endeavored to extend their cooperation to various fields of activity, particularly economically. Several semi-governmental economic conferences were held from 1949 and throughout the 1950s. A plan to establish an all-Islamic Development Bank was worked out in 1970 and endorsed several times in 1972–1975, and the Bank became operational in 1976. A separate Development Fund (to afford credit on easier, non-commercial terms) has been planned since the late 1970s. (These financial institutions, like all Islamic banks, face the problem of the Islamic ban on interest; it is usually solved by substituting other, equivalent payments—e.g. a share in profits and expenses.) An all-Islamic News Agency, agreed upon in 1972, has been operating since the mid-1970s, but does not seem to have much impact. An all-Islamic Court of Justice, repeatedly suggested, has not yet been established.

Generally, while the ideal of all-Islamic unity is a vision alive in the hearts of Muslims, recent waves of radical, assertive Islamism (such as the revolutionary Iranian effort to shape a thoroughly Islamic state, and attempts in other countries to make Islamic law, the SHARI'A, the dominant element in legislation and state and society practices) may have given it a fresh impetus. Pan-Islam aspirations do not entail, in pre-

sent-day realities, plans for an all-Islamic political entity (see ISLAMIC RADICALISM AND MOVEMENTS). They are directed toward the cultivation of strong all-Islamic cooperation. Organizations established for that purpose have remained loose and without much clout—the ICO, for instance, failed in its efforts to end the (inter-Islamic) IRAN-IRAQ WAR—but they have become part of the Islamic countries' international association and orientation.

PAN TURKISM   A movement aiming at the linguistic, cultural, and sometimes political unity of all Turkish-speaking peoples. The movement (also labelled Pan Turanism—after Turan, the name of the Turks' ancient homeland in Central Asia) sprang up amongst Turkish intellectuals in the Russian and Ottoman empires towards the end of the nineteenth century. It was influenced by efforts of Russification of Turkish speaking peoples as well as by nationalist ideas, the development of Turcology in Europe, and the increasing contacts between Turks within the OTTOMAN EMPIRE and those outside it. In TURKEY the movement, which numbered many Turkish migrants from Russia among its adherents, as well as the national philosopher Ziya GÖKALP, was particularly active during the period of the YOUNG TURKS. It exercised a strong influence upon some of their leaders. It gained momentum as the theories of Ottomanism and Pan-Islamism that were aimed at guarding the integrity of the Empire were regarded as ineffectual. Enver's decision to enter World War I against RUSSIA was partially motivated by his desire to free the Turkic peoples, as were his activities on the Russian front. ATATÜRK, who wanted to maintain good relations with the USSR, discarded Pan Turkism, preferring to foster loyalty to the Turks' Anatolian homeland. During World War II (and especially after the German victories in Russia) Pan Turkism circles resumed their activities, but they were suppressed when the tide of war turned.

In the post war period, Pan Turkist ideas continued to be expressed in Turkey by some intellectuals and writers and by circles of migrants from the Turkic world. Although not branded as Pan Turkism, solidarity with allegedly suppressed Turkish communities abroad (such as those of Cyprus, Bulgaria, Greece and IRAQ) had also been manifest in government policy and the attitudes of the Turkish public at large. The chauvinist Nationalist Action Party formed in 1965 by Alparslan Türkes, voiced a strong commitment toward the so-called Outside Turks, calling for more support to be given to their cause. When the Soviet Union collapsed at the end of 1991, Turkey was quick to foster relations with Turkic republics and communities formerly under Soviet rule and declared it a new sphere of its foreign policy. While consistently denying that this was a manifestation of Pan Turkism, Turkey emphasized that in its newly established relations with the Turkic world it was motivated not only by political and economic considerations, but also by strong feelings of Turkish brotherhood and solidarity.

PARTITION PLAN (UN Resolution 181) (see ARAB-ISRAEL PEACEMAKING).

PASDARAN (Revolutionary Guards of Iran) A military organization formed soon after the Islamic revolution in IRAN. It is similar in every way to a regular army, with land, sea and air forces, and 100,000 fighters. Its goal was to defend the revolution due to KHOMEINI's lack of confidence in the regular army, whose commanders had sworn allegiance to the Shah. The core of this army was made up of Iranian guerrilla fighters, who had been trained in Fatah camps in LEBANON in the 1970s.

In the last months of the Shah's regime, when the ranks of the army and official security forces were weakened, the Pasdaran took upon themselves policing functions and implementation of the orders of Khomenei. Following the revolution they set up branches of the *Komiteh* (see IRAN) throughout the country, in order to locate and crush any counter-revolutionary elements. Upon the outbreak of the war with Iraq (see IRAN-IRAQ WAR), the organization started to arm itself with heavy weapons and become institutionalized, and played an active role in defense activities and attacks. The number of its fighters reached 400,000, and it was placed in charge of enlisting volunteers (*Basij*) by means of the establishment of Khomeini's "20 million man army." The competition with the official army and the absence of coordination between the two forces led to many clashes.

The plan to merge the Pasdaran with the regular army was shelved, not only because of the active opposition of its commanders, but because the existence of the force was further institutionalized in that ranks of command were created, uniforms introduced, large budgets allocated, and a separate ministry established. Even though the Pasdaran and the army continue to exist separately, there is a common supreme command under the Ministry of Defense.

(P)DFLP (POPULAR) DEMOCRATIC FRONT FOR THE LIBERATION OF PALESTINE) see PALESTINIAN GUERRILLA ORGANIZATIONS.

PEACE NOW Israeli non-partisan, extra-parliamentary peace movement, established in the spring of 1978 (half a year before the Camp David Accords were signed), after 350 reserve officers wrote a letter to Prime Minister Menahem BEGIN demanding that he continue along the path to peace. Most of the movements' activities were implemented by means of public gatherings, demonstrations, letters and meetings.

Following the signing of the Egyptian-Israeli Peace Treaty (see ARAB-ISRAEL PEACEMAKING) Peace Now acted for the continuation of the peace process. From the beginning of its existence it argued that the continuation of the occupation of the WEST BANK and GAZA STRIP contradicted the goal of peace, and offered five principles on the basis of which peace negotiations between Israel and its neighbors should be held: (1) the principle of territorial compromise, according to which each side will surrender part of its historical claims; (2) recognition of the right of the State of Israel to a sovereign existence within secure and recognized borders that will be acceptable to both sides; (3) Israeli recognition of the right of the Palestinian people to national existence; (4) the need for arrangements that will ensure Israeli security requirements, including certain border changes; (5) the integrity of JERUSALEM as the capital of ISRAEL, while taking into account the totality of the religious and national interests in the city.

Peace Now stood at the head of the protest against the Lebanese War (see ARAB-ISRAEL CONFLICT) and was the major organizing force of the mass demonstration in Tel Aviv on 25 September 1982, following the massacre in Sabra and Shatilla, and in favor of the establishment of a national commission of inquiry to investigate the background to the massacre and demanding the resignation of Ariel SHARON as Defense Minister.

Even though Peace Now was never a pacifist movement and was patriotic in its views, it rapidly became a target for right-wing hatred in Israel, and was accused of defeatism and even treason. The movement's activists always comprised primarily university graduates of Ashkenazi origin, and thus failed to turn into a mass movement. During a Peace Now demonstration, held on 10 February 1983—the day on which the Kahan Commission of Inquiry published its report on the Sabra and Shatilla massacre—a Peace Now activist, Emil Grunzweig, was killed when a hand grenade was thrown at the demonstrators by a Jewish right winger.

Peace Now considered running in the elections to the eleventh Knesset (1984) but finally decided to remain extra-parliamentary. Until the end of the 1980s, Peace Now avoided holding direct contacts with official PLO representatives, but relations were established with various Palestinian personalities in the territories, such as Feisal al-HUSSEINI. In the course of the INTIFADA, the movement increased its activities and called for an end to the occupation. The movement supported all the peace moves of the government of Yitzhak RABIN established in July 1992, but protested against some of its activities, such as the expulsion of 415 HAMAS and Islamic JIHAD activists to LEBANON in December 1992. Following the establishment of the government of Binyamin NETANYAHU in June 1996; its apparent ambivalence toward the Oslo process with the Palestinian Authority; and settlement activity in East Jerusalem, Peace Now stood at the forefront of those calling for the government's resignation.

PEACE OF GALILEE OPERATION (1982)   see ARAB-ISRAEL CONFLICT.

PEACE-KEEPING FORCES (UNEF; UNIFIL UNTSO; UNDOF)   see ARAB-ISRAEL PEACEMAKING.

PEEL COMMISSION, PEEL REPORT   see ARAB-ISRAEL PEACEMAKING, PALESTINE ARABS.

PERES, SHIMON (b. 1923–)   Israeli statesman, chairman of the Israel Labor Party, 1977–1992 and from the end of 1995 to 1997, and Prime Minister, 1984–1986 and 1995–1996. Born in Poland, Peres immigrated with his family to Palestine in 1934 and studied in Tel Aviv and at the agricultur-

al school at Ben Shemen. In 1940 he was amongst the founders of Kibbutz Alumoth and was secretary of the youth movement *Tnu'at Hano'ar Ha'oved Vehalomed*. Peres started to work with David Ben GURION and Levi ESHKOL in the *Hagana* command (the defense force of the pre-state Jewish community in Palestine) in 1947, and continued to serve them after the establishment of the state. In 1949 he was appointed head of the Ministry of Defense mission to the US, which was engaged in purchasing military equipment. In 1952 he was appointed Deputy Director-General of the Ministry of Defense and the following year Director-General—a position in which he established strong ties with France, helped to establish Israel's nuclear capability and advanced the development of the Israeli Aircraft Industry.

In 1959 Peres was first elected to the Knesset on the *Mapai* ballot and was appointed Deputy Minister of Defense—a position he held until 1965. That year he left *Mapai*, together with Ben Gurion and Moshe DAYAN, and was one of the founders of *Rafi*, becoming the new party's Secretary-General. In 1969 he was appointed Minister of Immigration and Absorption by Prime Minister Golda MEIR and was responsible for the economic development of the occupied territories. The following year he was appointed Minister of Transportation and Communications. In 1974 Peres served as Minister of Information in the Meir government, and after Meir's resignation he failed in his first contest against Yitzhak RABIN for the Labor Party leadership. In the first government formed by Rabin in 1974 he served as Minister of Defense.

On 23 February 1977, Peres once again lost in a contest for the Labor Party leadership, but following Rabin's resignation, on 7 April 1977, became Party Chairman. Under his leadership the Labor-*Mapam Ma'arach* list (the Alignment) lost the elections to the ninth Knesset (1977) for the first time since the establishment of the state, and Peres led it in opposition until 1984. In 1978 Peres was elected one of the Vice-Presidents of the Socialist International. Following the elections to the eleventh Knesset (1984), Peres set up a National Unity government with the *Likud*, and in accordance with the rotation agreement with Yitzhak SHAMIR served as Prime Minister in the years 1984–1986 and as Minister of Foreign Affairs in the years 1986–1988. In April 1987 Peres concluded the London Agreement with King HUSSEIN of JORDAN, but the agreement was not approved by the cabinet (see ARAB-ISRAEL PEACE-MAKING). In the National Unity Government formed by Shamir in 1988 Peres was appointed Minister of Finance. In March 1990, following the stalemate in the peace process, Peres decided to bring down the government in a vote on a motion of no-confidence, and unsuccessfully tried to form an alternative government.

Following Peres's failure to establish a government, Rabin announced that he would once again contest the Labor Party leadership, and on 19 February 1992, replaced Peres as leader of the Labor Party. In the government formed by Rabin after the elections to the thirteenth Knesset (1992) Peres was appointed Minister of Foreign Affairs, and in cooperation with Rabin approved the process initiated by his deputy Yossi BEILIN, which led to Israel's recognition of the PALESTINE LIBERATION ORGANIZATION (PLO) and the signing of the Declaration of Principles on 13 September 1993 (see ARAB-ISRAEL PEACEMAKING). Together with Rabin and Yasser ARAFAT, Peres received the Nobel Prize for Peace on 10 December 1994. Following Rabin's assassination on 4 November 1995, Peres was appointed Prime Minister and Minister of Defense. In the direct election of the Prime Minister held simultaneously with the elections to the fourteenth Knesset (1996) Peres was defeated by Binyamin NETANYAHU by a small majority. In June 1997, Peres was replaced by Ehud BARAK as chairman of the Labor Party.

PERSIAN GULF (PG) (in Arab usage: Arab Gulf, in recent years often called "The Gulf"—to avoid dispute in political terminology) Gulf of the Indian Ocean/Arabian Sea, separating the Arabian Peninsula in the south-southwest and IRAN in the north-north-east. Connected with the Gulf of OMAN and the Arabian Sea by the shallow Straits of HORMUZ, the PG is rather shallow, its maximum depth not exceeding 328 feet (approximately 100 meters). It is about 500 miles (800 km.) long and of varying width (125-200 miles, 200-320 km.). Its area contributing about 90,000 sq.miles (235,000 sq. km.)

The PG contains a number of islands—near the Iranian coast the largest one of Qishn, the historically important Hormuz, and Sirri (all at its eastern end, near the Straits of Hormuz) and the small islet of Kharg (at its western end). Kharg and Sirri were de-

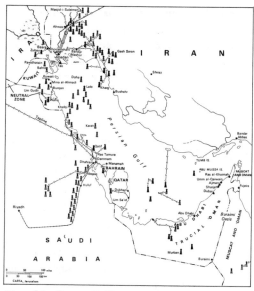

Map of the Persian Gulf

veloped in recent years as OIL loading terminals. Near the Arabian shore are the islands of BAHRAIN and, farther east, the small inlets of ABU MUSSA and the TANBS, both claimed and forcibly occupied by Iran in dispute with the UNITED ARAB EMIRATES (UAE), and Huwar and smaller islets nearby disputed by Bahrain and QATAR. At the north-western end of the PG, several Kuwaiti islands, e.g. Bubiyan and Warba, have been a matter of dispute between KUWAIT and IRAQ. Two large peninsulas jut into the PG from Arabia: Qatar, and TRUCIAL COAST (or Trucial Oman, now the UAE, with its tip, Ras Musandam, belonging to Oman);. The latter peninsula protrudes into the Straits of Hormuz and separates the PG and the Gulf of Oman, with its western coast on the former and its eastern coast on the latter.

The northern/north-eastern, Iranian shore of the PG is primarily mountainous, with very few streams. It does have a few inlets that are suitable for harbors—e.g. Bandar Khomeini (formerly Bandar Shahpur), Bushehr (Bushire) and, near the Straits of Hormuz, Bandar Abbas. The southern/southwestern, Arabian shore is sandy and mostly flat. It is unsuitable for harbors except for a few bays—e.g. at Kuwait, which has served for centuries as the chief port of the region, and at DUBAI. At most of the modern oil ports on the PG's Arabian shore ships anchor at a distance from the shore and the oil is conveyed to them by pipes. At the northern end of the PG only one major river flows into it: the SHATT

AL-ARAB. This is the joint estuary of the Euphrates and the Tigris (coming from TURKEY and Iraq), and the Karun and Karkheh (coming from Iran). The silt carried by the rivers has created a wide, marshy plain and encroaches on the sea in marshy tongues. Thus no ports can be built on the coast. The main ports (Basra, Khorramshahr) are inland, some distance up the river; but Iraq has built several artificial loading installations off the shore. The alignment of the Iraq-Iran border on the Shatt al-Arab and the adjacent PG coast is in dispute, as is the Iraq-Kuwait border.

The PG has served since antiquity as an important trade and marine route. From the sixteenth century, it lost some of its centrality in Europe's eastern trade, as it moved to the route around Africa and, in the nineteenth century, through the SUEZ CANAL. From the early sixteenth century, the PG was dominated by the Portuguese who captured Bahrain and Hormuz and established strongholds. Their rule ended in 1622, when Persia conquered Bahrain and Hormuz. Persia remained the dominant force in the PG, though most of the Arabian coast was ruled by local Arab sheikhs and tribes. Indeed, the Bahrain islands were also seized in 1783 by sheikhs of the al KHALIFA. From the seventeenth century, piracy and slave-trading were rampant in the PG. The suppression of piracy was one of the main reasons for Great BRITAIN's growing involvement in the PG from the end of the eighteenth and the early nineteenth century. Another reason was the need to protect the approaches to India—e.g. against French ambitions and plans clearly enunciated by Napoleon. From 1820, numerous agreements for the cessation of piracy were signed between Britain, via its governors and envoys in India, and the various sheikhs and amirs of the Arabian Gulf coast and islands. Gradually, throuthout the nineteenth century, these agreements established British protection over the various petty rulers, and the entire PG area became an area of British influence.

Concerning most of the Arabian PG sheikhs, the establishment of Britain's protectorates caused no major clash with the OTTOMAN EMPIRE, as the latter claimed no effective possession of the south-eastern reaches of the PG. It was different at the north-western end of the PG, where the Sultan claimed sovereignty over the al-Hassa coastal district (later part of SAUDI ARABIA), over Kuwait, and most decidedly

over the Shatt al-Arab and the coast of the province of Basra (later Iraq). Yet Britain was increasingly interested precisely in these north-western parts of the PG, as they were potential targets of great power ambitions and intrigues. RUSSIA's ambitions to establish a foothold in the PG, a warm-water port and an outlet to the southern seas, were thought to be evident. Its aspirations to expand in the direction of India (also perceived in Afghanistan) were a source of constant British apprehension. Moreover, a new player was appearing on the scene: imperial Germany. Turkey was, toward the end of the century, entering a close alliance with Germany. German enterprises were penetrating the Ottoman Empire, extending feelers towards the PG. German plans from 1899 for the Baghdad Railway, were opposed by Britain and its allies. After a long diplomatic struggle, they were transferred from a German-Ottoman scheme into an international one, so that the railway would not reach Basra, but would extend to the PG at Kuwait. Britain vigorously opposed that extension and persuaded Turkey to bar it.

In a treaty with Britain, the Sheikh of Kuwait in 1899 accepted British protection, promising not to grant any concessions to other powers without British consent. While the Sultan's claim to sovereignty was not formally denied, Kuwait had become a British protectorate. British interests in the region were further intensified when an oil exploration concession in south-western Iran, near the Shatt al-Arab, was granted to British interests in 1901; oil was discovered in 1908, and the British government in 1914 acquired control of the Anglo-Persian Oil Company, formed in 1909. The local Sheikh who de facto controlled the oil area, Sheikh Khaz'al of Muhammara (later Khorramshahr), in 1910 also accepted British protection, in return for his pledge to keep the oil operations secure. The sovereignty of the Shah of Iran was not formally denied, but the whole southern part of Iran, including its PG shores, were by now virtually a British zone of influence: the eastern section, with the coast of the Gulf of Oman, from Bandar Abbas eastwards, under a formal agreement of 1907 with Russia, and the western part, de facto and contrary to that agreement, through Britain's dominating influence on the tribes controlling the area (Bakhtiaris, Qashqais), though German agents were also active in the area. After the outbreak of World War I in 1914, Turkey joined

Britain's enemies. The British protectorate over Kuwait was further tightened and in 1915 IBN SA'UD, the ruler of the al-Hassa coast and the Najd hinterland, signed a treaty with Britain that was a veiled semi-protectorate. A British expeditionary force that conquered southern Iraq came from India through the PG.

After World War I Iraq was under a British MANDATE. There were British protectorates over all the sheikhdoms on the PG's Arabian coast, and southern Iran was under dominating British influence. The PG was almost completely under British control. A British "Political Resident" for the PG was stationed in Bushir, from 1946 in Bahrain. Political "Agents" or "Officers" resided in most local centers (Kuwait, Bahrain, Qatar, Dubai, ABU DHABI). Between the World Wars, the situation changed and British control diminished, as Iraq became independent (1932) and, despite the Anglo-Iraqi treaty of 1930, increasingly anti-British. Iran asserted its independence and established more effective control over its southern regions (including the liquidation of Sheikh Khaz'al's British-protected semi-autonomy in Muhammara). Yet, in World War II the PG remained a principal staging area for British and allied forces and operations—including a brief war against Iraq's rebellious RASHID AL's regime in May 1941 and the occupation (August 1941) of southern Iran (in co-ordination with the simultaneous occupation of its northern parts by Russia), to prevent Iran from allying itself with Germany or being occupied by it

After World War II, the PG had become one of the most crucial areas of conflict worldwide, along with the process of withdrawal of the British Empire, mainly due to its oil wealth—two thirds of the world's proven oil reserves and, by the 1950s, over half of the exported oil in the world produced by its riparian countries. There was an extreme discrepancy between oil wealth and military ability to protect it as in the case of Saudi Arabia and other Arab oil-producing sheikhdoms. With the erosion of Britain's dominating position in the PG, regional actors took over and political tension among and within them accelerated. Iraq was finally moving out of the orbit of British influence; British air bases—one of them in the Basra area, at the head of the PG—in 1955 became joint bases under the Baghdad Pact and were lost to Britain when Iraq seceded from that Pact in

1959. Iraq's alliance with Britain lapsed under Iraq's new, revolutionary regime (after the coup of July 1958). Relations with Iran were deeply disturbed by the nationalization of Iran's oil production by the radical MOSSADDEQ government that also clashed with the Shah. The dispute was settled in 1954, after the fall of the radical government and the restoration of the Shah's regime. The oil company was reshaped to include other foreign companies (thirty-five percent American) and Britain lost its exclusive control. From the 1960s, the Shah of Iran increasingly entertained great-power ambitions, presenting Iran as the principal power and main guardian of the Gulf. Since the 1930s Saudi Arabia has been linked chiefly to the UNITED STATES rather than to Britain. Kuwait, emboldened by the development and economic power created by its oil, demanded full independence—which Britain willingly granted in 1961.

Britain still acted, to some extent, as the policeman of the PG. It sometimes intervened in dynastic and succession disputes of the various sheikhs and rulers (mainly in the Trucial Coast, later to become the UAE). Sometimes it intervened in disputes between principalities, e.g. the BURAIMI dispute between Saudi Arabia, Abu Dhabi and Oman in the 1950s, and several territorial conflicts between Trucial sheikhdoms. Even after the withdrawal of its protectorate from Kuwait in 1961, it responded to Kuwait's appeal and sent troops when Iraq refused, the same year, to accept its independence and claimed all Kuwait as Iraqi territory. Britain also guided and aided the various Arab PG principalities to plan joint institutions (currency, communications, etc.) toward a future federation. But Britain felt since the 1950s and 1960s that the role of protector and policeman no longer fitted either world conditions or indeed its own diminishing wealth and strength as a great power. In 1968 it announced that by the end of 1971 it would withdraw its protectorates and bases.

When in 1971 the British Protectorates were abolished, the seven sheikhdoms of the Trucial Coast formed the UAE (prepared beforehand, under British guidance). Qatar and Bahrain refused to join, preferring to become separately independent. The states on the shores of the PG were now all independent—Iran, Iraq, Kuwait, Saudi Arabia, Bahrain, Qatar, the UAE and Oman. In great-power and global terms, a certain power vacuum was created by Britain's withdrawal. This greatly concerned the US. The security of the PG, and in particular the freedom of shipping, were by now even more vital than before since a large portion of the non-Soviet world's oil supply, and far more than one-half of its oil export trade, were being loaded in the PG ports and moving through its waters. It was not only the danger of Russian penetration that perturbed the US and the West, but the threat of destabilization by terrorist groups (such as a shady SOUTH YEMEN-based "Popular Front for the Liberation of the Occupied Arab Gulf," PFLOAG, that was already in rebellion in Oman's Dhofar region)—groups that the West suspected of being manipulated by Russia and, for some time, China (and perhaps also Iraq). Iran under the Shah, until 1979, cooperated with Oman to ensure the defense of the Gulf of Oman, i.e., the eastern extension of the PG, and the Straits of Hormuz, with US and British support. In 1974 a formal Iran-Oman agreement was concluded. Moreover, the US undertook, informally and to a limited extent, to protect the freedom of shipping in the PG and its stability. Together with Britain (to an even more limited extent), it arranged to receive certain naval and air "facilities"—e.g. in Bahrain and Oman. For some years, the US thought of more permanent arrangements, such as a "Rapid Deployment Force" based on the Indian Ocean, with equipment stored, ready for use, at agreed points ashore. The only country of the region willing to join the scheme and host US storage facilities was Oman (in an agreement of 1980).

In general, the newly independent PG countries were extremely reluctant to link themselves to the US. While they were eager to obtain a low-profile de facto protection, they refused to enter into any formal agreements. Saudi Arabia's position was quite unclear—and Iraq was anyway no ally of the US. Even the alliance with the Shah's Iran was informal only. The US encouraged the Shah in his stance as the chief guardian of the PG. Yet, in some respects Iran, even during the Shah's regime, encouraged disturbances for the principalities on the Arabian shore. It had renounced its old claim to Bahrain in 1970, accepting a poll conducted by the Secretary-General of the UN, according to which the majority of the population wanted independence. Yet with its power growing, there was no telling whether it would not reassert that claim. In 1971, Iran revived a claim to the ABU MUSSA and Tanb islands of SHARJA and RAS AL-

KHAIMA and forcibly occupied them when British protection was being withdrawn and the UAE emerged. An informal settlement was made—e.g. a reported sharing of the islands' offshore oil revenue between Iran and Sharja—but Iran remained in occupation. Iraq, in its anti-Iranian campaign, demanded the islands' return to the UAE—but the UAE remained cautiously silent. For beyond the specific case of Iranian forcible expansion, there was constant apprehension of Iran's assertion of control over the PG and potential claims to territory on the Arabian shore and islands close to it, and of Iranian subversion—using the considerable part of the population that was Shi'i, Iranian or of Iranian origin. These apprehensions grew after Iran was taken over, in 1979, by KHOMEINI's assertive Islamic regime that spoke of "exporting" its Islamic revolution. It was in large part in response to these new challenges and dangers that the six countries on the Arabian shore of the PG—Saudi Arabia, Kuwait, Qatar, Bahrain, the UAE and Oman (without Iraq)—formed the GULF COOPERATION COUNCIL, GCC, in 1981. Holding regular ministerial and "summit" meetings and with a permanent secretariat, the GCC has instituted (after initial hesitations and difficulties), a fairly wide range of measures to enhance cooperation and joint or co-ordinated action in many fields, including plans for a joint military force. It has also, however, taken a very cautious and low-profile line toward Iran. In the Iraq-Iran conflict the sympathies of the Arab PG countries were no doubt with Iraq (despite former apprehensions of Iraqi aggressive schemes and subversion, and a lack of empathy with its revolutionary regime). Some of them aided Iraq with huge funds, supporting its war-damaged oil exports and assuring its war-disrupted supplies. The GCC followed an official policy of neutrality during the war.

The IRAN-IRAQ WAR (1980–1988) gravely affected the PG, to such an extent that it was frequently called the "Gulf War." The original, and main arena of operations was the Shatt al-Arab, close to the shores of the Gulf, with Khorramshahr and territory around it taken by Iraq (reconquered by Iran in May 1982), Abadan destroyed, as was Basra under frequent Iranian shelling. An Iranian counter-offensive in February 1986 reached Iraq's oil-loading installations on the PG-shore at Fao (al-Faw) and offshore (Mina'al-Bakr). Moreover, in early 1984 the Iraqi airforce, superior to Iran's, extended its bombing operations not only to Kharg Island (Iran's main oil loading installation) but to shipping, and in particular oil tankers, mostly foreign, en route to or from Kharg. In 1985, Iran built additional or alternative facilities at Sirri Island, near the Straits of Hormuz, reached by shuttle tankers and thought to be beyond the Iraqi bombers' range (but bombed from August 1986). Iran retaliated by attacking oil tankers, nearly all of them foreign, en route to or from ports, on the PG's Arabian coast. Iran also intercepted and searched foreign ships in the PG, sometimes confiscating cargoes destined for Iraq. It effectively blocked the Straits of Hormuz, which led to a re-flagging of Kuwaiti oil-tankers, but frequently European and even great-power vessels were hit. The US, Britain, FRANCE and since 1986 the USSR sent naval patrols into the PG, indicating that they would protect their ships. Interference with their shipping diminished, though there were few actual confrontations.

The end of the Iran-Iraq war in 1988 left the reasons that led to it, primarily the Shatt al-Arab dispute, unresolved. Moreover, Iraqi access to the Gulf through this waterway remained blocked, and financial shortage played a primary role in pushing Iraq to the invasion of Kuwait in early August 1990 (see GULF WAR). The occupation of Kuwait began a regional crisis that lasted until February 1991, when Kuwait was liberated by the American-led international coalition. The liberation of Kuwait led to the setting ablaze of hundreds of Kuwaiti oil wells by the withdrawing Iraqi forces.

From the late 1980s Iran has been systematically developing its military power, including the purchase of missile-producing as well as nuclear technologies (see IRAN), reestablishing itself as the dominant power in the region. Iraq remained subjected to UN sanctions and restrictions in oil marketing and military movements in its own territory (see IRAQ), Iran's primacy in the Gulf, and its demonstrated willingness to establish normal relations with the Arab states of the Gulf. Nonetheless, American troops and naval units are still deployed in Kuwait and Saudi Arabia. From the mid-1990s these Arab oil-rich monarchies seem to have acquiesced in the restored Iranian centrality in the Gulf area. Iran's renewed legitimacy in the Arab world was demonstrated in the summit meeting of the ISLAMIC CONFERENCE ORGANIZATION, held in late 1997 in Tehran.

PFLOAG (POPULAR FRONT FOR THE LIBERATION OF THE ARAB GULF) see PERSIAN GULF.

PFLP (POPULAR FRONT FOR THE LIBERATION OF PALESTINE) see PALESTINIAN GUERRILLA ORGANIZATIONS.

PFLP-GC (POPULAR FRONT FOR THE LIBERATION OF PALESTINE—GENERAL COMMAND) see PALESTINIAN GUERRILLA ORGANIZATIONS.

PHALANGES (*hizb al-kata'ib*) Lebanese political Party and militia. Founded in 1936 as a paramilitary youth organization by Pierre JUMAYYIL, following his participation in the Olympic games in Berlin and deep inspiration by the *Hitler Ugend*—the Nazi Youth Movement. Other founders were Georges Naqqash, Charles Hilou (later President of LEBANON, 1964–1970) and other young Maronite leaders who advocated Lebanese independence and national spirit along with the example of totalitarian German and Italian nationalism of their time. Although this was not stated explicitly, the Phalanges were a Christian-Maronite organization primarily intended to defend the Maronite community, and preserve the Christian character of Lebanon against suspected Muslim schemes. Its motto "God, the fatherland, and the family,"reflected its conservative views, placing the Phalanges in the right, pro-Status Quo of the Lebanese political System. The Phalanges adopted a pro-French attitude, seeing FRANCE as the defender of Lebanon's separate independence and Christian character. However, it clashed with the French administration when France refused to ratify the Franco-Lebanese Treaty of 1936 and grant independence to Lebanon. It was dissolved in 1937 and again in 1942. In the crisis of 1943 the Phalanges participated in demonstrations and strikes in support of the Lebanese government. Afterwards, the Phalanges were recognized as a legal organization. While keeping their paramilitary structure, they also became a political party. In the 1940s they opposed President Bishara al-Khouri and his pan-Arab policies. In 1949 the organization was declared illegal, along with all other youth organizations, after violent clashes with the SYRIAN SOCIAL NATIONALIST PARTY (SSNP). Until May 1952, it operated under another name ("Lebanese Unity Party"). It then returned to operate under its present name, this time as a political party. In the civil war of 1958, the Phalanges supported President Camille CHAMOUN against the Muslim Nasserist rebels, this time together with the SSNP. After the settlement of that crisis, it foiled, by threatening armed resistance and a new civil war, the formation of a government dominated by the former rebels.

In the 1960s and early 1970s the Phalanges operated mainly as a political faction. It did not establish a fully organized and identified party. It appeared in elections as Independent, in shifting list-alliances with other factions. The Lebanese political system, inherently dominated by primordial loyalty to family and clan, did not do well with political-ideological parties, such as the Phalanges, which lacked support from Lebanon's traditional leaders (the Zua'ma). The Phalanges were thus usually represented in Parliament by a handful (three–seven) of deputies. In Parliament, the Phalanges representatives formed a loose alliance (the "Tripartite Bloc") with Raymond Edde's "National Bloc" and Camille Chamoun's "National Liberals."

The Phalanges published a paper of its own, al-Amal, from 1940—first as a fortnightly, then a weekly, and since the 1950s as a daily.

The ideology of the Phalanges rests on the premise that Lebanon constitutes a separate historic entity with an identity of its own and a continuity dating back to the Phoenicians (see PHOENICIANISM). The coexistence of Lebanon's various communities can be assured only by the continuation of a community-based regime. This institutes pluralism in constitutional terms. It affords the Christian communities, and especially the MARONITES, a measure of predominance (these views also led the Phalanges to defend the Jewish community in Beirut in the 1948 war and also in the crisis of 1958 and 1967 war). The Phalanges admit that Lebanon is culturally linked with the Arab countries. Yet it denies that these links should lead to a political attachment and opposes the integration of Lebanon in any plan of Arab unity (beyond the loose alliance of the Arab states in the ARAB LEAGUE). While it goes along with many all-Arab policies, it holds that Lebanese interests have precedence over all-Arab ones. Thus it conformed, in the decades since 1948, to general Arab policies towards Israel, at least in public, and officially supported Palestinian guerrilla activities. It opposed guerrilla

operations from Lebanese soil that would involve Lebanon in clashes or war with Israel contrary to its interests. It also opposed the growth of the increasingly powerful PALESTINE LIBERATION ORGANIZATION (PLO) establishment in Lebanon. This created in effect a state within the state. In fact, the Phalanges—or at least some of their commanders—maintained undercover links with Israel. This began as early as the late 1940s when the party leaders turned to the Jewish state for support purposes. Aid was received from Israel especially after the break of the civil war in 1975, reaching its peak in 1982.

In the Civil War (1975–1990), the Phalanges formed the mainstay of the Christian military power, sometimes in tacit or overt cooperation of Christian-dominated units of the Lebanese army. In this process, a younger generation of military leaders emerged, with Bashir JUMAYYIL, the younger son of the founder-leader, at the helm. Pierre Jumayyil officially remained the chairman but stayed in the background (and was considered more moderate). In 1976 Bashir Jumayyil established the Lebanese Forces (LF) as a new framework under his command and based on the Phalanges structure, under which all Christian militias were to become unified, by force if needed (for the violent clashes with rival Maronite militias—Franjiyeh's Marada, Chamoun's "Tigers,"1978–1980—see LEBANON, Maronites). From 1980, the Phalanges/Lebanese Forces controlled most of the Christian-dominated areas—East Beirut and central Mount Lebanon. The Phalanges set up a radio station, the "Voice of Lebanon," also "Voice of Free Lebanon." As it gained de facto control of the Christian "canton,"and as government services broke down, it began providing general services (health, communications etc.) It collected taxes and other fees and payments. Its main source of revenue was custom duties it levied on imports in several ports it controlled, including part of Beirut port, and Jounieh just north of Beirut.

The brutality of Bashir Juamyyil and other young Phalanges leaders in treating their Maronite rivals also marked much of their military actions against their Muslim and leftist civil war foes. There were many reports of mutual massacres. They particularly loathed the Palestinian military establishment and the refugee camps' population. During the civil war the Phalanges tried for many months to subdue the Palestinians' stronghold in East Beirut, the refugee camp of Tel al-Za'tar. They were able to eliminate it only in August 1976—during the period in which SYRIA turned against its Muslim, leftist and Palestinian allies who had rejected Syria's plan for a solution of the Lebanese crisis, and supported the conservative-Christian camp. The Lebanese Forces' de facto semi-alliance with Syria soon broke down as the civil war dragged on, despite its official termination in October-November 1976. They were able to hold most of the Christian-dominated areas at the cost of being involved in near-constant clashes wherever that Christian region bordered on areas held or disputed by Muslim, Druze or Syrian forces.

Under Bashir Jumayyil's leadership, the Phalanges tightened its clandestine links with Israel, receiving arms, training, and advice, and its leaders met Israeli leaders. The Israeli invasion of Lebanon in June 1982 was well received by the Lebanese Forces, which had been apparently confided in regarding the major Israeli plan, though not the timing of the operation. They were particularly pleased with Israel's determination to rid Lebanon of the Palestinian military presence and help the Phalanges attain a dominate position in Lebanon. However, the Lebanese Forces demonstrated cautious collaboration with Israel on the siege of Beirut, to prevent damage to Bashir's prospects of election as the next Lebanese President.

Thus, the Lebanese Forces frustrated the Israeli command which had expected them to take over Muslim and Palestinian-dominated West Beirut, making it unnecessary for Israeli forces to do so. They also disagreed to cooperate with Israel's other ally, Sa'ad Haddad (see SOUTH LEBANON ARMY), fearing to be branded as collaborators. Yet they became the dominant political-military force in most of Lebanon outside the Syrian-occupied zones. In August 1982 their chief, Bashir Jumayyil, always leaving open channels to Lebanon's Sunni-Muslim community (other Phalanges leaders maintained ties with the Syrians, not an uncommon phenomena among the Maronite-Christians), was elected President of Lebanon with Israeli support. On 14 September he was killed when the Phalanges headquarters was blown up by a member of the pro-Syrian SSNP. A week later, his brother Amin Jumayyil was elected to replace Bashir as President. During the week in between, Phalanges units, operating in full coordination with the Israel Defence Force's command, stormed the Palestinian camps of Sabra and Shatila in West Beirut which had been taken over by Israel on 14–15 September, and massacred hundreds of Palestinians, mostly civilians. They were reportedly commanded by Elie Hubeika, the head of the Phalanges secret services.

The Phalanges/Lebanese Forces leadership was much more militant than President Amin Jumayyil. It embarked on a campaign to expand the areas under its control, with Israeli connivance, in the Shuf region southeast of Beirut. However, once Israeli troops withdrew from that area in September 1983, the Phalanges were defeated by the Druze militia and driven northward. Later it lost most of its positions in the coastal plain and South Lebanon to Druze and SHI'A militias. In 1984—1985, the Phalanges also lost much of its political influence outside the Christian-dominated region of Mount Lebanon which it still dominated, as President Jumayyil, seeking a settlement with the Leftists and Shi'a militia with Syria's help, had to agree in 1984 to the formation of a national coalition government headed by his adversaries and to accept, in principle, a Syrian-based plan for constitutional reforms.

In the following years, and particularly since the death of Bashir Jumayyil, the Phalanges were deeply split. There was constant tension between its political leadership and its military establishment (coterminous and near-identical with the Lebanese Forces). The latter acted independently without the approval, and sometimes against the wishes, of the former. The (political) chairmanship was vacated in July 1984 by founder-leader Pierre Jumayyil, who died soon afterwards. The man he had nominated, Elie Karame (b. 1940), was duly elected chairman in September 1984, but was replaced in August 1986 by Georges Sa'adeh, long-time vice-chairman. In the military command there were frequent upheavals and changes—the veteran military leader Fadi Fram was replaced in 1984 by Fu'ad Abu Nader; Samir Ja'ja' (Geagea) rebelled in 1985 against President Jumayyil and the Phalanges leadership's policies, which he saw as a surrender to Syrian pressure, and usurped the top command. Ja'ja's clashed with Elie Hubeika over the latter's acceptance of the Syrian-sponsored agreement with the Druze and Shi'i militias of December 1985. The latter's defeat once again foiled Syria's efforts at forging a national conciliation in Lebanon (see LEBANON, MARONITES). The political Phalanges' leadership tried to mediate and end the clashes but to no avail. The situation in the Phalanges/Lebanese Forces command remained confused and weakened the organization's position, though it remained in de facto control of a Christian "canton" until late 1988. Then, a new actor, the Maronite leadership of the Lebanese army under General Michel AWN, tried to take control of the Maronite enclave (as a first step toward "liberating" Lebanon from foreign, mainly Syrian, occupation). This led to a bloody intra-communal struggle between the Lebanese army and the Lebanese Forces in 1989–1990. Meanwhile, the Phalanges' leadership, under Georges Sa'adeh, had maintained its more moderate positions. It participated in the Ta'if reconciliation conference in autumn 1989 (see LEBANON). Sa'adeh himself first was a candidate in the Presidential elections in November 1989 and then joined the new pro-Syrian government under Salim al-Huss, reflecting the Phalanges dilemma: the need to participate in Lebanese reconciliation on the one hand, while maintaining solidarity with fellow radical Maronites on the other.

Since the end of the civil war in 1990, the Phalanges became a political party. It accepted the dismantling of its militia and the new political order despite voicing opposition to Syria's domination (e.g., in 1992 they boycotted the Parliamentary elections. This move was criticized by some of the party leaders). Sa'adeh was re-elected as the party leader in June 1992. He defeated Ja'ja'—a move interpreted as a victory for the more moderate, accommodating line, over the militant one. Ja'ja' himself was later arrested and tried for having been involved in a bombing of a church in 1994. This led to the final dissolution of the Lebance Forces.

PHARAONISM Egyptian trend of thought in the early decades of the twentieth century, perceiving EGYPT as a distinct historic entity, defined by the ancient civilization and unique geography of the Nile valley. The leading spokesmen of this trend (Salama Mussa, Hussein Fawzi, Tah Hussein, and Tawfiq al-Hakim) were, by and large, intellectuals of the Turko-Egyptian elite. They were impressed by modern Western concepts of territorial, secular nationalism, and advocated a deep commitment to Egypt's ancient past, claiming that it constituted a separate unit from the Muslim-Arab world both culturally

and politically. Pharaonism regarded the Arabs as foreign conquerors and Islam as a passing stage, maintaining that Egypt retained, despite 1,300 years of its Arab and Muslim history, its distinct, "Pharaonic" genius—re-surfacing throughout history in aspirations to re-establish its separate independence. Pharaonism as a general trend in literature and thought peaked in the 1920s, blending other trends dissociating Egypt from its Arab-Islamic heritage—such as liberalism, ethnic-territorial nationalism, and Mediterranean cultural links. Pharaonism never crystallized as a clearly enunciated doctrine or ideology, let alone a political faction. During the 1930s this distinct territorial nationalism came increasingly under attack, losing most of its influence when supranational—Arab and Islamic—orientations became dominant and many of the prominent writers identified with it joined those trends.

PKK The initials of *Partiya Karkeran Kurdistan*, Kurdish for The Kurdistan Workers Party, a leftist-nationalist Kurdish organization. It was largely responsible for the Kurdish uprising and terrorism in TURKEY since 1984. The KURDS fought against Republican Turkey several times during the 1920s and 1930s but their revolts were largely suppressed. Kurdish grievances came to a head again during the late 1970s when the whole country was gradually being torn apart by social and political tensions, whilst moving toward a total breakdown of law and order. The Kurds had long complained about their generally lower socioeconomic conditions and Turkey's attempts to assimilate them, denying their separate identity. While some Kurds (in the hope of gaining their national rights) largely joined all-Turkish radical organizations, others established their own Kurdish ones.

The PKK was the strongest Kurdish group to emerge in Turkey. It was formed in 1978 (with roots going back to 1974) by a former student activist from Ankara University, Abdallah Ocalan (nicknamed "Apo"). Its goal was to create a leftist Kurdish state in the Southeastern Kurdish-inhabited parts of the country. It began recruiting supporters amongst the Kurdish youth and conducted occasional assaults on Turkish forces. After the military takeover in September 1980, Ocalan and his associates settled in Damascus, enjoying training bases in the Beqa valley. Their first congress was held in July

1981 on the Syrian-Lebanese border. In March 1984 the PKK declared an all-out open war against Turkey, and, smuggling men and arms through the borders with SYRIA, IRAQ and sometimes IRAN, considerably increased its guerilla activities in Turkish territory. Its targets included not only Turkish security forces, but also other Kurds suspected of collaborating with Turkish authorities. Whilst the south-eastern regions with their largely supportive Kurdish population became the hub of the guerilla war, the PKK had in time been able to extend its underground activities to other parts of Turkey, as well as to Western Europe.

The Kurdish insurgency led to serious problems. In its efforts to suppress it, Turkey placed the south-eastern provinces under martial law and increased its forces in the area to an estimated 160,000 troops. This put an enormous burden on the budget. Measures employed by the Turkish army included land and air assaults on PKK bases and hideouts (sometimes across the border); the employment of "village guards" against possible PKK attacks, the evacuation of many villages, and the harsh treatment of any PKK fighters or supporters who were caught. While Syria denied cooperation with the PKK or even the presence of Ocalan on its territory, a strain on the countries relations emerged and similar tensions evolved with Iraq and Iran. The Kurdish question—and the manner of suppressing the insurgency—negatively affected Turkey's relations with Europe and the West and became a major political issue in Turkey itself.

By 1997 the war against the PKK had already claimed well over 20,000 victims on both sides, but there were growing signs that the Turkish forces were finally gaining the upperhand in the struggle. The PKK, on its part, declared several times unilateral cease fires signalling its readiness to compromise on the basis of Turkey's territorial integrity. Turkish politicians, on their part, perceived the PKK as a terrorist organization, refusing to recognize it. Some Turkish politicians stressed the importance of economic development in Kurdish areas in order to alleviate the problem, and others even proposed the granting of some cultural rights to the Kurds. But the army (and virtually all mainstream leaders) remained determined about the necessity of suppressing the insurgency by force, without dealing with the PKK.

PLO   see PALESTINE LIBERATION ORGANIZATION, PALESTINE ARAB-GUERRILLA ORGANIZATIONS, PALESTINE ARABS.

POLISARIO   "People's Organization for the Liberation of Saguia al-Hamra and Rio del Oro"—a political and guerrilla organization founded in 1973–1975 to fight for the independence of Spanish Sahara. Between 1975–1976 it engaged in a guerrilla war against MOROCCO (and until 1979 also against MAURITANIA). In February 1976 POLISARIO proclaimed an independent "Sahara Arab Democratic Republic" (SADR). From the outset, POLISARIO was armed, supplied and financed mainly by ALGERIA, where it was concentrated and headquartered. This support was meant to cease with the establishment of the ARAB MAGHREB UNION in 1989, which indicated a *rapprochement* between Morocco and Algeria. LIBYA also supported the organization, providing funds and arms, which mostly ceased with the signing of the unity agreement with Morocco in 1984 (abrogated by Morocco in 1986). The ceased support to the organization from Morocco's regional rivals seems to have weakened POLISARIO although political, and possibly financial support, still comes from Algeria.

(POPULAR) DEMOCRATIC FRONT FOR THE LIBERATION OF PALESTINE   see PALESTINIAN GUERRILLA ORGANIZATION.

POPULAR FRONT FOR THE LIBERATION OF PALESTINE   see PFLP.

POPULAR FRONT FOR THE LIBERATION OF THE ARAB GULF (PFLOAG)   see PERSIAN GULF.

PROGRESSIVE SOCIALIST PARTY (PSP) (*al-Hizb al-Taqadumi al-Ishtiraki*) A Lebanese political party founded in 1949 by Kamal JUNBALAT, and, although not in doctrine is mainly DRUZE. Through the years, the PSP was mainly a vehicle for attaining Junbalat's political ambitions, and as such, was completely controlled by him. After his assassination in March 1977, his son Walid JUNBLAT became it's president. Since the mid-1970s it maintained a militia of its own which was the main fighting force of the Druze in the Civil War. In 1991, following the end of the Civil War and the establishment of the "Government of National Reconciliation," December 1990, most of the Lebanese militias, including that of the PSP, were dissolved and their members joined the Lebanese administration. The PSP, now solely a political party, has representatives in the Lebanese Parliament. see LEBANON, DRUZE, JUNBALAT.

PROTESTANTS   In contrast to the old-established "Eastern churches" (GREEK-ORTHODOX or MONO-PHYSITES *et al*) and the Catholic ones created since the Crusades (through UNIATES or conversion to the LATIN rite)—Protestant communities have grown in the ARAB countries only in fairly recent times. They therefore did not enjoy the ancient rights of com-

munal-religious semi-autonomy under the MILLET SYSTEM of the OTTOMAN EMPIRE. They have remained small communities.

Missionaries of various Protestant denominations—mainly from English-speaking countries, Germany and Scandinavia—began operating in the late eighteenth, and mainly nineteenth, centuries, creating small groups of Protestants, principally by the conversion of Eastern CHRISTIANS.

The number of Protestants in the Arab countries is estimated at 250,000–300,000—with significant communities only in EGYPT (approximately 100,000, mainly Presbyterians, most of them converted COPTS) and SUDAN (mainly Anglican Episcopalians, nearly all among the African tribes of south SUDAN).

Q

QABUS IBN SA'ID (b. 1940)   Sultan of OMAN since 1970. He is eighth in the direct line of the Al Busaidy dynasty, which was founded in 1744. Educated in England (Sandhurst Military Academy, one year with a Scottish regiment; social studies at a British university), Qabus returned to OMAN in the mid-1960s. He was kept in total seclusion at the Salala Palace by his father, Sultan Sa'id ibn Taimur (1910–1972), who objected to, and prevented, modernization of the country, maintaining an autocratic regime. In July 1970, Qabus overthrew his father, with active British encouragement, and became Sultan. (His father went into exile in England and died there.) As Sultan, Qabus fostered gradual economic and social development and a measure of reform, but maintained a strictly conservative regime. He implemented low-profile moderate policies in both international and inter-Arab affairs maintaining a close alliance with BRITAIN and the UNITED STATES. At the same time, he maintained close relations with IRAN, both before and after the Islamic revolution (see OMAN).

Qabus was the only Arab leader who overtly supported the late President Anwar al-SADAT's peace-making policy with ISRAEL with no qualms, adhering to his policy through the 1980s. Following the Israel-PLO Oslo Accord of September 1993, the Sultan fostered close and independent relations with Is-

rael, despite Egyptian and Syrian criticism. He hosted Prime Minister RABIN of Israel in October 1994. In the early 1980s, Qabus was among those Arab rulers willing to provide the US government strategic facilities for the defense of the Gulf following the Soviet invasion of Afganistan. In November 1995, responding to US emphasis on human rights in the wake of the GULF WAR, Qabus ordered an amnesty for all political prisoners.

QADDOUMI, FARUQ (b. 1934)   Palestinian politician, head of the PALESTINE LIBERATION ORGANI-ZATION (PLO) political department. Born in Qaddoum, near Nablus, in the WEST BANK, Qaddoumi graduated in Economics and Political Science from Cairo University, and was one of the founders of *Fatah*. He was a member of the PLO Executive Committee since 1969, and since 1973, head of its political department. Within this structure Qaddoumi led the more militant line regarding the conflict with ISRAEL and inter-Arab relations. He is seen to be close to SYRIA and in the 1980s his name was mentioned as a possible replacement to Yasser ARAFAT. This would be more convenient to Syria, which at that time had come into conflict with Arafat. He opposed the Oslo Accords, remaining in Tunis while most of the PLO leaders headed by Arafat moved to Gaza to found the PALESTINIAN AUTHORITY. Still in

Tunis, he is one of the most prominent opponents of Arafat in the PLO's mainstream.

al-QADHAFI, MU'AMMAR
(b. 1942) Libyan army officer and head of state since 1969. He was a member of a poor family in the Sirt desert and of the Qadhifa tribe. Qadhafi was imbued with a fighting tradition: his grandfather was reportedly killed in 1911 while resisting the Italian conquest, and his father, Abdel Salam Ibn Hamad, fought the Italians and was wounded. The family wandered in the Sirt-Fezzan area and was protected by its patron, Muhammad Saif al-Nasir, the younger brother of the Fezzan governor in the monarchial era. Qadhafi was the younger son in a family with three daughters. His brothers died and he was given the name Mu'ammar, which meant long life.

Qadhafi's way from the marginal nomad life into the center of the Libyan society was due to education. His father, who was illiterate, sent Qadhafi to a secondary school in Sirt, where he studied three years. This period exerted an important influence on the child, exposing him for the first time to the non-nomadic and non-tribal society. In 1957 he moved to Sebba, where he studied in a secondary school. He did not complete his studies as he was expelled due to his political activities. He moved to Misurata, where he completed secondary school. He enrolled at the University of Benghazi to study History and Geography, but transferred in 1963 to the Military Academy, from which he graduated in 1965. In 1966 the Army sent him to further officers' training in BRITAIN.

A fervent, revolutionary nationalist deeply influenced by Egypt's ABDEL NASSER, Qadhafi agitated and organized revolutionary cells within the army and was reportedly imprisoned, but reinstated. On 1 September 1969 Qadhafi, a young unknown army officer captain, launched a successful military coup and deposed the monarchy of King Idris al-SANUSI, while the latter was on holiday in Turkey. Qadhafi promoted himself to the rank of Colonel and became Commander in Chief of the Armed Forces and Chairman of the Revolutionary Council. In 1971, in another move inspired by Nasser, Qadhafi established a single political party, "The Arab Socialist Union."

Since his advent to power in 1969, Qadhafi renewed the idea of direct popular rule (*Sultat al-Sh'ab*)

in LIBYA. This direct rule idea apparently mirrored his disappointment with the Nasserite mode of the single party, and his disappointment over the Libyan Socialist Union Party's failure to rally the Libyan heterogeneous society around his leadership. Apparently also, his wish to establish direct rule attested to his aversion to political "middlemen" and heavy bureaucratic structures and stemmed from his Bedouin origin.

Since 1973, Qadhafi began to operate the "Popular Revolution." This ideological system reached its peak on 2 March 1977 with the declaration of the establishment of the "People's Power" system and the *Jamahiriyya*—the polity of the masses— which became part of the state's official name (*al-jamahiriyya al-Libiyya*).

Within this spirit of direct rule, Qadhafi allegedly separated "revolution" from "power" and ostensibly withdrew from active political leadership in March 1979. Nevertheless, Qadhafi remained the sole and supreme leader and he has continued since then to head the state.

During the late 1970s and 1980s, Qadhafi invested a lot of effort to implement his "Third International Theory" as presented in the three parts of his *Green Book*, published in 1976, 1978 and 1979. Yet throughout the 1980s, the passionate pursuit of his ideological principles subsided. He was compelled to cope with increasing manifestations of opposition, mainly the result of the relative domestic stagnation and the increasing austerity measures necessitated by the declining oil revenues since the beginning of the 1980s. Signs of growing opposition troubled him especially since his army was deeply involved in a military penetration in Chad (which ended in 1987, after seven years, in a most humiliating defeat).

Another problem, much more substantial to his political position, was the escalating conflict with the US. One of its peaks was the American air bombing of Tripoli and Benjhazi in mid-April 1986. Qadhafi's headquarters in the *Bab-al-Aziziya* barracks in Tripoli, which also served as his family's residence, was bombed and his adopted daughter was killed. Since then, the US hardened its policy toward Libya, aimed at curbing Qadhafi's alleged involvement and support of international TERRORISM.

In 1992, whilst celebrating his twenty-third anniversary in power, he faced the most serious threat to his regime, when the US and Britain claimed that Libya was responsible for the explosion of a Pan-American aircraft over Lockerbie (Scotland) in 1988. The US and Britain demanded that Qadhafi extradite the Libyans suspected of the explosion. Libya persistently refused, and the UN Security Council imposed sanctions that remained in effect until late 1997.

The UN sanctions strangled Libya economically and isolated Qadhafi regionally and internationally. The growing distress domestically strengthened the opposition activists who aimed at toppling his regime. Most challenging were the anti-regime operations launched by the Islamic militants in 1996–1997. Although after twenty-seven years in power the Libyan leader proved surprisingly resilient politically, the growing threats with the American hostile hard line policy, the Islamic challenge and growing socio-economic difficulties are endangering his rule. A foreign report, not refuted nor collaborated by any other sources, said in the summer of 1996 that Qadhafi had a serious heart attack. If true, one should add his health problem to the list of sources which are potentially menacing to his rule. During his reign, Qadhafi became notorious, especially in the United Sates and Western Europe, as an archetypal aggressor, an imbalanced, frantic, and unpredictable leader who would not disdain any means, including terrorism, to realize his aspirations.

QAMARAN ISLANDS Group of small islands in the Red Sea, off the coast of Yemen, with an area of 22 sq.miles (57 sq. km.) and a population of aprroximately 2,000. For some time, in the sixteenth century, the islands, a Portuguese strongpoint, were under nominal Ottoman-Turkish sovereignty. They also served as a quarantine station for Muslim pilgrims from the East on their way to Mecca. During World War I, in 1915, Qamaran was occupied by the British and administered from ADEN. In 1938, BRITAIN agreed with Italy not to claim British sovereignty and not to erect fortifications. In 1949, Britain reaffirmed its possession of Qamaran—reportedly in an agreement with Yemen (which Yemen later denied). When SOUTH YEMEN became independent, in 1967, it claimed Qamaran as part of the formerly British territory of Aden, but Yemen disputed that claim. Yemen's possession of the islands was more firmly established in 1972,

during the Yemen-South Yemen war, and though not specifically mentioned in the agreement that ended that war, was accepted by South Yemen.

QASSEM, ABDEL KARIM (1914–1963) Iraqi officer and politician, ruler of IRAQ, 1958–1963. Born in Baghdad of a SUNNI-Muslim lower middle-class family, Qassem became a professional army officer, commissioned in 1938. He served as a battalion commander with the Iraqi expeditionary forces in the Palestine War of 1948. In 1956, as a brigade commander, he became head of a group of "Free Officers" plotting to overthrow the monarchy and end Iraq's special relationship with BRITAIN. On 14 July 1958, the group carried out a bloody revolution, led by Qassem and his associate Colonel Abd al-Salam Aref, and proclaimed a republic. Contrary to his fellow conspirators' plans and expectations, Qassem declined to form a Revolutionary Command Council, but appointed himself Commander-in-Chief, Prime Minister and acting Minister of Defense. He did not assume the title of President but in effect became dictator and "Sole Leader" (which was for some time his semi-official title).

Though there were affinities beween Qassem's revolution and that of Egypt's ABDEL NASSER, Qassem did not wish to join the UNITED ARAB REPLUBLIC (UAR) and strove to keep Iraq independent of Nasser's dominating influence. Bitter hostility between the two men soon ensued, triggering tension between Qassem and Aref, who wanted a much closer cooperation with Egypt and apparently nurtured ill-disguised ambitions to replace Qassem. In September, Aref was dismissed and later tried and sentenced to death, but reprieved by Qassem. Nationalist-Nasserist disaffection soon escalated into a conspiracy, which culminated in a mutiny and coup attempt staged in March 1959 in Mosul by Colonel Shawwaf. In the suppression of that mutiny Qassem was aided by the Communists. This cooperation soured when the Communists began clamoring for a real share in power; when they increasingly infiltrated the administration in the summer of 1959, Qassem suppressed them. Qassem was interested in social affairs and in September 1958 enacted a major land reform law. Early in 1960 he tried to revive political parties; but the attempt failed, and it remains in doubt to what extent Qassem had taken it seriously in the first place. He became increasingly erratic—to an extent that he was nicknamed "The Mad Dictator". Endowed with an exalted sense of his own mission, he had not created a political base to his rule, and by 1961 he had no supporters left among the political groupings and was in serious political difficulties (a rebellion of the KURDS; his claim to KUWAIT; his breach with the oil company—see IRAQ). In February 1963, a combination of civilian BA'TH activists and nationalist anti-Communist officers conducted a successful coup during which Qassem and his closest collaborators were executed without a trial.

QATAR Emirate on the Arabian coast of the PERSIAN GULF, on a peninsula of the same name that juts northwards into the Gulf, approximately 105 miles (170 km.) long and 25–40 miles (40–65 km.) wide. Qatar borders, at the base of the peninsula, on SAUDI ARABIA. Historically, it also bordered on ABU DHABI (TRUCIAL OMAN, now UNITED ARAB EMIRATES UAE). In 1974 Abu Dhabi ceded the strip bordering on Qatar to Saudi Arabia. Qatar's population was 50,000–80,000 until the late 1960s. It then began rapidly growing, due mainly to the influx of foreign workers attracted by the expanding OIL economy. Over eighty percent of its population, estimated (1996) at 550,000, resides in the capital, Doha. The share of foreigners is estimated at least at fifty percent of the population or more. They include: Pakistanis, Indians and Iranians (some of whom are not recent migrants, Iranians having been for a long time an estimated fifteen to twenty percent of Qatar's population). With the mid-1980s crisis of the oil economy, the number of foreigners has begun decreasing. Qatar's indigenous inhabitants are Sunni Muslims, mostly of the WAHHABI school. The population subsisted, until the growth of the oil economy from the 1960s, on animal husbandry (semi-nomadic grazing), fishing, pearl-diving and some cultivation.

Qatar was traditionally ruled by sheikhs of the al-Thani family. Ottoman TURKEY sometimes claimed a nominal sovereignty, but never really controlled the area. When the British, from the 1820s, established a network of treaty relations with the Gulf rulers, originally to put an end to piracy, the sheikh of Qatar became part of that network. The British Protectorate was formalized in treaties of 1868, 1882 and 1916. A British political officer "guided" the ruler. In 1968, when Britain announced its decision to

withdraw from its Gulf commitments, the sheikh envisaged, with British encouragement, joining the federation of sheikhdoms then planned for Trucial Oman (the UAE). He abandoned that intention, favoring separate, complete independence for Qatar. In April 1970 he provisionally declared independence, at the same time proclaiming a provisional constitution that provided for government on a modern pattern and a semi-elected Consultative Council (the ruler selecting its twenty, later thirty members from among double that number elected by limited suffrage). Qatar formally declared its independence on 1 September 1971, when the British Protectorate lapsed. It was admitted the same month to the ARAB LEAGUE and the UN. Throughout the years Qatar became a member of the Islamic Conference Organization, the group of non-aligned states, and the GULF COOPERATION COUNCIL (of which Qatar was a founding member, 1981).

Oil was discovered in 1940 at Dukhan, on the west coast. Due to World War II production began only in 1949. In 1991 Qatar completed the devolpment of a major gas field which is one of the world's largest (see OIL). While productions and revenues were modest compared to other Gulf countries, they enabled Qatar to finance the development both of its economy, its communications (ports, roads), and its social infrastructure (a network of health and educational institutions covering all its inhabitants, including a university opened in 1977).

Most of Qatar's economic development remained directly linked to the oil sector. A small refinery operated from 1953 at Umm Sa'id. This later served as the nucleus for a major industrial area, including: an expanded refinery, petrochemical plants, mainly for the production of fertilizer, and steel and cement plants. Like other Gulf oil principalities, Qatar used part of its new riches to establish a fund dispensing development aid, in modest dimensions, mainly to Arab and Islamic countries. The fund cut back on donations with the developing recession of oil prices since the mid-1980s.

Internal politics were disturbed by conflicts and rivalries within the ruling family of the al-Thani sheikhs. None of the twentieth century rulers has left his position of his own free will. Sheikh Abdallah ibn QASSEM, (ruled 1913–1949), was compelled to abdicate. His son and successor, Ali ibn Abdallah, (ruled 1949–1960) suffered the same fate. His son and successor, Hamad ibn Ali (ruled 1960–1972), was ousted by his cousin, Crown Prince and Prime Minister Khalifa ibn Hamad (ruled 1972–1995). Khalifa was ousted by his son Hamad ibn Khalifa, who has ruled Qatar since 1995. Most key posts in the Cabinet continue to be held by members of the ruler's clan. Partial elections for a thirty member advisory council were once held (1970).

Qatar's foreign relations are marked by close relations with the US culminating in Qatar's participation in the coalition and war against IRAQ (1991). In spite of its low-profile foreign policy, Qatar managed to develop relations with ISRAEL without attracting hostile Arab reaction. Mutual visits were held and low-level diplomatic representation was instituted. Qatar also abolished its participation in the ARAB BOYCOTT OF ISRAEL.

QOM   A city with a population of 300,000, 62 miles (100 km.) south of Tehran—the most important spiritual center in IRAN. The burial place of Fatima, sister of Emam Reza, whose shrine can be found in the town of Mashhad, in northeast Iran,

which is also considered an important religious center. The city is the most important center for the study of Muslim theology and the training of Shi'te clergymen after Najaf in IRAQ. Almost all senior clerics of Iran and leaders of the Lebanese HIZBALLAH received their religious education at Qom, or spent several years there. The contacts established amongst them served later on as a basis for the creation of networks of ties and underground and political activities. It was always one of the important centers of opposition to the PAHLAVI dynasty. In the 1970s Qom turned into the headquarters of the supporters of KHOMEINI and his revolution (see IRAN). Since the revolution, the regime has invested a lot in the development of the city, and a highway was built between it and Tehran. The city has also become the center for the activity of fundamentalist Islamic organizations from various countries, and hundreds of foreign students have joined the Iranian students at the religious seminaries.

QUTB, al-SAYYID   see ISLAMIC RADICALISM AND MOVEMENTS.

R

RABIN, YITZHAK (1922–1995)   Israeli Chief of Staff, leader of the ISRAEL Labor Party and Prime Minister, 1974–1977 and 1992–1995. Born in JERUSALEM, Rabin studied at the Kadouri agricultural school. He joined the *Palmah* (the mobilized force of the *Hagana*—the pre-state defense force of the Jewish community) in 1941 and served within its ranks until the end of Israel's War of Independence (see ARAB-ISRAEL CONFLICT). Rabin participated in the armistice talks with EGYPT in Rhodes (see ARAB-ISRAEL PEACEMAKING) but rejected the agreement attained and returned to Israel before the signing ceremony. He served as Chief of Staff, 1964–1968, and was the leading architect of the Israeli victory in the Six-Day War (see, ARAB-ISRAEL CONFLICT.

Following his retirement from the IDF in 1968, Rabin was appointed Ambassador to Washington until March 1973. After being elected to the eighth Knesset (1973) on the Israel Labor Party list, he was appointed Minister of Labor in the second govern-

ment of Golda MEIR. Following Meir's resignation in April 1974, Rabin was elected Chairman of the Labor Party, after defeating Shimon PERES by a small majority, and became Prime Minister. During his first Premiership, Israel signed the Interim Agreement with Egypt (see ARAB-ISRAEL PEACEMAKING) and the first memorandum of understanding with the US, both in September 1975, and successfully performed an operation for the release of Israeli hostages from Entebbe in Uganda.

Toward the end of 1976 Rabin broke up Labor's historic alliance with the National Religious Party, after the latter had abstained in a vote on a motion of no-confidence over the alleged desecration of the Sabbath caused by a ceremony held at an air-force base. A second contest with Peres was held in February 1977, and once again Rabin won by a small majority. Despite his victory Rabin resigned from the Premiership as a result of the uncovering of a family bank account in the US.

When the Labor Party was in opposition Rabin once again contested the Labor Party leadership in December 1980, but received only twenty-nine percent of the votes. In the National Unity Government formed by Peres in September 1984 Rabin was appointed Minister of Defense, and continued to serve in this post until March 1990. During this period he took the IDF out of Lebanon (save for a "Security Zone" in Southern Lebanon), supported stopping the development of the "Lavi" plane, and was in charge of the struggle against the INTIFADA, which was portrayed as an "iron fist" policy.

In January 1989 Rabin formulated a plan for holding elections in the WEST BANK and GAZA STRIP, after which Israel would negotiate a settlement with the elected leadership—a plan that was adopted by the Government as the Shamir-Rabin initiative in May 1989. Even though he supported the National Unity Government with the *Likud*, he went along with Peres's initiative for bringing down the Government in a vote on a motion of no-confidence in March 1990, after he became convinced that the *Likud* would block any progress in the peace process. After Peres failed to form an alternative Government, he called the move "the stinking trick." In the primaries for the Labor Party leadership held in February 1992, Rabin beat Peres and two other contestants, with just over forty percent of the votes. Rabin ran Labor's campaign for the elections to the thirteenth Knesset (1992) under the slogan "Israel is waiting for Rabin," undertaking to reach an agreement on an interim autonomy agreement with the Palestinians within six to nine months. The Government he formed after Labor's victory acted vigorously to advance what he called "the peacemaking process." Despite his reservations regarding the PALESTINE LIBERATION OR-GANIZATION (PLO), after giving up on any prospect for progress in the bilateral talks between Israel and Palestinians from the territories in Washington, Rabin did not object to the Oslo Talks. On 13 September he signed the Declaration of Principles with the PLO and shook the hand of PLO chairman Yasser ARAFAT (see ARAB-ISRAEL PEACEMAKING). Rabin also signed the Peace Agreement with JORDAN in October 1994, and unofficially let it be understood that he would agree to an Israeli withdrawal from the GOLAN HEIGHTS in return for full peace and normalization with SYRIA. After years of power struggles Rabin and Peres finally reached a *modus vivendi*, and together with Arafat received the Nobel Prize for Peace on 10 December 1994. However, Rabin's peace policy won him the title of "traitor" by the extreme right in Israel, especially the nationalist-religious stream. Following a mass demonstration in Tel Aviv in favor of the peace and against violence on 4 November 1995, he was shot to death by a fanatic Jewish assassin. His funeral was attended by heads of state and prime ministers from over eighty states.

RAFSANJANI, HOJJAT OL-ESLAM ALI-AKBAR HASHEMI (b. 1934) President of IRAN (1989–1997) and one of the leaders of the Islamic regime in Iran. Rafsanjani was born in the town of Bahreman in the district of Rafsanjan in the south of the country, to a wealthy religious family that owns pistachio groves. As a youth, Rafsanjani studied in QOM, at a religious seminary, *inter alia* under KHOME-INI. In Qom he joined an extreme religious organization—the *Fadaiyan-e Eslam* (Self-Sacrificers of Islam), and in the 1960s participated in protest activities organized by Khomenei. In 1964 he was detained for allegedly supplying a pistol to a member of the *Fadaiyan*, who had murdered Prime Minister Hassan Ali-Mansour. Rafsanjani denied the charges, but after the revolution admitted to them. He was detained a few more times, most recently in 1975, and was accused of assisting the Mojahedin KHALQH. He was released at the end of 1978, together with many other clergymen, within the framework of the Shah's efforts to pacify the religious establishment. Following the victory of the Islamic revolution, Rafsanjani was appointed a member of the revolutionary council, and established together with KHAMENEI and other clergymen the Islamic Republic Party. In 1979 he was appointed Minister of the Interior. He was the target of an unsuccessful attempt on his life by an extreme religious group—the *Forghan*. In 1980 he was elected by a large majority as chairman of the *Majlis*; in 1981 as personal representative of Khomenei to the Supreme Defense Council; and in 1984 as a member of the Supreme Council of Cultural Revolution, which was assigned the task of Islamicizing the whole education system, especially the universities. Toward the end of the IRAN-IRAQ WAR in 1988, Rafsanjani was appointed by Khomenei Acting Supreme Commander of the Armed Forces (a post which according to the constitution is reserved for the supreme leader himself), with the goal of preventing a military collapse. Out of a pragmatic approach he convinced Khomenei to agree to a cease-fire in order to prevent total defeat. In July 1989 Rafsanjani was elected by a vast majority as President (to replace Khamenei who was elected heir to Khomenei) and announced that his goal was to implement economic reform, to stop inflation and increase production. In 1993 he was elected to a second term as President, but won a smaller majority. During his two terms he tried to realize a pragmatic policy both in domestic matters and foreign affairs, but encounted active opposition by the extreme camp, which managed to stifle many of his plans (see IRAN). Rafsanjani completed extensive projects for the development of the country's infrastructure, but failed to improve the economic condition of the citizens, which continued to deteriorate. The more established Khamanei became in his post as supreme leader, the more the influence of Rafsanjani eroded. Toward his retirement from the presidency, he was appointed by Khamenei head of "The Council for Determining the Interests of the Regime" (an institution for laying down a strategic policy) whose influence over the affairs of state is not clear.

RAJAVI, MAS'UD AND MARYAM   see IRAN.

RAS al-KHAIMA   The northern most of the seven sheikhdoms of TRUCIAL OMAN and strategically located just south of the STRAITS OF HORMUZ. Since 1971 a member of the UNITED ARAB EMIRATES, UAE, with an area of approximately 650 sq.miles (about. 1,700 sq.km.). The population, about 25,000 by the late 1960s, grew to over 140,000 in the mid-1990s as a result of the expanding economy in the 1970s. Most of the population lived in the port and main town of Ras al-Khaima. In the past, before the advent of modern development and the oil economy, the inhabitants engaged in fishing, pearl-diving and boat-building, and some nomadic animal husbandry.

Ras al-Khaima has been traditionally ruled by the sheikhs of the *al-Qassemi* (or also *al-Jawassemi*) clan which also rules nearby SHARJA. Since the nineteenth century the Sheikh was under British protection, along with the other sheikhs of the region. When BRITAIN withdrew that protection in 1971, Ras al-Khaima initially decided to stay out of the federation of the UAE then being formed, but eventually

joined it. The Sheikh—since 1948 Saqr ibn Muhammad—is a member of the UAE Council of Rulers, and Ras al-Khaima sends four Ministers to the Federal Government. In the protracted struggle between the advocates of a stronger federation and those of more power to the various sheikhdoms, Ras al-Khaima vigorously backed the latter, led by DUBAI—to a degree that the Sheikh contemplated seceding from the UAE. One of the reasons was his reluctance to integrate his small motorized military force in the federal army (an integration proclaimed in 1978).

An oil concession was granted in 1964 to American companies. Most of it (except for offshore areas) was relinquished after unsuccessful drillings, and later taken over by "Shell" and other companies. Oil discoveries have been announced several times since the 1970s, mainly offshore, and production was reported beginning in 1984. Though Ras al-Khaima had as yet no substantial oil income of its own and depended on federal UAE funds, some development began. An airport was constructed (1976) and the al-Saqr port was modernized. A cement factory was built and an oil refinery was planned (with KUWAIT).

Ras al-Khaima is involved in several border disputes with other sheikhdoms within the UAE, but also with other neighbors. A dispute with OMAN, which claimed the northern part of Ras al-Khaima's coast for its Ras Musandam exclave, was, after smoldering since the early 1950s, raised by Oman in 1974. It was resolved in 1979 in an agreement mediated by Saudi Arabia and Kuwait. Of greater impact is a dispute with IRAN over Ras al-Khaima's Tanb (Tumb) Islands. Iran's claim to these islands was pressed more strongly when offshore oil prospects became realistic, and in November 1971 (while the British protectorate was being removed and the UAE was in the process of formation), Iran forcibly occupied them, along with Sharja's ABU MUSSA ISLAND. The UAE, and Ras al-Khaima in particular, has since then demanded their return. While Ras al-Khaima would like to press that demand, the UAE pursues it with great caution.

RASHID, AL   (House of) A clan of sheikhs of the Shammar tribe in northern Najd, centering on al-Ha'il. In the late nineteenth century, the Rashids became rivals of the House of SA'UD—(see there for their struggle). In World War I, the Rashids were loyal to the Ottoman Sultan, or CALIPH.

After the war, the Saudis were victorious in renewed fighting, and in the fall of 1921 the Rashids surrendered, renouncing all claims to power. After winning, Ibn Sa'ud and his son and heir apparent, Sa'ud, followed a policy of reconciliation. In addition to hosting the leaders of the Rashid clan as guests (and practically hostages) at the court, they married two of the Shammar daughters (the King's wife bore him his son ABDALLAH—Crown Prince and First Deputy Prime Minister since 1982). The HASHEMITE regime in IRAQ tried in the 1940s to use one of the Rashidi Princes who had escaped to Iraq as a spearhead of diplomatic and propaganda attacks against the Saudis, but it never materialized.

RASTAKHIZ PARTY (Resurgence)   The name of a political Party established by the Shah in 1975. The goal was to turn the Party into a popular base of support for the regime, which would legitimize the implementation of the Shah's grandiose political-economic-social plans. The establishment of the Party reflected the patrimonial attitude of the Shah toward the Iranian people, which in his eyes was not ripe for democracy. After he failed to establish a bipartisan regime, the Shah adopted a single party system like the one in the Soviet Union, which in his opinion had gained great material and economic achievements thanks to political centralization. On 1 March 1975, the establishment of the new Party and the cancellation of all the existing parties was announced. The Shah called upon all the citizens, "who believe in the constitution, the monarchy and the white revolution, to join." Within eighteen months it was announced that 5 million citizens (out of a total population of 35 million) had joined.

On the surface, the structure of the Party was democratic. The members could elect their representatives from among whom a secretary general was chosen. Party members could raise any topic for debate and complain about any wrong, and the government was obliged to handle the issue and take the complaint into account. In fact, the Shah hoped that the Party would constitute an alternative to opposition parties. However, the power given to the Party opened the way to contests for power and a struggle over authority between the Party and the government. This political centralization and the

obligation of civil servants and all citizens to join the Party, caused much public frustration and harmed the image of the Shah, who refused to accept criticism about the single party system. The establishment of the Rastakhiz shattered the hopes of the liberals in IRAN that the Shah would lead the state in the direction of democracy, whilst implementing reform plans in the economic, social and cultural spheres.

Upon the mounting of public protest against the regime in 1978, part of the personalities who did not belong to the Shah's supporters left the Party, and it suffered an internal split. When the disturbances spread in Iran, the Party called for the extension of freedom, expressed loyalty to Islam and demanded a solution to economic problems. However, this effort was too late to save the Party from liquidation, since it lacked popular roots. The Party not only failed to realize the Shah's goals and expectations, it precipitated the collapse of his regime. Upon the announcement of the government of Sharif-Emami in September 1978 regarding freedom of political association within the framework of the national reconciliation, fifteen Parties announced the renewal of their activity, which resulted in the end of the Shah's Party.

REAGAN PLAN   see ARAB-ISRAEL PEACEMAKING.

RED CRESCENT   As the symbol of the cross was unacceptable to Muslim countries, they chose that of the Red Crescent to designate their humanitarian and welfare-in-war societies parallel to the Red Cross. First to do so was Ottoman TURKEY, in 1876. (IRAN chose the Red Lion and Sun.) The ARAB countries followed in the 1920s when they became independent or semi-independent. The International Red Cross recognized these Red Crescent societies as members of its international network—informally initially, and fully and formally since 1949. In October 1986, an international conference decided to rename the League of Red Cross Societies "League of Red Cross and Red Crescent Societies." Iran decided after its Islamic Revolution of 1979 to rename its "Lion and Sun" Red Crescent.

REFAH   see TURKEY.

REFUGEES   The Middle East has been affected by several issues of group migration and/or refugees.

Some concern past centuries—such as the migration of Spanish JEWS, as well as some from MOROCCO, in the fifteenth and mainly the sixteenth centuries, to the OTTOMAN EMPIRE; heterodox and minority groups finding refuge in Mount Lebanon; the migration of DRUZE from Mount Lebanon to south-eastern SYRIA ("Jabal Druze"—the Mountain of the Druze) in the eighteenth and nineteenth centuries. The Ottoman Empire allowed and encouraged Muslim refugees from the Balkan (*bushnaq*, i.e. Bosnians) and the Caucasus (CIRCASSIANS, Chechens) to settle in its realm.

The ARMENIANS of Eastern Anatolia were considered hostile and persecuted by the Turks. Many of them fled, particularly after the pogroms of 1895–1996. Between 1915–1918 most of the Armenian population of Eastern Anatolia was forced to leave—many hundreds of thousands of them died or were massacred by Muslim civilians and the Turkish troops. (They were thought to be supporting and aiding RUSSIA, TURKEY's enemy in World War I). The survivors of this community settled in most countries of the region, Syria and LEBANON in particular, and ceased to be refugees, though they preserved their separate identity and social and religious organization (see Armenians). Many ASSYRIANS (Nestorian Christians) also fled from Turkey during and immediately after World War I, mainly to IRAQ. After much friction, and massacres in 1933, many of them fled again, and while League of Nations efforts for a resettlement project overseas were only marginally successful, many of them settled in neighboring north-eastern Syria (the Jazira). The flight of Turkish refugees from the Balkans following the Balkan Wars (1912–1913) and World War I, and the exodus of Greeks and Bulgarians from Anatolia, were resolved in a Greek-Turkish Agreement of 1923 on an organized population exchange. However, further waves of emigration of Turks from the Balkans to Turkey took place in the 1930s from Rumania and Bulgaria, and again in the 1950s and mid-1990s, from Bulgaria.

Jewish refugees, mainly from Europe, strove to reach Palestine, but their entry was restricted by the British MANDATE authorities to a quota supposedly based on the economic absorptive capacity of the country but decisively influenced by political considerations.

The plight of survivors of the Nazi Holocaust, still in European camps after World War II, was an important moral and political factor in the deliberations on the future of Palestine, 1945–1947, and in world support for the establishment of a Jewish state. Independent ISRAEL, from 1948, instituted free and unlimited Jewish immigration. Under the "Law of Return," about 1.3 million people came to Israel in the 1950s and early 1960s. These included not only the remnants of European Jewry, but about 500,000 Jews from the Arab countries—with the largest groups coming from Morocco (approximately 140,000), Iraq (about 120,000), YEMEN (nearly 50,000), LIBYA and TUNISIA (about 40,000 each). (see JEWS.) From the early 1970s, Jews started to arrive from the Soviet Union as well, culminating in the wave of 1989–1996, when over 600,000 Jewish immigrants arrived in Israel. Another group of Jewish immigrants to Israel were the *Falasha* from Ethiopia in two major waves 1984–1985 and 1991, about 15,000 in each wave. By the late 1990s the number of Ethiopian Jews in Israel was estimated at over 60,000.

SUDAN has encountered a refugee problem—in both directions—since the 1960s: Sudanese refugees to the neighboring African countries (Uganda, Ethiopia, Zaire), and refugees from those countries in south Sudan. The Sudanese refugees were almost exclusively from south Sudan's black African tribes, fleeing the vicissitudes of the Civil War and the resulting destruction of their livelihood. Their number—excluding those who fled their domicile but remained in the bush, inside Sudan—has been variously estimated at up to 200,000–400,000. Refugees from the same African countries, and Chad, in Sudan were estimated at similar figures, with some estimates reaching 500,000–600,000 and even 1 million and over. However, these refugee movements, in both directions, fluctuated and remained sporadic, with the number of refugees constantly changing.

Refugee problems have emerged in several states as a result of political upheavals, rebellions, minority and community crises. Thus Kurdish populations—estimated by Kurdish sources at hundreds of thousands—have been removed by the Iraqi authorities from the Kurdish areas in northeast Iraq and forcibly resettled elsewhere.

Following the GULF WAR of 1991 and subsequent Kurdish rebellion, many thousands of Kurds left their homes and moved into Turkey, many of whom returned into the internationally secure zone (see IRAQ).

The ongoing armed clashes, raids, and bombings of southern Lebanon by Israel in retaliation to the attacks of the PALESTINIAN GUERRILLA ORGANIZATIONS across the Lebanese border from 1968; the Civil War in Lebanon that erupted in 1975, and the Israeli invasion, 1982, created waves of refugees—Shi'i Muslims from south Lebanon, mainly to west Beirut, and CHRISTIANS from the Shi'i south and the Druze-dominated Shuf to Christian-controlled East Beirut and Mount Lebanon. Parts of these refugee movements seem to be temporary, with the refugees returning after the acute crisis is over, but large parts, particularly of MARONITE-Christians that migrated abroad, seem to have turned into irreversible, permanent migration.

The end of French domination of ALGERIA and proclamation of the latter's independence in 1962, entailed a massive wave of refugees from this country, immigrating primarily to France. This wave of immigration represented the horrors of the Algerian war for national liberation and the abyss of ethnic and cultural hostility between the indigenous Muslim population and the French colonists, which surfaced amid mutual murderous fighting, especially toward the end of the long war for Algerian liberation (1955–1962). About 1 million of nearly all the originally French settlers (*pied noir*) had left Algeria shortly before it attained independence. Another group of refugees from Algeria during those few weeks before full authority was transferred to the Algerians was about 100,000 Jews, most of whom arrived in France. A third group of migrants was about 15,000 Muslim Algerians (*arki*) who had collaborated with French colonial rule and were allowed to migrate to France, amid the brutal massacre of tens of thousands of them by the Algerian national liberation front. Migration for labor purposes from Algeria to France increased following the former's independence, partly as a consequence of the agreement between the two parties. Until 1973, over 800,000 Muslim Algerians lived in France and transferred remittances to their relatives in Algeria. This wave of emigration to France was largely blocked due to the strong social and political response of French citizens against the new migrants.

From the 1980s, a trend of migration from Turkey and the MAGHREB countries to the European Union

(EU) has been increasingly on the rise, in the quest for higher wages and improved economic position. Reflecting the attractive force of the EU prosperity and the weak economies of the Middle Eastern countries, the number of North African and Turkish residents in the EU increased from 2.8 million in 1974, to close to 3.5 million in 1985, and 4.3 million in 1992 (divided as follows: 2.35 million Turks, mostly in Germany; 1 million Moroccans; 640,000 Algerians and 250,000 Tunisians). Other, smaller groups of migrants came from Egypt, Jordan, Lebanon, Syria and Libya. In 1993 there were 50,000 Egyptians in Greece. (These figures do not include immigrants from Middle Eastern countries who acquired European citizenship, or illegal immigrants.)

The primary phenomenon of voluntary migration in the Middle East has been linked to the economic gap between oil-rich countries (especially in the ARABIAN PENINSULA, Iraq, and Libya), and poor countries, with high rate of population growth. Egypt, for example, and Yemen—or countries with a large population of Palestinian refugees, such as Jordan, Syria and Lebanon—and the growing demand by the former states for additional manpower. Although selective and small scale labor migration to the Gulf countries began already in the early 1950s, primarily of Palestinians from Jordan, Egyptians, Syrians and Yemenis, it turned into a massive wave following the explosion of oil prices following the October 1973 war (see ARAB-ISRAEL CONFLICT, OIL). The skyrocketing demand for labor force in the oil-producing countries, especially for construction and menial jobs, attracted mainly Arab unskilled workers from poor countries such as Egypt, Sudan, Yemen, and others. By 1975 the number of Arab labor migrants in the oil-rich countries was estimated at over 1.3 million, with the leading groups originating from Egypt, Yemen, and Jordan (apparently, mostly Palestinians). The main absorbing countries then were Libya (primarily from Egypt) and Saudi Arabia (mainly from Yemen). This trend continued to accumulate momentum, reaching another turning point upward with the second boom of oil prices in 1979 following the Iranian Shi'i revolution, which doubled the income of the oil producing states in one year and boosted the demand for labor force for ambitious construction projects and welfare programs. By 1980, the number of labor migrants in Saudi Arabia and other Gulf countries increased by over 250%, reaching the figure of three million. Arab labor migrants, however, remained less than half of the total labor force of expatriates in the oil-producing countries and their share even decreased from 43% in the mid-1970s to about 37% in 1980. The other labor migrants were from India, Pakistan, Sri Lanka, and other Asian countries, who had been preferred by the employing countries, mainly because of the lesser likelihood that they might try to remain as permanent residents in those countries. The demand for labor migrants decreased by the mid-1980s as a result of the plunge of oil prices and necessary shortcuts in the expenditures of the oil states. The demand grew more selective once many infrastructural projects had come to their end. Still, the number of labor migrants, especially in the Gulf countries, continued to grow, reaching the figure of 5.2 million by the end of the 1980s. With the Iraqi invasion of KUWAIT and the GULF WAR, close to 1.5 million workers were forced to leave the oil-rich countries, or fled because of the war, significantly affecting the economies of labor-exporting states. Of this figure, some 750,000 Yemenis were expelled from Saudi Arabia and other Gulf countries; 350,000 Egyptians fled from Iraq, and close to 500,000 Jordanians and Palestinians were expelled from the Gulf countries. However, Egyptian labor migration was resumed shortly afterward, reaching by 1994 2.5 million, twenty-five percent more than in 1987. Some 200,000 Yemenis were allowed to return to Saudi Arabia in the aftermath of the Gulf War, while Jordanians and Palestinians have not been permitted again into the Gulf states, at least not in significant numbers.

The most persistent, and politically significant, refugee problem in the region is that of the Palestinian refugees of the 1948 Arab-Israel war who fled in, or were expelled by, the Israeli forces from their domiciles in the part of Palestine that became Israel, some to the Arab parts of Palestine and some to the neighboring Arab countries (see ARAB-ISRAEL CONFLICT, PALESTINE ARABS). The origins and precise circumstances that resulted in the Arab exodus from Palestine had been in dispute for a long time, with each of the parties to the Arab-Israeli conflict blaming each other. Arab spokesmen have largely maintained that the refugees were deliberately expelled by the Jews, to provide space for further Jewish immigration—a built-in element in ZIONISM—while Is-

rael has officially adhered to the claim that notwithstanding some cases of atrocities and expulsion in the course of military action, the bulk of the refugees fled on their own initiative, in the confusion and fear of military operations, and following the instructions, and even more so the example, of their leaders (as later described also by several individual Arab witnesses in the press and published memoirs). More recent studies, based on official Israeli archives, showed that there was no official policy or instruction intended to bring about that expulsion and that most of the Palestinians who became refugees had left their homes on their own initiative, before they faced the Israeli forces, especially in the period between late 1947 and June 1948. Later on, Israel's civil and military leadership became more decisive about preventing the refugees from returning to their homes, and more willing to use forceful expulsion of PALESTINE ARABS from their homes. This was not equally implemented in every sector of fighting and had much to do with decisions of local military commanders and circumstances, which might explain the remaining of some 160,000 Palestinians within Israel. The correct way in which to solve the Palestinian refugees problem was also disputed. From 1948, Israel had maintained that the return of that largely hostile population was inconceivable for the Jewish state, given the level of external threat posed by the neighboring Arab world and the Palestinian Arabs themselves. Furthermore, Israel argued that a solution to the problem should be compatible with similar cases in recent history (i.e., of India-Pakistan; Germany-Eastern Europe; Turkey-Greece), namely, that the refugees should be resettled in the Arab countries with international aid. After the War, Israel offered to pay compensation for landed property left behind by the refugees and to allow the repatriation of a limited, agreed number of refugees in the framework of a comprehensive peace accord. (In 1949 the figure of 100,000 was proposed, but hardly mentioned afterwards.) These offers, though never formally withdrawn, had been rejected by the Palestinian leaders or spokesmen as well as by most Arab states (the idea of resettlement was in principle acceptable to the Jordanian government in the early 1950s, but resented by its Palestinian citizens). The latter insisted that the refugees be allowed to return to their original places in Israel or at least be given the choice to return or to be compensated; UN votes annually endorsed that right. In view of the absorption of hundreds of thousands of Jews from the Arab countries in Israel, unofficial Israeli spokesmen made the argument that the establishment of the State of Israel in fact entailed an exchange of Jewish and Arab populations which should be considered as equitable and final.

The figures of the refugees of 1948 were also a matter of contention. UN agencies generally accepted an estimated total of 715,000–730,000 (usually accepted by the Arabs). Other estimates—more acceptable for Israel—maintained that the number of refugees was 600,000–650,000 (of the total Palestinian-Arab population of approximately 1.3 million, over 400,000 remained in the WEST BANK, 70,000–100,000 in the GAZA STRIP, and some 160,000 in Israel, including 23,000 internal refugees (see IS-RAEL ARAB CITIZENS) and the refugees cannot have been more than the balance). Most of these refugees stayed within Palestine—approximately 200,000 in the West Bank, and 120,000–160,000 in the Gaza Strip. Some 200,000 went to Transjordan; and 150,000 abroad mostly to Lebanon and Syria. By the mid-1990s the estimated number of refugees and their descendants, has reached over 2.5 million—due to a very high birth-rate plus a certain tendency to inflate the lists for the sake of rations and benefits, not to delete the deceased and not to take off the lists those who had found permanent employment and in effect ceased to be refugees in the economic sense. Of these refugees, 250,000–300,000 lived in the West Bank; 350,000–400,000 in the Gaza Strip; nearly 1,800,000–2,200,000 in JORDAN (including 200,000–300,000 who fled the West Bank during the 1967 War and shortly afterwards, and a further 400,000–500,000 who fled or were expelled from KUWAIT and other Gulf OIL-rich monarchies during and after the 1990–1991 Gulf crisis); about 300,000–350,000 in Lebanon and slightly fewer in Syria, and some 60,000 internal refugees in Israel. Of the 3 million refugees, some 800,000–900,000 lived in sixty-one refugee camps, many of which had in effect become fully grown townships. Most of these camps came under de facto control of the PALESTINE LIBERATION ORGANIZATION (PLO) in the course of the 1970s. Israeli statistics of the Palestinian refugees (including the bulk that resides out of the refugee camps) tend to be usually lower than those of UNRWA—often supported by Palestinian statistics as well, by between thirty and fifty percent. Much of this discrepancy derives from the different definition of the term "refugee," determined by socioeconomic or political conditions (which might be subject to the refugee's self-definition), or both.

UNRWA's relief operations, food supplies, and its health and education services were never in question and the UN General Assembly year after year endorsed the budgets needed. Effective action on resettlement or rehabilitation, on the other hand—though vaguely included in the mandate of UNRWA and the UN Palestine Conciliation Commission (PCC, see ARAB-ISRAEL PEACE MAKING)—never got off the ground. Several surveys and plans, usually combined with and based on general economic development schemes for the Arab countries, were drafted—such as the Report of a PCC-appointed Economic Survey Mission (the "Clapp Report") in December 1949, or that of the Carnegie Foundation's Joseph Johnson in 1962 (which was shelved by the PCC and not even submitted to the UN General Assembly). Yet none of them were acceptable to the parties. This was hardly surprising since the Arab states objected in principle to any resettlement. It was, indeed, basically a political issue that could not be solved by economic surveys. There was a head-on confrontation between the Arab and Israeli preferable solutions to the problem. The UN General Assembly in its annual resolutions consistently repeated, in accordance with its Resolution 194 of December 1948, the two alternatives: rehabilitation and absorption in the host countries—or repatriation (of those "willing to live in peace with their neighbors"), calling on Israel to allow the refugees free choice.

Since the 1960s it has become increasingly evident that most of the refugees have lost their rural and agricultural character and that their rehabilitation is primarily a matter of work and housing and must be mainly urban and industrial. Hence it does not require large-scale agricultural development and resettlement projects. A considerable number of refugees have indeed over the years de facto rehabilitated themselves, i.e., have found permanent employment and housing. Some have even built remarkable careers and enterprises—mainly in the oil countries. Since the early 1960s, the Commissioner of UNRWA has repeatedly estimated their number at about twenty percent of the refugees, maintaining that further thirty-forty percent may still be in need of "some" assistance by UNRWA, i.e., are semi-rehabilitated. The number of those rehabilitated and semi-rehabilitated is probably much higher—there is no way of determining facts or reliable estimates, since the refugees or former refugees concerned do not usually delete their names from the lists of refugees, so as not to lose the status of refugees and the benefits that go with it (and also for obvious political reasons). In the early 1980s only one-third of the refugees—estimated by UNRWA at 1.8 million—were qualified for the agency's relief. (see also UNRWA, PALESTINE ARABS).

REJECTION FRONT; STEADFASTNESS FRONT (Arabic: *jabhat al-rafd*) Informal description of a group of ARAB states and Palestinian groups that coalesced in the wake of the October 1973 War to propound a hard line of opposition to any ARAB-ISRAEL PEACEMAKING, whether direct, or internationally mediated. Although some elements of this group claimed that the conflict with ISRAEL could only end when the Jewish state was destroyed, the proponents of this coalition were motivated by ideological Pan-Arab nationalist considerations—determining the disappearance of Israel as a state—and a realistic perception as to the Arab strategic capability to impose such disappearance through diplomacy, among other means. Hence, their prime concern was the fear that under such conditions the diplomatic process would lead to effective legitimization of Israel by the Arab states, which seemed to be too high a cost for the former's withdrawal from the Arab territories it had occupied in June 1967. The leading forces of the Rejection Front were IRAQ and LIBYA, which, together with some Palestinian groups (primarily the Popular Front for the Liberation of Palestine) (PFLP), formed a rather loose and amorphous coalition. Particularly for Iraq and Libya, their rejectionist position also derived from individual self-interest, regional and domestic, to which the post-1973 peace process seemed to be detrimental. They rejected the transitory approach to the conflict with Israel—"a strategy of phases"—adopted by the hard core of Arab states (EGYPT, SAUDI ARABIA, SYRIA, and ALGERIA, as well as the PALESTINE LIBERATION ORGANIZATION (PLO's mainstream), arguing that the first phase in this strategy would probably limit the

freedom of action of the Arabs to the extent that the perceived Arab tactics might become a strategic reality, namely, the continued existence of Israel, and no redemption of Palestinian national rights.

A new radical Arab coalition opposed to the current Arab-Israel context emerged in the wake of President al-SADAT's historic visit to JERUSALEM in November 1977, formalized in a summit meeting convened by Libya's President QADHAFI, in December of that year. The participants in this meeting, Libya, Syria, Algeria, SOUTH YEMEN, the PLO and Iraq (though the latter refused to join the coalition formally, mainly because of its deepening dispute with Syria, demanding a total rejection of diplomacy as a means to resolve the conflict with Israel), established the "Steadfastness and Confrontation Front" (*jabhat al-sumud wal-tasaddi*). The "Steadfastness Front" clearly disassociated itself from its predecessor, "Rejection Front," by adopting a platform which did not entirely reject diplomacy and international mediation as a legitimate means in the Arab-Israeli encounter. It left the door open to renewed joint Arab action in this regard, based on hitherto established prohibitions of direct negotiations with Israel, its recognition, and the separate conduct of Arab states in this regard.

Henceforth, it took the lead in the moves to denounce and ostracize EGYPT. The Front held several separate summit meetings of its leaders (Damascus, September 1978; Tripoli, April 1980; Benghazi, September 1981), mainly to discuss its response to the ongoing Israel-Egypt peace process which culminated in the signing of the Camp David Accords in September 1978, and a peace treaty in March 1979. The signing of the Camp David Accords resulted in a temporary *rapprochement* between Syria and Iraq, following a decade of deep hostility, which shunned the "Steadfastness Front" and demonstrated its practical hollowness and declarative nature. The Iraqi-Syrian alignment collapsed shortly after the erruption of the IRAN-IRAQ WAR, which further drew Iraq away from any involvement in the conflict with Israel, when it needed Arab support, especially financial aid from the Gulf OIL countries, in its war with Iran, while Syria and Libya supported Iran. Algeria also toned down its support of the Steadfastness Front, and the PLO split in 1983 due to Syrian pressure on the PLO's mainstream of *Fatah*, with only the extremist, anti-ARAFAT factions continuing to back Syria. Nonetheless, in the 1980s, Syria, Libya,

Algeria and South Yemen continued to maintain their alignment on the issue of peacemaking with Israel. At Syria's behest, they boycotted the ARAB SUMMIT CONFERENCES of Amman (1980) and Casablanca (1985) and half-boycotted part of the twelfth summit, Fez, in November 1981, sending low-level representatives instead of the heads-of-state, and broke it up by vetoing the Fahd plan (see ARAB-ISRAEL PEACEMAKING), forming a block which opposed the return of Egypt to the ARAB LEAGUE until 1989.

The declining effect of the Front on regional Arab politics in the 1980s was to a large extent muted by IRAN's growing role in Middle Eastern regional politics, and especially in deterring the Gulf oil-producing monarchies from realigning with Egypt. As Syria's ally and its participation, despite its non-Arab identity, as an observer in summit meetings of the Steadfastness Front and summit meetings with Syria and Libya, and its involvement in supporting the Shi'i militant HIZBALLAH in LEBANON and its armed struggle against Israel, Iran became effectively influential in the Arab-Israeli peace process.

The radical or extremist factions within the PLO are also sometimes called "Rejection Front." They collaborated as an informal coalition from the 1970s and in 1984 formally set up a Syrian-supported "National Salvation Front" within the PLO.(see PALESTINE LIBERATION ORGANIZATION) Following the signing of the Oslo Agreement by Israel and the PLO in September 1993, a new Syrian-backed coalition of ten Palestinian opposition groups, combining radical leftist, national and Islamic militants, was proclaimed under the name "The Ten Front," a loose group of factions with little practical significance beyond issuing joint proclamations against the Oslo Agreement. The most important group taking part in the front is HAMAS whose massive presence in the PALESTINIAN AUTHORITY controlled areas and the WEST BANK and GAZA STRIP and military potential, exceeds all other groups' political and military potential altogether.

REVOLUTIONARY GUARDS OF IRAN   see IRAN.

REZA SHAH PAHLAVI   see PAHLAVI REZA SHAH.

al-RIFA'I, ZEID (b.1936)   Jordanian politician, Prime Minister 1973–1976; 1985–1989. The son of Samir al-Rifa'i , who also served as Jordanian Prime Minister (1944–1945; 1947; 1950–1951; 1956; 1958–1959; 1963). Married to the daughter of Prime Minister and former Senate Chairman Bahjat al-Talhuni. A member of the close circle of King HUSSEIN's confidants since they were classmates in college. A graduate of American Universities (Columbia, Harvard) in Political Science and International Relations, Rifa'i joined the Diplomatic Service and that of the Royal Court, also attending to the family's ramified business interests and land property (e.g., in the Jordan Valley development zone). He served at the Jordanian Embassies in EGYPT, LEBANON and at the UN, and in 1967 was appointed Private Secretary to the King. He was promoted in 1969 to Chief of the Royal Cabinet; a post he held during the Jordan-PLO crisis of 1970. In 1970 became Ambassador to BRITAIN, where he served until 1973. In 1972 an attempt was made on his life by "Black September;" a cover name for *Fatah*'s unit in charge of international guerrilla operations (see Palestinian Guerrilla Organizations), which culminated in Rifa'i's severe wounds. In May 1973, still in his thirties, Rifa'i became Prime Minister, taking also the Foreign Affairs portfolio. He held his position until 1976. Perceived by the PLO as hostile, during his first term of premiership a remarkable improvement in Jordan-Syria relations occurred, which was ascribed largely to his efforts. During his second term the BEDOUINS in the south went on riots on grounds of the government's austerity measures that had been taken as a result of a major economic crisis. Considering the Bedouins' loyalty a major imperative to his regime, King Hussein removed Rifa'i from his position (1989). Since 1978, whenever not a prime minister, Rifa'i served as a member of the Senate, becoming its Deputy-President (1984) and its Speaker (1997) .

RIYAD MAHMUD (b.1917)   Egyptian diplomat and politician. Foreign Minister 1964–1972; Secretary-General of the ARAB LEAGUE 1972–1979. A graduate of the Military College (1939) and a career officer, Riyad represented EGYPT in the Egypt-Israel Mixed Armistice Commission from 1949–1952 and headed the Foreign Minister's Department for Arab Affairs, 1954–1955. He was Ambassador to SYRIA, 1955–1958 (until the Egypt-Syria merger of 1958 as UNITED ARAB REPUBLIC (UAR) and Presiden-

tial Advisor on foreign affairs during the time of the UAR, 1958–1961. In 1961 he became Deputy Head of Egypt's permanent mission to the UN, and in 1962 its head and Ambassador. From 1964 to 1972 he served as Foreign Minister—from 1970 as Deputy Premier. He was considered an expert rather than a policy-making leader, but wielded considerable influence. Riyad was not as close a collaborator and confidant of President al-SADAT as he had been under ABDEL NASSER, and was removed by Sadat from the cabinet in January 1972, appointing him Special Advisor to the President as Deputy Premier (a nominal honorific rather than an actual function). In June 1972 Riyad was appointed Secretary-General of the Arab League, a post he held for nearly seven years. He represented the mainstream (as his predecessors had done) and worked to keep the League together, mediating between rival blocks. He resigned in March-April 1979, as Egypt's membership of the League was suspended and its relations with the Arab states severed, in the wake of its peace treaty with IS-RAEL.

Riyad did not go along with Sadat's peace policy, largely agreed with the Arab states' denunciation of that policy, publicly criticizing it. (This was bitterly resented in Egypt.) When the League began preparing steps against Egypt and the latter ceased attending its meetings, in 1978, he was torn by conflicting loyalties. He absented himself from the Foreign Ministers' Council in October 1978, but attended the ARAB SUMMIT CONFERENCE held in Baghdad in November and its follow-up meetings in March 1979. Eventually, he saw no way to resolve his loyalty conflict and continue as League Secretary. Since 1979 Riyad has not been politically active. He published his political memoirs (the English version entitled *The Struggle for Peace in the Middle East*) in 1981.

RUSHDIE, SALMAN (b. 1947) Muslim British writer of Indian origin, who became world famous after being sentenced to death, in abstentia, by the Ayatolla KHOMEINI in February 1989, following the the publication of his book *The Satanic Verses*. The book was boisterously criticized by Muslims in India and Pakistan because its content was considered blasphemous to ISLAM, and especially the prophet Muhammed.

The book was first published in Great Britain in September 1988 and was even given a favorable book review in one of the newspapers in Tehran. However, Khomenei considered the protests an opportunity to head the struggle of the Muslims. He published a FATWA, according to which the assassination of Rushdie was a religious duty for all Muslims. Khomenei rallied the various people around the Islamic revolution and revolutionary institutions, and offered a prize of 1 million dollars for Rushdie's head. The sum was doubled five years later, and in 1997 stood at 2.5 million dollars.

Many religious leaders in IRAN and outside Iran did not object to Khomenei's sentence. It had a grave effect on Iran's foreign relations, creating a serious crisis with the European states and especially with Great Britain. Even though KHAMENEI, who succeeded Khomenei as President of Iran, declared that the Fatwa would be canceled if Rushdie would retreat from what he had written and ask for the forgiveness of the Muslims in the world, he finally canceled this declaration. He announced that the death sentence would not be withdrawn under any circumstance.

Many approaches on the issue by the Council of Europe to Iran remained unanswered. In May 1995 Iran announced that it would not initiate Rushdie's murder. However, because of internal rivalries inside Iran, the government refused to accept the demand of the Council of Europe that it give this in writing, and therefore the crisis continued.

Rushdie, who lived underground for many years, came out of hiding in 1996 and started a public campaign in Europe and the US to mobilize international leaders and public opinion to have the Fatwa cancelled. However, Iran continues to object.

RUSSIA, RUSSIAN AND SOVIET INTERESTS Early Russian contacts with the Middle East in the sixteenth century were religion-based. From the seventeenth century, Czarist Russian searched for territorial expansion. Control of the Bosphorus-Dardanelles outlet to the Mediterranean and the Capsian Sea-PERSIAN GULF corridor leading to India, led to many wars with the OTTOMAN EMPIRE and Persia. From the late eighteenth century, there were also territorial gains at the expense of the latter declining powers. However, unilateral intervention of Great BRITAIN (which was meant to ensure the survival of these Muslim powers as a buffer zone between India and Russia to protect its continental and maritime communications to India through the Persian Gulf) or combinations of the major European powers, prevented the consolidation of those gains and the rise of Russia as a hegemonic power in the area next to its southern borders. Apart from territorial expansion Russia's penetration took the form of claiming special rights in the spheres of military, trade, and rights of protected Christian communities.

The historic watershed in the process of Russian expansion, at the expense of the Ottoman Empire was marked by the Treaty of Kuchuk Kainarji of 1774. This gave Russia direct territorial access to the Black Sea (hitherto an "Ottoman lake"); declaration of the Tatar Khanat of Crimea independent of Ottoman rule (which led after less than a decade to its annexation to Russia); protectorate over the Christian principalities of Moldavia and Wallachia; maritime and commercial rights in the Ottoman Empire. Henceforth, Russia diplomaticaly pressured the Ottoman borders southward, and intervened, on behalf of Orthodox Christian communities under the Muslim Ottoman rule, Pan-Slavic ideology and sheer military aggression. By the early nineteenth century Russia became a dominant Black Sea power. This became a springboard for further territorial claims and maritime rights, alarming Britain and other European powers concerned about Russia's gains, and culminating in the emergence of "The Eastern Question," namely, the problem of Ottoman weakness and the danger it posed to the European balance of power as an easy prey, mainly for Russia.

Russia played a primary role in the struggle of Christian communities for national liberation. Indeed, Serbia, Greece, Romania, Montenegro, and Bulgaria all became independent states during the course of the nineteenth century and early twentieth century. Ther transformation accelerated the disintegration and shrinking territories of the Ottoman Empire.

Parallel to the encroachment on the Ottoman Empire's territories, from the beginning of the nineteenth century Persia was obliged to make major territorial concessions to Russia in Caucasia—some as a result of military defeats, and others as a result of joint pressure by Russia and Great Britain. In the second half of the nineteenth century, Russia managed to expand its control to the Khanat of Central Asia (Buchara, Khiva, and Kokand), and get a foothold

in the Caspian Sea at Persia's expense. It also established a border line with Persia in Turkmenistan—east of the Caspian Sea—which had previously constituted a buffer zone under Persian influence.

Russia was interested primarily in territorial gains and less in commercial and economic concessions, as was Britain (the building of railways and roads, and the search for minerals). However, in the beginning of the twentieth century, Russia granted Persia two loans in return for the customs duties revenue of the state. From 1900, Russia became Persia's sole lender. Indeed it gave Persia additional economic rights at the expense of the Persian treasury. In 1907 Russia and Britain signed a treaty which *inter alia* called for the partition of Persia between them into influence zones. The northern area, including Tehran, was in Russia's influence zone, while Britain reserved for itself a dominant status in the southeastern territories. According to the treaty, Russia and Great Britain were to respect the independence and territorial integrity of Persia. Nonetheless, they continued to intervene directly and indirectly in its internal affairs, culminating in the takeover of the Persian part of Azerbaijan (including its capital, Tabriz) and forcing the dismissal of the Persian *Majlis* (its parliament). Russian influence in Persia was also reflected in the control of Persian elite military units commanded by Russian officers.

The ARAB region, under Ottoman rule until 1918, was affected by Russia only in some cases, e.g., Russia supported the Ottoman Sultan in 1833 against the rebellious Egyptian Viceroy Muhammad Ali. The Crimean War of 1854–1856 developed out of a quarrel between Russia and FRANCE over the holy places in Palestine and Russia's claim to protect all Orthodox CHRISTIANS in the Ottoman Empire.

In World War I, Russia, allied with Britain and France claimed, that after victory, it had the right to annex Constantinople (Istanbul) and the whole area of the Bosphorus and Dardanelles straits. These claims were accepted by Paris and London (in a secret agreement of March 1915) in a radical transformation of Western policy. Furthermore the Western powers gave Russia complete freedom of action in its zone of influence in Persia. In the secret SYKES-PICOT AGREEMENT, 1916, Russia obtained Western approval for the annexation of most of eastern Anatolia as well. In return, Russia consented to the partitioning of the Arab parts of the Ottoman Empire between its two European allies. However, by the time the Ottoman Empire was defeated, the revolutionary Bolshevik government in Moscow had renounced all Tsarist territorial claims and gains.

The Russian Revolution of 1917 facilitated another Ottoman advance toward the Caucasus: the peace treaty with the Soviets, concluded at Brest Litovsk in March 1918, secured the return of Kars, Ardahan—ceded to Russia in 1878—and Batum to the Ottoman domain. (Batum was returned to the Georgian Republic in 1919.) The Soviet-Turkish border was finally fixed in March 1921 in a Treaty of Friendship. This was after the end of the Turko-Armenian hostilities, in favor of TURKEY leaving the regions of Kars and Ardahan in Turkish hands. In October, the Soviet republics of Armenia, Georgia and Azerbaijan signed the Treaty of Kars with Nationalist Turkey. The Soviets were the first to recognize the Nationalist government, providing it with invaluable military and financial aid.

Similarly, the Bolshevik Revolution mitigated the Russian pressure on IRAN. In 1918 Bolshevik Russia canceled all the rights of the Czar's regime in Northern Iran and in 1921 signed an agreement with the government of Persia in this spirit, as part of its efforts to settle its relations with its southern neighbors and turn them into buffers between itself and imperialist Britain.

The Soviet Union obtained fishing rights in the Caspian Sea, but its real gain in the Agreement was the recognition of its right to introduce military forces into Persia in the event of intervention by a third party, which would pose a threat to the Soviet Union from the Persian territory.

During the interwar period, the Middle East did not figure prominently in Soviet foreign policy. That policy was conducted on two separate levels:

The USSR sought to maintain normal foreign relations, especially with its three immediate neighbors—Turkey, Persia and Afghanistan—with whom it concluded in 1921 treaties of friendship and non-aggression. The USSR was not a party to the Peace Treaty of LAUSANNE, 1923, but it was a signatory to the MONTREUX CONVENTION on the Straits, 1936, which permitted its re-fortification and restricted the right of warships to pass the Straits and enter the Black Sea. The USSR established commercial and diplomatic relations with SAUDI ARABIA and YEMEN, in 1925 and 1928 respectively, despite the reactionary nature of these traditionalist monarchies. Both missions were withdrawn in 1938.

On a different level, the USSR supported revolutionary activities in colonial countries, through the Communist International (Comintern). A Congress of the Peoples of the East, held in Baku in 1920 under the auspices of the Comintern, called on the inhabitants of the area to rise up against their colonial masters. COMMUNISM, however, had little appeal for the peoples of the Middle East. Its secularist, atheistic elements were anathema to the religious values and beliefs of Muslim society. Indeed, a proletarian industrial working class did not yet exist. Communist cells were suppressed by the existing semi-independent nationalist regimes—with the full support of their Western tutors, Britain and France, who prevented any contact between these regimes and Moscow.

The relations between the Soviet Union and Iran under REZA SHAH were tense, due to the constant Iranian fear of Soviet expansion at Iran's expense, and subversion efforts among ethnic minorities in northern Iranian provinces, mainly in the Iranian Azerbaijan region and Khurasan. The USSR was disturbed by the suppression of the Communists in Iran as well as by the granting of concessions to British and American companies to prospect for OIL in northern Iran. The Soviet Union also exerted pressure to attain preferred import conditions for agricultural produce from the northern regions of Iran and fishing rights in the Caspian Sea, whilst simultaneously trying to dump food products into Iran in a way that harmed local production. In 1940 the Soviet Union signed a Trade and Shipping Agreement with Iran.

As the USSR resumed its position of a Great Power, penetration of the Middle East once again became a major Russian concern. This caused the Soviet Union to exert pressure on Iran and Turkey, to attain strategic gains, territorial as well as economic. In secret negotiations with Nazi Germany in 1940, the USSR declared that it had territorial aspirations "south of the national territory of the Soviet Union in the direction of the Indian Ocean and the Persian Gulf." It also acknowledged its demand for "land and naval bases" within range of the Bosphorus and the Dardanelles. In August 1941, following the German invasion of Russia, the Soviet Union invaded the northern part of Iran, parallel to a similar action by

Britain in the southern provinces, in order to ensure a territorial bridge, used by the Allies to transfer strategic assistance to the Soviet Union. Despite the joint undertaking of Britain and the Soviet Union to Iran in their treaty of 1941 to respect the territorial integrity of Iran, its sovereignty and political independence and withdraw their forces within six months from the end of the War, Moscow used the occupation of northern Iran for pressures on the latter's government for political and economic blackmailing. The Russians continued their subversive activities in Azerbaijan and Kurdistan, while encouraging the demands of local groups for autonomy. Furthermore they demanded an oil concession in the area occupied by them and effectively prevented the Iranian government from exercising its administrative duties in Iranian Azerbaijan. They also pressured the government to allow the Iranian Communists freedom of action and to establish themselves as a party under the name TUDEH.

Soviet-Turkish relations, already strained following the German-Soviet Pact of 1939, further deteriorated after World War II. Angered by Turkish neutrality during the War (and by the wartime activities of Pan-Turkish circles), the USSR in the beginning of 1945 repudiated its treaty of 1925 with Turkey. Moscow conditioned the renewal of the treaty on sharing the defense of the Straits and the return of the Kars and Ardahan regions. These demands, rejected by Turkey (and renounced by the USSR only in 1953), placed it firmly in the Western bloc. Since Britain was unable to afford the necessary aid, the US stepped in, thereafter becoming Turkey's principal ally. In Iran, the Soviets continued to maintain military occupation of the northern provinces for a year after the end of the War, which led to an official Iranian complaint to the UN Security Council. The Soviets agreed to finally withdraw their forces under pressure of the Western powers, following a resolution by the Security Council in this regard. The entrance of Iranian forces into the northern region put an end to the Soviet-supported puppet governments of the "Republic of Azerbaijan," whose capital was Tabriz, and the "Republic of Kurdistan," whose capital was MAHABAD.

This policy of pressure on the "Northern Tier" states of the Middle East was one of the causes for a new American strategy entitled the "Truman Doctrine," proclaimed in March 1947, which promised assistance to states under external threat to their security, which sought American support. The announcement of the new American policy indicated growing US interests in the Middle East, especially regarding Turkey and Iran and efforts to contain the Soviet threat of penetration into the region. Nonetheless, in December 1954 the Soviet Union signed an agreement with Iran by which the former agreed to pay its debt to Iran for goods and services it had received during World War II. The two states also signed a map of their common border. Despite Iran's membership in a Western alliance (CENTO), the Soviets could maintain a measure of cooperation with Iran which, unlike Turkey, announced in 1962 that it would not allow the stationing of foreign missiles on its territory. In 1964–1965 a significant improvement in Soviet-Iranian relations occured, when a number of economic and commercial agreements were signed, and Moscow hosted three visits of the Shah culminating in increased technical cooperation between the two states.

During World War II, the USSR established full diplomatic relations with those Arab states that had previously been kept out of its reach by Britain and France, EGYPT, SYRIA, LEBANON, and IRAQ. In 1945 it sought a share in trusteeships to be imposed on the former Italian colonies, particularly LIBYA. Its proposals were, however, aborted by the West. The antagonism between Russia and the West clearly manifested itself in the Middle East. Russia encouraged Middle Eastern nations in conflict with the West (such as Syria and Lebanon, 1945–1946, Iran in its defiance of Western oil interest 1951–953, and Egyptian and Iraqi nationalist governments struggling with Britain). It endorsed the partition of Palestine, 1947, recognized ISRAEL and let Czechoslovakia assist it with arms in its crucial struggle for survival, and it was assumed that its wish to get Britain out was a major reason for this change of policy. (Indeed, in 1949–1950 the USSR reverted to the violent anti-ZIONISM that had been traditional with the Communist Party.)

Soviet relations with Turkey throughout the 1950s were marked by Russian hostility and tended to reflect the Cold War. Turkey's growing alignment with the West, culminating in its incorporation into NATO in 1952, left its imprint on its relations with the northern neighbor, which from the mid-1950s succeeded in outflanking Turkey by establishing close links with Egypt, Syria, and Iraq. By the mid-1960s the Soviet Union had already renounced its Stalinist demands from Turkey and was openly courting its friendship, while the beginning of US-Soviet *detente* in the early 1970s helped to ease traditional Turkish fears of the Russians. The new emphasis put by the Soviets on coexistence and economic cooperation was welcomed by the Turkish government, although it could hardly lose sight of Russia's long hostility and perceived the new overture as sheer scare tactics. Hence, while no significant change occurred in Turkey's commitment to the Western alliance, in the 1960s agreements on technical cooperation were concluded between the two countries.

In its growing support for the Arab nationalist governments, the USSR greatly diminished, or at least played down, its support for local Communist parties and for national minorities in conflict with these governments (such as the KURDS). As such support could not be completely abandoned, however, Soviet policy continued displaying shifts and contradictions. It was obviously determined by the strategic and political interests of an expanding Great Power rather than by considerations of Communist ideology or solidarity.

In the mid-1950s, the opportunity came for the USSR to make a major breakthrough. A revolutionary nationalist Egypt was locked in a bitter struggle with Britain and also increasingly isolated from the US, resisting American pressure for a Western-guided regional military alliance, first the MIDDLE EAST DEFENSE ORGANIZATION, and later the Baghdad Pact, which Egypt regarded as a means of continuing Western domination. Intensification of the ARAB-ISRAEL CONFLICT also engendered anti-Western feelings, to Moscow's profit. As of early 1954, the USSR consistently vetoed UN Security Council resolutions on the conflict that did not tally with the Arab position. A large-scale arms deal was concluded in May 1955, officially between Egypt and Czechoslovakia, but in fact included the sale of major items of weaponry directly by the USSR to Egypt. From this point on, the Soviet Union had a growing stake in the Arab world. Full political and diplomatic support for Egypt's stand in the Suez crisis of 1956 and similarly for Syria in 1957, accompanied in both cases by threats of military intervention, enhanced the USSR's position as the Arabs' chief strategic supporter against

Western imperialism and Israel. From 1957–1958, the USSR gave ever-increasing military and economic aid to Syria and Egypt. Subsequent revolutions in the Arab world enlarged the camp of the USSR's clients: Iraq 1958, ALGERIA 1962, Yemen 1962, SOUTH YEMEN 1967, SUDAN and Libya, 1969, and Somalia, 1974. However, Egypt remained the USSR's single most important client and ally, even though their relations too had undergone a period of cooling down from the late 1950s to the early 1960s, during which Moscow tightened its links with Iraq, Egypt's arch-Arab rival, especially in those years. Soviet aid was often directed to implement large-scale, ostentatious schemes of national prestige, such as the ASWAN HIGH DAM and steel plants in Egypt. The USSR also trained the officers of its Arab allies' armed forces, providing most of their military equipment, thus making them increasingly dependent on it. There was a growing presence of Soviet naval forces in the Mediterranean. By the end of the 1960s, these forces enjoyed the use of strategic ports in Egypt, Syria and Algeria. Soviet naval units were welcome guests in Sudan, Yemen, South Yemen and Iraq (although the closure of the SUEZ CANAL after June 1967 severed the sea link between the latter group of countries and the Soviet Mediterranean squadron).

The June 1967 War constituted another watershed in Soviet relations with the Arab Middle East. Soviet policies were among the chief factors determining the course of events that led to the eruption of war, and increasingly so as Moscow supported the Arab cause against Israel in the UN and in Great-Power talks on the Middle Eastern crisis after the war (see ARAB-ISRAEL CONFLICT). The war brought to the Soviet Union Western, notably US, recognition as a Middle Eastern power and for the first time US-Soviet relations included discussions of the Middle East, specifically the Arab-Israeli conflict. The USSR speedily more than replaced all military equipment lost in the conflict by the Arab states, both quantitatively and qualitatively. In 1969–1970 it went even further: it not only dispatched large numbers of Soviet officers to train and advise the Egyptian armed forces but after the Israelis demolished the Egyptian anti-aircraft system in the War of Attrition, Soviet crews manned SAM-2 and SAM-3 missile sites, while Soviet pilots were sent to Egypt to fly operational combat missions. The USSR had severed diplomatic relations with Israel in June 1967 and supported Arab demands for its total and unconditional withdrawal from the territories occupied in 1967. But since it accepted the existence of an independent Israel, it was at first hesistant about supporting the PALESTINE LIBERATION ORGANIZATION (PLO), which strove for the elimination of Israel. By the early 1970s, however, it was aiding and encouraging the PLO politically and militarily, without explicitly associating itself with its ultimate objective.

The USSR was also reportedly supporting insurgent movements in the Persian Gulf area and various leftist groupings in some of the conservative, Western-oriented Arab states. While aiding mainly the radical or revolutionary regimes, it also sought to increase contacts with such generally pro-Western countries as JORDAN, KUWAIT, MOROCCO and TUNISIA.

The early 1970s that saw the peak of the USSR's involvement in the Arab world also witnessed the beginning of a decline in its influence. Egypt, which under Nasser had been the main target and instrument of Soviet penetration, became under Anwar al-SADAT the first major trouble spot. Despite a Treaty of Friendship and Cooperation concluded in 1971, Sadat expelled the entire Soviet military units present in Egypt since April 1970 (estimated at 15,000–20,000) in 1972—allegedly in response to the Soviet refusal to meet his requirements for arms supplies that would enable a major Egyptian military initiative against Israel, but possibly as a signal to the US, inviting Washington to a political dialogue with Egypt. The Soviets, who were entering a period of *detente* summits with the US, did not wish to jeopardize their achievements on this plane as a result of Arab adventurism.

In a new agreement in early 1973, the USSR promised Sadat to supply military material that would change the Arab-Israeli military balance—without, however, inpeding the supply of the strategic weaponry that Sadat had been demanding. Most of the promised weapons arrived during the Ocober 1973 war in which the USSR stood by Egypt and Syria by operating an airlift supplying arms, ammunition and military equipment necessary for continuing the prolonged combat effort. After that war Sadat turned to the US in his endeavors to reach a political settlement that would restore the Sinai to Egypt, and Soviet influence in Egypt continued its decline. In 1976 Egypt unilaterally abrogated the 1971 treaty. In 1977

it also withdrew its Ambassador from Moscow and in 1981 expelled the Soviet Ambassador from Cairo. (Full ambassadorial relations were restored in 1984.)

Soviet relations with Iran under the Shah continued to fluctuate, maintaining a modest level of trade exchange and technical cooperation while basically affected by distrust and hostility. By maintaining such a level of cooperation with Moscow, Iran hoped to mitigate the latter's political subversion and minimize the threats to its regional security. In 1967, the Soviets signed a contract to sell Iran 40 million dollars worth of ammunition. The *rapprochement* between the two countries led to a reduction in Soviet propaganda against the Shah's regime. Moscow's policy toward him remained basically hostile, which was supported by opposition forces. In the mid 1970s "underground" propaganda was broadcasted from the Soviet Union, while the official Soviet media did not stop its criticism of the Iranian regime. The Soviet threat to Iran intensified as Moscow undertook to supply massive quantities of weapons to Iraq, and its growing military involvement in the Indian Ocean, southern Yemen and the Horn of Africa. Despite its resentment of the Shah's relentless efforts since the mid-1960s to turn Iran into a hegemonic military power in the Gulf, in October 1976 the Soviet Union signed a 550 million dollar contract with the Shah for the sale of SAM-7 anti-aircraft missiles, half-tracks and tank carriers. A year later, another contract was signed by the two parties for the supply of a million tons of Iranian oil to the Soviet Union in return for the supply of more Soviet military equipment to Iran. In the latter half of the 1970s Moscow enhanced its support for extreme left wing organizations, which by 1976 began waging guerrilla warfare against the regime and the murder of American advisors and company representatives, which constituted a declaration of war against the Shah and his contacts with the US. In the beginning of 1978 the Soviet media openly renewed its attacks against the Shah, supporting the demands of the Iranian opposition.

The ascendancy of the Islamic revolutionary regime in Iran led to a new chapter in Soviet relations with that country, primarily because the new regime in Tehran abrogated its links with the US and other Western-oriented alliances, such as CENTO. Contrary to the embargo by the West on the supplies of armaments to Iran, the Soviet bloc states sent it weapons, though indirectly, through Syria and Libya. Nevertheless, tension soon developed in the relations betwen Iran and the Soviet Union. Already in the course of 1979 the Iranian leaders accused the Soviet Union of subversion and the supply of arms to the Kurds and the Tudeh Party, criticizing it for its invasion of Afghanistan at the end of 1979. In February 1983, a crisis developed between the two countries as a result of the detention of the heads of the Tudeh Party in Iran and the expulsion of eighteen Soviet diplomats from Tehran. Nonetheless, from the late 1980s, the economically bankrupt Soviet Union was willing to meet Iran's interest in purchasing middle and long range missiles, and the technologies for manufacturing such missiles, as well as conventional arms systems. The purchase of three Russian submarines and their entry into the Gulf in the mid-1990s was viewed by the West as a possible threat to the export of oil through the Gulf, while its purchase of Russian nuclear reactors and technology became a constant source of concern within the region and in Washington, in light of estimates that Iran could have the capability to manufacture a nuclear device within five to ten years.

The decreasing Soviet strategic influence in Egypt under Sadat encouraged the Soviet Union to seek compensation by improving its ties with other Arab states and the PLO, so that it would retain clout with the US and a key role in any Middle Eastern settlement. Moscow was occasionally successful: it concluded further Friendship and Cooperation Treaties—with Iraq (1972), Somalia (1974—unilaterally abrogated by that country in 1977), South Yemen (1979), Syria (1980), Yemen (1984). No such treaty was signed with Libya—though Libya reportedly proposed it. Soviet influence with the PLO grew through intense political and military assistance.

There were sporadic breakthroughs with the US, such as a Soviet-American statement of October 1977 on the Middle East, designed to lead to a reconvening of the Geneva Peace Conference under joint Soviet-US aegis. However, the Soviet invasion of Afghanistan in January 1980 resulted not only in a crisis in US-Soviet relations, and resumption of the Cold War between the two Superpowers, but it also alienated the Muslim Middle East and aroused official resentment toward the Soviet Union by most Muslim states, save Syria and Libya.

On the whole, however, Soviet achievements in the Middle East were marginal. It registered apparent successes in the periphery—Afghanistan, Ethiopia—but even these turned out to be temporary, and, in the case of Afghanistan, a disastrous entanglement. Revolutionary Iran which ejected US influence did not replace the Shah's relationship with Washington with a partnership with the USSR. Moreover, the IRAN-IRAQ WAR increased Soviet predicaments. The radical states, Syria, Libya, South Yemen, with which its relations were closest and to which Moscow had far-reaching commitments, proved largely intractable and unmalleable as clients, while the PLO lost a great deal of its significance following its expulsion from Lebanon in 1982 and its internal dissensions. (The USSR helped efforts to mediate and reconcile those rifts.) Syria remained a strategic asset, and dependent on Soviet aid. The USSR needed its partnership with Damascus to ensure its participation in the Middle East peace process. However, such an intimate cooperation with states increasingly recognized as responsible for international terror cast doubts on the USSR's capabilities in restraining client states and its responsibility as a great power. Although the US also suffered a number of setbacks such as the rejection of the Reagan Plan (1982) and the withdrawal of the marines from Lebanon (1983–1984), these were not sufficient to reinstate the USSR as one of two world powers with more or less equal status in the region. In the mid-1980s, the USSR increasingly involved itself in the Persian Gulf, acting as a guardian of free shipping. In 1985, the USSR managed to establish diplomatic relations with several Gulf states that had refused them before—OMAN and the UNITED ARAB EMIRATES (UAE). (Kuwait had already established relations in 1963.)

By the mid-1980s, a host of domestic and global causes resulted in the declining stature of the Soviet Union in the Middle East. Growing economic difficulties and an inability to continue competing with the US and keep up the latter's strategic and technological progress, were primary in determining a profound change of the Soviet Union—manifested in the "Glasnost" and "Perestroika" policies of liberalization on both domestic and international levels—and its policies toward the Middle East. Other developments that contributed to the changing Soviet policies in the Middle East and cast doubts on the once brilliant specter of an alliance with the USSR were the declining Western dependence on Middle Eastern oil and the gradually diminishing importance of that commodity in the international arena. The obvious limitations of a Superpower whose chief claim to influence has traditionally been the supply of arms, especially when some of its client states are intent on peace, and the superpower itself is apprehensive of an outbreak of hostilities that might jeopardize its position; the failure to win Third World states in general and Arab states in particular as adherents of Marxist-Leninist ideology and "the non-capitalist path of development;" the growing tendency of social radicalism and nationalism to ally themselves with ISLAMIC RADICALISM and the technological gap between East and West and the USSR's evident economic difficulties. However, despite the USSR's collapse and disintegration in 1991, Russian posture in the Middle East as an influential power remains significant, especially due to the nature of this region as intrinsically conflict-ridden and highly suspicious of the US due to its special relations with Israel.

The late 1980s witnessed a discernible change in the policy of the Soviet Union under Gorbachev toward Israel and the Arab-Israeli conflict. Israel's willingness to accept the idea of an international peace conference with the Soviet Union's participation and other Israeli gestures, and the Soviet response in releasing Jewish dissenters from prison, helped breaking the icy relations between the two countries since 1967. In the second half of the 1980s, Soviet-Israeli contacts were made over issues such as the property of the Russian Churches in Israel and Jewish emigration from the Soviet Union.

In 1987 low-level diplomatic relations were resumed between Israel and the Soviet Union, becoming full diplomatic relations in 1991, toward the convening of the international peace conference in Madrid. From the late 1980s, a growing wave of Jewish immigration to Israel from the Soviet Union, turned into a massive tide after the fall of the Soviet Union in August 1991. By the mid-1990s this wave of immigration had reached over half a million JEWS from the former Soviet Union.

From the early 1990s, Israel-Russia relations witnessed beginnings of trade exchange and technological cooperation, including in military-applied spheres.

The new Soviet policy toward Israel was a diminishing commitment for continued military backing to Moscow's Arab allies, primarily Syria, in their conflict with Israel. Further, the Soviet Union encouraged a diplomatic settlement to the Arab-Israeli conflict.

Although the Soviet Union did not join the American-led international coalition against Iraq, it supported the UN Security Council resolutions that followed the Iraqi invasion of Kuwait. Once the ground offensive against Iraqi forces began, the Soviet Union attempted to end the war before Iraq finally accepted the US-based conditions. However, these differences regarding the Gulf War did not prevent US-Soviet cooperation in convening the Madrid peace confrence in late October 1991, with Russia's president as one of the co-sponsors of the renewed ARAB-ISRAEL PEACEMAKING. Russia also joined the multi-lateral talks (1992–1996) and supported the Israel-PLO Oslo Agreement of September 1993. From 1996, Russia enhanced its involvement in the deadlocked Arab-Israel peace process, especially in the Israel-Syria track which had been halted since the last negotiations held in the US in February 1996.

The disintegration of the Soviet Union and the emergence of six Muslim republics—some of which had once been ruled by Persia and others linked by historic, linguistic, and cultural ties to Turkey— paved the way for the emergence of new relations between part of the former Soviet Union's republics and the Middle Eastern countries. For Iran, these republics opened new opportunities for developing political and comercial ties as well as for spreading the Islamic Revolution. In February 1992 the republics of Kyrgyzstan, Tajikistan, Uzbekistan, Turkmenistan and Azerbaijan joined the framework of the ECONOMIC COOPERATION ORGANIZATION (ECO). In addition, a framework for cooperation between the states of the Caspian Sea was created with the participation of Iran, Russia, Azerbaijan, Turkmenistan and Kazakhstan. In the summer of 1996 the railways of Iran and Turkmenistan were connected and the "Silk Way," which in the past had connected Iran with central Asia, was reopened. However, the Iranian efforts in the economic sphere enjoyed only limited success, for the Islamic republics required, first and foremost, technological assistance and capital investments, which Iran was unable to provide, and in this sphere they preferred ties with the Western states and Israel.

Turkey also began to build bridges to the new republics that emerged on the ruins of the former Soviet Union. Particular attention was given to the Turkic republics with which Turkey had linguistic, cultural and historical bonds—Azerbaijan, Kazakhstan, Uzbekistan, Kyrgyzstan and Turkmenistan. Turkey, at the end of 1991, was quick to recognize them as independent states and established diplomatic relations. Frequent visits of leaders and officials were exchanged and a host of agreements of cooperation signed in all fields. Turkey was also the moving spirit behind several all-Turkic conferences convened with the participation of the Turkic republics and communities. Turkey has been primarily motivated by hopes of finding new outlets for Turkish trade and business in the new developing Turkish world, in addition to deep-seated ethnic solidarity. It also viewed this new opening toward "Eurasia" (*Avrasya*) as offering it opportunities of serving as a link with Europe and the West, thus increasing its standing in international relations. Turkey at the same time fostered cooperation with Black Sea countries establishing the Black Sea Cooperation with the participation of the riparian and Caucasian countries.

In a way, these developments have broadened the boundaries of the Middle East as a regional system by bringing in these newly independent Muslim states of central Asia.

Furthermore, the partial incorporation of these republics into the Middle East by economic and political interests has already contributed to further diversification of inter-state relations in the Middle East and the blurring of ethno-religious identities as major determinants of international behavior, best represented by the willingness of those central Asian republics to foster technological and economic relations with Israel.

S

EL-SAADAWI, NAWAL (b.1931) A leading Egyptian writer and outspoken feminist. After studing medicine at the University of Cairo, Saadawi began to work, in 1958, for the Ministry of Health serving as a village doctor. In 1972, following her writings on sexuality, especially with the publication of *Woman and Sex*, Saadawi was dismissed from her job as Egypt's national public health director. In 1978 she joined the United Nations in Addis Ababa as an advisor on Arab women's programs. In 1980 she resigned and returned to EGYPT. She was briefly imprisoned under Anwar al-SADAT in a round up of Egyptian intellectuals in 1981. A year later, Saadawi founded the Arab Women's Solidarity Association (AWSA) dedicated to improving the status of Arab women. The Egyptian government banned the AWSA in June 1991, following its stance on the GULF WAR. A prolific writer, El Saadawi has addressed the relations between power, medicine and gender, ranging from sexual violence to female circumcision, and has boldly denounced women's oppression. Some of her works translated into English include *The Hidden Face of Eve: Women in the Arab World*, the autobiographical *Memoirs from the Women's Prison*, and novels, *Memoirs of a Woman Doctor, Woman at Point Zero* and *The Fall of the Imam*.

SA'ADEH, ANTOUN see SYRIAN NATIONAL SOCIAL PARTY.

SABAEANS, SABIANS see MANDEAEANS.

AL-SABAH The ruling dynasty of Kuwait; the ruler using the title Sheikh, or in recent decades Amir. (see KUWAIT).

SABRI, ALI (b. 1920) Egyptian officer and politician, Prime Minister 1962–1965, Vice-President 1965–1967. Sabri was trained as a professional officer, graduating in 1939 from the military academy. He was not among the ten founding members of the "Free Officers" group that staged the coup d'état of July 1952, but was close to them and allegedly acted as their liaison to the US Embassy before and during the coup. He began his ascent to power as Director of President ABDEL NASSER's Office. When EGYPT merged with SYRIA in 1958 to form the UNITED ARAB REPUBLIC (UAR), Sabri became Minister for Presidential Affairs in the UAR government. He kept this post in the Egyptian government, when the UAR was dissolved in 1961. As he had become one of President Nasser's closest associates, he was appointed Prime Minister in September 1962, heading the government until October 1965. As Prime Minister he was also a member of the Presidential Council named in 1962. From 1965, when he had to give up the Premiership, until 1967, he was one of four (from 1966: three) Vice Presidents. In 1967–1968 he served briefly as Deputy Prime Minister and Minister of Local Government.

From 1965 Sabri held, concurrently with his Vice-Presidency, the chairmanship of the ARAB SOCIALIST UNION (ASU), Egypt's single party and the mass basis of its regime. He endeavored to reorganize that party into cadres, on the Soviet model, and turn it into an effective mass organization and a base for his own ascent to power. In the 1960s, Sabri headed the left wing of Eygpt's ruling junta—advocating ever closer relations with the Soviet Union and, at home, a speedier and more intense advance toward state socialism; the expansion of the state sector of the economy; more vigorous nationalizations and a stricter regime. As he came to be considered "Moscow's man," his position in the leadership team was seen as an index of the regime's shifting relations with the USSR. In June 1967 he was credited with the organization of the mass demonstrations that brought Nasser to withdraw his resignation. After 1967, however, when ABDEL NASSER felt compelled to moderate his policies in the internal, inter-Arab and international arenas, Sabri's influence declined. He remained, except for a few months between 1967–1968, without a government position, and in 1969 he was dismissed as Chairman of the ASU—apparently both because of his leftist radical tendencies and his power ambitions.

After Nasser's death, in September 1970, he was seen by many as a leading candidate for the succession, the one preferred by the Soviet Union. He lost out to Anwar al-SADAT, but was included in the new government as one of Sadat's two Vice Presidents. However, a power struggle continued behind the scenes, and in May 1971 he was accused, together with a group of other leaders and administrators from Nasser's days, of plotting, treason, and power abuse in his pre-1970 positions. He was dismissed from all governments and party posts and put on trial. In December 1971 he was sentenced to death, but the sentence was commuted to life imprisonment. He was pardoned and released by Sadat in May 1981, but did not resume activities in political or public affairs.

al-SADAT, (MUHAMMAD) ANWAR (1918–1981) Egyptian officer and statesman. President of EGYPT 1970–1981. Born in Mit Abul Kom in the Delta province of Minufiyya into a peasant family. (His father was a clerk with the army, his mother was Sudanese.) He graduated from the military academy in 1938 and became a professional officer. A keen nationalist of conservative Islamic tendency, he was close to, and for some time a member of, the MUSLIM BROTHERHOOD and the right-wing, pro-Fascist Misr al-*Fatah* (Young Egypt) Party. In 1941–1942, he became active in a pro-German underground group, and in October 1942 he was expelled from the army. He was detained for about two years. In 1944 he escaped and went underground until the detention order was lifted the following year. He was arrested in 1946 and charged with complicity in the murder of the former Finance Minister Amin Osman (Uthman) and also suspected of involvement in an attempt to assassinate ex-Premier Nahhas. In prison for over two years during the trial, he was acquitted in December 1948. He then worked as a journalist, but in January 1950 was readmitted to the army.

Restored to his officer's rank and position, Sadat soon joined the secret group of "Free Officers" headed by Gamal ABDEL NASSER and was active—then a Lieutenant-Colonel—in that group's coup of July 1952. He became a member of the twelve-man Revolutionary Council heading the new regime and remained, in various capacities, one of the leaders of the new team throughout the years of its rule—though he held no ministerial positions except for one term as Minister of State, 1954–1956. In the first years of the new regime, Sadat officially liaised between the Muslim Brotherhood and right-wing groups. After the Brotherhood was banned and suppressed in 1954 and the regime began turning to the left, he was no longer with Nasser's inner circle. (His appointment as Minister of State was a token appointment with no real power.) For some time he was editor of the regime's daily, *al-Gumhuriyya*. Sadat was a member of the Council of the National Rally, the regime's single party, serving as its Secretary-General from 1957. This post did not warrant much influence, particularly after Egypt's merger with SYRIA which led to the UNITED ARAB REPUBLIC (UAR) (1958). From 1959 to 1969 Sadat was Chairman of the National Assembly, including one year, 1960–1961, of that of the UAR. As he was among the "Free Officers," the closest to Islamic tendencies, he was sent on several missions to Muslim countries and represented Egypt at Islamic conferences. He was also Egypt's chief liaison with YEMEN.

In December 1969 Sadat was appointed Vice-President of Egypt, as Nasser's only deputy. This appointment was seen as a step to balance rightist and leftist tendencies within the ruling team and particularly to check the advance of the latter, led by Ali SABRI. Upon Nasser's death in September 1970, Sadat was appointed President of Eygpt, and also of the single party, the ARAB SOCIALIST UNION (ASU). He was thenceforth duly elected, as the only candidate, in October 1970. His selection by the ruling team was apparently intended to avoid a struggle for the succession by rightist and leftist candidates —it was assumed: Zakariyya Muhyi al-Din as opposed to Ali Sabri—and Sadat himself was seen as a rather colorless compromise candidate, a weak *primes inter pares*. Following his suppression of the semi-coup attempt by a group of central figures of the previous regime ("centers of power") in May 1971, and elimination of his rivals (see EGYPT), Sadat established his personal leadership with a firm grip on power and soon began to form his own policies.

At first he did so cautiously and without admitting that he was abandoning some of the principles of NASSERISM. Indeed he insisted that his measures were merely a "corrective revolution" (this is what he called the May 1971 episode), restoring the true principles of the 1952 revolution. Nonetheless, his policies were strongly marked by his departure from the Nasserist legacy. This was illustrated by his symbolic abolition of the anachronistic UAR as Egypt's name, replaced by "Egypt Arab Republic," indicating the primacy of Egypt as a separate entity over ARABISM. Domestically, he mitigated the repressive and arbitrary procedures of the security apparatuses in tackling opposition groups, and facilitated more freedom of speech, insisting on the return to con-

stitutional rule and operation through the formal institutions of the state. He released the political prisoners from jails and allowed the Muslim Brotherhood to renew its activity and publication of its newspapers and pamphlets, apparently as a counterbalance to his Nasserist rivals. Gradually, and mainly from 1973, he liberalized the economic regime (see EGYPT for details).

Simultaneously, Sadat's foreign policies changed gradually over time. His attitude toward inter-Arab affairs was moderate, abandoning attempts to impose Egyptian domination on other Arab states which he moved to closer to, especially SAUDI ARABIA. He went along with the plan for a federation with LIBYA and Syria, the Federation of Arab Republics, (FAR)— a scheme that never got off the ground—but resisted Libyan pressure for a full merger of Egypt and Libya (see EGYPT, LIBYA, ARAB NATIONALISM), putting up with the resulting deterioration in Egypt's relations with Libya.

Sadat's foreign policy was shaped by the overwhelming concern for Israel's occupation of Sinai and other Arab territories—a matter of vital priority and national honor. From the outset, Sadat set the goal of recovering occupied Sinai, forcefully or peacefully. Hence he declared that 1971 would be the "year of decision." He was ready to move toward peace negotiations following an Israeli withdrawal to the al-Arish-Ras Muhammad line, and parallel to works for reopening the Suez Canal for shipping. His initiative was a response to Israeli Defense Minister DAYAN's suggestion in that direction, though with much narrower Israeli withdrawal. Yet despite the positive response of Israeli Prime Minister MEIR to Sadat's message, it failed to get off the ground, mainly because Sadat insisted that his suggestions were to be an indivisible part of a comprehensive settlement toward which he needed Israeli commitment for such comprehensive withdrawal, with a timetable of its implementation. Also, in his talks with UN envoy Jarring, Sadat was still unwilling to meet Israel's essential demand for direct negotiations, and repeated insistence on a "just settlement" of the refugee problem, which was conceived in ISRAEL as tantamount to a claim for its elimination.

Sadat made intense efforts to prevent war and further exhaust the diplomatic avenues, which were remarkable in his changing relations with the great powers. He renewed the dialogue with the US in an attempt to use its offices for the recovery of Sinai and other territories occupied by Israel in 1967, seeking closer relations with Western European powers. In 1971 he hosted President Podgorny, signing a Treaty of Friendship with the Soviet Union. Yet this was viewed by observers as an effort to shore up uneasy relations rather than a sign of mutual confidence. Sadat visited Moscow in October 1971 and February 1972 to settle differences, mainly regarding Egypt's military needs for an offensive operation to liberate Sinai. The Soviet procrastination and reluctance to supply Egypt with its needs, combined with a growing grumbling among the officers' corps against the heavy presence and of Soviet military personnel within the military, were apparently the main driving forces behind his decision to reduce Egypt's dependence on the USSR (which had never cultivated Sadat and would probably have preferred in 1970 to see Ali Sabri elected). In July 1972 he unilaterally terminated the services of an estimated 15,000–20,000 Soviet experts, including all the military ones. He later explained that the main reason for that drastic step was the Russians' unwillingness to give him a free hand and unlimited support in his preparations for war against Israel and to remove their involvement in, or even control of, Egyptian decision-making. His surprising step, however, was also a message of goodwill toward the US, aimed at tempting Washington to come to terms with Cairo over possible settlement of the conflict with Israel, but to no avail. Washington was still unwilling to take an active role in such context, perceiving the gap between Israel and the Arabs too wide to bridge. Despite the blow to the Soviet stature in the Middle East, in 1972–1973 relations were improved and the USSR resumed full military aid especially during the War of 1973.

From a historical perspective, it is clear that Sadat had no illusions as to the inability of his armed forces to liberate Sinai. Yet almost three years of futile diplomacy, primarily aimed at bringing the US to play an active role in forcing Israel out of Sinai, brought him to the conclusion that only a major military operation could break the diplomatic stalemate and the "no war no peace" mode, would change the strategic balance with Israel, revitalizing the diplomatic process. Although preparations for war continued since 1971, specific steps toward an Egyptian-Syrian coordinated offensive began in early

1973. It was cemented in the spring-summer of that year. In his directives to the Egyptian top military command, Sadat underlined the need to cross the canal and retain a symbolic strip along its eastern bank, to serve him as a bargaining chip. (For the October 1973 War, see ARAB-ISRAEL CONFLICT.)

In military terms, the War was not an Egyptian victory. Yet from a wider perspective, and from the Egyptian and Arab perception, it was a great achievement: Egyptian forces had won battles, displayed impressive capabilities of military planning and leadership and thus restored their pride and honor. Furthermore they had forcibly recovered part of occupied Sinai, including the vital eastern shore of the SUEZ CANAL, and broken the political deadlock. A major achievement was the coordination with Saudi Arabia and imposition, in the midst of the OIL embargo on the US and Holland, threatening to reduce oil production unless Israel had withdrawn from all occupied Arab territories. This caused panic in the West, putting Israel under tremendous international pressure. This was Sadat's achievement, Sadat's victory, and his prestige was at its peak, both in Egypt and in other Arab countries.

Sadat now sought to resume, on the basis of the new situation created, negotiations with Israel. He did this increasingly and indeed almost exclusively with US mediation. However, after two partial and separate settlements reached in January 1974 and September 1975 following protracted, US-mediated negotiations, no further progress was achieved. The deadlock was broken in November 1977 by Sadat's dramatic visit to Israel. In his meetings with Israeli leaders and his public address to a solemn meeting of the Knesset, Sadat offered complete peace and normal relations against a total withdrawal from all territories occupied in 1967 and an agreed, negotiated solution to the problem of the PALESTINE ARABS. In substance, his proposals were thus not different from previous positions held by Egypt and other moderate Arab states. His great achievement was the psychological breakthrough of meeting the Israelis—longtime demonized and boycotted—face to face, his spelling out what before had at best been implied: his willingness for coexistence with Israel—though still not full peace—which he defined as "no more war." Indeed, Sadat sought to attain Israeli acceptance of the principle of withdrawal from all occupied Arab territories which would enable him to negotiate for Egypt alone, without waiting for an all-Arab consensus. He made it clear, though, that he would not conclude a separate peace with Israel but would consider an eventual agreement as a first step toward a general Arab-Israel settlement. (For the negotiations that followed, the "Camp David Agreements" of September 1978 and the Egypt-Israel peace Treaty of March 1979—see EGYPT and ARAB-ISRAEL PEACEMAKING.)

The official normalization of relations went into effect in January 1980 and Ambassadors were exchanged in February. Sadat did not live to see the completion of Israel's withdrawal in April 1982. He had received the Nobel Prize, jointly with Premier Menachem BEGIN of Israel, in December 1978 (after the Camp David Agreements, before the Peace Treaty), as well as several European and American medals and prizes, some of them posthumously. Sadat's relations with Israel's leaders soon cooled down, going through several crises. Negotiations on an interim autonomous regime for the Palestinians of the WEST BANK and GAZA STRIP soon stalled and were discontinued. Israel's formal annexation of East JERUSALEM, in July 1980, was resented by Sadat, as were Israel's air raids on the Iraqi nuclear reactor, in June 1981, and military escalation between Israel and the Palestinian military buildup in Lebanon in July of that year.

Sadat's moves toward peace with Israel led the Arab world to denounce and ostracize Egypt, and him personally (see EGYPT). Sadat bore this severance of Egypt from the Arab family of nations—which was never complete, relations in many fields continuing unofficially—and the personal defamation accompanying it with an angry disappointment and a show of pride. He refused with contempt to abrogate his agreements with Israel in return for the restoration of Egypt to its natural place within the Arab world and generous Arab financial aid, insisting that it was the Arab states who needed Egypt, and not vice versa.

After 1979, Sadat continued to enhance relations with the US, encouraging it to play a crucial, near-exclusive, mediating role in the peace process. During his rule, Egypt also became increasingly dependent on US aid. Sadat received US Presidents Nixon and Carter in Egypt, visiting the US in October 1975 and several times later. In 1979–1980 he became a partner to wider US strategy plans, agreeing to pro-

vide low-profile facilities for a planned US "Rapid Deployment Force" (which was not fully implemented). His relations with the USSR continued to decline and in 1976 Sadat abrogated the Treaty of Friendship. In 1977 he recalled Egypt's Ambassador, leaving it represented at a lower level. He later expelled several Soviet diplomats, and in September 1981 requested the withdrawal of the Soviet Ambassador and the closure of the Military Attache's office—all unfriendly gestures.

At home, Sadat continued his policy of the political and economic liberalization and de-Nasserization. He gradually dismantled the single-party system, allowing in 1975 the formation of "platforms," i.e., organized factions, within the Arab Socialist Union, and late in 1976 their transformation into full-fledged parties. In 1978 he formed his own party, the "National Democratic Party," which soon became the government and absorbed the ASU. In the executive, no further major upheavals occurred. Sadat served as his own Prime Minister in 1973–1974 and thereafter appointed loyal second-rank associates to that post. He dismissed Vice-President SHAFE'I in 1975, replacing him with the Commander of the Air Force, Husni MUBARAK. He replaced his Defense Minister — considered the most important man after the President—several times. Sadat himself was re-elected President in 1976, with no rival candidate.

The main issue that clouded Sadat's last years—and his record and memory—was the complex one of Egypt's economic and social problems, the inability of his liberalization to fulfill the high-pitched expectations pinned on it and solve the country's basic problems. The growing disappointment with Sadat's policies was aggravated by that policy's negative side-effects: an increasing relapse into the inequality of a free enterprise society; the emergence of a new class of profiteers flaunting their wealth in visible contrast to the poverty of large parts of the population; and a great deal of spreading corruption and nepotism.

Sadat and his policies, both socioeconomic and those concerning Israel, were denounced by the left, the Nasserists, the extreme Islamists, and various intellectuals. Sadat himself, aware of his inability to solve the socioeconomic problems facing Egypt, turned mainly to foreign affairs. In the last years of his presidency he tightened his regime, taking harsher measures against his adversaries on the leftists and Nasserist left and the Islamic right, including an extensive campaign of imprisonment and a purge in September 1981. (For Sadat's measures against his critics and the radical Islamic groups, see ISLAMIC FUNDAMENTALISM, EGYPT.)

By 1980, Sadat's charisma, his paternalistic leadership, his ebullient command of popular support, declined during his last years. He had also gradually abandoned the simple life style that had made him popular, adopting a more imperial style of grandeur. Ramified activities of his family were disliked. His wife, Jihan, whom he had married in 1951 after divorcing his first wife—Jihan's mother was of English origin—seemed personally popular—yet her increasing involvement in active public life was not. When Sadat was murdered in October 1981 by Islamic extremists during a parade on the anniversary of the October War of 1973, there were few signs of genuine mourning. His memory as a leader and a statesman who had shaped Egypt's history, seems to be dimmed and not very actively cultivated.

Sadat wrote a few books on the Revolution of 1952, with autobiographical features (*Revolt on the Nile*, 1957), an autobiography (*In Search of Identity*, 1977–1978), and other memoirs.

S.A.D.R. (SAHARAN ARAB DEMOCRATIC REPUBLIC) see WESTERN SAHARA CONFLICT.

al-SADR, MUSSA (1928–1978) Lebanese-Iranian Shi'i religious and political leader. Sadr triggered and led the social and political awakening of the Shi'i community in Lebanon since the 1960s. Born in QOM, IRAN, to a family of Shi'i religious scholars of Lebanese origin, Sadr received both a traditional Islamic and a secular education, graduating from Tehran University. He taught Islamic Law and Logic of the seminary at Qom, and in 1954 moved to IRAQ to continue his religious education. In 1959 he moved to Tyre, Lebanon, where he began mobilizing the local Shi'i population with the aim of enhancing the political influence of both the traditional Shi'i leadership and the leftist, ideological parties, which attracted many Shi'i youth. Sadr established orphanages, medical facilities and schools for his community, and in December 1967 established, for the first time in the modern history of SYRIA and LEBANON, a Shi'i-Islamic Higher Council, to which he was elected Chairman in May 1969 (only in March

1994 was it reported that his deputy since 1974, Shaykh Muhammad Mahdi Shams al-Din, replaced him as Chairman of the Council). These activities won Sadr wide support of the rank and file of Lebanon's Shi'is, and he was often referred to as IMAM. Politically, Sadr supported the integrity of the Lebanese state and its basic structure, but demanded modifications to accommodate the growing needs of the Shi'i community, considered by many to be the largest in Lebanon, and raise its status. To achieve this end he organized political strikes and rallies, employing, as a vehicle for social change, a powerful Shi'i historic-religious myth, namely the martyrdom of Hussein ben Ali in the Battle of Karbala (680), which he reinterpreted as a symbol of active resistance against the oppressors and not mere passivity and obedience, as it had been interpreted until then.

Sadr became an ally of Syria, facilitating in 1973 the recognition of the ALAWIS in Lebanon (and consequently, those in Syria) as Shi'ite Muslims, thus enhancing the political legitimacy of the Alawi-led regime in Syria (see SYRIA) and winning the Lebanese Shi'is' foreign patronage, for the first time in their history. Considering the harsh, at times even violent PLO rule in South Lebanon, an area with a clear Shi'i majority, Sadr opposed the PLO. In 1974 he founded and led a movement for the advancement and defense of the Shi'i community, originally conceived as a mainly social and non-political body called "The Disinherited" (*al-Mahrumin*). In 1975 this movement grew increasingly political and turned into the Shi'i AMAL organization, with its own militia, of which Sadr became the first and main leader. In August 1978 Sadr disappeared while on a mission in LIBYA. The Libyans claimed that he had departed for Italy, but the Lebanese Shi'is never accepted this explanation, believing that Sadr was either detained and still imprisoned in Libya, or murdered by the Libyans. His disappearance caused a grave crisis between Libya and Lebanon in general, and the Lebanese Shi'is in particular. The latter venerate Sadr's memory as a martyr.

al-SA'ID, NURI (1888–1958) Iraqi officer and politician, the most prominent figure in the HASHEMITE Iraqi oligarchy from the foundation of modern IRAQ in 1921 to the military coup that toppled the monarchy in 1958. Many times Prime Minister of Iraq, al-Sa'id's long political career, his ardent British orientation, statesmanship and image as "the strong man" of the Iraqi regime even when not in office, made him one of the most influential Arab leaders who left his imprint on the shaping of the Twentieth Century Middle East.

Born in Baghdad to a Muslim-Sunni family of mixed Arab-Kurdish descent, Nuri Sa'id graduated from the Istanbul Military Academy and became an officer in the Ottoman army. Active, but not prominent, in pre-World War I Arab nationalist associations, Nuri al-Sa'id deserted the Ottoman army during World War I, joined Sharif HUSSEIN's ARAB REVOLT in 1916 and became Chief of Staff in Amir Feisal's army (commanded by his brother-in-law, Ja'far al-Askari). He remained attached to Feisal after the war and became the first Chief of Staff of the Iraqi army in 1921. He was Minister of Defense 1922–1924 and 1926–1928. In 1930 he became Prime Minister for the first time, in which capacity he negotiated the Iraqi treaty of 1930 with BRITAIN which terminated the MANDATE, and founded a party—al-Ahd (The Covenant) to support him in Parliament. Nuri Sa'id was Prime Minister 1930–1932, 1939–1940, 1941–1944, 1946–1947, 1949, 1950–1952, 1954–1957, 1958, heading fourteen governments, and often held other or additional ministerial offices, particularly as Foreign or Defense Minister. After the defeat of the Rashid Ali movement in 1941, Nuri Sa'id was Iraq's strong leader, whether in or out of office, and the typical representative of the Hashemite royal family. In February 1958 he became Prime Minister of the short-lived ARAB UNITY of IRAQ and JORDAN. Nuri al-Sa'id was murdered in Baghdad during the coup of July 1958.

Nuri al-Sa'id persistently followed a policy which sought to establish a firm alliance with Britain, and loyally supported the Hashemite dynasty—though in the late 1930s he was allied for some time with the anti-British and anti-Hashemite junta of officers ruling Iraq behind the scene, and apparently flirted with Germany in 1940. He feared and hated Communism and distrusted the USSR. In Arab affairs he was keenly conscious of Iraq's age-old rivalry with EGYPT. In January 1943 he submitted to the British government his scheme for a Federation of the Fertile Crescent (excluding Egypt and the Arabian Peninsula) under the Iraqi throne (with a measure of autonomy for the Jews of Palestine and the Christians of LEBANON) but it met with strong Arab opposition,

particularly Egyptian, triggering inter-Arab talks on the essence and ways to implement the idea of Arab unity, which eventually led to the foundation of the League of Arab states in March 1945. Having lost regional leadership to Egypt, Sa'id kept trying to acquire a central role for Iraq by conducting antagonistic policies toward Egypt—primarily on the Palestine question—and nurturing the idea of an Iraqi-Syrian unity through links with Syrian supporters of such unity. As an ardent supporter of Britain and sworn enemy of Communism, Sa'id was the architect of the Baghdad Pact (see CENTO which he signed with Turkey in February 1958, throwing the Arab world into an unprecedented turmoil, ideological political struggle with Egypt over hegemony in the Fertile Crescent, and in fact, in the Arab world as a whole.)

In domestic affairs Nuri Sa'id promoted administrative efficiency and economic planning. He was a conservative, even an autocrat, and did not believe that parliamentary democracy was a suitable form of government for Iraq. In his heyday Iraq was in effect a police state—though his regime seems mild and rational compared to the situation under the Hashemite military successors. During his last years Nuri Sa'id was not in tune with the social and political forces sweeping the Arab world and seemed to have little understanding of them.

al-SA'IQA   see PALESTINIAN GUERRILLA ORGANIZATIONS.

SALEH, ALI ABDALLAH (b.1942)   Yemeni officer and politician, President of YEMEN since 1978. A son of the Hashed (ZEIDI) tribes, Saleh was a professional army officer who became prominent in 1977–1978. A battalion commander with the rank of major, and from 1977 military commander of the Ta'iz region, he helped Ali Hussuein Ghashmi, the Chairman of the Military Council, following the assassination of President Ibrahim al-Hamdi in October 1977, to become president in April 1978, and to consolidate his power by suppressing a rebellion of rival officers that same month. When Ghashmi was assassinated in June 1978, Saleh became a member of the Presidential Council as well as Chief of Staff and Deputy Commander-in-Chief. He was also promoted to the rank of Lieutenant-Colonel. A month later he was made President. He purged the officers' corps of opposing and rebellious elements, escaped several assassination attempts, and succeeded in consolidating his power and giving Yemen, torn for years by factional rivalries and internal violence, a period of relative stability until 1990. The establishment of united Yemen that year created a source of major friction between the former leaderships. Saleh managed to control this through military and political means. After suppressing the war with secessionist SOUTH YEMEN (1994), Saleh re-consolidated his rule over Yemen. In two parliamentary election rounds in united Yemen (1993 and 1997) Saleh managed to create the impression of popular support for his regime in both parts of Yemen.

At first considered dependent on and subservient to SAUDI ARABIA, and faced in February 1979 with a South Yemeni invasion and warlike activities, Saleh succeeded in restoring a delicate balance between Saudi Arabia (on whose financial aid Yemen remained dependent) and South Yemen (with whom he achieved a reconciliation). However, Saleh continued to regard South Yemen (PDRY) as a potential risk for the stability and security of Yemen. In foreign affairs Saleh followed a pronouncedly neutralist policy. Yemen remained balanced between the US, which supported it against South Yemen, and the USSR (which had in the past supplied most of Yemen's military equipment). He visited Moscow in October 1981 and concluded a Treaty of Friendship and Cooperation with the USSR in October 1984. In inter-Arab affairs he also followed a policy of low-profile neutrality. In domestic matters he endeavored to keep a balance between the conservative tribal federations and leftist urban factions. In his first two years in power he tried to reconcile the underground leftist "National Democratic Front" and even invited it to join the government. No final agreement was reached, and Saleh soon felt secure enough to drop the offer and continue on a more median course. After preparing the skeleton of a ruling party, in 1982 the General People's Congress (GPC) was announced and Saleh was nominated its Secretary-General. The formation of united Yemen (1990) (see YEMEN ARAB REPUBLIC) was to a large extent the result of Saleh's efforts aimed at eliminating threats from the south. In 1990 he took on the responsibilities of the financial and foreign relations difficulties of PDRY, resulting from the failure of its main sponsor, the USSR, to bring the long-yearned

for unity to realization. Saleh led the Yemen forces against the South Yemeni forces during the War (1994), securing the continued existence of a conservative united Yemen.

al-SALLAL, ABDALLAH (b. 1917) Yemeni officer and politician, leader of the 1962 revolution. President of the Yemen Republic 1962–1967. Son of a lower-class ZEIDI family, in the 1930s Sallal was sent to the Baghdad Military Academy, from which he graduated in 1938. Upon his return he was suspected of anti-regime activities and detained for some time, but was then allowed to resume his army career. He took part in the abortive coup of 1948 and was sentenced to death. The sentence was commuted to seven years imprisonment and he was released after a few years. In 1955 he was appointed Governor of Hudeida, fostered close links to Crown Prince al-Badr, who made him commander of his guard and of the newly established military academy in 1959. When al-Badr became IMAM-King in September 1962, Sallal, then a Major, became commander of the Royal Guard and also apparently, commander-in-chief of the army. He led the military coup that same month that toppled the monarchy, became President of the Republic and led the Republican camp in the Civil War that followed. He was concurrently also Prime Minister 1962–1963 and 1966–1967.

Sallal was strongly pro-Egyptian and depended on Egyptian support, not only in the conduct of the civil war, in which an Egyptian expeditionary force was the main guarantee of the Republic's survival, but also in the frequent factional struggles within the Republican camp and army. He advocated a union of YEMEN with EGYPT and concluded an agreement for Yemen to join the abortive Egypt-IRAQ federation of July 1964.

Sallal was immersed in factional controversies and had little influence on the officers' corps, and even less on the tribes, and was anathema to the Royalist camp. When the Egyptians felt compelled to seek a settlement of the Yemen conflict with the Royalists, they removed him in April 1965, and took him to Egypt, into house arrest. However, when in September 1966 he was needed in Yemen, to manifest Egypt's commitment to the Yemeni Revolution, he was reinstated in San'a and resumed power of the Premiership and the Presidency. When Egypt withdrew its expeditionary force in 1967, Sallal was over-thrown in a bloodless coup in November 1967. He went into exile to Baghdad and lost all influence on Yemeni affairs. Late in 1981, apparently no longer considered a dangerous rival, he was allowed to return to Yemen.

SANJABI, KARIM (1904–1995) Iranian politician. Son of Sardar Nasser Sanjalu, a leader of the Sanjabi tribes. In 1949 Sanjabi was a founding member of the NATIONAL FRONT OF IRAN (*Jebhe-ye Melli-e Iran*), a coalition of Parties and political groups. During the premiership of Dr. Muhammad MOSSADDEQ, Sanjabi served as Minister of Education. He was a member of the Iranian delegation to the International Court in the Hague during the Iranian-British oil concession dispute. In 1977, under his leadership, the NFI challenged the regime, demanding political freedom in December 1978. At the peak of the unrest, which ended with the victory of the Islamic revolution, Sanjabi was invited by the Shah and offered the post of Prime Minister. However, his demands for far reaching political reforms were turned down. Shortly after that, Sanjabi met KHOMEINI in Paris and declared his support for the plan to bring down the regime in Iran. Following the victory of Khomenei in February 1979, Sanjabi was appointed Foreign Minister in the interim government of Mehdi BAZARGAN. However, disagreement with the fundamentalist ideas of the new Islamic regime led Sanjabi to resign in April 1979 and dissociate himself from it. He left IRAN secretly in 1981 and settled in the US, where he published his memoirs in 1989.

SAN REMO CONFERENCE Convened in April 1920 by the principal allied powers victorious in World War I (BRITAIN, FRANCE, Italy, Japan, Greece and Belgium) to decide on the Turkish peace treaty and certain other matters. The San Remo Conference, *inter alia*, assigned the MANDATES which the nascent League of Nations had decided in 1919 to impose on Arab territories previously dominated by the OT-TOMAN EMPIRE. It gave to France the Mandate for SYRIA and LEBANON, to Britain those for Mesopotamia (IRAQ) and Palestine, the latter to be administered in accordance with the BALFOUR DECLARATION. The League of Nations formally confirmed these Mandates in 1922. Simultaneously with the San Remo Conference, Britain and France concluded an accord on

French participation in the future exploitation of OIL in Iraq. Arab spokesmen denounced the decisions of the San Remo Conference as contrary to previously promised independence to the Arabs by the Allied Powers during the war.

SANUSSIS, SANUSSIYYA Islamic religious order founded in Mecca in 1837 by Muhammad ibn Ali al-Sanussi, of Algerian origin. A Sunni order of the Maleki *madhhab* or school dominant in North Africa, it aimed at purging Islam of unorthodox accretions and returning to the original teachings of the Prophet and the Qur'an. Though orthodox-fundamentalist, the founder and the Sanussis were influenced by certain aspects of Islamic mysticism—but they kept their rituals simple and austere and discouraged ceremonies of ecstasy, dancing and singing, as practised by the DERVISH ORDERS.

In 1841, the founder went to EGYPT and from there to Benghazi and Tripoli to teach and spread his doctrine. He was more successful among the Bedouin, especially those of Cyrenaica, than among the peasants and town's people, and set up a network of lodges (singular: *zawiya*), i.e., centers of residence, prayer and teaching, for the Sanussi Brothers (*Ikhwan*). The Mother Lodge, *al-Zawiya al-Baida*, on the central Cyrenaican plateau, was founded in 1843; the center shifted to the Jaghbub oasis in the Western Desert when the founder settled there in 1856, and later, about 1895, to Kufra. The founder died in 1859 and was succeeded by his son, al-Sayyid al-Mahdi al-Sanussi, under whose leadership the Sanussis spread also in SUDAN and the Sahara. After his death, in 1902, the order was headed by al-Sayyid Ahmad al-Sharif al-Sanussi, the nephew of the founder.

In the early twentieth century the Sanussis, dominating the Cyrenaica countryside, developed into a political force, as well. When Italy invaded and occupied LIBYA in 1911, the Sanussis mounted strong resistance which continued as a guerrilla war and merged from 1914 until World War I, as TURKEY saw the Sanussis as allies and aided them. However, a rival Sanussi leader, al-Sayyid Muhammad Idris al-SANUSSI, the founder's grandson and the second leader's son, decided to support the British and their allies (including Italy), and raised a Sanussi force in Egypt to fight on their side. In 1916 he was recognized by BRITAIN as the "Grand Sanussi," the chief of the Sanussi order. Idris overcame the rival leadership, and Ahmad al-Sharif escaped to Turkey, never to return.

Idris al-Sanussi became King of independent Libya in 1951. His reign was ultra-conservative and while he continued to rely mainly on Sanussis in Cyrenaica, there was frequent friction between him and the nationalists in Tripolitania. Even with Idris as King, Libya was not a Sanussi country, the Sanussis were only one group of the population, and not the largest one; but they were the mainstay of the regime, particularly in Cyrenaica. The King's position was undermined in 1963 by the abolition of the federal structure of Libya and the imposition of a unitary regime dominated by Tripoli. The continuity of the Sanussi reign seemed fragile since Idris had no children. He was deposed by a military coup on 1 September 1969, led by Colonel Mu'ammar al-QADHAFI. In the years of independence the strength and influence of the Sanussis declined—perhaps inevitably, with the increasing modernization of Libya and the development of its OIL economy. This decline has accelerated and intensified since the revolution of 1969 and the disappearance of the King and the Sanussi establishment that had been prominent in government and the services. Qadhafi and his regime have not taken institutional steps formally to ban the Sanussis order, but the centralist character of the regime and its strict, all-embracing control seem to have eliminated the public-political influence of the Sanussis (see also LIBYA).

al-SANUSSI, al-SAYYID MUHAMMAD IDRIS

(1890–1983)   Head of the SANUSSI order in LIBYA-Cyrenaica, King of Libya 1951–1969. Born at Jaghbub, Cyrenaica, the grandson of the founder of the Sanussi order, Idris established contacts with the British in Egypt in 1914 and stayed in EGYPT during World War I, and while the Sanussi's guerrilla war against the Italians became part of Ottoman Turkey's war, he recruited in Egypt a Sanussi force on the side of Britain and its allies. In 1916 Britain recognized him as the "Grand Sanussi," the leader of the order—in place of his uncle al-Sayyid Ahmad Sharif al-Sanussi who fought on the other side. After the victory of the allies, Italy recognized him, in the Rajma Agreement of 1920, as Amir of Cyrenaica heading a self-governing regime in the interior centered on the Sanussi oases of Jaghbub and Kufra. In 1922

Sanussi accepted the additional title of Emir of Tripolitania offered to him by the nationalists of that region—against Italy's wish. His agreement with the Italians was anyway half-hearted and short-lived. While the Sanussis resumed their rebellion and guerrilla war, he left in 1922 for exile in Cairo, and remained there for twenty years.

When Italy entered World War II Sanussi called upon all Libyans to co-operate with the Allies in a joint effort to drive out the Italians and initiated the recruitment of a Sanussi force which took part in the North African campaign. In return the British recognized his claim to head an independent or autonomous Cyrenaica. After the allied victory, and while discussions on the future of Libya were still going on, he proclaimed himself in 1949 *amir* of Cyrenaica—with British support, and under a provisional British military government. In 1951 the crown of a united Libya was offered to him and on 7 October 1951 the National Assembly proclaimed him King of Libya. He ascended the throne on 24 December 1951 when Libya became independent.

His reign was ultra-conservative and while he continued relying on his Sanussis in Cyrenaica, there was frequent friction between him and the nationalists in Tripolitania. His position was weakened in 1963 by the abolition of the federal structure of Libya and the imposition of a Unitarian régime dominated by Tripoli. The stability of his reign seemed to depend on his person, since he had no children. King Idris al-Sanussi was deposed by a military coup on 1 September 1969; he was abroad at the time and did not fight for his throne. He spent the rest of his days in exile in Greece and Egypt.

SARKIS, ELIAS (1924–1985)   President of LEBANON 1976–1982. A MARONITE Christian jurist and economist, he served as Governor of the Central Bank 1967–1976 before being elected as President. Born to a middle-class non-prominent family, Sarkis was educated at French-Catholic institutions in Beirut. He graduated in Law at the Jesuit St. Joseph University. From 1953 he was a judge at the Audit Office (*cour des comptes*). Involved in an investigation of irregularities in the Defense Ministry, he came to the attention of President Fu'ad Shihab (1902–1973, 1958–1964). He was transferred to the President's Office in 1959. He played an important part in turning it into a powerful institution. He collaborated with the secret services developed by President Shihab. In 1962 he became its director-general and in 1967, Governor of the Central Bank for nine years during increasingly difficult economic times. In 1970 he was a candidate for the Presidency, supported by the "Shihabist" camp but lost to Suleiman Franjiyyeh by one vote. In 1976, SYRIA, then in de facto occupation of most of Lebanon, strongly supported his election as President in May, after the amendment of the Lebanese Constitution to allow early elections.

During his Presidency, the Civil War that had officially ended in October 1976 resumed and escalated. The rival armed militias and the Syrian army dominated most of the country. ISRAEL and the PALESTINE LIBERATION ORGANIZATION (PLO) were fighting bitterly in the south. In June 1982 this culminated in the Israeli invasion in the last months of his term. The Civil War had severe consequences for the Lebanese state:its army disintegrated; the government was unable to function properly, virtually losing control, and the President did not control much more than his own palace. Sarkis' main concern throughout his presidency was to bring about full implementation of the Riyad and Cairo summits' resolutions meant to put an end to the civil war, primarily by enforcing restrictions on armed Palestinian presence and activity in South Lebanon. However, he was not given much support from Syria, especially after SADAT's visit to JERUSALEM which made it incumbent on Asad to keep the PLO on his side in his efforts to isolate Egypt. Sarkis, while respected, was therefore not an effective President, although he managed to keep the government apparatus united and prevented the total collapse of the Lebanese state. Although he did his best to reconcile the warring factions and work out a peace settlement, he refrained from expressing forceful opinions or taking clear-cut positions in the constant struggle between the factions, coalitions and militias. However, toward the end of his term he demonstrated growing support for Bashir JU-MAYYIL as his successor. Out of frustration, he was on the verge of resigning several times (e.g., in July 1978). When his term expired in September 1982, he retired and in the three remaining years of his life took no further part in public affairs.

SA'UD, HOUSE OF AND DYNASTY The ruling dynasty in the largest country of the Arabian

Peninsula, SAUDI ARABIA, giving the country its name. The family, of the Anaiza tribe, first ruled the Dar'iyya area of Najd. Muhammad Ibn Sa'ud, who ruled Dar'iyya 1726-1765, adopted the WAHHABIYA doctrine and set up a Wahhabi state in 1745. As he expanded his area of control he spread the new faith over large parts of the Peninsula. His son, ABDEL AZIZ (ruled 1766–1803) and his grandson Sa'ud (ruled 1803–1814) extended their power as far as the Syrian and Iraqi borders, raided the border areas and ransacked also Mecca and Madina. Under Abdallah Ibn Sa'ud (ruled 1814–1818), the Saudis were defeated by Muhammad Ali of EGYPT, acting on behalf of the Ottoman Sultan, and Abdallah was captured, brought to Istanbul and executed there. With that the first Saudi state came to an end. Egyptian inability to control the heartland of the Arabian Peninsula enabled the Saudi House to continue ruling al-Riyadh area. This limited rule under the Egyptian shadow kept on until 1843. The main Saudi combatant against the Egyptian-Ottoman efforts of re-capturing the Saudi areas was Feisal ibn Turki (ruled: 1834–1837; 1843–1865). From 1843 under his leadership the House of Saud reasserted itself. After the death of Feisal and mainly due to fraternal rivalries, the dynasty declined again. This decline was also due to military efforts by the Ottomans and the rival House of RASHID of the Shammar tribe causing the Saudis to limit their control only to the Dar'iyya-Riyadh area.

In the 1880s the Rashid clan gained strength. In 1890–1891 it defeated the contemporary head of the Saudis, Abdel Rahman Al Saud, and conquered the Dar'iyya-Riyadh area. Survivors of the House of Sa'ud found refuge in KUWAIT, among them young SA'UD IBN ABDEL AZIZ (1880–1953, ruled 1902–1953). The latter resumed the fight and regained control of Riyadh in 1902. He soon began expanding his realm. In 1913 he took the al-Hassa region on the PERSIAN GULF and thus came into contact with the sphere of British interests and domination. In 1915 he made a pact with BRITAIN. In the course of his expansion, he beat the Rashidis, who surrendered in 1921, and clashed with HUSSEIN; the HASHEMITE Sharif of Mecca and King of HIJAZ. In 1924 Ibn Sa'ud conquered Hijaz and deposed the Hashemites. Henceforth the House of Sa'ud ruled most of the Arabian Peninsula (except the southern, south-eastern and some of the eastern parts).

Ibn Sa'ud, who named his Kingdom Saudi Arabia in 1932, died in 1953. His eldest son Sa'ud ibn Abdel Aziz (1902–1969) succeeded him. Sa'ud's reign was clouded by a deep rift with his half-brother FEISAL IBN ABDEL AZIZ (1904–1975). In 1958 he was forced to transfer substantial authority to Feisal. In 1964 he was deposed of and succeeded by Feisal. He went into exile and died in 1969. Feisal ruled until 1975, when he was assassinated by one of his nephews. He was succeeded by his half-brother Khaled ibn Abdel Aziz (1912–1982). Following Khaled's death, in 1982, his half-brother Fahd ibn Abdel Aziz (b. 1921) became King, with another half-brother, Abdallah ibn Abdel Aziz (b. 1923), as heir apparent. These four successions consolidated the principle laid down by Ibn Sa'ud—the Kingship was to pass on to his sons, by and large according to seniority.

Other key figures among Ibn Sa'ud's surviving sons (he had over forty) are Prince Sultan (b. 1924), Defense Minister since 1962 and one of the Deputy Prime Ministers since 1982, and Prince Na'if (b. 1934), Minister of Interior since 1975—both full brothers of King Fahd, members of a powerful group of brothers called, after their mother, the seven Sudairis. Other surviving sons of Ibn Sa'ud serve as Ministers, provincial governors etc. and some are active in business. Many members of the third generation, Ibn Sa'ud's grandsons, are also active, and some are prominent in business, government and army positions. Of King Feisal's sons, for instance, one, Abdallah (b. 1921), was Minister of Interior (1953–1960); one, Sa'ud (b. 1941), has been Foreign Minister since 1975; one, Turki (b. 1945) is Director of Foreign Intelligence.

Things are no doubt slowly changing in Saudi Arabia. New strata of educated professionals, "technocrats" and businessmen are growing and political influence is being spread more widely. Some members of the new elite belong to the House of Sa'ud and are waiting in the political wings for their turn in succession. In the future the current line of succession will exhaust itself, raising the issue of future successions. These undoubtedly will combine the old rules laid by Abdel Aziz with the demands of a modernizing country.

SA'UD, IBN ABDEL AZIZ (1902–1969) King of Saudi Arabia 1953–1964. Eldest son of King AB-

DALLAH Abdel Aziz (after the death of his brother Turki in 1919). With the consolidation of the Saudi Kingdom, his father named him heir apparent in 1932 (with the understanding that his half-brother Feisal would be second in line) and Viceroy of Najd. When Ibn Sa'ud died in 1953, Sa'ud mounted the throne and also became Prime Minister, despite reports of sharpening rivalry between him and Feisal. In 1958 Sa'ud was compelled by the council of leading princes to hand over actual executive power to Feisal after the eruption of fraternal succession rivalries drawing on several sources: a severe financial crisis, despite increasing oil revenues, as a result of extravagance and unbridled spending; deteriorating relations with EGYPT, and an official accusation made by President ABDEL-NASSER of an assassination attempt financed and designed by Sa'ud.

Sa'ud's poor health also made him travel abroad frequently. In spite of the change, Sa'ud continued struggling. He made a partial comeback and took the Premiership in 1960, but in 1962 he had to restore it to Feisal. In 1964, he demanded that Feisal surrender his powers. In the crisis that ensued, Feisal gained the upper hand. On 2 November 1964, the Council of "Ulama" (Muslim Sages) deposed Sa'ud and declared Feisal king in his place. Sa'ud went into exile, at first in Europe; in 1966 he settled in Egypt and allowed Nasser to use him in his conflict with Feisal. When Nasser toned down his inter-Arab activities after 1967 and strove for a reconciliation with Feisal, Sa'ud was pushed into the background and ceased public and political activities. He died in exile in 1969.

SAUDI ARABIA (al-Mamlaka al-Arabiyya al-Sa'udiyya). A Kingdom in the Arabian peninsula, informally also known as **Saudia**). Saudi Arabia borders on JORDAN, IRAQ, the PERSIAN GULF principalities (KUWAIT, BAHRAIN, QATAR, the UAE, OMAN), Yemen and SOUTH YEMEN. The country has two coasts: in the east, the Persian Gulf and in the west, the Red Sea. Saudi Arabia does not have an outlet to open water in the Arab sea. The borders with Kuwait were defined in the Uqair agreement of 1922, those with Iraq and Jordan in the Hadda and Bahra Agreements of 1925—all arranged with British help (as were several provisional accords preceding them). On the Kuwaiti and Iraqi borders there were two "Neutral Zones" where no agreement could be reached. In

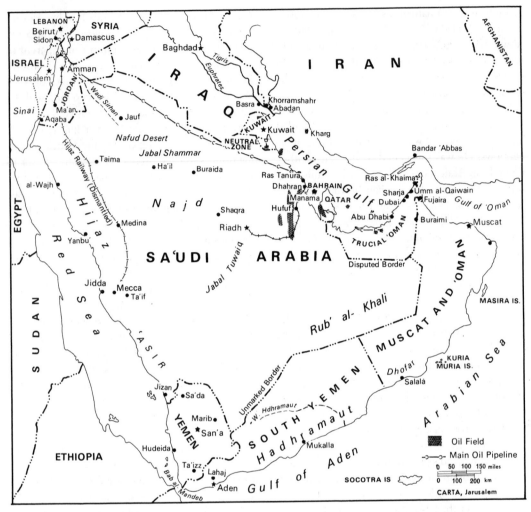

Map of the Arabian Peninsula

1969 and 1981 respectively it was agreed to abolish and divide these zones sharing the oil revenues. The border with YEMEN was settled in 1934, after a war, but some disagreements remain. Old disputes with South Yemen were added to the agenda with the Yemeni unification in 1990. On the borders with the Persian Gulf principalities there are also some disagreements. These are now dormant and have been deliberately played down in recent years.

Demographically, there were, until the 1960s, widely different estimates as to the total population in the kingdom. A census taken in 1964 was considered defective and was never published. A census of 1974 counted 7 million. In the late 1990s, the population has been estimated at some 19.5 million (including about 4.5 million foreign workers).

The indigenous population is Arabic speaking. The overwhelming majority are SUNNI-Muslims belonging to the Unitarian WAHHABI trend of the *Hanbali* school. An unknown number of Shi'ite Muslims live in the al-Hassa region (the north-eastern province). A small Yemenite *Zeidi* minority live in the Asir region. The majority of the population is of tribal background, and a decreasing part are still nomadic or semi-nomadic (estimated until the 1960s at twenty-five to thirty-five percent, but considered in the mid-1990s to be less than ten percent). The urban population is estimated at some seventy-five percent.

In the past, the economy was one of desert nomads engaged in camel raising (and raiding), with a few agricultural settlements near oases, and few towns with some commerce on the coasts and in the nearby hinterland. Fishing and shipping developed more on the Persian Gulf than on the Red Sea shore. For many years, a major source of income was the annual Muslim pilgrimage (*Hajj*) to the holy cities of Mecca and Medina (estimates as to the number of pilgrims from abroad in the 1920s and 1930s varied from 50,000 to over 200,000. In the 1960s it reached 200,000–375,000. From the late 1990s it has been approximately 2 million). Beginning with the 1940s, OIL production has become the major source of national and individual income and of development resources.

Political History: Saudi Arabia, under that name, emerged in 1932. In the earlier twentieth century the area now named Saudi Arabia was divided. In Najd, the central and northern part of the peninsula, the HOUSE OF SA'UD, which had re-established its rule of the central region, around al-Riyadh, in 1901–1902, was gradually expanding its domination (defeating the rival House of Rashid). In 1913 it had also added to its domain the al-Hassa region on the north-western coast of the Persian Gulf. The Saudi ruler, Abdel Aziz ibn Abdel Rahman "IBN SA'UD," was from 1915 allied with Great Britain, but stayed neutral in World War I. Since 1921 he assumed the title "Sultan of Najd and its Dependencies." The western part of what later became Saudi Arabia, HIJAZ, was under Turkish-Ottoman sovereignty. However, Turkey exercised actual control mainly in the towns and along the pilgrims' route to Mecca and Medina. In 1916, HUSSEIN Ibn Ali, the HASHEMITE Sharif of Mecca, rebelled with British aid and established himself as King of Hijaz. Clashes between Ibn Sa'ud and Hussein escalated into war in 1924. Ibn Sa'ud conquered Hijaz and deposed the Hashemites in 1925. In January 1926 he proclaimed himself King of Hijaz, too.

From 1926, Ibn Sa'ud consolidated his rule throughout most of the peninsula and integrated Hijaz. This was more developed than Najd and did not easily accept the Saudis' Wahhabi rules and customs. He appointed his son Sa'ud, the heir apparent Governor of Najd, and his son Feisal Viceroy as Governor of Hijaz. He set up a Consultative Council (*Majlis al-Shura*) of sheikhs and notables in Hijaz. BRITAIN recognized his independence in the Treaty of Jidda of 1927. In 1929–1930, he put down a rebellion of tribal chieftains and the *Ikhwan* ("Brethren"—the semi-settled military nuclei of the Wahhabis), who demanded the continuation of conquests beyond the northern borders.

Once stability had been achieved, Ibn Sa'ud proclaimed the union of the two parts of his kingdom, on 18 September 1932, as the "Kingdom of Saudi Arabia." In his continuing efforts to stabilize the country, he endeavored to settle the tribes, mainly around the oases. The establishment of Ikhwan settlements ceased after the suppression of their revolt. He allotted lands to sheikhs and wealthy merchants to encourage settlement. In 1947 he exempted them from paying rent on these lands. His attitude to the tribes was on the "carrot and the stick" pattern. He subsidized the sheikhs with large grants of money and took their women relatives for himself and his sons' wives. He harshly punished tribes which did not keep order, carried out traditional raids for plunder (*ghazzu*), or turned against him.

The conquest of Hijaz and the Holy Cities made the Saudi monarch the "Custodian of the Two Shrines" and Arabia a focus for all Islam. In 1926, Ibn Sa'ud convened an all-Islamic congress in Mecca. Nonetheless he rejected a proposal by Indian Muslims to turn Hijaz into an all-Islamic Protectorate and strained relations with EGYPT by barring the traditional Egyptian army escort for the Egyptian *Hajj* (pilgrimage) caravan, claiming there was no longer any need for such protection. In reality he was trying to prevent any competition with his rule over the Holy Places. Ibn Sa'ud concluded a series of friendship and non-aggression treaties with Britain conerning borders under the latter's rule: Transjordan (1933) and Bahrain (1936), as well as with Independent Iraq (1936) and Egypt (1936), settling also the 1926 dispute over the *Hajj* escort. But there was increasing tension between Saudi Arabia and Yemen. In the 1920s, Saudi Arabia gradually extended its protection to the Asir region, taking advantage of internal disputes in the ruling IDRISSI dynasty. In 1933, a revolt of Hassan al-Idrissi was put down and Ibn Sa'ud formally annexed Asir to his kingdom. Idrissi fled to Yemen where he received asylum as well as aid in organizing raids across its border. Yemen also disputed the Saudi annexation of Asir. In March 1934, Ibn Sa'ud declared war on Yemen and within a few weeks conquered large portions of the country, including the principal port of Hudeida. In June 1934, he signed a peace treaty agreeing to give up the occupied areas, evacuate Yemen and revert to the status quo. In 1937 he signed a friendship and non-aggression pact with Yemen.

In 1933, Ibn Sa'ud granted the first oil exploration rights to American companies against stiff British opposition: the Standard Oil Company of California, which was joined by the Texas Oil Company in 1934. The two companies jointly formed ARAMCO, the "Arabian American Oil Company." In 1948 two more giant companies joined—Standard of New Jersey, and Socony Vacuum. Oil was found in the Dhahran, Dammam, and Abqaiq areas. Commercial production began in 1938, but it increased significantly only after World War II, when it became the mainstay of the economy (see OIL).

In World War II Ibn Sa'ud was neutral, though he veered toward the Allies. Even when the Axis powers appeared victorious, he refused to support the anti-British revolt of Rashid Ali al-Kilani in Iraq (1941). He pointedly sent his son Mansur to Cairo on the eve of the battle of al-Alamein. He rejected German and Japanese requests for oil concessions. On account of the sharp decline in the number of pilgrims since the late 1930s, he requested—and received—financial aid from the Allies, mostly the USA (by September 1946 17.5 million in grants and loans). On 1 March 1945, Saudi Arabia joined the Allies, without formally declaring war, maintaining the neutrality of the Holy Places. This enabled it to join the UN as a charter member.

During this period, relations between Saudi Arabia and the US strengthened. A US diplomatic representation in the kingdom was established in 1940. Under a 1943 agreement the Americans in 1944–1946 built a large air base in Dhahran (with rights to use it for three years). In 1953 a US military mission began training the Saudi army and has not left the country since then. The US government also decided to lay an oil pipeline from Dhahran to the Mediterranean, in Lebanon (the Trans-Arabian Pipeline, or TAPLine. This was later built by the oil company and completed in 1950).

In February 1945, Ibn Sa'ud met President Roosevelt on board an American warship. At the meeting he stressed his attitude in support of the Palestinian Arab cause. Roosevelt seemed impressed. Saudi Arabia and the US continued to differ on the Palestine issue. Ibn Sa'ud opposed President Truman's proposal to permit the immigration to Pales-

tine of 100,000 Jewish survivors of the Holocaust (1946). Furthermore, he resented US support for the partition of Palestine (1947), and US aid to ISRAEL. He did not implement threats of retaliation against American interests, such as stopping the flow of oil. In 1949, the US representation in Jidda was raised to ambassadorial level. Under a defense treaty of 1951, US rights at the Dhahran base were extended for an additional five years. (These were extended again in 1956 until 1962.) The supply of American arms, training and military aid continued.

In increased inter-Arab relations Saudi Arabia took a moderately active part. In 1936, with the Palestinian issue becoming a focal point of Arab political and diplomatic activity, Saudi Arabia joined forces with Egypt. Together they created the non-Hashemite axis opposing any Iraqi and Transjordanian involvement in Palestinian affairs. Ibn Sa'ud had been among the Arab rulers calling the Palestine Arabs to suspend their rebellion, promising to struggle for their cause. In 1938–1939, and again in 1946–1947, Saudi Arabia was one of the Arab states invited by Britain to participate in the abortive London Conferences on the fate of Palestine. In 1945, Saudi Arabia was among the founders of the ARAB LEAGUE.

Ibn Sa'ud was absolute ruler of Saudi Arabia, restricted only by Islamic law and custom. Muslim law (the SHARI'A) was state law, administered by religious courts. The Consultative Council of Hijaz became progressively weaker. It was eventually replaced by the King's council, which had no real powers. There was no distinction between the national treasury and the private coffers of the king. This was changed only toward the end of Ibn Sa'ud's life. In 1951–1952 the first national budget was published. The first bank in Saudi Arabia opened shortly after. In October 1953, on the eve of his death, Ibn Sa'ud established the first council of ministers, but kept his right of veto. Despite opposition of the clergy to westernizing innovations, Ibn Sa'ud began a series of development programs—made possible by increasing oil revenues. A railroad was laid between Dammam on the Persian Gulf and Riyadh (completed 1951). A network of roads and internal air communications was developed; the number of cars increased, and radio stations were established, first by Aramco and then by the state. Ibn Sa'ud also somewhat curbed WAHHABI intolerance. The ban on smoking, for example, was never put into effect in Hijaz and was soon abolished throughout the country. The ban on music ended with the introduction of radio broadcasts.

Ibn Sa'ud died on 11 November 1953. Though many expected a struggle among his sons for the succession, Sa'ud, the designated heir apparent, smoothly mounted the throne, also assuming the position of Prime Minister.

King Sa'ud attempted to establish his own dynasty and make his eldest son Fahd his legal successor. However, faced with his brothers' opposition, he had to appoint his half-brother Feisal instead. Under Sa'ud, the pace of change increased. Income from oil passed the 300 million dollar mark in the mid-1950s. New social strata emerged including: college graduates; army officers; civil servants and clerks; technicians and skilled labor. The number of foreign technicians and experts increased. Modern schools, with mostly foreign teachers—Palestinians, Egyptians, Lebanese and Syrians—caused much ferment. In 1955 Sa'ud expelled many of them. The royal family itself was the source of much waste and corruption. The royal household alone consumed seventeen percent of the state revenues. Luxury began spreading also among a new class of entrepreneurs. The power of the Unitarian religious leaders declined and a way of life incompatible with its doctrine spread widely. In spite of the large oil earnings, the deficit in 1957 was 500 million dollars; state debts 5,400 million dollars, and the value of the rial plummeted.

Sa'ud was also experiencing difficulties in foreign affairs. Immediately after his ascendancy, a serious dispute with Britain (as the power protecting Oman) erupted over BURAIMI. Anglo-Saudi relations deteriorated until they were cut off completely in 1956 asserting it was a product of Britain's Suez War. Saudi Arabia's rulers had always taken an anti-HASHEMITE stand in the Arab League. They opposed, together with Egypt and SYRIA, all Hashemite plans to lead regional unity of the "Fertile Crescent" or "GREATER SYRIA" advocated respectively by the rulers of Iraq and Jordan. Saudi Arabia was one of the principal opponents of the Western-sponsored Baghdad Pact; worked against Iraqi influence in Syria and, together with Egypt, attempted to alienate Jordan from the West. However, an alliance with a radical-revolutionary Nasserist Egypt, along with its

aspirations to hegemony in the Arab world, could not last long. In 1957–1958, relations worsened to an extent that ABDEL NASSER accused Sa'ud in March 1958 of organizing an attempt on his life. The continuing tension in Egyptian-Saudi Arabian relations caused a major deviation from traditional Saudi policies in the inter-Arab arena. After a long alliance with Egypt since the mid-1920s, stemming from shared apprehension of Hashemite Jordan's and Iraq's regional aspirations, with the collapse of the Hashemite regime in Iraq in 1958 and rising threat of NASSERISM, Saudi Arabia shifted its Arab policy and concluded an alliance of conservative regimes with Jordan.

Nasser's charge added to the unrest in Saudi Arabia resulting from the financial crisis and the escalating quarrel between Sa'ud and his brother Feisal, the heir apparent and Deputy Prime Minister. On 3 March 1958, a coalition of princes representing the main branches of the royal family and the religious leaders forced Sa'ud to transfer to Feisal all executive authority. Feisal placated Nasser, introducing a number of reforms. He changed the composition of the government, bringing four ministries, including the Treasury, under his direct supervision. He cut royal household expenses from seventeen percent to five percent of the state budget. The financial situation recovered. In 1960 there was a surplus balance of 185 million dollars. The reforms aroused opposition, mainly within the royal family. Some of the princes objected to the curtailment of their purses, while others, led by Prince TALAL, turned radical, demanding more drastic reforms and savings. Aided by these princes, Sa'ud compelled Feisal to resign in December 1960, and resumed full authority. He promised Talal's group reforms and changes and even appointed him Minister of Finance. He did not keep his promises. In 1961 he dismissed Talal who later fled from the country and began cooperating with the enemy of Saudi Arabia at the time, President Nasser. Because of failing health, however, Sa'ud had to seek medical treatment in the US in November 1961, and authority reverted to Feisal. In March 1962, Sa'ud regained the upper hand. In the summer he was compelled to go abroad again for medical treatment. This struggle between the two brothers continued until 1964. In the meantime, Feisal succeeded in removing Sa'ud's supporters from key positions, and in March 1964

Feisal refused to hand over his power to Sa'ud. Finally the Council of religious leaders (ulama) deposed Sa'ud on 2 November 1964 and proclaimed Feisal king. His half-brother Khaled was made heir apparent.

Feisal made use of the machinery of absolute power to weaken power foci that had raised their head under Sa'ud—princes, the clergy, and foreigners. He encouraged energetic though gradual development. That progress was enabled during his reign by oil revenues. These reached 500 million dollars in 1964; 1,000 million dollars in 1969; 3,000 million dollars in 1972, and 25,000 million dollars in 1975. During Feisal's reign, Saudi Arabia introduced long range planning with successive five-year development plans based on oil revenues. Even though those plans were not very successful in diminishing Saudia dependence on oil, they still managed to dramatically improve the quality of life and defenses of the Kingdom. Additionally, Feisal continued efforts to settle the Bedouin. Telecommunications were developed and a third radio station was inaugurated in 1968 in Dammam. The army was strengthened, mainly the "National Guard"—tribal units, mostly of Najdi tribes particularly loyal to the king, in charge primarily of internal security. The development of modernized branches of advanced military technology also commenced. Though all this modernization was quite contrary to the inclinations of the religious establishment, Feisal took care not to affect their status more than necessary. The Shari'a remained the law of the land, including its code of punishments (such as the amputation of the hands of thieves, and public executions). A special "Religious Police" continued to enforce the performance of the obligatory prayer and other religious duties.

In his inter-Arab policies, Feisal attempted to thwart Egyptian attempts to penetrate the Arabian peninsula. When civil war broke out in Yemen in September 1962 and Egypt sent an expeditionary force to help the Republicans, Feisal gave moral and political support and increasing military and financial assistance to the Royalists. This hostile confrontation with Egypt led not only to a war of proxy but also to many warlike clashes. In ADEN and South Arabia, Saudi Arabia supported the underground "South Arabian League." This opposed the mainline Nasserist-inclined nationalist movement and Egyptian attempts to penetrate and control Aden.

Its relations with leftist-revolutionary South Yemen, from 1967, were tense and not too friendly. As relations with Egypt deteriorated, Egypt was even accused of activating a subversive underground in Saudi Arabia; the "Arabian Peninsula People's Union." This was held responsible for several sabotage attacks in Saudi cities and along the pipeline (several of its members, mostly from the Yemeni minority in Asir, confessed to having been trained and sent by the Egyptian army in Yemen. Some of them were executed in early 1967).

The deterioration of relations with Egypt and its allies in the leftist-Nasserist Pan-Arab camp induced Feisal in the early 1960s to cultivate the idea of Islamic unity, in effect an alliance of conservative Islamic states. But, while he drew closer to several conservative states, such as Jordan, IRAN, PAKISTAN, little resulted from the Islamic unity idea at that stage. (Closer, institutionalized cooperation between the Islamic states was gradually implemented later, from 1969–1970. Saudi Arabia was quite active in this but by then it no longer had pronounced anti-Nasserist inter-Arab implications and was in fact joined by all Islamic countries, not only the conservative ones.)

Efforts to mend relations with Egypt and devise a solution to the Yemen conflict were increased from the mid-1960s. As Egypt withdrew its expeditionary force from Yemen in 1967 and Nasser toned down his activist-interventionist Arab policies, relations began to improve. Egypt's involvement in the Six-Day War of 1967 also induced Saudi Arabia, like most Arab states, to disregard inter-Arab disputes and rally to Egypt's side against Israel. On the eve of the War, Saudi Arabia's declarations against Israel were extremist, but its participation in the war was minimal. It sent a brigade to Jordan, which did not arrive in time and took up positions in southern Jordan when the war was over. Saudi Arabian troops remained in Jordan for several years.

At the Khartoum Summit of September 1967, following the defeat, Saudi Arabia consented to grant an annual aid of 50 million dollars to Egypt and Jordan. Open enmity between Saudi and Egypt ceased after the war, with growing Egyptian dependency on Saudi subsidies. Broadcasts against Saudi Arabia from Radio Cairo ended. Underground groups also ceased their activities, which had been anyway sporadic and very limited in scope. Nonetheless some organizations claimed continued existence. (In 1969 a plot was reportedly suppressed, but it was not clear whether it was connected with them or a factional or officers' conspiracy.)

In the later 1960s and early 1970s Saudi Arabia endeavored to mend its relations with the other countries of the Arabian peninsula (including the settlement of various small border disputes) and stabilize the peninsula. In 1965 the border with Jordan in the Aqaba area was confirmed (with certain modifications, giving Jordan a somewhat longer shoreline). The same year it was agreed with Kuwait to divide the Neutral Zone (the agreement was finalized in 1969). A similar division of the Saudi-Iraqi Neutral Zone was agreed on with Iraq in 1975 and finalized in 1981. An end to the Yemen Civil War was negotiated with active Saudi involvement. In July 1970 Saudi Arabia recognized the Yemen Republic and soon resumed aid to Yemen (and a growing influence on Yemeni affairs). Late in 1971 Saudi Arabia, which had for years halfheartedly supported an Omani-Ibadi Imam rebellion against the Sultan of Oman, arranged a reconciliation with the Sultan. Official relations were established as it renounced its claims to the oasis of Buraimi. In 1974 a border agreement was reached with the UAE, finalizing the renunciation of Saudi claims to Buraimi. Modifications of the border with the UAE's ABU DHABI were provided. This meant that Saudi territory would extend to the coast of the Persian Gulf between Abu Dhabi and Qatar. King Feisal's campaign of reconciliation and stabilization extended also to Iran, even though certain conflicts of interest and a wide divergence of attitudes were not resolved. In 1975 the Shah paid a state visit to Saudi Arabia. The stabilization of Saudi relations in the peninsula was completed in 1976, when Saudi Arabia persuaded South Yemen to stop its support of the DHOFAR rebellion against Oman and of other subversive organizations in the Persian Gulf region. Normal relations with South Yemen accompanied by a measure of Saudi aid were also established. This line of Feisal's policy was brought to fruition after his death (1975).

King Feisal continued cultivating close relations with the US. He was considered by the US as a moderate and an ally. This relationship was shaken by the leading hard-line role played by the Saudi Oil Minister Abdallah Zaki Yamani in the oil crisis of 1973—the linking of supplies with political conditions; the boycott declared on the US and the West; the sudden replacement of agreed-on prices by the unilateral imposition of huge price increases. But even then, and more so later, the US continued seeing Saudi Arabia as the moderate and reasonable one among the oil-producing countries. It also endeavored to involve Saudi Arabia in the Middle East peace process after 1973. Yet on the Arab-Israel issue Saudi Arabia was certainly not "moderate"— at least in its publicly declared policies. It consistently refrained from any subsidies to countries participating in the peace process since its very first day in 1977. Secretary of State Kissinger paid several visits to Saudi Arabia from November 1973 through 1974 and 1975. President Nixon did so in June 1974. The Saudi princes and Ministers were frequent visitors to the US. A new agreement on economic and defense cooperation, including large-scale supplies of advanced American military equipment, was concluded in June 1974, and another one in January 1975. In his efforts to build up modern armed forces with advanced military technology, Feisal also concluded contracts with France and Britain, sometimes based on Saudi commitments to supply oil. West Germany joined the competition for Saudi contracts later, but was more restrictive, refusing to supply offensive weapons, e.g., armored tanks.

King Feisal was assassinated in March 1975 by his nephew Feisal ibn Musa'id ibn Abdel Aziz. He acted alone in revenge for the death for his brother in a demonstration against the opening of a television station in Saudi Arabia. The assassin blamed King Feisal for giving the orders to use live ammunition during that 1965 riot. Feisal's half-brother KHALED ascended smoothly to the throne, while Fahd became heir apparent. Khaled ruled for seven years but due to his poor health left most of the political decision to his second-in-the-hierarchy, Prince Fahd. During his reign, Feisal's policies were followed perhaps with a somewhat more conservative tinge. During those years oil production and oil revenues reached their peak. A recession in production and a fall of oil prices and of Saudi Arabia's revenue set in shortly before Khaled's death in 1982 and their impact was felt only after Fahd's succession. In 1979, Saudi Arabia completed the total take-over of the foreign oil company. Aramco continued operating on behalf of the state and its national oil company, "Petromin."

King Khaled maintained close relations with the US and the West. He received visits from President Carter in January 1978 and French President Giscard d'Estang in 1977. He concluded further large-scale contracts for advanced American arms in 1978 and 1981. However, these arms purchases in the US became more difficult. They aroused increasing opposition in the US Congress and public, fanned *inter alia* by pro-Israel circles who saw a danger to Israel in such sophisticated and advanced weapons going to an Arab country that had not signalled much readiness for a peaceful Arab-Israel settlement. These difficulties came to a head in 1981 around the sale of sophisticated American Surveillance aircraft ("AWACS") which the US House of Representatives voted to ban with only a narrow majority in the Senate, preventing a congressional veto. Saudi Arabia had to face similar difficulties in further large sales of American weapons systems after Khaled's time. It therefore increased its arms purchases in Europe, particularly FRANCE. King Khaled paid state visits to France and Britain in June 1981, and received French President Mitterand three months later. Yet, relations with the US administration remained close. When the US planned in 1980 to set up a "Rapid Deployment Force" to defend the Persian Gulf and the Middle East in emergency, it envisaged Saudi Arabia as hosting some of the potential storage and deployment bases. This, however, Saudi Arabia was not prepared officially and openly to grant. Instead it shied away from a formalized alliance and preferred whatever facilities it might grant to the US. According to various reports and rumors it did indeed grant some—to remain secret and informal. This Saudi policy was the result of traditional apprehension of the two strong actors in the Gulf area; Iraq and Iran. Both were very strongly anti-American since the 1980s. Thus Saudi Arabia kept a very low profile in its relations with the US. A dramatic change in this approach was forced upon Saudi Arabia by the Iraqi invasion of Kuwait in 1990. This was widely believed to be only a prelude to a full-scale takeover of Saudi Arabia by Iraq. During the period until actual fighting broke out in January 1991, the US used Saudia territory as a major basis for building the military might of the anti-Iraqi coalition. Military forces from many Arab and non-Arab countries were stationed in Saudi Arabia, among them those of former and potential enemies, like Egypt and Syria. A senior Saudia officer participated in the planning and implementation of the war along with senior officers of other participants in the coalition. With fighting in January and February 1991, Saudia land was used by all coalition members as staging ground for attacks against Iraq, which retaliated by firing scud missiles on Saudia targets inflicting scores of casualties among the Saudis and US troops stationed there. The war caused Saudi Arabia to openly manifest its reliance on US guarantees for its survival. This damaged its reputation among nationalist Arabs. Further damage had to do with the expense of the war. Saudi Arabia accrued a debt of 55 billion dollars as a result of the preparations and the actual fighting. In spite of continued close relations between Saudi Arabia and the US the two countries have played down their relations in the wake of the war.

Saudi Arabia's main concerns since the late 1950s focused on security of the regime. This was seen to be endangered by social and political radicalism embodied by Nasser's Egypt and low domestic stability of neighboring assertive regimes such as Iraq and Yemen. With the end of the Yemen war, Saudi hegemony in the Arabian Penninsula was to be reinforced. The post-1973 oil boom made the vulnerable Saudi regime even more susceptible to blackmailing pressures of radical Arab regimes. In 1967–1987 financial aid extended to the Arab confrontation states as well as to other states (including non-Arab states, such as Pakistan). This became a major international instrument in enhancing Saudi national security and regional stability. Saudi inter-Arab policies from the mid-1970s have been affected by three processes: the developing Civil War in Lebanon and its conclusion in 1990; the evolving peace processes between Israel and its Arab neighbors, mainly Egypt; and the growing threat of the Iranian revolution to the conservative regimes of the Arabian penninsula.

Based on its newly acquired prestige from the use of the oil weapon during the 1973 war, Saudi Arabia, in conjunction with Sadat's Egypt, assumed for a short while a leading position among the Arab nations. In this context, it assumed the role of a mediator in inter-Arab disputes. In October 1976 it first intervened in the Lebanese Civil War. It attempted to form an accepted formula among all interested parties, most notably among Syria, the PLO and Lebanon. Years of mediation led primarily by the heir apparent (since 1982) Prince Abdallah led to negotiated agreements among the rival Lebanese factions, culminating in the 1989 conciliation accord signed in the Saudi resort town of Ta'if, which was to serve as the basis for the post-civil war political order and reconstruction of Lebanon in the 1990s (see LEBANON).

The peace process with Israel involved many more actors and constituted a much greater potential danger to regional stability and Saudi national security due to its divisive impact on the Arab world. The crisis triggered in November 1977 by Egyptian President SADAT's visit to JERUSALEM and moves toward peace with Israel, was received with great concern about the future inter-Arab relaitions and possible drift to radicalism. Saudi Arabia was among those Arab states who attempted to prevent, or at least postpone, the Arab boycott of Egypt. This was strongly demanded by Syria, Libya and the PLO. However, once a decision in this regard was made at the ARAB SUMMIT CONFERENCE in Baghdad (November 1978), Saudi Arabia firmly fulfilled the collective decision. By succumbing to radical Arab states' pressures, Saudi Arabia signalled to other conservative states in the Gulf area as well as to Jordan, to join the sanctions against Egypt, turning the hard line into an all-Arab mainline. However, Saudi Arabia did not sever all links with Egypt. It did not, for instance, withdraw all its investments, trade and communications. They all continued, along with tourism. Egyptian technicians and workers stayed in Saudi Arabia and continued sending home their earnings—but official relations were broken and several joint ventures were suspended. Saudi Arabia endeavored to maintain a mainline, apparently moderate camp of Arab states; a plan for a comprehensive peace in the Middle East it presented, through its main policy maker at the time, heir apparent Fahd ("the Fahd Plan"), to the Arab summit in 1981, was adopted in 1982, albeit with modifications, as all-Arab guidelines towards a Middle East settlement. Throughout the 1980s Saudi Arabia encouraged a return to the peace process through the American broker, but refrained from overtly supporting separate efforts by individual Arab states, such as the PLO-Jordan accord of March 1985 on joint political action, which was denounced by Syria. The Saudis strongly supported the Madrid International Peace Conference

(October 1991) by encouraging the PLO and Syria to take part in it.

The Israeli-Palestinian DOP (September 1993) and the Israeli-Jordanian peace treaty (October 1994) were welcomed by the Saudi regime. Although Saudi Arabia itself remained reserved regarding direct contacts with Israel, its positive influence on the process was demonstrated by the decision made by the GULF COOPERATION COUNCIL (see below) immediately after the Israel-Jordan Peace Treaty was signed, to abolish the indirect boycott against Israel (see ARAB BOYCOTT). Moreover, with the changing times, the chief Saudia mufti issued in 1995 a religious scholarly opinion (*fatwa*) legitimizing peace with Israel as long as it would be based on the Islamic tradition practiced by the Prophet Muhammad in his dealing with non-Muslims, i.e., that it would be temporary.

In the last years of King Khaled's rule, the IRAQ-IRAN WAR caused Saudi Arabia much concern. It sympathized with Iraq, despite previous apprehensions about that country's revolutionary character and policies. Its relations with Iran, although never cordial, were deeply troubled since KHOMEINI's Islamic revolution. The growing dangers to Gulf security due to the Soviet invasion of Afghanistan (January 1980), the Islamic revolution in Iran, and growing Soviet agitation in the Horn of Africa and South Yemen, led the Gulf Arab monarchies under Saudi leadership to establish in May 1981 a regional cooperation organization (GCC). Initially designated for security purposes, the GCC became a functioning framework for shaping joint policies on economic and political issues as well. From 1981, several violent incidents occurred involving Iranian pilgrims who staged assertive radical-Islamic demonstrations; particularly bloody clashes occurred in 1987 leading to the death of more than 300 Iranian pilgrims.

Saudi Arabia came to sustain Iraq with substantial economic and financial aid, partly clandestine. It also allowed Iraq to ship oil through the Saudi pipeline to Yanbu' on the Red Sea, and exported some Saudi oil on Iraq's account. Officially, it followed—and made the GCC follow—a careful policy of neutrality between Iraq and Iran. But in spite of aiding Iraq in its war with Iran, Iraq was seen as a potential enemy to be appeased for as long as possible. However, with the Iraqi invasion of Kuwait and the formal request of military help from the US, Saudi

Arabia took the unprecedented position of asking for the support of a foreign power. This was usually considered problematic in Arab nationalist eyes, against another Arab country, which indicated the deep fear of an imminent collapse of the kingdom without this assistance. Jordan sided with Iraq during the crisis, re-flaming the old enmity and suspicion between the two monarchies. Even with the passing of time, and almost a decade after the war, Saudi Arabia is entrenched in its positions with regards to Iraq and Jordan.

Saudi domestic politics have developed since the mid-1960s along two parallel lines: the lingering process of developing political methods and institutions, and the sporadic, yet bloody, activities of still unorganized domestic opposition. In 1962 Feisal promised a series of political reforms culminating only about thirty years later under King Fahd and partly as a result of US pressure. In 1992 King Fahd announced a series of reforms in the Saudi system. First, he revived the Consultative Council (*majlis shura*), which had been devised by Prince Feisal in the Hijaz in the 1920s, but was dormant for most of the century. The current council consists of sixty appointed members, who swore their loyalty to the king who nominated them. The council does not have any legislative powers. In late 1993 King Fahd also issued by-laws for the routine operation of the council of ministers. Concurrently, new by-laws concerning the provincial system were issued and provincial councils were nominated for all thirteen provinces. Later in 1995 all non-royal ministers were replaced in a major cabinet re-shuffle.

Intrigues among the princes such as Talal's ventures, and the Sa'ud-Feisal struggle in the 1960s led to the first display of open opposition to the Saudia regime. The existence of a revolutionary underground organization had been repeatedly rumored in the 1960s; so had unrest and plots among officers. In 1969 a combined plot attempt had reportedly been suppressed. The days of King Khaled's rule also saw some internal unrest. In November 1979, there was a serious outbreak of violence when an underground group, apparently an organization of heretics, with only partly political and mainly radical-religious motivation, seized the Ka'ba Mosque in Mecca; they were bloodily suppressed. In November 1979 and February 1980 there was also some unrest among the Saudi Arabia's Shi'tes, on the Gulf coast. The regime,

in an attempt to discredit the opposition and minimize its impact, attributed most of the unrest to the influx of foreign workers. The precarious political position of Saudi Arabia after the Gulf War; the deployment of US troops on its soil; and its strained relations with its two militant neighbors have exposed it to opposition activity generated and supported from outside the kingdom. In November 1995 and again in June 1996 military targets in Saudi Arabia were bombed. In the latter incident, in which Iran was suspected of being involved, a bomb killed nineteen US servicemen at the Khobar Towers apartment complex, which was used for military housing. In the second half of the 1990s a Saudi millionaire publicly called from London for the destruction of the house of Sa'ud and several Saudi opposition movements began to extensively use the internet to disseminate anti-Saudi propaganda.

Another source of uncertainty has to do with the issue of succession. King Khaled died in June 1982, and his half-brother Fahd ibn Abdel Aziz smoothly ascended the throne. Another brother, Abdallah, was named heir apparent and First Deputy Premier, with Defense Minister Prince Sultan assumed to be next in line. King Fahd in general continued his predecessors' policies and there were no major changes. Yet the current line of succession dictated by Abdel Aziz decades ago is about to exhaust itself with the turn of the century, raising questions regarding the future course of the royal succession.

An additional source of concern for Saudi Arabia has to do with the former source of income and prosperity. The oil recession since the early 1980s and the resulting decline in oil production and prices made Saudi Arabia a borrowing country instead of a lending one. The huge expenses involved with the Gulf war contributed their share to the shrinking foreign currency reserves. From a high of about 150 billion dollars in the late 1970s, Saudi Arabia had in 1996 only some 11 billion dollars in hard currency reserves. Still, the war gave Saudi Arabia the right context to send back hundreds of thousands of foreign workers, especially Palestinian, thus minimizing to some extent its potential contribution to local opposition to the regime.

SAVAK Acronym for *Sazman-e Ettelaat Va Amniat-e Keshvar* (State Security and Intelligence Organization). The organization was an association of the internal and external security services of IRAN, but focused primarily on activities among citizens inside the state and outside of it. The organization was set up by advice of the Americans and their assistance after the military coup of 1953 that brought down MOSSADDEQ. This also returned the Shah to power, in order to fight primarily the spread of Communism, Soviet sabotage and the activity of the TUDEH PARTY. However, over the years, and due to the growing public demand for freedom of expression, the activities of the Savak expanded as a tool for political control. In the last years of its existence, the Savak also supervised all types of social, intellectual and cultural activities. Even the headlines of the newspapers were set by the Savak authorities.

The organization gradually gained control over the trade unions and workers' organizations; elections of its leaders became a matter determined by its approval. In the 1970s, the Shah intensified the means of political suppression upon the appearance of guerrilla groups and militias that operated underground. Reports on the suppression of human rights by the Savak caused great harm to the image of the Shah in the international scene (see IRAN, HUMAN RIGHTS). The demand to put an end to the mass arrests, torture and executions (whose dimensions were apparently exaggerated by opposition organizations and world media) were among the main targets of the criticism of the opposition organizations to the Shah's regime.

General Ne'matollah Nassiri, who was the Shah's confidant, was appointed to head the Savak in 1965, and greatly expanded the organization's activities in the 1970s. Simultaneously, with the increased activity of those opposed to the regime abroad, the Savak too expanded its activities in various countries (especially Europe and the US), establishing many branches throughout the world, which were usually located in the embassies of Iran.

In June 1978 upon the spread of the disturbances in Iran, the Shah deposed Nassiri together with his deputies and several senior officers in the service in response to the latter's inhumane conduct with the regimes opponents. In this deposition, the Shah wanted to demonstrate the degree of his liberalism to the citizens on the one hand, and to express his dissatisfaction with the performance of the Savak, which had failed to foresee many internal and external events (including the coup in Afghanistan),

on the other. Also, rumors about the financial corruption of Nassiri accelerated up his deposition. However, the expulsion of Nassiri constituted a serious blow to the Savak, which brought the organization to a state of paralysis, and further damaged the status of the Shah.

SECURITY COUNCIL RESOLUTIONS 242 AND 338   see ARAB ISRAEL PEACEMAKING.

SÈVRES, TREATY OF   Peace treaty signed in August 1920 between the OTTOMAN EMPIRE and its World War I enemies. It obliged the Ottoman government to surrender all non-Turkish provinces in Asia and Africa; to renounce all claims to them; to recognize the Allied arrangements for their disposal. The Ottoman government retained Istanbul and large parts of Anatolia (although some of them were divided by the Allies as spheres of influence, in a separate secret agreement at Sèvres). Some of Eastern Anatolia's provinces were to be ceded to an independent AR-MENIA. Moreover, the Kurdish areas of south-eastern Anatolia were to be granted autonomy, and later (if recommended by the League of Nations), full independence. Izmir and its surroundings remained under Ottoman sovereignty but were to be administered by Greece for five years, after which a local parliament or a plebiscite would be entitled to request their incorporation into Greece. The Islands of the Dodecanese were left in Italy's possession, while Imbros and Tenedos were given to Greece.

Under the terms of the Treaty, commercial vessels and warships were to be given complete freedom of navigation in the Straits of the Bosphorus and the Dardanelles in times of peace and war. An International Straits Commission was to control them. Representatives of BRITAIN, FRANCE and Italy would supervise the financial, economic and administrative policy of TURKEY.

The Treaty was never ratified. It dismembered not only the Ottoman Empire but also Anatolia, which constitutes Turkey proper. Furthermore, it considerably restricted its sovereignty. The nationalist movement led by Mustafa Kemal in central Anatolia totally rejected the Treaty and fought a successful war of independence. This enabled it to replace the Sultan's government and abolish his office, gaining full international recognition for its achievements by the TREATY OF LAUSANNE.

SHAFE'IS One of the four schools (*madhhab*, pl. *madhahib*) of SUNNI Islam (see ISLAM). Though it is not particularly significant to the standard Muslim life the *madhhab* to which he belongs, and one's *madhhab* is hardly used to describe or name a Sunni Muslim, it is different concerning the Shafe'is in YEMEN. There, the Sunni Muslims, nearly all of them Shafe'is, are usually called Shafe'is—an identity with clear socio-political significance which demonstrated itself through the modern political history of Yemen. They constituted almost half of North Yemen's population and following the union with SOUTH YEMEN in 1990 became a slight majority, though they remained the weaker political group *vis-a-vis* the Shi'i ZEIDIS that had constituted a narrow majority before 1990. The Shafe'is live mainly in the coastal plain (the *Tihama*), and in contrast to the Zeidis very few of them belong to tribes. Urban elements and the intelligentsia are somewhat stronger among the Shafe'is than among the Zeidis. In the past, the confrontation of Shafe'is and Zeidis was a significant element in Yemen's history. The Shafe'is had no military power comparable to the great and belligerent Zeidi tribes and were subjected to Zeidi hegemony. During the Ottoman period they tended, therefore, to co-operate with the Turkish authorities. In the independent Kingdom-Imamate of Yemen (1911 to 1962), they did not play a political and public administrative role equal to their share in the population. Some of the Shafe'is intelligentsia played leading roles in the revolution of 1962—e.g. Ahmad Muhammad Nu'man and Abdel Rahman al-Beidani. Shafe'is filled significant positions in the Yemen Republic from 1962. Shafe'is were members of the Presidential Council (A.M. Nu'man, Muhammad Ali Uthman 1965-1973, assassinated 1973) and Prime Ministers (Nu'man, Hassan al-Makki, Abdel Aziz Abdel Ghani), Ministers and senior officers. The republican regime endeavored to play down the difference between Shafe'is and Zeidis and even "abolished" *Shafe'iyya* and *Zeidiyya* as legally and officially significant categories. The Egyptian expeditionary force also helped to promote and foster young Shafe'is. Yet, while the distinction between Shafe'is and Zeidis has become less important, the Yemen Arab Republic remained Zeidi-led. No Shafe'i has become President or reached the top rank of the army leadership. While the issue had not erupted in recent decades into violence or public manifestations, a measure of dissatisfaction among Shafe'is, particularly army officers, was reported from time to time.

SHAMIR-RABIN INITIATIVE see ARAB ISRAEL PEACEMAKING.

SHAMIR, YITZHAK (b. 1915) One of the leaders of the *Lehi* underground movement, leader of the *Likud*, 1983–1993 and Israeli Prime Minister, 1983–1984 and 1986–1992. Born in Poland, Shamir studied at a Hebrew secondary school in Bialystock and was a member of *Beitar*. He interrupted his studies of law in Warsaw to immigrate to Palestine in 1935 and completed his studies at the Hebrew University of JERUSALEM. In 1937 Shamir joined the IZL underground movement and when it split in 1940 joined *Lehi* ("The Stern Gang"), becoming one of its three leaders after Avraham Stern was killed by the British secret service in 1942. Shamir was arrested twice by the British Mandatory authorities—in 1941 and 1946, and in both cases managed to escape—the second time from a detention camp in Eritrea.

In the years 1948–1955 Shamir was engaged in various commercial pursuits and during the following decade held a senior position in the *Mossad*, after which he returned to private business activities and was active in the struggle for Soviet Jewry. Shamir joined the *Herut* Movement in 1970 and was elected to its executive committee, directing the Immigration Department and later the Organization Department. In 1975 he was elected Chairman of the movement's Executive Committee.

Shamir served in the eighth Knesset and continued to serve until the thirteenth Knesset. Following the 1977 political upheaval he was elected Speaker of the Knesset, and in March 1980, after Moshe DAYAN resigned, was appointed Minister of Foreign Affairs. Following Menahem BEGIN's resignation from the Premiership, Shamir became Prime Minister in October 1983, holding the post of Foreign Minister as well. Following the elections to the eleventh Knesset (1984) a National Unity government was formed in 1984 by Shimon PERES, in which Shamir served as Deputy Prime Minister and Minister of Foreign Affairs. In October 1986 Peres and Shamir switched posts, in accordance with the rotation agreement, and Shamir once again became Prime Minister. In March 1987 he was formally elected chairman of the *Herut* Movement. Following the elections to the twelfth Knesset (1988) Shamir preferred the formation of another National Unity government, even though he could have formed a narrow government without the Labor Party. At the beginning of 1989 he formulated, together with Minister of Defense Yitzhak RABIN, a peace initiative, which *inter alia* provided for the holding of elections in the territories and Israeli willingness to negotiate with an elected Palestinian leadership (see ARAB-ISRAEL PEACEMAKING). However, in light of growing opposition within the *Likud* to the initiative, he adopted a more rigid position, and on 15 March 1990, his government was brought down in a vote on a motion of no-confidence, orchestrated by the Labor Party. Following an unsuccessful attempt by Shimon Peres to form a new government, Shamir formed a narrow government, headed by the *Likud*. The policy of restraint followed by his government during the GULF WAR was greatly appreciated by the US. Shamir's decision to participate in the Madrid Conference, and the opening of bilateral talks with SYRIA, LEBANON and a Jordanian-Palestinian delegation, resulted in three of his coalition partners—*Tehiya, Tsomet* and *Moledet*—leaving the government and a call for early elections. In the elections to the thirteenth Knesset (1992) the Likud lost and in March 1993, following Shamir's resignation from his Party's leadership, Binyamin NETANYAHU was elected in primaries as the new *Likud* leader. Shamir continued to serve in the Knesset, but decided not to run in the elections to the fourteenth Knesset (1996). He was strongly opposed to the Declaration of Principles signed by the Rabin government with the PALESTINE LIBERATION ORGANIZATION (PLO), and expressed his disapproval when the Netanyahu government continued to implement the Oslo Agreements (see ARAB-ISRAEL PEACEMAKING). Shamir was highly critical of Netanyahu, following the signing of the Hebron Agreement in January 1997, and announced that it was necessary to find "a new leader for the national camp."

SHARETT, MOSHE   see ISRAEL.

SHARI'A   (Islamic Law) Originally and ideally intended to regulate all spheres of life without differentiating between civil, public, criminal, personal status law etc., the areas covered by the *Shari'a* have in fact been shrinking in the past century—Islamic

law being superseded by secular legislation. From the mid-nineteenth century secular laws were enacted in various fields (commercial, criminal etc.), though initially not in matters of personal status. This was done either by the adoption of complete Western codes and the enactment of new Western-inspired laws, or the codification of Islamic laws by Western methods (e.g. the Ottoman Civil Code, *Mejelle*). Such secular legislation, and the establishment of civil, criminal, commercial courts outside the framework and jursidiction of the *Shari'a*, were ostensibly designed to supplement the *Shari'a*, not abrogate it. The area of *Shari'a* jurisdiction was gradually restricted, mainly to matters of personal status and the WAQF (religious endowment).

This process applied to the OTTOMAN EMPIRE and EGYPT as well as the French-ruled MAGHREB, and was taken over and continued by the Arab states (except for those of the Arabian Peninsula), when they became semi-independent after World War I and fully independent later.

In the twentieth century the secular legislator began interfering also with the laws of personal status. The area dominated by the *Shari'a* reforms were made in most Arab countries—e.g. the enhancement of women's status in cases of divorce and the prohibition of polygamy (as in TUNISIA in 1956) or its restriction by the imposition of conditions and/or the need to obtain the permission of the *Shari'a* judge, the *Qadi* (as in a Syrian law of 1953 or in various Egyptian laws). Such reforms were effected, usually by the secular legislator, in three principal ways: 1. The adoption of suitable elements from teachings of *Shari'a* jurists of various schools instead of such precepts of the dominant school that did not suit the purpose of the reformers. 2. Procedural devices denying legal recognition to certain acts even if valid under the *Shari'a* (e.g. Egyptian legislation prohibiting the registration of marriages below a minimal age). 3. Penal legislation to prevent acts permitted under the *Shari'a* (e.g. the prohibition or restriction of polygamy; Israel applies the same method). The Ottoman Family Law of 1917 is the first modern law of personal status based on this method; modern laws in the same direction have been adopted by most Arab countries. Modern legislation has also abolished or disregarded the harsh *Shari'a* code of punishments such as death for adultery, amputations for theft, etc. Other reforms concern the administration of the *Waqf*—up to its complete abolition in Egypt.

The Arab states also reorganized the *Shari'a* courts' system along more modern, and partly Western, patterns. They introduced, for instance, a hierarchy of judicial authorities and appellate *Shari'a* courts not previously reorganized in the *Shari'a* system. While the reforms mentioned considerably widened the *qadi's* discretionary power (e.g. concerning permission for polygamy or the dissolution of marriages), the *qadi* and the *Shari'a* court personnel were in most Arab countries integrated to a large extent in the state-appointed and state-directed service. Egypt abolished the *Shari'a* courts altogether in 1956, transferring their powers to the civil court—where *Shari'a* law still governs family matters and personal status but is applied by civil judges, with *Shari'a qadis* as advisers. TUNISIA has also abolished *Shari'a* jurisdiction. A similar process has affected Islamic institutions sanctioned by the *Shari'a* and their personnel (though its speed and extent vary from one Arab country to another): mosque functionaries—the *Imam*, the *Khatib*, the *Wa'iz*—are in many cases government-appointed and part of the civil service or at least placed under government control. (In Egypt, this process has been opposed in recent years by Muslim radicals and has led to numerous clashes.) Indeed even the MUFTI has lost some of his independence and usually implements the government's policies. Traditional Islamic institutions of education are in part being superseded by secular state schools, e.g. al-AZHAR University—modernized, adding secular subjects to their curricula and revising methods of instruction (coming under increasing state supervision).

On the other hand, secular legislation is inspired by the *Shari'a* in most Arab countries. As all Arab countries except LEBANON define themselves as Islamic countries, with Islam as the state religion, their constitutions lay down, in various versions, that Islamic law, the *Shari'a*, should be "the basis" or "a principal source" (in Egypt, since 1980, *the* main source) of all legislation. The extent to which these principles have been put into effect varies from country to country and cannot be precisely measured in any case. Radical Islamic groups inside and outside government have been pressing in recent years for a stronger enhancement of *Shari'a* influence on legislation. They demand, for instance, a systematic review of all existing laws as to their compatibility with the *Shari'a* and the revision of those found incompatible. (In Egypt, the National Assembly set up several committees to discuss possible legislation in that sphere—but the government seems to go deliberately slow.) There are efforts to devise a banking and financial system replacing the payment of interest, banned by the *Shari'a*, by different formulae such as sharing costs and profits. These experiments are borne mainly by the financial institutions of states that fully apply the *Shari'a* codes, such as SAUDI ARABIA, the PERSIAN GULF principalities, and Pakistan. Radical Islamists oppose the increasing control by government of mosques and their staff. Inspired by Iran's radical-Islamic regime, these circles pay much attention to matters like dress, women's deportment, separation of the sexes, the ban on alcohol, etc., and sometimes employ pressure or even violence to enforce what they hold to be *Shari'a* rules in these fields. Observers see an increase in the acceptance of these rules by growing parts of the public in Egypt and other Arab countries. Radicals also strive to impose on the state judicial systems the harsh *Shari'a* code of punishments (e.g. death for adultery, amputations for theft, floggings etc.) that are applied by none of the modern Arab states except for those of the Arabian peninsula (but are practiced by Iran and Pakistan). No Arab country seems to be willing to adopt that code. The exception is SUDAN, which under President NUMEIRI's decree, the *Shari'a* code of punishments was applied in September 1983, arousing wide-spread horrified opposition. After his fall in 1985, the new regime seemed to refrain from applying it but was reluctant about simply abolishing it. Since the advent of the Islamists to power in 1989, the *Shari'a* has become fully applied in Sudan.

SHARI'ATI, ALI (1933–1977) Iranian thinker, the outstanding ideologist of the Islamic Revolution outside the religious establishment. Born in Mazinan, a village near Mashhad, son of a well known preacher and commentator of Islamic law who had a great deal of influence on him. In the early 1950s, as a student at Mashhad University, he was active in groups linked with Muhammad MOSSADDEQ and was arrested. In 1960 he went to Paris to continue his studies and in 1964 received a Ph.D. in sociology and theology. In Paris he met writers, philosophers and Islamologists, and was much influenced by the

Algerian revolution which achieved success during his stay in Paris.

Upon his return to IRAN, he taught at Mashhad University, but was soon dismissed and went to Tehran. There he became a popular lecturer and in 1967 co-founded *Husseiniya Arashad*, a progressive religious and social institution. The SAVAK (secret police) soon closed that institute and arrested Shari'ati. He was jailed for a year and a half and endured house arrest for an additional two years. In June 1977 he was permitted to travel abroad and went to London. He died there and was buried in Damascus.

Shari'ati differed from KHOMEINI in many ways, but there were some similarities between the two. They both opposed the Shah's regime and any influence from the West. They preached activism to the masses, sought to use the religious establishment to spread their views, guide the public and prevent opposing views and activities, and saw Islam as the ideology of the revolution. They opposed imperialism (especially cultural imperialism, which alienates the people from its heritage), liberalism, capitalism, Marxism and socialism. But Shari'ati believed in Islamic humanism and rejected the determinist fatalism widespread in the Islamic establishment, because it deprived the individual of responsibility for his fate and that of society. According to Shari'ati, Muslims should not wait for Shi'i Islam's secret IMAM, but should act here and now, and an important precondition for action was preparing the soul and making an ideological change. He believed the ultimate goal was a society based on equality, a society that required leadership, but not necessarily a leader. Thus Shari'ati's tenets, though influential and respected, were not in accord with the official doctrine of Shi'i Islam and Khomeini's regime.

SHARIAT-MADARI, AYATOLLAH SEYYED KAZEM (1905–1986) The most senior religious leader in IRAN in the 1970s. Shariat-Madari was born in the district of Azerbaijan in northwest Iran, studied in the theological institutions in Tabriz and the religious town of QOM, and later enagaged in religious instruction in the two cities. He turned into a revered religious leader in Azerbaijan. After the death of the spiritual leader of Iran (the Ayatollah Borujedi in 1962), he gradually rose in rank and took his place, gaining many adherents in his home district and among the traders of the bazaar in Tehran. Even

though KHOMEINI also competed for the position of supreme religious leader, Shariat-Madari supported the struggle of Khomenei against the Shah's steps and even participated in it, including the bloody demonstrations, which took place in Tehran in June 1963 (see IRAN) under Khomenei's leadership. When Khomenei was arrested and the Shah considered having him executed for revolt, Shariat-Madari stood at the head of the senior clergymen who acted to save his life.

In the years 1977–1978, Shariat-Madari headed the struggle of the clergymen inside Iran, who demanded to strengthen the Islamic foundations of the state and appoint a team of five clergymen to supervise the legislation in the *Majlis* as laid down in the 1905 constitution. He objected to the demand of Khomenei to bring down the regime or to carry out an armed struggle against it. The supporters of Khomenei accused him of supporting the Shah, especially since he had risen to greatness during his regime. After the revolution, Shariat-Madari protested the vast use of coercion to impose the principles of Islam in the state and objected to the active intervention of the clergymen in state affairs. In April 1982 Shariat-Madari was accused by Khomenei of participating in a plot to bring down the Islamic regime, and ordered that he be deposed of his religious status, putting him under house arrest and placing the Muslim People Party (*Khalagh-e Mosalman*), which represented his positions and acted under his inspiration, outside the law. Shariat-Madari died in April 1986.

SHARIF (Arabic: noble.) A descendant of Hassan, the son of Fatima, the Prophet Muhammad's daughter, and the fourth CALIPH Ali, and thus a descendant of the Prophet. An especially honored position in the larger towns of the Arab-Muslim world was that of Naqib al-Ashraf, the Head of the Sharifs in the respective area; the position usually passed from father to son. A branch of Hassan's descendants bearing the title Sharif established itself in Mecca in the tenth century and ruled it independently or semi-independently until 1924, when Mecca and the HIJAZ were conquered by the IBN SA'UD. The HASHEMITES, rulers of JORDAN from 1921 (and until 1958 also of IRAQ) are descendants of the Sharifs of Mecca. The dynasty ruling MOROCCO since the seventeenth century (the House of al-Alawi or also

al-Filali or al-Hassani), also are of Sharifian descent. So are a number of other respected families throughout the Arab world.

Descendants of the Prophet Muhammad through his other grandson, al-Hussein ibn Ali, Hassan's younger brother, bear the title al-*Sayyid* (the master, the lord). But al-*Sayyid* is also used in Arabic as the ordinary address, "Mr." with no connotation of noble descent.

The centrality of Islamic values in Arab societies led to a tendency among strong families without genuine prestige of Sharifian descent, to claim such link, through innovation of pedigree back to the Prophet Muhammad. Such tendency, aimed at establishing one's legitimacy and prestige, has marked also modern Arab rulers.

AL-SHARIQA   see SHARJA.

SHARJA (Correct transliteration: *al-Sharqa*)   One of the seven sheikhdoms of TRUCIAL OMAN that federated in 1971 to form the UNITED ARAB EMIRATES (UAE). Area: approximately 1,000 sq. miles (2,600 sq. km.). The population, estimated until the 1960s at 15,000–20,000, engaged in fishing, boat-building, pearl-diving and some semi-nomadic animal husbandry. It increased rapidly after the discovery of oil and in the course of the general development of the UAE. A census of 1980 put it at 159,000, of which 111,000 were foreign workers. In 1985 this had increased to 269,000. The 1996 figures are a little over 400,000.

The sheikhs of Sharja, of the House of al-Qassemi, signed several treaties with BRITAIN in the nineteenth century and were under British protection, along with most of the other petty rulers of the Arabian coast of the PERSIAN GULF. Britain made Sharja a military base and the headquarters of the small paramilitary force it set up for the Trucial Coast, the Trucial scouts.

The British protectorate lapsed in 1971 and the region became independent as the (federated) UAE. Within the UAE, Sharja tended to side with the Dubai-led camp advocating weak federal institutions and more power to the federation's constituent units. It was also reluctant to integrate its paramilitary National Guard and its units of the Trucial scouts in the federal army. Eventually the integration was effected in 1986.

Sharja is proportionally represented on the Federal Council (six of forty) and the federal government. The governance of its own Sheikhdom has sometimes been troubled: Sheikh Saqr ibn Sultan, ruling since 1952, was overthrown in 1965, and the new Sheikh, Khaled ibn Muhammad, was killed in January 1972 in a coup attempt by the deposed Sheikh. Since 1972, the ruler has been Sheikh Sultan ibn Muhammad (b. 1942). He was challenged in 1987 by his brother, who tried to stage a coup d'état while the ruler was out of the country. After the other UAE rulers intervened, a compromise was reached. Under its conditions the ruler returned to his position while the contender became the Crown Prince, only to be removed by the ruler in 1990.

Sharja was involved in several border disputes, some of them concerning a number of exclaves it possessed in the interior of the Trucial Oman peninsula and on its eastern coast. Some of these disputes were with sheikhdoms that also joined the UAE (DUBAI, UMM AL-QAIWAIN) and were of little importance after the federal merger. Others concerned Oman which were settled in a UAE-Oman agreement of 1979 (of which no details were made known). A dispute with Iran over the island of ABU MUSSA acquired growing importance as offshore oil was discovered in the area. (The possession of the island was also in dispute between Sharja and Umm al-Qaiwain, and the two sheikhdoms had granted conflicting concessions to different US oil companies). In November 1971, when the British protectorate was withdrawn and the UAE was being formed, Iran forcibly occupied the island. While officially Sharja and the UAE protested and demanded the return of the island, some informal arrangements were made by Sharja and Iran, by which the latter endorsed the oil concession granted by Sharja and agreed to share the revenue derived from it.

Oil production, begun in 1974, is still modest even though it now comes from two fields; one of them has also commercial gas production. Accordingly, for its development plans, Sharja depended on its oil income and also drew on federal funds. Other sources of income include two ports and a prosperous tourism industry.

SHARON, ARIEL (b. 1928)   Israeli military commander and politician. Born in Moshav Kfar Malal, Sharon attended high school in Tel Aviv and joined the *Hagana* (the pre-state Jewish military force) in 1945. During Israel's War of Independence (see ARAB-ISRAEL CONFLICT) he was a platoon commander and was wounded in the unsuccessful battle over Latrun. In the years 1952–1953 Sharon studied history and oriental studies at the Hebrew University of JERUSALEM and was then appointed commander of the special 101 Commando Unit set up to carry out retaliatory operations against attacks by Palestinian infiltrators. In 1954 Unit 101 united with a paratroop regiment of which Sharon became the commanding officer, and continued to carry out unconventional operations across enemy lines, some of which occasionally resulted in the killing of innocent citizens. In the course of the 1956 Sinai Campaign (see ARAB-ISRAEL CONFLICT), in which Sharon served as commander of a paratroop brigade, he was accused of insubordination to his superiors in the attack on the Mitla Pass. The force under his command was entangled in a futile battle in which many men were killed, and as a result Sharon was released from his command. In 1957 he attended the Camberley Staff College in Great Britain. In the years 1958–1962, while continuing to serve as an army commander he attended law school at Tel Aviv University. After being promoted by Chief of Staff Yitzhak RABIN to Major-General in 1966 he participated in the Six-Day War (see ARAB-ISRAEL CONFLICT) as an armored division commander, and was acclaimed for his tactical brilliance. He was appointed Commander of the Southern Command in 1969, in which capacity he played an active role in the War of Attrition (see ARAB-ISRAEL CONFLICT). After the cease-fire along the SUEZ CANAL went into effect in August 1970, and throughout 1971, Sharon concentrated on repressing Palestinian terrorism in the GAZA STRIP and clearing Bedouins from northern Sinai. He proposed enabling the Egyptians to establish a civil administration in Sinai, while the IDF would remain in military occupation for fifteen years during which time the two countries would develop relations of trust. Perceiving that his chances of being appointed Chief of Staff were slim, Sharon retired from the IDF in June 1973 to run for the Knesset as a member of the Liberal Party within the *Likud* right-wing coalition which he helped to establish. During the Yom Kippur War (see ARAB-ISRAEL CONFLICT), which took place just before the elections, Sharon was recalled to active military service to command an ar-

mored division, with which he and other generals crossed the Suez Canal. Despite his success in military terms, Sharon's differences with other generals during the war and his repeated insubordination raised great controversy in military circles.

Sharon was first elected to the Knesset in the elections to the eighth Knesset (31 December 1973). In the course of 1974 he proposed that Israel negotiate with the PLO a solution to the Palestinian problem in Jordan. In December 1974, disgusted with political life, he resigned his Knesset seat and accepted an emergency appointment in the IDF. From June 1975 to March 1976 Sharon served as Special Advisor to Prime Minister Rabin and started to plan his return to politics, establishing his own political party—*Shlomzion*. The new party gained two Knesset seats in the elections to the ninth Knesset (1977), but soon after the elections merged with the *Herut* Movement within the *Likud*.

Sharon was appointed Minister of Agriculture and Chairman of the Ministerial Committee for Settlement by Menahem BEGIN. In this capacity he advocated the establishment of a dense network of Jewish urban and rural settlements in the WEST BANK. In this period Sharon also became a patron of GUSH EMUNIM. Sharon's relations with Begin deteriorated when Begin hesitated to appoint him Minister of Defense, following the resignation of Ezer WEIZMANN in 1980. Sharon was finally appointed Minister of Defense after the elections to the tenth Knesset (1981). He soon started to plan a major military operation in LEBANON, the main declared goals of which were to free Israel's northern settlements from Palestinian attacks; to destroy the PLO in Lebanon militarily and politically; to bring about the establishment of a friendly Maronite led government in Beirut, which would sign a peace treaty with Israel; and to force the Syrians out of Lebanon. In April 1982, in accordance with the terms of the peace treaty with EGYPT, Sharon carried out the last phase of the Israeli evacuation from northern Sinai, including the Israeli-founded town of Yamit, which he ordered to be demolished. Two months later Sharon embarked on "Operation Peace for Galilee" (see ARAB-ISRAEL CONFLICT), which soon caused him to clash with other government members, including Prime Minister Begin, over the war's course, and to carry out moves which were neither properly reported nor approved. Sharon personally approved the entry of the Phalange forces into the refugee camps of Sabra and Shatila on 15 September 1982, a day after the assassination of Lebanese President-elect Bashir JUMAYYIL, even though there was a perceived danger that these forces would perform a massacre in the camps. On these grounds the Kahan Commission of Inquiry, which examined the background of the massacre, forced Sharon to resign from his post as Minister of Defense, but he remained in the government as Minister without Portfolio.

In the National Unity Government formed after the elections to the eleventh Knesset (1984) Sharon was appointed Minister of Industry and Trade, and in this capacity continued to develop his plan for dense Jewish settlement in the West Bank, around eleven autonomous Palestinian areas. Following the government decision of 15 May 1989 to hold elections in the territories, Sharon stood at the head of an opposition group of ministers within the *Likud* who sought to prevent the implementation of the plan. After the National Unity government fell on 15 March following a vote on a motion of no-confidence, Sharon was appointed Minister of Construction and Housing in the new narrow government formed by Yitzhak SHAMIR. Within this framework he once again intensified Jewish settlement activities in the territories, and helped various private associations, which were engaged in the acquisition of houses in the Old City of Jerusalem and East Jerusalem. He was responsible for the purchase of tens of thousands of caravans and a vast construction effort, in order to house the mass immigration that started to pour into Israel from the Soviet Union in 1989. Sharon objected to the Madrid Conference (see ARAB-ISRAEL PEACEMAKING). He contended for the *Likud* leadership on 20 February 1992, but came in third after Shamir and David Levy. In the government formed by NETANYAHU in June 1996, a new ministry was formed especially for Sharon—the Ministry of National Infrastructures. Following the Hebron Agreement to which Sharon objected, he became a staunch supporter of the idea of establishing a new National Unity Government.

SHATT al-ARAB The joint estuary of the Euphrates and Tigris rivers in southern IRAQ, on the Iranian border. From the confluence, at Qurna, to the PERSIAN GULF, the length of the Shatt al-Arab is about 120 miles (190 km.). About fifty miles from its mouth, below Basra, the Shatt al-Arab receives on its left (eastern) bank the Karun River, from IRAN. The Shatt al-Arab creates on its lower course wide areas of swamps. It used to carry (until the Iraq-Iran war of 1980-1988) much of the foreign trade of Iraq (via Basra) and Iran (via Khorramshahr). It also provided the outlet for the southern Iraqi oil fields and the (Iranian) Abadan refineries.

The Shatt al-Arab has long been an object of strife between Iraq (previously the OTTOMAN EMPIRE) and Iran. According to an agreement of 1937 (based on previous Ottoman-Iranian accords), the Shatt al-Arab was wholly Iraqi territory except for a length of three miles opposite Abadan, where the frontier was considered to run along the thalweg (the line of greatest depth) of the river. This arrangement proved unsatisfactory to both sides, particularly to Iran, insisting that the boundary should be all along the thalweg or the median line. Questions of piloting, dues and general procedures caused sporadic outbursts of the conflict and grave crises in 1961, 1965 and 1969. In April 1969 Iran formally abrogated the agreement of 1937 and served notice that any future accord must be based on equal rights and the median line or thalweg. A period of crisis ensued, while Iran enforced shipping and piloting controls. In December 1971 Iraq even severed official relations (resumed in October 1973), and serious border clashes erupted in February 1974. The crisis was resolved with the March 1975 agreement that was finally signed in Algiers in June 1975. Iran, with the Shah at the height of his power, obtained full satisfaction of its demands concerning the Shatt al-Arab (in return, Iran stopped all support for the KURDS' rebellion—causing the collapse of that rebellion). Iraq, however, could not acquiesce in the disadvantageous Algiers accord of 1975 which, Iraq claimed, was imposed on it. Relations with Iran deteriorated following the Shi'i revolution of 1979 and in September 1980 Iraq abrogated the Algiers accord of 1975 and instigated an all out war against Iran. The IRAN-IRAQ WAR was triggered in large measure by the problem of the Shatt al-Arab. It focused on adjacent KHOZISTAN as the main area of operations in order to secure an Iraqi hold of both banks of the waterway. Iraqi forces speedily took most of the Iranian side of the Shatt al-Arab, including Khorramshahr, the main town. Abadan was cut off and besieged. In 1981–1982, however, Iranian forces recovered.

They broke the siege of Abadan in September 1981 and reconquered Khorramshahr (in ruins) in May 1982. Later they subjected Basra and the Iraqi side of the Shatt al-Arab to near-constant shelling. In February 1986 they crossed the River and occupied Faw on the Gulf coast and the area around it. As a shipping route, the Shatt al-Arab became totally unusable, as were the oil loading facilities which Iraq had constructed over many years at its mouth, and which were now for the most part destroyed. With Iran's consent to accept a cease-fire with Iraq in summer 1988, the disputed waterway remained mostly closed, a situation which aggravated Iraq's strategic predicament and in fact led to Saddam HUSSEIN's decision to invade KUWAIT in early August 1990. However, the Shatt remained closed to navigation.

SHI'A (Arabic: faction, party) The second largest branch of ISLAM after the SUNNI branch, comprising about ten percent of the Muslim world. Originally emerged in the mid-seventh century as Shi'at Ali (the faction, or partisans, of Ali), it strictly adhered to the right of Ali Ibn Abu Taleb, the Prophet's cousin and son-in-law, and fourth Caliph (656–661), to be the sole legitimate successor of the Prophet Muhammad (died 632 A.D.). According to the Shi'a, the right for Islamic leadership, embodied in the title "Commander of the Faithful" (amir al-mu'minin) was divinely vested in those in the lineage of the Prophet through Ali and his sons HASSAN and (martyred) HUSSEIN. The Shi'a members thus perceived the first three Caliphs as well as later leaders of the Muslim community (the Umayyad and Abbasid dynasties) as usurpers who deprived by force Ali's and his decendants' right for succession. The bloody struggle waged between the partisans of Ali and their adversaries during the seventh century, and especially the martyrdom of Ali's son Hussein in the battle of Karbala (in today's IRAQ) in 680, became a deeply rooted ethos in the Shi'a's historic consciousness of deprivation and discrimination by the adversary and stronger Sunni branch of Islam. Since then, the schism in Islam, which begun as a rivalry over succession, took on ethnic and geographic dimensions (most of the world's Shi'a population resides in IRAN, southern Iraq and the PERSIAN GULF eastern coasts).

From the outset, the Shi'a differed from the main stream of Islam in its idealism and strict adherence to the Qu'ran as a divine revelation, and to the Prophet's descendants as divinely blessed by mysterious abilities. Hence, the Shi'a tended to minimize the legitimacy of collective will of the community of believers, or the state, concerning both jurisprudence or the selection of its leader. The leader of the community in the Shi'a was called IMAM, marking his joint spiritual and political leadership, unlike the Sunni Islam where the clergy (ulama) have been subordinated to the political leaders. Not only that, in Shi'a Iran the clergy enjoyed more power in the community compared to Sunni Islam. They also established the custom of selecting a revered colleague to be the source of emulation (marja' al-taqlid) whose learned opinion on the compatibility of state decisions with Islam must be sought.

The Shi'a underwent several splits over the identity of the last Imam, with certain groups intermittently proclaiming the appearance of a living Imam. The main Shi'i stream is known as Imami (al-Imamiyya), or "Twelver" (thna-'ashariyya), also al-Ja'fariyya, holding a chain of twelve descending Imams from Ali, who was the first Imam, to the last, twelfth Imam (Muhammad al-Muntazar) who vanished in about 873. This invisible, hidden Imam is expected to return at the end of time as Mahdi, the Guided One, "to fill the earth with justice." The Twelver Shi'ism is the state religion and the faith of the decisive majority of the population since the sixteenth century. SHI'ITES constitute a majority in BAHRAIN (seventy percent); a marginal majority in Iraq (fifty-five percent) and DUBAI; a strong minority in Lebanon (over a third of the population, the largest Muslim community), and smaller minorities in SAUDI ARABIA (six percent) and several Persian Gulf principalities (e.g., in QATAR, where they constitute twenty percent of the population). See also ISLAM, MINORITIES.

The Zeidis grew out of a schism over the identity of the fifth Imam in the eighth century. They recognize a living Imam. Zeidis reside mainly in Yemen and rule that country. A schism over the seventh Imam gave birth to the ISMA'ILIYYA sect. One of their branches recognizes a living Imam, the "Aga Khan." It is disputed whether they are part of the Shi'a or on the fringes of, or outside, Islam. (Two other sects on the fringes of Islam grew out of the Isma'iliyya: the DRUZE and the ALAWIS.)

The Shi'ites in those Arab states where they are strongly represented have in general not enjoyed the status and share of power apportionate to their numbers. Even Iraq, with its Shi'a majority has, since becoming independent, been ruled mainly by Sunni Muslims. The Shi'tes of LEBANON have in recent decades begun to assert their strength and claim a larger share of power—partly inspired and encouraged by KHOMEINI's IRAN (as are underground groups of rebellious Iraqi Shi'ites). The post-Civil War settlement in Lebanon did not fulfil their wishes. It strengthened mainly the Sunnite community, although the power of the Speaker of Parliament, a post reserved to the Shi'ites according to the 1943 "National pact," has increased (see LEBANON).

In the religious-doctrinal field, both Sunni and Shi'a savants tend in recent decades to play down the differences and encourage a certain *rapprochement*; e.g., the (Sunni) Islamic University of al-AZHAR has been teaching Shi'a law doctrine (*fiqh*) since the 1950s. Generally the Shi'a Muslims have remained a distinct community cultivating its own customs and doctrines. Its main centers of learning are in Iran (QOM, Mashhad) and at the Shi'a holy cities of Iraq—Najaf (Ali's tomb), Karbalaa (Hussein's tomb) and al-Kazimein.

SHIHABI, HIKAMT (b. 1930) Syrian officer. Chief of Staff of the Syrian army from August 1974. General (Imad) Hikmat Shihabi is one of President Hafez al-ASAD's closest advisers and a prominent figure in the Syrian regime. He served first as head of the Syrian military Intelligence and then was promoted to his current post after proving his loyalty to Asad. As most of the officers surrounding Asad are ALAWITES and Asad's regime is based mainly on Alawite-commanded military power, Shihabi, a Sunni Moslem, is less of a threat to Asad than are other officers. Shihabi was in charge of the Syrian-Israeli Military Disengagement talks in the Golan in 1974 and was viewed by the Americans then as a moderate and balanced officer. In 1975, as Chief of Staff, he planned the dispatching of Syrian troops to LEBANON, a move that took place in June 1976. However, the Syrian involvement in Lebanon—not always a smooth and successful one—did not harm his status and he remained very close to Asad. Shihabi was also in charge —together with Syrian Defense Minister Mustafa TALAS—of negotiating arms deals with the USSR. In 1984, when Hafez Asad was recovering from a severe heart attack, General Shihabi ordered an armored unit to encircle Damascus in

order to deter Asad's younger brother, Rif'at, from taking power, thus proving himself loyal to the President in his most difficult hour. In 1994, during the peace negotiations with Israel, Shihabi was sent to Washington to meet the Israeli Chief of Staff, Ehud BARAK, and in 1995 met Barak's successor, Amnon Shahak. Considering his status and proximity to the Syrian President, and taking into account the American appreciation towards him, his mission was interpreted at the time as a signal of keenness on Asad's part. However, the talks did not produce a breakthrough in the peace negotiations between Syria and Israel.

In the struggle for Asad's succession, Shihabi is considered one of the potential contestants. His military background enhances his position and he enjoys support in the Syrian army and the Security services, but these are controlled mostly by Alawite officers, and being a Sunni-Moslem, he perhaps does not belong to the inner leadership core dominated by Alawite. He might be an acceptable compromise candidate.

SHULTZ PLAN see ARAB-ISRAEL PEACEMAKING.

al-SHUQEIRI, AHMAD (1908–1980) Palestinian Arab politician; founder and first chairman of the PALESTINE LIBERATION ORGANIZATION (PLO) 1964–1967. Born in Acre, the son of Sheikh As'ad al-Shuqeiri; a prominent Muslim scholar and political figure in mandatory Palestine. A lawyer by profession, trained at the Jerusalem Law School and the American University of Beirut, during World War II, Shuqeiri became a political adviser to the Syrian President Shukri al-Quwatli. In this capacity he was involved in the preliminary inter-Arab talks on Arab unity, which eventually led to the establishment of the ARAB LEAGUE. In 1945 Shuqeiri was assigned with establishment and leadership of the Arab Office in Washington to propagate the Palestinian-Arab cause to decision makers in the American capital, as a stopgap for the growing Zionist impact on American public opinion toward the end of World War II. In 1946, he was appointed to head the Arab Office in JERUSALEM, which he did until 1948. He was briefly a member of the Arab Higher Committee (March to June 1946); member of the Syrian delegation to the UN 1949–1950; Under Secretary for Political Affairs of the Arab League 1951–1957 (during which time he continued to represent Syria at the UN—from 1954 as Ambassador).

From 1957 Shuqeiri was Saudi Arabia's Minister of State for UN Affairs and Ambassador to the UN. This ended when in early 1963 he refused to submit an official complaint in the name of SAUDI ARABIA against EGYPT (officially, the UNITED ARAB EMIRATES (UAR)) for committing military aggression against Saudi territory during the Yemen War, and resigned his post. As Syrian and Saudi Ambassador to the UN he was the most active and vituperative spokesman for the Arab cause against ISRAEL. In April 1963 he became the representative of the PALESTINE ARABS at the Arab League and was asked to prepare a plan and statutes for an organization embodying the "Palestinian entity." This idea which had been advocated by ABDEL NASSER became a matter of debate on the inter-Arab arena since 1959. The first ARAB SUMMIT CONFERENCE, held in Cairo in January 1964, assigned Shuqeiri with holding consultations with the Arab governments and the Palestinians regarding the idea of establishing a political organization to represent their cause. On his initiative, with Nasser's backing and King Hussein's reluctant cooperation, Shuqeiri took the decision beyond its initial intention. In May 1964, he set up a Palestinian National Council which became the constituent assembly of the PLO under the auspices of the Arab League. Shuqeiri was the architect of the new organization, phrased the Palestinian National Charter and became the PLO's chairman. PLO leadership was controversial, on both inter-Arab and Palestinian levels. This reflected the fragmentation of Arab regional politics in the mid-1960s. Shuqeiri's image as a political instrument of Nasser's Arab policy backed his efforts to delay the strongly advocated war against Israel for the liberation of Palestine. In 1965 Shuqeiri assisted with the establishment of the Palestine Liberation Army. This was subordinated to the command of the Arab states which sponsored Palestinian military units. However, his assertiveness in demanding further financial resources and freedom of mobilization and organization for the Palestinians in the Arab countries led to growing tension with the Arab governments, particularly JORDAN. With the beginning of *Fatah's* guerrilla activities in January 1965, Shuqeiri's political PLO came under growing criticism, which apparently pushed him to further radicalize his statements against Arab rivals, and advocate war against Israel,

including speeches advocating the physical extermination of the JEWS of Israel. Following the 1967 War (see ARAB-ISRAEL CONFLICT), Shuqeiri participated in the Arab Summit Conference of Khartoum and played a leading role in formulating the three "nays" decided by the conference: no negotiation, no peace with Israel, and no recognition of Israel (see ARAB SUMMIT CONFERENCES). With the flourishing idea of guerrilla warfare against Israeli occupation of the WEST BANK and GAZA STRIP, Palestinian and Arab criticism of Shuqeiri's PLO leadership intensified. He was relieved of his post in December 1967 (formalized July 1968) and retired from the political scene. Shuqeiri published a number of memoirs in which he bitterly criticized the Arab regimes since 1948 for their insincere efforts to attain Arab unity; their insincere efforts on behalf of the Palestinian national movement; and their cynical use of the Palestinian cause for their own interests.

SINAI CAMPAIGN, SINAI WAR 1956 see ARAB-ISRAEL CONFLICT.

SINAI PENINSULA Triangle-shaped desert area which forms the land bridge between Asia and Africa, bordering in the west on the SUEZ CANAL and the Gulf of Suez, in the east on the Gulf of Aqaba. Area: approximately 23,000 sq.miles (59,000 sq.km.), until 1948 scarcely populated, mostly by BEDOUIN. After 1948 EGYPT stepped up the development of the peninsula after discovering minerals along the western shore—manganese at *Um Bugma* and OIL at Ras Sudar and Abu Rudeis—which became productive in the 1960s. By 1967 its population was estimated at over 125,000, including about 25,000 PALESTINE ARAB refugees. After the 1967 War, under Israeli occupation, the population shrunk to approximately 60,000 (of which 30,000–40,000 resided in the town of al-Arish, on the northern shore). Since Sinai was fully returned to Egypt in 1982, Egyptian investments in communication, infrastructure—linking Sinai to Egypt's mainland by tunnels under the Suez Canal—tourism and policy of encouraging settlement in the peninsula, brought about significant increase of its population, which is apparently over 250,000.

Sinai was part of the OTTOMAN EMPIRE since 1517. Having occupied Egypt, in 1882 BRITAIN made a claim for Egypt—and tried to establish—full rights of possession. British notes of 1892 and 1902 laid down the eastern boundary as a line drawn from al-Arish or Rafah to Aqaba. (A tentative plan to develop the al-Arish area for Jewish settlement was briefly discussed in 1902–1903, but was never put into practice.) When the Turks set up a garrison in Taba, south of Aqaba, in 1906, a sharp diplomatic clash with Britain ensued (the "Aqaba Incident"), and the Sultan, while not renouncing his claim, had to acquiesce the Rafah-Aqaba line as a border. This line became the boundary of British-Mandated Palestine (1922–1948) and—except for its northern extremity, where Egypt crossed it to occupy what became the GAZA STRIP—the armistice line between Egypt and ISRAEL (1949–1967) (see ARAB-ISRAEL CONFLICT).

Sinai was a main Egypt-Israel battle ground in 1956, 1967 and 1973 (see ARAB-ISRAEL CONFLICT). Most of it was occupied by Israel in 1956 (up to 10 miles [16 km.] east of the Suez Canal), but Israeli forces were withdrawn under international and Great Power pressure, while a UN Emergency Force (UNEF) was set up to guard the border and operated from 1957 to 1967. All Sinai was occupied by Israel in 1967, and Israel began exploiting the oil wells on its western coast, with considerable investment, developing tourism on its eastern coast, and also providing improved services for the Bedouin population. It also set up several settlements in the north and on the eastern coast.

In the War of October 1973, Egyptian forces crossed the Suez Canal and established a bridgehead about 6 miles (10 km.) wide. They were left in its possession by the cease-fire and a January 1974 "Disengagement Agreement" which added a 6 mile (10 km.) buffer zone to be held by a UN Emergency Force (UNEF) re-established in October 1973. An Egypt-Israel Interim Agreement, concluded in September 1975 under US auspices, provided for a further Israeli withdrawal of a few miles to the east and an expansion of the Egyptian-held area, and moved the buffer zone farther east. It also returned the Abu Rudais oil wells to an Egyptian civil administration, demilitarized and under UNEF supervision. The Suez Canal had been reopened in June 1975. In the Camp David Agreements of 1978 and the Egypt-Israel Peace Treaty of 1979, Israel had to agree to return all of Sinai to Egypt—as President SADAT rejected all proposals for the continued existence of Israeli set-

tlements and an Israeli presence, in one form or another, at Sharm al-Sheikh on the east coast. About half of Sinai, up to a line from al-Arish to the southern tip, was returned to Egypt in several stages, by January 1980. Israel's withdrawal from the rest—and thus the return of all Sinai—was completed in April 1982. What Israel had built on the east coast was handed over intact, while the settlements at the north-western end of the border were mostly demolished by the settlers. A "Multinational Force of Observers," agreed upon in 1978–1979, with personnel from eleven countries, was in place in March 1982; but there have been no crises calling for action on its part. A dispute that had remained unsolved concerned a tiny area at Taba near Eilat. It was finally submitted to an agreed international arbitration in 1986, whose verdict that the area belonged to Egypt was implemented without further argument.

SIX DAY WAR (JUNE 1967)   see ARAB-ISRAEL CONFLICT.

SOMALIA

A republic in northeast Africa, on the Horn of Africa, bounded by DJIBOUTI to northwest, and Ethiopia and Kenya to west and south. Its population is predominantly Muslim (ninety-nine percent of the population) but not Arab; the Somalis are, ethnically, of mixed Hamitic, Berber and Negro stock, and until the 1970s Arabic was used very little, mainly by traders.

Political History: The Republic of Somalia came into being as a result of a merger on 1 July 1960, a merger of two decolonized territories, namely, the former Italian-administered Trust Territory of Somalia and the British Protectorate of Somaliland. Italy had acquired control of the southern coastal and inland Somalia in the late 1880s, later made it a colony, lost it in World War II to British forces, received it back under a UN Trusteeship in 1950, and granted it independence on 30 June 1960. BRITAIN had acquired increasing influence in the northern part of Somalia during the nineteenth century, occupied it in the 1880s, made it a Protectorate in 1889, and granted it independence in late June 1960. (French Somalia, Djibouti, stayed out of the union and became separately independent.).

First elections, using universal adult suffrage, were held in the trust territory in March 1959, with the Somali Youth League (SYL) gaining the decisive power. Following the merger a coalition government was formed, led by the SYL, with Abdel Rashid Ali Shirmake as the first prime minister, constituting a balance of representation of the main northern and southern clans in the country. Shirmake pledged all clans an internal harmony at the price of external conflict, meaning expanding the borders to include Somali communities in Ethiopia, Djibouti and Kenya. Consequently, national liberation movements were established for these areas. A split within the ruling party as well as dificulties in foreign relations avoided the implementation of those commitments. Nonetheless, the SYL won the next elections in 1964 but a split in the party's dominant clan led to the election of Shirmake as president in 1967. Aware of its failure to stand up to its promises of unification of all claimed Somali lands, the government was willing to negotiate a settlement with Ethiopia and Kenya. However, domestic politics were marked by deep fragmentation along tribal lines. The legislative elections of 1969, which once again ended with the SYL victory, intensified clamors against the autocratic rule of the northern-based clan of the president and the prime minister, and the misrepresentation of both the government and the legislative assembly. In October 1969 Shirmake was assassinated in the course of factional violence, followed by a military coup. Mohamed Siad Barre, the chairman of the Supreme Revolutionary Council became president and the state was renamed "The Somali Democratic Republic."

Siad Barre ruled Somalia until 1991. During this period he implemented "scientific socialism" whose main goal was the nationalization of most of the economic resources, including land, services and institutions. In 1976, under the influence of the Soviet Union, the Somali Revolutionary Socialist Party was formed, to serve as a mechanism of control rather than as an ideological instrument of mass mobilization. Reforms of land holding rights effected in the mid-1970s turned into a severe source of inter-clan disputes. The regime waged a literacy campaign, adopting Somali as the official language in 1972 and using a modified Roman alphabet.

From the mid-1970s, the major part of the Somali people experienced displacement due to the severe drought of 1975–1976, which struck mainly the north, and led to resettlement of many in the south. In 1980–1988 Somalia was swept by waves of refugees from Ethiopia, which created an economic burden and serious refugee problem for Somalia, though repatriation of these refugees began in 1990. From the late 1980s further demographic changes occurred as a result of the ethnic dispute and civil strife. In 1989 after Siad Barre's economic policy collapsed, a group called the United Somali Congress was founded, led by General Mohamed Farah Idid. The USC, receiving military aid from Libya, started its activity against Siad Barre's regime from Ethiopia and assumed power in January 1991. Although USC had not initially intended to withhold a permanent government, a civil war broke and between September 1991 and March 1992 over 30,000 people were killed. In 1993, it was estimated that three-quarters of the population had been internally displaced by the civil war and by 1996, it was estimated that the internally displaced population was 250,000, while 475,000 became refugees in Ethiopia and Kenya.

The civil war between Siad Barre's and Idid's forces ended with no decision, indicating the collapse of the central government. This created a serious humanitarian problem in parts of the country and led to a UN-imposed arms embargo on Somalia in January; food and troops were airlifted to the violence and hunger-stricken country (it was estimated that close to 300,000 people died of starvation). In December 1992, a Unified Task Force (UNITAF) arrived in Mogadishu to ensure food deliveries to the needy areas, and to prevent looting. The force was comprised of troops from twenty-one countries, including those from Africa and Europe but mostly America. However, the international force became involved in disarmament of the disputed factions, in spite of the American intention to restore order and smooth delivery of food aid to those in need. During 1993, amid efforts to bring the warring parties to a negotiated settlement, the UN forces became engaged in armed clashes with local military forces, which involved hundreds of casualties and divided the states participating in the UN force. In November 1994 the UN forces began to withdraw from positions outside Mogadishu and in February 1995 UN forces began their departure from Somalia, amid intensified battles between local military factions over the abandoned UN key positions. The civil war continued throughout 1996 and early 1997, despite efforts by various African governments to bring a national conciliation and end of the armed clashes. Such agreements were signed in May 1997 by the Somali leaders in San'a (YEMEN) and Cairo.

While Somalia's relations with Kenya were mostly close since independence, relations with Ethiopia were marked by the Ogaden (a Somali inhabited area within Ethiopia) dispute. From 1977–1978, military clashes and unstable situations along the two states' borders remained a constant phenomenon in the Somalia-Ethiopia relations. Somalia joined the ARAB LEAGUE in February 1974 (one of three non-Arab countries to do so). Arabic has since been cultivated and used somewhat more in education and government administration. Within the Arab League, Somalia has not been very active. It belonged to a pragmatic camp, in particular since 1977, when it abrogated its Treaty of Friendship and Alliance with the USSR which it had concluded in 1974 and adopted Western orientation (in 1980 it also granted the US certain facilities for the latter's Rapid Deployment Force). In 1979 it was one of the three Arab states that maintained official relations with EGYPT, despite a collective decision of the Arab states, implemented by most of them, to sever diplomatic relations with Egypt after it had signed a peace treaty with Israel.

SOUTH ARABIA, FEDERATIONS OF see SOUTH YEMEN.

SOUTHEAST ANATOLIA PROJECT (GAP) see TURKEY, WATER POLITICS.

SOUTH LEBANON ARMY Since the mid 1960s, and especially after the deportation of the Palestinian fighters from JORDAN in "Black September" 1970, South LEBANON became a battleground for the PALESTINE LIBERATION ORGANIZATION (PLO) and ISRAEL. In the Cairo Agreement signed in November 1969 between the Lebanese government and the PLO under Nasir's auspices, Lebanon formally recognized the Palestinian Resistance's right to maintain political and military presence in specified Lebanese areas and to operate against Israel from south Lebanon, subject to coordination with the Lebanese army. Henceforth the PLO set up its bases there, and staged military operations against Israel, which responded in military operations carried out both against the Lebanese capital, Beirut (1968, 1973), and against

Palestinian bases in south Lebanon (termed "Fatahland" by Israel).

After the break of the civil war in Lebanon in 1975 and the disintegration of the Lebanese army in 1976, two Christian officers, major Saa'd Haddad (1937–1984), a Greek-Catholic from the southern town of Marj Ayun and supporter of former president Camille CHAMOUN, and Major Sami Shidyaq, were adduced by their factional superiors to move to south Lebanon. Their mission was to command the area, organize the local Christian militias and protect the Christian population, a minority in the south. Haddad's mission was discussed in the then-expanding dialogue between Israel and several Lebanese MARONITE-Christian leaders, although ties between CHRISTIANS in north and south Lebanon remained loose and Haddad's approximately 1500 men (mostly Christian, some Shi'ite) were all local recruits. Upon arriving in South Lebanon and realizing Israel's dominant role there, Haddad became its surrogate, receiving from it financial and military aid. Following the Litani Operation (see ARAB-ISRAEL CONFLICT) in March 1978, set to destroy Palestinian bases in South Lebanon, United Nations Security Council resolution 425 was adopted, calling for immediate withdrawal of Israeli forces from Lebanese territory. UNIFIL (United Nations Interim Force in Lebanon; see ARAB-ISRAEL PEACEMAKING) was sent to South Lebanon, remaining there ever since. Israel withdrew partly, leaving a 2-7 mile (4-12 km) wide, 50 mile (80 km.) long border strip linking three Christian enclaves under Israeli indirect control with Haddad's militia, in full control. Relations between Haddad and the Lebanese government deteriorated after his militia helped Israel prevent the advance of the Lebanese army into South Lebanon in July 1978; Haddad was tried *in absentia*, dismissed from the Lebanese army and deprived of his salary. In response, he declared in 1979 the areas under his control as "Free Lebanon" and received intensified Israeli aid, including the widening of its "Good Fence" policy adopted since 1976 (namely, extending humanitarian services to the South Lebanese population), enabling Lebanese citizens to cross the border to work in Israel, an act presented as humanitarian. In 1980 Haddad changed the name of his militia to the "South Lebanon Army" (SLA).

Between 1978–1982 South Lebanon remained a battleground of Israel and the PLO, although an

American-brokered cease-fire between the PLO and Israel had been in effect from summer 1981. In June 1982, Israel invaded Lebanon, declaring it had set out to remove the Palestinian terrorist threat from northern Israel. During the war, all attempts by Israel to include Haddad and his men in Israel's greater plans for Lebanon failed, due mainly to the refusal of the Lebanese PHALANGES leaders to cooperate with Haddad, branded as an Israeli collaborator. Israel pulled out from most occupied areas in Lebanon in 1983 and 1985, following intense guerrilla attacks by Shi'i groups—AMAL and HIZBALLAH—which took control of the South after the departure of the bulk of Palestinian fighters from Lebanon in 1982–1983. However, Israel still maintains a 10–20 km.–wide "Security Zone" in South Lebanon—and from 1985 has been facing the "Lebanese Resistance Movement"—a name used by Hizballah and Amal units fighting Israeli occupation.

Following Saa'd Haddad's death in January 1984, Major-General Antoine Lahad (b. 1929), a Christian-Maronite retired army officer from Dayr and al-Qamar, formerly commander of the Biqa' area, became head of the militia with Camille Chamoun's approval. The SLA was upgraded and expanded in 1985 (more than half of its men were Shi'is but many of them defected). Ever since, it has been engaged— together with the Israeli army—in almost daily fighting, especially with Hizballah, leading at times to major Israeli operations of shelling and air raids, such as in July 1993 and April 1996. The future awaiting the members of the militia after the conclusion of a formal Syrian-Israeli (and Lebanese-Israeli) peace settlement is problematic, constituting a major obstacle on the way to any settlement. While Israel demands the integration of the militia's members into the Lebanese army as a separate (maybe a territorial) unit, which would secure the well-being of the SLA members and families, perceiving it as a matter of credibility and accountability toward its protegé. On the other hand, the Lebanese government, which in the meantime sentenced Lahad to death *in absentia*, refuses to include sectarian units in its new, reorganized army which had eliminated sectarian-based formations since 1991.

SOUTH YEMEN, PEOPLE'S REPUBLIC OF

(since November 1970: People's Democratic Republic of Yemen), in South Arabia, independent be-

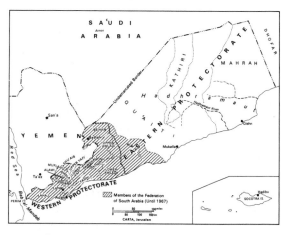

Map of South Yemen

tween 1967 and its unification with YEMEN in 1990, on the shores of the Indian Ocean (the Gulf of Aden), between the Red Sea and the Sultanate of Oman's Dhofar. South Yemen comprised the former Colony of ADEN and the Western and Eastern Aden Protectorates (including those that had not joined the Federation of South Arabia), and the offshore islands of Perim and Socotra. It gained independence in November 1967. South Yemen bordered on Yemen, SAUDI ARABIA and OMAN. The only demarcated frontier, existing between independence and unification, was a part of the Yemen border. The population was estimated at 1.59 million in the 1973 census, and at about 2.2 million in the mid–1980s. The main town is Aden, with a population of 562,000 in 1995. A new capital—*Madinat al-Sha'b* (Arabic: People's Town; former name: *al-Ittihad*) was built adjacent to Aden. The population is approximately seventy-five percent Arab and consists mainly of SHAFE'I SUNNI Muslims. Foreign workers—Yemenites, Indians, Pakistanis and Somalis—are all in Aden town (nearly all the Europeans and JEWS left after independence was gained). There is a sharp contrast between the modern Aden town and the underdeveloped, poor, tribal and partly nomadic hinterland. South Yemen derives its main revenues from Aden harbor and the city's oil refineries.

Political History BRITAIN briefly took control of Perim Island in 1799, to prevent Napoleon from moving to India through the Straits of Bab al-Mandab. In 1839, the government of Bombay Province, in British India, acquired Aden town from the Sultan of Lahaj, mainly for use as a coal depot. Aden remained under the jurisdiction of the Bombay government until 1932. As its significance developed, particularly following the opening of the SUEZ CANAL, 1869, Britain signed almost thirty separate treaties in which the Sultans, Sheikhs, Sharifs and Amirs of the town's hinterland accepted varying degrees of British protection. Most of these were Shafe'i Muslims who resisted the intrusions of both the ZEIDI Imams of Yemen and the OTTOMAN EMPIRE. Backed by Britain, these tribal leaders foiled Ottoman penetration of South Arabia in the 1870s and an attempt to conquer Aden in 1915 (although Ottoman troops succeeded in capturing Lahaj). The Yemeni IMAM Yahya claimed that South Arabia was an integral part of Yemen, but his demands were rejected by South Arabia's petty rulers. In 1932 the administration of Aden was transferred from Bombay Province to the Governor General of India. Five years later, in 1937, Aden became a Crown Colony, and the hinterland was termed the Western and Eastern Aden Protectorates.

Britain maintained stronger contacts with the chiefs of the Western Aden Protectorate, the immediate hinterland of Aden town. In the early 1950s the Colonial Office proposed to create in the Western Protectorate a federation which would later become a member of the British Commonwealth. This proposition was opposed by the tribal leaders who disliked the increasing British interference. But when Britain suggested a federation which would later become an independent Arab state linked with Britain only by a treaty, the Sultans, who were under growing leftist and Nasserist pressure, agreed.

In 1959, a "Federation of South Arabia" was formed. By 1965 it had seventeen members: fifteen from the Western Protectorate, one from the Eastern Protectorate and Aden town. One sultanate of the Western Protectorate and three of the Eastern Protectorate refused to join the Federation. A political party, the "United National Party," formed mainly by middle-class pro-British and Federalist Adenis, supported the Federation, but it had little influence and the Federation remained weak.

The Eastern Aden Protectorate—mostly deserts and barren hills, with some fertile valleys (of which the most important is the HADHRAMAUT)—consisted of the four sultanates of Wahidi, Qu'aiti, Kathiri and Mahra (including the island of Socotra), with Mukalla, in the Qu'aiti State, as the main town and harbor.

Saudi Arabia claimed the Hadhramaut as part of its territory. Britain was interested in pacifying the area and strengthening it against the Saudi claims. Between 1936 and 1939 Harold Ingrams, the British Political Officer in Mukalla, signed about 1,400 treaties with local tribal leaders obliging them to stop fighting among themselves. The chief sultans accepted the protection and tutelage of the British Governor of Aden. In 1940, Britain raised a military force of approximately 1,500 men, the Hadhramti Legion. Wahidi was the only one of the four Eastern Protectorate sultanates willing to join the Federation of South Arabia.

In Aden town, administered as a colony, the constitutional progress was that of paternalistic, British-guided gradualism. A Legislative Council, initially composed of "official" (i.e., colonial government officers) and non-official members, was established in 1946–1947. Reforms of 1955 and 1957 reduced the number of official members and increased, among the non-official ones, the number of elected members, until they formed a majority; the electorate, however, remained restricted. At the same time the Governor's Council, originally consisting of colonial officials only, was gradually enlarged to include representatives of local notables, and eventually members of the Legislative Council. It became a "Council of Ministers" in 1961, and its chairmanship passed from the Governor to a "Chief Minister" in 1963. The British wanted Aden to join the Federation— a highly controversial proposal, as the character and interests of the colony and the tribal sultanates were quite different: the latter were economically and socially backward, under the mediaeval autocracy of their desert chieftains, but enjoyed a larger degree of independence from Britain, while Aden town was economically more developed, socially sophisticated and politically active, but under a colonial form of government. Yet, in 1962–1963 Britain succeeded in persuading the Aden government and Legislative Council to approve Aden's entry into the Federation—with its weight in the Federation's councils much less than that merited by its population, strength and economic contribution. In January 1963, the Crown Colony became a Federal state and the British Governor's title was changed to that of High Commissioner.

Nationalists, both in the sultanates of the protectorates and particularly among the urban population of Aden, were dissatisfied and clamored for faster progress toward complete independence and the end of British tutelage and privileges. Most of them believed that violence was the only way to achieve their aims.

The first insurgent organization, formed in 1951 in the Lahaj Sultanate, was the "South Arabian League" (SAL), led by Muhammad Ali al-Jifri and Sheikhan al-Habshi and backed by EGYPT. Following the Yemen Revolution of 1962, Egyptian support was transferred to a new and more militant organization—the NATIONAL LIBERATION FRONT FOR OCCUPIED SOUTH YEMEN (NLF), founded in 1963 and led by Qahtan al-Sha'bi. On 14 October 1963, Sha'bi proclaimed, in the Radfan mountains north of Aden, an armed struggle against the Federation and any British presence. Later the main focus of the insurgency shifted to Aden town.

In February 1965, the British High Commissioner attempted to appease the insurgents and invited Abdel Qawi Makkawi, leader of the opposition in the Legislative Council, to form the Aden government. But insurgent activities increased, Makkawi gave them his open support, and in September 1965 the High Commissioner dismissed Makkawi, the government and the Legislative Council, suspended the constitution and ruled by decree. Makkawi became a voluntary exile.

The Yemeni minority, constituting almost half of Aden's population, and deprived of electoral rights, provided many insurgents. About 25,000 of them were members of the "Aden Trades Union Congress" (ATUC), led by Abdallah al-Asnaj. The first of these trade unions had been organized in 1953 with British support, but gradually ATUC had adopted a leftist and pro-Nasserist line. It also founded, in 1962, a political wing, the "People's Socialist Party" (PSP). In May 1965, the PSP joined the SAL to form the "Organization for the Liberation of the Occupied South" (OLOS). A few months later the SAL, which now supported the sultans and was considered conservative, seceded. Egypt sponsored a successful effort to unite all the insurgent organizations (excluding the SAL), and in January 1966, the OLOS—now made up mainly of PSP followers—and the NLF merged to form the FLOSY (Front for the Liberation of Occupied South Yemen). The deposed Prime Minister, Abdel Qawi Makkawi, headed the Political Bureau, and Abdallah Asnaj became Secretary-

General. FLOSY continued the armed struggle against Britain and the federation; it favored the union of South Arabia with Yemen and accepted Egyptian guidance. These two issues, and factional struggles, destroyed the recently achieved unity: late in 1966 the NLF split from FLOSY and the two organizations engaged each other in a struggle for supremacy. The NLF adopted an increasingly leftist, Marxist orientation and cultivated close links to the underground "Arab Nationalist Movement" (Harakat al-Qauwmiyyin al-Arab) and its Palestinian-Arab branch, the PFLF.

Between 1964 and 1967 insurgent activities greatly increased. Since the early 1960s, the South Arabian problem had also been raised at the UN—mainly by the Arab state, none of whom recognized the Federation. (The ARAB LEAGUE had denounced the Federation as "a creation of British imperialism and colonialism)." The UN Special Committee on Colonialism (the "Committee of 24"), and subsequently the General Assembly, endorsed in 1963 a report claiming that large parts of the South Arabian population disliked the existing regime and that the Federation was designed to prolong British rule in the area. British-Federal consultations in 1964 resulted in a British promise to grant independence, evacuate South Arabia and hand over power to the Federation by 1968. But in 1965 the UN General Assembly adopted a resolution urging elections, affirming the "inalienable right of the (South Arabian) people to self-determination and freedom from colonial rule" and demanding the "immediate and complete removal of the British bases." A similar resolution was adopted in 1966. Britain accepted the UN resolutions, again stating in February 1966 that it would withdraw by 1968, and agreed to some UN supervision of the election and self-determination process. In April 1967, a UN mission came to Aden for consultations on the organization of elections. Yet due to insurgent activities and a dispute with the British and federal authorities, the mission left after a few days. Both FLOSY and the NLF refused to meet the mission, because it would not forgo all contacts with the sultans. The UN mission thus played no part in the shaping of events. In February 1967 the British Foreign Secretary reiterated that Britain would leave South Arabia by 1968, transferring power to the Federal government, to whom financial and military support was also promised. During the summer of 1967, federal ministers held discussions with the UN mission (in Europe) and Britain, and made a (vain) attempt, supported by Britain, to contact the nationalists and arrange for a broad-based coalition of all groups.

Egyptian support for FLOSY was withdrawn following the 1967 war, together with the evacuation of the Egyptian expeditionary force from Yemen. Seizing this opportunity, the NLF took over most of the South Arabian sultanates. When the NLF emerged as the stronger force, the federal army and the ATUC backed it and those sultans and federal ministers who were not captured by the NLF fled the country. Egypt, which had previously ignored the NLF, now lent its support. On 5 September 1967, Britain had to acknowledge the collapse of the federal regime and to recognize the nationalists as the group with whom it would negotiate the transfer of power; in November it had to state that negotiations would be conducted with the NLF alone. Negotiations were held in Geneva that same month and it was agreed that independence would be granted to South Arabia at midnight on 29 November 1967. The new State was named the People's Republic of South Yemen, and Qahtan al-Sha'bi became its first President, Prime Minister and Commander of the Armed Forces. The Republic was immediately admitted to membership of the UN and the Arab League.

Independent South Yemen

Domestic Affairs The situation in South Yemen deteriorated during its first year of independence. It had few, if any, economic resources of its own; British aid was meager, and was soon stopped because of incessant disputes. Its only economic asset—Aden's position as a transit and refueling port—was placed in jeopardy by the closure of the Suez Canal. Government attempts to remedy the situation by tax increases and a reduction of salaries were unsuccessful. Moderate and extreme-leftist factions within the NLF were fighting for power. This led to instability and two unsuccessful rebellions during 1968.

In June 1969, a coup replaced President Qahtan al-Sha'bi and his government with a more extremist leftist Presidential Council and government under Muhammad Ali Haitham, Salem Rubai Ali and Abdel Fattah Isma'il.

During these first years efforts were made to abolish the traditional tribal South Yemen system by the liquidation of the former sultanates and the re-division of the country into six new governorates—but tribal allegiances remained strong. The former sultans, federal ministers, SAL and FLOSY leaders were purged, jailed or sentenced to death and their property was confiscated. In addition to their past political records they were accused of plotting and attempting rebellion against the new state—in collusion with Saudi Arabia and "the imperialists." In late 1969, South Yemen enacted far-reaching measures of nationalization.

In foreign and international affairs, South Yemen joined the leftist camp. It received economic and military aid from the USSR; and a close relationship developed between South Yemen and China, which also granted aid. According to reports never officially confirmed, the USSR enjoyed naval and air base facilities in Aden and Socotra. Relations with the US were severed by South Yemen in October 1969. South Yemen also recognized East Germany—which was at that stage still a demonstration of a leftist orientation. Later, in the 1970s, South Yemen joined COMECON, the economic association of the Soviet Bloc, as an observer. Its leaders visited the Soviet Union several times, and throughout the shifts and vicissitudes of South Yemen's politics and factional splits, close relations with the USSR and a strong Soviet influence remained constant. In October 1979 it signed a Treaty of Friendship and Cooperation with the USSR. Other Soviet Bloc countries like Cuba and East Germany also cultivated relations with South Yemen and aided it.

South Yemen's regime was troubled, as factional strife continued. This centered in part on doctrinal and ideological-political issues (there was, for instance, talk of pro-Chinese versus pro-Russian tendencies), but was determined by a struggle for power and by tribal allegiances and rivalries. In August 1971, Haitham was ousted and went into exile. Ali Nasser MUHAMMAD became Prime Minister and a member of the new Presidential Council, with Salem Rubai Ali and Abdel Fattah Isma'il. (It was to Ali Nasser's growing influence that the change to more pragmatic policies was ascribed. In June 1978, President Salem Rubai Ali was ousted and killed, and his supporters purged. A new 111-member Supreme People's Assembly was elected. The new Presidential Council had five, later ten, members, but two of them, Ali Nasser Muhammad and Abdel Fattah Isma'il, were the leading rulers. At first, Ali Nasser was Council Chairman, but in December 1978 he ceded that position to Abdel Fattah Isma'il, while continuing to hold the Premiership. Isma'il was also the Secretary-General of the ruling party, which had been re-formed in October 1978 as the "Yemen Socialist Party." Between the two men there was an increasingly bitter rivalry—with Isma'il as revolutionary-doctrinaire hard-liner (who also built up a party-dominated popular militia as the focus of his power), while Ali Nasser was seen as a pragmatist. Other members of the Presidential Council, the government and the party Politburo, such as Ali Nasser Antar and Ali Salem al-Baid, took shifting positions, maneuvering between the two principals.

In April 1980 Ali Nasser Muhammad gained the upper hand and took the Presidency in addition to the Premiership. He also became Secretary-General of the party. Isma'il went into exile to Russia. But while Ali Nasser was now the prime leader, factional struggles and purges continued. In 1985, an interfactional accommodation was reached—reportedly through Soviet mediation. It involved the return of Abdel Fattah Isma'il and the restoration of his faction to some power positions. Ali Nasser Muhammad gave up the Premiership (given to Haidar Abu Bakr al-Attas) and some of his dominating position in the Party. But this compromise did not achieve a full reconciliation and factional strife continued. In January 1986 it erupted in a major crisis, a bloody civil war whose details, related in conflicting versions, have not been fully clarified. In the fighting several top leaders were killed, including Abdel Fattah Isma'il and Ali Nasser Antar (who had joined Ali Nasser Muhammad's foes). Soviet and Arab attempts to mediate and restore a compromise had little success. Ali Nasser Muhammad's regime collapsed, and he himself escaped to Yemen and Ethiopia. Haidar al-Attas, heretofore a second-rank leader, not fully identified with either of the rival factions—was named President. Another second-rank official, Yassin Sa'id Nu'man, became Prime Minister, and Ali Salem al-Baid Secretary-General of the YSP. The new regime purged the state and party apparatus of the deposed leader's men and then endeavored to restore normal conditions. In October 1986 it held new elections to the Supreme People's Assembly. While continuing their predecessors' pragmatic policy of fostering normal relations with all Arab states and visiting to several of them, the new leaders rejected Ali Nasser Muhammad's proposals to work out a new compromise that would return him and his adherents to a position of shared power. In December 1986, he and about 140 of his men were put on trial, he and 48 others in *absentia*.

The former North and South Yemen were unified in May 1990. However, the continued independence of the two armies led to a south Yemeni attempt to secede from the union. Fighting began in the spring of 1994 and erupted into a full-scale civil war centered in the former southern capital city, Aden. The North Yemeni suppressed the civil war, and by July 1994 all independence attributes of the south disappeared. For the post-1990 unification, see YEMEN.

Foreign Affairs In inter-Arab affairs, too, South Yemen followed a radical-leftist line and became, with Syria and Libya, a mainstay of the REJECTION FRONT. Though it had adopted the name "South Yemen" to show that it regarded Yemen and South Yemen as parts of one country and wished to unite them, no practical steps were taken towards a merger and relations with Yemen remained cool and tense in South Yemen's first years. In November 1970 South Yemen renamed itself "People's Democratic Republic of Yemen" (without "South-")—a step resented by Yemen. Tension and sporadic clashes, aggravated by tribal and border disputes, soon escalated and in September 1972 clashes turned into warlike operations. These were halted by all-Arab, and particularly Libyan, mediation and renewed mutual endorsements of the decision in principle to unite the two Yemens. Such union pledges were reiterated at several meetings of the two Heads-of-State (changing ones in both countries), but relations did not significantly improve. In February 1979 clashes again escalated into warlike operations—again followed by declarations of unity and the resolve to merge that were not implemented.

Relations with Saudi Arabia were hostile from the first days; Saudia did not even recognize South Yemen and a border dispute soon arose. Relations with Egypt were correct but reserved; though South Yemen applied for assistance, Egypt gave it little help. South Yemen took a revolutionary stance regarding southeastern Arabia and the PERSIAN GULF, and particularly its neighbor Oman. It actively supported anti-Omani rebels fighting in adjacent Dhofar since the mid-1960s, providing them with arms and supplies and an operational base in its territory. It backed the rebels when they attempted to widen their scope and to subvert and "liberate" the Persian Gulf region as a whole (see OMAN, PERSIAN GULF). South Yemen also took an extreme anti-Israel line, and there were several reports, never fully confirmed, that it aided Egyptian efforts of the 1970s to block the Bab al-Mandab straits to Israel-bound shipping, put the islands of Perim and/or Qamaran (which it later claimed until 1972, when it acquiesced in Yemen's ownership) at the disposal of Palestinian-Arab guerrilla groups. It was also involved in a June 1971 bazooka attack on a Liberian oil tanker on its way to ISRAEL.

In the mid-1970s, South Yemen toned down its revolutionary zeal and adopted more pragmatic policies. This process was also connected with internal factional struggles (see below). As the Dhofar rebellion was declining and being defeated, South Yemen bowed in 1975-1976 to Saudi pressure, accompanied by promises of improved relations and substantial aid, and stopped its aid to the rebels and to subversive schemes in the Persian Gulf, thereby causing the virtual end of the rebellion. In 1976 South Yemen and Saudi Arabia established normal and official relations, and the cessation of South Yemen aid to the Dhofari rebels was formally agreed upon with Oman (after Saudi, Kuwaiti and UAE mediation). Normal relations with Oman were agreed in October 1982, though Ambassadors were not actually exchanged at the time. However, this gradual mitigation of South Yemen's inter-Arab policies and its growing dependence on aid from Saudia and the Arab Gulf states did not lead to a change either in its pro-Soviet orientation or in its membership of the Rejection Front. Thus, South Yemen refused to join the protest votes of the other Arab and Islamic countries against the Soviet intervention in Afghanistan, from December 1980, and sided with IRAN against IRAQ in the GULF WAR—together with South Yemen and LIBYA— though not very actively. In August 1981 it signed a Treaty of Friendship with Soviet-allied Ethiopia and Libya. This treaty, interpreted at first as an alliance and a defense pact, had little impact on political or defense realities. For the post-1990 unification, see YEMEN, ARAB REPUBLIC.

SOVIET POLICIES AND INTEREST see RUSSIA.

STEADFASTNESS FRONT see REJECTION FRONT.

SUDAN   Republic in northeast Africa, with the largest area among African states. Sudan borders in the east on Ethiopia and the Red Sea; in the south on Kenya, Uganda and Zaire; in the west on Chad, the Central African Republic and LIBYA; and in the north on EGYPT. Sudan has existed as a political entity in its present borders since 1899 (when it was re-conquered by Anglo-Egyptian forces, after the MAHDI's rule). Sudan attained independence in January 1956, and became a member of the UN in November of that year.

The Sudanese population remained largely rural. Its annual rate of urban growth between 1982–1992 was 3.9%. Main towns are the capital Khartoum, including Omdurman and Khartoum north; port Sudan on the Red Sea and Nad Madoni and al-Ulbayid in the center of the country. The population is not homogeneous. Ethnically, about fifty percent consider themselves Arab. (Some surveys list only forty percent or slightly less who claim "Arab origin.") More than ten percent are various non-Arab Muslim groups, mostly of "Hamitic" or "Nubian-Hamitic" descent—such as the NUBIANS in the north, the Beja in the north-east, the NUBA and the Fur in the west. All these populations, Arab and non-Arab alike, have strong negroid admixtures. About one third of the population, all in the south, are black Africans of "Nilo-Hamitic" origin—with Dinka and Nuer, Shilluk as the main tribes. Some surveys estimate the non-Arab populations of the north and the south together as more than fifty percent of the total. Arabic is the official language and a *lingua franca* for many of the non-Arab groups as well. Most of these groups have their own language—about 115 languages are counted, of which 26 are considered the main ones. In the non-Arab south, English is also used as a *lingua franca* and in a 1972 agreement with the southern rebels it was recognized as an official language for the south.

In terms of religion, more than half of the population are Muslims, although estimates vary from fifty to sixty percent to seventy-three percent. Christians are estimated at seven to nine percent, nearly all of them in the African south (where they comprise about twenty percent). Pagan animists are eighteen to twenty-four percent of the total population; all of them in the African south (where they constitute about eighty percent).

Sudan's population has, in recent years, also included large numbers of refugees from neighboring African countries—Uganda, Ethiopia, Chad and Zaire (Congo, since May 1997). Their number has sometimes been estimated at over one million, but is usually several hundred thousand. It fluctuates as groups move back and forth. There are also refugees from Sudan to the neighboring countries—mainly from the African south, in the context of the civil war. Their population, sometimes estimated at several hundred thousand, also keeps shifting.

Sudan's economy is almost entirely agricultural, and to a large extent pastoral. The most important cash crop is cotton. The state's antihouse agricultural-industrial projects, with those in Rahad and Jezira in the lead, failed to produce the desired results. Industry has been hampered by a lack of foreign investment, shortages of spare parts and lack of professional infrastructures. Efforts are made to explore and exploit oil and mineral deposits. The war has steadily exhausted the country's economic resources. Most crucially, the war blocked the exploitation of oil. For a country with complete dependency on oil import, this was a serious problem.

The state of the economy has constantly deteriorated during the 1990s, causing a severe distress for the government and society. Inflation ran at more than 100 percent in 1996, while the annual *per capita* income dropped to less than 500 dollars. The state of the economy appeared even more gloomy, with the 13 billion dollars external debt in 1996. Of this debt 1.6 billion dollars was due to the International Monetary Fund (IMF). Sudan, which has come closer than any other country in the mid-1990s to expulsion from the IMF, pays it an annual rate of 550 million dollars for servicing the debt, while the overall debt interest amounts to 650–780 million dollars a year. This amount far exceeds the value of all Sudanese exports.

According to IMF and World Bank sources, only 32.3% of the Sudanese population was economically active in 1992. The majority of the work force earned its living in the agricultural sector. The rate of unemployment was officially estimated in the mid-1980s at thirteen percent though in reality it appears to be much higher.

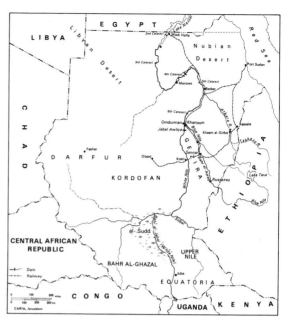

Map of Sudan

Political History

Pre-Independent Sudan *Bilad al-Sudan* (Arabic: "Land of the Blacks") was the name given by medieval Muslim geographers to the region lying south of the Sahara Desert and Egypt.

Muhammad Ali, the Ottoman Sultan's Viceroy in Egypt who became an autonomous ruler, conquered the north-central areas of the country, i.e., Nubia, Sennar and Kordofan, in 1820–1822. During the reign of the Khedive ISMA'IL (1863–1879), the provinces of Darfur, Bahr al-Ghazal and Equatoria and the Red Sea port of Suakin were added to Egypt's possessions. Egyptian rule impoverished Sudan, especially through the slave trade. The bitterness which the population felt towards the occupants was one of the reasons for the rebellion of the Mahdi.

The rebellion grew out of a fanatical Islamic-revivalist movement. Its leader, Muhammad Ahmad Ibn Abdallah, claimed to be the Mahdi (Arabic: The Guided One); the divine leader chosen by God at the end of time to fill the earth with justice. The Mahdi's followers (*al-Ansar*—Arabic: Helpers, after the first supporters of the Prophet Muhammad) defeated the troops sent against them in 1881 and conquered most of Kordofan, Darfur and Bahr al-Ghazal in 1882–1883. The British, who had occupied Egypt in 1882 (although nominally it remained part of the OTTOMAN EMPIRE), recommended the evacuation of the rest of Sudan and re-appointed the former Governor, General Gordon, to take care of it. Gordon negotiated with the Mahdi but failed to reach a compromise. In January 1885, the Mahdi's troops conquered Khartoum and massacred its garrison, including Gordon. The Mahdi died in the same year and his successor, the *Khalifa* Abdullahi, ruled until the liquidation of the Mahdist state in 1898.

In 1896, the British government decided to reconquer Sudan, mainly to prevent other powers (Germany, Italy, Belgium and especially FRANCE) from taking over the vital area of the sources of the Nile. The conquest was carried out in Egypt's name, to reimpose Egyptian control over what was described as Egyptian territory. The expeditionary force, composed of British and Egyptian troops under the command of Sir Herbert Kitchener, took Khartoum in September 1898 and by the end of that year the remaining *Mahdist* forces were defeated and the *Khalifa* Abdullahi was executed. The MAHDIYYA later became a peaceful sect, although still very influential. It was opposed by the MIRGHANIYYA or KHATMIYYA sect.

A "Condominium" agreement signed by BRITAIN and Egypt in January 1899 established their joint rule over Sudan. Britain wielded de facto control, and the regime it set up was colonial-type, the Anglo-Egyptian partnership being virtually fictitious. The administration was along military lines, because there were frequent uprisings. Pacification was completed only at the end of World War I. Sudan was governed by a Governor-General and appointed by the Egyptian Khedive on the recommendation of the British government. The Governor-General, who held both executive and legislative powers, was always British, and until 1926 the post was entrusted to the British Commander-in-Chief of the Egyptian army (the *Sirdar*). A March 1899 agreement with France ended a crisis over the occupation by French forces of Fashoda in South Sudan which had brought Britain and France to the brink of war: France relinquished the area. In 1901 and 1902, agreements with Italy and Ethiopia defined Sudan's borders with Eritrea and Ethiopia.

A nationalist movement appeared at a rather late stage, stimulated by the presence of Egyptian army officers and civil servants (generally of lower and middle rank). In 1921, Ali Abdel-Latif, a former army officer, created a "Sudanese United Tribes Society," which demanded independence for Sudan. He was imprisoned. On his release in 1929 he created a "White Flag League" aiming to establish Sudan as part of a Nile Valley united under the Egyptian Crown. Supported by Egyptian circles, it organized anti-British demonstrations in which military school cadets were active. The British imprisoned Abdel-Latif again and suppressed these beginnings of the national movement.

On 19 November 1924, Sir Lee Stack, the Governor-General of Sudan and *Sirdar* of the Egyptian army, was assassinated in Cairo by Egyptian nationalists. In retaliation, the British compelled all Egyptian troops and civil servants to evacuate Sudan. As anti-British agitation was mainly conducted by educated Sudanese in the cities, the British encouraged tribalism and tribal institutions and started ruling through local chiefs and sheikhs rather than creating a central bureaucracy based on urban educated Sudanese. Courses for training Sudanese administrators were discontinued; the Khartoum military college was closed down and harsh discipline was introduced at the Gordon Memorial College of Khartoum. This institution was opened in 1902 to train artisans and junior officials but had become a breeding-ground of Sudanese nationalism.

After 1924 Sudanese nationalism stagnated. From the mid-1930s its main organization was the "Graduates' Congress" based at Gordon College. Nationalist activity was revived after World War II when a decision concerning Sudan's future seemed imminent. The nationalists were now faced with the alternatives of an independent state or "Unity of the Nile Valley," i.e. union with Egypt (as Egypt demanded in its persistent struggle with Britain over Sudan— see EGYPT). Those favoring the latter appeared to have conceived this as a weapon against Britain rather than a permanent commitment unity with Egypt. Most of the supporters of independence joined the *Umma* (Nation) Party, under Abdallah al-Khalil, while the pro-Egyptian group, under Isma'il al-Azhari, formed the *Al-Ashiqqa"* (the Brethren), which grew out of the "Graduates' Congress." Both camps were continuously splitting into many rival factions. Of the Islamic orders, the Mahdiyya's al-Ansar supported independence, while the rival al-Mirghaniyya was pro-Egyptian.

The British started a gradual transition to partial autonomy in 1943 by establishing an Advisory Council for northern Sudan. In 1948 a Legislative Assembly was set up for the whole of Sudan. The transfer of power was slow, however, causing friction with Egypt which objected to any form of self-rule under British tutelage. The pro-Egyptian factions in Sudan also boycotted the legislative elections of 1948 and the consequent Assembly. The Sudanese members of the government—the Governor-General's Executive Council—were not, as a rule, political personalities.

A turning point was the July 1952 coup in Egypt. The new rulers agreed to grant the Sudanese the right of self-determination, as they were eager to get the British out of Sudan as soon as possible. Late in 1952 they concluded an accord with the Sudanese parties, and on 12 February 1953 Egypt and Britain signed an agreement about the future of Sudan. A transition period of three years was set to prepare the ground for the act of self-determination that would decide the future of Sudan (independence or union with Egypt). During the transition period the administration would be transferred to the Sudanese, and elections held under international supervision. British and Egyptian troops would be evacuated as soon as the elected Sudanese parliament decided that "Sudanization" was completed and the time for self-determination had come. Two international commissions were to assist that transition. Elections took place in November 1953, and al-Azhari's pro-Egyptian Party—which was now called "National Unionist Party" (NUP)—won. In January 1954, Azhari became the first Prime Minister of Sudan.

The Sudanization of the administration was considered complete in August 1955. Parliament demanded the evacuation of British and Egyptian troops which was effected by November 1955. Parliament and the government also demanded a simplification of the complicated constitutional procedure set for self-determination, and it was agreed that Sudan's future would be decided by a vote in Parliament. Azhari and his supporters had by now changed their minds about a union with Egypt and preferred complete independence. A resolution to that effect was unanimously adopted by Parliament on 19 December 1955. On 1 January 1956 Sudan became formally independent. As a Constitution, most of the British "Self-Government Statute" was taken over. This provided for an elected Parliament (elections being partially indirect, through tribal and village coun-

cils), and an Upper House three-fifths elected and two-fifths appointed. A Presidential Council, elected by Parliament, took over as Head of State.

Independent Sudan

Domestic Affairs Soon after achieving independence, Premier al-Azhari lost his parliamentary majority as his NUP split and lost the support of the pro-Egyptian Khatmiyya order. He had to form a coalition government that included Abdallah Khalil's *Umma* Party. In July 1956 a new coalition was formed by the *Umma* and the "People's Democratic Party" (PDP) founded by seceding members of the NUP and supported by the Khatmiyya. Abdallah Khalil became Prime Minister. The same coalition returned to power following the elections of February 1958, but its stability was threatened by disagreements between its partners over both domestic and foreign affairs. Thus the suggested appointment of the Mahdiyya leader Abdel-Rahman al-Mahdi as President of the Republic (instead of the five-member Presidency Council in office since independence) was strongly opposed by the PDP and had to be shelved. The *Umma* Party—pro-British and keen to strengthen ties with the West—also clashed with the PDP's pro-Egyptian and neutralist-leftist orientation. The threat of an economic crisis, caused mainly by a poor cotton crop, induced Premier Khalil to appeal for US economic aid. This was opposed by his coalition partners. To maintain his parliamentary majority, he had to win the support of the representatives of the south—in exchange for a pledge to discuss the transformation of Sudan's constitutional structure into a federal one. The coalition, and the Premier's position, were soon threatened again by feelers put out by some leaders of his own Party for a new coalition with the NUP. In October 1958, talks were held in Cairo between President ABDEL NASSER, al-Azhari and PDP leaders. This caused further concern to the Prime Minister and to a number of senior army officers who feared the increase of Egypt's political influence in Sudan. On 16 November the two main Parties—the *Umma* and the NUP—agreed to form a coalition. But their agreement was thwarted by a military coup on 17 November 1958.

The leader of the coup, General Ibrahim Abbud, abolished all political parties, "to save the country from the degeneration, chaos and instability" into which Party rivalries and the politicians' self-seeking intrigues had led it, and banned all political activity.

Parliament was dissolved and the constitution suspended. A "Supreme Council of the Armed Forces," composed of twelve officers, proclaimed General Abbud President and delegated to him all legislative, judicial and executive powers, as well as the command of the armed forces. A twelve-member cabinet headed by Abbud as Premier included seven officers.

Abbud's military dictatorship, which was rather mild and conservative, lasted for nearly six years. Several abortive military coups were crushed by Abbud in 1959. Fifteen prominent former politicians were arrested in 1961 for causing agitation and unrest, but they were released a year later. There was no progress toward constitutional rule or the resumption of political life; little economic advance—and the problem of southern Sudan (see below) appeared to be deteriorating. By September 1963, the southern tribes were in open rebellion.

A coup broke out in October 1964 sparked off by the troubles in the south and general discontent with the economic situation, inefficiency and corruption. Politicians, university students and workers had started campaigning for an end to military government and the restoration of democracy. On 21 October, police fired on demonstrators, killing one student. A general strike was called immediately. General Abbud was forced to negotiate with a common front comprised of all the old Parties and supported by the heads of the two Islamic orders. The Constitution of 1956 was reinstated. It was agreed that Abbud would remain President but hand over executive power to a transitional government composed of all parties and including, for the first time, the Communist Party and the MUSLIM BROTHERHOOD. Within four weeks, however, Abbud had to resign as President and Commander-in-Chief. The presidency reverted to a five-member Council.

The transitional government put much emphasis on the problem of southern Sudan and tried—unsuccessfully—to solve it with the help of supporters among southern leaders. The freedom of the press was restored and the ban on political parties abolished. In June 1965 elections were held, in which all parties, except the PDP, participated. As no Party won an absolute majority, a coalition was formed between the Umma Party, with seventy-six seats, and the NUP, fifty-three seats. Muhammad Ahmad Mahjoub (Umma) became Prime Minister and al-Azhari (NUP)

permanent chairman of the Presidential Council. The new regime was torn between rightist and leftist factions. In November 1965 the Communist Party was declared illegal. The decision was contested in court, which declared it null and void. However, after a protracted dispute with the judiciary, the court's judgement was overruled by the Assembly, which reimposed the ban.

In the meantime, the Umma Party was again split. A right wing under the leader of the Mahdiyya Order, the Imam al-Hadi al-Mahdi, supported the Premier, Mahjoub, while younger elements followed the Imam's nephew, the modernist-progressive Sadeq AL-MAHDI. The latter became Prime Minister after a vote of no confidence forced Mahjoub to resign in July 1966. The new government, also a coalition of the Umma and the NUP, was able to improve the economic situation owing to strict controls and loans from the World Bank. It also promised to solve the question of southern Sudan by a degree of regional autonomy. The drafting of a permanent constitution was speeded up. However, as the Imam withdrew his support from his nephew, one faction of the Umma Party voted against the government and it was defeated in the Assembly in May 1967. Mahjoub again became Premier, supported by a coalition of the NUP and the Imam al-Hadi faction of the Umma. The PDP now also joined (it merged, late in 1967, with the NUP, to form the "Democratic Unionist Party" (DUP). This government concluded an arms deal with the USSR and lifted the ban on the Communist Party. But the coalition was unstable: the presidency was claimed by both Azhari and al-Hadi al-Mahdi; the southern problem was unsolved; and the drafting of the constitution caused considerable controversy. The draft prepared was based on Islam, regionalism, decentralization and a strong presidential executive at the center. It was strongly opposed by the Communists and the PDP. In January 1968, the government decided to dissolve the Assembly. In new elections, in April 1968, the newly merged DUP won 101 seats, al-Hadi al-Mahdi's faction of the Umma thirty seats, and Sadeq al-Mahdi's Umma thirty-six. The two former groups again formed a government under Mahjoub. But this government, too, failed to tackle the three major problems—the economic situation, the permanent constitution and southern Sudan. Its position was undermined by disputes between the coalition partners and by reports that the two wings of the *Umma* had reunited and were about to re-establish their conservative rule.

On 25 May 1969 a group of army officers under Colonel Ja'far al-NUMEIRI staged a bloodless coup. The name of the state was changed to "Democratic Republic of the Sudan." The constitution was again suspended, and the Constituent Assembly and the Presidential Council were dissolved. Absolute powers were vested in a National Revolutionary Council. A former Chief Justice, Abu Bakr Awadallah, was appointed Prime Minister. His Cabinet contained several Communists. All political parties were abolished and several former ministers were brought to trial on charges of corruption. The new regime proclaimed a policy of "Sudanese Socialism," with the state participating in the economy, while maintaining freedom for foreign aid and local capital.

In October 1969, friction concerning the Communist Party came to a head. During a visit to East Germany, Awadallah declared that the Sudanese revolution could not function without the Communist Party (which had disregarded the ban imposed on political parties and conducted public meetings and propaganda activities). Numeiri prepared to cooperate with the Communists to achieve broader support for his regime, but striving to curtail their power, disavowed Awadallah and himself took over as Premier. He appointed Awadallah Foreign Minister and Minister of Justice.

In March 1970, Numeiri confronted the potentially most dangerous foes of his regime (and probably the strongest organized group in the country): the Mahdiyya and the *Ansar*. In Numeiri's official version, Mahdiyya demonstrations turned into a plot, a rebellion. He suppressed that "rebellion" in a military and security operation. Nuclei of Mahdiyya resistance forces, concentrated on Aba island in the White Nile, were liquidated—an operation in which the Imam, al-Hadi al-Mahdi, was killed. The rival, political Mahdiyya leader, Sadeq al-Mahdi, who was among the hundreds arrested, was deported to Egypt (as was the Communist leader Abdel Khaleq Mahjoub).

Relations with the Communists continued plaguing the regime and were at the root of several coup attempts, changes of government and purges. In November 1970, leading leftists were purged from the government and army, but other leftists continued

serving. The Communist Party itself was split on the question of collaboration with the regime (with the main faction, headed by Secretary-General Abdel Khaleq Mahjoub, opposing such collaboration). In July 1971, a group of leftist officers—of those purged in November—actually ousted Numeiri: they were, however, defeated after three days by loyal army units, and Numeiri was reinstated amidst bloody purges of leftists, summary trials and executions (including the top Communist leaders). The crisis also caused some upheaval in Sudan's foreign relations—the USSR was accused of supporting the coup, ambassadors were recalled, and relations came close to a breach; with Iraq, similarly accused, relations were severed. Libya and Egypt appear to have helped Numeiri.

The suppression of the Ansar and the Communists in 1970–1971 eliminated Numeiri's political rivals and enabled him to consolidate his regime. In August 1971 he proclaimed a transitional Constitution, and in September he was elected President, as the single candidate, also retaining the Premiership. In October he dissolved the Revolutionary Command Council. The same month he established a single Party, on the Egyptian pattern; the Sudanese Socialist Union (SSU). This held its first convention in January 1972. In February–March 1972, Numeiri attained the greatest achievement of his years in power: he reached agreement with the South rebels to end the civil war (see below). In September 1972, a People's National Assembly was elected (indirectly) and in April 1973 it adopted a permanent Constitution which proclaimed Sudan to be a "unitary, democratic, socialist and sovereign republic," with Islam as state religion (but provided for an autonomous regime in the south). In February 1974 a new National Assembly was elected.

But Sudan's stability continued to be shaken by plots and unrest. One nucleus of potential opposition was the officers' corps. An officers' plot and attempted coup was foiled in January 1973, and another in September 1975. At least the second was reportedly connected with and inspired by a political anti-Numeiri "National Front" (NF) that had been formed, in exile (mainly in Libya) or half-underground, from the early 1970s by a coalition of the Mahdiyya's *Umma* Party, the former NUP-DUP, and the Muslim Brotherhood. In July 1976 another coup attempt was staged by the NF, with active

Libyan support. It was suppressed only after serious fighting.

Numeiri responded by constant purges and an effort to tighten his government. He also tried to strengthen the SSU, with little success. In April 1977 Numeiri was re-elected, as the single candidate, for a second six-year term as President. He now felt secure enough to initiate a reconciliation with the NF. An amnesty was proclaimed in August 1977. Sadeq al-Mahdi returned to Sudan after over seven years of exile. Another faction of the NF, the Muslim Brothers led by Hassan Abdallah al-Turabi, also made its peace with the regime. The third faction of the NF, al-Sharif al-Hindi's DUP, reached an agreement with Numeiri in April 1978 on the dissolution of the NF (although the reconciliation process faced at the same time new obstacles because of Numeiri's tacit support of Egypt's peace policy towards ISRAEL). While promoting that reconciliation process, Numeiri continued reorganizing his government. In February 1978, elections to Sudan's Third People's National Assembly and the Southern People's Regional Assembly took place, with candidates sponsored by the *Umma*, the DUP and the Muslim Brothers successfully participating.

Meanwhile, Sudan was facing worsening economic problems, which caused further social and political unrest. The Numeiri regime had done very little to advance major development schemes. The only new projects were the start of work on the long-planned Jonglei Canal to drain the vast al-Sudd swamps of the White Nile (see WATER POLITICS) in 1978, with international aid and by foreign companies, and the beginning of oil production by the American Chevron company in south Sudan at about the same time. In general, the economy stagnated and production declined. When the government decided to devalue the currency in mid-1978, a wave of industrial trouble swept over Sudan. During 1979, there was further economic decline, and growing public resentment led to violent riots in August 1979. The reconciliation process suffered delays and was partially suspended. Renewed unrest in the south (see below) aggravated the situation. Reshuffles in the Cabinet and the SSU, as well as its the southern regional government, failed to calm the grousing unrest. During 1980–1981, Numeiri continued to struggle with the economic difficulties and growing pressures within the regime, facing a wave of vio-

lent riots which swept over the Darfur region. In October 1981 Numeiri dissolved the National Assembly. The new one he convened in February 1982 was appointed, not elected. In 1982, serious political-industrial unrest re-erupted in Khartoum; the army was summoned to crush the turbulence and the regime's prestige was eroded. Numeiri put the blame on the SSU's failure to win popular support and again made substantial changes at the top of the political hierarchy; dispersed the leading SSU institutions and purged the top echelons of the army command. General Abdel-Majid Hamed Khalil, since 1979 held the posts of First Vice-President, Minister of Defense, Commander-in-Chief, General Secretary of the SSU. He was regarded as Numeiri's chosen successor, and dismissed from all his posts (Numeiri had similarly dismissed in 1978 First Vice-President Abul-Qassem Muhammad Ibrahim and several times changed other Vice-Presidents).

Yet, despite this continuous political and economic predicament, and with the South Sudan crisis mounting, the Numeiri regime held on. In an April-May 1983 referendum Numeiri was elected, as the single candidate, for a third presidential term. In September 1983 he decreed the implementation of Islamic law (SHARI'A) and its code of punishments throughout Sudan—a step that was rejected by many, including both the major Islamic orders, the Mahdiyya and the Khatmiyya. This caused bitter resentment particularly in the non-Muslim south. The enforcement of the Islamic law, which was initiated by Numeiri to recover the regime's legitimacy, was perceived as a direct gain of the Muslim Brotherhood movement led by al-Turabi, enhancing its political position among Muslims in Sudan after years of being criticized for its collaboration with Numeiri.

The steady weakening of Numeiri's position came to a climax in March 1985, when massive civil disobedience erupted, paralyzing the country. On 6 April 1985, it brought about the regime's overthrow. Numeiri took refuge in Egypt. Power was taken over by the army command under General Abdel Rahman Muhammad Hassan Siwar-al-Dhahab, Defense Minister and Commander-in-Chief since March 1985. The government, the National Assembly, the Regional Assemblies, and the SSU were dissolved. In April a fifteen-member Transitional Military Council, with Siwar al-Dhahab as chairman, and a civilian government headed by Daf'allah Juzuli were formed.

This transitional government led Sudan until April 1986, when the first democratic elections since 1968 were held throughout the country (excluding large areas in the south—see below). The *Umma* Party under al-Sadeq al-Mahdi emerged as the strongest faction in the new Constituent Assembly with 99 of 260 seats, followed by the DUP with 63 and the Muslim Brothers' National Islamic Front (NIF), led by al-Turabi, with 51 seats. On 15 May 1986 Sadeq al-Mahdi formed a coalition government, comprising the *Umma*, the DUP and several southern groups. The NIF and the Communists (with three seats) formed the opposition. The Presidency was replaced by a Council of Sovereignty or State Supreme Council, chaired by Ahmad Ali al-Mirghani, the brother of the spiritual leader of the Khatmiyya sect (thus balancing al-Mahdi's position as Prime Minister). From summer 1986, the new government had to cope with Sudan's serious problems—with the economic crisis and the escalating civil war in the south as the most severe and urgent ones.

On 30 June 1989, a military coup d'état was launched in Khartoum by Brigadier General Urmar Hasan Ahmad al-Bashir. This ended the democratically elected government of al-Sadiq al-Mahdi. Bashir's government became the seventh to govern Sudan since its independence in 1956. Notwithstanding the new regime's promises to halt the country's headlong plunge into chaos, the crucial problems of Sudan have steadily aggravated, leading the country more deeply into political crisis, civil war and economic abyss.

A year after seizing power, the regime felt free to drop the mask which had hitherto camouflaged its true militant political Islamist character, the first one of its sort in the Sunni-Islamic countries. It became clear that the Bashir regime, with Hasan Abdallah al-Turabi as the power behind the throne, was the extension of the formally banned National Islamic Front (NIF) Party, the powerful group split from the Muslim Brotherhood in 1985.

The takeover by the NIF led to a systematic process of Islamization of the Sudanese public and institutional spheres, with the Front capturing the key bureaucratic and power positions in the country. On New Year's Eve of 1991, the Bashir regime reimplemented the SHARI'A (Islamic Holy Law) throughout the country, excluding the non-Muslim and non-Arab south. The Shari'a law, first implemented

by Numeiri in 1983 (see above), had been suspended and virtually shelved after the overthrow of Numeiri's regime in 1985, despite the NIF's persistent demand that it should be implemented. The Shari'a issue had been a steady source of a politcal and social controversy. The sourthern SPCA's major demand to repeal the Shari'a law formally, as a prerequisite to any negotiation with Khartoum, was one of the most important manifestations of this political-religious controversy.

Meanwhile, the ongoing civil war in the south of Sudan, which entered its fourteenth year in 1997, was a major source of concern for the regime, and continued to erode its political standing both at home and abroad. The war continued to take many lives from both warring sides, the government and the southern rebels with the Sudanese people's Liberation Army (SPLA) as the strong mainstream movement. Khartoum's government activated the Popular Defense Forces (PDF), a milita of mainly young Islamist zealots, to assist the army in warding off the rebels. It was not an easy task for the government; especially since it was urged to allocate growing resources for suppressing increasing popular socioeconomic and political turmoil in Khartoum.

The problem of Southern Sudan The most acute domestic problem is the question of the three southern provinces—Equatoria, Bahr al-Ghazal and the Upper Nile, populated by 6-7 million non-Arab and non-Muslim Negro tribes, mostly pagan and about twenty percent Christian. During the Condominium, the (British) government endeavored to preserve southern Sudan's special character and to close it to northern Muslim penetration and domination. In 1955, on the eve of independence, southerners, afraid of northern domination, rebelled, starting with a mutiny of southern troops. The rebellion was suppressed, but a further revolt broke out in 1963. In February 1964 the government decided to expel all foreign Christian missionaries operating in the south, accusing them of fostering the rebellion. Harsh military action against the rebels and villagers and tribes assisting them caused a great number of southern Sudanese to take refuge in neighboring countries. In July 1969 the UN estimated their number at over 150,000, while others spoke of up to 400,000. The rebellion and its suppression is said to have caused the death of hundreds of thousands of people.

The southerners were divided over their plans for the future. Some wanted a separate southern state independent of Sudan, whilst others favored a federation with the north. Some were prepared to cooperate with the existing unitary state, perhaps with increased local autonomy and decentralization, and collaborated with the government (in which some southerners, forming various shifting parties, usually held ministerial posts).

The new civilian government of October 1964 declared an amnesty in the south. A Round Table Conference on the constitutional future of the south was held in Khartoum in March 1965, attended by the government, representatives of southern and northern political parties and observers from seven African states. No agreement was reached, and the problem was referred to a committee. The latter recommended a measure of decentralization and regional autonomy—a recommendation endorsed by another conference of political parties. Elections postponed in the south in 1965 could be held in 1967. But the government was still unable to agree to a basic solution to the problem and the rebellion continued.

The rebellion was centered mainly in Equatoria province. Its forces were divided by tribal differences and antagonisms. It was, for instance, reported that the *Dinka*, the largest tribe, centered in Bahr al-Ghazal and Upper Nile provinces, took little part. But information about the internal organization and problems of the rebels was patchy and unreliable. In 1967–1968 the rebels established a Ugandan-based "Provisional Government" headed by Aggrey Jaden. Early in 1969 they proclaimed an independent "Nile Republic," headed now, after factional struggles and the ouster of Jaden, by Gordon Mayen. However, some of the rebels inside Sudan refused to recognize the Ugandan-based refugee government. In mid-1969 their military army, the Anyanya, proclaimed their own independent government, the Anyidi State. General Emidio Tafeng Lodongi formed a Revolutionary Council and government. In 1970–1971 Colonel Joseph Lagu emerged as the main leader.

After the coup of 1969, the new Numeiri regime resolved to find a solution to the problem of the south and opened secret negotiations with the rebels, in the Ethiopian capital Addis Ababa. In March 1972 an agreement was signed, thereby ending the civil war. The three southern provinces jointly were given a large degree of autonomy (later incorporated in the new provisional Constitution of 1973). The newly created Southern Region was to be ruled by a Higher Executive Council and an elected People's Regional Assembly. The chairman of the Council was to be appointed by the Head of State and serve also as Vice-President of Sudan. There was to be no discrimination on grounds of religion and ethnic background. The central governments remained responsible for defense, foreign policy, communications and several other matters of national concern. Education, housing, health etc., were left in the hands of the southern government. A first Regional Assembly was elected in November 1973. For several years the 1972 Agreement provided the basis for peace and cooperation in the south itself and between the south and north. But in the mid-1970s, circumstances began to change. The economic crisis aggravated the south's already serious economic problems. Sudan's realignment with Egypt was traditionally perceived in the south as a threat to southern autonomy and interests; the process of "national reconciliation," from 1977, seemed to strengthen the Arab-Islamic character of Sudan; and the government seemed to renege on its support for southern autonomy. There was also near-constant factional and tribal friction in the southern regional institutions and they were shaken by frequent changes in the executive and by the central (northern) government's attempts to use and manipulate these changes and frictions. Lagu, who had replaced Abel Alier, a Dinka, as chairman of the Executive Council in 1978, was out by February 1980 and Alier resumed his chairmanship. But in October 1981 the Council and the Assembly were dissolved, along with the dismissal of Sudan's National Assembly. From the early 1980s the south was much agitated by a proposal to dissolve the three-province region and reconstitute each province as a separate entity. This idea, evidently a breach of the agreement of 1972, was supported by Lagu and other Equatoria politicians (resenting Dinka predominance in the regional institutions), but strongly rejected by most of the south. Yet in June 1983, the dissolution of the three southern provinces was decreed by Numeiri, causing bitter resentment among its opponents. Even deeper anger was aroused in the south by Numeiri's September 1983 decree imposing Islamic law and its code of punishments on all Sudan without clearly exempting the non-Muslim south. These affronts and irritations brought much support to the rebellion that had re-erupted shortly before, in 1983.

The new rebellion was led by a "Sudan People's Liberation Movement" that emerged in 1983 out of splits in the renewed Anyanya organization, with a military wing, the "Sudan People's Liberation Army" (SPLA). The dominant leader of the rebels was a former Colonel in the Sudan army, John Garang, who claimed that he was fighting not only for the autonomy of the south but for a revolution in all of Sudan. The SPLA has had a considerable measure of military success.

During the late 1980s to 1990s, the SPLA, although suffering internal schisms and serious splits, appeared as a powerful movement, both politically and militarily. It achieved various political agreements with the northern elements of the NDA northern opposition. Most noteworthy was the Koba Dam Agreement of 1986. Its main articles were the repeal of the September 1983 Shari'a law; the adoption of the 1956 constitution as amended in 1964 with the incorporation of a regional government; and the abrogation of military pacts concluded between Sudan and other countries (implying Egypt and Libya). The SPLA persistently adhered to the "Koba Dam Declaration" urging all governments which had subsequented Numeiri's to implement the agreement and end the war, but to no avail.

During the 1990s, the SPLA and the Khartoum governments of Hasan Siwar al-Dahab (1985–1986), al-Sadiq al-Mahdi (1986–1989) and Bashir (1989–), reiterated their keen interest in reaching a political solution to the conflict, while launching a full-scale military offensive one against the other. During these years, none of the conflcting sides became closer to a military victory. Raging for the fourth successive year in 1997, the civil war continued to claim many lives from both sides and to drain the state's limited economic resources. Political contacts between the warring sides were completely deadlocked, as the Islamist regime in Khartoum could not meet the south's basic demands of repealing the Shari'a law and establish new political, economic, religious and social order in Sudan, to give the south and other deprived components of the society what they viewed as their fair share in the state's resources and key policies.

Foreign Affairs During its first years, Sudan's government followed a neutralist line, generally with pro-Western sympathies. After the 1958 coup, General Abbud carried on the same policy, although he was somewhat less friendly toward the West. The civilian government which succeeded Abbud in 1964 for some time allegedly supported revolutionary movements in southern Arabia, Congo and Eritrea. In 1965, relations with the German Federal Republic were severed after Bonn's decision to establish diplomatic relations with Israel (re-established in 1971), and those with Britain over Rhodesia (re-established in 1966). In June 1967, relations with the West deteriorated further as a result of the Six-Day War, and Sudan broke off relations with the US and UK; those with Britain were resumed in January 1968, and those with the US in July 1972. From 1967–1968, the Sudanese government strengthened relations with the USSR and the Soviet Bloc and accepted military and economic aid, including Soviet military advisers. After the May 1969 coup the Numeiri regime also recognized the German Democratic Republic. But relations with the Soviet Bloc suffered a heavy blow in the crisis of July 1971 (see above). In the 1970s military "facilities" the USSR enjoyed in Sudan were cut off. In 1977 all Soviet military advisers were reportedly expelled. Generally, the Numeiri regime followed, despite its officially neutralist stance, a pro-Western, pro-US orientation. It also grew increasingly dependent on US and Western aid. The post-1985 regime seemed to take a more reserved, neutralist line.

Sudan, admitted to the Arab League in 1956, upon attaining independence, followed a neutral policy between the rival Arab blocs. In 1958 a sharp conflict with Egypt arose when the latter tried to take over disputed border areas by force. Egypt was compelled to retreat following Kharoum's firm stand, including a complaint to the UN Security Council. Another, more permanent cause of friction with Egypt, the problem of the distribution of the Nile waters, was resolved in 1959 by a new agreement—see WATER POLITICS. Yet, during the first years of independence, Sudan remained suspicious of Egypt. It resented Egypt's "Big-Brother" attitude and reported intervention in Sudan politics, intrigues and the cultivation of pro-Egyptian factions. Gradually, however, relations normalized. After the Arab-Israeli Six-Day War, Sudan became more active in inter-

Arab affairs. The first Arab summit conference after the war was held in Khartoum in September 1967. A Sudanese contingent was left with the Egyptian army at the Suez front. Sudan's Premier was instrumental in successfully mediating between Egypt and Saudi Arabia in the Yemen war during the Khartoum summit.

Following the May 1969 coup, Numeiri initiated a policy of close cooperation with Egypt and Libya. Leaders of the three countries met several times to discuss cooperation in the military, economic and cultural spheres. In November 1970 they announced their decision to establish a tripartite federation of Egypt, Sudan and Libya. But when the federation was re-endorsed in April 1971 (with Syria as an additional member), Sudan was no longer among its members. It was not officially clarified why Sudan at the last minute opted out of the Federation. It may be assumed that it was due to the growing antagonism between it and Libya (see below). Sudan's relations with Egypt were not adversely affected. On the contrary, they were considerably strengthened during the 1970s and early 1980s and became so close that a trend towards an eventual Sudan-Egypt confederation was indicated. In February 1974, Presidents Numeiri and Sadat agreed on plans to "integrate" Sudan and Egypt. A Defense Pact was signed in January 1977 which was reconfirmed and renewed in December 1981. It was also decided that the two National Assemblies should meet in joint session, and from 1977 they did so several times. In 1979 Sudan dissented from the all-Arab denunciation and boycott of Egypt; supported its moves towards peace with Israel, and maintained official relations with it. All-Arab pressure compelled it to recall its Ambassador in December 1979, but it sent a new one in 1981. In October 1982 the idea of Sudanese-Egyptian integration was institutionalized in a formal agreement. As a token of that integration, a "Nile Valley Parliament," comprising sixty members from each National Assembly, first met in May 1983. From 1985, after the fall of Numeiri, the new regime visibly dissociated itself from Egypt. In February 1987 it signed a new Egypt-Sudan "Charter of Brotherhood," abolishing the integration agreements.

In Sudan's relations with Libya there were ups and downs, but the trend in the 1970s was toward increasing tension and a growing antagonism. Sudan always suspected Libyan subversion, intervention and plots; and indeed QADHAFI, resenting Numeiri's pro-Western orientation and his opposition to Libyan expansionist merger schemes (e.g., in Chad), seemed to have a hand in several attempts to topple or destabilize Sudan's regime. He granted asylum and operational bases to the Mahdiyya-plus-DUP opposition, and went as far as supporting and aiding the rebelling South Sudan African tribes, contrasting Qadhafi's own Arab nationalist and Islamic principles (since that was a rebellion of non-Arab and non-Muslim populations against an Arab-Muslim regime). Sudan also complained of breaches of its sovereignty by border incursions and overflights. Official relations were severed from 1976 to 1977, and from 1981 to the fall of Numeiri.

The post-1985 regime resumed relations and instituted a significant rapprochement with Libya (although it also complained of encroachments on Sudan's territory by Libyan operations in Chad). Relations with Ethiopia were also troubled. Ethiopia complained that Sudan was aiding the Eritrean rebels, or at least granting them asylum and operational bases. Sudan charged Ethiopia with affording similar support to the South Sudan African rebels. Since both countries were interested in normal relations, there were ups and downs, from acute tension and the recall of Ambassadors to solemn state visits. Sudan promised several times to end its aid to the Eritrean rebels (and did so to a certain extent). But the problem remained unresolved.

An additional irritant was the transit through Sudan of 10,000–15,000 escaping Ethiopian Jews, from 1981–1982 to a peak in 1984–1985; their reception in transit camps, and their transportation to Israel in an airlift organized by American institutions and tacitly allowed by Sudan. This issue also had internal repercussions in Sudan which led, after the fall of Numeiri, to the trial and condemnation of several leading officials, including one of Numeiri's Vice-Presidents.

Sudan's foreign affairs in the mid-1990s were complicated, suffering large dozes of hostility and even active oppostion in all of its major extenal scenes. The central threat was the imposition of sanctions by the UN Security Council in May 1996. The sanctions spearheaded by the US and Egypt were aimed at exerting pressure on Khartoum to extradite to Ethiopia three Egyptian nationals suspected of carrying out the attack on the life of Egypt's president, Husni MUBARAK in Addis Ababa in June 1995. The three allegedly stayed within Sudan's territory. According to Cairo, the Sudanese government was responsible for the assassination attempt. Egypt and the US were eager to see the Bashir Islamist regime toppled. The basic rejection toward the Sudanese regime stemmed from its radical Islamist nature and Cairo's and Washington's fears of Khartoum's violent activist policy, exporting the "Islamic revolution" to its regional arena. Such perceived Sudanese foreign policy, coupled by Khartoum's close relations with Iran's Islamic regime, seemed harmful to the governments in Egypt and other friendly governments to the US, while threatening, at the same time, the peace process in the Middle East.

Most alarming from Khartoum's point of view was the joining of Eritrea, Ethiopia and Uganda to the anti-Sudanese active hostile front, led by the US and Egypt. All of these countries wished to see the Sudanese regime eradicated. The animosity of the adjacent African countries toward the Khartoum government was exemplified by Eritrea's and Uganda's breaking off diplomatic relations with Sudan in 1995, and by Ethiopia's Eritrea's, and to a lesser degree also Uganda's military intervention in the Sudanese civil war, supporting the southern rebel movement.

These foreign policies further hightened Khartoum's already bitter enmity toward Washington, perceiving the US as the patron of Sudan's neighboring states and as responsible for all of Sudan's . woes. The Sudanese regime further considered the US as the enemy of Islam. Israel was viewed similarly and the regime adopted a rejectionist stand sometimes eclipsed by intentional political ambivalence toward the state of Israel and the Middle East peace process. The other side of the coin was Sudan's ardent commitment to the Palestinian cause.

From the early 1990s, Sudan's spirutal leader Hasan AL-TURABI has been active in bringing together radical Islamic movements into a continuous dialogue under his leadership. This dialogue, often mistakenly interpreted in the context of exporting the Islamic revolution, apparently intends to enhance Turabi's own status among radical Islamic movements and Sudan's position as an example of appled radical Islamism.

SUEZ CAMPAIGN see ARAB-ISRAEL CONFLICT.

SUEZ CANAL An artificial canal connecting the Mediterranean and the Red Sea stretching 101 miles (163 km.). Its northern outlet is at the city of Port Sa'id its southern outlet, at Suez. It passes through various lakes, the largest of which is the Great Bitter Lake. It had—until deepened and widened in a major 1,300 million dollar operation of 1976–1980, a depth of 43 ft. (13 meters) and a minimum width of 196 ft. (60 meters), able to accommodate vessels of up to 37 ft. (11 meters) draft and a load of up to 60,000 tons. Since that operation, it has been able to accommodate vessels with a load of up to 150,000 tons (or empty vessels up to 370,000 tons).

It was the French engineer Ferdinand de Lesseps who conceived the idea of the canal and was its driving force. FRANCE supported him in this endeavor while BRITAIN regarded the scheme as a French attempt to challenge its influence in the East, opposed it fiercely (and tried, as an alternative, to develop a land route from the Mediterranean to the Red Sea along with a railway from the Syrian coast to Mesopotamia, to link up with Euphrates and Tigris steamers). In November 1854, de Lesseps obtained from Sa'id—the governor of EGYPT—a concession for the "Universal Suez Canal Shipping Company" to dig the canal and operate it for ninety-nine years. Due to British pressure, the Ottoman Sultan, who was nominally the Suzerain of Egypt, refused to approve the concession.

A new concession, in January 1856, included an Egyptian undertaking to supply free of charge the labor required for digging. In 1858, despite British opposition, de Lesseps announced the formation of the Suez Canal Company. In November 1858, the company floated about 400,000 shares at the price of 500 francs each. Half of them were bought by France, with Egypt purchasing almost all the remainder.

Work began in 1859 under the guidance of French experts. Tens of thousands of Egyptian *fallahin* labored—and many of them perished. In 1866, the company dispensed, in an agreement with Isma'il, the new Viceroy, with most of the forced labor (*corvee*), against a substantial compensation. The agreement also stressed Egyptian sovereignty over the canal area and, in its wake, the Ottoman Sultan confirmed the concession. On 17 November 1869, the Suez canal was inaugurated with great pomp at a cost of 432.8 million francs.

The Egyptians held forty-four percent of the ordinary shares, in addition to preference shares entitling them to fifteen percent of the profits. However, the Khedive Isma'il got heavily into debt until he had to sell all his shares. The British government bought them in 1875, on Disraeli's initiative, for about 4 million dollars. In 1882, the British occupied Egypt, giving them control over the canal zone.

In 1888, the Maritime Powers and the OTTOMAN EMPIRE signed the Convention of Constantinople, in which they undertook to ensure the Suez canal was "always free and open in time of war as in time of peace, to every vessel of commerce or of war, without distinction of flag." With regard to some clauses of the convention, priority was given to Egyptian security needs, but this did not apply to the freedom of passage, which was established as an essential principle not limited by any conditions.

The Suez canal became profitable several years after its opening and, by 1920, its profits had paid eight times the original investment. On the eve of World War II, over 20 million tons per annum of shipping passed through the Canal. In the 1960s, the total tonnage reached 275 million; the annual income 150–200 million dollars. Until 1938, Egypt did not receive any of the company's revenues because in 1880 it had mortgaged its fifteen percent share of the profits to French banks. Under agreements in 1937 and 1949 this was corrected to some extent and Egypt began receiving seven percent of the profits. Similarly, in 1937 Egypt gained representation on the board of the company, which was enlarged in 1949.

The Suez canal was perceived as a highly important military and strategic asset. British reinforcements and equipment (mainly from India and Australia) passed through it during World War I. A Turkish-German attempt to capture the canal in 1915 was driven off. When Britain granted nominal independence to Egypt in 1922, it kept the right to station troops and bases in the canal Zone and to defend it. In the Anglo-Egyptian Treaty of 1936, Egypt recognized Britain's special interests with regard to the Suez canal and agreed to the stationing of British forces of a specified type and strength in the canal area. The treaty stressed that this would not be interpreted as occupation or an infringement of Egyptian sovereignty. During World War II, reinforcements for the Allied troops passed through the Suez canal. The Germans tried unsuccessfully to bomb it.

After World War II, Egypt demanded the evacuation of all British forces and bases from its soil, including the canal Zone. Negotiations were difficult, resulting in a severe crisis in 1951–1952 (see EGYPT). Under an October 1954 Agreement, Britain undertook to evacuate the canal Zone within twenty months. The bases was to be maintained with the help of British technicians, and British forces would be permitted to return to them in the event of an attack on a member state of the ARAB LEAGUE or on TURKEY (in other words, any Middle Eastern country with the exception of ISRAEL). The Agreement re-emphasized the freedom of passage, although for years Egypt had prevented the passage of ships to and from Israel. The last British forces evacuated the canal Zone in July 1956.

Meanwhile a crisis had emerged in the relations between Egypt and the UNITED STATES following the latter's retreat on its previous willingness to give Egypt financial aid for the construction of a high dam in Aswan. In response, on 26 July 1956, ABDEL NASSER announced the nationalization of the Suez canal. The West European countries, with Britain and France at the forefront, feared for the freedom of passage through the canal, and especially for their vital OIL supply route. They were also concerned that Egypt might not be able to maintain the canal or organize navigation through it. Egypt argued that it had only nationalized the company, as the canal itself was in any case Egyptian property, and no changes would occur in canal passage and arrangements. Negotiations on those arrangements and the safeguarding of international interests on compensation to the company and representation on the board of management, failed in late summer 1956. Discussions at the UN Security Council were to no avail.

At the beginning of November 1956, British and French troops moved into the canal Zone on the pretext of separating Egypt and Israel, then engaged in battles at Sinai (see ARAB-ISRAEL CONFLICT). In the course of the fighting, the Egyptians blocked the canal by sinking forty-seven ships. Intervention by the UN, and particularly the US and USSR, forced Britain and France to withdraw their forces from Egypt. In January 1957, Egypt abrogated the Anglo-

Egyptian Agreement of 1954 and denied Britain the right to return and operate its bases in the canal Zone. That same month the Egyptian "Suez canal Authority" began to clear the canal and in April it was re-opened for navigation. In 1957, Egypt also reiterated its undertaking to respect the freedom of navigation, detailing ways in which to pass through the canal. After lengthy negotiations with the company and shareholders, an agreement on compensation and the mutual settlement of accounts was reached in April 1958. Contrary to fears expressed in 1956, the Egyptians succeeded in running the canal, including navigation, without mishap. For a number of years after 1957, Egypt received loans and grants, mainly from the World Bank and KUWAIT, to widen and deepen the canal.

From 1948, Egypt prevented the passage of all ships on their way to or from Israel. Israel and many other countries deemed this blockade, which led to many incidents, which were contrary to the Constantinople Convention of 1888 and other international agreements (such as the Anglo-Egyptian Treaty and the Egypt-Israel Armistice). On 1 September 1951 it was condemned by the UN Security Council, which called on Egypt to "terminate the restrictions on passage," found to be "unjustified interference with the rights of nations to navigate the seas." Egypt ignored the decision, and attempts to get the Security Council to act again were frustrated by a Soviet veto.

The Suez canal was closed again during the June 1967 War and remained closed for eight years, as Israel occupied its east bank. The canal became the front line between Israeli and Egyptian forces which brought destruction and evacuation to most of the Egyptian population from the area, especially during the Israel-Egypt War of Attrition (1969–1970). Israel was willing in principle to accept the reopening of the canal on the condition that the freedom of navigation to and from Israel was assured. Egypt refused this and also opposed the reopening of the canal while Israeli forces were stationed on its east bank. Attempts in early 1971 to reach a separate interim agreement with Egypt through US offices on a partial Israeli withdrawal and the reopening of the Suez canal failed (see ARAB-ISRAEL PEACEMAKING).

In the October 1973 War, the Suez canal was a main battle arena. Egyptian forces succeeded in breaching the Israeli fortifications on the eastern bank (the "Bar-Lev Line") and crossed the canal. Israeli forces occupied a strip of territory on the western, Egyptian side (see ARAB-ISRAEL CONFLICT). The Disengagement Agreement of January 1974 provided for the evacuation of the Israeli-held beachhead on the Egyptian side of the canal, while it left Egypt holding a strip of territory on the eastern bank, with a UN Emergency Force manning a buffer zone. The agreement did not specifically speak of the reopening of the Suez canal, but in its wake Egypt began clearing and repairing the canal and rebuilding the destroyed cities on its shores (some of them, up to eighty percent): Port Said, Isma'iliyya, Suez. In 1979 construction of the Salem canal, bringing water from the Nile to Sinai, began and a year later the first tunnel under the Suez Canal 1 mile (1.6 km) was opened, directly linking Sinai into Egypt's mainland. By 1980, more than 1 million Egyptians had returned to these cities. Progress was achieved in a US-mediated Egypt-Israel Interim Agreement of 1 September 1975. Article seven declared: "Non-military cargoes destined for or coming from Israel shall be permitted through the Suez canal" (in foreign-flag vessels). Toward that agreement the Suez canal was reopened in June 1975. Finally, the Egypt-Israel Camp David agreements of September 1978 and the Peace Treaty of March 1979 provided for free passage of Israeli shipping through the canal. These were duly implemented.

The vicissitudes of the Suez canal problem had a significant impact on the world's oil economy, since most of the PERSIAN GULF oil used to pass through the canal. Its blocking during the crisis of 1956 caused an oil shortage in Europe. After the canal was reopened in 1957, the proportion of oil tankers among ships passing through it increased, reaching seventy percent of the tonnage of the approximately 21,000 vessels passing through it in 1966. After 1967, when most of the oil shipping had to take the route around Africa, giant oil tankers were built that would have been unable to pass through the canal. When the canal was again reopened in 1975, it could accommodate only twenty-three percent of the world's tankers (against seventy-four percent before 1967). This limitation was amended in part by the widening-and-deepening operation of 1976–1980. Following its completion, the canal could accommodate half of the world's tankers. From the early 1980s, oil tankers again constituted a large proportion of the canal traffic: 1,600-1,900 of the 22,000-23,000 vessels carried 100–135 million of the total 350 million tonnage passing through. However, the canal's economy continued to be affected by the fluctuations in the world oil market, and competition with the alternative road of giant tankers around the Cape of Good Hope, which forced the Canal Authority to adopt an attractive policy of rates and discounts to encourage large oil tankers and container vessels to use the canal. Income from the Suez canal was a vital source of revenue for Egypt—the third-largest (after oil exports and remittances from Egyptian workers abroad). It grew steadily from 676 million dollars in 1980 to over 1,000 million dollars in 1984, deriving mostly from transit tolls and the rest from services to vessels in transit.

The second half of the 1980s witnessed a new rise in the canal's revenues (over 1.3 billion dollars in 1988–1989), which peaked in 1990–1991 (1.66 billion dollars) as a result of the Iraqi invasion of KUWAIT and the GULF WAR. The number of vessels using the canal reached 17,312 (of which 3,185 were tankers) in 1993, but fell to 15,051 in 1995, generating total revenue of 1.94 billion dollars for that year.

SUNAY, CEVDET (1900–1982) Turkish officer, fifth President, of the Turkish Republic, 1966–1973. Born in Trabzon, Sunay graduated from the Military High School in Istanbul in 1917. He served on the Palestinian front and was caught by the British in the following year. He later joined the Nationalists participating in the War of Independence. After the war he completed his studies in the War College and Military Staff Academy and was given several assignments, rising through the ranks. In 1960 he was appointed Chief of the General Staff, and after the retirement of General GÜRSEL from the Presidency, was appointed senator and elected president in March 1966. He was succeeded in 1973 by Fahri KORUTÜRK.

SUNNIS The chief and major stream in ISLAM, adhering to the accepted *Sunna* ("Tradition"), in contrast to the SHI'A (the "Faction"), which reserved the leadership of the Muslim community to the descendants of Ali maintaining its own tradions. Several schools (*madhhab*, plural *madhahib*) developed within the framework of Sunni Islam. (For these

and Sunni Islam's marginal schools or sects as well as Sunni-Muslim mysticism and fundamentalist revivalist orders, see ISLAM, WAHHABIYYA, DERVISH ORDERS, MAHDIYYA, SANUSSIYYA.)

SYKES-PICOT AGREEMENT A secret exchange of notes, 1916, among BRITAIN, FRANCE and RUSSIA, the chief Allies of World War I, relating to the partition of the OTTOMAN EMPIRE after its defeat. Named after the chief British and French negotiators, Sir Mark Sykes and Charles Francois Georges-Picot.

According to the Sykes-Picot Agreement, the non-Turkish provinces of the Ottoman Empire were to be divided as follows: the Arabian Peninsula was to become independent. Palestine, west of the Jordan River (excluding the Negev), was to be placed under an international regime; Britain was to control Haifa, Acre and the region between them.

The French sphere was to include two zones. An "A" zone—the interior of, from and including Damascus, Homs, Hama and Aleppo in the west, up to and including the Mosul District in the east—was designated as a French zone of influence. A "Blue" zone—Cilicia in Asia Minor and all of coastal Syria and, west of the "A" zone—was to be placed under direct French control.

The British sphere included the "B" zone—the Negev desert in Palestine, the area east of the Jordan River, and central Mesopotamia with a northern arm reaching into Persia and a southern arm descending toward the Persian Gulf—designated as a British zone in influence. A "Red" zone—the provinces of Basra and Baghdad—was to be placed under direct British control (as were Haifa and Acre).

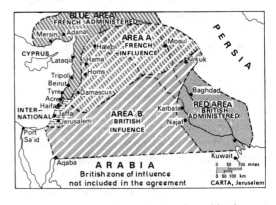

Partition of the Ottoman empire as planned by the Sykes-Picot Agreement

Zones "A" and "B" were envisaged as areas in which a semi-independent Arab state or a confederation of Arab states might be established, while France and Britain were to supply advisers and to be accorded economic privileges.

The Sykes-Picot Agreement was approved by Russia in return for Britain and France's recognition of Russia's right to annex Trabzon (Trebizond), Erzerum, Lake Van and Bitlis in Anatolia. The Sykes-Picot Agreement was published—and repudiated—in November 1917 by the Bolsheviks who found it in the Russian Foreign Office Archives. Both Arabs and Zionists strongly criticized the Sykes-Picot Agreement as being inconsistent with promises Britain had made to them (the MCMAHON-HUSSEIN CORESPONDENCE and the BALFOUR DECLARATION respectively).

The final distribution of the Ottoman territories partially reflected the Sykes-Picot Agreement, but was greatly modified by the system which abolished any formal, direct possession by the Powers—though it left them in de facto control. The Sykes-Picot Agreement's territorial provisions were also changed: Palestine became a British Mandate; Cilicia remained part of TURKEY and France ceded its rights in the Mosul region to Britain (see map), and conceded with annexation of Alexandretta (Hatai) to Turkey (1938–1939).

SYRIA Republic on the eastern shores of the Mediterranean, bordering TURKEY in the north, IRAQ in the east, JORDAN in the south, ISRAEL in the southwest, LEBANON and the Mediterranean in the west. Official name: Syrian Arab Republic. Arabic is the official language and commonly spoken. About ninety percent of the population are Arabs (i.e., Arabic is their mother-tongue). Some groups speak Kurdish, Armenian or Turkish, and there are remnants of Aramaic in some rural areas in northeastern Syria. On the whole, Syria's population is highly fragmented along ethno-religious divides, Muslim and non-Muslim. Close to seventy percent of the inhabitants of Syria are SUNNI Muslims. This number includes non-Arab KURDS, comprising six to seven percent of the population, mostly in the northeastern border region, the JAZIRA. The largest religious minority is the ALAWI or NUSSEIRI community, ten to twelve percent of the population, which is concentrated in the mountainous northwestern region. The DRUZE, of

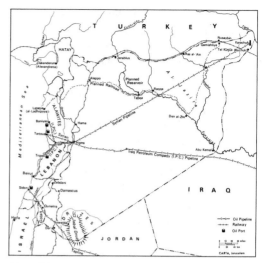

Map of Syria

which there are about three percent, dwell primarily in the Druze Mountains (*Jabal al-Druz*) in southern Syria with some in the Golan. Christians comprise 5-6 percent of Syria's population; about half of them are GREEK ORTHODOX, 400,000; GREEK CATHOLICS, (Melkites) 175,000; PROTESTANTS, 80,000; MARONITES, 35,000; non-Arab ARMENIANS, 25,000-30,000 (most of them Orthodox Gregorians, some Armenian Catholics), and smaller Christian communities (Syrian-Orthodox JACOBITES, Syrian Catholics, Assyrians-Nestorians, LATIN [Roman Catholics] and CHALDEANS). In addition, other religious minorities are the ISMAʿILIS and Shiʿis—about 1.5% YAZIDIS—and JEWS (a few hundred—down from over 25,000 in the 1940s). The number of nomadic BEDOUIN has dropped to 1.5–3% of the population.

Economy The Syrian economy is largely dependent upon agriculture, which accounts for approximately twenty-five percent of the labor force and contributes close to thirty percent of the GDP. Most of the manufacturing industry is in the public sector, although a significant section remains in private hands and has government approval. The industry has grown, and its share of the GDP is about twenty to twenty-three percent. It produces mainly consumption goods—textiles, leather, tobacco, edible oils and cement. The important industrial areas are Damascus, Aleppo, Homs and Ladhiqiyya. Since the late 1980s, various laws were passed that increased Syria's opening of and encouraged foreign investments (e.g., investment rule No. 10 from 1991).

Efforts were made to make the public sector more efficient while expanding the role played by the private sector without undermining the overall control of the government over the economy. However, foreign investments in Syria remain meager, and the bulk of Syria's economy remains centrally planned.

In the late 1950s, OIL was discovered in northeastern Syria. Commercial production for export, by the government-owned Syrian General Petroleum Corporation, began in the late 1960s. It produced nearly 1 million tons in 1968, 4.5 million in 1970, and since the mid-1970s stood at 8–10 million tons per annum, accounting for up to fifty-six percent of the exports in the mid 1990s. The oil sector is vital to Syria both as a source of governmental revenue and as a source of foreign currency. In the future, it is believed that the current oil production (600,000 barrels a day) may drop significantly unless exploration efforts, conducted by foreign companies, lead to discoveries of new oil fields.

In 1968, a 400 mile (620 km.), 5 million ton per annum pipeline was completed from the oil fields in the east to the refinery in Homs. (This was established in 1959 with a 1 million ton capacity, expanding in 1971 to 2.7 million tons) and thence to an oil port built at Tartous. There are other pipelines traversing Syrian territory. These are: one built by the Iraq Petroleum Company (IPC) in 1952, to Baniyas, branching out at Homs from the Kirkuk-Tripoli (Lebanon) line existing since 1934. Another oil pipeline crossing Syria is the "Tapline" from ARAMCO's fields in SAUDI ARABIA to Sidon in Lebanon (inoperative since 1975). The Syrian government received transit royalties from the producing companies. The Iraqi pipeline, with its 50–60 million ton per annum, also provided Syria with a substantial share of its needs. However, Syria's disputed relations with Iraq made this pipeline highly vulnerable to political crises between the two states. The pipeline was closed (by Iraq) from 1976–1979, and (by Syria) since 1982.

Syria's largest development project is the Tabaqa Dam (on the Euphrates), which created Lake Asad, completed in 1978 with Soviet aid. It is to irrigate 1.75 million acres, produce 600,000 kilowatts of electricity, and make possible large-scale settlement (see WATER POLITICS). However, despite the completion of the Euphrates Dam, Syria still suffers from shortages in electric power supply, and most of the population and industrial areas suffer from electricity cuts of up to four hours per day. The problem intensifies in the summer when a lowered level of water at the Tabaqa Dam disables part of the electricity turbines.

Political History The name Syria has existed since the Hellenistic period (fifth century B.C.), vaguely covering the area stretching from the Mediterranean to Mesopotamia. The Romans used the term Syria to refer to the area between Asia Minor and EGYPT which was dominated by the Roman Empire. This definition became the standard term, corresponding to the later Arabic term Bilad al-Sham (Land of the North) or Suria. Today's Syria was part of the OTTOMAN EMPIRE from 1517 until the end of World War I. Most of Syria was part of the three provinces (Vilayet) of Aleppo, Damascus and Beirut. The Ottoman administration was concentrated mainly in the cities, thus allowing local leaders to rule remote towns and villages, provided they pay their taxes and refrain from rebellion. With the continuing decline of the Ottoman Empire during the nineteenth century, Western influence grew—first through economic and cultural penetration, later through political and military intervention. FRANCE was the power with the most ramified interests in Syria, a result of steady commercial activity as well as ties with the Catholic, and especially the Maronite, community. Beginning in the 1830s, the Jesuits intensified their educational activity in Syria, opening many schools and, in 1875, a university in Beirut. American Protestants in 1834 established a modern printing press and in 1866 founded the Syrian Protestant College, later to be named the American University of Beirut (AUB). In the late nineteenth century the Ottoman government also opened a number of modern schools in Syria. A cultural revival resulted, which paved the way for the appearance of an ARAB NATIONAL MOVEMENT on the eve of World War I.

During World War I, when the British discussed future Arab independence with Sharif HUSSEIN of Mecca (with whom Syrian nationalists had also been in touch), in preparation for the Sharif's ARAB REVOLT of 1916, the future Arab state demanded by Hussein included Syria. However, the status and borders of the future state remained undetermined, and the British reserved the Western coast lands for a future French administration (see MCMAHON-HUS-

SEIN CORRESPONDENCE). The Syrian nationalists did not take participate in the Arab Revolt and there was no uprising in Syria. But the Turks suspected the nationalists and condemned several of them to death.

With the Ottoman collapse in 1918, Syria was conquered by Allied forces, including Arab troops commanded by Amir Feisal, son of Sharif Hussein. Feisal entered Damascus in October 1918 and, with the encouragement of the British, established an Arab government which gradually took over the administration in the interior of the country. However, the secret SYKES-PICOT AGREEMENT of 1916 between BRITAIN, France and RUSSIA designated the interior of the country as a French "area of influence," while the coastal areas were to be directly administered by France. With some flexibility and good will the two agreements might have been reconciled and a semi-independent Arab State established in the Syrian interior under French influence. However, Britain's interests in Europe and the uncompromising approach of the Arab nationalists surrounding Feisal in Damascus led to an early end of the Arab autonomous administration. The French became entrenched on the coast and antagonism between them and the nationalists intensified. In July 1919, a "General Syrian Congress" declared Syria's independence, and clashes soon erupted between Arab and French forces. In March 1920, the Congress proclaimed Feisal King of Syria (deliberately, with no borders precisely defined, practically refering to a "GREATER SYRIA" that would include Lebanon and Palestine). Britain and France did not recognize the declaration of independence and decided, at the SAN REMO CONFERENCE in April 1920, to confer upon France a MANDATE over Syria. French forces began moving toward Damascus and after a battle with Arab forces at Meisalun entered Damascus on 25 July 1920, ending Feisal's brief rule. In July 1922 the League of Nations endorsed the French Mandate over Syria and Lebanon.

From the start, the Syrians and particularly the Sunni-Muslim Arab majority (the mainstay of the nationalist movement) rejected the French rule imposed on them. The French on their part tried to weaken this majority and base their government upon the support of the ethnic and religious minorities, especially the Christians of Mount Lebanon. In September 1920 they set up a state of "Greater Lebanon" and added to the Christian majority area of Mount Lebanon, semi-autonomous since 1861, Muslim majority districts in the north (Akar, including the city of Tripoli), south, and east (al-Biqa`, the Valley), as well as mixed Beirut (see LEBANON). Furthermore, the very separation of Lebanon was contradictory to Syrian nationalists' conviction. The incorporation of predominantly Muslim areas into traditional Lebanon was to remain a source of Syrian resentment and revisionist claims.The French also divided the rest of Syria into separate administrative units, emphasizing separatist minority interests. The Ladhiqiyya region, inhabited chiefly by ALAWITES, became a separate administrative unit, as did Jabal Druze and the district of ALEXANDRETTA (with a sizeable Turkish minority). In the rest of Syria two different states (Aleppo and Damascus) were established, linked in a federation. In 1924–1925, these two states were united in the "State of Syria," but the three districts remained separate.

In the late 1920s the various Syrian states were given constitutions and councils, but real authority remained with the French High Commissioner in Beirut and his officials. The French Mandatory government improved public security and administration, communications, and the health and education systems. Syria even became a haven for refugees, e.g., Kurds and Armenians from Turkey, and later ASSYRIANS from Iraq. The people of Syria rejected the French administration as foreign rule. Their national opposition erupted into violence several times during the 1920s. In 1925, a local uprising in Jabal Druze, led by the Druze Sultan al-Atrash, spread to other areas of Syria and was supported by the nationalists of Damascus (see DRUZE). A nationalist Syrian government was formed in Jabal Druze by the nationalist leader, Dr. Abd al-Rahman Shahbandar. The rebels broke through to Damascus and the city was subsequently shelled by French guns and aircraft. The revolt was finally quelled in 1927.

The French government now agreed to grant Syria independence along with the manner of the Anglo-Iraqi Agreement of 1922—i.e., nominal independence based on a treaty granting the Mandatory Power special privileges and particularly the right to maintain troops and bases. Accordingly, France began to encourage increased self-government. In May 1926, Lebanon was declared a republic and granted a constitution and parliamentary institutions. In regard to Syria, however, similar progress was held up, mainly because nationalist demands far exceeded the concessions that France was willing to make. Only in 1928 did the French High Commissioner lift military government and allow the holding of elections for a constituent assembly. The elections of April 1928 were won by the "National Bloc" (*al-Kutla al-Wataniyya*)—a coalition of several nationalist groups united only by their opposition to the French Mandate. Hashem al-ATASSI, Prime Minister during Feisal's reign and now leader of the Bloc, was elected President of the Assembly.

The nationalists prepared a draft constitution, which demanded, *inter alia*, the re-unification of all Syria— implying: a "Greater Syria," mainly incorporating Lebanon. The French High Commissioner refused to endorse this draft; attempts to reach understanding failed, and the Assembly was dissolved in May 1930. The High Commissioner now unilaterally proclaimed a constitution. This established a Republican regime in Syria, providing for a Chamber of Deputies elected by male suffrage for a four-year term. The Chamber was to elect the President of the Republic, with limited powers. The government was to be responsible to the Chamber. "The obligations contracted by France in respect of Syria" were to take precedence, and in sensitive matters, the constitution was to be applied only with French approval.

The nationalists protested the imposition of this constitution, but public life began to follow its provisions. In January 1932 elections were held and the National Bloc lost much of its strength. New French proposals for a Franco-Syrian treaty to replace the Mandate with nominal independence for Syria, while safeguarding French interests, did not satisfy the nationalist members of the Chamber and were torpedoed by them. The Chamber was suspended *sine die* in 1934. Again tension increased in French-Syrian relations, and a general strike and rioting erupted early in 1936.

New efforts to find a political solution brought a Syrian delegation to Paris. The Popular Front government of Socialist Leon Blum was more inclined to compromise than its predecessors. In September 1936 a Franco-Syrian Treaty of Friendship and Alliance was initialled. Syria was to become independent and to be admitted to the League of Na-

tions within three years. The territories of Jabal Druze and Ladhiqiyya would be incorporated in the Syrian state, but maintain a certain degree of autonomy. France's economic status and educational institutions were guaranteed. France alone was to equip and train the Syrian army to be established. France was to maintain troops and military bases in Syria and aid in its defense in the case of war, while Syria was to provide France in that case with all facilities, communications, etc. The new Syrian Parliament endorsed the Treaty in December 1936 and it was formally signed the same month.

Elections were held in November 1936 and won by the National Bloc. Its leaders now took over the government: Hashem AL-ATASSI became President, Jamil Mardam Prime Minister, Shukri al-Quwwatli (1886–1967), Sa'dallah al-Jabiri, and Fares al-Khouri ministers. The Ladhiqiyya and Jabal Druze districts were incorporated into Syria, and many governmental posts were gradually given to the Syrians.

The Treaty turned out to be short-lived as power in France shifted to right-wing governments. Facing the escalating menace of Nazi Germany and Fascist Italy, the French government tarried, postponed the endorsement of the Treaty of 1936, and finally refused to ratify it. The quest for political settlement with France was again deadlocked. The nationalists insisted on the ratification of the Treaty and full independence, but were not united as to how to achieve this. The National Bloc suffered from splits and instability. Dr. Abdel-Rahman Shahbandar, never a trusted member of the Bloc's dominant faction (he was seen as pro-Hashemite and pro-British), withdrew in 1939 establishing a "Popular Organization" as an opposition. He was assassinated in 1940. It was apparently a political murder, which shocked the country dealing a heavy blow to the beginnings of a parliamentary tradition.

Separatist movements grew with French support in the Jazira and Jabal Druze areas. French-Syrian relations deteriorated as a result of the Alexandretta affair: the French surrendered to Turkey's increasing demands and pressure, and after a brief League of Nations-sponsored autonomy, the district was annexed by Turkey in July 1939. Furious protests and riots followed in Syria and President al-Atassi and the government resigned. The French dissolved the Chamber of Deputies, appointed a government of officials, and announced that the Franco-Syrian draft treaty would not be submitted to Parliament for ratification. The administration of the Jabal Druze and Ladhiqiyya districts was again separated from Syria. The question of Syria's territorial claims in Lebanon was discussed in the Franco-Syrian Negotiations, but remained unresolved due to the French refusal to ratify the Franco-Syrian draft treaty. Nevertheless, it is quite clear that the Syrian leaders accepted the idea of Lebanon remaining an independent state, although insisted it remained an integral part of the Arab World (see LEBANON).

After the defeat of France, June 1940, French officials in Syria remained loyal to the pro-German Vichy government. The Italians and the Germans stationed a cease-fire supervision commission in Syria and Lebanon and began preparing airfields and bases and organizing cells of agents and supporters. Their growing domination brought the British to invade Syria and Lebanon together with Free French forces in June 1941. General Georges Catroux, as Free France's new "Delegate-General" (no longer "High Commissioner"), proclaimed the termination of the Mandate and the independence of Syria, but made actual independence conditional on the conclusion of a new treaty. This gave France a privileged position—which Syria's nationalists no longer accepted. The French therefore delayed transferring the government to the Syrians and re-establishing parliamentary institutions. Under British and American pressure, they agreed in 1943 to hold free elections. The National Bloc once again triumphed, and its leader, Shukri al-Quwwatli, was elected President.

Power was now gradually transferred to the Syrian government and administration. The article of the constitution restricting Syria's sovereignty and granting special privileges to France (Article 116), was annulled in January 1944 without a struggle (after a fierce battle over the same issue in Lebanon in November 1943). The separatist autonomy of the Druze and Alawite districts was ended. But Franco-Syrian differences re-erupted when the French refused to transfer the "Troupes Speciales" (Syrian units within the framework of the French Middle East forces), to the jurisdiction of the Syrian government and to withdraw their own troops unless a preferential treaty was signed. However, the Syrians remained adamant in their refusal to do so, winning increasing international support.

In 1944, both the USSR and the US recognized Syria, and Britain followed suit in 1945. The newly-founded ARAB LEAGUE unequivocally supported Syria, who began to act like a sovereign state. In January 1945, the establishment of a national army was announced. In February, Syria declared war on the "Axis" powers and thus became, in April, one of the founding members of the United Nations. In May 1945, anti-French riots erupted because France still refused to withdraw its troops, and the French bombarded Damascus. However, a British ultimatum forced them to cease fire, and by the end of the year the British and French had agreed on the withdrawal of their troops. This agreement did not satisfy Syria, as its wording implied a privileged status for France in Syria and Lebanon, and (together with Lebanon) in February 1946, Syria lodged a complaint with the UN Security Council. The USSR vetoed a resolution calling for negotiations and a speedy withdrawal; but the parties settled the matter between themselves, and by mid-April 1946 France had withdrawn all its garrisons from Syria—"Withdrawal Day" (*id al-jala*) 17 April—became Syria's national holiday.

It soon emerged that Syria had no strong leadership. The "National Bloc," the major political force on the road to independence, disintegrated soon after that aim had been realized. Aleppo leaders, centered around the "People's Party," competed with the Damascus leadership and its "National Party." The minorities were loyal first and foremost to their communities, and the tribes to their own leaders. The 1947 elections resulted in a parliament without any strong party or leadership. Many independent deputies stood for local and clan interests. In this environment of instability, fundamental problems re-surfaced. Should Syria build separate independence, or should it unite with its Arab neighbors, Hashemite Jordan or Iraq? In general the Aleppo leadership supported union schemes. This reflected its long-lived traditional trade links with Iraq and Anatolia, as well as the political rivalry with Damascus. On the other hand, the Damascus leadership, which led most of the governments that opposed the Hashemite schemes of regional unity, together with Egypt, Lebanon and Saudi Arabia. Syria became a stage and subject for both inter-Arab and international struggles, which aggravated its political instability and shaped its regional Arab politics. This impact is best demonstrated in Syria's policy regarding the question of Palestine toward and during the 1948 war.

In 1946, after Transjordan was granted independence and Emir ABDALLAH became King, relations between Syria and the Hashemite Jordanian regime grew tense, due to Abdallah's announced policy of unifying Greater Syria (*suria al-kubra*) under his leadership. Abdallah's contacts and subversive efforts with opposition groups in Syria (Alawites, Druze, and tribes of the Jazira), who allegedly supported his scheme, led to deep enmity between Damascus and Amman. Damascus objected to establishing diplomatic relations with Jordan. The fear of Abdallah's scheme resulted from Damascus' assumption that it was backed by Britain. It thus became the leading factor determining Syrian policy on Palestine toward the end of the British Mandate in this country. Specifically, Damascus feared that a Jordanian takeover of the Arab part of Palestine following the British withdrawal from that country, would facilitate Abdallah in his implementation of his Greater Syria scheme. The United Nations General Assembly resolved on 29 November 1947, that Palestine should be partitioned into two independent states (Resolution 181). Prior to this Syrian President Quwwatly took the initiative to establish an Arab volunteer force assigned with salvaging Palestine. Syria's effort in organizing, training, equipping, and manning of the "Army of Deliverance" (*jaish al-inqadh*—see ARAB-ISRAEL CONFLICT), was commanded by Fawzi al-Qawaqji. The force, which assumed an all-Arab form, was meant to preempt King Abdallah's plan to take advantage of his alliance with Britain. This would give him a free hand in Palestine once the Mandate was completed and secure the annexation of Arab Palestine into his kingdom east of River Jordan. During the war, Damascus retained its control of the "Army of Deliverance," which served as the main military Arab force operating in Palestine in the period of the civil war (December 1947 to May 1948), and as of June 1948, as the main Arab force in the Galilee, until its defeat in October of that year. On 15 May 1948, Syrian regular units invaded Palestine south of Lake Tiberias, in a coordinated Arab invasion plan, but were repelled by the Israelis. In June, the Syrian forces succeeded in capturing an Israeli settlement west of Upper Jordan, which they managed to retain until the end of the war (the occupied territory was evacuated as a result of the Is-

rael-Syria Armistice Agreement—the last one between Israel and its neighbors—signed in July 1949).

Despite its relative success, the Syrian army's performance in the war was seen as a defeat. This resulted in intensified internal crisis of trust between the military and the politicians. Political and military leaders accused each other of responsibility for the debacle. On 30 March 1949, the Commander-in-Chief of the armed forces, General Husni al-Za'im, carried out a *coup d'état* and deposed the President, Parliament and government. A professional soldier born 1889 in Aleppo to a family of Kurdish origin, Za'im was elected President in a referendum in June 1949. He announced plans to eliminate widespread corruption and institute development schemes. In the inter-Arab arena he set about maintaining Syria's alliance with Egypt and Saudi Arabia, opposing unification with Iraq. During the Armistice negotiations with Israel in spring 1949, Za'im proposed to meet with Israeli Premier David BEN GURION, and sign a peace treaty with Israel in return for territorial concessions, including the division of Lake Tiberias between Israel and Syria, and settle 300,000 Palestinian refugees in the Syrian Jazira area. However, Ben Gurion refused to meet Za'im. He wanted to first of all conclude the armistice agreement and questioned both Za'im's dubious personality and the viability of his regime.

In August, Za'im was deposed in another coup by Sami al-Hinnawi and executed with his Prime Minister, Muhsin al-Barazi, also of Kurdish origin (the man chosen to shoot Za'im was a member of the SSNP, whose leader, Antoun Sa'adeh, was betrayed by Za'im and extradited to Lebanon where he was tried and executed in the same night). Hinnawi, an army officer born 1898 to an Arab-Kurdish family from Idlib, favored union with Iraq. He restored parliament, which was dominated, under his protection, by the Aleppo leadership and adherents of union. Hashem al-Atassi was elected to the presidency. But officers opposing union with Iraq rebelled. On 19 December, 1949 Hinnawi was deposed by Colonel Adib al-Shishakli. Shishakli, born in 1909 in Hamah to a family of landowners and intellectuals that had played a role in the Arab National Movement from the beginning of the century, served, like his two predecessors, in the "Troupes Speciales." In the 1948 war he was a high-ranking officer in the "Army of Deliverance." At first, Shishakli wanted to leave the President, Parliament and government intact and rule from behind the scenes as Deputy Chief of Staff. But the clash between army officers, whose intervention in state affairs increased, along with the civilian leadership, which wanted to return the officers to their barracks, created constant tension. In December 1951, Shishakli staged a second coup, establishing a dictatorial regime. He dissolved Parliament, abolishing all Parties, establishing a single political organization of his own, "The Arab Liberation Movement" (which, however, did not take root). In July 1953, a referendum approved a new constitution, which granted the President extensive powers, and Shishakli himself was elected to the post. The leaders of all factions were now united in their opposition to Shishakli. In February 1954, a new coup was carried out with the help of a military junta. Shishakli's government collapsed and he fled Syria. In 1964 he was assassinated in Brazil by a Druze militant in revenge for the shelling of Jabal Druze during his rule. Like Za'im, Shishakli also offered Israel a non-aggression pact, hoping to put an end to border clashes and to remove the Israeli Issue from the Syrian political agenda. In this, he was motivated by hopes to receive military and economic aid from the United States. However, Syrian hard-liners, like Akram Hourani and others, opposed any agreement with the west or with Israel, and the attempt did not bear fruit. After Shishakli's overthrow, the 1949 Parliament and President Hashem al-Atassi (dismissed by Shishakli in December 1951), were restored. But political stability was still lacking, and one government followed another. In 1955 Shukri al-Quwwatli was elected by Parliament to replace Atassi as President.

From the early 1950s radical nationalist and leftist elements, especially the "Arab Socialist Renaissance Party" (al-BA'TH) and the Communists, gained increasing influence in Syrian politics. This trend was enhanced by the intensifying Egyptian-Iraqi strife over the Baghdad Pact signed by Iraq and Turkey in February 1955, which Jordan and Syria were courted to join. The growing impact of the radical political movements in Syria had a direct impact on this country's regional policy, bringing Damascus closer to Egypt and the USSR. In October 1955, a Syro-Egyptian defense pact was signed and a joint command established. Between 1954–1956 Syria and Lebanon held talks on signing a mutual security agreement, but the Lebanese feared a Syrian cooptation and refrained from signing such an agreement. The USSR began fostering relations with Syria, concluding economic aid agreements and supplying arms (since February 1956). The tripartite offensive of Israel, Britain and France against Egypt in October–November 1956 reinforced Syrian links with Egypt. By 1957 the Ba'th Party was the leading agitator of Nasser's Arab nationalism and anti-imperialism, carrying the message of Syrian-Egyptian unity as the Party's goal. During the hostilities in Egypt, the Syrians blew up the oil pipelines from Iraq and Sa'udi Arabia passing through Syria, which resulted in tension between Syria and these two countries. The pipelines were repaired in March 1957, but Syria's relations with its pro-Western neighbors remained strained. Domestically, power came increasingly to rest in the military officers of primarily Ba'th or Communist leanings. These two Parties sometimes collaborated, but late in 1957 relations between them deteriorated to the point that a dangerous confrontation seemed imminent. Factional disputes also led to increasing violence, assassinations (such as that of Deputy Chief-of-Staff Adnan Maliki in April 1955), alleged plots and trials. The state of domestic fragmentation and disarray was aggravated by external pressures and attempts at shaping Syria's regional and international policies. The Ba'th leadership found itself in a double danger. It feared a Communist take-over or a general de-stabilization, and the intervention of pro-Western forces (Iraq, Jordan, Turkey, Israel) from outside. Admiration of Nasser by the Syrian military echelons, a deep sense of insecurity of the Ba'th leaders regarding their very future as a leading political force in Syria, and growing Ba'th-Communist competition in driving Syria toward unity with Egypt, led Syria's high military command in January 1958 to initiate a dramatic step by traveling to Cairo and appealing to Nasser to accept unity with Syria. The initiative which took place behind the back of the government and the President, was tantamount to a military coup, supported by the Ba'th and the Communist parties and their respective fellow officers. Nasser was prodded to "save Syria" by merging the two countries. It was an attempt to enlist Nasser to support the military's goal of ridding itself from the politicians, while the Ba'th and Communist parties perceived the initiative as a step that would serve each of them in the context of Syrian domestic politics.

The union came into force in February 1958 after Syria's politicians accepted all Nasser's conditions. Full merger of Syria and Egypt; dismantling of all parties and incorporation into the "National Union," the sole, ruling party, was allowed. The Egyptian President became the President of the UNITED ARAB REPUBLIC (UAR), and Syria became the "Syrian Region" of the UAR. At first Syria was to a certain extent treated as a distinct entity. Foreign affairs, security, education and industry were handled by the central government, separate governments of the two "regions" dealt with financial, economic and many internal matters. Integration tightened and the regime centralized. The provisional constitution (on the Egyptian pattern) granted extensive powers to the President. Early in 1960, local committees of the "National Union" were set up, and in the summer a single National Assembly—appointed from members of the defunct Syrian Parliament (one-third) and the Egyptian National Assembly (two-thirds). In October the authority of the central government was considerably expanded. In effect, Egypt, the bigger, more developed country, increasingly took over control of the Union.

The union soon became unpopular in Syria. The dissolved Ba'th Party was disappointed at the meager representation its leaders had in the regime. The upper classes were apprehensive of the socialist policies the UAR government was preparing to impose on Syria, while left-wing circles were disappointed at the slow pace of the socialist reforms. Above all, Syrian army officers felt that Egyptian officers were taking over key positions, relegating them to less important posts. A further step toward full integration was made in August 1961, when the separate governments of the two regions were abolished. Similarly, far-reaching steps were taken toward nationalization and reform (see UAR).

In September 1961, a Syrian officers' *junta* carried out a coup which resulted in Syria's withdrawal from the UAR and restorating its full independence. In November, a new temporary constitution was proclaimed and elections were held in December. The Constituent Assembly chosen elected Nazem al-Qudsi, a leader of the "People's Party," as President of the Republic. The new regime, which returned to the pre-union pattern of Syrian politics and did

not lead to stability, turned to the right, abolishing many of the UAR government reforms. This policy caused renewed ferment among the army officers and in March 1962 a group of officers carried out a further coup. President al-Qudsi and his civilian administration were dismissed; but due to disunity among the various officer factions and unrest in the cities, they were restored to power. The government was now more leftist—and still less stable. Ministers changed frequently and the government was more than ever under pressure by the army commanders, who were themselves divided into rival factions (pro-Egyptian against anti-Egyptian; *Ba'th* against right-wing, etc.,). Egypt refused to recognize Syria's secession, claimed the Union still existed and continued to call itself the "United Arab Republic." Mutual complaints shook the Arab League. When the League readmitted Syria as an independent member in 1962 and attacked Egypt, the latter boycotted the League's sessions for six months.

On 8 March 1963, *Ba'th*-linked officers staged another coup. Many of these officers were Alawites and Druze, but a strong man emerged there, after several months of factional struggle, the Sunni General Amin al-Hafez. Born 1920–1921 in Aleppo to a poor family, Hafez also served in the "Troupes Speciales" and was a veteran of the *Ba'th* officers group. The *Ba'th* began to purge the army and government of pro-Nasserist elements, resulting in an abortive Nasserist attempt to overthrow the regime in July 1963, which was responded to with ruthless repression and mass executions of Nasserists in Damascus.

In April 1963 Syria's *Ba'th* regime, together with Iraq (where the *Ba'th* had come to power a month earlier) and Nasser, concluded a federative "Tripartite Unity Charter" following talks in Cairo. However, the agreement was aborted. It turned out to be a step to win Nasser's legitimacy and an attempt to gain time for entrenching in power (see PAN-ARABISM, ARAB UNITY, BA'TH). The *Ba'th* regime in Syria endeavored to establish a united front with the *Ba'th* Iraqi Ba'thi regime but had little success.

Relations with Egypt, which had improved slightly with the discussions of federative union, deteriorated again following the massacre of Nasserists in July 1963 and following systematic purges of the Nasserists in the military and administration. The deteriorating relations with Egypt brought Damascus' rulers to embark on an increasingly militant policy against Israel, using the imminent completion of its National Water Carrier (from Lake Tiberias to the Negev) as a pretext to expedite war against Israel. The Syrian militant drive meant to embarass Nasser, whose military intervention in Yemen and economic strains all but prohibited an entanglement in war with Israel, forcing him to recognize the *Ba'th* regime in Damascus. It was under Syria's pressure that Nasser was obliged to convene all-Arab summit conferences—Syria included—and adopt a collective Arab plan for the diversion of the Jordan's tributaries from their natural flow to Lake Tiberias, thus preventing them from reaching Israel. In the course of 1964 and 1965 Syria continued to haunt Nasser with its military actions against the Israeli Water Carrier and propaganda against Nasser's shorthandedness in backing those actions in the face of Israeli military blows inflicted on the Arab diversion plan. In 1965 Syria also became the main sponsor of *Fatah,* as an implementation of its adherence to the idea of "long-term popular struggle" for the liberation of Palestine, which had been officially adopted by the ruling *Ba'th* Party.

Inside Syria, the *Ba'th* government began implementing a socialist policy of nationalizing banks and factories and distributing land to the peasants. Merchants' and landowners' protest demonstrations and riots in February-April 1964 were brutally suppressed. In April 1964, a new temporary constitution was proclaimed, defining Syria as a "Democratic Socialist Republic, constituting an integral part of the Arab nation." The *Ba'th* leadership had by now split into two rival factions. One, based on the veteran party leadership, was more moderate. The other comprised younger party leaders, many of them Alawites and Druze who pressed for speedy implementation of socialist principles and were hostile to Nasser and Nasserism. This won greater support among the army officers and was called the "military wing." Late in 1965, the moderate, "civilian" faction ousted the extremists from their positions. But in February 1966 a military coup brought to power an ultra-radical neo-*Ba'th* faction, which imprisoned and later exiled the previous military rulers as well as the old *Ba'th* leaders, including Michel AFLAQ, the founder and ideologist of the party, *Salah-ul-Din al-Bitar* (1912–1980), co-founder of the party and head of the deposed government, and General Amin al-

Hafez, Chairman of the Presidential Council. The exiled faction claimed to retain the "national" (all-Arab) leadership of the *Ba'th* and left to Baghdad, where its supporters seized power in 1968, paving the way to a bitter Syro-Iraqi ideological rift.

The power behind the coup was the Alawite General Salah JADID. He was supported by another Alawite, General Hafez al-ASAD, the airforce commander who became Minister of Defense and soon Jadid's rival, and the "regional' (Syrian) leadership of the *Ba'th* Party—Yussuf Zu'ayyin (who became Prime Minister) and Nur al-Din al-Atassi (who became President). The elimination of the moderate faction further restricted the public base of the regime, and drove it to collaborate with the Communists and to grant them, for the first time, representation in the government. It conducted purges, planted supporters in all key positions and gained control of all "Popular organizations" such as trade unions and associations of students, farmers and women. The regime also relied on powerful and ubiquitous secret services. Nationalization was stepped up. In 1967 the ruling party claimed that one-third of the cultivated land had already been redistributed.

The new Syrian regime tightened its relations with the Soviet Union and tried to improve its relations with Egypt. Syria's militant policy toward Israel, manifested in the use of Syrian territory as a staging ground for Palestinian attacks on Israel, turned the Israel-Syria border into an arena of violent clashes and constant tension which threatened to drag Nasser into the fray against his best judgement. The Egypt-Syria rapprochement was facilitated by Nasser's renewed strife with the Arab conservative regimes and deepening mistrust in his relations with the United States. In November 1966, following Soviet lobbying, a military pact was signed between the two states. Yet if the pact meant to bestow on Syria's rulers a sense of security and reduce their militancy, in effect it imposed on Nasser a military commitment to a regime which continued to sponsor Palesinian guerrilla attacks against Israel, forcing Israel to retaliate militarily. In mid-May 1967, Soviets allegations—which turned out to be unbased—that Israel had concentrated forces on its Syrian border, resulted in the introduction of massive Egyptian forces into Sinai, dragging Nasser into war which he had tried to avoid, bringing on Egypt a disastrous defeat (see ARAB ISRAEL CONFLICT).

The 1967 war resulted in the occupation of the Golan (the GOLAN HEIGHTS) by Israeli forces and their advance to within thirty-eight miles (sixty-one km.) of Damascus. Syria agreed to a cease-fire supervised by the United Nations, but continued to oppose any political settlement of the ARAB-ISRAEL CONFLICT. Syria also denounced the all-Arab mainstream led by Nasser as too moderate, and refused to participate in the Arab summit at Khartoum in August-September 1967 on grounds of rejecting any sort of collaboration with the "Arab Reaction." Syria rejected the United Nations Security Council resolution 242 of 22 November 1967. This called to work for a just and lasting peace in the Middle East based on Israel's withdrawal from occupied territories and acknowledgement of the sovereignty and territorial integrity of "every state in the area and their right to live in peace within secure and recognized boundaries." Syria refused to cooperate with UN envoy Gunar Jarring.

Militarily, Syria adhered to its antagonistic inter-Arab policy, advocating a "revolutionary" strategy in the conflict with Israel. At the same time, however, Syria avoided activating its own front against Israel within the concept of an "Eastern Command" as advocated by Nasser to support Egypt's War of Attrition which began in March 1969. Instead, it continued its overt military support for the armed Palestinian organizations, encouraging them to stage attacks against Israel from Jordan and Lebanon while tightening its political control over their establishment. In 1968 Syria sponsored the establishment of an armed Palestinian guerrilla group comprised of its own Parlestinian Ba'thists as a means to acquire a foothold within the PLO. As of summer 1968 this became an umbrella organization to all Palestinian guerrilla and civilian factions.

Meanwhile, the loss of the Golan Heights in the war intensified the internal struggle for power within the ruling elite. The leftist faction led by Jadid, Zu'ayyin, Atassi, and Foreign Minister Makhus, maintained the upper hand, accounting for Syria's isolation in the Arab world. On the other hand, a rival "nationalist" group, led by Defense Minister Asad, aimed at reducing Syria's dependence upon the USSR, improving relations with the other Arab states and putting more emphasis on the struggle against Israel. In October 1968, the "nationalist" group began to get the upper hand in the Ba'th Party. In Febru-

ary 1969 Asad took control in a semi-coup, but accepted a compromise (reportedly instigated by Egypt and the USSR) and agreed to the continuing participation in the government of the leftist faction, with Atassi as President and Zu'ayyin as Premier. In the growing conflict between the Fida'iyyin organizations and the governments of Lebanon and Jordan, 1969–1970, Syria consistently supported the Fida'iyyin, and relations with these countries deteriorated. Syria threatened intervention on several occasions. In September 1970, Syrian forces moved into Jordan to aid the Fida'iyyin but were repulsed (among the factors leading to their withdrawal were the threat of American and Israeli involvement). Later it was reported that Hafez al-Asad, then Minister of Defense, refused to provide an air support thus exposing the armored column to Jordanian air raids.

In November 1970 Asad completed his takeover. He dismissed President Atassi and provisionally replaced him with Ahmad al-Khatib (not a prominent leader), while Asad himself became Prime Minister. His opponents of the Jadid-Zu'ayyin faction were removed from their government and party posts, and most of them were arrested. In February 1971, a 173-member "People's Council" was appointed, which nominated Asad, in March, as President of the Republic. His nomination was endorsed, that same month, in a plebiscite (as the only candidate, 96% voting, 99.2% of the votes in favor). In April, Asad divested himself of the Premiership, appointing a loyal follower to the post. In May 1971 Asad was also elected Secretary-General of the Ba'th Party. He was reelected President, for a seven year term, by plebiscites in February 1978, in February 1985 and in December 1991. He was nominated, as the only candidate, by the Ba'th and approved by the People's Council (National Assembly).

Asad's regime at first emphasized a new "openness' in its internal policies—a slightly more liberal economic policy and an effort to associate certain non-Ba'th but "Socialist-Unionist" factions with the regime. A new, permanent Constitution was passed by the People's Council in January 1973 and endorsed by a plebiscite in March. It defined the "Syrian Arab Republic" as a "popular-democratic and socialist" state, "part of the Arab homeland," and its people as "part of the Arab nation, struggling for the realization of its total unity." Islamic Law (the SHARI'A) was to be the "principal base of legislation."

This last definition caused protest among Sunni Muslims who considered it insufficient. To assuage that Muslim opposition—the only force both capable and ready to resist the *Ba'th* regime—a clause was added providing that the President must be a Muslim (which raised another problem: as Asad was an Alawi, his endorsement as President implied the recognition of the Alawi community as Muslim—and many Sunni Muslims refused to accept that ruling). The President was to be proposed by the *Ba'th*, nominated by the People's Council, and elected for a seven-year term by plebiscite. The People's Council was to be chosen for a four-year term in general elections. At least half of its members were to be workers and peasants.

Elections for the People's Council were duly held in May 1973—the first general elections since 1961—and again in 1977, 1981, 1986, 1990 and 1994. Toward the 1973 elections, the *Ba'th* Party set up, in March 1972, a "National Progressive Front" with the Communists and several "Socialist Unionist" factions prepared to accept *Ba'th* guidance and primacy. Candidates usually appeared on behalf of that "Front," most of them *Ba'th* men, but independent candidates were not ruled out.

President Asad succeeded in giving Syria many years of a stable regime—the longest-ruling President and the most stable government the country had known since independence. The regime was, despite its various outward paraphernalia of democracy (elections, National Assembly), a harsh totalitarian rule of an army junta and the inner core of the *Ba'th* leadership (in most cases—the same people), reinforced by a ubiquitous secret service, with all media state- and party-directed, and with limited and tightly-controlled expression in political and social issues. The only group resisting openly were Sunni Muslim conservatives and fundamentalists, mainly the MUSLIM BROTHERHOOD. Depressed economy toward the late 1970s which was apparent especially among the rural, more conservative Sunni areas of northern Syria, intensified popular resentment toward the *Ba'th* regime. The Muslim Brotherhood's underground resistance took an increasingly violent form in the late 1970s, primarily against high-ranking party and government officials. In June 1979 it massacred sixty young officer cadets, most of them Alawis. Revenge attacks and killings by security personnel culminated in a massacre of several hundreds

of Brotherhood prisoners in the Tadmor (Palmyra) detention camp. New attacks and reprisal killings took place in April 1981 in Hamah, considered a stronghold and center of the Brotherhood. In February 1982, what amounted to an undeclared war between the regime and the Brotherhood came to a head in a week-long battle in Hamah, involving the use of artillery and aircraft. The government reported approximately 1,200 had been killed. Other sources (including senior government officials) spoke of up to 38,000. The events of Hamah broke the back of the Brotherhood's armed resistance, though its underground cells continued to exist and sporadic acts of violence occasionally took place.

Except for that Muslim struggle against the regime, whatever internal struggles were going on were conducted within a small group of *Ba'th* leaders and senior army officers, and behind a veil of secrecy. The chiefs of Jadid's defeated "military" faction were released after many years of detention without trial. They were not permitted to resume public-political activities. (Jadid himself died in a Damascus prison in 1993 and Atassi died in 1992, shortly after his release from prison). There were new power struggles; "inside" reports of plots or even armed clashes between rival formations abounded, but usually they remained unconfirmed. By and large, Asad seemed able to resolve or suppress such crises and to keep the reins firmly in his hands. In 1983–1984, after Asad suffered from a severe heart attack, a struggle for Asad's succession was reported. This struggle often revolved around the unconventional figure of his younger brother Rif'at al-Asad (b. 1937). He was reputedly a man without strong ideological convictions and not a loyal *Ba'th*ist, a master of intrigue, thirsting for power, and a wire-puller in economic enterprises (including illegal ones), residing for much of his time abroad, in France or Switzerland. Rif'at was for years the commander of the "Defense Brigades," a semi-secret formation for special operations and with special privileges, used to suppress internal unrest (e.g., that of the Muslim Brothers). He seemed bent on using his Brigades to pave his way to power. However, a coalition of rival senior officers barred his way. Early in 1984, an armed confrontation between the rival army factions was reported, but the President succeeded in defusing the crisis. During that crisis he appointed three Vice-Presidents—his loyal Deputy Premier Abd al-Halim

KHADDAM, his brother Rif'at, and the *Ba'th* functionary Zuhair Masharqa. However, the problem of Asad's succession, and the struggle between rival army and leadership factions, seemed to remain unsolved. In the early 1990s, President Asad was reported to be training his son, Basil (b. 1962), as his successor, giving him an increasing role in Syrian politics, including Syrian relations with Lebanon. However, Basil died in January 1994, allegedly in a car accident. Asad's younger son, Bashar (b. 1965), is reported to have become the prominent candidate to replace Asad.

Asad's foreign policy was shaped by two major considerations. First, Syria's internal issues deriving from its multi-communal structure. Given his minority-led regime, foreign policy had to be formulated in a manner that would not alienate the Sunni-Muslim majority and endanger Syrian integration. Secondly, Syria's national security, primarily in the context of the conflict with Israel, but also in terms of the regime security *vis-a-vis* rival Arab actors, especially the Iraqi *Ba'th* regime.

Syria's international policy was marked by Asad's endeavor to mitigate the doctrinaire leftism of his predecessor. While remaining an ally of the Soviet Union, he tried to tone down that alliance and to mend his fences with the West. He was reported, for instance, to have declined for ten years a Soviet offer of a formal treaty of friendship (like the one Egypt and Iraq had signed). Yet, over the years Syria's dependence on Soviet aid and support reasserted itself and Asad reverted to an outspoken pro-Soviet policy. He often visited Moscow. In October 1980, in view of Egypt's peace treaty with Israel and the eruption of full-scale war between Iraq and Iran, he finally signed a formal treaty of friendship and alliance with the USSR. Syria also refused to denounce Russia's military intervention in Afghanistan—almost alone in the Arab and Islamic world. Yet, Syria did not accept Soviet guidance in all respects. It did not support Iran in the IRAN-IRAQ WAR, or its position in the Arab-Israel Conflict, its policy toward the PALESTINE LIBERATION ORGANIZATION (see below) and toward Lebanon (especially Syria's invasion in 1976).

Asad's regime also endeavored to improve its relations with the West. Relations with Britain and the US, severed since 1967, were resumed—the first in May 1973, and the latter in June 1974, after Syria had accepted Secretary of State Kissinger's ac-

tive mediation in the wake of the October War. President Nixon visited Syria in June 1974. The rapprochement did not go very far. In the 1970s and 1980s, Syria resisted all American efforts to associate it in further negotiations toward a Middle East settlement (see ARAB-ISRAEL PEACEMAKING) . While it tried to foster better relations with the countries of the EEC, it took a generally anti-US line. The West also bitterly resented its support for extremist Palestinian organizations and its reported involvement in terrorism in Europe, as well as in hijackings and kidnappings by pro-Syrian groups in Lebanon. In October 1986, after a wave of Syrian terrorist attacks in Europe, Britain severed relations with Syria. Other Western countries, while refusing to go that far, took various diplomatic steps against Syria. Its involvement in international terrorism led to its inclusion in the US State Department list of countries supporting terrorism and giving shelter to terrorist groups, depriving it of American economic aid.

In his regional inter-Arab policies, Asad at first endeavored to end Syria's isolation. He strengthened relations particularly with Egypt. In April 1971 Syria joined with Egypt and LIBYA in the Federation of Arab Republics (see ARAB NATIONALISM). The FAR, although formally set up, did not evolve into a functioning body. Nonetheless, Syria continued fostering cooperation with Egypt, especially in the military field. This culminated in the October war of 1973 waged by Syria and Egypt jointly (see ARAB-ISRAEL CONFLICT). In that war Syria also received help from Iraqi and Jordanian contingents. Trust and cooperation between Egypt and Syria fluctuated along with the course of events on each country's front and the level of satisfaction of their respective interests. Obviously, Anwar al-SADAT and Asad had different understandings and definitions of the 1973 war aims which surfaced during the war and brought them to conflict over the conditions of terminating hostilities (similar problems arose with Iraq). Syria did not share Sadat's post-1973 US-supported endeavors to progress towards a peaceful settlement by separate and partial settlements ("step by step") led by Secretary of State Henry Kissinger. This was despite the fact that Damascus accepted the latter's mediation in order to reach a military disengagement with Israel in the Golan. Asad's disagreement with Sadat's peace policy reached a crisis following Egypt's Interim Agreement in Sinai (Sinai II, see ARAB-ISRAEL

PEACEMAKING) signed in September 1975. However, Syria and Egypt restored their cooperation in October 1976 following Syria's invasion of Lebanon and armed clashes with the PLO's armed forces. The restored cooperation represented Egyptian recognition of Syria's dominant role in Lebanon in return for Syria's participation in the collective Arab leadership, together with Egypt and Saudi Arabia, in order to work for a comprehensive peace settlement of the conflict with Israel.

The newly established Syro-Egyptian cooperation proved to be short-lived. The gulf between the two states in terms of their domestic, political and economic constraints, and opportunities to regain territory by peaceful means, soon revealed their separate strategies once the collective Arab effort to advance a comprehensive peace settlement (that would include the Palestinian issue with the PLO as its sole legitimate representative) came to an impasse. The Syria-Egypt conflicting approaches to the peace making process culminated in Sadat's November 1977 visit to JERUSALEM, and later in the Camp David Agreements of 1978 and the Egypt-Israel Peace Treaty of 1979. Syria was in the forefront of those ostracizing Egypt and severing relations with it (relations with Egypt were re-established in 1989).

Following Egypt's peace treaty with Israel, which had left Syria isolated in the conflict with Israel and exposed to its military threat, Asad embarked on a militant inter-Arab policy in an attempt to isolate Egypt and prevent other Arab actors, primarily Jordan and the PLO, from adopting Sadat's strategy. Already in December 1977, Asad joined Libya, AL-GERIA, SOUTH YEMEN (PDRY) and the PLO in establishing the "Front of Steadfastness and Confrontation" at the end of a summit meeting of the radical Arab actors in Tripoli (Iraq took part in the conference but refused to participate).

Syria's relations with Iraq had its ups and downs. Their mutual antagonism—with the rift between the two hostile wings of the *Ba'th* added to the deeply rooted rivalry for predominance in the Fertile Crescent, sharing the Euphrates waters and over Syria's intervention in Lebanon—led Iraq in 1976 to shut down the oil pipeline to and through Syria and close their common border. With the signing of the Camp David Accords in September 1978, Asad appealed to Iraq, as the only realistic ally able to balance Israel's military preponderance. In October Presidents Asad

and Hassan al-Bakr signed "Charter of Joint National Action" which was portrayed as a historic step toward Arab unity, leading to reopening of the border and pipeline, and renewal of trade and diplomatic relations between the two states. However, Syria's interest in the rapprochement was instrumental and talks between the two regimes on implementation of their unity plans broke down the following year. Their relations soon reverted to bitter hostility which surfaced along with their deteriorating domestic security. There was growing agitation of Muslim Brotherhood in Syria and radical SHI'A opposition in Iraq. They blamed each other for this and became increasingly involved in it. Relations between the two regimes reached a point of clear rupture when Iraq opened an all-out war against Iran in September 1980. This resulted in the elimination of Syria's military operation against Israel, further exposure of Syria's weakness and isolation in confronting the Israeli threat. Syria's weakness and isolation were demonstrated during Israel's Lebanon war (see ARAB-ISRAEL CONFLICT).

Although in 1971 Asad accepted Security Council Resolution 242—conditional on restoring the Palestinians' rights—Syria's approach to peaceful settlement and co-existence with Israel remained at best uncertain and non-committal, throughout the 1970s and 1980s. During these decades Asad's regime continued to resist direct negotiations with Israel, considering diplomacy a means to regain occupied Arab territories without necessarily committing Syria to establishing normal relations with Israel. Syria perceived another military confrontation with Israel as the main strategy for recovering the occupied territories, at least publicly. Even in the post-Gulf war era, Syria's participation in the Madrid peace conference and consequent bilateral negotiations with Israel, still had not clarified Syria's position regarding its willingness to estabish full normal relations with Israel other than end of the state of war. Egypt's defection from the Arab confrontation with Israel obliged Asad to seek what became the regime's primary national aim, succinctly defined as the achievement of a "Strategic Parity" with Israel. This was to include military equilibrium but also economic and social capabilities which were to equip the regime with legitimacy to impose its needs on the domestic and regional arenas alike. Such parity would put Syria on an equal bargaining footing with Israel. This was thus interpreted as a precondition for any settlement.

However, in 1987 Soviet leader Gorbachev advised Asad to seek a political settlement instead. He made it clear that the USSR would not support Syria indefinitely in its quest for a "Strategic Parity." The disintegration of the Soviet Union in 1991 left Syria without superpower backing. This forced Syria to seek help elsewhere, in the Western camp (another source of strategic support was Iran). When Iraq invaded KUWAIT in August 1990, Syria joined the multinational anti-Iraqi coalition and participated in the GULF WAR, paving the way for Syria's inclusion into the pro-Western, pro-American camp and the Arab-Israel Peace Process: the Madrid conference in 1991 and the bilateral Syrian-Israeli talks that followed. These talks, conducted since 1991, not only had not yielded a peace accord, they also failed to reach agreed upon principles for future agreement between the two states. Still, some progress had been made on the formal level, including two meetings between the Chiefs-of-Staffs of both armies in 1994–1995, and talks between the two countries' ambassadors in Washington. During the negotiations, the Syrians did not refrain from applying indirect military pressure on Israel in South Lebanon through the Lebanese pro-Iranian group, HIZBALLAH. The peace talks were interrupted in 1996, following the Syrian refusal to denounce terrorist bombings in Israel. The election of a new right-wing Israeli Governent led by Binyamin NETANYAHU in May 1996, led to the weakening of the peace negotiations despite some efforts to resume them.

Since the late 1970s, Syria has cultivated close relations with Libya in the framework of the Front of Steadfastness and Confrontation established in Tripoli in December 1977 following Sadat's visit to Jerusalem. Syria's expected gains from closer relations with Libya were mainly in the context of financial and military aid—which turned out to be meager, despite QADHAFI's bombastic promises. In 1980 Asad agreed to Qadhafi's urgent demands and proclaimed a full union of the two countries. This merger remained declaratory and was not implemented. Despite differences regarding Syria's role in Lebanon, the two states maintained close cooperation until the late 1980s on two main issues: preserving Egypt's isolation in the Arab world and preventing its return to the Arab League, and extending support to

Iran during its war with Iraq (1980–1988, see IRAN-IRAQ WAR).

Between 1980–1982 Syria interpreted its hostile relations with Iraq as a tightening of relations with Iran. Shortly after Iraq invaded Iran in September, Syria and Libya, apparently with Soviet consent, operated an air-lift to supply Iran with Soviet arms. Syria explained its pro-Iranian policy as the wrong war that the Iraqi regime initiated against the wrong enemy. There was hostility to Iraq and interest in shifting its potential westward. Syria collaborated further with Iran. These two events culminated in an official alliance signed between the two states in April 1982. They derived from Damascus' urgent need for a strategic ally which was also willing to provide Syria with cheaper oil. Moreover, given the Iranian political and Islamic threat to the Gulf Arab monarchies, Syria's collaboration with Iran provided the former with influence on those vulnerable oil monarchies which would be instrumental for extracting financial support from the Gulf oil-rich states. In 1982 Iran sent to Lebanon 1500 members of the "Revolutionary Guard" (PASDARAN, see IRAN) to serve as a nucleus for the establishment of a Lebanese Shi'a revolutionary movement. Despite some Iranian-Syrian disagreement concerning the Middle East Peace Process and Lebanese Hizballah, Iraq severed relations in October 1980 and the borders were again closed, as was the pipeline in April 1982.

In 1986–1987, efforts at mediation—mainly by Saudi Araba and Jordan—seemed to have scored some improvement in Iraq-Syria relations. However, Iraq and Syria found themselves repeatedly at loggerheads. The end of the Iraq-Iran war in 1988 with Iraq maintaining a huge army, along with Saddam HUSSEIN's declared intention to settle the account with Syria for its alliance with Iran during its war with Iraq, brought Baghdad's renewed subversion in Lebanon against Syria, extending arms to the rebelious Maronite Prime Minister General Michel AWN. He proclaimed a war of liberation against Syria. Relations between Syria and Iraq quickly deteriorated, drawing them to the verge of war. Two years later, following the Iraqi invasion of Kuwait, Syria joined Egypt and the Gulf Arab states in condemnation of Iraq and participating in the international coalition against Iraq. This move earned Syria substantial financial aid from the Gulf states. Iraq got a free hand in Lebanon and pulled it close to the United States and the West. At the same time it deepened its animosity with Iraq. Signs of a change in their relations were indicated in mid-1997 with the reopening of the border and renewed trade relations on a limited scale.

Syria's relations with Jordan also had ups and downs. The 1970 confrontation between the two countries led to Syria's decision to sever its diplomatic relations with Jordan. However, Jordan's military support for Syria in the 1973 war improved relations between the two countries. In 1975–1976 the two states reconciled, establishing close political and economic relations, more than had ever existed between them, with mutual visits of their heads of state and an agreement in principle to set up a strategic alliance and federative union. In 1978–1980 relations between the two regimes deteriorated again, reaching a crisis. This was due to Jordan's shifting alliance to Iraq—mainly for economic reasons—which grew tight in the course of the Iraq-Iran war. King Hussein's quest for a renewal of the peace process with Israel in which he would play a key role regarding the West Bank and GAZA STRIP meant support for the Muslim Brotherhood in Syria. In November 1980, Syria—together with other member of the "Front of Steadfastness and Confrontation"— boycotted the all-Arab summit conference held in Amman after failing to bring to a postponement of the summit. By this requirement Syria intended to prevent a demonstration of support for Iraq's war effort against Iran and an all-Arab empowerment of Jordan to seek a peaceful settlement for the occupied Palestinian territories. As its demands were rejected, two Syrian divisions were massed along the Jordanian border, posing a threat to the gathering Arab heads of state— which refrained from decisions detrimental to Syria— and to Jordan's sovereign territory. Another period of rapprochement began in 1986, following the collapse of the Amman Accord (between Arafat and Hussein) and crisis in PLO-Jordan relations. King Hussein actively endeavored to mediate between Syria and Iraq, and to associate it with concerted all-Arab policies on a Middle East settlement. Despite their different positions on the Kuwait crisis (Jordan objected to an international intervention and seemed to have supported Iraq), the two states took part in the Madrid peace conference after the Gulf war. Together with the PLO and Lebanon, they conducted on-going consultations regarding the peace talks with Israel. However, the façade of all-Arab coordination was shattered in October 1994 when Jordan signed a separate peace agreement with Israel, following the Israel-PLO Oslo Agreement of September 1993. Syria responded with overt criticism of the Jordan-Israel agreement, but King Hussein, unlike past consideration of its mighty northern neighbor, dismissed Syria's charges, maintaining that it should mind its own business.

During the 1970s and the 1980s, Syria's inter-Arab relations were burdened by its policies toward the PLO and its ever-deepening involvement in Lebanon. Syria, the patron of Fatah and other Palestinian guerrilla movements since the mid-1960s, moved under the reign of Hafez al-Asad on a trajectory of collision with the PLO, and particularly with its mainstream, Fatah. Syria's policy on the Palestinian issue had always been a reflection of selfish national interests camouflaged by its fierce pan-Arab nationalism. Syria charged the Palestinian guerrilla groups with a high price in return for the strategic support it extended them (logistic and headquarters bases, military and politicaal assistance, and occasionally also a staging ground for attacks against Israel); namely, their subordination to its own political considerations and narrow national needs. In addition to establishing its own guerrilla group in 1968 (al-SA'IQA), Syria maintained close links with other small Palestinian factions by which it secured effective domination of the PLO. As long as the PLO had focused on an armed struggle against Israel, differences with Syria were tactical and minor. Thus, in the early 1970s Syria repeatedly intervened to prevent the Lebanese army's attempts to impose restrictions on the Palestinians' military presence and activity. However, in view of the peace making process after the October 1973 war, Syria was anxious to coopt the PLO into its orbit. Unity was offered between them, "since Palestine is the southern part of Greater Syria" in order to prevent its isolation by Sadat's separate peace diplomacy. In April 1973, when battles erupted between Lebanese army units and the Palestinian forces following Israel's raid on PLO headquarters in Beirut, Syria extended military suport to the PLO and exerted political pressures on the Lebanese government, including the closure of their common border. Similarly, Syria initially supported militarily the Palestinian organizations in the Lebanese civil war that erupted in April 1975 (see LEBANON). However, in early 1976 Syria became involved in mediating a new political order in Lebanon, for which it needed the PLO's collaboration. The PLO, on its part, refused to accept the Syrian plans, adhering instead to its Lebanese leftist allies which would secure the Palestinian political and military independence. This rejection and growing power of the Palestinians and Lebanese leftist groups was at the backdrop of the Syrian military intervention in Lebanon in early June 1976. In this the Syrian and Palestinian forces clashed with each other, culminating in the latter's defeat in October of that year. Although Syria and the PLO restored their alignment, the Syrian regime developed deep animosity towards Yasser ARAFAT and on several occasions it was reported that Syria was seeking his replacement by a more obedient leader.

The mistrust between Syria and the PLO's mainstream assumed a particularly extreme form in the late 1970s and early 1980s in view of Egypt's peace agreement with Israel and Arafat's independent diplomacy in the international arena. This was meant to bring about a renewal of the peace process on the Palestinian issue. The ruptures in Syria-PLO relations were clearly manifested during the Israeli siege of Beirut in June-August 1982 and expulsion of the PLO armed personnel from the city. Not only did Syria collaborate with Saudi Arabia and the United States in facilitating the expulsion, but it also posed conditions regarding those Palestinians who would be welcome to find refuge on its soil. *Fatah*'s leadership, however, chose to go to Tunis rather than to Syria, sending a message of alienation to Damascus. The hostility between the PLO and Syria culminated in the following year with Syria's supervision and support of, first, a rebellion within al-Fatah in May 1983 (see ABU MUSSA), followed by systematic expulsion of Arafat's loyalists from Syria and to aid military operations that evicted Arafat's forces from eastern Lebanon's Biqa'. Secondly, a military effort to oust Arafat and his loyalists from Tripoli, his last attempt to defend an autonomous Palestinian stronghold in Lebanon. In 1983–1984 Syria also employed Abu Nidal's terrorist group to assassinate Palestinian figures known for their suport of peaceful settlement with Israel. Syria also supported militarily the Shi'a militia, AMAL, encouraging it to use military means to restrict the Pales-

tinian military presence in Lebanon by putting their refugee camps along the Lebanese shore south of Beirut under long siege. This was lifted only in late 1987 as a gesture of respect to the INTIFADA. It was under these circumstances that Syrian-based PLO factions reached an agreement with the PLO mainstream in 1987 and mediatory efforts to effect a reconciliation between Syria and Arafat's PLO were made. However, the PLO refused to accept Syrian domination and to adopt Syria's positions toward Israel and the Middle East peace process. Syria, although would not interfere with the PLO's efforts to conduct its independent peace diplomacy—including the 1988–1989 PLO-American dialogue—refused to resume full ties with the PLO or to allow renewed Palestinian presence in South Lebanon. This two-edged policy toward the PLO stemmed from Syria's hopes to be helped by the PLO in future negotiations with Israel, in the absence of Soviet (or even Iraqi) backing.

The Oslo Agreement in 1993 came as a blow to Syria and its calculations regarding the procedures and nature of progress of the peace negotiations, namely, the need for Syrian-sponsored coordination between the Arab partners and the separate tracks (see ARAB-ISRAEL PEACEMAKING). The Syrians responded, as they had done in the past on several occasions, by employing proxies in order to undermine the PLO-Israeli accord. In January 1994, a new front comprised of ten radical Palestinian organizations was proclaimed in Damascus, committed to combatting the Oslo Agreement and Arafat, who was portrayed as a traitor. The new rejectionist front consisted of both religious and leftist groups, mostly small and marginal. This indicated Syria's declining veto power *vis-a-vis* the PLO (and Jordan), remaining with Lebanon as the only subordinate client regarding relations with Israel. In this respect, Syria not only forced Lebanon to boycott the multi-lateral Middle East peace talks but also prevented Lebanon from handling independently the issue of Israel's presence in south Lebanon.

Syria's relations with Turkey deteriorated since the late 1980s, mainly due to the latter's threats to deny Syria's water share in the Euphrates (see WATER POLITICS) and Syria's growing support for Turkish opposition groups (the Kurdish PKK and the Armenian Asala—see TERRORISM). The tightening links between Israel and Turkey in the mid-1990s, elevated in 1997 to the level of strategic cooperation between the two countries, became a major source of concern for Syria, aggravating its already tense relations with Turkey (see also TURKEY).

Syria's political and military involvement in Lebanon since the mid-1970s has been a major issue on Syria's regional agenda, affecting its international relations as well. Since then Syria's involvement in Lebanon has grown consistently, from military intervention in 1976 to the establishment of an "Arab Deterrent Force" that was in reality Syrian; Syria's de facto occupation of eastern and northern Lebanon; its increasing role in affecting a national Lebanese reconciliation and putting an end to the Lebanese Civil War.

SYRIAC A branch of the Aramaic language, still used in the liturgy of several Eastern Christian churches. Western Syriac is used by the MARONITES and the MONOPHYSITIC Syrian Orthodox (usually called JACOBITES) and the Syrian Catholics (see UNIATE); Eastern Syriac—by the ASSYRIANS-NESTORIANS and the CHALDEANS. As a spoken tongue, Syriac has died out, although remnants still survive in a dialect partially spoken in a few villages in SYRIA and Eastern TURKEY.

SYRIAN SOCIAL NATIONALIST PARTY (Arabic: *al-hizb al-qawmi al-suri*) Renamed in 1947–1948 "Syrian Social Nationalist Party" (*al-hizb al-suri al-qawmi al-ijtima'i*, SSNP). A group founded in LEBANON in 1932 by the Greek-Orthodox Christian Antoun Sa'adeh (1902–1949), propounding the existence of a distinctive Syrian nation—as against both Syria's Arab and Pan-Arab nationalism and Lebanon's separate national entity and state. The Party agitated for the creation of a "Natural, GREATER SYRIA" to include SYRIA, LEBANON, JORDAN, Palestine (and ultimately also IRAQ, KUWAIT and Cyprus). It stood for a totalitarian regime and had pro-Fascist tendencies, but did not hold racist views.

Antoun Sa'adeh, the son of a Lebanese doctor who had emigrated to Brazil, returned to Lebanon in 1930 and taught German in the American University of Beirut. He gathered around him a group of students, mainly Greek-Orthodox Christians, and formed his party, of which he became leader (*Za'im*), in 1932–1934. Because of its agitation for the immediate termination of the French Mandate, the SSNP was banned in the late 1930s. Sa'adeh himself,

after being harassed by the authorities, left Lebanon, reportedly first to Italy and Germany, and then to South America. As Syria and Lebanon became independent, the Party became Lebanese, working for its objectives in Lebanon only (other branches in "Greater Syria" did the same). It was legalized in Lebanon in 1944, but was suspected and harassed in both Syria and Lebanon. Sa'adeh returned to Lebanon in 1947. He resumed his political activity, adding the word "social" to the name of his Party and temporarily dropping the controversial word "Syrian" from it, but, suspected by the authorities, he was kept under surveillance and was arrested on several occasions. In 1949, after the "Jummaizeh incident," violent clashes between the SSNP and its arch enemy, the PHALANGES, the Party was accused of a plot against the Lebanese state and was outlawed. Sa'adeh was summarily tried and executed. He failed to win support from Syria's dictator, Husni Za'im, who betrayed him and extradited him to Lebanon. Sixty-eight other members were tried; twelve were sentenced to death and six of them were executed.

To his followers, Sa'adeh became a martyr, and in revenge, a hit squad of the Party assassinated Riyad al-Sulh, the Prime Minister at the time of Sa'adeh's execution, in July 1951. (Another member, a Syrian officer, killed Za'im in August 1949 during his deposition in a coup.) In the 1950s, the Party, never strong or influential and by now half-underground, illegal and leaderless, was further weakened by splits. However, it managed to send one deputy to the Lebanese Parliament in 1957. In this period it was regarded as right-wing and pro-West and even connected with the HASHEMITE dynasty and Jordan. (Its original Greater Syria conception had been anti-Hashemite.) In Syria, several of its members were purged and were tried as plotters against the leftist regime.

In 1958, the Party supported Lebanon's President CHAMOUN against the Nasserist rebels and provided some of the fighters in the Civil War; as a reward, the outgoing President allowed it to operate legally. But late in 1961 it was accused of a new plot to seize power through a military coup and its leaders were arrested, or fled and went underground. Seventy-nine were sentenced to death; most of them in absentia (those in detention had their sentences commuted). The Party was again legalized in Lebanon in 1970.

After the break of the Civil War in 1975, the SSNP changed its basic orientation. It joined the Muslim-led "leftist" camp, providing one of its fighting militias. Nevertheless, it maintained its separate identity, and sometimes its militia clashed with other factions of the camp, such as the DRUZE fighters or Franjiyyeh's "Marada" militia.

While the alliance's main leaders accepted it as a freak group, mainly Christian, on their side, they could not fully trust it. The SSNP leaders—Asad Ashqar, Georges Abdel-Massih, In'aam Ra'd and Issam al-Maha'iri —reacted to the crisis in conflicting ways. Following the shift in Syria's position in the civil war in 1976, the SSNP split into two factions, one led by Georges Abdel-Massih and the other, emerging as the main one, led by In'aam R'ad (b. 1929), a Greek-Orthodox Christian from Ayn Zhalta.

This last faction regarded Syria's President Hafez al-ASAD as a leader capable of advancing the Party's goals. (It was reported that some of the people close to him were followers of the Party). The SSNP thus moved closer to Syria and became its proxy. After the Israeli invasion in 1982, a member of the SSNP assassinated President-elect Bashir JUMAYYIL. The Party's military wing implemented military operations against the Israeli army in Lebanon, including suicide car-bombings and assassination attempts. After 1985, it continued to occasionally attack Israel's self-proclaimed "Security Zone" in South Lebanon.

In December 1990, and for the first time in Lebanon's history, a member of the SSNP, Asa'd Marwan, became a member of the National Unity government formed after the end of the Civil War. It was created with a view to implement the Ta'if Agreement and disband the various Lebanese militias, including that of the SSNP. In 1992, In'aam R'ad was elected President of the Party.

In recent years, the SSNP remained a Syrian proxy on the one hand, and an almost-exclusive club for Greek-Orthodox Christians on the other. Despite its dogmatic ideals and the considerable devotion of its members, it is considered a small, marginal—and maybe even archaic—political group.

SYRTE, GULF OF   see SIRTE.

T

TABA AGREEMENT   see ARAB-ISRAEL PEACEMAKING.

TABA   see ARAB-ISRAEL PEACEMAKING.

TALABANI, JALAL (b. 1933) Leader of The Patriotic Union of Kurdistan (PUK), one of the two main Kurdish political organizations in northern Iraq alongside with the Kurdish Democratic Party (KDP) led by Mas'ud BARZANI. Talabani was born in the village of Kelkan, near the Dokan lake in Northern IRAQ. A lawyer by profession, he joined the KDP in 1947 and was elected a member of the party's central committee in 1951. Together with his father in-law, Ibrahim Ahmed (who served as general al secretary on and off during the 1950s), he led a Marxist line that opposed the more conservative wing led by Mulla Mustafa Barzani. Talabani opposed the 1966 treaty between Barzani and the Iraqi government and established his own KDP, but was defeated by Barzani. In 1970, following an agreement between Barzani and the BA'TH regime, Talabani returned to the KDP, serving as its envoy in Damascus. Talabani's rivalry with Barzani surfaced again following the collapse of the Kurdish rebellion in 1975 and Barzani's decision to find refuge in Iran. That year, Talabani split from the KDP, establishing the Kurdish Workers League. In 1976, the League joined the Social Democratic Movement, forming the Patriotic Union of Kurdistan (PUK).

In addition to the ideological struggles between Talabani and Barzani, there are more significant domestic issues facing the KURDS. Talabani and his followers came from the southern region of Kurdistan, where they speak Sorani and Barzani and his clan (associated with the Kurmanji or Bahdinani-speaking areas in the North) as less developed and more conservative. That the Barzani and Talabani factions also associate, respectively, with one of the two major—rival—Sufi orders in the Kurdish region of Iraq, the *Naqshbandiyya* and the *Qadiriyya*, possibly provids us with further impetus to their rivalry. The two parties have been battling over dominance in Iraqi Kudistan since the 1950s, resulting in a severe impediment to the Kurdish national struggle for independence.

Talabani has known different patrons during his years of activity but since the GULF WAR he has enjoyed a close relationship with IRAN and SYRIA. He maintains ties with additional regional forces such as TURKEY and JORDAN. Talabani has close ties with a number of Iraqi opposition elements such as the Supreme Council for Islamic Revolution in IRAQ, a Shi'ite group led by Ayatollah Baqer al-Hakim.

TALAL IBN ABDALLAH (1909–1972) King of JORDAN 1951–1952. The elder son of King ABDALLAH IBN HUSSEIN, born in Mecca, Talal ascended the Jordanian throne in 1951, after the assassination of his father. His reign was short-lived and there was no lasting mark of his reign. Nonetheless, he was popular as being supposedly nationalist and democratic. Talal suffered from a mental illness and was dethroned in August 1952. His son HUSSEIN, still too young to ascend the throne, succeeded him after a short period during which the Kingdom had been ruled by a council of regents. Talal spent the remaining twenty years of his life in a mental institution in Istanbul.

TALAS, MUSTAFA (b. 1932) Syrian SUNNI-Muslim army officer and politician; since 1972 Deputy Prime Minister and Minister of Defence. He is also Deputy Supreme Commander of the Syrian Army and a member of the ruling BA'TH Party. Born in the town of Rastan in the Governorate of Homs, Talas joined the Ba'th Party in 1947, while in high school. After working as a sports instructor and a scoutmaster, 1950–1952, he joined the military academy, where he made friends with another cadet, Hafez AL-ASAD. He graduated in 1954 and served as a commander of an armored unit. In 1958–1961, the UNITED ARAB REPUBLIC (UAR) period, he was sent to EGYPT. After the Syrian secession from the Union, Talas was dismissed from the army and arrested in 1962, but following the Ba'th coup in 1963 was returned to military service as commander of the fifth armored brigade and Chairman of the National Security Court in the central military region. In the intra-Ba'th factional struggle he was a follower of General Hafez

AL-ASAD. He implemented important missions—in the Hamat uprising in 1964; in the struggle against the "national" all-Arab command in 1966 and in the trial of the rebelling DRUZE officers led by Salim Hatum in 1967. He proved himself efficient and loyal. In 1965 he was elected member of the Regional (Syrian) Command of the Ba'th. In 1968 he was promoted exceptionally from the rank of Lieutenant-Colonel to the rank of Major-General. He became First Deputy Minister of Defence as well as Chief of Staff of the army and the Armed Forces.

When Hafez al-Asad assumed power in November 1970, Talas assured him the support of the Army. He was rewarded in March 1972 when he became Minister of Defence and first deputy Commander-in-Chief of the army and the Armed Forces. He has held these posts ever since, and the position of First Deputy Prime Minister since March 1984. In August 1973 he participated in the Syrian-Egyptian coordination talks prior to the Yom Kippur War as Deputy Chief of the Higher Military Council of the two Armies. As Minister of Defence, he oversaw the massive build-up of the Syrian Army with Soviet assistance. In 1983, when President Asad was recovering from a severe heart attack, he was one of the members of the committee called by him to run the country's everyday matters (among the five others were two other Sunnis: Chief of Staff Hikmat SHIHABI and Foreign Minister Abdel Halim KHADDAM). He stood by his side during the challenge posed by Asad's younger brother, Rif'at.

Although Talas is a high-ranking officer and very close to Asad, being a Sunni he does not belong to the inner leadership core dominated by ALAWIS. Furthermore, he does not have a power base in the Syrian Army which is also dominated by Alawis. Therefore, he preforms mainly ceremonial tasks. In Syria's foreign relations, Talas is a hard liner, delivering tough speeches against the PLO leadership and ISRAEL.

In addition to his official duties, Talas owns a publishing house that bears his name. Established in 1983, he was written or published more than forty books on various topics, including military thought and practice, studies of the JEWS and the conflict with ISRAEL, and the official Syrian account of the 1982 Lebanon War. In 1980 Talas obtained a Ph.D. degree from the Vorshelov Military Academy of General Staff in the USSR.

al-TALL, WASFI (1920–1971) Jordanian officer and politician. Born in Irbid. A graduate of the American University of Beirut, Tall worked as a teacher from 1942 to 1945 and served in the British army, reaching the rank of captain. In 1945 he became a member of Mussa al-Alami's team (see PALESTINE ARABS) and worked until 1947 in his propaganda offices in London and JERUSALEM. During Israel's 1948 War of Independence he joined Qawuqji's "Army of Deliverance" (see ARAB-ISRAEL CONFLICT) and served as a staff officer and battalion commander that operated in the Galilee. In 1949 he joined JORDAN's diplomatic and civil service. After rising in its ranks, he was Ambassador to IRAQ from 1961 to 1962.

Tall became Prime Minister and Minister of Defense in 1962 for one year, and was again Prime Minister in 1965–1967 and 1970–1971. An able administrator, he was considered loyal to the King HUSSEIN and a rigid anti-Nasserist. He assumed his last Premiership during the crisis between the Hussein regime and the PALESTINE LIBERATION ORGANIZATION (PLO) in 1972. Under his leadership the Jordanian army continued and completed the liquidation of the PLO military establishment in Jordan that had begun in September 1970. He was assassinated in November 1971 by Palestinian terrorists, while on a visit to Cairo; his murder was the first appearance of the "Black September" group, which was in fact a cover name of Fatah's international guerrilla apparatus.

TANB ISLANDS see ABU MASSA ISLANDS, PERSIAN GULF, RAS AL-KHAIMA, UAE.

TANGIER (also Tanger; Arabic: Tanya) Town and port in MOROCCO, on the Strait of Gibraltar. The population, mostly Muslim Moroccan, was estimated in the 1930s at 50,000–60,000; in the 1950s at 140,000, and in the mid-1990s at over 400,000. In the late nineteenth century, Tangier became the gate of entry into Morocco for European interests as well as the center for foreign diplomats who conferred upon it a special status and increasingly intervened in its administration, beginning with health control and law and order. In 1904 and 1905 FRANCE and Spain allotted Tangier a "special status" which the International Conference of Algeirs, 1906, endorsed, (against Germany). This was upheld by the Protectorate Treaty with Morocco, 1912, and reconfirmed

between France and Spain, though Tangier was within the Spanish Protectorate zone.

In December 1923, France, Spain and BRITAIN concluded a convention establishing a neutralized and demilitarized International Zone of Tangier and the area around the town, about 225 sq. miles (583 sq. km.) This convention was, amended and reconfirmed, in 1925 and 1928, joined by Italy in 1928, and accepted by most European countries. It enabled Tangier to be administered by a "Committee of Control," composed of the representatives of eight European states and the UNITED STATES (the US at first refused to associate itself, but later joined). A twenty-six to twenty-seven member "International Legislative Assembly" was to consist of sixteen to seventeen foreigners appointed by their governments (four French, four Spanish, three British, two Italian, and one each from the USA, Belgium, the Netherlands and Portugal), and nine local representatives (six Muslims and three JEWS) appointed by a "Commissioner" or Envoy (*Mandoub*) of the Sultan of Morocco. The *Mandoub* was to preside, and three Vice-Presidents of the Assembly were to establish a kind of executive. These arrangements were renewed in 1936 for twelve years. But during World War II, Spain seized control of Tangier in 1940, annexed it and dissolved its administrative bodies.

After the War, Spain was forced by the victorious allies to withdraw its occupation and was excluded from participation in the international regime that was re-established in October 1945. In 1952–1953, the statute was changed somewhat, enlarging US and Italian representation. Tangier prospered as a customs-free international entrepot and financial center. But as Morocco approached complete independence and the French and Spanish Protectorates were abolished (March 1956), Tangier's international regime could not continue either. In October 1956, an international conference abrogated Tangier's international status and agreed with Morocco on new arrangements to maintain its position as an international commercial and financial center, whilst remaining part of Morocco. These arrangements were proclaimed by Morocco in a new charter for Tangier in August 1957. However, in October 1959 the King of Morocco repealed that charter effective from April 1960. Tangier's free economy was ended, taxes and customs were introduced and Tangier was fully integrated in Morocco. As many international enterprises withdrew, a rapid decline in Tangier's economy set in. In July 1961, the King tried to repair the damage and announced the creation of a free port in Tangier from January 1962 and the re-introduction of certain limited tax and customs privileges. But Tangier's "golden" days were over. While its port and economic enterprises revived to some extent, it did not regain the lively prosperity it had once enjoyed as an international city.

TERRORISM   From the late 1960s the Middle East has become recognized as a center of regional and international terrorism, linked mainly to the ARAB-ISRAEL CONFLICT and emergence of Palestinian nationalism. From the 1980s terrorism turned to be increasingly identified with the resurgence of IS-LAMIC RADICALISM in this region, and its offshoots in the West.

Despite general disagreement as to the definition of terrorism, it is regarded here as an action involving the systematic use of extreme violence against civilians as a means of domestic or international coercion for political purposes. While terrorism is conducted usually by individuals and small autonomous groups, it is often secretly sponsored or backed by sovereign states against other states. Although terrorism has existed for centuries, it is only in recent decades that acts of terrorism have become a major political weapon in international and internal affairs, employed for political blackmail and publicity. Indeed, the strongest single factor explaining the proliferation and effectiveness of terrorism is the globalization of electronic media, and especially television.

Persia (see IRAN) and SYRIA were the cradle of the Assassins (eleventh-twelfth centuries), an offshoot of the ISLMA'ILIS—a Shi'i sect of ISLAM—the first group in history that planned and implemented systematic use of murder as a political weapon against the dominating Sunni order in Islam in an attempt to replace it with their own order. Motivated by religious fanaticism, the sect used dramatic political murders of Islamic rulers, but also of Crusaders, who brought their name to the West as the epitome of politically-motivated murderers. However, the frequent presence of terrorism in the contemporary Middle East and its offshoots in the Western Hemisphere can be explained by several specific aspects of the region's modern political and social history.

Political violence has been a prevalent manifestation during periods of radical social and political transition that the Middle East has been undergoing for over a century, marked by normative and ideological disorientation, political disorder, and the weakening of authoritative and legal institutions. In the absence of legal and institutional mechanisms of representation and regulation to which the deprived and weak can present their grievances and frustrations and to expect for justice, individuals and groups tend to accelerate the tendency to employ violence as a means of survival.

Political violence was particularly intensified by the relatively long struggle for national liberation from Western domination, which often assumed also social and economic protest and political struggle for power within the indigenous society. In this context, terrorism was employed by the Jewish dissident underground groups of the *Irgun Zva'i Le'umi* (IZL) and *Lohamei Herut Israel* (LHI—the "Stern Gang"), variably directed against Arab civilians (in the late 1930s and late-1940s), as well as against British military personnel and officials (mainly from 1944 to 1948).

The transition of Arab-Muslim peoples to full independence from the late 1940s witnessed the rise of revolutionary ideologies, which pretended to be a panacea to social and political maladies. Social and political messianic doctrines ostensibly justified the use of excessive and indiscriminate violence, bloody military coups, assassination of political leaders, and oppression or massacres of ethnic minorities as well as of rival political movements. Moreover, domestic instability and struggle of new elites for legitimacy and survival often generated assertive regional policies such as subversive interference across borders. LEBANON's long, bitter civil war demonstrated the costly results of such collapse of political and social order, generating much internal and international violence, with kidnappings, assassinations, and massacres of civilians by all sides. Loyalty to family and community broke any empathy with other groups. Palestinians massacred CHRISTIANS at Damour; the Christians massacred Palestinians at Sabra and Shatila; DRUZE massacred Christians in the Shuf and Christians did the same to Druze in Mount Lebanon. The identification of the state with the ruling elite, and more specifically, with the leading figure, made political assassination of leaders appear as an effective way to bring political change. Indeed, the higher in the hierarchy of power the assassinated figure was, the more meaningful was the act of terrorism meant to be, as an elimination of a symbol of a way of life, of a political doctrine and policy. The assassinations of Jordan's King ABDALLAH, Egyptian President Anwar al-SADAT, and Israeli Prime Minister Yitzhak RABIN all belonged to this category, though they had not been entirely bereft of power politics. Other cases, such as the assassination of Egyptian Prime Minister Nuqrashi Pasha in late 1948 and consequent murder of the founder and leader of the MUSLIM BROTHERHOOD society, Hasan al-Banna, shortly afterwards; the assassination of Lebanese Prime Minister Riyad al-Sulh in 1951 in revenge for the execution of Antoun Sa'adeh in 1949; and the attempt on the life of ABDEL NASSER in 1954 by a Muslim Brother; all represented a sheer struggle for power.

Terrorism has been a strategic choice often motivated by a radical group's political and military failures or weaknesses, ranging from terrain hostile to rural guerrilla warfare (compared to Asian or Latin American mountains and jungles) to difficulties in creating disciplined parties and mass organizations, to defeats in combatting armies. For instance, the PALESTINE LIBERATION ORGANIZATION's (PLO) inability to launch a "people's war" on the WEST BANK in the 1967–1970 period made attacks on Israeli civilians seem easier and more likely to be successful.

For decades, the Jewish *Yishuv* (the Zionist community in Palestine during the British MANDATE)— and later the state of ISRAEL—drew the attention of political radicalism in the Middle East. Sporadic acts of murder of civilian Jewish settlers by Arabs were an ongoing phenomenon, albeit not proliferated except for periods of riots and rebellion on the Arab part (see ARAB-ISRAEL CONFLICT; PALESTINE ARABS).

The emergence of the State of Israel and exile of over half of the Palestinian Arab population from their home was at the backdrop of a vast tendency of those refugees until the mid-1950s to infiltrate into the Israeli territory, mainly for the purpose of thefts, but also for sabotage and murder driven by sense of vengeance and nationalist zeal. From 1955 EGYPT organized and sponsored Self-Sacrificers (*fida'iyyun*) squads from residents of the GAZA STRIP which accounted for espionage, sabotage and murder activities against Israeli civilians. This activity generated repeated Israeli military retaliations against the neighboring Arab states which often caused casualties among civilians as well. The 1960s witnessed the emergence of revolutionary PALESTINIAN GUERRILLA ORGANIZATIONS that adopted the idea of armed struggle for the liberation of Palestine. The Arab military defeat of 1967 boosted this doctrine of guerrilla warfare whose targets came to be primarily Israeli civilians through three main arenas of action: rural, urban, and international, which despite attempts to describe them as a struggle for national liberation, and as an effort aimed at the destruction of the State of Israel and not against its civilians, was nothing but a classical form of terrorism. The timing, pace, and center of gravity of the Palestinian political violence shifted occasionally in accordance with operational opportunities and political considerations, though attacks through the borders and sea, and internal terrorism always remained the lion's share of the effort of violence.

Rural terrorism assumed the form of infiltration into Israel from the neighboring Arab states for the purpose of killing Israelis-officially targeting soldiers, but in fact focusing against the easier target of civilians. Conspicuous examples of such terrorism were the attacks on a children bus of Avivim on the Lebanese border in May 1970 perpetrated by the Popular Front for the Liberation of Palestine-General Command (PFLP-GC), and the attack on a school in Ma'alot in April 1974, perpetrated by the Democratic Front for the Liberation of Palestine in which 32 children were massacred during the rescue operation (see PALESTINIAN GUERRILLA ORGANIZATIONS).

This sort of operations also included shelling and launching rockets on Israeli settlements and towns. This was the most prevalent form of Palestinian terrorism-launched primarily from JORDAN (until 1971) and Lebanon (which by the mid-1980s was replaced by the Lebanese Shi'i movements of AMAL and HIZBALLAH. From the mid-1970s the successful sealing of the borders from Jordan and Lebanon, and the involvement of the Palestinian organizations in the Lebanese Civil War, motivated *Fatah* to initiate spectacular naval attacks on Israeli civilian centers, which climaxed in the hijacking of a bus and driving it with its passengers toward Tel Aviv in an attempt to bargain the release of Palestinian prisoners, which ended with 34 Israelis dead. Many of the post-1973 attacks across the border or by the sea, involved taking hostages with the attempt to bargain the release of Palestinian prisoners in Israel's hands. However, except for the case of the El Al airliner hijacked to Algiers in 1968 in which Israel was forced to give up, its government strongly adhered to the principle that there should be no surrender to the terrorists. However, Israel was alone in the international community inasmuch as West European countries usually preferred to refrain from strictly fulfilling the law against Middle East terrorist operating on their soil or captured by them. Israel itself gave up again in 1985 in the largest deal of exchanging three Israeli soldiers taken prisoners by the PFLP-GC in Lebanon for 1150 Palestinian and foreign prisoners held in Israel for crimes of political violence.

Urban terrorism became proliferated due to the free flow of Palestinian workers from the WEST BANK and Gaza Strip into Israel among whom were recruits to the guerrilla groups. The acts of terrorism they employed included mostly the placement of bombs in schools, marketplaces, theaters, and other public facilities in Israel, as well as shooting and killing civilians. The emergence of the armed Islamic movements—the Islamic JIHAD and HAMAS—in the mid and late 1980s brought to the perpetration of far more lethal forms of terrorism such as suicidal bombings of buses and public places, and attacks from ambush.

Palestinian resistance groups played a leading role in the sphere of international terrorism. Beginning in 1968, the PFLP hijacked an Israeli airliner to Algiers were the passengers were held hostages, and forced Israel to free Palestinian prisoners in return to the release of the passengers. Henceforth, Palestinian attacks abroad expanded their scope and targets, hijacking and blowing up (sometimes while in the air) Israeli and Western planes; sabotaging Israeli embassies, Jewish immigration to Israel and Jewish community centers, and murdering Israeli tourists and officials abroad. The PFLP's air terrorism peaked in September 1970 when the organization brought to Zarqa in Jordan three hijacked airplanes and threatened to bomb them with their passengers unless members of the organization be released, which instigated a full-scale military collision between the Palestinian organizations and the Jordanian army. (see JORDAN).

Although other Palestinian groups followed the PFLP, Palestinian international terrorism assumed significantly larger scale only when *Fatah*, the largest

Palestinian guerrilla group adopted this arena of operations in 1971 under the cover-name of "Black September," following the bloody events in Jordan that brought to an end armed Palestinian presence on and attacks from Jordanian territory. *Fatah* attacked mainly Israeli targets (most spectacular of which was the massacre of Israeli athletes at the Munich Olympic games in September 1972), but also Arab and American, which aimed at bringing up the Palestinian issue to the world's political consciousness as a problem of national rights of a people. Palestinian international terrorism peaked in 1971–1973, during which an effective cease-fire prevailed on the Israeli-Egyptian and Israeli-Jordanian fronts, which led Israel's government to wage active anti-terror warfare, including the assassination of Palestinian operational and political figures in Europe, but also to take comprehensive security precautions to defend the presence of Israelis and Israeli missions abroad. During these years operational collaboration between Palestinian organizations, especially the PFLP, and other terrorist groups (the Baader Meinhof gang and the Red Army in Germany; the Japanese Red Army; the Red Brigades in Italy; *l'Action Directe* in France, and many others), tightened. This collaboration was demonstrated in the massacre perpetrated by the Japanese Red Army in the terminal of Tel Aviv Airport in May 1972 on behalf of the PFLP; the kidnapping of the ministers of the ORGANIZATION OF PETROLEUM-EXPORTING COUNTRIES (OPEC) in Vienna in December 1975, led by the most notorious exponent of international terrorism in the 1970s and 1980s, reputed to be a Latin American named Illych Ramirez Sanchez, code-named Carlos; and the hijack of Entebbe, Uganda, in July 1976, executed by the PFLP-Special Operations Group (SOG) led by Wadi' Haddad in collaboration with German terrorists.

While the share of Palestinian international terrorism was marginal—never to exceed five percent of the global terrorist actions—it had an immense impact on international terrorism as a whole, much beyond its quantitative share. Indeed, its worldspread image reflected the innovative and quality of the Palestinian international terrorist operations in terms of the choice of targets, the net results in terms of damage and public echo, and the *modus operandi*, turning into a role model for many other similar organizations in the world. Moreover, the support they received from the Arab states enabled the Palestinian guerrilla groups-especially the PFLP and *Fatah*—to provide various services to international underground and terrorist organizations, such as weapons, training, documentation, international contacts and secure haven for the perpetrators. Furthermore, the plunge of Lebanon into civil war and anarchy in 1975 turned this country into a virtual free zone for terrorist groups, including European, Armenian, Middle Eastern and Japanese, with Palestinian factions playing the role of hosts and collaborators. Such links of cooperation with other guerrilla and terrorist groups remained valid well into the 1980s and their scope was revealed in 1982 by the Israeli invasion of Lebanon and capture of the PLO's headquarters and training camps. The most conspicuous result of the Lebanese anarchy during the 1980s was the large number of Western people taken hostages by small groups, primarily *Hizballah*, clearly sponsored by IRAN. In many cases the kidnappings ended in murder. This trend came to its end only by the late 1980 and early 1990s.

The most active Palestinian organizations in international terrorism during the 1970s and 1980s were the PFLP, *Fatah*, and the ABU NIDAL group, a semi-mercenary terrorist organization headed by an ex-*Fatah* member-Sabri al-Banna-whose targets were Palestinian, Arab, and foreign, and whose operations continued till the early 1990s. Other Palestinian organizations involved in international terrorism were the Syrian-backed Sa'iqa organization, and the PFLP-GC. Palestinian international terrorism received secret but indispensable support from the Soviet Block, despite repeated denials of its respective East European governments. The scope and depth of that support-providing arms, shelters, passports, intelligence, and communication-revealed after the collapse of the Iron Curtain, indeed exceeded the assumptions made earlier in the West. Many terrorists, especially but not only Palestinian ones, acquired their skills in Eastern Europe or from Soviet advisers in training camps within the region.

Pseudonyms disguised the involvement of state sponsors or groups in specific attacks. *Fatah* used "Black September," while the Palestinian mercenary terrorist group of Abu Nidal (officially called *Fatah* Revolutionary Council) employed such aliases as the "Arab Revolutionary Brigades" (in April 1986 Syria-backed bombing of a TWA airliner), " The

Revolutionary Organization of Socialist Muslims" (attacks on British targets), and "The Arab Revolutionary Organization" (a June 1985 bombing at Frankfurt airport). Syrian-controlled al-Sa'iqa bombed Jewish community centers, stores, and restaurants in FRANCE under the cover-names "Eagles of the Palestinian Revolution" and "Alliance for Palestinian Justice"). Iran's minions such as *Hizballah* were called "Islamic Jihad," "Guardians of the Islamic Revolution," or "Organization of the Oppressed on Earth"; Libyan surrogates employed "Egypt's Revolution" among other names.

Why did Palestinian groups use terrorism and under what considerations did this weapon lose its effectiveness? A major reason for the adoption of indiscriminate violence was the lack of attractive alternative strategies since neither conventional nor classical guerrilla warfare within the occupied territories of the West Bank and Gaza Strip proved to be feasible and mass mobilization was impracticable in the absence of sovereignty. As a deprived and marginal group, on both the Arab-regional and international arenas, the choice of "popular armed struggle," that is, political violence, as a strategy was meant to be first and foremost an instrument of nation building. Boosting Palestinian nationalism and reaching out the world public opinion, especially in the West, was by far more realistic than destroying or demoralizing Israel by such attacks. Finally, the Palestinian masses approved of this type of warfare, which has been congruent with the Arab-Muslim ethos of resistance to foreign domination. Violence against Israel has remained highly effective value among the Palestinians, determining a group's political position and prestige within the community. Thus, factions competed each other in carrying out attacks, and moderates were intimidated or even assassinated. Violent activism-defined as "armed struggle" —indeed helped the PLO's leadership headed by ARAFAT to maintain the PLO as a loose coalition, or umbrella of various Palestinian activist groups, despite the price it entailed in terms of continued Israeli and American rejection of the PLO as a partner in the Middle East peacemaking process.

Yet although the armed struggle was defined by the Palestinian National Charter as a "strategy," the employment of violence, particularly in the international arena, appeared to be increasingly controlled and subordinated to political calculations of cost and benefit that such strategy might produce. While gaining publicity and support, the PLO was never able to gain military victory or a diplomatic role as long as it used terrorism as a major instrument. That strategy damaged the PLO's standing in the United States and West Europe while making Israel adamant in refusing to negotiate with the PLO or yield territory. Moreover, the deployment of terrorism also affected the PLO itself, tending to give a veto power and added prestige to the most extreme factions and individuals.

Still, Palestinian organizations were unique in their combined nationalist and international activity, and ability to maintain both violence and diplomacy due to the growing international recognition of the PLO. However, this combination grew impracticable along time, inasmuch as the PLO strove for recognition and inclusion for which even the Arab oil weapon was insufficient. With the beginning of the ARAB-IS-RAEL PEACEMAKING in the aftermath of the October 1973 War, the benefit of international terrorism was reconsidered in view of the PLO's effort to attain recognition as an equal partner in the Middle East peace process. Hence, as of late 1974 the Palestinian mainstream led by *Fatah*-and followed by the PFLP—decided to cease using this sort of international terrorism, explaining that it had turned to be counter-effective to the PLO's political aims. The abandonment of international terrorism by the PLO factions, however, was far from being complete. A salient example-which also demonstrated the unwillingness of a West European state to take strict measures against Palestinian terrorism even when it had been directed against its own interest-was the incident of the Achille Lauro, an Italian cruise ship seized in October 1985 by four Palestinian gunmen of the Palestine Liberation Front (PLF), one of the PLO's constituent groups headed by Abu Abbas, then a member of the PLO Executive Committee. The gunmen shot a sixty-nine year-old wheelchair-bound American, and threw his body overboard. The PLO spokesmen defended the perpetrators' deed and extended full diplomatic support for their release after they had been forced by American navy fighter planes to land in Sicily, together with Abu Abbas himself who joined to end the failed operation thank to an Egyptian military transport. Italy, trying to avoid a clash with the PLO, ignored a US request to arrest Abu Abbas and he was allowed to

leave, following which he continued to fulfil his membership on the PLO Executive Committee. Following this incident and consequent international pressure, Arafat declared in Cairo that the PLO would renounce terrorism except in the occupied territories, though his organization continued to undertake violent actions in Israel itself and not only in the West Bank and Gaza Strip. Further step toward departure from terrorism was made by Arafat's declaration in December 1988 in Geneva in which he renounced terrorism and accepted Security Council Resolution 242. The new declaration was given under heavy international pressure in order to meet an American prerequisite to opening a dialogue with the PLO. However, the poor results of the dialogue and the PLO's growing frustration at the diminishing impact of the Palestinian uprising (INTIFADA) in the West Bank and Gaza Strip, stood at the backdrop of Arafat's refusal to denounce a terrorist attack by the PLF (Abu Abbas group) on Israeli civilians by landing from the sea on the shore of Nitzanim, even at the cost of suspension of the US-PLO dialogue. A final end of the use of violence against Israeli targets came only with the Israel-PLO Oslo Agreement, though it committed only *Fatah* and those factions identifying with the PALESTINIAN AUTHORITY, while most other groups, especially the Islamic ones (*Hamas* and the Islamic Jihad) accelerated their attacks on Israel in an attempt to foil the implementation of the Oslo agreement (see ARAB-ISRAEL PEACEMAKING).

Ex-PLO activist factions continued to maintain and even intensify international terrorism against "imperialist," "capitalist," and "Zionist" targets. Primary among them were Abu Nidal's *Fatah* Revolutionary Council and the PFLP-SOG led by Wadi' Haddad. The latter was, until 1974, the head of the PFLP international operations branch who refused to accept the decision to cease violent operations abroad and seceded from the organization. In 1976 he sponsored the hijacking of an Air France airliner designated to Tel Aviv, which was flown to Entebbe, where over 100 Israeli passengers had been held hostages before being rescued by an Israeli commando force. Following Haddad's death in 1978, his faction split to three sub-groups: The May 15 Organization, led by Hussein al-Umari (supported by IRAQ), the PFLP-Special Command (backed by the PDRY), and The Lebanese Armed Revolutionary Faction (LARF) led by George Ibrahim Abdallah, (notorious for conducting a series of bombings in Paris, that left 15 killed and 150 wounded), which continued to operate against Western targets. Palestinian international terrorism thus turned to be increasingly conducted by esoteric groups supervised by radical Arab states, such as Iraq, Syria, Libya and the PDRY, representing their own shared goals rather than Palestinian national interests.

From the mid-1970s the lion's share of Palestinian international terrorism was claimed, however, by the Abu Nidal group, which was successively supported by Iraq, Syria, and Libya. The dissident group first became the executive instrument of Iraqi subversive policy till the end of the 1970s, mainly against Syria and the PLO, in addition to its commitment to fight Israel, traditional Arab regimes, and Western countries involved in the Arab-Israel peacemaking. From 1978 it turned to fight the growing trend of pragmatism within *Fatah*'s ranks, expressed by the willingness to accept a Palestinian state in the West Bank and Gaza Strip, alongside Israel and not on its wreckage. In 1978 alone the group assassinated three prominent PLO officials who had led the PLO's diplomatic offensive in Europe in this direction. In 1979 Abu Nidal left Baghdad against the backdrop of rapprochement between the Iraqi regime and the PLO, and moved to Damascus to serve as an instrument in the latter's subversive activity against Iraq, Jordan (accused by Damascus of supporting the Syrian MUSLIM BROTHERHOOD) and the PLO for its independent diplomatic overtures in Europe. The political dialogue conducted between Jordan and the PLO (1982–1986) was another target of Abu Nidal. Palestinian and Jordanian diplomats were among the victims of the terrorist activity of the group, as well as Alia, the Royal Jordanian Airlines. In early June 1982 the Abu Nidal group made an attempt on the life of Israel's ambassador in London, which gave the Israeli government the pretext it had been looking for to justify a major military operation against the Palestinian presence in Lebanon. In 1985 Abu Nidal began his contacts with Libya while still holding bases in the Biqa' (under Syrian control) and Palestinian refugee camps in Lebanon, and also in Sudan. The main financial sources of the organization came from patron states, graft and blackmail and also its own network of business companies and front organizations. Although the group was successively supported by Iraq, Syria and Libya,

it apparently maintained a level of financial and operational independence. While many of its operations may have coincided with the interests of the hosting states, the group also conducted its independent operations. Since the mid-1970s the Abu Nidal group committed dozens of major atrocities, which claimed the lives of many officials and innocent peoples in the Middle East, Western Europe, Rumania, Turkey, Austria, and India (for more details on the group's activities, see ABU NIDAL).

The PLO's self-sustained restrictions on terrorism, the decline of radical Arab nationalism, and most of all, the collapse of the Soviet Block in the late 1980s, all brought to a shift in the course of nationally-motivated Palestinian political violence. Indeed, with the end of the GULF WAR terrorism became increasingly identified with Islamic radical movements, although the latter's involvement in the sphere of political violence was by no means a new phenomenon (see ISLAMIC RADICALISM AND MOVEMENTS).

From the early 1970s Turkey has been the target of internal terrorism motivated by nationalist and revolutionary causes. The major organization involved in such activities against the government has been the Kurdish Workers Party (PKK), whose objective is to set up a Marxist Kurdish state in eastern Anatolia, which is heavily inhabited by 10-12 million KURDS. Established in 1973, the organization was initially supported financially by the Soviet Union and from 1987, by Syria and Iran. The PKK has training camps in the Syrian-controlled Biqa' area of Lebanon, as well as covert offices in the major cities of Turkey, as well as overt political offices in Tehran, Baghdad, Damascus, Nicosia and in some European capitals. The organization conducted assassinations and armed attacks against personnel and government's installations, including the army and police, as well as against civilian authorities and tourism (which in 1990–1991 deprived the country of fifty percent of its income from tourism). During the years the PKK's terrorist attacks and counter-attacks by the Turkish government, which were particularly intensified since the GULF WAR of 1991 and included deep raids into Iraq's territory, claimed the lives of over 27,000 people, mostly Kurds. One of the most notorious operations of the PKK was a slaughter of 33 unarmed soldiers in east Anatolia in 1993, performed amidst a truce that had been declared by the organization's leader Abdallah Ocalan.

Other terrorist organizations, usually small in number (a few dozens to a few hundreds) are:

a. Dev Sol (Revolutionary Left), advocating a popular democratic revolution in Turkey. Established in 1979, the group implemented tens of political assassinations, particularly of senior Turkish security officials.

b. Another terrorist group is The Armenian Secret Army for the Liberation of Armenia (ASALA), which since 1975 has been active in fighting against Turkish officials and Turkish interests worldwide. A Marxist-Leninist group, ASALA aspires to restore the historical Armenian homeland that includes north-eastern Turkey, north-western Iran and the ex-soviet Republic of Armenia. It also demands admission of Turkish responsibility for the massacre of hundreds of thousands of Armenians during World War I. It maintained close relations with Abu Nidal group, the PFLP-GC, and some Kurdish opposition groups, and supported by Iran's and Syria's intelligence services, with reported bases in the Biqa' area of Lebanon until 1982. The killing of the movement's leader Bedron Ohanessian, code-named Hagop Hagopian, in 1988 led to the decline of its activity and split to three sub-groups. However, from the early 1990s the movement witnessed a revitalization, apparently due to the proclamation, and apparently support, of the independent republic of Armenia. Since its foundation ASALA committed murders of over 30 Turkish diplomats and officials, and attacks on Turkish missions abroad.

c. *Hizballah*, an extreme Islamist group that began its activity in the early 1990s, calling for the Islamization of Turkey and full implementation of the Islamic Law. The group has been active in Europe among Turkish migrants, and maintains close links with other Middle East fanatic Islamic movements of the KHOMEINI's school, including the Lebanese *Hizballah* movement.

From the 1970s the main states sponsoring terrorism as an instrument of foreign policy in the Middle East have been Libya, Syria and Iraq, and since the early 1980s, Iran as well. From the early 1990s Sudan has also been accused of sponsoring Islamic terrorism. Sharing the goal of eliminating US influence in the region, the use of terrorism offered these regimes a low-cost, low-risk way of waging conflict, hiding behind shadowy connections or front groups that victims could not easily deter or punish. Their motives included Libya's efforts to promote its regional status as a leading radical power and to overthrow all moderate regimes; Syria's attempts to control Lebanon and lead a hard line toward Israel that would secure its national interests and prevent Jordan and the PLO from making separate peace agreements with Israel; Iran's goals of sparking Islamic fundamentalist revolutions and gaining hegemony over the PERSIAN GULF, and supporting radical Islamic movements in Lebanon and the Palestinian occupied territories to promote Iran's image as a sworn enemy of Israel and the US.

These regimes provided various terrorist groups with necessary facilities, such as money, safe havens, logistical help, training, weapons, diplomatic support, and protection against retaliation, without which international terrorism could not have been implemented at the scope and effectiveness it has been conducted. The ability to obtain genuine passports, send arms and explosives via diplomatic pouches, enjoy lavish financing and good training facilities let Middle East terrorists operate in a more frequent, deadly manner than counterparts elsewhere. The proliferation of inter-state conflicts in the Middle East has been manifested in the numerous subversive and terrorist groups sponsored by states: ALGERIA backed the POLISARIO movement against MOROCCO; Iraq supports the Mujahidin-i-Khalk against Iran; Iran sponsored groups trying to expand Islamic revolution throughout the region. Libya and SUDAN used terrorists against EGYPT, Arab states backed Palestinian terrorism against Israel, Jordan for a long time helped the MUSLIM BROTHERHOOD against Syria, and Syria stood behind ASALA and the PKK against TURKEY.

Intimidating or killing opponents also enhanced sponsoring regimes' stability. Iraq's government, for example, ordered the murders of overseas critics during the 1970s and 1980s in BRITAIN, SOUTH YEMEN, KUWAIT and Sudan. Iran's minions also murdered opponents abroad. In the 1980s, Ali Akbar Tabatabai was assassinated in Washington DC; ex-Premier Shahpour BAKHTIAR was slain in Paris. In 1987 alone, eight anti-Khomeini activists were murdered in Pakistan, West Germany, Britain, Turkey and Switzerland. Syria did the same to its opponents. Apart from murdering opponents in exile, Syria is considered responsible to the assassinations of Lebanese leaders Kamal JUNBLAT (1977) and Bashir JUMAYYIL (1982).

The Lebanese populace was frightened into acquiescence. Critical coverage of Syrian domestic politics or foreign policy was silenced by terrorizing Arab and Western journalists. In 1980, one of the most outspoken emigre editors, Salim al-Lawzi, was kidnapped, horrendously tortured, and murdered. In April 1982 a car bomb exploded in front of the office of *al-Watan al-Arabi* in Paris killed two and wounded sixty-two. The French expelled two Syrian diplomats for involvement in the attack. Syria recruited suicide bombers to attack the Israelis and allowed Iranian-backed squads to operate freely in attacking the US Embassy and Marines in Beirut, as well as against the IDF headquarter of the civil administration in Tyre.

To avoid attacks, European countries often made concessions to states or groups using terrorism. For example, France refused in 1977 to hold Palestinian terrorist leader Abu Daoud for extradition and let terrorists function freely there as long as they did not act violently on its territory. Relatives of George Abdallah, a Lebanese and leader of the LARF terrorist group imprisoned in France, planted bombs in Paris to force his release. Britain reopened relations with Libya just a year after Libyan diplomats openly murdered a British police-women in London.

In January 1987, two West Germans were abducted in Beirut by Abbas Ali Hamadi to prevent West Germany from extraditing his brother, Muhammad Ali Hamadi to the United States for air piracy and murder in bombing a TWA plane. This ploy worked but Abbas himself was later caught and tried by West German authorities. Yugoslavia would not detain the terrorist "Carlos." The killers of US Ambassador Cleo Noel and Deputy Chief of mission George Moore (Sudan, 1973), ambassador Roger Davies (Cyprus, 1974), and Ambassador Francis Meloy Jr., and diplomat Roger Waring (Beirut, 1976) were either released from prison or never prosecuted in those countries.

The United States rejected the idea of concessions to terrorists but made them in practice on several occasions. Despite proclaiming a tough line against Iran, President Ronald Reagan sold Tehran arms trying to free Americans held hostage in Lebanon. Economic and strategic considerations also inhibited Western action. Despite the Reagan administration's condemnation of Libya, the United States was still buying forty percent of Libya's oil production until 1982 when it imposed a boycott. As late as 1985 US exports to Libya (including service contracts) still ran between 800 million dollars to 1 billion dollars. Until a further tightening of US sanctions in 1996, US companies were still Iran's biggest customer as well.

The tendency to surrender to blackmail under terrorist threat was also demonstrated in regard to Americans who, despite obvious danger and warning, insisted on staying in Beirut and kidnapped by Iranian-sponsored Lebanese factions. Humanitarian concern and political calculation that failure to free the hostages damaged his public standing, persuaded Reagan to abandon his most cherished principle. Even these extraordinary efforts which almost wrecked his administration only succeeded in freeing three hostages. And the terrorists' success at gaining US concessions encouraged them to seize more Americans. This and many other events showed the incredible leverage that small groups of terrorists could have on public attention, national policies, and the international agenda.

Yet states or movements deploying terrorism were also internationally tarnished by that choice, sometimes suffering international isolation, economic sanctions or even military retaliation. The function and fortunes of terrorism in the region can be seen by examining how Syria, Iran, and Libya used terrorism as a strategy with varying degrees of effectiveness. Syria played a critical role in the mid-1960s initiating Palestinian guerrilla warfare against Israel but in the late 1970s and 1980s used terrorism against the PLO when trying to control that organization.

Lebanon provided another test for Syria's strategic sponsorship of terrorism. After its army entered Lebanon in 1976, Damascus built up surrogate groups or allies who sometimes engaged in terrorist acts including the SYRIAN SOCIAL NATIONALIST PARTY (SSNP) and al-Sai'qa, Abu Nidal, and PFLP-GC. After 1983, more Palestinian groups including the ABU MUSSA (*Fatah*'s splinter faction) were added. As of the early 1990s Syria became the center of ten Palestinian groups that oppose the Oslo agreement and the Palestinian Authority, some of whom are involved in terrorism.

The guiding line of Syrian-sponsored terrorism in Lebanon was to force the withdrawal of Israeli troops and US Marines in 1982-1984. The Islamic Jihad claimed responsibility for those operations, which were actually performed by Iranian-backed Islamic factions that later consolidated in *Hizballah* and received support from Syria in terms of the freedom to train, operate, and transport bombs through Syrian-held territory.

Having forced a US pull-out, Syrian intelligence then turned its attention to Southern Lebanon. While much of the armed activity was organized by Shi'i groups (*Hizballah* and, to a lesser extent, *Amal*), Damascus assisted these as well as Palestinian factions it controlled to strike against Israel. Goals included destroying the May 1983 Lebanon-Israel peace accord which gave Israel free hand in Lebanon and force Israeli withdrawal from this country.

Some suicide bombers were even more closely tied to Syria. In July 1985, for example, a twenty-three year-old Lebanese named Haytham Abbas blew up himself and his car at a checkpoint of the Israel-backed SOUTH LEBANON ARMY. The previous day, Abbas had given a television interview praising ASAD (whose picture could be seen on the table and wall), calling him" "the symbol of resistance in the Arab homeland and the first struggler." He was a member of the Lebanese branch of Syria's ruling BA'TH Party. Other suicide terrorists belonged to the Syrian-controlled SSNP.

When it appeared possible that Jordan might negotiate with Israel in 1983-1986 Syria organized numerous attacks on Jordanian diplomats and airline offices to deter any peace process. In April 1983, PLO moderate Issam Sartawi was murdered in Portugal by Abu Nidal. In October, the Jordanian ambassadors to India and Italy were wounded. The next month, a Jordanian security man in Athens was killed and another embassy employee was wounded. In December, an attack in Spain killed one and wounded another diplomat. As soon as King HUSSEIN gave up the idea, the assaults ceased.

Syria sponsored the elimination of moderate PLO officials and demonstrate that Jordan could not protect anyone from its wrath. In December 1984, PLO Executive Committee member Fahd Qawasmeh, who took a softer line on cooperation with Jordan, was assassinated in Amman. In April 1985 a rocket was fired at a Jordanian airliner taking off from Athens. In July the Jordanian airline's office in Madrid was attacked and a diplomat was killed in Ankara.

In September a Jordanian publisher was murdered in Athens. The 1986 murders of Palestinian moderate Aziz Shehadeh in Ramallah, and Nablus Mayor Zafir al-Masri, were traced to PFLP operations from Damascus. The perpetrators included Abu Nidal's group, Syrian-sponsored PLO splinters led by Abu Musa, and the Damascus-based PFLP. Arafat pledged to revenge al-Masri but in April 1987 the PLO leader was again allied to the PFLP whose gunmen had done the murder. Arafat also periodically patched up ties with Abu Nidal despite his previous record of anti-PLO terrorism.

While Syria wanted to strike at Israel, it also did not want to provoke Israeli a war that it would likely loose. Consequently, after 1973, Syria was careful not to strike directly against Israel through the GOLAN HEIGHTS since this might prompt direct Israeli retaliation. Instead, it routed operations through proxies operating in Lebanon, Jordan, or even Europe.

An April 1986 bomb attempt against an El Al plane in London was another such operation. Nizar Hindawi convinced his pregnant, unwitting Irish girlfriend to carry the suitcase which contained a bomb that would have killed nearly 400 people. Fortunately, an Israeli security man discovered the bag's false bottom. Hindawi had entered England on a Syrian government employees' passport. His bomb was similar to those employed in 1983 bomb attempts against El Al and an explosion that killed four Americans on a TWA plane over Greece. Hindawi had come to London on a special passport issued to Syrian government employees, and received the sophisticated explosive device directly from the Syrian embassy there. His confession implicated the Syrian ambassador to Britain, two Syrian diplomats, and the deputy director of Syria's air force intelligence. London only briefly severed ties with Damascus.

The balance sheet for Syrian terrorism has on the whole been successful, because, first, Damascus used terrorism for limited, well-defined goals: gaining hegemony in Lebanon, breaking US and Israeli leverage there, discouraging Jordan from making peace with Israel, constraining PLO action contrary to Syrian objectives, and blackmailing wealthy Arab oil-producing states into providing subsidies. Second, it used terrorism as part of a broader strategy incorporating diplomatic and military leverage. Third, despite some errors, Syria was far more cautious than Libya or Iran in covering its tracks and refraining from boasting about its involvement. Since it was hard to find ironclad proof of responsibility for terrorist acts, this policy discouraged Western states from applying sanctions. Finally, Syria was strong enough in its own right and close enough to the USSR to deter military retaliation, a luxury Iran and Libya did not enjoy.

Iran employed terrorism starting with holding US diplomats as hostages in 1979. The radical Islamic faction used this act and the ensuing crisis in an extremely practical way to displace moderates in the leadership unite the country around itself, and destroy relations with the United States in order to eliminate its influence within Iran. In trying to spread revolution, Iran's agents made a number of attacks. September 1980, an Iran-sponsored group fired rocket grenades at the US embassy in Beirut. In December 1981 the Iraqi embassy was bombed as part of Iran's war effort against Baghdad. Thirty people including the ambassador died. Iran-backed the bombing of the French embassy in May 1982 by *Hizballah*-acting under the name Islamic Jihad-to punish that country for selling arms to Iraq, Iran's enemy. The US embassy was attacked in April 1982, while Iranian-backed group used suicide bombers with devastating effect against the US Marine and French camps in Beirut, and the Israeli headquarters in Tyre in 1983. Evidence indicated that explosives for all the bombings in Kuwait and Lebanon were furnished by Iran and moved through Syria.

On the Gulf front, Iran used terrorism as an extension of its war against Iraq and to strike at neutral countries helping it, primarily Kuwait that had given vital transport and financial help to Baghdad. In December 1983, Iranian-based Islamic Jihad terrorists used explosives against the US embassy, a foreign residential complex, the airport, an industrial park, and power station in Kuwait city. A great deal of hostage-taking and terrorism ensued in the attempt to free seventeen Shi'i imprisoned for these crimes in Kuwait.

In May 1985, Iranian-backed terrorists tried to assassinate Kuwait's Emir al-Sabah, killing six bystanders. In May 1986, Islamic Jihad attacked the al-Ahmadi and Mukawwa oil refineries. In July 1987, two Kuwaiti Shi'is were killed while trying to place bombs in a shopping area. The men had disappeared nine months earlier while fishing in the Gulf and

were trained as saboteurs. Iran always used Lebanese, Iraqi, or Kuwaiti Shi'is to cloak its involvement in such attacks. And Kuwait's imprisonment of them led to new kidnappings and attacks demanding their release.

Similar activities continued in later years. In 1988, France obtained the release of two of its citizens held hostage in Lebanon by repaying a 330 million dollars Shah-era loan, letting an Iranian embassy official wanted for involvement in terrorism leave the country, and expelling anti-Khomeini activities. A German court found that high Iranian officials ordered the 1992 murder of four Kurdish leaders in Berlin. An Iran's government demanded the assassination of writer Salman RUSHDIE, while being the sponsor of the Lebanese *Hizballah* movement and Palestinian groups using terror to oppose the ARAB-ISRAEL PEACE MAKING. In 1994 *Hizballah* was apparently responsible to the bombing of the Jewish community center in Buenos Aires and the Zionist office in London.

Iranian-backed terrorism did not bring Islamic fundamentalist regimes to the Gulf or Lebanon, destroy Israel, or defeat Iraq. But Iran gained a foothold and weakened Western influence in Lebanon, intimidated Gulf Arabs, and regained assets from the West and France. In Tehran, at least, it seemed the Islamic republic had confronted great powers on an equal basis, raised its prestige in the Islamic world, and foiled plots against itself. Terrorism had been integrated into Iranian foreign policy.

Compared to Syria, Libya's Muammar QADHAFI tried to use terrorism in too much of a grandiose unfocused manner while being in a far weaker position to defend himself afterwards. He openly campaigned to murder opponents abroad, of whom eleven were killed in 1980–1981 and five such assassination attempts occurred in 1985. In March 1984, a bomb planted against Libyan emigres injured twenty-four people in England. The following month Libyans fired from the embassy building in London at a peaceful demonstration. A British police woman was killed, eleven exiles were wounded. Due to Libyan pressure, the suspects were allowed to leave Britain.

In early 1985, a Libyan intelligence officer and a Palestinian working for Abu Nidal met in Rome to plan setting off a truckbomb carrying 200 pounds of explosives outside the US embassy in Cairo. The

Libyans offered 500,000 dollars for the operation. The contact man went to Syria for training, picked up explosives in Lebanon, and took them to Cairo, but an informant tipped off the Egyptians who rounded up the conspirators just before they executed their plan on 22 May 1985. After two efforts to murder Libyan exiles in Egypt the Egyptians, in November 1984 faked pictures of the bloody "victim" and gave them to Libyan agents. Libya's official media celebrated the murder only to be confronted with Egyptian audio/video tapes and confessions from four arrested Libyan agents of its involvement. Another hit team planning to kill MUBARAK and others, including US diplomats, was captured in Cairo in November 1985.

Abu Nidal also had Libya as a patron. On 27 December 1985, his men launched simultaneous attacks at the airports of Rome—twelve killed (including five Americans) and seventy-four wounded—and Vienna—two killed and over forty wounded. Libya's official news agency praised this as "heroic." TUNISIA reported that Tunisian passports used by the Vienna terrorists had been confiscated by Libya from workers it had expelled earlier that year. By providing material support to terrorist groups which attack US citizens. As a result, President Reagan held Libya an against the United States under established principles of international law, just as if it had used its own armed forces.

US intelligence found a similar trail in the bombing of a disco frequented by American servicemen in West Berlin in March 1986 and in the murder of American hostage Peter Kilburn in Beirut the next month shortly after the US reprisal raid on Libya. A Libyan military attache in Syria arranged for a Libyan-financed group to purchase Kilburn from his kidnappers and then to kill him. While Qadhafi retreated a while from supporting terrorism after the US bombing of Libya in 1986, Libya was also found responsible for the destruction of a Pan American passenger plane over Lockerbie, Scotland, in 1988 and other attacks in later years.

Iraq used terrorism in similar ways: against dissidents abroad, in efforts to take over the PLO, and to hit at Israel, Iran, and other enemies. Perhaps the most significant such operation was when Nawaf Russan, an Iraqi intelligence colonel who also served as Abu Nidal's deputy, led a three-man hit team that seriously wounded Israeli Ambassador Shlomo Argov in London on June 3 1982. Three days later, Israel invaded Lebanon and four days after that, Iraq offered a unilateral cease-fire in the GULF WAR arguing that the Arabs and Iranians should unite against Israel. Russan was a Jordanian officer recruited by Iraqi intelligence. In London, his group reconnoitered and prepared to attack the embassies of the UNITED ARAB EMIRATES Jordan, SAUDI ARABIA, Egypt and Kuwait if Iraqi interests so dictated. The attack on Argov was designed to provoke an Israeli attack on Syrian forces in Lebanon. Syria, Iraq's enemy and an ally of Iran, would suffer while a new crisis gave Baghdad a good excuse to demand—unsuccessfully, however—that Iran should end the IRAN-IRAQ WAR.

The concept of terrorism can also be applied to certain types of internal repression, including large-scale torture and executions. For example, Iraq deported over 200,000 ethnic Persians and shot about 600 clerics and activists including the popular Ayatollah Bakir al-Sadr and his sister in 1978. In 1988, it used poison gas and mass shootings against its Kurdish citizens. Syrian destroyed large parts of its own city of Hama and killed tens of thousands of rebelling Muslim Brotherhood civilians in February 1982.

Terrorism continued to be an important regional factor in the 1990s. Under an Islamic radical regime, Sudan became a new sponsor and the locale of training camps once located in Lebanon. It was linked to the 1996 assassination attempt against Egyptian President Husni Mubarak and the bombing of the World Trade Center in New York. The latter incident revealed the dangerous links between Islamist organizations in the Middle East and their followers-immigrants in the US (see ABDEL RAHMAN, ISLAMIC RADICALISM). As revenge for its defeat in the 1991 war over Kuwait, Iraq attempted to kill former US President George Bush.

In terms of revolutionary movements, Algerian Islamists used bombs, political assassinations, and the mass killing of civilians as central instruments in their attempts to seize power. Groups in Egypt also targeted foreign tourists and local COPTS (see EGYPT). A few bombings were also carried out in Saudi Arabia, probably with Iranian help. Syria continued to sponsor a Kurdish insurgency against Turkey and *Hizballah's* cross-border attacks on Israel.

As of the 1980s acts of terrorism were increasingly committed by Islamic radical groups in Egypt,

Algeria, and Lebanon seeking to foment religious as well as social and political revolution. From the late 1980s, Palestinian Islamic groups such as the Islamic Jihad and *Hamas* took the lead in perpetrating terrorism against Israel. Although these Palestinian Islamic movements operated violently during the *Intifada*, their main impact, described by Israeli leaders as "a strategic threat to the peace process" was manifested after the signing of the Israel-PLO Oslo Agreement, and particularly following the massacre of Muslim worshipers in the Patriarchs' Cave of Hebron perpetrated by a Jewish fanatic (February 1994). Since then, the two movements adopted suicidal attacks on Israeli targets, mostly civilian, in city centers, buses and coffee shops, with a proclaimed goal of undermining the Oslo process, but in fact also to maintain their own survival and status under the newly established Palestinian Authority. The suicidal bombings reached their peak in a series of attacks in Jerusalem, Ashkelon and Tel Aviv in February-March 1966, claiming the lives of over 60 Israelis, which apparently decided the fall of the Labor-led government of Shimon PERES and paved the way to the victory of Binyamin NETANYAHU and the emergence of a right-wing government in Israel in May of that year.

Yet even here terrorism was not an altogether authentic process. Already by the late 1980s *Hamas* fostered links of collaboration with Iran, receiving financial and military support which became significant in the movement's operational considerations. While *Amal* was an authentic Lebanese movement interested in promoting the Shi'is' conditions of life and share in government, the civil war in this country instigated its turn to arms as militia as well, and even before Israel invaded Lebanon it was the Iranian intervention that gave rise to an ideological and personal process of radicalization that brought to the emergence of *Hizballah*. *Hizballah* used anti-Israel terrorism to pursue its desire to turn Lebanon into a state and society ruled solely by the Shari'a.

Terrorist strategies were often presented as a magical way to achieve otherwise unobtainable goal, as explained by *Hizballah*'s mentor, Muhammad Hussein Fadlallah. Faced with the threat from *Hizballah*, the relatively moderate *Amal* had to prove itself equally tough and anti-Western to compete for the community's allegiance. When radicals hijacked a TWA plane to Beirut in June 1985, *Amal* seized con-

trol of the action to win credit for gaining the release of Shi'ites captured by Israel in southern Lebanon. Once terrorism is grated legitimacy within a community, competition among groups will escalate its use.

Terrorism also involved criminal activities carried out within a political framework. Some of Arafat's rivals, most notably Abu Nidal, ran mercenary terrorist services. In Lebanon, too, kidnappings were carried out for ransom by nominally political groups. Many of the recruits to terrorist groups were ordinary people, sometimes devastated refugees, or teenagers with no ideological commitment. Even suicide bombers were often hired from people desperate to obtain money for their families. Participation in a terrorist activity under social and lawless conditions could achieve high status and material benefits. The career of gunmen was a well-paid one in Lebanon during the 1975–1990 civil war. Among the Islamic groups, those killed, even after committing the most brutal murders, became glorified martyrs, a particularly comforting thought for Islamic fundamentalists. Relatively few, though, are called on to risk their lives and those captured had firm precedents for believing they would soon be released by some new terrorist action.

Despite some continuity, Middle Eastern international terrorism seemed to have declined since the early 1990s. A major contribution to that has been the process of political and economic reconstruction that the Lebanese state has undergone under tight Syrian supervision. This process led to the formation of better organized and more efficient armed forces; disarmament of all militias (except *Hizballah*) and their incorporation in the political system; release of all foreign hostages; and determined enforcement of law and order, by force if needed (see LEBANON).

Although Lebanon is still the basis of Syrian-backed Palestinian, Turkish (mainly Kurdish), and Lebanese guerrilla and terrorist groups, mostly in the Biqa' area, this country ceased to be a free zone for uncontrolled anarchist and terrorist groups.

TIGRIS RIVER   see WATER POLITICS.

TIRAN STRAITS   A narrow passage connecting the Gulf of Aqaba/ Eilat to the Red Sea. Approaching the SINAI COAST for a distance of 4.5 miles (7 km.), are a string of uninhabited and barren islands, culminating with the westenmost island of Tiran.

The Islands, considered Saudi Arabian territory, were taken over by EGYPT in 1949–1950, with Saudi permission. From the early 1950s Egypt used its presence in the island to justify the closure of the Straits of Tiran to shipping to and from the Israeli port of Eilat, claiming that they were entirely within its territorial waters. While this claim was questioned, most countries (as well as most legal experts), consider straits connecting the high seas with another country's territorial waters and ports to be international waterways through which the right of innocent passage overrides the territorial-water rights of the riparian country. An International Convention on the Law of the Sea, adopted in 1958, confirmed this principle in articles four and sixteen, but the particular problem of the Straits of Tiran and the Gulf of Aqaba were never submitted to international judicial ruling. The closure of the Tiran Straits twice resulted in war for ISRAEL. In 1956, Israeli penetration of Sinai was meant, among other aims, to break the blockade on its southern outlet to the sea. Its reclosure in May 1967 was the catalyst for the Six-Day War. The peace treaty between Israel and Egypt in 1979 secured the maintenance of the Tiran Strait as an international waterway. (For Egypt's blockade, until 1956, and subsequent events concerning the Straits of Tiran, see ARAB-ISRAEL CONFLICT.)

TRANSJORDAN   see JORDAN HASHEMITE KINGDOM OF.

TRUCIAL COAST OR TRUCIAL OMAN   A large peninsula on the southern (Arabian) shores of the PERSIAN GULF, mostly desert. The population, estimated in the late 1960s at 150,000–200,000 (for later figures see UNITED ARAB EMIRATES (UAE)). The economy was comprised mainly of nomadic fishers, pearl-divers, boat-builders, and maritime commerce, until the beginning of the OIL boom in the 1960s. Most of the Trucial Coast consisted of seven Arab sheikhdoms—ABU DHABI, DUBAI, SHARJA, RAS AL-KHAIMA, UMM AL-QAIWAIN, AJMAN, AND FUJAIRA. The tip of the peninsula, Ras Musandam is an enclave which belongs to OMAN.

From the early nineteenth century, BRITAIN took military measures against the piracy which was rife in the area, and in 1820 it imposed an agreement by

coastal chiefs to end it. In 1853 this became a perpetual maritime truce, and the area, previously known as the "Pirate Coast," was named the "Trucial Coast". These treaties, and others which followed, provided protection and subsidies for the British. Subsequently, British political officers were stationed in Abu Dhabi and Dubai, under the Political Resident for the Persian Gulf at Bushire in IRAN (and from 1946 in BAHRAIN).

In the early 1950s Britain began to organize cooperation between the seven sheikhdoms through a quasi-federal permanent council headed by the British Resident. Britain also established a small British-commanded military police force jointly for the seven—the "Trucial Scouts," with headquarters at SHARJA. In 1959, Britain decided to create a common currency, the Gulf Rupee, to replace the Indian Rupee that had, until then, been the currency. This plan did not fully materialize, as several sheikhdoms preferred other currencies, such as the Saudi Rial, the Bahrain Dinar or a new Qatar Rial. In 1966, Britain established a naval base in Sharja, destined to replace the British base in ADEN then due to be evacuated. But in 1968 Britain relinquished its foothold in the Gulf area and removed its protection in 1971. In December 1971 the rulers, with British encouragement, formed an independent federal state, the United Arab Emirates (UAE). (see UNITED ARAB EMIRATES).

TUDEH PARTY   also known as (Hezb-e Tudeh-ye Iran) Party of the Iranian masses. Tudeh was created in Septemeber 1941 to be the COMMUNIST PARTY of IRAN. Throughout its years of its activity, it represented Soviet Marxism and passionately defended the attitudes and interests of the Soviet Union in Iran. In the 1940s and 1950s, the Party enjoyed great popularity among the intellectuals in Iran and had a major influence over political events. For years it was the only well organized Party in Iran and its members numbered more than 100,000. Its founder was Taqi Arani, who was born in 1901 in Tabriz (the capital of Iran's Azerbaijan province) and concluded his studies in chemistry in Germany. The first conference of the Party was held in August 1944 and many activists were arrested in 1945 due to the Party's support for the separatist movement of Azerbeijan (see IRAN). The Party was further crippled by a new wave of arrests which occurred in 1949 after the Shah accused the Party of being responsible for the planning of an unsuccessful attempt on his life. The Party managed to recover and in 1951, upon the appointment of Muhammad MOSSADDEQ as Prime Minister, it carried on full overt activities, despite the fact that the prohibition was not formally canceled. The Party supported the nationalization of the oil industry by Mossaddeq, but opposed his approach to the US to solve the problem. Until the fall of Mossaddeq in 1953, the Party took advantage of anti-Western feelings in order to set up many organizations to mobilize the sympathy of various groups such as youth, women, and peace supporters. Upon the fall of the government of Mossaddeq and the rehabilitation of the Shah in 1953, the Party once again went underground and dozens of its leaders escaped to East Germany, where they set up headquarters for their activities. In 1965, in light of the improvement of the relations between Iran and the Soviet Union, the Party announced a more moderate platform. This tactical change brought about an ideological split and the breaking away of the Ma'oist section that supported guerrilla activities to bring down the Shah's regime. The Maoist group soon split into two organizations: the pro-Chinese Tudeh Party Revolutionary Organization and the Toufan (the Storm), which had a Marxist-Leninist orientation. Neither of these gained much support.

In the years that preceded the Islamic revolution in Iran, the activity of the party concentrated primarily in organzing demonstrations and exciting Iranian student organizations abroad. Upon the weakening of the Shah's regime and of the political suppression, the Party renewed its activity inside Iran as well. It announced its support of Ayatullah KHOMEINI's struggle to bring down the Shah, and even placed its organizational infrastructure at his disposal.

The Party announced overt activity in March 1979—one month after the establishment of the Islamic regime. This activity continued until April 1983, when the Secretary General of the Party, Nour-ed-Kia-Nouri, and about a thousand activists were arrested simultaneously in a well planned operation. Kia-Nouri was the first among those arrested to admit on television that the Party had engaged in espionage for the benefit of the Soviet Union. Hundreds of its members were executed. Since then the Party's prestige has waned, and the tempo of its ac-

tivity has been greatly slowed down, both in and outside of Iran. This blow, together with the crumbling of the Soviet Union, led to the departure of many of the Party's members and to the creation of various communist groups, particularly in Europe. The Party continues to publish its mouthpiece *Nameh-e Mardom* (People's Herald), which is published in Europe.

TUMB OR TUNB ISLANDS see ABU MASSA ISLANDS, PERSIAN GULF, RAS AL-KHAIMA, UNITED ARAB EMIRATES.

TUNISIA Republic in Northwest Africa, on the southern shore of the Mediterranean Sea, bordering on LIBYA in the east and ALGERIA in the west and south. Area: 63,170 sq. miles (163,610 sq. km.). Population: 8.79 million (1994 census) of which ninety-eight percent are Muslim. Most of the population is Arab; there are some BERBERS in the south, who retain a distinctive Berber identity. Its capital is Tunis (estimated population: 1 million).

Colonial History Tunisia was under Ottoman sovereignty since 1574, ruled by a local Bey. In April 1881 the country was occupied by FRANCE, which had ruled Algeria since 1830. France prevented Tunisia's imminent financial collapse and put an end to raids by Tunisian tribes in Algeria. France, who had obtained European agreement to its takeover, concluded two treaties with the Bey which established a French Protectorate: (1) the Treaty of Bardo or Qasr Sa'id (1881) (under which the Bey remained the nominal ruler while France became responsible for military, financial and foreign affairs); (2) the Treaty of Mersa (1883) (which transferred the real power to the French Resident-General and his French advisers). French law and administration were applied and land was registered as a step toward colonization and agricultural development by French companies. Grants of large plots of land encouraged the influx of settlers, mainly from France and Italy, until they numbered some 150,000 on the eve of World War I (out of some. 2 million inhabitants), and about 200,000 in the 1920s.

In the 1890s France established a Consultative Council, composed only of Frenchmen. The council only had advisory authority with regard to financial matters, and members were appointed. Beginning in 1907, the French representatives were elected by the French inhabitants, while fourteen Muslim representatives and one Jew were added, nominated by the Bey.

Early in the twentieth century, Islamic and nationalist organizations began to emerge amid grievances at the French policy of discriminating against native Tunisians in educational and economic spheres as well as political representation in favor of the French settlers. In 1906, the *Jeunes Tunisians*, an activist elite group inspired by the YOUNG TURKS, presented the Protectorate authorities with a list of grievances, demanding that it fulfill its promise of revitalizing Tunisia. A year later, this group organized itself in the *Parti evolutioniste* and started to publish a newspaper, which aimed not at independence but equality, through collaboration with the French Protectorate. Violent riots followed the Italian invasion of Libya in 1911, resulting in a declaration of Martial Law that same year by the Protectorate Government. The Martial Law remained in force until 1921, and shortly after its declaration the *Parti evolutioniste* collapsed. Following World War I, national consciousness in Tunisia intensified, and in 1920 the *Parti Liberal Constitutionel Tunisien*, commonly known as the *Destour* (after the Arabic word *dustur* for constitution) was founded, headed by Abdel-Aziz al-Tha'alibi. It advocated a constitutional regime with an elected legislative assembly, which would lead to the implicitly expressed goal of independence.

The French tried to placate the *Destour* by introducing partial administrative reforms. In 1922, regional councils were established, as well as a "Grand Council" with limited consultative authority, mainly in financial matters. The separation between a French-European section and an indigenous Tunisian one in these councils remained. In elections to the grand and regional councils, 1922, the *Destour* failed and only few of its candidates were elected.Although it had set the sage and laid the organizational struggle for independence, by the late 1920s the *Destour* was dying. The only remaining members were memebrs oft he bourgeoisie families. In the 1920s, with growing immigration from the rural provinces to the cities, a new elite emerged, represented by young, educated men originally from the hinterland, many of whom joined the *Destour*. In 1932, a group of young educated party members, led by the lawyer Habib BOURGUIBA, established their own newspaper,

l'Action Tunissienne, and two years later, following a decree of the French governor which dissolved the party and suspended its newspapers, they founded the *Neo-Destour* Party (ND), with Bourguiba as their secretary general. The ND advocated a more nationalist agenda, demanding independence, but also socioeconomic reforms to alter the inequities of the Protectorate and elevate the depressed conditions of the rural population. The new Party challenged the Protectorate, calling for disobedience and refusal to pay taxes. At the end of 1934 the Party was outlawed and many of its leaders were arrested. Nevertheless, it continued to expand and flourish due to the growing socioeconomic role it played in the lives of many Tunisians', particularly in the provincial areas. The Party came to be regarded as a leading national movement, reflecting its appeal to landowners, traditional artisans, and merchants in the periphery and, after World War II, also to the labor union. Following the establishment of the Popular Front Government in France in 1936 the activity of the ND was renewed. But after the government's demise, together with the demonstrations of 1938, it was again outlawed and many of its leaders arrested.

In 1940 Tunisia came under Vichy rule, and German and Italian forces were stationed in Tunisia. While the Vichy government was reluctant to fulfill the nationalists' requests for more independence, the Germans supported the nationalists' demands, released their leaders from prison and allowed some of them to go to Rome for political training. Bey Muhammad al-Munsif (June 1942–June 1943) supported the nationalists and collaborated with the Axis forces. Following the Allies' conquest of Tunisia in early 1943, the Bey was dismissed and replaced by Muhammad al-Amin (1943–1957), and the government was handed to the Free French. In mid-1944 the special rights of the Italian inhabitants were abolished.

Toward the end of the war, political restrictions in Tunisia were eased and local political activity increased, but was once again repressed by France. In 1945 Bourguiba moved to Cairo and joined the "Front for the Defense of the Maghreb," established in late 1944. In 1945 the French introduced political reforms. The council of ministers and the Grand Council (composed now of fifty-three members in each of the French and the Tunisian sections) were re-organized and an elected municipality was granted to Tunis. The nationalists were not satisfied and their congress in the summer of 1946 demanded full independence. In early 1947, the French decided to establish a "National Government;" but the ND refused to participate until wider self-rule be granted.

In late 1949, Bourguiba returned from EGYPT to head the nationalists in their negotiations with the French. In April 1950 he presented "Seven Demands" of the ND, most of which were granted during 1950–1951. This gave rise to a new government in August 1950 headed by Muhammad Chenik with an equal number of Tunisian and French ministers. Among the ministers Salah Ben Youssef (a ND leader) as Minister of Justice. However, negotiations for Tunisian self-rule were opposed by the French Right and the colonists, who opposed any concessions to the Tunisians and more radical Muslim nationalists. Demonstrations were renewed and led to violent clashes in early 1952, mainly between Tunisian "gangs," the *Fellagha*, and their French counterpart, the "Red Hand". Several ND leaders, including Bourguiba, were arrested, Chenik was removed from power and all power was resumed by the French authorities. The new ruling power continued to decree reforms intended to lead to the establishment of an indigenous autonomy. The ND, meanwhile, took their case to the UN; in 1952 and 1953 the General Assembly rejected resolutions calling for speedy independence, but adopted a compromise formula which recommended gradual progress toward that goal.

In July 1954 the Pierre Mendis government of France offered Tunisia "internal sovereignty," with France retaining responsibility for defense and foreign affairs only. It also legalized the ND. In autumn 1954 a cease-fire was reached, though some of the *Fellagha* refused to accept it. On 21 April 1955, a preliminary agreement was signed, accepting the "internal sovereignty" offered. This was finalized and worked out in detail on 3 June 1955. Bourguiba, who had been released from prison in 1953, participated in the negotiations. He returned to Tunisia in June 1955 as a national leader of great influence, though holding no official position. The more radical nationalist ND leaders, headed by Salah Ben Youssef, demanded complete independence and violently rejected the agreement—but the majority endorsed it. Ben Youssef was ousted from the party in October 1955 and went into exile in Cairo, where he agitated against Bourguiba and the ND leadership.

In September 1955 Taher Ben-Ammar formed a new government composed only of Tunisians, six of whom belonged to the ND. In November 1955, the party congress re-elected Bourguiba as ND President and endorsed the agreements, but demanded complete independence and the election of a constituent assembly, a demand enhanced by the renewal of *Fellagha* activity and the fact that Morocco was reaching full independence. France cooperated and an agreement on 20 March 1956 granted Tunisia full independence, including authority over foreign affairs, defense and internal security. It was, however, agreed that there would be an "interdependence" between France and Tunisia, which in fact meant that the former would retain its domination through "cooperation" in foreign and defense affairs, to be regulated in separate agreements. French forces were to remain in the strategic naval base of Bizerte and other camps.

Tunisia Under Bourguiba Elections for a Constituent Assembly were held on 25 March 1956 and all ninety-eight seats were won by a National Front, of which the ND was the main component. On 11 April, Bourguiba became Prime Minister, with sixteen of the seventeen ministers belonging to the ND. During the next year the authority of the Bey was curtailed, and on 25 July 1957, the Assembly abolished the monarchy and proclaimed Tunisia a republic, with Bourguiba as Head-of-State. On 1 June 1958, a new Constitution was promulgated. It provided for the election of a President for a five-year term, re-eligible for three consecutive terms and endowed with wide powers, and a National Assembly elected for five years.

Relations with France dominated Tunisia's politics in the late 1950s and early 1960s. The financial-economic cooperation was abolished by 1957 and renewed on a different footing in 1959. The nationalization of French property (e.g., transport and power companies, and cultivated lands—French settlers held 2 million acres, over twenty percent of all cultivated lands) remained a source of much friction between Tunisia and its former colonial ruler. By the early 1960s most of the nearly 200,000 French settlers had left Tunisia. A final agreement on compensation was reached between Tunis and Paris in 1965.

The domestic politics of independent Tunisia were negatively affected by power struggles within the ND, particularly between Bourguiba and Ben Youssef's followers. The first few years of Tunisian independence witnessed a systematic effort on Bourguiba's past to consolidate his authoritarian control of the country by expelling Ben Youssef's supporters from the Party and weakening their social and economic bases (such as the religious establishment and the absentee landlords). At the same time, government intervention in the economy increased, together with social and economic grievances, large-scale unemployment and inflation. The exclusion of institutionalized opposition was underlined by the elimination of political rivals through court trials. Among those ousted, during Bourguiba's first year were Prince Chadly, the eldest son of the ex-Bey, and two former Prime Ministers, Taher Ben Ammar and Salah al-Din Baccouche (Baqush); ex-Prime Minister Saleh Mzali was tried in early 1959. Exiled Salah Ben Youssef was tried *in absentia* and sentenced to death in January 1957 and again in October 1959, along with many of his followers (eight were executed; Ben Youssef was assassinated in West Germany in August 1961). The fact that Ben Youssef operated from Cairo was partly why relations between Bourguiba and Gamal ABDEL NASSER deteriorated. Political purges continued throughout the early 1960s. Following a plot discovered late in 1962, thirteen were sentenced to death in January 1963, including seven army officers.

In November 1959 elections were held. Communist candidates challenged the ND, but the latter won all ninety seats. In 1963 the Communist Party was banned, leaving the ND completely unchallenged. Bourguiba was both President and Prime Minister until November 1969, when he nominated Bahi al-Adgham to the latter post, replacing him in October 1970 by Hedi Nouira, a staunch Bourguiba follower who served until April 1980 and was followed by Muhammad Mzali. Bourguiba himself was re-elected to the presidency in 1964, 1969 and 1974. In 1975 he was proclaimed President for life. Bourguiba's old age and failing health made his succession one of Tunisia's main political problems.

The increased intervention of the government in the economy soon led to the adoption of the so-

cialist model with the first development plan proclaimed in 1961. In 1964 the ND was restructured, its commitment to Tunisian socialism was emphasized and its name was changed to *Parti Socialiste Destourien* (PSD). In the elections of November 1964 the PSD won all ninety seats unchallenged.

From 1958 the regime maintained a "National Work Service," under which men reaching the age of twenty were to work in a development project for one year. Some 120,000–300,000 men served annually in this framework. In 1964–1969 this was instrumental in the attempt to collectivize agriculture, carried out by the Minister of Finance and Planning, Ahmad Ben Salah. Massive land nationalization was undertaken and small independent farms were forcibly merged into some 1000 agricultural cooperatives, encompassing over twenty-five percent of the rural population. But the project met massive opposition, which finally forced Bourguiba to dismiss Ben Salah (September 1969) and put him on trial for treason. He was sentenced in May 1970 to ten years in prison. In 1973 he escaped to Europe where he conducted anti-Bourguiba propaganda in the name of a new opposition *"Mouvement de l'Uniti Populaire"* (MUP). After Ben Salah's fall most of the cooperatives were abolished and many plots returned to their owners.

The growing emphasis on socioeconomic and social affairs and Tunisian Socialism, led to a growing conflict between the government and the strong Labor Union movement. As early as 1956, the ND regarded the *Union Generale Tunisienne du Travail* (UGTT) too independent and forced the replacement of its Secretary-General, Ahmad Ben Salah, by Ahmad Tlili, who was himself replaced in 1963 by Habib Ashour. Ashour was ousted in 1965, but returned to his post in 1970.

Labor relations remained relatively stable until the mid-1970s. In 1976, large-scale strikes forced the government to conclude a social contract with the UGTT in 1977. However, strikes continued, and the UGTT became a vocal critic of the government and a rallying point of opposition.

Students and unemployed youth also participated in demonstrations. Opposition leaders like Muhammad Masmoudi (a former Foreign Minister in exile in Libya) declared their support of the UGTT, and the crisis caused a split in the government. While Prime Minister Nouira took a hard line, the Minister of the Interior, Taher Belkhodja, advocated reforms. Bourguiba supported Nouira and Belkhodja was dismissed in late 1977; six other ministers resigned in sympathy. Nouira's new government comprised mainly "technocrats".

In early 1978, Ashour resigned from the politbureau and the central committee of the PSD in order to have a free hand and to dissassociate himself from the ruling establishment. The UGTT then demanded changes in the system of government and an end to the harsh suppression of strikes and demonstrations. In January 1978 the UGTT called a general strike. The regime used troops to suppress the strike, mainly in the cities, with some fifty killed and several hundred wounded. Hundreds were arrested, and Ashour and other UGTT leaders were charged with Libya-backed subversion. Ashour was sentenced to ten years imprisonment with hard labor, and other leaders were also imprisoned. A new UGTT Secretary-General, Tijani Abid (appointed in March 1978), and his colleagues disavowed the unions' previous militant opposition and promised to cooperate with the government. Ashour was pardoned by Bourguiba in 1979, but remained under house arrest until December 1981. Most of the others were pardoned as well, but only after it was evident that the UGTT had lost its power as a center of opposition. At the UGTT congress of April 1981, for the first time a non-PSD person, Tayyeb Baccouche (Baqqush), was elected Secretary-General. Furthermore, of the thirteen members elected to the executive committee, eleven were former members imprisoned in 1978. Following his release in late 1981, Ashour was elected UGTT President—a post created for him. In December 1984 he was re-elected Secretary-General and in November 1985 again ousted, sentenced and imprisoned. The increase in social and political protest achieved liberalization in the election system and, gradually, competing parties were permitted to operate. In July 1979, an amendment to the electoral law enabled two candidates to compete for each seat in the assembly. The idea of a multi-party system was, however, still rejected by the PSD congress of September 1979. In the November 1979 elections (the first multi-candidate contest) only the PSD participated, because the opposition boycotted them.

In January 1980 the town of Gafsa in western Tunisia was attacked, apparently by militant political exiles backed by Libya. It was occupied for a week, until the Tunisian Army regained control. More than forty were killed in the clashes; some sixty were brought to trial and thirteen were executed. Opposition groups condemned the "Tunisian Armed Resistance" for resorting to violence in collaboration with a foreign power.

Premier Nouira resigned in February 1980 and was replaced by the Minister of Education, Muhammad Mzali. Mzali's government included ministers who had resigned or been dismissed in 1977 and the government. During 1980 most political prisoners were released and in 1981 some 1,000 UGTT members who had been involved in the 1978 riots were pardoned. The activity of parties other than the PSD was tolerated. In July 1980 the "*Mouvement des Democrates Socialistes*" (MDS) (founded in 1978 by former PSD leader Ahmad Mestiri) was permitted to publish two weeklies. In February 1981 an amnesty was granted to most MUP members, causing the latter's split, mainly by a local-based faction striving to legalize its political activity as a party, and the leaders in exile who opposed conciliation with the regime. In April 1981 the PSD was reformed and new blood was infused: 75% of the 80 central committee members were new. Bourguiba now declared that he would not rule out the establishment of other political parties, though he continued objecting to Communism and Muslim fundamentalism, as well as to groups linked to a foreign power. The Communist Party, banned since 1963, was officially recognized in July 1981, ending the one-party system. Unofficial political groupings were permitted to participate in the November 1981 elections, with the provision that any party which received 5% of the votes would be recognized as a party. The Communists, MDS and MUP competed in the elections; but the "National Front," composed of the PSD and UGTT won 94.6% of the votes and all 136 seats. Since none of the other groups won the minimum 5% of the votes, they were not officially recognized until November 1983.

In January 1984, rioting and looting erupted in protest against the abolition of subsidies on basic foodstuffs. The 115% increase in the price of bread added to long-standing dissatisfaction and unemployment, especially among educated youth. The rioting spread from the south all over Tunisia, a state of emergency was declared and the army was called in. Approximately 150 were killed, more than 900 wounded and over 1,000 arrested. After a turbulent week, Bourguiba intervened and canceled the price hikes, reestablishing order. An official inquiry blamed the Minister of the Interior, Driss Guiga. He was dismissed and replaced by Premier Mzali (whose position was thus strengthened). Guiga went into exile and was later tried *in absentia* and sentenced to fifteen years imprisonment. Further strikes in the public sector in early 1984 (in demand of higher pay), subsided following an agreement between the government and the UGTT. Local elections, in May 1985, were boycotted by all groups except the PSD; even the UGTT did not form a common list with the ruling party.

As Premier Mzali consolidated his power (following six years of heading the government), he seemed to groom himself as the eventual successor to Bourguiba. Even though the president was old andsick, he still dominated Tunisia. In July 1986 Mzali was dismissed and replaced by Rashid Sfar, and Mzali narrowly escaped arrest by fleeing the country. Tunisia was regarded as a Westernized country, where traditional Islam was weak. State and religion were officially separated, law courts secularized, religious endowments (*waqf; habus*) abolished (public *habus* lands nationalized and private habus lands sold), and women enjoyed equal rights. Until the late 1960s, reaction against that secularism was generally limited to older, traditionally-minded individuals, mainly in the countryside. In the 1970s, however, urban Islamic movements began to emerge, demanding a society based on Islamic principles.

Realizing the explosive potential of Islamic fundamentalism, the government at first, in June 1981, tried to channel Islamic agitation into a legalized *"Mouvement de Tendance Islamique"* (MTI); but the attempt to separate moderate and extremist Islamists was ineffective, and the government soon turned against the MTI, too, mprisoning some fifty of its leaders in September 1981. The rapid rise of radical Islam turned it into the main challenge for the regime, which culminated in confrontation in the late 1980s.

International Relations There are many disagreements between France and Tunisia over military issues. Tunisia opposed the use of its own soil for operations against the Algerian rebels and from 1956 to 1961 was in near-permanent conflict with France on this issue, which erupted at times in violent clashes. Finally, Tunisia resolved to prevent France altogether from using land and naval military bases in Tunisia, including Bizerte. The Bizerte crisis reached its climax in July 1961 when Tunisia blockaded the base and fighting ensued with heavy casualties. Following Tunisia's complaint to the UN, the General Assembly supported Tunisia's right to demand the withdrawal of French troops. After lengthy bilateral negotiations, during which Algeria reached independence, the crisis ended with the evacuation of Bizerte by the French in October 1963. No French forces remained in Tunisia. Despite its conflict with France in the late 1950s and early 1960s Tunisia aligned itself with the West, and especially with France, largely reflecting Bourguiba's secular and liberal creed. Tunisia also fostered relations with the USSR, China and the other Communist countries. Tunisia's close relations with the West represented not only Bourguiba's pragmatic and liberal political approach but also economic considerations. Foreign aid came mainly from France, the UNITED STATES, West Germany, the World Bank and European monetary institutions, and SAUDI ARABIA, and Tunisia's foreign trade was mainly with (France, Italy, Germany, Greece).

Regional and Inter-Arab Affairs Tunisia's involvement in Arab affairs, although increased over the years, focused on its immediate neighbors in the Maghrib, while core Arab concerns remained secondary on its agenda. After joining the ARAB LEAGUE in 1958, Tunisia boycotted its sessions until 1961 because of its conflict with Nasser's EGYPT. Tunisia accused Egypt of trying to impose its domination by subversive and forcible means, of hosting leading Tunisian opposition figures and constituting a center of hostile propaganda and subversion against Bourguiba. That same year Tunisia's relations with Egypt were severed, to be resumed only in 1961. Tunisian-Arab relations were also troubled by Bourguiba's divergent, independent position on the ARAB-ISRAEL CONFLICT. Throughout the Arab world public opinion was enraged in spring 1965 when Bourguiba (who had voiced similar ideas earlier) during a visit to a Palestinian refugee camp near Jericho (in Jordan's WEST BANK), called for Arab acceptance of the existence of ISRAEL based on the UN partition plan of 1947 and the return of the Palestinian-Arab refugees and a settlement of the conflict by peaceful means through direct negotiations with Israel. His demands from Israel were hardly different from the mainline positions of the Arab state, but his call for recognition and peace, and his willingness for direct negotiations particularly in the face of peaking commitment to Pan-Arabism were indeed revolutionary. Bourguiba's statements caused a storm of protest in the Arab world. He was fiercely denounced as a traitor. Tunisia's expulsion from the Arab League was demanded, and several Arab ambassadors were recalled. These attacks later continued with Egyptian inspiration. In May 1965, Tunisia also refused to sever diplomatic relations with West Germany following the latter's establishment of relations with Israel, as most other Arab states did. As a result of these conflicts and Tunisia's rift with Egypt, Tunisia again boycotted the Arab League meetings in 1965 and in 1966, severing diplomatic relations with Egypt. In the weeks before the 1967 Arab-Israel conflict Tunisia re-establied relations with Egypt, sending troops to the war front (they did not arrive in time). Tunisia's relations in the Arab world continued to improve after the 1967 war, despite its open clash with SYRIA, which in May 1968 denounced Tunisia for betraying the Arab cause. During 1969–1970 Tunisia's relations with Algeria improved and on 6 January 1970 a treaty of friendship and cooperation was signed, leading *inter alia* to collaboration in the exploitation of oil fields along the common border.

Relations with neighboring Libya since the revolution in 1969 were volatile, reflecting apprehensive concern. Nonetheless, there was a desire to foster good neighborly relations, mainly due to Mu'ammar QADHAFI's erratically expansionist and aggressive regional policy. In June 1970, with Muhammad Masmoudi as the new Foreign Minister, Tunisia became more active in Arab affairs and closer to Libya. This trend culminated in a surprising announcement on 12 January 1974, that Tunisia and Libya would form unity of merger, a step previously rejected by Bourguiba. This step was apparently engineered by Masmoudi while Prime Minister Nouira was absent, and Bourguiba appeared somewhat in the dark about the negotiations. Nouira forced Masmoudi into exile, and the Libyian-Tunisian merger plan was shelved, harming Tunisian-Libyan relations. A conflict over the continental shelf, widely believed to contain oil, was submitted to the International Court of Justice in 1977 and an agreement

was reached in February 1982. But Libya was harboring Tunisian political exiles, and backing subversive activities of Tunisian oppositionaries. Tunisia believed that the Gafsa attack of January 1980 was supported, even initiated, by Libya, and charged Libya with continuous military infiltrations. Near conflict erupted when Libya expelled nearly one-third of the 100,000 Tunisian workers in Libya in August 1985. This led to bitter mutual accusations, and Tunisia severed relations with Libya. Tunisia was also worried by the announcement of Moroccan-Libyan unity in August 1984.

Relations with Algeria further improved after 1977, after Tunisia stopped siding with Morocco in the dispute over Western Sahara. In March 1983 Tunisia and Algeria signed a new border and friendship agreement. They achieved further rapprochement due to their common concern regarding the Libya-Morocco union of August 1984. Following its abolition in 1986, Algeria tried to mediate and heal the rift between Tunisia and Libya.

Tunisia's relations with Libya began to improve in March 1987, when President Bourguiba met with a Libyan official to discuss the issue of compensation for Tunisian workers, along with the restoration of capital to Tunisian companies expelled from Libya two years earlier. A written Libyan pledge (produced in early 1987) not to interfere in Tunisian internal affairs, facilitated the September 1987 Tunisian announcement that the dispute with Libya over the expulsion of Tunisian workers had been resolved. Consular ties between the two countries were resumed a month later, when the border between Tunisia and Libya reopened.

Tunisia's involvement in core Arab affairs became evident following various events: the transfer of the Arab League headquarters from Cairo to Tunis in 1979, the appointment of Tunisian Chedly KLIBI as Secretary-General of the League, and the convening of an Arab Summit Conference in Tunis in November of that year. Tunisia became further involved in further politics when the PLO headquarters and armed units moved to Tunis after their expulsion from Beirut in August 1982. Tunisia's involvement and vulnerability were further demonstrated by the Israeli bombing of PLO installations in Tunisia in October 1985 (and by its near-involvement in, the aftermath of the terrorist hijack of the Italian cruise ship *Achille Lauro*, that month). From 1985 to 1986,

Tunisia requested that the PLO remove from Tunisia all military personnel and installations and confine its presence to administrative and political departments. Yasser ARAFAT reportedly agreed, and a considerable number of PLO men were transferred to other Arab countries.

Tunisia after Bourguiba In the second half of 1987, President Bourguiba's behavior became increasingly erratic, raising doubts about his ability to govern. In September 1987, Bourguiba named BEN-ALI ZEIN AL-ABIDIN as Prime Minister. Ben-Ali was also responsible for internal affairs and served as Secretary-General of the ruling PSD Party. Ben-Ali, (who was appointed as Minister of the Interior in April 1986) had, in fact, been controlling the government for some time. Concern amongst government ministers about Bourguiba's conduct led, after a discrete examination of the constitutional provisions, to a declaration by seven doctors (on 7 November 1987), that President Bourguiba was unfit to govern, due to senility and ill health. In accordance with the constitution, Prime Minister Ben-Ali, whose appointment had apparently been approved by the majority of the ministers and senior military officers, was sworn in as President, while Bourguiba was officially retired. The "Change of 7 November," as the coup was to be called by government officials, was widely welcomed by most segments of the Tunisian public, and marked, in many ways, the end of an era in Tunisian's contemporary history. Under the leadership of President Ben-Ali, Tunisia distanced itself from its struggle for independence, which had overshadowed Bourguiba's rule, preparing for contemporary and future challenges often overlooked during Bourguiba's latter years as President. Ben-Ali declared that existing foreign and economic policies would continue to be pursued, but the constitution would be revised to allow greater political freedom. Ben-Ali formed a new cabinet, in which four ministers closely associated with Bourguiba were not included. A National Security Council, which included himself, the Prime Minister, together with the Defence, Foreign and Interior ministers was also established. This council was created in order to safeguard internal security. At the outset of his tenure, Ben-Ali attempted to effect a policy of national reconciliation, granting the opposition parties a greater role, and increasing civil liberties within Tunisian society. Opposition newspapers (which had been suspended by the Bourguiba administration) were permitted to resume publication.

In late November the Tunisian National Assembly approved legislation which limited the length of time during which a person could be held in police custody without the approval of a public prosecutor, to four days. It also limited the amount of time during which a person could be held on reprimand to six months for most offences. Thousands of political and common-law detainees were released during the first months of the Ben-Ali administration, including Islamic fundamentalists such as Rashed Ghanoushi and opposition party leaders such as Ahmed Mestiri, the leader of the MDS. As part of these legislative measures, a multi-party system was instituted in April 1988 by the National Assembly. In order to gain recognition however, parties had to work within the constitution, and were not allowed to pursue purely religious, racial, regional or linguistic objectives. In July 1988 the Assembly approved a series of amendments, which, among other items, abolished the post of President-for-life and limited the term of a President to a maximum of two five-year terms. A maximum age of seventy was imposed on Presidential candidates. The reforms redefined the role of the Prime Minister as a coordinator of government activities and not as a government leader. Further internal reforms were implemented in the July 1988 modification of the Tunisian press code along with the ratification of the UN convention against torture and other inhumane or degrading acts.

The new Tunisian President also sought to improve relations with the UGTT. As a result of Ben-Ali's initiatives, the two rival leaders of the Union, Habib Achour and Abdel-Aziz Bouraoui, agreed to renounce their union responsibilities in an attempt to reconciliate between rivalling factions. Ben-Ali implemented measures intended to steer Tunisia toward greater political pluralism. As a prelude to a multi-party political system, Ben-Ali attempted to differentiate between the state and party apparatus, by excluding RCD officials from the cabinet, who hitherto had participated in its sessions. A year after the 7 November coup, Ben-Ali announced a "National Pact," securing basic Tunisian rights. The President eased the pressure on the Islamic opposition, attempting to establish better relations with these groups. A more Islamic and Arab identity was advocated by the regime, which, as concessions to the Islamists, offered televised prayers and promoted the status of the Zeitouna religious college to that of a university. In spite of this, the political Islamist party, now renamed *Hizb al-Nahdah*, or *Parti de la Renaissance*, was not given official recognition.

Multi-party elections for the National Assembly and the Presidency were held in April 1989. This was the first such plebiscite in Tunisia since 1981, in which seventy-six percent of eligible voters participated. The ruling RCD party won all 141 seats in the Assembly, while the Islamic candidates, who ran as independents, emerged as the major opposition force, winning a total of thirteen percent of the total votes cast, and receiving in some areas up to twenty-five percent of the votes. Opposition allegations of fraud during the vote were denied. Ninety-nine percent of the voters endorsed Ben-Ali as President. These measures of democratization, however, failed to decrease the internal dissent and dissatisfaction that prevailed within various sectors of Tunisian society, who continued to advocate a more liberal political system. President Ben-Ali was viewed as becoming more autocratic, while the Islamic movement, which failed to win official recognition, expressed its frustration by organizing and inciting demonstrations by student groups. Clashes between students and security authorities erupted in early 1990, along with a municipal workers strike. The government, on its part, was keen on promoting the June 1990 municipal elections as a harbinger of a future multi-party system. In spite of an amendment which introduced a form of proportional representation (dividing fifty percent of the seats between all parties), in lieu of the number of votes received, these elections were boycotted by all opposition movements, who claimed that they were unfair.

By the end of 1990, international human rights organizations argued that even though a large number of prisoners had been freed since Ben-Ali came to power, human rights abuses, primarily of suspected members of *Al-Nahda*, were reported to be pervasive. Following the 1989 elections, *Al-Nahda's* leader, Rashed GHANOUSHI, left Tunisia and went into voluntary exile in London. Pro-Iraqi demonstrations in Tunis during the GULF WAR, led to further clashes between security authorities and Islamic militants, who were accused of planning an Islamist revolution and of planning to assassinate President

Ben-Ali in October 1991. This was in addition to the May arrest of approximately 300 people, including 100 members of the security forces, in connection with an alleged Islamic fundamentalist plot. While the Islamic movement appeared to be a growing threat to the Tunsian government, attempts were made by the regime to continue the efforts aimed at establishing a more liberal political system, allowing for the participation of the legalized opposition. In late 1991, Ben-Ali announced his intention to change the electoral code over the course of the coming year in order to encourage further political representation for other parties. A dialogue between legal opposition parties and the government began in January 1992. At the same time, widespread measures were taken against the Islamic opposition, resulting in numerous arrests and two publicized trials of over 200 Islamist and *Al-Nahda* activists, accused in the summer of 1992 of plotting a takeover of the government. The defendants were sentenced to long prison terms, including life sentences imposed on Ghanoushi and the leaders. *Al-Nahda's* exiled leaders, among them Rashed Ghanoushi. These trials were the final stage of what amounted to be a government campaign against *Al-Nahda*, effectively removing it from public life. Critics of the Tunisian regime accused President Ben-Ali of departing from his promised democratic reforms.

The early 1990s witnessed a significant improvement in the Tunisian economy, further weakening the Islamic opposition. At the time of Ben-Ali's rise to power, the Tunisian economy suffered a high deficit on its balance of payments, coupled with an increase in external debt, which by the end of 1985 totalled over 4,880 million dollars. With the assistance of the International Monetary Fund, the Tunisian government embarked on an economic program designed to liberalize trade, (strengthening the financial sector); a restruction of state enterprises; and the introduction of tax reforms.

Tunisia's policy regarding private investment has changed, moving from the Socialist-oriented policies dominant during the Bourguiba era, to incentives geared to attract foreign investment and capital. By 1989, significant progress had been made in the economy. The 1990 to 1991 Gulf crisis marked a setback in the country's economic recovery, reflected by a drop in exports and in tourism revenues. Planned investments of Gulf states in Tunisia were halted, due to its ambivalent positions toward the Iraqi conquest of Kuwait and the international coalition that was established to contain Iraq. Foreign aid to Tunisia was curtailed as well. The Tunisian economy, however, quickly recovered after the war, and by 1992 GDP growth was recorded at 8.6%. A 1993 World Bank estimate put Tunisia's GNP per capita at 1,780 dollars, a relatively high figure compared to the average in the Arab world, reflecting the emergence of a growing middle class that played an active role in Tunisian economy and society. On its part, the government, committed to fostering foreign investments and revised the foreign investment law in 1994. The law updated existing legislation, emphasizing the main tenets of the government's economic policy: job creation, decentralization and technology transfer. The implementation of these objectives, however, has been rather slow and cumbersome. A new trade agreement signed with the European Union in 1995 exposed Tunisian manufactures to strong competition. This new economic reality added new dimensions to Tunisia's economy, which evolved to a more liberal and competitive form.

In preparation for the scheduled 1994 Presidential and Parliamentary elections, President Ben-Ali promised a revised electoral law that would consolidate the political pluralism which the President had promised since his rise to power in 1987. Under the terms of the new system, the number of seats in the National Assembly was to be increased by an additional 19 seats, which would be distributed amongst the parties proportionally, according to the national vote to the current 163 member National Assembly. This would allow the opposition parties some level of Parliamentary representation. In spite of these modest electoral reforms (which still left the overwhelming majority of the Assembly in the hands of the ruling RCD party), the non-Islamist opposition parties accepted the new formula, raising doubts about their ability to pose a serious alternative to an increasingly authoritarian regime. The Islamic movements retained their illegal status and were barred from participating in the political system. Under these circumstances, the results of the March 1994 elections were not surprising. President Ben-Ali, the sole presidential candidate, officially won 99.9% of the vote. The RCD Party won 97.73% of the vote in the parliamentary elections, but in the wake of the changes in the electoral code, the op-

position parties divided the additional 19 seats in the National Assembly amongst themselves. While few complaints against the voting process were filed by the opposition parties after the elections, serious doubts were raised regarding the sincerity of the Tunisian regime to encourage genuine political pluralism. The government's power and apparent unwillingness to tolerate internal dissent appeared to be more significant in the wake of the election results. Tunisian officials however, continued, to claim that democracy would have to be gradually implemented ino Tunisia, in order to avoid the instability and violence that engulfed neighboring Algeria.

The government continued to suppress *Al-Nahda* activists and supporters, as well as other opposition leaders and human rights activists. It also seemed willing to endure the mounting international criticism of its repressive policies, reiterating its principle of supporting a more democratic system, yet pointing to the difficulties it saw in creating such an order. Local elections held in 1995 did little to change the impression of the regime's authoritarian nature. The RCD Party won control of all municipal councils, while opposition party candidates won only 6 out of the 4,090 seats in municipal bodies throughout the country. These results appeared to embarrass some Tunsian officials, who again restated their support for a more democratic system. 1996 was a year of unprecedented suppression of opposition parties in Tunisia, clearly manifested in the harsh prison sentences imposed on MDS Party leaders Muhammad Mouada (allegedly for having received money from a foreign country—Libya) and his deputy Khemais Chemari, were sentenced to imprisonment for having passed on information regarding Mouada's trial to human rights activists abroad. As the year drew on, however, the government again signaled its intent on promoting political pluralism in the country, and securing a place for the opposition. The imprisoned MDS leaders were released at the beginning of 1997, in what was considered a gesture of goodwill by the government toward the opposition.

Foreign Relations Under Ben-Ali's Presidency, Tunisia's foreign relations reflected continuity rather than change of Bourguiba's era. Tunisia sought to promote relations with the United States, advancing military cooperation and negotiating the rescheduling of Tunisia's 400 million dollar military debt to the US Similar ties were fostered with European countries, such as Spain and the Federal Republic of Germany. Tunisia strengthened its relations with France, primarily in the economic sphere. French President François Mitterand visited Tunisia in June 1989, a visit that was followed by the signing of four agreements concerning financial aid to the country. Bilateral relations with TURKEY progressed with the signing of a military cooperation agreement in March 1990.

The Iraqi invasion of KUWAIT in August 1990 and the unfolding Gulf crisis, clouded Tunisian-Western relations. Affected by strong public support for IRAQ within Tunisia, Ben-Ali condemned the deployment of the US-led military force in the Gulf, and refused to attend an emergency Arab summit meeting which convened in Cairo. Tunisia's position during the crisis damaged relations with the West in the aftermath of the Gulf War. The US reduced the level of its economic aid to Tunisia in February 1991, easing its military aid altogether. However, bilateral investment agreements signed between Tunisia and the US, along with a visit of French President Mitterand to Tunisia, served as signs of an improvement in the relations between Tunisia and the West. Amidst growing international concern over the rise of militant Islamist groups in North Africa, Western leaders were quite keen on reiterating their support for the Tunisian government. The containment of Islamic extremists became, therefore, a high priority on the agenda of Tunisian-Western relations, encouraging further economic cooperation as an instrument to achieve this goal. A new cooperation agreement between Tunisia and the European Union (the first of its kind between a North African country and the Union), signed in 1995, marked the beginning of a new era in Tunsian-European relations.

Relations with Tunisia's North African neighbors improved, most significantly with Libya. Full diplomatic relations with Libya were resumed in December 1987, following a Libyan consent to pay 10 million dollars to Tunisian workers who had been expelled in 1985, and to free Tunisian assets frozen in Libya. A summit meeting of Ben-Ali and Qadhafi, held on the island of Djerba in May 1988, concluded an agreement to establish a socioeconomic union between the two countries, and allowing unlimited passage across their common border. Fol-

lowing the summit, a number of Tunisian-Libyan joint projects commenced, a large number of Libyan tourists visited Tunisia and many Tunisians found employment in Libya. Tunisia's bilateral relations with Morocco, on the other hand, remained cool, primarily as a result of Tunisia's reserved position *vis-a-vis* the war in Western Sahara and a close alliance with Algeria.

Tunisia's improved relations with Libya led President Ben-Ali to explore the possibility of including Libya in regional frameworks such as the Maghreb Treaty of Fraternity and Cooperation of 1983. Efforts were also made to establish stronger regional political organs. The first summit meeting of the five heads of Maghrebi states took place in Algiers during the Arab Summit Conference held in June 1988. Tunisia was instrumental in the formation of the Arab Maghreb Union (AMU), advocating the need to promote economic cooperation and to strengthen the Union's institutions. At a preliminary meeting of the Maghreb foreign ministers held in January 1990, Tunisia proposed a series of measures which included the creation of a permanent secretariat, along with the expansion of the Union's Consultative Council, and the establishment of commissions charged with advancing regional cooperation in various arenas. Another Tunisian initiative aimed at promoting regional cooperation was the proposal to create a common energy market for the Maghreb, allowing free trade in electricity, petroleum and natural gas between North African nations. A regional television service, serving the entire North African region, was established in Tunis in March 1990. Special passport control lines for North African nationals were set up at the Tunis airport as well. Tunisian officials also expressed their interest in discussing within the AMU the possibility of rescheduling North African debts to European countries, and raising the issue of racial attacks against North African nationals working in Europe in talks with the European Union. However, these initiatives failed to materialize or vitalize the AMU, which did not evolve into a strong regional economic body as Tunisia had hoped.

Relations with other Arab states also improved following Bourguiba's dismissal in November 1987. In January 1988 Tunisia resumed its diplomatic relations with Egypt, which had been severed in 1979 following the Egyptian-Israeli peace treaty. This step was accompanied by bilateral agreements signed between the two countries, and an official visit of President Ben-Ali to Cairo in March 1990, the first visit by a Tunisian President in twenty-five years. The assassination of PLO military commander Abu Jihad at his home near Tunis in April 1988, allegedly by Israeli commandos, served as a source of embarrassment to the Tunisian government, which lodged a complaint to the UN Security Council, which condemned the "Israeli aggression against Tunisian territory." Tunisia continued to maintain its role as a moderate Arab state, securing its ties with the Gulf states and with Saudi Arabia as well. Yet Tunisia's involvement in Arab affairs somewhat diminished in 1990, when, following Egypt's return to the Arab League, the latter's headquarters moved back to Cairo despite Tunisia's protest, resulting in the resignation of Klibi as Secretary-General and his replacement by the Egyptian Ismat Abdel Majid. In the aftermath of the Gulf War, Tunisia sought to defuse quickly the strained relations that its tacit support of Iraq in the Gulf crisis caused with some Arab states. Seeking to distance Tunisia from Iraq, President Ben-Ali refused to meet the Iraqi Vice-President Tareq Aziz in April 1991, and toured the Gulf states in November of that year. Relations with Egypt were bolstered amidst their mutual attempts to contain domestic Islamist agitation and subsequent cooperation in confronting this threat. Tunisia also withdrew its Ambassador from Khartoum in October 1991, claiming that Sudan had supported Islamic terrorists. Bilateral ties with Kuwait, which had been damaged after the Gulf war, returned slowly to a normal level by 1994, when the Kuwaiti Foreign Minister and First Deputy Prime Minister visited Tunis, announcing that diplomatic relations between the two countries would be restored and that Kuwait would resume investments in Tunisia.

The Madrid Peace Conference held in late October 1991 was openly supported by Tunisia, which became an active participant in the multi-lateral talks and in regional work groups established as part of these negotiations. Tunisia welcomed the Israel-PLO Oslo agreement signed in September 1993. Following the establishment of the PALESTINIAN AUTHORITY in May 1994, PLO officials and headquarters left Tunisia. Their departure, coupled with the progress achieved in the peace talks, helped pave the road to the establishment of diplomatic relations between Tunisia and Israel. Moves in this direction included issuing visas to Israeli tourists, and visits of Israeli officials to Tunis. In October 1994 the Tunisian and Israeli Foreign Ministers met in New York and agreed in principle to open interest sections in the Belgian embassies in Tunis and Tel Aviv, as a first step toward full diplomatic relations between the two countries. However, the implementation of this agreement was slow, as Tunisian officials repeatedly linked the opening of these bureaus to further progress in the Middle East peace process. An agreement regarding the opening of these bureaus, which, contrary to the initial plan, were to be independent diplomatic missions, was reached at a meeting between Tunisian Foreign Minister Ben Yahya and his Israeli counterpart Ehud BARAK in Washington in January 1996.

Israel opened its Interest Bureau in Tunis in April 1996, and the Tunisian office in Tel Aviv was opened shortly afterward. Tunisia also opened a liaison office in Gaza at the same time. There was little criticism within Tunisia of such normalization moves with Israel. The Tunisian government nonetheless remained cautious about further developing of its ties with Israel, stating that these relations depended on further progress of the Arab-Israeli peacemaking endeavor.

Tunisia can be perceived as an oasis of stability in the turbulent North African region, along and its successful economic performance has led to a high standard of living. The controlled and limited nature of democratization conducted began in the late 1980s was accompanied by constant efforts at creating regional frameworks of political and economic cooperation, and further trade exchange with the European Union. However, in the future the development of the private sector might increase pressure for a more pluralistic political and social system. Creating such an order, without endangering domestic internal stability, is a challenge that still faces the Tunisian government.

al-TURABI, HASSAN (b. 1932) A Sudanese political leader and thinker, one of the most prominent leaders in contemporary SUNNI radical ISLAM; leader of the Sudanese Islamic movement since 1964.

Turabi was born in Kassla, eastern SUDAN. He received a traditional Islamic education (his father was a *Qadi*). After studying law at the University of Khartoum, where he graduated in 1955, Turabi continued his academic training abroad. Turabi holds a Masters degree in Law from London University (1957) and a Ph.D in Law from the Sorbonne (1964). His travels afforded him with great knowledge of Western culture and thought, as well as fluency in French and English.

After his return to Sudan, he was appointed Dean of Khartoum's Law Faculty but soon became involved in politics. In 1964, he was elected as leader of the MUSLIM BROTHERHOOD, a post he still holds. In 1965, following the fall of the military regime of Abbud, he formed the FIC (Front for Islamic Constitution). The FIC included several Islamic sects and movements aiming at an Islamic constitution for Sudan. Turabi served as its Secretary-General until its disbanding in 1969 following NUMEIRI's military coup.

Turabi was arrested following the 1969 coup led by Numeiri and spent a few years in jail. Following the national reconciliation of the Muslim Brotherhood with Numeiri's regime in 1977 and its joining the government, Turabi held several posts mostly of a judicial nature. He served as General-Attorney (1979–1982) and as advisor to the President on legal and foreign policy issues (1983–1985). During this period he strengthened the holdings of his Party in key power loci in the country including the armed forces. This was a major factor in the success of the military coup of General BASHIR in 1989 that brought Turabi and his Party to power. In fact, Turabi is the main figure behind the development of the political dogma of the Muslim Brotherhood in Sudan. He was responsible for its breakaway from the founding organization of the Muslim Brotherhood in EGYPT and the emphasis on Sudanese identity. He was the architect of the process in which the movement developed from a negligible political entity to a major popular force. Turabi displayed impressive political manouvering skills and missed no opportunity to strengthen the movement.

With the fall of Numeiri's regime in 1985, Turabi established the National Islamic Front (NIF). Between December 1988 and March 1989, he held a number of positions in Sadek al-MAHDI's coalition government: Attorney General, Foreign Minister, and Minister of Justice.

To a great degree, Turabi and his Party, were behind the military coup of General Bashir in June 1989 after they had despaired of coming to power

democratically. From 1989 until 1996, Turabi did not fill an official post in Bashir's regime. Even so, he was the key figure behind the scenes and dictated the ideological and political dogma of the regime. In March 1996 he was chosen to be Chairman of Parliament.

Turabi is considered one of the most important leaders in Sunni Radical Islam and is admired by other radical Islamic leaders such as Rashed al-GHANOUSHI, (leader of the Tunisian Islamic Movement) and Ishak al-Farhan, leader of Muslim Brotherhood in Jordan who regard him and his movement's rise to power as a model. On the other hand, rivalry exists between Turabi and the Muslim Brotherhood in Egypt as to who will lead the world Muslim Brotherhood. In 1991 Turabi established a Pan-Islamic body, named the "Popular Arabic Islamic Conference" (PAIC) that includes various Islamic movements and other political trends in the Arab world. The organization was slated as an alternative to the world Muslim Brotherhood organisation that is dominated by the Egyptians.

Despite his radical Islamic views and alleged involvement in the domestic affairs of neighboring countries, it is remarkable that Turabi made an effort to convince Yasser arafat to recognize Resolution 242 (see ARAB-ISRAEL PEACEMAKING) in late 1988. Ever since 1989, Turabi and his followers have been accused by rulers of Arab and African states, such, as Egypt, Tunisia and Ethiopia, of undermining their regimes and providing military and financial support to Islamic movements in those countries. Turabi was accused of directly assisting the Islamic group that attempted to assassinate President Husni MUBARAK of Egypt in June 1995 during his visit to Ethiopia.

In addition to his political role, Turabi is considered one of the central and original Islamic thinkers of his generation. He published numerous books and articles in various languages on subjects such as Ancient Islamic Heritage, Democracy, Women's rights and the relationship between state and society. His most famous book to date is "The Renewal of Islamic Thought" (Tadjdid al-Fikr al-Islami) published in 1985. Another acclaimed work is The Islamic Movement in Sudan that outlines the development of the Muslim Brotherhood in Sudan .

In his writings and activities, Turabi emphasises the importance of transforming the Islamic movements into mass political movements, relinquished the elitist character of the past as advocated by Sayyid Qutb. In fact, Turabi, together with Rashed al-Ghanoushi, leader of *Al-Nahda* movement in Tunisia, are widely recognized as leaders of a new political trend in radical Islam.

TURKEY (Türkiye Cumhuriyeti). Republic on the eastern Mediterranean, representing the nucleus of the OTTOMAN EMPIRE after its collapse in World War I.

Population and Land—Over ninety-nine percent of the population is Muslim (and the vast majority, approximately eighty-five percent ethnic Turks). The state does not officially recognize any sub-division of Muslim minorities. The majority are Sunni, but there is a strong Shi'i minority with estimates ranging from seven percent to thirty percent, most of whom are of the ALEVI denomination. The KURDS are the strongest ethnic minority, estimated at between ten percent and twenty percent, mostly SUNNI. About 1 to 1.5% are Arabs, mostly Alevi. In the past members of these religious and ethnic groups tended to live in highly concentrated geographical areas, with Shi's in central and eastern Anatolia, Kurds in the southeastern provinces, and Arabs along the Syrian border. However, due to extensive urbanization and migration, these groups are now dispersed throughout the country, particularly in the large cities. Non Muslim groups, which were quite considerable in Ottoman times, have greatly dwindled in the republican period, totaling less than 0.2% of the population. The largest ethnic-religious groups are ARMENIANS estimated at 45,000-50,000; JEWS, around 25,000; and Roman CATHOLICS who number 27,000-30,000. The GREEK ORTHODOX also number a few thousands perhaps as many as 20,000. The non-Muslims are largely concentrated in Istanbul.

Turkey is situated on the eastern Mediterranean, connecting the two continents of Europe and Asia. The only waterways connecting the Black Sea and the Mediterranean, the Straits of the Bosphorus and the Dardanelles and the Sea of Marmara, are controlled by Turkey. It is thus strategically situated at a vital land and sea junction. Most of Turkey is in Asia, comprising the Anatolian peninsula (Asia Minor). European Turkey forms a small region called Thrace at the south eastern tip of the Balkans. Turkey's boundaries are mostly natural sea borders: the Black

Sea in the north, the Aegean in the west and the Mediterranean in the south. On land, Turkey is bordered in the west by Bulgaria and Greece, in the east by Georgia, Armenia, Azerbaijan and IRAN, and in the south by IRAQ and SYRIA.

Turkey has a large variety of topographic features. An extensive plateau in central Anatolia, slopes down toward the western coast but is bounded by long mountain ranges to the north and south, and rises into the mountainous highlands in the east. Climatic conditions are marked by variations between the regions: The coastal areas and the western valleys have cool rainy winters and hot, moderately dry summers; the central plateau has cold winters and dry hot summers; and the mountain ranges and the eastern highlands have extremely hot and dry summers with bitter cold winters. The interior plateau and the eastern region are less suitable for human habitation and cultivation and have remained relatively undeveloped.

Economy For many years agriculture was the basis of the Turkish economy, and the primary source of income for most Turks. But the growth of industrial and the service sectors have changed this. In 1995 agruliculture accounted for approximately fifteen percent of the GDP, providing employment to around forty-four percent of the labor force. Turkey raises a wide range of crops and livestock, which satisfies almost all domestic need. These include grain, fruits and vegetables, olives, sugar beets, pulses, a variety of animal products, tobacco and cotton. Foodstuffs are also an important part (twenty-three percent in 1993) of the country's exports. The agricultural sector suffers from low yields caused by inefficient methods of cultivation, an inadequate amount of arable land, poor irrigation and weather conditions. This has led to undesired poverty among the peasant population, and many have left their villages to seek better opportunities and higher incomes in the cities both at home and abroad. Cities in Turkey have grown enormously in recent years. In an effort to accelerate agricultural productivity, increase exports, and raise the living standards of the rural population, Turkey has, over the years devoted considerable efforts and financial resources to the expansion of irrigation, the education of farmers, mechanization, loans and a variety of other supports and incentives. Yet generally agriculture still lags behind the other economic sectors. The greatest current project for the development of agriculture (as well as industry) is the Southeast Anatolia Project (GAP) designed to increase the area under cultivation and produce hydroelectric power for the entire region.

Mining and industry now occupy (undeveloped in Ottoman times), an important and growing role in the Turkish economy, accounting in 1995 for thirty-four percent of the GDP (including construction), and engaging fifteen percent of the labor force. Industries include: textiles, food processing, cement, chemicals, lumber, paper, iron and steel. Manufactured goods accounted in 1993 for seventy-two percent of exports value. Construction is an important sector, and large construction firms have been successfully engaged in large scale projects both at home and abroad. Turkey has rich and varied mineral deposits, (the most important being coal, lignite, iron and chrome), and mining products also feature in the country's exports (four percent). Turkey produces oil and natural gas, but quantities are limited and do not meet domestic needs. The development of mining and industry has been regarded as a primary objective in republican Turkey in her drive for modernization, self-sufficiency and eradication of rural underemployment.

From the 1930s to the end of the reign of the Republican People's Party in the 1940s Turkey followed a policy of state enterprise and control (étatism). This was regulated by a five year plan, resulting in an impressive (if limited) degree of industrialization. Since the 1950s, this policy has given way to a relaxation of state control of the economy, and the encouragement of private (including foreign) investment. By the end of the 1970s, Turkey had already developed capital goods and high technology industries. The most recent phase, associated with the policy of Prime Minister (later President) Turgut ÖZAL in the 1980s has been a change from import substitution approach to an export oriented one, increasing efficiency and competitiveness. There has also been a growing movement in favor of privatization. The growth of the industrial sector has largely been responsible for the impressive economic growth of recent years.

The growth of the services sector throughout the republican period, and notably in the last few decades, has been remarkable. Indeed this sector accounted in 1995 for about fifty-one percent of the GDP and employs about forty percent of the labor force. The network of roads and railroads, which Turkey inherited from the Ottoman period was very poor. Nonetheless, today it efficiently covers most areas of the country, also connecting it to all its neighbors. Railroads, all publicly owned, extend a total of 6,476 miles (10,413 km.), while highways total 199,385 miles (320,611 km.). Turkey also maintains good coastal maritime communications. The major ports are Istanbul, Mersin, Izmir and Iskenderun. Major cities in Turkey are connected by the fast growing Turkish Airlines, as well as many destinations in the Middle East, Europe, Central Asia, the Far East and the United States. Additionally there are a number of new privately owned airlines. Along with the development of transportation, there has been an expansion and modernization of the telecommunications system. The tourism industry has been greatly facilitated by this "opening up" of Turkey to the world, in addition to large investments made in building new and modern tourist facilities. In 1996, 8.6 million people visited Turkey and earnings from tourism amounted to some 6 billion dollars.

In 1995 Turkish exports stood at 21.98 billion dollars and imports at 35.19 billion dollars. Exports (fifty-one percent of which went to the EU countries), included textiles, iron, steel, other metals, and foodstuffs, while imports (forty-seven percent from the EU) included mainly machinery, fuels, minerals and foodstuffs. Turkey has traditionally suffered from a deficit in its foreign trade and balance of payments. This was caused by its imports (mostly capital goods for development and industrialization as well as for military purposes), which far exceeded its exports. Strong controls and protective tariffs were necessary, and the country had to resort to borrowing in large amounts in order to meet its requirements in foreign currency. Substantial aid was received from the OECD as well as other sources and Turkey was often in need of rescheduling her foreign debts. Since the 1960s there has been some relief from the remittances sent home by the hundreds of thousands of Turkish workers employed in Europe, but this was insufficient and unreliable. The increased oil prices led to a particularly severe financial crisis in the 1970s. Several reform packages were tried and strong measures taken after 1980 to increase exports. Results were impressive, leading to a sharp rise in exports and, helped by the reduction of oil prices, to a considerable improvement in the country's foreign reserves. There was also a change in the structure of exports now no longer based on agricultural products and raw materials, but on manufactured goods. The improved balance of payments allowed Turkey to increase imports, leading in the early 1990s to rising deficits once more. In recent years the main problem facing the Turkish economy has been the uncontrolled government expenditure and low tax revenues. This has caused an enormous deficit in the budget as well as high inflation, (about eighty percent in 1997).

Political History The present borders with the exception of Hatay, i.e., ALEXANDRETTA province, and the border with IRAQ in the Mosul area) were determined by the TREATY OF LAUSANNE in 1923 between Turkey and the victorious allies of World War I. The Mosul border was established by the League of Nations arbitration late in 1925. In 1939 the province of Alexandretta, then part of Mandatory SYRIA, was annexed to Turkey in agreement with France, and renamed, in Turkish, Hatay. Turkey became a member of the League of Nations in 1932, and was a founding member of the UN. Turkey is also a member of the Council of Europe and NATO and an associate of the EU and the WEU.

Foreign Relations. The area which today comprises the Turkish Republic (with the exception of the Kars and Ardahan regions ceded to Russia in 1878) was until the end of World War I part of the Ottoman Empire. Owing to nationalist uprisings and the encroachment of the great powers the Ottoman Empire by the end of the nineteenth century, had lost most of its previous possessions in the Balkans and North Africa. Though the period of Sultan ABDEL HAMID II (1876–1909) was mostly peaceful, European pressure continued, and lacking he support of the Western Powers, the Sultan turned more and more toward cooperation with Germany. Nationalist ferment among the various ethnic groups in the Empire also continued, occasionally resulting in armed revoltion. Abdel Hamid took tough measure to suppress these revolts while upholding the Ottoman principle of equality for the CHRISTIANS as initiated by the nineteenth century reformers. Toward the Muslim population of the Empire, also beginning to be attracted by ideas of nationalism and separatism, he promoted the idea of Pan-Islamism

designed to foster loyalty to the Ottoman Sultan-Caliph, in the name of religion.

In 1908, a military coup brought the YOUNG TURKS to power. One of their chief aims was the preservation of the Empire's sovereignty and integrity. Yet within a few years they were forced to fight several wars and suffer considerable territorial losses. In 1908, Bosnia and Herzegovina were formally annexed by Austria. Bulgaria declared its independence and Crete was incorporated into Greece. The Italian-Ottoman War of 1911–1912 resulted in the loss of Tripolitania and the Dodecanese Islands, and in the Balkan Wars of 1912–1913 Turkey lost Macedonia and Western Thrace. Albania declared its independence in 1912. The direct rule of the Empire now extended only to Anatolia, Eastern Thrace and the Arab provinces of Asia.

The decision to enter World War I on the side of the Central Powers was made by a small group of military leaders headed by Enver Pasha. The decision proved fatal, though Ottoman arms were not entirely unsuccessful. The Empire suffered severe losses on the Caucasian front and failed in an attempted invasion of Egypt (1915), but put up a strong defense at Gallipoli, forcing the Allied expeditionary force to evacuate the peninsula (1915–1916). The Ottoman army also stopped the British advance in Mesopotamia at Kut al-Amara (1916) winning several battles against Russia in Armenia and Persia (1916). However, new British offensives from EGYPT and Mesopotamia (the former helped by the troops of Ibn Ali Sharif Hussein of Mecca who had proclaimed the ARAB REVOLT) resulted in the loss of most of the Fertile Crescent by the end of 1918. In October 1918, Turkey was compelled to sign the Armistice of Mudros.

The Russian Revolution of 1917 had opened the way for another Ottoman advance towards the Caucasus, and the peace with the Soviets, concluded at Brest Litovsk in March 1918, secured the return of Kars, Ardahan, and Batum to the Ottoman domain. Batum was returned to the Georgian Republic in a treaty of June 1919 with the Trans-Caucasian Republics; Kars and Ardahan remained Turkish.

In 1918 Anatolia and the region of Istanbul were still under the control of the Ottoman government. Shortly afterward the Allied armistice forces occupied the Straits and the Istanbul region and, within the next year, British and French forces occupied parts of south-eastern Anatolia. The Italians landed at Antalya, and the Greeks at Izmir. At the same time Armenian forces controlled sections of Eastern Anatolia. The occupation of the Istanbul area and various parts of Anatolia conformed ostensibly to the provision of the armistice. However, these steps were meant to produce *fait accomplis* in line with the secret agreements concluded earlier between the Allies for the partition of Anatolia. The Ottoman government of Sultan Mehmed VI Vahideddin was powerless to prevent this. In August 1920 it was forced to sign the Treaty of Sèvres. This reduced the Ottoman Empire's territory to some middle and northern parts of Anatolia and Istanbul, and considerably limited its sovereignty, including the continued enforcement of the CAPITULATIONS, by which foreign residents had extra territorial rights, and the opening of the Straits to "every vessel of commerce or war" under the supervision of an International Commission.

However, resistance to Allied schemes and the dictated treaty had sprung up in the Turkish provinces, with mass meetings, the organization of societies "for the Defense of Rights," and sporadic guerrilla warfare. Turkish national consciousness had already been developed by writers and intellectuals, notably Ziya GÖKALP, during the last years of the Empire. But it was the experience of foreign, invasion, Christian and particularly Greek, which gave the resistance its driving force.

Organization and leadership were provided by the wartime hero, Mustafa Kemal (ATATÜRK). Two congresses, one in Erzurum in July 1919, and the other in Sivas in September of that year, were convened under his leadership. They called for the preservation of the integrity of Turkish territory and full independence.

Elections to the Ottoman Parliament in October were won by the Nationalists, and in January 1920 Parliament adopted the National Pact, based on the resolutions of the two congresses. The growing power of the Nationalists precipitated a confrontation with the Allies and the Ottoman government. In March of that year some of the Nationalist leaders in Istanbul were arrested and exiled by the Allies, who had dominated Istanbul, while the Sultan dissolved Parliament and had the Nationalists declared rebels. The Nationalists convened in Ankara (the center of their activities) the Grand National Assembly, with Mustafa Kemal as its President, forming a temporary government.

After this open Nationalist defiance of the Ottoman government the Allies and the Greeks (encouraged by Britain) began a successful offensive into Anatolia in June 1920, capturing Bursa and Usak and occupying Adrianople in Thrace. But the Nationalists were successful against their other adversaries. They defeated an Army of the Caliphate sent against them by the Sultan, and in May they concluded an armistice with the French. They also drove the Armenians eastward following Turko-Armenian hostilities that ended in December 1920 in a peace favorable to the Turks. The eastern frontier, leaving the regions of Kars and Ardahan in Turkish hands, was finally fixed in March 1921 in a Treaty of Friendship with the Soviets. In October Nationalist Turkey signed the Treaty of Kars with the Soviet republics of Armenia, Georgia and Azerbaijan. The Soviets were the first to recognize the Nationalist government and provided invaluable military and financial aid. Dissension among the Allied Powers also helped the Nationalists. Italy, realizing the futility of the struggle, agreed, in March 1921, to withdraw in return for economic concessions. The French followed suit in October with the Franklin-Bouillon Agreement, which fixed the border between Turkey and Syria.

The next main struggle was between Turkey and Greece. The Greeks had resumed their offensive early in 1921, but their advance was twice halted by Ismet Pasha (INÖNÜ). After another Greek advance, Mustafa Kemal, the supreme commander, defeated the Greeks on the Sakarya River in September. In August 1922 a Turkish counter-offensive began, and within two weeks the Greeks were swept out of Anatolia. The Turkish forces turned towards Thrace which was still in Greek hands. War between the British and the Nationalist Turks appeared imminent when the latter approached the Straits, still under Allied occupation. Yet both sides agreed to negotiate, and at the Armistice of Mudanya signed in October 1922, the Allied Powers agreed to a restoration of Turkish sovereignty in Thrace, Istanbul and the Straits.

A new peace conference opened in Lausanne in November. As the Sultanate had been abolished in November 1922 (see below), the Nationalists alone represented Turkey. Bargaining was difficult and protracted, but in the end the Nationalists, led at the conference by Ismet Pasha (Inönü), obtained most of their demands. By the Treaty of Lausanne, signed in July 1923, Turkey managed to keep practically all of the Turkish provinces, and abolished virtually all restrictions on her independence, including the capitulations. The Straits were to remain open to all vessels of commerce and war, but with certain limitations of the latter; an international commission was to supervise the Straits. In October the last foreign troops evacuated Istanbul and this Republic of Turkey was proclaimed with Mustafa Kemal as its first elected President.

Turkey's foreign policy during and after the Kemalist period was based on its desire to preserve the hard-won independence and integrity of the state. Kemal's motto, "Peace at home, peace in the world," was regarded as the guarantee of Turkish security, and Turkey made a great effort to promote good relations with neighbors and world powers alike. Mustafa Kemal gave up all ideas of retaking the Empire's non-Turkish provinces or of pursuing Pan-Islamic or Pan-Turkish policies.

Turkey's claim to the province of Mosul, demanded by Britain for mandatory Iraq, continued for a time to upset Turko-British relations. But in 1926, following arbitration and a decision by the Council of the League of Nations, Turkey agreed to renounce its claim in return for a share in Iraq's oil revenues. Relations with the USSR were further strengthened when the two countries signed a Treaty of Friendship and Neutrality in December 1925. Relations with Greece showed a steady improvement. By a special agreement annexed to the Treaty of Lausanne, Turkey and Greece effected an exchange of population. After its completion in 1930, a Treaty of Friendship and Arbitration was signed.

Turkey reacted to the growing menace from Germany and Italy in the 1930s by contracting various alliances. In August 1932 Turkey joined the League of Nations; two years later, it concluded with Greece, Yugoslavia and Rumania the Balkan Pact. In 1937 it signed at Saadabad, a non-aggression pact with Iraq, Iran and Afghanistan. The rising Fascist menace also brought about a *rapprochement* with the Western Powers, resulting in their consent (in the Montreux Convention of 1936) to the fortification of the Straits that had been banned under the Treaty of Lausanne. France also consented in 1939, to the annexation by Turkey of the Syrian district of Alexandretta, partly populated by Turks. To consolidate the ties between Turkey and the Western Powers, an Anglo-Turkish Declaration of Mutual Assistance was issued in May 1939, and was followed shortly afterwards by a Non-Aggression Pact with France. In October a tripartite pact was signed between Britain, France and Turkey. Turkish efforts to enter into an alliance with the USSR failed owing to the German-Soviet pact.

During World War II Turkey maintained its neutrality. Fearing German superiority Turkey remained inactive even after Italy's entry into the war although her treaty with the Western Powers specified Turkish intervention if the war reached the Mediterranean. Furthermore, German victories induced Turkey to conclude a Non-Aggression Pact with Germany in June 1941 and to consent to the sale of chrome ore to Germany. Nevertheless, Turkey did not renounce its Western alliance, continued to sell chrome to Britain and resisted Nazi pressure for closer collaboration. The change in the course of the war did not bring an immediate formal shift in Turkish foreign policy, although economic relations with the West increased. Meetings between President Inönü, Churchill and Roosevelt in the course of 1943 failed to persuade Turkey to cooperate fully with the West. Turkey insisted that it was not prepared for war. Its fears of Nazi invasion were compounded by the fear of subsequent Soviet liberation. Only in 1944, after the tide of war had turned strongly in favor of the allies, did Turkey break off relations with Germany. In February 1945 Turkey declared war on Germany, thus qualifying it to participate in the United Nations Conference in San Francisco.

Immediately after the war, Soviet-Turkish relations, (already strained following the German-Soviet Pact of 1939) further deteriorated. Angered by Turkish neutrality during the war (and by the wartime activities of Pan-Turkish circles), the USSR, early in 1945, repudiated her treaty of 1925 with Turkey. Moscow conditioned the renewal of the treaty in sharing the defense of the Straits and return of the Kars and Ardahan regions. These demands, rejected by Turkey (and renounced by the USSR only in 1953), placed it firmly in the Western bloc. Since Britain was unable to provide the necessary aid, the US stepped in—Turkey's principal ally. Beginning in 1947, the US (within the framework of the Truman Doctrine, the Marshall Plan, and later NATO) gave Turkey massive military, economic and technical aid. In 1949 Turkey became a member of the Council of Europe. A year later, to prove its loyalty to Western interests, it despatched a brigade to join the UN forces in the Korean war. In 1952 Turkey was admitted to NATO as a full member, with Izmir becoming the headquarters of the European South-Eastern Command. Subsequently Turkey and the USA signed several bilateral agreements which provided for American aid and granted the USA bases and installations in the country. In 1959 the two countries signed a formal defense agreement. Turkey also participated in regional alliances, with the approval of the Western Powers. A project to set up a Middle East Defence Organization in 1951 failed due to Egyptian objection. But in 1955 Turkey signed a defence alliance with Iraq, known as the Baghdad Pact, which later included Pakistan, Iran and Britain. Upon Iraq's withdrawal from the treaty following the military coup of 1958, the headquarters of the Pact moved to Ankara. In 1960 its name was changed to Central Treaty Organization (CENTO). In 1954 Turkey also signed a Treaty of Alliance, Political Cooperation and Mutual Assistance with Greece and Yugoslavia. Although Turkey had voted against the partition of Palestine in 1947, it later established diplomatic relations with Israel and in the late 1950s the two countries reached a close level of cooperation.

In the late 1950s the Cyprus question became increasingly vital in Turkish foreign policy. In the face of growing Greek terrorism and British plans to leave the island, Turkey adamantly opposed exclusive Greek rule of the island or union (enosis) with Greece. Its motivation was both national (the existence of a Turkish minority in the island) and strategic (the danger of a communist take-over). Prolonged discussions resulted in the agreements of Zurich and London (1959). According to these Cyprus was granted independence and a constitution containing strict safeguards for Turkish minority rights. Order was restored in the island, and Greek-Turkish relations improved. But tension arose again at the end of 1963, when President Makarios of Cyprus revealed plans for constitutional changes, resulting in riots between Turkish and Greek Cypriots. Direct Turkish intervention, with the possibility of war be-

tween Greece and Turkey was averted in the summer of 1964 only by American pressure. A resemblance of order was restored when the UN sent a peace-keeping force to the island.

There has been no final settlement on the Cyprus issue since then, regardless of intermittent talks between the Turkish and Greek communities and numerous attempts made by outside mediators to help reach a solution. Additionally the unresolved question of Cyprus has had a most adverse effect on Turkish-Greek relations. Relations have remained cool, and occasionally have almost led to a war. A crisis flared up again in November 1967 when Turkey blamed Greek troops (which joined the Cypriot National Guard, with the backing of the Junta government in Greece), of fresh violence on the island. Full war was averted only by American mediation leading to the pull out of all Greek troops. In the summer of 1974 war was once again imminent when a *pro enosis* coup carried out by the National Guard and led by Nikos Sampson ousted President Makarios. After attempting to bring about intervention by Britain (a guarantor power) Turkey in July landed its troops on the north Cyprus coast and went on to occupy some forty percent of the island's territory. Although Sampson and the Greek Junta supporting him were soon overthrown, Turkey has continued its occupation of the northern part. Turkey insists now on a solution based on the establishment of a federated bizonal, bi-communal Cypriot state. The island itself has remained partitioned between the Greek led state of Cyprus and the Turkish zone. Both absorbed thousands of refugees from the other side, turning into virtually homogenous areas. In November 1983 the Turkish zone declared itself the Turkish Republic of Northern Cyprus, with Ra'uf Denktas as President, but it is not recognized by any state other than Turkey. The border between the zones has remained quiet, but occasional incidents have brought about renewed tension. A new crisis occurred in early 1997 when it became known that Cyprus had ordered long range surface to air missiles from Russia able to hit Turkish territory. The situation was defused only when Cyprus agreed to hold off deployment for sixteen months.

A number of other issues tended to cloud Turkish Greek relations from time to time increasing tensions between the two countries. The question of territorial water in the Aegean Sea in which the presence of numerous Greek islands made it difficult to determine mutual rights. This was particularly important at a time when both countries wished to explore and exploit possible natural resources on the sea bed. Turkey's exploratory missions into the Aegean were strongly opposed by Greece, while Turkey objected to Greece's attempts to extend its territorial waters and to Greek militarization of the islands. A dangerous crisis erupted between the two countries in January 1996 over sovereignty in Kardak (Imia in Greek). Kardak was an uninhabited small rocky islet off the Turkish southern coast, and landed by a Turkish naval force and the dispute only diffused through American pressure on Turkey to leave the island. Another bone of contention between the two countries was the alleged cases of infringements on the rights of Turkish and Greek minorities in each other's country.

The 1950s were regarded as the "honeymoon" period in Turkey's relations with the West, and particularly with the United States. In the 1960s foreign policy shifted toward a more flexible approach in its relations with the superpowers. Several factors played a role in this development. The close relations developed earlier with the United States led to a number of disputes, and some disappointment was felt on the Turkish side with the degree and terms of American economic, political and military support. The removal of the Jupiter missiles from Turkish soil in the wake of the Cuban crisis early in 1963 was also greatly resented by Turkey who considered it as a unilateral act weakening its own defenses. Most harmful to Turkish American relations was a letter written by President Johnson to Prime Minister Inönü in June 1964 warning him against military intervention in Cyprus and the use of American arms. The letter was seen as contrary to the Turkish American alliance and friendship and as proof of the unreliability of American aid. Public opinion in Turkey was opposed to the large presence of American personnel in the country and influenced by anti-Americanism abroad and by the growing leftist movements in the country. Hence the mood in the country became increasingly hostile toward the Turkish-American alliance. This caused a discernible impact on government policy. In its more extreme manifestations, anti-Americanism witnessed frequent assaults on Americans in Turkey from members of radical youth organizations.

Along with the new tensions arising between Turkey and the United States in the 1960s, a new approach developed in Turkey towards its relations with the Soviet bloc and with the non aligned countries. The Soviet Union had already renounced its Stalinist demands from Turkey and openly courted its friendship, while the beginning of US-Soviet *détente* in the early 1970s helped to ease traditional Turkish fears of the Russians. Turkey began to respond to Soviet feelers, attempting to mobilize Soviet support for its cause in Cyprus as well as diversify its trade and economic aid opportunities. For the same reasons Turkey began to pursue an active policy toward the non-aligned countries, too. Although generally unsuccessful in changing the position of either the Soviet Block or the non-aligned countries on the Cyprus issue, (they generally favored the non aligned Cyprus to NATO member Turkey). Turkey's new "multilateral" approach opened up many new avenues for international cooperation.

Among the non-aligned countries, Turkey showed particular regard to Arab and Muslim countries. Turkey's relations with most Arab countries had earlier been beset by such obstacles as its strong identification with Western interests in the Middle East, its attempts to incorporate the Arab countries in the Western system of alliance, and by its recognition of ISRAEL. But in the 1960s Ankara began to systematically court the friendship of the Arab world, taking care not to interfere in inter-Arab squabbles and adopting a more pro-Arab position on the ARAB ISRAEL CONFLICT. In September 1969 Turkey for the first time participated officially in the Islamic Conference meeting in Rabat and it later became a fully fledged member of the organization. With the oil crisis in 1973, and the severe problems encountered by the Turkish economy in the following years, Turkey showed even greater zeal in building bridges with the countries of the Middle East, particularly with the oil producing countries, such as Iraq, LIBYA and Iran. While these countries were not always willing to meet Turkey's requirements for special terms, cooperation between Turkey and the Arab world in such fields as trade, investment and the export of labor grew substantially. A corollary to this process was a significant cooling in Turkish-Israeli relations. In October 1979 Turkey allowed the PLO to open an office in Ankara and in July the following year, when an Israeli law proclaimed unified Jerusalem as the eternal capital of the state of Israel, lowered its diplomatic representation in Israel to the level of second-secretary. Trade and other forms of cooperation between the two countries were "frozen" and virtually stopped.

Nevertheless, notwithstanding the *rapprochement* between Turkey, the Soviet block and the non aligned world, Turkey remained faithful to its alliance with the West. But relations with the United States were tense. American pressure seeking to cease the production of opium, led in August 1971 to a Turkish ban on growing poppies which was a major crop in Turkey. The Turkish government in the face of public pressure revoked the ban in 1974. A serious conflict erupted in February 1975 when the American Congress declared an embargo on the shipment of arms to Turkey following its occupation of northern Cyprus. Turkey responded by suspending the Defence Cooperation Agreement signed between the two countries in 1969 and closing down some American installations on its soil. Relations remained strained until 1980 when the Defence and Economic Co-operation Agreement was signed, and Congress had repealed its restrictions on arms shipments. Other strains on the relationship between American-Turkish relationsship included periodic resolutions adopted in the American Congress to commemorate the Armenian massacres of World War I. But Turkey has never renounced its alliance and cooperation with the United States and America remains its chief arms supplier and the chief guarantor of its security in times of need. The relationship was further strengthened after the 1979 Soviet invasion of Afghanistan and the Islamic revolution in Iran. These events demonstrated to both sides the importance of their alliance for the security and stability of the region.

Turkey's interest in cooperation with Europe likewise remained strong due to the requirements of the alliance and also to its trade with European countries which was developing fast. The presence of large numbers of Turkish workers in Germany and other West European countries—some 2.5 million Turks by the end of the 1970s—was another consideration, as was Turkey's natural desire to belong to the "family" of Western-European countries. In September 1963 Turkey reached an agreement of association with the European Community envisaging several preliminary phases along a seventeen year road until Turkey could apply for full membership. The process met various delays, but in April 1987, Turkey made a formal application for membership. However, much to its disappointment, the decision on admittance was deferred until 1993 but by early 1997, the European Union had still to consider Turkey's application. Additionally it had become evident that not only was Turkey's membership uncertain, but other countries applying later (such as East European countries) might gain membership prior to Turkey. Reasons for European hesitation to admit Turkey include Turkey's poor economic performance; European fears of being flooded by Turkish workers; Turkey's troublesome relationship with Greece; its record on human rights, and—and in the Turkish mind—the cultural and religious differences that distinguish it from the rest of Europe. European bodies such as the European Community or the Council of Europe have not refrained from applying sanctions against Turkey after the military intervention against Cyprus in 1980 and other occasions but Turkey continued to actively pursue its goal, and in December 1995 signed a Customs Union agreement with the EU, granting it at least some of the full member benefits.

When the Soviet Union disintegrated and the Cold War came to an end in 1991, Turkey was presented with the problem of maintaining strategic importance in Western eyes, especially given the danger of continued instability in the Middle East and the area formerly comprising the Soviet Union. Turkey was generally on good terms with Iraq, due to its dependency on Iraqi OIL imports and both countries' common interest in suppressing Kurdish aspirations. But Turkey had long been apprehensive about Iraqi leader Saddam HUSSEIN's military build up and when the Gulf crisis erupted following Iraq's invasion of KUWAIT in August 1990, Turkey placed itself squarely on the side of the American led coalition. Turkey was first to respond to the UN resolution applying sanctions on Iraq by shutting off the flow of Iraqi oil through its territory. Turkey also deployed a large army on its border with Iraq and once the GULF WAR began, in January 1991, it allowed American warplanes to attack Iraqi targets from bases in its territory. For all its help Turkey was a major contributor to the success of the American coalition. Following the war Turkey showed great concern with the fate of Northern Iraq, providing a base for operation "Provide Comfort" and for supervising the no-fly zone imposed by the coaliton. Turkey strongly opposed a settlement which might lead to the creation of a Kurdish state and the dissolution of Iraq, because Turkey lost billions of dollars as a result of the santions against Iraq. Turkey also showed interest in the early lifting of the sanctions.

With the final collapse of the Soviet Union, Turkey began to establish relations with the new republics emerging on the ruins of the former Soviet Empire. Particular attention was given to the Turkic republics with which Turkey had linguistic, cultural and historical bonds—Azerbaijan, Kazakhstan, Uzbekistan, Kyrgyzstan and Turkmenistan. Turkey, at the end of 1991, was quick to recognize them as independent states, establishing diplomatic relations with them. Frequent visits of leaders and officials were exchanged and a host of agreements of cooperation signed in all fields. Turkey was also the moving spirit behind several all-Turkic conferences convened with the participation of the Turkic republics and communities. Turkey was motivated in part by strong sentiments of solidarity with her newly-found brethren, but primarily by hopes of finding new outlets for Turkish trade and business in the new developing Turkish world. It also viewed this new opening toward "Eurasia" (*Avrasya*) as an opening to opportunities for links with Europe and the West, thus increasing its standing in international relations.

Turkey at the same time fostered cooperation with such Black Sea countries—and established a forum for Black Sea Cooperation with the participation of the riparian and Caucasian countries. An important development in Turkey's foreign policy since the early 1990s was the improvement of relations with Israel. Several factors brought the two countries together: such as the oil glut and the lessening of Turkish dependency on Arab oil; Turkish concern over TERRORISM and instability in the Middle East (involving such countries as Syria, Iraq and Iran); and the peace process between Israel and its neighbors. Signs of improvement had begun in the 1980s, but the process was accelerated after Turkey and Israel exchanged ambassadors in December 1991. Visits of Turkish President Süleyman DEMIREL to Israel in late 1995 and Israeli President Ezer WEIZMANN to Turkey in mid-1996 cemented the tightening relations. Most significant were two agreements on military cooperation signed in 1995 and 1996, one for airforce

training in each other's country and the other for the upgrading of Turkish F-4 fighter bombers by the Israeli aircraft industry. There was also an increase in trade between the two countries, as well as a rise in the number of Israeli tourists visiting Turkey.

Following the rise to power of the Islamic Welfare Party headed by Necmettin ERBAKAN in July 1996, there was widespread speculation that Turkey might choose to strengthen its relations with the Muslim world and disassociate itself from Europe and the West as recommended by the ruling Party's platform. Erbakan began his term of office with trips to several Muslim countries, signed a multi-billion contract with Iran for the supply of natural gas, and initiated plans for forming an organization of the eight most developed Muslim countries. However, no significant change was made in Turkey's foreign policy orientation. Ankara continued to express her loyalty to NATO and her close association with the United States and Europe. Even the military cooperation with Israel, which caused much resentment and criticism among Arab regimes and Iran, continued to develop despite the Prime Minister's reservations, mainly due to the military's adherence to this policy.

Domestic Political History In the past 125 years, Turkey twice has witnessed radical changes in its political regime. In 1878 Sultan Abdel Hamid (1876–1909), suspended the first Ottoman Constitution and dissolved Parliament. His reign, which ended with the Young Turks' revolution in 1908, was a heavy-handed personal autocracy. It also put renewed emphasis on the Islamic character of the state, although the nineteenth century reforms towards secularization and modernization were not discarded. The Young Turks forced the Sultan to reactivate the Constitution and convene a new parliament. He was accused of an attempted counter-coup and deposed in 1909, replaced by Mehmet V. Reshad.

The Young Turks, western oriented in education and outlook, introduced political, economic and social reforms. However, various wars and insurrections prevented them from implementing their reform program. Though the semblance of democratic procedure remained, the regime soon drifted into a new authoritarianism, let by a triumvirate of Cemal (Jamal), Enver and Talat. They limited the power and hold of the traditional religious institutions, but due to the dictates of their Islamic policy (trying to keep the Arabs within the framework of the empire) they were not abolished entirely.

The defeat of the Ottoman Empire in World War I ended the Young Turk regime and the traditional foundations on which the state had rested. This paved the way for the establishment of the modern Turkish national state. The achievement of full independence and territorial integrity made it possible for Nationalist Turkey, under the leadership of Mustafa Kemal (Atatürk), to embark on a far-reaching program of political economic and social reform. With the old regime discarded, and the country destitute, Mustafa Kemal resolved to create a new Turkey on the Western secular pattern.

The first steps towards reform had been taken during the war of independence when, in April 1920, the Grand National Assembly convened to replace the dissolved Ottoman Parliament. Under the law of Fundamental Organization adopted in January 1921, the Assembly was given executive and legislative powers in the name of the sovereign nation. Loyalty was still professed to the Ottoman Sultan, but in November 1922, in the face of the Sultan's fight against the Nationalists, the Sultanate was abolished altogether. However, a spiritual Caliphate was to remain in the Ottoman dynasty. As Sultan Mehmed VI Vahideddin fled the country, his cousin Abdülmecid was elected to this office. In October 1923 the Turkish Republic was announced, Mustafa Kemal elected as its first President, and Ismet Pasha (Inönü) as Premier. Ankara was made its capital. In March 1924 Mustafa Kemal, as part of his growing program of secularization, had the Assembly abolish the Caliphate, and the Ottoman dynasty was exiled from the country. In April 1924 the first Turkish Constitution was announced, incorporating and extending the constitutional steps already taken. Kemal's chief political instrument in Parliament was the People's Party, later renamed Republican People's Party (RPP, *Cümhuriyet Halk Partisi*), formed in August 1923 out of the League for the Defence of the Right of Anatolia and Rumelia. Following these political reforms other measures of departure from the Ottoman-Islamic past were taken. Along with the Caliphate, the office of the *Seyh (Sheikh)-ul-Islam*, i.e., (the head of the religious hierarchy), the Ministry of Religious Affairs and *Evkaf* (religious endowments, see WAQF), were abolished in 1924. All schools were placed under the supervision of the Ministry of Public Instruction, which soon closed all the religious seminaries (*Medrese*). Muslim courts were also closed (see SHARI'A) as, later, were religious orders (*Tarikat*) (see DERVISH ORDERS), monasteries (*Tekke*) and holy tombs *Türbe*). In 1925 the traditional headgear (*tarbush, fez*) was prohibited and the international calendar and time systems were adopted. New civil, criminal and commercial codes, based on European models were introduced in 1926. Two of the most radical and far-reaching reforms were made in 1928. One abolished the clause in the Constitution declaring Islam to be the state religion, whilst the other discarded the old Arabic script used in Turkey in favor of a new one based on the Latin alphabet. The change of alphabet was to proceed further in the 1930s, when the Turkish Language Society initiated an ambitious project of purifying the language of all its foreign forms and of most of its Arabic and Persian words. Foreign words which had become part of the vocabulary were replaced by pure Turkish words taken from local dialects, other Turkic languages, or invented. The emancipation of women already advanced by the introduction of the new civil code, was completed in 1935, when women were accorded full political rights. Other reforms included the requirement that citizens adopt family names (1934), and the proclamation of Sunday as the weekly day of rest instead of Friday (1935).

In the economic sphere, Kemal concentrated on developing Turkey's rich mineral resources, industry and communications. With the memory of the Capitulations still alive, and unwilling to risk Turkey's political independence by the importation of foreign capital, he initiated the policy of *tatism*, in which the state was to be the chief investor and owner of large enterprises and to exercise close control over planning and development. Industrializing was at its height in the 1930s especially during the first Five-Year Plan from 1934.

Despite Kemal's charismatic leadership, he encountered serious opposition to his rule and reforms from the outset. At the end of 1924, some of his previous collagues, such as Rauf (Orbay) and Ali Fuad (Cebesoy), organized the conservative Progressive People's Party. Early in 1925 a Kurdish insurrection broke out in the eastern provinces (motivated by displeasure with Kemal's secularism and by Kurdish nationalist sentiments), and was put down by the middle of the year. The rebellion's leaders were sentenced to death by a special Independent Tribunal, although further disturbances occurred. Accused of complicity in the revolt, the Progressive Party was disbanded. In 1930 former premier Fethi (Okyar) founded the Liberal Republican Party, with the approval of Kemal. However, this experiment in opposition politcs was short lived: and failing in municipal elections, and accused variously of reactionary leanings and communism, the Party was soon dissolved. The RPP continued to rule for the next fifteen years unopposed, though a measure of criticism was allowed in the press and in Parliament. In 1937 the six major principles of the RPP—republicanism, nationalism, populism, *étatism*, secularism, and reformism—were incorporated into the state constitution. The Party made great efforts to inculcate the people with its ideas. One of its methods was the establishment of People's Houses in urban areas, or People's Rooms in villages, to serve as centers of cultural activity and indoctrination. But large segments of the population were not won over by Kemal's policies and reforms. The conservative elements, particularly the peasants, rejected secularism. The commercial classes resented the heavy hand of the government on the economy, while still others opposed the authoritarianism of the RPP and the personal rule of its chief.

Signs of opposition increased after Atatürk's death in 1938, under the rule of his successor, President Ismet Inönü. Conditions in Turkey during World War II accentuated existing grievances. Shortages and rising prices, the levying of a capital tax with punitive measures (directed mainly against minorities), and repressive measures against the press, all contributed to growing dissatisfaction and a demand for liberalization. This coincided with increasing support for democracy following the victory of the Western Powers in the war.

At the end of 1945, Inönü announced his support for a multiparty system and several new parties were established. The most important (as it turned out), was the Democratic Party, (DP) founded in January 1946 by previous members of RPP, such as Celal BAYAR, Adnan Menderes and Refik Koraltan. The Party advocated free enterprise and political freedom, and its popular support was soon demonstrated in the 1946 elections. Concern at the

DP's success and desire to block its progress brought about a rift in RPP and the replacement of authoritarian Premier Recep Peker by Hasan Saka in 1947. It also brought about some liberalization toward the economy and religion. However, in the elections of May 1950, the DP (despite a split in its own ranks in 1948 and the formation of a rival National Party) won by a large majority. The transfer of power occurred peacefully, and Celal Bayar was elected President and Adnan Menderes formed the government.

The victory of the DP was largely due to the support from the peasant population in Turkey, which remained its chief support throughout its rule. Although outwardly committed to secularism and curbing reactionary manifestations, the DP relaxed the secularist anti-religious attitude of the previous regime. It also assisted the peasants economically with loans, public works, etc. Its supporters among the business classes benefited from a relaxation in government controls and the encouragement of local and foreign investment. Helped by increasing foreign aid and favorable weather conditions for agriculture, the economy was booming in the early 1950s.

The government failed however, to implement its liberal principles in the political arena. In 1953 it confiscated the property of the RPP and closed the People's Houses. Rigid new Press Laws were adopted in 1954 and 1956. Critical journalists were prosecuted and newspapers suspended. Politically motivated interference in the judiciary, civil service and academic appointments, all became commonplace. A turn for the worse in the economic situation, inflation and the growing public debt made the government increasingly unpopular, as did anti-Greek and anti-minority riots in Istanbul in September 1955. In 1955 the DP itself split, and the seceding faction founded the Freedom Party. The decline in the popularity of the DP and its government was illustrated in the 1957 elections. The DP was returned to power, but with a smaller margin of votes and the RPP made considerable gains. However, the government did not change its policies and growing criticism by the opposition was met with further repression.

During this period unrest had spread to the army. Kept out of politics by Atatürk (but in fact loyal to Kemalist), army officers became anxious in the face of the deterioration of the economy; the growing internal tensions, and the government's failure to preserve Kemalist principles. In 1959 and early 1960 the confrontation between the RPP and the DP and its government became critical, with violent repercussions. The most serious incident occurred in April 1960 when troops were ordered to prevent Ismet Inönü (leader of the opposition) from conducting a political tour. Following the arrest of several officers, General Cemal Gürsel (Commander of the Land Forces who had been in contact with army conspirators) resigned. The government set up a commission of inquiry into the activities of the opposition, and subsequently banned all political activities. By the end of the month, students held demonstrations, resulting in clashes, casualties and the imposition of martial law. The use of the army in supressing the opposition deepened the crisis. On 27 May 1960, the army staged a bloodless coup that brought the ten-year rule of the DP to an end.

From May 1960 until October 1961 Turkey was ruled by a National Unity Committee, composed of the leading rebel officers. Cemal Gürsel was President of the Republic, Premier and Minister of Defence. The DP was banned and its leaders put on trial, charged with breaches of the constitution, responsibility for the 1955 riots and corruption. In the trial (held from October 1960 to May 1961 on the island of Yassiada near Istanbul) 15 leaders were sentenced to death and about 430 imprisoned (including 31 to life terms). Menderes and 2 of his ministers were executed, while 12 death sentences were commuted to life imprisonment (including Bayar); 138 were acquitted. The NUC ruled through a largely civilian cabinet and declared its aim to be the return of the country to democratic rule. Fourteen radical members of the NUC who favored long-term military rule and wide reform were purged in November 1960. In January political parties were permitted to resume their activities and several new parties emerged. The same month, a Constituent Assembly was convened (with the NUC as the Upper House), to draft a new constitution that would prevent future governments from such abuses of power as those perpetrated by the old regime. The new constitution drafted with the help of a special commission of experts and professors was approved by a national referendum in July 1961. Elections were held in October 1961 and gave the RPP 173 seats in the 450-member Assembly and 36 in the 150-member Senate. Second in the elections came the newly

formed Justice Party (*Adalet Partisi*), founded by General Ragip Gümüşpala and seen as the successor of the outlawed DP, with 158 seats in the Assembly, and 70 in the Senate. Cemal Gürsel was elected President, and Ismet Inönü formed a RPP-JP coalition government.

The first years of the Second Republic failed to produce civilian rule and political stability. The army still kept an eye on political developments. The NUC members became partners in the regime by being nominated life members of the Senate, and when in May 1966, Gürsel's health deteriorated, the Chief-of-Staff General Cevdet SUNAY, was elected President. Two abortive coups in February 1962 and May 1963, both led by Colonel Talat Aydemir, proved that some officers' groups still wanted to take the reins of power into their own hands. As no single Party had a majority in the Assembly, coalition governments were necessary, and frequent crises ensued.

The RPP-JP coalition (supported by the army) fell in May 1962, over a heated debate on a proposed amnesty for the political prisoners of the Yassiada trials. The issue was later settled by a second Inönü cabinet which was formed in coalition with the minor parties and without the JP. This was done by the deduction of four years from the jail sentences, leading to the release of many convicts. (Subsequently all the prisoners, including Celal Bayar, were released on various grounds.) The government also adopted a five-year plan, providing for a wide-scale development program. Disenchantment with the RPP and their own failure in local elections in November 1963, induced the minor parties to leave the government. A third Inönü government had to rely on the support of independents and it collapsed in February 1965. This time an independent senator, Suat Ürgüplü, formed an interim government until the elections, composed of all Parties except the RPP, with the leading role assumed by the JP whose leader, Süleyman Demirel, became Deputy Premier.

The JP returned to power in October 1965 gaining an absolute majority of 240 seats, and Demirel formed a JP government. The RPP, with only 134 seats, was once again pushed to the back benches. The JP's growth and overwhelming election sucess showed that it had gained the votes of many who had previously supported the DP particularly the conservative, religiously-minded masses and the peasant, who had been indifferent or hostile to the 1960 revolution. In the general election of October 1969, the Party increased its number of seats in the Assembly from 240 to 256, compared to the 143 held by the RPP. The remaining seats were held by minor parties and independents.

As Prime Minister, Demirel tried to steer a careful course and avoid the excesses and mistakes of the DP. He committed himself to furthering economic development and social reform, whilst maintaining political liberalism and freedom of expression. Nevertheless, criticism of Demirel and his government became increasingly severe. Frequent splits in his Justice Party (both for political and personal reasons) gradually reduced his majority in Parliament. The most serious split occurred with the defection of the right-wing deputies under the leadership of Saadettin Bilgic in February 1970 (forcing Demirel to resign and form a new government). The most vehement critics of the government came from among the intellectual classes who clung to Kemalist and Socialist principles. They accused the government of ruinous economic policies (entailing inflation and a worsening balance of payments), a failure to introduce social (particularly land) reform and yielding to foreign capitalism and American domination. These critics belonged to the RPP, the newly formed Marxist Workers' Party, student and youth organizations, and Leftist labor unions. Militant youth organizations became a continuous embarrassment to the government, striking or rioting on issues of university reform as well as internal and foreign policy. By 1970, student riots and clashes between rightist and leftist groups had become the order of the day, resulting in bloodshed, the closure of the universities and the imposition of martial law. Matters came to a head in the early months of 1971 when militant leftist youth organizations carried out a series of explosions, bank robberies and kidnappings of US servicemen (subsequently released) and the government appeared unable to curb the violence.

Signs were once more evident of the army's displeasure with the government and its increasing determination to intervene in a decisive manner. Impelled partly by these motives (and partly from fear of a more radical army coup), on 12 March 1971 Commander-in-Chief, General Memduh Tagmac, along with three other prominent military of-ficers, gave the President and leaders of Parliament an ultimatum, that unless a strong national government was formed which would end the anarchy and initiate economic and social reforms, the army would takeover. Demirel resigned at once, and the whole event was termed a "coup by memorandum".

Complying with the army's wishes, a national, non-partisan cabinet was formed by Nihat Erim, a member of the right wing of the RPP (who duly resigned his membership), and made up of a majority of non political technocrats (later replaced by JP politicians). The government adopted a program for the restoration of law and order and social and economic reform. With the army given virtually a free hand, it cracked down on terrorism by proclaiming martial law in eleven provinces and conducting massive arrests among radical leftist groups. Repression became particularly heavy after the abduction and assassination in May of the Israeli consul general in Istanbul, Ephraim Elrom. Arrests became more widespread and the freedoms of the universities, the media and other organizations were curtailed by constitutional amendments. The Islamist National Order Party and the Marxist Workers Party were closed. Finding his position tenuous because of the withdrawal of Demirel's support, Erim resigned in April 1972 and was succeeded by Ferit Melen of the Republican Reliance Party. Although repression largely continued, politicians were gradually reasserting their position *vis-a-vis* the army. A major battle was fought between them in 1973 over the election of a new president, and in the face of the politicians' objection to the army's candidate, former Chief of Staff Faruk Gürler, the retired admiral Fahri KORUTÜRK, was elected in April. This was regarded as a compromise and was accepted by all sides. Naim Talu was appointed Prime Minister and the country prepared for the general elections to be held in October 1973.

The elections of 1973 did not give any party an absolute majority. The RPP emerged as the biggest party with 185 seats (and thirty-three percent of the vote), a result seen partly as a protest against the military intervention and partly as the success of the new leader Bülent Ecevit (who had ousted Inönü in 1972) to appeal to wide sections of the public with his social democratic platform. The JP came second with 149 seats, and the rest were divided between smaller parties. Third place was won by the National

Salvation Party (a reincarnation of the National Order Party), under Necmettin Erbakan. After lengthy negotiations Ecevit formed a government in January 1974 with the National Salvation Party and with Erbakan as his deputy. Although ideologically dissimilar, the two Parties found common ground in their support for small enterprise and their commitment to social justice. But Ecevit resigned in September in the hope that his rise in popularity over the Cyprus invasion would bring him victory in early elections. This proved a miscalculation since, after an interim period when a national non-partisan cabinet was formed by Sadi Irmak, Demirel's JP succeeded in March 1975 in forming a "National Front" coalition with smaller rightist and centrist parties including Erbakan's Salvation Party—which sustained until the elections in 1977.

The general situation in the country had meanwhile significantly deteriorated. The oil crisis in 1973 had a most adverse effect on the Turkish economy as the country struggled to safeguard its supply of energy and pay the high prices demanded by world market. Turkey, with imports far exceeding its exports, had traditionally suffered from a negative balance of trade, but had succeeded in covering at least part of its deficit by remittances received by migrant Turkish workers and external loans and credits. However, the burden on the country's foreign exchange reserves now became intolerable and Turkey found it increasingly difficult not only to pay for the cost of energy, but to allocate the sums for the importation of necessary machinery, spare parts and consumer goods. Industry and development suffered greatly gave rise to unemployment as well as shortages and rising prices. Europe's economic depression also meant that remittances from Turkish workers were decreasing and opportunities for work abroad were widely curtailed.

The economic crisis had its own effect in adding to social discontent and restlessness which was already manifest among the poorer members of society—workers, urban migrants, students and the vast number of unemployed. Members of minority groups such as the Kurds and the Alevis were also among the disaffected, combining their socioeconomic grievances with their feelings of alienation and discrimination by the majority. These feelings deepened in the course of the 1970s, leading once again to expanded radicalism and violence. Some of the radical groups (mainly on the extreme right) were, under the patronage of official parties such as the so called Grey Wolves (the "Commandos") which was affiliated with Türkes' Nationalist Action Party. These became the source of increasing violence, which the government (with Türkes as a leading member), was powerless to curb. Opposing the rightists on the left were a host of splinter groups and factions from the left who increasingly used terrorism as a policical tactic. Rallies, demonstrations and strikes organized by leftist trade unions added to the anarchy.

In the face of these worsening conditions, both major Parties agreed on early elections in June 1977. Results favored both (at the expense of the smaller parties), but still did not result in an absolute majority. Ecevit came out strongest from the polls but failed to gain the parliament's confidence. Demirel who formed a second "National Front" government, was himself defeated in the Assembly shortly afterwards. In January 1978 Ecevit formed yet another Government, only to be replaced again by Demirel in November. These frequent governmental changes were a reflection of the Parties' failure to cope with Turkey's acute problems, as well as their inability to come together for the sake of the country. A coalition between the two major Parties proved impossible because of the great personal rivalry between Ecevit and Demirel. When President Korutürk's term of office came to an end in April 1980, these parties could not even agree on a successor in 100 rounds in the Assembly. By that time the crisis in the country had assumed alarming proportions. Desperate efforts to reform the economy along lines proposed by the IMF were being made, and a stabilization program was announced by Demirel in January 1980—under the supervision of Turgut Özal. But a second "wave" of the oil crisis following the Iranian revolution had brought much suffering to the population resulting in the industry's virtual standstill due to oil and electricity shortages. In addition, terrorism raged claiming nearly twenty victims a day. Terrorist targets were well known public figures (like Erim). Kurdish underground groups, such as Abdallah Ocalan's PKK participated in the carnage, and Armenian groups, notably ASALA, assassinated Turkish officials abroad. Sectarianism also (formed by ultra nationalists and fundamentalists) resulted in the a series of bloody riots between Sunnis and Alevis in different parts of the country.

Under these circumstances an army coup once again seemed inevitable. Precipitating the army's move was a rally under the slogan "save Jerusalem" held in early September 1980 by the National Salvation Party in Konya. The actual coup was staged on 12 September by a group of top commanders appointing themselves to the National Security Council (NSC). Justifying their move by their concern for the integrity and unity of the country and their loyalty to Kemalism, they resolved to restructure governmental institutions. The head of the NSC, Chief of Staff Kenan Evren, became head of state, and the cabinet was replaced by one of bureaucrats and retired officers, headed by Bülent Ulusu and including Özal as deputy Prime Minister. The constitution was suspended and the National Assembly dissolved. All political Parties (as well as radical trade unions) were banned and their leaders arrested. (Ecevit and Demirel were eventually released without trial and Türkes and Erbakan were released only following trial.) Many governors, mayors and municipal councils were also dismissed. Strikes were prohibited, as were all political activities. The press was heavily censored and the universities put under strict control.

Although the army vowed to re-institute democracy, the country would undergo a thorough clean up in the process. Tens of thousands of "dangerous" public figures and officials were arrested, but the army saved its most severe treatment for suspected terrorists, from all sides of the political spectrum. Martial law was declared, and thousands were rounded up, tried, and given harsh sentences. Many were executed.

Repeating the acts of the 1960 generals, Evren and his colleagues began proceedings toward a new constitution aimed at preventing the recurrence of anarchy. A constituent assembly was convened and a constitutional committee charged with formatting a draft constitution. After review by the NSC the draft was approved by referendum in November 1982, simultaneously confirming Evren's position as the next President. Presidential powers were increased and some political freedoms were limited in order to provide for a new kind of political order marked by stability. With a new Political Party Law adopted, the ban on political activity was removed in April 1983, and several new parties emerged after approval by the NSC. These were the centrist Na-

tionalist Democracy Party (NDP) headed by Turgut Sunalp, a retired general; the Kemalist Populist Party (PP), headed by Necdet Calp; and the right of center Motherland Party (MP), headed by Turgut Özal. Old party leaders had been banned from political activity for a period of ten years (other veteran politicians for five) but they were quick to establish "new" parties officially led by others.

Although the army supported the NDP, Özal won the October 1983 elections. He was popular due to his anti-statist posture and successful economic policies; and veteran politicians were still unable to challenge him. Although he was short of an absolute majority from the popular vote, the new electoral system benefited large parties, and gave him a comfortable majority—212 out of 400 seats in the National Assembly. He formed a government composed largely of engineers—his own recruits—and in the following years proved his ability to maintain a firm grip on his government and his Party.

The army's campaign of repression, resulted in a sharip decline of terrorism. However, Özal faced two major problems in office. One was the economy, in which he continued to follow the liberal policies initiated by him under Demirel and the military regime. These had already begun to bring about a remarkable economic growth rate, a dramatic increase in exports, and an improvement in the balance of payments, although his free interest policy caused prices to rise once again. The other was the ongoing Kurdish insurgency in the southeast which in 1984 took an ominous turn with the declaration of an all out war against the authorities by the PKK, with a growing number of casualties on both sides. The policy adopted by Özal was basically to follow the army's prescription of suppression by force. But Özal did give importance to economic development in the area, in which the Southeast Anatolia Project (GAP) was progressing in full swing. Özal went as far as conceding the need to grant the Kurds certain cultural rights, but little was done in this direction.

Responding to internal and outside pressure, Özal put the matter of restoring the political rights of the old party leaders to a referendum. This took place in September 1987, and was approved by a close vote, passing by a margin of one percent. To prevent his rivals from organizing elections, Özal called for early elections in November, which he won again with an overwhelming majority of 292 seats (out of 450) but a reduced share (36.29%) of the popular vote. This was a clear sign that the power of the MP was already being successfully challenged by some of the old names in Turkish politics. The Social Democratic Populist Party (SODEPOP), led by Professor Erdal Inönü, son of Ismet, won ninety-nine seats with a quarter of the popular vote; the True Path Party (TPP), led by the veteran Demirel, came third with fifty-nine seats. Not so successful were the Democratic Left Party (DLP), led by Ecevit, and the Welfare Party (WP), led by Erbakan, both of which failed to clear the ten percent threshold required for representation in the Assembly.

Dwindling support for the MP was also due to various corruption scandals and the fact that inflation was once again on the rise. This may have played a role in Özal's decision to run for the Presidency when Evren's term ended in November 1989. Özal calculated that his failures and his dwindling support might soon end his political career, but that the majority he had in Parliament could still secure him seven years in office. Having been elected—the second civilian President in the history of the Republic after Celal Bayar—he was succeeded in the premiership by Yildirim Akbulut, who was in turn replaced by Mesut YILMAZ in June 1991 head of the Liberal wing of the Party. All along Özal continued to interfere in state affairs and was largely responsible for the position Turkey took during the Gulf War. But criticism of Özal at home, as well as continued economic difficulties which the government failed to overcome, led to the defeat of the MP in the October 1991 general elections. Although short of an absolute majority, Demirel's TPP won 178 seats, the MP 115 seats, and the SODEPOP 88 seats. Ecevit's DLP, with seven seats suffered—like the Social Democrats themselves—from the split in the left. On the other hand, Erbakan's WP showed clear signs of a political comeback taking 62 seats.

Personal rivalry between Demirel and Özal agreed to joint the of the two major parties, and a coalition was formed between the TPP and the SODEPOP, with Inönü becoming deputy Prime Minister. Still eager for power, Özal continued his active role in state affairs but, with a strong Demirel, a delicate balance had to be maintained. There were no core policy differences that divided the two major Parties since Demirel basically followed Özal's policies

of loyalty to the Western alliance and liberalization of the economy, whilst adopting a harsher line toward the Kurdish insurgency. When Özal suddenly died in April 1993 Demirel decided to run for President viewing this as an appropriate culmination of a long political career in which he bounced back after two military coups. After his election, his associate Tansu ÇILLER was elected as leader of the Party and was appointed by him as Prime Minister. She became the first woman Party leader and Prime Minister in Turkish history.

Çiller retained the coalition with the Social Democrats and advanced Demirel's policies. But her term of office was beset by many problems. On the personal side, Çiller had to continuously confront charges of corruption and demands for the investigation of her personal wealth. Inflation continued to spiral and with the limited sources of revenue (stemming partly from inefficient taxation and the high costs of services and state enterprises), there was a growing deficit in national coffers. The Kurdish insurgency continued unabated and claimed over 20,000 victims between 1984. Furthermore, Kurdish opposition appeared in Parliament when leftist and Kurdish members associated with the Social Democrats became organized as a political Party under the name of the People's Labor Party (PLP). It was closed by the constitutional court in 1993 and again in 1994—under its new name Democracy Party (DEP)—when its deputies were arrested and tried. Increasingly, human rights were becoming a public issue and a subject of great pressure from the West, but the process of democratization promised by Çiller proved to be a slow one. There were also disagreements on this issue with her coalition partners, the Social Democrats, who, in 1995, dissolved their Party and incorporated with Deniz Baykal's newly founded Republican People's Party (RPP). In September Baykal withdrew his Party's support from the government and agreed to rejoin only on condition that early elections be held and that an amendment to the Prevention of Terrorism Law be passed.

The results of the elections held in December 1995 failed to resolve the country's chronic political crisis. In an Assembly expanded to 550, members the WP won 158 seats (21.4% of the vote), TPP–135 (19.2%), MP–132 (19.7%), DLP–76 (14.6%) and the newly formed RPP–49 (10.7%). Other Parties including the People's Democratic Party (PDP) (an incarnation of the Kurdish DEP), failed to win enough votes to enter the Assembly. The emergence of Erbakan's Islamist WP as the largest political power caused enormous shock waves in Turkey and abroad, given the secular character of the state and the Kemalist legacy. Yet this was hardly surprising given the Party's rising appeal amongst the voters. With wide sections of the public still adhering to religious and conservative norms, the "Islamist solution" attracted many of the disaffected classes of society—peasants, lower and middle class town dwellers, Kurds and the like—as a possible way out of their daily hardships. The major secularist parties had all opportunities in government, but no real improvement had occurred, and their leaders seemed to be infested by corruption and self-serving material gains. The WP, by contrast, had already made impressive gains in municipal elections, and their record in governing cities like Istanbul and Ankara seemed clean, efficient and compassionate.

Erbakan was the first to try his hand at forming a government. He failed due to the professed determination of both TPP and MP to keep the Islamists out of power. Subsequently, after much haggling, and in spite of the personal antipathy between Çiller and Yilmaz, both Parties joined together forming a coalition, based on the principle of a rotating premiership. (Mesut Yilmaz became Prime Minister, to be replaced by Tansu Çiller after one year in office, and then returning after two years for the last part). The coalition was supported from the outside by the DLP. But the government did not remain empowered for long for two reasons. Firstly, the MP supported a WP motion to investigate an alleged corruption by Çiller. Secondly, there was a constitution court ruling which invalidated the vote of confidence. With no other real alternative in sight Erbakan was called once again to form a government and in July received the vote of confidence for a coalition government with the TPP—the first Islamist-led government in secular Turkish history. Çiller became deputy Prime Minister and Foreign Minister, and it was agreed again to apply the principle of a rotating premiership—Erbakan for the first two years, followed by Çiller.

By the spring of 1997 the new government seemed fairly stable and it was widely believed that what kept the two partners together was their mutual commitment to refrain from investigations into each other's affairs. With the Kurdish insurgency slowly placed under control, the main internal issue confronting the government was the economy which remained fragile, particularly in terms of the budget deficit and high inflation. Curiously, given the rhetoric of the WP in the past, no major changes in internal public policy, or in foreign policy, occurred and it was clear that Erbakan was trying not to alienate his partners and particularly the army. The army however, seemed to have accepted the voters' choice only for lack of any practical alternative, and kept close watch on the government's actions. It soon became apparent that some WP members at least were defiantly planning to allow religious garb for women in the public service, to build a grand mosque, in the heart of Istanbul, and to enhance the position of religious education. In response the National Security Council, (including top military commanders), convened to "advise" Erbakan of the need to curb all extreme religious manifestations in the country. Erbakan complied, but other dividing issues, as well as Erbakan's clear reluctance to implement some of the army's demands, triggered growing pressure on him. Seeing his position undermined, Erbakan resigned in June 1977 in the hope that new elections would strengthen his party. His partner Çiller was to head an interim government, but a new coalition was formed instead, headed by MP leader Mesut Yilmaz. This coalition included the DLP and the new Democratic Turkey Party and was backed by the RPP from outside. Erbakan's WP and Çiller's TPP (reduced in power from many defections) were driven into the opposition. In January 1998 the constitutional court resolved to closed down the Islamic Welfare Party on grounds of violating the principle of secularization.

Constitution, Government and Politics

Turkey's Constitution of 1982, superseding the one promulgated in 1961, reflected the wish to uphold Turkey's democratic regime while introducing stronger safeguards against instability and anarchy of the kind which led to the 1980 military intervention. It proclaimed the Turkish Republic as a democratic, secular and social state, governed by the rule of law, respecting human rights and loyal to the nationalism of Atatürk. Like its predecessor, it detailed the fundamental rights and duties of the individual citizens, which were all declared equal before the law. Rights and freedoms were inviolable and inalienable, but it was possible to restrict them by law for the sake of ensuring "the integrity of the state" and "the public interest". The Legislative Power was vested in the Grand National Assembly composed of 400 deputies (later increased to 450 and again to 550), elected every five years by all citizens over twenty-one (reduced to 18). The Executive Power is exercised and implemented by the President and the Council of Ministers. The president is elected for a period of seven years by the Grand National Assembly from among its members or those qualified to be deputies. He cannot be reelected. The constitution elevates the president's position from his previous largely ceremonial role, by increasing his powers. He can, for example, return laws to the Assembly for reconsideration or challenge their constitutionality in the Constitutional Court, summon the Assembly or call for new elections; and preside over the Council of Ministers. He appoints the Prime Minister from among the members of the Assembly and has the authority of appointing many other officials in various bodies. Judicial power is exercised by independent courts, which include the Constitutional Court and Courts of the Security of the State. Other bodies prescribed by the constitution are a National Security Council (which has advisory powers and is composed of the President, the Prime Minister, certain ministers and top commanders); a Higher Education Council; and the Atatürk High Institution of Culture, Language and History. The promulgation of the constitution was followed by an electoral law, which upholds the proportional system stipulating that only parties which obtained at least ten percent of the national vote may be represented in the Assembly. The Political Parties Law regulates the organization and activities of the parties. These laws as well as some stipulations of the constitution itself have been the subject of much debate since 1983, objections resting on their restrictive and rather authoritarian character. Several amendments have already been adopted.

Public life in Turkey has always been marked by the existence of many vociferous political parties, which have also been subject to frequent splits, usually on personal grounds. The high ten percent threshold in national elections has greatly restricted the number of parties represented in the Grand National Assembly, and favors the major parties. But the proportional system accounts for the make up of the Assembly which is very fragmented. This has been further enhanced by frequent defections. No political party holds an absolute majority, and it is extremely difficult to form a stable government. The parties represented in November 1997 in the Assembly are: The Welfare Party (*Refah Partisi*) which is reformist in nature and reserved toward the West, advocating Islamist solutions for Turkey's external and internal problems (150 seats, leader—Necmettin Erbakan); the True Path Party (*Dogru Yol Partisi*), center right, pro west (91 seats, leader—Tansu Çiller); Motherland Party (*Anavatan Partisi*), center right (139 seats, leader—Mesut Yilmaz); the Democratic Left Party (*Demokrat Sol Partisi*), center left (63 seats, leader—Devlet Bahçeli); Republican People's Party (*Cumhuriyet Halk Partisi*), center left (54 seats, leader —Deniz Baykal); the Democratic Turkey Party (*Demokrat Türkiye Partisi*) center right (21 seats, leader—Husamettin Cindoruk. Smaller parties are the Nationalist Action Party (*Milliyets' Hareket Partisi*) nationalist rightist; the Grand Unity Party (*Büyük Birlik Partisi*), nationalist-Islamist and the Democratic Party (*Demokrat Partisi*). There are also 19 independents. The People's Democratic Party (*Halkin Demokrasi Partisi*), advocating democratization and Kurdish rights failed to gain representation in the Assembly.

Media Turkey has a lively press devoting much space to political criticism and public affairs. The freedom of the press is guaranteed by the constitution. However, certain restrictions relating to the security, the indivisible integrity of the state and the like apply. There are over thirty dailies, most appearing in Istanbul and Ankara. They are mostly independent, but often have their own political leanings. The largest ones are *Hürriyet* (Freedom), with a circulation of close to a million, *Sabah* (Morning) and *Milliyet* (Nationality). The smaller daily *Cumhuriyet* (Republic) is considered of high standard and read by the more educated classes. So are *Yeni Yüzyil* (New Century) and *Radikal* (Radical). There is also a variety of periodicals, popular magazines and journals which are ideological and intellectual. Like the press, active publishing houses—issuing both original and translated books—are concentrated mainly in Istanbul and Ankara. Radio and television broadcasting is spread throughout the country with stations in the major cities. In the past the public Radio and

Television Corporation (TRT) had a monopoly over all broadcastings but new legislation allowed the establishment of a host of new private and commercial stations.

Higher Education There has been substantial increase in the number of universities in recent years, in an attempt to absorb the growing numbers of high school graduates wishing to acquire higher education.

The number of universities in 1997 was sixty, educating a total of around half a million students.

Most of the universities are public, but there are also a number of private universities, established by foundations, as well as hundreds of higher professional schools. Institutions of higher learning are today spread throughout the country, but the older universities and schools in the major cities Istanbul, Ankara and Izmir are still considered the best. As a result of student and intellectual unrest in the 1960s and 1970s, institutions of higher learning were constitutionally placed under the close control of the Higher Education Council (Yök).

UAE   see UNITED ARAB EMIRATES.

UAR   see UNITED ARAB REPUBLIC.

UMM al-QAIWAIN   The smallest of the seven sheikhdoms of the TRUCIAL COAST, which by 1971 became the UNITED ARAB EMIRATES (UAE). Area: approximately 290 sq. miles (750 sq. km.). The population—until the development of the UAE's oil economy since the 1960s mostly nomadic—was given in a census of 1985 as 20,300, of whom 7,200 were indigenous and 13,100 foreigners. Estimates (1996) quote a number of a little over 35,000. Umm al-Qaiwain was, along with the other Trucial sheikhdoms, a British Protectorate until 1971, when it joined the Federation of the UAE being formed and becoming independent. Within the UAE, the ruler of Umm al-Qaiwain—of the Mu'alla clan—belongs to the Dubai-led camp that seeks less federal authority and more power for individual sheikhdoms. Since the late 1960s, Umm al-Qaiwain has granted several oil concessions to Shell and American companies. No major oil strikes have yet been reported. Lacking large revenues, Umm al-Qaiwain has tried to develop non-oil sources, among them: a free trade zone (established 1988) and tourist attraction, scheduled to begin operation in 1998.

UN RESOLUTION 242 AND 338   see ARAB-ISRAEL PEACEMAKING.

UNDOF   see ARAB-ISRAEL PEACEMAKING.

UNEF   see ARAB-ISRAEL PEACEMAKING.

UNIATE   The union of parts of Eastern churches, *en bloc*, with the Catholic Church, and the Catholic communities thus created. The uniate was based on the acceptance of the dogmas of the Catholic Church and the supreme authority of the Pope, while allowing the uniate communities to maintain their own liturgy, including language (instead of LATIN), and a measure of autonomy, including the uniate community's administrative structure and hierarchy, headed by a Patriarch. Sometimes it was a process in stages so that no precise dates can be given, and dates indicated are in some doubt. The uniate communities in the Middle East (with their previous church in parentheses) are MARONITES (Monothelites, 1182, 1445, 1736); GREEK-CATHOLICS (GREEK ORTHODOX, 1730, 1775); CHALDEANS (NESTORIAN-ASSYRIANS, 1552); ARMENIAN-Catholics (MONOPHYSITE Armenian-Orthodox Gregorians, twelfth century, 1375, 1439); COPT-Catholics (Monophysite Copts, 1741); Syrian Catholics (Monophysite Syrian-Orthodox, 1662). Of these uniate communities, the Maronites, Greek-Catholics and Chaldeans are sizable groups (see entries); the rest are small communities. See also CHRISTIANS.

UNIFIL   see ARAB-ISRAEL PEACEMAKING.

UNITED ARAB EMIRATES (UAE)   A Federation set up and becoming independent, in December 1971, by the seven of the TRUCIAL COAST or Trucial

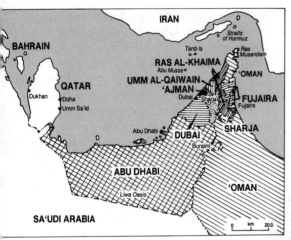

Map of the United Arab Emirates

Oman on the southern, Arabian coast of the PERSIAN GULF—ABU DHABI, DUBAI, SHARJA, RAS AL-KHAIMA, UMM AL-QAIWAIN, AJMAN and al-FUJAIRA. The area of the UAE is 32,000 sq. miles (83,600 sq. km.). The population, estimated at approximately 200,000 when the UAE was first formed, grew rapidly with the development of the country's OIL economy, mainly by the influx of foreign workers from other Arab countries, Pakistan and India. In the mid-1970s it was estimated at approximately 800,000. Official census figures (1992) put the total population of the Emirates at about 2,250,000. Seventy to seventy five percent of them are foreigners. A 1996 law limiting employment for foreigners has already begun to cause a decrease in the number of manual workers.

The seven sheikhdoms had been under British protection since the 1820s. Preparations for independence and the creation of a federation began in earnest in 1968, when BRITAIN announced its decision to abolish its protectorate. Negotiations on the federation were difficult. BAHRAIN and QATAR, which had planned to join it, withdrew. Even when the UAE was established, one of the seven sheikhdoms, Ras al-Khaima, refused to join, joining instead in 1972. The new independent UAE was immediately admitted to the ARAB LEAGUE and the UN in December 1971, and began setting up its federal constitution and administration. In July 1972 a draft constitution was proclaimed. It provided for a Supreme Council of the seven rulers and a Federal National Council composed of representatives of the seven sheikhdoms appointed by their rulers. (Representation does account somewhat for the

varying size of the sheikhdoms but it is not entirely proportional: Abu Dhabi and Dubai have eight representatives each, Sharja and Ras al-Khaima six each, and the three remaining ones, four each). Abu Dhabi and Dubai were to have a veto power in both these councils. To this day, the UAE does not have an elected parliament, but a consultative council which has the right to review federation laws, though not to veto them.

The Supreme Council was to elect one of its members as President of the UAE for a five-year term, and he was to form a government in consultation with the other rulers and with all seven sheikhdoms represented in it. Currency and customs were to be united. Federal institutions were to be gradually established and unified. But the sheikhdoms were to retain their separate identity and to control their own economy, with the federal budget financed not by direct taxation but by contributions of the Sheikhdoms. (There were to be no quotas fixed; de facto, Abu Dhabi and Dubai alone financed the federal budget, with Abu Dhabi paying the bulk.)

The ruler of Abu Dhabi, Sheikh Zayed ibn Sultan Al-Nuhayan, was elected by the seven rulers as President of the UAE, and the ruler of Dubai, Sheikh Rashed ibn Sa'id al-MAKTUM, as Vice-President. The latter's son, Maktum ibn Rashed al-Maktum, became Prime Minister, and other sons took on other key positions.

The new federation was troubled from the start by a continuous struggle over its constitutional-political structure. The rulers of Dubai wanted federal powers to be restricted and the main powers to remain vested in the individual sheikhdoms. This debate of principles was aggravated by the old and continuous rivalry between Dubai and Abu Dhabi. Dubai, supported by Ras al-Khaima, Umm al-Qaiwain and sometimes by Sharja, obstructed or delayed the development and final endorsement of most federal institutions. When the term of the provisional constitution of 1971 ended in 1976, a permanent constitution was worked out, but Dubai and its supporters insisted on a postponement and a further five-year extension of the provisional arrangements. After five years, in 1981, the same thing happened again, and in 1986 the provisional constitution was extended for a further five years.

Sheikh Zayed of Abu Dhabi has been re-elected President every five years since independence. He had a decisive impact on the UAE's policy of arms and technology procurement. In this context, it is worth noting the rivalry between his sons, the Crown Prince and a younger half-brother, over a 6 billion dollar aircraft deal.

The creation of a federal army and the dissolution of the various armed formations of the sheikhdoms in the early 1970s met similar obstacles. Decisions to this effect taken in May 1976 caused a crisis and could not be implemented. In 1978 it was again decided to merge and establish all armed formations and federal forces. Yet attempts to enforce the dissolution of the separate formations caused a new crisis in 1979. In the context of that crisis, Dubai had to be compensated by the appointment of its ruler as Prime Minister, in addition to the position of Vice-President. Since then the UAE unified army has consisted of the former six separate armies, with Dubai contributing token units and the rest of the forces maintaining their independence.

The rapid economic development of the UAE since the early 1970s, which has transformed it into one of the world's richest countries, was the result of its growing oil production. The bulk of the oil production is centered in Abu Dhabi, which began producing in 1962. Dubai exported its first oil in 1969; Sharja began producing, in more modest quantities, in 1974; and Ras al-Khaima in 1984. Oil production and export are not federal matters and the oil revenue is the producing sheikhdom's, not the UAE's—for details see OIL. Compared with other oil-producing countries, the UAE was less hit by the oil glut and its per capita GDP is one of the highest in the world (see TABLE OF BASIC DATA).

In its foreign and international policies the UAE takes a rather cautious and low-profile stance. Within the Arab League it belongs to the moderate mainstream camp, refrains from spectacular initiatives, and usually follows the lead of Saudi Arabia. The UAE was one of the founding members of the GULF COOPERATION COUNCIL, GCC, in 1981. From the outbreak of the IRAQ-IRAN WAR throughout the Gulf crisis of 1990–1991, the UAE's main concern centered around the security of the Persian Gulf shipping lanes professing strict neutrality in the IRAN-IRAQ WAR. In spite of it joining the American-led coalition against IRAQ, it later returned to low-profile support of US policies in the Gulf, at times not avoiding crit-

icism of US harsh policies with regard to Iraq and IRAN. Similar caution is also applied to its territorial disputes with Iran: the forcible seizure by Iran of the ABU MUSSA and Tanb Islands in 1971, and the Iranian attempt at controlling the entry to the UAE part of Abu Mussa Island (1992). The UAE success in resolving the last dispute with Iran was a reflection of the varying policies of the GCC member states with Iran, even at times of hostility with other members at times of crisis. The UAE was officially neutralist in world affairs as long as the two superpowers competed for influence over the Gulf. In November 1985 the UAE became the third Gulf country to establish official relations with the USSR.

UNITED ARAB REPUBLIC (UAR) (Arabic: *al-jumhuriyya al-arabiyya al-muttahida*) A merger between EGYPT and SYRIA in February 1958 became the UAR. It collapsed in September 1961, when Syria seceded following a military coup. The initiative for the merger came from Syrian BA'TH military and political leaders (for the Syrian motivation, see SYRIA).

Egypt, though ideologically adhering to ARAB UNITY, was seeking political coordination and a dominating influence, as opposed to a full-fledged merger. President ABDEL NASSER agreed to the merger on condition that it would be based on his terms and on the pattern of Egypt's regime, including its one-party system. A provisional constitution was proclaimed by Presidents Nasser and Quwwatli and endorsed on 21 February 1958 by a plebiscite in both countries. A UAR National Assembly of 300 Egyptians and 100 Syrians was to be appointed by the President, with at least half of its members chosen from among members of the dissolved Egyptian and Syrian Assemblies. A small UAR government was to deal with defense, foreign affairs, industrialization, education and "national guidance," and two "regional" governments with all domestically related issues. A single political entity, the "National Union" on the Egyptian pattern, was to replace the parties active in Syria, including the *Ba'th*, that espoused the Unity Agreement.

The February 1958 referendum that endorsed the union and its constitution also elected Gamal Abdel Nasser President, as the only candidate. He appointed four Vice-Presidents—two Egyptians (Abdel Hakim Amer and Abdel Latif Baghdadi) and two Syrians (Akram Hourani and Sabri al-Assali). Amer was also to command the joint military forces and an eight-member UAR Government (seven Egyptians and one Syrian). In October 1958 the central government was expanded (fourteen Egyptians, seven Syrians) and its sphere of activities and authority widened.

The UAR government did not work well, and there were frequent reshuffles. But Syrian dissatisfaction went much deeper. The "National Union" failed to take root in Syria, and the disbandment of the existing parties caused unrest. It was in particular the *Ba'th* leaders who were disaffected. They had pressed for the union, hoping that they would become the ideological mentors of the UAR and the effective power in Syria. However, Nasser was unwilling to share power or accept guidance. In 1959, *Ba'th* leaders unitedly resigned from their government positions and went into opposition, increasingly underground. That same year, the national all-Arab command of the Party resumed its activity at a conference in LEBANON. However, resentment grew in much wider Syrian circles based on the posting of Egyptian officers in key positions in the Syrian armed forces; the growing trend toward centralization which put increasing power in the hands of the central government; the efforts to impose Egyptian patterns on Syria's body politic; and the application of Egyptian economic policies. This began with land reform and some nationalization, and culminated in July 1961 in far-reaching nationalization measures and a turn to full state socialism. This very much undermined the social and economic interests of the Syrian bourgeoisie, indicating to them that Syria had effectively lost its independence and was losing its identity.

Nasser responded by tightening Egypt's grip. The economic measures of 1961 were accompanied, in August, by the abolition of the two regional governments. A new central government was headed by seven Vice-Presidents, only two of whom were Syrians. (Abdel Hamid Sarraj was seen as Nasser's commissar with near-dictatorial powers and was soon involved in a struggle with Amer, who wanted that position for himself.) In September 1961 a group of Syrian officers took power in Syria. They were initially prepared to discuss changes in the structure of government and a proper division of powers. But Nasser was not willing to compromise, and the officers proclaimed Syria's secession and the dissolution of the UAR.

The collapse of the first merger of Arab states had far-reaching repercussions on the behavior of Arab states toward each other, especially concerning unity. Indeed, the immediate result of the Syrian secession was Nasser's intensified ideological warfare and subversion against the conservative Arab regimes ("the Reaction") whom he held responsible for the UAR failure, together with Western imperialism. In 1962, he openly took the liberty to intervene in the domestic affairs of other Arab states in the name of Arab socialist revolution, now presented as a prerequisite to Arab unity. Egypt regarded the secession as an illegal act of rebellion, refused to recognize Syria's renewed independence (though it did not object to its re-acceptance to the Arab League in 1962) and continued to call itself UAR until it was abolished by al-SADAT in 1971. There was a partial reconciliation in the spring of 1963, when Syria, now under a *Ba'th* government, began, together with *Ba'th* IRAQ, discussions with Egypt on a renewed union—also to be called UAR, but on a federal triangular pattern. This scheme failed (see ARAB UNITY, EGYPT, SYRIA). Official Egypt-Syria relations were resumed only in November 1966, together with the conclusion of a defense pact and significant *rapprochement* between the two states.

UNITED STATES OF AMERICA, US INTERESTS AND POLICIES

Except for a brief period between 1786 and 1805 when the US took diplomatic and military measures to protect its maritime rights from the Barbary rulers of the North African coast, Washington initially showed no interest in the "Eastern Question." At the same time, private US philanthropists, primarily Presbyterian missionaries, were active, establishing the Syrian Protestant College in 1866 (later the American University of Beirut); the American University of Cairo; Robert College in Istanbul and a network of smaller colleges and hospitals throughout the LEVANT, TURKEY and EGYPT. With overseas commercial interests expanding at the turn of the century, the US began to assert its "Open Door" policy for equal economic treatment with the European powers in MOROCCO—at the Algiers Conference in 1906—and elsewhere in the Middle East.

US involvement in the Middle East increased at the close of World War I. While the US had not declared war against the OTTOMAN EMPIRE, President

Wilson expressed American preferences concerning the future disposition of Ottoman territories occupied by the Allies. Point twelve of his Fourteen Points defining US war aims called for self-determination for these territories. American pressure led to the development of the MANDATE concept as a compromise between independence and European COLONIALISM. An appreciation of American, especially American Jewish, public opinion had also influenced Britain's support of Zionist aspirations in the BALFOUR DECLARATION of 1917. Independent American study groups were sent by President Wilson in 1919 to SYRIA-Palestine (the King-Crane Mission) and to Armenia (the Harbord Mission), but their recommendations were not followed. After the US Senate refused to ratify the Treaty of Versailles and the Covenant of the League of Nations, American interest in the Middle East declined.

In the inter-war period, the US, pursuing its Open Door principle, concluded agreements to protect its cultural and economic interests in Syria-Palestine (with FRANCE, 1924) and in Palestine and IRAQ (with Great BRITAIN, 1924 and 1930 respectively). In 1928, a consortium of seven US OIL companies led by Standard Oil of New Jersey succeeded in gaining a 23.75 percent share in the Turkish Petroleum Company (from 1929: Iraq P.C.) concessions in Iraq and other former Ottoman territories. Standard Oil of California (SOCAL) acquired exploration rights in the British-protected sheikhdom of BAHRAIN in 1930, and a total American concession to SAUDI ARABIA in 1933, substantially expanded in 1939. The American Gulf Oil Company, in equal partnership with the British government-owned Anglo-Persian Oil Company, secured a concession in KUWAIT in 1934.

World War II raised the level of American involvement in the Middle East. Great Britain held the supreme allied command for the region, and the US initially established only supply missions in North Africa and IRAN (September 1941). Joint Anglo-American forces occupied French North Africa (November 1942 to May 1943). American pressure against restrictive British regulations and suspicions of British imperial ambitions caused tension in the British-directed Middle East Supply Center and American efforts to establish closer ties with the Middle East. By the end of 1943, the US had initiated direct lend-lease aid programs with Egypt, Iran,

Saudi Arabia, and Turkey. Rumors that Britain sought to displace American oil companies in the region led to a drive to increase US influence in Saudi Arabia. This culminated in February 1945 in the meeting between President Roosevelt and King Abdel Aziz IBN SA'UD and the latter's agreement several months later to grant the US an airbase at Dhahran.

American public interest in the Palestine question grew during the war. In 1944, the Zionist movement brought its Biltmore Program, which called for the establishment of a Jewish state, before both houses of Congress. Resolutions calling for the abolition of the 1939 White Paper were introduced; the War Department and State Department intervention precluded a vote. In 1944 both presidential candidates pledged support for Jewish statehood. The Roosevelt Administration attempted to construct a neutral policy on Palestine based on prior "consultation with both ARABS and JEWS," but its pledges and commitments were contradictory. In his meeting with Ibn Sa'ud, President Roosevelt made a commitment to consult the Saudi king before any change in the current American policy on the Palestine question. President Truman introduced a pro-Zionist tilt in American policy by his August 1945 endorsement of the Harrison Report determining that displaced Jewish survivors of the Holocaust had pro-Zionist preferences. He called for the immediate admission of 100,000 Jews into Palestine, intensifying the struggle for Palestine and causing Britain to seek coordination with Washington on this matter. Attempts to establish a coordinated Anglo-American policy on Palestine, however, failed (the Anglo-American Committee of Inquiry and the Morrison-Grady Plan), mainly because the President's decision making on Palestine was motivated by electoral considerations, which frequently adversed the policy recommended by the Departments of State and Defense.

US strategic interests in the Middle East reached a turning point in the wake of World War II, when the region became a focal point of Soviet agitation and efforts to establish its influence over Greece, Turkey and Iran, countries bordering with it or with the "Iron Curtain." This led to US resistance to the continued Soviet presence in Iran as well as Soviet territorial demands from Turkey. The Truman Doctrine, announced on 12 March 1947, promised assistance to states under external threat to their security, who sought American support. The statement indicated an American take over—albeit in agreement with Britain—of the latter's responsibilities of economic and military assistance to Greece and Turkey.

Beginning in 1947, the US gave Turkey massive military, economic and technical aid. In 1949 Turkey became a member of the Council of Europe and a year later, to prove its loyalty to Western interests, it dispatched a brigade to join the UN forces in the Korean War. In 1952 Turkey was admitted to NATO as a full member, with Izmir becoming the headquarters of the European South Eastern Command. Subsequently, Turkey and the US signed several bilateral agreements which provided for American aid and granted the US bases and installations in the country. In 1959 the two countries signed a formal defense agreement.

The Truman Doctrine became a prelude to building an alliance with Iran, replacing the weakened traditional influence of the Soviet Union and Great Britain. In October 1947 the first Military Agreement between the US and Iran was concluded and American military experts arrived in Iran to reorganize the army. In the early 1950s the US granted Iran an initial 25 million dollar loan. The US added Iran to the states receiving economic aid within the framework of "Point Four," giving it a grant of half a million dollars. A transient US naval presence was transformed into the US Sixth Fleet in 1948, and a smaller US naval contingent, the US Middle East Force, was permanently stationed in the PERSIAN GULF.

US Middle East policy was premised on the renewal of Anglo-American strategic cooperation, with primary responsibility for the defense of the region assigned to Britain. Yet frequent Anglo-American discord, primarily on Palestine, embittered the relations between these allies, affecting the Western posture in the region. In Palestine, the Truman Administration did not follow the British lead (though both the Departments of State and Defense largely supported the British position). In November 1947, the US supported the partition of Palestine into Jewish and Arab states. Indeed, once the state of Israel was declared on 15 May 1948, the US granted it immediate de facto recognition. By May 1950, Anglo-American cohesion on Palestine was to some extent achieved by the Tripartite Declaration (US-Britain-France) which announced a semi-guarantee of the sovereignty and borders of all Middle Eastern states and the coordination of arms supplies that would not endanger the regional status quo.

From the 1950s on, US basic interests and strategy have remained relatively steady, focusing on access to petroleum resources, free shipping and communications, containing Soviet expansion and influence, bringing the ARAB-ISRAEL CONFLICT to an end, and, as of the late-1970s, developing normal relations with both Israel and the Arab states.

Anglo-American differences also emerged elsewhere in the Middle East. The US tended to come to terms with the new nationalist forces, while the British sought to preserve the political and economic status quo. US and British oil interests were in constant rivalry. Divergences became evident in the American acceptance of Saudi Arabian demands for an equal sharing of oil profits in 1950; the attitude toward the Egyptian "Free Officers" junta of 1952, and the Iranian oil crisis of 1952–1953. US interests and the ARAMCO oil consortium at least particularly supported border disputes between Saudi Arabia and the Trucial sheikhdoms (ABU DHABI) and OMAN (see BURAIMI). Following the 1951–1953 oil crisis between Iran and Great Britain, an international consortium was established in 1954 to export Iranian oil, forty percent of whose shares were given to the Anglo-Iranian oil company (which had now become British Petroleum). The remainder was divided amongst several oil companies, including Dutch "Shell" and five American companies (see OIL).

In the 1950s, Washington initiated efforts to create a MIDDLE EAST DEFENSE ORGANIZATION. In October 1951, the Truman Administration, joined by Britain, France and Turkey, proposed to Egypt membership in a Middle East command ("SACME"), which would also take over the British base in the SUEZ CANAL Zone as an allied enterprise. After repeated Egyptian refusals to join the command as well as a less ambitious Middle East Defense Organization, the new Eisenhower Administration shifted its alliance-building schemes toward the "Northern Tier" states more directly threatened by the Soviet Union. Among the Arab states, only Iraq showed a realization of such a Soviet threat and agreed to join the US efforts. In April 1954, the US agreed to give military aid to Baghdad. In May, a US Military Aid Agreement was signed with Pakistan. Turkey (having become a full NATO member in 1952), signed a series of agreements with Pakistan (April 1954) and Iraq (February 1955). Thus a regional pro-Western bloc consisting of Turkey, Iraq, Pakistan, and Iran emerged as the Baghdad Pact. Britain joined, while the US gave decisive political support and sat in on the Pact's committees. Hopes that other Arab states would join were not fulfilled. Indeed, the Pact antagonized Egypt, Syria and other Arab states, creating much anti-US and anti-Western sentiment. Attempts by the Eisenhower Administration to advance a settlement of the Arab-Israel dispute through a solution of the refugee problem and perhaps Israeli territorial concessions in the Negev, also failed. An effort to devise an agreed integrated plan for the Jordan River development was also aborted (see WATER POLITICS).

US policy before and during the Suez crisis of 1956 was contradictory. After Egypt made an arms deal with the Soviet Bloc in May 1955, Secretary Dulles reneged on a promise to aid its major development project, the construction of the ASWAN HIGH DAM, and also ensured that international aid would be denied. This led President ABDEL NASSER to nationalize the SUEZ CANAL. But when Britain and France prepared military action against Egypt, Eisenhower and Dulles refused to associate the US with the former imperial powers. In October-November 1956, the US pressured Britain and France to withdraw from Egypt at the outset of their military operations. Simultaneous pressure on ISRAEL compelled it to evacuate the SINAI with uncertain political assurances and no guarantees. The US was not thanked much for its position on that matter.

From 1957, the US moved to fill the Western great power vacuum that it had brought about. On 5 January 1957, President Eisenhower issued an EISENHOWER DOCTRINE, approved by Congress on 9 March. It pledged US armed aid "to secure and protect the territorial integrity and political independence of such nations" (in the Middle East) "requesting aid against any armed aggression from any nation controlled by international Communism" (it said nothing about the principal danger: internal subversion). When it was actually applied, it was against threats from Nasserist Egypt rather than the USSR. In April 1957 the Sixth Fleet was deployed during an attempted coup against the Hashemite monarchy in JORDAN, and in July 1958 the US landed Marine and Army units in LEBANON to help President CHAMOUN, at his request, against a Nasserist

Rebellion aided by UNITED ARAB REPUBLIC (UAR) intervention. In March 1959, after revolutionary Iraq's secession from the Baghdad Pact, now renamed CENTO, the US concluded bilateral executive agreements with the remaining members, Turkey, Iran and Pakistan, pledging "appropriate action including the use of armed force" in their defense in case of aggression. The Agreements derived were explicitly authorized by the Eisenhower Doctrine.

Several other bilateral arrangements in the Middle East served US nuclear strategic interests in the 1950s and early 1960s. In March 1959 a Defense Agreement was signed between the US and Iran, granting the Americans the right of military intervention in Iran in the event of external aggression. That same year Iran joined CENTO, of which Turkey, Pakistan, Great Britain and the US were also members. Besides military assistance, the intensifying ties with the US also manifested themselves in financial assistance, which by 1960 reached the total sum of about 800 million dollars. US airbase rights in Morocco (1950–1956 under French rule; 1956–1963 agreed with independent Morocco) and LIBYA (1954–1970) were of special importance to the American Strategic Air Command (SAC) before the introduction of the intercontinental range B-52. The Dhahran airbase in Saudi Arabia (1946–1962) never became a full Strategic Air Command base, but was an important US Air Force transit stop. In the late 1950s, the US deployed intermediate range ballistic missiles in Turkey. With the introduction of Polaris missile-firing submarines in the early 1960s, the Mediterranean itself inceasingly became an arena of superpower strategic competition. However, by the end of the 1960s, the increasing ranges of both Superpowers' nuclear delivery systems caused a shift: US bomber forces and US land-based missiles no longer needed Middle East bases because US missile-firing submarines could hit their targets from the Indian Ocean. Intelligence monitoring from space satellites also somewhat reduced American dependence on intelligence gathering facilities based in the Northern Tier states (Turkey, Iran and Pakistan). US military-strategic interests in the Middle East were thus declining in the late 1960s.

Under Kennedy, less stress was placed on establishing a Middle East alliance system, and more emphasis was given to preemption of Soviet-supported insurgencies by encouraging economic aid and development, such as food aid to Egypt. The US strove to attract the Arab nationalists to the West by taking new diplomatic initiatives towards Nasserist Egypt—such as the exchange of letters between Kennedy and Nasser—and its allies, including the new republican regime in YEMEN, in power since September 1962 and recognized by the US in December. During the Egyptian-Saudi conflict in the context of the Yemen Civil War, the US initially served in a mediatory capacity and avoided overidentification with the conservative Saudis supporting the Yemeni royalists. Egyptian air attacks against Saudi border towns, however, soon forced increased American pro-Saudi alignment. In July 1963, a US Air Force fighter squadron was deployed in Saudi Arabia for six months, signalling America's commitment to the integrity of the Kingdom.

Alongside its attempted dialogue with the "progressive" regimes of the Arab world, the Kennedy Administration significantly deepened US ties to Israel. Kennedy personally described the US-Israel connection as a "special relationship" and gave private assurances of coming to Israel's defense. He approved the sale of the first major American weapon-system (defensive) to Israel: the Hawk anti-aircraft missile. A Kennedy initiative to seek a resolution of the Palestinian refugee problem through the US-sponsored Joseph Johnson mission (1962) was aborted (see REFUGEES).

US efforts to draw Nasserist Egypt closer to the American orbit ended during the Johnson Administration and US ties with the Arab conservative regimes as well as with Israel tightened, among other reasons, because of Nasser's continued involvement in the Yemen war and championing the collective Arab plan of diverting the headwaters of the Jordan River (see WATER POLITICS). From 1965 to 1966 the cash value of US military sales to Saudi Arabia increased more than tenfold; US arms transfers to Lebanon, LIBYA, Morocco, and TUNISIA increased as well. Offensive arms were sold to Israel for the first time (tanks in 1965 and Skyhawk fighter-bombers in 1966). Johnson's sympathetic attitude toward Israel became evident in the crisis of May-June 1967 and the war that followed. As US attempts to defuse the crisis over the STRAITS OF TIRAN by the formation of a multilateral naval force floundered, Washington's position was interpreted by Israel as a tacit "green light" to a military action. Suspicion of US-

Israel military collusion led seven Arab states, including Egypt, Syria and Iraq, to sever diplomatic relations with the US. On 19 June, Johnson formulated a principle on the Arab-Israel situation that guided US policy for successive administrations: Israeli withdrawal from the territories taken in the war was conditional on a peace settlement. The US interpreted Security Council Resolution 242 of November 1967, which it co-sponsored, in the same framework, and was increasingly drawn into Arab-Israel diplomacy (see ARAB-ISRAEL PEACEMAKING).

The Nixon Administration entered office in 1969 determined to introduce a more evenhanded American policy in the region. During 1969, with the escalating Egypt-Israel "War of Attrition" and increasing Soviet involvement, Nixon agreed to discuss the Arab-Israel conflict in two power talks with the USSR and four power talks with the USSR, Britain and France. These talks were abortive. In December, Secretary of State William Rogers publicly announced a plan discussed since October through diplomatic channels. The "Rogers Plan" called for an Israeli return to the pre-1967 borders with only minor alterations, in return for Arab-Israel agreements that were short of full peace. It was rejected by both Israel and the Arab states, but later efforts for more limited disengagement arrangements ("Rogers Plan II," 1970) were accepted, and facilitated the end of the War of Attrition. However, they entirely failed in bringing the disputed parties to the negotiating table. Nixon's policies changed when Soviet ties with Egypt and Syria deepened and Israel emerged as an American regional ally balancing Soviet proxies, especially after 1970. Israel's new role was demonstrated in September 1970 when the US and Israel made contingency plans to use Israeli forces to block a Syrian invasion of Jordan (see JORDAN). The end of the crisis, with a more secure and stable Hashemite regime, led to increased American military and economic aid to Jordan.

New strategic dilemmas were posed for US Middle East policy with Britain's announcement in 1968 of its plan to withdraw from the Persian Gulf, which it executed in 1971. With excessive military commitments elsewhere, particularly in Vietnam, the US fashioned a "Twin Pillar Policy" (1970) which, consistent with the global "Nixon Doctrine," placed the burden of Gulf security on two pro-Western regional powers—Iran and Saudi Arabia. In May 1972,

Nixon and his National Security adviser Henry Kissinger agreed to let the Shah of Iran purchase the most advanced American military equipment in order to build a large army, designed to turn Iran into a regional power. Between the years 1970–1977 Iran purchased from the US arms and military equipment worth 12 billion dollars and its orders until 1980 stood at a similar sum. US arms transfers to Iran and to a lesser extent to Saudi Arabia increased dramatically. As their needs for increased revenues contributed to their demands for a larger share of oil profits, the US had to accept these demands in 1972 (see OIL).

The 1973 war raised US aid to Israel to unprecedented levels, whilst throwing into sharp profile the need for active US diplomacy in the Arab-Israel conflict. Threats of unilateral Soviet intervention at the war's end, and Nixon's decision to initiate a nuclear alert, underlined the dangers which the conflict posed. The Arab oil embargo (though not fully implemented) and skyrocketing prices that accompanied the war underlined the linkage of Western access to Arab oil and Arab demands concerning the Arab-Israel conflict. The US needed Middle East oil only to a limited degree (though the share of Middle East oil in its consumption had grown from approximately three percent in 1970 to over seven percent in 1973. Yet it considered the regular supply of Middle East oil to its allies in Europe and Japan, which constituted a major part of their oil import a vital US interest.

Through the step-by-step negotiating strategy of Secretary of State Kissinger, his pressure, and his tireless shuttle diplomacy, separation of forces agreements were reached between Israel and its Egyptian and Syrian neighbors on the Sinai and the GOLAN in January and May 1974, respectively. In November 1973 the US and Egypt renewed their diplomatic relations, severed since 1967, and a similar step was effected with Syria in June 1974. A second Sinai Agreement that involved further Israeli withdrawal and the inclusion of elements tantamount to ending the state of belligerency was achieved by Kissinger under the Ford Administration in September 1975. American civilian technicians were stationed in three Sinai warning stations. An accompanying Memorandum provided for the supply of advanced weaponry, including F-16 aircraft to Israel and contained new political assurances, including a US commit-

ment not to recognize the PALESTINE LIBERATION OR-GANIZATION (PLO) or negotiate with it as long as it did not recognize Israel's right to exist, until it renounced TERRORISM and accepted UN resolutions 242 and 338.

After 1973, Egypt increasingly shifted from the Soviet to the American orbit. By early 1975, the administration agreed to sell Cairo C-130 military transport aircraft, thereby beginning a new US arms sales relationship with Egypt. In June 1974, a wide-ranging agreement for Saudi-US military and economic cooperation re-established and deepened their relations. The Carter Administration inherited its predecessor's assumption that the Arab-Israel conflict was the main problem for the US in the region. However, perceiving the Palestinian issue as the core of the Arab-Israeli conflict, the Carter-Vance-Brzezinski team replaced Kissinger's step by step strategy by striving for a comprehensive settlement. This shift led to US efforts to revive the Geneva Peace Conference, suspended since December 1973, to bring the Soviet Union into the peace process and to tackle the Palestinian problem (including informal, mostly indirect, talks with Palestinian representatives). In March 1977, Carter called for the establishment of a "Palestinian homeland," though he later explained that he did not mean an independent Palestinian state. In October 1977, in a joint communiqué with the USSR, the US recognized for the first time "the legitimate rights of the Palestinians." Through Saudi mediation, the Administration sought to bring about a change in the PLO position on Resolution 242 and thereby open up a direct US-PLO link. US-Israel relations in this period witnessed tension due to differences over the peacemaking efforts as well as over the new Israeli settlements in the occupied WEST BANK and GAZA STRIP.

The deadlock confronting the American peacemaking efforts by summer-fall 1977, paved the road to al-SADAT's bold peace initiative, demonstrated in his visit to JERUSALEM in November 1977. However, both Egypt and Israel elected to pursue their newly established direct negotiation track, but also to seek US offices and mediation once their efforts deadlocked shortly after that visit. US and Egyptian positions converged after Carter's January 1978 visit to Aswan. The Carter team sought to bolster the ongoing peace process, and to secure Saudi moderation on the price of oil, by proposing in early

1978 to link unprecedented advanced fighter air-craft sales to Saudi Arabia (60 F-15), Egypt (50 F-5E) and Israel (75 F-16 and 15 F-15) in one package. In 1978, as the Egyptian-Israeli dialogue floundered, Carter invited President Sadat and Prime Minister BEGIN to the US presidential retreat at Camp David and, tying up his Presidency from 5 to 17 September, acted as a "full partner" in the negotiations that culminated in two frameworks for peace—Egypt-Israel, and general Arab-Israel—known as the Camp David Agreements. As the Egyptians and Israelis disagreed in subsequent months over how to translate the frameworks into a peace treaty, Carter again directly intervened and personally engaged in his own shuttle-diplomacy (March 1979) which led, at the end of the month, to the signing of the Egyptian-Israeli Peace Treaty on the White House lawn.

The second area on which US Middle East activity during the Carter Administration was focused ran from Afghanistan through Iran to the Horn of Africa. In 1977, the Administration showed little concern for the growing Soviet intervention in the Horn of Africa, supporting the de-militarization of the Indian Ocean. The deterioration in the political position of the Shah of Iran in late 1978, led to his fall in January 1979. This demonstrated that the West could no longer rely on an Iranian surrogate to protect its interests. During the Carter Presidency criticism in the US public and government circles escalated over human rights violations in Iran by the regime, which soon constrained further American financial and military aid to the Shah. At the end of 1978, at the peak of the political crisis in Iran, President Carter visited Tehran and declared the US' unreserved support for the Shah's regime. However, the American administration misperceived the real domestic danger to the Shah, identifying it with the left and the COMMUNISTS rather than with the Islamic leadership. The crisis over Iran—the seizure of the US Embassy in Tehran on 4 November 1979 by revolutionary Iranians, its staff taken as hostages, and the failure of an attempted rescue mission in late April 1980—demonstrated the limits of American military strength in the region. The US was unable to act on the scene against the Soviet invasion of Afghanistan in late December 1979. Concerned that the Soviets might move into Iran, the US tried to fill the vacuum. The "Carter Doctrine," issued on 23 January 1980, declared that "any attempt by

any outside force to gain control of the Persian Gulf region will be regarded as an assault on the vital interests of the US and such an assault will be repelled by any means necessary, including military force." In March the US established a Rapid Deployment Joint Task Force (RDJTF)—a 100,000 man intervention force to back up the new presidential doctrine. Having lost its Middle East bases some fifteen years earlier, the US concluded agreements with Oman, SOMALIA and Kenya on lower profile facilities and with Egypt on increased use of Egyptian airfields.

The Reagan Administration (1981–1988) emphasized even more the military-strategic factors in US Middle Eastern policy. The Reagan team facilitated the implementation of the Egyptian-Israeli peace treaty, overseeing Israel's final withdrawal from Sinai in April 1982, and establishing the "Multinational Force and Observers" (MFO) to patrol the Sinai. Reagan was personally warmer and more attentive toward Israel than any previous president. He described Israel as a strategic asset and was the first president to call Israel an "ally," despite the lack of any formal Treaty of Alliance. These views were generally shared by his Secretaries of State Alexander Haig and George Shultz, but reportedly not by his Secretary of Defense Caspar Weinberger. US policy on Israel was marked by ups and downs in accordance with intra-cabinet feuds. Reagan's strategic policies sometimes conflicted with Israeli interests. Thus the Administration's drive in the fall of 1981 to sell Airborne Warning and Control System aircraft (AWACS) to Saudi Arabia—a decision inherited from Carter and opposed by Israel which also objected to advanced arms sales to Jordan. The Israeli attack on the Iraqi nuclear reactor earlier in June 1981, air attacks in Lebanon, and the decision to apply the Israeli law on the GOLAN HEIGHTS (December 1981) were seen as frustrating American attempts to reach a "strategic consensus" with the ARAB world, for the sake of Western interests in the region. Thus an essentially friendly administration suspended temporarily American arms deliveries to Israel after the latter's attack on the Iraqi nuclear reactor. In December 1981, after Israel's Golan Law, talks on a US-Israel Strategic Cooperation Agreement were suspended. The Lebanon War, from June 1982, brought about further Israeli-US differences, despite Secretary Haig's sympathy for Israel's need to take a limited military action. Haig's removal in the middle of the war seemed to further tip the scales against US-Israeli cooperation, as reflected also by American television and press coverage. Israel's war against the PLO and the plight of the Palestinian refugees raised issues that had been dormant in recent years.

On 1 September 1982, a Reagan speech launched the "Reagan Plan," arguing that "self-government by the Palestinians of the West Bank and Gaza Strip together with Jordan offers of the best chance for a durable, just and lasting peace." With the unveiling of this Plan, the US expected greater Jordanian involvement in the peace process. Despite US attempts to assure Syria's cooperation, however, the newly announced American policy effectively ignored Syria's concerns and national security needs. Not only had the Reagan Plan excluded Syria, but Israel's insistence on maintaining its freedom of action in large parts of Lebanon and attempts to legitimize it by an American-backed formal agreement (signed on 17 May 1983) with a subordinate Lebanese administration and demand that Syria withdraw from Lebanon, turned Syria into an active enemy of the new American policy.

As the US was drawn into the politics of Lebanon and disappointed with the responses of Syria to its efforts, US policy reverted to greater coordination with Israel. By November 1983, a US-Israel Strategic Cooperation Agreement was worked out and put into effect. Further peace initiatives, the Administration recognized from 1983 onward, would have to come from the parties to the conflict themselves and not from Washington. Yet the US remained deeply involved in efforts to advance such peace initiatives.

The Reagan Administration was militarily involved in the Middle East more than previous ones, especially in its second term. In Lebanon, Reagan approved the deployment of the US Marines in a peacekeeping capacity. From 25 August to 10 September 1982, 800 Marines joined a Multinational Peacekeeping Force that oversaw the evacuation of the PLO from Beirut. By 29 September, 1200 marines returned to Beirut—along with French and Italian forces—to assist the Lebanese government to take control of the city. In early 1983, the Marines found themselves confronting warring Lebanese militias. Furthermore, suicidal attacks were committed by members of the Shi'i Lebanese HIZBALLAH against

the American Embassy and the multinational force in Beirut, in April, August and October, claiming the lives of hundreds of American troops. US naval and air forces operated against Syrian and related Lebanese militia positions but retreated from Lebanon before the end of the year. Relations with Syria remained troubled because of Syria's involvement with terrorism. The frustrated American involvement in Lebanon was partly linked to its deteriorating relations with Iran as a result of the latter's inspired subversive and sabotage activities in the oil monarchies of the Gulf, and its encouragement of the terrorist attacks on the American and Multinational Force in Beirut in the course of 1983, and systematic efforts of its Shi'i protege, namely, *Hizballah*, to take Western hostages (see ISLAMIC RADICALISM AND MOVEMENTS).

The US confronted Libya as well. Growing tensions led the US to close the Libyan Embassy in Washington in May 1981. In August of that year US Navy F-14s shot down two Libyan SU-22 warplanes over the Gulf of Sirte (*Sidra*), claimed by Libya as territorial waters. In his second term, Reagan increasingly blamed Libya for international terrorism, including the 27 December 1985 bombing of the Rome and Vienna airports. In March 1986, US naval aircraft exercising over the Gulf of Sirte came under a Libyan missile attack, and US ships and planes destroyed two Libyan ships, damaged three others and raided an SA-5 missile-radar site on shore. After linking Libya to a terrorist bomb in West Berlin that left two persons dead including a US soldier, thirteen F-11 US fighter-bombers flying out of Britain and naval carrier-launched fighters bombed military and intelligence targets in Libya, including Colonel QAD-HAFI's command and communications center, on 14-15 April 1986.

While the Reagan Administration identified Iran besides Syria and Libya as a sponsor of international terrorism, US policy became more complex due to the intense interest of both superpowers in the Persian Gulf. Reagan inherited the Carter Doctrine without reservation; he deepened American commitments to the Gulf region when he declared that he would not allow Saudi Arabia to fall the same way as Iran. The RDJTF he inherited from his predecessor, was upgraded on 1 January 1983 to the US Central Command (CENTCOM) which became the first US unified command for the Middle East in the post-war period. In the Iraq-Iran GULF WAR itself, the US initially observed strict neutrality. Iraq seemed eager to improve its relations with the US, resuming official ties (severed in 1967) in November1984. Late in 1983 the US began to deepen its slight tilt to Iraq as Iran threatened to close the Straits of HORMUZ and repeatedly attacked foreign ships, especially oil tankers serving the Arab Gulf ports. US token naval forces in the Gulf escorted some US merchant ships and oil tankers to protect them against Iran's threats of attack and its practice of seizure and boarding. In 1987, the US extended such protection to Kuwaiti shipping, and US-Iran tension escalated. While the Departments of State and Defense continued to support a firm stance against Iran in the Gulf, the National Security Council initiated new contacts with Iran in 1985, supporting limited arms sales to Tehran. US interest in re-establishing relations with Iran became mixed with the wish to secure the release of American hostages held by Iranian-backed militants in Lebanon. (The American hostages at the Tehran US Embassy were released in January 1981). The arms-for-hostages arrangements became entwined with illegal attempts to conduit American funds to anti-Nicaraguan rebel ("Contra") forces in Central America. As information about these schemes became public from November 1986, it became into a major affair in the US—"Irangate"—in which Israeli intelligence and arms dealers were also involved. In any case, Iran troubled the Reagan Administration as much as its predecessor with additional emphasis on Iran's involvement in the Gulf, and in terrorism in Lebanon and elsewhere. In April 1988, the US Navy destroyed two Iranian oil platforms in the Persian Gulf, sank two frigates and a guided missile boat in retaliation for the planting of naval mines by Iran in the Gulf, one of which damaged an American frigate. In July the Americans mistakenly brought down an Iranian passenger plane over the Gulf, killing all its 290 passengers.

The American involvement in the Arab-Israeli peacemaking effort was on a low burner during most of the 1980s. The Jordan-PLO dialogue, and the Amman Agreement signed by King HUSSEIN and ARAFAT in February 1985, were direct results of the expulsion of the PLO from Lebanon and the Reagan Plan. The Agreement reached a deadlock when Arafat failed to accept Resolution 242, and Israel stated its clear objection to the participation of PLO-affiliated delegates in the peace process. The eruption of the Palestinian uprising (INTIFADA) in December 1987 led to a new high-ranking US involvement in peacemaking diplomacy by Secretary of State Shultz, based on elements from the Palestinian self-rule part of the Camp David Agreement, the Reagan Plan, and the Hussein-Arafat Agreement. However, the sweeping national atmosphere in the uprising Palestinian community, demonstrated by the revitalization of the PLO and further decline of the Jordanian posture in the West Bank, meant that the American initiative could not get off the ground. With the announcement of Jordan's legal and administrative disengagement from the West Bank by King Hussein on 31 July 1988, the American initiative was finally decimated. The proclamation of a Palestinian independent state by the PNC session in Algiers in November, the growing pragmatization on the part of the PLO's mainstream leadership under the influence of the West Bank and Gaza Strip *intifada* leaders, intensive diplomatic contacts and Arafat's official acceptance of Resolution 242 and renouncing terrorism, caused the US government to announce the beginning of a low-ranking political dialogue with the PLO in December 1988. The new US administration of George Bush tried to support the Israeli government's peace initiative of May 1989, which suggested holding elections in the West Bank and Gaza Strip for a political delegation with which Israel would hold talks on implementation of the Camp David Agreement on Palestinian transitory self-rule in the occupied Palestinian territories. Yet this initiative remained futile, as was the US-PLO dialogue, which ended in May 1990 when Arafat refused to renounce an aborted terrorist attempt against Israel by a small Palestinian guerrilla group and member of the PLO.

The radically changing global setting as a result of the collapse of the Soviet bloc in the late 1980s and early 1990s, came to the fore in the US response to the Iraqi invasion of Kuwait in early August 1990. The American response took the form of passing resolutions in the UN Security Council that imposed a total embargo on Iraq until it evacuated Kuwait, deploying its forces on Saudi Arabia's soil and the Persian Gulf, forging an international military coalition which also included, in addition to the Gulf Arab monarchies, other leading Arab states such as Egypt and Syria. To encourage the latter's participation, the US government made diplomatic efforts to enable Egypt to write off part of its national debt (paid mainly by the Gulf oil states). Further, it gave its tacit consent for a free Syrian action in Lebanon— facilitating Syria's final take over of Beirut and elimination of the last MARONITE-based resistance to Syrian hegemony in Lebanon. From the beginning of the crisis, the US led the international effort against Iraq, initially using economic sanctions, and later, when Iraq refused to abide by the Security Council ultimatum, operating the international military build-up of over half a million troops—most of whom were American—to drive Iraq out of Kuwait by force. (For the war itself, see GULF WAR; IRAQ.)

Another issue tackled between the potential Arab allies and the US during the Kuwait crisis was the long-dormant Arab-Israel peacemaking process. Although the Gulf crisis was a purely Arab-Arab dispute, it became linked to the Arab-Israel conflict by virtue of the US need for legitimizing the Syrian and Egyptian participation in the anti-Iraq coalition, and the latter's requirement for active American involvement in resuming the peacemaking process. Indeed, the American and Soviet governments undertook to resume the peacemaking effort when the Gulf crisis had been settled, within the framework of an international peace conference and with the aim of reaching a comprehensive settlement.

However, despite the sweeping victory of the international coalition over Iraq—albeit without seriously affecting the regime's survivability—and the rise of the US as the leading superpower following the end of the Cold War, US Secretary of State James Baker launched seven shuttle rounds of visits to the Middle East capitals to ensure the concerned parties would accept the American formula for an international peace conference to be held in Madrid, under joint US-Soviet auspices. Particularly difficult was getting Israel to consent to such a formula, especially against the tension that had marked their relations due to the policy of increased settlement in the occupied territories of the right-wing Israeli government headed by Yitzak SHAMIR. One of the bargaining chips used by Washington in this regard was the Israeli request for American financial guarantees for a 10 billion dollar loan designated for the absorption of the new immigrants from the former Soviet Union.

The Madrid Conference that commenced on 31 October 1991 was ceremonial, as had been long in-

sisted on by Israel. Following this, bilateral negotiations between Israel and each of the Arab parties— including a Palestinian representation from the West Bank and Gaza Strip being part of a Jordanian-Palestinian delegation—began, as a way of reaching contractual peace settlements. The US not only provided the negotiating parties with the required facilities in Washington and the venue for the talks, but also offered its mediation. Together with Russia, the US supervised the multilateral track of Arab-Israeli negotiations, together with West European delegates, Japan, Canada, and others states on regional cooperation, mainly economic and infrastructural development, arms control and the refugee problem (for the development of these negotiations see ARAB-ISRAEL PEACEMAKING, SYRIA, JORDAN, ISRAEL, PLO). It was in this context, with the advent of a center-left government in Israel in June 1992, that the Clinton Administration became actively involved in mediation efforts between Israel and Syria, with numerous visits of Secretary of State Christopher, and a presidential visit of Clinton himself, to Damascus for talks with President ASAD. This did not conclude an agreement, though it certainly contributed to the promotion of the level of negotiators on both sides, allegedly bringing them closer than ever to agree on the principles of a peaceful agreement in late 1995 and early 1996.

On the other hand, the Israel-PLO Oslo Agreement demonstrated that when the regional parties concerned were willing and able to reach mutual understanding, the US role would diminish to a status of facilitator rather than of full partner. The US came into the scene of the Agreement only after it had essentially been concluded between Israeli and PLO delegates. However, the widely attended and media-covered official ceremony of the signing on the White House lawn on September 13, 1993, led by US President Clinton, with Arafat and Prime Minister RABIN shaking hands, not only meant to bestow on Clinton the prestige of successful peacemaker, but also underlined the US commitment for the implementation of the Agreement, along with a new era in US-PLO relations.

The wave of terrorist attacks by HAMAS on Israeli citizens in February-March 1996, triggered an American initiative for holding an international conference for combating terrorism in the Sinai resort of Sharm al-Sheikh in March, with the participation of Israeli, Arab and other international delegations. This was seen as a gesture of support for Israel and the peace-making efforts.

The election of Binyamin NETANYAHU as Israel's Prime Minister in the May 1996 elections and the advent of a right-wing coalition government, presented the American government with a dilemma regarding the continued peacemaking efforts. Israel's proclaimed policies on the Golan precluded, at least from the Syrian viewpoint, the resumption of the talks with Israel. On the Israeli-Palestinian track, the US President intervened when armed clashes erupted in October 1996, following the opening of the Hasmonean Tunnel in the Old City of Jerusalem, by inviting Netayahu, Arafat, and King Hussein to Wahsington to an urgent summit. However, it took another four months until the awaited Israeli deployment in the city of Hebron could be agreed upon, with active American diplomatic involvement. This, however, has indicated the limits—domestic as well as international—of US diplomatic brokerage in the Arab-Israeli peace process, as demonstrated by the failure of all attempts to effect another Israeli redeployment in the West Bank as stipulated by the Oslo Agreement and reaffirmed in the Hebron Agreement.

US-Iran relations remained in crisis, despite secret efforts by both sides to overcome the differences between them following the death of KHOMEINI in 1989, due to the internal strife between the pragmatic government of RAFSANJANI and the conservative-radical faction, led by KHAMENEI, which had vested interest in nurturing the image of the US as an enemy, as part of its radical Islamist policy. Iran conditioned any *rapprochement* with Washington on the release of 12 billion dollars deposited in American banks that had been frozen by President Carter's instructions after the takeover of the US Embassy in Tehran; the end of US support for the Middle East peace process; and an end to Washington's hostile attitude towards the Islamic regime in Tehran. In May 1990 the two states reached an Agreement to enable the International Court in the Hague to deal with mutual financial claims. In 1996, the two states reached an agreement regarding the payment of compensation to the families of 290 persons killed in an Iranian commercial airline accidentally shot down by the Americans over the Persian Gulf.

Nevertheless, during the Clinton Presidency, relations once again deteriorated after the US began, in the middle of 1993, to adopt a strategy of "Double Containment" toward Iraq and Iran. In addition to preservation of the UN-imposed economic embargo on Iraq since August 1990, this strategy included the exertion of economic pressure on Iran and required its allies to limit and even stop trading with it. The US accused Iran of nurturing Islamic terrorist activities in the US itself, acting against the Middle East peace process and developing mass destruction weapons, including nuclear weapons. The Clinton Administration prohibited American companies and their subsidiaries abroad to maintain trade relations with Iran. Even though the West European states refused to join the US call for an economic boycott of Iran, the Americans managed to stop other states investing in development programs in Iran or engaging in economic deals with it.

With the election of KHATAMI as Iran's new President in 1997, Washington sent clear messages as to its willingness to open a new era in its relations with Iran. This was reciprocated to some extent by the new Iranian President. However, continuing Iranian support for militant Islamists elsewhere in the Middle East, its efforts to attain nuclear capability, and the ongoing power struggle between the dogmatic clerical establishment led by Khamenei, and the more pragmatic Iranian elite, still blocked a rapid shift in the relations between the two countries.

UNRWA United Nations Relief and Works Agency for Palestine Refugees in the Near East, established by the UN General Assembly in December 1949 to aid and rehabilitate the Palestinian-Arab-REFUGEES. Various agencies, primarily the International Red Cross, immediately began to aid the refugees in 1948, but as the problem seemed to be continuing, the Western powers, especially BRITAIN, sought to mitigate the ARAB nationalist wrath by institutionalizing the aid to the Palestinian refugees. The task of the UNRWA was to take care of half a million refugees qualified for its relief. It has done so throughout the years. (Indeed, due to its services, public health and the level of schooling, vocational and academic education among the refugees was usually superior to that of the surrounding Arab populations.) The Agency provided aid, mainly in housing. (In specified areas this was allotted by the hosting state, mostly in the vicinity of large cities, starting as tent camps, and then becoming constructed areas.) Also food rations, health services and education, were provided through a widespread network of its own schools and grants for studying in other institutions. Efforts toward rehabilitation and resettlement were hampered for political reasons, mainly the objection of the Palestinian leaders themselves (who did not live in refugee camps) and the Arab states as a matter of principle, strictly insisting on repatriation. Its budget, voluntarily contributed by member-states of the UN (with the US always paying the largest share), was initially 20 million dollars per annum. This figure gradually increased to 40 million dollars after 1960, passed the 100 million dollar mark in the 1970s, and peaked in 1981 at 230 million dollars. Beset by constant deficits, it had to be reduced in the 1980s.

UNRWA employs a large staff (teachers, administrators etc.)—about 17,000 in the mid-1980s—most of them Palestinians, with the top echelons manned by foreigners. (see REFUGEES.) After the initial outlay for the construction of camps, forty-forty-five percent of this budget paid for food rations—approximately 1,500 calories per capita, forty-two to forty-six percent for education (UNRWA maintaining, by the 1970s, some 640 schools of its own), and thirteen to fourteen percent for health services (administration costs included).

In 1980 UNRWA operated in sixty-one camps throughout the WEST BANK (twenty), GAZA STRIP (eight), JORDAN (ten), LEBANON (thirteen), and SYRIA (ten), and served over 600,000 refugees qualified for its services. (For estimates as to the number of Palestinian refugees and their geographical distribution, see REFUGEES.)

UNTSO   see ARAB-ISRAEL CONFLICT.

VELAYATI, ALI-AKBAR (b. 1945)   Iranian Foreign Minister 1981–1997. Velayati was born in a northern suburb of Tehran. He completed his studies of medicine at the University of Tehran in 1971, and in 1977 completed his specialization in pediatrics in the US. Before the Islamic revolution in 1979 he served as Associate Professor in the faculty of Health Sciences in Tehran. Following the revolution he was appointed Deputy Minister of Health. Was a member of the Islamic Republic Party and was elected to the *Majlis*. In 1981 he was appointed Minister of Foreign Affairs. Since then he was in charge primarily of implementing the policy laid down by the leaders of the regime, and especially RAFSANJANI. Velayati, who demonstrates moderation in his declarations, has done a lot to improve the relations between Iran and the Arab and European states. However, he remained faithful to the political-ideological line of the regime against renewal of relations with the UNITED STATES, the Middle East peace process and the existence of the State of ISRAEL. Following the election of Khatami as President in May 1997, Velayati was removed from office.

VENICE DECLARATION   see ARAB-ISRAEL PEACE-MAKING.

WAFD (Arabic: Delegation: Also New *Wafd*)   EGYPT's principal nationalist Party from the 1920s to 1953. It emerged following the 1919 anti-British riots and consequent delegation of Egyptian nationalist leaders sent to BRITAIN to negotiate Egypt's independence. The delegation was led by Ahmad Sa'ad Zaghlul, as was the Party until Zaghlul's death in 1927, when Mustafa al-Nahhas became its leader. The *Wafd*, with nationalism and the completion of Egypt's independence as its main goal, was modernistic and liberal-democratic in internal matters and for many years fought the King and his Court because of their attempts to reduce Parliament's power. While the *Wafd* was a school and transition stage for most Egyptian politicians, many left it in the early 1920s to establish rival, mostly more conservative parties. The *Wafd* won the elections of 1924, 1925 (a partial win), 1926, 1929, 1936, 1942 and 1950—usually when a *Wafdist* or neutral government held the elections. But it was in power only for short periods in 1924, 1928 and 1930—and later in 1936–1937, 1942–1944 and 1950 to January 1952, with the King and his Court repeatedly finding ways to dissolve parliament or end the *Wafd's* rule by other means. The *Wafd* split in 1937 when it expelled a group of younger leaders headed by M.F. Nuqrashi and Ahmad Maher, who later founded the *Sa'adist* Party, and in 1942 when it expelled the Coptic *Wafd* leader Makram Ubeid who founded an "Independent Wafdist Bloc." In the 1940s, a reformist, moderately leftist faction developed inside the *Wafd*. In the early 1930s, the Party also established para-military formations (the "Blue Shirts"), but they had little impact.

Initially considered extremist and anti-British, the *Wafd* came to be regarded by the British as the group most representative of Egyptian nationalism, the one with which an agreement should, and could, be reached. Indeed, the Anglo-Egyptian Treaty of 1936 was concluded while Egypt was led by the *Wafd*. In February 1942 the British compelled King Farouq to dismiss his government and appoint Nahhas Prime Minister, hoping a *Wafd* government would cooperate with the British war effort more willingly than the King's men. Farouq dismissed Nahhas in October 1944 (shortly after he had established the basis for the ensuing League of Arab states), after the British toned down their interference in Egyptian politics. Eventually, it was a *Wafd* government which in 1951 precipitated a severe crisis in Anglo-Egyptian relations; it had to resign in January 1952.

In 1952 the new officers' regime compelled the *Wafd* to "purge" its leadership. But in 1953 it was banned altogether, along with all other political parties. When President al-SADAT reintroduced a multiparty system in 1976–1977, some twenty-four to twenty-eight members of the National Assembly joined to reestablish the *Wafd*. The application of the "New *Wafd*" to be licensed as a Party was at first rejected because the new party law banned the reactivation of pre-1952 leaders and parties. In 1978

the license was granted; but it was hedged in by so many restrictions, including the disqualification of the Party's main leader, Fu'ad Siraj al-Din, as a pre-1952 man, that the *Wafd* redissolved itself the same year. However, in 1983, the Administrative Court allowed its re-constitution and lifted the disqualification of Siraj al-Din. In the elections of May 1984, the combined list of New Wafd and theMUSLIM BROTHERHOOD won fifty-seven to fifty-eight seats in the 448-seat National Assembly, becoming the only opposition group represented in the Assembly as a recognized faction. Its deputies included eight of the Muslim Brotherhood movement—itself not licensed to present candidates. This election alliance of New *Wafd* and the Brotherhood was terminated toward the elections of 1987.

In 1987, the *Wafd* began publishing a daily paper (*al-wafd al-jadid*), the first opposition licensed daily since 1952. In the April 1987 elections, the *Wafd* won thirty-six seats, losing its position as the principal opposition group and the only one represented in the Assembly. The New *Wafd* Party boycotted the 1990 elections to the People's Assembly, like most of the opposition parties, and had no representation in the house.

WAHHABIS, WAHHABIYYA Puritan, ultra-conservative movement founded in the 1740s in the Arabian Peninsula by Muhammad ibn Abdel Wahhab from Uweina in Najd. His teaching was adopted and spread from about 1745 by Muhammad Ibn Sa'ud of the Anaiza tribe who ruled the Dar'iyya region. The Wahhabiyya, SUNNI Muslims of the Hanbali school, greatly influenced by the teachings of Ibn Taimiyya (d. 1328), claimed that Islam had been distorted by innovations, and strove to restore it to the purity of the *Quran* and the early Sunna. They rejected most later interpretations of Islamic theology and mysticism (*Sufiyya*), and objected especially to the popular veneration of saints and tombs. They forbade the decoration of mosques, and banned all luxuries, including coffee and tobacco. They regarded all Muslims who did not accept their teachings as heretics.

After the Saudis had spread the Wahhabiyya in Najd, they began raiding other regions in the peninsula (HIJAZ, Yemen) and along the northern borders. Their zealous rejection of the cult of tombs led them, in the course of these raids, to destroy the mosque of the tomb of Hussein ibn Ali in Karbala in southern Iraq in 1802–1803, the Ka'ba in Mecca and the mosque of the tomb of the Prophet Muhammad in Medina in 1803–1804. They also harassed the annual *Hajj* pilgrims' caravans. The Ottoman Sultan then took action against them, mainly through Muhammad Ali, the Governor of EGYPT, and his troops. ¨For the changing fortunes, and decline, of the Saudi Wahhabis in the nineteenth century and their resurgence from 1902 see House of SA'UD, IBN SA'UD, SAUDI ARABIA).

After Ibn Sa'ud consolidated his conquests by the incorporation of Hijaz in 1924–1925, the Wahhabiyya doctrine of ISLAM was imposed as the state religion in his realm, called Saudi Arabia from 1932. Ibn Sa'ud also tried to settle an order of Wahhabiyya "Brethren" (*Ikhwan*) in fortified villages. These efforts were abandoned after a rebellion by the *Ikhwan* had to be suppressed in 1929–1930. Moreover, Wahhabiyya practices and interdicts were gradually mitigated. Indeed, some of them were even eroded by modernization and technological developments (e.g., the strict Wahhabiyya's objection to movies and television), and some of them went out of use. Also, far removed from the original Wahhabiyya's destruction of holy tombs and their mosques, the Saudi Kings began calling themselves "Guardian of the Two Shrines" (namely, of Mecca and Medina) and the protectors and organizers of the *Hajj*.

Outside Saudi Arabia, there are some Wahhabis in the PERSIAN GULF sheikhdoms, particularly in QATAR, where they are the majority of the indigenous population.

Wahhabi teachings had some influence on other fundamentalist trends or sects such as the MAHDIYYA and the SANUSSIYYA, and on reformist-revivalist Islamic thinkers such as Muhammad Abduh and Rashid Rida (see ISLAMIC FUNDAMENTALISM).

WAQF (Pl.: *Awqaf*; in North Africa also called *Habous*) Muslim religious endowment, or trust. Property dedicated as Waqf is given for all time and not subject to any transaction, inheritance or sale. Its income is used for the purpose indicated in the Waqf deed, which may be the welfare of the dedicator's family (Waqf *dhurri* or *ahli*), or support for public worship site, education, or social relief (Waqf *kheiri*). Each Waqf is administered by a custodian (*mutawalli*, nazir) named by the dedicator, and Muslim Law

(SHARI'A) courts have exclusive jurisdiction over Waqf matters.

For over a millenium, Waqf developed into a central institution in Muslim societies, providing welfare and education purposes. At the same time, the accumulation of religiously endowed landed property, which constituted a significant share of the market, and inefficient management and rigidity in the face of changing social and economic conditions, caused Waqf to have a negative economic impact. In the late nineteenth century Waqfs constituted almost three quarters of the agricultural land, in the OTTOMAN EMPIRE, and in the mid-1930s Waqf estates were one seventh of the cultivated land in EGYPT and one sixth in IRAN. It was against this backdrop that modernizing national elites in the Middle Eastern Muslim countries regarded this institution as an obstacle to the consolidation of state power and control of the economy and society; hence they pointed to the backwardness of this institution and need to be reformed, centrally controlled by the government, or even abolished. Yet the religious Islamic establishment opposed far-reaching reforms that would weaken its social status and influence. Reforms in the direction of central administration of Waqf properties began in Egypt in 1851, formalized in the establishment of a particular ministry for that purpose in 1913. In TURKEY all *Awqaf* properties which had been under the supervision of the Ministry of *Awqaf* were transferred in 1924 to "The General Administration of Awqaf" which also controlled the historical and religious institutions and sites. The establishment of new funds for support of public institutions or private enterprises became subjected to the civil code with no connection to the traditional religious Waqf procedure. The League of Nations MANDATES over IRAQ, LEBANON, SYRIA and Palestine, instructed the mandatory powers to administer the *Awqaf* in accordance with the SHARI'A. In British-Mandatory Palestine, the government refrained from interfering with Muslim affairs, and established the Supreme Muslim Council to which the administration of all Waqf matters—among other matters related to the Muslim community—were handed. No reforms were instituted by this body which had been presided by a cleric, al-Hajj Amin al-HUSSEINI. Once attaining independence, the governments of all Arab states—all with a SUNNI Muslim majority, except Iraq—took over the administration of *Awqaf*, But the traditional ruling elites in these states, until the end of the 1940s, confined their reforms, if any, to marginal and minor matters, applying them only to future dedications, not to existing *awqaf*. The military regimes took more radical steps. Syria abolished the family Waqf in 1949 and prohibited the founding of new *awqaf* altogether. Egypt also abolished the family Waqf in 1952, nationalized the administration of *awqaf kheiriyya* (with certain exceptions) in 1953 and authorized the Ministry of Awqaf to use the income of Waqf properties for purposes other than those indicated in their Waqf deed. In 1957, Egypt wholly nationalized Waqf properties, to be distributed within the framework of the agrarian reform, with proceeds of sales earmarked for development projects. TUNISIA also nationalized all Waqf properties in 1961. In Iraq, reforms in the Waqf system have not been similarly far-reaching. In Iran under the PAHLAVI dynasty, the administration of *Awqaf* was traditionally conducted by senior clergy who used the income for religious educational and charity institutions. By the Civil Code of 1928, the Waqf Organization of the Ministry of Education was authorized to transform a Waqf into a private property or prohibit such a change, to control the budgets of *Awqaf*, and take over a Waqf with unknown administrators. With the advent of the Islamic revolution in 1979, however, this code was abolished.

ISRAEL was faced by the special problem that many beneficiaries or administrators of *awqaf* had become absentees in 1948. As the properties were administered by a custodian, changes had to be introduced. In 1965, family *awqaf* were transferred to the beneficiaries' full ownership, and Waqf *kheiri* properties—to Muslim boards of trustees. (see also SHARI'A)

WASHINGTON TALKS see ARAB ISRAEL PEACE-MAKING.

WATER POLITICS Water resources in the Middle East are scarce as a result of the arid and semi-arid climate. Besides insufficiency of water resources, water demand is steadily increasing due to the growing population. Currently, all Middle Eastern water resources are fully utilized and those which have not yet been used are very expensive to develop.

Another major problem of the region is that most of the scarce water resources have been diverted to irrigated farming, which is extremely important in the region's economies. Many regional governments have chosen to pursue policies of encouraging both population growth and agricultural development, which were often crystallized in a policy of "food security." Such a policy promotes food production at any expense, resulting in water wastage.

Additionally, much of the water resources of the Middle East are common to more than one state as Tables 1 and 2 indicate. Not only rivers such as the Nile, Tigris-Euphrates and Jordan-Yarmuk are international or transboundary in their nature. Many of the ground water resources such as those which lie deep below the Sahara in the desert areas between SAUDI ARABIA and JORDAN or which lie below the border areas between Syria and Jordan, are also international water resources. There is a tendency to over-utilize these shared groundwater resources—thus they become lowered very rapidly. But, perhaps, the most important factor which shapes the fate of international water resources is their geopolitical setting and the legal stance of the co-basin countries that share a certain international water resource. Issues of national sovereignty appear as the decisive factors in formulating state policies in relation to their shared water resources.

The most important factor to shape relations amongst states is power-asymmetry or the relative power (hegemonic power) of one country in an international river basin. States may exercise their powers in order to impose a solution to a conflict over water resources. But water is only one of many issues which link countries together. As a result, there is a trade-off between policies concerning the shared water resources and other foreign policy matters. States (even regional powers), are concerned about their image in the international environment and tend to adopt conciliatory stances toward co-basin states. Depending on the history of relations between states (especially that of conflicts and their resolutions), states will tend to use conflict management techniques such as negotiation, adjudication and mediation in their water conflicts and will seek help through international law.

The four major legal doctrines which evolved over the years in relation to sovereignty over water resources use are:

1) The Harmon Doctrine or the principle of absolute territorial sovereignty. According to this, a

Table 1. Shared Water Resources in the Middle East

COUNTRY	Annual River Flow		Total Water Resources in million cubic m/yr	Percentage of Total Flow Originating Outside the Boundaries
	From other countries in million cubic m/yr	To other countries in million cubic m/yr		
Egypt	55.5	0.0	58.1	97
Sudan	119.0	56.5	154.0	77
Iran	x	x	117.5	39
Iraq	66.0	x	109.2	66
Israel	0.5	0	2.2	21*
Jordan	0.4	X	1.7	-
Lebanon	0.6	0.9	5.6	10
Saudi Arabia	0.0	X	4.6	-
Syria	27.9	30	53.7	79
Turkey	7.0	69	193.1	3.5

x No information
Sources: World Resources 1996-7; Gleick, 1993; Bakour and Kolars, 1994.

Table 2. International Rivers in the Middle East

RIVER	Catchment Area in thousand km²	Length in km	Average flow in billion cubic m/yr	Riparians
Nile	3,100,000	6,895	85	Ethiopia, Eritrea,Uganda, Tanzania, Kenya, Zaire, Rwanda, Burzundi, Egypt, Sudan
Tigris	375,000	1,850	48.7	Turkey, Iraq, Iran
Euphrates	444,000	3,000	31.8 (Hit)	Turkey, Syria, Iraq
Jordan-Yarmuk	17,665	2,501	0.9 (Jordan+ Yarmuk)	Lebanon, Syria, Israel, Jordan
Orontes-Asi	16,900	571	2.0	Syria, Turkey, Lebanon
Kabir	98,000	90	0.32	Syria, Turkey
Afrion	278,000	149	0.28	Syria, Turkey

x Riparian, by the tributaries of the Tigris
Sources: Gischler, 1979; Kliot, 1994; Gleick, 1993

state may use the fluvial waters which lie within its territory without any limitation whatsoever, regardless of the effects that this utilization has on other states. This doctrine has often been adopted by upper riparian states.

2) Lower riparians often favor the principles of absolute territorial integrity. According to this, states cannot utilize the waters of an international river in a way which might cause any detrimental effects on co-riparian territory. This doctrine is often tied to prior appropriation of water (or historically acquired rights) in which existing water rights of lower riparians (EGYPT in the Nile, and IRAQ in the Euphrates) must first be respected and satisfied before any claims can be met. Israel claims acquired rights in both the Jordan drainage basin and in the mountain aquifer (see below).

3) Condominium or common jurisdiction of all riparians over the whole international river aims at limiting a state's freedom of action over the utilization of international rivers. The application of this principle would mean that a state has to obtain prior consent from co-riparians for all projects concerned with the utilization of the waters. The emphasis is placed on the mutual development of a river's waters by all riparian states.

4) Finally, there is the principle of equitable utilization which permits the use of a river's waters to the extent that this does no harm to other riparian countries. This principle has become the most widely advocated by the international legal community as evinced by treaties, judicial decisions and international bodies such as the International Law Association (ILA) which postulated the eleven Helsinki

Rules (1967). Most of the ILA rules were adopted by the International Law Commission (ILC), a UN affiliated body which is preparing, on behalf of the United Nations, a multilateral treaty on the peaceful non-navigational uses of fresh water. ILC rules call for equitable and reasonable utilization and participation in the international river basin, specifying the factors relevant to this use.

ILC rules adopted the Helsinki principles in relation to the application of equitable utilization of

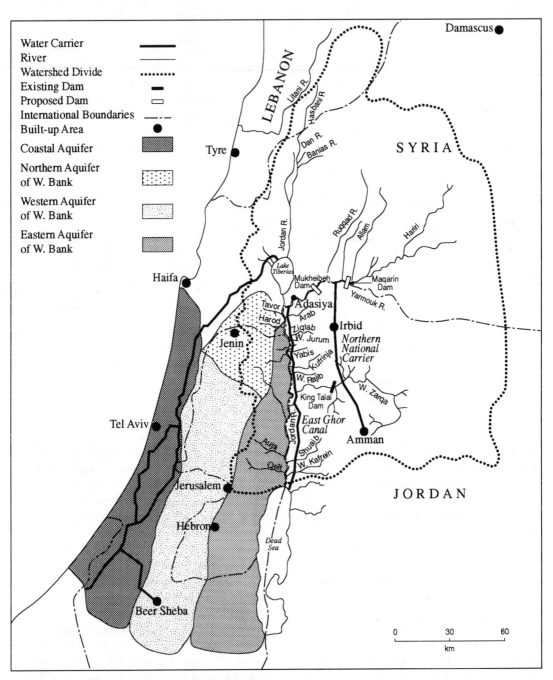

The Jordan River basin and the Israeli–Palestinian shared groundwater resources

water resources of international river basins. These principles are:

1) Geographic, hydrographic, hydrological, climatic and other natural factors.

2) The socioeconomic needs of the water course states concerned.

3) The effects of the use or uses of the international water course caused by one water course state to other water course state.

4) The existing and the potential uses of the international water course.

5) Conservation, protection, development and economy of use of the water resources of the international water course.

6) The availability of alternatives of corresponding value, for a particular planned or existing use.

Most of these principles are used by the partners to transboundary water course in the Middle East to justify their claim for their utilization. Examples are:

economic and agricultural future potential: the SUDAN, TURKEY, SYRIA, Ethiopia

existing use: Egypt, ISRAEL, Iraq

per capita water availability: Syria, Turkey

equity, national security: Turkey, LEBANON, Egypt, Israel.

Equity is difficult to measure and each state selects different aspects of equity in water utilization. In addition, ILC rules advocate another principle in which states are asked not to cause "appreciable harm" to other co-basin states when they develop common water resources. The two principles, that of equitable and reasonable utilization and the "no appreciable harm," are accepted in the customary international law but may contradict each other. Governments insist on a narrow interpretation of the principle of "no appreciable harm," arguing that any action that another riparian takes which may affect the water quantity or quality should be prohibited. This is *the* Egyptian position in relation to a possibility that Ethiopia may use the water of the Blue Nile and thus reduce the flow of the Nile to Egypt. Finally, it should be stated that for the most part water disputes in the Middle East have remained below the military level. One case in which the dispute became militarized is the 1964 Arab diversion plan. The Arab states planned to divert the headwaters of the Jordan into the Yarmuk and to utilize the planned Mukheiba Dam in Jordan (which has

not been built) for storage of the diverted waters. The plan was a response to Israel's construction of the National Water Carrier. The Arab states were motivated not by water needs but by hostility to the Israeli project, claiming that the Carrier would strengthen Israeli capability to support more immigrants—which would be of disadvantage to the Palestinians. Israel launched some military strikes against the diversion works. No matter how acute the crises that may emerge in coming years over water supply in the Middle East, armed conflict is not likely to be an outcome.

The Nile The Nile drainage basin is shared by ten countries. Its catchment area of 1,152 sq. miles (3 million sq. km.) stretches from the wet equatorial climate of Rwanda and Zaire up to the arid areas of Egypt and the Sudan. About eighty-six percent of the Nile's flow originates in Ethiopia and fourteen percent comes from the Equatorial countries: Kenya, Uganda, Tanzania, Zaire, Rwanda, and Burundi. Egypt and the Sudan, (which do not contribute any water to the Nile), have monopolized all its water supply and use practically the whole amount. Ethiopia, which contributes eighty-six percent of its water, uses only one to two percent of its water.

Egypt, the downstream riparian, was the first to develop the Nile for its own needs, and has been doing so for more than 3000 years. Based on history and the doctrine of absolute territorial integrity or prior appropriation of water, Egypt claims that any attempt by other upper riparians, (such as Ethiopia and the Equatorial states to block the Nile's flow to Egypt), would cause Egypt to go to war and would be considered as *casus belli* as declared by the late President SADAT.

For centuries Egypt established its hegemonic stance in the Nile Basin. Under British rule and British protection, Egypt and the Sudan signed the first Nile Agreement of 1929 according to which Egypt received 48 billion m3 of the Nile's water and the Sudan only 4 billion m3. There is no doubt that this agreement reflected not only Egypt's dominance in the Nile basin, but also the weakness of Ethiopia and the powerlessness of the other Equatorial states which were then all colonies of Britain or Belgium. This situation of monopolizing the Nile's water for Egyptian needs changed somewhat after the Sudan became independent in 1956 and demanded a larger share in the Nile's water. The 1959 Nile Agree-

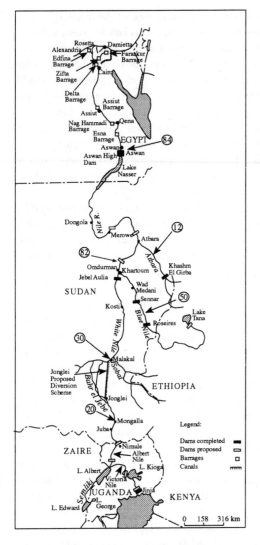

Map 1: The Nile - Sources and Tributaries, Control and Discharge

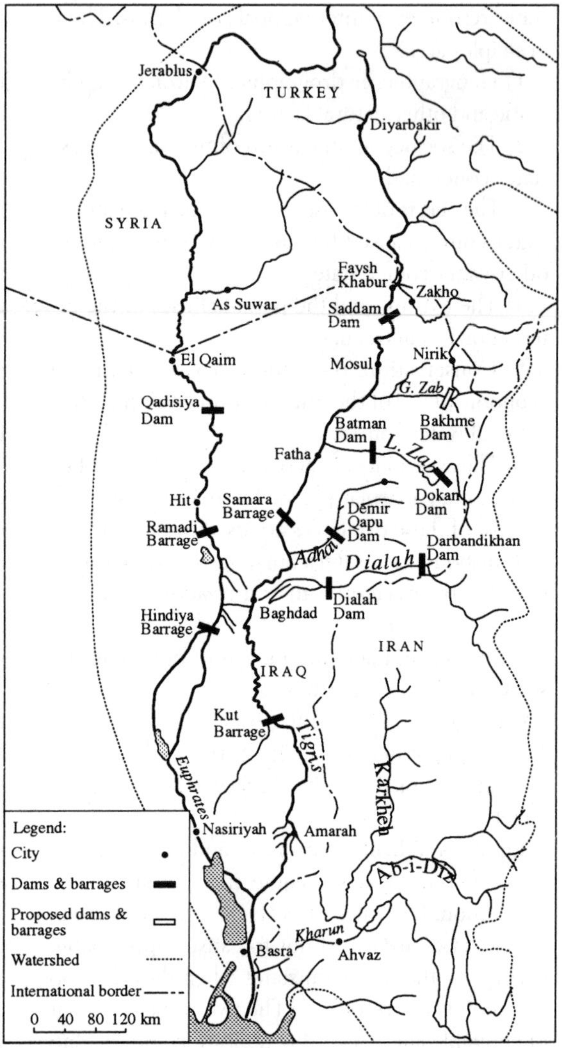

Map 2: The Tigris - Euphrates River Basin

ment between the two (but with the exclusion of all other riparians) acknowledged Egypt's "historic rights" and needs as fixed at 48 billion m3 of water whereas Sudan's needs were determined as 6.0 billion m3. The two countries decided to build a high dam at Aswan to store water for them both. Altogether, the water stored at the dam will be divided as follows: 55.0 billion m3 for Egypt and 18.5 billion m3 for the Sudan. The upper riparians of the Nile have declared on various occasions that they reserve their rights on the Nile. Ethiopia and the Equatorial states do not recognize the validity of the 1929 and 1959 Agreements. Throughout the years the upper

riparians hardly expanded their Nile usage: Ethiopia uses about 1 billion m3 of water and all the other Equatorial states use 1.7 billion m3 of water. They would like to increase this usage because of a combination of factors, such as population growth, droughts and food shortages. Egypt's greatest fear over the years has been that Ethiopia might undertake development of the Blue Nile watershed without Egyptian acquiescence. In 1956 and in 1977 Ethiopia adopted the Harmon Doctrine in relation to its rights to the Nile. But in 1991 the new Ethiopian Arab states drafted an accord of Friendship and Peace with the Sudan. In this both sides affirmed their commitment to equitable shares in the Nile waters with the mutual avoidance of appreciable harm. Based on the principles of ILC rules for equitable allocation, there is no doubt that Ethiopia and the other Equatorial states are entitled to expand their use of the Nile. Based on their geography and hydrological contribution to the Nile (together with their socioeconomic needs and their potential for future development), they are entitled to a larger water allotment of the Nile. Egypt, and to a lesser extent Sudan, can claim in the name of the same principle of equity, their existing uses, socioeconomic needs and lack of alternatives, as the basis for continuing the existing patterns of use. As ILC Rules do not give priority to any of the principles for equitable and reasonable utilization, all the riparians may claim that they are justified in their demands. Egypt and Sudan may also use the "no harm" stipulation to justify the status quo, claiming that any redistribution efforts would be harmful to their existing and future use of the Nile River. Egypt is sustaining a policy of cooperation with its co-basin partners by promoting exchange of data in a network of hydrometereological stations or by promoting Undugu—a voluntary forum of coordination and consultation on socioeconomic affairs including water issues with its partners.

Egypt was able to postpone the moment of truth in which it will have to give away some of the Nile's water it is using in favor of its partners, by exercising a policy based on its dominance and the great power asymmetry in the basins. Egypt is also concerned about its image as a leader amongst African states. Egypt always perceived its foreign relations with neighbors as complex and founded on trade-offs; hence the need to facilitate and benefit the other co-basin members in spheres such as trade. The most significant obstacle to the Nile's integrative cooperation and development is the poverty of its co-basin states and their level of dependence on agrarian economies and food security. Also, the long political instability of the region, its civil and ethnic wars, autocratic regimes and limited foreign aid, have blocked any cooperative efforts. It is not at all certain that altered circumstances will lead to rapid change.

The Tigris-Euphrates The Euphrates originated in the mountains of eastern Turkey and has a discharge of 30.0 billion m3 at the Turkish-Syrian border and 32.0 billion m3 at the Syrian-Iraqi border. Turkey's contribution to the Euphrates flow is estimated at eighty-eight to ninety-eight percent. Syria contributes to the flow of the river by the Khabur and Balikh tributaries, but the sources of these tributaries are also in Turkey.

The Tigris' sources are also located in the high mountains of eastern Turkey, and it flows on the Syrian border to Iraq. The Tigris is joined by the Greater and Lesser Zab, Diyalah and Adhaim tributaries. Turkey contributes thirty-eight percent of the water to the main channel of the Tigris, and an additional eleven percent of the water comes from tributaries which also rise in Turkey. The total amount of the Tigris and its tributaries flow is 52.7 billion m3 per year . The combined natural flow of the Euphrates-Tigris was 81.9 billion m3, but removal of water for irrigation and other uses reduced this flow in recent years.

The old civilization of Mesopotamia, inherited by modern Iraq, was the major beneficiary of the Euphrates water. Similarly to Egypt and Iraq, the downstream riparian has developed the water resources of the Euphrates since time immemorial. As with Ethiopia in the Nile basin, Turkey (the upperstream riparian), found that although it contributed most of the water to the Euphrates, Iraq was the major user of the Euphrates flow and Syria followed suit. Since the late 1980s and early 1990s, Turkey has expanded its use of the Euphrates flow for irrigation and for water storage in its new dams. Turkey is poor in energy sources and intends to use the enormous energy of the Euphrates and Tigris to produce electric power for industry and electricity. In the early 1990s, Turkey initiated a very large development project called the Southeastern Anatolia Project (GAP). This incorporated twenty-two dams and nineteen hydropower projects on the Euphrates and Tigris. Upon completion, the hydropower stations are expected to supply 26 billion kilowatt hours of energy—a quantity which equals almost half of Turkey's current energy needs, and opens up 1.6 million hectares of land to irrigated farming. In 1996, the Keban, Karakaya and Atatürk dams were completed and large amounts of water have accumulated from them, especially at Atatürk Dam. It has been estimated that currently Turkey has reduced the Euphrates flow by 2–3 billion m3 of water. However, when the GAP is fully implemented, depletion of flow due to irrigation and evaporation of water from reservoir surfaces and evapotranspiration will reach 16 billion m3 of the Euphrates flow. Turkey guaranteed its co-riparians on the Euphrates, Syria and Iraq, that it will release a constant flow of the Euphrates water—15.7 billion m3 for their needs. This, however, proved insufficient for reassuring Syria and Iraq.

Syria has modest water resources outside the Euphrates and its tributaries, the Balikh and Khabour. More problematic is the fact that many of the other Syrian water resources are also internationally shared. The Orontes is shared by Lebanon and Turkey, and the Yarmuk with Jordan and Israel. Syria constructed a dam on the Euphrates, the Tabaqa Dam for irrigation and power production. Syria's current use of the Euphrates flow is estimated as 4.0–4.5 billion m3 of water (for irrigation, domestic and evaporation losses). In December 1994, Syria formally protested against Turkey's dam construction programme on the Euphrates, claiming it would prevent Syria from receiving its rightful allocation of water. The flow of the Euphrates to Syria will no doubt be sufficient for Syria's needs in the next decade but insufficient for both Syria and Iraq. Iraq was already using 16.0–17.0 billion m3 of Euphrates flow in the late 1980s. If Syria leaves only 10 billion m3 of Euphrates flow (out of the 16 billion m3 Turkey will leave for it) for Iraq, it will not satisfy Iraq's needs.

The legal and geopolitical setting in the Tigris-Euphrates is very complex. There is no agreement among the riparians of the Tigris-Euphrates. Iraq and Syria combined forces on their common border in 1975 when Syria impounded Tabaqa Dam. Tension between Syria and Turkey soared in early 1990 when Turkey impounded Atatürk Dam. Turkey pledged a Euphrates flow of 15.7 billion m3 of water to its lower co-riparians in 1987 and, again in 1990, and Iraq and Syria signed a bilateral agreement for sharing the Euphrates water at fifty-eight and forty-two percent, respectively.

The legal positions of the co-riparians reflect both their interests and the region's sensitive geopolitical setting. Turkey has adopted a doctrine of absolute sovereignty (Harmon Doctrine) in relation to the Tigris-Euphrates. Therefore, Turkey cannot expect to receive international funding for the GAP which has been implemented by Turkish self-financing. In August 1991, Süleyman DEMEREL, then the

Turkish Prime Minister, summed up the Turkish position as follows: "Water is an upstream resource and downstream users cannot tell us how to use our resource. By the same token, oil is an upstream resource in many Arab countries and we do not tell them how to use it." More recently, Turkey adopted a new legal stance and proclaimed its right to develop the Tigris-Euphrates based on the principle of "equitable utilization." Turkey specified that, based on its enormous water contribution to the Tigris-Euphrates and the fact that Iraq has an alternative source to the Euphrates in the form of the Tigris waters, it is entitled to expand its use of the Euphrates. Other claims which Turkey raised also followed the principles of ILC rules for equitable utilization. It pointed to water wastage in both Iraq and Syria and insisted that it comply with international law by providing early notification of the GAP plan to its co-riparians and also that its dams would provide a regulated water supply to its co-basin states.

Syria once adopted the doctrine of absolute sovereignty in relation to the Yarmuk-Jordan. This effectively abandoned any legal basis for claims against Turkey in relation to the Euphrates. However, more recently, Syria changed its mind and adopted the limited sovereignty doctrine. Syria now claims that it is entitled to Euphrates water in order to take advantage of its economic potential and increase food production. Syria also supports demands for equitable utilization based on its low per capita water availability. Syrian adherence to the principle of equitable and reasonable utilization is also reflected in its agreement to share the Euphrates flow with Iraq at the border: fifty-eight percent to Iraq and the remainder to Syria. Syria and Iraq also cooperate and coordinate their positions in negotiations with Turkey—not an easy task for two hostile regimes.

Iraq first adopted a claim to the Euphrates based on its "acquired rights" and thus adopted a similar position to that of Egypt. Iraq invoked the principle of "appreciable harm" emphasizing the principle of prior use in all its discussions with Turkey and Syria. Turkey rejected Iraqi claims for "acquired rights," insisting that this was only one of many factors to be considered in reaching equitable utilization of an international river.

Indeed, the principle of equitable apportionment might expect states such as Iraq and Egypt to modify their patterns of water use in order to permit upstream states such as Turkey and Ethiopia to develop their hydro-electric and agricultural potential.

As in other parts of the world, water conflicts are not divorced from the various geopolitical settings. In the Tigris-Euphrates basin the conflict that surrounds tensions between Syria and Turkey affects issues other than water. Syria demands the return of the Alexandretta-Hatai which was detached from Syria in 1939 (then under French mandate) and integrated into Turkey. Turkey has been aggrieved by Syria's full utilization of the Orontes—another international river shared by the two—but with very little water remaining for Turkish usage. Turkey also overtly links the Euphrates flow and Syria's support of the Kurdish guerrilla terrorist actions in Turkey. Turkey threatened Syria that if it does not stop this support, the Euphrates flow will be curtailed.

Turkey and Iraq shared many interests such as trade and oil and there is a genuine desire to solve the water conflict because of the multilateral interests of both countries. Iraq's Syria relations, on the other hand, are strained, due to political competition and rivalry between the two regimes. Yet they were able to cooperate in the water sector in their struggle against Turkish hegemony though without much efficiency. Despite the conflict among the Euphrates riparian states, in theory they could benefit from cooperation and trade-offs: Iraqi oil for Turkish water or Turkish water for Syrian gas is one example of how to promote regional stability. The exchange of water and food for oil might be a future formula for regional stability and security. Turkey may supply its southern neighbors with food and technology in return for oil. The question remains as to the level of attraction of all these goods in the complex bargaining process over the Tigris-Euphrates basin.

The Jordan-Yarmuk Basin The Jordan River and its tributary, the Yarmuk, are shared by the states of Lebanon, Syria, Israel and Jordan. In the Lower Jordan Valley, the Palestinians could also be considered as co-riparians. The total flow of the upper Jordan River is 540 million m3 and about 450–500 million m3 is used by Israel in its National Water Carrier. The Yarmuk has a discharge of 400-500 million m3 of water. Syria uses about half of it, whereas the Hashemite Kingdom of Jordan is using 130 million m3 by the East Ghor Canal (King Abdullah Canal). In the last decade Israel has been using about 70–100 MCM a year. Israel and the Pales-

tinians also share groundwater resources: the mountain aquifer with 679 million m3 of water of which the most important is the western sub aquifer with 300–335 million m3 of water. Israel utilizes 483 MCM of the mountain aquifer, whereas the Palestinians are using 130–138 million m3 from it. All the above water resources are over-utilized, far beyond their natural recharge, and there is a chronic water shortage in the Palestinian areas and in Jordan. Until 1994, there was neither agreement on water allocation, nor cooperation in the use of common water resources between Israel and its Arab co-riparian neighbors.

In the early 1990s the peace process between Israel, Jordan and the Palestinians included intensive discussions in the water sector. The Israeli-Jordanian peace treaty, signed on 26 October 1994, addressed matters relating to water resources shared by these parties. Israel and Jordan agreed to mutually recognize the rightful allocations of both sides in Jordan-Yarmuk's waters and also in the groundwater resources of Wadi Araba which was utilized by Israel and which were transferred to Jordan as part of the Peace Treaty. Israel agreed to provide Jordan with 30 million m3 of water from Lake Tiberias in the short term and to provide 20 million m3 of water from the Beisan Valley. In the long term, after the construction of storages on the Lower Jordan and the Yarmuk and after the saline water of the Lower Jordan is treated, Jordan will gain about 100 million m3 of Jordan's Yarmuk water. Currently Israel delivers to Jordan each year 30 million m3 of water which is conveyed by a pipe specifically constructed for that purpose. Israel was allowed to continue using the wells it used in Wadi Araba which provide 5–6 million m3 of water. Israel and Jordan also established a joint water committee which discussed all the common water issues and future projects. The water agreement between Israel and Jordan could be interpreted as equitable as it tries to improve water scarcity in Jordan. Israel, though it has a midstream position in the Jordan-Yarmuk, was able to dictate its priorities in water use of the Jordan-Yarmuk because of the power asymmetry in that basin and because of Israel's role as a dominant power in the basin. However, a recognition by Jordan (and the Palestinians) gives Israel benefits outside the water sector, but it reinforces its readiness for minor concessions there. Moreover, there is always an emphasis on mutualism, namely that each concession Israel makes will be reciprocated by one from the "other" side. There is significant external influence in the negotiations on water issues. In addition to Israelis and Jordanians, the Americans and the World Bank were deeply involved and ready to assist with financial aid for some of the planned projects.

On 18 September 1995, Israel and the Palestinians signed an Agreement on Water and Sewage. In this Agreement Israel recognized Palestinian water rights in the West Bank and agreed to expand Palestinian water supply during an interim period by 28.6 million m3/year for supply of urgent needs in the domestic sector. In the long run, an additional quota of 41–51 million m3 will be developed from the mountain aquifer for Palestinian needs. Many of the expressions and arrangements in that agreement point to leniency in the direction of more equitable utilization of the common water resources. Examples are the agreement to develop additional water for various uses; the prevention of water quality deterioration; reuse and treatment of sewage water; and the establishment of a Joint Water Committee. Israel agreed on parity in managing the shared water resources and sewage in order to secure responsible process of management. However, the water agreements between Israel and Jordan and Israel and the Palestinians are subject to geopolitical fluctuations in the region. Especially on the Israeli-Palestinian front, the recurrent breakdowns and standstills deriving mainly from deep territorial disagreements, mean that understanding certain cooperation between Israel and the Palestinian authority is closely linked to the peacemaking process.

WEAPONS OF MASS DESTRUCTION see NON CONVENTIONAL WEAPONS.

WEIZMANN, EZER (b. 1924)   Israeli soldier, politician and the seventh President of the State of Israel. Born in Tel Aviv, nephew to Haim WEIZMANN. In the course of World War II he served in the RAF and was stationed in EGYPT and India. From 1946 to 1948 Weizmann was a member of the IZL underground movement. He served in the "Aviation Service" that preceded the establishment of the Israeli Air Force. During Israel's War of Independence (see ARAB-ISRAEL CONFLICT) he flew ammunition and supplies to the Negev and Gush Etzion and in

1948 was sent to Czechoslovakia to learn to fly the Messerschmidt planes and fly one of them back to Israel. Weizmann served in the Air Force until 1966 and from 1958 served as Commander of the force. In the years 1966–1969 he was head of the Operations Branch and Deputy Chief of Staff.

In 1969 Weizmann retired from the IDF to become Minister of Transportation on behalf of *Gahal* in the second National Unity Government formed by Golda MEIR. In the years 1971–1972 he served as Chairman of the *Herut* Movement Executive and resigned in December 1972 due to differences of opinion with party leader Menahem BEGIN. He returned to *Herut* in May 1973 and was elected to the ninth Knesset (1977). Weizmann was appointed Minister of Defense in Begin's first Arab states, and played an important role in the peace process with Egypt. In March 1978 he was responsible for the performance of the Litani Operation in Lebanon, and after that advocated the formation of a National Unity Government to advance the peace process—an idea rejected by Begin. During this period a major metamorphosis occurred in his opinions and he became increasingly critical of the rigid and uncompromising policy of his party regarding the peace process, while clashing with Minister of Agriculture Ariel SHARON over the issue of the government's settlement policy in the occupied territories. In May 1980 Weizmann resigned from the Arab states, and in November was expelled from *Herut*.

In the years 1980–1984 Weizmann engaged in business. In March 1984 he formed a new party *Yahad*, which ran in the elections to the eleventh Knesset (1984). *Yahad* won three seats and joined the bloc which formed around the *Ma'arach* (Alignment) toward the establishment of the National Unity Government. In the Arab states formed by Shimon PERES he was appointed Minister without Portfolio and a member of the Inner Cabinet. In January 1985 he was appointed minister responsible for coordinating the affairs of Israel's Arab population.

In October 1986, Weizmann joined the Labor Party. In the National Unity Government formed by Yitzhak SHAMIR in 1988 he was appointed Minister of Science. At the end of 1989 Shamir threatened to expel him from the Arab states for allegedly holding contacts with members of the PALESTINE LIBERATION ORGANIZATION (PLO). After the National

Unity Government was dismantled he decided to leave politics and resigned from the Knesset in February 1992.

In 1993 Weizmann was elected President of the State, and was frequently criticized for his political expressions, his refusal to reduce the sentences of several life prisoners, his chauvinistic attitude on women's issues and homophobic statements. Following the election of Binyamin NETANYAHU to the Premiership in June 1996 and the sense of crisis in the relations with the Palestinians, Weizmann occasionally played a diplomatic role with Israel's Arab partners in an effort to restore the peacemaking process.

WEIZMANN, HAIM (1874–1952)   Chemistry professor, Zionist leader and first President of the State of ISRAEL. Born in RUSSIA, he was active in the Zionist Movement (see ZIONISM) from its very beginning. In 1903 he was one of the founders of the Democratic Faction, which favored "practical Zionism." In 1904 Weizmann migrated to Great BRITAIN, where he received a professorship in chemistry at Manchester University. With the help of contacts with British statesmen and journalists, and thanks to his contribution to the British war effort, Weizmann was largely responsible for the issuing of the BALFOUR DECLARATION on 2 November 1917. On 4 June 1918, with British encouragement, he met with the Emir Feisal, who later became King of SYRIA and after that of IRAQ, and reached an agreement on Jewish-Arab cooperation with him.

Weizmann was President of the Zionist Organization and its main representative in talks with the British Arab states from 1921 to 1946, with a break in the years 1931–1935. His support of full cooperation with the British Arab states was the main reason for his defeat in the 1931 Zionist Congress. Weizmann also advocated a moderate policy toward the Arabs. Until 1937 he supported a plan for political parity between JEWS and Arabs in Palestine, irrespective of their numerical balance. After 1937 he started to support the partition idea and the establishment of two separate states for Jews and Arabs, even though he did not object to the Jewish state joining a Middle Eastern federation (see ARAB-ISRAEL PEACEMAKING).

Even though Weizmann supported the 1942 Biltmore Program, which called for the establishment of a Jewish commonwealth in Palestine, tension developed between himself and David Ben GURION, after Ben Gurion accused him of excessive independence. In addition, Weizmann's moderate policy did not suit the struggle which started to develop within the Jewish community against the British policy in Palestine after 1939. His absence from Palestine increased his detachment from the rest of the members of the Zionist Executive, and weakened his influence. However, his personal weight and prestige were crucial in convincing US President Harry Truman to support the establishment of a Jewish state during the crucial years 1947–1948.

In May 1948 Weizmann was chosen as the first President of the State of Israel and he was sworn in on 16 February 1949. Due to his poor health and the largely ceremonial nature of the office of President, Weizmann did not play an important role in formulating the policies of the new state. The enterprises which he supported most warmly were those of the Hebrew University of Jerusalem, which was inaugurated in 1925, and the Weizmann Institute for Science in Rehovot, opened in 1934, where he established his private residence.

WELFARE PARTY (Tur. Refah Partisi)   see ERKABAN, NECMETTIN.

WEST BANK   The eastern part of Palestine occupied by JORDAN during the 1948 War (see ARAB-ISRAEL CONFLICT and formally annexed in April 1950. The term "West Bank" was coined by the Jordanian regime as part of its effort to blur the Palestinian identity, hence adopting the idea of "Unity of the Two Banks" (*wahdat al-daffatein*) of the River Jordan, in which former Transjordan, east of the River, formed the "East Bank." The appellation soon became universally used. The WEST BANK—including East JERUSALEM—comprised an area of approximately 2,200 sq. miles (5,700 sq. km.). In 1948, the population was about 400,000 plus a futher 200,000 REFUGEES from the ISRAEL-held areas. Jordanian statistics put it at over 800,000 in the 1960s. In the June 1967 War the West Bank was occupied by Israel. The population at that time—after considerable migration to the East Bank during the nineteen years of Jordanian rule, and a wave of refugees during and in the immediate aftermath of the 1967 War (200,000–300,000—see PALESTINE ARABS)—was about 600,000 (without the 70,000 inhabitants of East Jerusalem, which was incorporated in Israel), including 245,000 refugees (65,000 of them in camps), according to UNRWA records. In the late 1990s the total Palestinian population of the West Bank was estimated at approximately 1.2 million (without East Jerusalem). In addition, the Jewish population in the area grew steadily, mainly by new settlers and settlements, reaching in late 1997 155,000 in 128 settlements.

Economy Under Israel's occupation, the West Bank's economy developed rapidly until 1977–1978 as a result of the link to the Israeli market, and increasing labor opportunities in Israel. Israel remained the largest market for the West Bank produce and services and is the dominant exporter to the West Bank, creating relations of dependence on the Israeli economy. From the late 1970s, this growth slowed down and reached severe crisis in the mid-1980s, coupled with the shrinking labor opportunities in, and remittances from, the OIL producing countries, resulting in economic depression which was much behind the eruption of the INTIFADA in late 1987.

In 1992, over 35% of the total labor force was employed in Israel, mostly in construction (73.7%) and other menial, low-paid jobs. Agriculture has been the West Bank's largest economic sector, constituting in 1991 sixteen to seventeen percent of the area's GDP and employing twenty-nine percent of the labor force. Extensive cultivation of land shrunk over the years due to severe restrictions on water consumption by the Israeli authorities. In the early 1990s the irrigated land made up less than 5% of the West Bank area. Other economic sectors contributing to the GDP were: small industry (6.5%), construction (10.7%), public and community services (10.5%).

Despite the Palestinian attempts to disengage from and minimize the links with the Israeli economy during the *intifada*, the economy of the West Bank remained largely dependent on Israel. This has been demonstrated primarily by the employment of Palestinians across the "green line" separating Israel and the West Bank. Opportunities of employment in Israel have shrunk since the GULF WAR of 1991 due to Israel's restrictions, which assumed occasionally to impose full closure on the Palestinian-inhabited areas since 1993, due to serious terrorist attacks against Israelis. The economic cost of those

closures to the Palestinian economy in the West Bank and Gaza Strip have been approximately estimated at 1.2 million dollars a day and over. Pressures by Israeli employers and foreign governments and economic agencies to lift the repeated closures led to the increase of the labor force allowed to work in Israel from 22,000 in 1996 to 37,000 in mid-1997 (for other economic aspects, see also PALESTINIAN AUTHORITY).

Under Jordanian rule the inhabitants of the West Bank constituted about one-half of the total population of Jordan. The West Bank provided thirty-five-forty percent of Jordan's GDP and its government revenue, nearly one-half of its industrial and sixty–eighty percent of its agricultural production. It was represented in both houses of Parliament by one-half of the members, and many of its inhabitants occupied senior positions in Jordan's administration and public life. Politically active, volatile and more sophisticated than the East Bankers, the Arabs of the West Bank were an element of unrest and ferment in Jordan and a growing ground for much opposition, but throughout the years of Jordanian rule there was no movement for secession nor for the creation of an independent Palestinian-Arab state separate from Jordan.

In June 1967, the West Bank was occupied by Israel and put, in accordance with International Law and practice, under military government, with the laws of the previous government for occupying country remaining in force. This rule was not applied to East Jerusalem which had after the war immediately been declared "united" with Israeli West Jerusalem, i.e., incorporated in Israel, an act formally finalized in July 1980. From early 1982, Israel replaced its military government of the West Bank and Gaza with "civil administration" subordinated to the regional military command of the Israel Defense Force. The change was meant to enable Israel to maintain its overall control of the region by identifying the military command as the "source of authority" for a future Palestinian self-governing authority to be established in accordance with the Camp David Agreements. Practically, the "civil administration" continued to be manned by military personnel and was never applied to the Israeli settlements in the occupied territories on which the Israeli Law was applied. Under Israel's military rule, two election campaigns to the local government authorities were held (1972 and 1976), as an act manifesting normalcy aimed at validating Israel's claim to continue its control of this occupied area. While the first elections by and large reaffirmed the status of the traditional leadership of notables, the second elections brought a generation shift, and the rise of a new stratum of politically radical mayors linked to the PALESTINIAN GUERRILLA ORGANIZATIONS, which gradually challenged Israel's continued occupation through the establishment of the "Committee of National Guidance." This culminated in the head-on collision in 1982 over the refusal of most of them to recognize the newly established "civil administration" by Israel. Consequently, Israel decided to postpone further elections to local government in the West Bank indefinitely.

From 1967, Israel adopted a policy of "open bridges," with Jordan (and through its other Arab states) tacitly complying with that policy; mutual visits between the West Bank and Jordan were allowed, though under strict control, as was the movement of goods and funds—permitting an export of the agricultural produce of the West Bank to Jordan, and through it, to other Arab countries as well. Jordan also retained considerable influence in the West Bank, continuing to pay salaries of former officials of its government, channelling funds to public and semi-public institutions—thanks to Arab financial aid allotted by the Khartoum ARAB SUMMIT CONFERENCE of September 1967, to serve the steadfastness (sumud) of the Palestinians in the Israeli-occupied territories—and being consulted by West Bank (and, in the 1970s, increasingly so also by GAZA STRIP) notables and political leaders on steps and positions to be taken. Some institutions, such as the Muslim Council in East Jerusalem (a religious-political body established shortly after the war by leading Jordan-oriented figures), were directly linked to Jordan. The West Bank continued to be represented in Jordan's Parliament; but the one-half ratio was no longer maintained. No elections were held in the kingdom as a whole, including the West Bank from 1967, and new representatives of the West Bank to the Parliament could only be nominated by the Jordanian regime, some of them being East Bank residents.

However, HASHEMITE Jordan and King HUSSEIN increasingly lost support in public opinion, especially after the bloody clashes between the Jordanian armed forces and the Palestinian Guerrilla Organizations in September 1970 and again in July 1971. Although the Hashemite regime cultivated links and channels and continued claiming the West Bank as part of its territory, it did little to organize its supporters, mainly due to financial constraints, but also as a result of Israel's strict forbidding of any political activity in the West Bank and Gaza Strip.

In March 1972, King Hussein proposed a federal structure for a future reunited Jordan and the West Bank—unpopular amongst the Palestinian residents of the West Bank and Gaza Strip. From 1978, Arab aid funds (an annual 100 million dollars for ten years) were allotted to the Palestinians in the occupied territories by the Arab summit conference held in Baghdad, to be distributed by a joint Jordanian-PLO committee in Amman. However, only half of the expected funds were actually transferred to the joint committee, because most Arab oil-rich states failed to implement their share in the aid. The joint committee promoted coordination between Jordan and the PLO on other political issues, culminating in the Amman Agreement signed by PLO chairman Yasser ARAFAT and King Hussein, on joint political action aimed at establishing a Jordanian-Palestinian confederation.

In 1986, following the suspension of the Amman Agreement by King Hussein, Jordan reinforced its posture among the Palestinians in the occupied territories at the expense of the PLO (with the tacit support of Israel), announcing a five-year economic and social development plan for the inhabitants of the West Bank, tentatively set at 1,300 million dollars. However, a shortage of financial resources rendered this project impracticable, and despite a growing effort of the Hashemite regime to enhance the status of its supporters in the West Bank in 1986–1987 by establishing a new daily newspaper in Jerusalem (al-Nahar), with the eruption of the IN-TIFADA in December 1987, the Palestinians in the West Bank manifested unchallenged support for the PLO, with growing resentment toward Jordan's attempts to maintain its image as an involved party in determining the political future of this region.

On July 31 1988 King Hussein announced the legal and administrative disengagement of Jordan from the West Bank, and in November of that year the Palestinian National Council session in Algiers proclaimed the independence of the Palestinian state based on the UN partition resolution of 29 November 1947.

In accordance with the Declaration of Principles (see ARAB-ISRAEL PEACEMAKING) on the establishment of a Palestinian self-governing authority, of 13 September 1993, and the Cairo Agreement on the Gaza Strip and Jericho, the PLO assumed control of the Jericho enclave in the Jordan Valley on 17 May 1994. In November and December 1995, under the terms of the Interim Agreement on the West Bank and Gaza Strip between Israel and the PALESTINIAN AUTHORITY signed in Taba on 28 September 1995, Israeli armed forces withdrew from all Palestinian towns in the West Bank (Nablus, Ramallah, al-Bireh, Jenin, Tulkarm, Qalqilya, Bethlehem), save Hebron, the withdrawal from which was postponed to the aftermath of Israel's general elections of May 1996. In September 1996 bloody clashes erupted between Israeli soldiers and Palestinian police in the West Bank and Gaza Strip, in the wake of the opening of the Hasmonean Tunnel by Israel in the Old City of Jerusalem. Eventually, the withdrawal was implemented only in January 1997, the IDF retaining responsibility for the security of some 400 Jewish settlers occupying some fifteen percent of the town (see also PALESTINIAN AUTHORITY). The Hebron Agreement reaffirmed Israel's commitment to redeploy (namely, withdraw) its military forces from the rural Palestinian areas in the West Bank in two phases, to be completed in October 1997 and August 1998. However, differences soon surfaced regarding the interpretation of the scope of Israel's withdrawal: ninety percent according to the PA; forty percent according to the Israeli government, and even this was only in the context of the permanent settlement and not prior to it. From the beginning of 1997, Israeli projects of building new Jewish neighborhoods in East Jerusalem and renewed suicide bombings in the summer of that year in Jerusalem, perpetrated by HAMAS activists in Jerusalem, further deepened the stalemate in the peacemaking process.

In the Israel-occupied West Bank, though without Israeli aid, several post-secondary colleges have turned into universities (Bir Zeit, 1975; al-Najah, Nablus, 1977; Bethlehem—a Catholic institution—1973; Hebron Islamic College, 1972). A lively press in East Jerusalem, including several dailies (al-Quds, al-Fajr, al-Sha'b, al-Liwa'al-Nahar), served the West Bank and Gaza, too—and, though subject to Israeli censorship, vigorously expressed their views. In the aftermath of the Gulf War, al-Fajr and al-Sha'bwere closed down due to financial shortage of the PLO, and in 1997 the Jordan-oriented al-Nahar was also closed due to inability to compete with the newly established papers of the PA al-Ayyam and al-Hayat al-Jaidida.

WESTERN SAHARA CONFLICT A territorial dispute over formerly Spanish Sahara—the western extremities of the Sahara, on the Atlantic Ocean—since the end of Spain's rule in 1976, involving primarily MOROCCO, MAURITANIA, ALGERIA, LIBYA and the indigenous inhabitants of the disputed territory.

The disputed territory was a Spanish possession from the nineteenth century. In 1958 the Spanish Sahara province was formally created, encompassing the Spanish colonies of Saguia al-Hamra and Rio del Oro, with al-Ayun as its capital, with an area of approximately 100,000 sq.miles (260,000 sq.km). There were no precise data on the population of the province, a mixture of Moorish-BERBER and African stock, including some Arab elements. The sedentary population was assumed to be approximately 25,000 maximum, and the number of nomads estimated at 30,000–40,000, although some sources cited figures of 50,000–80,000. Nonetheless, Saharan activists since the 1970s declared far higher figures. Since the late 1970s, during the Moroccan-Sahara War (see below), most of these nomads allegedly crossed the border into Algeria. Western Sahara's main and only economic asset is large phosphate deposits developed by Spain in the recent decades of its rule of the territory.

Once independent, Morocco claimed a large part of Western Sahara, including areas in the then French-dominated Algeria, as well as territories of Spanish Sahara that had been a Spanish Protectorate and were handed over in the 1950s and 1960s, perceiving them as part of the historic Moroccan homeland. Hence, Morocco refused to recognize the independent status of MAURITANIA once it had been decolonized in 1960. Spain rejected Morocco's claims, envisaging instead a gradual increase in local self-government within a Spanish commonwealth. In 1963 the Western Sahara for the first time took part in elections to the Spanish Cortes (males only, three deputies, of whom two were tribal chiefs). In 1967 a local Assembly (Jama'a) was set up—forty tribal chiefs, and forty elected. Spain also continued investing in Spanish Sahara and developing the phosphate mines, including a sixty-mile conveyor belt to the coast and loading facilities, opened in 1972-73.

From the mid-1960s the UN General Assembly was discussing the problem of Spanish Sahara. Faced with Morocco's claims versus Spain's concepts and local demands for independence, it recommended a referendum. Spain accepted that recommendation in principle and reiterated that acceptance several times, but took no action to prepare such a referendum. Morocco opposed this, insisting that the Western Sahara was part of its national territory. Algeria, a powerful and assertive neighbor, in competition with Morocco over Maghrebi leadership, rejected Morocco's claims, favoring independence. Mauritania, involved in its own conflict with Morocco, wavered. Several Moroccan-Algerian-Mauritanian summit meetings failed to reach an agreement. Local organizations, most of them advocating independence, emerged in the 1970s, and around 1973–1975 the "Popular Organization for the Liberation of al-Saguia al-Hamra and Rio del Oro" (POLISARIO) became the leading one.

Before the official end of the Spanish government in Western Sahara, and in order to stress its claim over the territory, in October 1975 the Moroccan regime initiated the "Green March" in which tens of thousands of Moroccans entered the Spanish-ruled territory, ostensibly as a manifestation of popular will of the Moroccan people. In February 1976, Spain handed the territory over to Morocco and Mauritania, following their agreement to divide the area between them, with Morocco annexing the northern part, including the phosphate mines of Bou Craa. The POLISARIO, backed by Algeria, responded by initiating armed resistance against both Morocco and Mauritania, and proclaiming the establishment of "Saharan Arab Democratic Republic". In August 1979, Mauritania renunced its share of the Western Sahara, which was immediately annexed by Morocco as a new province, Oued al-Dahab. This aggravated the conflict and turned it into an ongoing war between the POLISARIO and Morocco. (For details, see MOROCCO.) From the mid-1970s on, the armed conflict over the Western Sahara became the pivot of inter-Arab relations in the MAGHREB, with Algeria (and to a lesser extent, Libya too), extending military and financial support, including

military bases on its soil, from which raids on Moroccan garrison forces in the Western Sahara were launched.

Algeria-based SADR was recognized, gradually, by several countries —mainly of the leftist-revolutionary African group (not the Soviet Bloc). By 1979, twenty-three countries had done so, sixteen of which were African; by the mid-1980s some sixty-five, among them the four radical Arab states Algeria, Libya, SYRIA andSOUTH YEMEN, including Mauritania, which recognized SADR in 1984. The UN refused to accept as final Morocco's annexation and continued to call for a referendum, as did the Organization for African Unity (OAU). (For the resulting Morocco-OAU crisis see MOROCCO.) After a protracted wrangle over the admission of SADR to the OAU, half measures and postponements, SADR was officially admitted and seated at the twentieth Summit, November 1984.

WESTERN WALL   see HOLY PLACES, ARAB-ISRAEL CONFLICT.

WOMEN, GENDER AND POLITICS   During the past two decades, women in the Middle East have elevated issues of gender, the family and women's rights to the center of debate. This debate is hardly new, as it has surfaced during previous periods of political struggle and social reform. In late nineteenth-century EGYPT, women writers in the press campaigned for women's education and questioned their integration into the work force. In 1923, Huda Sha'arawi founded the Egyptian Feminist Union, which sought to achieve political, social and legal rights for women in the belief that women's emancipation and equality were fundamental to Egyptian independence. Turkish women demanded suffrage during the rise to power of the YOUNG TURKS in 1908. Thousands of Algerian women participated in their country's battle for liberation from French colonialism. More recently, Palestinian women actively demonstrated for their civil and political rights during the INTIFADA (1987–1993), while Iranian women were equally involved in implementing the Islamic Revolution.

Any discussion of women in the Middle East should take into consideration ISLAM and its influence on women's lives and gender. Islam is not monolithic; it takes on many forms and variations, and is affected by differences of region, culture, social tradition, generation, education and class. Thus, women in Muslim societies embrace a multitude of positions and beliefs towards Islam. As there is no universal interpretation of Islam and its religious sources, it is impossible to draw up a quintessential Muslim woman. Perhaps the best example of this diversity is the various interpretations on veiling. While some evoke the Qur'an which enjoins women to "cover their adornments," others argue that veiling was intended only for the wives of the Prophet. Still others have suggested that the veil was adopted from pre-Islamic cultures, and is not indigenous to Islam. Moreover, the term "veil" has come to mean a whole range of attire, differing in fabric and design, according to regional and socioeconomic differences. For some women, veiling signifies a religious conservatism, while for others, it is a means of asserting national liberation, or cultural authenticity in the face of a dominant culture. It is important to recognize, however, that neither gender nor Islam are the only defining factors in the lives and identities of Middle Eastern women, but that class, ethnicity, race, kin, education and age are also significant variables.

Throughout the Middle East, women have better access to education than they did twenty years ago. In elementary and secondary educational levels, female enrollment in 1990 had reached between ninety-three and ninety-eight percent in BAHRAIN, ISRAEL, JORDAN, QATAR and the UNITED ARAB EMIRATES (UAE). High illiteracy rates, however, still prevail among both older and rural women throughout the region. Family pressures and the need for subsistence agricultural labor are factors that limit girls' education in rural areas. According to 1990 statistics, forty-six percent of Egyptian women between ages fifteen and twenty-four were illiterate. In SAUDI ARABIA the female literacy rate has risen dramatically from only two percent in 1970 to forty-eight percent in 1990. Similar increases have also occurred in Jordan, Iraq and Syria.

Women have also entered the work force in greater numbers. During the 1970s, employment for women increased, as states such as EGYPT and TURKEY expanded state-funded industries in pursuit of import-substitution economies. The migration of male laborers from Jordan, LEBANON, SYRIA and Yemen to the oil-rich Gulf states also opened up job oppor-

tunities for women. During the late 1980s, Turkey and Israel boasted the highest female participation rate in the economy, above thirty percent, with TUNISIA, Lebanon, KUWAIT and Egypt not far behind. The majority engaged in professional work, such as teaching or nursing, fields which women have traditionally been encouraged to enter. A high percentage of women also worked in the informal sector, in agriculture and family businesses, with little or no salary. Nearly seventy percent of the economically active women in Turkey in 1989 were unpaid family workers, similar to women in IRAQ and Egypt.

Despite some gains in education and employment, women continue to struggle against gender inequalities and for greater participation in the political process. Women and gender are a central issue in the current debate on citizenship and the degree to which Middle Eastern governments are willing to empower their citizens to participate in the political process. Governments, state institutions and political groups inaccurately tend to define the citizen to be male, while relegating women to a second-class status. In many states, this notion is further reinforced by the fact that the right to citizenship is granted only if the father is a citizen. This has created a serious problem particularly among Kuwaiti women married to non-Kuwaitis, whose children cannot enjoy the rights and state benefits of Kuwaiti citizens. Women still do not have the right to vote in Bahrain, Libya, Saudi Arabia, OMAN, Qatar, UAE, and Kuwait. Moreover, in countries where women are enfranchised, the number of women government officials and decision makers tends to be extremely low. Women in government, however, have not always been willing to raise gender issues, and have more often pursued the lines of the ruling party, as in the case of Egypt.

More important than enfranchisement is the basic right of both men and women to organize without state interference. In Egypt and Kuwait, for example, the state would like to have more control over non-governmental groups whose constituents are women, as well as minorities and other marginalized groups, and circumscribe their freedom to organize around issues that might challenge state ideology and policy. In Tunisia, where women's rights have been promoted by the government, all women's groups are affiliated with the ruling party, government—co-opted trade unions, or organized by the Ministry of Women's and Family Affairs. Thus Tunisian women have little choice but to support government policy and to negotiate for better terms for themselves.

The inequalities that women face extend beyond voting and political rights. Throughout the Middle East, with the exception of Turkey and Tunisia, personal status laws, such as marriage, divorce, inheritance and child custody, are governed by religious law. These laws most often legitimize men's rights over women's, and reinforce patriarchal control over women. Women are not seen as equals, but rather are defined by their roles as wives, mothers, and daughters. The discrimination against women and the inequality they experience under these laws also tend to contradict women's rights as citizens of the state. In ALGERIA, for example, its constitution guarantees political, economic, social and cultural rights to Algerian women. In contrast, Algeria's 1984 Family Code relegates adult women to the status of minors. Throughout the region, many women's groups have petitioned the state to replace religious law with secular civil law, whereas Islamist women's groups insist on maintaining religious law, but with modern, critical interpretations that would eliminate gender inequality and discrimination.

Women are also at the center of the discourse on identity. Recognized as a fluid and historical construct, identity is the key component in the struggle between religious and secular forces. Women have become the symbolic battleground, as they are perceived as the most vulnerable segment of society when it comes to issues of honor, chastity and modesty. Although Islamist groups are not identical in their aims and political agendas, they tend to agree that Westernization has destroyed Islamic culture and a return to the pillars of Islam will restore Muslim pride and integrity. In the Islamic Republic of Iran, the "Westernized" *gharbzadegi* woman was depicted as representing society's ills, intent on corrupting the moral fabric of society. In contrast, the Islamist woman is portrayed as upholding traditional Islamic values, and wearing the *hijab* (veil), hailed as the symbolic demarcation line between the Muslim and the Other. Like Islamists, secular nationalists have also fabricated an ideal woman, depicted as the defender of the nation, as the transmitter of group values and traditions, whose role as wife and mother is exalted.

For the past two decades, writer and feminist Nawal El-SAADAWI has challenged women's prescribed role in society, and has led the movement for women's rights in Egypt. In 1971 Saadawi wrote *al-Mara wa al-Jins* (Woman and Sex), describing women's sexual oppression, especially female circumcision, which she observed while working as a doctor. Because her writing engaged a subject of cultural taboo, Saadawi found herself the subject of intense criticism from Egyptians and Arabs alike. In the early 1980s, with a group of feminists and intellectuals, she formed the Arab Women's Solidarity Association (AWSA), registered as a non-governmental organization in 1985. The AWSA espoused that the liberation of women is complimentary to the liberation of the land and economy. It supported women's participation in political, social, economic and cultural life, demanded an end to gender discrimination in public and private spheres, and sought to improve women's lives and working conditions among all sectors of the population. The AWSA held several international conferences on women and gender, and published a quarterly journal entitled *Noon*. In June 1991, after publicly opposing both Iraq's invasion of Kuwait and the US-led military intervention, the Egyptian government dissolved the organization and transferred its assets to a religious women's charity group. Clearly, government officials felt threatened by the secular feminism of the AWSA and its potential for mobilizing women against the state. Saadawi's visibility and determination have angered many, particularly conservative Islamists who have issued death threats against her. Since 1992 she has been living in Europe and the US where she continues her activism and writing.

Islamist women in Egypt also are redefining women's roles in society. Prominent among them is veteran Islamist Zainab AL-GHAZALI, who formed the Muslim Women's Society in 1936, and later joined forces with Hassan al-Banna's MUSLIM BROTHERS in 1948. Al-Ghazali has maintained that women can find liberation within Islam, and should exercise their power through their traditional family roles. Others, such as writer and activist Safinaz Kazim, also praise such conventional roles, yet, at the same time, support women's right to work. Imprisoned under SADAT, Kazim envisions a gender-free society, in which men and women are simply Muslims, and not gendered beings. Some women, such as political scientist Heba Ra'uf Ezzat, support the creation of an Islamic women's liberation movement. Ezzat refutes the dichotomy drawn between public and private spheres, which relegates women to the private sphere, and believes that women should and can take on roles in both raising a family and participating in public life.

Following their active role in their country's struggle for independence, Algerian women freedom fighters, the *moudjahidat*, came to symbolize the nationalist aspirations of the Algerian people and the Arabs as a whole. A new image of Algerian women, that of a modern, militant woman, emerged. In the post-independence years, despite demands and expectations, the state made few attempts to advance women in political, economic and social spheres. The number of women working outside the home, for example, has remained extremely low, and was less than seven percent in 1990. Women's representation in the National Assembly also never exceeded three percent. Only in education have women made some strides. Since 1992, Algerian women have been entrenched in a struggle for daily survival, as Algeria has become the battleground between secularist and Islamists, following the imposition of military rule on the heels of the victory of the Islamic Salvation Front (FIS) in the 1991 national elections. While Algerian women span the political spectrum, expressing support for both Islamist and secularist forces, women have been particularly susceptible to the violence of the armed Islamist factions. Many of the women who work, who do not veil, and who are active in political and social organizations have paid with their lives. These women continue to insist on their individual identities and rights, and pose a threat to the Algerian Islamists.

Nearly two decades after the Islamic Revolution, Iranian women have begun to question their position. While the Republic's leaders and ideologues were unanimous in their campaign against the Westernized woman, they have been unable to reach a consensus on what constitutes an Islamic woman, and what kind of role she should play in society. Early visions of a completely gender-segregated society, with women in the home, have since been challenged by socioeconomic realities and women's resistance. The mobilization of the male population in the eight-year-long war with Iraq helped to push women into the workplace. The phenomenon of women-headed households, a consequence of the war, has further necessitated women's economic integration. The 1986 census data, which indicated that women were only ten percent of the labor force, does not accurately reveal the extent Iranian women participate in the economy, as it overlooks the large number of economically active rural women. While employment has increased, women's education still lags behind that of men's, with the greatest disparity at the post-secondary level. Since the early 1990s, the regime has placed even greater importance on female education and economic integration as part of a grand scheme to reduce the country's extremely high birth rate.

Women have been particularly critical of government attempts to limit their participation in society and political life. The few women elected to parliament, such as Azam Taleqani and Maryam Behrouzi, have successfully lobbied for some reforms, particularly concerning marriage and family law. In an attempt to expand women's roles, President RAFSANJANI created the Women's Bureau in 1993. Although many have dismissed the organization as powerless, the Women's Bureau has been successful in campaigning for legal amendments to lift restrictions on female enrollment in certain university programs such as law and engineering. The last few years have also witnessed the appearance of several women's journals, such as *Farzaneh* and *Zenan*, which have questioned the restrictions on women and the imposition of the *hijab*. One interesting development has been the prominence of women directors in Iran's booming film industry. Although subject to censorship and modesty codes, film has provided an alternative and, most important, international medium for Iranian women to express their visions of social and political change.

In contrast to Iranian women, Turkish women enjoy formal equality under the 1926 Civil Code, which guaranteed equal rights to divorce and inheritance, abolished polygamy and instituted civil marriage. Replacing the Islamic *Shari'a* law, the Civil Code attempted to create a "new woman," in a symbolic break from the past. The Civil Code, however, still reinforces patriarchal relations between women and their fathers or husbands, such as by recognizing the husband as the head of the family and by giving preference to men in custody cases. The position of Turkish women is further reflected in educational statistics. 1990 figures indicate that thirty-one percent of Turkish women are illiterate. Among rural women and older women, illiteracy is double. Only forty-one percent of secondary school graduates are women. Women with higher degrees are even fewer, reaching only thirty-five percent. Women's political participation is also minimal, despite the fact that Turkish women have been enfranchised since 1934. In the 1995 elections, only thirteen women were elected to the 550-member parliament, representing a mere 2.3 percent.

Gender and citizenship issues are the focus of both Islamists and feminists in Turkey. Since the mid-1980s, Islamist women have actively confronted the state for the right to cover their heads in public institutions, especially universities. Although the Turkish Islamist movement lauds the importance of the family and conventional roles for women, it also supports women in more public roles, and will not hesitate to call upon the state's secular Civil Code to defend their rights. Feminist activists have pushed for a revision of clauses in the Civil Code which reinforce patriarchy and women's subordination, especially in the private sphere. Of particular concern is domestic violence, in which the state has been reluctant to intervene. During the past few years, women activists have established a foundation to fund and shelter victims of domestic violence, as well as a women's library and information center in Istanbul.

While many women have figured prominently in the history of the Palestinian nationalist movement, the Intifada had particular effect in politically mobilizing all segments of Palestinian women living under Israeli occupation. In the tradition of Algerian women nationalists, Palestinian women were prominent in demonstrations and many assumed leadership positions in the Popular Committees. As many women realized that their own emancipation was only secondary to national liberation, they began to develop a feminist consciousness. In an attempt to empower women and to elevate their roles and rights to that of national importance, several independent, feminist-oriented organizations have since been established. The Women's Affairs Center in Nablus, founded by novelist Sahar Khalifa in 1988, provides women with vocational and educational training and conducts research on women's issues. The Women's Studies Center in Jerusalem seeks to foster social change through research programs directed at women. In 1991 it held a conference on domestic violence, leading other women's groups to place this issue on their agendas. The Women Studies Committee of the Bisan Center for Research and Development in Ramallah aims to raise the level of women's involvement in national decision-making processes and to develop a feminist thinking compatible with Palestinian society.

Palestinian women have begun to shift their focus away from the nationalist struggle and towards defining their roles and rights as citizens in a future Palestinian state. In particular, Palestinian women have expressed concern that they will become increasingly marginalized from the political process, and that their integration in national development will be minimal. The Palestinian Authority has not been entirely receptive to the aims and needs of women. It has made proposals for social legislation that would link rights to welfare, pension, and medical benefits to one's participation in the labor force. Palestinian women who are unemployed would be forced to depend on husbands and fathers for access to such rights. Special provisions for birth allowances have also been suggested, indicating a pro-natalist policy when fertility rates are already high. The Palestinian Authority also has demonstrated its insistence on exercising state control over non-governmental organizations; state control would severely circumscribe the activities of the various women's groups, which have been key players in promoting women's equality and integration into the political process. These proposals merely reinforce women's traditional role in the family, whereas Palestinian women have clearly demonstrated that they would like to be fully integrated in the political and state-building processes.

Similarly, women in Kuwait also have struggled for basic rights and state recognition. The Kuwaiti state promotes the preservation of the patriarchal family and limited roles for women as part of an attempt to reinforce social control and national cohesion. At the same time, the 1962 constitution guarantees all Kuwaiti nationals the right to an education and a job. Thus, women are encouraged to assume both the role of mother and worker. Kuwaiti women, however, still lack the basic right to vote and to run for office; as a result, their political voice has been severely circumscribed. Without full citizenship rights, Kuwaiti women cannot easily challenge wage discrimination or demand social benefits denied to them because they are women. The only arena in which they can officially express themselves is within women's organizations, which are state-controlled and funded, and do not provide for a wide scope of political expression. Although the Women's Cultural and Social Society and the Girl's Club have advocated women's suffrage and political rights, and even have enjoyed the support of some members of the ruling family, these two groups have refrained from challenging the patriarchal family unit and the existing gender inequalities.

Whether they champion traditional women's roles or create new roles for themselves, women in the Middle East have raised their voices. Amidst crises of political and cultural identity, together with economic dislocation, the struggle of women for political and civil rights will become all the more significant as the region enters the twenty-first century.

YARMUK RIVER   see WATER POLITICS.

YAZDI, IBRAHAM   see IRAN.

YAZIDIS   A small religious community whose members, estimated at 100,000, live in northern IRAQ, northern SYRIA and the Trans-Caucasian republics. The Yazidis are apparently of Kurdish descent, but opinions on their origin differ. They speak a Kurdish dialect, but use ARABIC in their religious rites. Their religion comprises SABAEAN, Muslim, Christian, Zoroastrian and pagan elements. The founding father of the Yazidi sect—perceived by them a saint—is believed to be Sheikh Adi, a Muslim mystic who lived in the twelfth century and acquired a divine status through the transmigration of his soul. His tomb is located in Jabal Sinjar, north of Mosul, and is a site of annual pilgrimage. The Yazidis' divine figure is Peacock Angel, the supreme angle of the seven angels who ruled the world after it had been created by God, as a strong force contending with God and to be appeased by man. The Yazidis, who do not believe in evil, sin and the devil, are wrongly described as Devil-Worshippers.

YEMEN ARAB REPUBLIC   In southwest Arabia, bordering with SAUDI ARABIA in the north and northeast, OMAN in the southeast, and the Red Sea in the west. Until 1990 Yemen was comprised of two separate republics: Yemen and the People's Democratic Republic of Yemen (PDRY), or SOUTH YEMEN (SY).

Yemen consists largely of a high plateau broken in the north by deep, fertile valleys. The western, narrow coastal strip is called the Tihama. About forty-five percent of the population earn their living from agriculture. Industry and business are still very new. In the 1960s and 1970s, several modern roads between the major cities were constructed with foreign aid—the US, the USSR and China each promoting and financing several development projects. In the 1980s oil was struck in Yemen, and in addition to other discoveries in the former SY the country began to export oil, valued at about 1 billion dollars in 1995. Yemen has large reserves of gas, and an agreement to develop this new source of income was signed with a French firm in 1995.

The population of unified Yemen was approximately 14 million in 1996 (of the 1.5–2 million who used to work abroad, mainly in Saudi Arabia, about 850,000 workers were expelled during the GULF WAR because of the pro-IRAQ position of the Yemen government; the 1996 estimate of expatriates is approximately 700,000). Most Yemenis are Arab, except for a small group of Hamitic and Negroid origin from eastern Africa, located in the Tihama. SUNNI Muslims of the SHAFE'I school comprise about fifty-three percent. Forty-six percent belong to the Zeidi sect of SHI'A Islam. There are also some Shi'ite ISMA'ILIS (but statistics are unreliable and estimates vary). About ten percent of the population live in towns. Most of the rural population belongs to about seventy-five tribes nominally affiliated to tribal confederations, of which the most important are those of Hashed and Bakil.

Most of the tribes claim descent from Qahtan, the legendary father of the ancient tribes of South

Arabia. The rest are related to the north Arabian Adnani tribes which migrated to Yemen following the rise of ISLAM. The Yemeni tribe under its sheikh is an almost independent political unit with its own armed forces and judicial system. As approximately eighty percent of the tribes, including the strongest ones, are ZEIDIS, the Zeidi IMAM—who is nominally elected by the Zeidi Sada (plural of Sayyid; descendants of the fourth CALIPH Ali and his son Hussein (see Shi'a)—was able to establish, since the eleventh century, his hegemony over the non-militant Shafe'is, and maintain an autonomous political center.

Political History

Yemen until The Revolution (1962)
The OT-TOMAN EMPIRE claimed sovereignty over Yemen and officially considered it an Ottoman province. Yet the Empire only controlled and garrisoned the coast. In the interior, since the 1890s, a continuous rebellion erupted, which intensified after 1904 under a new Imam, Yahya Hamid al-Din. In 1911 the Turks were forced to conclude an agreement with the Imam granting the interior de facto autonomy under nominal Ottoman sovereignty. During World War I, Yemen remained loyal to the Ottoman Khalifa (Caliph) and the Imam refrained from hindering Turkish operations from Yemen against the British in ADEN. The dismemberment of the Ottoman Empire after the war automatically gave Yemen complete independence.

The Imams Yahya Hamid al-Din (1904–1948) and Ahmad Bin Yahya (1948–1962) endeavored to keep Yemen isolated from the modern world. Foreigners were forbidden to enter the country and modernization and economic development was forbidden. Relations with neighboring Saudi Arabia were hostile, culminating in a war in 1934, over Asir (a fertile area located between the two states). The Imam's tribal army was defeated. In the south, border disputes led to a permanent conflict with the British in Aden. This continued, despite the 1934 Anglo-Yemeni Treaty of San'a (the first British diplomatic representative was sent to San'a in 1951), until the British evacuation of South Arabia in 1968. The Anglo-Yemen conflict enabled fascist Italy to become the main foreign power to have real contact with Yemen with treaties signed in 1926 and 1927. Britain was disturbed both by Italian penetration—especially after Italy's conquest of Ethiopia, 1936—and by the official relations Yemen established with

the USSR, 1928. However, the Soviet mission was withdrawn in 1938, and Italy lost its special interest in the Red Sea following the loss of Ethiopia, 1941, in World War II (in which Yemen remained neutral). In the 1950s, Yemen attempted to introduce some degree of modernization by improving relations with the USSR and the People's Republic of China and accepting their aid. In 1958 Yemen under Imam Ahmad, formally joined the UNITED ARAB REPUBLIC (UAR), the newly established union of EGYPT and SYRIA, in a federation that was never implemented, reflecting its hostile relations with Saudi Arabia.

The Imams established a centralist, patrimonial regime in San'a, paying subsidies to strong allying tribes and subduing rebellious ones by military expeditions in the 1920s and 1930s. They built a tribal army mobilized in rotation for short periods, encamped near San'a and used mainly to pacify Zeidi tribes and enforce taxation in Shafe'i areas. They used the detribalized Zeidi elite of notables and religious dignitaries—the Sada—as the administrative backbone of their regime.

This political structure, built almost exclusively on the strictly controlled Zeidi tribes, began to fall apart in the 1940s and 1950s. Tribal unrest increased, erupting into several tribal rebellions. Two coup attempts were finally staged in 1948 and 1955. During the former, Imam Yahya was assassinated, but his son Ahmad subdued the rebels and assumed the Imamate. In the second coup Imam Ahmad was forced to leave San'a, but he was saved by his eldest son Muhammad al-Badr, who mobilized the northern Bakil tribes. Two princes, Abdallah and Abbas, who had been involved in the 1955 coup, were executed. These attempted coups, launched mainly by disappointed royal princes, would-be reformers among the Sada and young officers, hastened the establishment of a new central, non-tribal army. Young officers were sent abroad for their military education, mainly to Baghdad (among them Abdallah al-SALLAL, Hamud al-Ja'ifi, Hassan al-Amri, who were to play a leading role in the 1962 Revolution and post-monarchic regime). The urban elite, encouraged by Shafe'i unrest, began to demonstrate its interest in modernization. Some of its members went into exile and began a propaganda campaign against the Imam's regime—prominent among them were the Zeidi notables Mahmud al-Zubeiri and Qadi Abdel Rahman al-Iryani and the Shafe'i Ahmad

Muhammad Nu'man. The last three years of Imam Ahmad's reign were marked by intensive unrest. Seven days after Ahmad's death, on 26 September 1962, the new Imam Muhammad al-Badr was overthrown by a military coup. He escaped to the northern mountains and mobilized resistance among the Zeidi tribes. Henceforth, Yemen was embroiled in a civil war, which soon assumed an inter-Arab dimension when it became involved in support of the revolutionaries, and Saudi Arabia. This counterbalanced the Egyptian intervention by supporting the Royalists.

Revolution and Civil War (1962–1970)

Domestic Affairs The young officers who overthrew al-Badr proclaimed a "People's Republic." Motivated by Nasserist aspirations, they called for a total change in Yemen's economic, social and religious structure and asked Egypt for help. A few days after the coup, an Egyptian expeditionary force landed in Hudeida. The revolutionaries appointed Abdallah al-Sallal President of a Revolutionary Council, and re-elected an Executive Council. A temporary constitution was proclaimed in April 1963.

The non-militant Shafe'i population was encouraged by the anti-tribalism of the Republican Government as well as by the presence of the Egyptian forces, which became increasingly involved in the tribal and factional intrigues and struggle for power, in addition to their military operations against the Royalists. A young member of their intelligentsia, Abdel Rahman al-Beidani, became prominent in the Government and, as Foreign Minister and economic expert, began to rival Sallal. But in September 1963 the Egyptians, realizing that the Zeidis were the real power in Yemen, detained Beidani in Cairo. He never returned to Yemeni politics. If the Shafe'is hoped to abolish Zeidi hegemony and take over the leadership of the Republic, their hopes were frustrated. The Republican regime underwent frequent personal and factional changes—resulting largely from shifting Egyptian support. When on the offensive, the Egyptians supported the leftist officers, such as Sallal, Hassan al-Amri, Abdallah Juzeilan, Hamud al-Ja'ifi. When on the defensive and seeking to appease the Zeidi tribes, they invited Sallal for protracted "medical treatment" in Cairo and appointed non-revolutionary moderates like Nu'man, Iryani and Zubeiri to lead the Republic. Thus, Sallal held office until August 1963, when he was flown

to Cairo (nominally retaining the Presidency), while Iryani became a Vice-President and endeavored, with Nu'man, to win over the Zeidi tribes, organizing a pro-Republican tribal conference (Amran, September 1963). In January 1964 Sallal returned and Amri was appointed Prime Minister. In April 1965, following Egyptian defeats and attempts to reach conciliation with Saudi Arabia, Nu'man was again appointed Prime Minister and organized, together with Iryani (Zubeiri had been murdered in April), a pro-Republican conference of Zeidi tribes at Khamir. But in June 1965 Iryani and Nu'man were forced to resign and the leadership of the government was again taken over by Sallal. A month later he had to transfer the office to Hassan al-Amri, and following the Jidda Agreement in August (see below) he was again flown to Cairo. Amri then headed the San'a regime with Iryani and Nu'man, thus appeasing the Zeidi tribes. In September 1966, with the collapse of Nasser's truce with Saudi Arabia, Sallal was returned to San'a and the above three leaders were flown to Cairo where they were detained until October 1967, when Egypt ceased its military involvement in Yemen.

Under the blow of its defeat in the Six Day War of June 1967, as Egypt had been preparing its evacuation of Yemen in agreement with Saudi Arabia, it released Amri, Nu'man and Iryani. Sallal was toppled in October 1967 and left Yemen for exile in November. The new regime, with Iryani as Head of a new Republican Council and Amri as Prime Minister, was supported by the military power of the tribes, especially the Hashed. The paramount chief of this tribal confederation, Sheikh Hussein al-Ahmar, had been executed by Imam Ahmad. His son and successor, Abdallah al-Ahmar, had refused to join either the Royalists or Sallal's Egyptian-backed regime. Al-Ahmar's newly acclaimed support was one of the main reasons that San'a did not fall to a Royalist assault in late 1967 and early 1968. Together with Iryani, al-Ahmar became the real leader in San'a and many Zeidi tribes, under their hitherto pro-Royalist sheikhs, followed him and joined the new Republic. Hassan al-Amri, who organized the defense of the besieged capital, thereby acquiring a considerable reputation, cooperated with Iryani and Ahmar in the policy of compromise with Zeidi tribalism. The Shafe'is, on the other hand, who had for five years fought with the Republican Army and provided it some of its best commanders, resented the Egyptian evacuation and the new regime.

Their bitterness erupted into two intra-army clashes (also described as coup attempts) in March and August 1968. In these, Ahmar's tribal warriors joined Zeidi soldiers against leftist Shafe'i officers. The latter were subdued and some forty under former Chief-of-Staff Abdel Raqib Abdel Wahhab were expelled from Yemen. (Abdel Raqib was killed in 1969 when he returned from his exile and resumed plotting.) However, since the settlement of 1970 (see below) the Zeidi-Shafe'i antagonism has been mitigated and the differences between the two communities have been deliberately played down by the regime.

From 1962 to 1969–1970, the Royalists maintained their own regime in various parts of the country. After the September 1962 coup, Imam al-Badr was initially believed to be dead and his uncle Prince Hassan bin Yahya, formerly a rival of Imam Ahmad and opposed to al-Badr's succession, declared himself Imam. However, when Badr emerged alive, Prince Hassan recognized him as Imam and was appointed Prime Minister and Commander-in-Chief. A Royalist government emerged in October 1962 which included some of the Sada, e.g. Qadi Ahmad al-Siyyaghi and Ahmad al-Shami. Princes Muhammad and Abdallah bin Hussein, and Hassan and Abdallah bin Hassan, were sent to the northern mountains to lead the tribes in the campaign. Zeidi tribes began to join the Royalist camp. This led to increasing power of the young princes in command of the tribes; the ablest among them, Prince Muhammad bin Hussein, began in 1964 to train a semi-regular tribal army of his own. Imam Badr often left Yemen for medical treatment, and Prince Hassan bin Yahya was old. All this led to a certain division of power, and pressure for some democratization within the Royalist camp. In January 1965 the Imam promised to establish a legislative assembly to limit the power of the Imamate. In August 1966 Imam al-Badr was virtually deposed when a new "Imamate Council" was formed. Prince Muhammad bin Hussein was appointed Vice-President of this Council, and since Imam al-Badr was in Saudi Arabia (April 1965–October 1968), he was now the real leader of the Royalists. Prince Muhammad commanded the Royalist offensive against San'a in late 1967 and early 1968. In June 1968 he appointed the members of a new Imamate Council and a new government under his premiership. Nonetheless, after failing to achieve further military successes, he was ousted early in 1969 by the Imam who had returned to Yemen in October 1968.

The Civil War between the Royalist and Republican camps also involved foreign powers, turning it into an inter-Arab dispute, involving primarily Egypt and Saudi Arabia. The Egyptian expeditionary force— the war's main protagonist—was estimated at about 15,000 in late October 1962; 25,000 in January 1963; 50,000 in November 1963 and 70,000 in August 1965. Following the Egypt-Saudi Jidda Agreement of August 1965, this number was reduced to about 30,000. The force was finally evacuated in 1967. The last soldier officially departed from Hudeida on 15 December 1967. This foreign military intervention attracted much support to the Royalists. The belligerent Zeidi tribes fought the Republicans and joined the Royal princes not because they wanted to restore the Imam's rule, but because the Royal family was a unifying element in the war against the Egyptians. The Saudi government supplied the Royalists with war materials and gold. The Egyptian forces campaigned to cut off the two sources of Royalist strength: the tribes, and the Saudi supplies. (It did this by closing Yemen's northern and eastern borders and by bombing centers and communications in southern Saudi Arabia. This turned the conflict into an Egyptian-Saudi war.)

In response to a UN initiative, Saudi Arabia and Egypt signed, on 29 April 1963, the "Bunker Agreement" to end foreign intervention. UN observers were posted along the Yemen-Saudi border. This did not end foreign intervention. The war continued, and as no effort was made to supervise and end Egyptian intervention, Saudi Arabia denounced the agreement in November of that year. Fighting continued during 1964 with partial Egyptian successes. A Yemen reconciliation congress in October 1964 proved abortive. Both sides insisted on their original demands—the Royalists on the revival of the Imamate under the Hamid al-Din's family and the evacuation of Egyptian troops, and the Republicans on the "continuation of the revolutionary way" and the exclusion of the Imamic Hamid al-Din family. In the spring and summer of 1965 the Royalists gained the upper hand. They captured Harib and Marib in February and defeated large Egyptian forces in Jabal al-Akhdar. This isolated the Egyptian garrison in the al-Jauf area.

In August 1965, President ABDEL NASSER and King FEISAL signed the "Jidda Agreement" to end the war. Saudi supplies were to end and Egyptian forces to be evacuated within a year. The future regime of Yemen was to be determined by a plebiscite in November 1966. Royalist and Republican delegates were to discuss a regime for the transition period. In November 1965 delegates of both sides met in the northwestern town of Harad but failed to reach agreement. This was mainly due to a change in Egyptian Arab policy, reflecting the growing competition with Saudi Arabia over regional leadership. Egypt had stopped conciliating Saudi Arabia, and following reports of British plans to withdraw from Aden (officially announced in February 1966), decided to remain in Yemen in order to achieve its long-term plans.

In March-April 1966, Egypt evacuated its forces except for a number of strongholds to the San'a-Hudeida-Ta'iz triangle. This left the main tribal areas to their own rule, and to the new moderate Republican regime simultaneously established. When the Egyptian army was evacuated from the Saudi southern border and northern Yemen, King Feisal stopped giving subsidies and supplies to the young Yemen princes. This led to many Zeidi tribes switching their allegiance to the Republican Government. The Royalists managed to organize only small scale and ineffective operations. The Egyptians concentrated on bombing the Royalist tribes. The bombing was intensified following Sallal's return to power in September 1966, including, according to several reports (confirmed by the International Red Cross on 2 June 1967), the use of poison gas. Following this many of the tribes returned to the Royalist camp.

After the Six Day War, King Feisal and President Nasser agreed at the Khartoum Summit Conference of August-September 1967 to end the war. Soon after, the Egyptian army was removed from San'a and Ta'iz and concentrated in Hudeida, from which its evacuation began in October 1967. The Royalists, under the command of Prince Muhammad bin Hussein, marched on San'a and laid siege to it in early December 1967. Since the Egyptian intervention forces were gone and the regime in San'a had changed, many Yemeni tribes, mainly of the Hashed Confederation, were mobilized in an effort to save the capital. The Republican Army, which had previously left the main conduct of the war to the Egyptians, demonstrated its fighting ability, supported by civilian volunteers, and the siege was lifted.

After the Egyptian evacuation, the Yemen War became a local, civil war. In many cases it was also a diplomatic one, in which various tribes continued to shift sides, and to obtain rewards and subsidies from both sides without much fighting. It began to peter out in 1969. Inter-Arab efforts to end the war were resumed, mainly by a Tripartite Committee established by the Khartoum agreement. Again these were abortive and ceased early in 1968. In 1969, however, the policy of conciliating Saudi Arabia followed by Iryani and Amri was successful and Saudi support for the Royalists was reduced. Drought and starvation, intense in 1970, also greatly weakened the Royalist tribes. In March 1970, the Republican Prime Minister visited Jidda for the Islamic Foreign Ministers' Conference, and a general reconciliation agreement was prepared. In May, the former Royalist Foreign Minister Ahmad al-Shami—who had previously advocated reconciliation with San'a and agreed to exclude the Hamid al-Din family (thus following Saudi policy)—came to San'a with thirty Royalist leaders, none of whom were members of the Royal Family. An agreement was reached that amounted to the adhesion of the Royalists to the Republic and the exclusion of the Imamic family, i.e. the abolition of the Imamate. The Royal princes and some of their tribal supporters continued to resist, and the Imam al-Badr refused to abdicate. But the war was ended. The Imam and the princes went into exile. Former Royalists were admitted to the Republican regime. Shami joined the Republican, i.e. Presidential, Council (as did the moderate Republican Ahmad Muhammad Nu'man). Four Royalists joined the government, and twelve were co-opted to the National Council. (Shami and Nu'man were not included when the Republican Council was re-formed in April 1971, with three members only, under Iryani. Nu'man became Prime Minister, but resigned in July.)

Foreign Affairs The Republican victory also ended a diplomatic struggle between the two camps over world recognition and international relations. After the September 1962 coup, the Republic was immediately recognized by almost all the Arab states—except Saudi Arabia and JORDAN (the latter recognized the Republic in 1964)—and the Soviet Bloc, which also gave the Republic military aid, mainly through Egypt. In December 1962, the US also recognized the Republic. The same month, the UN accepted the credentials of the Republican delegation as the true representatives of Yemen. Britain and France refrained from recognizing the Republic. Despite US recognition, US-Yemen relations were not warm and the Republic severed relations with Washington in spring 1967. Saudi Arabia continued to recognize the Royalists, its aid enabling them to continue their struggle. After the Royalist defeat, the establishment of the new post-1967 Republican regime and the settlement of 1970, most of the countries still recognizing the Royalists withdrew that recognition in favor of the Republic. Saudi Arabia extended its recognition in July 1970, as did Britain and France. Later in 1970, Saudi Arabia and the Republic of Yemen exchanged ambassadors and the Saudis resumed economic aid and soon acquired considerable influence in Yemen. A state visit by President Iryani and his Prime Minister in March 1973 cemented close Saudi-Yemeni relations.

Republican Yemen (1970–1990)

Domestic Affairs Post-1970, Yemen's chief problem was how to establish a reasonable, functioning balance between forces and pressures pulling in conflicting directions—both in foreign and internal affairs. The internal power struggles were aggravated by the absence of well established constitutional and political traditions of modern state governance. The Republic had tried several times to proclaim provisional constitutional rules and set up representative-consultative councils, but none of these had taken root. In December 1970, a Constitution was promulgated by President Iryani. Yemen was declared an "Islamic Arab Republic"; part of the Arab nation, with Islam as the state religion and the SHARI'A as the foundation of its laws. The regime was to be a "parliamentary democracy," with equal rights for all (including women). There was to be a Consultative Council (*Majlis al-Shura*), elected for four year terms (with between twenty and thirty members appointed by the President). This would be given legislative powers. Political parties were banned. Elections for the Council were held March 1971. The Council was dominated by the tribal-conservative element. It elected Abdallah al-Ahmar, the chief of the Hashed tribes, as its

chairman. It named a new Republican (i.e. Presidential) Council Iryani as Chairman, with Amri and the Shafe'i leader Muhammad Ali Othman. After three months, Amri took the Premiership, too—but he was ousted after a few days, because he was involved in, or guilty of, a murder. (The real reason for him being ousted was allegedly his opposition to the Consultative Council and its tribal leaders.) He went into exile and did not return to Yemeni politics. Thus disappeared a man who had been for years one of the top leaders of the Republic. Nu'man became a member of the Presidential Council for a few months in 1973–1974, but then he, too, was ousted and removed from the political scene. Muhammad Ali Othman was assassinated in May 1973. The Presidential Council now consisted only of Iryani and Premier Abdallah Hajri, co-opted in 1972. Iryani was the only one to remain out of all the grand old men of the Republic.

These frequent changes reflected a general lack of stability. The condominium of the Zeidi tribal leaders, the officers' corps and the modernist-leftist Shafe'i intelligentsia was uneasy. The Iryani-Amri-Nu'man team had collapsed. There was growing unrest among the officers. Groups of leftists were going underground. This later emerged as a "National Democratic Front" (from about 1976), erupting in a rebellion. It was only by a series of shifting tactical maneuvers that Iryani was able to preserve a certain equilibrium. Maneuvering concerning Yemen's foreign orientation did not stop either (see below). In December 1972, Iryani replaced Premier Muhsin al-Aini with Abdallah al-Hajri; an ex-Royalist who was considered strongly right-wing, pro-Saudi and anti-South Yemen. But in February 1974 he dismissed Hajri, who had gone too far to the right, and appointed the Shafe'i Hassan al-Makki, a moderate leftist. (Hajri was assassinated in 1977.)

In June 1974, Iryani and his regime were overthrown in a military coup led by Lieutenant-Colonel Ibrahim Hamdi. The new ruler dissolved the Presidential Council and governed as Commander-in-Chief with a "Military Revolutionary Command Council" which he chaired. He also suspended the Constitution of 1970; dissolved the Consultative Council and declared new provisional constitutional arrangements. Initially seen to be a right-winger and closely linked with Saudi Arabia, Hamdi endeavored to establish himself as a strong leader, keeping in check both the tribes and the leftists—thus reverting to his predecessor's policy of balancing maneuvers. He tried to mend relations with South Yemen, for some time gaining the support of the underground "National Democratic Front." He was soon confronted by growing tribal resistance, in particular by the Hashed tribes (he was himself linked with the rival Bakil tribes). In 1977 this resistance turned into a virtual rebellion. Hamdi was assassinated in October 1977. The identity of the murderers was never established, but it was assumed that they came either from the tribal right wing or from a group of officers plotting for power.

Lieutenant-Colonel Ahmad Hussein Ghashmi became Commander-in-Chief and Chairman of the Military Council. In February 1978 he revived a representative body by appointing a "People's Constituent Assembly," responding to tribal demands. (Ghashmi himself was of Hashed tribal origin.) In April 1978 the Assembly replaced the Military Council by a Presidential Council, electing Ghashmi President. An officers' coup attempt was suppressed. But Ghashmi was assassinated in June 1978 by an envoy from South Yemen (who was killed by his own bomb in a strange episode never fully clarified). Power was taken over by Lieutenant-Colonel Ali Abdallah SALEH, as Chief-of-Staff and member of the Presidential Council. A month later, in July 1978, he was appointed President. He purged the Army of rebellious officers; suppressed another coup (October 1978), and survived several assassination attempts. Saleh, himself of the Hashed tribes, succeeded in establishing the balance of power sought in vain by his predecessors and giving Yemen, after so many years of upheavals and instability, a remarkably stable regime. The leftist underground "National Democratic Front" faded out, its rebellion collapsed in 1982, and the officers' corps ceased to form a restive political force. Saleh was re-elected President in May 1983 for an additional five-year term.

Foreign Affairs One of the main elements affecting Yemen internal and foreign policies has been relations with neighboring South Yemen. In spite of centuries-long political division, emanating largely from British interests, many tribes and families maintained connections with their relatives across the border. Even differences in the nature of the respective regimes after 1967 did not put an end to these contacts. However, relations with South Yemen

were problematic from the start. Yemen had always regarded South Yemen—in the past, the port-town of Aden and the Aden Protectorates, and later the South Arabia Federation—as part of its territory; and the South Yemen nationalists had taken the same position. When South Yemen became independent, in November 1967, the envisioned union of Yemen and South Yemen became the official policy, and an unquestioned principle of both. But the realization of that vision was a very complex matter. The two states were socially and politically very different, and antagonistic. South Yemen—known since 1970 as the "People's Democratic Republic of Yemen"—was a virulently leftist-revolutionary, Marxist-Maoist country. A merger with it was feared by many in Yemen as a virtual take-over of conservative Yemen by that revolutionary Left, or at least the introduction of a dangerous conflict into Yemen's society. Yemen, therefore, procrastinated over any actual steps toward union—and was encouraged in that policy by Saudi Arabia—while South Yemen was pressing for the consummation of the merger.

Meanwhile, South Yemen actively aided subversive and revolutionary elements in Yemen while Yemen gave asylum and support to South Yemen opponents of the regime—conservatives, or members of defeated factions of the leftist regime. As the borders were largely unmarked, there were border clashes and intrusions (mainly from South Yemen. Yemen claimed, for instance, several times, that in clashes with leftist rebels inside Yemen, the rebels were men from South Yemen). This led to a state of constant tension. Border clashes in 1972 escalated in September into serious battles. Arab mediation efforts achieved a cease-fire and a reconciliation. In October the two Prime Ministers signed an agreement in Cairo, confirming the decision to merge the two countries. This was solemnly re-endorsed by the two Presidents, meeting in Tripoli in November 1972. Joint committees were to work out details. However, despite occasional meetings, no progress was made and the merger issue remained dormant, the conservative-tribal partner in Yemen's power structure blocking any advance. In February 1979, border incidents again escalated into warlike operations (the "Ten Day War"). A mediation again arranged a cease-fire and a reconciliation, and the two Presidents met in March, in KUWAIT, and re-endorsed the decision to merge ("within one year"). Since that time there have been occasional clashes, and committee sessions and meetings at various levels, including Presidential summit meetings in 1981 (in Kuwait and Aden) and 1986 (Tripoli). But the union of the two Yemens—always reconfirmed, and unquestioned as a principle and goal—was never realized. Negotiations on the settlement of border disputes regarding oil-rich areas produced in 1989 an agreement on unification. This was implemented in 1990.

The achievement of an equilibrium was Yemen's chief aim in its foreign policies, too. On the international scene it followed a neutralist policy. It resumed official relations with the US in June 1972 and again began receiving US aid, both economically and in military supplies. At the same time it cultivated good relations with the USSR and also received considerable aid from it. President Saleh visited Moscow in 1981, and concluded a Treaty of Friendship and Cooperation with the USSR in October 1984 (without turning Yemen into a close ally of the USSR). US aid to Yemen, resulting in part from the disappearance of Soviet presence, declined dramatically due to the pro-Iraqi positions of Yemen in the Gulf Crisis. In 1995 US foreign aid returned to past allocations.

In the inter-Arab arena, Yemen belonged to the main stream identified with Egypt and Saudi Arabia, and refrained from taking sides regarding inter-Arab disputes. Its main problem in foreign and inter-Arab affairs was how to balance its position between Saudi Arabia and South Yemen. This issue had important internal repercussions. Saudi Arabia, whose economic and political aid was a mainstay of Yemen's survival, and which absorbed a large number of Yemeni workers (estimated in the 1970s and 1980s at about 2 million, with their remittances providing Yemen's main source of revenue and foreign currency), was always exerting its influence for conservative policies, and particularly in support of the tribal federations, its clients, and against a full *rapprochement* between Yemen and South Yemen. Keeping relations with Saudi Arabia on an even keel was therefore always vital for Yemen. Since 1970 and Iryani's March 1973 visit (which also yielded a border agreement in which Yemen for the first time accepted the 1930 loss of Asir and its annexation to Saudi Arabia) Yemen had succeeded in that task.

However, Yemen's exclusion from the GCC (established in 1981) left Yemen on the margins of the Peninsular political scene. This remained a cause of bitterness among Yemeni leaders. In the late 1980s Yemen's relations with Saudi Arabia and other oil-rich Gulf monarchies deteriorated due to the decreasing financial support from the latter. In February 1989, Yemen joined the newly established ARAB CO-OPERATION COUNCIL, which also included Iraq, Egypt, and Jordan.

Unified Yemen (1990–)

Domestic Affairs The first years of unification saw increased violence and numerous killings by opponents of the new political structure on both sides of the (former) border. Still, North Yemen elite took the lead and South Yemen figures had to be satisfied with lesser positions. Shortly after the merge a new set of laws, including a new constitution (1991, amended after the civil war, 1994) were adopted. The Political Parties Law of 1991 led to multi-party parliamentary elections (1993), but also to the demonstration of continued political weakness of the former South Yemenis. Difficulties in forming a new balanced political structure, and feelings of discrimination among the southerners, along with traditional tribal rivalries, led to the establishment of a secessionist movement by elements of the southern elite. Early attempts at finding a solution failed. The signing in February 1994 in Amman of an agreement to settle the dispute only aggravated the crisis when the signatories refused to shake hands. In late April 1994 fighting began in earnest, involving tank and air units of the former armies which until that point had not been integrated. In May a new Democratic Republic of Yemen was declared in the south. The new state received limited diplomatic and military support from most Peninsular countries led by Saudi Arabia, apprehensive of the possibility of a strong united Yemen, which might become a new regional power. Yemen could not muster any meaningful degree of support due to its siding with Iraq, the enemy of the GCC countries during the 1991 Gulf Crisis. The introduction of the free election system did not help Yemen either due to the challenge it presented for the Saudi regime.

After several months of fierce fighting and fruitless intervention of the UN Security Council (which passed two resolutions), during which the city of Aden was invaded and bombarded, causing many civilian casualties, the war ended in July 1994. The North Yemeni military superiority brought about a clear victory and the continued union of Yemen. Following the conclusion of fighting, Yemen took steps to re-integrate South Yemen into the union, including the designation of Aden as the economic capital of Yemen. Still, no political concessions were made to the former South Yemeni elite. On the contrary, Saleh became, in October 1994, the President, with no presidential council (with South Yemeni politicians participating) which existed at that time. The legal reforms were strongly influenced by Muslim law. They became the only source of legislation, reflecting the rising power of the Islamic movement in the country. The Muslim Party increased its representation in the cabinet concurrent with its growing popularity among Yemenis.

Upon his victory, President Saleh tried first to re-consolidate his rule over the south by a wave of purges of civil servants. Later, he tried to implement more openness in his domestic and foreign policies. In April 1995 he released 50,000 from the Army and later that year he reorganized his own Party, relinquishing some of his powers. Nonetheless, two major obstacles continued to block the road to national stability and reconciliation: relations between north and south and the growing influence of the Muslim radical elements on Yemeni politics. Disaffection from the north remained after the Civil War due to the lack of government investments in the rehabilitation process of the south. The economic conditions in those areas continued to worsen, causing sporadic popular demonstrations and governmental counter-measures. The Islamic challenge was even more serious.

The reform Muslim party, established in 1990, has quickly acquired a position of influence among decisionmakers and the public. Their main demands have been the institution of the Muslim law (*shari'a*) as the law of the country, and keeping their growing separate education system intact. Being part of the Yemeni political system, they have tried several different approaches to government—from boycott to full participation—all for the cause of eventually seizing power in Yemen.

Among other steps, Saleh established the principle of parliamentary elections open to all, including women (not to the liking of the Islamists). During the 1997 parliamentary elections a rather representative parliament was elected. Following these elections, a technocrat, economist of the former South

Yemen, Farag Bin Ghanem, became the first non-politician to head the cabinet. This was a further indication of the Saleh government's determination to heal the wounds of the Civil War. This move highlighted the conciliatory approach adopted by Saleh after the Civil War.

Foreign Affairs During the 1990 Gulf crisis, Yemen became a member of the UN Security Council, and abstained on several draft resolutions regarding the Iraqi invasion of Kuwait. This reflected its tense relations with the oil-rich Arab Gulf monarchies. Moreover, Yemen took a clear declarative stand for Iraq—conceived as an outcry of the poor against the rich—though refraining from actively participating or assisting it. The Yemen disposition put Iraq in direct conflict with Saudi Arabia, causing the expulsion of hundreds of thousands of Yemeni workers. The immediate Yemen deep economic depression was caused by the expulsion and the Saudi economic sanctions. Iraq halted its trade with Yemen due to its own crisis resulting from the war. In the late 1990s Yemen has recovered from that crisis and has one of the region's most sound economies. This is due in part to its cooperation with the IMF and a five-year program of economic reforms initiated after the end of the 1994 civil war.

In the years following the war, Yemen made a major diplomatic effort to improve relations with Saudi Arabia and the other members of the GCC. This resulted in a border agreement with Oman and negotiations with Saudi Arabia on border issues began. There was also the possibility of a return of some Yemenis to work in Saudi Arabia (1996). The more relaxed posture on the regional level was also projected to the Western countries. As a result of the unification process and the freedom of political activity, as reflected in the 1993 and 1997 parliamentary elections, relations with the US and EC were dramatically improved.

YEMEN, PEOPLE'S DEMOCRATIC REPUBLIC OF see SOUTH YEMEN.

YILMAZ, MESUT (b. 1947) Turkish politician, Prime Minister (1991, 1996, and 1997). Yilmaz was born in Istanbul in 1947 and graduated from the Faculty of Political Science at Istanbul University in 1971. He completed his studies at the University of Koln and returned to TURKEY where he was employed in various positions in the private sector. He joined the center right Motherland Party led by Turgut ÖZAL in 1983 and became deputy chairman. The same year he was elected member of the Grand National Assembly from Rize, and served in Özal's government as Minister of State and government spokesman, and as Minister of Tourism and Culture. He was elected again to the Assembly in 1987 and was appointed Foreign Minister. He went on to serve in Yildirim Akbulut's cabinet in 1989, but resigned in 1990 over President Özal's continued interference in foreign affairs. Upon the resignation of Akbulut the following year, Yilmaz was elected Party leader in what was considered a victory for its liberal wing. He was appointed Prime Minister in June 1991, but, following the victory of the True Path Party in the October 1991 elections, went on to lead his Party in opposition.

In the elections of December 1995, Yilmaz's Motherland Party came in third place, with 132 seats (out of 550) in the Grand National Assembly and 19.7% of the vote after Necmettin Erbakan's Welfare Party (158 seats, 21.4%) and Tansu ÇILLER's True Path Party (135 seats, 19.2%). In order to keep the winning Islamists out of power, in March 1996 Yilmaz and Çiller (despite their mutual antipathy) formed a government based on a rotation system of premiership. In this Yilmaz became Prime Minister for the first year (due to return to this post in 1999). He was forced to resign, however, after three months when Çiller pulled out of the coalition because of Yilmaz's lack of support in a parliamentary vote which ordered an investigation of corruption charges against her. A new coalition government led by ER-BAKAN followed and Yilmaz returned to the opposition.

In June 1997 Prime Minister Erbakan resigned under growing pressure of the high military command and the opposition. Defections from the True Path Party, the co-partner of the WP, made it impossible to reestablish the previous coalition. Instead, Yilmaz, in July 1997, succeeded in forming an alternative coalition made up of his Motherland Party, the Democratic Left Party and the Democratic Turkey Party. It was backed from the outside by the Republican People's Party.

YOM KIPPUR WAR (1973)   see ARAB-ISRAEL CONFLICT.

YOUNG TURKS   The movement, largely comprised of Ottoman military officers, officials and intellectuals who opposed the tyrannical regime of Sultan ABDEL HAMID II and brought about its downfall in the 1908 revolution. Made up of several factions and streams of thought, its strongest organization was the Committee of Union and Progress (CUP), dominated by Turks and concerned with the preservation of Ottoman independence and territorial integrity. In one form or another, it ruled the OTTOMAN EMPIRE for most of the following decade.

The movement began in 1889 when a secret society was formed by students of the military medical school to fight the Sultan's absolutist and tyrannical regime. Students from other institutions joined the society, but the police began to crack down on the revolutionaries and many of them had to flee abroad. In European capitals and in Cairo, the exiles (the most prominent of whom were Ahmed Riza and Murad Bey) formed a number of societies and published periodicals which were smuggled into the Ottoman Empire. In 1899 they were joined by the Sultan's own brother and two of his sons (one of whom, Sabahettin, later rose to a position of leadership). After 1906, many new secret societies were organized by officers and officials within the Empire itself.

The revolution was carried out by a group of officers affiliated with the CUP. Military unrest reached its peak in summer 1908, when several high-ranking officers in Macedonia defected. The Sultan failed to prevent the mutiny from spreading. On 24 July he yielded to the officers' demands by reactivating the Constitution of 1876 and Parliamentary institutions. The CUP's hold was further stregthened when a conservative counterrevolution failed in April 1909. The Sultan was deposed and replaced by his compliant brother Mehmed Resad.

The Young Turks' revolution gave rise to great hopes for solidarity and equality among all the nations of the Empire; but the CUP gradually became centralistic and authoritarian. It was committed to the preservation of the Empire and tried to achieve this by a harsh policy of Ottomanization, the prohibition of nation-oriented organizations and the compulsory dissemination of the Turkish language. It was therefore opposed by more liberal groups and non-Muslim, non-Turkish elements that supported decentralization. In 1911, liberal opposition in Parliament came together in the Liberal Union. Parliament was dissolved and new elections were won by the CUP; but an officers' coup in July 1912 ousted the Party. In a counter coup, in January 1913, led by ENVER Pasha, the CUP regained power, and from then until 1918 the state was in fact ruled by a military dictatorship headed by a triumvirate of Enver, Cemal and Tal'at.

Despite their efforts, the Young Turks failed to preserve the integrity of the Empire. In 1908, soon after the Revolution, Austria-Hungary annexed Bosnia and Herzegovina; Bulgaria declared its independence; and Greece incorporated Crete. The Ottoman-Italian War of 1911–1912 led to the loss of Tripolitana and the Dodecanese Islands. Albania rebelled (1910), gaining independence two years later. In the Balkan Wars of 1912–1913 Turkey lost almost all its European territories. The Young Turks' decision to join World War I against the Entente powers hastened the final dissolution of the Empire. Though promoting Pan-Islamist ideas, the government was unable to prevent the Arab revolt of Sharif Hussein of Mecca in 1916. By the end of the war the Arab provinces occupied by Allied and Arab troops had been irrevocably detached from the Empire. The Young Turks' leaders fled the country, and though they later tried to re-establish their rule, the new nationalist forces had the upper hand.

The Young Turks introduced a significant measure of modernization. They organized provincial administration in 1913 and passed new laws encouraging local industry and economic development. They were educated in military and secular schools and attempted to reduce the influence of religion on state affairs, adopting, for example, a new liberal family law in 1917. By maintaining at least the outward forms of parliamentarianism, elections and Party life, they permeated the country with the principles of democratic procedure. Finally, the relative freedom of expression allowed by them led to the crystallization of various ideologies, among which were those of secularism and Turkish nationalism (the latter founded by Ziya GÖKALP). In many ways they paved the road for the radical reforms of ATATÜRK.

Z

ZAKARIYYA, FU'AD (b. 1927) Egyptian scholar and liberal thinker. Born in Port-Sa'id, he completed his Ph.D. studies in Philosophy at Ain Shams University (1956), where he taught philosophy. Between 1957 and 1962, he taught in New York, and was later appointed as Head of the Philosophy Department of Kuwait University. In his books on contemporary Islamic movements he vehemently attacked the Islamic militant groups, especially on the grounds of their demand to establish a state of SHARI'A in EGYPT. At the same time he called for conducting a real dialogue with the young generation, to strenghthen its awareness about the dangers of establishing such a state. He strongly criticizes the rigid Arab nationalist opposition to Egypt's peace with ISRAEL.

ZAYED IBN SULTAN see NUHAYAN, AL.

ZEIDIS, ZEIDIYYA Offshoot of SHI'A ISLAM whose believers constitute the majority population of YEMEN.

The Zeidis split from the bulk of the Shi'a on grounds of recognizing Zeid Ibn Ali—the grandson of Hussein Ibn Ali—as the fifth IMAM. Zeid was defeated in 740 by the Umayyad forces. Unlike the mainstream of the Shi'a, the Zeidis recognize a continuing line of living Imams, who must be descendants of the Khalifa Ali through his sons al-Hassan and al-Hussein. Their Imam is elected by the *Sada* (plural of Sayyid, descendants of the Khalifa Ali and his son Hussein). The election of the Imam caused repeated schisms. In recent decades the Yemeni Imams Yahya Hamid al-Din and Ahmad Ibn Yahya broke the rule of election by appointing their elder sons to succeed them. The Zeidis established two states: one on the CASPIAN SEA up to 1126, and Yemen from the early days of ISLAM.

In modern times the Zeidis of Yemen often fought with the Ottoman Turks. While the latter controlled the coast, the Zeidis usually maintained a measure of autonomy in the interior or else rebelled. The founder of modern Yemen, Yahya Hamid al-Din, elected

Imam in 1904, rebelled and secured his autonomy in the interior. He obtained full independence in 1918 and ruled until 1948, re-establishing Zeidi hegemony.

The Zeidis form about fifty-five percent of the population of Yemen (though there are conflicting estimates)—the rest are mainly Sunni SHAFE'IS—and about eighty percent of the powerful, belligerent tribes, of whom the strongest are the confederations of Hashed and Bakil tribes. The Zeidis were the military and social elite of the Kingdom. The administrative, judicial and religious backbone of the state was mostly provided by non-tribal Zeidiyya Sada, whose number is estimated at 300,000. Some Sada families claimed that the Imamate, e.g. the al-Wazir clan, was behind the abortive coup of 1948 in which the Imam Yahya was killed.

The Republican regime set up by the revolution of 1962 abolished the Imamate and the Sada hegemony. However, as the Zeidiyya tribes were the strongest element in the civil war ensuing, the new regime had to reach some agreement with them and gradually revive and recognize their leading position. The Republican-Royalist reconciliation of 1970 endorsed the abolition of the Imamate, although the Imam, Muhammad al-Badr, in exile, did not formally renounce it. Some Sada attempts to revive the Imamate were reported but not substantiated, and since 1970 there has been no recognized Imam.

ZEROUAL, LIAMINE (al-Amin Zerwal) (b. 1941) Algerian politician, born in 1941 in Batna, where his father was an IMAM. After a long military career reaching the rank of Major General, he retired, and following his opposition to the brutal manner in which the 1988 riots were suppressed, President BEN JEDID took his position. He later served as Ambassador in Romania until the January 1992 military takeover, following the overwhelming victory of the ISLAMIC SALVATION FRONT in the December 1991 Parliamentary elections.

Zeroual was appointed Minister of Defense in 1993, replacing the military regime's strongman, Khalid Nizar. On 31 January 1994 the mandate of the five-man presidential council (*Haute Conseil d'Etat*), HCE, expired. The National Dialogue Conference in January which was convened to decide on the succession to the council collapsed. The ruling Higher Security Council (*Haut Conseil de Securite*), i.e., the

Military High Command, decided to appoint Zeroual as President for a three year transitional period. Reportedly reluctant to assume the Presidency after Nizar refused the post, he was convinced that the alternative would be a power vacuum, since rival factions in the high command had failed to agree on another candidate. Zeroual's ascension signified that military rule (which had been the real but hidden power in ALGERIA since independence) had come into the open.

Zeroual faced two challenges: bitter civil strife and financial and economic crisis. He advocated a dialogue with the Islamists in order to seek a political solution that would avert a civil war while retaining the military's dominant role in politics, against the military hard-liners who rejected any compromise with the Islamists. Following the failure of the talks with the imprisoned leaders of the Islamic Salvation Front (FIS), Zeroual scheduled Presidential elections for November 1995. Zeroual won the elections (which were held in a relatively free atmosphere) against three other candidates, with a sixty-one percent majority. In 1996 he introduced constitutional amendments which enhanced the Presidency's powers and prohibited parties to use ISLAM and Berber identity as their banner. While the amendments were approved by an eighty-five percent majority, his political initiatives did not solve the Algerian crisis. Zeroual sought to liberalize the inefficient state-controlled economy. This was marginally successful in view of the ongoing violence and opposition of the bureaucracy. In foreign policy, he sought to improve Algeria's relations with the US and European Community. While maintaining close relations with the mainstream Arab states, he maintained tense relations with MOROCCO.

ZIONISM The movement for the national renaissance and political independence of the Jewish People in *Eretz Yisrael* (Palestine), which emerged toward the end of the nineteenth century. The name is derived from one of the biblical names of Jerusalem—Zion.

Religious yearning for the return to *Eretz Yisrael* existed ever since the JEWS were exiled at the end of the first and beginning of the second centuries A.D., following the failure of their revolts against the Romans. Throughout the years of exile, this yearning, in conjunction with periods of persecution and hardship, resulted in numerous messianic awakenings. The difference between the new movement and the previous yearning was in that the content of Zionism was essentially secular. Modern Zionism developed in Europe, in an atmosphere of virulent anti-Semitism. This anti-Semitism was not limited to the reactionary countries of Eastern Europe, where repeated waves of suppression and pogroms took place, but was also to be found in the enlightened countries of Central and Western Europe, in which the Jews appeared to enjoy equal rights and in which Jewish thinkers were influenced by the current nationalist and socialist doctrines and philosophies.

The Zionist thinkers were preceded by several pre-Zionist ones: the Jewish-German socialist Moses Hess (1918–1975), who in his book *Rome and Jerusalem* (1862) advocated the establishment of an independent Jewish state by the Jews, that would be based on socialist principles, and would lead to the social and economic normalization of the Jewish people; Rabbi Zvi Hirsch Kalischer (1798–1874), who argued that the Messiah would only arrive after a large part of the Jewish people would return to and settle in *Eretz Yisrael*; and Rabbi Yehuda Ben Shlomo Alkelai (1798–1879), who after the blood libel against the Jews of Damascus in 1894, preached for a return to Zion, first within the framework of the traditional religious thinking, but later on the basis of contemporary national thinking. The first two Zionist thinkers were Yehuda Leib Pinsker (1821–1891), who in his book *Auto-Emancipation* (1882), argued that emancipation (equal rights) granted by others cannot resolve the problems of the Jewish people, and that only its territorial concentration and sovereignty can create normal conditions for its existence; and Dr. Theodor HERZL (1860–1904), who after considering various solutions to the Jewish problem, concluded that the Jews must leave their places of exile and concentrate in a sovereign state.

In his famous book *The Jewish State* (1896), Herzl explained that due to the prevalence of anti-Semitism on the one hand, and the Jewish desire to survive on the other, the Jewish problem cannot be resolved by means of assimilation. The grave situation of the Jews can only be turned into a positive force by means of a political solution—the establishment of an independent Jewish state with the consent of the great powers. Herzl described the

ideal state which he envisioned in his book *Altneuland* ("Old-New State," 1902).

Herzl initiated the first practical attempt to translate Zionism into political action by establishing the World Zionist Organization, which held its first congress in Basel in 1897. The Basel Program, drafted at that Congress, stated that "the aim of Zionism is to create for the Jewish people a home in Palestine secured by public law." Herzl also engaged in diplomatic efforts amongst the leaders of states, especially the OTTOMAN EMPIRE and Germany, in a position to help realize the Zionist goals.

The institutionalization of Zionism resulted in regular congresses with the participation of representatives from all over the world, and a permanent apparatus, which operated in-between congresses, and has persisted to the present day, even though its importance decreased after the establishment of the State of ISRAEL in 1948.

It was the settlement activities of "*Hovevei Zion*" ("Lovers of Zion") in *Eretz Yisrael*, which began in 1881, that heralded the beginning of the "practical Zionism." The two Zionist approaches, political and practical, continued to play an important role in the Zionist development and efforts in *Eretz Yisrael*. The combined approach was called "Synthetic Zionism," which is associated with Professor Haim WEIZMANN, who played an important role in the attainment of the BALFOUR DECLARATION from Great Britain in 1917, and the establishment of the British Mandate in Palestine under the auspices of the League of Nations. To the Zionists who belonged to the socialist movements, practical settlement and agricultural work was of supreme importance. The political Zionists, on the other hand, argued that while ninety percent of Zionism was made up of actual settlement, it was the political work which constituted the condition for success.

Even though there were only a few Zionists who believed that most of the Jews would actually immigrate to *Eretz Yisrael*, the majority believed that eventually, as a result of immigration, the Jews would constitute a majority in the country. "Catastrophic Zionism," connected with Max Nordau (1849–1923), argued that if the Jews would not come to *Eretz Yisrael*, a catastrophe would befall them.

While most of the Zionists regarded the goal of the movement to be the establishment of a Jewish state (even though for tactical reasons they did not use the term "state," but "homeland," "national home" and "commonwealth,") there were Zionists who believed that the establishment of a Jewish state was a pipe dream, and that it would be better if the goal were the establishment of a Jewish "spiritual center" in *Eretz Yisrael*. The term "spiritual center," which was associated with Ahad Ha'am, regarded Zionism as a solution to the problem of Judaism rather than of the Jewish people. There were also Zionists who advocated the establishment of a binational (Jewish-Arab) state (see ARAB-ISRAEL PEACE-MAKING), believing that there was no other moral solution to the clash between the national aspirations and demands of the Jews and Arabs in *Eretz Yisrael*-Palestine. However, both spiritual Zionism and bi-nationalism were minority views within the Zionist movement.

In its early years, the Zionist movement had to contend with the question: should the Jews insist on establishing their state in Eretz Yisreal, or should other alternatives be considered? Finally, the seventh Congress, which convened in 1905, decided to reject the "Uganda Plan," which proposed establishing the Jewish state in the British African colony, and to strive to establish it in *Eretz Yisrael* only. As a result, several personalities, led by the British Jewish playwright Israel Zangwill, left the Zionist Organization, and set up the Territorial Zionist Organziation. Some of the "territorialists" argued that the "stateless" Jewish people requires a "peopleless" territory, but that unfortunately *Eretz Yisrael* could not fulfill this need, maintaining that the problem was urgent and the Jews had to accept any available territory.

From the very beginning the Zionist endeavor consisted of immigration (*Aliyah*), the purchase of land, settlement and economic development. Throughout its history, Zionism had to choose from various options and make difficult decisions. The decisions adopted by the majority were almost always preceded by stormy debates, though there were decisions dictated by events or taken by individual leaders. When World War I broke out, the Zionist offices were transferred from Berlin to Copenhagen, in order to preserve the movement's neutrality. However, the leaders of the Zionist Movement in BRITAIN, the most prominent of whom was Haim Weizmann, started already in 1915 to follow a moderately pro-British policy, with the intention of gaining British

support for the Zionist idea. This angered the American Zionists, many of whom sympathized with Germany (until the US joined the war on the side of the Allies), while the Zionists in Central Europe and *Eretz Yisrael* were extremely worried by it. However, even amongst the pro-British Zionists, there were marked differences of opinion between the activists who wanted Jewish soldiers to fight in the war on the British side, or at least support the British war effort, and those who feared that direct involvement would endanger the 60,000 Jews living in *Eretz Yisrael*.

Three years after the end of World War I a debate developed between the American Zionists and the leadership of the Zionist Organization (which was made up primarily of Russian Jews). The Americans, led by Supreme Court Justice Louis Brandeis (1856–1942), felt that upon the attainment of international recognition and the expected approval of the British Mandate by the League of Nations, the political chapter of Zionism had been achieved, and that all future efforts should concentrate on economic development based on private initiative and solid business principles. This approach was rejected by Weizmann, with the support of most of the Zionist Organization, as a result of which Brandeis and his colleagues left the movement.

Another important Zionist debate occurred in 1935, following the failure to bring about a rapprochement between *Mapai*, led by David Ben GURION and the Revisionists, led by Ze'ev Jabotinsky, who demanded a revision of the Mandate to apply its Jewish national home clauses on Transjordan. The Zionist Actions Committee adopted a "discipline clause," the aim of which was to prohibit any independent political action by individual Zionist parties, especially the Revisionists, who sought to implement a more activist policy than that implemented by the official leadership. As a result the Revisionists decided to leave the Zionist Organization and established the new Zionist Organization. Even though the Revisionists returned to the fold of the Zionist Organization in 1946, the IZL and *Lehi* underground movements, ideologically associated with the Revisionists, never accepted the authority and discipline of the majority, which was represented by the Jewish Agency, the *Va'ad Le'umi* (the self-administration body of the Jewish community in Palestine) and the *Hagana* (the pre-state Jewish defense force), and until the establishment of the state the two sides lived essentially in a state of conflict. It was primarily Menahem BEGIN, IZL Commander after 1943, who made sure that the split regarding the short term goals and the means of attaining them, would not lead to civil war. Only after the establishment of the state did the struggle turn political, within the democratic framework of the state.

Following the publication of the Peel Commission Report in 1937 (see ARAB-ISRAEL PEACEMAKING), the Zionist movement had to contend, for the first time in its existence, with the question of whether to consider the establishment of a Jewish state in only part of western *Eretz Yisrael*. Despite the fact that some important Zionist factions opposed partition, the twentieth Zionist Congress decided, in 1937, to enable the Executive to consider the possibility positively. In late 1938 the British retreated from the idea of partition, due to strong Arab opposition, though partition remained an option in British thinking and planning during and after World War II. In 1946, the Zionist Executive adopted the idea of partition and the establishment of "a viable Jewish state" in Palestine, as the only realistic way to secure a state. In 1947, following the publication of the UNSCOP partition plan, the Zionist Movement agreed in principle to the establishment of a Jewish state in only part of western Palestine.

Unlike World War I, in the course of World War II there was no question of Jewish neutrality. Despite the disappointment with the 1939 White Paper, issued by the British government, which limited Jewish immigration and land purchases, Ben Gurion announced that the Jews would fight with the British against the Nazis as if there were no White Paper, and fight the White Paper as if there were no war going on. However, as the war progressed and the dimensions of the Holocaust became known, the "dissidents" (IZL and *Lehi*) refused to refrain from an armed struggle against the British, who continued to prevent the entry of immigrants into the country, beyond the set quota. As a result, in 1944, Britain's Minister Resident in Cairo, Lord Moyne, was assassinated by the *Lehi* and IZL leader Menahem Begin announced the revolt against Britain. The official Zionist institutions and those of the Jewish community in Palestine reacted sharply to these measures, but their position on the issue was usually ambivalent, except for a short period in which mem-

bers of the IZL were disclosed to the British authorities within the framework of what came to be known as the "*saison*."

Additional issues with which Zionism contended throughout the years related to the relations between Jews and Arabs (see ARAB-ISRAEL CONFLICT); relations with the British authorities, which became increasingly hostile (until 1948); and the appropriate ways for developing Zionism in *Eretz Yisrael*. The various Zionist parties had different approaches to these issues. The dominant position (which, after 1931, swung strongly in the direction of the workers' parties) was that one ought to seek a *modus vivendi* with the Arabs, but not at the expense of immigration and land purchases; that formally the Zionists must continue to cooperate with the British, but at the same time develop an independent defense force and continue with settlement and immigration activities, even if the British regarded them as "illegal"; and that the Zionist development must be mixed—national and personal, socialist and capitalist, secular and religious.

Following the establishment of the State of Israel there were many who felt that the Zionist movement and the Zionist Organization had completed their tasks, even though Zionist endeavors, such as immigration (especially from countries of distress, but also from prosperous countries), requisition of lands and settlement activities, continued. In fact, after the establishment of the state the term "Zionism" was extended to include the identification of Diaspora Jews with the State of Israel, and the concern of the State of Israel to prevent assimilation among the Jews of the Diaspora.

Throughout the history of Zionism the Zionists have found cooperation with the "non-Zionists"— those Jews, who sympathized with the Zionist effort but had no intention of settling in *Eretz Yisrael* themselves. Such cooperation manifested itself in joint involvement in specific projects, and since 1929 in joint membership of the Zionists and non-Zionists in the Jewish Agency. In contrast, there were constant clashes, at various levels, between the Zionists and the various groups of "anti-Zionists," who objected to the Zionist ideology. Until World War II these included the Jewish Bund and the *Volkspartei*, the extreme *Haredi* (ultra-religious) Judaism, Reform Judaism and assimilated Jews. The Bund and *Volkspartei*—movements that developed at the end of the nineteenth century and beginning of the twentieth century and which believed that the Jews, even though they are a nation, should seek national autonomy in the countries where they live, and not in a separate state in *Eretz Yisrael*. The *Haredim* perceived Zionism as a threatening secular movement trying to speed up the redemption, while according to their belief only God, not man, could bring the redemption. The Reform movement, based on its interpretation of Judaism in the past, claimed that *Eretz Yisrael* should be excluded from the Jewish frame of reference, and that the Jews themselves should not be regarded as a separate people. The assimilated Jews felt that Jewish nationalism would sabotage their status in the countries in which they live. There were also individuals who objected to Zionism because of the injustice it had caused to the Arabs, arguing that Zionism was immoral. Today only the extreme *Haredim* may still be defined as anti-Zionist, even though extensive Jewish circles are non-Zionist.

The Arabs always opposed Zionism totally, as a matter of principle, seeing in it an imperialist movement that came to usurp Arab lands and dispossess their inhabitants. Since the beginning of the Arab-Israeli peacemaking process, most of the Arab states have been willing to recognize the existence of the State of Israel as a fact, but their basic attitude to Zionism has not changed.

After 1947 most of the Muslim states, and several states with a large Muslim minority, such as India, supported the Arab cause. After 1973, the Arabs managed to spread anti-Zionism throughout the Third World, as a spearhead of their political struggle to delegitimize the State of Israel. This effort reached its peak when on 10 November 1975, the UN General Assembly passed a resolution that equated Zionism with racism. The Soviet Union also adopted for most of its existence an anti-Zionist policy, which was basically ideological, but included elements of traditional anti-Semitism. Nevertheless, the Soviet Union supported the establishment of the State of Israel and backed the state in its first years.

Since the 1980s there have been some intellectual circles in Israel that argue that Israel has reached its "post-Zionist" period, since Zionism has realized itself in that the Jewish state was established and fortified. Many of the "post-Zionists" are inclined to view Zionism and its enterprise critically, arguing that Zionism developed many myths and lies in order to justify itself and its activities.

Typesetting and Layout: Shimmy Carlebach
Copyediting: Emma Corney
Printing and Binding: Sun Fung Offset Binding Limited